ELEVENTH EDITION

THE ECONOMY TODAY

BRADLEY R. SCHILLER
American University

Boston Burr Ridge, IL Dubuque, IA New York San Francisco St. Louis
Bangkok Bogotá Caracas Kuala Lumpur Lisbon London Madrid Mexico City
Milan Montreal New Delhi Santiago Seoul Singapore Sydney Taipei Toronto

THE ECONOMY TODAY
Published by McGraw-Hill/Irwin, a business unit of The McGraw-Hill Companies, Inc., 1221 Avenue of the Americas, New York, NY, 10020.

This book is printed on acid-free paper.

1 2 3 4 5 6 7 8 9 0 DOW/DOW 0 9 8 7

ISBN 978-0-07-351126-9
MHID 0-07-351126-9

Executive editor: *Douglas Reiner*
Developmental editor: *Angela Cimarolli*
Marketing manager: *Melissa Larmon*
Senior project manager: *Harvey Yep*
Lead production supervisor: *Michael R. McCormick*
Senior designer: *Kami Carter*
Photo research coordinator: *Lori Kramer*
Lead media project manager: *Brian Nacik*
Cover design: *Kami Carter*
Interior design: *Kami Carter*
Typeface: *10/12 Times New Roman*
Compositor: *Aptara*
Printer: *R. R. Donnelley*

Library of Congress Cataloging-in-Publication Data

Schiller, Bradley R., 1943–
The economy today / Bradley R. Schiller.—Eleventh ed.
p. cm.
Includes index.
ISBN-13: 978-0-07-351126-9 (alk. paper)
ISBN-10: 0-07-351126-9 (alk. paper)
1. Economics. I. Title.
HB171.5.S292 2008
330—dc22

2007025926

www.mhhe.com

ABOUT THE AUTHOR

Bradley R. Schiller has over three decades of experience teaching introductory economics at American University, the University of California (Berkeley and Santa Cruz), and the University of Maryland. He has given guest lectures at more than 300 colleges ranging from Reno, Nevada, to Istanbul, Turkey. Dr. Schiller's unique contribution to teaching is his ability to relate basic principles to current socioeconomic problems, institutions, and public policy decisions. This perspective is evident throughout *The Economy Today.*

Dr. Schiller derives this policy focus from his extensive experience as a Washington consultant. He has been a consultant to most major federal agencies, many congressional committees, and political candidates. In addition, he has evaluated scores of government programs and helped design others. His studies of discrimination, training programs, tax reform, pensions, welfare, Social Security, and lifetime wage patterns have appeared in both professional journals and popular media. Dr. Schiller is also a frequent commentator on economic policy for television, radio, and newspapers.

Dr. Schiller received his PhD from Harvard in 1969. He earned a B.A. degree, with great distinction, from the University of California (Berkeley) in 1965. He is now a professor of economics in the School of Public Affairs at American University in Washington, DC.

PREFACE

FIBER OPTICS SET THE PACE

The world does seem to be moving faster. News travels at amazing speeds. Financial markets move with lightning reflexes. Technology advances at an astonishing pace. New products appear daily.

Fiber optics play a key role in this harried and hurried pace. The strands of fiber optics that appear on the cover of this book remind us how and why the economic pace has accelerated. They also remind us of how our productive capacity keeps expanding.

The increased pace of our tech-driven world hasn't made teaching economics any easier. Sure, the *tools* of teaching (e.g., "smart" classrooms, course-management software, distance learning, electronic chat rooms) have increased our productivity. But the *content* has become more complex, largely due to the globalization of production, financial markets, and even market psychology. What happened to interest rates, stock prices, or currency values in China and Europe while you were sleeping may have significant impact on today's action in U.S. markets, on Fed policy decisions, and ultimately on the performance of the U.S. economy. It's hard enough just keeping track of all this action. Teaching students to think in globally interactive terms is an even greater challenge.

At the micro level, globalization and technological advances create similar problems. Market structures are continuously evolving, as are the products themselves. With those changes, even market boundaries are on the move. Is your local cable franchise really a monopoly when satellite, Internet, and telephone companies offer virtually identical products? Will Apple Computer, Inc., behave more like a monopolist or like a perfect competitor in the newly defined iPhone and iTV markets? With the Internet creating *global* shopping malls, how should industry concentration ratios be calculated? The Federal Trade Commission and the Antitrust Division of the U.S. Justice Department are vexed by ever-changing market boundaries and structures.

Coping with Change

So how do we cope with all this flux in the classroom? Or, for that matter, in a textbook that will be in print for 3 years? We could ignore the complexities of the real world and focus exclusively on abstract principles, perhaps "enlivening" the presentation with fables about the Acme Widget Company or the Jack and Jill Water Company. That approach not only bores students, but it also reinforces the misperception that economics is irrelevant to their daily life. Alternatively, we could spend countless hours reporting and discussing the economic news of the day. But that approach transforms the principles course into a current-events symposium.

The Economy Today pursues a different strategy. I am convinced that economics is an exciting and very relevant field of study. I have felt this way since I attended my first undergraduate principles course. Despite an overbearing, boring textbook and a super-sized class (over 1,000 students!), I somehow discerned that economics could be an interesting topic. All it needed was a commitment to merging theoretical insights with the daily realities of shopping malls, stock markets, global integration, and policy development. Whew!

What Makes Economies Tick

How does this lofty ambition translate into the nuts and bolts of teaching? It starts by infusing the textbook and the course with a purposeful theme. Spotlighting scarcity and the necessity for choice is not enough; there's a much bigger picture. It's really about why some nations prosper while others languish. As we look around the world, how can we explain why millionaires abound in the United States, Hong Kong, the United Kingdom, and Australia, while 2.8 *billion* earthlings live on less than $2 a day? How is it that affluent consumers in developed nations carry around camphones while one-fourth of the world's population has never made a phone call? Surely, the way an economy is structured has something to do with this. At the micro level, Adam Smith taught us long ago that the degree of competition in product markets affects the quantity, quality, and price of consumer products.

Markets vs. Government

At the aggregate level, we've also seen that macro structure matters. Specifically, we recognize that the degree of government intervention in an economy is a critical determinant of its performance. The Chinese Communist Party once thought that central control of an economy would not only reduce income inequalities but also accelerate growth. Since decentralizing parts of its economy, freeing up some markets, and even legalizing private property (see World View, p. 17), China has become the world's fastest-growing economy. India has heeded China's experience and is also pursuing a massive privatization and deregulation strategy. At the same time, some of the world's poorest nations remain economically imprisoned by excessive regulation, undeveloped markets, high taxes, unsecured property rights, and pervasive corruption.

This doesn't imply that *laissez faire* is the answer to all of our economic problems. What it does emphasize, however, is how important the choice between market reliance and government dependence can be.

We know that the three core questions in economics are WHAT, HOW, and FOR WHOM to produce. Instead of discussing them in a political and institutional void, we should energize these issues with more real-world context. We should also ask who should resolve these core questions, the governments or the marketplace? Where, when, and why do we expect market failure—suboptimal answers to the WHAT, HOW, and FOR WHOM questions? Where, when, and why can we expect government intervention to give us better answers—or to fail? This theme of market reliance versus government dependence runs through every chapter of *The Economy Today.*

Real-World Concerns

Within the two-dimensional framework of three core questions and markets-versus-governments decision making, *The Economy Today* pursues basic principles in an unwavering real-world context. The commitment to relevance is evident from the get-go. At the outset, the very serious trade-offs between arms spending and food production in North Korea (p. 9) put the concept of opportunity costs into a meaningful context. Chapter 1 pursues the nature of opportunity cost into the future by examining the earthbound sacrifices we'll have to make for the proposed Lunar and Martian settlements (Chapter 1's "Economy Tomorrow" section, p. 19). These kinds of concrete, page one examples motivate students *to learn and retain* core economic principles.

Chapter 2 gives students a quick economic tour of the world. It shows how different nations have resolved the WHAT, HOW, and FOR WHOM questions. Students see how rich the USA is—and how poor other nations are (see World Views, pp. 27 and 28). They also see that inequality is not an ailment unique to "rich" nations (e.g., World View, p. 39). Chapter 37 pursues this perspective even further by examining the urgent problem of global poverty—its unfathomable dimensions, its principal causes, and its remedial policy options. These two chapters give students an empirically based global perspective on economic outcomes that can spark a motivated search for explanations, that is, economic theory.

Macro Realities

In macro, most instructors emphasize the cyclical problems of unemployment and inflation. But students don't get motivated to learn the origins or solutions for these problems just by citing the latest economics statistics (yawn). Most students don't have enough personal experience to know why 6 percent unemployment or 3.7 percent inflation are *serious* concerns. To fill that void, *The Economy Today* takes students on a tour of unemployment and inflation. In Chapter 6, they see unemployment statistics translate into personal tragedies and social tensions. They see who loses their job when the unemployment rate rises (p. 109) and how devastating the experience can be (pp. 113–114). In Chapter 7, the devastation wrought by hyperinflation drives home the realization that price-level changes matter. These two chapters lay a global, historical, and personal foundation that gives purpose to the study of macro theory. Few other texts lay this foundation.

In the core macro chapters (8–18), *The Economy Today* constantly reminds students of the real-world relevancy of core concepts. The potential instability of aggregate demand, for example, is illustrated with data on quarterly variance in consumption and investment (p. 179) as well as News accounts on investment decisions (p. 178) and consumer confidence (pp. 175, 207). The impacts of terrorism (News, p. 178) and "oil shocks" (News, p. 359) on

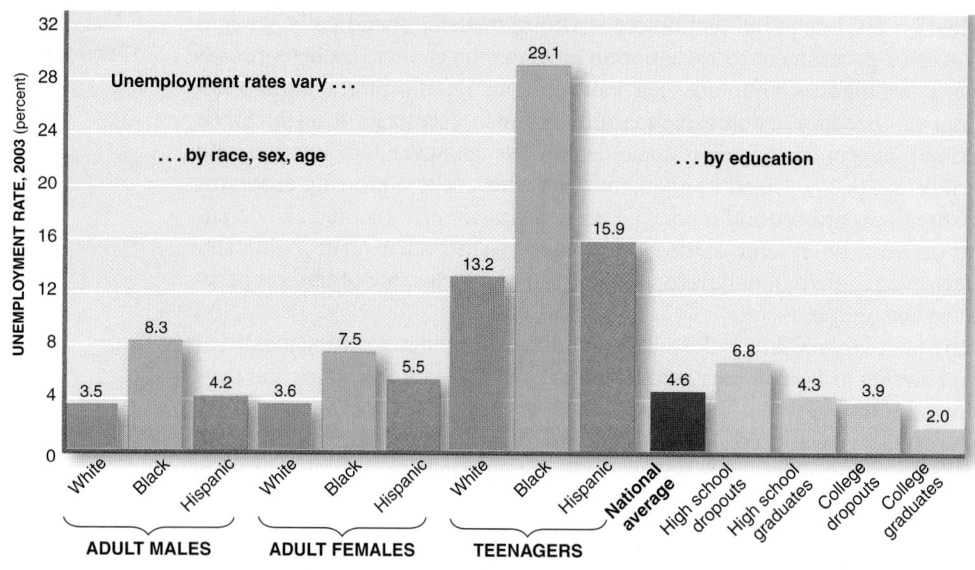

FIGURE 6.4
Unemployment Isn't Experienced Equally by Race, Sex, or Education

Minority groups, teenagers, and less-educated individuals experience higher rates of unemployment. Teenage unemployment rates are particularly high, especially for black and other minority youth.
Source: U.S. Department of Labor (2006 data).

both AD and AS get timely recognition, as do the successive tax cuts of 2001, 2002, 2003, and 2004. By tying core AS/AD concepts to real-world events, the textbook highlights the importance and relevance of macro theory.

When we peer into the long run, it's important to ask what makes economies grow and what institutions or policies can accelerate that growth. But students won't pay much attention until you demonstrate that economic growth is both *important* and *desirable.* Chapter 17 attempts this by reviewing the payoffs to growth and by directly confronting concerns about the limits to growth. Chapter 37 illustrates how the *absence* of economic growth can fulfill Malthus's vision of human misery.

Nowhere is the commitment to a real-world context more evident than in Chapter 19. The very title of the chapter ("Theory versus Reality") reveals its purpose. The chapter not only confronts but also *explains* the gap between the promise of macro theory and the reality of economic outcomes. The section entitled "Why Things Don't Always Work" (starting on p. 375) is a nice bridge between the blackboard and the boardroom for your students. Every macro course should include this chapter.

Micro Realities

The emphasis on real-world applications continues in the micro section. Nowhere is this more evident than in the discussion of market structure. Chapter 22 offers the typical depiction of the perfectly competitive firm in static equilibrium (albeit illustrated with real-world catfish farmers). Then comes a *second* chapter on perfect competition that turns the spotlight on the competitive dynamics that power market-based economies. The reality of market structures is that they typically evolve—sometimes at lightening speed. In 1977, Apple Computer, Inc., had a virtual monopoly on personal computers; in 2001 it had a lock on portable, digital music players (iPods). In 2007, it had the new iPhone and iTV markets to itself. In all these cases, a swarm of wannabes transformed the market into more competitive structures. In the process, the products improved, sales volumes increased, and prices fell at extraordinary rates of speed. By emphasizing the *behavior* of a competitive market rather than just the *structure* of static equilibrium, Chapter 23 injects excitement into the discussion of market structures. The "Economy Tomorrow" section at the end of Chapter 23 explains why iPods are likely to cost only $29 within a few years and why iPhones may be selling for only $99. Understanding how competitive markets make this happen is probably the most important insight in microeconomics. By building on student experience with music downloads and MP3 players, *The Economy Today* helps students acquire that insight.

The central theme of government dependence versus market reliance is particularly evident in Chapter 27, "(De)Regulation of Business." When the lights went out in California and later in the Midwest, a lot of people blamed "power pirates." They wanted the government to more closely regulate electricity markets. Others protested that government regulation (e.g., price controls, environmental standards) had *caused* the brownouts and blackouts. They advocated *less* government intervention and more reliance on the market mechanism. Chapter 27 uses the experience of (de)regulation in the rail, air, electricity, and telecommunications industries to highlight unique features of natural monopoly and the possibilities of both market and government failure.

The FOR WHOM question is one of the three core issues in economics, but it typically gets scant treatment in a principles course. *The Economy Today* tries to remedy this shortfall with companion chapters on taxes (Chapter 33) and income transfers (34). The chapters emphasize the key economic concepts (e.g., marginal tax rates, tax elasticity of labor supply, moral hazard) that are common to both sides of the tax-transfer redistribution system. By examining President George W. Bush's 2006 tax return (p. 666) students see the distinction between nominal and effective tax rates. By reviewing trends in aging and labor-force participation (pp. 683–688), they may realize how Social Security alters work incentives and behavior.

International Realities

International trade (35) and finance (36) chapters not only explain the core concepts of comparative advantage and exchange-rate determination but also assess the *resistance* to free trade and flexible exchange rates. By identifying the vested interests that resist trade, *The Economy Today* bridges the gap between free-trade models and real-world trade disputes. Students see not only why trade is desirable but also how and why we pay for trade barriers. This is a lot more interesting than simply reciting the mathematics of comparative advantage in cloth and wine.

No chapter brings home the notion of a global community more than Chapter 37. This new chapter focuses on the pervasiveness of material deprivation in scores of poor nations. The chapter is designed not only to raise student consciousness of global poverty but also to stimulate more interest in the core issue of what makes economies really "tick"—or not.

The bottom line here is simple and straightforward: ***By infusing the presentation of core concepts with a unifying theme and pervasive real-world application,* The Economy Today *offers an exciting and motivated introduction to economics.***

EFFECTIVE PEDAGOGY

Clean, Clear Theory

Despite the abundance of real-world applications, this is at heart a *principles* text, not a compendium of issues. Good theory and interesting applications are not mutually exclusive. This is a text that wants to *teach economics,* not just increase awareness of policy issues. To that end, *The Economy Today* provides a logically organized and uncluttered theoretical structure for macro, micro, and international theory. What distinguishes this text from others on the market is that it conveys theory in a lively, student-friendly manner.

Assurance-of-Learning Ready

Many educational institutions today are focused on the notion of assurance of learning, an important element of some accreditation standards. *The Economy Today* is designed specifically to support your assurance-of-learning initiatives with a simple, yet powerful, solution.

Each test bank question for *The Economy Today* maps to a specific chapter learning objective listed in the text. You can use our test bank software, EZ Test, to easily query for learning outcomes/objectives that directly relate to the learning objectives for your course. You can then use the reporting features of EZ Test to aggregate student results in similar fashion, making the collection and presentation of assurance-of-learning data simple and easy.

Concept Reinforcement

Student comprehension of core theory is facilitated with careful, consistent, and effective pedagogy. This distinctive pedagogy includes the following features:

Chapter Learning Objectives. New to this edition, each chapter contains a set of chapter-level Learning Objectives. Students and professors can be confident that the organization of each chapter surrounds common themes outlined by three to five learning objectives listed on the first page of each chapter. End-of-chapter material including the chapter summary, discussion questions, and problem sets is tagged to these objectives as is the supplementary material, which includes the Test Bank, Instructor's Manual, Study Guide, and PowerPoint Presentations.

Self-Explanatory Graphs and Tables. Graphs are *completely* labeled, colorful, and positioned on background grids. Because students often enter the principles course as graph-phobics, graphs are frequently accompanied by synchronized tabular data. Every table is also annotated. This shouldn't be a product-differentiating feature but, sadly, it is. Putting a table in a textbook without an annotation is akin to writing a cluster of numbers on the board, then leaving the classroom without any explanation.

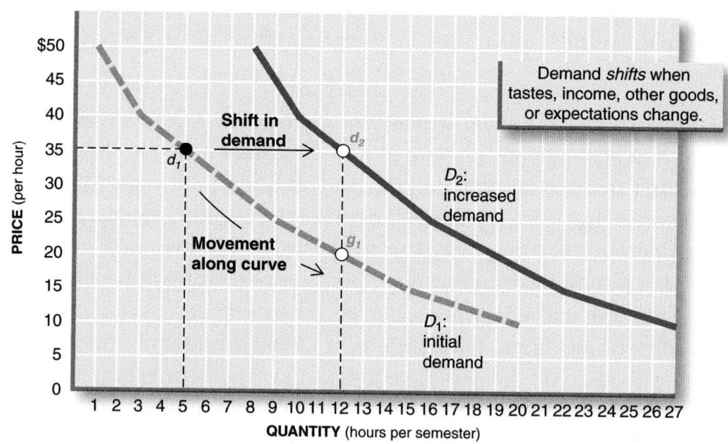

FIGURE 3.3
Shifts vs. Movements

A demand curve shows how a consumer responds to price changes. If the determinants of demand stay constant, the response is a *movement* along the curve to a new quantity demanded. In this case, the quantity demanded increases from 5 (point d_1), to 12 (point g_1), when price falls from $35 to $20 per hour.

If the determinants of demand change, the entire demand curve *shifts*. In this case, an increase in income increases demand. With more income, Tom is willing to buy 12 hours at the initial price of $35 (point d_2), not just the 5 hours he demanded before the lottery win.

		Quantity Demanded (hours per semester)	
	Price (per hour)	Initial Demand	After Increase in Income
A	$50	1	8
B	45	2	9
C	40	3	10
D	35	5	12
E	30	7	14
F	25	9	16
G	20	12	19
H	15	15	22
I	10	20	27

Reinforced Key Concepts. Key terms are defined in the margin when they first appear and, unlike in other texts, redefined in the margin as necessary in subsequent chapters. Web site references are directly tied to the book's content, not hung on like ornaments. End-of-chapter discussion questions use tables, graphs, and boxed news stories from the text, reinforcing key concepts, and are linked to the chapter's learning objectives.

Boxed and Annotated Applications. In addition to the real-world applications that run through the body of the text, *The Economy Today* intersperses boxed domestic (In the News) and global (World View) case studies. Although nearly every text on the market now offers boxed applications, *The Economy Today*'s presentation is distinctive. First, the sheer number of In the News (106) and World View (78) boxes is unique. Second, and more important, *every* boxed application is referenced in the body of the text. Third, *every* News and World View comes with a brief, self-contained explanation. Fourth, the News and World View boxes are the explicit subject of the end-of-chapter Discussion Questions and Student Problem Set exercises. In combination, these distinctive features assure that students will actually *read* the boxed applications and discern their economic content. The *Test Bank* provides subsets of questions tied to the News and World View boxes so that instructors can confirm student use of this feature.

Photos and Cartoons. The text presentation is also enlivened with occasional photos and cartoons that reflect basic concepts. The photos on page 38 are much more vivid testimony to the extremes of inequality than the data in Figure 2.5 (p. 37). The contrasting photos of the original Apple I (p. 473), the iMac, and the iPhone (p. 482) underscore how the "animal spirits" of competitive markets spur innovation. Every photo and cartoon is annotated and referenced in the body of the text. These visual features are an integral part of the presentation, not diversions.

Readability

The one adjective invariably used to describe *The Economy Today* is "readable." Professors often express a bit of shock when they realize that students actually enjoy reading the book. (Well, not as much as a Stephen King novel, but a whole lot better than most textbooks they've had to plow through.) The writing style is lively and issue-focused. Unlike any other textbook on the market, every boxed feature, every graph, every table, and every cartoon is explained and analyzed. Every feature is also referenced in the text, so students actually learn the material rather than skipping over it. Because readability is ultimately in the eye of the beholder, you might ask a couple of students to read and compare a parallel chapter in *The Economy Today* and in another text. This is a test *The Economy Today* usually wins.

Student Problem Set

I firmly believe that students must *work* with key concepts in order to really learn them. Weekly homework assignments are *de rigueur* in my own classes. To facilitate homework assignments, I have prepared the *Student Problem Set,* which includes built-in numerical and graphing problems that build on the tables, graphs, and boxed material that aligns with

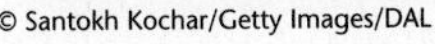

© Santokh Kochar/Getty Images/DAL

Gene Alexander, USDA Natural Resources Conservation Service/DAL

Analysis: An abundance of capital equipment and advanced technology make American farmers and workers far more productive than workers in poor nations.

each chapter's learning objectives. Grids for drawing graphs are also provided. Each chapter's problem set is detachable and includes answer boxes that facilitate grading. (Answers are available in the *Instructor's Resource Manual* on the book's Web site). The *Student Problem Set* is located behind the tab at the end of this book.

All of these pedagogical features add up to an unusually supportive learning context for students. With this support, students will learn and retain more economic concepts—and maybe even enjoy the educational process.

DISTINCTIVE MACRO

The macro section of *The Economy Today* is well known for its balanced presentation of different theoretical perspectives, its consistent use of the AS/AD framework, its global perspective, and its explicit juxtaposition of theory and reality.

Balanced Macro Theory

This isn't a highly opinionated text. It doesn't assert that only long-run issues matter or that monetary policy is the only effective lever of short-run stabilization. Rather, *The Economy Today* strives to offer students a *balanced* introduction to both short- and long-run macro concerns as well as an array of competing viewpoints. Keynes isn't dead, nor are supply-side policy options ignored. Instead, competing theories are presented in their best possible light, and then subjected to comparative scrutiny. This approach reflects my belief that students need to be exposed to a variety of perspectives if they're to understand the range and intensity of ongoing debates. The benefits of such an eclectic and balanced approach were strikingly evident in the aftermath of the September 11, 2001, terrorist attacks. Not only did policy discussion shift abruptly from long-run issues (e.g., productivity growth and "saving Social Security") to short-run issues (stabilizing the economy), but even Milton Friedman and Alan Greenspan endorsed countercyclical fiscal policy! Shouldn't students have a broad foundation of principles that enables them to follow these developments? *The Economy Today* offers such breadth of coverage.

Consistent AS/AD Framework

Too many textbooks still treat the aggregate supply/aggregate demand (AS/AD) framework as a separate theory. The AS/AD model is *not* a separate theory; it is just a convenient framework for illustrating macro theories in a world of changing prices. And it's a much more useful tool than the "Keynesian cross," which always leads to an inflation dead end, forcing instructors to backtrack and pull the AS/AD model out of the closet. This outdated two-model approach isn't necessary: ***Keynesian theory can be fully developed without the Keynesian cross.***

In this text, *only* the AS/AD framework is used. I still develop the consumption and investment functions to ascertain how much real output will be demanded at the existing price level. These GDP components, along with government spending and net exports, are added *horizontally* to determine a point on the AD curve (instead of adding them vertically to construct a Keynesian aggregate expenditure curve). The slope of the AD curve is then explained by the real balances, interest-rate, and foreign-trade responses to changing price levels.

The core multiplier concept is also explicitly illustrated. In the AS/AD framework this is accomplished with sequential *shifts* of the AD curve, propelled by induced changes in consumption (derived from the traditional consumption function). Notice in Figures 10.6 (p. 203) and Figure 10.9 (p. 205) how the multiplier is illustrated by sequential AD shifts and measured along a horizontal plane (the prevailing price level, *not* an AS curve).

These AD multiplier effects are summarized again in Figure 11.4 (p. 217). This depiction of multiplier effects in the AS/AD framework spotlights the fact that AD shifts have both price and output effects (e.g., Figure 11.3, p. 215). Shouldn't students *start* their macro tour with this real-world perspective?

In view of this upfront AS/AD depiction of the multiplier, the core macro presentation is exclusively rendered in the context of the AS/AD model. This greatly simplifies the presentation for students, who often got lost shuttling between two distinct models, sometimes in the same chapter. Since students have never encountered the Keynesian cross model, they won't miss it in *The Economy Today.* For instructors who still want to use it, the Keynesian cross is now contained in the appendix to Chapter 9. As that appendix explains, the two models are simply different paths for reaching the same conclusions. The advantage of the AS/AD framework is that it generates more useful policy guidelines in a world of changing price levels. The single framework also facilitates contrasts of competing macro theories (see Figure 16.1, p. 314, for example) and time perspectives (long-run versus short-run).

Global Macro Constraints

The Economy Today incorporates not only the reality of changing price levels but also the constraints of global linkages. The Fed's Board of Governors always looks over its collective shoulder at global markets when making decisions on domestic monetary policy. The impact of changing interest rates on the value of the dollar and global money flows is always discussed. Likewise, the effectiveness of fiscal-policy initiatives is always sensitive to potential export "leakage" and other trade effects. I have tried to convey a sense of how these global links constrain policy decisions and impacts in the "Global Macro" chapter. This unique chapter (18) is intended to introduce a dose of global reality into the macro course without delving into theories of trade or finance (Chapters 35 and 36). Chapter 18 is a stand-alone chapter in the macro section. It is designed for instructors who sense the need to offer more of a global perspective in the macro course, but don't have time to cover trade and finance theories.

Theory and Reality

The final chapter in the macro section serves two purposes. First, it brings together the various Keynesian, monetarist, supply-side, and growth theories into a convenient review format. No other text brings all the macro material into such a course-ending overview.

The second purpose of Chapter 19 is to examine why economic performance so often falls short of economic theory. This is a fun section, because it delves into the institutional and political constraints that shape and limit macro policy. Fiscal policy debates come alive when Republicans and Democrats start arguing over the size and content of antiterrorism stimulus policy (see News, p. 384). The chapter ends the macro course with the suggestion that the real world offers choices between *imperfect* markets and *imperfect* government intervention.

DISTINCTIVE MICRO

The micro section of *The Economy Today* focuses on the performance of specific companies and government programs to showcase the principles of market structure, labor-market functioning, redistribution, and regulation.

Competitive Market Dynamics

The real power of the market originates in competitive forces that breed innovation in products and technology. Other texts treat the competitive firm as a lifeless agent buffeted by larger market forces, but this book provides a very different perspective. *The Economy Today* is the only principles text that has *two* chapters on perfect competition: Chapter 22 on firm behavior and Chapter 23 on industry behavior. Chapter 23 traces the actual evolution of the computer industry from the 1976 Apple I to the iMac. It gives students a real-world sense of how market structure *changes* over time and lets them see how dynamic, even revolutionary, competitive markets can be. The rise and fall of "dot.coms" and the ongoing plunge in MP3 player (iPod) prices reinforce the notion that competitive markets move with lightning speed to satisfy consumer demand.

(De)Regulation

As mentioned earlier, Chapter 27 focuses on the (de)regulation of private industry. The chapter first examines the qualities of natural monopoly and the rationale for regulating its behavior. The trade-offs inherent in any regulatory strategy are highlighted in the review of the railroad, cable TV, airline, telephone, and electricity industries. As in so many areas, the choice between imperfect markets and imperfect regulation is emphasized.

Taxes and Transfers

The Economy Today offers parallel chapters on taxes and transfers. Chapters 33 and 34 emphasize the central trade-offs between equity and efficiency that plague tax and transfer policies. The varying distributional effects of specific taxes and transfers are highlighted. Examples are drawn from the Bush tax-cut packages of 2001–2004, President Bush's own 2006 tax return (p. 666), as well as the tax and benefit sides of Social Security. Taken together, the two chapters underscore the government's role in reshaping the market's answer to the FOR WHOM question.

Average College Cost Breaks $30,000

NEW YORK (CNNMoney.com)—The average cost of a four-year private college jumped to $30,367 this school year, the first time the average has broken the $30,000 mark.

As they have for the past 11 years, average college costs rose faster than inflation, according to the latest report from the College Board, a non-profit association of 4,500 schools, colleges and universities.

The rate of growth in tuition at four-year private colleges was the same as last year—5.9 percent—and the average tuition reached $22,218.

Of course college costs don't just end at tuition. Room and board costs grew at around 5 percent for both public and private schools this year, with public schools at $6,960 and private schools $8,149 a year.

With room and board, four-year public colleges average $12,796 for in-state residents.

College Costs

	Tuition	Total Cost
Four-year public	$5,836	$12,796
Four-year private	$22,218	$30,367

Source: CollegeBoard.

—Rob Kelley

Source: CNNMoney.com, October 27, 2006.

Analysis: Tuition increases reduce the real income of students. How much you suffer from inflation depends on what happens to the prices of the products you purchase.

Financial Markets

Chapter 32 emphasizes the *economic* rather than the institutional role of financial markets, a topic rarely found in competing texts. The stock and bond markets are viewed as arbiters of risk and mechanisms of resource allocation. The mechanisms of present value discounting are also covered. The chapter starts with the financing of Columbus's New World expedition and ends with a look at the role today's venture capitalists play in promoting growth and technology (highlighting Google's IPO).

Real Companies, Real Products

Although real-world content is a general attribute of *The Economy Today,* the level of detail in the micro section is truly exceptional. Table 25.2 (p. 512) offers concentration ratios for specific *products* (e.g., video game consoles), not the abstract industries (e.g., electronic equipment) that inhabit other texts. No other text provides such specific data, though this is the kind of detail that students can relate to. The oligopoly chapter (25) reviews a slew of recent price-fixing cases (music CDs, perfume, auction houses) and mergers. The chapter on monopolistic competition (26) starts with an examination of Starbucks and ends with a look at the growing market for "branded" bottled waters. Students will recognize these names and absorb the principles of market structure. Baseball fans will gain a greater appreciation of labor-demand principles after examining the multimillion-dollar salary of New York Yankees third baseman Alex Rodriguez.

> Another highly concentrated industry that advertises heavily is the $10 billion-per-year breakfast cereals industry. Although the Federal Trade Commission has suggested that "a corn flake is a corn flake no matter who makes it," the four firms (Kellogg, General Mills, Philip Morris, and Quaker Oats) that supply more than 90 percent of all ready-to-eat breakfast cereals spend over $400 million a year—about $1 per box!—to convince consumers otherwise. During the last 20 years, more than 200 brands of cereal have been marketed by these companies. As the FTC has documented, the four companies "produce basically similar RTE [ready-to-eat] cereals, and then emphasize and exaggerate trivial variations such as color and shape. . . . [They] employ trade-marks to conceal such basic similarities and to differentiate cereal brands."[3]

DISTINCTIVE INTERNATIONAL

The global economy runs through every chapter of *The Economy Today.*

World Views

The most visible evidence of this globalism is in the 78 World View boxes that are distributed throughout the text. As noted earlier, these boxed illustrations offer specific global illustrations of basic principles. To facilitate their use, every World View has a brief caption that highlights the theoretical relevance of the example. The *Test Bank* and Student Problem Set also offer questions based on the World Views.

Global Macro

As noted earlier, Chapter 18 offers a unique global perspective on domestic macro policy. The global macro chapter is intended as a substitute for the traditional trade and finance chapters. It is designed for instructors who want to offer some international perspectives in the macro course but don't have time to cover trade and finance theory. In courses with more scope for international coverage, the global macro chapter can be used as a capstone to the more traditional chapters.

Vested Trade Interests

Consistent with the reality-based content of the entire text, the discussions of trade and finance theory go beyond basic principles to policy trade-offs and constraints. It's impossible to make sense of trade policy without recognizing the vested interests that battle trade principles. Chapters 35 and 36 emphasize that there are both winners and losers associated with every change in trade flows or exchange rates. Because vested interests are typically highly concentrated and well organized, they can often bend trade rules and flows to their advantage. Trade disputes over Mexican trucks, "dumped" steel, and sugar quotas help illustrate the realities of trade policy. The ongoing protest against the World Trade Organization is also assessed in terms of competing interests.

Global Poverty

The new chapter (37) on global poverty reminds us all that economic performance is of paramount importance to the well-being of the global community. Unfortunately, population growth has exceeded GDP growth in many nations, driving over a billion people to the edge of Malthusian subsistence. Chapter 37 explores the depths of that deprivation, examines its causes, and surveys alternative policy strategies for fulfilling the World Bank's "Millennium Goal" of halving the incidence of global poverty.

DISTINCTIVE WEB SUPPORT

The eleventh edition of *The Economy Today* continues to set the pace for Web applications and support of the principles course.

WebNotes

A mini Web site directory is provided in each chapter's marginal WebNotes. These URLs aren't random picks; they were selected because they let students extend and update adjacent in-text discussions.

www.mhhe.com/economics/schiller11e

The Economy Today's Web site now includes even more features that both instructors and students will find engaging and instructive. The Online Learning Center is user-friendly. Upon entering the site at **www.mhhe.com/schiller11e,** students and instructors will find three separate book covers: one for *The Economy Today,* one for *The Macroeconomy Today,* and one for *The Microeconomy Today.* By clicking on the appropriate cover, users will link to a specific site for the version of the book they are using.

Proceeding into the Student Center, students will find lots of brand-new interactive study material. Raymond E. Polchow of Zane State College has revised 20 self-grading multiple-choice and five true-or-false questions per chapter, which are ideal for self-quizzing before a test. In addition, Professor Polchow has enhanced the supplementary Student Problem Set for the site by creating extra problems for added practice. Professors can assign the additional 10 problems per chapter as homework or students can access them for additional skills practice. Answers can be found on the password-protected Instructor's Edition of the Web site. Professor Polchow also revised and created new Web Activities for each chapter to accompany 15 Collaborative Activities, unique to the site. On top of all that, students have access to my periodic NewsFlashes, a User's Manual for the site, and links to Econ Graph Kit, Economics on the Web, and Career Opportunities. They will also have the option of purchasing PowerWeb access with their book, which supplies them with three to five news articles per week on the topics they are studying.

The password-protected Instructor Center includes some wonderful resources for instructors who want to include more interactive student activities in their courses. The downloadable *Instructor's Manual* and PowerPoints, auxiliary Student Problem Set and answers, and Instructor's Notes for the Collaborative Activities and Web Activities are available to provide guidance for instructors who collect these assignments and grade them. John Min of Northern Virginia Community College has created Online Lecture Launchers for each chapter. These interactive PowerPoint presentations highlight current events relevant to key macro, micro, and international topics. They serve as excellent "jumping-off points" for in-class discussion and lectures and will be updated quarterly to provide the most current information.

Premium Content. The Online Learning Center now offers students the opportunity to purchase premium content. Like an electronic study guide, the OLC Premium Content enables students to take pre- and post-tests for each chapter as well as to download Schiller-exclusive iPod content including pod casts by Brad Schiller, narrated PowerPoint presentations, practice quizzes, Paul Solman videos, and chapter summaries—all accessible through the students' MP3 device.

McGraw-Hill's Homework Manager Plus™

McGraw-Hill's Homework Manager Plus is a complete, Web-based solution that includes and expands upon the actual problem sets found at the end of each chapter. It features algorithmic technology that provides a limitless supply of auto-graded assignments and graphing exercises, tied to the learning objectives in the book. McGraw-Hill's Homework Manager can be used for student practice, graded homework assignments, and formal examinations; the results easily integrated with your course management system, including WebCT and Blackboard, or stored in your personalized Homework Manager-provided grade book.

WHAT'S NEW IN THE ELEVENTH

To previous users of *The Economy Today,* all of its distinctive features have become familiar—and, hopefully, welcome. For those instructors already familiar with *The Economy Today,* the more urgent question is, What's new? The answer is *a lot.* By way of brief summary, you may want to note the following:

Global Poverty

The all-new chapter on global poverty should excite and motivate students to learn what makes economies "tick." The photo of Bono from U2 and Eddie Vedder from Pearl Jam at a Live-Aid concert (p. 733) will spark instant recognition and a bit of excitement. Although the chapter has been placed at the end of the text, it can easily be used earlier in the course, even as an introductory issue. To facilitate that flexibility, the chapter emphasizes basic key terms, leaving more advanced concepts for other chapters. There is a lot of descriptive information about the dimensions of global poverty, followed by a survey of growth problems and growth strategies. The Jeff Sachs "Big Money, Big Plan" approach is contrasted with the new emphasis on microfinance.

AD Development

The exclusive use of the AS/AD framework to illustrate Keynesian and other macro theories continues to distinguish *The Economy Today.* In this eleventh edition, more space is devoted to constructing the AD curve from the individual spending components of GDP (see Figure 9.9 on p. 181).

New Economy Tomorrows

The chapter-ending Economy Tomorrow feature continues to challenge students with future-looking applications of core concepts. Many of these have been updated; some are completely new. In Chapter 3, the organ-transplant market is used to illustrate the unintended consequences of government-set price ceilings and the contrast with market-driven outcomes. Chapter 2 offers a first glimpse of the global poverty problem; Chapter 37 peers into the future of alternative strategies for alleviating world poverty.

New In the News

There are 25 all-new In the News applications. In micro, these cover everything from the proposed XM-Sirius Satellite merger (p. 503) to Hawaiian beach closings (p. 569) and Wal-Mart job applicants (p. 601). In macro, they range from consumer dissaving (p. 169) to Hurricane Katrina's impacts on aggregate supply (p. 319) and consumer confidence (p. 175).

New World Views

World Views have also been updated throughout the text; 30 are new to this edition. In macro, these include new World Views on Zimbabwe's 1500 percent inflation (p. 129), the Argentine bank crisis (p. 269), and China's monetary-policy restraint. In micro, new World Views include global competition in flat-panel TVs (p. 472) and India's wireless market (p. 483), OPEC's pricing power (p. 522) and the United Nations' ominous 2007 warning about global warming. In the international section, everything from U.S. nontariff barriers to Mexican trucking (p. 711), to China's burgeoning foreign-exchange reserves (p. 729) and contrasting strategies for fighting global poverty (p. 746) get World View exposure.

Built-in Student Problem Set

The Economy Today's set of arithmetic and graphing problems has proven to be an extremely valuable tool for homework and quizzes. In fact, it has become so widely used that it is now packaged in the text itself, at the back. As before, it offers quantitative and graphing problems (with grids!) explicitly tied to the text, including each chapter's figures, tables, In the News, and World Views. There are more than 100 new problems, as well as improvements to old ones. Answers are in the print *Instructor's Resource Manual,* also available on the password-protected instructor's section of the Web site.

New Questions for Discussion

There are at least 40 new end-of-chapter Questions for Discussion. As always these draw explicitly on the content of their respective chapters, including boxed applications and figures.

Previous WebNotes have been checked for currency and edited as needed. These are designed to enable students to update and extend in-text discussions.

Thorough Updating

Besides all these salient updates, the entire text has been rendered up-to-date with the latest statistics and case studies. ***This unparalleled currency is a distinctive feature of* The Economy Today**.

NEW AND IMPROVED SUPPLEMENTS

Instructor Aids

Test Bank. Linda Wilson and Jane Himarios of the University of Texas at Arlington and Robert Shoffner of Central Piedmont Community College have thoroughly revised the *Test Bank* for the eleventh edition. This team assures a high level of quality and consistency of the test questions and the greatest possible correlation with the content of the text as well as the *Study Guide,* which was prepared by Linda Wilson with Mark Maier. All questions are coded according to chapter learning objectives, AACSB Assurance of Learning, and Bloom's Taxonomy guidelines. The computerized *Test Bank* is available in EZ Test, a flexible and easy-to-use electronic testing program that accommodates a wide range of question types including user-created questions. Tests created in EZ Test can be exported for use with course management systems such as WebCT, BlackBoard, or PageOut. The program is available for Windows, Macintosh, and Linux environments. Test banks are offered in micro and macro versions, each of which contains nearly 4,000 questions including over 200 essay questions.

PowerPoint Presentations. Anthony Zambelli of Cuyamaca College created new presentation slides for the eleventh edition. Developed using Microsoft PowerPoint software, these slides are a step-by-step review of the key points in each of the book's 37 chapters. They are equally useful to the student in the classroom as lecture aids or for personal review at home or the computer lab. The slides use animation to show students how graphs build and shift. Narration to the slides was created by Paul Kubik of Loyola University.

Overhead Transparencies. All of the text's tables and graphs have been reproduced as full-color overhead transparency acetates.

Instructor's Resource Manual. Peggy Pelt of Gulf Coast Community College has prepared the *Instructor's Resource Manual.* The *Instructor's Resource Manual* is available online, and it includes chapter summaries and outlines, "lecture launchers" to stimulate class discussion, and media exercises to extend the analysis. New features include the complete integration of chapter Learning Objectives, AACSB, and Bloom's Taxonomy guidelines.

News Flashes. As up-to-date as *The Economy Today* is, it can't foretell the future. As the future becomes the present, however, I write two-page News Flashes describing major economic events and relating them to specific text references. These News Flashes provide good lecture material and can be copied for student use. Adopters of *The Economy Today* have the option of receiving News Flashes via fax or mail. They're also available on the Schiller Web site. Four to six News Flashes are sent to adopters each year. (Contact your local McGraw-Hill/Irwin sales representative to get on the mailing list.)

Student Aids

At the instructor's discretion, students have access to the News Flashes described above. In addition, the following supplements can facilitate learning.

Built-in Student Problem Set. The built-in *Student Problem Set* is found at the back of every copy of *The Economy Today.* Each chapter has 8 to 10 numerical and graphing problems tied to the content of the text. Graphing grids are provided. The answer blanks are formatted to facilitate grading and all answers are contained in the *Instructor's Resource Manual.* For convenience, the *Student Problem Set* pages are also perforated.

Study Guide. The new *Study Guide* has been completely updated by Linda Wilson and Mark Maier. The *Study Guide* develops quantitative skills and the use of economic terminology, and enhances critical thinking capabilities. Each chapter includes a Quick Review that lists the key points in an easy-to-read bulleted format, Learning Objectives for the chapter, a crossword puzzle using key terms, 10 true-false questions with explanations, 20 multiple-choice questions, problems and applications that relate directly back to the text, and common student errors. Answers to all problems, exercises, and questions are provided at the end of each chapter.

ACKNOWLEDGMENTS

This eleventh edition is unquestionably the finest edition of *The Economy Today,* and I am deeply grateful to all those people who helped develop it. Angela Cimarolli did a superlative job in orchestrating the development process and Douglas Reiner provided energetic and insightful editorial leadership. Harvey Yep, the Project Manager, did an exceptional job in assuring that every page of the text was visually pleasing, properly formatted, error-free, and timely produced. Douglas, Angie, and Harvey are the best production team an author could hope for. The design team, led by Kami Carter, created a lively pallette of colors and features that enhanced *The Economy Today*'s readability. My thanks to all of them and their supporting staff. Also to Eamon Monahan for critical research assistance.

I also want to express my heartfelt thanks to the professors who have shared their reactions (both good and bad) with me. Direct feedback from these users and reviewers has been a great source of continuing improvements in *The Economy Today:*

Reviewers

James L. Allen, Jr.
Wharton County Junior College
Louis H. Amato
University of North Carolina, Charlotte
Nejat Anbarci
Florida International University
Hamid Bastin
Shippensburg University
David Bernotas
University of Georgia
John Bockino
Suffolk County Community College

Peter Boelman
Riverside Community College, Norco
Nancy Brooks
University of Vermont, Burlington
Taggert J. Brooks
University of Wisconsin, La Crosse
M. Neil Browne
Bowling Green State University
J. M. Callan
University of Cincinnati
Regina Cassady
Valencia Community College
Kwang Soo Cheong
Johns Hopkins University
Chul Chung
Georgia Institute of Technology
Joy Clark
Auburn University, Montgomery
Robert H. Collins
University of South Carolina, Lancaster
Barbara Connolly
Westchester Community College
Zach Cronin
Hillsborough Community College
Anthony Davies
Duquesne University
Gregg Davis
Flathead Valley Community College, Kalispell
Diana Denison
Red Rocks Community College
David Doorn
University of Minnesota, Duluth
Eric Drabkin
Hawaii Pacific University, Honolulu
David H. Eaton
Murray State University
Vince Enslein
Clinton Community College
Russell Evans
Oklahoma State University
Nick Feltovich
University of Houston
Kaya Ford
Northern VA Community College
Diana Fortier
Waubonsee Community College
Charles Fraley
Cincinnati State Technical and Community College
William Ganley
Buffalo State College
Lisa Giddings
University of Wisconsin, La Crosse
Scott Gilbert
Southern Illinois University, Carbondale
Stephen Gillespie
George Mason University
Chiara Gratton-Lavoie
Buffalo State College
Homer Guevara, Jr.
Northwest Vista College
Rik Hafer
Southern Illinois University, Edwardsville
Simon Hakim
Temple University
Richard B. Hansen
Hillsborough Community College
Dave Hickman
Frederick Community College
George E. Hoffer
Virginia Commonwealth University
Yu Hsing
Southeastern Louisiana University
Mofidul Islam
Columbia Southern University
Miren Ivankovic
Southern Wesleyan University
Louis Johnston
Saint John's University
Paul Jorgensen
Linn Benton Community College
David E. Kalist
Shippensburg University
Elizabeth Sawyer Kelly
University of Wisconsin, Madison
Kevin Kelley
Northwest Vista College
James Lacey
Hesser College
Daniel Lawson
Drew University
Jose Lopez-Calleja
Florida International University
Georgios Marketakis
Queens College
Matthew Marlin
Duquesne University
Fred May
Trident Technical College
Bill McLean
Oklahoma State University
Michael Meeropol
Western New England College
Stan Mitchell
McLennan Community College
Barbara A. Moore
University of Central Florida

Louise Nordstrom
Nichols College
Alan Osman
Ohio State University, Columbus
Peggy Pelt
Gulf Coast Community College
Michael C. Petrowsky
Glendale Community College
Paul J. Pontillo
Genesee Community College
Daniel Powroznik
Chesapeake College
Prosper Raynold
Miami University of Ohio, Oxford
Mitchell Redlo
Monroe Community College
Micahel Reksulak
Georgia Southern University
Brian Rosario
University of California, Davis
Rochelle Ruffer
Youngstown State University
Julia Sampson
Malone College
William C. Schaniel
University of West Georgia
Ted Scheinman
Mt. Hood Community College
Jerry Schwartz
Broward Community College North
Robert Shoffner
Central Piedmont Community College
Garvin Smith
Daytona Beach Community College, Daytona Beach
Karen J. Smith
Columbia Southern University
Noel S. Smith
Palm Beach Community College, Boca Raton
Carol O. Stivender
University of North Carolina, Charlotte
Daniel A. Talley
Dakota State University
Eric C. Taylor
Central Piedmont Community College
Lea Templer
College of the Canyons
Wendine Thompson-Dawson
University of Utah, Salt Lake City
Mariano Torras
Adelphi University
Brian M. Trinque
The University of Texas, Austin
Joe Turek
Lynchburg College
Nora Underwood
University of Central Florida
Paul R. Watro
Jefferson Community & Technical College
James Wetzel
Virginia Commonwealth University
Katherine Willey Wolfe
University of Pittsburgh, Pittsburgh
Andrea Zanter
Hillsborough Community College

Finally, I'd like to thank all the professors and students who are going to use *The Economy Today* as an introduction to economics principles. I welcome any responses (even the bad ones) you'd like to pass on for future editions.

—Bradley R. Schiller

AACSB STATEMENT

The McGraw-Hill Companies is a proud corporate member of AACSB International. Recognizing the importance and value of AACSB accreditation, the author of *The Economy Today* has linked select questions in the test bank to the general knowledge and skill guidelines found in the AACSB standards for business accreditation.

The statements contained in *The Economy Today* are provided only as a guide for the users of this text. The AACSB leaves content coverage and assessment clearly within the realm and control of individual schools, the mission of the school, and the faculty. The AACSB also charges schools with the obligation of doing assessment against their own content and learning goals. While *The Economy Today* and its teaching package make no claim of any specific AACSB qualification or evaluation, this eleventh edition identifies select questions according to the six general knowledge and skills areas. There are, of course, many suitable questions within the test bank, the text, and the teaching package that may also be used as "standards" for your course.

CONTENTS IN BRIEF

CONTENTS

PART 7: POLICY CONSTRAINTS

PART 8: PRODUCT MARKETS: THE BASICS

PART 9: MARKET STRUCTURE

CHAPTER 37: GLOBAL POVERTY 733

IN THE NEWS BOXES

WORLD VIEW BOXES

Rank	Country	2006 GDP Estimate (in billions)
	World's Largest Economies	
1	United States	$ 12,980
2	European Union	$ 12,820
3	China	$ 10,000
4	Japan	$ 4,220
5	India	$ 4,042
6	Germany	$ 2,585
7	United Kingdom	$ 1,903
8	France	$ 1,871
9	Italy	$ 1,727
10	Russia	$ 1,723
11	Brazil	$ 1,616
12	Korea, South	$ 1,180
13	Canada	$ 1,165
14	Mexico	$ 1,134
15	Spain	$ 1,070
16	Indonesia	$ 935
17	Taiwan	$ 668
18	Australia	$ 666
19	Turkey	$ 627
20	Iran	$ 610
21	Argentina	$ 599
22	Thailand	$ 585
23	South Africa	$ 576
24	Poland	$ 542
25	Netherlands	$ 512
26	Philippines	$ 443
27	Pakistan	$ 427
28	Saudi Arabia	$ 374
29	Colombia	$ 366
30	Ukraine	$ 355
31	Bangladesh	$ 330
32	Belgium	$ 330
33	Egypt	$ 328
34	Malaysia	$ 308
35	Sweden	$ 285
36	Austria	$ 279
37	Vietnam	$ 258
38	Algeria	$ 253
39	Hong Kong	$ 253
40	Switzerland	$ 252
	World's Smallest Economies	
219	Anguilla	$ 0.110
220	Falkland Islands (Islas Malvinas)	$ 0.085
221	Nauru	$ 0.070
222	Wallis and Futuna	$ 0.070
223	Saint Pierre and Miquelon	$ 0.052
224	Montserrat	$ 0.032
225	Saint Helena	$ 0.020
226	Tuvalu	$ 0.017
227	Niue	$ 0.008
228	Tokelau	$ 0.002

Source: CIA, *The World Factbook*. GDP measured in purchasing power parity; estimates for smallest nations updated by author.

Analysis: National economies vary greatly in size (i.e., total output produced).

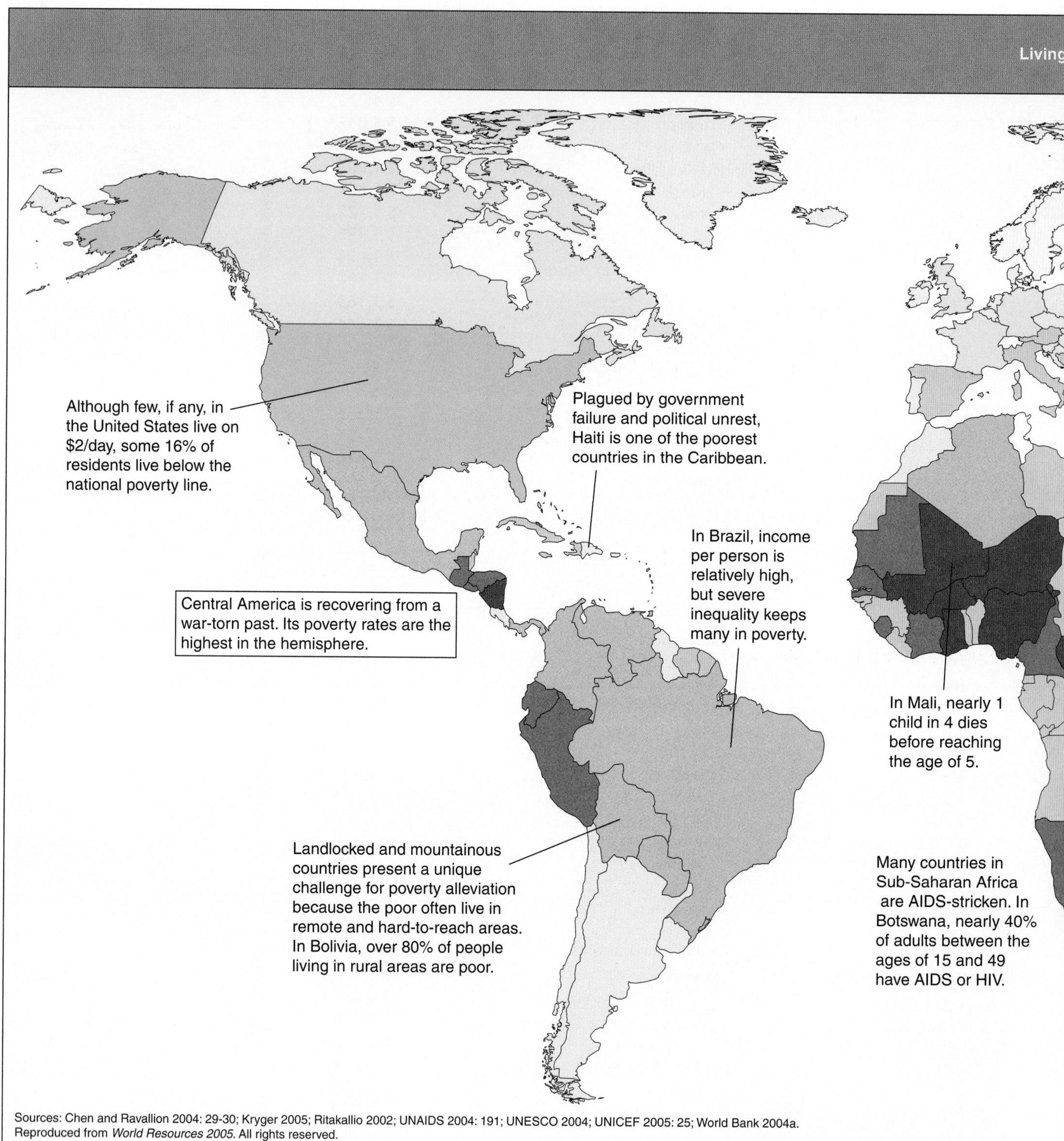

Living
Although few, if any, in the United States live on $2/day, some 16% of residents live below the national poverty line.
Plagued by government failure and political unrest, Haiti is one of the poorest countries in the Caribbean.
In Brazil, income per person is relatively high, but severe inequality keeps many in poverty.
Central America is recovering from a war-torn past. Its poverty rates are the highest in the hemisphere.
In Mali, nearly 1 child in 4 dies before reaching the age of 5.
Landlocked and mountainous countries present a unique challenge for poverty alleviation because the poor often live in remote and hard-to-reach areas. In Bolivia, over 80% of people living in rural areas are poor.
Many countries in Sub-Saharan Africa are AIDS-stricken. In Botswana, nearly 40% of adults between the ages of 15 and 49 have AIDS or HIV.
Sources: Chen and Ravallion 2004: 29-30; Kryger 2005; Ritakallio 2002; UNAIDS 2004: 191; UNESCO 2004; UNICEF 2005: 25; World Bank 2004a.
Reproduced from *World Resources 2005*. All rights reserved.

Analysis: Poverty is distributed unevenly across the world.

Per Day

Percentage of People Living Under $2/day

- < 15%
- 15-35%
- 35-75%
- > 75%
- No Data

Poverty Rates in Developed Countries

- < 4%
- 5-12%
- 13-18%

Much of Eastern Europe is still in transition from Soviet rule. Poverty exists in countries where it was extremely rare 20 years ago.

No poverty data are available for Afghanistan, where only 5% of rural residents have access to improved sanitation.

China has seen 300 million people emerge from poverty in the last two decades. However, these gains are largely in the east, close to the coast

In the Middle East, gender inequality remains an obstacle to growth. For example, 70% of men in Yemen are literate, compared with only 29% of women.

India is home to the most people living on an income of less than $2/day, over 800 million.

Some countries, such as Somalia, are mired in conflict, and accurate data on human well-being cannot be collected.

Sub-Saharan Africa remains the biggest challenge in poverty alleviation. More than 2/3 of all inhabitants are poor.

Poverty in Australia ranges widely by locale–from 2% to 15%. The nationwide average is 9%.

Analysis: International trade is a vital part of the global economy.

Rank	Country	2006 Estimate (in billions)
	World's Largest Exporters	
1	European Union	$ 1,330
2	Germany	$ 1,133
3	United States	$ 1,024
4	China	$ 974
5	Hong Kong	$ 611
6	Japan	$ 590
7	France	$ 490
8	United Kingdom	$ 468
9	Italy	$ 450
10	Netherlands	$ 413
11	Canada	$ 405
12	Belgium	$ 335
13	Korea, South	$ 326
14	Russia	$ 317
15	Singapore	$ 283
16	Mexico	$ 248
17	Spain	$ 222
18	Taiwan	$ 215
19	Saudi Arabia	$ 204
20	Sweden	$ 173
	World's Largest Importers	
1	United States	$ 1,869
2	European Union	$ 1,466
3	Germany	$ 916
4	China	$ 777
5	United Kingdom	$ 603
6	France	$ 529
7	Japan	$ 524
8	Italy	$ 445
9	Netherlands	$ 373
10	Canada	$ 353
11	Belgium	$ 333
12	Hong Kong	$ 329
13	Spain	$ 324
14	Korea, South	$ 309
15	Mexico	$ 253
16	Singapore	$ 246
17	Taiwan	$ 205
18	India	$ 187
19	Russia	$ 171
20	Switzerland	$ 162

Source: CIA, *The World Factbook*. Exports and Imports

PART 1 The Economic Challenge

People around the world want a better life. Whether rich or poor, everyone strives for a higher standard of living. Ultimately, the performance of the economy will determine who attains that goal.

These first few chapters examine how the *limits* to output are determined and how the interplay of market forces and government intervention utilize and expand those limits.

1

Economics: The Core Issues

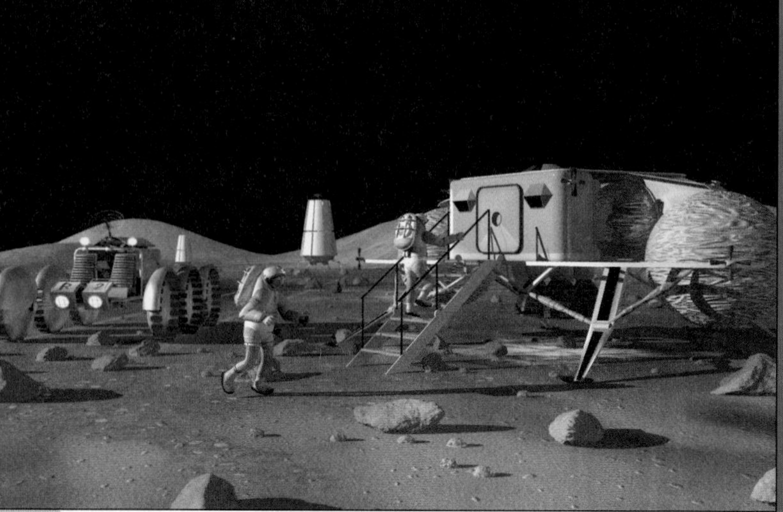

LEARNING OBJECTIVES

After reading this chapter, you should know:

LO1. The role scarcity plays in defining economic choices.

LO2. The core economic issues that nations must resolve.

LO3. How nations resolve these issues.

Water was in the headlines a lot in early 2007. The good news was that NASA had discovered traces of water on Mars, raising the possibility of life on that planet. The bad news was that the United Nations discovered that millions of people here on Earth die each year because they don't have access to clean water. NASA used the good news to jump-start a space program that will put a permanent human settlement on the moon by 2020 (see World View). The United Nations used its bad news to warn that 135 million humans will die of water-related diseases by the year 2020.

These are both major economic stories. To colonize the moon, we'll have to mobilize over $100 billion of resources and the very best technologies. To bring safe water and sanitation to the world's poorest inhabitants, we'll likewise need billions of dollars' worth of land, labor, and capital, together with the best available technologies.

What makes these problems emphatically *economic* issues is their common dependence on the use of scarce resources. The list of projects we want to complete is always longer than the amount of money, resources, or time we have available. That forces us to make difficult choices about how best to use our resources—whether it's a *global* choice between colonizing the moon or building water systems or a *personal* choice about how best to spend the rest of the day.

In this first chapter we explore the nature of scarcity and the kinds of choices it forces us to make. As we'll see, ***three core issues must be resolved:***

- ***WHAT to produce with our limited resources.***
- ***HOW to produce the goods and services we select.***
- ***FOR WHOM goods and services are produced;*** that is, who should get them.

We also have to decide *who* should answer these questions. Should we let market participants decide how much water to supply and who gets it? Or should the government intervene to assure adequate water supplies for everyone? Should people take care of their own health and retirement, or should the government provide a safety net of health care and pensions? Should the government regulate airfares or let the airlines set prices? Should Microsoft decide what features get included in a computer's operating system, or should the government make that decision? Should interest rates be set by private banks alone, or should the government try to control interest rates? The battle over *who* should answer the core questions is often as contentious as the questions themselves.

WORLD VIEW

NASA Plans Lunar Outpost

NASA unveiled plans yesterday to set up a small and ultimately self-sustaining settlement of astronauts at the south pole of the moon sometime around 2020—the first step in an ambitious plan to resume manned exploration of the solar system.

The long-awaited proposal envisions initial stays of a week by four-person crews, followed by gradually longer visits until power and other supplies are in place to make a permanent presence possible by 2024.

The effort was presented as an unprecedented mission to learn about the moon and places beyond, as well as an integral part of a long-range plan to send astronauts to Mars. The moon settlement would ultimately be a way station for space travelers headed onward, and would provide not only a haven but also hydrogen and oxygen mined from the lunar surface to make water and rocket fuel.

—Marc Kaufman

Source: *Washington Post,* December 5, 2006, p. A01. **© 2006, The Washington Post, excerpted with permission.**

Analysis: The National Aeronautics and Space Administration (NASA) plans to spend $100 billion to establish a manned station on the moon, then continue on to Mars. What are the opportunity costs of such a venture?

THE ECONOMY IS US

To learn how the economy works, let's start with a simple truth: *The economy is us.* "The economy" is simply an abstraction referring to the grand sum of all our production and consumption activities. What we collectively produce is what the economy produces; what we collectively consume is what the economy consumes. In this sense, the concept of "the economy" is no more difficult than the concept of "the family." If someone tells you that the Jones family has an annual income of $42,000, you know that the reference is to the collective earnings of all the Joneses. Likewise, when someone reports that the nation's income is $14 trillion per year—as it now is—we should recognize that the reference is to the grand total of everyone's income. If we work fewer hours or get paid less, both family income *and* national income decline. The "meaningless statistics" (see accompanying cartoon) often cited in the news are just a summary of our collective market behavior.

The same relationship between individual behavior and aggregate behavior applies to specific outputs. If we as individuals insist on driving cars rather than taking public

"Meaningless statistics were up one-point-five per cent this month over last month."

Analysis: Many people think of economics as dull statistics. But economics is really about human behavior—how people decide to use scarce resources and how those decisions affect market outcomes.

transportation, the economy will produce millions of cars each year and consume vast quantities of oil. In a slightly different way, the economy produces billions of dollars of military hardware to satisfy our desire for national defense. In each case, the output of the economy reflects the collective behavior of the 300 million individuals who participate in the U.S. economy.

We may not always be happy with the output of the economy. But we can't ignore the link between individual action and collective outcomes. If the highways are clogged and the air is polluted, we can't blame someone else for the transportation choices we made. If we're disturbed by the size of our military arsenal, we must still accept responsibility for our choices (or nonchoices, if we failed to vote). In either case, we continue to have the option of reallocating our resources. We can create a different outcome the next day, month, or year.

SCARCITY: THE CORE PROBLEM

Although we can change economic outcomes, we can't have everything we want. If you go to the mall with $20 in your pocket, you can buy only so much. The money in your pocket sets a *limit* to your spending.

The output of the entire economy is also limited. The limits in this case are set not by money but by the resources available for producing goods and services. Everyone wants more housing, new schools, better transit systems, and a new car. We also want to explore space and bring safe water to the world's poor. But even a country as rich as the United States can't produce everything people want. So, like every other nation, we have to grapple with the core problem of **scarcity**—the fact that there aren't enough resources available to satisfy all our desires.

scarcity: Lack of enough resources to satisfy all desired uses of those resources.

Factors of Production

factors of production: Resource inputs used to produce goods and services, such as land, labor, capital, and entrepreneurship.

The resources used to produce goods and services are called **factors of production.** ***The four basic factors of production are***

- ***Land***
- ***Labor***
- ***Capital***
- ***Entrepreneurship***

These are the *inputs* needed to produce desired *outputs.* To produce this textbook, for example, we needed paper, printing presses, a building, and lots of labor. We also needed people with good ideas who could put it together. To produce the education you're getting in this class, we need not only a textbook but a classroom, a teacher, a blackboard, and maybe a computer as well. Without factors of production, we simply can't produce anything.

Land. The first factor of production, land, refers not just to the ground but to all natural resources. Crude oil, water, air, and minerals are all included in our concept of "land."

Labor. Labor too has several dimensions. It's not simply a question of how many bodies there are. When we speak of labor as a factor of production, we refer to the skills and abilities to produce goods and services. Hence, both the quantity and the quality of human resources are included in the "labor" factor.

capital: Final goods produced for use in the production of other goods, e.g., equipment, structures.

Capital. The third factor of production is capital. In economics the term **capital** refers to final goods produced for use in further production. The residents of fishing villages in southern Thailand, for example, braid huge fishing nets. The sole purpose of these nets is to catch more fish. The nets themselves become a factor of production in obtaining the final goods (fish) that people desire. Thus, they're regarded as *capital.* Blast furnaces used to make steel and desks used to equip offices are also capital inputs.

Entrepreneurship. The more land, labor, and capital available, the greater the amount of potential output. A farmer with 10,000 acres, 12 employees, and six tractors can grow more crops than a farmer with half those resources. But there's no guarantee that he will. The farmer with fewer resources may have better ideas about what to plant, when to irrigate, or how to harvest the crops. ***It's not just a matter of what resources you have but also of how well you use them.*** This is where the fourth factor of production—**entrepreneurship**—comes in. The entrepreneur is the person who sees the opportunity for new or better products and brings together the resources needed for producing them. If it weren't for entrepreneurs, Thai fishermen would still be using sticks to catch fish. Without entrepreneurship, farmers would still be milking their cows by hand. If someone hadn't thought of a way to miniaturize electronic circuits, you wouldn't have a cell phone.

entrepreneurship: The assembling of resources to produce new or improved products and technologies.

The role of entrepreneurs in economic progress is a key issue in the market versus government debate. The Austrian economist Joseph Schumpeter argued that free markets unleash the "animal spirits" of entrepreneurs, propelling innovation, technology, and growth. Critics of government regulation argue that government interference in the marketplace, however well intentioned, tends to stifle those very same animal spirits.

Limits to Output

No matter how an economy is organized, there's a limit to how much it can produce. The most evident limit is the amount of resources available for producing goods and services. One reason the United States can produce so much is that it has over 3 *million* acres of land. Tonga, with less than 500 acres of land, will never produce as much. The U.S. also has a population of over 300 million people. That's a lot less than China (1.3 *billion*), but far larger than 200 other nations (Tonga has a population of less than 125,000). So an abundance of "raw" resources gives us the potential to produce a lot of output. But that greater production capacity isn't enough to satisfy all our desires. We're constantly scrambling for more resources to build more houses, make better movies, and colonize the moon. With so many desires, how can we possibly feed the world's poor and bring them safe water at the same time?

The science of **economics** helps us frame these choices. In a nutshell, economics is the study of how people use scarce resources. How do you decide how much time to spend studying? How does Google decide how many workers to hire? How does Chrysler decide whether to use its factories to produce sports utility vehicles or sedans? What share of a nation's resources should be devoted to space exploration, the delivery of health care services, or pollution control? In every instance, alternative ways of using scarce labor, land, and capital resources are available, and we have to choose one use over another.

economics: The study of how best to allocate scarce resources among competing uses.

Opportunity Costs

The earthly sacrifices implied by an expedition to Mars go to the heart of the decision-making dilemma. ***Every time we use scarce resources in one way, we give up the opportunity to use them in other ways.*** If we use more resources to explore space, we have fewer resources available for producing earthly goods. The forgone earthly goods represent the **opportunity costs** of a Mars expedition. ***Opportunity cost is what is given up to get something else.*** Even a so-called free lunch has an opportunity cost (see cartoon). The resources

opportunity cost: The most desired goods or services that are forgone to obtain something else.

"There's no such thing as a free lunch."

Analysis: All goods and services have an opportunity cost. Even the resources used to produce a "free lunch" could have been used to produce something else.

used to produce the lunch could have been used to produce something else. A trip to Mars has a much higher opportunity cost.

Your economics class also has an opportunity cost. The building space used for your economics class can't be used to show movies at the same time. Your professor can't lecture (produce education) and repair motorcycles simultaneously. The decision to use these scarce resources (capital, labor) for an economics class implies producing less of other goods.

Even reading this book is costly. That cost is not measured in dollars and cents. The true (economic) cost is, instead, measured in terms of some alternative activity. What would you like to be doing right now? The more time you spend reading this book, the less time you have available for that alternative use of your time. The opportunity cost of reading this text is the best alternative use of your scarce time. If you are missing your favorite TV show, we'd say that show is the opportunity cost of reading this book. It is what you gave up to do this assignment. Hopefully, the benefits you get from studying will outweigh that cost. Otherwise this wouldn't be the best way to use your scarce time.

Guns vs. Butter

One of the persistent national choices about resource use entails defense spending. After the September 11, 2001, terrorist attacks on the World Trade Center and Pentagon, American citizens overwhelmingly favored an increase in military spending. But where were the extra resources going to come from? Any resources employed in national defense must be taken from other industries. The 1.4 million men and women already serving in the armed forces aren't available to build schools, program computers, or teach economics. Similarly, the land, labor, capital, and entrepreneurship devoted to producing military hardware aren't available for producing civilian goods. An *increase* in national defense implies still more sacrifices of civilian goods and services. This is the "guns versus butter" dilemma that all nations confront.

webnote

To see how the share of output allocated to national defense has changed in recent decades, visit the Congressional Budget Office Web site at www.cbo.gov and search for "discretionary outlays."

PRODUCTION POSSIBILITIES

The opportunity costs implied by our every choice can be illustrated easily. Suppose a nation can produce only two goods, trucks and tanks. To keep things simple, assume that labor (workers) is the only factor of production needed to produce either good. Although other factors of production (land, machinery) are also needed in actual production, ignoring them for the moment does no harm. Let us assume further that we have a total of only 10 workers available per day to produce either trucks or tanks. Our initial problem is to determine the *limits* of output. How many trucks or tanks *can* be produced in a day with available resources?

Before going any further, notice how opportunity costs will affect the answer. If we use all 10 workers to produce trucks, no labor will be available to assemble tanks. In this case, forgone tanks would become the *opportunity cost* of a decision to employ all our resources in truck production.

We still don't know how many trucks could be produced with 10 workers or exactly how many tanks would be forgone by such a decision. To get these answers, we need more details about the production processes involved—specifically, how many workers are required to manufacture trucks or tanks.

The Production Possibilities Curve

production possibilities: The alternative combinations of final goods and services that could be produced in a given time period with all available resources and technology.

Table 1.1 summarizes the hypothetical choices, or **production possibilities,** that we confront in this case. Row *A* of the table shows the consequences of a decision to produce trucks only. With 10 workers available and a labor requirement of 2 workers per truck, we can manufacture a maximum of five trucks per day. By so doing, however, we use all available workers, leaving none for tank assembly. If we want tanks, we have to cut back on truck production; this is the essential choice we must make.

The remainder of Table 1.1 describes the full range of production choices. By cutting back truck production from five to four trucks per day (row *B*), we reduce labor use from 10 workers to 8. That leaves 2 workers available for other uses.

TABLE 1.1
Production Possibilities Schedule

As long as resources are limited, their use entails an opportunity cost. In this case, resources (labor) used to produce trucks can't be used for tank assembly at the same time. Hence, the forgone tanks are the opportunity cost of additional trucks. If all our resources were used to produce trucks (row *A*), no tanks could be assembled.

	Truck Production							Tank Production			
	Total Available Labor	Output of Trucks per Day	×	Labor Needed per Truck	=	Total Labor Required for Trucks	Labor Not Used for Trucks	Potential Output of Tanks per Day		Increase in Tank Output
A	10	5		2		10	0	0		
B	10	4		2		8	2	2.0	>	2.0
C	10	3		2		6	4	3.0	>	1.0
D	10	2		2		4	6	3.8	>	0.8
E	10	1		2		2	8	4.5	>	0.7
F	10	0		2		0	10	5.0	>	0.5

If we employ these remaining 2 workers to assemble tanks, we can build two tanks a day. We would then end up with four trucks and two tanks per day. What's the opportunity cost of these two tanks? It's the one additional truck (the fifth truck) that we could have produced but didn't.

As we proceed down the rows of Table 1.1, the nature of opportunity costs becomes apparent. Each additional tank built implies the loss (opportunity cost) of truck output. Likewise, every truck produced implies the loss of some tank output.

These trade-offs between truck and tank production are illustrated in the production possibilities curve of Figure 1.1. ***Each point on the production possibilities curve depicts an alternative mix of output*** that could be produced. In this case, each point represents a

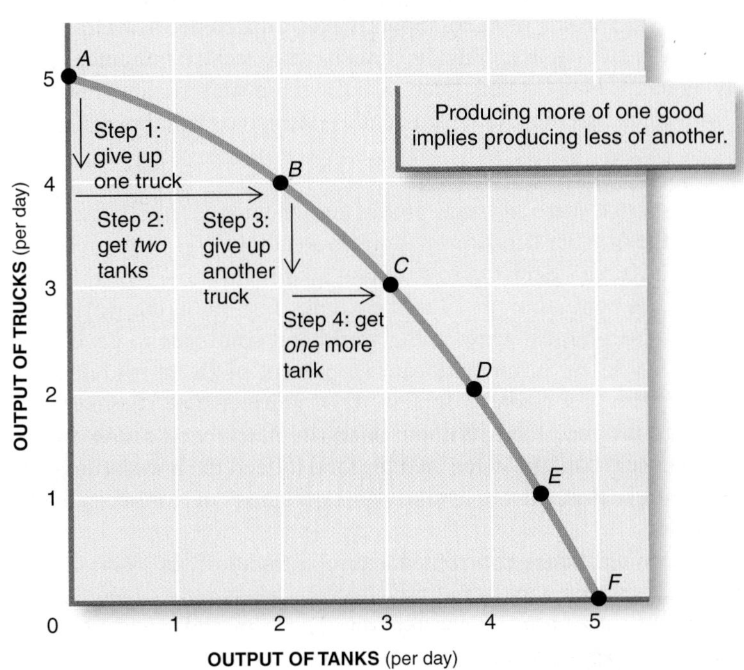

FIGURE 1.1
A Production Possibilities Curve

A production possibilities curve (PPC) describes the various output combinations that could be produced in a given time period with available resources and technology. It represents a menu of output choices an economy confronts.

Point *B* indicates that we could produce a *combination* of four trucks and two tanks per day. By producing one less truck, we could assemble a third tank, and thus move to point *C*.

Points *A, D, E,* and *F* illustrate still other output combinations that could be produced. This curve is a graphic illustration of the production possibilities schedule in Table 1.1.

different combination of trucks and tanks that we could produce in a single day using all available resources (labor in this case).

Notice in particular how points *A* through *F* in Figure 1.1 represent the choices described in each row of Table 1.1. At point *A*, we're producing five trucks per day and no tanks. As we move down the curve from point *A* to point *B*, truck production drops from five to four vehicles per day while tank assembly increases from zero to two. In other words, we're giving up one truck to get two tanks assembled. The opportunity cost of those tanks is one truck that is given up. A production possibilities curve, then, is simply a graphic summary of production possibilities, as described in Table 1.1. It illustrates the alternative goods and services we could produce and the implied opportunity costs of each choice. In other words, ***the production possibilities curve illustrates two essential principles:***

- ***Scarce resources.*** There's a limit to the amount we can produce in a given time period with available resources and technology.
- ***Opportunity costs.*** We can obtain additional quantities of any desired good only by reducing the potential production of another good.

Increasing Opportunity Costs

The shape of the production possibilities curve reflects another limitation on our choices. Notice how opportunity costs increase as we move along the production possibilities curve. When we cut truck output from five to four (step 1, Figure 1.1), we get two tanks (step 2). When we cut truck production further, however (step 3), we get only one tank per truck given up (step 4). The opportunity cost of tank production is increasing. This process of increasing opportunity cost continues. By the time we give up the last truck (row *F*), tank output increases by only 0.5: We get only half a tank for the last truck given up. These increases in opportunity cost are reflected in the outward bend of the production possibilities curve.

Why do opportunity costs increase? Mostly because it's difficult to move resources from one industry to another. It's easy to transform trucks to tanks on a blackboard. In the real world, however, resources don't adapt so easily. Workers who assemble trucks may not have the same skills for tank assembly. As we continue to transfer labor from one industry to the other, we start getting fewer tanks for every truck we give up.

The difficulties entailed in transferring labor skills, capital, and entrepreneurship from one industry to another are so universal that we often speak of the *law* of *increasing opportunity cost.* This law says that we must give up ever-increasing quantities of other goods and services in order to get more of a particular good. The law isn't based solely on the limited versatility of individual workers. The *mix* of factor inputs makes a difference as well. Truck assembly requires less capital than tank assembly. In a pinch, wheels can be mounted on a truck almost completely by hand, whereas tank treads require more sophisticated machinery. As we move labor from truck assembly to tank assembly, available capital may restrict our output capabilities.

The Cost of North Korea's Military

The kind of opportunity costs that arise in truck production or tank assembly takes on even greater significance in the broader decisions nations make about WHAT to produce. Consider, for example, North Korea's decision to maintain a large military. North Korea is a relatively small country: Its population of 24 million ranks fortieth in the world. Yet North Korea maintains the fourth-largest army in the world and continues to develop a nuclear weapons capability. To do so, it must allocate 16 percent of all its resources to feeding, clothing, and equipping its military forces. As a consequence, there aren't enough resources available to produce food. Without adequate machinery, seeds, fertilizer, or irrigation, Korea's farmers can't produce enough food to feed the population (see World View). As Figure 1.2 illustrates, the opportunity cost of "guns" in Korea is a lot of needed "butter."

During World War II, the United States confronted a similar trade-off. In 1944, nearly 40 percent of all U.S. output was devoted to the military. Civilian goods were so scarce that they had to be rationed. Staples like butter, sugar, and gasoline were doled out in small quantities. Even golf balls were rationed. In North Korea, golf balls would be a luxury even

webnote

The International Institute for Strategic Studies compiles data on national military forces (www.iiss.org). To determine what percentage of a nation's population is in the armed forces, try the Central Intelligence Agency (www.odci.gov/cia/publications/factbook).

WORLD VIEW

Food Shortages Plague N. Korea

BEIJING, Feb. 13—A severe food shortage has crippled the U.N. feeding program that sustains North Korea's most vulnerable and undernourished people, according to Masood Hyder, the U.N. humanitarian aid coordinator and World Food Program representative in Pyongyang.

He said his organization can now feed fewer than 100,000 of the 6.5 million people it normally does, many of them kindergarten-age children and pregnant women who cannot get what they need to stay healthy from the country's distribution system. . . .

Food shortages already produce stunted growth in four out of 10 North Korean students and allow pregnant women to gain only half of the 22 pounds they are expected to gain to give birth to healthy babies.

Some orphanages have started serving two meals a day instead of three because of the shortages, Masood said.

—Edward Cody

Source: *Washington Post,* February 14, 2004. © **2004 The Washington Post, excerpted with permission.** www.washingtonpost.com

North Korea Expanding Missile Programs

Despite international pressure to curtail its missile program, North Korea is building at least two new launch facilities for the medium-range Taepo Dong 1 and has stepped up production of short-range missiles, according to U.S. intelligence and diplomatic sources.

The projects, and a conclusion by U.S. intelligence agencies that North Korea intends to test-fire a second missile capable of striking Japan, are inflaming regional tensions, U.S. officials and Korea experts said.

—Dana Priest and Thomas W. Lippman

Source: *Washington Post,* November 20, 1998. © **1998 The Washington Post, excerpted with permission.** www.washingtonpost.com

A/P Wide World

Analysis: North Korea's inability to feed itself is partly due to maintaining its large army: Resources used for the military aren't available for producing food.

without a military buildup. As the share of North Korea's output devoted to the military increased, even basic food production became more difficult.

Figure 1.3 illustrates how other nations divide up available resources between military and civilian production. The $530 billion the United States now spends on national defense absorbs only 4 percent of total output. This made the opportunity costs of the war in Iraq and post-9/11 military buildup less painful.

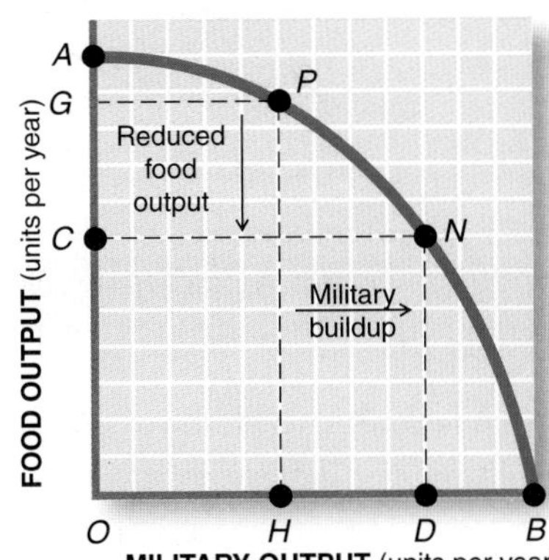

FIGURE 1.2
The Cost of War

North Korea devotes 16 percent of its output to the military. The opportunity cost of this decision is reduced output of food. As the military expands from *OH* to *OD,* food output drops from *OG* to *OC.*

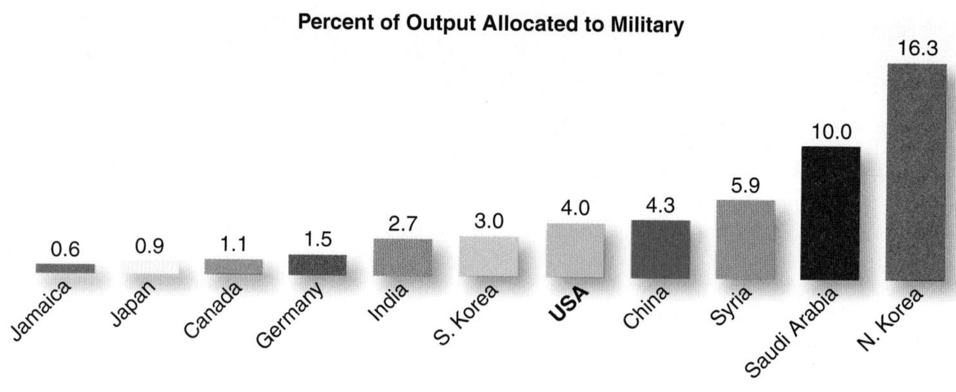

FIGURE 1.3
The Military Share of Output

The share of output allocated to the military is an indication of the opportunity cost of maintaining an army. North Korea has the highest cost, using 16 percent of its resources for military purposes. Although China and the United States have much larger armies, their military *share* of output is much smaller.

Source: U.S. Central Intelligence Agency (2005–2006 data).

Efficiency

Not all of the choices on the production possibilities curve are equally desirable. They are, however, all *efficient*. Efficiency means squeezing *maximum* output out of available resources. Every point of the PPC satisfies this condition. Although the *mix* of output changes as we move around the production possibilities curve (Figures 1.1 and 1.2), at every point we are getting as much *total* output as physically possible. Since **efficiency** in production means simply "getting the most from what you've got," every point on the production possibilities curve is efficient. At every point on the curve we are using all available resources in the best way we know how.

efficiency: Maximum output of a good from the resources used in production.

Inefficiency

There's no guarantee, of course, that we'll always use resources so efficiently. ***A production possibilities curve shows* potential *output, not necessarily* actual *output.*** If we're inefficient, actual output will be less than that potential. This happens. In the real world, workers sometimes loaf on the job. Or they call in sick and go to a baseball game instead of working. Managers don't always give the clearest directions or stay in touch with advancing technology. Even students sometimes fail to put forth their best effort on homework assignments. This kind of slippage can prevent us from achieving maximum production. When that happens, we end up *inside* the PPC rather than *on* it.

Point *Y* in Figure 1.4 illustrates the consequences of inefficient production. At point *Y*, we're producing only three trucks and two tanks. This is less than our potential. We could assemble a third tank without cutting back truck production (point *C*). Or we could get an extra truck without sacrificing any tank output (point *B*). Instead, we're producing *inside* the production possibilities curve at point *Y*. Such inefficiencies plagued centrally planned economies. Government-run factories guaranteed everyone a job regardless of how much output he or she produced. They became bloated bureaucracies; as much as 40 percent of the workers were superfluous. When communism collapsed, many of these factories were "privatized," that is, sold to private investors. The privatized companies were able to fire

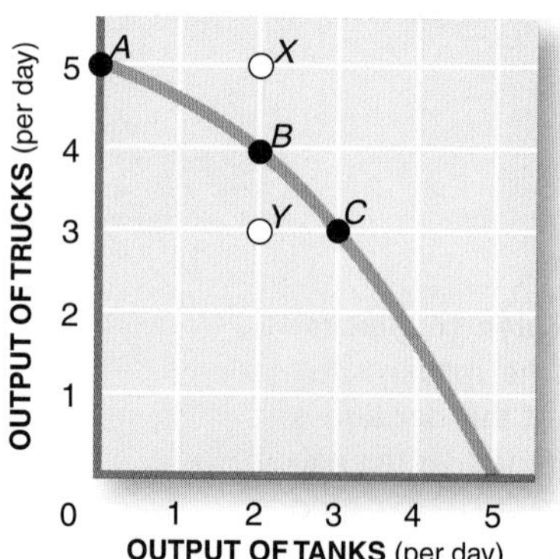

FIGURE 1.4
Points Inside and Outside the PPC Curve

Points outside the production possibilities curve (point *X*) are unattainable with available resources and technology. Points inside the PPC (point *Y*) represent the incomplete use of available resources. Only points on the PPC (*A*, *B*, *C*) represent maximum use of our production capabilities.

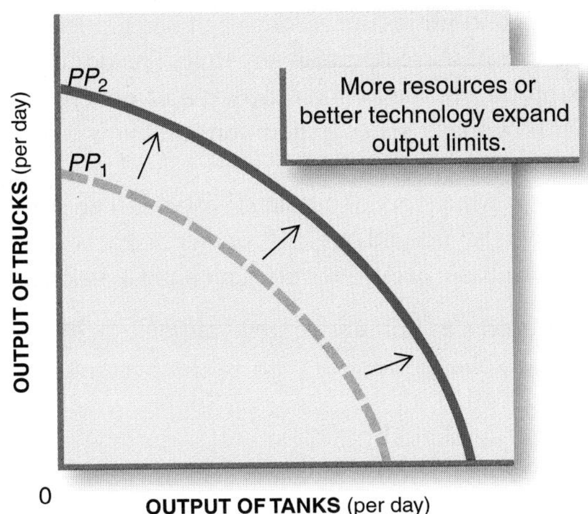

FIGURE 1.5
Growth: Increasing Production Possibilities

A production possibilities curve is based on *available* resources and technology. If more resources or better technology becomes available, production possibilities will increase. This economic growth is illustrated by the *shift* from PP_1 to PP_2.

thousands of workers and *increase* output. Governments in Europe and Latin America have also sold off many of their state-owned enterprises in the hopes of increasing efficiency and reaching the production possibilities curve.

Unemployment

Countries may also end up inside their production possibilities curve if all available resources aren't used. In 2003, for example, as many as 8 million Americans were looking for work each week, but no one hired them. As a result, we were stuck *inside* the PPC, producing less output than we could have. A basic challenge for policymakers is to eliminate unemployment and keep the economy on its production possibilities curve. In 2007, the United States was closer to this goal.

Economic Growth

Figure 1.4 also illustrates an output mix that everyone would welcome. Point *X* lies *outside* the production possibilities curve. It suggests that we could get *more* goods than we're capable of producing! Unfortunately, point *X* is only a mirage: ***All output combinations that lie outside the production possibilities curve are unattainable with available resources and technology.***

Things change, however. Every year, population growth and immigration increase our supply of labor. As we continue building factories and machinery, the stock of available capital also increases. The *quality* of labor and capital also increase when we train workers and pursue new technologies. Entrepreneurs may discover new products or better ways of producing old ones. All these changes increase potential output. This is illustrated in Figure 1.5 by the outward *shift* of the PPC. Before the appearance of new resources or better technology, our production possibilities were limited by the curve PP_1. ***With more resources or better technology, our production possibilities increase.*** This greater capacity to produce is represented by curve PP_2. This outward shift of the production possibilities curve is the essence of **economic growth.** With economic growth, countries can have more guns *and* more butter. Without economic growth, living standards decline as the population grows. This is the problem that plagues some of the world's poorest nations, where population increases every year but output often doesn't (see Table 2.1).

economic growth: An increase in output (real GDP); an expansion of production possibilities.

BASIC DECISIONS

Production possibilities define the output choices that a nation confronts. From these choices every nation must make some basic decisions. As we noted at the beginning of this chapter, the three core economic questions are

- ***WHAT to produce***
- ***HOW to produce***
- ***FOR WHOM to produce***

WHAT

There are millions of points along a production possibilities curve, and each one represents a different mix of output. We can choose only *one* of these points at any time. The point we choose determines what mix of output gets produced. That choice determines how many guns are produced, and how much butter. Or how many space expeditions and how many water-treatment facilities.

The production possibilities curve doesn't tell us which mix of output is best; it just lays out a menu of available choices. It's up to us to pick out the one and only mix of output that will be produced at a given time. This WHAT decision is a basic decision every nation must make.

HOW

Decisions must also be made about HOW to produce. Should we generate electricity by burning coal, smashing atoms, or transforming solar power? Should we harvest ancient forests even if that destroys endangered owls or other animal species? Should we dump municipal and industrial waste into nearby rivers, or should we dispose of it in some other way? Should we use children to harvest crops and stitch clothes or should we use only adult labor? There are lots of different ways of producing goods and services, and someone has to make a decision about which production methods to use. The HOW decision is a question not just of efficiency but of social values as well.

FOR WHOM

After we've decided what to produce and how, we must address a third basic question: FOR WHOM? Who is going to get the output produced? Should everyone get an equal share? Should everyone wear the same clothes and drive identical cars? Should some people get to enjoy seven-course banquets while others forage in garbage cans for food scraps? How should the goods and services an economy produces be distributed? Are we satisfied with the way output is now distributed?

THE MECHANISMS OF CHOICE

Answers to the questions of WHAT, HOW, and FOR WHOM largely define an economy. But who formulates the answers? Who actually decides which goods are produced, what technologies are used, or how incomes are distributed?

The Invisible Hand of a Market Economy

Adam Smith had an answer back in 1776. In his classic work *The Wealth of Nations,* Smith said the "invisible hand" determines what gets produced, how, and for whom. The invisible hand he referred to wasn't a creature from a science fiction movie but, instead, a characterization of the way markets work.

Consider the decision about how many cars to produce in the United States. Who decides to produce over 16 million cars and trucks a year? There's no "auto czar" who dictates production. Not even General Motors can make such a decision. Instead, the *market* decides how many cars to produce. Millions of consumers signal their desire to have a car by browsing the Internet, visiting showrooms, and buying cars. Their purchases flash a green light to producers, who see the potential to earn more profits. To do so, they'll increase auto output. If consumers stop buying cars, profits will disappear. Producers will respond by reducing output, laying off workers, and even closing factories. These interactions between consumers and producers determine how many cars are produced.

Notice how the invisible hand moves us along the production possibilities curve. If consumers demand more cars, the mix of output will include more cars and less of other goods. If auto production is scaled back, the displaced autoworkers will end up producing other goods and services, which will change the mix of output in the opposite direction.

market mechanism: The use of market prices and sales to signal desired outputs (or resource allocations).

Adam Smith's invisible hand is now called the **market mechanism.** Notice that it doesn't require any direct contact between consumers and producers. Communication is indirect, transmitted by market prices and sales. Indeed, ***the essential feature of the market mechanism is the price signal.*** If you want something and have sufficient income, you can buy it. If enough people do the same thing, the total sales of that product will rise, and perhaps its price will as well. Producers, seeing sales and prices rise, will want to exploit this profit potential. To do so, they'll attempt to acquire a larger share of available resources and use it to produce the goods we desire. That's how the "invisible hand" works.

The market mechanism can also answer the HOW question. To maximize their profits, producers seek the lowest-cost method of producing a good. By observing prices in the marketplace, they can identify the cheapest method and adopt it.

The market mechanism can also resolve the FOR WHOM question. A market distributes goods to the highest bidder. Individuals who are willing and able to pay the most for a product tend to get it in a pure market economy.

Adam Smith was so impressed with the ability of the market mechanism to answer the basic WHAT, HOW, and FOR WHOM questions that he urged government to "leave it alone" **(laissez faire).** In his view, the price signals and responses of the marketplace were likely to do a better job of allocating resources than any government could.

laissez faire: The doctrine of "leave it alone," of nonintervention by government in the market mechanism.

Government Intervention and Command Economies

The laissez-faire policy Adam Smith favored has always had its share of critics. Karl Marx emphasized how free markets tend to concentrate wealth and power in the hands of the few, at the expense of the many. As he saw it, unfettered markets permit the capitalists (those who own the machinery and factories) to enrich themselves while the proletariat (the workers) toil long hours for subsistence wages. Marx argued that the government not only had to intervene but had to *own* all the means of production—the factories, the machinery, the land—in order to avoid savage inequalities. In *Das Kapital* (1867) and the *Communist Manifesto* (1848), he laid the foundation for a communist state in which the government would be the master of economic outcomes.

The British economist John Maynard Keynes offered a less drastic solution. The market, he conceded, was pretty efficient in organizing production and building better mousetraps. However, individual producers and workers had no control over the broader economy. The cumulative actions of so many economic agents could easily tip the economy in the wrong direction. A completely unregulated market might veer off in one direction and then another as producers all rushed to increase output at the same time or throttled back production in a herdlike manner. The government, Keynes reasoned, could act like a pressure gauge, letting off excess steam or building it up as the economy needed. With the government maintaining overall balance in the economy, the market could live up to its performance expectations. While assuring a stable, full-employment environment, the government might also be able to redress excessive inequalities. In Keynes's view, government should play an active but not all-inclusive role in managing the economy.

webnote

For more information on Smith, Malthus, Keynes, and Marx, visit the Federal Reserve Bank of San Francisco at www.frbsf.org/education and click on "Great Economists and Their Times" under "Publications"

Continuing Debates

These historical views shed perspective on today's political debates. The core of most debates is some variation of the WHAT, HOW, or FOR WHOM questions. Much of the debate is how these questions should be answered. Conservatives favor Adam Smith's laissez-faire approach, with minimal government interference in the markets. Liberals, by contrast, think government intervention is needed to improve market outcomes. Conservatives resist workplace regulation, price controls, and minimum wages because such interventions might impair market efficiency. Liberals argue that such interventions temper the excesses of the market and promote both equity and efficiency.

The debate over how best to manage the economy is not unique to the United States. Countries around the world confront the same choice, between reliance on the market and reliance on the government. Public opinion clearly favors the market system, as the accompanying World View documents. Yet, few countries have ever relied exclusively on either the markets or the government to manage their economy. Even the former Soviet Union, where the government owned all the means of production and central planners dictated how they were to be used, made limited use of free markets. In Cuba, the government still manages the economy's resources but encourages farmers' markets and some private trade and investment.

The World View on page 15 categorizes nations by the extent of their market reliance. Hong Kong scores high on this "Index of Economic Freedom" because its tax rates are relatively low, the public sector is comparatively small, and there are few restrictions on private investment or trade. By contrast, North Korea scores extremely low because the government owns all property, directly allocates resources, sets wages, and limits trade.

Markets vs. Government Reliance?

A new poll of 20 countries from around the world finds a striking global consensus that the free market economic system is best. In all but one country polled, a majority or plurality agreed with the statement that "the free enterprise system and free market economy is the best system on which to base the future of the world."

Source: GlobeScan 2005 poll for Program on International Policy Attitudes, University of Maryland.

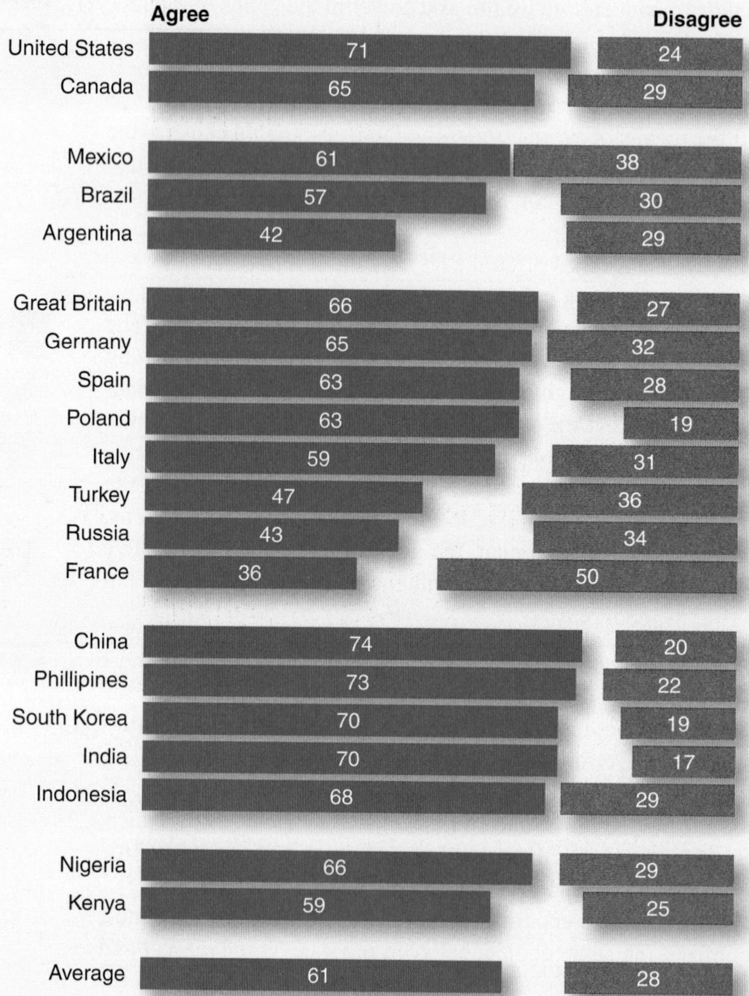

Analysis: People around the world believe that markets can do a good job of fostering economic growth.

The rankings shown in the following World View are neither definitive nor stable. In 1989, Russia began a massive transformation from a state-controlled economy to a more market-oriented economy. Some of the former republics (e.g., Estonia) became relatively free, while others (e.g., Turkmenistan) still rely on extensive government control of the

WORLD VIEW

Index of Economic Freedom

Hong Kong ranks number one among the world's nations in economic freedom. It achieves that status with low tax rates, free-trade policies, minimal government regulation, and secure property rights. These and other economic indicators place Hong Kong at the top of the Heritage Foundation's 2007 country rankings by the degree of "economic freedom." The "most free" and the "least free" (repressed) economies on the list of 157 countries are

Greatest Economic Freedom	Least Economic Freedom
Hong Kong	North Korea
Singapore	Cuba
Australia	Libya
United States	Zimbabwe
New Zealand	Myanmar (Burma)
United Kingdom	Turkmenistan
Ireland	Iran
Luxembourg	Angola
Switzerland	Guinea-Bissau
Canada	Belarus

Source: Heritage Foundation, *2007 Index of Economic Freedom*, Washington, DC, 2007. Used with permission. www.heritage.org

Analysis: All nations must decide whether to rely on market signals or government directives to determine economic outcomes. Nations that rely the least on government intervention score highest ("most free") on this Index of Economic Freedom.

economy. China has greatly expanded the role of private markets and Cuba is moving in the same direction in fits and starts. Even Libya—the third "least-free" nation on the Heritage list—is just now experimenting with some market reforms.

In the United States, the changes have been less dramatic. The most notable shift was President Franklin Roosevelt's New Deal, which greatly expanded the government's role in the economy. In more recent times, the tug-of-war between laissez faire and government intervention has been much less decisive. Although President Reagan often said that "government *is* the problem," he hardly made a dent in government growth during the eight years of his presidency. Likewise, President Clinton's very different conviction that the government can *fix* problems, not cause them, had only minor effects on the size and scope of government activity. President George W. Bush not only lowered taxes but also lessened government regulation of HOW goods are produced.

webnote

To learn how the Heritage Foundation defines economic freedom, visit its Web site at www.heritage.org

A Mixed Economy

Even if President Bush had gotten all the tax cuts and deregulation he wanted, the government would still play a large role in the U.S. economy. No one wants to rely exclusively on Adam Smith's invisible hand. Nor is anyone willing to have the economy steered exclusively by the highly visible hand of the government. ***The United States, like most nations, uses a combination of market signals and government directives to select economic outcomes.*** The resulting compromises are called **mixed economies.**

mixed economy: An economy that uses both market signals and government directives to allocate goods and resources.

The reluctance of countries around the world to rely exclusively on either market signals or government directives is due to the recognition that both mechanisms can and do fail on occasion. As we've seen, market signals are capable of answering the three core questions of WHAT, HOW, and FOR WHOM. But the answers may not be the best possible ones.

Market Failure

market failure: An imperfection in the market mechanism that prevents optimal outcomes.

When market signals don't give the best possible answers to the WHAT, HOW, and FOR WHOM questions, we say that the market mechanism has *failed.* Specifically, **market failure** means that the invisible hand has failed to achieve the best possible outcomes. If the market fails, we end up with the wrong (*sub*optimal) mix of output, too much unemployment, polluted air, or an inequitable distribution of income.

In a market-driven economy, for example, producers will select production methods based on cost. Cost-driven production decisions, however, may lead a factory to spew pollution into the environment rather than to use cleaner but more expensive methods of production. The resulting pollution may be so bad that society ends up worse off as a result of the extra production. In such a case we may need government intervention to force better answers to the WHAT and HOW questions.

We could also let the market decide who gets to consume cigarettes. Anyone who had enough money to buy a pack of cigarettes would then be entitled to smoke. What if, however, children aren't experienced enough to balance the risks of smoking against the pleasures? What if nonsmokers are harmed by secondhand smoke? In this case as well, the market's answer to the FOR WHOM question might not be optimal.

Government Failure

government failure: Government intervention that fails to improve economic outcomes.

Government intervention may move us closer to our economic goals. If so, the resulting mix of market signals and government directives would be an improvement over a purely market-driven economy. But government intervention may fail as well. **Government failure** occurs when government intervention fails to improve market outcomes or actually makes them worse.

The collapse of communism revealed how badly government directives can fail. But government failure also occurs in less spectacular ways. For example, the government may intervene to force an industry to clean up its pollution. The government's directives may impose such high costs that the industry closes factories and lays off workers. Some cutbacks in output might be appropriate, but they could also prove excessive. The government might also mandate pollution control technologies that are too expensive or even obsolete. None of this has to happen, but it might. If it does, government failure will have worsened economic outcomes.

webnote

Comparative data on the percentage of goods and services the various national governments provide are available from the Penn World Tables at www.pwt.econ.upenn.edu

The government might also fail if it interferes with the market's answer to the FOR WHOM question. For 50 years, communist China distributed goods by government directive, not market performance. Incomes were more equal, but uniformly low. To increase output and living standards, China has turned to market incentives (see World View on the next page). As entrepreneurs respond to these incentives, everyone may become better off—even while inequality increases.

Excessive taxes and transfer payments can also worsen economic outcomes. If the government raises taxes on the rich to pay welfare benefits for the poor, neither the rich nor the poor may see much purpose in working. In that case, the attempt to give everybody a "fair" share of the pie might end up shrinking the size of the pie. If that happened, society could end up worse off.

Seeking Balance

None of these failures has to occur. But they might. The challenge for society is to minimize failures by selecting the appropriate balance of market signals and government directives. This isn't an easy task. It requires that we know how markets work and why they sometimes fail. We also need to know what policy options the government has and how and when they might work.

WHAT ECONOMICS IS ALL ABOUT

Understanding how economies function is the basic purpose of studying economics. We seek to know how an economy is organized, how it behaves, and how successfully it achieves its basic objectives. Then, if we're lucky, we can discover better ways of attaining those same objectives.

End vs. Means

Economists don't formulate an economy's objectives. Instead, they focus on the *means* available for achieving given *goals.* In 1978, for example, the U.S. Congress identified "full employment" as a major economic goal. Congress then directed future presidents (and their economic

WORLD VIEW 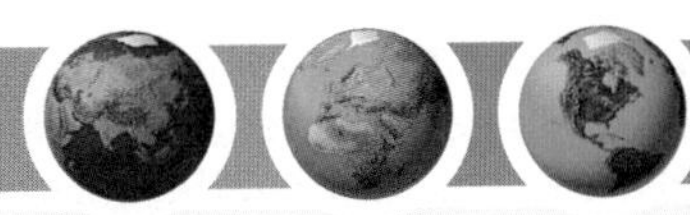

China's Leaders Back Private Property

SHANGHAI, Dec. 22—China's Communist Party leaders on Monday proposed amendments to the nation's constitution that would enshrine a legal right to private property. . . .

Virtually assured of adoption in the party-controlled National People's Congress, the amendments constitute a significant advance in China's ongoing transition from communism to capitalism. They amount to recognition that the economic future of the world's most populous country rests with private enterprise—a radical departure from the political roots of this land still known as the People's Republic of China.

Not since the Communist Party swept to power in 1949 in a revolution built on antipathy toward landowners and industrialists have Chinese been legally permitted to own property. Under the leadership of Chairman Mao, millions of people suffered persecution for being tainted with "bad" class backgrounds that linked them to landowning pasts.

But in present-day China the profit motive has come to pervade nearly every area of life. The site in Shanghai where the Communist Party was founded is now a shopping and entertainment complex anchored by a Starbucks coffee shop. From the poor villages in which most Chinese still live to the cities now dominated by high-rises, the market determines the price of most goods and decisions about what to produce. Business is widely viewed as a favored, even noble, undertaking.

The state-owned firms that once dominated China's economy have traditionally been sustained by credit from state banks, regardless of their balance sheets. Today, many are bankrupt, and banks are burdened by about $500 billion in bad loans, according to private economists. The government has cast privatization as the prescription for turning them around, creating management incentives to make them profitable.

—Peter S. Goodman

Source: *Washington Post,* December 23, 2003. www.washingtonpost.com

Analysis: Government-directed production, prices, and incomes may increase equalities but blunt incentives. Private property and market-based incomes motivate higher productivity and growth.

advisers) to formulate policies that would enable us to achieve full employment. The economist's job is to help design policies that will best achieve this and other economic goals.

Macro vs. Micro

The study of economics is typically divided into two parts: macroeconomics and microeconomics. Macroeconomics focuses on the behavior of an entire economy—the "big picture." In macroeconomics we worry about such national goals as full employment, control of inflation, and economic growth, without worrying about the well-being or behavior of specific individuals or groups. The essential concern of **macroeconomics** is to understand and improve the performance of the economy as a whole.

macroeconomics: The study of aggregate economic behavior, of the economy as a whole.

Microeconomics is concerned with the details of this big picture. In microeconomics we focus on the individuals, firms, and government agencies that actually compose the larger economy. Our interest here is in the behavior of individual economic actors. What are their goals? How can they best achieve these goals with their limited resources? How will they respond to various incentives and opportunities?

microeconomics: The study of individual behavior in the economy, of the components of the larger economy.

A primary concern of *macro*economics, for example, is to determine how much money, *in total,* consumers will spend on goods and services. In *micro*economics, the focus is much narrower. In micro, attention is paid to purchases of *specific* goods and services rather than just aggregated totals. Macro likewise concerns itself with the level of *total* business investment, while micro examines how *individual* businesses make their investment decisions.

Although they operate at different levels of abstraction, macro and micro are intrinsically related. Macro (aggregate) outcomes depend on micro behavior, and micro (individual) behavior is affected by macro outcomes. One can't fully understand how an economy works until one understands how all the individual participants behave. But just as you can drive a car without knowing how its engine is constructed, you can observe how an economy runs without completely disassembling it. In macroeconomics we observe that the car goes faster when the accelerator is depressed and that it slows when the brake is applied. That's all we need to know in most situations. At times, however, the car breaks down. When it does, we have to know something more about how the pedals work. This leads us into micro studies. How does each part work? Which ones can or should be fixed?

Our interest in microeconomics is motivated by more than our need to understand how the larger economy works. The "parts" of the economic engine are people. To the extent that we care about the well-being of individuals, we have a fundamental interest in microeconomic behavior and outcomes. In this regard, we examine how individual consumers and business firms seek to achieve specific goals in the marketplace. The goals aren't always related to output. Gary Becker won the 1992 Nobel Prize in economics for demonstrating how economic principles also affect decisions to marry, to have children, to engage in criminal activities—or even to complete homework assignments in an economics class.

Theory vs. Reality

The distinction between macroeconomics and microeconomics is one of many simplifications we make in studying economic behavior. The economy is much too vast and complex to describe and explain in one course (or one lifetime). Accordingly, we focus on basic relationships, ignoring annoying detail. In so doing, we isolate basic principles of economic behavior and then use those principles to predict economic events and develop economic policies. This means that we formulate theories, or *models,* of economic behavior and then use those theories to evaluate and design economic policy.

Our model of consumer behavior assumes, for example, that people buy less of a good when its price rises. In reality, however, people *may* buy *more* of a good at increased prices, especially if those high prices create a certain snob appeal or if prices are expected to increase still further. In predicting consumer responses to price increases, we typically ignore such possibilities by *assuming* that the price of the good in question is the *only* thing that changes. This assumption of "other things remaining equal" (unchanged) (in Latin, ***ceteris paribus***) allows us to make straightforward predictions. If instead we described consumer responses to increased prices in any and all circumstances (allowing everything to change at once), every prediction would be accompanied by a book full of exceptions and qualifications. We'd look more like lawyers than economists.

ceteris paribus: The assumption of nothing else changing.

Although the assumption of *ceteris paribus* makes it easier to formulate economic theory and policy, it also increases the risk of error. If other things do change in significant ways, our predictions (and policies) may fail. But, like weather forecasters, we continue to make predictions, knowing that occasional failure is inevitable. In so doing, we're motivated by the conviction that it's better to be approximately right than to be dead wrong.

Politics. Politicians can't afford to be quite so complacent about economic predictions. Policy decisions must be made every day. And a politician's continued survival may depend on being more than approximately right. George H. Bush's loss in the 1992 election resulted in part from his repeated predictions that the economy was "turning around." When this optimistic forecast proved wrong, voters lost faith in President Bush's ability to direct the economy. Ironically, his son gained a critical advantage in the superclose 2000 presidential election because of another economic slowdown and a slumping stock market. Once again, voters sought a new economic policy team.

After he took office, President George W. Bush immediately sought to change the mix of output. Even before the September 11, 2001, terrorist attacks, he wanted more "guns," as reflected in added defense spending. He also secured tax cuts to boost private consumption and investment. Were these the right choices? Economic theory can't completely answer that question. Choices about the mix of output are ultimately political—decisions that must take into account not only economic trade-offs (opportunity costs) but also social values. "Politics"—the balancing of competing interests—is an inevitable ingredient of economic policy.

Imperfect Knowledge. One last word of warning before you read further. Economics claims to be a science, in pursuit of basic truths. We want to understand and explain how the economy works without getting tangled up in subjective value judgments. This may be an impossible task. First, it's not clear where the truth lies. For more than 200 years economists have been arguing about what makes the economy tick. None of the competing theories has performed spectacularly well. Indeed, few economists have successfully predicted major economic events with any consistency. Even annual forecasts of inflation, unemployment, and output are regularly in error. Worse still, never-ending arguments about what caused a major economic event continue long after it occurs. In fact, economists are still arguing over the primary causes of the Great Depression of the 1930s!

In part, this enduring controversy reflects diverse sociopolitical views on the appropriate role of government. Some people think a big public sector is undesirable, even if it improves economic performance. But the controversy has even deeper roots. Major gaps in our understanding of the economy persist. We know how much of the economy works, but not all of it. We're adept at identifying all the forces at work, but not always successful in gauging their relative importance. In point of fact, we may *never* find an absolute truth, because the inner workings of the economy change over time. When economic behavior changes, our theories must be adapted.

In view of all these debates and uncertainties, don't expect to learn everything there is to know about the economy today in this text or course. Our goals are more modest. We want to develop a reasonable perspective on economic behavior, an understanding of basic principles. With this foundation, you should acquire a better view of how the economy works. Daily news reports on economic events should make more sense. Congressional debates on tax and budget policies should take on more meaning. You may even develop some insights that you can apply toward running a business or planning a career, or—if the Nobel Prize–winning economist Gary Becker is right—developing a lasting marriage.

THE ECONOMY TOMORROW

THE JOURNEY TO MARS

AFP/Getty Images

January 3, 2004, was a milestone in space exploration. That was the day the first robotic space vehicle—*Spirit*—landed on Mars. The pictures *Spirit* transmitted back to Earth unveiled a whole new boundary for human exploration. It created a challenge President Bush was quick to confront. Within days he announced an ambitious new agenda for America's space program:

- By 2010 the United States is to complete the International Space Station.
- By 2008, a new Crew Exploration Vehicle, capable of ferrying astronauts and scientists to the Space Station, will be developed and ready for use.
- By 2015, the Crew Exploration Vehicle will begin extended human missions to the moon.
- After 2015, human missions to Mars will begin.

Scientists and ordinary citizens around the world cheered both *Spirit*'s accomplishments and President Bush's vision. People heard echoes of President Kennedy's May 1961 promise that mankind would soon set foot on the moon—a promise that seemed equally implausible at the time, but ultimately proved to be attainable.

Opportunity Costs. The journey to Mars is not only a technological commitment but an economic commitment as well. The resources used to complete the Space Station, to colonize the moon, and to journey onto Mars and worlds beyond all have alternative uses here on Earth. Some of the same scientists could be developing high-speed *rail* systems, safer domestic flights, or more eco-friendly technologies. The technological resources being poured into space exploration could be perfecting cell phone quality or simply accelerating online data transmissions. If we devoted as many resources to medical research as space research, we might find more ways to extend and improve life here on Earth. Or we could use all those resources to develop safe water and sanitation systems for the globally poor. In other words, the journey to Mars will entail opportunity costs, that is, the sacrifice of earthly goods and services that could be produced with those same resources.

webnote

Review NASA's budget at www.whitehouse.gov or www.cbo.gov. For more information on the space program, visit www.nasa.gov

The journey to Mars won't be cheap. President Kennedy's *Apollo* program cost over $100 billion in today's dollars. Cost estimates for the journey to Mars run as high as $1 *trillion,* spread out over 20 years. That much money would fund a lot of earthly programs.

Earthly Benefits. NASA says the benefits of the Mars journey would outweigh those opportunity costs. Space exploration has already generated tangible benefits for us earthlings. NASA cites advances in weather forecasting, in communications technology, in robotics, in computing and electronics, and in search and rescue technology. The research behind the space program has also helped create the satellite telecommunications network and the Global Positioning System (GPS). Medical technologies such as the image processing used in CAT scanners and MRI machines also trace their origins to engineering work for space exploration. President Bush said we should expect still further benefits from the journey to Mars: not only tangible benefits like new resources and technological advance but also intangibles like the spiritual uplifting and heightened quest for knowledge that exploration promotes.

Resource Allocations. As a society, we're going to have to make important choices about the economy tomorrow. Do we want to take the journey to Mars? If so, how fast do we want to get there? How many earthly goods and services do we want to give up to pay for the journey? Every year, the President and the U.S. Congress have to answer these questions. Their answers are reflected in the funds allocated to NASA (rather than other programs) in each year's federal budget. If you were in charge of the budget, how would you allocate scarce resources between space exploration and earthly activities?

SUMMARY

- Scarcity is a basic fact of economic life. Factors of production (land, labor, capital, entrepreneurship) are scarce in relation to our desires for goods and services. LO1
- All economic activity entails opportunity costs. Factors of production (resources) used to produce one output cannot simultaneously be used to produce something else. When we choose to produce one thing, we forsake the opportunity to produce some other good or service. LO1
- A production possibilities curve (PPC) illustrates the limits to production—the alternative combinations of final goods and services that could be produced in a given period if all available resources and technology are used efficiently. The PPC also illustrates opportunity costs—what is given up to get more of something else. LO1
- The bent shape of the PPC reflects the law of increasing opportunity costs. This law states that increasing quantities of any good can be obtained only by sacrificing ever-increasing quantities of other goods. LO1
- Inefficient or incomplete use of resources will fail to attain production possibilities. Additional resources or better technologies will expand them. This is the essence of economic growth. LO1
- Every country must decide WHAT to produce, HOW to produce, and FOR WHOM to produce with its limited resources. LO2
- The WHAT, HOW, and FOR WHOM choices can be made by the market mechanism or by government directives. Most nations are mixed economies, using a combination of these two choice mechanisms. LO3
- Market failure exists when market signals generate suboptimal outcomes. Government failure occurs when government intervention worsens economic outcomes. The challenge for economic theory and policy is to find the mix of market signals and government directives that best fulfills our social and economic goals. LO3
- The study of economics focuses on the broad question of resource allocation. Macroeconomics is concerned with allocating the resources of an entire economy to achieve aggregate economic goals (e.g., full employment). Microeconomics focuses on the behavior and goals of individual market participants. LO3

Key Terms

scarcity
factors of production
capital
entrepreneurship
economics
opportunity cost
production possibilities
efficiency
economic growth
market mechanism
laissez faire
mixed economy
market failure
government failure
macroeconomics
microeconomics
ceteris paribus

Questions for Discussion

1. What opportunity costs did you incur in reading this chapter? If you read four more chapters of this book today, would your opportunity cost (per chapter) increase? Explain. LO1
2. How much time could you spend on homework in a day? How much do you spend? How do you decide? LO1
3. What's the real cost of the food in the "free lunch" cartoon on page 5? LO1
4. How might a nation's production possibilities be affected by the following? LO2
   a. A decrease in taxes.
   b. An increase in government regulation.
   c. An increase in military spending.
   d. An increase in college tuition.
   e. Faster, more powerful electronic chips.
5. Markets reward individuals according to their output; communism rewards people according to their needs. How might these different systems affect work effort? LO3
6. How does government intervention affect college admissions? Who would go to college in a completely private (market) college system? LO3
7. How will the Chinese economy benefit from private property? (See World View, page 17.) Is there any downside to greater entrepreneurial freedom? LO3
8. How many resources should we allocate to space exploration? How will we make this decision? LO2
9. What is the connection between North Korea's missile program and its hunger problem? (World View, page 9) LO3

problems The Student Problem Set at the back of this book contains numerical and graphing problems for this chapter.

web activities to accompany this chapter can be found on the Online Learning Center: **http://www.mhhe.com/economics/schiller11e**

APPENDIX

USING GRAPHS

Economists like to draw graphs. In fact, we didn't even make it through the first chapter without a few graphs. This appendix looks more closely at the way graphs are drawn and used. The basic purpose of a graph is to illustrate a relationship between two *variables*. Consider, for example, the relationship between grades and studying. In general, we expect that additional hours of study time will lead to higher grades. Hence, we should be able to see a distinct relationship between hours of study time and grade-point average.

Suppose that we actually surveyed all the students taking this course with regard to their study time and grade-point averages. The resulting information can be compiled in a table such as Table A.1.

According to the table, students who don't study at all can expect an F in this course. To get a C, the average student apparently spends 8 hours a week studying. All those who study 16 hours a week end up with an A in the course.

These relationships between grades and studying can also be illustrated on a graph. Indeed, the whole purpose of a graph is to summarize numerical relationships.

We begin to construct a graph by drawing horizontal and vertical boundaries, as in Figure A.1. These boundaries are called the *axes* of the graph. On the vertical axis (often called the *y*-axis) we measure one of the variables; the other variable is measured on the horizontal axis (the *x*-axis).

TABLE A.1
Hypothetical Relationship of Grades to Study Time

Study Time (hours per week)	Grade-Point Average
16	4.0 (A)
14	3.5 (B+)
12	3.0 (B)
10	2.5 (C+)
8	2.0 (C)
6	1.5 (D+)
4	1.0 (D)
2	0.5 (F+)
0	0.0 (F)

In this case, we shall measure the grade-point average on the vertical axis. We start at the *origin* (the intersection of the two axes) and count upward, letting the distance between horizontal lines represent half (0.5) a grade point. Each horizontal line is numbered, up to the maximum grade-point average of 4.0.

The number of hours each week spent doing homework is measured on the horizontal axis. We begin at the origin again, and count to the right. The *scale* (numbering) proceeds in increments of 1 hour, up to 20 hours per week.

When both axes have been labeled and measured, we can begin illustrating the relationship between study time and grades. Consider the typical student who does 8 hours of homework per week and has a 2.0 (C) grade-point average. We illustrate this relationship by first locating 8 hours on the horizontal axis. We then move up from that point a distance of 2.0 grade points, to point *M*. Point *M* tells us that 8 hours of study time per week is typically associated with a 2.0 grade-point average.

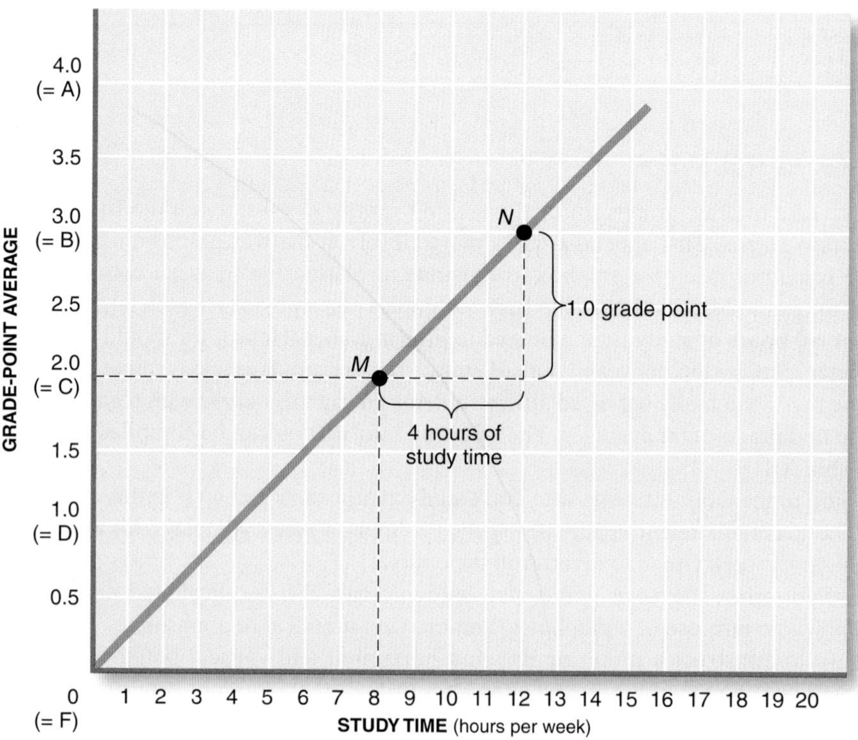

FIGURE A.1
The Relationship of Grades to Study Time

The upward (positive) slope of the curve indicates that additional studying is associated with higher grades. The average student (2.0, or C grade) studies 8 hours per week. This is indicated by point *M* on the graph.

The rest of the information in Table A.1 is drawn (or *plotted*) on the graph the same way. To illustrate the average grade for people who study 12 hours per week, we move upward from the number 12 on the horizontal axis until we reach the height of 3.0 on the vertical axis. At that intersection, we draw another point (point *N*).

Once we've plotted the various points describing the relationship of study time to grades, we may connect them with a line or curve. This line (curve) is our summary. In this case, the line slopes upward to the right—that is, it has a *positive* slope. This slope indicates that more hours of study time are associated with *higher* grades. Were higher grades associated with *less* study time, the curve in Figure A.1 would have a *negative* slope (downward from left to right).

Slopes

The upward slope of Figure A.1 tells us that higher grades are associated with increased amounts of study time. That same curve also tells us *by how much* grades tend to rise with study time. According to point *M* in Figure A.1, the average student studies 8 hours per week and earns a C (2.0 grade-point average). To earn a B (3.0 average), students apparently need to study an average of 12 hours per week (point *N*). Hence an increase of 4 hours of study time per week is associated with a 1-point increase in grade-point average. This relationship between *changes* in study time and *changes* in grade-point average is expressed by the steepness, or *slope,* of the graph.

The slope of any graph is calculated as

$$\text{Slope} = \frac{\text{vertical distance between two points}}{\text{horizontal distance between two points}}$$

In our example, the vertical distance between *M* and *N* represents a change in grade-point average. The horizontal distance between these two points represents the change in study time. Hence the slope of the graph between points *M* and *N* is equal to

$$\text{Slope} = \frac{3.0\text{ grade} - 2.0\text{ grade}}{12\text{ hours} - 8\text{ hours}} = \frac{1\text{ grade point}}{4\text{ hours}}$$

In other words, a 4-hour increase in study time (from 8 to 12 hours) is associated with a 1-point increase in grade-point average (see Figure A.1).

Shifts

The relationship between grades and studying illustrated in Figure A.1 isn't inevitable. It's simply a graphical illustration of student experiences, as revealed in our hypothetical survey. The relationship between study time and grades could be quite different.

Suppose that the university decided to raise grading standards, making it more difficult to achieve every grade other than an F. To achieve a C, a student now would need to study 12 hours per week, not just 8 (as in Figure A.1). Whereas students could previously expect to get a B by studying 12 hours per week, now they'd have to study 16 hours to get that grade.

Figure A.2 illustrates the new grading standards. Notice that the new curve lies to the right of the earlier curve. We say that the curve has *shifted* to reflect a change in the relationship between study time and grades. Point *R* indicates that 12 hours of study time now "produce" a C, not a B (point *N* on the old curve). Students who now study only 4 hours per week (point *S*) will fail. Under the old grading policy, they could have at least gotten a D. ***When a curve shifts, the underlying relationship between the two variables has changed.***

A shift may also change the slope of the curve. In Figure A.2, the new grading curve is parallel to the old one; it therefore has the same slope. Under either the new grading policy or the old one, a 4-hour increase in study time leads to a 1-point increase in grades. Therefore, the slope of both curves in Figure A.2 is

$$\text{Slope} = \frac{\text{vertical change}}{\text{horizontal change}} = \frac{1}{4}$$

FIGURE A.2
A Shift

When a relationship between two variables changes, the entire curve *shifts*. In this case a tougher grading policy alters the relationship between study time and grades. To get a C, one must now study 12 hours per week (point *R*), not just 8 hours (point *M*).

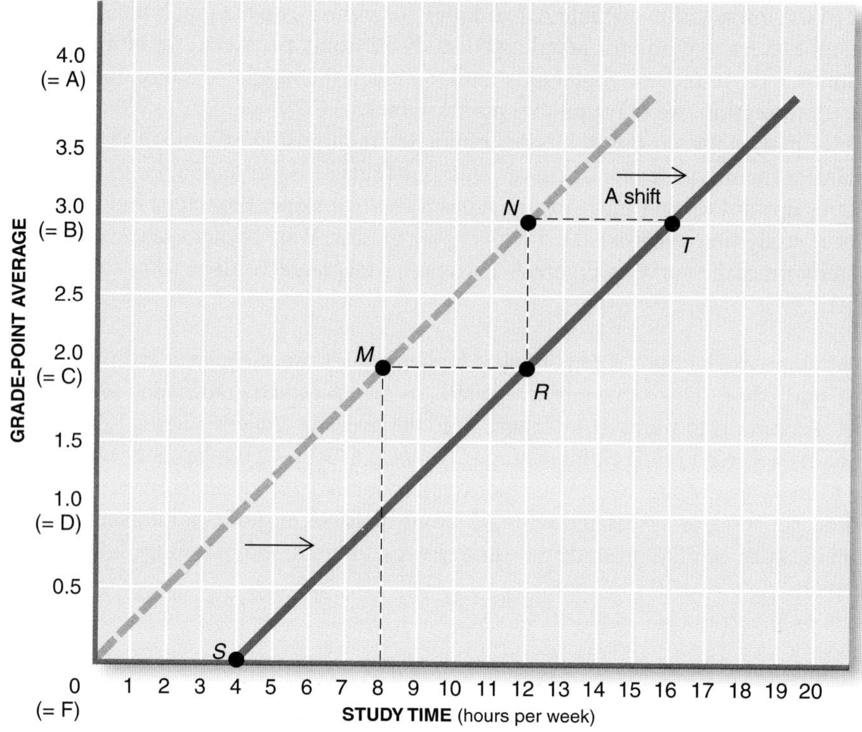

This too may change, however. Figure A.3 illustrates such a possibility. In this case, zero study time still results in an F. But now the payoff for additional studying is reduced. Now it takes 6 hours of study time to get a D (1.0 grade point), not 4 hours as before. Likewise, another 4 hours of study time (to a total of 10) raise the grade by only two-thirds of a point. It takes 6 hours to raise the grade a full point. The slope of the new line is therefore

$$\text{Slope} = \frac{\text{vertical change}}{\text{horizontal change}} = \frac{1}{6}$$

The new curve in Figure A.3 has a smaller slope than the original curve and so lies below it. What all this means is that it now takes a greater effort to *improve* your grade.

Linear vs. Nonlinear Curves

In Figures A.1–A.3 the relationship between grades and studying is represented by a straight line—that is, a *linear curve.* A distinguishing feature of linear curves is that they have the same (constant) slope throughout. In Figure A.1, it appears that *every* 4-hour increase in study time is associated with a 1-point increase in average grades. In Figure A.3, it appears that every 6-hour increase in study time leads to a 1-point increase in grades. But the relationship between studying and grades may not be linear. Higher grades may be more difficult to attain. You may be able to raise a C to a B by studying 4 hours more per week. But it may be harder to raise a B to an A. According to Figure A.4, it takes an additional 8 hours of studying to raise a B to an A. Thus the relationship between study time and grades is *nonlinear* in Figure A.4; the slope of the curve changes as study time increases. In this case, the slope decreases as study time increases. Grades continue to improve, but not so fast, as more and more time is devoted to homework. You may know the feeling.

Causation

Figure A.4 doesn't by itself guarantee that your grade-point average will rise if you study 4 more hours per week. In fact, the graph drawn in Figure A.4 doesn't prove that additional study ever results in higher grades. The graph is only a summary of empirical observations. It says nothing about cause and effect. It could be that students who study a lot are smarter to begin with. If so, then less-able students might not get higher grades if they studied harder. In other words, the *cause* of higher grades is debatable. At best, the

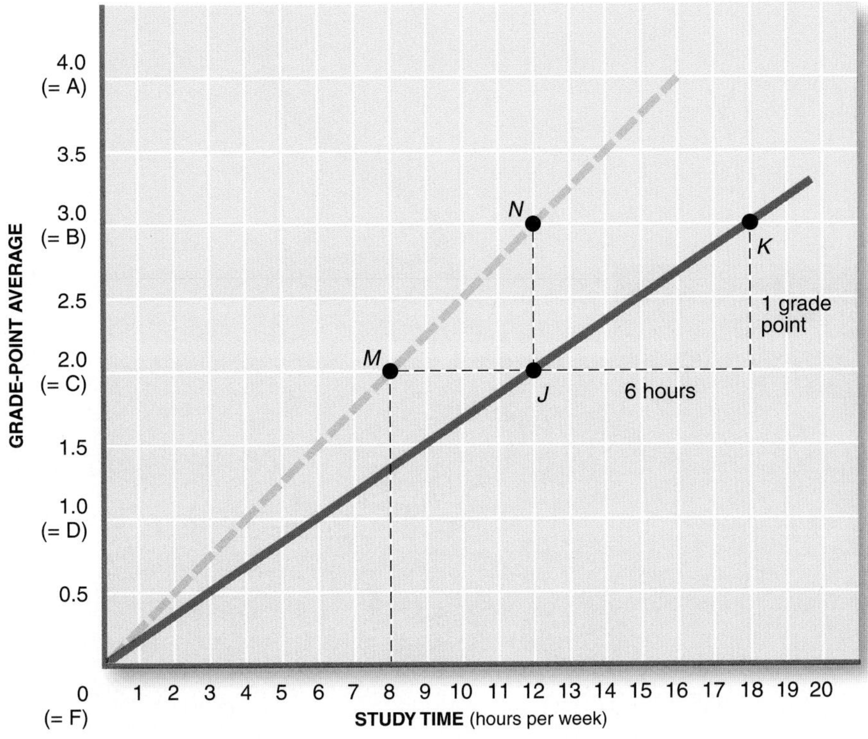

FIGURE A.3

A Change in Slope

When a curve shifts, it may change its slope as well. In this case, a new grading policy makes each higher grade more difficult to reach. To raise a C to a B, for example, one must study 6 additional hours (compare points *J* and *K*). Earlier it took only 4 hours to move the grade scale up a full point. The slope of the line has declined from 0.25(= 1 ÷ 4) to 0.17(= 1 ÷ 6).

empirical relationship summarized in the graph may be used to support a particular theory (e.g., that it pays to study more). Graphs, like tables, charts, and other statistical media, rarely tell their own story; rather, they must be *interpreted* in terms of some underlying theory or expectation.

webnote

For online practice with graphs, visit "Math Skills for Introductory Economics" at syllabus.syr.edu/cid/graph/book.html

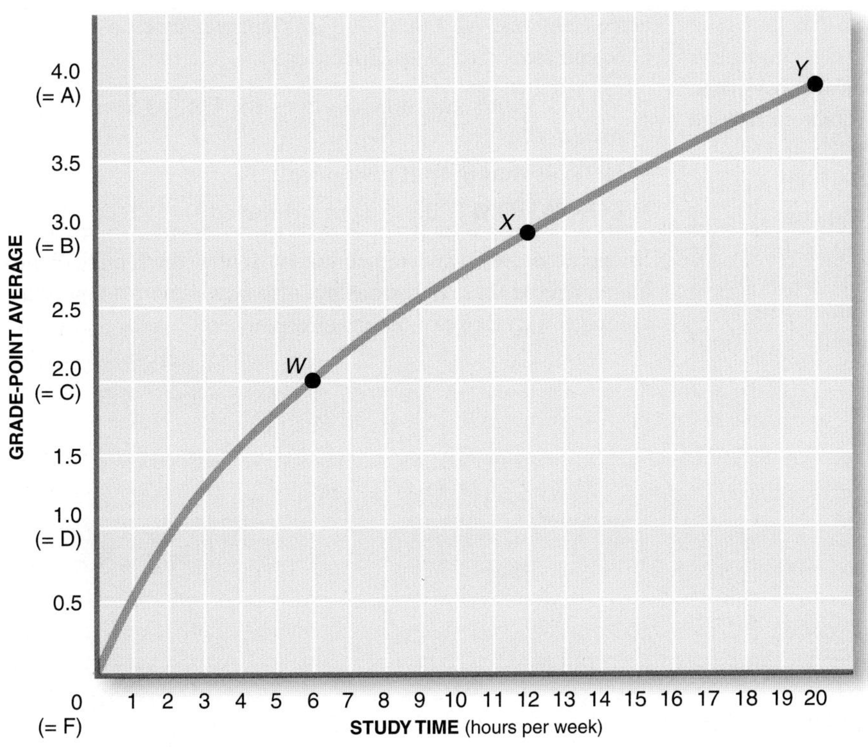

FIGURE A.4

A Nonlinear Relationship

Straight lines have a constant slope, implying a constant relationship between the two variables. But the relationship (and slope) may vary. In this case, it takes 6 extra hours of study to raise a C (point *W*) to a B (point *X*) but 8 extra hours to raise a B to an A (point *Y*). The slope decreases as we move up the curve.

The U.S. Economy:
A Global View

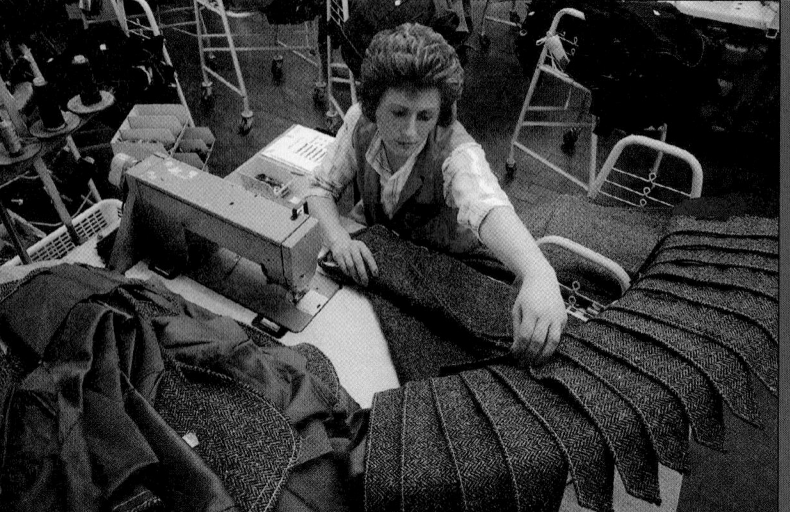

LEARNING OBJECTIVES

After reading this chapter, you should know:

LO1. The relative size and content of U.S. output (GDP).

LO2. How America is able to produce so much output.

LO3. How incomes are distributed in the U.S. and elsewhere.

All nations must confront the central economic questions of WHAT to produce, HOW to produce, and FOR WHOM to produce it. However, the nations of the world approach these issues with vastly different production possibilities. China, Canada, the United States, and Brazil have more than *3 million* acres of land each. All that land gives them far greater production possibilities than Dominica, Tonga, Malta, or Lichtenstein, each of which has less than 500 acres of land. The population of China totals more than 1.3 billion people, nearly five times that of the United States, and 25,000 times the population of Greenland. Obviously, these nations confront very different output choices.

In addition to vastly uneven production possibilities, the nations of the world use different mechanisms for deciding WHAT, HOW, and FOR WHOM to produce. Belarus, Romania, North Korea, and Cuba still rely heavily on central planning. By contrast, Singapore, New Zealand, Ireland, and the United States permit the market mechanism to play a dominant role in shaping economic outcomes.

With different production possibilities and mechanisms of choice, you'd expect economic outcomes to vary greatly across nations. And they do. This chapter assesses how the U.S. economy stacks up. Specifically,

- **WHAT goods and services does the United States produce?**
- **HOW is that output produced?**
- **FOR WHOM is the output produced?**

In each case, we want to see not only how the United States has answered these questions but also how America's answers compare with those of other nations.

WHAT AMERICA PRODUCES

The United States has less than 5 percent of the world's population and only 12 percent of the world's arable land, yet it produces more than 20 percent of the world's output.

GDP Comparisons

gross domestic product (GDP): The total market value of all final goods and services produced within a nation's borders in a given time period.

The World View shows how total U.S. production compares with that of other nations. These comparisons are based on the total market value of all the goods and services a nation produces—what we call **gross domestic product (GDP).**

In 2005, the U.S. economy produced nearly $13 trillion worth of output. The second-largest economy, China, produced only two-thirds that much. Japan came in third, with about a third of U.S. output. Cuba, by contrast, produced only $1.6 *billion* of output, less than the state of South Dakota. Russia, which was once regarded as a superpower, produced only $1.5 trillion, about as much as New York State. The entire 27-member European Union produces less output than the United States.

Per Capita GDP. What makes the U.S. share of world output so remarkable is that we do it with so few people. The U.S. population amounts to only 5 percent of the world's total. Yet we produce over 20 percent of the world's output. That means we're producing a lot of output *per person.* China, by contrast, has the opposite ratios: 20 percent of the world's population producing less than 14 percent of the world's output. So China is producing a lot of output but relatively less *per person.*

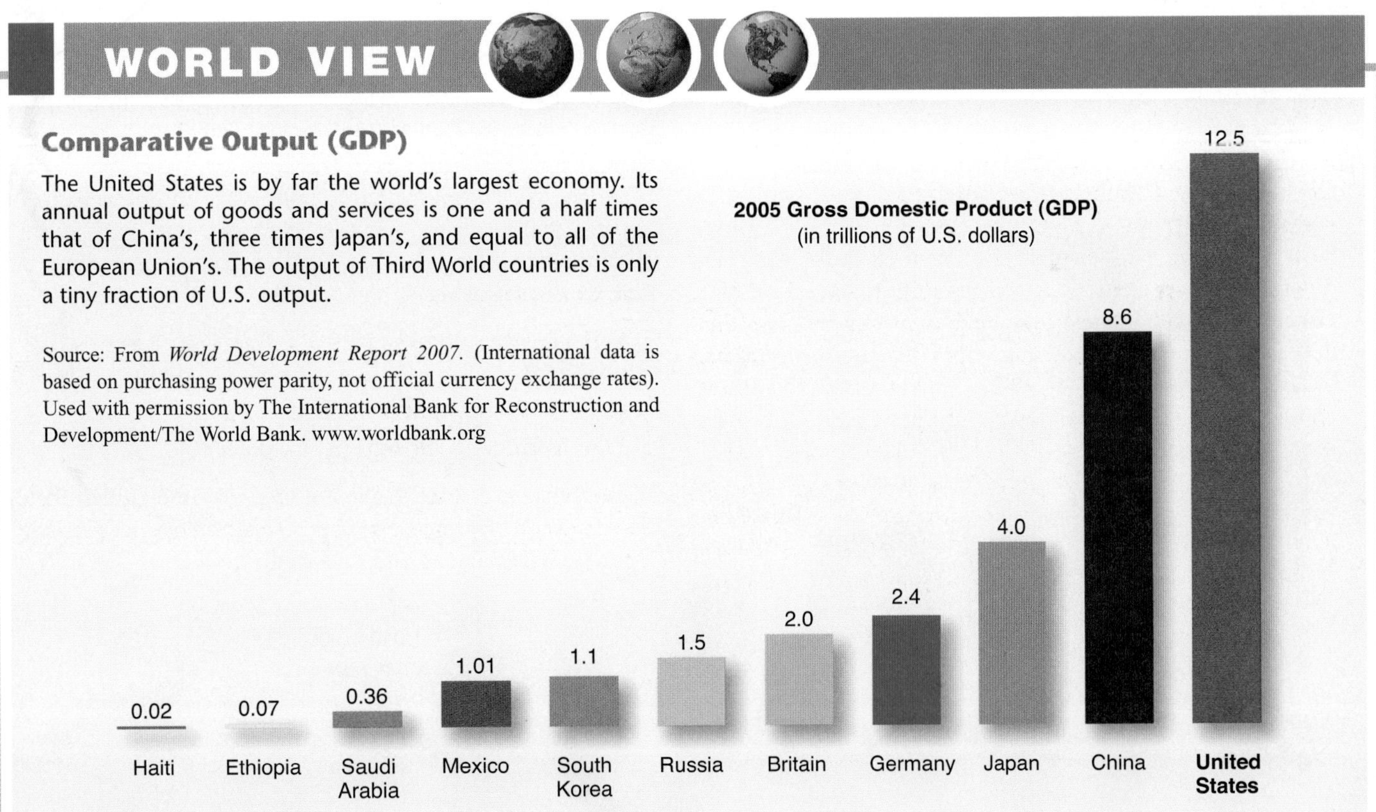

Comparative Output (GDP)

The United States is by far the world's largest economy. Its annual output of goods and services is one and a half times that of China's, three times Japan's, and equal to all of the European Union's. The output of Third World countries is only a tiny fraction of U.S. output.

Source: From *World Development Report 2007.* (International data is based on purchasing power parity, not official currency exchange rates). Used with permission by The International Bank for Reconstruction and Development/The World Bank. www.worldbank.org

Analysis: The market value of output (GDP) is a basic measure of an economy's size. The U.S. economy is far larger than any other and accounts for over one-fifth of the entire world's output of goods and services.

per capita GDP: The dollar value of GDP divided by total population; average GDP.

This people-based measure of economic performance is called **per capita GDP.** Per capita GDP is simply total output divided by total population. Per capita GDP doesn't tell us how much any specific person gets. ***Per capita GDP is an indicator of how much output the average person would get if all output were divided up evenly among the population.***

In 2005, per capita GDP in the United States was roughly $42,000—nearly five times larger than the world average. The following World View provides a global perspective on just how "rich" America is. Some of the country-specific comparisons are startling. China, which produces the world's second-largest GDP, has such a low *per capita* income that most of its citizens would be considered "poor" by official American standards. Yet people in other nations (e.g., Haiti, Ethiopia) don't even come close to that low standard. According to the World Bank, nearly half of the people on Earth subsist on incomes of less than $2 a day—a level completely unimaginable to the average American. Seen in this context, why the rest of the world envies (and sometimes resents) America's prosperity is easy to understand.

GDP Growth. What's even more startling about global comparisons is that the GDP gap between the United States and the world's poor nations keeps growing. The reason for that

WORLD VIEW

GDP Per Capita around the World

The American standard of living is nearly five times higher than the world average. People in the poorest nations of the world (e.g., Haiti, Ethiopia) barely survive on per capita incomes that are a tiny fraction of U.S. standards.

Source: From *World Development Report 2007*. Used with permission by the International Bank for Reconstruction and Development/The World Bank. www.worldbank.org

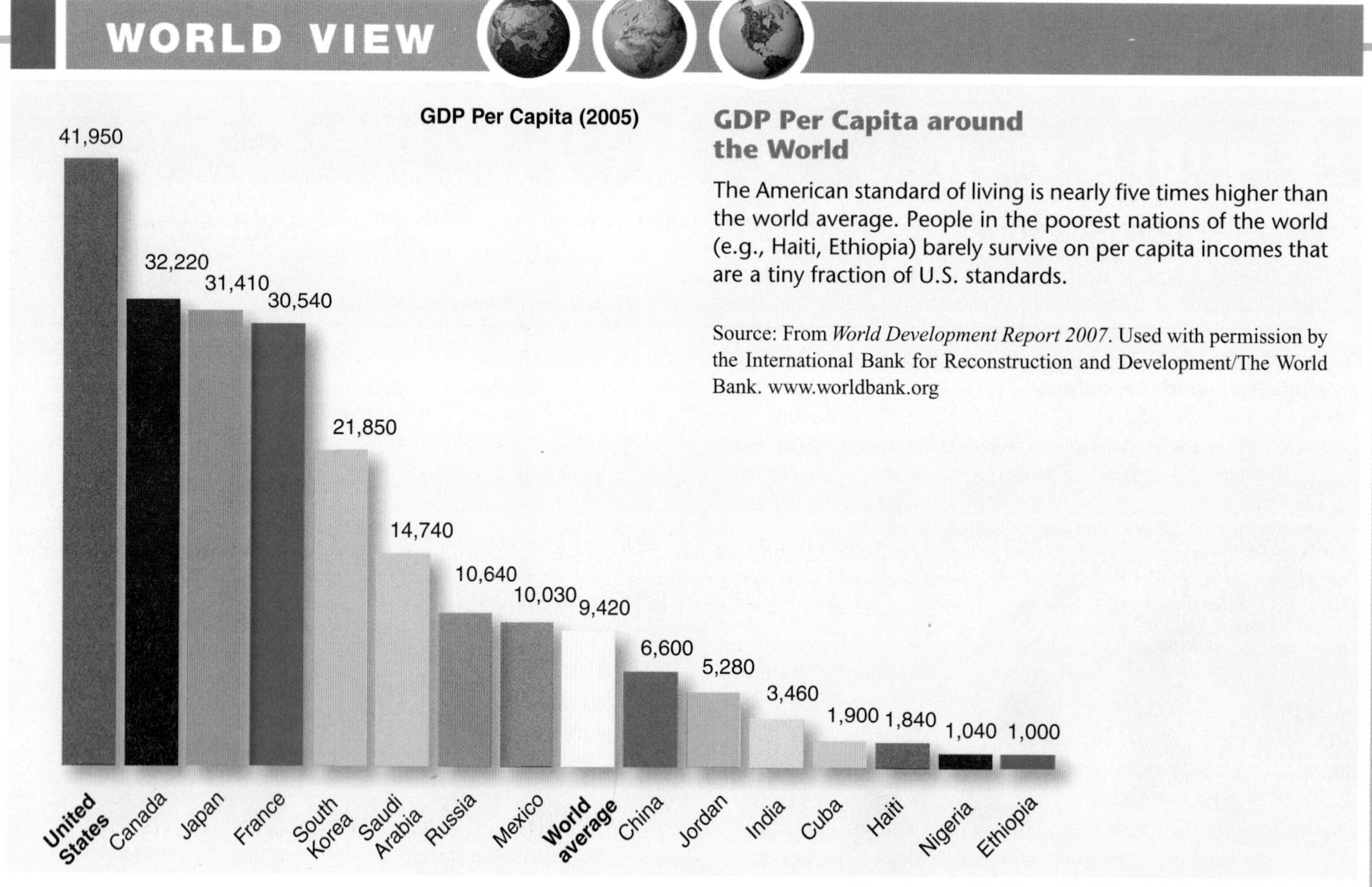

Analysis: Per capita GDP is a measure of output that reflects average living standards. America's exceptionally high GDP per capita implies access to far more goods and services than people in other nations have.

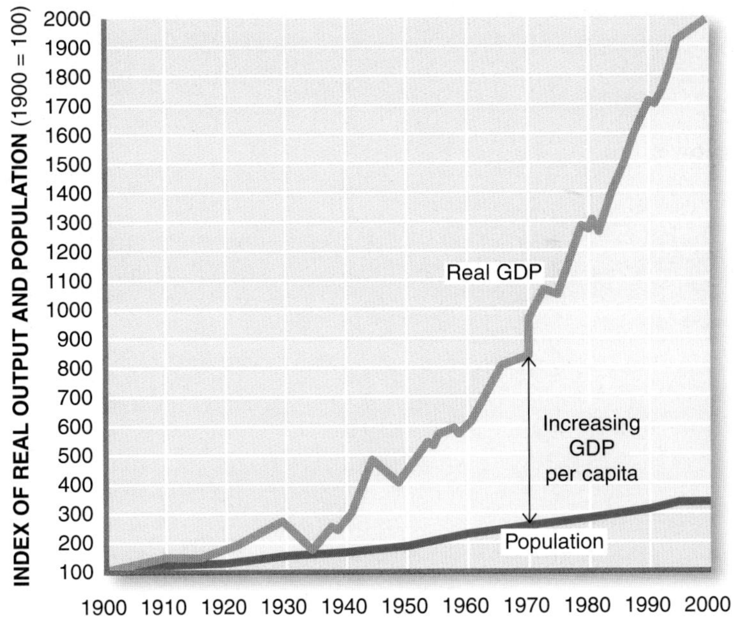

FIGURE 2.1
U.S. Output and Population Growth since 1900

Over time, the growth of output in the United States has greatly exceeded population growth. As a consequence, GDP per capita has grown tremendously. GDP per capita was five times higher in 2000 than in 1900.

Source: U.S. Department of Labor.

is **economic growth.** With few exceptions, U.S. output increases nearly every year. ***On average, U.S. output has grown by roughly 3 percent a year, nearly three times faster than population growth (1 percent).*** Hence, not only does *total* output keep rising, but *per capita* output keeps rising as well (see Figure 2.1).

economic growth: An increase in output (real GDP); an expansion of production possibilities.

Poor Nations. People in the world's poorest countries aren't so fortunate. China's economy has grown exceptionally fast in the last 20 years, propelling it to second place in the global GDP rankings. But in many other nations total output has actually *declined* year after year, further depressing living standards. Notice in Table 2.1, for example, what's been happening in Haiti. From 2000 to 2005, Haiti's output of goods and services (GDP) *declined* by an average of 0.5 percent a year. As a result, total Haitian output in 2005 was 3 percent *smaller* than in 2000. During those same years, the Haitian population kept growing—by 1.4 percent a year. With *negative* economic growth and fast population growth, Haiti's per capita GDP fell below $2,000 a year. That low level of per capita GDP left nearly two-thirds of Haiti's population undernourished.

webnote

Data on the output of different nations are available from the Central Intelligence Agency at www.odci.gov/cia/publications/factbook

As Table 2.1 shows, the economic situation deteriorated even faster in Zimbabwe. Even some poor nations that had *positive* GDP growth in recent years (e.g., Burundi, Paraguay) didn't grow fast enough to raise living standards. As a result, they fell even further behind America's (rising) level of prosperity.

The Mix of Output

Regardless of how much output a nation produces, the *mix* of output always includes both *goods* (such as cars, plasma TVs, potatoes) and *services* (like this economics course, visits to a doctor, or a professional baseball game). A century ago, about two-thirds of U.S. output consisted of farm goods (37 percent), manufactured goods (22 percent), and mining (9 percent). Since then, over 25 *million* people have left the farms and sought jobs in other sectors. As a result, today's mix of output is reversed: ***Nearly 75 percent of U.S. output consists of services, not goods*** (see Figure 2.2).

TABLE 2.1
GDP Growth vs. Population Growth

The relationship between GDP growth and population growth is very different in rich and poor countries. The populations of rich countries are growing very slowly, and gains in per capita GDP are easily achieved. In the poorest countries, population is still increasing rapidly, making it difficult to raise living standards. Notice how per capita incomes are *declining* in many poor countries (such as Paraguay, Zimbabwe, and Haiti).

	Average Growth Rate (2000–2005) of		
	GDP	Population	Per Capita GDP
High-income countries			
United States	2.8	1.0	1.8
Canada	2.6	1.0	1.6
Japan	1.3	0.2	1.1
France	1.5	0.6	0.9
Low-income countries			
China	9.6	0.6	9.0
India	6.9	1.5	5.4
Kenya	2.8	2.2	0.6
Paraguay	1.8	2.4	−0.6
Madagascar	2.0	2.8	−0.8
Burundi	2.2	3.1	−0.9
Haiti	−0.5	1.4	−1.9
Zimbabwe	−6.1	0.6	−6.7

Source: From *World Development Report, 2007.* Used with permission by the International Bank for Reconstruction and Development/The World Bank.

webnote

Data on the mix of output in different nations are compiled in the World Bank's annual World Development Report, available at www.worldbank.org

The *relative* decline in goods production (manufacturing, farming) doesn't mean that we're producing *fewer* goods today than in earlier decades. Quite the contrary. While some industries such as iron and steel have shrunk, others, such as chemicals, publishing, and telecommunications equipment, have grown tremendously. The result is that manufacturing output has increased fourfold since 1950. The same kind of thing has happened in the farm sector, where output keeps rising even though agriculture's *share* of total output has declined. It's just that output of *services* has increased so much faster.

Development Patterns. The transformation of the United States into a service economy is a reflection of our high incomes. In Ethiopia, where the most urgent concern is still to keep people from starving, over 50 percent of output comes from the farm sector. Poor people don't have enough income to buy dental services, vacations, or even an education, so the mix of output in poor countries is weighted toward goods, not services.

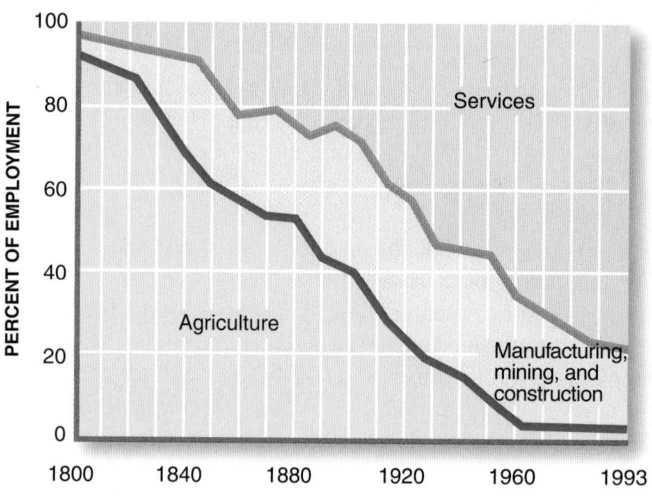

FIGURE 2.2
The Changing Mix of Output

Two hundred years ago, almost all U.S. output came from farms. Today, 75 percent of output consists of services, not farm or manufactured goods.

Source: U.S. Department of Commerce.

Today's Mix of Output

Services have become such a dominant share of the economy's output that we can say that ***America is primarily a service economy and will become increasingly so in the future.*** This generalization doesn't provide much detail, however, about exactly WHAT America produces. What kinds of services are being produced? Which goods?

We can develop a clearer picture of our answer to the WHAT question by examining the uses to which our output is put. ***The four major uses of total output (GDP) are***

- ***Consumption***
- ***Investment***
- ***Government services***
- ***Net exports***

Consumer Goods and Services. Most of America's output consists of consumer goods and services. This output includes everything from breakfast cereals (a good) to movie rentals (a service) and college education (another service)—anything and everything households buy for their own use. As Figure 2.3 illustrates, such consumption goods and services account for over two-thirds of all output.

Investment Goods and Services. Investment goods are a completely different type of output. **Investment** goods are the plant, machinery, equipment, and structures that are produced for the business sector. These investment goods are used to (1) replace worn-out equipment and factories, thus *maintaining* our production possibilities, and (2) increase and improve our stock of capital, thereby *expanding* our production possibilities. Presently the United States devotes 17 percent of output to investment.

investment: Expenditures on (production of) new plant, equipment, and structures (capital) in a given time period, plus changes in business inventories.

Poor countries need capital investment desperately. Their incomes are so low, however, that they can't afford to cut back much on consumer goods. When Stalin wanted to make Russia an industrial power, he cut output of consumer goods and forced Russian households to scrape by with meager supplies of food, clothing, and even shelter for decades. Today, most poor nations have to depend on foreign aid and other capital inflows to finance needed investment. Without more investment, they run the risk of continuing stagnation or even a decline of living standards.

Government Services. The third type of output every nation produces is government services. Federal, state, and local governments purchase resources to police the streets, teach classes, write laws, and build highways. The resources the government sector uses for these purposes are unavailable for either consumption or investment. At present, the production of government services absorbs roughly one-fifth of total U.S. output (see Figure 2.3).

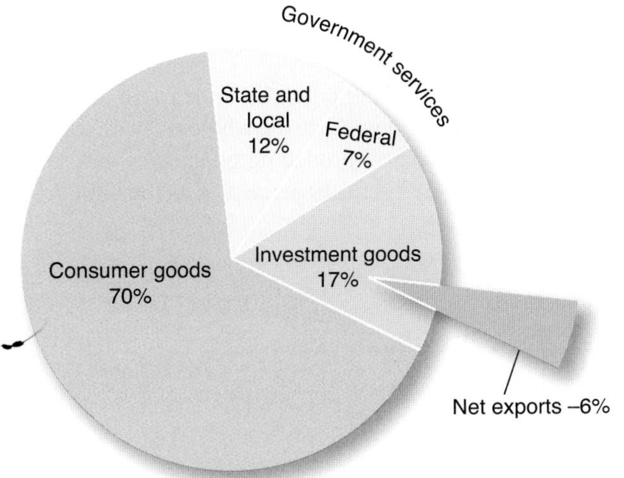

FIGURE 2.3
What America Produces

Over two-thirds of America's output consists of consumer goods and services. Investment (such as plant, equipment, buildings) claims about 17 percent of total output. The public sector gets nearly 19 percent. Although we export more than 10 percent of domestic output, we import an even larger share of goods and services; *net* exports are negative.

Source: *Economic Report of the President, 2007.*

income transfers: Payments to individuals for which no current goods or services are exchanged, e.g., Social Security, welfare, unemployment benefits.

Notice the emphasis again on the production of real goods and services. The federal government now *spends* about $3 trillion a year. Much of that spending, however, consists of income transfers, not resource purchases. **Income transfers** are payments to individuals for which no direct service is provided. Social Security benefits, welfare checks, food stamps, and unemployment benefits are all transfer payments. This spending is *not* part of our output of goods and services. ***Only that part of federal spending used to acquire resources and produce services is counted in GDP.***

Federal purchases (production) of goods and services account for only 7 percent of total output. What state and local governments lack in size, they make up for in sheer numbers. In addition to the 50 state governments, there are 3,000 counties, 18,000 cities, 17,000 townships, 21,000 school districts, and over 20,000 special districts. These are the government entities that build roads; provide schools, police, and firefighters; administer hospitals; and provide social services. The output of all these state and local governments accounts for roughly 12 percent of total GDP.

exports: Goods and services sold to foreign buyers.

imports: Goods and services purchased from foreign sources.

Net Exports. Finally, we should note that some of the goods and services we produce each year are used abroad rather than at home. In other words, we **export** some of our output to other countries.

International trade isn't a one-way street. While we export some of our own output, we also **import** goods and services from other countries. These imports may be used for consumption (sweaters from New Zealand, Japanese DVDs, travel), investment (German ball bearings, Lloyds of London insurance), or government (French radar screens). Theoretically, imports wouldn't affect the value of GDP since GDP includes only goods and services produced within a nation's borders. In practice, however, estimates of GDP are based on market *purchases,* not surveys of production. As a result, consumption, investment, and government purchases include imports as well as domestically produced goods. To get an accurate reading of *domestic* production, imports must be subtracted out.

net exports: The value of exports minus the value of imports.

Table 2.2 summarizes America's trade flows. In 2006, we exported $1,023 billion worth of goods (e.g., airplanes, farm machinery, tobacco, food) and another $414 billion of services (e.g., movies, travel, engineering). These exports amounted to approximately 10 percent of total output. We imported even more goods and services, however, and so ended up with negative **net exports** (a trade deficit).

Comparative Advantage

You might wonder why we trade so much. Most of the goods we import could be produced in the United States. In fact, most imported goods have domestically produced substitutes, for example, cars, computers, and tomatoes. Our decision to import them is not based on our inability to produce them but instead on the *efficiency* of importing them. International trade allows a nation to produce goods in which it has a cost advantage and then trade them for imported goods in which it has a cost disadvantage. This principle of **comparative advantage** entails exporting goods with low opportunity cost and importing goods with high opportunity cost. In other words, **international trade allows countries to produce and export what they do best and import goods they don't produce as efficiently.**

comparative advantage: The ability of a country to produce a specific good at a lower opportunity cost than its trading partners.

Although all nations gain from international trade, smaller countries are most in need of specialization. With few resources, a small economy can't produce the whole array of goods and services consumers want. So they need to *specialize*—producing goods they can sell (export) in world markets. Saudi Arabia, for example, exports 40 percent of its total output,

TABLE 2.2
U.S. Trade Flows

The U.S. is the world's largest exporter *and* the world's largest importer. When imports exceed exports, net exports are negative: we are consuming more output than we are producing.

EXPORTS of U.S.-made goods and services	:	$ 1,437 billion
− IMPORTS of foreign-made goods and services	:	2,202 billion
NET EXPORTS		−$ 765 billion

Source: U.S. Department of Commerce (2006 data).

mostly in the form of crude oil. It then uses its export earnings to buy desired cars, engineering services, and food that it can't produce efficiently itself. China exports textiles, dolls, and linens that are produced with cheap labor, then imports airplanes, telecommunications equipment, and oil rigs that are more capital-intensive. U.S. consumers get cheaper consumer goods while China gets needed investment goods.

HOW AMERICA PRODUCES

Our trade patterns offer some clues into How America produces. All nations must use the same **factors of production** to produce goods and services. But the quantity and quality of those factors varies greatly.

factors of production: Resource inputs used to produce goods and services, such as land, labor, capital, entrepreneurship.

Human Capital

We've already observed that America's premier position in global GDP rankings isn't due to the number of humans within our borders. We have far fewer bodies than China, India, Indonesia, and Brazil, yet produce far more output. What counts for production purposes is not just the *number* of workers a nation has, but the *skills* of those workers—what we call **human capital.**

human capital: The knowledge and skills possessed by the workforce.

Over time, the United States has invested heavily in human capital. In 1940, only 1 out of 20 young Americans graduated from college; today, over 30 percent of young people are college graduates. High school graduation rates have jumped from 38 percent to over 85 percent in the same time period. In the less developed countries, only 1 out of 2 youth ever *attend* high school, much less graduate (see World View). As a consequence, the United Nations estimates that 1.2 billion people—a fifth of humanity—are unable to read a book or even write their own names. Without even functional literacy, such workers are doomed to low-productivity jobs. Despite low wages, they are not likely to "steal" many jobs from America's highly educated and trained workforce.

Capital Stock

America has also accumulated a massive stock of capital—over $40 *trillion* worth of machinery, factories, and buildings. As a result of all this prior investment, U.S. production tends to be very **capital-intensive.** The contrast with *labor-intensive* production in poorer countries is striking. A Chinese farmer mostly works with his hands and crude

capital-intensive: Production processes that use a high ratio of capital to labor inputs.

WORLD VIEW

The Education Gap between Rich and Poor Nations

Virtually all Americans attend high school and roughly 85 percent graduate. In poor countries, relatively few workers attend high school and even fewer graduate. Half the workers in the world's poorest nations are illiterate.

Source: From *World Development Indicators, 2006.* Used with permission by the International Bank for Reconstruction and Development/The World Bank. www.worldbank.org

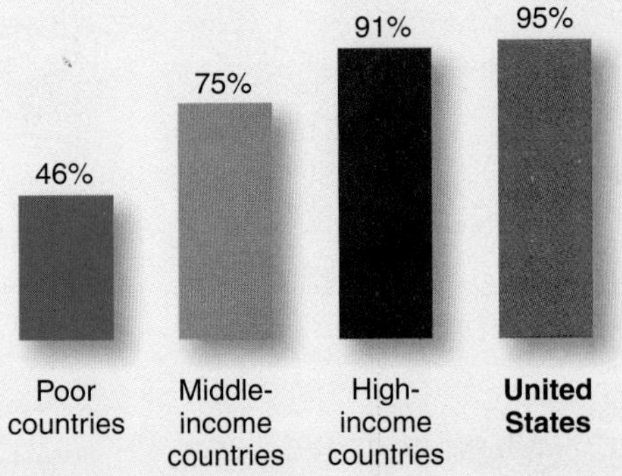

Enrollment in Secondary Schools (percent of school-age youth attending secondary schools)

Poor countries	Middle-income countries	High-income countries	**United States**
46%	75%	91%	95%

Analysis: The high productivity of the American economy is explained in part by the quality of its labor resources. Workers in poorer, less developed countries get much less education and training.

implements, whereas a U.S. farmer works with computers, automated irrigation systems, and mechanized equipment (see photos below). Russian business managers don't have the computer networks or telecommunications systems that make U.S. business so efficient. In Haiti and Ethiopia, even telephones, indoor plumbing, and dependable sources of power are scarce.

High Productivity

productivity: Output per unit of input, such as output per labor-hour.

When you put educated workers together with sophisticated capital equipment, you tend to get more output. This relationship largely explains why the United States has such a lead in worker **productivity**—the amount of output produced by the average worker. ***American households are able to consume so much because American workers produce so much.*** It's really that simple.

The huge output of the United States is thus explained not only by a wealth of resources but by their quality as well. ***The high productivity of the U.S. economy results from using highly educated workers in capital-intensive production processes.***

Factor Mobility. Our continuing ability to produce the goods and services that consumers demand also depends on our agility in *reallocating* resources from one industry to another. Every year, some industries expand and others contract. Thousands of new firms start up each year and almost as many others disappear. In the process, land, labor, capital, and entrepreneurship move from one industry to another in response to changing demands and technology. In 1975, Federal Express, Compaq Computer, Staples, Oracle, and Amgen didn't even exist. Wal-Mart was still a small retailer. Starbucks was selling coffee on Seattle street corners, and the founders of Google and YouTube weren't even born. Today, these companies employ over a million people. These workers came from other firms and industries that weren't growing as fast.

Technological Advance. One of the forces that keeps shifting resources from one industry to another is continuing advances in technology. Advances in technology can be as sophisticated as microscopic miniaturization of electronic circuits or as simple as the reorganization of production processes. Either phenomenon increases the productivity of the workforce and potential output. ***Whenever technology advances, an economy can produce more output with existing resources.***

Outsourcing and Trade. The same technological advances that fuel economic growth also facilitate *global* resource use. Telecommunications has become so sophisticated and inexpensive that phone workers in India or Grenada can answer calls directed to U.S. companies.

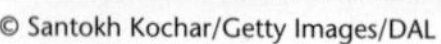

© Santokh Kochar/Getty Images/DAL

Gene Alexander, USDA Natural Resources Conservation Service/DAL

Analysis: An abundance of capital equipment and advanced technology make American farmers and workers far more productive than workers in poor nations.

Likewise, programmers in India can work online to write computer code, develop software, or perform accounting chores for U.S. corporations. Although such "outsourcing" is often viewed as a threat to U.S. jobs, it is really another source of increased U.S. output. By outsourcing routine tasks to foreign workers, U.S. workers are able to focus on higher-value jobs. U.S. computer engineers do less routine programming and more systems design. U.S. accountants do less cost tabulation and more cost analysis. By utilizing foreign resources in the production process, U.S. workers are able to pursue their *comparative advantage* in high-skill, capital-intensive jobs. In this way, both productivity and total output increase. Although some U.S. workers suffer temporary job losses in this process, the economy overall gains.

Role of Government

In assessing HOW goods are produced and economies grow, we must also take heed of the role the government plays. As we noted in Chapter 1, the amount of economic freedom varies greatly among the 200-plus nations of the world. Moreover, the Heritage Foundation has documented a positive relationship between the degree of economic freedom and economic growth (see Figure 2.4). Quite simply, when entrepreneurs are unfettered by regulation or high taxes, they are more likely to design and produce better mousetraps. When the government owns the factors of production, imposes high taxes, or tightly regulates output, there is little opportunity or incentive to design better products or pursue new technology.

Recognizing the productive value of economic freedom isn't tantamount to rejecting all government intervention. No one really advocates the complete abolition of government. On the contrary, the government plays a critical role in establishing a framework in which private businesses can operate.

- *Providing a legal framework.* One of the most basic functions of government is to establish and enforce the rules of the game. In some bygone era maybe a person's word was sufficient to guarantee delivery or payment. Businesses today, however, rely more on written contracts. The government gives legitimacy to contracts by establishing the rules for such pacts and by enforcing their provisions. In the absence of contractual rights, few companies would be willing to ship goods without prepayment (in cash). Even the incentive to write textbooks would disappear if government copyright laws didn't forbid unauthorized photocopying. By establishing ownership rights, contract rights, and other rules of the game, the government lays the foundation for market transactions.

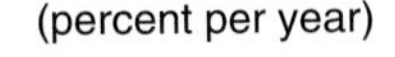

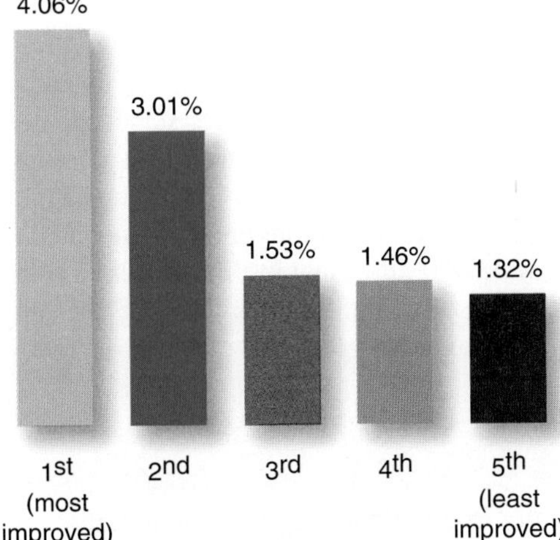

FIGURE 2.4
Economic Freedom and Growth

The extent of economic freedom (market reliance) affects a nation's ability to grow. The Heritage Foundation shows that as nations become "freer" (rely more on markets and less on government), output (real GDP) grows more quickly.

Source: Heritage Foundation, *2006 Index of Economic Freedom,* Washington, DC. Used with permission.

- *Protecting the environment.* The government also intervenes in the market to protect the environment. The legal contract system is designed to protect the interests of a buyer and a seller who wish to do business. What if, however, the business they contract for harms third parties? How are the interests of persons who *aren't* party to the contract to be protected?

  Numerous examples abound of how unregulated production may harm third parties. Earlier in the century, the steel mills around Pittsburgh blocked out the sun with clouds of sulfurous gases that spewed out of their furnaces. Local residents were harmed every time they inhaled. In the absence of government intervention, such side effects would be common. Decisions on how to produce would be based on costs alone, not on how the environment is affected. However, such **externalities**—spillover costs imposed on the broader community—affect our collective well-being. To reduce the external costs of production, the government limits air, water, and noise pollution and regulates environmental use.

externalities: Costs (or benefits) of a market activity borne by a third party.

- *Protecting consumers.* The government also uses its power to protect the interests of consumers. One way to do this is to prevent individual business firms from becoming too powerful. In the extreme case, a single firm might have a **monopoly** on the production of a specific good. As the sole producer of that good, a monopolist could dictate the price, the quality, and the quantity of the product. In such a situation, consumers would likely end up with the short end of the stick—paying too much for too little.

  To protect consumers from monopoly exploitation, the government tries to prevent individual firms from dominating specific markets. Antitrust laws prohibit mergers or acquisitions that would threaten competition. The U.S. Department of Justice and the Federal Trade Commission also regulate pricing practices, advertising claims, and other behavior that might put consumers at an unfair disadvantage in product markets.

  Government also regulates the safety of many products. Consumers don't have enough expertise to assess the safety of various medicines, for example. If they rely on trial and error to determine drug safety, they might not get a second chance. To avoid this calamity, the government requires rigorous testing of new drugs, food additives, and other products.

monopoly: A firm that produces the entire market supply of a particular good or service.

- *Protecting labor.* The government also regulates how labor resources are used in the production process. In most poor nations, children are forced to start working at very early ages, often for minuscule wages. They often don't get the chance to go to school or to stay healthy. In Africa, 40 percent of children under age 14 work to survive or to help support their families. In the United States, child labor laws and compulsory schooling prevent minor children from being exploited. Government regulations also set standards for workplace safety, minimum wages, fringe benefits, and overtime provisions.

Striking a Balance

All these government interventions are designed to change the way resources are used. Such interventions reflect the conviction that the market alone might not select the best possible way of producing goods and services. There's no guarantee, however, that government regulation of HOW goods are produced always makes us better off. Excessive regulation may inhibit production, raise product prices, and limit consumer choices. As noted in Chapter 1, *government* failure might replace *market* failure, leaving us no better off—possibly even worse off. This possibility underscores the importance of striking the right balance between market reliance and government regulation.

FOR WHOM AMERICA PRODUCES

As we've seen, America produces a huge quantity of output, using high-quality labor and capital resources. That leaves one basic question unanswered: FOR WHOM is all this output produced?

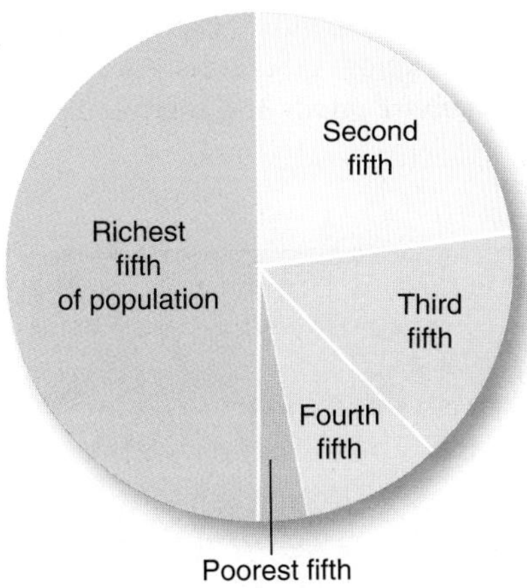

FIGURE 2.5
The U.S. Distribution of Income

The richest fifth of U.S. households gets half of all the income—a huge slice of the income pie. By contrast, the poorest fifth gets only a sliver.

Income Quintile	2005 Income	Average Income	Share of Total Income (%)
Highest fifth	above $92,000	$160,000	50.4
Second fifth	$58,000–92,000	$ 73,000	23.0
Third fifth	$36,000–58,000	$ 46,000	14.6
Fourth fifth	$19,000–36,000	$ 27,000	8.6
Lowest fifth	$0–19,000	$ 11,000	3.4

Source: U.S. Department of Commerce, Bureau of the Census (averages rounded to thousands of dollars; 2005 data).

How many goods and services one gets largely depends on how much income one has to spend. The U.S. economy uses the market mechanism to distribute most goods and services. Those who receive the most income get the most goods. This goes a long way toward explaining why millionaires live in mansions and homeless people seek shelter in abandoned cars. This is the kind of stark inequality that fueled Karl Marx's denunciation of capitalism. Even today, people wonder how some Americans can be so rich while others are so poor.

webnote

The most current data on the U.S. income distribution are available from the U.S. Bureau of the Census at www.census.gov/hhes/www/income.html

U.S. Income Distribution

Figure 2.5 illustrates the actual distribution of income in the United States. For this illustration the entire population is sorted into five groups of equal size, ranked by income. In this depiction, all the rich people are in the top **income quintile;** the poor are in the lowest quintile. To be in the top quintile in 2005, a household needed at least $92,000 of income. All the households in the lowest quintile had incomes under $19,000.

income quintile: One-fifth of the population, rank-ordered by income (e.g., top fifth).

The most striking feature of Figure 2.5 is how large a slice of the income pie rich people get: ***The top 20 percent (quintile) of U.S. households get half of all U.S. income.*** By contrast, the poorest 20 percent (quintile) of U.S. households get only a sliver of the income pie—less than 4 percent. Those grossly unequal slices explain why nearly half of all Americans believe the nation is divided into "haves" and "have nots."

Global Inequality

As unequal as U.S. incomes are, income disparities are actually greater in many other countries. Ironically, income inequalities are often greatest in the poorest countries. The richest *tenth* of U.S. families gets 30 percent of America's income pie. The richest tenth of Sierra Leone's families gets 45 percent of that nation's income (see World View on page 39). Given the small size of Sierra Leone's pie, the *bottom* tenth of Sierra Leone families is left with mere crumbs. As we'll see in Chapter 37, 75 percent of Sierra Leone's population live in "severe poverty," defined by the World Bank as an income of less than $2 a day.

Comparisons across countries would manifest even greater inequality. As we saw earlier, Third World GDP per capita is far below U.S. levels. As a consequence, even **poor *people in the United States receive far more goods and services than the* average *household in most low-income countries.***

RF/CORBIS/DAL

Analysis: The market distributes income (and, in turn, goods and services) according to the resources an individual owns and how well they are used. If the resulting inequalities are too great, some redistribution via government intervention may be desired.

WORLD VIEW

Income Share of the Rich

Inequality tends to diminish as a country develops. In poor, developing nations, the richest tenth of the population typically gets 40 to 50 percent of all income. In developed countries, the richest tenth gets 20 to 30 percent of total income.

Source: From *World Development Indicators, 2006.* Used with permission by the International Bank for Reconstruction and Development/The World Bank. www.worldbank.org

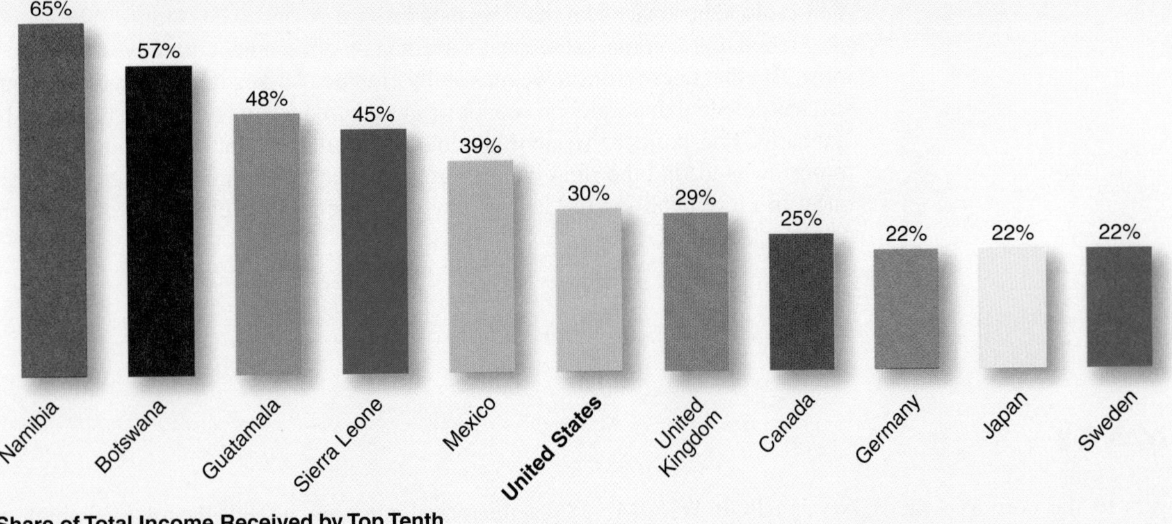

Analysis: The FOR WHOM question is reflected in the distribution of income. Although the U.S. distribution is very unequal, inequalities loom even larger in most Third World countries.

THE ECONOMY TOMORROW

ENDING GLOBAL POVERTY

Global answers to the basic questions of WHAT, HOW, and FOR WHOM have been shaped by market forces and government intervention. Obviously, the answers aren't yet fully satisfactory.

Millions of Americans still struggle to make ends meet. Worse yet, nearly 3 *billion* people around the world live in abject poverty—with incomes of less than $2 a day. Over a fourth of the world's population is illiterate, nearly half has no access to sanitation facilities, and a fifth is chronically malnourished.

The World Bank thinks we can do a lot better. In fact, it has set ambitious goals for the economy tomorrow. In the Millennium Declaration of October 2000, the 180 nation-members of the World Bank set specific goals for world development. By 2015, they agreed to

- Reduce extreme poverty and hunger by at least half.
- Achieve universal primary education.
- Reduce child and maternal mortality by two-thirds.
- Reduce by half the number of people without access to potable water.

Achieving these goals would obviously help billions of people. But how will we fulfill them?

People in rich nations also aspire to higher living standards in the economy tomorrow. They already enjoy more comforts than people in poor nations even dream of. But that doesn't stop us from wanting more consumer goods, better schools, improved health care, a cleaner environment, and greater economic security. How will we get them?

A magic wand could transform the economy tomorrow into utopia. But short of that, we're saddled with economic reality. All nations have limited resources and technology. To get to a better place tomorrow, we've got to put those resources to even better uses. Will the market alone head us down the right path? As we've observed (Figure 2.4), economies that have relied more on market mechanisms than on government directives have prospered the most. But that doesn't mean we must fully embrace laissez faire. Government intervention still has potential to accelerate economic growth, reduce poverty, raise health and education standards, and protect the environment. The challenge for the economy both today and tomorrow is to find the right balance of market and government forces. We'll explore this quest in more detail as the text proceeds and revisit the challenge of global poverty in Chapter 37.

SUMMARY

- Answers to the core WHAT, HOW, and FOR WHOM questions vary greatly across nations. These differences reflect varying production possibilities, choice mechanisms, and values. LO1
- Gross domestic product (GDP) is the basic measure of how much an economy produces. The United States produces over $14 trillion of output per year, more than one-fifth of the world's total. The U.S. GDP per capita is five times the world average. LO1
- The high level of U.S. per capita GDP reflects the high productivity of U.S. workers. Abundant capital, education, technology, training, and management all contribute to high productivity. The relatively high degree of U.S. economic freedom (market reliance) is also an important cause of superior economic growth. LO2
- Over 75 percent of U.S. output consists of services, including government services. This is a reversal of historical ratios and reflects the relatively high incomes in the United States. Poor nations produce much higher proportions of food and manufactured goods. LO2
- Most of America's output consists of consumer goods and services. Investment goods account for only 17 percent of total output, and government purchases about 20 percent. LO2
- Incomes are distributed very unequally among households, with households in the highest income class (quintile) receiving over 10 times more income than low-income households. Incomes are even less equally distributed in many poor nations. LO3
- The mix of output, production methods, and the income distribution continues to change. The WHAT, HOW, and FOR WHOM answers in tomorrow's economy will depend on the continuing interplay of (changing) market signals and (changing) government policy. LO3

Key Terms

gross domestic product (GDP)
per capita GDP
economic growth
investment
income transfers
exports
imports
net exports
comparative advantage
factors of production
human capital
capital-intensive
productivity
externalities
monopoly
income quintile

Questions for Discussion

1. Americans already enjoy living standards that far exceed world averages. Do we have enough? Should we even try to produce more? LO1
2. Why is per capita GDP so much higher in the United States than in Mexico? LO2
3. Why do people suggest that the United States needs to devote more output to investment goods? Why not produce just consumption goods? LO2
4. The U.S. farm population has shrunk by over 25 million people since 1900. Where did all the people go? Why did they move? LO2
5. How might the following government interventions affect a nation's economic growth? LO2
   a. Mandatory school attendance.
   b. High income taxes.
   c. Copyright and patent protection.
   d. Political corruption.
6. How many people are employed by your local or state government? What do they produce? What is the opportunity cost of that output? LO1
7. Why should the government regulate how goods are produced? Can regulation ever be excessive? LO1
8. Should the government try to equalize incomes more by raising taxes on the rich and giving more money to the poor? How might such redistribution affect total output and growth? LO3
9. Why are incomes so much more unequal in poor nations than in rich ones? LO3
10. How might free markets help reduce global poverty? How might they impede that goal? LO3

problems The Student Problem Set at the back of this book contains numerical and graphing problems for this chapter.

web activities to accompany this chapter can be found on the Online Learning Center: **http://www.mhhe.com/economics/schiller11e**

Supply and Demand

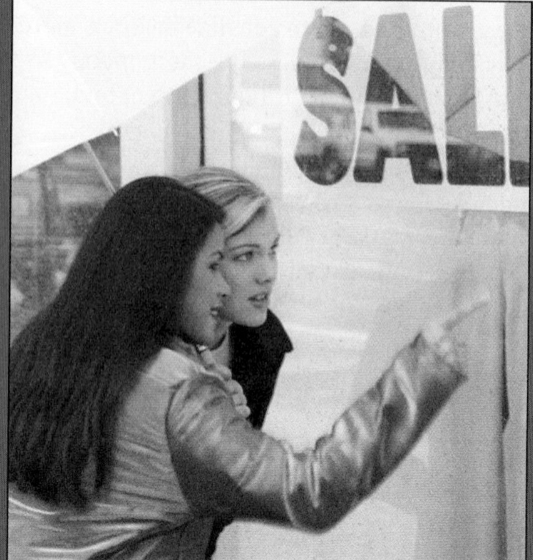

LEARNING OBJECTIVES

After reading this chapter, you should know:

LO1. The meaning of market demand and supply.

LO2. How market prices are established.

LO3. What causes market prices to change.

LO4. How government price controls affect market outcomes.

The lights went out in California in January 2001. With only minutes of warning, sections of high-tech Silicon Valley, San Francisco, the state capital of Sacramento, and a host of smaller cities went dark. Schools closed early, traffic signals malfunctioned, ATM machines shut down, and elevators abruptly stopped. "It's like we're living in Bosnia," said Michael Mischer, an Oakland, California, baker. "How could this happen?"[1]

California's then governor, Gray Davis, had a ready answer. He said out-of-state power company "pirates" were gouging California residents with exorbitant prices they could not pay. As he saw it, the electricity crisis was a classic example of market-driven greed. To resolve the crisis, the governor proposed stiff price controls, the state purchase of transmission lines, and state-ordered customer refunds from "profiteering" power companies. As he saw it, only the state government could keep the lights on.

Critics said the governor's explanation made for good politics but bad economics. Government intervention, not the market, was the cause of the electricity crisis, they said. Supply and demand were out of balance in California and only *higher* prices and *less* government intervention could keep the lights on. U.S. Treasury Secretary Paul O'Neill criticized the governor for trying "to defeat economics… I mean, you don't have to have an economics degree to understand that this is an unworkable situation." One of UC–Berkeley's Nobel-winning economists, Daniel McFadden, echoed that sentiment, blaming the state's "rigid regulation" for its energy woes.

California's 2001 energy crisis is a classic illustration of why the choice between market reliance and government intervention is so critical and often so controversial. The goal of this chapter is to put that choice into a coherent framework. To do so, we'll focus on how unregulated markets work. How does the market mechanism decide WHAT to produce, HOW to produce, and FOR WHOM to produce? Specifically,

- **What determines the price of a good or service?**
- **How does the price of a product affect its production and consumption?**
- **Why do prices and production levels often change?**

Once we've seen how unregulated markets work, we'll observe how government intervention may alter market outcomes—for better or worse. Hopefully, the lights won't go off before we finish.

[1]Rene Sanchez and William Booth, "California Forced to Turn the Lights Off," *Washington Post,* January 18, 2001, p. 1.

MARKET PARTICIPANTS

A good way to start figuring out how markets work is to see who participates in them. The answer is simple: just about every person and institution on the planet. Domestically, over 300 million consumers, about 20 million business firms, and tens of thousands of government agencies participate directly in the U.S. economy. Millions of international buyers and sellers also participate in U.S. markets.

Maximizing Behavior

All these market participants enter the marketplace to satisfy specific goals. Consumers, for example, come with a limited amount of income to spend. Their objective is to buy the most desirable goods and services that their limited budgets will permit. We can't afford *everything* we want, so we must make *choices* about how to spend our scarce dollars. Our goal is to *maximize* the utility (satisfaction) we get from our available incomes.

Businesses also try to maximize in the marketplace. In their case, the quest is for maximum *profits.* Business profits are the difference between sales receipts and total costs. To maximize profits, business firms try to use resources efficiently in producing products that consumers desire.

The public sector also has maximizing goals. The economic purpose of government is to use available resources to serve public needs. The resources available for this purpose are limited too. Hence, local, state, and federal governments must use scarce resources carefully, striving to maximize the general welfare of society. International consumers and producers pursue these same goals when participating in our markets.

Market participants sometimes lose sight of their respective goals. Consumers sometimes buy impulsively and later wish they'd used their income more wisely. Likewise, a producer may take a 2-hour lunch, even at the sacrifice of maximum profits. And elected officials sometimes put their personal interests ahead of the public's interest. In all sectors of the economy, however, ***the basic goals of utility maximization, profit maximization, and welfare maximization explain most market activity.***

Specialization and Exchange

We are driven to buy and sell goods and services in the market by two simple facts. First, most of us are incapable of producing everything we want to consume. Second, even if we *could* produce all our own goods and services, it would still make sense to *specialize,* producing only one product and *trading* it for other desired goods and services.

Suppose you were capable of growing your own food, stitching your own clothes, building your own shelter, and even writing your own economics text. Even in this little utopia, it would still make sense to decide how *best* to expend your limited time and energy, relying on others to fill in the gaps. If you were *most* proficient at growing food, you would be best off spending your time farming. You could then *exchange* some of your food output for the clothes, shelter, and books you wanted. In the end, you'd be able to consume *more* goods than if you'd tried to make everything yourself.

Our economic interactions with others are thus necessitated by two constraints:

1. Our absolute inability as individuals to produce all the things we need or desire.
2. The limited amount of time, energy, and resources we have for producing those things we could make for ourselves.

Together, these constraints lead us to specialize and interact. Most of the interactions that result take place in the market.

THE CIRCULAR FLOW

Figure 3.1 summarizes the kinds of interactions that occur among market participants. Note first that the figure identifies four separate groups of participants. Domestically, the rectangle labeled "Consumers" includes all 300 million consumers in the United States. In the "Business firms" box are grouped all the domestic business enterprises that buy and sell goods and services. The third participant, "Governments," includes the many separate agencies of the federal government, as well as state and local governments. Figure 3.1 also illustrates the role of global actors.

FIGURE 3.1
The Circular Flow

Business firms supply goods and services to product markets (point *A*) and purchase factors of production in factor markets (*B*). Individual consumers supply factors of production such as their own labor (*C*) and purchase final goods and services (*D*). Federal, state, and local governments acquire resources in factor markets (*E*) and provide services to both consumers and business (*F*). International participants also take part by supplying imports, purchasing exports (*G*), and buying and selling factors of production (*H*).

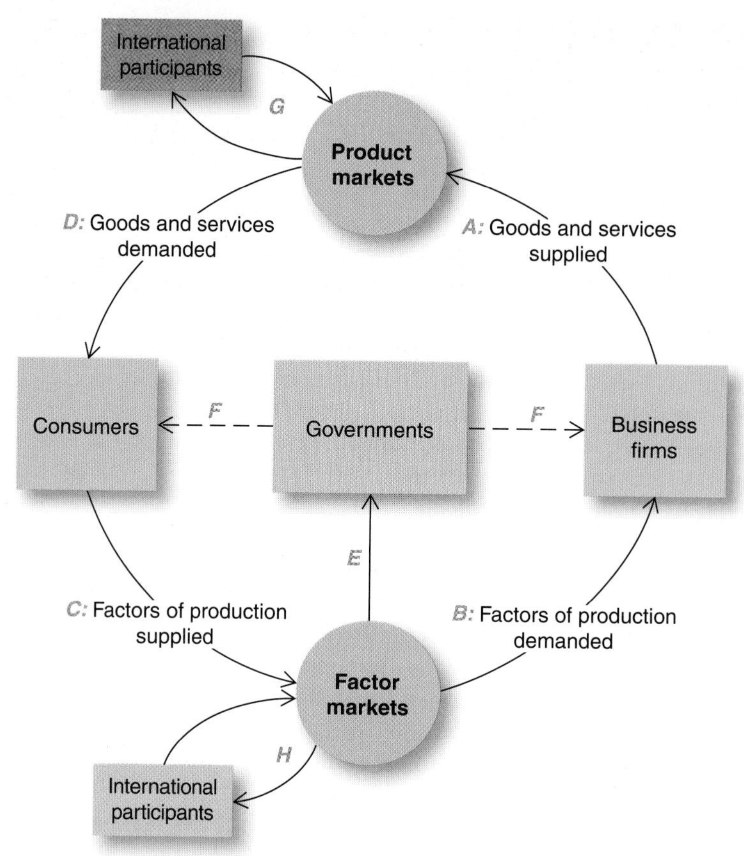

The Two Markets

factor market: Any place where factors of production (e.g., land, labor, capital) are bought and sold.

The easiest way to keep track of all this activity is to distinguish two basic markets. Figure 3.1 makes this distinction by portraying separate circles for product markets and factor markets. In **factor markets,** factors of production are exchanged. Market participants buy or sell land, labor, or capital that can be used in the production process. When you go looking for work, for example, you're making a factor of production—your labor—available to producers. The producers will hire you—purchase your services in the factor market—if you're offering the skills they need at a price they're willing to pay. The same kind of interaction occurs in factor markets when the government enlists workers into the armed services or when the Japanese buy farmland in Montana.

product market: Any place where finished goods and services (products) are bought and sold.

Interactions within factor markets are only half the story. At the end of a hard day's work, consumers go to the grocery store (or to a virtual store online) to buy desired goods and services—that is, to buy *products.* In this context, consumers again interact with business firms, this time purchasing goods and services those firms have produced. These interactions occur in **product markets.** Foreigners also participate in the product market by supplying goods and services (imports) to the United States and buying some of our output (exports).

opportunity cost: The most desired goods or services that are forgone in order to obtain something else.

The government sector also supplies services (e.g., education, national defense, highways). Most government services aren't explicitly sold in product markets, however. Typically, they're delivered "free," without an explicit price (e.g., public elementary schools, highways). This doesn't mean government services are truly free, though. There's still an **opportunity cost** associated with every service the government provides. Consumers and businesses pay that cost indirectly through taxes rather than directly through market prices.

In Figure 3.1, the arrow connecting product markets to consumers (point *D*) emphasizes the fact that consumers, by definition, don't supply products. When individuals produce goods and services, they do so within the government or business sector. For instance, a doctor, a dentist, or an economic consultant functions in two sectors. When selling services in the market, this person is regarded as a "business"; when away from the office, he or she is regarded as a "consumer." This distinction is helpful in emphasizing that ***the consumer is the final recipient of all goods and services produced.***

Locating Markets. Although we refer repeatedly to two kinds of markets in this book, it would be a little foolish to go off in search of the product and factor markets. Neither market is a single, identifiable structure. The term *market* simply refers to a place or situation where an economic exchange occurs—where a buyer and seller interact. The exchange may take place on the street, in a taxicab, over the phone, by mail, or in cyberspace. In some cases, the market used may in fact be quite distinguishable, as in the case of a retail store, the Chicago Commodity Exchange, or a state employment office. But whatever it looks like, ***a market exists wherever and whenever an exchange takes place.***

Dollars and Exchange

Figure 3.1 provides a useful summary of market activities, but it neglects one critical element of market interactions: dollars. Each arrow in the figure actually has two dimensions. Consider again the arrow linking consumers to product markets: It's drawn in only one direction because consumers, by definition, don't provide goods and services directly to product markets. But they do provide something: dollars. If you want to obtain something from a product market, you must offer to pay for it (typically, with cash, check, or credit card). Consumers exchange dollars for goods and services in product markets.

The same kinds of exchange occur in factor markets. When you go to work, you exchange a factor of production (your labor) for income, typically a paycheck. Here again, the path connecting consumers to factor markets really goes in two directions: one of real resources, the other of dollars. Consumers receive wages, rent, and interest for the labor, land, and capital they bring to the factor markets. Indeed, nearly ***every market transaction involves an exchange of dollars for goods (in product markets) or resources (in factor markets).*** Money is thus critical in facilitating market exchanges and the specialization the exchanges permit.

Supply and Demand

In every market transaction there must be a buyer and a seller. The seller is on the **supply** side of the market; the buyer is on the **demand** side. As noted earlier, we *supply* resources to the market when we look for a job—that is, when we offer our labor in exchange for income. We *demand* goods when we shop in a supermarket—that is, when we're prepared to offer dollars in exchange for something to eat. Business firms may *supply* goods and services in product markets at the same time they're *demanding* factors of production in factor markets. Whether one is on the supply side or the demand side of any particular market transaction depends on the nature of the exchange, not on the people or institutions involved.

supply: The ability and willingness to sell (produce) specific quantities of a good at alternative prices in a given time period, *ceteris paribus.*

demand: The ability and willingness to buy specific quantities of a good at alternative prices in a given time period, *ceteris paribus.*

DEMAND

To get a sense of how the demand side of market transactions works, we'll focus first on a single consumer. Then we'll aggregate to illustrate *market* demand.

Individual Demand

We can begin to understand how market forces work by looking more closely at the behavior of a single market participant. Let us start with Tom, a senior at Clearview College. Tom has majored in everything from art history to government in his 3 years at Clearview. He didn't connect to any of those fields and is on the brink of academic dismissal. To make matters worse, his parents have threatened to cut him off financially unless he gets serious about his course work. By that, they mean he should enroll in courses that will lead to a job after graduation. Tom thinks he has found the perfect solution: Web design. Everything associated with the Internet pays big bucks. Plus, the girls seem to think Webbies are "cool." Or at least so Tom thinks. And his parents would definitely approve. So Tom has enrolled in Web-design courses.

Unfortunately for Tom, he never developed computer skills. Until he got to Clearview College, he thought mastering Sony's latest alien-attack video game was the pinnacle of electronic wizardry. Tom didn't have a clue about "streaming," "interfacing," "animation," or the other concepts the Web-design instructor outlined in the first lecture.

Given his circumstances, Tom was desperate to find someone who could tutor him in Web design. But desperation is not enough to secure the services of a Web architect. In a market-based economy, you must also be willing to *pay* for the things you want. Specifically, ***a demand exists only if someone is willing and able to pay for the good***—that is, exchange dollars for a good or service in the marketplace. Is Tom willing and able to *pay* for the Web-design tutoring he so obviously needs?

Let us assume that Tom has some income and is willing to spend some of it to get a tutor. Under these assumptions, we can claim that Tom is a participant in the *market* for Web-design services.

But how much is Tom willing to pay? Surely, Tom is not prepared to exchange *all* his income for help in mastering Web design. After all, Tom could use his income to buy more desirable goods and services. If he spent all his income on a Web tutor, that help would have an extremely high *opportunity cost.* He would be giving up the opportunity to spend that income on other goods and services. He'd pass his Web-design class but have little else. It doesn't sound like a good idea.

It seems more likely that there are *limits* to the amount Tom is willing to pay for any given quantity of Web-design tutoring. These limits will be determined by how much income Tom has to spend and how many other goods and services he must forsake in order to pay for a tutor.

Tom also knows that his grade in Web design will depend in part on how much tutoring service he buys. He can pass the course with only a few hours of design help. If he wants a better grade, however, the cost is going to escalate quickly.

Naturally, Tom wants it all: an A in Web design and a ticket to higher-paying jobs. But here again the distinction between *desire* and *demand* is relevant. He may *desire* to master Web design, but his actual proficiency will depend on how many hours of tutoring he is willing to *pay* for.

demand schedule: A table showing the quantities of a good a consumer is willing and able to buy at alternative prices in a given time period, *ceteris paribus.*

We assume, then, that when Tom starts looking for a Web-design tutor he has in mind some sort of **demand schedule,** like that described in Figure 3.2. According to row *A* of this schedule, Tom is willing and able to buy only 1 hour of tutoring service per semester if he must pay $50 an hour. At such an outrageous price he will learn minimal skills and just pass the course.

At lower prices, Tom would behave differently. According to Figure 3.2, Tom would purchase more tutoring services if the price per hour were less. At lower prices, he would not have to give up so many other goods and services for each hour of technical help. Indeed, we see from row *I* of the demand schedule that Tom is willing to purchase 20 hours per semester—the whole bag of design tricks—if the price of tutoring is as low as $10 per hour.

Notice that the demand schedule doesn't tell us anything about *why* this consumer is willing to pay specific prices for various amounts of tutoring. Tom's expressed willingness to pay for Web-design tutoring may reflect a desperate need to finish a Web-design course, a lot of income to spend, or a relatively small desire for other goods and services. All the demand schedule tells us is what the consumer is *willing and able* to buy, for whatever reasons.

Also observe that the demand schedule doesn't tell us how many hours of design help the consumer will *actually* buy. Figure 3.2 simply states that Tom is *willing and able* to pay for 1 hour of tutoring per semester at $50 per hour, for 2 hours at $45 each, and so on. How much tutoring he purchases will depend on the actual price of such services in the market. Until we know that price, we cannot tell how much service will be purchased. Hence ***"demand" is an expression of consumer buying intentions, of a willingness to buy, not a statement of actual purchases.***

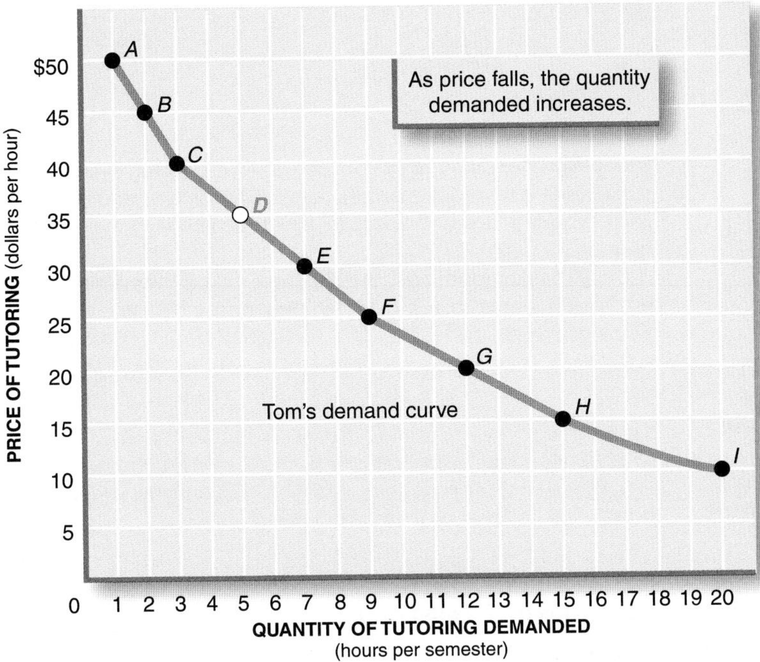

FIGURE 3.2
A Demand Schedule and Curve

A demand schedule indicates the quantities of a good a consumer is able and willing to buy at alternative prices (*ceteris paribus*). The demand schedule below indicates that Tom would buy 5 hours of Web tutoring per semester if the price were $35 per hour (row *D*). If Web tutoring were less expensive (rows *E–I*), Tom would purchase a larger quantity.

A demand curve is a graphical illustration of a demand schedule. Each point on the curve refers to a specific quantity that will be demanded at a given price. If, for example, the price of Web tutoring were $35 per hour, this curve tells us the consumer would purchase 5 hours per semester (point *D*). If Web tutoring cost $30 per hour, 7 hours per semester would be demanded (point *E*). Each point on the curve corresponds to a row in the schedule.

Tom's Demand Schedule

	Price of Tutoring (per hour)	Quantity of Tutoring Demanded (hours per semester)
A	$50	1
B	45	2
C	40	3
D	35	5
E	30	7
F	25	9
G	20	12
H	15	15
I	10	20

A convenient summary of buying intentions is the **demand curve,** a graphical illustration of the demand schedule. The demand curve in Figure 3.2 tells us again that this consumer is willing to pay for only 1 hour of tutoring per semester if the price is $50 per hour (point *A*), for 2 if the price is $45 (point *B*), for 3 at $40 an hour (point *C*), and so on. Once we know what the market price of tutoring actually is, a glance at the demand curve tells us how much service this consumer will buy.

demand curve: A curve describing the quantities of a good a consumer is willing and able to buy at alternative prices in a given time period, *ceteris paribus.*

What the notion of *demand* emphasizes is that ***the amount we buy of a good depends on its price.*** We seldom if ever decide to buy only a certain quantity of a good at whatever price is charged. Instead, we enter markets with a set of desires and a limited amount of money to spend. How much we actually buy of any good will depend on its price.

A common feature of demand curves is their downward slope. ***As the price of a good falls, people purchase more of it.*** In Figure 3.2 the quantity of Web-tutorial services demanded increases (moves rightward along the horizontal axis) as the price per hour

IN THE NEWS

Auto Makers Return to Deep Discounts

GM's Problems Prompt Price Cuts of up to $10,000; Ford, Chrysler Likely to Follow

General Motors reintroduced heavy incentives on many of its 2005 and 2006 models yesterday, slashing sticker prices by as much as $10,000 on some cars and trucks.

The huge price cuts come after General Motors Corp.'s sales plunged in October and are an acknowledgment that the world's largest auto maker needs to boost sales as it grapples with a $1.6 billion loss in the third quarter and decreasing market share. Some of the new discounts are even better deals for car buyers than this summer's popular employee-discount program.

All three U.S. car makers enjoyed a surge in sales this summer when they offered customers the same prices they had previously given their own employees. That boosted sales but cut deeply into profit margins, especially for GM and Ford. Each reported massive losses in North America in the third quarter.

More than a month ago, the Big Three cut off the employee-pricing discounts in a bid to set new prices that are above employee levels.

—Gina Chon

Source: *The Wall Street Journal,* November 15, 2005, p. D1.

Analysis: The law of demand predicted that General Motors would sell fewer cars if it raised its price and more cars if it reduced their price. That is exactly what happened.

law of demand: The quantity of a good demanded in a given time period increases as its price falls, *ceteris paribus.*

decreases (moves down the vertical axis). This inverse relationship between price and quantity is so common we refer to it as the **law of demand.** General Motors used this law to increase auto sales in 2005–2006 (see News).

Determinants of Demand

The demand curve in Figure 3.2 has only two dimensions—quantity demanded (on the horizontal axis) and price (on the vertical axis). This seems to imply that the amount of tutoring demanded depends only on the price of that service. This is surely not the case. A consumer's willingness and ability to buy a product at various prices depend on a variety of forces. ***The determinants of market demand include***

- ***Tastes*** (desire for this and other goods).
- ***Income*** (of the consumer).
- ***Other goods*** (their availability and price).
- ***Expectations*** (for income, prices, tastes).
- ***Number of buyers.***

Tom's "taste" for tutoring has nothing to do with taste buds. *Taste* is just another word for desire. In this case Tom's taste for Web-design services is clearly acquired. If he didn't have to pass a Web-design course, he would have no desire for related services, and thus no demand. If he had no income, he couldn't *demand* any Web-design tutoring either, no matter how much he might *desire* it.

substitute goods: Goods that substitute for each other; when the price of good *x* rises, the demand for good *y* increases, *ceteris paribus.*

Other goods also affect the demand for tutoring services. Their effect depends on whether they're *substitute* goods or *complementary* goods. A **substitute good** is one that might be purchased instead of tutoring services. In Tom's simple world, pizza is a substitute for tutoring. If the price of pizza fell, Tom would use his limited income to buy more pizzas and cut back on his purchases of Web tutoring. When the price of a substitute good falls, the demand for tutoring services declines.

complementary goods: Goods frequently consumed in combination; when the price of good *x* rises, the demand for good *y* falls, *ceteris paribus.*

A **complementary good** is one that's typically consumed with, rather than instead of, tutoring. If textbook prices or tuition increases, Tom might take fewer classes and demand *less* Web-design assistance. In this case, a price increase for a complementary good causes the demand for tutoring to decline.

Expectations also play a role in consumer decisions. If Tom expected to flunk his Web-design course anyway, he probably wouldn't waste any money getting tutorial help; his demand for such services would disappear. On the other hand, if he expects a Web tutor to determine his college fate, he might be more willing to buy such services.

Ceteris Paribus

ceteris paribus: The assumption of nothing else changing.

If demand is in fact such a multidimensional decision, how can we reduce it to only the two dimensions of price and quantity? In Chapter 1 we first encountered this ***ceteris paribus*** trick. To simplify their models of the world, economists focus on only one or two forces at a time and *assume* nothing else changes. We know a consumer's tastes, income, other goods, and expectations all affect the decision to hire a tutor. But we want to focus on the relationship between quantity demanded and price. That is, we want to know what *independent* influence price has on consumption decisions. To find out, we must isolate that one influence, price, and assume that the determinants of demand remain unchanged.

The *ceteris paribus* assumption is not as farfetched as it may seem. People's tastes, income, and expectations do not change quickly. Also, the prices and availability of other goods don't change all that fast. Hence, a change in the *price* of a product may be the only factor that prompts an immediate change in quantity demanded.

The ability to predict consumer responses to a price change is important. What would happen, for example, to enrollment at your school if tuition doubled? Must we guess? Or can we use demand curves to predict how the quantity of applications will change as the price of college goes up? ***Demand curves show us how changes in market prices alter consumer behavior.*** We used the demand curve in Figure 3.2 to predict how Tom's Web-design ability would change at different tutorial prices.

Shifts in Demand

Although demand curves are useful in predicting consumer responses to market signals, they aren't infallible. The problem is that ***the determinants of demand can and do change.*** When they do, a specific demand curve may become obsolete. A ***demand curve (schedule) is valid only so long as the underlying determinants of demand remain constant.*** If the *ceteris paribus* assumption is violated—if tastes, income, other goods, or expectations change—the ability or willingness to buy will change. When this happens, the demand curve will **shift** to a new position.

shift in demand: A change in the quantity demanded at any (every) given price.

Suppose, for example, that Tom won $1,000 in the state lottery. This increase in his income would greatly increase his ability to pay for tutoring services. Figure 3.3 shows the effect of this windfall on Tom's demand. The old demand curve, D_1, is no longer relevant. Tom's lottery winnings enable him to buy *more* tutoring at any price, as illustrated by the new demand curve, D_2. According to this new curve, lucky Tom is now willing and able to buy 12 hours per semester at the price of $35 per hour (point d_2). This is a large increase in demand; previously (before winning the lottery) he demanded only 5 hours at that price (point d_1).

With his higher income, Tom can buy more tutoring services at every price. Thus, ***the entire demand curve shifts to the right when income goes up.*** Figure 3.3 illustrates both the old (prelottery) and the new (postlottery) demand curves.

Income is only one of the basic determinants of demand. Changes in any of the other determinants of demand would also cause the demand curve to shift. Tom's taste for Web tutoring might increase dramatically, for example, if his parents promised to buy him a new car for passing Web design. In that case, he might be willing to forgo other goods and spend more of his income on tutors. ***An increase in taste (desire) also shifts the demand curve to the right.***

webnote

Priceline.com is an online service for purchasing airline tickets, vacation packages, and car rentals. The site allows you to specify the *highest* price you're willing to pay for air travel between two cities. In effect, you reveal your demand curve to Priceline. If you use the price-naming option and they find a ticket that costs no more than the price you're willing and able to pay, you must buy it. Priceline makes a profit by matching demand and supply. Try it at www.priceline.com

Pizza and Politics. A similar demand shift occurs at the White House when a political crisis erupts. On an average day, White House staffers order about $180 worth of pizza from the nearby Domino's. When a crisis hits, however, staffers work well into the night and their demand for pizza soars. On the days preceding the March 2003 invasion of Iraq, White House staffers ordered more than $1,000 worth of pizza

FIGURE 3.3
Shifts vs. Movements

A demand curve shows how a consumer responds to price changes. If the determinants of demand stay constant, the response is a *movement* along the curve to a new quantity demanded. In this case, the quantity demanded increases from 5 (point d_1), to 12 (point g_1), when price falls from \$35 to \$20 per hour.

If the determinants of demand change, the entire demand curve *shifts*. In this case, an increase in income increases demand. With more income, Tom is willing to buy 12 hours at the initial price of \$35 (point d_2), not just the 5 hours he demanded before the lottery win.

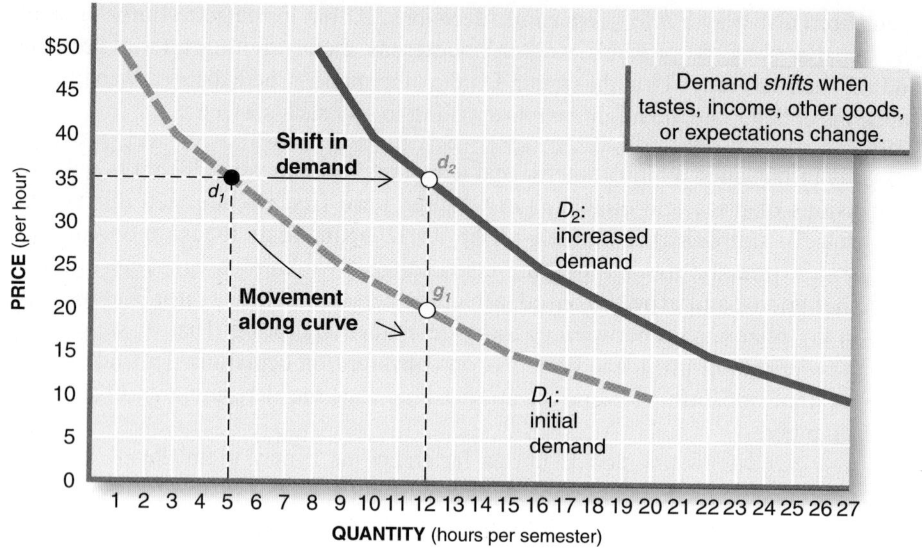

	Price (per hour)	Quantity Demanded (hours per semester) Initial Demand	After Increase in Income
A	\$50	1	8
B	45	2	9
C	40	3	10
D	35	5	12
E	30	7	14
F	25	9	16
G	20	12	19
H	15	15	22
I	10	20	27

per day! Political analysts now use pizza deliveries to predict major White House announcements.

Movements vs. Shifts

It's important to distinguish shifts of the demand curve from movements along the demand curve. ***Movements along a demand curve are a response to price changes for that good.*** Such movements assume that determinants of demand are unchanged. By contrast, ***shifts of the demand curve occur when the determinants of demand change.*** When tastes, income, other goods, or expectations are altered, the basic relationship between price and quantity demanded is changed (shifts).

For convenience, movements along a demand curve and shifts of the demand curve have their own labels. Specifically, take care to distinguish

- ***Changes in quantity demanded:*** movements along a given demand curve, in response to price changes of that good.
- ***Changes in demand:*** shifts of the demand curve due to changes in tastes, income, other goods, or expectations.

Tom's behavior in the Web-tutoring market will change if either the price of tutoring changes (a movement) or the underlying determinants of his demand are altered (a shift).

Notice in Figure 3.3 that he ends up buying 12 hours of Web tutoring if either the price of tutoring falls (to $20 per hour) or his income increases. Demand curves help us predict those market responses.

Market Demand

Whatever we say about demand for Web-design tutoring on the part of one wannabe Web master, we can also say about every student at Clearview College (or, for that matter, about all consumers). Some students have no interest in Web design and aren't willing to pay for related services: They don't participate in the Web-tutoring market. Other students want such services but don't have enough income to pay for them: They too are excluded from the Web-tutoring market. A large number of students, however, not only have a need (or desire) for Web tutoring but also are willing and able to purchase such services.

What we start with in product markets, then, is many individual demand curves. Fortunately, it's possible to combine all the individual demand curves into a single **market demand.** The aggregation process is no more difficult than simple arithmetic. Suppose you would be willing to buy 1 hour of tutoring per semester at a price of $80 per hour. George, who is also desperate to learn Web design, would buy 2 at that price; and I would buy none, since my publisher (McGraw-Hill) creates a Web page for me (try mhhe.com/economics/Schiller11). What would our combined (market) demand for hours of tutoring be at that price? Clearly, our individual inclinations indicate that we would be willing to buy a total of 3 hours of tutoring per semester if the price were $80 per hour. Our combined willingness to buy—our collective market demand—is nothing more than the sum of our individual demands. The same kind of aggregation can be performed for all consumers, leading to a summary of the total market demand for a specific good or service. Thus ***market demand is determined by the number of potential buyers and their respective tastes, incomes, other goods, and expectations.***

market demand: The total quantities of a good or service people are willing and able to buy at alternative prices in a given time period; the sum of individual demands.

The Market Demand Curve

Figure 3.4 provides the basic market demand schedule for a situation in which only three consumers participate in the market. It illustrates the same market situation with demand curves. The three individuals who participate in the market demand for Web tutoring at Clearview College obviously differ greatly, as suggested by their respective demand schedules. Tom's demand schedule is portrayed in the first column of the table (and is identical to the one we examined in Figure 3.2). George is also desperate to acquire some job skills and is willing to pay relatively high prices for Web-design tutoring. His demand is summarized in the second column under Quantity Demanded in the table.

The third consumer in this market is Lisa. Lisa already knows the nuts and bolts of Web design, so she isn't so desperate for tutorial services. She would like to upgrade her skills, however, especially in animation and e-commerce applications. But her limited budget precludes paying a lot for help. She will buy some technical support only if the price falls to $30 per hour. Should tutors cost less, she'd even buy quite a few hours of design services. Finally, there is my demand schedule (column 4 under Quantity Demanded), which confirms that I really don't participate in the Web-tutoring market.

The differing personalities and consumption habits of Tom, George, Lisa, and me are expressed in our individual demand schedules and associated curves in Figure 3.4. To determine the *market* demand for tutoring from this information, we simply add these four separate demands. The end result of this aggregation is, first, a *market* demand schedule and, second, the resultant *market* demand curve. These market summaries describe the various quantities of tutoring that Clearview College students are *willing and able* to purchase each semester at various prices.

How much Web tutoring will be purchased each semester? Knowing how much help Tom, George, Lisa, and I are willing to buy at various prices doesn't tell you how much we're actually going to purchase. To determine the actual consumption of Web tutoring, we have to know something about prices and supplies. Which of the many different prices illustrated in Figures 3.3 and 3.4 will actually prevail? How will that price be determined?

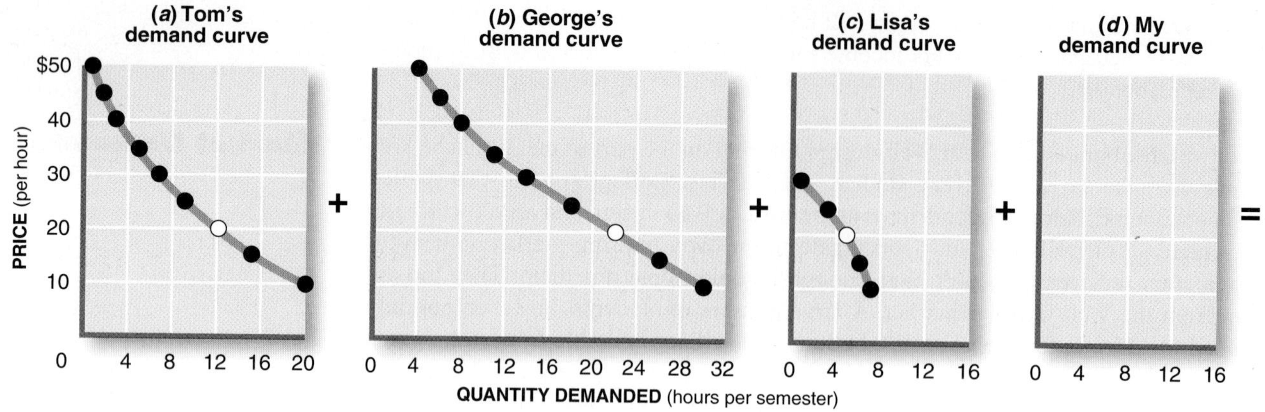

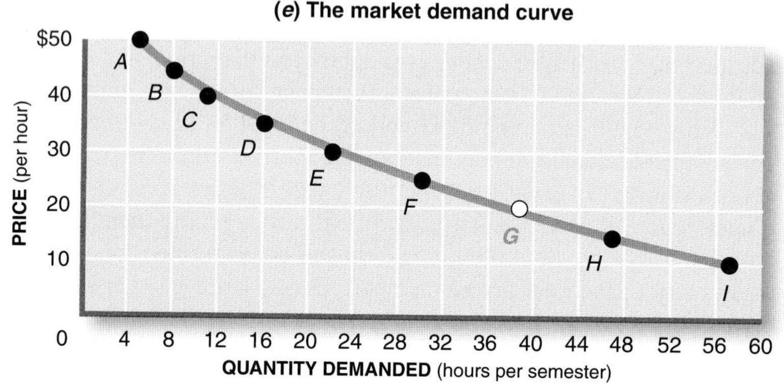

FIGURE 3.4
Construction of the Market Demand Curve

Market demand represents the combined demands of all market participants. To determine the total quantity of Web tutoring demanded at any given price, we add the separate demands of the individual consumers. Row *G* of this schedule indicates that a *total* quantity of 39 hours per semester will be demanded at a price of $20 per hour. This same conclusion is reached by adding the individual demand curves, leading to point *G* on the market demand curve (see above).

		Quantity of Tutoring Demanded (hours per semester)								
	Price (per hour)	Tom	+	George	+	Lisa	+	Me	=	Market Demand
A	$50	1		4		0		0		5
B	45	2		6		0		0		8
C	40	3		8		0		0		11
D	35	5		11		0		0		16
E	30	7		14		1		0		22
F	25	9		18		3		0		30
G	20	12		22		5		0		39
H	15	15		26		6		0		47
I	10	20		30		7		0		57

SUPPLY

To understand how the price of Web tutoring is established, we must also look at the other side of the market: the *supply* side. We need to know how many hours of tutoring services people are willing and able to *sell* at various prices, that is, the **market supply.** As on the demand side, the *market supply* depends on the behavior of all the individuals willing and able to supply Web tutoring at some price.

market supply: The total quantities of a good that sellers are willing and able to sell at alternative prices in a given time period, *ceteris paribus.*

Determinants of Supply

Let's return to the Clearview campus for a moment. What we need to know now is how much tutorial help people are willing and able to provide. Generally speaking, Web-page design can be fun, but it can also be drudge work, especially when you're doing it for someone else. Software programs like PhotoShop, Flash, and Fireworks have made Web-page design easier and more creative. And Wi-Fi laptops have made the job more convenient. But teaching someone else to design Web pages is still work. So why does anyone do it? Easy answer: for the money. People offer (supply) tutoring services to earn income that they, in turn, can spend on the goods and services they desire.

How much income must be offered to induce Web designers to do a job depends on a variety of things. The ***determinants of market supply include***

- ***Technology***
- ***Factor cost***
- ***Other goods***
- ***Taxes and subsidies***
- ***Expectations***
- ***Number of sellers***

The technology of Web design, for example, is always getting easier and more creative. With a program like PageOut, for example, it's very easy to create a bread-and-butter Web page. A continuous stream of new software programs (e.g., Fireworks, DreamWeaver) keeps stretching the possibilities for graphics, animation, interactivity, and content. These technological advances mean that Web-design services can be supplied more quickly and cheaply. They also make *teaching* Web design easier. As a result, they induce people to supply more tutoring services at every price.

How much Web-design service is offered at any given price also depends on the cost of factors of production. If the software programs needed to create Web pages are cheap (or, better yet, free), Web designers can afford to charge lower prices. If the required software inputs are expensive, however, they will have to charge more money per hour for their services.

Other goods can also affect the willingness to supply Web-design services. If you can make more income waiting tables than you can tutoring lazy students, why would you even boot up the computer? As the prices paid for other goods and services change, they will influence people's decision about whether to offer Web services.

webnote

Sellers of books and cars post asking prices for their products on the Internet. With the help of search engines such as autoweb.com consumers can locate the seller who's offering the lowest price. By examining a lot of offers, you could also construct a supply curve showing how the quantity supplied increases at higher prices.

In the real world, the decision to supply goods and services is also influenced by the long arm of Uncle Sam. Federal, state, and local governments impose taxes on income earned in the marketplace. When tax rates are high, people get to keep less of the income they earn. Once taxes start biting into paychecks, some people may conclude that tutoring is no longer worth the hassle and withdraw from the market.

Expectations are also important on the supply side of the market. If Web designers expect higher prices, lower costs, or reduced taxes, they may be more willing to learn new software programs. On the other hand, if they have poor expectations about the future, they may just sell their computers and find something else to do.

Finally, we note that the number of potential tutors will affect the quantity of service offered for sale at various prices. If there are lots of willing tutors on campus, a lot of tutorial service will be available at reasonable prices.

All these considerations—factor costs, technology, expectations—affect the decision to offer Web services and at what price. In general, we assume that Web architects will be willing to provide more tutoring if the per-hour price is high and less if the price is low. In other words, there is a **law of supply** that parallels the law of demand. ***The law of supply says that larger quantities will be offered for sale at higher prices.*** Here again, the laws rest on the *ceteris paribus* assumption: The quantity supplied increases at higher prices *if*

law of supply: The quantity of a good supplied in a given time period increases as its price increases, *ceteris paribus.*

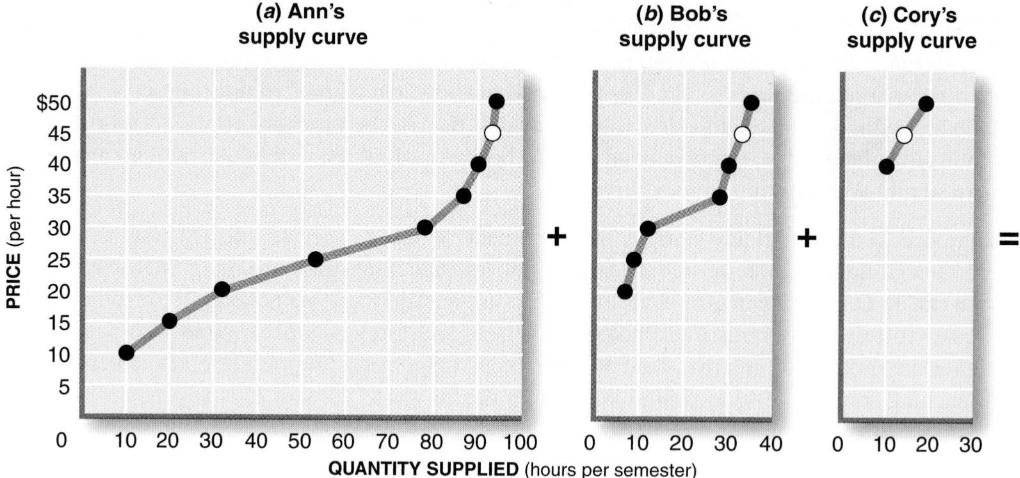

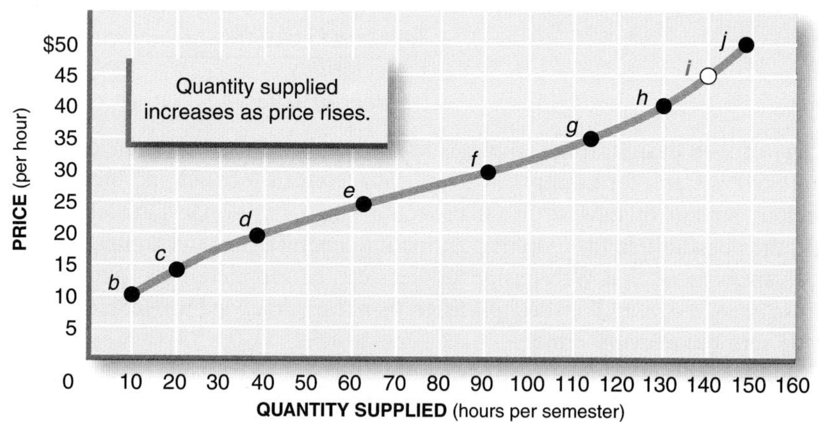

FIGURE 3.5
Market Supply

The market supply curve indicates the *combined* sales intentions of all market participants. If the price of tutoring were $45 per hour (point *i*), the *total* quantity of services supplied would be 140 hours per semester. This quantity is determined by adding the supply decisions of all individual producers. In this case, Ann supplies 93 hours, Bob supplies 33, and Cory supplies the rest.

	Price (per hour)	Quantity of Tutoring Supplied by Ann	+	Bob	+	Cory	=	Market
j	$50	94		35		19		148
i	45	93		33		14		140
h	40	90		30		10		130
g	35	86		28		0		114
f	30	78		12		0		90
e	25	53		9		0		62
d	20	32		7		0		39
c	15	20		0		0		20
b	10	10		0		0		10

the determinants of supply are constant. ***Supply curves are upward-sloping to the right,*** as in Figure 3.5. Note how the *quantity supplied* jumps from 39 hours (point *d*) to 130 hours (point *h*) when the price of Web service doubles (from $20 to $40 per hour).

Market Supply

Figure 3.5 also illustrates how market supply is constructed from the supply decisions of individual sellers. In this case, only three Web masters are available. Ann is willing to

IN THE NEWS

Another Storm Casualty: Oil Prices

The region that produces and refines a major portion of the nation's oil and natural gas was largely shut down by Hurricane Katrina yesterday, further tightening strained energy markets and sending prices to new highs.

As oil companies evacuated offshore operations throughout the Gulf of Mexico, oil production in that region was reduced by 92 percent and gas output was cut by 83 percent.

The latest interruptions in oil supplies are likely to send retail gasoline prices even higher than the current average of $2.60 a gallon. . . .

The Gulf of Mexico, which produces 27 percent of the nation's oil and a fifth of its natural gas, is dotted with nearly 4,000 platforms linked by 33,000 miles of underwater pipelines. Over the weekend, oil companies withdrew their workers from 615 platforms and 96 drilling rigs in the gulf.

—Jad Mouawad and Simon Romero

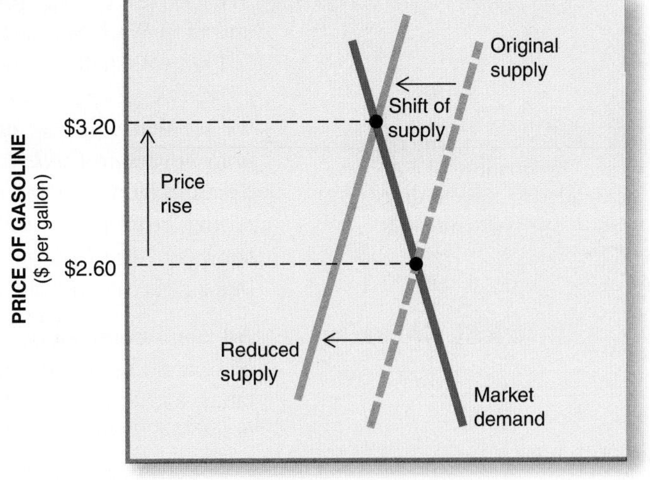

Source: From "Another Storm Casualty: Oil Prices" by Jad Mouawad and Simon Romero, *The New York Times*, August 30, 2005, p. 1. Copyright © 2005 by The New York Times Co. Reprinted with permission.

Analysis: When factor costs or availability worsen, the supply curve shifts to the left. Such leftward supply-curve shifts push prices up the market demand curve.

provide a lot of tutoring at low prices, whereas Bob requires at least $20 an hour. Cory won't talk to students for less than $40 an hour.

By adding the quantity each Webhead is willing to offer at every price, we can construct the market supply curve. Notice in Figure 3.5, for example, how the quantity supplied to the market at $45 (point *i*) comes from the individual efforts of Ann (93 hours), Bob (33 hours), and Cory (14 hours). ***The market supply curve is just a summary of the supply intentions of all producers.***

None of the points on the market supply curve (Figure 3.5) tells us how much Web tutoring is actually being sold on the Clearview campus. ***Market supply is an expression of sellers' intentions—an offer to sell—not a statement of actual sales.*** My next-door neighbor may be willing to sell his 1994 Honda Civic for $8,000, but most likely he'll never find a buyer at that price. Nevertheless, his *willingness* to sell his car at that price is part of the *market supply* of used cars. (See Webnote for more detail on the market supply of used cars.)

Shifts of Supply

As with demand, there's nothing sacred about any given set of supply intentions. Supply curves *shift* when the underlying determinants of supply change. Thus, we again distinguish

- ***Changes in quantity supplied:*** movements along a given supply curve.
- ***Changes in supply:*** shifts of the supply curve.

Our Latin friend *ceteris paribus* is once again the decisive factor. If the price of a product is the only variable changing, then we can ***track changes in quantity supplied along the supply curve.*** But if *ceteris paribus* is violated—if technology, factor costs, the profitability of producing other goods, tax rates, expectations, or the number of sellers change—then ***changes in supply are illustrated by shifts of the supply curve.***

The accompanying News illustrates how a supply shift sent gasoline prices soaring in 2005. When Hurricane Katrina shut down oil-producing facilities in the Gulf of Mexico, the gasoline supply curve shifted leftward and price jumped.

EQUILIBRIUM

The abrupt spike in oil prices offers some clues as to how the forces of supply and demand set—and change—market prices. For a closer look at how those forces work, we'll return to Clearview College for a moment. How did supply and demand resolve the WHAT, HOW, and FOR WHOM questions in that Web-tutoring market?

Figure 3.6 helps answer that question by bringing together the market supply and demand curves we've already examined (Figures 3.4 and 3.5). When we put the two curves together, we see that ***only one price and quantity are compatible with the existing intentions of both buyers and sellers.*** **This equilibrium occurs at the intersection of the supply and demand curves,** as in Figure 3.6. Once it's established, Web tutoring will cost $20 per hour. At that **equilibrium price,** campus Webheads will sell a total of 39 hours of tutoring per semester—the same amount that students wish to buy at that price. Those 39 hours of tutoring service will be part of WHAT is produced.

equilibrium price: The price at which the quantity of a good demanded in a given time period equals the quantity supplied.

Market Clearing

An equilibrium doesn't imply that everyone is happy with the prevailing price or quantity. Notice in Figure 3.6, for example, that some students who want to buy Web-design assistance services don't get any. These would-be buyers are arrayed along the demand curve *below* the equilibrium. Because the price they're *willing* to pay is less than the equilibrium

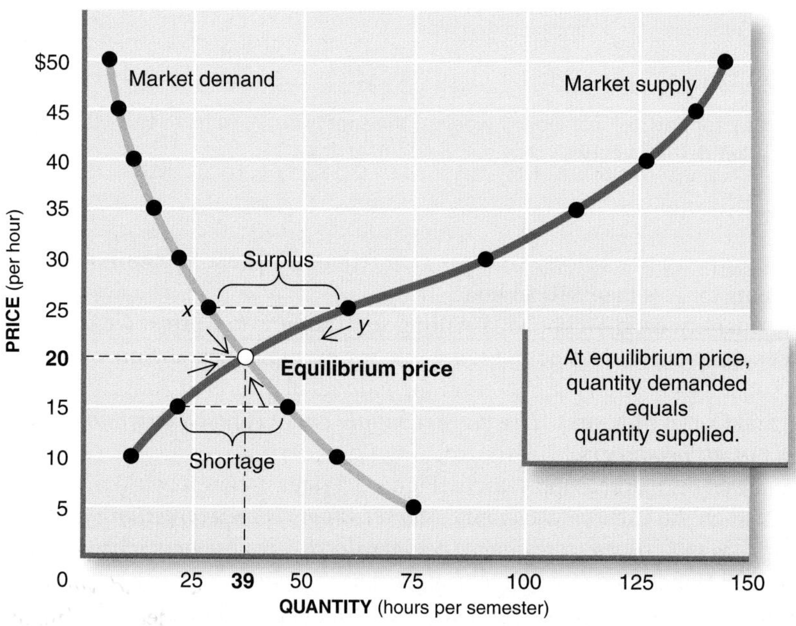

FIGURE 3.6
Equilibrium Price

The intersection of the demand and supply curves establishes the *equilibrium* price and output. Only at equilibrium is the quantity demanded equal to the quantity supplied. In this case, the equilibrium price is $20 per hour, and 39 hours is the equilibrium quantity.

At above-equilibrium prices, a market surplus exists—the quantity supplied exceeds the quantity demanded. At prices below equilibrium, a market shortage exists.

Price (per hour)	Quantity Supplied (hours per semester)		Quantity Demanded (hours per semester)
$50	148	market surplus	5
45	140		8
40	130		11
35	114		16
30	90		22
25	62		30
20	39	equilibrium	39
15	20	market shortage	47
10	10		57

*Non*equilibrium prices create surpluses or shortages

price, they don't get any Web-design help. The market's FOR WHOM answer includes only those students willing and able to pay the equilibrium price.

Likewise, some would-be sellers are frustrated by this market outcome. These people are arrayed along the supply curve *above* the equilibrium. Because they insist on being paid *more* than the equilibrium price, they don't actually sell anything.

Although not everyone gets full satisfaction from the market equilibrium, that unique outcome is efficient. The equilibrium price and quantity reflect a compromise between buyers and sellers. No other compromise yields a quantity demanded that's exactly equal to the quantity supplied.

The Invisible Hand. The equilibrium price isn't determined by any single individual. Rather, it's determined by the collective behavior of many buyers and sellers, each acting out his or her own demand or supply schedule. It's this kind of impersonal price determination that gave rise to Adam Smith's characterization of the market mechanism as "the invisible hand." In attempting to explain how the **market mechanism** works, the famed eighteenth-century economist noted a remarkable feature of market prices. The market behaves as if some unseen force (the invisible hand) were examining each individual's supply or demand schedule and then selecting a price that assured an equilibrium. In practice, the process of price determination isn't so mysterious: It's a simple process of trial and error.

market mechanism: The use of market prices and sales to signal desired outputs (or resource allocations).

Surplus and Shortage

To appreciate the power of the market mechanism, consider interference in its operation. Suppose, for example, that campus Webheads banded together and agreed to charge a minimum price of $25 per hour. By establishing a **price floor,** a minimum price for their services, the Webheads hope to increase their incomes. But they won't be fully satisfied. Figure 3.6 illustrates the consequences of this *dis*equilibrium pricing. At $25 per hour, campus Webheads would be offering more tutoring services (point *y*) than Tom, George, and Lisa were willing to buy (point *x*) at that price. A **market surplus** of Web services would exist in the sense that more tutoring was being offered for sale (supplied) than students cared to purchase at the available price.

price floor: Lower limit set for the price of a good.

market surplus: The amount by which the quantity supplied exceeds the quantity demanded at a given price; excess supply.

As Figure 3.6 indicates, at a price of $25 per hour, a market surplus of 32 hours per semester exists. Under these circumstances, campus Webheads would be spending many idle hours at their keyboards waiting for customers to appear. Their waiting will be in vain because the quantity of Web tutoring demanded will not increase until the price of tutoring falls. That is the clear message of the demand curve. As would-be tutors get this message, they'll reduce their prices. This is the response the market mechanism signals.

As sellers' asking prices decline, the quantity demanded will increase. This concept is illustrated in Figure 3.6 by the movement along the demand curve from point *x* to lower prices and greater quantity demanded. As we move down the market demand curve, the *desire* for Web-design help doesn't change, but the quantity people are *able and willing to buy* increases. When the price falls to $20 per hour, the quantity demanded will finally equal the quantity supplied. This is the *equilibrium* illustrated in Figure 3.6.

An Initial Shortage. A very different sequence of events would occur if a market shortage existed. Suppose someone were to spread the word that Web-tutoring services were available at only $15 per hour. Tom, George, and Lisa would be standing in line to get tutorial help, but campus Web designers wouldn't be willing to supply the quantity demanded at that price. As Figure 3.6 confirms, at $15 per hour, the quantity demanded (47 hours per semester) would greatly exceed the quantity supplied (20 hours per semester). In this situation, we may speak of a **market shortage,** that is, an excess of quantity demanded over quantity supplied. At a price of $15 an hour, the shortage amounts to 27 hours of tutoring services.

market shortage: The amount by which the quantity demanded exceeds the quantity supplied at a given price; excess demand.

When a market shortage exists, not all consumer demands can be satisfied. Some people who are *willing* to buy Web help at the going price ($15) won't be able to do so. To assure themselves of sufficient help, Tom, George, Lisa, or some other consumer may offer to pay a *higher* price, thus initiating a move up the demand curve in Figure 3.6. The higher prices

IN THE NEWS

All the Web's a Stage for Ticket Sales

The Internet has become the ultimate selling bazaar for ticket scalpers.

No longer confined to hanging outside of coliseums or local turnkey operations, professional scalpers—along with thousands of small-time entrepreneurs—now use the Internet to sell hard-to-get tickets to concerts and sporting events.

Justin Aglialoro, 31, started his own ticket selling business at his Swedesboro. N.J., home. He now has season tickets for 22 professional baseball teams, 21 football teams and two NBA teams. He resells them on his website, sportseventsintl.com, and through online ticket clearinghouses such as StubHub and auctioneer eBay. . . .

With sports and concert fans willing to pay hundreds above face value for tickets, Aglialoro doesn't mind being called a scalper. He hopes to clear $100,000 this year, three times what he made as an assistant bank manager, a job he quit earlier this month.

Like Aglialoro, Mike Domek credits the Internet for jump-starting a new lucrative career. Domek used to scalp Chicago Cubs tickets in the early 1990s. He launched TicketsNow—which has become one of the Internet's largest clearinghouses for concert and sport tickets—in 1999.

Domek's company has since developed computer software that's licensed to scalpers, allowing them to link to central ticket-selling databases. Domek expects his company to do $100 million in business this year.

"The Internet made reselling efficient for sellers and secure for buyers," says Domek, 36. "It's become mainstream."

—Gary Strauss

Source: *USA TODAY,* June 17, 2005, p. 2A. Reprinted with permission.

Analysis: When tickets are sold initially at below-equilibrium prices, a market shortage is created. Scalpers resell tickets at prices closer to equilibrium, reaping a profit in the process.

offered will in turn induce other enterprising Webheads to tutor more, thus ensuring an upward movement along the market supply curve. Notice, again, that the *desire* to tutor Web design hasn't changed; only the quantity supplied has responded to a change in price. As this process continues, the quantity supplied will eventually equal the quantity demanded (39 hours in Figure 3.6).

Self-Adjusting Prices. What we observe, then, is that ***whenever the market price is set above or below the equilibrium price, either a market surplus or a market shortage will emerge.*** To overcome a surplus or shortage, buyers and sellers will change their behavior. Webheads will have to compete for customers by reducing prices when a market surplus exists. If a shortage exists, buyers will compete for service by offering to pay higher prices. Only at the *equilibrium* price will no further adjustments be required.

Sometimes the market price is slow to adjust, and a disequilibrium persists. This is often the case with tickets to rock concerts, football games, and other one-time events. People initially adjust their behavior by standing in ticket lines for hours, or hopping on the Internet, hoping to buy a ticket at the below-equilibrium price. The tickets are typically resold ("scalped"), however, at prices closer to equilibrium (see News).

Business firms can discover equilibrium prices by trial and error. If consumer purchases aren't keeping up with production, a firm may conclude that price is above the equilibrium price. To get rid of accumulated inventory, the firm will have to lower its price (a Grand End-of-Year Sale, perhaps). In the happier situation where consumer purchases are outpacing production, a firm might conclude that its price was a trifle too low and give it a nudge upward. In either case, the equilibrium price can be established after a few trials in the marketplace.

Changes in Equilibrium

No equilibrium price is permanent. The equilibrium price established in the Clearview College tutoring market, for example, was the unique outcome of specific demand and supply schedules. Those schedules themselves were based on our assumption of *ceteris paribus*. We assumed that the "taste" (desire) for Web-design assistance was given, as were consumers' incomes, the price and availability of other goods, and expectations. Any of these determinants of demand could change. When one does, the demand curve has to be redrawn. Such a shift of the demand curve will lead to a new equilibrium price and quantity. Indeed, ***the equilibrium price will change whenever the supply or demand curve shifts.***

A Demand Shift. We can illustrate how equilibrium prices change by taking one last look at the Clearview College tutoring market. Our original supply and demand curves, together with the resulting equilibrium (point E_1), are depicted in Figure 3.7. Now suppose that all

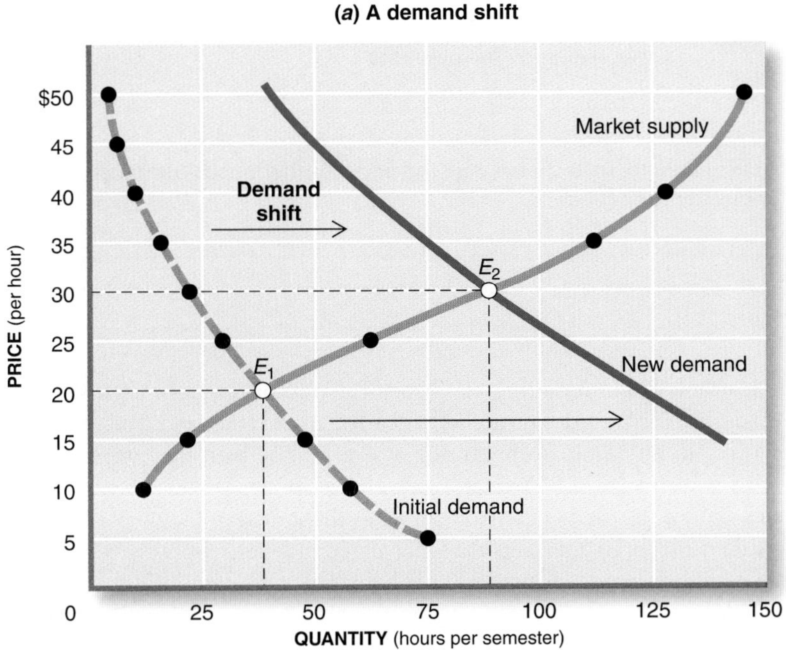

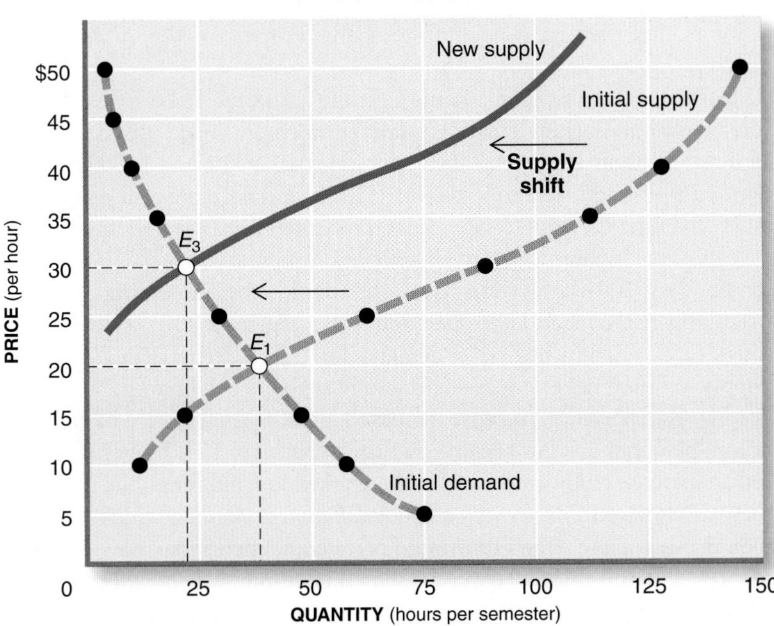

FIGURE 3.7
Changes in Equilibrium

If demand or supply changes (shifts), market equilibrium will change as well.

Demand shift. In (*a*), the rightward shift of the demand curve illustrates an increase in demand. When demand increases, the equilibrium price rises (from E_1 to E_2).

Supply shift. In (*b*), the leftward shift of the supply curve illustrates a decrease in supply. This raises the equilibrium price to E_3.

Demand and supply curves shift only when their underlying determinants change, that is, when *ceteris paribus* is violated.

WORLD VIEW

As Gas Nears $7 a Gallon, More Britons Take the Bus

LONDON, April 27—David Graham pulled up to the gas pump in his shiny black sport-utility vehicle with a "for sale" sign taped in the window.

Graham, 48, a London building contractor, pointed at the price on the pump—the equivalent of $6.62 a gallon, which means it costs him $125 to fill his tank. "That's why this is for sale," Graham said. "I can't afford it anymore. I have to walk everywhere. Things have gone mad."

The average gasoline price in Britain has risen 19 percent since January 2005. Many stations are charging well above the $6.48 national average; at least one in London's chic Chelsea neighborhood was charging nearly $8 a gallon last weekend.

"It's disgusting," said Elizabeth Jones, 50, a pharmacy assistant, who was pumping $40 worth of gas—for half a tank—into her little Ford Fiesta in a working-class neighborhood in west London.

Jones said she now takes the bus to the grocery store instead of driving. She and her husband sold their second car because they couldn't afford to fill two tanks.

—Kevin Sullivan

Source: *Washington Post,* April 28, 2006, p. A12. **© 2006, The Washington Post, excerpted with permission.**

Analysis: When a determinant of demand changes, the demand curve shifts. In this case the price of other goods (driving) increased, causing a rightward shift of market demand for bus transportation.

the professors at Clearview begin requiring class-specific Web pages from each student. The increased need (desire) for Web-design ability will affect market demand. Tom, George, and Lisa will be willing to buy more Web tutoring at every price than they were before. That is, the *demand* for Web services has increased. We can represent this increased demand by a rightward *shift* of the market demand curve, as illustrated in Figure 3.7*a*.

Note that the new demand curve intersects the (unchanged) market supply curve at a new price (point E_2); the equilibrium price is now $30 per hour. This new equilibrium price will persist until either the demand curve or the supply curve shifts again.

A Supply Shift. Figure 3.7*b* illustrates a *supply* shift. The decrease (leftward shift) in supply might occur if some on-campus Webheads got sick. Or approaching exams might convince would-be tutors that they have no time to spare. ***Whenever supply decreases (shifts left), price tends to rise,*** as in Figure 3.7*b*.

The rock band U2 learned about changing equilibriums the hard way. Ticket prices for the band's 1992 tour were below equilibrium, creating a *market shortage.* So U2 raised prices to as much as $52.50 a ticket for their 1997 tour—nearly double the 1992 price. By then, however, demand had shifted to the left, due to a lack of U2 hits and an increased number of competing concerts. By the time they got to their second city they were playing in stadiums with lots of empty seats. The apparent *market surplus* led critics to label the 1997 "Pop Mart" tour a disaster. For their 2001 "Elevation Tour," U2 offered "festival seating" for only $35 in order to fill stadiums and concert halls. Demand shifted again in 2005. Buoyed by a spike of new hit songs (e.g., "Beautiful Day"), demand for U2's "Vertigo Tour" far outstripped available supply, sending ticket prices soaring (and scalpers celebrating).

British demand for bus transportation likewise increased in 2006. As the price of gasoline approached $7 a gallon, personal driving became awfully expensive. This higher price for "other goods" caused an increase (rightward shift) in the market demand for public transportation (see World View). Britons still *preferred* cars, but *demanded* more bus rides.

The World View on the next page shows how rapid price adjustments can alleviate market shortages and surpluses. In this unusual case, a restaurant continuously adjusts its prices to ensure that everything on the menu is ordered and no food is wasted.

MARKET OUTCOMES

Notice how the market mechanism resolves the basic economic questions of WHAT, HOW, and FOR WHOM.

WHAT

The WHAT question refers to the amount of Web tutorial services to include in society's mix of output. The answer at Clearview College was 39 hours of tutoring per semester. This decision wasn't reached in a referendum, but instead in the market equilibrium (Figure 3.6). In the same way but on a larger scale, millions of consumers and a handful of auto producers decide to include 16 million or so cars and trucks in each year's mix of output. Auto manufacturers use rebates, discounts, and variable interest rates to induce consumers to buy the same quantity that auto manufacturers are producing.

HOW

The market mechanism also determines HOW goods are produced. Profit-seeking producers will strive to produce Web designs and automobiles in the most efficient way. They'll use market prices to decide not only WHAT to produce but also what resources to use in the production process. If new software simplifies Web design—and is priced low enough—Webheads will use it. Likewise, auto manufacturers will use robots rather than humans on the assembly line if robots reduce costs and increase profits.

FOR WHOM

Finally, the invisible hand of the market will determine who gets the goods produced. At Clearview College, who got Web tutoring? Only those students who were willing and able to pay $20 per hour for that service. FOR WHOM are all those automobiles produced each year? The answer is the same: those consumers who are willing and able to pay the market price for a new car.

Optimal, Not Perfect

Not everyone is happy with these answers, of course. Tom would like to pay only $10 an hour for a tutor. And some of the Clearview students don't have enough income to buy any tutoring. They think it's unfair that they have to design their own Web pages while rich students can have someone else do their design work for them. Students who can't afford cars are even less happy with the market's answer to the FOR WHOM question.

WORLD VIEW

Dining on the Downtick

Americans aren't the only consumers who fall for packaging. Since late January, Parisians (not to mention TV crews from around the world) have been drawn to 6 rue Feydeau to try La Connivence, a restaurant with a new gimmick. The name means "collusion," and yes, of course, La Connivence is a block away from the Bourse, the French stock exchange.

What's the gimmick? Just that the restaurant's prices fluctuate according to supply and demand. The more a dish is ordered, the higher its price. A dish that's ignored gets cheaper.

Customers tune in to the day's menu (couched in trading terms) on computer screens. Among a typical day's options: *forte baisse du haddock* ("precipitous drop in haddock"), *vif recul de la côte de boeuf* ("rapid decline in beef ribs"), *la brochette de lotte au plus bas* ("fish kabob hits bottom"). Then comes the major decision—whether to opt for the price that's listed when you order or to gamble that the price will have gone down by the time you finish your meal.

So far, only main dishes are open to speculation, but co-owners Pierre Guette, an ex-professor at a top French business school, and Jean-Paul Trastour, an ex-journalist at *Le Nouvel Observateur*, are adding wine to the risk list.

La Connivence is open for dinner, but the midday "session" (as the owners call it) is the one to catch. That's when the traders of Paris leave the floor to push their luck *à table.* But here, at least, the return on their $15 investment (the average price of a meal) is immediate—and usually good.

—Christina de Liagre

Source: *New York,* April 7, 1986. www.newyorkmag.com

Analysis: A market surplus signals that price is too high; a market shortage suggests that price is too low. This restaurant adjusts price until the quantity supplied equals the quantity demanded.

Although the outcomes of the marketplace aren't perfect, they're often optimal. Optimal outcomes are the best possible *given* our incomes and scarce resources. Sure, we'd like everyone to have access to tutoring and to drive a new car. But there aren't enough resources available to create such a utopia. So we have to ration available tutors and cars. The market mechanism performs this rationing function. People who want to supply tutoring or build cars are free to make that choice. And consumers are free to decide how they want to spend their income. In the process, we expect market participants to make decisions that maximize their own welfare. If they do, then we conclude that everyone is doing as well as possible, given their available resources.

THE ECONOMY TOMORROW

DEADLY SHORTAGES: THE ORGAN-TRANSPLANT MARKET

As you were reading this chapter, dozens of Americans were dying from failed organs. More than 100,000 Americans are waiting for life-saving kidneys, livers, lungs, and other vital organs. They can't wait long, however. Every day at least 20 of these organ-diseased patients die. The clock is always ticking.

Modern technology can save most of these patients. Vital organs can be transplanted, extending the life of diseased patients. How many people are saved, however, depends on how well the organ "market" works.

The Supply of Organs. The only cure for liver disease and some other organ failures is a replacement organ. Over 50 years ago, doctors discovered that they could transplant an organ from one individual to another. Since then, medical technology has advanced to the point where organ transplants are exceptionally safe and successful. The constraint on this life-saving technique is the *supply* of transplantable organs.

Although over 2 million Americans die each year, most deaths do not create transplantable organs. Only 20,000 or so people die in circumstances—such as brain death after a car crash—that make them suitable donors for life-saving transplants. Additional kidneys can be "harvested" from live donors (we have two, but can function with only one; not true for liver, heart, or pancreas).

You don't have to die to supply an organ. Instead, you become a donor by agreeing to release your organs after death. The agreement is typically certified on a driver's license and sometimes on a bracelet or "dog tag." This allows emergency doctors to identify potential organ supplies.

People become donors for many reasons. Moral principles, religious convictions, and humanitarianism all play a role in the donation decision. It's the same with blood donations: People give blood (while alive!) because they want to help save other individuals.

Market Incentives. Monetary incentives could also play a role. When blood donations are inadequate, hospitals and medical schools *buy* blood in the marketplace. People who might not donate blood come forth to *sell* blood when a price is offered. In principle, the same incentive might increase the number of *organ* donors. If offered cash now for a postmortem organ, would the willingness to donate increase? The law of supply suggests it would. Offer $1,000 in cash for signing up, and potential donors will start lining up. Offer more, and the quantity supplied will increase further.

Zero Price Ceiling. The government doesn't permit this to happen. In 1984 Congress forbade the purchase or sale of human organs in the United States (the National Organ Transplantation Act). In part, the prohibition was rooted in moral and religious convictions. It was also motivated by equity concerns—the For Whom question. If organs could be bought and sold, then the rich would have a distinct advantage in living.

price ceiling: Upper limit imposed on the price of a good.

The prohibition on market sales is effectively a **price ceiling** set at zero. As a consequence, the only available organs are those supplied by altruistic donors. The quantity

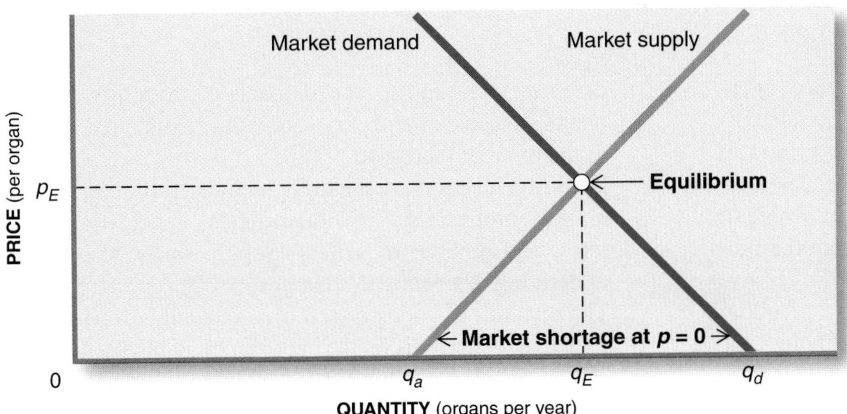

FIGURE 3.8
Organ-Transplant Market

A market in human organs would deliver the quantity q_E at a price of p_E. The government-set price ceiling ($p = 0$) reduces the quantity supplied to q_a.

supplied can't be increased with price incentives. In general, ***price ceilings have three predictable effects; they***

- ***Increase the quantity demanded.***
- ***Decrease the quantity supplied.***
- ***Create a market shortage.***

webnote

The United Network for Organ Sharing (www.UNOS.org) maintains data on organ waiting lists and transplants.

The Deadly Shortage. Figure 3.8 illustrates the consequence of this price ceiling. At a price of zero, only the quantity q_a of "altruistic" organs is available (roughly one-third of the potential supply). But the quantity q_d is demanded by all the organ-diseased individuals. The market shortage $q_d - q_a$ tells us how many patients will die. To escape this fate, many rich patients use the Internet to search for organs around the world (see World View).

Without the government-set price ceiling, more organ-diseased patients would live. Figure 3.8 shows that q_E people would get transplants in a market-driven system rather than only q_a in the government-regulated system. But they'd have to pay the price p_E—a feature regulators say is unfair. In the absence of the market mechanism, however, the government must set rules for who gets the even smaller quantity of organs supplied.

WORLD VIEW

Growing Organ-Supply Shortfall Creates Windfall for Online Brokers

Growing demand for organ transplants world-wide is bringing new clout to online middlemen who charge ailing customers enormous fees to match them with scarce body parts.

These brokers have stepped in to fill a breach created by steep shortfall in supply. In rich nations, people are living longer at the same time that a drop in deaths from automobile accidents has shrunk a key source of donated organs. Since buying and selling of organs is illegal almost everywhere, brokers say they match prospective patients with sources outside their own country's health system. Forbes located offers of transplants online priced at anywhere from 60% to 400% more than their typical costs. One California broker arranges kidney transplants for $140,000, and hearts, livers and lungs for $290,000. Most of these transplants are being carried out in hospitals in developing countries where medical and ethical standards "don't rise to Western levels."

—Wendy Pollack

Source: *The Wall Street Journal,* January 12, 2007.

Analysis: Where shortages exist, the market mechanism will try to find an equilibrium. The *global* market in human organs favors the rich, however.

SUMMARY 

- Individual consumers, business firms, government agencies, and foreigners participate in the marketplace by offering to buy or sell goods and services, or factors of production. Participation is motivated by the desire to maximize utility (consumers), profits (business firms), or the general welfare (government agencies) from the limited resources each participant has. LO1
- All market transactions involve the exchange of either factors of production or finished products. Although the actual exchanges can occur anywhere, they take place in product markets or factor markets, depending on what is being exchanged. LO1
- People willing and able to buy a particular good at some price are part of the market demand for that product. All those willing and able to sell that good at some price are part of the market supply. Total market demand or supply is the sum of individual demands or supplies. LO1
- Supply and demand curves illustrate how the quantity demanded or supplied changes in response to a change in the price of that good, if nothing else changes *(ceteris paribus)*. Demand curves slope downward; supply curves slope upward. LO2
- Determinants of market demand include the number of potential buyers and their respective tastes (desires), incomes, other goods, and expectations. If any of these determinants change, the demand curve shifts. Movements along a demand curve are induced only by a change in the price of that good. LO3
- Determinants of market supply include factor costs, technology, profitability of other goods, expectations, tax rates, and number of sellers. Supply shifts when these underlying determinants change. LO3
- The quantity of goods or resources actually exchanged in each market depends on the behavior of all buyers and sellers, as summarized in market supply and demand curves. At the point where the two curves intersect, an equilibrium price—the price at which the quantity demanded equals the quantity supplied—is established. LO3
- A distinctive feature of the market equilibrium is that it's the only price-quantity combination acceptable to buyers and sellers alike. At higher prices, sellers supply more than buyers are willing to purchase (a market surplus); at lower prices, the amount demanded exceeds the quantity supplied (a market shortage). Only the equilibrium price clears the market. LO3
- Price ceilings are disequilibrium prices imposed on the marketplace. Such price controls create an imbalance between quantities demanded and supplied, resulting in market shortages. LO4

Key Terms

factor market
product market
opportunity cost
supply
demand
demand schedule
demand curve
law of demand
substitute goods
complementary goods
ceteris paribus
shift in demand
market demand
market supply
law of supply
equilibrium price
market mechanism
price floor
market surplus
market shortage
price ceiling

Questions for Discussion

1. In our story of Tom, the student confronted with a Web-design assignment, we emphasized the great urgency of his desire for Web tutoring. Many people would say that Tom had an "absolute need" for Web help and therefore was ready to "pay anything" to get it. If this were true, what shape would his demand curve have? Why isn't this realistic? LO1
2. With respect to the demand for college enrollment, which of the following would cause (1) a movement along the demand curve or (2) a shift of the demand curve? LO3
   a. An increase in incomes.
   b. Lower tuition.
   c. More student loans.
   d. An increase in textbook prices.
3. What would have happened to gasoline production and consumption if the government had prohibited post-Katrina price increases (see News, page 55)? LO4
4. Which determinants of pizza demand change when the White House is in crisis (page 49)? LO3
5. Why do Internet ticket resellers make so much money (News, p. 58)? How else might tickets be (re)distributed? LO2

6. In Figure 3.8, why is the organ demand curve downward-sloping rather than vertical? LO1
7. The shortage in the organ market (Figure 3.8) requires a nonmarket rationing scheme. Who should get the available (q_a) organs? Is this fairer than the market-driven distribution? LO4
8. What would happen in the apple market if the government set a *minimum* price of $2.00 per apple? What might motivate such a policy? LO4
9. The World View on page 61 describes the use of prices to achieve an equilibrium in the kitchen. What happens to the food at more traditional restaurants? LO2
10. Is there a shortage of on-campus parking at your school? How might the shortage be resolved? LO2

problems The Student Problem Set at the back of this book contains numerical and graphing problems for this chapter.

web activities to accompany this chapter can be found on the Online Learning Center: **http://www.mhhe.com/economics/schiller11e**

The Public Sector

4

LEARNING OBJECTIVES

After reading this chapter, you should know:

LO1. The nature and causes of market failure.

LO2. How government budgets are financed and spent.

LO3. The meaning of government failure.

> The market has a keen ear for private wants, but a deaf ear for public needs.
>
> —Robert Heilbroner

Markets do work: The interaction of supply and demand in product markets *does* generate goods and services. Likewise, the interaction of supply and demand in labor markets *does* yield jobs, wages, and a distribution of income. As we've observed, the market is capable of determining WHAT goods to produce, HOW, and FOR WHOM.

But are the market's answers good enough? Is the mix of output produced by unregulated markets the best possible mix? Will producers choose the production process that protects the environment? Will the market-generated distribution of income be fair enough? Will there be enough jobs for everyone who wants one?

In reality, markets don't always give us the best-possible outcomes. Markets dominated by a few powerful corporations may charge excessive prices, limit output, provide poor service, or even retard technological advance. In the quest for profits, producers may sacrifice the environment for cost savings. In unfettered markets, some people may not get life-saving health care, basic education, or even adequate nutrition. When markets generate such outcomes, government intervention may be needed to ensure better answers to the WHAT, HOW, and FOR WHOM questions.

This chapter identifies the circumstances under which government intervention is desirable. To this end, we answer the following questions:

- **Under what circumstances do markets fail?**
- **How can government intervention help?**
- **How much government intervention is desirable?**

As we'll see, there's substantial agreement about how and when markets fail to give us the best WHAT, HOW, and FOR WHOM answers. But there's much less agreement about whether government intervention improves the situation. Indeed, an overwhelming majority of Americans are ambivalent about government intervention. They want the government to "fix" the mix of output, protect the environment, and ensure an adequate level of income for everyone. But voters are equally quick to blame government meddling for many of our economic woes.

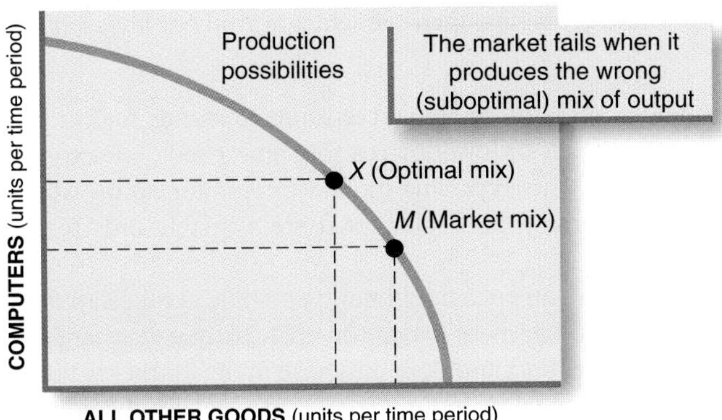

FIGURE 4.1
Market Failure

We can produce any mix of output on the production possibilities curve. Our goal is to produce the optimal (best-possible) mix of output, as represented by point *X*. Market forces, however, might produce another combination, like point *M*. In that case, the market fails—it produces a *sub*optimal mix of output.

MARKET FAILURE

We can visualize the potential for government intervention by focusing on the WHAT question. Our goal here is to produce the best-possible mix of output with existing resources. We illustrated this goal earlier with production possibilities curves. Figure 4.1 assumes that of all the possible combinations of output we could produce, the unique combination at point *X* represents the most desirable one. In other words, it's the **optimal mix of output,** the one that maximizes our collective social utility. We haven't yet figured out how to pinpoint that optimal mix; we're simply using the arbitrary point *X* in Figure 4.1 to represent that best-possible outcome.

optimal mix of output: The most desirable combination of output attainable with existing resources, technology, and social values.

Ideally, the **market mechanism** would lead us to point *X*. Price signals in the marketplace are supposed to move factors of production from one industry to another in response to consumer demands. If we demand more computers—offer to buy more at a given price—more resources (labor) will be allocated to computer manufacturing. Similarly, a fall in demand will encourage producers to stop making computers and offer their services in another industry. ***Changes in market prices direct resources from one industry to another, moving us along the perimeter of the production possibilities curve.***

market mechanism: The use of market prices and sales to signal desired outputs (or resource allocations).

Where will the market mechanism take us? Will it move resources around until we end up at the optimal point *X*? Or will it leave us at another point on the production possibilities curve, with a *sub*optimal mix of output? (If point *X* is the *optimal,* or best-possible, mix, all other output mixes must be *sub*optimal.)

We use the term **market failure** to refer to situations where the market generates less than perfect (suboptimal) outcomes. If the invisible hand of the marketplace produces a mix of output that's different from the one society most desires, then it has failed. ***Market failure implies that the forces of supply and demand haven't led us to the best point on the production possibilities curve.*** Such a failure is illustrated by point *M* in Figure 4.1. Point *M* is assumed to be the mix of output generated by market forces. Notice that the market mix (*M*) doesn't represent the optimal mix, which is assumed to be at point *X*. The market in this case *fails;* we get the wrong answer to the WHAT question.

market failure: An imperfection in the market mechanism that prevents optimal outcomes.

Market failure opens the door for government intervention. If the market can't do the job, we need some form of *nonmarket* force to get the right answers. In terms of Figure 4.1, we need something to change the mix of output—to move us from point *M* (the market mix of output) to point *X* (the optimal mix of output). Accordingly, ***market failure establishes a basis for government intervention.*** We look to the government to push market outcomes closer to the ideal.

Causes of Market Failure. Because market failure is the justification for government intervention, we need to know how and when market failure occurs. ***The four specific sources of market failure are***

- ***Public goods***
- ***Externalities***
- ***Market power***
- ***Equity***

We will first examine the nature of these problems, then see why government intervention is called for in each case.

Public Goods

The market mechanism has the unique capability to signal consumer demands for various goods and services. By offering to pay higher or lower prices for some goods, we express our preferences about WHAT to produce. However, this mode of communication works efficiently only if the benefits of consuming a particular good are available only to the individuals who purchase that product.

Consider doughnuts, for example. When you eat a doughnut, you alone get the satisfaction from its sweet, greasy taste—that is, you derive a private benefit. No one else benefits from your consumption of a doughnut: The doughnut you purchase in the market is yours alone to consume; it's a **private good.** Accordingly, your decision to purchase the doughnut will be determined only by your anticipated satisfaction, your income, and your opportunity costs.

private good: A good or service whose consumption by one person excludes consumption by others.

No Exclusion. Most of the goods and services produced in the public sector are different from doughnuts—and not just because doughnuts look, taste, and smell different from "star wars" missile shields. When you buy a doughnut, you exclude others from consumption of that product. If Dunkin' Donuts sells you a particular pastry, it can't supply the same pastry to someone else. If you devour it, no one else can. In this sense, the transaction and product are completely private.

The same exclusiveness is not characteristic of national defense. If you buy a missile defense system to thwart enemy attacks, there's no way you can exclude your neighbors from the protection your system provides. Either the missile shield deters would-be attackers or it doesn't. In the former case, both you and your neighbors survive happily ever after; in the latter case, we're all blown away together. In that sense, you and your neighbors consume the benefits of a missile shield *jointly*. National defense isn't a divisible service. There's no such thing as exclusive consumption here. The consumption of nuclear defenses is a communal feat, no matter who pays for them. Accordingly, national defense is regarded as a **public good** in the sense that ***consumption of a public good by one person doesn't preclude consumption of the same good by another person.*** By contrast, a doughnut is a private good because if I eat it, no one else can consume it.

public good: A good or service whose consumption by one person does not exclude consumption by others.

The Free-Rider Dilemma. The communal nature of public goods creates a dilemma. If you and I will *both* benefit from nuclear defenses, which one of us should buy the missile shield? I'd prefer that *you* buy it, thereby giving me protection at no direct cost. Hence, I may profess no desire for a missile shield, secretly hoping to take a **free ride** on your market purchase. Unfortunately, you too have an incentive to conceal your desire for national defenses. As a consequence, neither one of us may step forward to demand a missile shield in the marketplace. We'll both end up defenseless.

free rider: An individual who reaps direct benefits from someone else's purchase (consumption) of a public good.

Flood control is also a public good. No one in the valley wants to be flooded out. But each landowner knows that a flood-control dam will protect *all* the landowners, regardless of who pays. Either the entire valley is protected or no one is. Accordingly, individual farmers and landowners may say they don't *want* a dam and aren't willing to *pay* for it. Everyone is waiting and hoping that someone else will pay for flood control. In other words, everyone wants a *free ride.* Thus, if we leave it to market forces, no one will *demand* flood control and all the property in the valley will be washed away.

The difference between public goods and private goods rests on *technical considerations* not political philosophy. The central question is whether we have the technical capability to exclude nonpayers. In the case of national defense or flood control, we simply don't have that capability. Even city streets have the characteristics of public goods. Although theoretically we could restrict the use of streets to those who paid to use them, a tollgate on every corner would be exceedingly expensive and impractical. Here again, joint or public consumption appears to be the only feasible alternative. As the accompanying News on Napster emphasizes, the technical capability to exclude nonpayers is the key factor in identifying "public goods."

IN THE NEWS

Napster Gets Napped

Shawn Fanning had a brilliant idea for getting more music: download it from friends' computers to the Internet. So he wrote software in 1999 that enabled online file-sharing of audio files. This peer-to-peer (P2P) online distribution system became an overnight sensation: in 2000–01 nearly 60 million consumers were using Napster's software to acquire recorded music.

At first blush, Napster's service looked like a classic "public good." The service was free, and one person's consumption did not impede another person from consuming the same service. Moreover, the distribution system was configured in such a way that nonpayers could not be excluded from the service.

The definition of *"public good"* relies, however, on whether nonpayers *can* be excluded, not whether they *are* excluded. In other words, technology is critical in classifying goods as "public" or "private." In Napster's case, encryption technology that could exclude nonpayers was available, but the company had *chosen* not to use it. After being sued by major recording companies for copyright infringement, Napster changed its tune. In July 2001, it shut down its free download service. Two years later it re-opened with a *fee-based* service that could exclude nonpayers. Although free downloads are still available from offshore companies (e.g., Kazaa), fee-based services have sprung up all over (e.g., Apple's iTunes Music Store, Wal-Mart). For most consumers, music downloads are now a private good.

Source: "Napster Is Back!" *NewsFlash,* October 2003.

Analysis: A product is a "public good" only if nonpayers *cannot* be excluded from its consumption. Napster had the technical ability to exclude nonpayers but initially chose not to do so. Fee-based music downloads are a private good.

To the list of public goods we could add snow removal, the administration of justice (including prisons), the regulation of commerce, the conduct of foreign relations, airport security, and even Fourth of July fireworks. These services—which cost tens of *billions* of dollars and employ thousands of workers—provide benefits to everyone, no matter who pays for them. In each instance it's technically impossible or prohibitively expensive to exclude nonpayers from the services provided.

Underproduction of Public Goods. The free riders associated with public goods upset the customary practice of paying for what you get. If I can get all the national defense, flood control, and laws I want without paying for them, I'm not about to complain. I'm perfectly happy to let you pay for the services while we all consume them. Of course, you may feel the same way. Why should you pay for these services if you can consume just as much of them when your neighbors foot the whole bill? It might seem selfish not to pay your share of the cost of providing public goods. But you'd be better off in a material sense if you spent your income on doughnuts, letting others pick up the tab for public services.

Because the familiar link between paying and consuming is broken, public goods can't be peddled in the supermarket. People are reluctant to buy what they can get free. Hence, ***if public goods were marketed like private goods, everyone would wait for someone else to pay.*** The end result might be a total lack of public services. This is the kind of dilemma Robert Heilbroner had in mind when he spoke of the market's "deaf ear" (see quote at the beginning of this chapter).

The production possibilities curve in Figure 4.2 illustrates the dilemma created by public goods. Suppose that point *A* represents the optimal mix of private and public goods. It's the mix of goods and services we'd select if everyone's preferences were known and reflected in production decisions. The market mechanism won't lead us to point *A*, however, because the *demand* for public goods will be hidden. If we rely on the market, nearly everyone will withhold demand for public goods, waiting for a free ride to point *A*. As a result, we'll get a smaller quantity of public goods than we really want. The market mechanism will leave

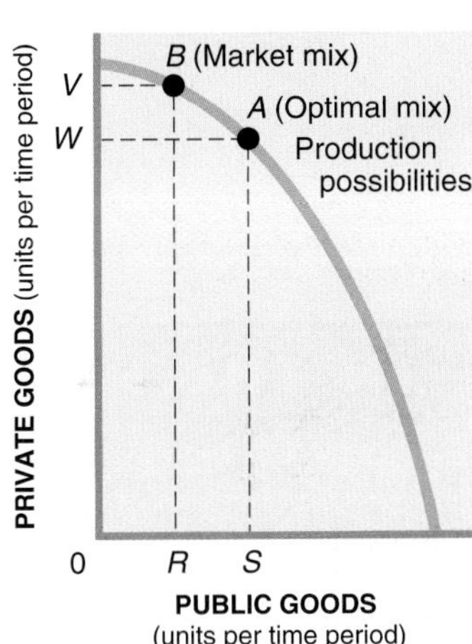

FIGURE 4.2
Underproduction of Public Goods

Suppose point *A* represents the optimal mix of output, that is, the mix of private and public goods that maximizes society's welfare. Because consumers won't demand purely public goods in the marketplace, the price mechanism won't allocate so many resources to their production. Instead, the market will tend to produce a mix of output like point *B*, which includes fewer public goods (0*R*) than is optimal (0*S*).

us at point *B*, with few, if any, public goods. Since point *A* is assumed to be optimal, point *B* must be *suboptimal* (inferior to point *A*). The market fails: We can't rely on the market mechanism to allocate enough resources to the production of public goods, no matter how much they might be desired.

Note that we're using the term "public good" in a peculiar way. To most people, "public good" refers to any good or service the government produces. In economics, however, the meaning is much more restrictive. The term "public good" refers only to those nonexcludable goods and services that must be consumed jointly, both by those who pay for them and by those who don't. Public goods can be produced by either the government or the private sector. Private goods can be produced in either sector as well. The problem is that ***the market tends to underproduce public goods and overproduce private goods.*** If we want more public goods, we need a *nonmarket* force—government intervention—to get them. The government will have to force people to pay taxes, then use the tax revenues to pay for the production of national defense, flood control, snow removal, and other public goods.

Externalities

The free-rider problem associated with public goods is one justification for government intervention. It's not the only justification, however. Further grounds for intervention arise from the tendency of costs or benefits of some market activities to "spill over" onto third parties.

Consider the case of cigarettes. The price someone is willing to pay for a pack of cigarettes reflects the amount of satisfaction a smoker anticipates from its consumption. If that price is high enough, tobacco companies will produce the cigarettes demanded. That is how market-based price signals are supposed to work. In this case, however, the price paid isn't a satisfactory signal of the product's desirability. The smoker's pleasure is offset in part by nonsmokers' *dis*pleasure. In this case, smoke literally spills over onto other consumers, causing them discomfort and possibly even ill health (see News below). Yet their loss isn't reflected in the market price: The harm caused to nonsmokers is *external* to the market price of cigarettes.

IN THE NEWS

U.S. Details Dangers of Secondhand Smoking

Secondhand smoke dramatically increases the risk of heart disease and lung cancer in nonsmokers and can be controlled only by making indoor spaces smoke-free, according to a comprehensive report issued yesterday by U.S. Surgeon General Richard H. Carmona.

"The health effects of secondhand smoke exposure are more pervasive than we previously thought," Carmona said. "The scientific evidence is now indisputable: Secondhand smoke is not a mere annoyance. It is a serious health hazard that can lead to disease and premature death in children and nonsmoking adults."

According to the report, the government's most detailed statement ever on secondhand smoke, exposure to smoke at home or work increases the nonsmokers' risk of developing heart disease by 25 to 30 percent and lung cancer by 20 to 30 percent. It is especially dangerous for children living with smokers and is known to cause sudden infant death syndrome, respiratory problems, ear infections and asthma attacks in infants and children. . . .

The report does not present new scientific data but is an analysis of the best research on secondhand smoke. It said, for instance, that the Centers for Disease Control and Prevention estimated last year that exposure to secondhand smoke kills more than 3,000 nonsmokers from lung cancer, approximately 46,000 from coronary heart disease, and as many as 430 newborns from sudden infant death syndrome.

—Marc Kaufman

Source: *Washington Post,* June 28, 2006 p. 1. **© 2006, The Washington Post, excerpted with permission.**

Analysis: The health risks imposed on nonsmokers via "passive smoke" represent external costs. The market price of cigarettes doesn't reflect these costs borne by third parties.

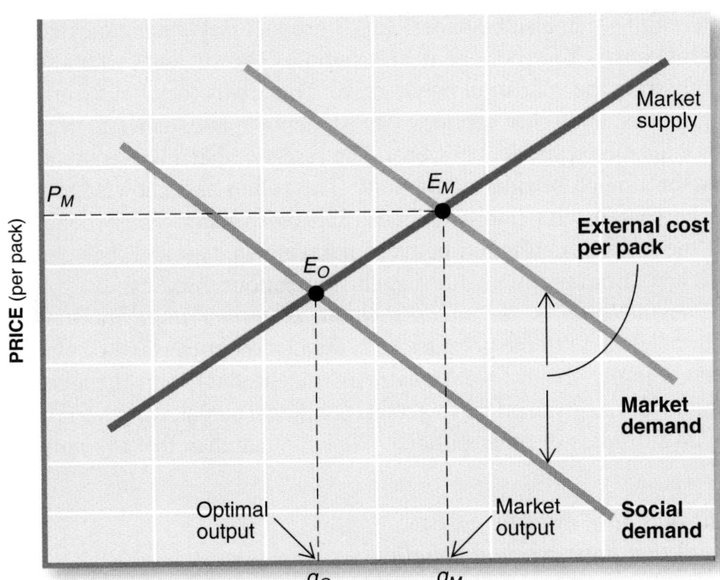

FIGURE 4.3
Externalities

The market responds to consumer demands, not externalities. Smokers demand q_M cigarettes. But external costs on nonsmokers imply that the *social* demand for cigarettes is less than (below) *market* demand. The socially optimal level of output is q_O, less than the market output q_M.

The term **externalities** refers to all costs or benefits of a market activity borne by a third party, that is, by someone other than the immediate producer or consumer. ***Whenever externalities are present, market prices aren't a valid measure of a good's value to society.*** As a consequence, the market will fail to produce the right mix of output. Specifically, ***the market will underproduce goods that yield external benefits and overproduce those that generate external costs.***

externalities: Costs (or benefits) of a market activity borne by a third party; the difference between the social and private costs (benefits) of a market activity.

External Costs. Figure 4.3 shows how external costs cause the market to overproduce cigarettes. The market demand curve includes only the wishes of smokers, that is, people who are willing and able to purchase cigarettes. The forces of market demand and supply result in an equilibrium at E_M in which q_M cigarettes are produced and consumed. The market price P_M reflects the value of those cigarettes to smokers.

The well-being of *non*smokers isn't reflected in the market equilibrium. To take the *non-smoker's* interests into account, we must subtract the external costs imposed on *them* from the value that *smokers* put on cigarettes. In general,

$$\text{Social demand} = \text{market demand} \pm \text{externalities}$$

In this case, the externality is a *cost,* so we must *subtract* the external cost from market demand to get a full accounting of social demand. The "social demand" curve in Figure 4.3 reflects this computation. To find this curve, we subtract the amount of external cost from every price on the market demand curve. What the *social* demand curve tells us is how much society would be willing and able to pay for cigarettes if the preferences of both smokers and nonsmokers were taken into account.

The social demand curve in Figure 4.3 creates a social equilibrium at E_O. At this juncture, we see that the socially *optimal* quantity of cigarettes is q_O, not the larger market-generated level at q_M. In this sense, the market produces too many cigarettes.

Externalities also exist in production. A power plant that burns high-sulfur coal damages the surrounding environment. Yet the damage inflicted on neighboring people, vegetation, and buildings is external to the cost calculations of the firm. Because the cost of such pollution is not reflected in the price of electricity, the firm will tend to produce more electricity (and pollution) than is socially desirable. To reduce this imbalance, the government has to step in and change market outcomes.

webnote

Check out the pollution problems in your neighborhood at www.epa.gov/epahome/commsearch.htm

External Benefits. Externalities can also be beneficial. A product may generate external *benefits* rather than external *costs.* Your college is an example. The students who attend your school benefit directly from the education they receive. That's why they (and you) are willing to *pay* for tuition, books, and other services. The students in attendance aren't the only beneficiaries of this educational service, however. The research that a university conducts may yield benefits for a much broader community. The values and knowledge students acquire may also be shared with family, friends, and co-workers. These benefits would all be *external* to the market transaction between a paying student and the school. Positive externalities also arise from immunizations against infectious diseases.

If a product yields external benefits, the social demand is greater than the market demand. In this case, the social value of the good *exceeds* the market price (by the amount of external benefit). Accordingly, society wants *more* of the product than the market mechanism alone will produce at any given price. To get that additional output, the government may have to intervene with subsidies or other policies. We conclude then that ***the market fails by***

- ***Overproducing goods that have external costs.***
- ***Underproducing goods that have external benefits.***

If externalities are present, the market won't produce the optimal mix of output. To get that optimal mix, we need government intervention.

Market Power

In the case of both public goods and externalities, the market fails to achieve the optimal mix of output because the price signal is flawed. The price consumers are willing and able to pay for a specific good doesn't reflect all the benefits or cost of producing that good.

The market may fail, however, even when the price signals are accurate. The *response* to price signals, rather than the signals themselves, may be flawed.

monopoly: A firm that produces the entire market supply of a particular good or service.

market power: The ability to alter the market price of a good or a service.

Restricted Supply. Market power is often the cause of a flawed response. Suppose there were only one airline company in the world. This single seller of airline travel would be a **monopoly**—that is, the only producer in that industry. As a monopolist, the airline could charge extremely high prices without worrying that travelers would flock to a competing airline. At the same time, the high prices paid by consumers would express the importance of that service to society. Ideally, such prices would act as a signal to producers to build and fly more planes—to change the mix of output. But a monopolist doesn't have to cater to every consumer's whim. It can limit airline travel and obstruct our efforts to achieve an optimal mix of output.

Monopoly is the most severe form of **market power.** More generally, market power refers to any situation in which a single producer or consumer has the ability to alter the market price of a specific product. If the publisher (McGraw-Hill) charges a high price for this book, you'll have to pay the tab. McGraw-Hill has market power because there are relatively few economics textbooks and your professor has required you to use this one. You don't have power in the textbook market because your decision to buy or not won't alter the market price of this text. You're only one of the million students who are taking an introductory economics course this year.

The market power McGraw-Hill possesses is derived from the copyright on this text. No matter how profitable textbook sales might be, no one else is permitted to produce or sell this particular book. Patents are another common source of market power because they also preclude others from making or selling a specific product. Market power may also result from control of resources, restrictive production agreements, or efficiencies of large-scale production.

Whatever the source of market power, the direct consequence is that one or more producers attain discretionary power over the market's response to price signals. They may use that discretion to enrich themselves rather than to move the economy toward the optimal mix of output. In this case, the market will again fail to deliver the most desired goods and services.

The mandate for government intervention in this case is to prevent or dismantle concentrations of market power. That's the basic purpose of **antitrust** policy. Another option is to *regulate* market behavior. This was one of the goals of the antitrust case against Microsoft. The government was less interested in breaking Microsoft's near monopoly on operating systems than in changing the way Microsoft behaved.

antitrust: Government intervention to alter market structure or prevent abuse of market power.

In some cases, it may be economically efficient to have one large firm supply an entire market. Such a situation arises in **natural monopoly,** where a single firm can achieve economies of scale over the entire range of market output. Utility companies, local telephone service, subway systems, and cable all exhibit such scale (size) efficiencies. In these cases, a monopoly *structure* may be economically desirable. The government may have to regulate the *behavior* of a natural monopoly, however, to ensure that consumers get the benefits of that greater efficiency.

natural monopoly: An industry in which one firm can achieve economies of scale over the entire range of market supply.

Inequity

Public goods, externalities, and market power all cause resource misallocations. Where these phenomena exist, the market mechanism will fail to produce the optimal mix of output in the best-possible way.

Beyond the questions of WHAT and HOW to produce, we're also concerned about FOR WHOM output is produced. The market answers this question by distributing a larger share of total output to those with the most income. Although this result may be efficient, it's not necessarily equitable. As we saw in Chapter 2, the market mechanism may enrich some people while leaving others to seek shelter in abandoned cars. If such outcomes violate our vision of equity, we may want the government to change the market-generated distribution of income.

Taxes and Transfers. The tax-and-transfer system is the principal mechanism for redistributing incomes. The idea here is to take some of the income away from those who have "too much" and give it to those whom the market has left with "too little." Taxes are levied to take back some of the income received from the market. Those tax revenues are then redistributed via transfer payments to those deemed needy, such as the poor, the aged, the unemployed. **Transfer payments** are income payments for which no goods or services are exchanged. They're used to bolster the incomes of those for whom the market itself provides too little.

transfer payments: Payments to individuals for which no current goods or services are exchanged, like Social Security, welfare, and unemployment benefits.

Merit Goods. Often, our vision of what is "too little" is defined in terms of specific goods and services. There is a widespread consensus in the United States that everyone is entitled to some minimum levels of shelter, food, and health care. These are regarded as **merit goods,** in the same sense that everyone merits at least some minimum provision of such goods. When the market does not distribute that minimum provision, the government is called on to fill in the gaps. In this case, the income transfers take the form of *in-kind* transfers (e.g., food stamps, housing vouchers, Medicaid) rather than *cash* transfers (e.g., welfare checks, Social Security benefits).

merit good: A food or service society deems everyone is entitled to some minimal quantity of.

Some people argue that we don't need the government to help the poor—that private charity alone will suffice. Unfortunately, private charity alone has never been adequate. One reason private charity doesn't suffice is the "free-rider" problem. If I contribute heavily to the poor, you benefit from safer streets (fewer muggers), a better environment (fewer slums and homeless people), and a clearer conscience (knowing fewer people are starving). In this sense, the relief of misery is a *public* good. Were I the only taxpayer to benefit substantially from the reduction of poverty, then charity would be a private affair. As long as income support substantially benefits the public at large, then income redistribution is a *public* good, for which public funding is appropriate. This is the *economic* rationale for public income-redistribution activities. To this rationale one can add such moral arguments as seem appropriate.

Macro Instability

The micro failures of the marketplace imply that we're at the wrong point on the production possibilities curve or inequitably distributing the output produced. There's another basic question we've swept under the rug, however. How do we get to the production possibilities curve in the first place? To reach the curve, we must utilize all available resources and technology. Can we be confident that the invisible hand of the marketplace will use all available resources? Or will some people face **unemployment**—that is, be willing to work but unable to find a job?

unemployment: The inability of labor-force participants to find jobs.

And what about prices? Price signals are a critical feature of the market mechanism. But the validity of those signals depends on some stable measure of value. What good is a doubling of salary when the price of everything you buy doubles as well? Generally, rising prices will enrich people who own property and impoverish people who rent. That's why we strive to avoid **inflation**—a situation in which the *average* price level is increasing.

inflation: An increase in the average level of prices of goods and services.

Historically, the marketplace has been wracked with bouts of both unemployment and inflation. These experiences have prompted calls for government intervention at the macro level. ***The goal of macro intervention is to foster economic growth—to get us on the production possibilities curve (full employment), maintain a stable price level (price stability), and increase our capacity to produce (growth).***

GROWTH OF GOVERNMENT

The potential micro and macro failures of the marketplace provide specific justifications for government intervention. The question then turns to how well the activities of the public sector correspond to these implied mandates.

Federal Growth

Until the 1930s the federal government's role was largely limited to national defense (a public good), enforcement of a common legal system (also a public good), and provision of postal service (equity). The Great Depression of the 1930s spawned a new range of government activities, including welfare and Social Security programs (equity), minimum wage laws and workplace standards (regulation), and massive public works (public goods and externalities). In the 1950s the federal government also assumed a greater role in maintaining macroeconomic stability (macro failure), protecting the environment (externalities), and safeguarding the public's health (externalities and equity).

These increasing responsibilities have greatly increased the size of the public sector. In 1902 the federal government employed fewer than 350,000 people and spent a mere $650 *million.* Today the federal government employs nearly 4 million people and spends roughly $3 *trillion* a year.

Direct Expenditure. Figure 4.4 summarizes the growth of the public sector since 1930. World War II caused a massive increase in the size of the federal government. Federal purchases of goods and services for the war accounted for over 40 percent of total output during the 1943–44 period. The federal share of total U.S. output fell abruptly after World War II, rose again during the Korean War (1950–53), and has declined slightly since then.

The decline in the federal share of total output is somewhat at odds with most people's perception of government growth. This discrepancy is explained by two phenomena. First, people see the *absolute* size of the government growing every year. But we're focusing here on the *relative* size of the public sector. Since the 1950s the public sector has grown a bit more slowly than the private sector, slightly reducing its relative size.

Income Transfers. Second, Figure 4.4 depicts only government spending on goods and services, not *all* public spending. Direct expenditure on goods and services absorbs real resources, but income transfers don't. Hence, income transfers don't directly alter the mix of output. Their effect is primarily *distributional* (the FOR WHOM question), not *allocative* (the WHAT question). Were income transfers included, the relative size and growth of the federal government would be larger than Figure 4.4 depicts. This is because ***most of the growth in federal spending has come from increased income transfers, not purchases of goods and services.***

State and Local Growth

State and local spending on goods and services has followed a very different path from federal expenditure. Prior to World War II, state and local governments dominated public-sector spending. During the war, however, the share of total output going to state and local governments fell, hitting a low of 3 percent in that period (Figure 4.4).

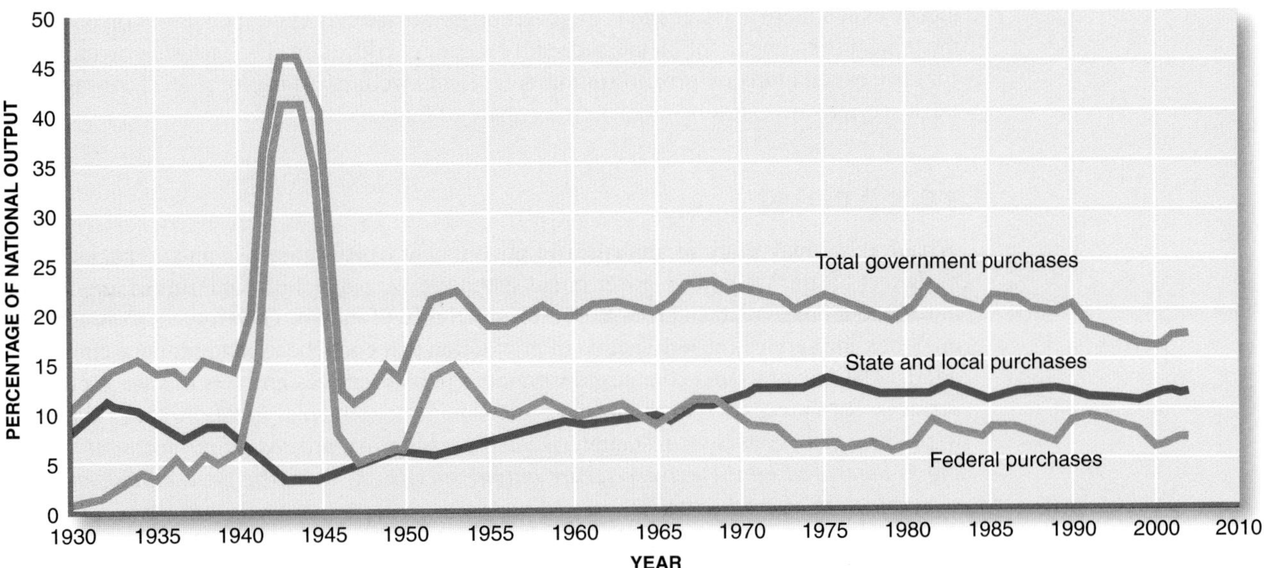

FIGURE 4.4
Government Growth

During World War II the public sector purchased nearly half of total U.S. output. Since the early 1950s the public-sector share of total output has been closer to 20 percent. Within the public sector, however, there's been a major shift: State and local claims on resources have grown, while the federal share has declined significantly.

Source: *Economic Report of the President, 2007.*

State and local spending caught up with federal spending in the mid-1960s and has exceeded it ever since. Today more than 80,000 state and local government entities buy much more output than Uncle Sam and employ five times as many people.

Figure 4.5 provides an overview of federal, state, and local budgets. National defense and health care absorb most federal expenditure (other than income transfers). Education is

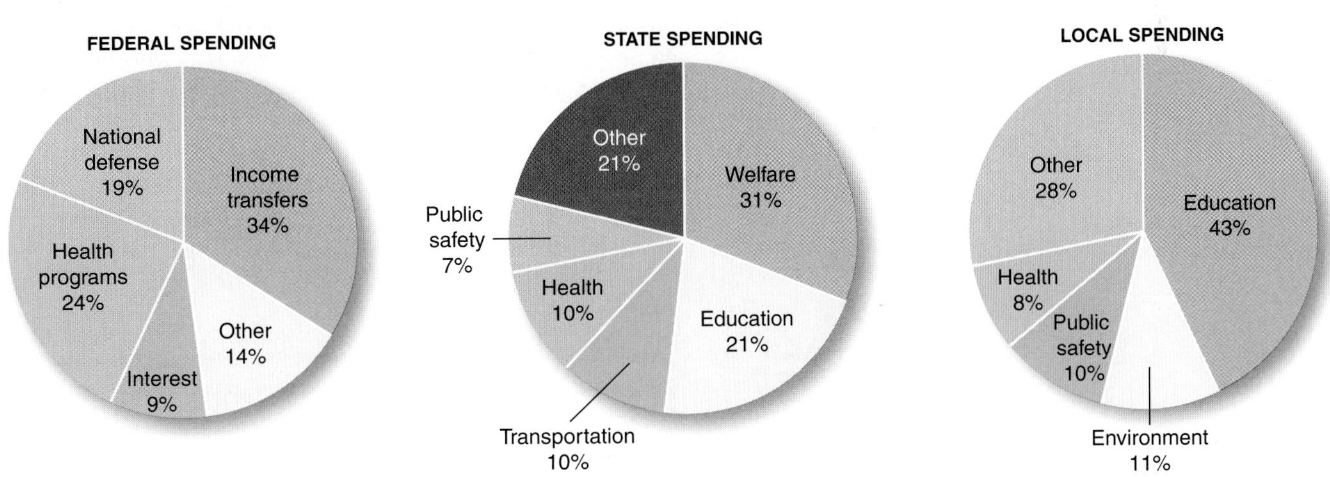

FIGURE 4.5
Government Spending

Over half of federal spending consists of cash and in-kind income transfers (the FOR WHOM question). Among direct purchases (the WHAT question) national defense dominates. State budgets focus on education (colleges) and transportation. Local purchases are dominated by school expenditures.

Source: U.S. Census Bureau and Office of Management and Budget (FY2006 data).

a huge expenditure at lower levels of government. Most direct state spending is on colleges; most local spending is for elementary and secondary education. The fastest-growing areas for state expenditure are prisons (public safety) and welfare. At the local level, sewage and trash services are claiming an increasing share of budgets.

TAXATION

Whatever we may think of any specific government expenditure, we must recognize one basic fact of life: We pay for government spending. We pay not just in terms of tax *dollars* but in the more fundamental form of a changed mix of output. Government expenditures on goods and services absorb factors of production that could be used to produce consumer goods. The mix of output changes toward *more* public services and *less* private goods and services. Resources used to produce missile shields or elementary schools aren't available to produce cars, houses, or restaurant meals. In real terms, ***the cost of government spending is measured by the private-sector output sacrificed when the government employs scarce factors of production.***

opportunity costs: The most desired goods or services that are forgone in order to obtain something else.

The **opportunity costs** of public spending aren't always apparent. We don't directly hand over factors of production to the government. Instead, we give the government part of our income in the form of taxes. Those dollars are then used to buy factors of production or goods and services in the marketplace. Thus, ***the primary function of taxes is to transfer command over resources (purchasing power) from the private sector to the public sector.*** Although the government sometimes also borrows dollars to finance its purchases, taxes are the primary source of government revenues.

Federal Taxes

As recently as 1902, much of the revenue the federal government collected came from taxes imposed on alcoholic beverages. The federal government didn't have authority to collect income taxes. As a consequence, *total* federal revenue in 1902 was only $653 million.

Income Taxes. All that has changed. The Sixteenth Amendment to the U.S. Constitution, enacted in 1915, granted the federal government authority to collect income taxes. The government now collects over $1 *trillion* in that form alone. Although the federal government still collects taxes on alcoholic beverages, the individual income tax has become the largest single source of government revenue (see Figure 4.6).

progressive tax: A tax system in which tax rates rise as incomes rise.

In theory, the federal income tax is designed to be **progressive**—that is, to take a larger *fraction* of high incomes than of low incomes. In 2006, for example, a single person with less than $8,500 of income paid no federal income tax. The next $7,550 of income was taxed at 10 percent, however. People with incomes of $50,000–$70,000

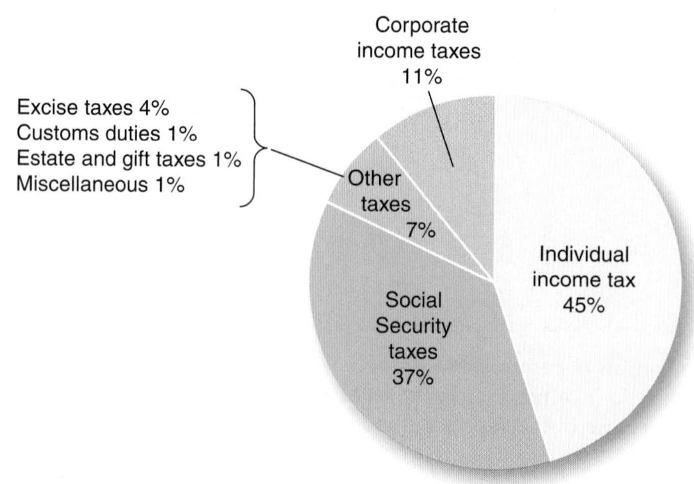

FIGURE 4.6
Federal Taxes

Taxes transfer purchasing power from the private sector to the public sector. The largest federal tax is the individual income tax. The second-largest source of federal revenue is the Social Security payroll tax.

Source: Office of Management and Budget, FY2007 data.

confronted a 25 percent tax rate on their additional income. The marginal tax rate got as high as 35 percent for people earning more than $350,000 in income. Thus ***people with high incomes not only pay more taxes but also pay a larger* fraction *of their income in taxes.***

Social Security Taxes. The second major source of federal revenue is the Social Security payroll tax. People working now transfer part of their earnings to retired workers by making "contributions" to Social Security. There's nothing voluntary about these "contributions"; they take the form of mandatory payroll deductions. In 2007, each worker paid 7.65 percent of his or her wages to Social Security and employers contributed an equal amount. As a consequence, the government collected nearly $900 billion.

At first glance, the Social Security payroll tax looks like a **proportional tax,** that is, a tax that takes the *same* fraction of every taxpayer's income. But this isn't the case. The Social Security (FICA) tax isn't levied on every payroll dollar. Incomes above a certain ceiling ($97,500 in 2007) aren't taxed. As a result, workers with *really* high salaries turn over a smaller fraction of their incomes to Social Security than do low-wage workers. This makes the Social Security payroll tax a **regressive tax.**

proportional tax: A tax that levies the same rate on every dollar of income.

regressive tax: A tax system in which tax rates fall as incomes rise.

webnote

The Office of Management and Budget's "A Citizen's Guide to the Federal Budget" provides convenient charts and data on federal revenues. See www.whitehouse.gov/omb/budget or www.access.gpo.gov.su_docs/budgetguide.html

Corporate Taxes. The federal government taxes the profits of corporations as well as the incomes of consumers. But there are far fewer corporations (less than 4 million) than consumers (300 million), and their profits are small in comparison to total consumer income. In 2007, the federal government collected only $270 billion in corporate income taxes, despite the fact that it imposed a top tax rate of 38 percent on corporate profits.

Excise Taxes. The last major source of federal revenue is excise taxes. Like the early taxes on whiskey, excise taxes are sales taxes imposed on specific goods and services. The federal government taxes not only liquor ($13.50 per gallon) but also gasoline (18.4 cents per gallon), cigarettes (39 cents per pack), air fares, and a variety of other goods and services. Such taxes not only discourage production and consumption of these goods—by raising their price and thereby reducing the quantity demanded—they also raise a substantial amount of revenue.

webnote

Current excise tax rates are available from the U.S. Bureau of Alcohol, Tobacco, and Firearms. See www.atf.treas.gov

State and Local Revenues

Taxes. State and local governments also levy taxes on consumers and businesses. In general, cities depend heavily on property taxes, and state governments rely heavily on sales taxes. Although nearly all states and many cities also impose income taxes, effective tax rates are so low (averaging less than 2 percent of personal income) that income tax revenues are much less than sales and property tax revenues.

"I can't find anything wrong here, Mr. Truffle . . . you just seem to have too much left after taxes."

Analysis: Taxes are a financing mechanism that enable the government to purchase scarce resources. Higher taxes imply less private-sector purchases.

IN THE NEWS

Perpetuating Poverty: Lotteries Prey on the Poor

A recently released Gallup survey confirms the fears of many who oppose government-promoted gambling: the poorest among us are contributing much more to lottery revenues than those with higher incomes. The poll found that people who played the lottery with an income of less than $20,000 annually spent an average of $46 per month on lottery tickets. That comes out to more than $550 per year and it is nearly double the amount spent in any other income bracket.

The significance of this is magnified when we look deeper into the figures. Those with annual incomes ranging from $30,000 to $50,000 had the second-highest average—$24 per month, or $288 per year. A person making $20,000 spends three times as much on lottery tickets on average than does someone making $30,000. And keep in mind that these numbers represent average spending. For every one or two people who spend just a few bucks a year on lotteries, others spend thousands.

—Jordan Ballor

Source: Action Institute, March 3, 2004. From "Perpetuating Poverty: Lotteries Prey on the Poor" by Jordan Ballor, www.action.org. Used with permission by the author.

Analysis: Poor people spend a larger percentage of their income on lottery tickets than do rich people. This makes lotteries a regressive source of government revenue.

Like the Social Security payroll tax, state and local taxes tend to be *regressive*—that is, they take a larger share of income from the poor than from the rich. Consider a 4 percent sales tax, for example. It might appear that a uniform tax rate like this would affect all consumers equally. But people with lower incomes tend to spend most of their income on goods and services. Thus, most of their income is subject to sales taxes. By contrast, a person with a high income can afford to save part of his or her income and thereby shelter it from sales taxes. A family that earns $40,000 and spends $30,000 of it on taxable goods and services, for example, pays $1,200 in sales taxes when the tax rate is 4 percent. In effect, then, they are handing over 3 percent of their *income* ($1,200 ÷ $40,000) to the state. By contrast, the family that makes only $12,000 and spends $11,500 of it for food, clothing, and shelter pays $460 in sales taxes in the same state. Their total tax is smaller, but it represents a much larger *share* (3.8 versus 3.0 percent) of their income.

webnote

The U.S. Census Bureau compiles the most comprehensive data on state and local government finances. For details visit www.census.gov/ftp/pub

Local property taxes are also regressive because poor people devote a larger portion of their incomes to housing costs. Hence, a larger share of a poor family's income is subject to property taxes. State lotteries are also regressive, for the same reason (see News). Low-income players spend 1.4 percent of their incomes on lottery tickets while upper-income players devote only 0.1 percent of their income to lottery purchases.

GOVERNMENT FAILURE

Some government intervention in the marketplace is clearly desirable. The market mechanism can fail for a variety of reasons, leaving a laissez-faire economy short of its economic goals. But how much government intervention is desirable? Communist nations once thought that complete government control of production, consumption, and distribution decisions was the surest path to utopia. They learned the hard way that ***not only markets but governments as well can fail.*** In this context, **government failure** means that government intervention fails to move us closer to our economic goals.

government failure: Government intervention that fails to improve economic outcomes.

In Figure 4.7, the goal of government intervention is to move the mix of output from point M (failed market outcome) to point X (the social optimum). But government intervention might unwittingly move us to point G_1, making matters worse. Or the government might overreact, sending us to point G_2. Red tape and onerous regulation might even force us to point G_3, *inside* the production possibilities curve (with less total output than at point M). All those possibilities (G_1, G_2, G_3) represent government failure. Government

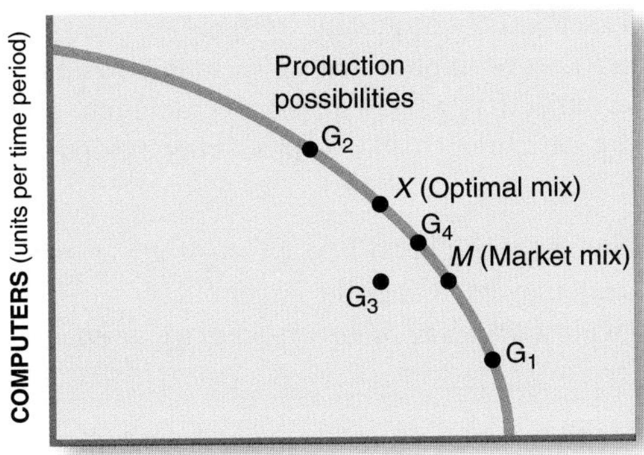

FIGURE 4.7
Government Failure

When the market produces a suboptimal mix of output (point M), the goal of government is to move output to the social optimum (point X). A move to G_4 would be an improvement in the mix of output. But government intervention *may* move the economy to points G_1, G_2, or G_3—all reflecting government failure.

intervention is desirable only to the extent that it *improves* market outcomes (e.g., G_4). Government intervention in the FOR WHOM question is desirable only if the distribution of income gets better, not worse, as a result of taxes and transfers. Even when outcomes improve, government failure may occur if the costs of government intervention exceeded the benefits of an improved output mix, cleaner production methods, or a fairer distribution of income.

Perceptions of Waste

Taxpayers seem to have strong opinions about government failure. When asked whether the government "wastes" their tax dollars or uses them well, the majority see waste in government (see News on "Persistent Doubts"). The average taxpayer now believes that state governments waste 29 cents out of each dollar, while the federal government wastes 42 cents out of each tax dollar!

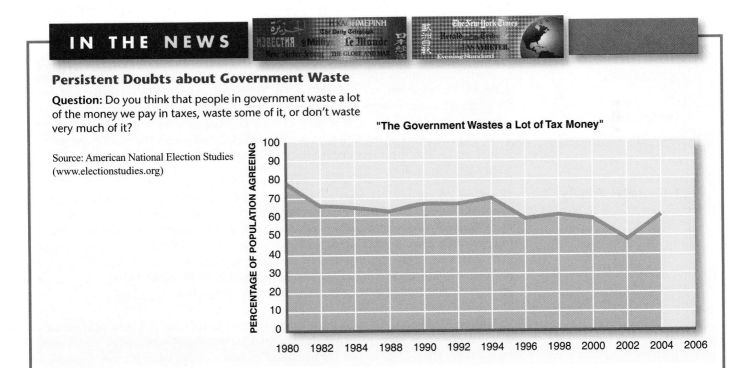

IN THE NEWS

Persistent Doubts about Government Waste

Question: Do you think that people in government waste a lot of the money we pay in taxes, waste some of it, or don't waste very much of it?

Source: American National Election Studies (www.electionstudies.org)

"The Government Wastes a Lot of Tax Money"

PERCENTAGE OF POPULATION AGREEING
100
90
80
70
60
50
40
30
20
10
0
1980 1982 1984 1988 1990 1992 1994 1996 1998 2000 2002 2004 2006

Analysis: Market failure justifies government intervention. If the government wastes resources, however, it too may fail to satisfy our economic goals.

Government "waste" implies that the public sector isn't producing as many services as it could with the sources at its disposal. Such inefficiency implies that we're producing somewhere *inside* our production possibilities curve rather than on it (e.g., point G_3 in Figure 4.7). If the government is wasting resources this way, we can't possibly be producing the optimal mix of output.

Opportunity Cost

Even if the government weren't wasting resources, it might still be guilty of government failure. As important as efficiency in government may be, it begs the larger question of how many government services we really want. In reality, ***the issue of government waste encompasses two distinct questions:***

- ***Efficiency:*** Are we getting as much service as we could from the resources we allocate to government?
- ***Opportunity cost:*** Are we giving up too many private-sector goods in order to get those services?

If the government is producing goods inefficiently, we end up *inside* the production possibilities curve, with less output than attainable. Even if the government is efficient, however, the *mix* of output may not be optimal, as points G_1 and G_2 in Figure 4.7 illustrate. ***Everything the government does entails an opportunity cost.*** The more police officers or schoolteachers employed by the public sector, the fewer workers available to private producers and consumers. Similarly, the more computers, pencils, and paper consumed by government agencies, the fewer accessible to individuals and private companies.

webnote

For more public opinion on the role of government, visit the University of Michigan's National Election Studies site at www.umich.edu/~nes/nesguide/gd-index.htm

When assessing government's role in the economy, ***we must consider not only what governments do but also what we give up to allow them to do it.*** The theory of public goods tells us only what activities are appropriate for government, not the proper *level* of such activity. National defense is clearly a proper function of the public sector. Not so clear, however, is how much the government should spend on tanks, aircraft carriers, and missile shields. The same is true of environmental protection or law enforcement.

The concept of opportunity costs puts a new perspective on the whole question of government size. Before we can decide how big is "too big," we must decide what we're willing to give up to support the public sector. A military force of 1.4 million men and women is "too big" from an economic perspective only if we value the forgone private production and consumption more highly than we value the added strength of our defenses. The government has gone "too far" if the highway it builds is less desired than the park and homes it implicitly replaced. In these and all cases, the assessment of bigness must come back to a comparison of what is given up with what is received. The assessment of government failure thus comes back to points on the production possibilities curve. Has the government moved us closer to the optimal mix of output (e.g., point G_4 in Figure 4.7) or not?

Cost-Benefit Analysis

This is a tough question to answer in the abstract. We can, however, use the concept of opportunity cost to assess the effectiveness of specific government interventions. From this perspective, ***additional public-sector activity is desirable only if the benefits from that activity exceed its opportunity costs.*** In other words, we compare the benefits of a public project to the value of the private goods given up to produce it. By performing this calculation repeatedly along the perimeter of the production possibilities curve, we could locate the optimal mix of output—the point at which no further increase in public-sector spending activity is desirable.

Valuation Problems. Although the principles of cost-benefit analysis are simple enough, they're deceptive. How are we to measure the potential benefits of improved police services, for example? Should we estimate the number of robberies and murders prevented, calculate the worth of each, and add up the benefits? And how are we supposed to calculate the worth of a saved life? By a person's earnings? value of assets? number of friends? And what about the increased sense of security people have when they know the police are patrolling in their neighborhood? Should this be included in the benefit calculation? Some people will attach great value to this service; others will attach little. Whose values should be the standard?

When we're dealing with (private) market goods and services, we can gauge the benefits of a product by the amount of money consumers are willing to pay for it. This price signal isn't available for most public services, however, because of externalities and the nonexclusive nature of pure public goods (the free-rider problem). Hence, ***the value (benefits) of public services must be estimated because they don't have (reliable) market prices.*** This opens the door to endless political squabbles about how beneficial any particular government activity is.

The same problems arise in evaluating the government's efforts to redistribute incomes. Government transfer payments now go to retired workers, disabled people, veterans, farmers, sick people, students, pregnant women, unemployed people, poor people, and a long list of other recipients. To pay for all these transfers, the government must raise tax revenues. With so many people paying taxes and receiving transfer payments, the net effects on the distribution of income aren't easy to figure out. Yet we can't determine whether this government intervention is worth it until we know how the FOR WHOM answer was changed and what the tax-and-transfer effort cost us.

Ballot Box Economics

In practice, we rely on political mechanisms, not cost-benefit calculations, to decide what to produce in the public sector and how to redistribute incomes. ***Voting mechanisms substitute for the market mechanism in allocating resources to the public sector and deciding how to use them.*** Some people have even suggested that the variety and volume of public goods are determined by the most votes, just as the variety and volume of private goods are determined by the most dollars. Thus, governments choose that level and mix of output (and related taxation) that seem to command the most votes.

Sometimes the link between the ballot box and output decisions is very clear and direct. State and local governments, for example, are often compelled to get voter approval before building another highway, school, housing project, or sewage plant. *Bond referenda* are direct requests by a government unit for voter approval of specific public-spending projects (e.g., roads, schools). In 2006, for example, governments sought voter approval for $80 billion of new borrowing to finance public expenditure; over 80 percent of those requests were approved.

webnote

The National Conference of State Legislatures tracks bond referenda and other ballot issues. Visit them at www.ncsl.org to review recent ballots.

Bond referenda are more the exception than the rule. Bond referenda account for less than 1 percent of state and local expenditures (and none of federal expenditures). As a consequence, voter control of public spending is typically much less direct. Although federal agencies must receive authorization from Congress for all expenditures, consumers get a chance to elect new representatives only every 2 years. Much the same is true at state and local levels. Voters may be in a position to dictate the general level and pattern of public expenditures but have little direct influence on everyday output decisions. In this sense, the ballot box is a poor substitute for the market mechanism.

Even if the link between the ballot box and allocation decisions were stronger, the resulting mix of output might not be optimal. A democratic vote, for example, might yield a 51 percent majority for approval of new local highways. Should the highways then be built? The answer isn't obvious. After all, a large minority (49 percent) of the voters have stated that they don't want resources used this way. If we proceed to build the highways, we'll make those people worse off. Their loss may be greater than what proponents gain. Hence, the basic dilemma is really twofold. ***We don't know what the real demand for public services is, and votes alone don't reflect the intensity of individual demands.*** Moreover, real-world decision making involves so many choices that a stable consensus is impossible.

Public-Choice Theory

In the midst of all this complexity and uncertainty, another factor may be decisive—namely, self-interest. In principle, government officials are supposed to serve the people. It doesn't take long, however, before officials realize that the public is indecisive about what it wants and takes very little interest in government's day-to-day activities. With such latitude, government officials can set their own agendas. Those agendas may give higher priority to personal advancement than to the needs of the public. Agency directors may foster new programs that enlarge their mandate, enhance their visibility, and increase their prestige or income. Members of Congress may likewise pursue legislative favors like tax breaks for supporters more diligently than they pursue the general public interest. In such cases, the probability of attaining the socially optimal mix of output declines.

public choice: Theory of public-sector behavior emphasizing rational self-interest of decision makers and voters.

The theory of **public choice** emphasizes the role of self-interest in public decision making. Public-choice theory essentially extends the analysis of market behavior to political behavior. Public officials are assumed to have specific personal goals (for example, power, recognition, wealth) that they'll pursue in office. ***A central tenet of public-choice theory is that bureaucrats are just as selfish (utility maximizing) as everyone else.***

Public-choice theory provides a neat and simple explanation for public-sector decision making. But critics argue that the theory provides a woefully narrow view of public servants. Some people do selflessly pursue larger, public goals, such critics argue, and ideas can overwhelm self-interest. Steven Kelman of Harvard, for example, argues that narrow self-interest can't explain the War on Poverty of the 1960s, the tax revolt of the 1970s, or the deregulation movement of the 1980s. These tidal changes in public policy reflect the power of ideas, not simple self-interest.

Although self-interest can't provide a complete explanation of public decision making, it adds important perspectives on the policy process. James Buchanan of George Mason University (Virginia) won the 1986 Nobel Prize in economics for helping develop this public-choice perspective. It adds a personal dimension to the faceless mechanics of ballot box economics, cost-benefit analysis, and other "objective" mechanisms of public-sector decision making.

THE ECONOMY TOMORROW

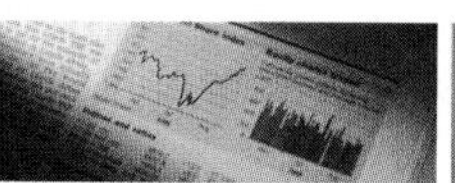

DOWNSIZING GOVERNMENT

The Great Depression of the 1930s devastated the world economy. For many people, it was compelling evidence that the market alone couldn't be trusted to answer the WHAT, HOW, and FOR WHOM questions. With unemployment, hunger, and homelessness at record levels, people everywhere turned to government for help. In the United States, Franklin Roosevelt's New Deal envisioned a more activist government, restoring full employment and assuring everyone some minimal level of economic security. In Eastern Europe, the Communist Party advanced the notion that outright government *control* of the economy was the only sure way to attain economic justice for all.

Confidence in the ability of government to resolve core economic issues continued to increase in the post–World War II era. Securing national defenses during the Cold War (1948–89) justified the maintenance of a large military establishment, both in the United States and elsewhere. The War on Poverty that began in the mid-1960s brought about a huge increase in government social programs and income transfers. As the U.S. population has aged, the government's health care and retirement programs (e.g., Social Security, Medicare) have grown rapidly. In each case, there was a political consensus that expanded public services would enhance society's welfare. That consensus helped grow *total* federal spending (including purchases and income transfers) from 17 percent of GDP in 1965 to over 23 percent in 1982.

Public opinion didn't keep pace with the growth of government. Opinion polls revealed that people weren't convinced that government intervention was the surest way to resolve economic problems. President Reagan campaigned successfully on the promise of *reducing* government interference in the marketplace. With massive tax cuts and deregulation he tried to curb government growth in social programs.

The end of the Cold War created a unique opportunity to reduce military spending as well. Between 1991 and 1998 military spending declined every year and the armed forces shrank by nearly 500,000 personnel. In the process, the federal share of output gradually declined (see Figure 4.4). By 2000 total government spending had declined to 18 percent of GDP.

The decline in government spending wasn't confined to the United States. The collapse of the Soviet Union motivated market-oriented reforms throughout eastern Europe and

IN THE NEWS

Little Confidence in Government

Public-opinion polls reveal that Americans have little confidence in government, as the following responses illustrate.

Question: How much of the time do you think you can trust the government in Washington to do what is right—just about always, most of the time, or only some of the time?

Source: Conducted by CBS News/New York Times poll, September 2006.

Answers	
Just about always	1%
Most of the time	26%
Some of the time	65%
Never (vol.)	6%
Don't know/No answer	1%

Analysis: In principle, governments intervene to remedy market failure. But the public has little confidence in government performance.

Asia. In Europe and Latin America governments downsized by privatizing government-owned railroads, airlines, telephone service, and even postal service. In the process, the global economy became more market-driven and less government-directed.

The Post-9/11 Defense Buildup. The terrorist attacks of 9/11 reversed the slow downtrend in U.S. government spending. Defense expenditures increased by 50 percent in only 3 years (2002–4). Homeland security and the war in Iraq also expanded the government's claim on the economy's resources.

The longer-run trend in government growth isn't clear. Despite lingering doubts about government performance (see News), the worldwide war against terrorism is likely to keep defense expenditures at a high level for many years. The aging of the population in the United States, Europe, and Asia will also increase demands for public pensions and health care. Accordingly, governments aren't likely to resume shrinking. Whatever the size of the public sector turns out to be, the continuing challenge will be to promote optimal WHAT, HOW, and FOR WHOM outcomes in the economy tomorrow.

SUMMARY

- Government intervention in the marketplace is justified by market failure, that is, suboptimal market outcomes. LO1
- The micro failures of the market originate in public goods, externalities, market power, and an inequitable distribution of income. These flaws deter the market from achieving the optimal mix of output or distribution of income. LO1
- Public goods are those that can't be consumed exclusively; they're jointly consumed regardless of who pays. Because everyone seeks a free ride, no one demands public goods in the marketplace. Hence, the market underproduces public goods. LO1
- Externalities are costs (or benefits) of a market transaction borne by a third party. Externalities create a divergence between social and private costs or benefits, causing suboptimal market outcomes. The market overproduces goods with external costs and underproduces goods with external benefits. LO1
- Market power enables a producer to thwart market signals and maintain a suboptimal mix of output. Antitrust policy seeks to prevent or restrict market power. The government may also regulate the behavior of powerful firms. LO1
- The market-generated distribution of income may be unfair. This inequity may prompt the government to intervene with taxes and transfer payments that redistribute incomes. LO1
- The macro failures of the marketplace are reflected in unemployment and inflation. Government intervention is intended to achieve full employment and price stability. LO1
- The federal government expanded greatly after 1930. More recent growth has been in transfer payments, defense spending and health programs. LO2
- State and local governments purchase more output (12 percent of GDP) than the federal government (7 percent) and employ five times as many workers. LO2

- Income and payroll taxes provide most federal revenues. States get most revenue from sales taxes; local governments rely on property taxes. LO2
- Government failure occurs when intervention moves us away from rather than toward the optimal mix of output (or income). Failure may result from outright waste (operational inefficiency) or from a misallocation of resources. LO3
- All government activity must be evaluated in terms of its opportunity cost, that is, the *private* goods and services forgone to make resources available to the public sector. LO2
- Allocation decisions within the public sector may be based on cost-benefit analysis or votes. The self-interests of government agents may also affect decisions of when and how to intervene. LO2

Key Terms

optimal mix of output
market mechanism
market failure
private good
public good
free rider
externalities
monopoly
market power
antitrust
natural monopoly
transfer payments
merit good
unemployment
inflation
opportunity cost
progressive tax
proportional tax
regressive tax
government failure
public choice

Questions for Discussion

1. Why should taxpayers subsidize public colleges and universities? What external benefits are generated by higher education? LO1
2. If everyone seeks a free ride, what mix of output will be produced in Figure 4.2? Why would anyone voluntarily contribute to the purchase of public goods like flood control or snow removal? LO1
3. Could local fire departments be privately operated, with their services sold directly to customers? What problems would be involved in such a system? LO1
4. Why might Fourth of July fireworks be considered a public good? Who should pay for them? What about airport security? LO1
5. What is the specific market-failure justification for government spending on (*a*) public universities, (*b*) health care, (*c*) trash pickup, (*d*) highways, (*e*) police? Would a purely private economy produce any of these services? LO1
6. If smoking generates external costs, why shouldn't smoking simply be outlawed? How about cars that pollute? LO1
7. The government now spends over $500 billion a year on Social Security benefits. Why don't we leave it to individuals to save for their own retirement? LO1
8. What government actions might cause failures like points G_1, G_2, and G_3 in Figure 4.7? Can you give examples? LO3
9. How does XM Satellite deter nonsubscribers from listening to its transmissions? Does this make radio programming a private good or a public good? LO1
10. Should the government be downsized? Which functions should be cut back? LO2

problems The Student Problem Set at the back of this book contains numerical and graphing problems for this chapter.

web activities to accompany this chapter can be found on the Online Learning Center: **http://www.mhhe.com/economics/schiller11e**

PART 2 Measuring Macro Outcomes

Macroeconomics focuses on the performance of the entire economy rather than on the behavior of individual participants (a micro concern). The central concerns of macroeconomics are (1) the short-term business cycle and (2) long-term economic growth. In the long run, the goal is to expand the economy's capacity to produce goods and services, thereby raising future living standards. In the short run, the emphasis is on fully using available capacity, thereby maximizing output and minimizing unemployment. Chapters 5 through 7 focus on the measurement tools used to gauge the nation's macroeconomic performance (both short run and long run). Also examined are the social and economic damage caused by the problems of unemployment and inflation.

National-Income Accounting

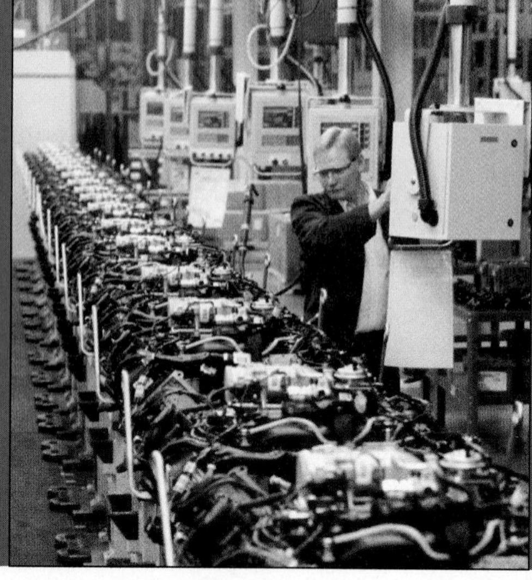

LEARNING OBJECTIVES

After reading this chapter, you should know:

L01. What GDP measures—and what it doesn't.

L02. Why aggregate income equals aggregate output.

L03. The major submeasures of output and income.

A favorite cliché of policymakers in Washington is that government likes to tackle only those problems it can measure. Politicians need visible results. They want to be able to brag to their constituents about the miles of new highways built, the number of students who graduated, the number of families that left welfare, and the number of unemployed workers who found jobs. To do this, they must be able to measure economic outcomes.

The Great Depression of the 1930s was an abject lesson in the need for better measures of economic performance. There were plenty of anecdotes about factories closing, farms failing, and people selling apples on the streets. But nobody knew the dimensions of the nation's economic meltdown until millions of workers had lost their jobs. The need for more timely information about the health of the national economy was evident. From that experience a commitment to **national-income accounting**—the measurement of aggregate economic activity—emerged. During the 1930s the economist Simon Kuznets (who later received a Nobel Prize for his work) and the U.S. Department of Commerce developed an accounting system that gauges the economy's health. That national-accounting system now churns out reams of data that are essential to tracking the economy's performance. They answer such questions as

- **How much output is being produced? What is it being used for?**
- **How much income is being generated in the marketplace?**
- **What's happening to prices and wages?**

It's tempting, of course, to ignore all these measurement questions, especially since they tend to be rather dull. But if we avoid measurement problems, we severely limit our ability to understand how the economy works or how well (or poorly) it's performing. We also limit our ability to design policies for improving economic performance.

National-income accounting also provides a useful perspective on the way the economy works. It shows how factor markets relate to product markets, how output relates to income, and how consumer spending and business investment relate to production. It also shows how the flow of taxes and government spending may alter economic outcomes.

MEASURES OF OUTPUT

national-income accounting: The measurement of aggregate economic activity, particularly national income and its components.

The array of goods and services we produce is truly massive, including everything from professional baseball to guided-missile systems. All these things are part of our total output; the problem is to find a summary measure.

Itemizing the amount of each good or service produced each year won't solve our measurement problems. The resulting list would be so long that it would be both unwieldy and meaningless. We couldn't even add it up, since it would contain diverse goods measured in a variety of units (e.g., miles, packages, pounds, quarts). Nor could we compare one year's output to another's. Suppose that last year we produced 2 billion oranges, 2 million bicycles, and 700 rock concerts, whereas this year we produced 3 billion oranges, 4 million bicycles, and 600 rock concerts. Which year's output was larger? With more of some goods, but less of others, the answer isn't obvious.

Gross Domestic Product

To facilitate our accounting chores, we need some mechanism for organizing annual output data into a more manageable summary. The mechanism we use is price. ***Each good and service produced and brought to market has a price. That price serves as a measure of value for calculating total output.*** Consider again the problem of determining how much output was produced this year and last. There's no obvious way to answer this question in physical terms alone. But once we know the price of each good, we can calculate the *value* of output produced. The total dollar value of final output produced each year is called the **gross domestic product (GDP).** GDP is simply the sum of all final goods and services produced for the market in a given time period, with each good or service valued at its market price.

gross domestic product (GDP): The total market value of all final goods and services produced within a nation's borders in a given time period.

Table 5.1 illustrates the use of prices to value total output in two hypothetical years. If oranges were 20 cents each last year and 2 billion oranges were produced, then the *value* of orange production last year was $400 million ($0.20 × 2 billion). In the same manner, we can determine that the value of bicycle production was $100 million and the value of rock

Output	Amount
a. Last Year's Output	
In physical terms:	
Oranges	2 billion
Bicycles	2 million
Rock concerts	700
Total	?
In monetary terms:	
2 billion oranges @ $0.20 each	$ 400 million
2 million bicycles @ $50 each	100 million
700 rock concerts @ $1 million each	700 million
Total	$1,200 million
b. This Year's Output	
In physical terms:	
Oranges	3 billion
Bicycles	4 million
Rock concerts	600
Total	?
In monetary terms:	
3 billion oranges @ $0.20 each	$ 600 million
4 million bicycles @ $50 each	200 million
600 rock concerts @ $1 million each	600 million
Total	$1,400 million

TABLE 5.1
The Measurement of Output

It's impossible to add up all output when output is counted in *physical* terms. Accordingly, total output is measured in *monetary* terms, with each good or service valued at its market price. GDP refers to the total market value of all goods and services produced in a given time period. According to the numbers in this table, the total *value* of the oranges, bicycles, and rock concerts produced "last" year was $1.2 billion and $1.4 billion "this" year.

concerts was $700 million. By adding these figures, we can say that the value of last year's production—last year's GDP—was $1,200 million (Table 5.1*a*).

Now we're in a position to compare one year's output to another's. Table 5.1*b* shows that the use of prices enables us to say that the *value* of this year's output is $1,400 million. Hence, *total output* has increased from one year to the next. ***The use of prices to value market output allows us to summarize output activity and to compare the output of one period with that of another.***

GDP vs. GNP. The concept of GDP is of relatively recent use in U.S. national-income accounts. Prior to 1992, most U.S. statistics focused on gross *national* product or GNP. Gross *national* product refers to the output produced by American-owned factors of production regardless of where they're located. Gross *domestic* product refers to output produced within America's borders. Thus, GNP would include some output from an Apple computer factory in Singapore but exclude some of the output produced by a Honda factory in Ohio. In an increasingly global economy, where factors of production and ownership move easily across international borders, the calculations of GNP became ever more complex. It also became a less dependable measure of the nation's economic health. ***GDP is geographically focused, including all output produced within a nation's borders regardless of whose factors of production are used to produce it.*** Apple's output in Singapore ends up in Singapore's GDP; the cars produced at Honda's Ohio plant are counted in America's GDP.

International Comparisons. The geographic focus of GDP facilitates international comparisons of economic activity. Is Japan's output as large as that of the United States? How could you tell? Japan produces a mix of output different from ours, making *quantity*-based comparisons difficult. We can compare the *value* of output produced in each country, however. The World View "Comparative Output" in Chapter 2 (page 27) shows that the value of America's GDP is three times larger than Japan's.

GDP per capita: Total GDP divided by total population; average GDP.

GDP per Capita. International comparisons of total output are even more vivid in *per capita terms*. **GDP per capita** relates the total value of annual output to the number of people who share that output; it refers to the average GDP per person. In 2006, America's total GDP of $13 trillion was shared by 300 million citizens. Hence, our average, or *per capita,* GDP was more than $43,000. By contrast, the average GDP for the rest of the world's inhabitants was less than $10,000. In these terms, America's position as the richest country in the world clearly stands out.

Statistical comparisons of GDP across nations are abstract and lifeless. They do, however, convey very real differences in the way people live. The accompanying World View examines some everyday realities of living in a poor nation, compared with a rich nation. Disparities in per capita GDP mean that people in low-income countries have little access to telephones, televisions, paved roads, or schools. They also die a lot younger than do people in rich countries.

But even the World View fails to fully convey how tough life is for people at the *bottom* of the income distribution in both poor and rich nations. Per capita GDP isn't a measure of what every citizen is getting. In the United States, millions of individuals have access to far more goods and services than our average per capita GDP, while millions of others must get by with much less. Although per capita GDP in Kuwait is three times larger than that of Brazil's, we can't conclude that the typical citizen of Kuwait is three times as well off as the typical Brazilian. The only thing these figures tell us is that the average Kuwaiti *could have* almost three times as many goods and services each year as the average Brazilian *if* GDP were distributed in the same way in both countries. ***Measures of per capita GDP tell us nothing about the way GDP is actually distributed or used: they're only a statistical average.*** When countries are quite similar in structure, institutions, and income distribution, however—or when historical comparisons are made within a country—per capita GDP can be viewed as a rough-and-ready measure of relative living standards.

webnote

Global data on per capita incomes and other social indicators are available from the United Nations at www.un.org/depts/unsd/social/inc-eco.htm

WORLD VIEW

Global Inequalities

The 2.4 billion residents of the world's low-income nations have comparatively few goods and services. Their average income (per capita GDP) is only $2,500 a year, a *fourteenth* of the average income in high-income nations such as the United States, Japan, and Germany. It's not just a colossal *income* disparity; it's also a disparity in the quality and even the duration of life. Some examples:

	Low-income nations	High-income nations
Total population	2.4 billion	1.0 billion
Per capita income	$2,486	$32,524
Life expectancy (years)	59	78
Child mortality (per 1,000)	122	7
Access to sanitation	43%	93%
Paved roads (% of total)	19%	94%
Energy use per capita (kilograms of oil per year)	501	5,410
Cars (per 1,000 people)	6	433
Televisions (percent of households)	16%	98%
Cell phones (per 1,000 people)	42	771
Personal computers (per 1,000 people)	11	574
Public health spending (% of GDP)	1.3	6.7

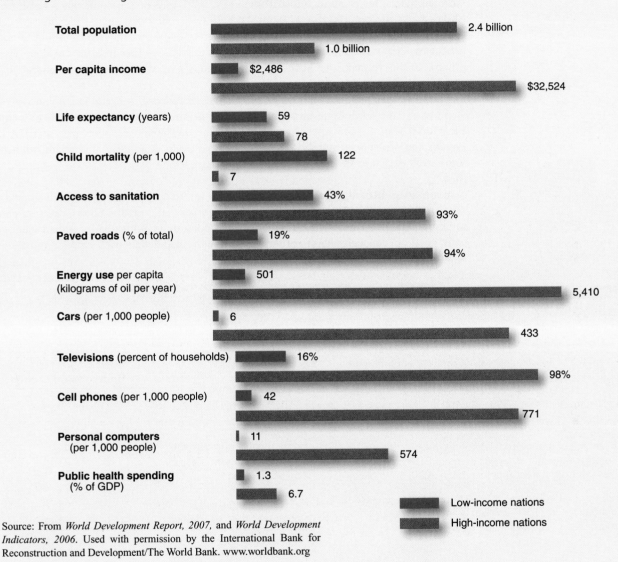

Source: From *World Development Report, 2007,* and *World Development Indicators, 2006.* Used with permission by the International Bank for Reconstruction and Development/The World Bank. www.worldbank.org

Analysis: Hidden behind dry statistical comparisons of per capita GDP lie very tangible and dramatic differences in the way people live. Low GDP per capita reflects a lot of deprivation.

Measurement Problems

Nonmarket Activities. Although the methods for calculating GDP and per capita GDP are straightforward, they do create a few problems. For one thing, ***GDP measures exclude most goods and services that are* produced *but not* sold *in the market.*** This may appear to be a trivial point, but it isn't. Vast quantities of output never reach the market. For example, the homemaker who cleans, washes, gardens, shops, and cooks definitely contributes to the output of goods and services. Because she's not paid a market wage for these services, however, her efforts are excluded from the calculation of GDP. At the same time, we do count the efforts of those workers who sell identical homemaking services in the marketplace. This seeming contradiction is explained by the fact that a homemaker's services aren't sold in the market and therefore carry no explicit, market-determined value.

The exclusion of homemakers' services from the GDP accounts is particularly troublesome when we want to compare living standards over time or between countries. In the United States, for example, most women now work outside the home. As a result households make greater use of *paid* domestic help (e.g., child care, house cleaning). Accordingly, a lot of housework and child care that were previously excluded from GDP statistics (because they were unpaid family help) are now included (because they're done by paid help). In this respect, our historical GDP figures may exaggerate improvements in our standard of living.

Homemaking services aren't the only output excluded. If a friend helps you with your homework, the services never get into the GDP accounts. But if you hire a tutor or engage the services of a term paper–writing agency, the transaction becomes part of GDP. Here again, the problem is simply that we have no way to determine how much output was produced until it enters the market and is purchased.[1]

Unreported Income. The GDP statistics also fail to capture market activities that aren't reported to tax or census authorities. Many people work "off the books," getting paid in unreported cash. This so-called underground economy is motivated by tax avoidance and the need to conceal illegal activities. Although illegal activities capture most of the

IN THE NEWS

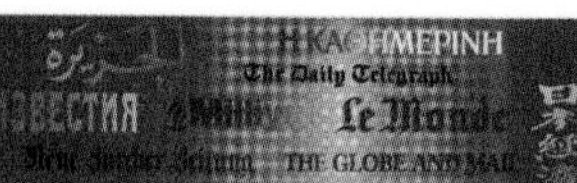

A Lot Going On under the Table

- Percentage of households making untaxed or unmeasured "underground" purchases: 83
- Estimated unreported income per person in 2000, excluding illegal activities: $4,300
- Percentage of unreported income from wages and salaries: 18
- Percentage of unreported income from capital gains: 13
- Unreported income as a percentage of GDP: 12
- Taxes lost from unreported income in 2000: $195 billion

The underground economy—transactions that are untaxed or unaccounted for in GDP—involves a lot more than nannies and drug deals.

	Estimated Percentage of Services Supplied by the Underground Economy
Lawn maintenance	90
Domestic help	83
Child care	49
Home repair/improvements	34
Laundry/sewing services	25
Appliance repair	17
Car repairs	13
Haircuts/beauty service	8
Catering	8

Data from University of Michigan Institute for Social Research, U.S. Department of Labor.

Source: U.S. Internal Revenue Service. www.irs.gov

Analysis: GDP statistics include only the value of reported market transactions. Unreported transactions in the underground economy can't be counted and may therefore distort perceptions of economic activity.

[1]The U.S. Commerce Department does, however, *estimate* the value of some nonmarket activities (e.g., food grown by farmers for their own consumption, the rental value of homeownership) and includes such estimates in GDP calculations.

Stages of Production	Value of Transaction	Value Added
1. Farmer grows wheat, sells it to miller	$0.12	$0.12
2. Miller converts wheat to flour, sells it to baker	0.28	0.16
3. Baker bakes bagel, sells it to bagel store	0.60	0.32
4. Bagel store sells bagel to consumer	0.75	0.15
Total	$1.75	$0.75

TABLE 5.2
Value Added in Various Stages of Production

The value added at each stage of production represents a contribution to total output. Value added equals the market value of a product minus the cost of intermediate goods.

headlines, tax evasion on income earned in otherwise legal pursuits accounts for most of the underground economy. The Internal Revenue Service estimates that over two-thirds of underground income comes from legitimate wages, salaries, profits, interest, and pensions that simply aren't reported. As the accompanying News indicates, unreported income is particularly common in the service sector. People who mow lawns, clean houses, paint walls, or provide child care services are apt to get paid in cash that isn't reported. The volume of such mundane transactions greatly exceeds the underground income generated by drug dealers, prostitutes, or illegal gambling.

Value Added

Not every reported market transaction gets included at full value in GDP statistics. If it did, the same output would get counted over and over. The problem here is that the production of goods and services typically involves a series of distinct stages. Consider the production of a bagel, for example. For a bagel to reach Einstein's or some other bagel store, the farmer must grow some wheat, the miller must convert it to flour, and the baker must make bagels with it. Table 5.2 illustrates this chain of production.

Notice that each of the four stages of production depicted in Table 5.2 involves a separate market transaction. The farmer sells to the miller (stage 1), the miller to the baker (stage 2), the baker to the bagel store (stage 3), and finally, the store to the consumer. If we added up the separate value of each market transaction, we'd come to the conclusion that $1.75 of output had been produced. In fact, though, only one bagel has been produced, and it's worth only 75 cents. Hence, we should increase GDP—the value of output—only by 75 cents.

To get an accurate measure of GDP we must distinguish between *intermediate* goods and *final* goods. **Intermediate goods** are goods purchased for use as input in further stages of production. Final goods are the goods produced at the end of the production sequence, for use by consumers (or other market participants).

intermediate goods: Goods or services purchased for use as input in the production of final goods or in services.

We can compute the value of *final* output in one of two ways. The easiest way would be to count only market transactions entailing final sales (stage 4 in Table 5.2). To do this, however, we'd have to know who purchased each good or service in order to know when we had reached the end of the process. Such a calculation would also exclude any output produced in stages 1, 2, and 3 in Table 5.2 but not yet reflected in stage 4.

Another way to calculate GDP is to count only the **value added** at each stage of production. Consider the miller, for example. He doesn't really contribute $0.28 worth of production to total output, but only $0.16. The other $0.12 reflected in the price of his flour represents the contribution of the farmer who grew the wheat. By the same token, the baker *adds* only $0.32 to the value of output, as part of his output was purchased from the miller. By considering only the value *added* at each stage of production, we eliminate double counting. We don't count twice the *intermediate* goods and services that producers buy from other producers, which are then used as inputs. As Table 5.2 confirms, we can determine that value of final output by summing up the value added at each stage of production. (Note that $0.75 is also the price of a bagel.)

value added: The increase in the market value of a product that takes place at each stage of the production process.

Real vs. Nominal GDP

Although prices are a convenient measure of market value, they can also distort perceptions of real output. Imagine what would happen to our calculations of GDP if all prices were to double from one year to the next. Suppose that the price of oranges, as shown in Table 5.1, rose from $0.20 to $0.40, the price of bicycles to $100, and the price of rock concerts to $2 million each. How would such price changes alter measured GDP? Obviously, the price increases would double the dollar *value* of final output. Measured GDP would rise from $1,400 million to $2,800 million.

Such a rise in GDP doesn't reflect an increase in the *quantity* of goods and services available to us. We're still producing the same quantities shown in Table 5.1; only the prices of those goods have changed. Hence, ***changes in GDP brought about by changes in the price level give us a distorted view of real economic activity.*** Surely we wouldn't want to assert that our standard of living had improved just because price increases raised measured GDP from $1,400 million to $2,800 million.

To distinguish increases in the quantity of goods and services from increases in their prices, we must construct a measure of GDP that takes into account price-level changes. We do so by distinguishing between *real* GDP and *nominal* GDP. **Nominal GDP** is the value of final output measured in *current* prices, whereas **real GDP** is the value of output measured in *constant* prices. ***To calculate real GDP, we adjust the market value of goods and services for changing prices.***

nominal GDP: The value of final output produced in a given period, measured in the prices of that period (current prices).

real GDP: The value of final output produced in a given period, adjusted for changing prices.

Note, for example, that in Table 5.1 prices were unchanged from one year to the next. When prices in the marketplace are constant, interyear comparisons of output are simple. But if all prices double, the comparison becomes more complicated. If all prices doubled from last year to this year, this year's nominal GDP would rise to $2,800 million. But these price increases wouldn't alter the quantity of goods produced. In other words, *real* GDP, valued at constant prices, would remain at $1,400 million. Thus, ***the distinction between nominal and real GDP is important whenever the price level changes.***

Because the price level does change every year, both real and nominal GDP are regularly reported. Nominal GDP is computed simply by adding the *current* dollar value of production. Real GDP is computed by making an adjustment for changes in prices from year to year.

Consider the GDP statistics for 2005 and 2006, as displayed in Table 5.3. The first row shows nominal GDP in each year: Nominal GDP increased by $789 billion between 2005 and 2006 (row 2). This 6.3 percent increase looks impressive. However, some of that gain was fueled by higher prices, not increased output. Row 3 indicates that the price level rose by 3.3 percent during that same period.

Row 4 in Table 5.3 adjusts the GDP comparison for the change in prices. We deflate the 2006 nominal GDP by factoring out the 3.3 percent price increase. Simple division is all we need to compute *real* GDP in 2006 as being $12,822 billion. Hence, *real* GDP increased by only $366 billion in 2006 (row 5), not by the larger inflation-exaggerated amount in row 2.

base period: The time period used for comparative analysis; the basis for indexing, for example, of price changes.

Notice in Table 5.3 that in 2005 real and nominal GDP are identical because we're using that year as the basis of comparison. We're comparing performance in 2006 to that of the 2005 **base period.** Real GDP can be expressed in the prices of a particular year; that year

TABLE 5.3
Computing Real GDP

Real GDP is the inflation-adjusted value of nominal GDP. Between 2005 and 2006, *nominal* GDP increased by $789 billion (row 2). Some of this gain was due to rising prices (row 3). After adjusting for inflation, *real* GDP increased only by $366 billion (row 5).

	2005	2006
1. Nominal GDP (in billions)	$12,456	$13,245
2. Change in nominal GDP		+$789
3. Change in price level, 2005 to 2006		3.3%
4. Real GDP in 2005 dollars	$12,456	$12,822
		$\left(= \dfrac{\$13,245}{\dfrac{103.3}{100.0}}\right)$
5. Change in real GDP		+$366

serves as the base for computing price-level and output changes. The general formula for computing real GDP is

$$\text{Real GDP in year } t = \frac{\text{nomical GDP in year } t}{\text{price index}}$$

The price index shows how average prices have changed between the base year and year *t*. Between 2005 and 2006, average prices rose 3.3 percent. This price-level change is indexed as 103.3. Thus, real GDP in 2006 is calculated as

$$\begin{array}{c}\text{Real GDP in 2006} \\ \text{(2005 prices)}\end{array} = \frac{13{,}245 \text{ billion}}{\frac{103.3}{100.0}} = \$12{,}822 \text{ billion}$$

This is the figure shown in row 4, Table 5.3.

The distinction between nominal and real GDP becomes critical when more distant years are compared. Between 1933 and 2006, for example, prices rose by 1,300 percent. Table 5.4 shows how such price-level changes can distort our views of how living standards have

webnote

Find out how much real GDP fell per year during the Great Depression (1929–40) at www.bea.doc.gov/bea/dn/0898nip3/table1.htm

Suppose we want to determine how much better off the average American was in 2003, as measured in terms of new goods and services, than people were during the Great Depression. To do this, we'd compare GDP per capita in 2003 with GDP per capita in 1933. The following data make that comparison.

	GDP	Population	Per Capita GDP
1933	$ 56 billion	126 million	$ 444
2003	10,988 billion	291 million	37,760

In 1933, the nation's GDP of $56 billion was shared by 126 million Americans, yielding a *per capita* GDP of $444. By contrast, GDP in 2003 was almost 200 times larger, at $10,988 billion. This vastly larger GDP was shared by 291 million people, giving us a per capita GDP of $37,760. Hence, it would appear that our standard of living in 2003 was 85 times higher than the standard of 1933.

But this increase in *nominal* GDP vastly exaggerates our material well-being. The average price of goods and services—the *price level*—increased by 1,300 percent between 1933 and 2003. The goods and services you might have bought for $1 in 1933 cost $14 in 2003. In other words, we needed a lot more dollars in 2003 to buy any given combination of real goods and services.

To compare our *real* GDP in 2003 with the real GDP of 1933, we have to adjust for this tremendous jump in prices (inflation). We do so by measuring both years' output in terms of *constant* prices. Since prices went up, on average, fourteenfold between 1933 and 2003, we simply divide the 2003 *nominal* output by 14. The calculation is

$$\begin{array}{c}\text{Real GDP} \\ \text{in 2003} \\ \text{(1933 prices)}\end{array} = \text{nominal 2003 GDP} \times \frac{\text{1933 price level}}{\text{2003 price level}}$$

By arbitrarily setting the level of prices in 1933 at 100 and noting that prices have increased fourteenfold since then, we can calculate

$$\begin{array}{c}\text{Real GDP} \\ \text{in 2003} \\ \text{(1933 prices)}\end{array} = \$10{,}988 \text{ billion} \times \frac{100}{1{,}400}$$
$$= \$785 \text{ billion}$$

With a population of 291 million, this left us with real GDP per capita of $2,698 in 2003—as measured in 1933 dollars. This was more than six times the *real* per capita GDP of the depression ($444), but not nearly so great an increase as comparisons of *nominal* GDP suggest.

TABLE 5.4
Real vs. Nominal GDP: A Historical View

FIGURE 5.1
Changes in GDP: Nominal vs. Real

Increases in *nominal* GDP reflect higher prices as well as more output. Increases in *real* GDP reflect more output only. To measure these real changes, we must value each year's output in terms of common base prices. In this figure the reference year is 2000. Nominal GDP rises faster than real GDP as a result of inflation.

Source: *Economic Report of the President, 2007.*

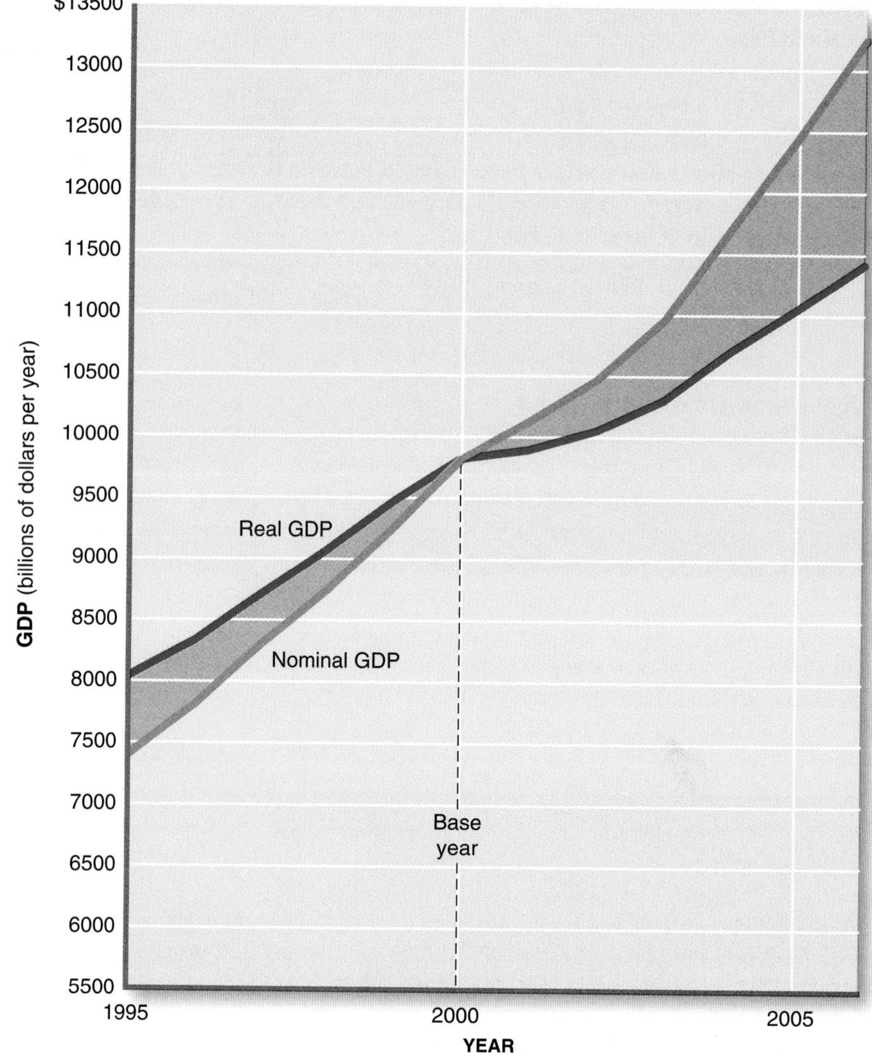

changed since the Great Depression: In *nominal* terms, our per capita income has risen a whopping 85 times over; in *real* terms, however, the income gain is a much less spectacular 6 times over.

Figure 5.1 shows how nominal and real GDP have changed since 1995. Real GDP is calculated here on the basis of the level of prices prevailing in 2000. (Note that real and nominal GDP are identical in that base year.) The dollar value of output produced each year has risen considerably faster than the quantity of output, reflecting persistent increases in the price level—that is, **inflation.**

inflation: An increase in the average level of prices of goods and services.

Notice also how inflation can obscure actual *declines* in real output. Real GDP actually declined in 1991 (by 0.2 percent), though nominal GDP kept rising (by 3.3 percent). Although the dollar *value* of final output continued to rise in that year, the actual production of goods and services was falling; nominal and real GDP moved in opposite directions (see data on inside front cover).

Chain-Weighted Price Adjustments. Although the distinction between real and nominal GDP is critical in measuring the nation's economic health, the procedure for making inflation adjustments isn't perfect. When we use the prices of a specific year as the base for computing real GDP, we're implicitly freezing *relative* prices as well as *average* prices.

Over time, however, relative prices change markedly. Computer prices, for example, have fallen sharply in recent years in both absolute and relative terms. During the same period, unit sales of computers have increased by 20 to 25 percent a year. If we used the higher computer prices of 5 years ago to compute that sales growth, we'd greatly exaggerate the *value* of today's computer output. If we use today's prices, however, we'll underestimate the value of output produced in the past. To resolve this problem, the U.S. Department of Commerce uses a *chain-weighted* price index to compute real GDP. Instead of using the prices of a *single* base year to compute real GDP, ***chain-weighted indexes use a* moving average *of price levels in consecutive years as an inflation adjustment.*** When chain-weighted price adjustments are made, real GDP still refers to the inflation-adjusted value of GDP but isn't expressed in terms of the prices prevailing in any specific base year. All official estimates of real GDP are now based on chain-weighted price indexes.

webnote

If you want to see some great charts on GDP and other economic statistics, visit Dr. Ed Yardeni's Web site at www.prudential.com/yardeni

Net Domestic Product

Changes in real GDP from one year to the next tell us how much the economy's output is growing. Some of that growth, however, may come at the expense of future output. Recall that our **production possibilities** determine how much output we can produce with available factors of production and technology. If we use up some of these resources to produce this year's output, future production possibilities may shrink. ***Next year we won't be able to produce as much output unless we replace factors of production we use this year.***

production possibilities: The alternative combinations of final goods and services that could be produced in a given time period with all available resources and technology.

We routinely use up plant and equipment (capital) in the production process. To maintain our production possibilities, therefore, we have to at least replace what we've used. The value of capital used up in producing goods and services is commonly called **depreciation.**[2] In principle, it's the amount of capital worn out by use in a year or made obsolete by advancing technology. In practice, the amount of capital depreciation is estimated by the U.S. Department of Commerce.

depreciation: The consumption of capital in the production process; the wearing out of plant and equipment.

By subtracting depreciation from GDP we get **net domestic product (NDP).** This is the amount of output we could consume without reducing our stock of capital and therewith next year's production possibilities.

net domestic product (NDP): GDP less depreciation.

The distinction between GDP and NDP is mirrored in a distinction between *gross* investment and *net* **investment. Gross investment** is positive as long as some new plant and equipment are being produced. But ***the stock of capital—the total collection of plant and equipment—won't grow unless gross investment exceeds depreciation.*** That is, the *flow* of new capital must exceed depreciation, or our *stock* of capital will decline. Whenever the rate of gross investment exceeds depreciation, **net investment** is positive.

investment: Expenditures on (production of) new plant, equipment, and structures (capital) in a given time period, plus changes in business inventories.

gross investment: Total investment expenditure in a given time period.

net investment: Gross investment less depreciation.

Notice that net investment can be negative as well; in such situations we're wearing out plant and equipment faster than we're replacing it. When net investment is negative, our capital stock is shrinking. This was the situation during the Great Depression. Gross investment fell so sharply in 1932–34 (see front endpaper of book) that it wasn't even replacing used-up machinery and structures. As a result, the economy's ability to produce goods and services declined.

THE USES OF OUTPUT

The role of investment in maintaining or expanding our production possibilities helps focus attention on the uses to which GDP is put. It's not just the total value of annual output that matters, it's also the use that we make of that output. ***The GDP accounts also tell us what mix of output we've selected, that is, society's answer to the core issue of WHAT to produce.***

Consumption

The major uses of total output conform to the four sets of market participants we encountered in Chapter 2, namely, consumers, business firms, government, and foreigners. Those goods and services used by households are called *consumption goods* and range all the way

[2]The terms *depreciation* and *capital consumption allowance* are used interchangeably. The depreciation charges firms commonly make, however, are determined in part by income tax regulations and thus may not accurately reflect the amount of capital consumed.

from doughnuts to wireless computer services. Included in this category are all goods and services households purchase in product markets. As we observed in Chapter 2, all this consumer spending claims over two-thirds of our annual output (see Figure 2.3).

Investment

Investment goods represent another use of GDP. Investment goods are the plant, machinery, and equipment we produce. Net changes in business inventories and expenditures for residential construction are also counted as investment. To produce any of these investment goods, we must use scarce resources that could be used to produce something else. Investment spending claims about one-sixth of our total output.

Government Spending

The third major use of GDP is the *public sector*. Federal, state, and local governments purchase resources to police the streets, teach classes, write laws, and build highways. The resources purchased by the government sector are unavailable for either consumption or investment purposes. At present, government spending on goods and services (*not* income transfers) claims roughly one-fifth of total output.

Net Exports

exports: Goods and services sold to international buyers.

Finally, remember that some of the goods and services we produce each year are used abroad rather than at home. That is, we **export** some of our output to other countries, for whatever use they care to make of it. Thus, GDP—the value of output produced—will be larger than the sum of our own consumption, investment, and government purchases to the extent that we succeed in exporting goods and services.

imports: Goods and services purchased from international sources.

We **import** goods and services as well. A flight to London on British Air is an imported service; a Jaguar is an imported good. These goods and services aren't part of America's GDP since they weren't produced within our borders (even though Jaguar is owned by Ford, the cars are produced in England). In principle, these imports never enter the GDP accounts. In practice, however, it's difficult to distinguish imports from domestic-made products, especially when goods include value added from both foreign and domestic producers. Even "American-made" cars typically incorporate parts manufactured in Japan, Mexico, Thailand, Britain, Spain, or Germany, with final assembly here in the United States. Should that car be counted as an "American" product or as an import? Rather than try to sort out all these products and parts, the U.S. Commerce Department simply subtracts the value of all imports from the value of total spending. Thus, exports are *added* to GDP and *imports* are subtracted. The difference between the two expenditure flows is called **net exports.**

net exports: The value of exports minus the value of imports.

GDP Components

Once we recognize the components of output, we discover a simple method for computing GDP. ***The value of GDP can be computed by adding up the expenditures of market participants.*** Specifically, we note that

$$\text{GDP} = C + I + G + (X - M)$$

where C = consumption expenditure
I = investment expenditure
G = government expenditure
X = exports
M = imports

This approach to GDP accounting emphasizes the fact that ***all the output produced in the economy must be claimed by someone.*** If we know who's buying our output, we know how much was produced and what uses were made of it.

MEASURES OF INCOME

There's another way of looking at GDP. Instead of looking at who's *buying* our output, we can look at who's *being paid* to produce it. Like markets themselves. ***GDP accounts have two sides: One side focuses on expenditure (the demand side), the other side focuses on income (the supply side).***

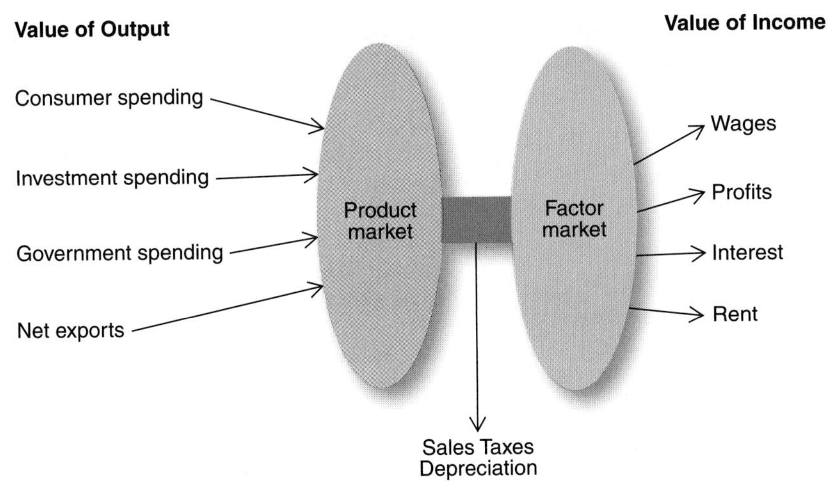

FIGURE 5.2
Output = Income

The spending that establishes the value of output also determines the value of incomes. With minor exceptions, the market value of incomes must equal the market value of output.

We've already observed (see Figure 3.1) that every market transaction involves an *exchange* of dollars for a good or resource. Moreover, the *value* of each good or resource is measured by the amount of money exchanged for it (its market price). Hence, ***the total value of market incomes must equal the total value of final output, or GDP.*** In other words, one person's expenditure always represents another person's income.

Figure 5.2 illustrates the link between spending on output and incomes. This is a modified version of the circular flow we saw in Chapter 3. The spending that flows into the product market gets funneled into the factor market, where resources are employed to produce the goods people want. The expenditure then flows into the hands of business owners, workers, landlords, and other resource owners. With the exception of sales taxes and depreciation, all spending on output becomes income to factors of production.

The equivalence of output and income isn't dependent on any magical qualities possessed by money. Were we to produce only one product—say, wheat—and pay everyone in bushels and pecks, total income would still equal total output. People couldn't receive in income more wheat than we produced. On the other hand, all the wheat produced would go to *someone*. Hence, one could say that the production possibilities of the economy define not only the limits to *output,* but also the limits to real *income.* The amount of income actually generated in any year depends on the production and expenditure decisions of consumers, firms, and government agencies.

Table 5.5 shows the actual flow of output and income in the U.S. economy during 2006. Total output is made up of the familiar components of GDP: consumption, investment, government goods and services, and net exports. The figures on the left side of Table 5.5 indicate that consumers spent $9,269 billion, businesses spent $2,212 billion on plant and equipment, governments spent $2,527 billion, and net imports were $763 billion. Our total output value (GDP) was thus more than $13 trillion in 2006.

The right-hand side of Table 5.5 indicates who received the income generated from these markets transactions. ***Every dollar spent on goods and services provides income to someone.*** It may go to a worker (as wage or salary) or to a business firm (as profit and depreciation allowance). It may go to a landlord (as rent), to a lender (as interest), or to government (as sales or property tax). None of the dollars spent on goods and services disappears into thin air.

National Income

Although it may be exciting to know that we collectively received over $13 trillion of income in 2006, it might be of more interest to know who actually got all that income. After all, in addition to the 300 million pairs of outstretched palms among us, millions of businesses and government agencies were also competing for those dollars and the goods and

TABLE 5.5
The Equivalence of Expenditure and Income (in billions of dollars)

The value of total expenditure must equal the value of total income. Why? Because every dollar spent on output becomes a dollar of income for someone.

Expenditure			Income	
C: Consumer goods and services	$ 9,269		Wages and salaries	$ 7,489
I: Investment in plant, equipment, and inventory	2,212		Corporate profits	1,616
G: Government goods and services	2,527		Proprietors' income	1,015
X: Exports	1,466		Rents	77
M: Imports	(2,229)		Interest	509
			Sales taxes	913
			Depreciation	1,576
			Miscellaneous	47
			Statistical discrepancy	3
GDP: Total value of output	$13,245	=	Total value of income	$13,245

Source: U.S. Department of Commerce (2006 data).

services they represent. By charting the flow of income through the economy, we can see FOR WHOM our output was produced.

Depreciation. The annual income flow originates in product-market sales. Purchases of final goods and services create a flow of income to producers and, through them, to factors of production. But a major diversion of sales revenues occurs immediately, as a result of depreciation charges made by businesses. As we noted earlier, some of our capital resources are used up in the process of production. For the most part, these resources are owned by business firms that expect to be compensated for such investments. Accordingly, they regard some of the sales revenue generated in product markets as reimbursement for wear and tear on capital plant and equipment. They therefore subtract *depreciation charges* from gross revenues in calculating their incomes. Depreciation charges reduce GDP to the level of *net* domestic product (NDP) before any income is available to current factors of production. As we saw earlier,

$$\text{NDP} = \text{GDP} - \text{depreciation}$$

Net Foreign Factor Income. Remember that some of the income generated in U.S. product markets belongs to foreigners. Wages, interest, and profits paid to foreigners are not part of U.S. income. So we need to subtract that outflow.

Recall also that U.S. citizens own factors of production employed in other nations (e.g., a Ford plant in Mexico; a McDonald's outlet in Singapore). This creates an *in*flow of income to U.S. households. To connect the value of U.S. output to U.S. incomes, we must add back in the net inflow of foreign factor income.

national income (NI): Total income earned by current factors of production: GDP less depreciation and indirect business taxes, plus net foreign factor income.

Once depreciation charges are subtracted from GDP and net foreign factor income added, we're left with **national income (NI),** which is the total income earned by U.S. factors of production. Thus,

$$\text{NI} = \text{NDP} + \text{net foreign factor income}$$

As Table 5.6 illustrates, our national income in 2006 was $11.7 trillion, nearly 90 percent of GDP.

Personal Income

There are still more revenue diversions as the GDP flow makes its way to consumer households.

TABLE 5.6
The Flow of Income, 2006

The revenue generated from market transactions passes through many hands. Households end up with disposable income equal to about 70 percent of GDP, after depreciation and taxes are taken out and net interest and transfer payments are added back in. Disposable income is either spent (consumption) or saved by households.

Income Flow	Amount (in billions)
Gross domestic product (GDP)	$13,245
Less depreciation	(1,576)
Net domestic product (NDP)	11,669
Plus net foreign factor income	30
Less statistical discrepancy	3
National income (NI)	11,702
Less indirect business taxes	(1,012)
Less corporate taxes	(475)
Less retained earnings*	(499)
Less Social Security taxes	(945)
Plus transfer payments	1,602
Plus net interest	511
Personal income (PI)	10,884
Less personal taxes	(1,361)
Disposable income (DI)	9,523

*Retained earnings are net of inventory valuation changes and depreciation.
Source: U.S. Department of Commerce.

Indirect Business Taxes. Another major diversion of the income flow occurs at its point of origin. When goods are sold in the marketplace, their purchase price is typically encumbered with some sort of sales tax. Thus, some of the revenue generated in product markets disappears before any factor of production gets a chance to claim it. These *indirect business taxes,* as they're called, must be deducted from national income because they don't represent payment to factors of production.

Corporate Taxes and Retained Earnings. Theoretically, all the income corporations receive represents income for their owners—the households who hold stock in the corporations. But the flow of income through corporations to stockholders is far from complete. First, corporations may pay taxes on their profits. Accordingly, some of the income received on behalf of a corporation's stockholders goes into the public treasury rather than into private bank accounts. Second, corporate managers typically find some urgent need for cash. As a result, part of the profits is retained by the corporation rather than passed on to the stockholders in the form of dividends. Accordingly, both *corporate taxes* and *retained earnings* must be subtracted from national income before we can determine how much income flows into the hands of consumers.

Still another deduction must be made for *Social Security taxes*. Nearly all people who earn a wage or salary are required by law to pay Social Security "contributions." In 2007, the Social Security tax rate for workers was 7.65 percent of the first $97,500 of earnings received in the year. Workers never see this income because it is withheld by employers and sent directly to the U.S. Treasury. Thus, the flow of national income is reduced considerably before it becomes **personal income (PI),** the amount of income received by households before payment of personal taxes.

personal income (PI): Income received by households before payment of personal taxes.

Not all of our adjustments to national income are negative. Households receive income in the form of transfer payments from the public treasury. More than 47 million people receive monthly Social Security checks, for example, and another 14 million receive some form of public welfare. These income transfers represent income for the people who receive them. People also receive interest payments in excess of those they pay (largely because of interest payments on the government debt). This *net* interest is another source of personal income. Accordingly, our calculation of personal income is as follows:

National income (= income earned by factors of production)
less indirect business taxes
corporate taxes
retained earnings
Social Security taxes
plus transfer payments
net interest
Equals ***personal income*** (= income received by households)

As you can see, the flow of income generated in production is significantly reduced before it gets into the hands of individual households. But we haven't yet reached the end of the reduction process. We have to set something aside for personal income taxes. To be sure we don't forget about our obligations, Uncle Sam and his state and local affiliates usually arrange to have their share taken off the top. Personal income taxes are withheld by the employer, who thus acts as a tax collector. Accordingly, to calculate **disposable income (DI),** which is the amount of income consumers may themselves spend (dispose of), we reduce personal income by the amount of personal taxes:

disposable income (DI): After-tax income of households; personal income less personal taxes.

Disposable income = personal income − personal taxes

Disposable income is the end of the accounting line. As Table 5.6 shows, households end up with roughly 70 percent of the revenues generated from final market sales (GDP). Once consumers get this disposable income in their hands, they face two choices. They may choose to *spend* their disposable income on consumer goods and services. Or they may choose to *save* it. These are the only two choices in GDP accounting. **Saving,** in this context, simply refers to disposable income that isn't spent on consumption. In the analysis of income and saving flows, we don't care whether savings are hidden under a mattress, deposited in the bank, or otherwise secured. All we want to know is whether disposable income is spent. Thus, ***all disposable income is, by definition, either consumed or saved; that is,***

saving: That part of disposable income not spent on current consumption; disposable income less consumption.

Disposable income = consumption + saving

webnote

For the latest data on GDP and its components visit the Bureau of Economic Analysis at www.bea.doc.gov

THE FLOW OF INCOME

Figure 5.3 summarizes the relationship between expenditure and income. The essential point again is that every dollar spent on goods and services flows into somebody's hands. Thus, ***the dollar value of output will always equal the dollar value of income.*** Specifically, total income (GDP) ends up distributed in the following way:

- To *households,* in the form of disposable income.
- To *business,* in the form of retained earnings and depreciation allowances.
- To *government,* in the form of taxes.

Income and Expenditure

The annual flow of income to households, businesses, and government is part of a continuing process. Households rarely stash their disposable income under the mattress; they spend most of it on consumption. This spending adds to GDP in the next round of activity, thereby helping to keep the flow of income moving.

Business firms also have a lot of purchasing power tied up in retained earnings and depreciation charges. This income, too, may be recycled—returned to the circular flow—in the form of business investment.

Even the income that flows into public treasuries finds its way back into the marketplace, as government agencies hire police officers, soldiers, and clerks, or they buy goods and services. Thus, ***the flow of income that starts with GDP ultimately returns to the market in the form of new consumption (C), investment (I), and government purchases (G).*** A

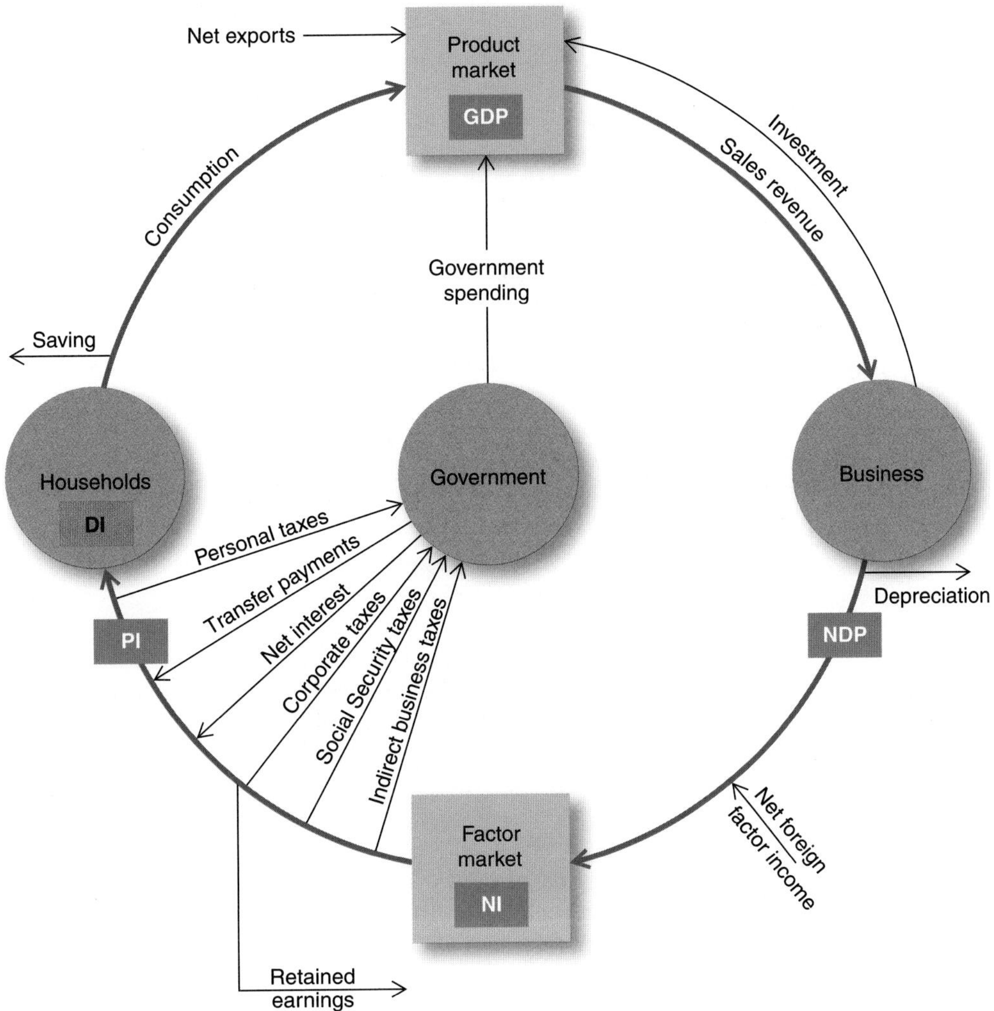

FIGURE 5.3
The Circular Flow of Spending and Income

GDP represents the dollar value of final output sold in the product market. The revenue stream flowing from GDP works its way through NDP, NI, and PI before reaching households in the form of smaller DI. DI is in turn either spent or saved by consumers. This consumption, plus investment, government spending, and net exports, continues the circular flow.

new GDP arises, and the flow starts all over. In later chapters we examine in detail these *expenditure* flows, with particular emphasis on their ability to keep the economy producing at its full potential.

THE ECONOMY TOMORROW

THE QUALITY OF LIFE

Money, money, money—it seems that's all we talk about. Why don't we talk about important things like beauty, virtue, or the quality of life? Will the economy of tomorrow be filled with a glut of products but devoid of real meaning? Do the GDP accounts—either the expenditure side or the income side—tell us anything we really want to know about the quality of life? If not, why should we bother to examine them?

Analysis: GDP includes *everything* produced and sold in the product market, no matter how much each good or service contributes to our social well-being.

Intangibles. All the economic measures discussed in this chapter are important indexes of individual and collective welfare; they tell us something about how well people are living. They don't, however, capture the completeness of the way in which we view the world or the totality of what makes our lives satisfying. A clear day, a sense of accomplishment, even a smile can do more for a person's sense of well-being than can favorable movements in the GDP accounts. Or, as John Kenneth Galbraith put it, "In a rational lifestyle, some people could find contentment working moderately and then sitting by the street—and talking, thinking, drawing, painting, scribbling, or making love in a suitably discreet way. None of these requires an expanding economy."[3]

The emphasis on economic outcomes arises not from ignorance of life's other meanings but from the visibility of the economic outcomes. We all realize that well-being arises from both material and intangible pleasures, but the intangibles tend to be elusive. It's not easy to gauge individual happiness, much less to ascertain the status of our collective satisfaction. We have to rely on measures we can see, touch, and count. As long as the material components of our environment bear some positive relation to our well-being, they at least serve a useful purpose.

In some situations, however, more physical output may actually worsen our collective welfare. If increased automobile production raises congestion and pollution levels, the rise in GDP occasioned by those additional cars is a misleading index of society's welfare. In such a case, the rise in GDP might actually mask a *decrease* in the well-being of the population. We might also wonder whether more casinos, more prisons, more telemarketing, more divorce litigation, and more Prozac—all of which contribute to GDP growth—are really valid measures of our well-being (see cartoon). Exclusive emphasis on measurable output would clearly be a mistake in many cases.

[3]Cited in Leonard Silk, *Nixonomics,* 2nd ed. (New York: Praeger, 1973), p. 163.

IN THE NEWS

America's Declining Social Health

National-income accounts are regularly reported and widely quoted. They do not, however, adequately reflect the nation's *social* performance. To measure more accurately the country's social health, a Fordham University team of social scientists has devised an Index of Social Health with 16 indicators, including infant mortality, drug abuse, health-insurance coverage, and poverty among the aged. According to this index, America's social health deteriorated sharply in the mid-1970s. The index of social health stayed flat in the 1980s, despite a sustained rise in the nation's economy. It rose with GDP after 1993 but peaked again in 1999 at a level far below that of 1973.

Source: Fordham Institute, *2003 Index of Social Health,* Tarrytown, NY.

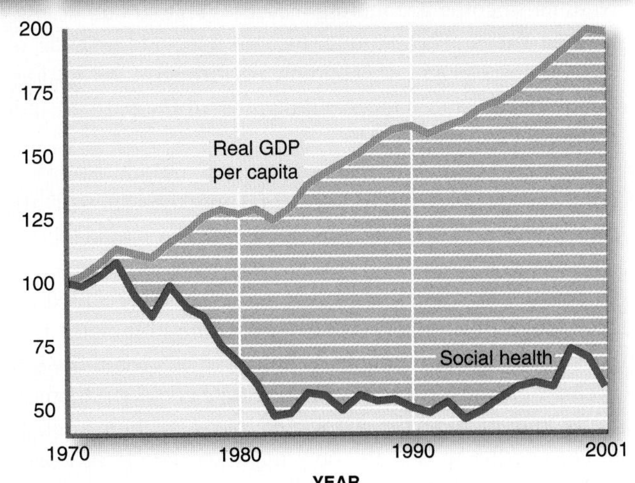

Analysis: The national-income accounts emphasize material well-being. They are an important, but not complete, gauge of our societal welfare.

What is true of automobile production might also be true of other outputs. Increased development of urban areas may diminish social welfare if that development occurs at the expense of space, trees, and tranquillity. Increased mechanization on the farm may raise agricultural output but isolate and uproot farmers. So, too, increased productivity in factories and offices might contribute to a sense of alienation. These ill effects of increased output needn't occur; but if they do, indexes of output tell us less about social or individual well-being.

Index of Well-Being. Researchers at Fordham University devised an alternative index of well-being. Their Index of Social Health includes a few economic parameters (such as unemployment and weekly earnings) but puts more emphasis on sociological behavior (such as child abuse and teen suicides). They claim that this broader view points to stagnation in societal well-being over the past two decades, even though GDP was rising (see News).

Not everyone would accept Fordham's dour view of our collective social health. Their index, however, does underscore the fact that *social welfare* and *economic welfare* aren't always synonymous. The GDP accounts tell us whether our economic welfare has increased, as measured by the value of goods and services produced. They don't tell us how highly we value additional goods and services relative to nonmarket phenomena. Nor do they even tell us whether important social costs were incurred in the process of production. These judgments must be made outside the market; they're social decisions.

Finally, note that any given level of GDP can encompass many combinations of output. Choosing WHAT to produce is still a critical question, even after the goal of *maximum* production has been established. The quality of life in the economy tomorrow will depend on what specific mix of goods and services we include in GDP.

webnote

The United Nations has constructed a Human Development Index that offers a broader view of social well-being than GDP alone. For details and country rankings, visit www.undp.org. Also check the Genuine Progress Indicator at www.rprogress.org

SUMMARY 

- National-income accounting measures annual output and income flows. The national-income accounts provide a basis for assessing our economic performance, designing public policy, and understanding how all the parts of the economy interact. LO1
- The most comprehensive measure of output is gross domestic product (GDP), the total market value of all final goods and services produced within a nation's borders during a given time period. LO1
- In calculating GDP, we include only the value added at each stage of production. This procedure eliminates the possibility of the double counting that would result because business firms buy intermediate goods from other firms and include the associated costs in their selling price. For the most part, only marketed goods and services are included in GDP. LO1
- To distinguish physical changes in output from monetary changes in its value, we compute both nominal and real GDP. Nominal GDP is the value of output expressed in *current* prices. Real GDP is the value of output expressed in *constant* prices (the prices of some *base* year). LO1
- Each year some of our capital equipment is worn out in the process of production. Hence, GDP is larger than the amount of goods and services we could consume without reducing our production possibilities. The amount of capital used up each year is referred to as *depreciation*. LO3
- By subtracting depreciation from GDP we derive net domestic product (NDP). The difference between NDP and GDP is also equal to the difference between *gross* investment—the sum of all our current plant and equipment expenditures—and *net* investment—the amount of investment over and above that required to replace wornout capital. LO3
- All the income generated in market sales (GDP) is received by someone. Therefore, the value of aggregate output must equal the value of aggregate income. LO2
- The sequence of flows involved in this process is

  GDP
  less depreciation
  equals **NDP**
  plus net foreign factor income
  equals national income (**NI**)
  less indirect business taxes,
  corporate taxes,
  retained earnings, and
  Social Security taxes
  plus transfer payments and
  net interest
  equals personal income (**PI**)
  less personal income taxes
  equals disposable income (**DI**) LO2
- The incomes received by households, business firms, and governments provide the purchasing power required to buy the nation's output. As that purchasing power is spent, further GDP is created and the circular flow continues. LO3

Key Terms

national-income accounting
gross domestic product (GDP)
GDP per capita
intermediate goods
value added
nominal GDP
real GDP
base period
inflation
production possibilities
depreciation
net domestic product (NDP)
investment
gross investment
net investment
exports
imports
net exports
national income (NI)
personal income (PI)
disposable income (DI)
saving

Questions for Discussion

1. The manuscript for this book was typed by a friend. Had I hired a secretary to do the s ame job, GDP would have been higher, even though the amount of output would have been identical. Why is this? Does this make sense? LO1
2. GDP in 1981 was $2.96 trillion. It grew to $3.07 trillion in 1982, yet the quantity of output actually decreased. How is this possible? LO1
3. If gross investment is not large enough to replace the capital that depreciates in a particular year, is net investment greater or less than zero? What happens to our production possibilities? LO3
4. Can we increase consumption in a given year without cutting back on either investment or government services? Under what conditions? LO3

5. Why is it important to know how much output is being produced? Who uses such information? LO1
6. What jobs are likely part of the underground economy? LO1
7. How might the quality of life be adversely affected by an increase in GDP? LO1
8. Is the Fordham Index of Social Health, discussed in the News on page 103, a better barometer of well-being than GDP? What are its relative advantages or disadvantages? LO1
9. Over 4 million Web sites sell a combined $50 billion of pornography a year. Should these sales be included in (a) GDP and (b) an index of social welfare? LO1

problems The Student Problem Set at the back of this book contains numerical and graphing problems for this chapter.

web activities to accompany this chapter can be found on the Online Learning Center: **http://www.mhhe.com/economics/schiller11e**

Unemployment

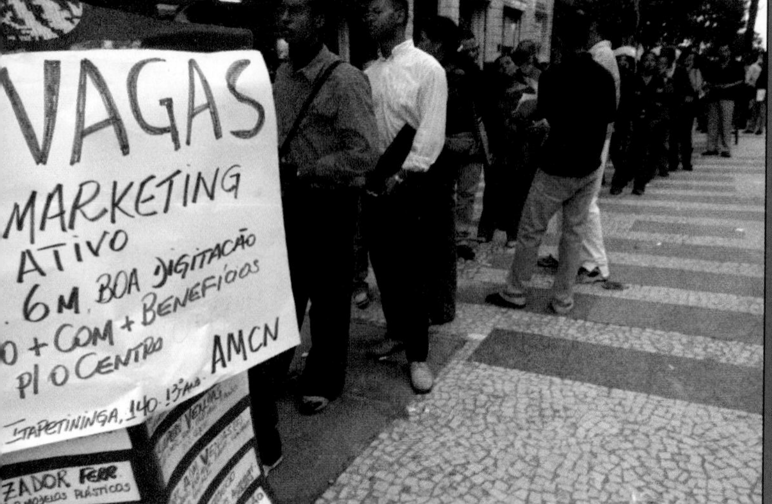

LEARNING OBJECTIVES

After reading this chapter, you should know:

LO1. How unemployment is measured.

LO2. The major types of unemployment.

LO3. The meaning of "full employment."

George H. had worked at the textile mill in Kannapolis, North Carolina, for 18 years. Now he was 46 years old, with a wife and three children. With his base salary of $38,200 and the performance bonus he received nearly every year, he was doing pretty well. He had his own home, two cars, company-paid health insurance for the family, and a growing nest egg in the company's pension plan. The H. family wasn't rich, but they were comfortable and secure.

Or so they thought. Overnight the H. family's comfort was shattered. With little warning, the mill was closed in July 2003. George H., along with 4,800 fellow workers, was permanently laid off. The weekly paychecks and the company-paid health insurance stopped immediately; the pension nest egg was in doubt. Within a few weeks, George H. was on the street looking for a new job—an experience he hadn't had since high school. The unemployment benefits the state provided didn't come close to covering the mortgage payment, groceries, insurance, and other necessities. And even those benefits soon ran out. The H. family quickly used up its savings, including the $5,000 they'd set aside for the children's college education.

George H. stayed unemployed for nearly 2 years. His wife found a part-time waitressing job, and his oldest son went to work rather than college. George himself ultimately found a warehousing job that paid only half as much as his previous job.

In the recession of 2001 and its aftermath nearly 2 *million* workers lost their jobs as companies "downsized," "restructured," or simply closed. Not all these displaced workers fared as badly as George H. and his family. But the job loss was a painful experience for every one of those displaced workers. That's the human side of an economic downturn.

The pain of joblessness is not confined to those who lose their jobs. In recessions, students discover that jobs are hard to find in the summer. No matter how good their grades are or how nice their résumés look, some graduates just don't get any job offers in a recession. Even people with jobs feel some economic pain: Their paychecks shrink when hours or wages are scaled back.

In this chapter we take a closer look at the problem of unemployment, focusing on the following questions:

- **When is a person "unemployed"?**
- **What are the costs of unemployment?**
- **What's an appropriate policy goal for "full employment"?**

As we answer these questions, we'll develop a sense of why full employment is a major goal of macro policy and begin to see some of the obstacles we face in achieving it.

THE LABOR FORCE

To assess the dimensions of our unemployment problems, we first need to decide who wants a job. Millions of people are jobless, yet they're not part of our unemployment problem. Full-time students, young children playing with their toys, and older people living in retirement are all jobless. We don't expect them to be working, so we don't regard them as part of the unemployment problem. We're not concerned that *everybody* be put to work, only with ensuring jobs for all those persons who are ready and willing to work.

To distinguish those people who want a job from those who don't, we separate the entire population into two distinct groups. One group consists of *labor-force participants;* the other group encompasses all *nonparticipants.*

The **labor force** includes everyone age 16 and older who is actually working plus all those who aren't working but are actively seeking employment. Individuals are also counted as employed in a particular week if their failure to work is due to vacation, illness, labor dispute (strike), or bad weather. All such persons are regarded as "with a job but not at work." Also, unpaid family members working in a family enterprise (farming, for example) are counted as employed. ***Only those people who are either employed or actively seeking work are counted as part of the labor force.*** People who are neither employed *nor* actively looking for a job are referred to as *nonparticipants.* As Figure 6.1 shows, only half the U.S. population participates in the labor force.

labor force: All persons age 16 and over who are either working for pay or actively seeking paid employment.

Note that our definition of labor-force participation excludes most household and volunteer activities. People who choose to devote their energies to household responsibilities or to unpaid charity work aren't counted as part of the labor force, no matter how hard they work. Because they are neither in paid employment nor seeking such employment in the marketplace, they are regarded as outside the labor market (nonparticipants). But if they decide to seek a paid job outside the home, we'd say that they are "entering the labor force." Students too are typically out of the labor force until they leave school. They *"enter"* the labor force when they go looking for a job, either during the summer or after graduation. People *"exit"* the labor force when they go back to school, return to household activities, go to prison, or retire. These entries and exits keep changing the size and composition of the labor force.

Since 1960, the U.S. labor force has more than doubled in size. As Figure 6.2 indicates, this labor-force growth has come from two distinct sources: population growth and a rising **labor-force participation rate.** The U.S. population has increased by only 70 percent since 1960, while the labor force has more than doubled. The difference is explained by the rapid increase in the labor-force participation of women. Notice in Figure 6.2 that only 1 out of

labor-force participation rate: The percentage of the working-age population working or seeking employment.

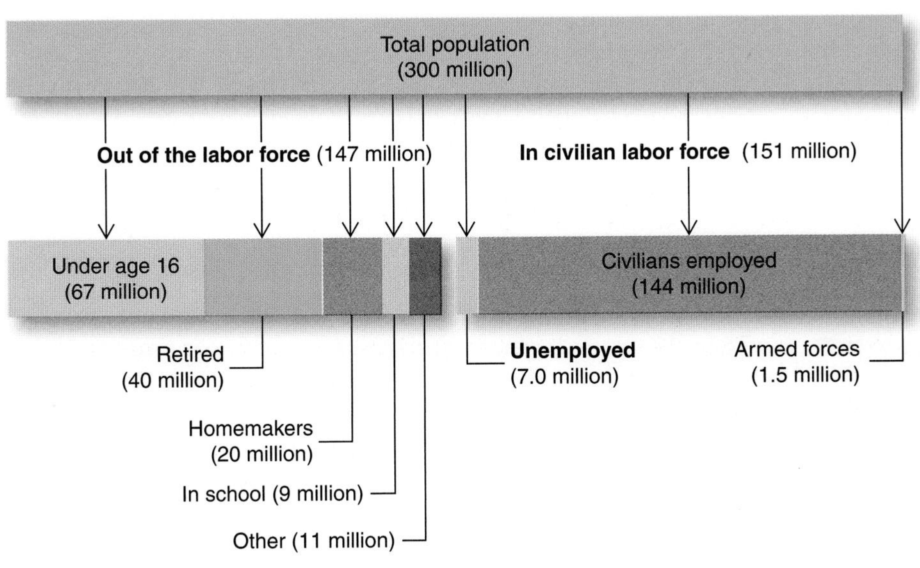

FIGURE 6.1
The Labor Force, 2006

Only half the total U.S. population participates in the civilian labor force. The rest of the population is too young, in school, at home, retired, or otherwise unavailable.

Unemployment statistics count only those participants who aren't currently working but are actively seeking paid employment. Nonparticipants are neither employed nor actively seeking employment.

Source: U.S. Bureau of Labor Statistics.

FIGURE 6.2
A Growing Labor Force

The labor force expands as births and immigration increase. A big increase in the participation rate of women after 1950 also added to labor-force growth.

Source: *Economic Report of the President, 2007*

Participation Rates (age 16 and older)

Year	Men	Women
1950	86.4	33.9
1960	83.3	37.7
1970	79.7	43.3
1980	77.4	51.5
1990	76.4	57.5
2000	74.7	60.0
2006	73.5	59.4

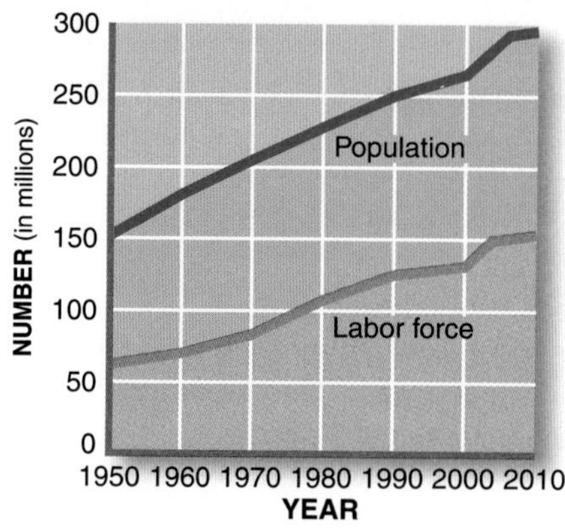

3 women participated in the labor force in 1950–60, whereas 6 out of 10 now do so. The labor-force participation of men actually declined during the same period, even though it remains higher than that of women.

Growth of Production Possibilities

Future growth of the U.S. labor force will come primarily from population growth and immigration. These two sources add about 2 million persons to the labor force each year. This labor-force growth is an important source of the nation's economic growth. As we first saw in Chapter 1, the quantity of goods and services an economy can produce in any time period is limited by two factors:

- ***Availability of factors of production.***
- ***Our technological know-how.***

production possibilities: The alternative combinations of final goods and services that could be produced in a given time period with all available resources and technology.

economic growth: An increase in output (real GDP); an expansion of production possibilities.

As the available labor force has grown, the nation's **production possibilities** curve has shifted outward, as in Figure 6.3. With those shifts has come an increased capacity for producing goods and services, the essence of long-run **economic growth.**

Institutional Constraints. We could grow the economy even faster if we used more labor and natural resources. But we've chosen to impose institutional constraints on resource exploitation. Child labor laws, for example, prohibit small children from working, no matter how much they or their parents yearn to contribute to total output. Yet we could produce more output this year if we put all those little bodies to work. In fact, we could produce a little more output this year if you were to put down this book and get a job. To the extent that small children, students, and others are precluded from working, both the size of our labor force (our *available* labor) and our potential output shrink.

Constraints are also imposed on the use of material resources and technology. We won't cut down all the forests this year and build everybody a wooden palace. We've collectively decided to preserve some natural habitat for owls and other endangered species. Therefore,

FIGURE 6.3
Labor-Force Growth

The amount of labor available for work—the *labor force*—is a prime determinant of a nation's production possibilities. As the labor force grows, so does the capacity to produce. To produce at capacity, however, the labor force must be fully employed. At point *F*, resources are unemployed.

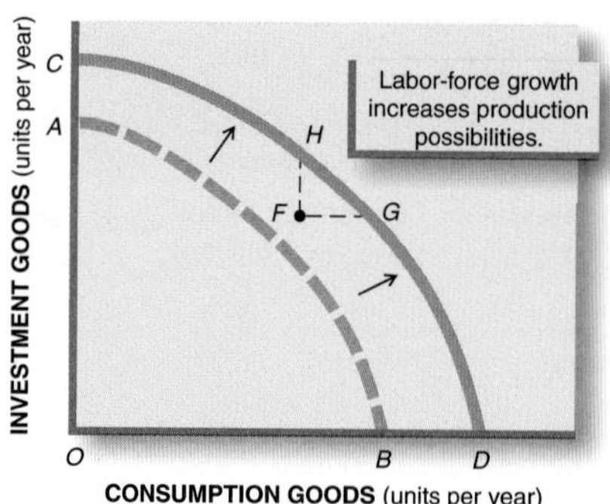

the federal government limits each year's tree harvest on public lands. The federal government also restricts the use of nuclear technology. In both cases, the need for environmental protection constrains the use of resources or technology and limits annual output. These are *institutional* constraints on our productive capacity. Without such constraints, we could produce more output. ***Our production possibilities in any year depend not only on what resources and technology are available but also on how we choose to restrict their use.***

Unemployment

An expanding labor force not only increases our capacity to produce but also implies the need to keep creating new jobs. Even in the short run (with given resources and technology), we have to confront the issue of job availability.

We can't reach points beyond the production possibilities curve, but we can easily end up somewhere inside that curve, as at point *F* in Figure 6.3. When that happens, we're not producing at (short-run) capacity, and some available resources remain underused. ***To make full use of available production capacity, the labor force must be fully employed.*** If we fail to provide jobs for all labor-force participants, we end up with less than capacity output and the related problem of **unemployment.** With the labor force growing by 2 million people a year, the challenge of keeping all labor-force participants employed never disappears.

unemployment: The inability of labor-force participants to find jobs.

Okun's Law; Lost Output. Arthur Okun quantified the relationship between unemployment and the production possibilities curve. According to the original formulation of **Okun's Law,** each additional 1 percent of unemployment translated into a loss of 3 percent in real output. More recent estimates of Okun's Law put the ratio at about 1 to 2, largely due to the changing composition of both the labor force (more women and teenagers) and output (more services). Using that 1-to-2 ratio allows us to put a dollar value on the aggregate cost of unemployment. In 2003, high unemployment left us $450 billion short of our production possibilities. That output shortfall implied a loss of $1,500 of goods and services for every American.

Okun's Law: 1 percent more unemployment results in 2 percent less output.

MEASURING UNEMPLOYMENT

To determine how many people are actually unemployed, the U.S. Census Bureau surveys about 60,000 households each month. The Census interviewers first determine whether a person is employed—that is, worked for pay in the previous week (or didn't work due to illness, vacation, bad weather, or a labor strike). If the person isn't employed, he or she is either *unemployed* or *out of the labor force.* To make that distinction, the Census interviewers ask whether the person actively looked for work in the preceding 4 weeks. ***If a person is not employed and actively seeking a job, he or she is counted as unemployed.*** Individuals neither employed nor actively seeking a job are counted as outside the labor force (nonparticipants).

The Unemployment Rate

In 2006, an average of 7 million persons were counted as unemployed in any month. As Figure 6.1 shows, these unemployed individuals accounted for 4.6 percent of our total labor force. Accordingly, the average **unemployment rate** in 2006 was 4.6 percent.

unemployment rate: The proportion of the labor force that is unemployed.

$$\frac{\text{Unemployment}}{\text{rate}} = \frac{\text{number of unemployed people}}{\text{labor force}}$$

The monthly unemployment figures indicate not only the total amount of unemployment in the economy but also which groups are suffering the greatest unemployment. Typically, teenagers just entering the labor market have the greatest difficulty finding (or keeping) jobs. They have no job experience and relatively few marketable skills. Employers are reluctant to hire them, especially if they must pay the federal minimum wage. As a consequence, teenage unemployment rates are typically three times higher than adult unemployment rates (see Figure 6.4).

Minority workers also experience above-average unemployment. Notice in Figure 6.4 that black and hispanic unemployment rates are much higher than white worker's unemployment rates.

webnote

Data on unemployment by race and gender from 1948 to the present are available from the Bureau of Labor Statistics at www.bls.gov

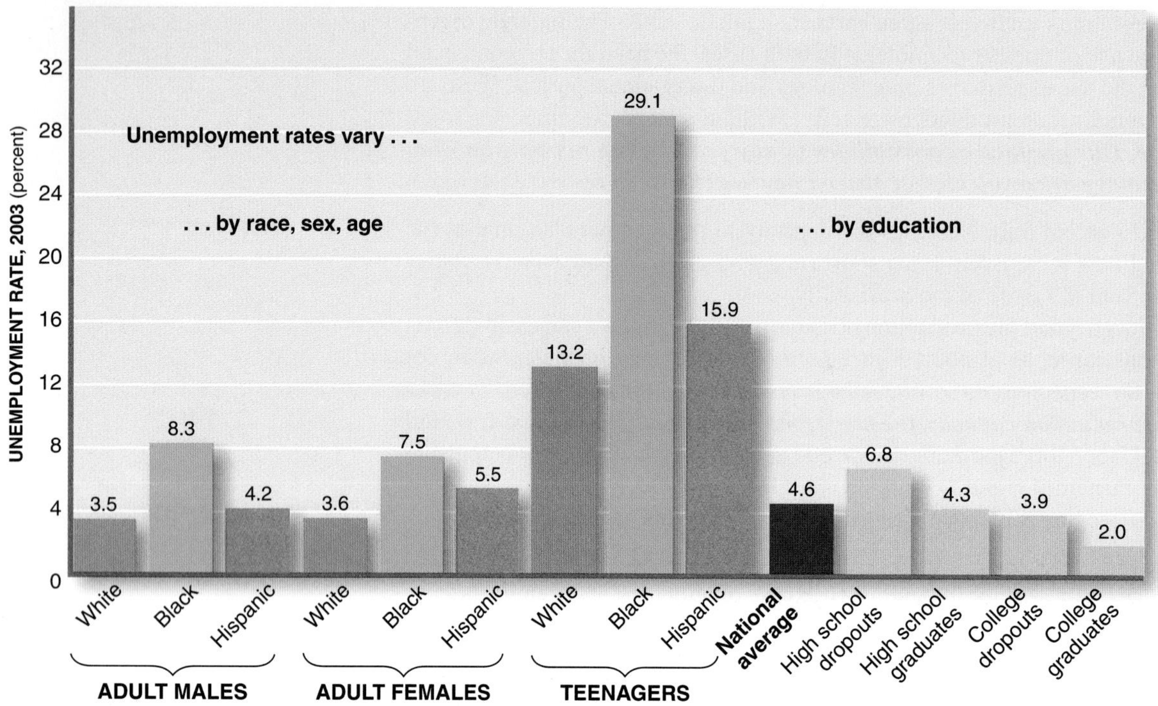

FIGURE 6.4
Unemployment Isn't Experienced Equally by Race, Sex, or Education

Minority groups, teenagers, and less-educated individuals experience higher rates of unemployment. Teenage unemployment rates are particularly high, especially for black and other minority youth.
Source: U.S. Department of Labor (2006 data).

Education also affects the chances of being unemployed. If you graduate from college, your chances of being unemployed drop sharply, regardless of gender or race (Figure 6.4). Advancing technology and a shift to services from manufacturing have put a premium on better-educated workers. Very few people with master's or doctoral degrees stand in unemployment lines.

The Duration of Unemployment

Although high school dropouts are more likely to be unemployed than college graduates, they don't *stay* unemployed. In fact, most people who become unemployed remain jobless for a relatively brief period of time. As Table 6.1 indicates, the median spell of unemployment in 2006 was 8 weeks. Less than one out of five unemployed individuals had been

TABLE 6.1
Duration of Unemployment

The severity of unemployment depends on how long the spell of joblessness lasts. About one-third of unemployed workers return to work quickly, but many others remain unemployed for 6 months or longer.

Duration	Percent of Unemployed
Less than 5 weeks	37.3%
5 to 14 weeks	30.3
15 to 26 weeks	14.7
27 weeks or more	17.6
Median duration	8.3 weeks

Source: U.S. Bureau of Labor Statistics (2006 data).

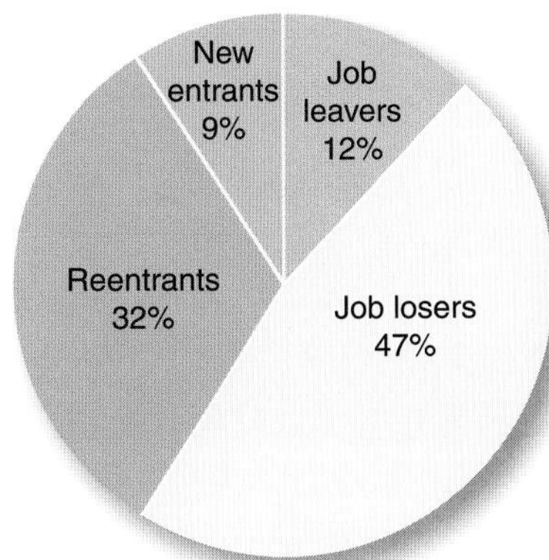

FIGURE 6.5
Reasons for Unemployment

People become unemployed for various reasons. Roughly half of the unemployed were job losers in 2006. About 40 percent of the unemployed were entering or reentering the labor market in search of a job. In recessions, the proportion of job losers shoots up.

Source: U.S. Labor Department.

jobless for as long as 6 months (27 weeks or longer). People who lose their jobs do find new ones. ***When the economy is growing, both unemployment rates and the average duration of unemployment decline.*** Recessions have the opposite effect—raising the costs of unemployment significantly.

Reasons for Unemployment

The reason a person becomes unemployed also affects the length of time the person stays jobless. A person just entering the labor market might need more time to identify job openings and develop job contacts. By contrast, an autoworker laid off for a temporary plant closing can expect to return to work quickly. Figure 6.5 depicts these and other reasons for unemployment. In 2006, nearly half the unemployed were job losers (laid off or fired), and 1 in 8 were job leavers (quit). The rest were new entrants (primarily teenagers) or reentrants (primarily mothers returning to the workforce). Like the duration of unemployment, the reasons for joblessness are very sensitive to economic conditions. In really bad years, most of the unemployed are job losers, and they remain out of work a long time.

Discouraged Workers

Unemployment statistics don't tell the complete story about the human costs of a sluggish economy. When unemployment persists, job seekers become increasingly frustrated. After repeated rejections, job seekers often get so discouraged that they give up the search and turn to their families, friends, or public welfare for income support. When the Census Bureau interviewer asks whether they're actively seeking employment, such **discouraged workers** are apt to reply no. Yet they'd like to be working, and they'd probably be out looking for work if job prospects were better.

discouraged worker: An individual who isn't actively seeking employment but would look for or accept a job if one were available.

Discouraged workers aren't counted as part of our unemployment problem because they're technically out of the labor force (see cartoon on next page). The Labor Department estimates that nearly 400,000 individuals fell into this uncounted class of discouraged workers in 2006. In years of higher unemployment, this number jumps sharply.

Underemployment

Some people can't afford to be discouraged. Many people who become jobless have family responsibilities and bills to pay: They simply can't afford to drop out of the labor force. Instead, they're compelled to take some job—any job—just to keep body and soul together. The resultant job may be part-time or full-time and may pay very little. Nevertheless, any paid employment is sufficient to exclude the person from the count of the unemployed, though not from a condition of **underemployment.**

underemployment: People seeking full-time paid employment who work only part-time or are employed at jobs below their capability.

Underemployed workers represent labor resources that aren't being fully utilized. They're part of our unemployment problem, even if they're not officially counted as *unemployed.* In 2006, nearly 1.3 million workers were underemployed in the U.S. economy.

The Phantom Unemployed

Although discouraged and underemployed workers aren't counted in official unemployment statistics, some of the people who *are* counted probably shouldn't be. Many people report that they're actively seeking a job even when they have little interest in finding

"I've stopped looking for work, which, I believe, helps the economic numbers."

Analysis: People who stop searching for a job aren't officially counted as "unemployed." They are called "discouraged workers."

employment. To some extent, public policy actually encourages such behavior. For example, welfare recipients are often required to look for a job, even though some welfare mothers would prefer to spend all their time raising their children. Their resultant job search is likely to be perfunctory at best. Similarly, most states require people receiving unemployment benefits (see News) to provide evidence that they're looking for a job, even though some recipients may prefer a brief period of joblessness. Here again, reported unemployment may conceal labor-force nonparticipation. More generous benefits in European nations are thought to create similar problems (see the following World View).

webnote

For the most recent data on unemployment in the United States, visit the U.S. Bureau of Labor Statistics at www.bls.gov

IN THE NEWS

Unemployment Benefits Not for Everyone

In 2006, more than 7 million people collected unemployment benefits averaging $277 per week. But don't rush to the state unemployment office yet—not all unemployed people are eligible. To qualify for weekly unemployment benefits you must have worked a substantial length of time and earned some minimum amount of wages, both determined by your state. Furthermore, you must have a "good" reason for having lost your last job. Most states will not provide benefits to students (or their professors!) during summer vacations, to professional athletes in the off-season, or to individuals who quit their last jobs.

If you qualify for benefits, the amount of benefits you receive each week will depend on your previous wages. In most states the benefits are equal to about one-half of the previous weekly wage, up to a state-determined maximum. The maximum benefit in 2006 ranged from $210 in Mississippi to a high of $826 in Massachusetts.

Unemployment benefits are financed by a tax on employers and can continue for as long as 26 weeks. During periods of high unemployment, eligibility may be extended another 13 weeks or more by the U.S. Congress.

Source: U.S. Employment and Training Administration. www.workforcesecurity.doleta.gov

Analysis: Some of the income lost due to unemployment is replaced by unemployment insurance benefits. Not all unemployed persons are eligible, however, and the duration of benefits is limited.

Europe's Unemployment Woes

Years of sluggish economic growth (low demand) raised unemployment rates in Europe to levels rarely seen in the United States. Generous unemployment benefits cushion the personal losses from this joblessness, however. Those same benefits also discourage European workers from accepting new jobs (less supply).

Source: U.S. Department of Labor (2006 data). http://stats.bls.gov/fls

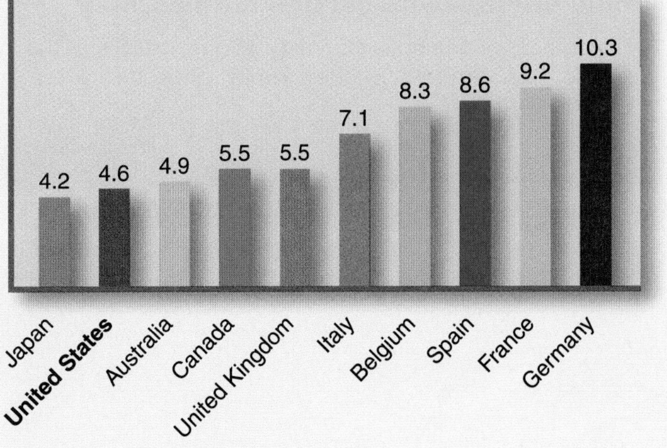

Analysis: Unemployment rates are typically significantly higher in Europe than in the United States. Analysts blame both sluggish economic growth and high unemployment benefits.

THE HUMAN COSTS

webnote

Compare unemployment rates of different countries at stats.bls.gov/fls/home.htm

Although our measures of unemployment aren't perfect, they're a reliable index to a serious macro problem. Unemployment statistics tell us that millions of people are jobless. That may be all right for a day or even a week, but if you need income to keep body and soul together, prolonged unemployment can hurt.

Lost Income. The most visible impact of unemployment on individuals is the loss of income. For workers who've been unemployed for long periods of time, such losses can spell financial disaster. Typically, an unemployed person must rely on a combination of savings, income from other family members, and government unemployment benefits for financial support. After these sources of support are exhausted, public welfare is often the only legal support left.

Lost Confidence. Not all unemployed people experience such a financial disaster, of course. College students who fail to find summer employment are unlikely to end up on welfare the following semester. Similarly, teenagers and others looking for part-time employment won't suffer great economic losses from unemployment. Nevertheless, the experience of unemployment—of not being able to find a job when you want one—can still be painful. This sensation isn't easily forgotten, even after one has finally found employment.

Social Stress. It is difficult to measure all the intangible effects of unemployment on individual workers. Studies have shown, however, that joblessness causes more crime, more health problems, more divorces, and other problems (see News on next page). Such findings underscore the notion that prolonged unemployment poses a real danger. Like George H., the worker discussed at the beginning of this chapter, many unemployed workers simply can't cope with the resulting stress. Thomas Cottle, a lecturer at Harvard Medical School, stated the case more bluntly: "I'm now convinced that unemployment is *the* killer disease in this country—responsible for wife beating, infertility, and even tooth decay."

IN THE NEWS

How Unemployment Affects the Family

Percentages of unemployed adults who reported that the following had occurred in their family since they were last employed.

—Stephanie Armour

Source: *USA Today,* June 27, 2003. USA TODAY. Copyright 2003. Reprinted with permission.

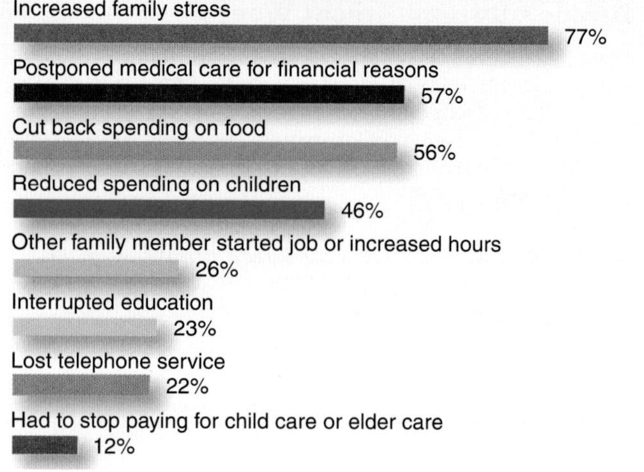

Analysis: The cost of unemployment is not measured in lost wages alone. Prolonged unemployment also impairs health, social relationships, and productivity.

Ill Health. German psychiatrists have also observed that unemployment can be hazardous to your health. They estimate that the anxieties and other nervous disorders that accompany 1 year of unemployment can reduce life expectancy by as much as 5 years. In Japan, the suicide rate jumped by more than 50 percent in 1999 when the economy plunged into recession. In New Zealand, suicide rates are twice as high for unemployed workers than for employed ones.

DEFINING FULL EMPLOYMENT

In view of the economic and social losses associated with unemployment, it's not surprising that *full employment* is one of our basic macroeconomic goals. You may be surprised to learn, however, that *"full"* employment isn't the same thing as *"zero"* unemployment. There are in fact several reasons for regarding some degree of unemployment as inevitable and even desirable.

Seasonal Unemployment

seasonal unemployment: Unemployment due to seasonal changes in employment or labor supply.

Some joblessness is virtually inevitable as long as we continue to grow crops, build houses, or go skiing at certain seasons of the year. At the end of each such season, thousands of workers must go searching for new jobs, experiencing some **seasonal unemployment** in the process.

Seasonal fluctuations also arise on the supply side of the labor market. Teenage unemployment rates, for example, rise sharply in the summer as students look for temporary jobs. To avoid such unemployment completely, we'd either have to keep everyone in school or ensure that all students went immediately from the classroom to the workroom. Neither alternative is likely, much less desirable.[1]

[1]Seasonal variations in employment and labor supply not only create some unemployment in the annual averages but also distort monthly comparisons. Unemployment rates are always higher in February (when farming and housing construction come to a virtual standstill) and June (when a mass of students go looking for summer jobs). The Labor Department adjusts monthly unemployment rates according to this seasonal pattern and reports "seasonally adjusted" unemployment rates for each month. Seasonal adjustments don't alter *annual* averages, however.

Frictional Unemployment

There are other reasons for expecting a certain amount of unemployment. Many workers have sound financial or personal reasons for leaving one job to look for another. In the process of moving from one job to another, a person may well miss a few days or even weeks of work without any serious personal or social consequences. On the contrary, people who spend more time looking for work may find *better* jobs.

The same is true of students first entering the labor market. It's not likely that you'll find a job the moment you leave school. Nor should you necessarily take the first job offered. If you spend some time looking for work, you're more likely to find a job you like. The job-search period gives you an opportunity to find out what kinds of jobs are available, what skills they require, and what they pay. Accordingly, a brief period of job search may benefit labor market entrants and the larger economy. The unemployment associated with these kinds of job searches is referred to as **frictional unemployment.**

frictional unemployment: Brief periods of unemployment experienced by people moving between jobs or into the labor market.

Three factors distinguish frictional unemployment from other kinds of unemployment. First, enough jobs exist for those who are frictionally unemployed—that is, there's adequate *demand* for labor. Second, those individuals who are frictionally unemployed have the skills required for available jobs. Third, the period of job search will be relatively short. Under these conditions, frictional unemployment resembles an unconventional game of musical chairs. There are enough chairs of the right size for everyone, and people dance around them for only a brief period of time.

No one knows for sure just how much of our unemployment problem is frictional. Most economists agree, however, that friction alone is responsible for an unemployment rate of 2 to 3 percent. Accordingly, our definition of *"full employment"* should allow for at least this much unemployment.

Structural Unemployment

For many job seekers, the period between jobs may drag on for months or even years because they don't have the skills that employers require. Imagine, for example, the predicament of steelworkers. During the 1980s, the steel industry contracted as consumers demanded fewer and lighter-weight cars and as construction of highways, bridges, and buildings slowed. In the process, over 300,000 steelworkers lost their jobs. Most of these workers had a decade or more of experience and substantial skill. But the skills they'd perfected were no longer in demand. They couldn't perform the jobs available in computer software, biotechnology, or other expanding industries. Although there were enough job vacancies in the labor market, the steelworkers couldn't fill them: These workers were victims of **structural unemployment.**

structural unemployment: Unemployment caused by a mismatch between the skills (or location) of job seekers and the requirements (or location) of available jobs.

The same kind of structural displacement hit the defense industry in the 1990s. Cutbacks in national defense spending forced weapons manufactures, aerospace firms, and electronics companies to reduce output and lay off thousands of workers. The displaced workers soon discovered that their highly developed skills weren't immediately applicable in nondefense industries.

Teenagers from urban slums also suffer from structural unemployment. Most poor teenagers have an inadequate education, few job-related skills, and little work experience. For them, almost all decent jobs are "out of reach." As a consequence, they remain unemployed far longer than can be explained by frictional forces.

Structural unemployment violates the second condition for frictional unemployment: that the job seekers can perform the available jobs. Structural unemployment is analogous to a musical chairs game in which there are enough chairs for everyone, but some of them are too small to sit on. It's a more serious concern than frictional unemployment and incompatible with any notion of full employment.

Cyclical Unemployment

The fourth type of unemployment is **cyclical unemployment**—joblessness that occurs when there simply aren't enough jobs to go around. Cyclical unemployment exists when the number of workers demanded falls short of the number of persons supplied (in the labor force). This isn't a case of mobility between jobs (frictional unemployment) or even of job seekers' skills (structural unemployment). Rather, it's simply an inadequate level of demand for goods and services and thus for labor. Cyclical unemployment resembles the most familiar form of musical chairs, in which the number of chairs is always less than the number of players.

cyclical unemployment: Unemployment attributable to a lack of job vacancies, that is, to an inadequate level of aggregate demand.

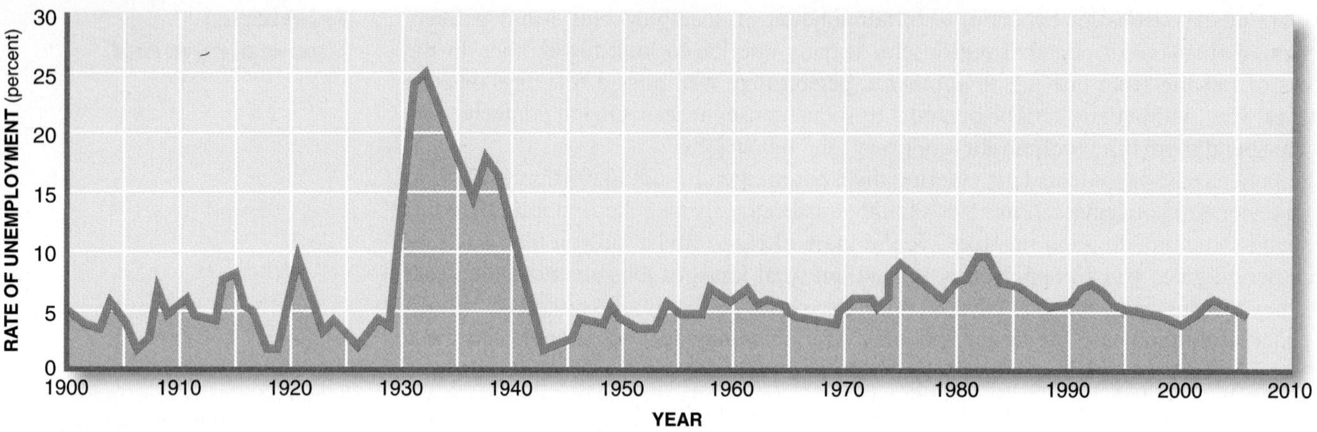

FIGURE 6.6
The Unemployment Record

Unemployment rates reached record heights (25 percent) during the Great Depression. In more recent decades, the unemployment rate has varied from 4 percent in full-employment years to over 10 percent in recession years. Keeping the labor force fully employed is a primary macro policy goal.

Source: U.S. Department of Labor.

The Great Depression is the most striking example of cyclical unemployment. The dramatic increase in unemployment rates that began in 1930 (see Figure 6.6) wasn't due to any increase in friction or sudden decline in workers' skills. Instead, the high rates of unemployment that persisted for a *decade* were caused by a sudden decline in the market demand for goods and services. How do we know? Just notice what happened to our unemployment rate when the demand for military goods and services increased in 1941!

Slow Growth. Cyclical unemployment can emerge even when the economy is expanding. Keep in mind that the labor force is always growing, due to population growth and continuing immigration. If these additional labor-force participants are to find jobs, the economy must grow. Specifically, ***the economy must grow at least as fast as the labor force to avoid cyclical unemployment.*** When economic growth slows below this threshold, unemployment rates start to rise.

The Full-Employment Goal

In later chapters we examine the causes of cyclical unemployment and explore some potential policy responses. At this point, however, we just want to establish a macro policy goal. In the Employment Act of 1946, Congress committed the federal government to pursue a goal of "maximum" employment but didn't specify exactly what that rate was. Presumably, this meant avoiding as much cyclical and structural unemployment as possible while keeping frictional unemployment within reasonable bounds. As guidelines for public policy, these perspectives are a bit vague.

Inflationary Pressures. The first attempt to define *full employment* more precisely was undertaken in the early 1960s. At that time the Council of Economic Advisers (itself created by the Employment Act of 1946) decided that our proximity to full employment could be gauged by watching *prices.* As the economy approached its production possibilities, labor and other resources would become increasingly scarce. As market participants bid for these remaining resources, wages and prices would start to rise. Hence, ***rising prices are a signal that employment is nearing capacity.***

After examining the relationship between unemployment and inflation, the Council of Economic Advisers decided to peg full employment at 4 percent unemployment. The unemployment rate could fall below 4 percent. If it did, however, price levels would begin to rise. Thus, 4 percent unemployment was regarded as an acceptable compromise of our employment and price goals.

Changes in Structural Unemployment. During the 1970s and early 1980s, this view of our full-employment potential was considered overly optimistic. Unemployment rates stayed far above 4 percent, even when the economy expanded. Moreover, inflation began to accelerate at higher levels of unemployment. Critics suggested that structural barriers to full employment had intensified due to

- ***More youth and women.*** Between 1956 and 1979, the proportion of teenagers and adult women in the labor force grew tremendously (see Figure 6.2). Their relative lack of work experience increased frictional and structural unemployment.
- ***Liberal transfer payments.*** Higher benefits and easier rules for unemployment insurance, food stamps, welfare, and Social Security made unemployment less painful. As a result, more people were willing and able to stay unemployed rather than work.
- ***Structural changes in demand.*** Changes in consumer demand, technology, and trade shrank the markets in steel, textiles, autos, and other industries. The workers dislocated from these industries couldn't be absorbed fast enough in new high-tech and other service industries.

In view of these factors, the Council of Economic Advisers later raised the level of unemployment thought to be compatible with price stability. In 1983, the Reagan administration concluded that the "inflation-threshold" unemployment rate was between 6 and 7 percent (see cartoon).

Declining Structural Pressures. The structural barriers that intensified inflationary pressures in the 1970s and early 1980s receded in the 1990s. The number of teenagers declined by 3 million between 1981 and 1993. The upsurge in women's participation in the labor force also leveled off. High school and college attendance and graduation rates increased. And welfare programs were reformed in ways that encouraged more work. All these structural changes made it easier to reduce unemployment rates without increasing inflation. In 1991, the first Bush administration concluded that **full employment** was equivalent to 5.5 percent unemployment. In 1999, the Clinton administration suggested the full-employment threshold might have dropped even further, to 5.3 percent. In reality, the national unemployment rate stayed below even that benchmark for 4 years (Figure 6.6) without any upsurge in inflation. In 2004 the Bush administration set the full-employment threshold at 5.1 percent.

full employment: The lowest rate of unemployment compatible with price stability; variously estimated at between 4 percent and 6 percent unemployment.

"I don't like six-per-cent unemployment, either. But I can live with it."

Analysis: So-called full employment entails a compromise between employment and inflation goals. That compromise doesn't affect everyone equally.

The "Natural" Rate of Unemployment

The ambiguity about which rate of unemployment might trigger an upsurge in inflation has convinced some analysts to abandon the inflation-based concept of full employment. They prefer to specify a "natural" rate of unemployment that doesn't depend on inflation trends. In this view, the natural rate of unemployment consists of frictional and structural components only. It's the rate of unemployment that will prevail in the long run. In the short run, both the unemployment rate and the inflation rate may go up and down. However, the economy will tend to gravitate toward the long-run **natural rate of unemployment.**

natural rate of unemployment: Long-term rate of unemployment determined by structural forces in labor and product markets.

Although the natural rate concept avoids specifying a short-term inflation trigger, it too is subject to debate. As we've seen, the *structural* determinants of unemployment (e.g., age and composition of the labor force) change over time. When structural forces change, the level of natural unemployment presumably changes as well.

Congressional Targets

Although most economists agree that an unemployment rate of 4 to 6 percent is consistent with either natural or full employment, Congress has set tougher goals for macro policy. According to the Full Employment and Balanced Growth Act of 1978 (commonly called the Humphrey-Hawkins Act), our national goal is to attain a 4 percent rate of unemployment. The act also requires a goal of 3 percent inflation. There was an escape clause, however. In the event that both goals couldn't be met, the president could set higher, provisional definitions of full employment.

webnote

To see the Fed's annual Humphrey-Hawkins report to Congress, go to www.federalreserve.gov/boarddocs/hh

webnote

To get a more vivid image of the Great Depression than unemployment statistics provide, see the photo collection of the Farm Security Administration at memory.loc.gov/ammem/fsowhome.html

THE HISTORICAL RECORD

Our greatest failure to achieve full employment occurred during the Great Depression. As Figure 6.6 shows, as much as one-fourth of the labor force was unemployed, in the 1930s.

Unemployment rates fell dramatically during World War II. In 1944, virtually anyone who was ready and willing to work quickly found a job: The civilian unemployment rate hit a rock-bottom 1.2 percent.

Since 1950, the unemployment rate has fluctuated from a low of 2.8 percent during the Korean War (1953) to a high of 10.8 percent during the 1981–82 recession. From 1982 to 1989 the unemployment rate receded, but it shot up again in the 1990–91 recession.

During the last half of the 1990s the unemployment rate fell steadily and hit the low end of the full-employment range in 2000. Slow GDP growth in 2000–01 and the economic stall caused by the September 11, 2001, terrorist attacks, pushed the unemployment rate sharply higher in late 2001 (see News). The subsequent recovery of the U.S. economy pushed the unemployment rate down into the "full-employment" range in 2005 (causing policymakers to worry more about inflation again than joblessness).

IN THE NEWS

Unemployment Soars by 700,000

The U.S. jobless rate surged to 5.4 percent last month, the highest level in almost five years, as companies laid off hundreds of thousands of workers in the wake of the Sept. 11 terrorist attacks, the Labor Department reported yesterday.

The rate jumped from 4.9 percent in September, for the biggest monthly increase since the recession of 1980.

As the economy deteriorated, jobless rates rose significantly for every major demographic group—adult men and women, teens, whites, blacks and persons of Hispanic origin—as the ranks of the unemployed soared to 7.7 million from 7 million.

The number of people working part time, either because their workweeks were cut back or because they could not find full-time jobs, is also growing. Over the past two months, this group has increased by 1.1 million, to 4.5 million.

—John M. Berry

Source: *Washington Post,* November 3, 2001, p. 1. www.washingtonpost.com

Analysis: A slowdown in economic growth causes the unemployment rate to rise—sometimes sharply.

THE ECONOMY TOMORROW

OUTSOURCING JOBS

To keep unemployment rates low in the economy tomorrow, job growth in U.S. product markets must exceed labor-force growth. As we've observed, this will require at least 2 million *new* jobs every year. Achieving that net job growth is made more difficult when U.S. firms shut down their U.S. operations and relocate production to Mexico, China, and other foreign nations. Even in the absence of plant shutdowns, **outsourcing** of U.S. production to workers in India, Poland, Malaysia, and elsewhere can limit U.S. job growth.

outsourcing: The relocation of production to foreign countries

Cheap Labor. Low wages are the primary motivation for all this outsourcing. As the accompanying World View documents, telephone operators and clerks in India are paid a tenth that of their U.S. counterparts. Indian accountants and paralegals get paid less than half that of their U.S. counterparts. Polish workers are even cheaper. With cheap, high-speed telecommunications, that offshore labor is an attractive substitute for U.S. workers. Over the next 10 years, over 3 million U.S. jobs are expected to move offshore in response to such wage differentials.

Small Numbers. In the short run, outsourcing clearly worsens the U.S. employment outlook. But there's a lot more to the story. To begin with, the total number of outsourced jobs averages less than 300,000 per year. That amounts to only .002 of all U.S. jobs, and only 3–5 percent of total U.S. *un*employment. So even in the worst case, outsourcing can't be a major explanation for U.S. unemployment.

WORLD VIEW

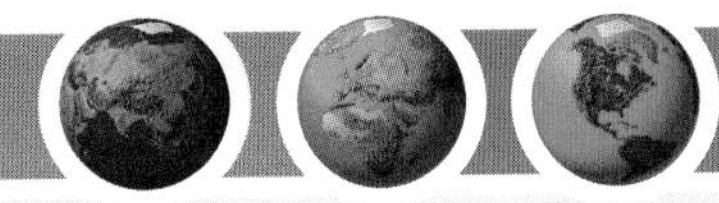

Salary Gap

Programmers' Pay

A Hungarian computer programmer starts at a salary of $4,800 per year; an American programmer begins at $60,000.

Average Salaries of Computer Programmers

Country	Salary Range
Poland and Hungary	$4,800–8,000
India	$5,880–11,000
Philippines	$6,564
Malaysia	$7,200
Russian Federation	$5,000–7,500
China	$8,952
Canada	$28,174
Ireland	$23,000–34,000
Israel	$15,000–38,000
United States	$60,000–80,000

Wages, India versus U.S.

Wages in the United States in some occupations are twice as high as in India, and in others 12 times as high.

Hourly Wages for Selected Occupations, U.S. and India, 2002–2003

Occupation	U.S.	India
Telephone Operator	$12.57	Under $1.00
Health Record Technologist/ Medical Transcriptionist	$13.17	$1.50–2.00
Payroll Clerk	$15.17	$1.50–2.00
Legal Assistant/Paralegal	$17.86	$6.00–8.00
Accountant	$23.35	$6.00–15.00
Financial Researcher/Analyst	$33.00–35.00	$6.00–15.00

Source: Ashok Deo Bardhan and Cynthia Kroll, "The New Wave of Outsourcing" (November 2, 2003). *Fisher Center for Real Estate and Urban Economics. Fisher Center Reports*: Report # 1103. http://repositories.cdlib.org/iber/fcrene/reports/1103

Analysis: Cheap foreign labor is a substitute for U.S. labor. These and similar salary gaps encourage U.S. firms to relocate production offshore.

IN THE NEWS

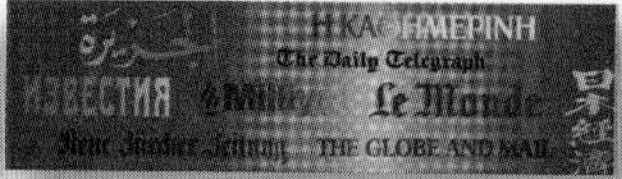

Outsourcing May Create U.S. Jobs

Higher Productivity Allows For Investment in Staffing, Expansion, a Study Finds

WASHINGTON—U.S. companies sending computer-systems work abroad yielded higher productivity that actually boosted domestic employment by 90,000 across the economy last year, according to an industry-sponsored study. . . .

Expected to be released today, the study's premise is that U.S. companies' use of foreign workers lowers costs, increases labor productivity and produces income that companies can use to expand both in the U.S. and abroad. . . .

The study claims that twice the number of U.S. jobs are created than displaced, producing wage increases in various sectors. . . .

Demand for U.S. exports is expected to increase due to the relatively lower prices of U.S.-produced goods and services and higher incomes in foreign countries where U.S. work is done.

—Michael Schroeder

Source: *The Wall Street Journal,* March 30, 2004. WALL STREET JOURNAL. Copyright 2004 by DOW JONES & COMPANY, INC. Reproduced with permission of DOW JONES & COMPANY, INC. in the format Textbook via Copyright Clearance Center.

More Jobs

Estimated new U.S. jobs created from outsourcing abroad, according to an industry study

	2003	2008
Natural Resources & Mining	1,046	1,182
Construction	19,815	75,757
Manufacturing	3,078	25,010
Wholesale Trade	20,456	43,359
Retail Trade	12,552	30,931
Transportation & Utilities	18,895	63,513
Publishing, Software & Communications	−24,860	−50,043
Financial Services	5,604	32,066
Professional & Business Services	14,667	31,623
Education & Health Services	18,015	47,260
Leisure, Hospitality & Other Services	4,389	12,506
Government	−3,393	4,203
Total Employment	**90,264**	**317,367**

Source: Global Insight and North American Industry Classification System.

Analysis: Outsourcing increases U.S. productivity and profits while reducing U.S. production costs and prices. These outcomes may increase demand for U.S. jobs by more than the immediate job loss.

Insourcing. We also have to recognize that outsourcing of U.S. jobs has a counterpart in the "insourcing" of foreign production. The German BMW company builds cars in Alabama to reduce production and distribution costs. In the process German autoworkers lose some jobs to U.S. autoworkers. In addition to this direct investment, foreign nations and firms hire U.S. workers to design, build, and deliver a wide variety of products. In other words, ***trade in both products and labor resources is a two-way street.*** Looking at the flow of jobs in only one direction distorts the jobs picture.

Productivity and Growth. Even the gross flow of outsourced jobs is not all bad. The cost savings realized by U.S. firms due to outsourcing increases U.S. profits. Those profits may finance new investment or consumption in U.S. product markets, thereby creating new jobs. The accompanying News suggests more jobs are gained than lost as a result. Outsourcing routine tasks to foreign workers also raises the productivity of U.S. workers by allowing U.S. workers to focus on more complex and high-value tasks. In other words, outsourcing promotes specialization and higher productivity both here and abroad. ***Production possibilities expand, not contract, with outsourcing.***

Creating Jobs. Greater efficiency and expanded production possibilities don't guarantee jobs in the economy tomorrow. The challenge is still to *use* that expanded capacity to the fullest. To do so, we have to use macroeconomic tools to keep output growing faster than the labor force. Stopping the outsourcing of jobs won't achieve that goal—and may even worsen income and job prospects in the economy tomorrow.

SUMMARY 

- To understand unemployment, we must distinguish the labor force from the larger population. Only people who are working (employed) or spend some time looking for a job (unemployed) are participants in the labor force. People neither working nor looking for work are outside the labor force. LO1
- The size of the labor force affects production possibilities. As the labor force grows, so does the capacity to produce goods and services. LO1
- Unemployment implies that we're producing inside the production possibilities curve rather than on it. LO1
- The macroeconomic loss imposed by unemployment is reduced output of goods and services. Okun's Law suggests that 1 percentage point in unemployment is equivalent to a 2 percentage point decline in output. LO1
- The human cost of unemployment includes not only financial losses but social, physical, and psychological costs as well. LO1
- Unemployment is distributed unevenly; minorities, teenagers, and the less educated have much higher rates of unemployment. Also hurt are discouraged workers—those who've stopped looking for work at part-time or menial jobs because they can't find full-time jobs equal to their training or potential. LO1
- There are four types of unemployment: seasonal, frictional, structural, and cyclical. LO2
- Because some seasonal and frictional unemployment is inevitable and even desirable, full employment is not defined as zero unemployment. These considerations, plus fear of inflationary consequences, result in full employment being defined as an unemployment rate of 4 to 6 percent. LO3
- The economy (output) must grow at least as fast as the labor force to keep the unemployment rate from rising.
- The natural rate of unemployment is based on frictional and structural forces, without reference to short-term price (inflation) pressures. LO1
- Unemployment rates got as high as 25 percent in the 1930s. Since 1960, the unemployment rate has ranged from 3.4 to 10.8 percent. LO1
- Outsourcing of U.S. production directly reduces domestic employment. But the indirect effects of higher U.S. productivity, profits, and global competitiveness may create even more jobs. LO1

Key Terms

labor force
labor-force participation rate
production possibilities
economic growth
unemployment
Okun's Law
unemployment rate
discouraged worker
underemployment
seasonal unemployment
frictional unemployment
structural unemployment
cyclical unemployment
full employment
natural rate of unemployment
outsourcing

Questions for Discussion

1. Is it possible for unemployment rates to increase at the same time that the number of employed persons is increasing? How? LO1
2. If more teenagers stay in school longer, what happens to (*a*) production possibilities? (*b*) unemployment rates? LO1
3. What factors might explain (*a*) the rising labor-force participation rate of women and (*b*) the declining participation of men? (See Figure 6.2 for trends.) LO1
4. Why might job (re)entrants have a harder time finding a job than job losers? LO2
5. If the government guaranteed some income to all unemployed persons, how might the unemployment rate be affected? Who should get unemployment benefits? (See News, page 112) LO2
6. Can you identify three institutional constraints on the use of resources (factors of production)? What has motivated these constraints? LO2
7. Why is frictional unemployment deemed desirable? LO2
8. Why do people expect inflation to heat up when the unemployment rate approaches 4 percent? LO3

9. Identify (*a*) two jobs at your school that could be outsourced and (*b*) two jobs that would be hard to outsource. LO3

10. How can the outsourcing of U.S. computer jobs generate new U.S. jobs in construction or retail trade? (See News, page 120) LO3

problems The Student Problem Set at the back of this book contains numerical and graphing problems for this chapter.

web activities to accompany this chapter can be found on the Online Learning Center: **http://www.mhhe.com/economics/schiller11e**

7 Inflation

LEARNING OBJECTIVES

After reading this chapter, you should know

L01. How inflation is measured.

L02. How inflation redistributes income and wealth.

L03. The meaning of "price stability."

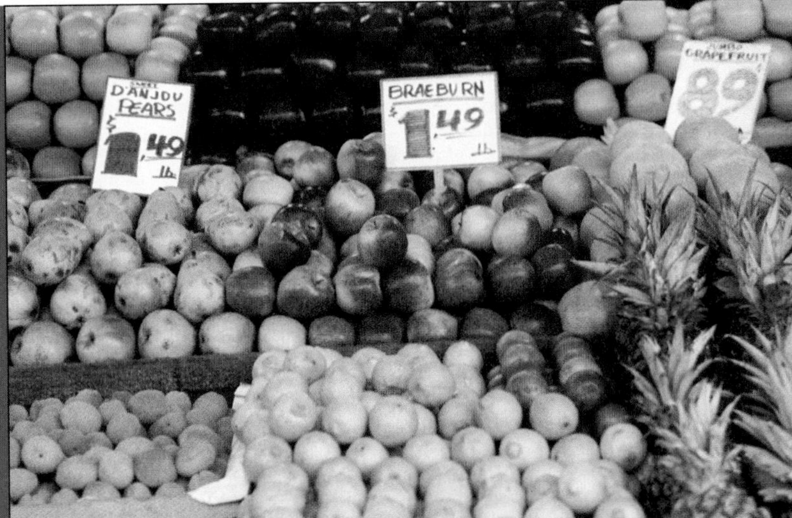

Germany set a record in 1923 that no other nation wants to beat. In that year, prices in Germany rose a *trillion* times over. Prices rose so fast that workers took "shopping breaks" to spend their twice-a-day paychecks before they became worthless. Menu prices in restaurants rose while people were still eating! Accumulated savings became worthless, as did outstanding loans. People needed sacks of currency to buy bread, butter, and other staples. With prices more than doubling every *day,* no one could afford to save, invest, lend money, or make long-term plans. In the frenzy of escalating prices, production of goods and services came to a halt, unemployment rose tenfold, and the German economy all but collapsed.

Hungary had a similar episode of runaway inflation in 1946, as did Japan. More recently, Russia, Bulgaria, Brazil, Zaire, Yugoslavia, Argentina, Uruguay, and Zimbabwe have all witnessed at least a tenfold jump in prices in a single year.

The United States has never experienced such a price frenzy. During the Revolutionary War, prices did double in 1 year, but that was a singular event. In the last decade, U.S. prices have risen just 1 to 4 percent a year. Despite this enviable record, Americans still *worry* a lot about inflation. In response to this anxiety, every president since Franklin Roosevelt has expressed a determination to keep prices from rising. In 1971, the Nixon administration took drastic action to stop inflation. With prices rising an average of only 3 percent, President Nixon imposed price controls on U.S. producers to keep prices from rising any faster. For 90 days all wages and prices were frozen by law—price increases were prohibited. For 3 more years, wage and price increases were limited by legal rules.

In 1990, U.S. prices were rising at a 6 percent clip—twice the pace that triggered the 1971–74 wage and price controls. Calling such price increases "unacceptable," Federal Reserve Chairman Alan Greenspan set a goal of *zero* percent inflation. In pursuit of that goal, the Fed slowed economic growth so much that the economy fell into a recession. The Fed did the same thing again in early 2000.

In later chapters we'll examine how the Fed and other policymakers slow the economy down or speed it up. Before looking at the levers of macro policy, however, we need to examine our policy goals. Why is inflation so feared? How much inflation is unacceptable? To get a handle on this basic issue, we'll ask and answer the following questions:

- **What kind of price increases are referred to as *inflation*?**
- **Who is hurt (or helped) by inflation?**
- **What is an appropriate goal for *price stability*?**

As we'll discover, inflation is a serious problem, but not for the reasons most people cite. We'll also see why deflation—falling prices—isn't so welcome either.

WHAT IS INFLATION?

inflation: An increase in the average level of prices of goods and services.

Most people associate **inflation** with price increases on specific goods and services. The economy isn't necessarily experiencing an inflation, however, every time the price of a cup of coffee goes up. We must distinguish the phenomenon of inflation from price increases for specific goods. ***Inflation is an increase in the average level of prices, not a change in any specific price.***

The Average Price

Suppose you wanted to know the average price of fruit in the supermarket. Surely you wouldn't have much success in seeking out an average fruit—nobody would be quite sure what you had in mind. You might have some success, however, if you sought out the prices of apples, oranges, cherries, and peaches. Knowing the price of each kind of fruit, you could then compute the average price of fruit. The resultant figure wouldn't refer to any particular product but would convey a sense of how much a typical basket of fruit might cost. By repeating these calculations every day, you could then determine whether fruit prices, *on average,* were changing. On occasion, you might even notice that apple prices rose while orange prices fell, leaving the *average* price of fruit unchanged.

The same kinds of calculations are made to measure inflation in the entire economy. We first determine the average price of all output—the average price level—then look for changes in that average. A rise in the average price level is referred to as inflation.

deflation: A decrease in the average level of prices of goods and services.

The average price level may fall as well as rise. A decline in average prices—a **deflation**—occurs when price decreases on some goods and services outweigh price increases on all others. This happened in Japan in 1995, and again in 2003. Such deflations are rare, however: The United States has not experienced any general deflation since 1940.

Relative Prices vs. the Price Level

relative price: The price of one good in comparison with the price of other goods.

Because inflation and deflation are measured in terms of average price levels, it's possible for individual prices to rise or fall continuously without changing the average price level. We already noted, for example, that the price of apples can rise without increasing the average price of fruit, so long as the price of some other fruit, such as oranges, falls. In such circumstances, **relative prices** are changing, but not *average* prices. An increase in the *relative* price of apples simply means that apples have become more expensive in comparison with other fruits (or any other goods or services).

Changes in relative prices may occur in a period of stable average prices, or in periods of inflation or deflation. In fact, in an economy as vast as ours—in which literally millions of goods and services are exchanged in the factor and product markets—***relative prices are always changing.*** Indeed, relative price changes are an essential ingredient of the market mechanism. Recall from Chapter 3 what happens when the market price of Web-design services rises relative to other goods and services. This (relative) price rise alerts Web architects (producers) to increase their output, cutting back on other production or leisure activities.

A general inflation—an increase in the average price level—doesn't perform this same market function. If all prices rise at the same rate, price increases for specific goods are of little value as market signals. In less extreme cases, when most but not all prices are rising, changes in relative prices do occur but aren't so immediately apparent. Table 7.1 reminds us that some prices do fall even during periods of general inflation.

REDISTRIBUTIVE EFFECTS OF INFLATION

The distinction between relative and average prices helps us determine who's hurt by inflation—and who's helped. Popular opinion notwithstanding, it's simply not true that everyone is worse off when prices rise. ***Although inflation makes some people worse off, it makes other people better off.*** Some people even get rich when prices rise! The micro consequences of inflation are reflected in redistributions of income and wealth, not general declines in either measure of our economic welfare. These redistributions occur because people buy different combinations of goods and services, own different assets,

Item	Early Price	2007 Price
Long-distance telephone call (per minute)	$ 6.90 (1915)	$ 0.03
Pocket electronic calculator	200.00 (1972)	2.99
Digital watch	2,000.00 (1972)	1.99
Polaroid camera (color)	150.00 (1963)	29.95
Pantyhose	2.16 (1967)	1.29
Ballpoint pen	0.89 (1965)	0.29
Transistor radio	55.00 (1967)	5.99
Videocassette recorder	1,500.00 (1977)	59.00
DVD player	800.00 (1997)	69.00
Laptop computer	3,500.00 (1986)	700.00
Airfare (New York–Paris)	490.00 (1958)	328.00
Microwave oven	400.00 (1972)	69.00
Contact lenses	275.00 (1972)	39.00
Television (19-inch, color)	469.00 (1980)	169.00
Compact disk player	1,000.00 (1985)	29.00
Digital camera	748.00 (1994)	140.00
Digital music player	399.00 (2001)	99.00

TABLE 7.1
Prices That Have Fallen

Inflation refers to an increase in the *average* price level. It doesn't mean that *all* prices are rising. In fact, many prices fall, even during periods of general inflation.

and sell distinct goods or services (including labor). The impact of inflation on individuals therefore depends on how prices change for the goods and services each person actually buys or sells.

Price Effects

Price changes are the most visible consequence of inflation. If you've been paying tuition, you know how painful a price hike can be. Ten years ago, the average tuition at public colleges and universities was $1,000 per year. Today the average tuition exceeds $5,800. At private universities, tuition has increased eightfold in the past 10 years, to over $22,000 (see News). You don't need a whole course in economics to figure out the implications of

IN THE NEWS

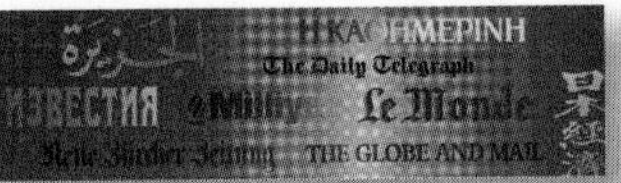

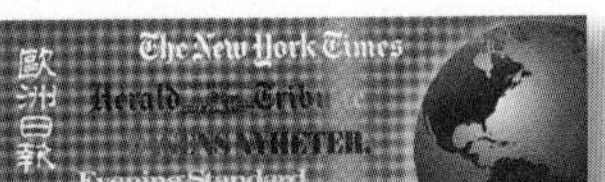

Average College Cost Breaks $30,000

NEW YORK (CNNMoney.com)—The average cost of a four-year private college jumped to $30,367 this school year, the first time the average has broken the $30,000 mark.

As they have for the past 11 years, average college costs rose faster than inflation, according to the latest report from the College Board, a non-profit association of 4,500 schools, colleges and universities.

The rate of growth in tuition at four-year private colleges was the same as last year—5.9 percent—and the average tuition reached $22,218.

Of course college costs don't just end at tuition. Room and board costs grew at around 5 percent for both public and private schools this year, with public schools at $6,960 and private schools $8,149 a year.

With room and board, four-year public colleges average $12,796 for in-state residents.

College Costs

	Tuition	Total Cost
Four-year public	$5,836	$12,796
Four-year private	$22,218	$30,367

Source: CollegeBoard.

—Rob Kelley

Source: CNNMoney.com, October 27, 2006.

Analysis: Tuition increases reduce the real income of students. How much you suffer from inflation depends on what happens to the prices of the products you purchase.

these tuition hikes. To stay in college, you (or your parents) must forgo increasing amounts of other goods and services. You end up being worse off since you can't buy as many goods and services as you could before tuition went up.

nominal income: The amount of money income received in a given time period, measured in current dollars.

real income: Income in constant dollars; nominal income adjusted for inflation.

The effect of tuition increases on your economic welfare is reflected in the distinction between nominal income and real income. **Nominal income** is the amount of money you receive in a particular time period; it's measured in current dollars. **Real income,** by contrast, is the purchasing power of that money, as measured by the quantity of goods and services your dollars will buy. If the number of dollars you receive every year is always the same, your *nominal income* doesn't change—but your *real income* will rise or fall with price changes.

Suppose your parents agree to give you $6,000 a year while you're in school. Out of that $6,000 you must pay for your tuition, room and board, books, and everything else. The budget for your first year at school might look like this:

FIRST YEAR'S BUDGET

Nominal income	$6,000
Consumption	
Tuition	$3,000
Room and board	2,000
Books	300
Everything else	700
Total	$6,000

After paying for all your essential expenses, you have $700 to spend on clothes, entertainment, or anything else you want. That's not exactly living high, but it's not poverty.

Now suppose tuition increases to $3,500 in your second year, while all other prices remain the same. What will happen to your nominal income? Nothing. Unless your parents take pity on you, you'll still be getting $6,000 a year. Your nominal income is unchanged. Your *real* income, however, will suffer. This is evident in the second year's budget:

SECOND YEAR'S BUDGET

Nominal income	$6,000
Consumption	
Tuition	$3,500
Room and board	2,000
Books	300
Everything else	200
Total	$6,000

You now have to use more of your income to pay tuition. This means you have less income to spend on other things. Since room and board and books still cost $2,300 per year, there's only one place to cut: the category of "everything else." After tuition increases, you can spend only $200 per year on movies, clothes, pizzas, and dates—not $700, as in the "good old days." This $500 reduction in purchasing power represents a *real* income loss. Even though your *nominal* income is still $6,000, you have $500 less of "everything else" in your second year than you had in the first.

Although tuition hikes reduce the real income of students, nonstudents aren't hurt by such price increases. In fact, if tuition *doubled,* nonstudents really wouldn't care. They could continue to buy the same bundle of goods and services they'd been buying all along. Tuition increases reduce the real incomes only of people who go to college.

Two basic lessons about inflation are to be learned from this sad story:

- ***Not all prices rise at the same rate during an inflation.*** In our example, tuition increased substantially while other prices remained steady. Hence, the "average" price increase wasn't representative of any particular good or service. Typically, some prices rise rapidly, others only modestly, and some actually fall.

Prices That Rose (%)		Prices That Fell (%)	
Apples	+12.8%	New cars	−0.2%
Gasoline	+12.0	Cereal	−1.8
College tuition	+6.7	Chicken	−2.5
Textbooks	+6.4	Computers	−15.6
Coffee	+2.5	Televisions	−16.2
	Average inflation rate: +3.2%		

Source: U.S. Bureau of Labor Statistics.

TABLE 7.2
Price Changes in 2006

The average rate of inflation conceals substantial differences in the price changes of specific goods and services. The impact of inflation on individuals depends in part on which goods and services are consumed. People who buy goods whose prices are rising fastest lose more real income. In 2006, drivers and college students were particularly hard-hit by inflation.

- ***Not everyone suffers equally from inflation.*** This follows from our first observation. Those people who consume the goods and services that are rising faster in price bear a greater burden of inflation; their real incomes fall further. Other consumers bear a lesser burden, or even none at all, depending on how fast the prices rise for the goods they enjoy.

Table 7.2 illustrates some of the price changes that occurred in 2006. The average rate of inflation was only 3.2 percent. This was little solace to college students, however, who confronted tuition increases of 6.7 percent, and 6.4 percent price hikes on textbooks (sorry!). On the other hand, price reductions on televisions and computers spared consumers of these products from the pain of the *average* inflation rate.

Income Effects

Even if all prices rose at the *same* rate, inflation would still redistribute income. The redistributive effects of inflation originate not only in *expenditure* patterns but also *income* patterns. Some people have fixed incomes that *don't* go up with inflation. Fixed-income groups include those retired people who depend primarily on private pensions and workers with multiyear contracts that fix wage rates at preinflation levels. Lenders (like banks) that have lent funds at fixed interest rates also suffer real income losses when price levels rise. They continue to receive interest payments fixed in *nominal* dollars that have increasingly less *real* value. All these market participants experience a declining share of real income (and output) in inflationary periods.

Not all market participants suffer a real income decline when prices rise. Some people's nominal income rises *faster* than average prices, thereby boosting their *real* incomes. Keep in mind that there are two sides to every market transaction. ***What looks like a price to a buyer looks like an income to a seller.*** If students all pay higher tuition, the university will take in more income. When the nominal incomes colleges receive increase faster than average prices, they actually *benefit* from inflation. They end up being able to buy *more* goods and services (including faculty, buildings, and library books) after a period of inflation than they could before. Their real income rises. When the price of this textbook goes up, my *nominal* income goes up. If the text price rises faster than other prices, my *real* income increases as well. In either case, you lose (sorry!).

Once we recognize that nominal incomes and prices don't all increase at the same rate, it makes no sense to say that "inflation hurts everybody." ***If prices are rising, incomes must be rising too.*** In fact, on *average,* incomes rise just as fast as prices (see Figure 7.1). That fact is of little comfort, however, to those who end up losing real income in the inflation game.

Wealth Effects

Still more winners and losers of the inflation game are selected on the basis of the assets they hold. Suppose you deposit $100 in a savings account on January 1, where it earns 5 percent interest. At the end of the year you'll have more nominal wealth ($105) than you started with ($100). But what if all prices have doubled in the meantime? In that case, your $105 will buy you no more at the end of the year than $52.50 would have bought you at the

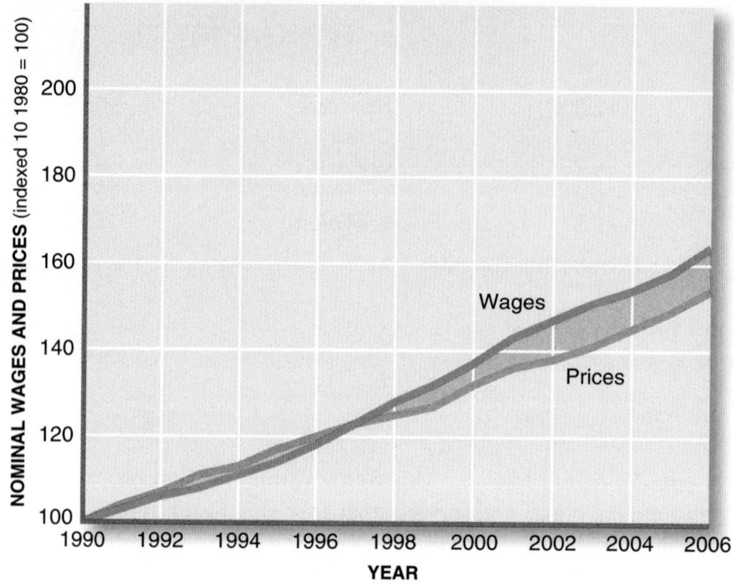

FIGURE 7.1
Nominal Wages and Prices

Inflation implies not only higher prices but higher incomes as well. Hence, inflation can't make *everyone* worse off. In fact, average wages increase along with average prices. They rise faster than prices when productivity increases. Wages rise slower than prices when fringe benefits or payroll taxes are increasing.

Source: *Economic Report of the President, 2007.*

beginning. Inflation in this case reduces the *real* value of your savings, and you end up worse off than those individuals who spent all their income earlier in the year!

Table 7.3 shows how the value of various assets has changed. Between 1991 and 2001, the average price level increased 32 percent. The average value of stocks, diamonds, and homes rose much faster than the price level, increasing the *real* value of those assets. Farmland prices rose too, but just a bit more than average prices. People who owned bonds, silver, and gold weren't so lucky; their *real* wealth declined.

Redistributions

By altering relative prices, incomes, and the real value of wealth, inflation turns out to be a mechanism for redistributing incomes and wealth. ***The redistributive mechanics of inflation include:***

- ***Price effects.*** People who prefer goods and services that are increasing in price the fastest end up with fewer goods and services.
- ***Income effects.*** People whose nominal incomes rise more slowly than the rate of inflation end up with fewer goods and services.
- ***Wealth effects.*** People who own assets that are declining in real value end up with less real wealth.

TABLE 7.3
The Real Story of Wealth

Households hold their wealth in many different forms. As the value of various assets changes, so does a person's wealth. Between 1991 and 2001, inflation was very good to people who held stocks. By contrast, the real value of bonds, gold, and silver fell.

Asset	Change in Value (%), 1991–2001
Stocks	+250%
Diamonds	+71
Oil	+66
Housing	+56
U.S. farmland	+49
Average price level	+32
Silver	+22
Bonds	+20
Stamps	−9
Gold	−29

WORLD VIEW 

Zimbabwe's Inflation Rate Skyrockets

JOHANNESBURG, South Africa (AP)—Huge price increases for bread, electricity and meat drove Zimbabwe's annual inflation rate to 1,593.6 percent, the Central Statistical Office was quoted Tuesday as saying.

The figure for January 2007 represents a 312.5 percent increase on the December rate, the biggest leap in 17 months. Economists have said there could be hourly price increases in stores by May or June, the Zimbabwe Independent newspaper reported last week. . . .

Consumers struggle to keep up with daily price changes for goods, while the government accuses businesses of sabotaging the economy by adjusting prices. . . .

A wave of discontent is sweeping through the public sector. For seven weeks, nurses and doctors have been on strike at four hospitals in the capital, Harare, and in Bulawayo.

A civil servants' union this weekend gave the government until Friday to agree to a 400 percent wage hike for its 180,000 members or face unspecified "action."

Source: *The Guardian,* February 14, 2007.

Analysis: Hyperinflation forces market participants to focus on the very short run and increases sociopolitical tensions.

On the other hand, people whose nominal incomes increase faster than inflation end up with larger shares of total output. The same thing is true of those who enjoy goods that are rising slowest in price or who hold assets whose real value is increasing. In this sense, ***inflation acts just like a tax, taking income or wealth from one group and giving it to another.*** But we have no assurance that this particular tax will behave like Robin Hood, taking from the rich and giving to the poor. In reality, inflation often redistributes income in the opposite direction.

Social Tensions

Because of its redistributive effects, inflation also increases social and economic tensions. Tensions—between labor and management, between government and the people, and among consumers—may overwhelm a society and its institutions. As Gardner Ackley of the University of Michigan observed, "A significant real cost of inflation is what it does to morale, to social coherence, and to people's attitudes toward each other." "This society," added Arthur Okun, "is built on implicit and explicit contracts. . . . They are linked to the idea that the dollar means something. If you cannot depend on the value of the dollar, this system is undermined. People will constantly feel they've been fooled and cheated."[1] This is how the middle class felt in Germany in 1923 and in China in 1948, when the value of their savings was wiped out by sudden and unanticipated inflation. A surge in prices also stirred social and political tensions in Russia as it moved from a price-controlled economy to a market-driven economy in the 1990s. The same kind of sociopolitical tension arose in Zimbabwe in 2007 when prices skyrocketed (see World View). On a more personal level, psychotherapists report that "inflation stress" leads to more frequent marital spats, pessimism, diminished self-confidence, and even sexual insecurity. Some people turn to crime as a way of solving the problem.

Money Illusion

Even those people whose nominal incomes keep up with inflation often feel oppressed by rising prices. People feel that they *deserve* any increases in wages they receive. When they later discover that their higher (nominal) wages don't buy any additional goods, they feel cheated. They feel worse off, even though they haven't suffered any actual loss of real income. This phenomenon is called **money illusion.** People suffering from money illusion are forever reminding us that they used to pay only $5 to see a movie or $20 for a textbook. What they forget is that nominal incomes were also a lot lower in the "good old days" than they are today.

money illusion: The use of nominal dollars rather than real dollars to gauge changes in one's income or wealth.

[1]Quoted in *BusinessWeek,* May 22, 1978, p. 118.

MACRO CONSEQUENCES

Although microeconomic redistributions of income and wealth are the primary consequences of inflation, inflation has *macroeconomic* effects as well.

Uncertainty

webnote

To see how much the cost of college or any product will change at different inflation rates, use the CPI inflator provided by the Federal Reserve Bank of Minneapolis at woodrow.mpls.frb.us/research/data/us/calc

One of the most immediate consequences of inflation is uncertainty. When the average price level is changing significantly in either direction, economic decisions become more difficult. As the accompanying cartoon suggests, even something as simple as ordering a restaurant meal is more difficult if menu prices are changing (as they did during Germany's 1923 runaway inflation). Longer-term decisions are even more difficult. Should you commit yourself to 4 years of college, for example, if you aren't certain that you or your parents will be able to afford the full costs? In a period of stable prices you can be fairly certain of what a college education will cost. But if prices are rising, you can't be sure how large the bill will be. Under such circumstances, some individuals may decide not to enter college rather than risk the possibility of being driven out later by rising costs.

Price uncertainties affect production decisions as well. Imagine a firm that wants to build a new factory. Typically, the construction of a factory takes 2 years or more, including planning, site selection, and actual construction. If construction costs change rapidly, the firm may find that it's unable to complete the factory or to operate it profitably. Confronted with this added uncertainty, the firm may decide not to build a new plant. This deprives the economy of new investment and expanded production possibilities.

Speculation

webnote

Want a "down-under" view of inflation? The Reserve Bank of New Zealand offers insights into the problems of inflation at www.rbnz.govt.nz/statistics/0135595.html

hyperinflation: Inflation rate in excess of 200 percent, lasting at least 1 year.

Inflation threatens not only to reduce the level of economic activity but to change its very nature. If you really expect prices to rise, it makes sense to buy goods and resources now for resale later. If prices rise fast enough, you can make a handsome profit. These are the kinds of thoughts that motivate people to buy houses, precious metals, commodities, and other assets. But such speculation, if carried too far, can detract from the production process. If speculative profits become too easy, few people will engage in production; instead, everyone will be buying and selling existing goods. People may even be encouraged to withhold resources from the production process, hoping to sell them later at higher prices. Such speculation may fuel **hyperinflation,** as spending accelerates and production declines. This happened in Germany in the 1920s, China in 1948–49, and in Russia in the early 1990s. Russian prices rose by 200 percent in 1991 and by another 1,000 percent in 1992. These price increases rendered the Russian ruble nearly worthless. No one wanted to hold rubles or trade for them. Farmers preferred to hold potatoes rather than sell them. Producers of shoes and clothes likewise decided to hold rather than sell their products. The resulting contraction in supply caused a severe decline in Russian output. The 2007 hyperinflation in Zimbabwe (see previous World View) caused similar disruptions.

"DO I HAVE YOUR ASSURANCE THAT PRICES WILL NOT BE INCREASED BEFORE WE ARE SERVED?"

Analysis: The uncertainty caused by rising prices causes stress and may alter consumption and investment decisions.

Bracket Creep

Another reason that savings, investment, and work effort decline when prices rise is that taxes go up, too. Federal income tax rates are *progressive;* that is, tax rates are higher for larger incomes. The intent of these progressive rates is to redistribute income from rich to poor. However, inflation tends to increase *everyone's* income. In the process, people are pushed into higher tax brackets and confront higher tax rates. The process is referred to as **bracket creep.** In recent years, bracket creep has been limited by the inflation indexing of personal income tax rates and a reduction in the number of tax brackets. However, Social Security payroll taxes and most state and local taxes aren't indexed.

bracket creep: The movement of taxpayers into higher tax brackets (rates) as nominal incomes grow.

Deflation Dangers

Ironically, a *falling* price level—a deflation—might not make people happy either. In fact, a falling price level can do the same kind of harm as a rising price level. When prices are falling, people on fixed incomes and long-term contracts gain more *real* income. Lenders win and creditors lose. People who hold cash or bonds win: Homeowners and stamp collectors lose. A deflation simply reverses the kinds of redistributions caused by inflation.

A falling price level also has similar macro consequences. Time horizons get shorter. Businesses are more reluctant to borrow money or to invest. People lose confidence in themselves and public institutions when declining price levels deflate their incomes and assets.

MEASURING INFLATION

In view of the macro and micro consequences of price-level changes, the measurement of inflation serves two purposes: to gauge the average rate of inflation and to identify its principal victims.

Consumer Price Index

The most common measure of inflation is the **Consumer Price Index (CPI).** As its name suggests, the CPI is a mechanism for measuring changes in the average price of consumer goods and services. It's analogous to the fruit price index we discussed earlier. The CPI doesn't refer to the price of any particular good but to the average price of all consumer goods.

Consumer Price Index (CPI): A measure (index) of changes in the average price of consumer goods and services.

By itself, the "average price" of consumer goods isn't a very useful number. But once we know the average price of consumer goods, we can observe whether that average rises—that is, whether inflation is occurring. By observing the extent to which prices increase, we can calculate the **inflation rate.**

inflation rate: The annual percentage rate of increase in the average price level.

We can get a better sense of how inflation is measured by observing how the CPI is constructed. The process begins by identifying a market basket of goods and services the typical consumer buys. For this purpose, the Bureau of Labor Statistics surveys a large sample of families every year to determine what goods and services consumers actually buy. Figure 7.2 summarizes the results of the 2005 survey, which reveal that 32.7 cents out of every consumer dollar is spent on housing (shelter, furnishings, and utilities), 13.7 cents on food, and another 18 cents on transportation. Only 5.1 cents of every consumer dollar is spent on entertainment.

Within these broad categories of expenditure, the Bureau of Labor Statistics itemizes specific goods and services. The details of the expenditure survey show, for example, that private expenditures for reading and education account for only 3 percent of the typical consumer's budget, less than is spent on alcoholic beverages, tobacco, and gambling. It also shows that we spend 7 cents out of every dollar on fuel, to drive our cars (3.2 cents) and to heat and cool our houses (3.8 cents).

Once we know what the typical consumer buys, it's relatively easy to calculate the average price of a market basket. The Bureau of Labor Statistics actually goes shopping in 85 cities across the country, recording the prices of the 184 items that make up the typical market basket. Approximately 19,000 stores are visited, and 60,000 landlords, renters, and homeowners are surveyed—every month!

webnote

At the U.S. Bureau of Labor Statistics, www.bls.gov, you can find the CPI for the most recent month and the same month last year.

As a result of these massive, ongoing surveys, the Bureau of Labor Statistics can tell us what's happening to consumer prices. Suppose, for example, that the market basket cost \$100 last year and that the same basket of goods and services cost \$110 this year. On the basis of those two shopping trips, we could conclude that consumer prices had risen by 10 percent in 1 year.

FIGURE 7.2
The Market Basket

To measure changes in average prices, we must first know what goods and services consumers buy. This diagram, based on consumer surveys, shows how the typical urban consumer spends each dollar. Housing, transportation, and food account for over two-thirds of consumer spending.

Source: U.S. Bureau of Labor Statistics, Consumer Expenditure Survey (2005 data).

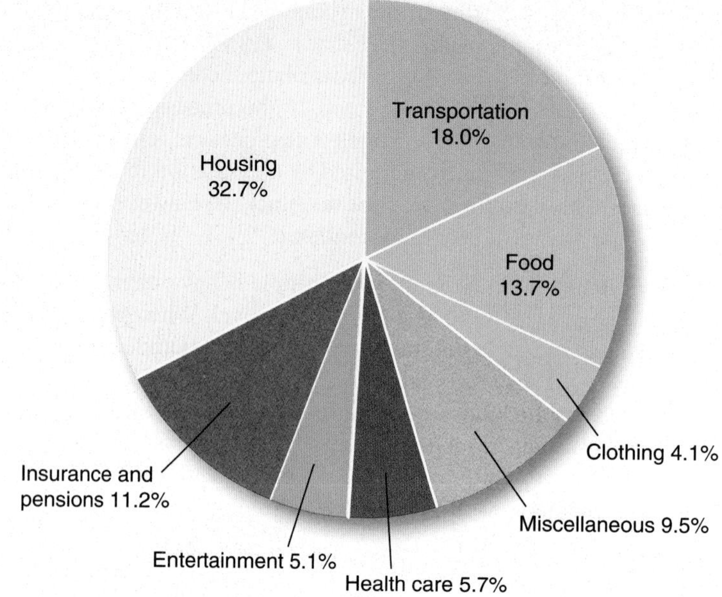

base period: The time period used for comparative analysis: the basis for indexing, for example, of price changes.

In practice, the CPI is usually expressed in terms of what the market basket cost in a specific **base period.** The price level in the base period is arbitrarily designated as 100. In the case of the CPI, the average price level for the period 1982–84 is usually used as the base for computing price changes. Hence, the price index for that base period is set at 100. In January 2007, the CPI registered 202. In other words, it cost $202 in 2007 to buy the same market baskets that cost only $100 in the base period. Prices had increased by an average of 102 percent over that period. Each month the Bureau of Labor Statistics updates the CPI, telling us how the current cost of that same basket compares to its cost between 1982 and 1984.[2]

Table 7.4 illustrates how changes in the official CPI are computed. Notice that all price changes don't have the same impact on the inflation rate. Rather, ***the effect of a specific price change on the inflation rate depends on the product's relative importance in consumer budgets.***

item weight: The percentage of total expenditure spent on a specific product; used to compute inflation indexes.

The relative importance of a product in consumer budgets is reflected in its **item weight,** which refers to the percentage of a typical consumer budget spent on the item. Table 7.4 shows the item weights for college tuition and housing. College tuition may loom very large in your personal budget, but only 1.5 percent of *all* consumer expenditure is spent on college tuition. Hence, the item weight for college tuition in the *average* consumer budget is only 0.0152.

Housing costs absorb a far larger share of the typical consumer budget. As Table 7.4 shows, the item weight for housing is 0.327. Accordingly, rent increases have a much larger impact on the CPI than do tuition hikes.

core inflation rate: Changes in the CPI, excluding food and energy prices.

The Core Rate. Every month the Labor Department reports the results of its monthly price surveys. In its news releases, the department distinguishes changes in the "core" price level from the broader, all-inclusive CPI. The **core inflation rate** excludes changes in food and energy prices, which have a lot of month-to-month variation. A freeze in California or Florida can cause a temporary spike in produce prices; a hurricane in the Gulf can do the

[2]Since January 1978, the Bureau of Labor Statistics has actually been computing two CPIs, one for urban wage earners and clerical workers and the second and larger one for all urban consumers (about 80 percent of the population). A third index, which uses rent rather than ownership costs of shelter, was introduced in 1983. The "urban/rental" index is most commonly cited.

The Consumer Expenditure Survey of 2005 revealed that the average household spends 1.52 cents of every consumer dollar on college tuition. Households without college students don't pay any tuition, of course. And your family probably devotes *more* than 1.52 cents of each consumer dollar to tuition. On *average,* however, 1.52 cents is the proportion of each dollar spent on tuition. This figure is the *item weight* of tuition in computing the CPI.

The impact on the CPI of a price change for a specific good is calculated as follows:

Item weight × percentage change in price of item = percentage change in CPI

Suppose that tuition prices suddenly go up 20 percent. What impact will this single price increase have on the CPI? In this case, where tuition is the only price that increases, the impact on the CPI will be only 0.30 percent (0.0152 × 20) as illustrated below. Thus, a very large increase in the price of tuition (20 percent) has a tiny impact (0.30 percent) on the *average* price level.

Housing, on the other hand, accounts for 32.7 percent of consumer expenditure. Thus if housing prices increase 20 percent, and housing is the only price that increases, the impact on the CPI will be 6.54 percent, as shown below.

The relative importance of an item in consumer budgets—its item weight—is a key determinant of its inflationary impact.

Item	Item Weight	×	Price Increase for the Item	=	Impact on the CPI
College tuition	0.0152		20%		0.30%
Housing	0.327		20		6.54

TABLE 7.4

Computing Changes in the CPI

The impact of any price change on the average price level depends on the importance of an item in the typical consumer budget.

webnote

The U.S. Bureau of Labor Statistics updates the CPI and PPI every month. For the latest inflation data visit the bureau at stats.bls.gov/cpi. Visit stats.bls.gov/ppi for an explanation of how the PPI and CPI differ.

webnote

The importance of housing prices is emphasized in Steven Cecchetti's "Inflation Updates" at http://people.brandeis.edu/~cecchett

same thing to oil prices. These temporary price shocks, however, may not reflect average price trends. By excluding volatile food and energy prices from the core rate, we hope to get a more accurate monthly reading of consumer price trends.

Producer Price Indexes

In addition to the Consumer Price Index, there are three Producer Price Indexes (PPIs). The PPIs keep track of average prices received by *producers.* One index includes crude materials, another covers intermediate goods, and the last covers finished goods. The three PPIs don't include all producer prices but primarily those in mining, manufacturing, and agriculture. Like the CPI, changes in the PPIs are identified in monthly surveys.

Over long periods of time, the PPIs and the CPI generally reflect the same rate of inflation. In the short run, however, the PPIs usually increase before the CPI, because it takes time for producers' price increases to be reflected in the prices that consumers pay. For this reason, the PPIs are watched closely as a clue to potential changes in consumer prices.

The GDP Deflator

The broadest price index is the GDP deflator. The GDP deflator covers all output, including consumer goods, investment goods, and government services. Unlike the CPI and PPIs, the **GDP deflator** isn't based on a fixed "basket" of goods or services. Rather, it allows the contents of the basket to change with people's consumption and investment patterns. The GDP deflator therefore isn't a pure measure of price change. Its value reflects both price changes and market responses to those price changes, as reflected in new expenditure patterns. Hence, the GDP deflator typically registers a lower inflation rate than the CPI.

GDP deflator: A price index that refers to all goods and services included in GDP.

Real vs. Nominal GDP. The GDP deflator is used to adjust nominal GDP statistics for changing price levels. Recall that **nominal GDP** refers to the *current*-dollar value of output, whereas **real GDP** denotes the *inflation-adjusted* value of output. These two measures of output are connected by the GDP deflator:

nominal GDP: The value of final output produced in a given period, measured in the prices of that period (current prices).

real GDP: The value of final output produced in a given period, adjusted for changing prices.

$$\text{Real GDP} = \frac{\text{nominal GDP}}{\text{GDP deflator}} \times 100$$

The nominal values of GDP were $10 trillion in 2000 and $5.7 trillion in 1990. At first blush, this would suggest that output had increased by 75 percent. However, the price level rose by 24 percent between those years. Hence, *real* GDP in 2000 in the base-period prices of 1990 was

$$\frac{\text{2000 real GDP}}{\text{(in 1990 prices)}} = \frac{\text{nominal GDP}}{\text{price deflator}} = \frac{\$10\text{ trillion}}{\frac{124}{100}} = \frac{\$10\text{ trillion}}{1.24} = \$8.06\text{ trillion}$$

In reality, then, output increased by only 41 percent in the 1990s. Changes in real GDP are a good measure of how output and living standards are changing. Nominal GDP statistics, by contrast, mix up output and price changes.

THE GOAL: PRICE STABILITY

In view of the inequities, anxieties, and real losses caused by inflation, it's not surprising that price stability is a major goal of economic policy. As we observed at the beginning of this chapter, every U.S. president since Franklin Roosevelt has decreed price stability to be a foremost policy goal. Unfortunately, few presidents (or their advisers) have stated exactly what they mean by "price stability." Do they mean *no* change in the average price level? Or is some upward creep in the price index acceptable?

A Numerical Goal

An explicit numerical goal for **price stability** was established for the first time in the Full Employment and Balanced Growth Act of 1978. According to that act, the goal of economic policy is to hold the rate of inflation under 3 percent.

Unemployment Concerns

price stability: The absence of significant changes in the average price level; officially defined as a rate of inflation of less than 3 percent.

Why did Congress choose 3 percent inflation rather than zero inflation as the benchmark for price stability? One reason was concern about unemployment. To keep prices from rising, the government might have to restrain spending in the economy. Such restraint could lead to cutbacks in production and an increase in joblessness. In other words, there might be a trade-off between declining inflation and rising unemployment. From this perspective, a little bit of inflation might be the "price" the economy has to pay to keep unemployment rates from rising.

Recall how the same kind of logic was used to define the goal of full employment. The fear there was that price pressures would increase as the economy approached its production possibilities. This suggested that some unemployment might be the "price" the economy has to pay for price stability. Accordingly, the goal of "full employment" was defined as the lowest rate of unemployment *consistent with stable prices.* The same kind of thinking is apparent here. The amount of inflation regarded as tolerable depends in part on the effect of anti-inflation strategies on unemployment rates. After reviewing our experiences with both unemployment and inflation, Congress concluded that 3 percent inflation was a safe target.

Quality Changes

The second argument for setting our price-stability goal above zero inflation relates to our measurement capabilities. The Consumer Price Index isn't a perfect measure of inflation. In essence, the CPI simply monitors the price of specific goods over time. Over time, however, the goods themselves change, too. Old products become better as a result of *quality improvements.* A plasma TV set costs more today than a TV did in 1955, but today's television also delivers a bigger, clearer picture, in digital sound and color, and with a host of on-screen programming options. Hence, increases in the price of TV sets tend to exaggerate the true rate of inflation: Most of the higher price represents more product.

The same is true of automobiles. The best-selling car in 1958 (a Chevrolet Bel Air) had a list price of only $2,618. That makes a 2008 Ford Taurus look awfully expensive at $20,605. The quality of today's cars is much better, however. Improvements since 1958 include seat belts, air bags, variable-speed windshield wipers, electronic ignitions, rear-window

IN THE NEWS

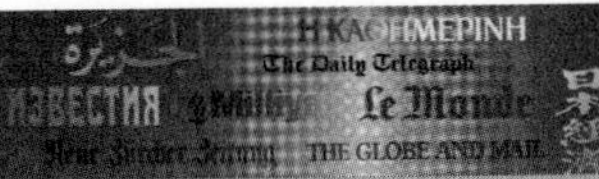

Ignoring Cell Phones Biases CPI Upward

Cellular telephones have been in commercial operation in the United States for 13 years. Beginning in Chicago in late 1983, and then at the Los Angeles Olympic Games in 1984, cellular telephone usage spread first to the top 30 Metropolitan Statistical Areas (MSAs), then to the other 300 or so MSAs, and finally to rural areas. At year-end 1996, there were over 40 million cellular subscribers in the United States. . . .

Yet the cellular telephone will not be included in the calculation of the Consumer Price Index (CPI) until 1998 or 1999. "This neglect of new goods leads to an upward bias in the CPI," NBER Research Associate Jerry Hausman concludes.

The CPI estimates that since 1988, telecommunications prices have increased by 8.5 percent, or 1.02 percent per year. A corrected index that includes cellular service decreased 1.28 percent per year since 1988, Hausman figures. "Thus, the bias in the BLS [Bureau of Labor Statistics] telecommunications services CPI equals approximately 2.3 percentage points per year."

Source: National Bureau of Economic Research, *NBER Digest,* June 1997. www.nber.org/digest

Analysis: Since the CPI tracks prices for a fixed basket of goods, it misses the effects of falling prices on new goods that appear between survey periods.

defrosters, radial tires, antilock brakes, emergency flashers, remote-control mirrors, crash-resistant bodies, a doubling of fuel mileage, a 100-fold decrease in exhaust pollutants, and global positioning systems. As a result, today's higher car prices also buy cars that are safer, cleaner, and more comfortable.

The U.S. Bureau of Labor Statistics does adjust the CPI for quality changes. Such adjustments inevitably entail subjective judgments, however. Critics are quick to complain that the CPI overstates inflation because quality improvements are undervalued.

New Products

The problem of measuring quality improvements is even more difficult in the case of new products. The computers and word processors used today didn't exist when the Census Bureau conducted its 1972–73 survey of consumer expenditure. The 1982–84 expenditure survey included those products but not still newer ones such as the cellular phone. As the News above explains, the omission of cellular phones caused the CPI to overstate the rate of inflation. The consumer expenditure survey of 1993–95 included cell phones but not digital cameras, DVD players, flat-screen TVs, or MP3 players—all of which have had declining prices. As a result, there's a significant (though unmeasured) element of error in the CPI insofar as it's intended to gauge changes in the average prices paid by consumers. The goal of 3 percent inflation allows for such errors.

THE HISTORICAL RECORD

In the long view of history, the United States has done a good job of maintaining price stability. On closer inspection, however, our inflation performance is very uneven. Table 7.5 summarizes the long view, with data going back to 1800. The base period for pricing the market basket of goods is again 1982–84. Notice that the same market basket cost only $17 in 1800. Consumer prices increased 500 percent in 183 years. But also observe how frequently the price level *fell* in the 1800s and again in the 1930s. These recurrent deflations held down the long-run inflation rate. Because of these periodic deflations, average prices in 1945 were at the same level as in 1800!

Figure 7.3 provides a closer view of our more recent experience with inflation. In this figure we transform annual changes in the CPI into percentage rates of inflation. The CPI

TABLE 7.5
Two Centuries of Price Changes

Before World War II, the average level of prices rose in some years and fell in others. Since 1945, prices have risen continuously. The Consumer Price Index has more than doubled since 1980.

Year	CPI	Year	CPI	Year	CPI	Year	CPI
1800	17.0	1900	8.3	1940	14.0	1980	82.4
1825	11.3	1915	10.1	1950	24.1	1982–84	100.0
1850	8.3	1920	20.0	1960	29.6	1990	130.5
1875	11.0	1930	16.7	1970	38.8	2000	172.8

Note: Data from 1915 forward reflect the official all-items Consumer Price Index, which used the pre-1983 measure of shelter costs. Estimated indexes for 1800 through 1900 are drawn from several sources.

Source: U.S. Bureau of Labor Statistics.

increased from 72.6 to 82.4 during 1980. This 9.8-point jump in the CPI translates into a 13.5 percent rate of inflation ($9.8 \div 72.6 = 0.135$). This inflation rate, represented by point *A* in Figure 7.3, was the highest in a generation. Since then, prices have continued to increase, but at much slower rates.

As the accompanying World View documents, the low rates of inflation the United States has experienced are far below the pace in other nations. In 2006, for example, the inflation rate in the United States was lower than in Europe and incomprehensibly low to Zimbabweans, who saw their prices rise 300 percent in one *month* (earlier World View, page 129).

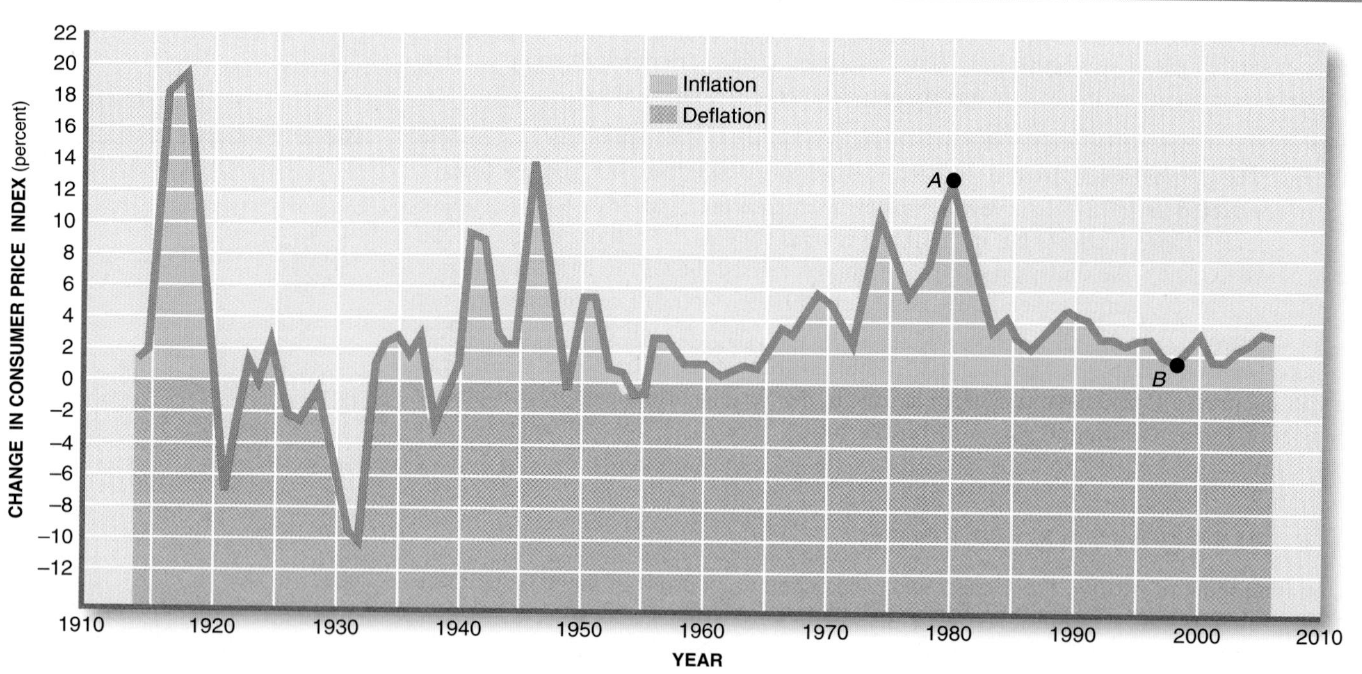

FIGURE 7.3
Annual Inflation Rates

During the 1920s and 1930s, consumer prices fell significantly, causing a general deflation. Since the Great Depression, however, average prices have risen almost every year. But even during this inflationary period, the annual rate of price increase has varied widely. In 1980, the rate of inflation was 13.5 percent (point *A*); in 1998, average prices rose only 1.6 percent (point *B*).

Source: U.S. Bureau of Labor Statistics.

WORLD VIEW 

Worldwide Inflation

In many countries prices rise at rates much higher than those in the United States. In 2006, the inflation rate in Zimbabwe was so high that prices rose 80 percent every *month.*

In the United States the inflation rate for the entire *year* was only 3.2 percent. In Japan, the price level hardly changed at all. What are the implications of such wildly different inflation rates?

Country	Inflation Rate	Country	Inflation Rate
Zimbabwe	1,593.6	Mexico	3.5
Guinea	24.1	**United States**	3.2
Costa Rica	13.1	China	2.0
Venezuela	11.7	Canada	1.8
Sierra Leone	11.7	Germany	1.8
Russia	10.4	Japan	0.3

Source: International Monetary Fund, *World Economic Outlook,* 2007. www.imf.org

Analysis: Although inflation is regarded as a major macro problem in the United States, American inflation rates are comparatively low. Many developing countries have extraordinarily fast price increases.

CAUSES OF INFLATION

The evident variation in year-to-year inflation rates requires explanation. So do the horrifying bouts of hyperinflation that have erupted in other nations at various times. What causes price levels to rise or fall?

In the most general terms, this is an easy question to answer. Recall that all market transactions entail two converging forces, namely, *demand* and *supply.* Accordingly, any explanation of changing price levels must be rooted in one of these two market forces.

Demand-Pull Inflation

Excessive pressure on the demand side of the economy is often the cause of inflation. Suppose the economy was already producing at capacity but that consumers were willing and able to buy even more goods. With accumulated savings or easy access to credit, consumers could end up trying to buy more output than the economy was producing. This would be a classic case of "too much money chasing too few goods." As consumers sought to acquire more goods, store shelves (inventory) would begin to empty. Seeing this, producers would begin raising prices. The end result would be a demand-driven rise in average prices, or demand-pull inflation.

Cost-Push Inflation

The pressure on prices could also originate on the supply side. When hurricanes Katrina and Rita destroyed oil-producing facilities in the Gulf (August 2005), oil prices increased abruptly, raising transportation and production costs in a broad array of industries. To cover these higher costs, producers raised output prices. When a tsunami devastated Sri Lanka in December 2004, it destroyed a huge portion of that country's production capacity, including its vital fishing industry. As market participants scurried for the remaining output, prices rose across the board.

Inflationary pressures could also originate in higher wages. If labor unions were able to abruptly push up wage rates, the costs of production would increase, putting pressure on product prices.

webnote

For current news stories on inflation, check out the Excite server money.excite.com/ht/nw/tbeconomy.html. Search for "inflation."

PROTECTIVE MECHANISMS

Whatever the *causes* of inflation, market participants don't want to suffer the consequences. Even at a relatively low rate of inflation, the real value of money declines over time. If prices rise by an average of just 4 percent a year, the real value of $1,000 drops to $822 in

Year	Annual Inflation Rate 2%	4%	6%	8%	10%
2007	$1,000	$1,000	$1,000	$1,000	$1,000
2008	980	962	943	926	909
2009	961	925	890	857	826
2010	942	889	840	794	751
2011	924	855	792	735	683
2012	906	822	747	681	621
2013	888	790	705	630	564
2014	871	760	665	584	513
2015	853	731	627	540	467
2016	837	703	592	500	424
2017	820	676	558	463	386

TABLE 7.6
Inflation's Impact, 2007–2017

In the past 20 years, the U.S. rate of inflation ranged from a low of 1 percent to a high of 13 percent. Does a range of 12 percentage points really make much difference? One way to find out is to see how a specific sum of money will shrink in real value in a decade.

Here's what would happen to the real value of $1,000 from January 1, 2007, to January 1, 2017, at different inflation rates. At 2 percent inflation, $1,000 held for 10 years would be worth $820. At 10 percent inflation that same $1,000 would buy only $386 worth of goods in the year 2017.

5 years and to only $676 in 10 years (see Table 7.6). ***Low rates of inflation don't have the drama of hyperinflation, but they still redistribute real wealth and income.***

COLAs

cost-of-living adjustment (COLA): Automatic adjustments of nominal income to the rate of inflation.

Market participants can protect themselves from inflation by *indexing* their nominal incomes, as is done with Social Security benefits, for example. In any year that the rate of inflation exceeds 3 percent, Social Security benefits go up *automatically* by the same percentage as the inflation rate. This **cost-of-living adjustment (COLA)** ensures that nominal benefits keep pace with the rising prices.

Landlords often protect their real incomes with COLAs as well, by including in their leases provisions that automatically increase rents by the rate of inflation. COLAs are also common in labor union agreements, government transfer programs (like food stamps), and many other contracts. In every such case, ***a COLA protects real income from inflation.***

ARMs

real interest rate: The nominal interest rate minus the anticipated inflation rate.

Cost-of-living adjustments have also become more common in loan agreements. As we observed earlier, debtors win and creditors lose when the price level rises. Suppose a loan requires interest payments equal to 5 percent of the amount (principal) borrowed. If the rate of inflation jumps to 7 percent, prices will be rising faster than interest is accumulating. Hence, the **real interest rate**—the inflation-adjusted rate of interest—will actually be negative. The interest payments made in future years will buy fewer goods than can be bought today.

The real rate of interest is calculated as

$$\text{Real interest rate} = \text{nominal interest rate} - \text{anticipated rate of inflation}$$

In this case, the nominal interest rate is 5 percent and inflation is 7 percent. Hence, the *real* rate of interest is *minus* 2 percent. The following World View illustrates how inflation can make even sky-high (nominal) interest rates look pretty mundane.

The distinction between real and nominal interest rates isn't too important if you're lending or borrowing money for just a couple of days. But the distinction is critical for long-term loans like home mortgages. Mortgage loans typically span a period of 25 to 30 years. If the inflation rate stays higher than the nominal interest rate during this period, the lender will end up with less *real* wealth than was initially lent.

WORLD VIEW 

Sky-High Interest Rates in Africa

Fed up with those measly interest payments the bank pays on your hard-earned savings? Why not move your savings account to Zimbabwe, where banks were paying interest rates of 400 percent or more on savings accounts in 2007? That's right, 400 percent!

These sky-high interest rates look tempting, but there's a catch. The inflation rate in Zimbabwe in 2006 was 1,593 percent (see World View, page 129). So those high interest payments didn't keep up with rising prices. After inflation, savers had less buying power than when they first put money in the bank. The *real* interest rate—the nominal interest rate minus inflation was actually *negative.* That hardly justifies a trip to Africa.

Source: International Monetary Fund. www.imf.org

Analysis: The appropriate measure of a return on savings is the *real* interest rate. The real rate equals the *nominal* rate minus anticipated inflation.

To protect against such losses, the banking industry offers home loans with adjustable interest rates. An **adjustable-rate mortgage (ARM)** stipulates an interest rate that changes during the term of the loan. A mortgage paying 5 percent interest in a stable (3 percent inflation) price environment may later require 9 percent interest if the inflation rate jumps to 7 percent. Such an adjustment would keep the real rate of interest at 2 percent. These and other inflation-indexing mechanisms underscore the importance of measuring price changes accurately.

adjustable-rate mortgage (ARM): A mortgage (home loan) that adjusts the nominal interest rate to changing rates of inflation.

THE ECONOMY TOMORROW

THE END OF INFLATION?

The earth spins, the sun shines, prices rise: two generations have grown up believing that inflation is an unalterable fact of life. No wonder. A dollar today is worth only 13 cents in 1945 money; a pound is worth only 6p. Much of the damage was done in the 1970s and early 1980s, and much has improved since then. In the OECD countries inflation is now hovering around its 1960s level of 3–4 percent. That gives governments the best chance they have had for decades to kill it off and achieve price stability. Sadly, they may fluff it.

Historical Stability. Price stability is not as extraordinary as it sounds. It does not mean that all prices stay the same: some will fall, others rise, but the average price level remains constant. Anyway, inflation, in the sense of continuously rising prices, is historically the exception, not the rule. On the eve of the first world war, prices in Britain were on average no higher than at the time of the fire of London in 1666. . . . During those 250 years, the longest unbroken run of rising prices was six years. Since 1946, by contrast, prices in Britain have risen every year, and the same is true of virtually every other OECD country.

It is easy to say that double-digit inflation is bad, but harder to agree on the ideal rate. Should governments aim for 5 percent, 3 percent, or 0 percent? Some claim that the extra benefits of zero inflation are tiny and would be outweighed by the short-term cost—lost output, lost jobs—of pushing inflation lower. A little bit of inflation, they say, acts like a lubricant, helping relative prices and wages to adjust more efficiently, since all wages and most prices are hard to cut in absolute terms. But a little inflation sounds like "a little drink" for an alcoholic. It can too easily accelerate. That is the lesson of the past 40 years—that and the fact that the economies with the lowest inflation have tended to be the ones with the least unemployment. Beyond the short term governments cannot choose to have a bit faster growth in exchange for a bit more inflation. The choice does not exist.

The Virtue of Zero. The rewards of reducing inflation from 5 percent to 0 percent may be smaller than those from crunching inflation from 5,000 percent to 5 percent, but they are still highly desirable. The best inflation rate is one that least affects the behaviour of companies, investors, shoppers and workers. That means zero, because anything higher interferes with the most fundamental function of prices—their ability to provide information about relative scarcities. If prices in general are rising by 5 percent a year, the fact that the price of one particular product rises by 8 percent goes largely unnoticed. Yet that product's relative 3 percent increase ought to attract the attention of potential new producers, and to encourage buyers to look elsewhere—in short, to set in train the changes that maximize economic efficiency. It would do that if the 3 percent rise was like a hillock in an otherwise flat landscape; but, in the mountains of generalized inflation, nobody notices a crag. Even with an annual inflation rate of 5 percent, the general price level doubles every 14 years, obscuring changes in relative prices.

Now imagine a world without inflation. Once it was believable, it would transform the way people behave. Companies would be confident about borrowing long-term money, and lenders confident about providing it. Real interest rates would fall. Firms would invest more because the probable pay-out would be clearer; the same would be true of individuals investing time and money on their education. Governments could budget for infrastructural projects, knowing that their plans would not be derailed by unexpected surges in prices. In general, everyone would think more about the long term because the long term would be easier to see.

Source: *The Economist,* January 22, 1992. www.economist.com

SUMMARY

- Inflation is an increase in the average price level. Typically it's measured by changes in a price index such as the Consumer Price Index (CPI). LO1
- At the micro level, inflation redistributes income by altering relative prices, income, and wealth. Because not all prices rise at the same rate and because not all people buy (and sell) the same goods or hold the same assets, inflation doesn't affect everyone equally. Some individuals actually gain from inflation, whereas others suffer a loss of real income or wealth. LO2
- At the macro level, inflation threatens to reduce total output because it increases uncertainties about the future and thereby inhibits consumption and production decisions. Fear of rising prices can also stimulate spending, forcing the government to take restraining action that threatens full employment. Rising prices also encourage speculation and hoarding, which detract from productive activity. LO2
- Fully anticipated inflation reduces the anxieties and real losses associated with rising prices. However, few people can foresee actual price patterns or make all the necessary adjustments in their market activity. LO1
- The U.S. goal of price stability is defined as an inflation rate of less than 3 percent per year. This goal recognizes potential conflicts between zero inflation and full employment as well as the difficulties of measuring quality improvements and new products. LO3
- From 1800 to 1945, prices both rose and fell, leaving the average price level unchanged. Since then, prices have risen nearly every year but at widely different rates. LO3
- Inflation is caused by either excessive demand (demand-pull inflation) or structural changes in supply (cost-push inflation). LO1
- Cost-of-living adjustments (COLAs) and adjustable-rate mortgages (ARMs) help protect real incomes from inflation. Universal indexing, however, wouldn't eliminate inflationary redistributions of income and wealth. LO2
- Worldwide inflation rates have diminished in recent years. Experience with inflation and changing patterns of asset ownership are creating political pressure for greater price stability. LO3

Key Terms

inflation
deflation
relative price
nominal income
real income
money illusion
hyperinflation
bracket creep
Consumer Price Index (CPI)
inflation rate
base period
item weight
core inflation rate
GDP deflator
nominal GDP
real GDP
price stability
cost-of-living adjustment (COLA)
real interest rate
adjustable-rate mortgage (ARM)

Questions for Discussion

1. Why would farmers rather store their output than sell it during periods of hyperinflation? How does this behavior affect prices? LO2
2. How might rapid inflation affect college enrollments? LO2
3. Who gains and who loses from rising house prices? LO2
4. Whose real wealth (see Table 7.3) declined in the 1990s? Who else might have lost real income or wealth? Who gained as a result of inflation? LO2
5. If *all* prices increased at the same rate (i.e., no *relative* price changes), would inflation have any redistributive effects? LO2
6. Would it be advantageous to borrow money if you expected prices to rise? Would you want a fixed-rate loan or one with an adjustable interest rate? LO2
7. Are people worse off when the price level rises as fast as their income? Why do people often feel worse off in such circumstances? LO2
8. Identify two groups that benefit from deflation and two that lose. LO2
9. Could demand-pull inflation occur before an economy was producing at capacity? How? LO3
10. Why would anyone borrow money at 400 percent interest, as was the case in Zimbabwe in 2007? (See World View, "Sky-High Interest Rates in Africa" (page 139). Why would a bank lend money in that situation? LO3
11. How much do higher gasoline prices contribute to inflation? LO1

problems The Student Problem Set at the back of this book contains numerical and graphing problems for this chapter.

web activities to accompany this chapter can be found on the Online Learning Center: **http://www.mhhe.com/economics/schiller11e**

PART

Cyclical Instability

One of the central concerns of macroeconomics is the short-run business cycle—recurrent bouts of expansion and contraction of the nation's output. These cycles affect jobs, prices, economic growth, and international trade and financial balances. Chapters 8 through 10 focus on the nature of the business cycle and the underlying market forces.

The Business Cycle

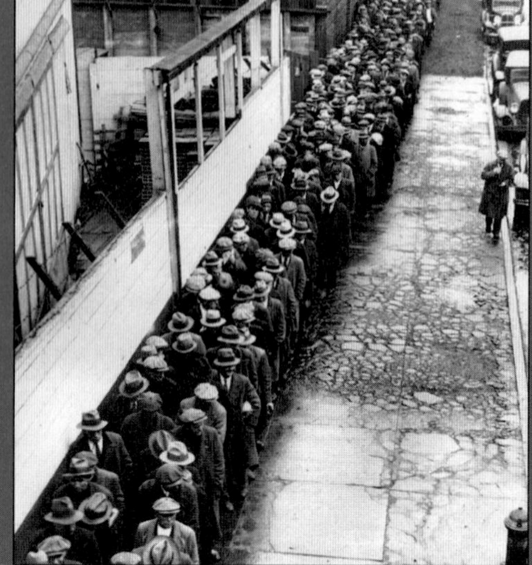

LEARNING OBJECTIVES

After reading this chapter, you should know:

LO1. The major macro outcomes and their determinants.

LO2. The nature of aggregate demand (AD) and aggregate supply (AS).

LO3. How AD and AS affect market outcomes.

In 1929 it looked as though the sun would never set on the U.S. economy. For 8 years in a row, the U.S. economy had been expanding rapidly. During the Roaring Twenties, the typical American family drove its first car, bought its first radio, and went to the movies for the first time. With factories running at capacity, virtually anyone who wanted to work found a job readily.

Everyone was optimistic. In his Acceptance Address in November 1928, President-elect Herbert Hoover echoed this optimism by declaring: "We in America today are nearer to the final triumph over poverty than ever before in the history of any land. . . . We shall soon with the help of God be in sight of the day when poverty will be banished from this nation."

The booming stock market seemed to confirm this optimistic outlook. Between 1921 and 1927 the stock market's value more than doubled, adding billions of dollars to the wealth of U.S. households and businesses. The stock market boom accelerated in 1927, causing stock prices to double again in less than 2 years. The roaring stock market made it look easy to get rich in America.

The party ended abruptly on October 24, 1929. On what came to be known as Black Thursday, the stock market crashed. In a few short hours, the market value of U.S. corporations tumbled, in the most frenzied selloff ever seen (see News). The next day President Hoover tried to assure America's stockholders that the economy was "on a sound and prosperous basis." But despite his assurances and the efforts of leading bankers to stem the decline, the stock market continued to plummet. The following Tuesday (October 29) the pace of selling quickened. By the end of the year, more than $40 billion of wealth had vanished in the Great Crash. Rich men became paupers overnight; ordinary families lost their savings, their homes, and even their lives.

The devastation was not confined to Wall Street. The financial flames engulfed the farms, the banks, and industry. Between 1930 and 1935, millions of rural families lost their farms. Automobile production fell from 4.5 million cars in 1929 to only 1.1 million in 1932. So many banks were forced to close that newly elected President Roosevelt had to declare a "bank holiday" in March 1933 to stem the outflow of cash to anxious depositors.

Throughout these years, the ranks of the unemployed continued to swell. In October 1929, only 3 percent of the workforce was unemployed. A year later the total was over 9 percent, and millions of additional workers were getting by on lower wages and shorter hours. But things got worse. By 1933, over one-fourth of the labor force was unable to find work. People slept in the streets, scavenged for food, and sold apples on Wall Street.

The Great Depression seemed to last forever. In 1933, President Roosevelt lamented that one-third of the nation was ill-clothed, ill-housed, and ill-fed. Thousands of unemployed workers marched to the Capitol to demand jobs and aid. In 1938, 9 years after Black Thursday, nearly 20 percent of the workforce was still idle.

IN THE NEWS

Market in Panic As Stocks Are Dumped in 12,894,600 Share Day; Bankers Halt It

Effect Is Felt on the Curb and throughout Nation—Financial District Goes Wild

The stock markets of the country tottered on the brink of panic yesterday as a prosperous people, gone suddenly hysterical with fear, attempted simultaneously to sell a record-breaking volume of securities for whatever they would bring.

The result was a financial nightmare, comparable to nothing ever before experienced in Wall Street. It rocked the financial district to its foundations, hopelessly overwhelmed its mechanical facilities, chilled its blood with terror.

In a society built largely on confidence, with real wealth expressed more or less inaccurately by pieces of paper, the entire fabric of economic stability threatened to come toppling down.

Into the frantic hands of a thousand brokers on the floor of the New York Stock Exchange poured the selling orders of the world. It was sell, sell, sell—hour after desperate hour until 1:30 P.M.

—Laurence Stern

Source: *The World,* October 25, 1929.

Analysis: Stock markets are a barometer of confidence in the economy. If people have doubts about the economy, they're less willing to hold stocks. The crash of 1929 mirrored and worsened consumer confidence.

The Great Depression shook not only the foundations of the world economy but also the self-confidence of the economics profession. No one had predicted the Depression, and few could explain it. The ensuing search for explanations focused on three central questions:

- **How stable is a market-driven economy?**
- **What forces cause instability?**
- **What, if anything, can the government do to promote steady economic growth?**

macroeconomics: The study of aggregate economic behavior, of the economy as a whole.

The basic purpose of **macroeconomics** is to answer these questions—to *explain* how and why economies grow and what causes the recurrent ups and downs of the economy that characterize the **business cycle.** In this chapter we introduce the theoretical model economists use to describe and explain the short-run business cycle. We'll also preview some of the policy options the government might use to dampen those cycles.

business cycle: Alternating periods of economic growth and contraction.

STABLE OR UNSTABLE?

Classical Theory

Prior to the 1930s, macro economists thought there could never be a Great Depression. The economic thinkers of the time asserted that a market-driven economy was inherently stable. There was no need for government intervention.

laissez faire: The doctrine of "leave it alone," of nonintervention by government in the market mechanism.

This **laissez-faire** view of macroeconomics seemed reasonable at the time. During the nineteenth century and the first 30 years of the twentieth, the U.S. economy experienced some bad years in which the nation's output declined and unemployment increased. But most of these episodes were relatively short-lived. The dominant feature of the Industrial Era was *growth:* an expanding economy, with more output, more jobs, and higher incomes nearly every year.

A Self-Regulating Economy. In this environment, classical economists, as they later became known, propounded an optimistic view of the macro economy. ***According to the classical view, the economy "self-adjusts" to deviations from its long-term growth trend.*** Producers might occasionally reduce their output and throw people out of work, but these dislocations would cause little damage. If output declined and people lost their jobs, the internal forces of the marketplace would quickly restore prosperity. Economic downturns were viewed as temporary setbacks, not permanent problems.

The cornerstones of classical optimism were flexible prices and flexible wages. If producers couldn't sell all their output at current prices, they had two choices. They could reduce the rate of output and throw some people out of work, or they could reduce the price of their output, thereby stimulating an increase in the quantity demanded. According to the **law of demand,** price reductions cause an increase in unit sales. If prices fall far enough, all the output produced can be sold. Thus, flexible prices—prices that would drop when consumer demand slowed—virtually guaranteed that all output could be sold. No one would have to lose a job because of weak consumer demand.

law of demand: The quantity of a good demanded in a given time period increases as its price falls, *ceteris paribus.*

Flexible prices had their counterpart in factor markets. If some workers were temporarily out of work, they'd compete for jobs by offering their services at lower wages. As wage rates declined, producers would find it profitable to hire more workers. Ultimately, flexible wages would ensure that everyone who wanted a job would have a job.

These optimistic views of the macro economy were summarized in Say's Law. **Say's Law**—named after the nineteenth-century economist Jean-Baptiste Say—decreed that "supply creates its own demand." Whatever was produced would be sold. All workers who sought employment would be hired. ***Unsold goods and unemployed labor could emerge in this classical system, but both would disappear as soon as people had time to adjust prices and wages.*** There could be no Great Depression—no protracted macro failure—in this classical view of the world.

Say's Law: Supply creates its own demand.

Macro Failure. The Great Depression was a stunning blow to classical economists. At the onset of the Depression, classical economists assured everyone that the setbacks in production and employment were temporary and would soon vanish. Andrew Mellon, Secretary of the U.S. Treasury, expressed this optimistic view in January 1930, just a few months after the stock market crash. Assessing the prospects for the year ahead, he said: "I see nothing. . . . in the present situation that is either menacing or warrants pessimism. . . . I have every confidence that there will be a revival of activity in the spring and that during the coming year the country will make steady progress."[1] Merrill Lynch, one of the nation's largest brokerage houses, was urging that people should buy stocks. But the Depression deepened. Indeed, unemployment grew and persisted *despite* falling prices and wages (see Figure 8.1). The classical self-adjustment mechanism simply didn't work.

The Keynesian Revolution

The Great Depression effectively destroyed the credibility of classical economic theory. As the British economist John Maynard Keynes pointed out in 1935, classical economists

> were apparently unmoved by the lack of correspondence between the results of their theory and the facts of observation:—a discrepancy which the ordinary man has not failed to observe. . . .
>
> The celebrated optimism of [classical] economic theory . . . is . . . to be traced, I think, to their having neglected to take account of the drag on prosperity which can be exercised by an insufficiency of effective demand. For there would obviously be a natural tendency towards the optimum employment of resources in a Society which was functioning after the manner of the classical postulates. It may well be that the classical theory represents the way in which we should like our Economy to behave. But to assume that it actually does so is to assume our difficulties away.[2]

Inherent Instability. Keynes went on to develop an alternative view of the macro economy. Whereas the classical economists viewed the economy as inherently stable, ***Keynes asserted that a market-driven economy is inherently unstable.*** Small disturbances in output, prices, or unemployment were likely to be magnified, not muted, by the invisible hand

[1]David A. Shannon, *The Great Depression* (Englewood Cliffs, NJ: Prentice Hall, 1960), p. 4.
[2]John Maynard Keynes, *The General Theory of Employment, Interest and Money* (London: Macmillan, 1936), pp. 33–34.

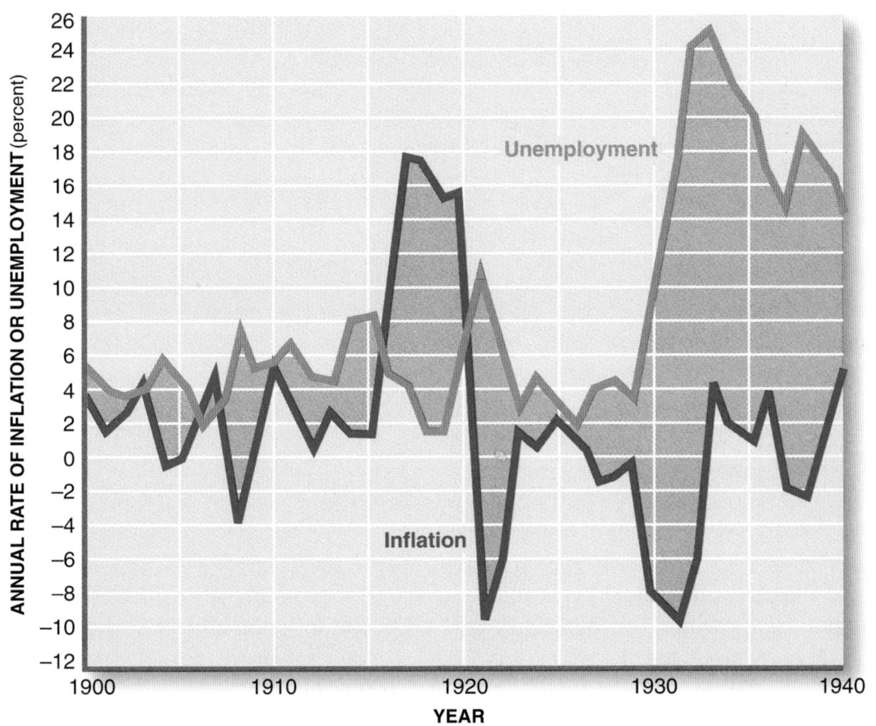

FIGURE 8.1
Inflation and Unemployment, 1900–1940

In the early 1900s, falling price levels (deflation) appeared to limit increases in unemployment. Periods of high unemployment also tended to be brief. These experiences bolstered the confidence of classical economists in the stability of the macro economy. Say's Law seemed to work.

In the 1930s, unemployment rates rose to unprecedented heights and stayed high for a decade. Falling wages and prices did not restore full employment. This macro failure prompted calls for new theories and policies to control the business cycle.

Source: U.S. Bureau of the Census, *The Statistics of the United States,* 1957.

of the marketplace. The Great Depression was not a unique event, Keynes argued, but a calamity that would recur if we relied on the market mechanism to self-adjust.

Government Intervention. In Keynes's view, the inherent instability of the marketplace required government intervention. When the economy falters, we can't afford to wait for some assumed self-adjustment mechanism but must instead intervene to protect jobs and income. The government can do this by "priming the pump": buying more output, employing more people, providing more income transfers, and making more money available. When the economy overheats, the government must cool it down with higher taxes, spending reductions, and less money.

Keynes's denunciation of classical theory didn't end the macroeconomic debate. On the contrary, economists continue to wage fierce debates about the stability of the economy. Those debates fill the pages of the next few chapters. But before examining them, let's first take a quick look at the economy's actual performance.

HISTORICAL CYCLES

The upswings and downturns of the business cycle are gauged in terms of changes in total output. An economic upswing, or expansion, refers to an increase in the volume of goods and services produced. An economic downturn, or contraction, occurs when the total volume of production declines. Changes in employment typically mirror these changes in production.

Figure 8.2 depicts the stylized features of a business cycle. Over the long run, the output of the economy grows at roughly 3 percent per year. There's a lot of year-to-year variation around this growth trend, however. The short-run cycle looks like a roller coaster, climbing steeply, then dropping from its peak. Once the trough is reached, the upswing starts again.

In reality, business cycles aren't as regular or as predictable as Figure 8.2 suggests. The U.S. economy has experienced recurrent upswings and downswings, but of widely varying length, intensity, and frequency.

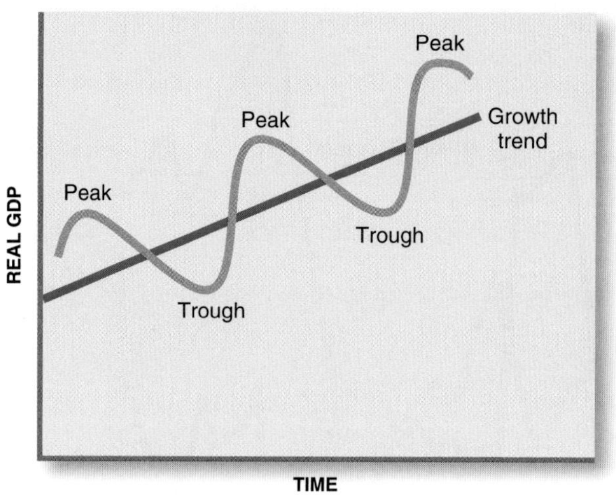

FIGURE 8.2
The Business Cycle

The model business cycle resembles a roller coaster. Output first climbs to a peak, then decreases. After hitting a trough, the economy recovers, with real GDP again increasing.

A central concern of macroeconomic theory is to determine whether a recurring business cycle exists and, if so, what forces cause it.

real GDP: The value of final output produced in a given period, adjusted for changing prices.

Figure 8.3 illustrates the actual performance of the U.S. economy since 1929. Changes in total output are measured by changes in **real GDP,** the inflation-adjusted value of all goods and services produced. From a long-run view, the growth of real GDP has been impressive: Real GDP today is 15 times larger than it was in 1929. Americans now consume a vastly greater variety of goods and services, and in greater quantities, than earlier generations ever dreamed possible.

Our long-term success in raising living standards is clouded, however, by a spate of short-term macro setbacks. On closer inspection, ***the growth path of the U.S. economy isn't a***

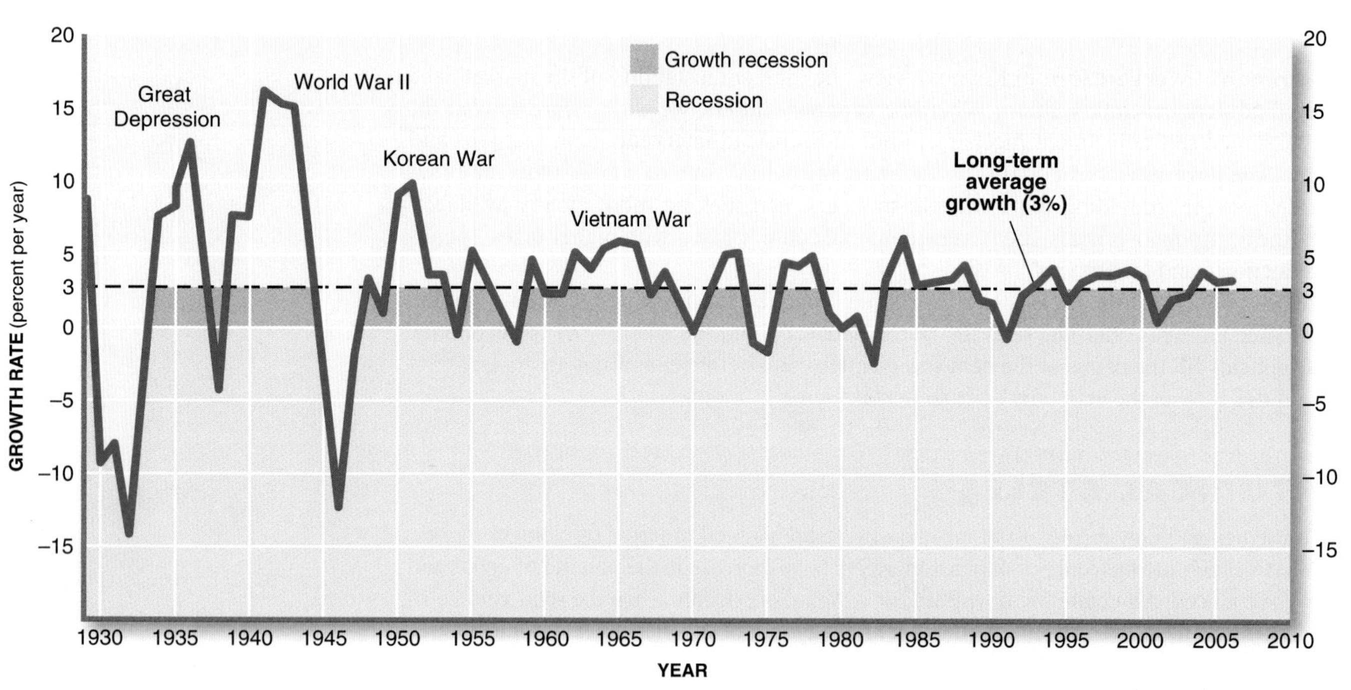

FIGURE 8.3
The Business Cycle in U.S. History

From 1929 to 2007, real GDP increased at an average rate of 3 percent a year. But annual growth rates have departed widely from that average. Years of above-average growth seem to alternate with years of sluggish growth (*growth recessions*) and actual decreases in total output (*recessions*).

Source: U.S. Department of Commerce (2007).

smooth, rising trend but a series of steps, stumbles, and setbacks. This short-run instability is evident in Figure 8.3. The dashed line represents the long-term *average* growth rate of the U.S. economy. From 1929 through 2007, the U.S. economy expanded at an average rate of 3 percent per year. But Figure 8.3 clearly shows that we didn't grow so nicely every year. There were lots of years when real GDP grew by less than 3 percent. Worse still, there were many years of *negative* growth, with real GDP *declining* from one year to the next. These successive short-run contractions and expansions are the essence of the business cycle.

The Great Depression

The most prolonged departure from our long-term growth path occurred during the Great Depression. Between 1929 and 1933, total U.S. output steadily declined. Notice in Figure 8.3 how the growth rate is negative in each of these years. During these 4 years of negative growth, real GDP contracted a total of nearly 30 percent. Investments in new plant and equipment virtually ceased. Economies around the world came to a grinding halt (see World View).

The U.S. economy rebounded in April 1933 and continued to expand for 3 years (see positive growth rates in Figure 8.3). By 1937, however, the rate of output was still below that of 1929. Then things got worse again. During 1938 and 1939 output again contracted and more people lost their jobs. At the end of the decade GDP per capita was lower than it had been in 1929.

webnote

The National Archives provides a wealth of information on the Great Depression in the Hoover Presidential Library. Visit www.hoover.nara.gov and click on "Research Our Collection" and "research/historical materials."

World War II

World War II greatly increased the demand for goods and services and ended the Great Depression. During the war years, real GDP grew at unprecedented rates—almost 19 percent in a single year (1942). Virtually everyone was employed, either in the armed forces or in the factories. Throughout the war, America's productive capacity was strained to the limit.

The Postwar Years

After World War II, the U.S. economy resumed a pattern of alternating growth and contraction. The contracting periods are called *recessions.* Specifically, we use the term **recession** to mean a decline in real GDP that continues for at least two successive quarters. As Table 8.1 indicates, there have been 11 recessions since 1944. The most severe postwar recession occurred immediately after World War II ended. Sudden cutbacks in defense production caused GDP to decline sharply in 1945. That postwar recession was relatively brief, however. Pent-up demand for consumer goods and a surge in investment spending helped restore full employment.

recession: A decline in total output (real GDP) for two or more consecutive quarters.

WORLD VIEW

Global Depression

The Great Depression wasn't confined to the U.S. economy. Most other countries suffered substantial losses of output and employment over a period of many years. Between 1929 and 1932, industrial production around the world fell 37 percent. The United States and Germany suffered the largest losses, while Spain and the Scandinavian countries lost only modest amounts of output.

Some countries escaped the ravages of the Great Depression altogether. The Soviet Union, largely insulated from Western economic structures, was in the midst of Stalin's forced industralization drive during the 1930s. China and Japan were also relatively isolated from world trade and finance and so suffered less damage from the Depression.

Country	Decline in Industrial Output
Chile	−22%
France	−31
Germany	−47
Great Britain	−17
Japan	−2
Norway	−7
Spain	−12
United States	−46

Analysis: International trade and financial flows tie nations together. When the U.S. economy tumbled in the 1930s, other nations lost export sales. Such interactions made the Great Depression a worldwide calamity.

TABLE 8.1
Business Slumps

The U.S. economy has experienced 13 business slumps since 1929. In the post–World War II period, these downturns have been much less severe. The typical recession lasts around 10 months.

When will the next recession occur, and how long will it last?

Dates	Duration (months)	Percentage Decline in Real GDP	Peak Unemployment Rate
Aug. '29–Mar. '33	43	53.4%	24.9%
May '37 –June '38	13	32.4	20.0
Feb. '45 –Oct. '45	8	38.3	4.3
Nov. '48–Oct. '49	11	9.9	7.9
July '53–May '54	10	10.0	6.1
Aug. '57–Apr. '58	8	14.3	7.5
Apr. '60–Feb. '61	10	7.2	7.1
Dec. '69–Nov. '70	11	8.1	6.1
Nov. '73–Mar. '75	16	14.7	9.0
Jan. '80–July '80	6	8.7	7.6
July '81–Nov. '82	16	12.3	10.8
July '90–Feb. '91	8	2.2	6.5
Mar. '01–Nov. '01	8	0.6	5.6

The 1980s

growth recession: A period during which real GDP grows, but at a rate below the long-term trend of 3 percent.

The 1980s started with two recessions, the second lasting 16 months (July 1981–November 1982). Despite the onset of a second recession at midyear, real GDP actually increased in 1981. But the growth rate was so slow (1.9 percent) that the number of unemployed workers actually rose that year. This kind of experience is called a **growth recession**—the economy grows, but at a slower rate than the long-run (3 percent) average: Thus,

- ***A growth recession occurs when the economy expands too slowly.***
- ***A recession occurs when real GDP actually contracts.*** A depression is an extremely deep and long recession—or when you don't even get socks for Christmas (see cartoon).

In November 1982, the U.S. economy began an economic expansion that lasted over 7 years. During that period, real GDP increased by over $1 trillion and nearly 20 million new jobs were created.

The 1990s and 2000–

The 1990s started poorly. Beginning in July 1990, real GDP started declining. Although the recession officially ended 8 months later (February 1991), subsequent growth was so slow

Analysis: Recessions occur when total output in the economy declines. In recessions, household income and spending fall.

that unemployment kept increasing. By the end of 1991, the recession had destroyed 2 million jobs and reduced total output by nearly 2 percent.

Economic growth accelerated in the late 1990s, again creating millions of new jobs. In the fall of 2000, the national unemployment rate fell to 3.9 percent, the lowest in over three decades, and the economic expansion set a longevity record. Shortly thereafter, however, GDP growth slowed so much that the United States experienced another brief recession in 2001, which was extended by the 9/11 terrorist attacks on New York City and Washington, DC. GDP growth resumed in 2002 and accelerated in 2003–2005.

A MODEL OF THE MACRO ECONOMY

The bumpy growth record of the U.S. economy lends some validity to the notion of a recurring business cycle. Every decade seems to contain at least one boom or bust cycle. But the historical record doesn't really answer our key questions. Are business cycles *inevitable?* Can we do anything to control them? ***Keynes and the classical economists weren't debating whether business cycles occur but whether they're an appropriate target for government intervention.*** That debate continues.

To determine whether and how the government should try to control the business cycle, we first need to understand its origins. What causes the economy to expand or contract? What market forces dampen (self-adjust) or magnify economic swings?

Figure 8.4 sets the stage for answering these questions. This diagram provides a bird's-eye view of how the macro economy works. This basic macro model emphasizes that the performance of the economy depends on a surprisingly small set of determinants.

On the right side of Figure 8.4 the primary measures of macroeconomic performance are arrayed. These basic ***macro outcomes include***

- ***Output:*** total value of goods and services produced (real GDP).
- ***Jobs:*** levels of employment and unemployment.
- ***Prices:*** average price of goods and services (inflation).

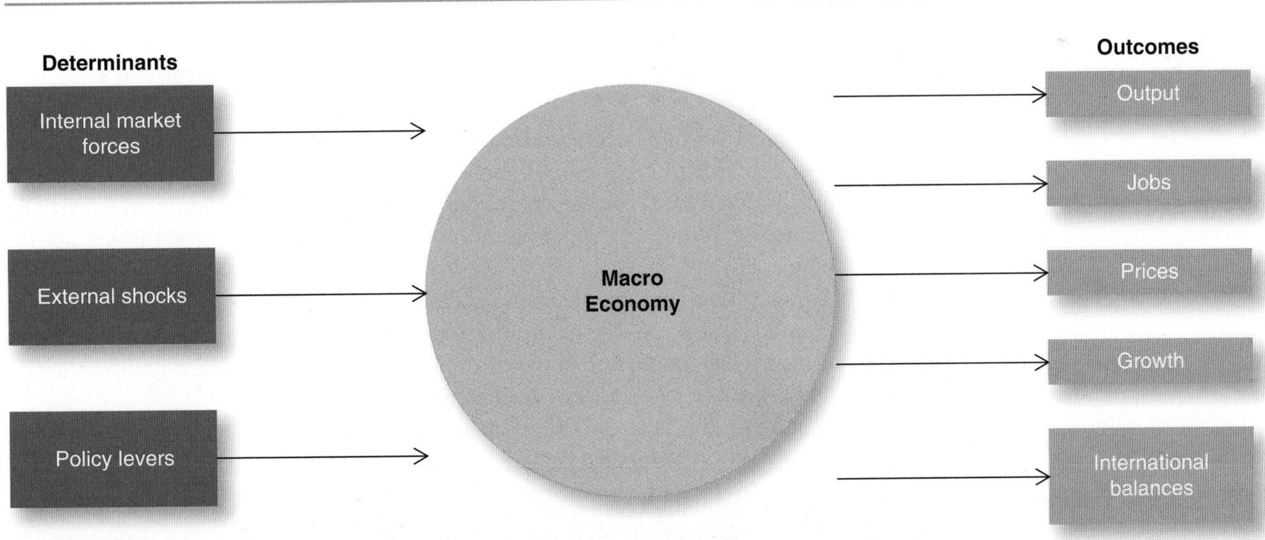

FIGURE 8.4
The Macro Economy

The primary outcomes of the macro economy are output of goods and services (GDP), jobs, prices, economic growth, and international balances (trade, currency). These outcomes result from the interplay of internal market forces such as population growth, innovation, and spending patterns; external shocks such as wars, weather, and trade disruptions; and policy levers such as tax, budget, and regulatory decisions.

- ***Growth:*** year-to-year expansion in production capacity.
- ***International balances:*** international value of the dollar; trade and payment balances with other countries.

These macro outcomes define our economic welfare; we measure our economic well-being in terms of the value of output produced, the number of jobs created, price stability, and rate of economic expansion. We also seek to maintain a certain balance in our international trade and financial relations. The economy's performance is rated by the "scores" on these five macro outcomes.

On the left side of Figure 8.4 three very broad forces that shape macro outcomes are depicted. These ***determinants of macro performance are***

- ***Internal market forces:*** population growth, spending behavior, invention and innovation, and the like.
- ***External shocks:*** wars, natural disasters, terrorist attacks, trade disruptions, and so on.
- ***Policy levers:*** tax policy, government spending, changes in the availability of money, and regulation, for example.

In the absence of external shocks or government policy, an economy would still function: It would still produce output, create jobs, develop prices, and maybe even grow. The U.S. economy operated with minimal government intervention for much of its history. Even today, many less developed countries operate in relative isolation from government or international events. In these situations, macro outcomes depend exclusively on internal market forces.

The crucial macro controversy is whether pure, market-driven economies are inherently stable or unstable. Classical economists viewed internal market forces as self-stabilizing and saw no need for the box in Figure 8.4 labeled "Policy levers." Keynes argued that policy levers were both effective and necessary. Without such intervention, Keynes believed, the economy was doomed to bouts of repeated macro failure.

Modern economists hesitate to give policy intervention that great a role. Nearly all economists recognize that policy intervention affects macro outcomes. But there are great arguments about just how effective any policy lever is. Some economists even echo the classical notion that policy intervention may be either ineffective or, worse still, inherently *de*stabilizing.

AGGREGATE DEMAND AND SUPPLY

To determine which views of economic performance are valid, we need to examine the inner workings of the macro economy. All Figure 8.4 tells us is that macro outcomes depend on certain identifiable forces. But the figure doesn't reveal *how* the determinants and outcomes are connected. What's in the mysterious circle labeled "Macro Economy" at the center of Figure 8.4?

When economists peer into the mechanics of the macro economy they see the forces of supply and demand at work. All the macro outcomes depicted in Figure 8.4 are the result of market transactions—an interaction between supply and demand. Hence, ***any influence on macro outcomes must be transmitted through supply or demand.***

By conceptualizing the inner workings of the macro economy in supply and demand terms, economists have developed a remarkably simple model of how the economy works.

Aggregate Demand

aggregate demand: The total quantity of output (real GDP) demanded at alternative price levels in a given time period, *ceteris paribus.*

Economists use the term *aggregate demand* to refer to the collective behavior of all buyers in the marketplace. Specifically, **aggregate demand** refers to the various quantities of output (real GDP) that all people, taken together, are willing and able to buy at alternative price levels in a given period. Our view here encompasses the collective demand for *all* goods and services rather than the demand for any single good.

To understand the concept of aggregate demand better, imagine that everyone is paid on the same day. With their incomes in hand, people then enter the product market. The question becomes: How much output will people buy?

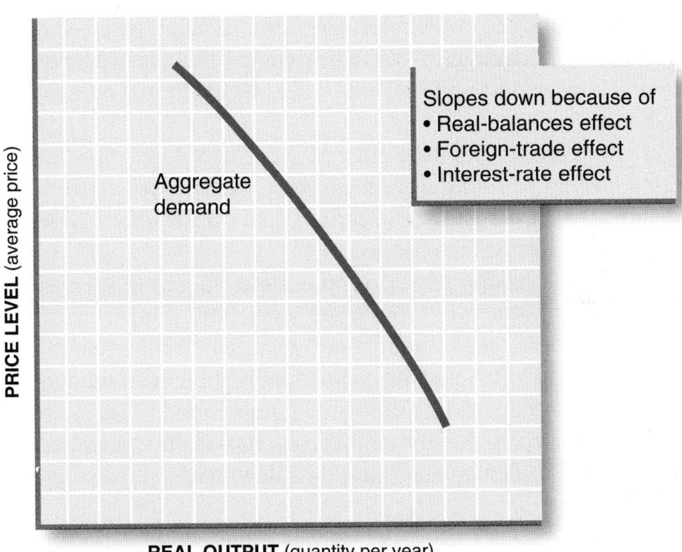

FIGURE 8.5
Aggregate Demand

Aggregate demand refers to the total output (real GDP) demanded at alternative price levels, *ceteris paribus*. The vertical axis measures the average level of all prices rather than the price of a single good. Likewise, the horizontal axis refers to the real value of all goods and services, not the quantity of only one product.

The downward slope of the aggregate demand curve is due to the real-balances, foreign-trade, and interest-rate effects.

To answer this question, we have to know something about prices. If goods and services are cheap, people will be able to buy more with their available income. On the other hand, high prices will limit both the ability and willingness to purchase goods and services. Note that we're talking here about the *average* price level, not the price of any single good.

Figure 8.5 illustrates this simple relationship between average prices and real spending. The horizontal axis depicts the various quantities of (real) output that might be purchased. The vertical axis shows various price levels that might exist.

The aggregate demand curve illustrates how the real value of purchases varies with the average level of prices. The downward slope of the aggregate demand curve suggests that with a given (constant) level of income, people will buy more goods and services at lower price levels. Why would this be the case? ***Three separate reasons explain the downward slope of the aggregate demand curve:***

- ***The real-balances effect.***
- ***The foreign-trade effect.***
- ***The interest-rate effect.***

Real-Balances Effect. The most obvious explanation for the downward slope of the aggregate demand curve is that cheaper prices make dollars more valuable. Suppose you had \$1,000 in your savings account. How much output could you buy with that savings balance? That depends on the price level. At current prices, you could buy \$1,000 worth of output. But what if the price level rose? Then your \$1,000 wouldn't stretch as far. ***The real value of money is measured by how many goods and services each dollar will buy.*** When the *real* value of your savings declines, your ability to purchase goods and services declines as well.

Suppose inflation pushes the price level up by 25 percent in a year. What will happen to the real value of your savings balance? At the end of the year, you'll have

$$\text{Real value of savings at year-end} = \frac{\text{savings balance}}{\dfrac{\text{price level at year-end}}{\text{price level at year-start}}}$$

$$= \frac{\$1{,}000}{\dfrac{125}{100}} = \frac{\$1{,}000}{1.25}$$

$$= \$800$$

In effect, inflation has wiped out a chunk of your purchasing power. At year's end, you can't buy as many goods and services as you could have at the beginning of the year. The quantity of output you demand will decrease. In Figure 8.5 this would be illustrated by a movement up the aggregate demand curve.

A declining price level (deflation) has the opposite effect. Specifically, lower price levels make you "richer": ***The cash balances you hold in your pocket, in your bank account, or under your pillow are worth more when the price level falls.*** As a result, you can buy *more* goods, even though your *nominal income* hasn't changed.

Lower price levels increase the purchasing power of other dollar-denominated assets as well. Bonds, for example, rise in value when the price level falls. This may tempt consumers to sell some bonds and buy more goods and services. With greater real wealth, consumers might also decide to save less and spend more of their current income. In either case, the quantity of goods and services demanded at any given income level will increase. These real-balances effects create an inverse relationship between the price level and the real value of output demanded—that is, a downward-sloping aggregate demand curve.

Foreign-Trade Effect. The downward slope of the aggregate demand curve is reinforced by changes in imports and exports. Consumers have the option of buying either domestic or foreign goods. A decisive factor in choosing between them is their relative price. If the average price of U.S.-produced goods is rising, Americans may buy more imported goods and fewer domestically produced products. Conversely, falling price levels in the United States may convince consumers to buy more "Made in the USA" output and fewer imports.

International consumers are also swayed by relative price levels. When U.S. price levels decline, overseas tourists flock to Disney World. Global consumers also buy more U.S. wheat, airplanes, and computers when our price levels decline. Conversely, a rise in the relative price of U.S. products deters foreign buyers. These changes in import and export flows contribute to the downward slope of the aggregate demand curve.

Interest-Rate Effect. Changes in the price level also affect the amount of money people need to borrow. At lower price levels, consumer borrowing needs are smaller. As the demand for loans diminishes, interest rates tend to decline as well. This "cheaper" money stimulates more borrowing and loan-financed purchases. These interest-rate effects reinforce the downward slope of the aggregate demand curve, as illustrated in Figure 8.5.

Aggregate Supply

Although lower price levels tend to increase the volume of output demanded, they have the opposite effect on the aggregate quantity *supplied.* As we observed, our production possibilities are defined by available resources and technology. Within those limits, however, producers must decide how much output they're *willing* to supply. Their supply decisions are influenced by changes in the price level.

Profit Effect. The primary motivation for supplying goods and services is the chance to earn a profit. Producers can earn a profit so long as the prices they receive for their output exceed the costs they pay in production. Hence, ***changing price levels will affect the profitability of supplying goods.***

If the price level declines, profits tend to drop. In the short run, producers are saddled with some relatively constant costs like rent, interest payments, negotiated wages, and inputs already contracted for. If output prices fall, producers will be hard-pressed to pay these costs, much less earn a profit. Their response will be to reduce the rate of output.

Higher output prices have the opposite effect. Because many costs are relatively constant in the short run, higher prices for goods and services tend to widen profit margins. As profit margins widen, producers will want to produce and sell more goods. Thus, ***we expect the rate of output to increase when the price level rises.*** This expectation is reflected in the

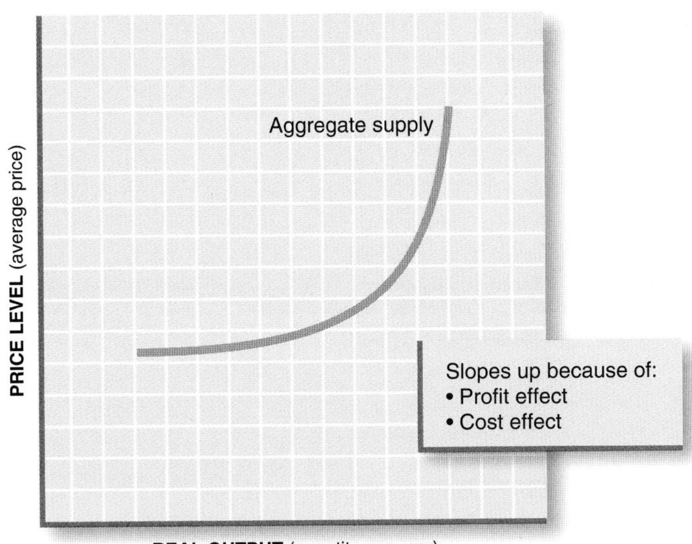

FIGURE 8.6
Aggregate Supply

Aggregate supply is the real value of output (real GDP) producers are willing and able to bring to the market at alternative price levels, *ceteris paribus*. The upward slope of the aggregate supply curve reflects both profit effects (the lure of widening profit margins) and cost effects (increasing cost pressures).

upward slope of the aggregate supply curve in Figure 8.6. **Aggregate supply** reflects the various quantities of real output that firms are willing and able to produce at alternative price levels, in a given time period.

aggregate supply: The total quantity of output (real GDP) producers are willing and able to supply at alternative price levels in a given time period, *ceteris paribus*.

Cost Effect. The upward slope of the aggregate supply curve is also explained by rising costs. The profit effect depends on some costs remaining constant when the average price level rises. Not all costs will remain constant, however. Producers may have to pay overtime wages, for example, to increase output, even if *base* wages are constant. Tight supplies of other inputs may also unleash cost increases. Such cost pressures tend to multiply as the rate of output increases. As time passes, even costs that initially stayed constant may start creeping upward.

All these cost pressures will make producing output more expensive. Producers will be willing to supply additional output only if prices rise at least as fast as costs.

The upward slope of the aggregate supply curve in Figure 8.6 illustrates this cost effect. Notice how the aggregate supply curve is practically horizontal at low rates of aggregate output and then gets increasingly steeper. At high output levels the aggregate supply curve almost turns straight up. This changing slope reflects the fact that ***cost pressures are minimal at low rates of output but intense as the economy approaches capacity.***

webnote

The slope of the aggregate supply curve depends in part on what producers pay for their inputs. Find out about producer prices at www.bls.gov/ppi

Macro Equilibrium

When all is said and done, what we end up with here is two rather conventional-looking supply and demand curves. But these particular curves have special significance. Instead of describing the behavior of buyers and sellers in a single product market, ***aggregate supply and demand curves summarize the market activity of the whole (macro) economy.*** These curves tell us what *total* amount of goods and services will be supplied or demanded at various price levels.

These graphic summaries of buyer and seller behavior provide some important clues about the economy's performance. The most important clue is point E in Figure 8.7, where the aggregate demand and supply curves intersect. This is the only point at which the behavior of buyers and sellers is compatible. We know from the aggregate demand curve that people are willing and able to buy the quantity Q_E when the price level is at P_E. From the aggregate supply curve we know that businesses are prepared to sell quantity Q_E at the price level P_E. Hence, buyers and sellers are willing to trade exactly the same quantity (Q_E) at that price level. We call this situation **macro equilibrium**—the unique combination of prices and output compatible with both buyers and sellers' intentions.

equilibrium (macro): The combination of price level and real output that is compatible with both aggregate demand and aggregate supply.

FIGURE 8.7
Macro Equilibrium

The aggregate demand and supply curves intersect at only one point (E). At that point, the price level (P_E) and output (Q_E) combination is compatible with both buyers' and sellers' intentions. The economy will gravitate to those equilibrium price (P_E) and output (Q_E) levels. At any other price level (e.g., P_1), the behavior of buyers and sellers is incompatible.

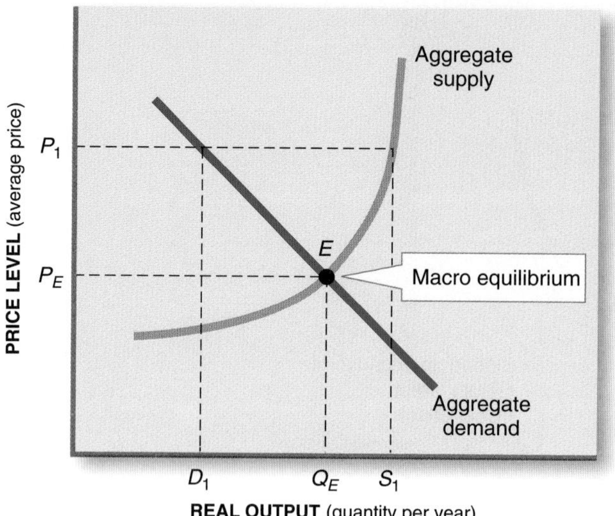

To appreciate the significance of macro equilibrium, suppose that another price or output level existed. Imagine, for example, that prices were higher, at the level P_1 in Figure 8.7. How much output would people want to buy at that price level? How much would business want to produce and sell?

The aggregate demand curve tells us that people would want to buy only the quantity D_1 at the higher price level P_1. In contrast, business firms would want to sell a larger quantity, S_1. This is a *dis*equilibrium situation in which the intentions of buyers and sellers are incompatible. The aggregate *quantity supplied* (S_1) exceeds the aggregate *quantity demanded* (D_1). Accordingly, a lot of goods will remain unsold at price level P_1.

To sell these goods, producers will have to reduce their prices. As prices drop, producers will decrease the volume of goods sent to market. At the same time, the quantities that consumers seek to purchase will increase. This adjustment process will continue until point E is reached and the quantities demanded and supplied are equal. At that point, the lower price level P_E will prevail.

The same kind of adjustment process would occur if a lower price level first existed. At lower prices, the aggregate quantity demanded would exceed the aggregate quantity supplied. The resulting shortages would permit sellers to raise their prices. As they did so, the aggregate quantity demanded would decrease, and the aggregate quantity supplied would increase. Eventually, we would return to point E, where the aggregate quantities demanded and supplied are equal.

Equilibrium is unique; it's the only price-level-output combination that is mutually compatible with aggregate supply and demand. In terms of graphs, it's the only place the aggregate supply and demand curves intersect. At point E there's no reason for the level of output or prices to change. The behavior of buyers and sellers is compatible. By contrast, any other level of output or prices creates a *dis*equilibrium that requires market adjustments. All other price and output combinations, therefore, are unstable. They won't last. Eventually, the economy will return to point E.

Macro Failures

There are two potential problems with the macro equilibrium depicted in Figure 8.7. The ***two potential problems with macro equilibrium are***

- ***Undesirability:*** The equilibrium price or output level may not satisfy our macroeconomic goals.
- ***Instability:*** Even if the designated macro equilibrium is optimal, it may not last long.

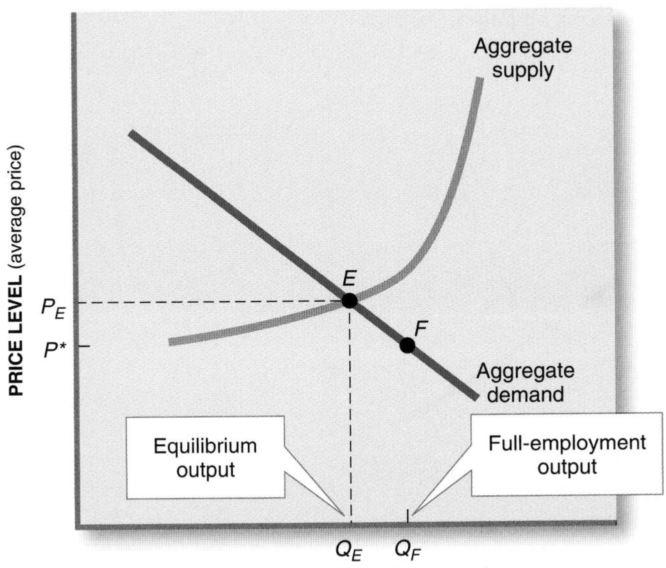

FIGURE 8.8
An Undesired Equilibrium

Equilibrium establishes only the level of prices and output that are compatible with both buyers' and sellers' intentions. These outcomes may not satisfy our policy goals. In this case, the equilibrium price level is too high (above P^*) and the equilibrium output rate falls short of full employment (Q_F).

Undesirability. The macro equilibrium depicted in Figure 8.7 is simply the intersection of two curves. All we know for sure is that people want to buy the same quantity of output that businesses want to sell at the price level P_E. This quantity (Q_E) may be more or less than our full-employment capacity. This contingency is illustrated in Figure 8.8. The output level Q_F represents our **full-employment GDP** potential. In this case, the equilibrium rate of output (Q_E) falls far short of capacity production. We've failed to achieve our goal of full employment.

full-employment GDP: The total market value of final goods and services that could be produced in a given time period at full employment; potential GDP.

Similar problems may arise from the equilibrium price level. Suppose that P^* represents the most desired price level. In Figure 8.8, we see that the equilibrium price level P_E exceeds P^*. If market behavior determines prices, the price level will rise above the desired level. The resulting increase in the average level of prices is what we call **inflation.**

inflation: An increase in the average level of prices of goods and services.

It could be argued, of course, that our apparent macro failures are simply an artifact. We could have drawn the aggregate supply and demand curves to intersect at point *F* in Figure 8.8. At that intersection we'd have both price stability and full employment. Why didn't we draw them there, instead of intersecting at point *E*?

On the graph we can draw curves anywhere we want. In the real world, however, ***only one set of aggregate supply and demand curves will correctly express buyers' and sellers' behavior.*** We must emphasize here that these "correct" curves may *not* intersect at point *F*, thus denying us price stability or full employment, or both. That is the kind of economic outcome illustrated in Figure 8.8.

Instability. Figure 8.8 is only the beginning of our macro worries. Suppose, just suppose, that the AS and AD curves actually intersected in the perfect spot. That is, imagine that macro equilibrium yielded the optimal levels of both employment and prices. If this happened, could we stop fretting about the state of the economy?

Unhappily, even a "perfect" macro equilibrium doesn't ensure a happy ending. The AS and AD curves aren't permanently locked into their respective positions. They can *shift*—and they will, whenever the behavior of buyers and sellers changes.

AS Shifts. Suppose the Organization of Petroleum Exporting Countries (OPEC) increased the price of oil, as it did in early 2006. These oil price hikes directly increased the cost of production in a wide range of U.S. industries, making producers less willing and able to

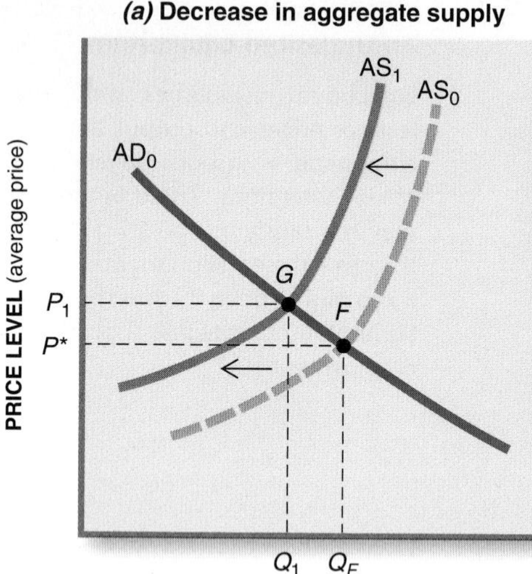

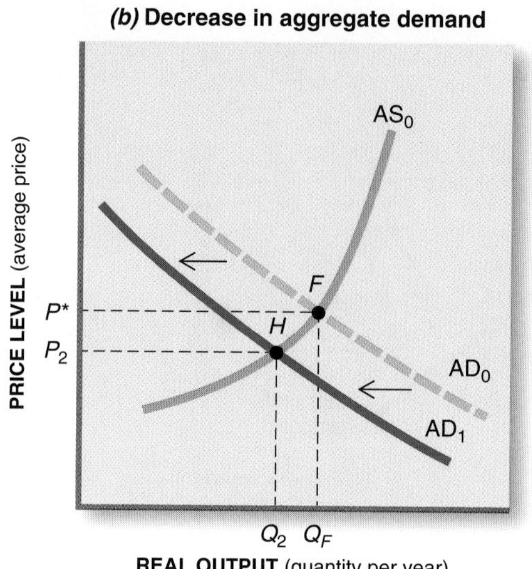

FIGURE 8.9
Macro Disturbances

(a) **Aggregate supply shifts** A decrease (leftward shift) of the aggregate-supply curve tends to reduce real GDP and raise average prices. When supply shifts from AS_0 to AS_1, the equilibrium moves from *F* to *G*. At *G*, output is lower and prices are higher than at *F*. Such a supply shift may result from higher import prices, natural disasters, changes in tax policy, or other events.

(b) **Aggregate demand shifts** A decrease (leftward shift) in aggregate demand tends to reduce output and price levels. When demand shifts from AD_0 to AD_1, both real output and the price level decline. A fall in demand may be caused by decreased export demand, changes in expectations, higher taxes, or other events.

supply goods at prevailing prices. Thus, the aggregate supply curve *shifted to the left,* as in Figure 8.9*a*.

The September 11, 2001, terrorist strikes against the World Trade Center and Pentagon also caused a leftward shift of aggregate supply. Physical destruction and fear of further terrorism kept some producers out of the market. Intensified security of transportation systems and buildings also increased the costs of supplying goods and services to the market.

The impact of a leftward AS shift on the economy is evident in Figure 8.9. Whereas macro equilibrium was originally located at the optimal point *F*, the new equilibrium is located at point *G*. At point *G*, less output is produced and prices are higher. Full employment and price stability have vanished before our eyes.

AD Shifts. A shift of the aggregate demand curve could do similar damage. In the wake of the September 11, 2001, terrorist attacks, Americans were worried about their physical and economic security. Consumers were afraid to go shopping at the mall, and even more afraid to board airplanes. Businesses were also fearful of starting new projects. As a result, the AD curve shifted left, as illustrated in Figure 8.9*b*. As the accompanying News relates, the slow recovery of confidence kept the AD curve from shifting back to the right in a timely manner.

Multiple Shifts. The situation gets even crazier when the aggregate supply and demand curves shift repeatedly in different directions. A leftward shift of the aggregate demand curve can cause a recession, as the rate of output falls. A later rightward shift of the aggregate demand curve can cause a recovery, with real GDP (and employment) again increasing. Shifts of the aggregate supply curve can cause similar upswings and downswings.

IN THE NEWS 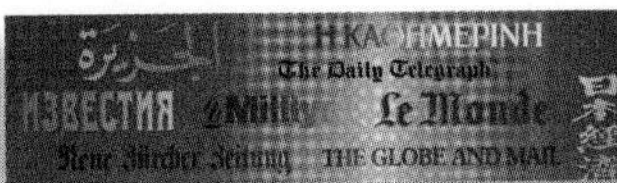 

Slack Demand Hinders Economy

Businesses Have Few Incentives to Expand or Hire, Economists Say

To understand why the U.S. economy can't seem to muster a stronger recovery, it helps to look for clues in Victorville, Calif., where 500 unused and unwanted passenger jets—some of them brand new—sit wingtip to wingtip in the desert.

Or in Detroit, where the Big Three continue to churn out large numbers of passenger cars that they sell at little or no profit, just to keep their factories busy.

Or in nearly every major metropolitan area, where office vacancy rates are still rising after 18 months, and have reached 25 percent in Dallas, 24 percent in Raleigh-Durham, N.C., and 18 percent in San Francisco.

But perhaps the best explanation can be found in those falling prices shoppers find for clothing, televisions, hotel rooms and cellular phone service. While the bargains are great for American consumers, they are being paid in the form of continued corporate layoffs, lackluster stock prices and a sky-high trade deficit—in short, an economy that's having trouble building up a head of steam.

Economists refer to this phenomenon as overcapacity, which is really nothing more than too much supply chasing too little demand....

To be sure, overcapacity is a feature of every recession. A slowdown in consumer spending and a decline in business investment suddenly leave too many companies with too many workers, underutilized plants and underperforming stores. In most cases, it is only after most of that excess is cut back, and supply and demand get back into some rough balance, that businesses begin hiring and investing again, laying the foundation for another period of economic expansion.

This time, however, that process is turning out to be longer and more drawn out than in the past, making for a slower and weaker recovery than forecasters, executives and policymakers had expected.

—Steven Pearlstein

Source: *Washington Post,* August 25, 2002.

Analysis: When AD shifts left, goods remain unsold, workers are laid off, and prices fall. The longer full-employment supply exceeds aggregate demand, the greater the economic pain.

Thus, ***business cycles are likely to result from recurrent shifts of the aggregate supply and demand curves.***

COMPETING THEORIES OF SHORT-RUN INSTABILITY

Figures 8.8 and 8.9 hardly inspire optimism about the macro economy. Figure 8.8 suggests that the odds of the market generating an equilibrium at full employment and price stability are about the same as finding a needle in a haystack. Figure 8.9 suggests that if we're lucky enough to find the needle, we'll probably drop it again.

The classical economists had no such worries. As we saw earlier, they believed that the economy would gravitate toward full employment. Keynes, on the other hand, worried that the macro equilibrium might start out badly and get worse in the absence of government intervention.

The AS/AD model doesn't really settle this controversy. It does, however, provide a convenient framework for comparing these and other theories about how the economy works. Essentially, ***macro controversies focus on the shape of aggregate supply and demand curves and the potential to shift them.*** With the right shape—or the correct shift—any desired equilibrium could be attained. As we'll see, there are differing views as to whether and how this happy outcome might come about. These differing views can be classified as demand-side explanations, supply-side explanations, or some combination of the two.

Demand-Side Theories

Keynesian Theory. Keynesian theory is the most prominent of the demand-side theories. Keynes argued that a deficiency of spending would tend to depress an economy. This

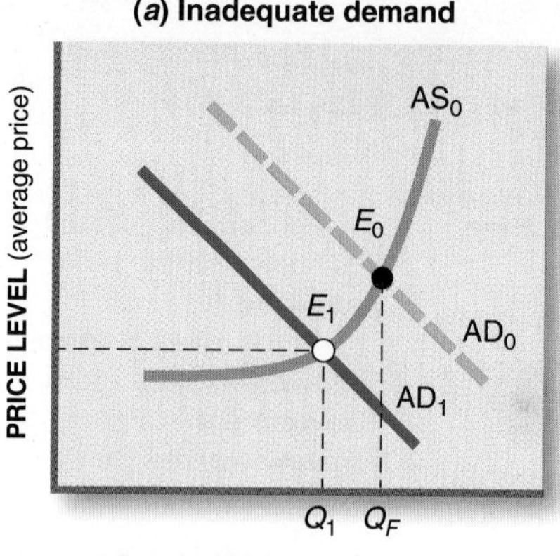

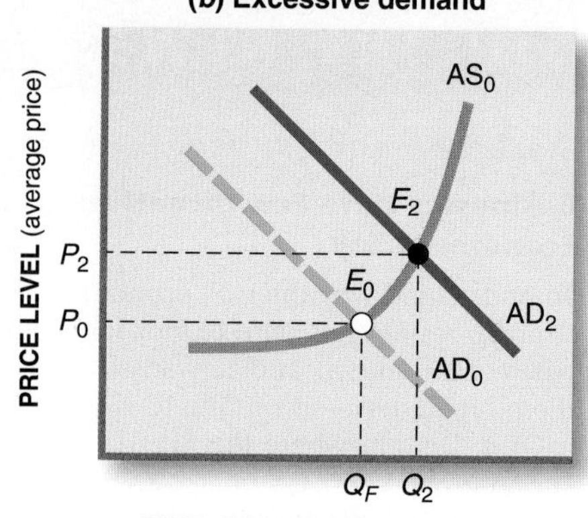

FIGURE 8.10
Demand-Side Theories

Inadequate demand may cause unemployment. In part (*a*), the demand AD_1 creates an equilibrium at E_1. The resulting output Q_1 falls short of full employment Q_F.

In part (*b*), excessive aggregate demand causes inflation. The price level rises from P_0 to P_2 when aggregate demand expands to AD_2. Demand-side theories emphasize how inadequate or excessive AD can cause macro failures.

deficiency might originate in consumer saving, inadequate business investment, or insufficient government spending. Whatever its origins, the lack of spending would leave goods unsold and production capacity unused. This contingency is illustrated by point E_1 in Figure 8.10*a*. Notice that the equilibrium at E_1 leaves the economy at Q_1, below its full-employment potential (Q_F). Thus, ***Keynes concluded that inadequate aggregate demand would cause persistently high unemployment.***

Keynes developed his theory during the Great Depression, when the economy seemed to be stuck at a very low level of equilibrium output, far below full-employment GDP. The only way to end the Depression, he argued, was for someone to start demanding more goods. He advocated a big hike in government spending—a rightward AD shift—to start the economy moving toward full employment. At the time his advice was largely ignored. When the United States mobilized for World War II, however, the sudden surge in government spending shifted the aggregate demand curve sharply to the right, restoring full employment (e.g., a reverse shift from AD_1 to AD_0 in Figure 8.10*a*). In times of peace, Keynes also advocated changing government taxes and spending to shift the aggregate demand curve in whatever direction is desired.

Monetary Theories. Another demand-side theory emphasizes the role of money in financing aggregate demand. Money and credit affect the ability and willingness of people to buy goods and services. If credit isn't available or is too expensive, consumers won't be able to buy as many cars, homes, or other expensive products. "Tight" money might also curtail business investment. In these circumstances, aggregate demand might prove to be inadequate, as illustrated in Figure 8.10*a*. In this case, an increase in the money supply and/or lower interest rates might help shift the AD curve into the desired position.

Both the Keynesian and monetarist theories also regard aggregate demand as a prime suspect for inflationary problems. In Figure 8.10*b*, the curve AD_2 leads to an equilibrium at E_2. At first blush, that equilibrium looks desirable, as it offers more output (Q_2) than the full-employment threshold (Q_F). Notice, however, what's happening to prices: The price level rises from P_0 to P_2. Hence, ***excessive aggregate demand may cause inflation.***

The more extreme monetary theories attribute all our macro successes and failures to management of the money supply. According to these *monetarist* theories, the economy will tend to stabilize at something like full-employment GDP. Thus, only the price level will be affected by changes in the money supply and resulting shifts of aggregate demand. We'll examine the basis for this view in a moment. At this juncture we simply note that ***both Keynesian and monetarist theories emphasize the potential of aggregate-demand shifts to alter some macro outcomes.***

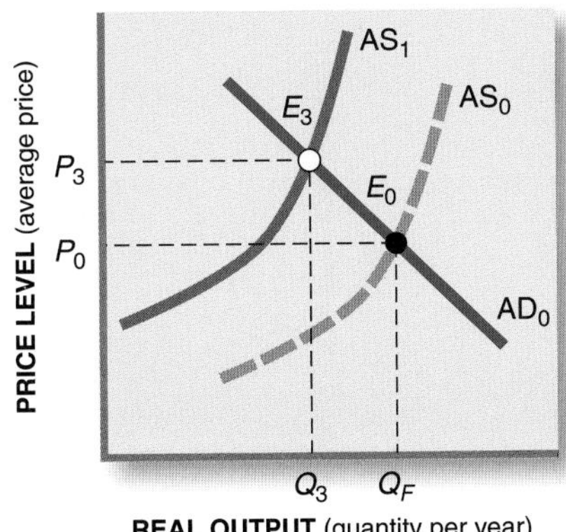

FIGURE 8.11
Supply-Side Theories

Inadequate supply can keep the economy below its full-employment potential and cause prices to rise as well. AS_1 leads to output Q_3 and increases the price level from P_0 to P_3. Supply-side theories emphasize how AS shifts can worsen or improve macro outcomes.

Supply-Side Theories

Figure 8.11 illustrates an entirely different explanation of the business cycle. Notice that the aggregate *supply* curve is on the move in Figure 8.11. The initial equilibrium is again at point E_0. This time, however, aggregate demand remains stationary, while aggregate supply shifts. The resulting decline of aggregate supply causes output and employment to decline (to Q_3 from Q_F).

Figure 8.11 tells us that aggregate supply may be responsible for downturns as well. Our failure to achieve full employment may result from the unwillingness of producers to provide more goods at existing prices. That unwillingness may originate in simple greed, in rising costs, in resource shortages, or in government taxes and regulation. Inadequate investment in infrastructure (e.g., roads, sewer systems) or skill training may also limit supply potential. Whatever the cause, if the aggregate supply curve is AS_1 rather than AS_0, full employment will not be achieved with the demand AD_0.

The inadequate supply illustrated in Figure 8.11 causes not only unemployment but inflation as well. At the equilibrium E_3, the price level has risen from P_0 to P_3. Hence, a decrease in aggregate supply can cause multiple macro problems. On the other hand, an increase—a rightward shift—in aggregate supply can move us closer to both our price-stability and full-employment goals. Chapter 16 examines the many ways of inducing such a shift.

webnote

The U.S. Bureau of Economic Analysis compiles data on gross domestic product. Using data from its Web site at www.bea.doc.gov, determine the GDP growth rate for each of the last six quarters. What supply or demand shifts might explain recent quarterly fluctuations in real GDP?

Eclectic Explanations

Not everyone blames either the demand side or the supply side exclusively. ***The various macro theories tell us that either AS or AD can cause us to achieve or miss our policy goals.*** These theories also demonstrate how various shifts of the aggregate supply and demand curves can achieve any specific output or price level. One could also shift *both* the AS and AD curves to explain unemployment, inflation, or recurring business cycles. Such eclectic explanations of macro failure draw from both sides of the market.

LONG-RUN SELF-ADJUSTMENT

Some economists argue that these various theories of short-run instability aren't only confusing but also pointless. As they see it, what really matters is the *long*-run trend of the economy, not *short*-run fluctuations around those trends. In their view, month-to-month or quarter-to-quarter fluctuations in real output or prices are just statistical noise. The *long*-term path of output and prices is determined by more fundamental factors.

This emphasis on long-term outcomes is reminiscent of the classical theory: the view that the economy will self-adjust. A decrease in aggregate demand is only a *temporary* problem. Once producers and workers make the required price and wage adjustments, the economy will return to its long-run equilibrium growth path.

The monetarist theory we encountered a moment ago has a similar view of long-run stability. According to the monetarist theory, the supply of goods and services is determined by institutional factors such as the size of the labor force and technology. These

FIGURE 8.12
The "Natural" Rate of Output

Monetarists and neoclassical theorists assert that the level of output is fixed at the natural rate Q_N by the size of the labor force, technology, and other institutional factors. As a result, fluctuations in aggregate demand affect the price level but not real output.

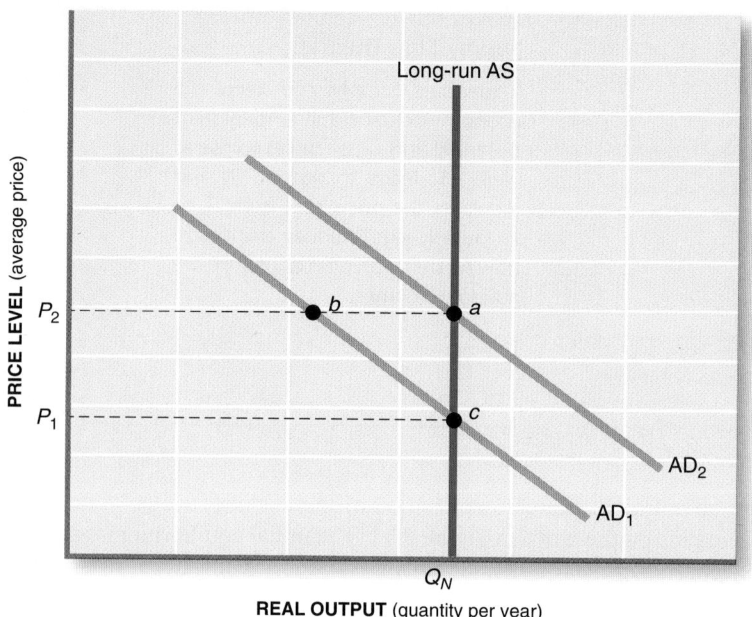

factors determine a natural rate of output that's relatively immune to short-run fluctuations in aggregate demand. If this argument is valid, the long-run aggregate supply curve is vertical, not sloped.

Figure 8.12 illustrates the classical/monetarist view of long-run stability. The vertical long-run AS curve is anchored at the natural rate of output Q_N The natural rate Q_N is itself determined by demographics, technology, market structure, and the institutional infrastructure of the economy.

If the long-run AS curve is really vertical, as the classical and monetarist theories assert, some startling conclusions follow. The most startling implication is that ***aggregate demand shifts affect prices but not output in the long run.*** Notice in Figure 8.12 how the shift from AD_1 to AD_2 raises the price level but leaves output anchored at Q_N.

What has happened here? Didn't we suggest earlier that an increase in aggregate demand would spur producers to increase output? And aren't rising prices an extra incentive for doing so?

Monetarists concede that *short-run* price increases tend to widen profit margins. This profit effect is an incentive to increase the rate of output. In the *long run,* however, costs are likely to catch up with rising prices. Workers will demand higher wages, landlords will increase rents, and banks will charge higher interest rates as the price level rises. Hence, a rising price level has only a *temporary* profit effect on supply behavior. In the *long run,* cost effects will dominate. In the *long run,* a rising price level will be accompanied by rising costs, giving producers no special incentive to supply more output. Accordingly, output will revert to its natural rate Q_N.

Classical economists use the vertical AS curve to explain also how the economy self-adjusts to temporary setbacks. If AD declines from AD_2 to AD_1 in Figure 8.12, the economy may move from point *a* to point *b*, leaving a lot of unsold output. As producers respond with price cuts, however, the volume of output demanded increases as the economy moves from point *b* to point *c*. At point *c*, full employment is restored. Thus flexible prices (and wages) enable the economy to maintain the natural rate of output Q_N.

Short- vs. Long-Run Perspectives

All this may well be true. But as Keynes pointed out, it's also true that "in the long run we are all dead." How long are we willing to wait for the promised "self-adjustment"? In the Great Depression, people waited for 10 years—and still saw no self-adjustment.

Whatever the long run may hold, it's in the short run that we must consume, invest, and find a job. However stable and predictable the long run might be, short-run variations in macro outcomes will determine how well we fare in any year. Moreover, ***the short-run aggregate supply curve is likely to be upward-sloping,*** as shown in our earlier graphs. This implies that both aggregate supply and aggregate demand influence short-run macro outcomes.

By distinguishing between short-run and long-run aggregate supply curves, competing economic theories achieve a standoff. Theories that highlight the necessity of policy intervention emphasize the importance of short-run macro outcomes. People *care* about short-run changes in job prospects and prices. If inflation or unemployment is too high, voters insist that "Washington" fix the problem—now.

Theories that emphasize the "natural" stability of the market point to the predictability of long-run outcomes. They prefer to let the economy self-adjust rather than risk government intervention that might worsen macro outcomes. Even if true, however, the duration of acceptable "short-" and "long-" run periods remains controversial.

THE ECONOMY TOMORROW

TAMING THE CYCLE

The AS/AD model is a convenient summary of how the macro economy works. The model raises more questions than it answers, however. Sure, the intersection of the AS/AD curves determines macro equilibrium. But how do we know we'll get the right equilibrium? And how can we forecast unfavorable shifts of the AS/AD curves—or reverse them when needed?

We've already seen that there are different theories about whether or how we can tame the business cycle. As we explore those theories, we need to establish our macro goals and policy options.

Setting Macro Goals. As we saw in Figure 8.4, there are many distinct macro outcomes. The first step in policy development is to decide which of those outcomes—output, jobs, prices, etc.—is most worrisome. Is our first priority jobs, or are we more concerned with inflation? Is the trade deficit or the value of the dollar our most urgent concern? Naturally, we'd like to hit *all* our macro targets. But this is rarely possible, as we'll see. Hence, we've got to establish priorities.

Adopting a Policy Strategy. Once the policy goal is established, a strategy for achieving it must be formulated. In the AS/AD framework, there are really only ***three strategy options for macro policy:***

- ***Shift the aggregate demand curve.*** Find and use policy tools that stimulate or restrain total spending.
- ***Shift the aggregate supply curve.*** Find and implement policy levers that reduce the cost of production or otherwise stimulate more output at every price level.
- ***Laissez faire.*** Don't interfere with the market; let markets self-adjust.

The first two strategies assume some government intervention is needed to tame the business cycle. The third strategy places more faith in the market's ability to self-adjust.

Selecting Policy Tools. There are a host of different policy tools available for implementing any given AS/AD strategy.

Classical Laissez Faire. The laissez-faire strategy advocated by classical economists requires no tools, of course. Classical economists counted on the self-adjustment mechanisms of the market—flexible prices and wages—to bring a quick end to recessions. In this view, AS and AD curves "naturally" shift back into an optimal position, where full-employment (Q_F) prevails.

Fiscal Policy. Keynes rejected this hands-off approach. He advocated using the federal budget as a policy tool. The government can shift the AD curve to the right by spending more money. Or it can cut taxes, leaving consumers with more income to spend. The government can shift the AD curve to the left by cutting spending or raising taxes. These budgetary tools are the hallmark of fiscal policy. Specifically, **fiscal policy** is the use of government tax and spending powers to alter economic outcomes.

fiscal policy: The use of government taxes and spending to alter macroeconomic outcomes.

Monetary Policy. The budget isn't the only tool in the interventionist tool box. Interest rates and the money supply can also shift the AD curve. Lower interest rates encourage consumers to buy more big-ticket items like cars, homes, and appliances—purchases typically financed with loans. Businesses also take advantage of lower interest rates to buy more loan-financed plant and equipment. **Monetary policy** refers to the use of money and credit controls to alter economic outcomes.

monetary policy: The use of money and credit controls to influence macroeconomic outcomes.

Supply-Side Policy. Fiscal and monetary tools are used to fix the AD side of the macro economy. **Supply-side policy** pursues a different strategy: It uses tools that shift the aggregate supply curve. Tax incentives that encourage more work, saving, or investment are in the supply-side tool box. So are deregulation actions that make it easier or cheaper to supply products.

supply-side policy: The use of tax incentives, (de)regulation, and other mechanisms to increase the ability and willingness to produce goods and services.

Trade Policy. International trade and money flows offer yet another option for shifting aggregate supply and demand. A reduction in trade barriers makes imports cheaper and more available. This shifts the aggregate supply to the right, reducing price pressures at every output level. Changing the international value (exchange rate) of the dollar alters the relative price of U.S.-made goods, thereby shifting both aggregate demand and supply. Hence, trade policy is another tool in the macroeconomic toolbox.

Getting It Right. The array of tools in the macro-policy toolbox is impressive. But there are still heated arguments about which tool—if any—to use in any given situation. In the following chapters we examine these policy tools more closely. Hopefully, we'll get some more clues about how to "get it right"—to tame the business cycle—in the economy tomorrow.

SUMMARY

- The long-term growth rate of the U.S. economy is approximately 3 percent a year. But output doesn't increase 3 percent every year. In some years, real GDP grows much faster than that; in other years growth is slower. Sometimes total output actually declines. LO1
- These short-run variations in GDP growth are a central focus of macroeconomics. Macro theory tries to explain the alternating periods of growth and contraction that characterize the business cycle; macro policy attempts to control the cycle. LO1
- The primary outcomes of the macro economy are output, prices, jobs, and international balances. The outcomes result from the interplay of internal market forces, external shocks, and policy levers. LO1
- All the influences on macro outcomes are transmitted through aggregate supply or aggregate demand. Aggregate supply and demand determine the equilibrium rate of output and prices. The economy will gravitate to that unique combination of output and price levels. LO3
- The market-driven macro equilibrium may not satisfy our employment or price goals. Macro failure occurs when the economy's equilibrium isn't optimal. LO1
- Macro equilibrium may be disturbed by changes in aggregate supply (AS) or aggregate demand (AD). Such changes are illustrated by shifts of the AS and AD curves, and they lead to a new equilibrium. LO2
- Competing economic theories try to explain the shape and shifts of the aggregate supply and demand curves, thereby explaining the business cycle. Specific theories tend to emphasize demand or supply influences. LO2
- In the long run the AS curve tends to be vertical, implying that changes in aggregate demand affect prices but not output. In the short run, however, the AS curve is sloped, making macro outcomes sensitive to both supply and demand. LO3
- Macro policy options range from laissez faire (the classical approach) to various strategies for shifting either the aggregate demand curve or the aggregate supply curve. LO1

Key Terms

macroeconomics
business cycle
laissez faire
law of demand
Say's Law
real GDP
recession
growth recession
aggregate demand
aggregate supply
equilibrium (macro)
full-employment GDP
inflation
fiscal policy
monetary policy
supply-side policy

Questions for Discussion

1. If business cycles were really inevitable, what purpose would macro policy serve? LO1
2. What events might prompt consumers to demand fewer goods at current prices? LO2
3. If equilibrium is compatible with both buyers' and sellers' intentions, how can it be undesirable? LO1
4. The stock market plunge following the September 11, 2001, terrorist attacks greatly reduced the wealth of the average U.S. household. How might this have affected aggregate demand? Aggregate supply? LO2
5. What exactly did Say mean when he said "supply creates its own demand"? LO1
6. What's wrong with the classical theory of self-adjustment? Why didn't sales and employment increase in 1929–33 in response to declining prices and wages (see Figure 8.1)? LO2
7. What might have caused real GDP to decline so dramatically in (*a*) 1929 and (*b*) 1946 (see Figure 8.3)? What caused output to increase again in each case? LO3
8. How would a sudden jump in U.S. prices affect (*a*) imports from Mexico, (*b*) exports to Mexico, and (*c*) U.S. aggregate demand? LO3
9. Why might rising prices stimulate short-run production but have no effect on long-run production? LO3
10. How might a tax cut affect both AD *and* AS? LO3

problems The Student Problem Set at the back of this book contains numerical and graphing problems for this chapter.

web activities to accompany this chapter can be found on the Online Learning Center:
http://www.mhhe.com/economics/schiller11e

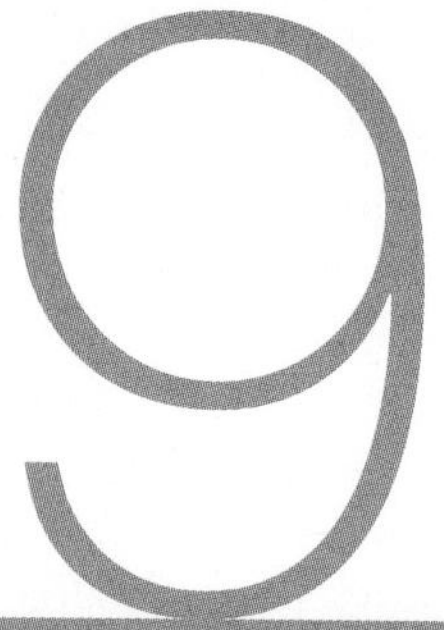

Aggregate Demand

LEARNING OBJECTIVES

After reading this chapter, you should know:

L01. The components of aggregate demand and their determinants.

L02. How and why AD shifts occur.

L03. How and when macro failure occurs.

The terrorist attacks of September 11, 2001, destroyed billions of dollars' worth of capital and killed nearly 3,000 people. As terrible as this devastation was, however, that physical damage made only a tiny dent in the $11 *trillion* production capacity of the U.S. economy. The *supply* of goods and services was relatively unscathed.

On the *demand* side of the economy the damage was much greater. The 9/11 terrorist strike instilled fear of further attacks. So much fear that Americans were hesitant to go shopping, much less travel. Businesses, too, were fearful of building new factories or equipment. As a result, aggregate demand shifted left, prolonging a recession.

Should the government have waited for the economy to self-adjust? Or should it have intervened to increase aggregate demand? We know how the British economist John Maynard Keynes would have answered this question. The Great Depression revealed the undependability of the classical self-adjustment process. Who knows how long another "self-adjustment" process might last. Rather than wait forever—until, as Keynes put it, we're all "dead"—the government should intervene to boost total spending and get the economy back on track.

In this and the next two chapters we focus on the demand side of the macro economy. We start with the same questions Keynes posed:

- **What are the components of aggregate demand?**
- **What determines the level of spending for each component?**
- **Will there be enough demand to maintain full employment?**

By working through the demand side of the macro economy, we'll get a better view of what might cause business cycles and what might cure them. Later on we'll examine the aggregate supply side more closely as well.

MACRO EQUILIBRIUM

In Chapter 8 we got a bird's-eye view of how macro equilibrium is established. Producers have some notion of how much output they're willing and able to produce at various price levels. Likewise, consumers, businesses, governments, and foreign buyers have some notion of how much output they're willing and able to buy at different price levels. These forces of **aggregate demand** and **aggregate supply** confront each other in the marketplace. Eventually, buyers and sellers discover that only one price level and output combination is acceptable to *both* sides. This is the price-output combination we designate as **(macro) equilibrium.** At equilibrium, the aggregate quantity of goods demanded exactly equals the aggregate quantity supplied. In the absence of macro disturbances, the economy will gravitate toward equilibrium.

aggregate demand: The total quantity of output demanded at alternative price levels in a given time period, *ceteris paribus.*

aggregate supply: The total quantity of output producers are willing and able to supply at alternative price levels in a given time period, *ceteris paribus.*

The Desired Adjustment

Figure 9.1 illustrates again this general view of macro equilibrium. In the figure, aggregate supply (AS) and demand (AD_1) establish an equilibrium at E_1. At this particular equilibrium, the value of real output is Q_E, significantly short of the economy's full-employment potential at Q_F. Accordingly, the economy depicted in Figure 9.1 is saddled with excessive unemployment. This is the kind of situation the U.S. economy confronted in 2001.

equilibrium (macro): The combination of price level and real output that is compatible with both aggregate demand and aggregate supply.

All economists recognize that such a *short-run* macro failure is possible. We also realize that the unemployment problem depicted in Figure 9.1 would disappear if either the AD or AS curve shifted rightward. A central macro debate is over whether the curves *will* shift on their own (self-adjust). If not, the government might have to step in and do some heavy shifting.

Components of Aggregate Demand

To assess the possibilities for self-adjustment, we need to examine the nature of aggregate demand more closely. Who's buying the output of the economy? What factors influence their purchase decisions?

We can best understand the nature of aggregate demand by breaking it down into its various components. ***The four components of aggregate demand are***

- ***Consumption (C)***
- ***Investment (I)***
- ***Government spending (G)***
- ***Net exports (X − M)***

Each of these components represents a stream of spending that contributes to aggregate demand. What we want to determine is how these various spending decisions are made. We also want to know what factors might *change* the level of spending, thereby *shifting* aggregate demand.

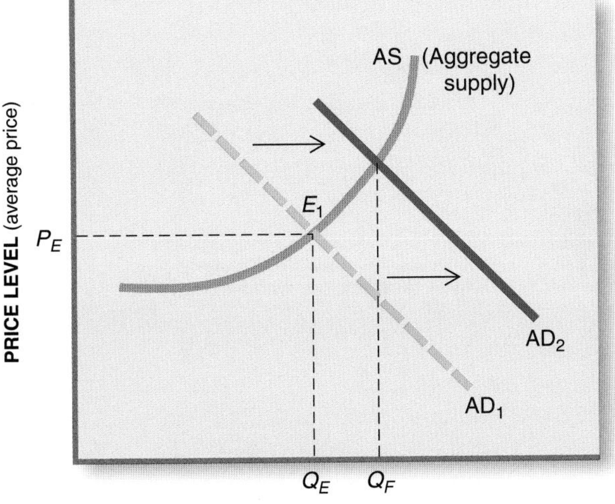

FIGURE 9.1
Escaping a Recession

Aggregate demand (AD) might be insufficient to ensure full employment (Q_F), as illustrated by the intersection of AD_1 and the aggregate supply curve. The question is whether and how AD will increase—that is, *shift* rightward—say, to AD_2. To answer these questions, the components or demand must be examined.

CONSUMPTION

consumption: Expenditure by consumers on final goods and services.

Consider first the largest component of aggregate demand, namely, **consumption.** Consumption refers to expenditures by households (consumers) on final goods and services. As we observed in Chapter 2, ***consumer expenditures account for over two-thirds of total spending.*** Hence, whatever factors alter consumer behavior are sure to have an impact on aggregate demand.

Income and Consumption

The aggregate demand curve tells us that consumers will buy more output at lower price levels with a *given* amount of income. But what if *incomes* themselves were to change? If incomes were to increase, consumers would have *more* money to spend at any given *price* level. This could cause a rightward *shift* of the AD curve, exactly the kind of move a recessionary economy (e.g., Figure 9.1) needs.

As far as Keynes was concerned, this was a no-brainer. Experience shows that ***consumers tend to spend most of whatever income they have.*** This is apparent in Figure 9.2: Year after year, consumer spending has risen in tandem with income. Hence, with *more* income, we expect *more* spending at any given price level.

disposable income: After-tax income of consumers; personal income less personal taxes.

Disposable income is the key concept here. As noted in Chapter 5, **disposable income** is the amount of income consumers actually take home after all taxes have been paid, transfers (e.g., Social Security benefits) have been received, and depreciation charges and retained earnings have been subtracted (see Table 5.6).

saving: That part of disposable income not spent on current consumption; disposable income less consumption.

What will consumers do with their disposable income? There are only two choices: They can either spend their disposable income on consumption, or they can save (not spend) it. At this point we don't care what form household **saving** might take (e.g., cash under the mattress, bank deposits, stock purchases); all we want to do is distinguish that share of disposable income spent on consumer goods and services from the remainder that is *not*

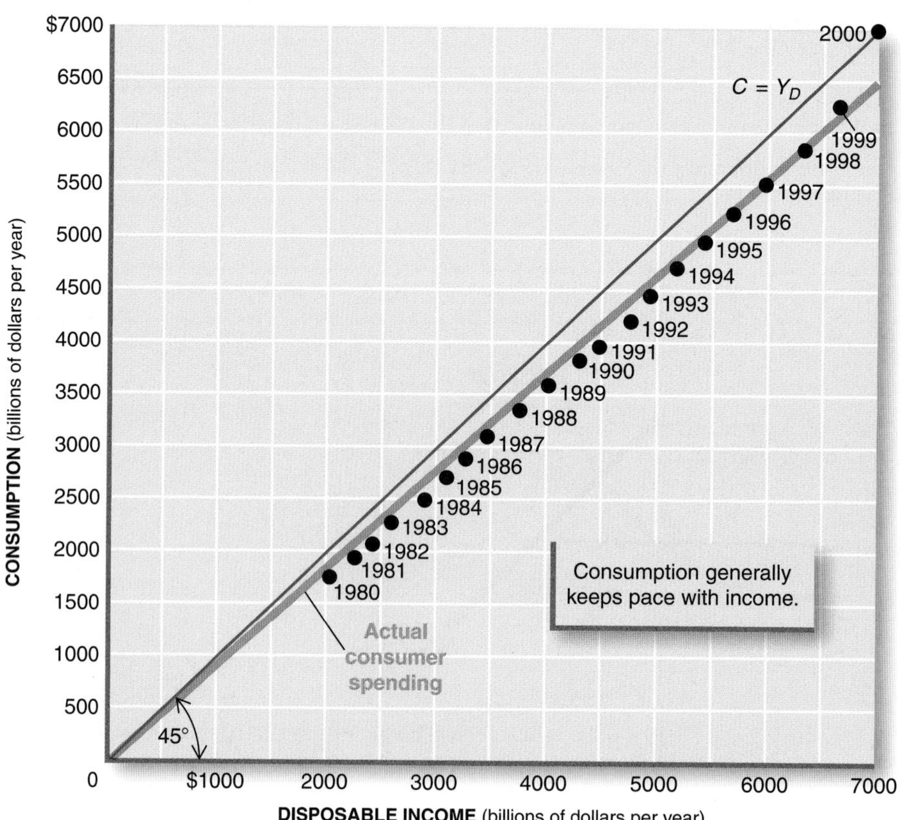

FIGURE 9.2
U.S. Consumption and Income

The points on the graph indicate the actual rates of U.S. disposable income and consumption for the years 1980–2000. By connecting these dots, we can approximate the long-term consumption function. Clearly, consumption rises with income. Indeed, consumers spend almost every extra dollar they receive.

spent. By definition, then, ***all disposable income is either consumed (spent) or saved (not spent);*** that is,

$$\underset{(Y_D)}{\text{Disposable income}} = \underset{(C)}{\text{consumption}} + \underset{(S)}{\text{saving}}$$

Consumption vs. Saving

To figure out how much consumer spending will add to aggregate demand, we need to know how much disposable income will be consumed and how much will be saved. There are two ways of looking at this decision.

APC. The proportion of *total* disposable income spent on consumer goods and services is referred to as the **average propensity to consume (APC).** To determine the APC, we simply observe how much consumers spend in a given time period out of that period's disposable income. In 2001, for example, the disposable income of U.S. households amounted to $7,469 billion. Out of this amount, consumers spent $7,342 billion and saved only $127 billion. Accordingly, we may calculate the *average* propensity to consume as

average propensity to consume (APC): Total consumption in a given period divided by total disposable income.

$$\text{APC} = \frac{\text{total consumption}}{\text{total disposable income}} = \frac{C}{Y_D}$$

For 2001 this works out to

$$\text{APC} = \frac{\$7{,}342\text{ billion}}{\$7{,}469\text{ billion}} = 0.98$$

In other words, U.S. consumers spent just about every penny they received in 2001. Specifically, consumers spent, on average, 98 cents out of every dollar of income. Only 2 cents out of every disposable dollar was saved.

The relatively high APC in the United States distinguishes our consumer-oriented economy. In recent years, the U.S. APC has even *exceeded* 1.0 on occasion, forcing U.S. households to finance some of their consumption with credit or past savings. Prior to 9/11, a lot of U.S. households were doing exactly that, as the accompanying News reports. The APC exceeded 1.0 again in 2005–2007 as consumers financed their purchases with both income and credit (see News, page 175)

The Marginal Propensity to Consume

If the APC can change from year to year, then consumers aren't always spending the same fraction of every dollar received (the APC is just an average). This led Keynes to develop a second measure of consumption behavior, called the *marginal* propensity to consume. The

IN THE NEWS

Livin' Large

Some 40% of Americans admit they live beyond their means. Seniors are the most likely to match their spending to their income, while young adults are most likely to overspend.

Source: *BusinessWeek,* August 27, 2001. Reprinted by permission. Copyright 2001 by The McGraw-Hill Companies.

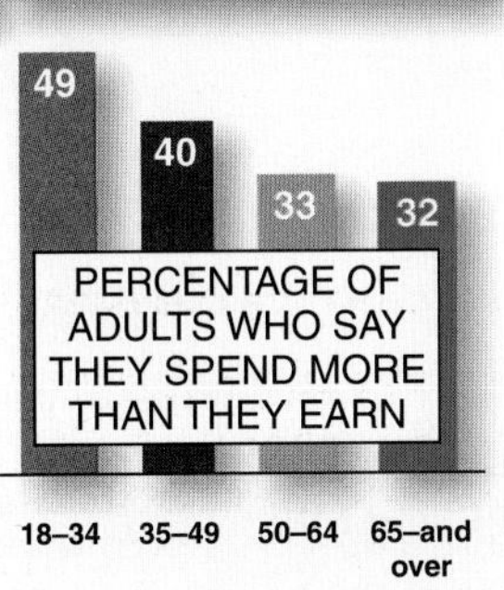

PERCENTAGE OF ADULTS WHO SAY THEY SPEND MORE THAN THEY EARN

18–34	35–49	50–64	65–and over
49	40	33	32

Data: Lutheran Brotherhood/Yankelovich Partners Survey of 1,010 Adults in January, 2001.

Analysis: When consumer spending exceeds disposable income, consumer saving is negative; households are *dis*saving. Dissaving is financed with credit or prior savings.

marginal propensity to consume (MPC): The fraction of each additional (marginal) dollar of disposable income spent on consumption; the change in consumption divided by the change in disposable income.

marginal propensity to consume (MPC) tells us how much consumer expenditure will *change* in response to *changes* in disposable income. With the delta symbol, Δ, representing "change in," MPC can be written as

$$\text{MPC} = \frac{\text{change in consumption}}{\text{change in disposable income}} = \frac{\Delta C}{\Delta Y_D}$$

To calculate the marginal propensity to consume, we could ask how consumer spending in 2001 was affected by the *last* dollar of disposable income. That is, how did consumer spending change when disposable income increased from \$7,468,999,999 to \$7,469,000,000? If consumer spending increased by 80 cents when this last \$1.00 was received, we'd calculate the *marginal* propensity to consume as

$$\text{MPC} = \frac{\Delta C}{\Delta Y_D} = \frac{\$0.80}{\$1.00} = 0.8$$

Notice that the MPC in this particular case (0.8) is lower than the APC (0.98). Suppose we had incorrectly assumed that consumers would always spend \$0.98 of every dollar's income. Then we'd have expected the rate of consumer spending to rise by 98 cents as the last dollar was received. In fact, however, the rate of spending increased by only 80 cents. In other words, consumers responded to an *increase* in their income differently than past averages implied.

No one would be upset if our failure to distinguish the APC from the MPC led to an error of only 18 cents in forecasts of consumer spending. After all, the rate of consumer spending in the U.S. economy now exceeds \$9 *trillion* per year! But those same trillion-dollar dimensions make the accuracy of the MPC that much more important. Annual *changes* in disposable income entail hundreds of billions of dollars. When we start playing with those sums—the actual focus of economic policymakers—the distinction between APC and MPC is significant.

The Marginal Propensity to Save

marginal propensity to save (MPS): The fraction of each additional (marginal) dollar of disposable income not spent on consumption; 1 − MPC.

Once we know how much of their income consumers will spend, we also know how much they'll save. Remember that all ***disposable income is, by definition, either consumed (spent on consumption) or saved.*** Saving is just whatever income is left over after consumption expenditures. Accordingly, if the MPC is 0.80, then 20 cents of each additional dollar is being saved and 80 cents is being spent (see Figure 9.3). The **marginal propensity to save (MPS)**—the fraction of each additional dollar saved (that is, *not* spent)—is simply

$$\text{MPS} = 1 - \text{MPC}$$

As Table 9.1 illustrates, if we know how much of their income consumers spend, we also know how much of it they save.

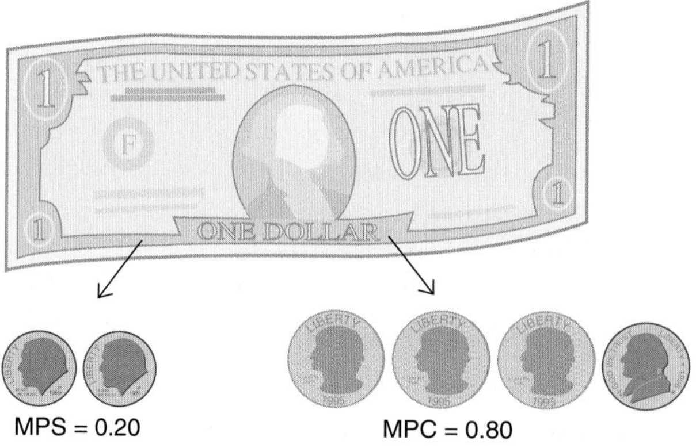

FIGURE 9.3
MPC and MPS

The marginal propensity to consume (MPC) tells us what portion of an extra dollar of income will be spent. The remaining portion will be saved. The MPC and MPS help us predict consumer behavior.

MPC. The marginal propensity to consume (MPC) is the *change* in consumption that accompanies a *change* in disposable income; that is,

$$MPC = \frac{\Delta C}{\Delta Y_D}$$

MPS. The marginal propensity to *save* (MPS) is the fraction of each additional (marginal) dollar of disposable income *not* spent—that is, saved. This is summarized as

$$MPS = \frac{\Delta S}{\Delta Y_D}$$

MPS equals 1 − MPC, since every additional dollar is either spent (consumed) or not spent (saved).

APC. The *average* propensity to consume is the proportion of *total* disposable income that's spent on consumption. It is computed:

$$APC = \frac{C}{Y_D}$$

APS. The average *propensity* to save is $\frac{S}{Y_D}$ and must equal 1 − APC.

TABLE 9.1
Average and Marginal Propensities

webnote

Go to the U.S. Bureau of Economic Activity (BEA) Web site at www.bea.doc.gov, and determine the rate of disposable income and consumer spending in the most recent two quarters. What was the APC in the most recent quarter? What was the MPC between the two quarters?

THE CONSUMPTION FUNCTION

The MPC, MPS, APC, and APS are simply statistical measures of observed consumer behavior. What we really want to know is what drives these measures. If we know, then we'll be in a position to *predict* rather than just *observe* consumer behavior. This ability would be of immense value in anticipating and controlling short-run business cycles.

Autonomous Consumption

Keynes had several ideas about the determinants of consumption. Although he observed that consumer spending and income were highly correlated (Figure 9.2), he knew consumption wasn't *completely* determined by current income. In extreme cases, this is evident. People who have no income in a given period continue to consume goods and services. They finance their purchases by dipping into their savings accounts (past income) or using credit (future income) instead of spending current income. We also observe that people's spending sometimes *changes* even when income doesn't, suggesting that income isn't the *only* determinant of consumption. Other, *non*income determinants of consumption include

- ***Expectations:*** People who anticipate a pay raise, a tax refund, or a birthday check often start spending more money even before the extra income is received. Conversely, workers who anticipate being laid off tend to save more and spend less. Hence, *expectations* may alter consumer spending before income itself changes.
- ***Wealth effects:*** The amount of wealth an individual owns also affects a person's ability and willingness to consume. A homeowner may take out a home equity loan to buy a flat-screen TV, a vacation, or a new car. In this case, consumer spending is being financed by wealth, not current income. *Changes* in wealth will also *change* consumer behavior. When the stock market rises, stockholders respond by saving less and spending more of their current income. This **wealth effect** was particularly evident in the late 1990s, when a persistent rise in the stock market helped fuel a consumption spree (and a negative savings rate). When the stock market reversed direction in 2000, consumers cut back their spending.

  Changes in housing prices have a similar effect. A 4-year surge in housing prices made consumers feel rich in 2002–5. Many homeowners tapped into those higher

wealth effect: A change in consumer spending caused by a change in the value of owned assets.

prices with home-equity loans in order to increase their consumption. When housing prices declined in 2006, this source of consumer finance dried up.

- ***Credit:*** The availability of credit allows people to spend more than their current income. On the other hand, the need to repay past debts may limit current consumption. Here again, *changes* in credit availability or cost (interest rates) may alter consumer behavior.
- ***Taxes:*** Taxes are the link between total and disposable income. The tax cuts enacted in 2001–3 put more income into consumer hands immediately (via tax rebates) and left them with more income from future paychecks (via tax-rate cuts). These tax reductions stimulated more aggregate demand at existing price levels. Were income taxes to go up, disposable incomes and consumer spending would decline.

Income-Dependent Consumption

In recognition of these many determinants of consumption, Keynes distinguished between two kinds of consumer spending: (1) spending *not* influenced by current income and (2) spending that *is* determined by current income. This simple categorization is summarized as

$$\text{Total consumption} = \begin{array}{c}\text{autonomous}\\ \text{consumption}\end{array} + \text{income-dependent consumption}$$

where *autonomous* consumption refers to that consumption spending independent of current income. The level of autonomous spending depends instead on expectations, wealth, credit, taxes, and other nonincome influences.

These various determinants of consumption are summarized in an equation called the **consumption function**, which is written as

consumption function: A mathematical relationship indicating the rate of desired consumer spending at various income levels.

$$C = a + bY_D$$

where C = current consumption
a = autonomous consumption
b = marginal propensity to consume
Y_D = disposable income

At first blush, the consumption function is just a mathematical summary of consumer behavior. It has important *predictive* power, however: ***The consumption function tells us:***

- ***How much consumption will be included in aggregate demand at the prevailing price level.***
- ***How the consumption component of AD will change (shift) when incomes change.***

One Consumer's Behavior

To see how the consumption function works, consider the plight of Justin, a college freshman who has no income. How much will Justin spend? Obviously he must spend *something,* otherwise he'll starve to death. At a very low rate of income—in this case, zero—consumer spending depends less on current income than on basic survival needs, past savings, and credit. The a in the consumption function expresses this autonomous consumption: Let's assume it's \$50 per week. Thus, the weekly rate of consumption expenditure in this case is

$$C = \$50 - bY_D$$

Now suppose that Justin finds a job and begins earning \$100 per week. Will his spending be affected? The \$50 per week he'd been spending didn't buy much. Now that he's earning a little income, Justin will want to improve his lifestyle. That is, ***we expect consumption to rise with income.*** The marginal propensity to consume tells us how fast spending will rise.

Suppose Justin responds to the new-found income by increasing his consumption from \$50 per week to \$125. The *change* in his consumption is therefore \$75. Dividing this *change* in his consumption (\$75) by the *change* in income (\$100) reveals that his marginal propensity to consume is 0.75.

Once we know the level of autonomous consumption (\$50 per week) and the marginal propensity to consume (0.75), we can predict consumer behavior with uncanny accuracy. In this case, Justin's consumption function is

$$C = \$50 + 0.75Y_D$$

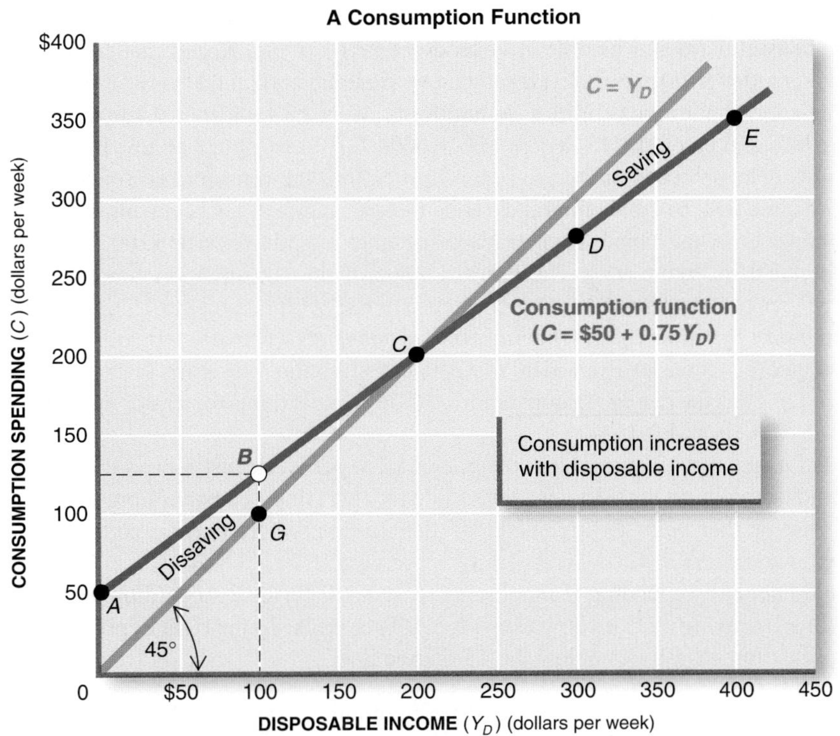

FIGURE 9.4
Justin's Consumption Function

The rate of consumer spending (C) depends on disposable income (Y_D). The marginal propensity to consume indicates how much consumption will increase with each added dollar of income. In this case, when disposable income rises from \$100 to \$200, consumption increases by \$75 (from point B to point C). The MPC = 0.75.

The consumption function can be expressed in an equation, a table, or a graph. Point B on the graph, for example, corresponds to row B in the table. Both indicate that this consumer desires to spend \$125 per week when his income is \$100 per week. The difference between income and consumption equals (dis)saving.

		Consumption (C = \$50 + 0.75 Y_D)				
	Disposable Income (Y_D)	Autonomous Consumption	+	Income Dependent Consumption	=	Total Consumption
A	\$ 0	\$50		\$ 0		\$ 50
B	100	50		75		125
C	200	50		150		200
D	300	50		225		275
E	400	50		300		350
F	500	50		375		425

With these numerical values we can advance from simple *observation* (what he's spending now) to *prediction* (what he'll spend at different income levels). Figure 9.4 summarizes this predictive power.

We've already noted that Justin will spend \$125 per week when his income is only \$100. This observation is summarized in row *B* of the table in Figure 9.4 and by point *B* on the graph. Notice that his spending exceeds his income by \$25 at this point. The other \$25 is still being begged, borrowed, or withdrawn from savings. Without peering further into Justin's personal finances, we simply say that he's **dissaving** \$25 per week. ***Dissaving occurs whenever current consumption exceeds current income.*** As the News on page 169 revealed, dissaving is common in the United States, especially among younger people who are "livin' large."

dissaving: Consumption expenditure in excess of disposable income; a negative saving flow.

If Justin's income continues to rise, he'll stop dissaving at some point. Perhaps he'll even start saving enough to pay back all the people who have sustained him through these difficult months. Figure 9.4 shows just how and when this will occur.

The 45-Degree Line. The green line in Figure 9.4, with a 45-degree angle, represents all points where consumption and income are exactly equal ($C = Y_D$). Recall that Justin currently has an income of \$100 per week. By moving up from the horizontal axis at $Y_D = \$100$, we see all the consumption possibilities he confronts. Were he to spend exactly \$100 on consumption, he'd end up on the 45-degree line at point *G*. But we already know he doesn't stop there. Instead, he proceeds further, to point *B*. At point *B* the consumption function lies above the 45-degree line, so consumption exceeds income; dissaving is occurring.

Observe, however, what happens when his disposable income rises to \$200 per week (row *C* in the table in Figure 9.4). The upward slope of the consumption function (see graph) tells us that consumption spending continues to rise with income. In fact, ***the slope of the consumption function equals the marginal propensity to consume.*** In this case, we see that when income increases from \$100 to \$200, consumption rises from \$125 (point *B*) to \$200 (point *C*). Thus the *change* in consumption (\$75) equals three-fourths of the *change* in income. The MPC is still 0.75.

Point *C* has further significance. At an income of \$200 per week Justin is no longer dissaving but is now breaking even—that is, disposable income equals consumption, so saving equals zero. Notice that point *C* lies on the 45-degree line, where current consumption equals current income.

What would happen to spending if income increased still further? According to Figure 9.4, Justin will start *saving* once income exceeds \$200 per week. To the right of point *C*, the consumption function always lies below the 45-degree line.

The Aggregate Consumption Function

Repeated studies of consumers suggest that there's nothing remarkable about Justin. The consumption function we've constructed for him can be used to depict all consumers simply by changing the numbers involved. Instead of dealing in hundreds of dollars per week, we now play with trillions of dollars per year. But the basic relationship is the same. This aggregate relationship between consumption spending and disposable income was already observed in Figure 9.2, and is confirmed again in the News at the top of the next page.

Shifts of the Consumption Function

Although the consumption function is a handy device for predicting consumer behavior, it's not infallible. People change their behavior. Neither autonomous consumption (the *a* in the consumption function) nor the marginal propensity to consume (the *b* in $C = a + bY_D$) is set in stone. Whenever one of these parameters changes, the entire consumption function moves. A change in *a shifts* the consumption function up or down; a change in *b* alters the *slope* of the function.

Consider first the value for *a*. We noted earlier that autonomous consumption depends on wealth, credit, expectations, taxes, and price levels. If any of these nonincome determinants changes, the value of the *a* in the consumption function will change as well.

We noted earlier how the 9/11 terrorist attacks heightened fears for both physical and economic security. Market disruptions and job layoffs added to the sense of insecurity. All these pressures derailed consumer confidence. Hurricane Katrina also shook consumer confidence, as the News at the bottom of the next page reports. As a result of plunging confidence, the value of autonomous consumption declined from a_1 to a_2 and the consumption function *shifted* downward, as in Figure 9.5 on page 176.

Shifts of Aggregate Demand. Shifts of the consumption function are reflected in shifts of the aggregate demand curve. Consider again the October 2001 downward shift of the consumption function. A decrease in consumer spending at any given income level implies a decrease in aggregate demand as well. Recall that the aggregate demand curve depicts how much real output will be demanded at various price levels, *with income held constant.* When the consumption function shifts downward, households spend less of their income. Hence, less real output is demanded at any given price level. To summarize,

- ***A downward shift of the consumption function implies a leftward shift of the aggregate demand curve.***
- ***An upward shift of the consumption function implies an increase (a rightward shift) in aggregate demand.***

IN THE NEWS

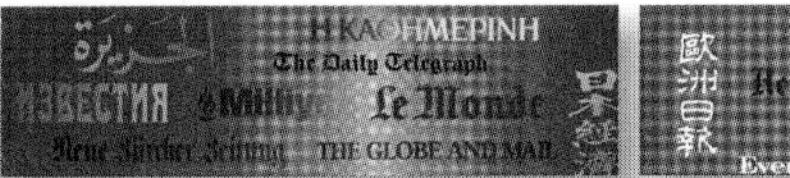
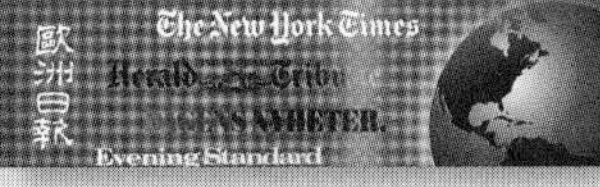

News Release: Personal Income and Outlays

Personal Income and Outlays: January 2007

Personal income increased $108.1 billion, or 1.0 percent, and disposable personal income (DPI) increased $73.0 billion, or 0.8 percent, in January, according to the Bureau of Economic Analysis. Personal consumption expenditures (PCE) increased $51.9 billion, or 0.5 percent.

Personal saving—DPI less personal outlays—was a negative $116.4 billion in January, compared with a negative $134.2 billion in December. Personal saving as a percentage of disposable personal income was a negative 1.2 percent in January, compared with a negative 1.4 percent in December. Negative personal saving reflects personal outlays that exceed disposable personal income. Saving from current income may be near zero or negative when outlays are financed by borrowing (including borrowing financed through credit cards or home equity loans), by selling investments or other assets, or by using savings from previous periods. For more information, see the FAQs on "Personal Saving" on BEA's Web site.

	December 2006	January 2007
Personal income	11,117	11,225
Disposable personal income	9,720	9,793
Personal outlays	9,854	9,910
Personal savings	–134	–117

Source: U.S. Bureau of Economic Analysis, March 1, 2007

Analysis: When household incomes increase, consumer spending increases as well. The marginal propensity to consume summarizes this relationship.

IN THE NEWS

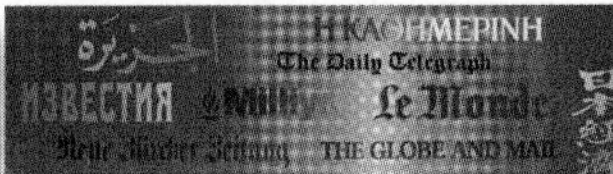
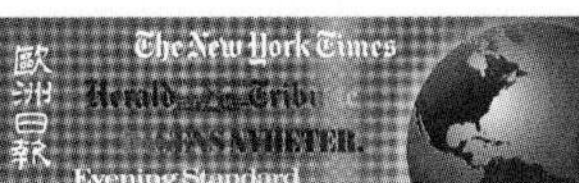

Consumer Confidence Takes Big Dive

WASHINGTON—Consumer confidence took the biggest tumble in 15 years in September, as Americans grappled with soaring energy prices after Hurricane Katrina, the New York-based Conference Board said Tuesday.

Economists said that while the September consumer confidence figures were not good news, they did not necessarily mean a dramatic slowdown in consumer spending, about two-thirds of the economy. The outlook depends on the pace of job growth and how far gasoline prices decline from recent highs of more than $3 a gallon.

"Accept this for what it is: an emotional reaction to tragic circumstances. But are people going to stop spending? No," says Ken Mayland of ClearView Economics.

But in one particularly worrying sign, the Consumer Confidence gauge of expected inflation showed the biggest jump since it was started in 1987.

Overall, the index plunged to 86.6, from August's 105.5—the sixth-largest drop in index history. The percentage of consumers calling business conditions "good" fell to 25.2% from 29.7% in August. The largest erosion was in future expectations, with 19.8% expecting the business environment to sour, up from 10%, and 25% expecting fewer jobs ahead, up from 17.3% in August.

—Sue Kirchhoff

Source: *USA TODAY*, September 28, 2005, p. B1. Reprinted with permission

Analysis: When consumer confidence declines, autonomous spending drops and the consumption function shifts downward (as in Figure 9.5). This causes a leftward shift of the AD curve (as in Figure 9.6).

These relationships are illustrated in Figure 9.6.

AD Shift Factors

Keep in mind that we need to know how much consumer spending will contribute to AD at any given price level. We get that information from the consumption function. That information helps us position the AD curve correctly. Then we want to know what might cause the AD curve to *shift*. We now know that ***the AD curve will shift if consumer incomes***

FIGURE 9.5
A Shift in the Consumption Function

Consumers' willingness to spend current income is affected by their confidence in the future. If consumers become more worried or pessimistic, autonomous consumption may decrease from a_1 to a_2. This change will shift the entire consumption function downward.

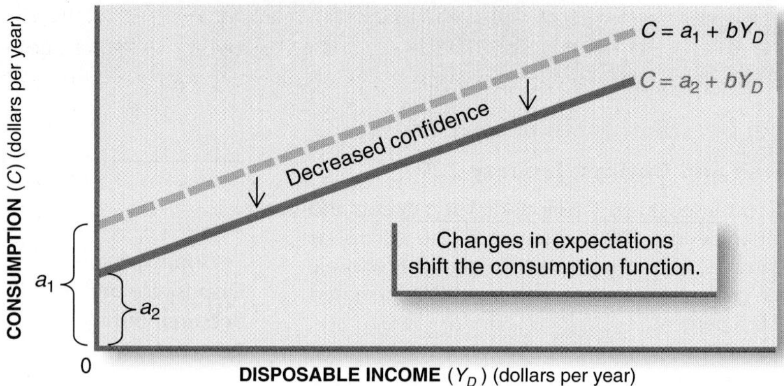

change or autonomous consumption changes. The shift factors that can alter autonomous consumption include

- Changes in expectations (consumer confidence).
- Changes in wealth.
- Changes in credit conditions.
- Changes in tax policy.

As we've observed, consumer expectations can change in a heartbeat (e.g., 9/11 attacks, Hurricane Katrina). The value of consumer wealth can also change dramatically. From mid-1997 to mid-2006, the real value of home prices rose by an astonishing \$6.5 *trillion.* With greater wealth, consumers were willing to spend more at every income level (an upward shift of the consumption function). According to a 2007 study by the Congressional Budget Office, this wealth effect added \$130–\$460 billion to annual consumption (and drove the marginal propensity to save into negative territory).

Shifts and Cycles

Shifts of aggregate demand can be a cause of macro instability. As we first observed in Chapter 8, recurrent shifts of aggregate demand may cause real output to alternately expand

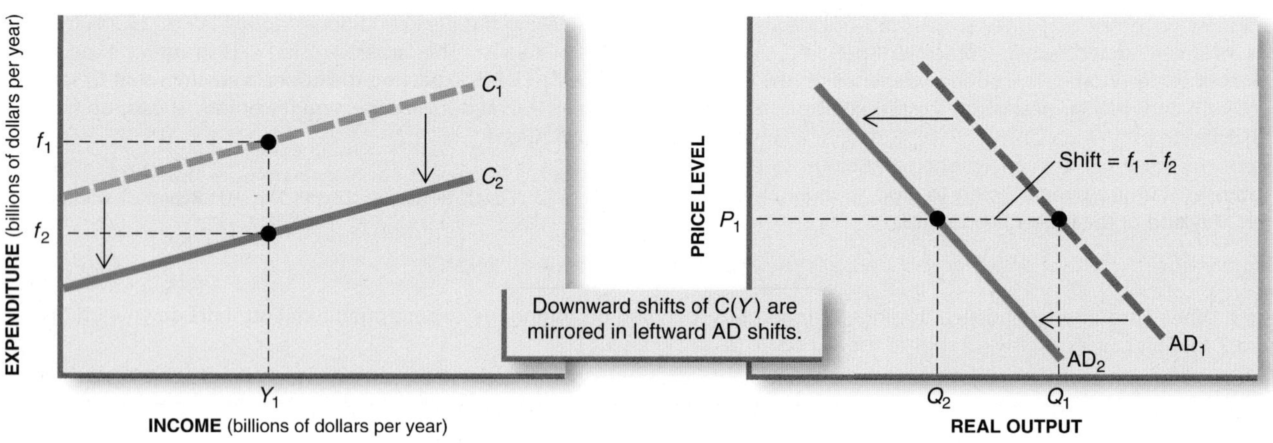

FIGURE 9.6
AD Effects of Consumption Shifts

A downward shift of the consumption function implies that households want to spend less of their income. Here consumption at the income level Y_1 decreases from f_1 to f_2. This decreased expenditure is reflected in a leftward shift of the aggregate demand curve. At the initial price level P_1 consumers demanded Q_1 output. At that same price level, consumers now demand less output, Q_2 [$= Q_1 - (f_1 - f_2)$].

and contract, thereby giving rise to short-run business cycles. What we've observed here is that those aggregate demand shifts may originate in consumer behavior. Changes in consumer confidence, in wealth, or in credit conditions alter the rate of consumer spending. If consumer spending increases abruptly, demand-pull inflation may follow. If consumer spending slows abruptly, a recession may occur.

Knowing that consumer behavior *might* cause macro problems is a bit worrisome. But it's also a source of policy power. What if we *want* AD to increase in order to achieve full employment? Our knowledge of consumer-based AD shift factors gives us huge clues about which macro policy tools to look for.

INVESTMENT

Consumption is only one of four AD components. To determine where AD is and when it might shift, we need to examine the other components of spending as well.

Determinants of Investment

As we observed in Chapter 5, investment spending accounts for roughly 15 percent of total output. That spending includes not only expenditures on new plant, equipment, and business software (all referred to as *fixed investment*) but also spending on inventories (called *inventory investment*). Residential construction is also counted in investment statistics because houses and apartment buildings continue to produce housing services for decades. All these forms of **investment** represent a demand for output.

investment: Expenditures on (production of) new plant, equipment, and structures (capital) in a given time period, plus changes in business inventories.

Expectations. Expectations play a critical role in investment decisions. No firm wants to purchase new plant and equipment unless it is convinced people will later buy the output produced by that plant and that equipment. Nor do producers want to accumulate inventories of goods unless they expect consumers to eventually buy them. Thus, ***favorable expectations of future sales are a necessary condition for investment spending.***

Interest Rates. A second determinant of investment spending is the rate of interest. Business firms typically borrow money in order to purchase plant and equipment. The higher the rate of interest, the costlier it is to invest. Accordingly, we anticipate a lower rate of investment spending when interest rates are high, more investment at lower rates, *ceteris paribus.*

Technology and Innovation. A third determinant of investment is changes in technology and innovation. When scientists learned how to miniaturize electronic circuitry, an entire new industry of electronic calculators, watches, and other goods sprang to life. In this case, the demand for investment goods shifted to the right as a result of improved miniaturized circuits and imaginative innovation (the use of the new technology in pocket calculators). More recently, technological advances and cost reductions have stimulated an investment spree in digital music players, laptop computers, cellular phones, video conferencing, fiber-optic networks, and anything associated with the Internet.

The curve I_1, in Figure 9.7, depicts the general shape of the investment function. To find the rate of investment spending in this figure, we simply have to know the rate of interest. At an interest rate of 8 percent, for example, we expect to see \$150 billion of investment (point *A* in Figure 9.7). At 6 percent interest, we'd expect \$300 billion of investment (point *B*).

Shifts of Investment

These predictions about investment spending depend on a critical assumption; namely, that investor expectations are stable. In truth, that's a very tenuous assumption. While no one is entirely sure what shapes investors' expectations, experience shows that they are often quite volatile.

Altered Expectations. Business expectations are essentially a question of confidence in future sales. An upsurge in current consumer spending could raise investor expectations for future sales, shifting the investment function rightward (to I_2). New business software might induce a similar response. New business tax breaks might have the same effect. If

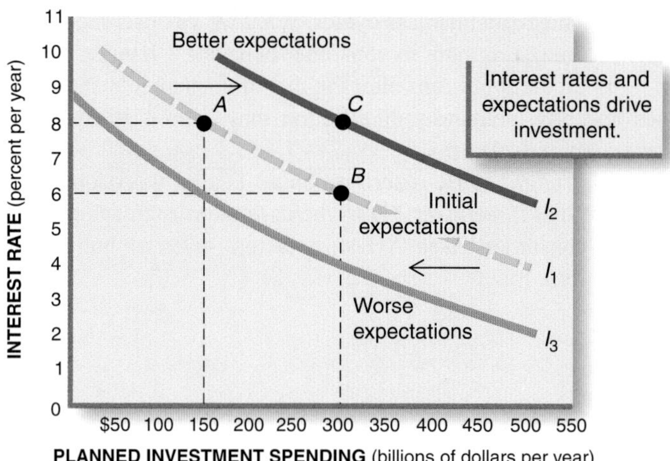

FIGURE 9.7
Investment Demand

The rate of desired investment depends on expectations, the rate of interest, and innovation. A *change* in expectations will *shift* the investment-demand curve. With given expectations, a change in the rate of interest will lead to *movements* along the existing investment-demand curve. In this case, an increase in investment beyond $150 billion per year (point *A*) may be caused by lower interest rates (point *B*) or improved expectations (point *C*).

any of these things happened, businesses would be more eager to invest. They'd borrow *more* money at any given interest rate (e.g., point *C* in Figure 9.7) and use it to buy more plant, equipment, and inventory.

Business expectations could worsen as well. The terrorist strikes of September 11, 2001, put a lot of investment plans on hold (see News). A transportation strike or spike in oil prices might worsen sales expectations as well. These kinds of events will shift the investment function leftward, as to I_3 in Figure 9.7.

AD Shifts. As was the case with consumer behavior, we are looking at investor behavior to help us understand aggregate demand. From Figure 9.7 we see that knowledge of investor expectations and interest rates will tell us how much investment will be included in aggregate demand at the current price level. We also see that a change in expectations will alter investment behavior and thereby *shift* the AD curve. ***When investment spending declines, the aggregate demand curve shifts to the left.***

IN THE NEWS

Small-Business Owners Pare Spending, Fearing Sales Will Dwindle After Attacks

Small-business owners expect the Sept. 11 terrorist attacks will sap fourth-quarter sales and have cut back fast on hiring and other spending plans. . . .

A survey by the National Federation of Independent Business, a small-business lobbying group in Washington, found during the days after the attacks on the World Trade Center and Pentagon a sharp downturn in expectations of sales growth for the next three months. . . .

The lower sales expectations led business owners to pare plans to hire workers, invest in capital equipment and in inventory, the NFIB said. That collective hunkering down would, of course, contribute further to recessionary pressures. . . .

Capital-spending plans in the post-Sept. 11 period were at their lowest level in the survey's 15-year history, and hiring plans were at the lowest level since 1993.

—Jeff Bailey

Source: *The Wall Street Journal,* October 3, 2001.

Analysis: Business investment is based more on expected future sales than on current sales and income. When expectations for future sales growth diminish, investment spending on plant, equipment, and inventory drops.

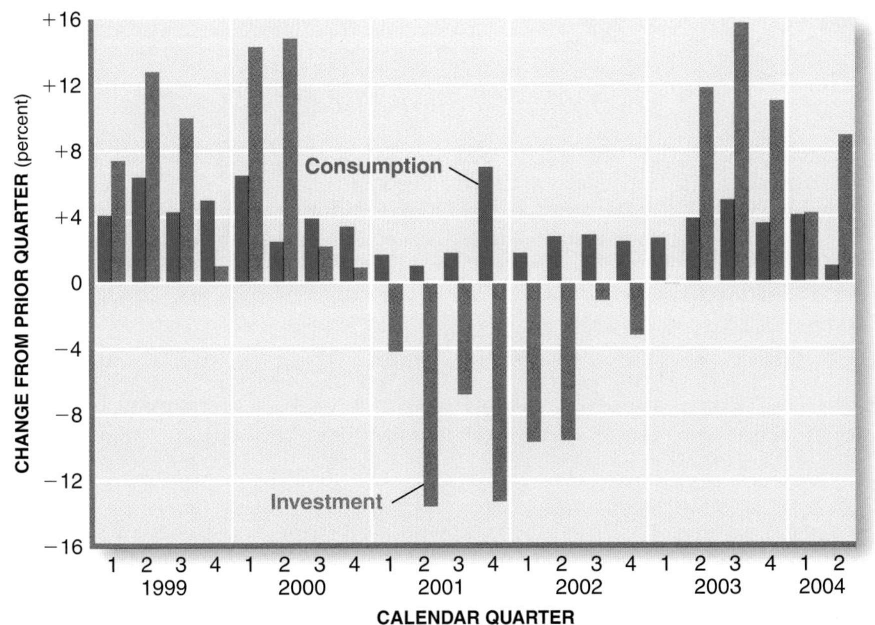

FIGURE 9.8
Volatile Investment Spending

Investment spending fluctuates more than consumption. Shown here are the quarter-to-quarter changes in the real rate of spending for fixed investment (excluding residential construction and inventory changes) and total consumption. Notice the sharp drops in investment spending just prior to the recession that began in March 2001 and again after the 9/11 attacks.

Source: *U.S. Bureau of Economic Analysis* (quarterly data seasonally adjusted).

Empirical Instability. Figure 9.8 shows that unstable investment is more than just a theoretical threat to macro stability. What is depicted here are the quarter-to-quarter changes in both consumer spending and investor spending for the years 1999–2004. Quarterly changes in *consumer* spending never exceeded 7 percent and never became negative. By contrast, *investment* spending plummeted by 13.3 percent in the post-9/11 quarter and jumped by over 14 percent in three other quarters. Those abrupt changes in investment (and related AD shifts) were a major cause of the 2001 recession and also an important source of subsequent recovery.

webnote

Check the U.S. Bureau of Economic Activity (BEA) Web site at www.stat-usa.gov to see how much seasonally adjusted investment has varied in percentage terms over the past six quarters.

GOVERNMENT AND NET EXPORT SPENDING

The apparent volatility of investment spending heightens rather than soothes anxiety about short-run macro instability. Together, consumption and investment account for over 80 percent of total output. As we have seen, the investment component of aggregate demand can be both uncertain and unstable. The consumption component of aggregate demand may shift abruptly as well. Such shifts can sow the seeds of macro failure. Will the other components of aggregate demand improve the odds of macro success? What determines the level of government and net export spending? How stable are they?

Government Spending

At present, the government sector (federal, state, and local) spends over $2 trillion on goods and services, all of which is part of aggregate demand (unlike income transfers, which are not). As we observed in Chapter 2, about two-thirds of this spending occurs at the state and local levels. That nonfederal spending is limited by tax receipts, because state and local governments can't deficit-spend. As a consequence, state and local spending is slightly procyclical, with expenditure rising as the economy (and tax receipts) expands and declining when the economy (and tax receipts) slumps. This doesn't auger well for macro stability, much less "self-adjustment." ***If consumption and investment spending decline, the subsequent decline in state-local government spending will aggravate rather than offset the leftward shift of the AD curve.***

Federal spending on goods and services isn't so constrained by tax receipts. Uncle Sam can *borrow* money, thereby allowing federal spending to exceed tax receipts. In fact, the federal government typically operates "in the red," with large annual budget deficits. This gives the federal government a unique *counter*-cyclical power. If private-sector spending

WORLD VIEW

Canada Forecasts Slower 2001 Growth, Citing U.S. "Spillover"

OTTAWA—Citing the impact of the slowing U.S. economy, the Bank of Canada lowered its forecast of gross domestic product growth this year to about 3 percent from a previous range of 3 percent to 4 percent.

In a revision of its monetary-policy report of last November, Canada's central bank said "the slowdown of the U.S. economy has been more abrupt than anticipated," and has had a "spillover effect" on Canada. More than 85 percent of Canadian exports go to the U.S.

Bank of Canada governor David Dodge said yesterday the economy is now likely to grow at the low end of the bank's 3–4 percent forecast made in November. The bank said that it estimates the Canadian economy grew last year by 5 percent.

The bank also said it expects total consumer price inflation to ease to an annual pace of 2 percent by the end of this year, reflecting declines in oil prices.

—Joel Baglole

Analysis: Most Canadian exports go to the United States. So when the U.S. economy slows, Canada experiences a decline in export demand—a leftward shift in that country's aggregate demand.

and incomes decline, federal tax revenues will fall in response. Unlike state and local governments, however, the federal government can *increase* its spending despite declining tax revenues. In other words, Uncle Sam can help reverse AD shifts by changing its own spending. This is exactly the kind of government action that Keynes advocated. We examine its potential more closely in Chapter 11.

Net Exports

The fourth and final source of aggregate demand is net exports. Our gross exports depend on the spending behavior of foreign consumers and businesses. If foreign consumers and investors behave like Americans, their demand for U.S. products will be subject to changes in *their* income, expectations, wealth, and other factors. In the Asian currency crisis of 1997–99, this was alarmingly evident: Once incomes in Asia began falling, U.S. exports to Asia of rice, corn, lumber, computers, and other goods and services fell sharply. So did the number of Asian students applying to U.S. colleges (a demand for U.S.-produced educational services). This decline in export spending represented a leftward shift of U.S. aggregate demand. The same kind of shift occurred in Canada's aggregate demand when the U.S. economy slowed in early 2001 (see World View).

Imports, too, can be unstable, and for the same reasons. Most U.S. imports are consumer goods and services. Imports, therefore, just get caught up in the ebb and flow of consumer spending. When consumer confidence slips or the stock market dips, import spending declines along with the rest of consumption (and investment). As a consequence, *net* exports can be both uncertain and unstable, creating further shifts of aggregate demand.

The AD Curve

Figure 9.9 illustrates how the four components of spending come together to determine aggregate demand. From the consumption function we determine how much output consumers will demand at the prevailing price level P_O. In this case, they demand Q_C of output. To that amount, we add investment demand Q_I, as revealed in Figure 9.7 and investor surveys. Local, state, and federal budgets will tell us how much output (Q_G) the government intends to buy. Net exports complete the computation. When we add them all up, we see that output Q_O will be demanded at the prevailing price level P_O. Hence, the AD curve must go through point *d.* The rest of the AD curve reflects how the quantity of output demanded will change if the price level rises or falls (i.e., the real-balances, interest-rate, and foreign-trade effects).

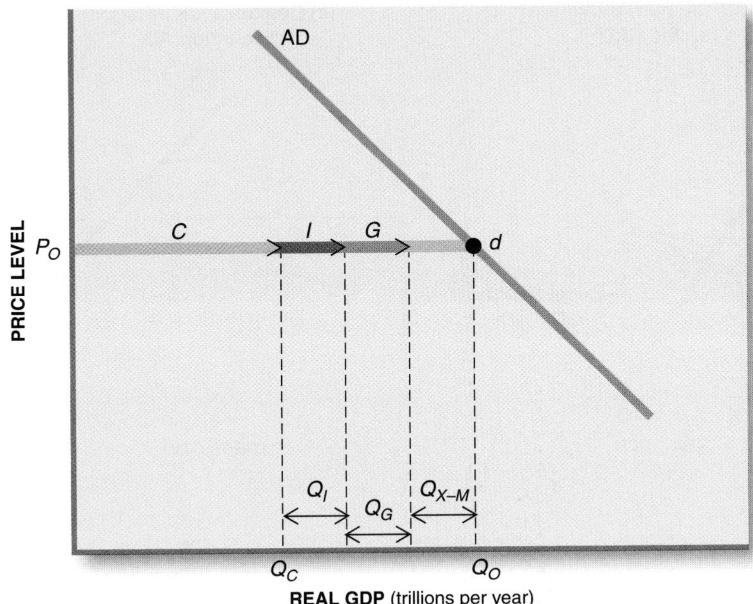

FIGURE 9.9
Building an AD Curve

The quantity of output demanded at the prevailing price level originates in the spending decisions of consumers (*C*), investors (*I*), government (*G*), and net exports (*X* – *M*). By adding up the intended spending of these market participants we can see how much output (Q_O) will be demanded at the current price level (P_O).

The slope of the AD curve above and below point *d* is based on the real-balances, interest-rate, and foreign-trade responses to changing price levels (see pages 152–154).

MACRO FAILURE

In principle, the construction of the AD curve is simple. In practice, it requires an enormous amount of information about the intentions and behavior of market participants. Let's assume for the moment, however, that we have all that information and can therefore accurately depict the AD curve. What then?

Once we know the shape and position of the AD curve we can put it together with the AS curve and locate macro equilibrium. Here's where our macro problems may emerge. As we noted earlier, ***there are two chief concerns about macro equilibrium, namely,***

1. ***The market's macro equilibrium might not give us full employment or price stability.***
2. ***Even if the market's macro equilibrium were perfectly positioned (i.e., with full employment and price stability), it might not last.***

Undesired Equilibrium

Figure 9.10*a* depicts the perfect macro equilibrium that everyone hopes for. Aggregate demand and aggregate supply intersect at E_1. At that macro equilibrium we get both full employment (Q_F) and price stability (P^*)—an ideal situation.

Keynes didn't think such a perfect outcome was likely. Why should aggregate demand intersect with aggregate supply exactly at point E_1? As we've observed, consumers, investors, government, and foreigners make independent spending decisions, based on many influences. Why should all these decisions add up to just the right amount of aggregate demand? Keynes didn't think they would. ***Because market participants make independent spending decisions, there's no reason to expect that the sum of their expenditures will generate exactly the right amount of aggregate demand.*** Instead, there's a high likelihood that we'll confront an imbalance between desired spending and full-employment output levels—that is, too much or too little aggregate demand.

Recessionary GDP Gap. Figure 9.10*b* illustrates one of the undesired equilibriums that Keynes worried about. **Full-employment GDP** is still at Q_F and stable prices are at the level P^*. In this case, however, the rate of output demanded at price level P^* is only Q_2, far short of full-employment GDP (Q_F). How could this happen? Quite simple: The spending plans of consumers, investors, government, and export buyers don't generate enough aggregate demand at current (P^*) prices.

full-employment GDP: The value of total output (real GDP) produced at full employment.

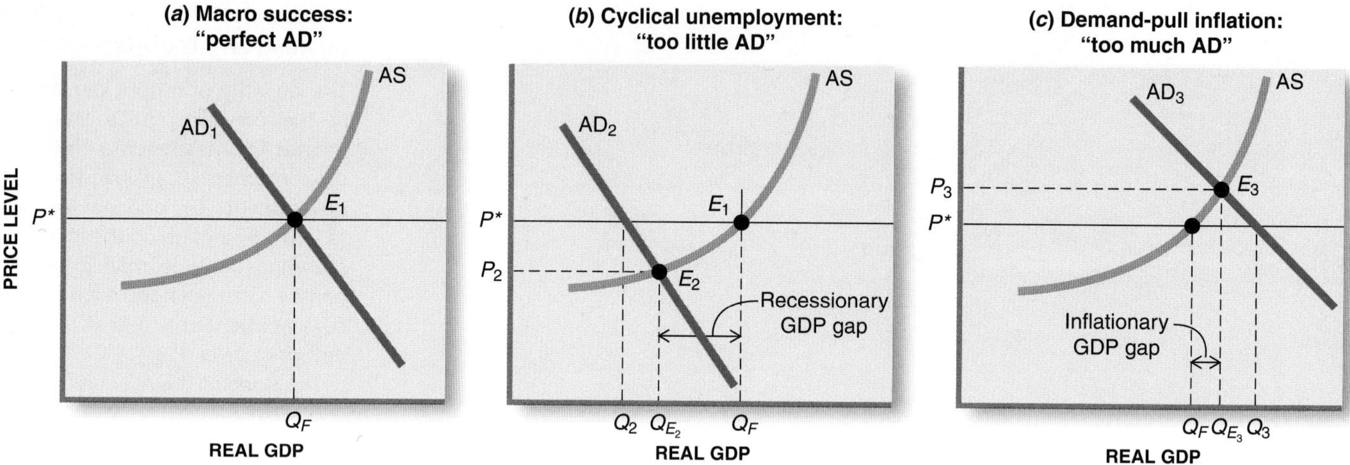

FIGURE 9.10
Macro Failures

Keynesian theory emphasizes that the combined spending decisions of consumers, investors, governments, and net exporters may not be compatible with the desired full employment (Q_F)–price stability (P^*) equilibrium (as they are in Figure *a*). Aggregate demand may be too small (Figure *b*) or too great (Figure *c*) causing cyclical unemployment (*b*) or demand-pull inflation (*c*). Worse yet, even a desirable macro equilibrium (*a*) may be upset by abrupt *shifts* of aggregate demand.

The economy depicted in Figure 9.10*b* is in trouble. At full employment, a lot more output would be produced than market participants would be willing to buy. As unsold inventories rose, production would get cut back, workers would get laid off, and prices would decline. Eventually, the economy would settle at E_2, where AD_2 and AS intersect. **Equilibrium GDP** would be equal to Q_{E2} and the equilibrium price level would be at P_2.

equilibrium GDP: The value of total output (real GDP) produced at macro equilibrium (AS = AD).

E_2 is clearly not a happy equilibrium. What particularly concerned Keynes was the **recessionary GDP gap,** the amount by which equilibrium GDP falls short of full-employment GDP. In Figure 9.10*b*, the recessionary GDP gap equals Q_F minus Q_{E2}. This gap represents unused productive capacity: lost GDP and unemployed workers. It is the breeding ground of **cyclical unemployment.**

recessionary GDP gap: The amount by which equilibrium GDP falls short of full-employment GDP.

cyclical unemployment: Unemployment attributable to a lack of job vacancies; that is, to inadequate aggregate demand.

Figure 9.11 illustrates this dilemma with more details on aggregate demand. The table depicts the demand for GDP at different price levels by consumers, investors, government, and net export buyers. Full-employment GDP is set at $10 trillion and the price level at 100. As is evident, however, the quantity of output demanded at that price level is only $8 trillion. This shortfall of aggregate demand will lead to output and price reductions, pushing the economy downward to equilibrium GDP, at point *E*. At that AS = AD intersection, the *equilibrium* GDP is at $9 trillion, with a price level of 90. The recessionary GDP gap is therefore $1 trillion ($Q_F - Q_E$).

Inflationary GDP Gap. Aggregate demand won't always fall short of potential output. But Keynes saw it as a distinct possibility. He also realized that aggregate demand might even *exceed* the economy's full-employment/price stability capacity. This contingency is illustrated in Figure 9.10*c*.

In Figure 9.10*c*, the AD_3 curve represents the combined spending plans of all market participants. According to this aggregate demand curve, market participants demand more output (Q_3) at current prices than the economy can produce (Q_F). To meet this excessive demand, producers will use overtime shifts and strain capacity. This will push prices up. The economy will end up at the macro equilibrium E_3. At E_3 the price level is higher (inflation) and short-run output exceeds sustainable levels.

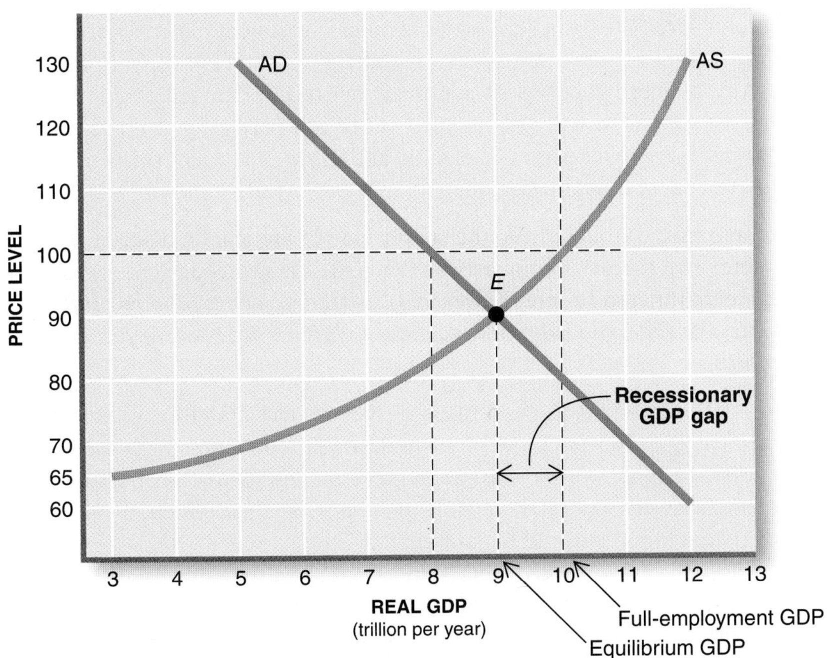

FIGURE 9.11

A Recessionary GDP Gap

The level of aggregate demand depends on the spending behavior of market participants. In this case, the level of GDP demanded at current prices (P = 100) ($8 trillion) is less than full-employment GDP ($10 trillion). This results in a lower equilibrium GDP ($9 trillion) and a recessionary GDP gap ($1 trillion). The price level also declines from 100 to 90.

	Real GDP Demanded (in $ trillions) by:					
Price Level	Consumers +	Investors +	Government +	Net Exports =	Aggregate Demand	Aggregate Supply
130	3.0	0.25	1.5	0.25	5.0	12.0
120	3.5	0.50	1.5	0.50	6.0	11.5
110	4.0	0.75	1.5	0.75	7.0	11.0
100	4.5	1.00	1.5	1.0	8.0	10.0
90	5.0	1.25	1.5	1.25	9.0	9.0
80	5.5	1.50	1.5	1.50	10.0	7.0
70	6.0	1.75	1.5	1.75	11.0	5.0
60	6.5	2.0	1.5	2.0	12.0	3.0

What we end up with in Figure 9.10*c* is another undesirable equilibrium. In this case we have an **inflationary GDP gap,** wherein equilibrium GDP (Q_{E3}) exceeds full-employment GDP (Q_F). This is a fertile breeding ground for **demand-pull inflation.**

inflationary GDP gap: The amount by which equilibrium GDP exceeds full-employment GDP.

demand-pull inflation: An increase in the price level initiated by excessive aggregate demand.

The GDP gaps illustrated in Figure 9.10*b* and *c* are clearly troublesome. In a nutshell,

- ***The goal is to produce at full employment, but***
- ***Equilibrium GDP may be greater or less than full-employment GDP.***

Whenever equilibrium GDP differs from full-employment GDP, we confront a macro failure (unemployment or inflation).

Unstable Equilibrium

Things need not always work out so badly. Although Keynes thought it improbable, the spending plans of market participants *might* generate the perfect amount of aggregate demand, leaving the economy at the desired macro equilibrium depicted in Figure 9.10*a*. In Figure 9.10*a*, equilibrium GDP equals full-employment GDP. Unfortunately, that happy outcome might not last.

As we've observed, market participants may change their spending behavior abruptly. The stock market may boom or bust, shifting the consumption component of aggregate demand. Changed sales forecasts (expectations) may alter investment plans. Crises in foreign economies may disrupt export sales. A terrorist attack or outbreak of war may rock everybody's boat. Any of these events will cause the aggregate demand curve to shift. When this happens, the AD curve will get knocked out of its "perfect" position in Figure 9.10*a*, sending us to undesirable outcomes like 9.10*b* and 9.10*c*. Recurrent shifts of aggregate demand could even cause a **business cycle.**

business cycle: Alternating periods of economic growth and contraction.

Macro Failures

Economies can get into macro trouble from the supply side of the market place as well, as we'll see later (Chapter 16). Keynes's emphasis on demand-side inadequacies serves as an early warning of potential macro failure, however. ***If aggregate demand is too little, too great, or too unstable, the economy will not reach and maintain the goals of full employment and price stability.***

Self-Adjustment?

As we noted earlier, not everyone is as pessimistic as Keynes was about the prospects for macro bliss. The critical question is not whether undesirable outcomes might *occur* but whether they'll *persist.* In other words, the seriousness of any short-run macro failure depends on how markets *respond* to GDP gaps. If markets self-adjust, as classical economists asserted, then macro failures would be temporary.

How might markets self-adjust? If investors stepped up *their* spending whenever consumer spending faltered, the right amount of aggregate demand could be maintained. Such self-adjustment requires that some components of aggregate demand shift in the right direction at just the right time. In other words, self-adjustment requires that any shortfalls in one component of aggregate demand be offset by spending in another component. If such offsetting shifts occurred, then the desired macro equilibrium in Figure 9.10*a* could be maintained. Keynes didn't think that likely, however, for reasons we'll explore in the next chapter.

THE ECONOMY TOMORROW

ANTICIPATING AD SHIFTS

The Index of Leading Indicators. Keynes's theory of macro failure gave economic policymakers a lot to worry about. If Keynes was right, abrupt changes in aggregate demand could ruin even the best of economic times. Even if he was wrong about the ability of the economy to self-adjust, sudden shifts of aggregate demand could cause a lot of temporary pain. To minimize such pain, policymakers need some way of peering into the future—to foresee shifts of aggregate demand. With such a crystal ball, they might be able to take defensive actions and keep the economy on track.

Market participants have developed all kinds of crystal balls for anticipating AD shifts. The Foundation for the Study of Cycles has identified 4,000 different crystal balls people use to foretell changes in spending. They include the ratio of used-car to new-car sales (it rises in economic downturns); the number of divorce petitions (it rises in bad times); animal population cycles (they peak just before economic downturns); and even the optimism/pessimism content of popular music (a reflection of consumer confidence).

One of the most widely used crystal balls is the Index of Leading Indicators. What's appealing about that index is the plausible connection between its components and future spending. Equipment orders, for example, is one of the leading indicators (number 6 in Table 9.2). This seems eminently reasonable, since businesses don't order equipment unless they later plan to buy it. The same is true of building permits (indicator 10); people obtain permits only if they plan to build something. Hence, both indicators appear to be dependable signs of future investment.

Unfortunately, the Leading Indicators aren't a perfect crystal ball. Equipment orders are often canceled. Building plans get delayed or abandoned. Hence, shifts of aggregate

TABLE 9.2
The Leading Economic Indicators

Everyone wants a crystal ball to foresee economic events. In reality, forecasters must reckon with very crude predictors of the future. One of the most widely used predictors is the Index of Leading Economic Indicators, which includes 11 factors believed to predict economic activity 3 to 6 months in advance. Changes in the leading indicators are used to forecast changes in GDP.

The leading indicators rarely move in the same direction at the same time. They're weighted together to create the index. Up-and-down movements of the index are reported each month by the nonprofit Conference Board.

Indicator	Expected Impact
1. Average workweek	Hours worked per week typically increase when greater output and sales are expected.
2. Unemployment claims	Initial claims for unemployment benefits reflect changes in industry layoffs.
3. Delivery times	The longer it takes to deliver ordered goods, the greater the ratio of demand to supply.
4. Credit	Changes in business and consumer borrowing indicate potential purchasing power.
5. Materials prices	When producers step up production they buy more raw materials, pushing their prices higher.
6. Equipment orders	Orders for new equipment imply increased production capacity and higher anticipated sales.
7. Stock prices	Higher stock prices reflect expectations of greater sales and profits.
8. Money supply	Faster growth of the money supply implies a pickup in aggregate demand.
9. New orders	New orders for consumer goods trigger increases in production and employment.
10. Building permits	A permit represents the first step in housing construction.
11. Inventories	Companies build up inventory when they anticipate higher sales.

demand still occur without warning. No crystal ball could predict a terrorist strike or the timing and magnitude of a natural disaster. Compared to other crystal balls, however, the Index of Leading Indicators has a pretty good track record—and a very big audience. It helps investors and policymakers foresee what aggregate demand in the economy tomorrow might look like.

SUMMARY

- Macro failure occurs when the economy fails to achieve full employment and price stability. LO3
- Too much or too little aggregate demand, relative to full employment, can cause macro failure. Too little aggregate demand causes cyclical unemployment; too much aggregate demand causes demand-pull inflation. LO3
- Aggregate demand reflects the spending plans of consumers (C), investors (I), government (G), and foreign buyers (net exports $= X - M$). LO1
- Consumer spending is affected by nonincome (autonomous) factors and current income, as summarized in the consumption function: $C = a + bY_D$. LO1
- Autonomous consumption (a) depends on wealth, expectations, taxes, credit, and price levels. Income-dependent consumption depends on the marginal propensity to consume (MPC), the b in the consumption function. LO1
- Consumer saving is the difference between disposable income and consumption (that is, $S = Y_D - C$). All disposable income is either spent (C) or saved (S). LO1
- The consumption function shifts up or down when autonomous influences such as wealth and expectations change. LO1
- The AD curve shifts when consumer income or autonomous consumption changes. LO2
- Investment spending depends on interest rates, expectations for future sales, and innovation. *Changes* in investment spending will also shift the AD curve. LO2
- Government spending and net exports are influenced by a variety of cyclical and noncyclical factors and may also change abruptly. LO1
- Even a "perfect" macro equilibrium may be upset by abrupt shifts of spending behavior. Recurrent shifts may cause a business cycle. LO2

Key Terms

aggregate demand
aggregate supply
equilibrium (macro)
consumption
disposable income
saving
average propensity to consume (APC)
marginal propensity to consume (MPC)
marginal propensity to save (MPS)
wealth effect
consumption function
dissaving
investment
full-employment GDP
equilibrium GDP
recessionary GDP gap
cyclical unemployment
inflationary GDP gap
demand-pull inflation
business cycle

Questions for Discussion

1. What percentage of last month's income did you spend? How much more would you spend if you won a $1,000 lottery prize? Why might your average and marginal propensities to consume differ? LO1
2. Why do rich people have a higher marginal propensity to save than poor people? LO1
3. How do households dissave? Where do they get the money to finance their extra consumption? Can everyone dissave at the same time? LO1
4. Why would a hurricane depress consumer confidence (see News, page 175)? LO2
5. According to the News on page 178, why did businesses cut investment spending in October 2001? Was this a rational response? LO2
6. For how long can the APC remain negative (as in News, page 175)? LO2
7. What factors influence the level of (a) U.S. exports to Mexico and (b) U.S. imports from Mexico? LO2
8. Why wouldn't market participants always want to buy all the output produced? LO3
9. If an inflationary GDP gap exists, what will happen to business inventories. How will producers respond? LO3
10. How might a "perfect" macro equilibrium (Figure 9.10a) be affected by (a) a stock market crash, (b) the death of a president, (c) a recession in Canada, and (d) a spike in oil prices? LO3

problems The Student Problem Set at the back of this book contains numerical and graphing problems for this chapter.

web activities to accompany this chapter can be found on the Online Learning Center: **http://www.mhhe.com/economics/schiller11e**

APPENDIX

THE KEYNESIAN CROSS

The Keynesian view of the macro economy emphasizes the potential instability of the private sector and the undependability of a market-driven self-adjustment. We have illustrated this theory with shifts of the AD curve and resulting real GDP gaps. The advantage of the AS/AD model is that it illustrates how both real output and the price level are simultaneously affected by AD shifts. At the time Keynes developed his theory of instability, however, inflation was not a threat. In the Great Depression prices were *falling*. With unemployment rates reaching as high as 25 percent, no one worried that increased aggregate demand would push price levels up. The only concern was to get back to full employment.

Because inflation was not seen as an immediate threat, early depictions of Keynesian theory didn't use the AS/AD model. Instead, they used a different graph, called the "Keynesian cross." ***The Keynesian cross focuses on the relationship of total spending to the value of total output, without an explicit distinction between price levels and real output.*** As we'll see, the Keynesian cross doesn't change any conclusions we've come to about macro instability. It simply offers an alternative, and historically important, framework for explaining macro outcomes.

Focus on Aggregate Expenditure

Keynes said that in a really depressed economy we could focus exclusively on the rate of *spending* in the economy, without distinguishing between real output and price levels. All he worried about was whether **aggregate expenditure**—the sum of consumer, investor, government, and net export buyers' spending plans—would be compatible with the dollar value of full-employment output.

aggregate expenditure: The rate of total expenditure desired at alternative levels of income, *ceteris paribus.*

For Keynes, the critical question was how much each group of market participants would spend at different levels of nominal *income.* As we saw earlier, Keynes showed that consumer spending directly varies with the level of income. That's why the consumption function in Figure 9.4 had *spending* on the vertical axis and nominal *income* on the horizontal axis.

Figure 9A.1 puts the consumption function into the larger context of the macro economy. In this figure, the focus is exclusively on *nominal* incomes and spending. Y_F indicates the dollar value of full-employment output at current prices. In this figure, \$3,000 billion is assumed to be the value of Y_F. The 45-degree line shows all points where total spending equals total income.

The consumption function in Figure 9A.1 is the same one we used before, namely

$$C = \$100 + 0.75(Y_D)$$

Notice again that consumers *dissave* at lower income levels but *save* at higher income levels.

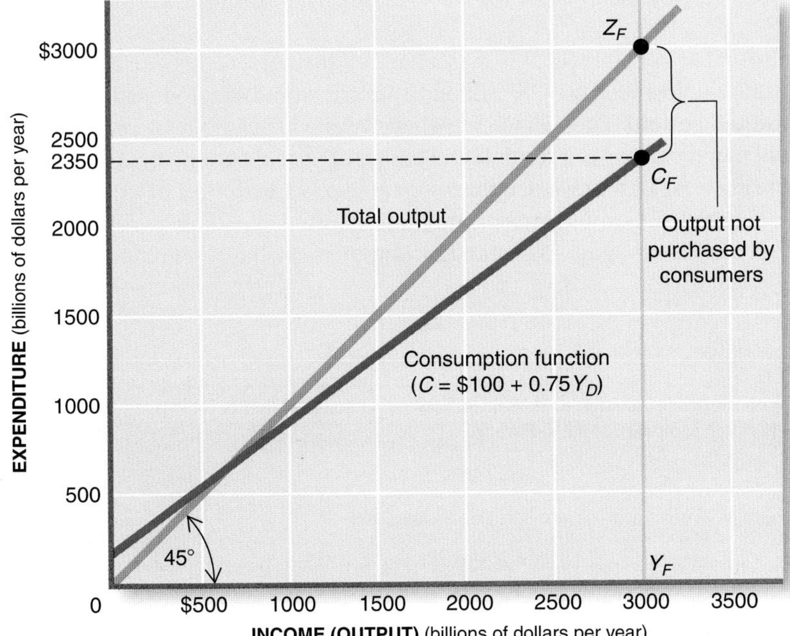

FIGURE 9A.1
The Consumption Shortfall

To determine how much output consumers will demand at full-employment output (Y_F), we refer to the consumption function. First locate full-employment output on the horizontal axis (at Y_F). Then move up until you reach the consumption function. In this case, the amount C_F (equal to \$2,350 billion per year) will be demanded at full-employment output (\$3,000 billion per year). This leaves \$650 billion of output not purchased by consumers.

The Consumption Shortfall

What particularly worried Keynes was the level of intended consumption at full employment. At full employment, \$3 trillion of income (output) is generated. But consumers plan to spend only

$$C = \$100 + 0.75(\$3{,}000 \text{ billion}) = \$2{,}350 \text{ billion}$$

and save the rest (\$650 billion).[1] Were product-market sales totally dependent on consumers, this economy would be in trouble: Consumer spending falls short of full-employment output. In Figure 9A.1, this consumption shortfall is the vertical difference between points Z_F and C_F.

Nonconsumer Spending

The evident shortfall in consumer spending need not doom the economy to macro failure. There are other market participants, and their spending will add to aggregate expenditure. Keynes, however, emphasized that the spending decisions of investors, governments, and net export buyers are made independently. They *might* add up to just the right amount—or they might *not.*

To determine how much other market participants might spend, we'd have to examine their behavior. Suppose we did so and ended up with the information in Figure 9A.2. The data in that figure reveal how many dollars will be spent at various income levels. By vertically stacking these expenditure components, we can draw an *aggregate* (total) expenditure curve as in Figure 9A.2. The aggregate expenditure curve shows how *total* spending varies with income.

A Recessionary Gap

Keynes used the aggregate expenditure curve to assess the potential for macro failure. He was particularly interested in determining how much market participants would spend if the economy were producing at full-employment capacity.

With the information in Figure 9A.2, it is easy to answer that question. At full employment (Y_F), total income is \$3,000 billion. From the table, we see that total spending at that income level is:

Consumer spending at	$Y_F = \$100 + 0.75(\$3{,}000)$	=	\$2,350
Investment spending at	Y_F	=	150
Government spending at	Y_F	=	200
Net export spending at	Y_F	=	50
Aggregate spending at	Y_F	=	\$2,750

In this case, we end up with less aggregate expenditure in product markets (\$2,750 billion) than the value of full-employment output (\$3,000 billion). This is illustrated by point *f* in Figure 9A.3.

The economy illustrated in Figure 9A.3 is in trouble. If full employment were achieved, it wouldn't last. At full employment, \$3,000 billion of output would be produced. But only \$2,750 of output would be sold. There isn't enough aggregate expenditure at current price levels to sustain full employment. As a result, \$250 billion of unsold output piles up in warehouses and on store shelves. That unwanted inventory pileup is a harbinger of trouble.

The difference between full-employment output and desired spending at full employment is called a **recessionary gap.** Not enough output is willingly purchased at full

recessionary gap: The amount by which aggregate spending at full employment falls short of full-employment output.

[1] In principle, we first have to determine how much *disposable* income is generated by any given level of *total* income, then use the consumption function to determine how much consumption occurs. If Y_D is a constant percentage of Y, this two-step computation boils down to

$$Y_D = dY$$

where d = the share of total income received as disposable income, and

$$C = a + b(dY)$$
$$= a + (b \times d)Y$$

The term $(b \times d)$ is the marginal propensity to consume out of *total* income.

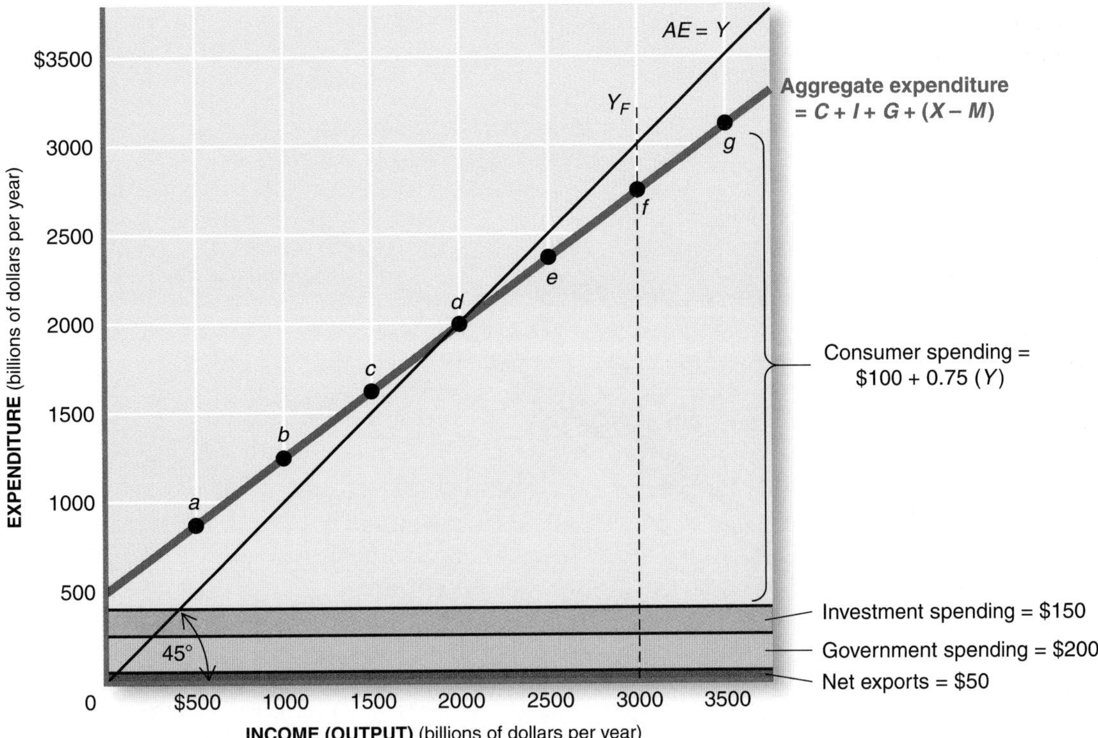

FIGURE 9A.2
Aggregate Expenditure

The aggregate expenditure curve depicts the desired spending of market participants at various income (output) levels. In this case, *I*, *G*, and (*X* – *M*) don't vary with income, but *C* does. Adding these four components gives us total desired spending. If total income were $1,000 billion, desired spending would total $1,250 billion, as shown in row *b* in the table and by point *b* in the graph.

	At Income (output) of	Consumers Desire to Spend	+	Investors Desire to Spend	+	Governments Desire to Spend	+	Net Export Spending	=	Aggregate Expenditure
a	$ 500	$ 475		$150		$200		$50		$ 875
b	1,000	850		150		200		50		1,250
c	1,500	1,225		150		200		50		1,625
d	2,000	1,600		150		200		50		2,000
e	2,500	1,975		150		200		50		2,375
f	3,000	2,350		150		200		50		2,750
g	3,500	2,725		150		200		50		3,125

employment to sustain the economy. Producers may react to the spending shortfall by cutting back on production and laying off workers.

A Single Equilibrium. You might wonder whether the planned spending of market participants would ever be exactly equal to the value of output. It will, but not necessarily at the rate of output we seek.

Figure 9A.3 illustrates where this **expenditure equilibrium** exists. Recall the significance of the 45-degree line in that figure. The 45-degree line represents all points where expenditure *equals* income. At any point on this line there would be no difference between total spending and the value of output.

expenditure equilibrium: The rate of output at which desired spending equals the value of output.

FIGURE 9A.3
Expenditure Equilibrium

There's only one rate of output at which desired expenditure equals the value of output. This expenditure equilibrium occurs at point *E*, where the aggregate expenditure and 45-degree lines intersect. At this equilibrium, $2,000 billion of output is produced and willingly purchased.

At full-employment output (Y_F = $3,000), aggregate expenditure is only $2,750 billion. This spending shortfall leaves $250 billion of output unsold. The difference between full-employment output (point *h*) and desired spending at full employment (point *f*) is called the recessionary gap.

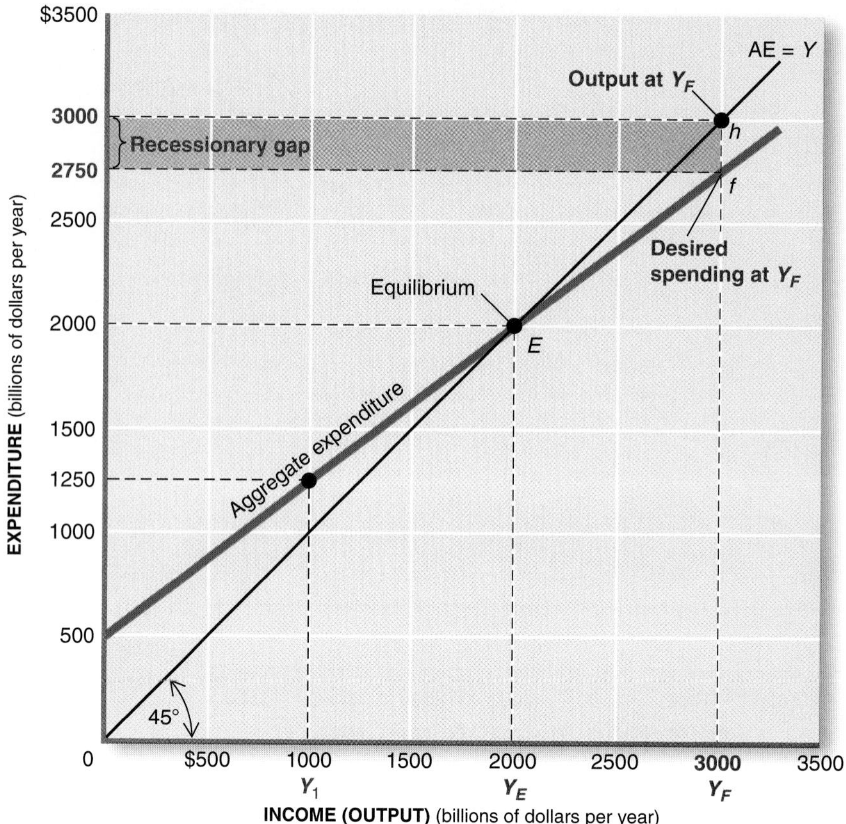

The juxtaposition of the aggregate expenditure function with the 45-degree line is called the Keynesian cross. ***The Keynesian cross relates aggregate expenditure to total income (output), without explicit consideration of (changing) price levels.*** As is evident in Figure 9A.3, the aggregate expenditure curve crosses the 45-degree line only once, at point *E*. At that point, therefore, desired spending is *exactly* equal to the value of output. In Figure 9A.3 this equilibrium occurs at an output rate of $2,000 billion. Notice in the accompanying table how much market participants desire to spend at that rate of output. We have

Consumer spending at	Y_E = $100 + 0.75($2,000)	= $1,600
Investment spending at	Y_E	= 150
Government spending at	Y_E	= 200
Net export spending at	Y_E	= 50
Aggregate spending at	Y_E	= $2,000

At Y_E we have spending behavior that's completely compatible with the rate of production. At this equilibrium rate of output, no goods remain unsold. At that one rate of output where desired spending and the value of output are exactly equal, an expenditure equilibrium exists. ***At macro equilibrium producers have no incentive to change the rate of output because they're selling everything they produce.***

Macro Failure

Unfortunately, the equilibrium depicted in Figure 9A.3 isn't the one we hoped to achieve. At Y_E the economy is well short of its full-employment goal (Y_F).

inflationary gap: The amount by which aggregate spending at full employment exceeds full-employment output.

The expenditure equilibrium won't always fall short of the economy's productive capacity. Indeed, market participants' spending desires could also *exceed* the economy's full-employment potential. This might happen if investors, the government, or foreigners wanted to buy more output or if the consumption function shifted upward. In such circumstances an **inflationary gap** would exist. An inflationary gap arises when market participants want to *spend more* income than can be produced at full employment. The resulting scramble for goods may start a bidding war that pushes price levels even higher. This would be another symptom of macro failure.

Two Paths to the Same Conclusion

The Keynesian analysis of aggregate *expenditure* looks remarkably similar to the Keynesian analysis of aggregate *demand.* In fact, it is: Both approaches lead to the same conclusions about macro instability. The key difference between the "old" (expenditure) analysis and the "new" (AD) analysis is the level of detail about macro outcomes. In the old aggregate-expenditure analysis, the focus was simply on total spending, the product of output and prices. ***In the newer AD analysis, the separate effects of macro instability on prices and real output are distinguished.***[2] In a world where changes in both real output and price levels are important, the AD/AS framework is more useful.

[2]This distinction is reflected in the differing definitions for the traditional *recessionary gap* (the *spending* shortfall at full-employment income) and the newer *recessionary GDP gap* (real output gap between full-employment GDP and equilibrium GDP).

Self-Adjustment or Instability?

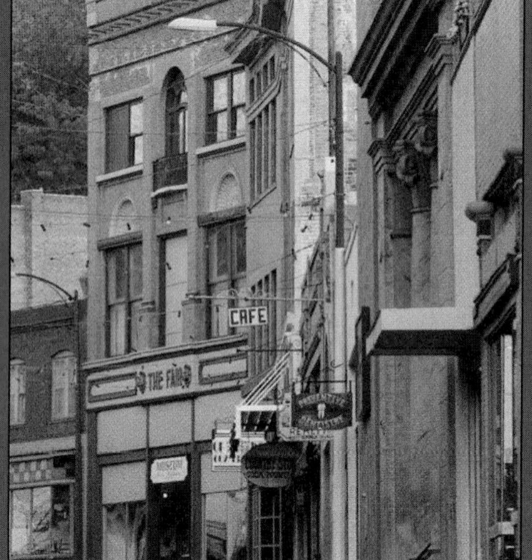

LEARNING OBJECTIVES

After reading this chapter, you should know:

LO1. The source of circular flow leakages and injections.

LO2. What the multiplier is and how it works.

LO3. How recessionary and inflationary GDP gaps arise.

John Maynard Keynes took a dim view of a market-driven macro economy. He emphasized that (1) macro failure is likely to occur in such an economy, and, worse yet, (2) macro failure isn't likely to go away. As noted earlier, the first prediction wasn't all that controversial. The classical economists had conceded the possibility of occasional recession or inflation. In their view, however, the economy would quickly self-adjust, restoring full employment and price stability. Keynes's second proposition challenged this view. The most distinctive, and frightening, proposition of Keynes's theory was that there'd be no automatic self-adjustment; the economy could stagnate in *persistent* unemployment or be subjected to *continuing* inflation.

President Herbert Hoover was a believer in the market's ability to self-adjust. So was President George H. Bush. As Hoover and Bush Sr. waited for the economy to self-adjust, however, they both lost their reelection bids. President George W. Bush wasn't willing to take that chance. As soon as he was elected, he pushed tax cuts through Congress that boosted consumer disposable incomes and helped bolster a sagging economy. After the terrorist attacks of September 11, 2001, he called for even greater government intervention.

These different presidential experiences don't resolve the self-adjustment debate; rather, they emphasize how important the debate is. In this chapter we'll focus on the *adjustment process,* that is, how markets *respond* to an undesirable equilibrium. We're especially concerned with the following questions:

- **Why does anyone think the market might self-adjust (returning to a desired equilibrium)?**
- **Why might markets *not* self-adjust?**
- **Could market responses actually *worsen* macro outcomes?**

LEAKAGES AND INJECTIONS

Chapter 9 demonstrated how the economy could end up at the wrong macro equilibrium—with too much or too little aggregate demand. Such an undesirable outcome might result from an initial imbalance between **aggregate demand** at the current price level and full-employment GDP. Or the economy could fall into trouble from a shift in aggregate demand that pushes the economy out of a desirable full-employment–price-stability equilibrium. Whatever the sequence of events might be, the bottom line is the same: Total spending doesn't match total output at the desired full-employment–price-stability level.

aggregate demand (AD): The total quantity of output demanded at alternative price levels in a given time period, *ceteris paribus.*

The Circular Flow. The circular flow of income illustrates both how such an undesirable outcome comes about and how it might be resolved. Recall that all income originates in product markets, where goods and services are sold. If the economy were producing at **full-employment GDP,** then enough income would be available to buy everything a fully employed economy produces. As we've seen, however, aggregate demand isn't so certain. It could happen that market participants opt *not* to spend all their income, leaving some goods unsold. Alternatively, they might try to buy *more* than full-employment output, pushing prices up.

full-employment GDP: The value of total output (real GDP) produced at full employment.

To see how such imbalances might arise, Keynes distinguished *leakages* from the circular flow and *injections* into that flow, as illustrated in Figure 10.1.

Consumer Saving

As we observed in Chapter 9, consumers typically don't spend *all* the income they earn in product markets; they *save* some fraction of it. This is the first leak in the circular flow. Some income earned in product markets isn't being instantly converted into spending. This circular flow **leakage** creates the potential for a spending shortfall.

leakage: Income not spent directly on domestic output but instead diverted from the circular flow, for example, saving, imports, taxes.

Suppose the economy were producing at full employment, with $3,000 billion of output at the current price level, indexed at $P = 100$. This initial output rate is marked by point F

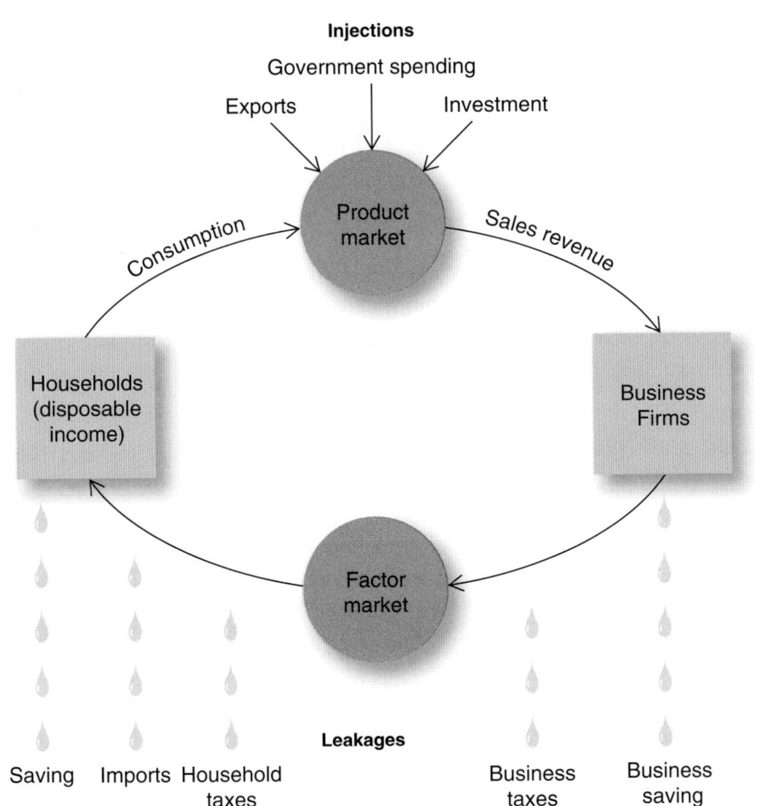

FIGURE 10.1
Leakages and Injections

The income generated in production doesn't return completely to product markets in the form of consumer spending. Consumer saving, imports, taxes, and business saving all leak from the circular flow, reducing aggregate demand. If this leakage isn't offset, some of the output produced will remain unsold.

Business investment, government purchases of goods and services, and exports inject spending into the circular flow, adding to aggregate demand. The focus of macro concern is whether desired injections will offset desired leakage at full employment.

FIGURE 10.2
Leakage and AD

The disposable income consumers receive is only about 70 percent of total income (GDP), due to taxes and income held by businesses. Consumers also tend to save some of their disposable income and buy imported products. As a result of these leakages, consumers will demand less output at the current price level ($P = 100$) than the economy produces at full-employment GDP (Q_F). In this case, consumers demand only $2,350 billion of output at the price level $P = 100$ (point C_F) when $3,000 billion of output (income) is produced (point F).

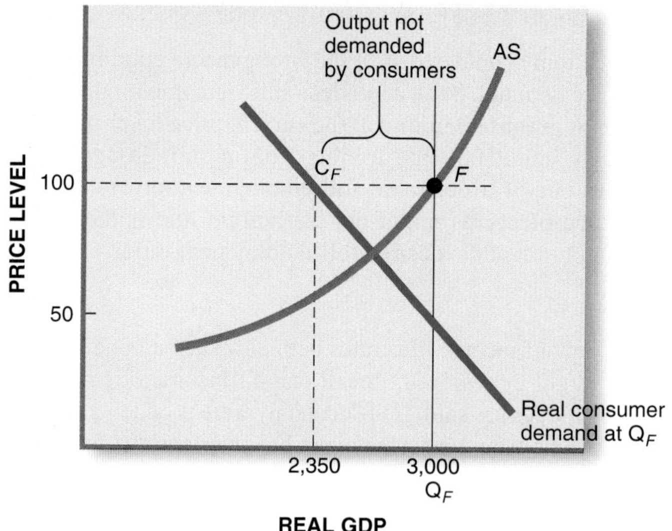

in Figure 10.2. Suppose further that *all* of the income generated in product markets went to consumers. In that case, would consumers *spend* enough to *maintain* full employment? We already observed in Chapter 9 that such an outcome is unlikely. Typically, consumers *save* a small fraction of their incomes.

If the consumption function were $C_F = \$100 \text{ billion} + 0.75Y$, consumers will spend only

$$C_F = \$100 \text{ billion} + 0.75(\$3{,}000 \text{ billion})$$
$$= \$2{,}350 \text{ billion}$$

at the current price level. This consumption behavior is illustrated in Figure 10.2 by the point C_F. Consumers would demand more real output with their current income if prices were to fall. Hence, the consumption component of aggregate demand slopes downward from point C_F. Our immediate concern, however, focuses on how much (real) output consumers will purchase at the *current* price level. At the price level $P = 100$ consumers choose to save $650 billion, leaving consumption ($2,350 billion) far short of full-employment GDP ($3,000 billion).

The decision to save some fraction of household income isn't necessarily bad, but it does present a potential problem. Unless other market participants, such as business, government, and foreigners, buy this unsold output, goods will pile up on producers' shelves. As undesired inventory accumulates, producers will reduce the rate of output and unemployment will rise.

Imports and Taxes

Saving isn't the only source of leakage. ***Imports also represent leakage from the circular flow.*** When consumers buy imported goods, their spending leaves (that is, leaks out of) the domestic circular flow and goes to foreign producers. As a consequence, income spent on imported goods and services is not part of the aggregate demand for domestic output.

In the real world, ***taxes are a form of leakage as well.*** A lot of revenue generated in market sales gets diverted into federal, state, and local government coffers. Sales taxes are taken out of the circular flow in product markets. Then payroll taxes and income taxes are taken out of paychecks. Households never get the chance to spend any of that income. They start with disposable income, which is much less than the total income generated in product markets. In 2006, disposable income was only $9.5 trillion while total income (GDP) was $13 trillion. Hence, consumers couldn't buy everything produced with their current incomes even if they saved nothing.

Business Saving

The business sector also keeps part of the income generated in product markets. Some revenue is set aside to cover the costs of maintaining, repairing, and replacing plant and equipment. The revenue held aside for these purposes is called a depreciation allowance. In addition, corporations keep some part of total profit (retained earnings) for continuing business uses rather than paying all profits out to stockholders in the form of dividends. The total value of depreciation allowances and retained earnings is called **gross business saving.** Whatever businesses save in these forms represents further leakage from the circular flow—income that doesn't automatically flow directly back into product markets.

gross business saving: Depreciation allowances and retained earnings.

Although leakage from the circular flow is a potential source of unemployment problems, we shouldn't conclude that the economy will sink as soon as consumers start saving some of their income, buy a few imports, or pay their taxes. Consumers aren't the only source of aggregate demand; business firms and government agencies also contribute to total spending. So do international consumers who buy our exports. So before we run out into the streets screaming "The circular flow is leaking!" we need to look at what other market participants are doing.

Injections into the Circular Flow

The top half of Figure 10.1 completes the picture of the circular flow by depicting **injections** of new spending. When businesses buy plant and equipment, they add to the dollar value of product market sales. Government purchases and exports also inject spending into the product market. These ***injections of investment, government, and export spending help offset leakage from saving, imports, and taxes.*** As a result, there may be enough aggregate demand to maintain full employment at the current price level, even if consumers aren't spending every dollar of income.

injection: An addition of spending to the circular flow of income.

The critical issue for macro stability is whether spending injections will actually equal spending leakage at full employment. If so, the economy will stabilize at full employment and we can stop worrying about short-run macro problems. If not, we've still got some work to do.

Self-Adjustment?

As we noted earlier, classical economists had no worries. They assumed that spending injections would always equal spending leakage. That was the foundation of their belief in the market's self-adjustment. The mechanism assuring the equality of leakages and injections was the interest rate.

webnote

Check the U.S. Bureau of Economic Analysis (BEA) Web site at www.bea.gov to see how much investment varied in the last year. Click on "Gross Domestic Product," then "Selected NIPA Tables."

Flexible Interest Rates. Ignore all other injections and leakages for the moment and focus on just consumer saving and business investment (Figure 10.3). If consumer saving (a leakage) exceeds business investment (an injection), unspent income must be piling up somewhere (in bank accounts, for example). These unspent funds will be a tempting lure for business investors. Businesses are always looking for funds to finance expansion or modernization. So they aren't likely to leave a pile of consumer savings sitting idle. Moreover, the banks and other institutions that are holding consumer savings will be eager to lend

Leakages	Injections
Consumer saving	Investment
Business saving	Government spending
Taxes	Exports
Imports	

FIGURE 10.3
Leakages and Injections

Macro stability depends on the balance between injections and leakages. Of these, consumer saving and business investment are the primary sources of (im)balance in a wholly private and closed economy. Hence the relationship between saving and investment reveals whether a market-driven economy will self-adjust to full employment and price stability.

more funds as consumer savings piles up. To make more loans, they can lower the interest rate. As we observed in Chapter 9 (Figure 9.7), lower interest rates prompt businesses to borrow and invest more. Hence, ***classical economists concluded that if interest rates fell far enough, business investment (injections) would equal consumer saving (leakage).*** From this perspective, any spending shortfall would soon be closed by this self-adjustment of leakage and injection flows. Aggregate demand would be maintained at full-employment GDP, because investment spending would soak up all consumer saving. The *content* of AD would change (less C, more I), but the *level* would remain at full-employment GDP.

Changing Expectations. Keynes argued that classical economists ignored the role of expectations. As Figure 9.7 illustrated, the level of investment *is* sensitive to interest rates. But the whole investment function *shifts* when business expectations change. Keynes thought it preposterous that investment spending would *increase* in response to *declining* consumer sales. A decline in investment is more likely, Keynes argued.

Flexible Prices. There is another way the economy could self-adjust. Look at Figure 10.2 again. It says consumers will demand only \$2,350 billion of output *at the current price level.* But what if prices *fell*? Then consumers would buy more output. In fact, if prices fell far enough, consumers might buy *all* the output produced at full employment. In Figure 10.2, the price level $P = 50$ elicits such a response.

Expectations (again). Keynes again chided the classical economists for their naiveté. Sure, a nationwide sale might prompt consumers to buy more goods and services. But how would businesses react? They had planned on selling Q_F amount of output at the price level $P = 100$. If prices must be cut in half to move their merchandise, businesses are likely to rethink their production and investment plans. Keynes argued that declining (retail) prices were likely to prompt investment cutbacks, as the accompanying News also suggests.

IN THE NEWS

The Bogeyman of Deflation

WELL, WE FACE A NEW DANGER: DEFLATION. So says the FOMC, the Federal Reserve's main policymaking body. It's astonishing what a few words can do, and these words riveted attention on something that, until recently, seemed a historic curiosity. Deflation signifies a general decline of prices; it hasn't happened in the United States since the Great Depression. . . .

Deflation would arise from too much supply (of everything from computer chips to airplane seats) chasing too little demand. Prices would drop as companies competed for buyers. . . . Why would that be bad? Lower prices would allow people to buy more with their wages: the economy could benefit.

But what's also true is that deflation poses dangers: (1) lower prices could squeeze corporate profits, hurt the stock market and pressure companies to fire workers and cut wages; (2) falling prices could lower overnight interest rates to near zero, making it harder for the Fed to stimulate the economy; (3) companies and farmers may default on loans, which are fixed while the prices they receive fall, and (4) consumers might delay purchases, believing future prices will be lower.

In the Depression, the dangers materialized. From 1929 to 1933, retail prices dropped 24 percent. Thousands of businesses and farmers went bankrupt. About 40 percent of banks failed. By 1933, unemployment was 25 percent. Although the Fed cut interest rates, the economy didn't respond. (In the summer of 1931, the Fed's discount rate was 1.5 percent; but prices were down 9 percent, making the price-adjusted interest rate almost 11 percent.)

—Robert J. Samuelson

Source: Washington Post Writers Group, May 19, 2003.

Analysis: Deflation does make products cheaper for consumers. But declining prices also reduce business revenues, profits, and sales expectations.

THE MULTIPLIER PROCESS

Keynes not only rejected the classical notion of self-adjustment, he also argued that things were likely to get *worse,* not better, once a spending shortfall emerged. This was the scariest part of Keynes's theory.

To understand Keynes's fears, imagine that the economy is initially at the desired full-employment GDP equilibrium, as represented again by point *F* in Figure 10.4. Included in that full-employment equilibrium GDP is

Consumption	=	$2,350 billion
Investment	=	400 billion
Government	=	150 billion
Net exports	=	100 billion
Aggregate demand at current price level	=	$3,000 billion

Everything looks good in this macro economy. This is pretty much how the U.S. economy looked from 1993 until early 2001.

A Decline in Investment

Now suppose that business expectations for future sales worsen. In early 2001, business forecasts of consumer spending were already declining. After the terrorist attacks of September 11, expectations fell even further. As expectations worsened, businesses cut back on investment spending (see News on next page).

Undesired Inventory. When business investment was cut back, unsold capital goods started piling up. Unsold trucks, office equipment, machinery, and airplanes quickly reached worrisome levels.

Ironically, this additional inventory is counted as part of investment spending. (Recall that our definition of investment spending includes changes in business inventories.) This additional inventory is clearly undesired, however, as producers had planned on selling these goods.

To keep track of these unwanted changes in investment, we ***distinguish*** **desired** ***(or planned) investment from*** **actual** ***investment.*** *Desired* investment represents purchases of new plant and equipment plus any *desired* changes in business inventories. By contrast,

webnote

At the Economics Briefing Room of the White House at www.whitehouse.gov/fsbr/output.html, find current data on output.

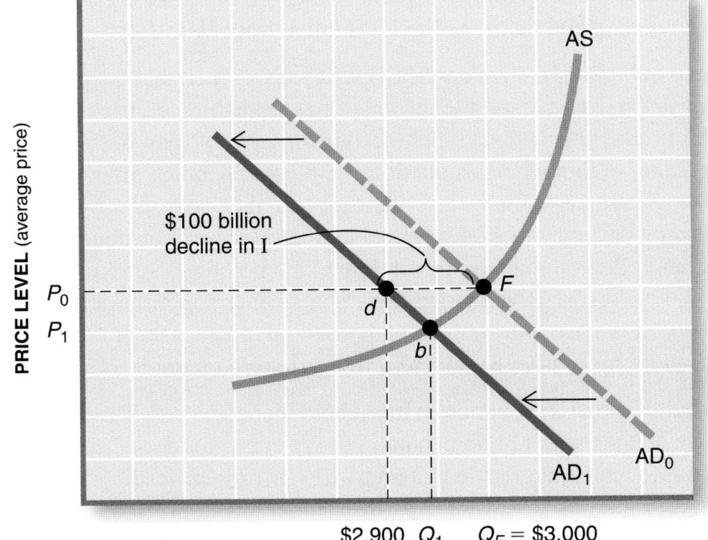

FIGURE 10.4
AD Shift

When investment spending drops, aggregate demand shifts to the left. In the short run, this causes output and the price level to fall. The initial equilibrium at *F* is pushed to a new equilibrium at point *b*.

IN THE NEWS

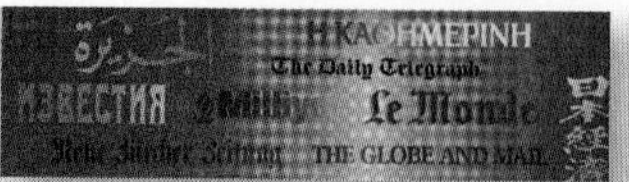

Small Businesses Hold Off on Big Purchases

Capital Spending Helps Drive Economy, So Drop-off May Hurt

SAN FRANCISCO—Small companies are buying fewer trucks, computers and other big-ticket items—the capital purchases that could lift the U.S. economy.

About 28% of small firms plan big purchases, a major survey out Monday said. That's down from about 32% before the terrorist attacks.

Capital spending by small firms is critical. It helps them be more productive and boosts sales at big companies like Ford Motor and Dell Computer. . . .

—Jim Hopkins

Source: *USA Today,* October 16, 2001. USA TODAY. Copyright 2001. Reprinted with permission. www.usatoday.com

Analysis: Worsened sales expectations may cause a decline in investment spending that shifts the AD curve to the left, leading to pileups of unwanted inventory.

actual investment represents purchases of new plant and equipment plus *actual* changes in business inventories, desired or otherwise. In other words,

$$\text{Actual investment} = \text{desired investment} + \text{undesired investment}$$

Falling Output and Prices. How are business firms likely to react when they see undesired inventory piling up on car lots and store shelves? They could regard the inventory pileup as a brief aberration and continue producing at full-employment levels. But the inventory pileup might also set off sales alarms, causing businesses to alter their pricing, production, and investment plans. If that happens, they're likely to start cutting prices in an attempt to increase the rate of sales. Producers are also likely to reduce the rate of new output.

equilibrium GDP: The value of total output (real GDP) produced at macro equilibrium (AS = AD).

Figure 10.4 illustrates these two responses. Assume that investment spending declines by \$100 billion at the existing price level P_0. This shifts the aggregate demand curve leftward from AD_0 to AD_1 and immediately moves the economy from point *F* to point *d*. At *d*, however, excess inventories prompt firms to reduce prices. As prices fall, the economy gravitates toward a new **equilibrium GDP** at point *b*. At point *b*, the rate of output (Q_1) is less than the full-employment level (Q_F) and the price level has fallen from P_0 to P_1.

Household Incomes

The decline in GDP depicted in Figure 10.4 isn't pretty. But Keynes warned that the picture would get uglier when *consumers* start feeling the impact of the production cutbacks.

So far we've treated the production cutbacks that accompany a GDP gap as a rather abstract problem. But the reality is that when production is cut back, people suffer. When producers decrease the rate of output, workers lose their jobs or face pay cuts, or both. Cutbacks in investment spending on September 2001 (prior News) led to layoffs at Honeywell, Advanced Micro Devices, and other capital-equipment manufacturers (see News on next page). An abrupt decline in travel caused even larger layoffs at airlines and aircraft manufacturers. As workers get laid off or have their wages cut, household incomes decline. Thus, ***a reduction in investment spending implies a reduction in household incomes.***

Income-Dependent Consumption

We saw in Chapter 9 the kind of threat a reduction in household income poses. Those consumers who end up with less income won't be able to purchase as many goods and services as they did before. As a consequence, aggregate demand will fall further, leading to still larger stocks of unsold goods, more job layoffs, and further reductions in income. It's this sequence of events—called the *multiplier process*—that makes a sudden decline in aggregate demand so frightening. ***What starts off as a relatively small spending shortfall quickly snowballs into a much larger problem.***

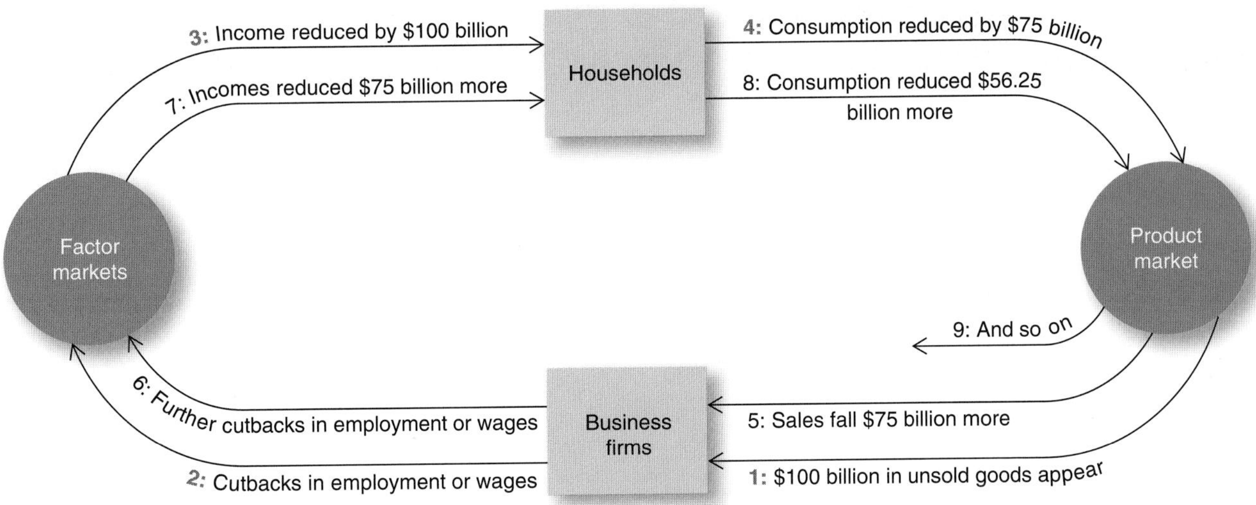

FIGURE 10.5
The Multiplier Process

A decline in investment (step 1) may lead to a cutback in production and income (step 2). A reduction in total income (step 3) will in turn lead to a reduction in consumer spending (step 4). These additional cuts in spending cause a further decrease in income, leading to additional spending reductions, and so on. This sequence of adjustments is referred to as the *multiplier process.*

We can see the multiplier process at work by watching what happens to the $100 billion decline in investment spending as it makes its way around the circular flow (Figure 10.5). At first (step 1), the only thing that happens is that unsold goods appear (in the form of undesired inventories). Producers adjust to this problem by cutting back on production and laying off workers or reducing wages and prices (step 2). In either case, consumer income falls $100 billion per year shortly after the investment cutbacks occur (step 3).

How will consumers respond to this drop in disposable income? ***If disposable income falls, we expect consumer spending to drop as well.*** In fact, the consumption function tells us just how much spending will drop. The **marginal propensity to consume (MPC)** is the critical variable in this process. Since we've specified that $C = \$100$ billion $+ 0.75Y$, we anticipate that consumers will reduce their spending by $0.75 for every $1.00 of lost income. In the present example, the loss of $100 billion of annual income will induce consumers to reduce their rate of spending by $75 billion per year (0.75 × $100 billion). This drop in spending is illustrated by step 4 in Figure 10.5.

marginal propensity to consume (MPC): The fraction of each additional (marginal) dollar of disposable income spent on consumption; the change in consumption divided by the change in disposable income.

The multiplier process doesn't stop here. A reduction in consumer spending quickly translates into more unsold output (step 5). As additional goods pile up on producers' shelves, we anticipate further cutbacks in production, employment, and disposable income (step 6).

As disposable incomes are further reduced by job layoffs and wage cuts (step 7), more reductions in consumer spending are sure to follow (step 8). Again the marginal propensity to consume (MPC) tells us how large such reductions will be. With an MPC of 0.75, we may expect spending to fall by another $56.25 billion per year (0.75 × $75 billion) in step 8.

The Multiplier

The multiplier process continues to work until the reductions in income and sales become so small that no one's market behavior is significantly affected. We don't have to examine each step along the way. As you may have noticed, all the steps begin to look alike once we've gone around the circular flow a few times. Instead of examining each step, we can look ahead to see where they are taking us. Each time the multiplier process works its way around the circular flow, the reduction in spending equals the previous drop in income multiplied by the MPC. Accordingly, by pressing a few keys on a calculator, we can produce a sequence of events like that depicted in Table 10.1 on page 201.

The impact of the multiplier is devastating. The ultimate reduction in real spending resulting from the initial drop in investment isn't $100 billion per year but $400 billion! Even if one is accustomed to thinking in terms of billions and trillions, this is a huge drop in demand.

webnote

Do sports teams create multiplier effects for cities? Read about this at www.brookings.edu/press/review/summer97/holl.htm

IN THE NEWS

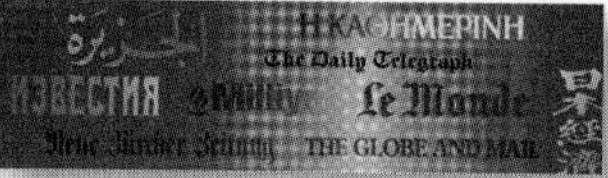

Terror's Aftermath: Layoffs

Who knows how many of these might have come anyway? But since Sept. 11, companies have cut more than 160,000 jobs. Airlines were the hardest hit, but other industries were also affected. Here are some of the biggest.

Company	Cuts	Industry
Boeing	30,000	Aerospace
American Airlines	20,000	Airline
United	20,000	Airline
Delta	13,000	Airline
Continental	12,000	Airline
Starwood Hotels & Resorts	12,000	Hotel
US Airways	11,000	Airline
Northwest	10,000	Airline
British Airways	7,000	Airline
Air Canada	5,000	Airline
Honeywell International	3,800	Aerospace/Diversified materials
Swissair	3,000	Airline
Alitalia	2,500	Airline
Textron	2,500	Aircraft manufacturing
EMC	2,400	Data storage
Advanced Micro Devices	2,300	Microprocessors
America West	2,000	Airline
Applied Materials	2,000	Semiconductors

Source: *BusinessWeek,* October 8, 2001. Reprinted with permission. Copyright 2001 by The McGraw-Hill Companies. www.businessweek.com

Analysis: Cutbacks in production cause employee layoffs. The newly unemployed workers curtail *their* spending, causing sequential layoffs in other industries. These "snowball" effects give rise to the multiplier.

What the multiplier process demonstrates is that the dimensions of an initial spending gap greatly understate the severity of the economic dislocations that will follow in its wake. ***The eventual decline in spending will be much larger than the initial (autonomous) decrease in aggregate demand.*** This was evident in the recession of 2001, when layoffs snowballed from industry to industry (see News), ultimately leaving millions of people unemployed.

multiplier: The multiple by which an initial change in spending will alter total expenditure after an infinite number of spending cycles; 1/(1 − MPC).

The ultimate impact of an AD shift on total spending can be determined by computing the change in income and consumption at each cycle of the circular flow, for an infinite number of cycles. This is the approach summarized in Table 10.1, with each row representing a spending cycle. The entire computation can be simplified considerably by using a single figure, the multiplier. The **multiplier** tells us the extent to which the rate of total spending will change in response to an initial change in the flow of expenditure. The multiplier summarizes the sequence of steps described in Table 10.1.[1] In its simplest form, the multiplier can be computed as:

$$\text{Multiplier} = \frac{1}{1 - \text{MPC}}$$

[1]The multiplier summarizes the geometric progression $1 + \text{MPC} + \text{MPC}^2 + \text{MPC}^3 + \cdots + \text{MPC}^n$, which equals $1/(1 - \text{MPC})$ when n becomes infinite.

Spending Cycles	Change in This Cycle's Spending and Income (billions per year)	Cumulative Decrease in Spending and Income (billions per year)	
First cycle: recessionary gap emerges	$100.00	$100.00	} ΔI
Second cycle: consumption drops by MPC × $100	75.00	175.00	ΔC
Third cycle: consumption drops by MPC × $75	56.25	231.25	
Fourth cycle: consumption drops by MPC × $56.25	42.19	273.44	
Fifth cycle: consumption drops by MPC × $42.19	31.64	305.08	
Sixth cycle: consumption drops by MPC × $31.64	23.73	328.81	
Seventh cycle: consumption drops by MPC × $23.73	17.80	346.61	
Eighth cycle: consumption drops by MPC × $17.80	13.35	359.95	
⋮	⋮	⋮	
*n*th cycle and beyond		400.00	

TABLE 10.1
The Multiplier Cycles

The circular flow of income implies that an initial change in income will lead to cumulative changes in consumer spending and income. Here, an initial income loss of $100 billion (first cycle) causes a cutback in consumer spending in the amount of $75 billion (second cycle). At each subsequent cycle, consumer spending drops by the amount MPC × prior change in income. Ultimately, total spending (and income) falls by $400 billion, or 1/(1 − MPC) × initial change in spending.

IN THE NEWS

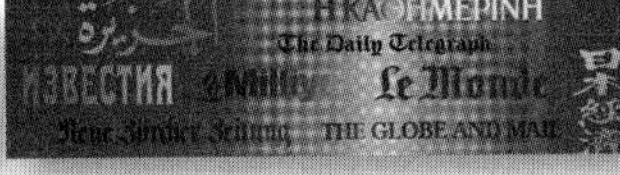

Companies Begin Another Round of Job Cuts

Even More Layoffs Could Threaten If Recession Closes In

When it comes to layoffs, employers are finding once is not enough.

The ongoing economic downturn means companies that have already laid off workers are cutting again. For example:

- Compaq Computer last week reported that it was laying off about 4,000 additional workers. That's in addition to about 4,500 cuts earlier this year. . . .
- Even though 8,500 workers at Lucent Technologies have accepted an early retirement offer, CEO Henry Schacht said last week that the beleaguered company plans its third round of job cuts since January. . . . The Murray Hill, N.J.–based company announced in January that it would eliminate 10,000 jobs and sell facilities employing an additional 6,000 workers as part of a restructuring and cost-cutting program.
- Santa Clara, Calif.–based Exodus Communications in June announced an unspecified number of layoffs. That follows the announcement in May that the web-hosting company would shed 675 positions, or about 15 percent of its workforce.
- Santa Clara–based equipment maker 3Com in May announced it was laying off 3,000 employees. That follows job cuts of about 1,200 in March.

This may just be the beginning of what's to come if the economy slides closer to a recession, some experts say.

—Stephanie Armour

Source: *USA Today,* July 17, 2001. USA TODAY. Copyright 2001. Reprinted with permission. www.usatoday.com

Analysis: Few industries escape damage from a recession. Spending slowdowns spread from industry to industry in a multiplier-like way. Job layoffs reduce disposable income and consumption.

In our example, the initial change in aggregate demand occurs when investment drops by $100 billion per year at full-employment output ($3,000 billion per year). Table 10.1 indicates that this investment drop-off will lead to a $400 billion reduction in the rate of total spending at the current price level. Using the multiplier, we arrive at the same conclusion by observing that

$$\begin{aligned}\text{Total change in spending} &= \text{multiplier} \times \text{initial change in aggregate spending}\\ &= \frac{1}{1 - \text{MPC}} \times \$100 \text{ billion per year}\\ &= \frac{1}{1 - 0.75} \times \$100 \text{ billion per year}\\ &= 4 \times \$100 \text{ billion per year}\\ &= \$400 \text{ billion per year}\end{aligned}$$

webnote

JWT Communications tracks ongoing layoffs. To see how widespread layoffs are in any time period, visit www.jwtec.com/hrlive/layoffs.php

In other words, ***the cumulative decrease in total spending ($400 billion per year) resulting from a shortfall in aggregate demand at full employment is equal to the initial shortfall ($100 billion per year) multiplied by the multiplier (4).*** More generally, we may observe that the larger the fraction (MPC) of income respent in each round of the circular flow, the greater the impact of any autonomous change in spending on cumulative aggregate demand. The cumulative process of spending adjustments can also have worldwide effects. As the World View illustrates, Asia's economic growth slowed when the U.S. economy slumped in 2001.

WORLD VIEW

U.S. Slowdown Helps Derail Asia

High-Tech Firms Suffer Vicious Circle

SAN FRANCISCO—Waves from the U.S. high-tech and economic slump continue to crash onto Asian shores: Analysts fear the onset of a global recession and Japanese tech giant Fujitsu said Monday that it will cut 16,400 workers.

"The U.S. economy—especially the technology sector—was the primary locomotive for the export economies of Japan, Korea, Taiwan and Malaysia," says Sung Won Sohn, chief economist at Wells Fargo Bank. "Now that the bubble has burst here, it's having a devastating effect on Asia."

Among the dire signs:

- Fujitsu, the No. 2 maker of personal computers in Japan and a leading maker of flash-memory chips, will lay off 10 percent of its workers, including 5,000 employees in Japan and 11,400 employees at plants in Thailand, Vietnam and the Philippines. . . .
- The economy of Taiwan, a leading manufacturer and exporter of high-tech parts and goods, officially has entered a recession. In the first year-to-year drop in 26 years, Taiwan's gross domestic product plunged 2 percent in the second quarter. . . .
- When the U.S. economy started limping last year, Asia's economies were still dashing ahead at double-digit growth rates. Now, export-oriented Asia is expected to grow only 2 percent this year, with Japan's economy flat-lining. . . .

Like a boomerang, the economic chill in Asia is circling back and hurting the USA. Economists call it the "international-multiplier effect."

Cash-poor Asian nations can no longer buy high-tech goods and other products from U.S. companies, which also rely heavily on overseas trade.

—Edward Iwata

Source: *USA Today*, August 21, 2001. USA TODAY. Copyright 2001. Reprinted with permission. www.usatoday.com

Analysis: Multiplier effects can spill over national borders. The 2001 economic slump in the United States reduced U.S. demand for Asian exports, setting off a sequence of spending cuts in Japan, Taiwan, and other Asian nations.

MACRO EQUILIBRIUM REVISITED

The key features of the Keynesian adjustment process are

- ***Producers cut output and employment when output exceeds aggregate demand at the current price level (leakage exceeds injections).***
- ***The resulting loss of income causes a decline in consumer spending.***
- ***Declines in consumer spending lead to further production cutbacks, more lost income, and still less consumption.***

Sequential AD Shifts

Figure 10.6 illustrates the ultimate impact of the multiplier process. Notice that the AD curve shifts *twice.* The first shift—from AD_0 to AD_1—represents the $100 billion drop in investment spending. As we saw earlier in Figure 10.4, this initial shift of aggregate demand will start the economy moving toward a new equilibrium at point *b.*

Along the way, however, the multiplier kicks in and things get worse. ***The decline in household income caused by investment cutbacks sets off the multiplier process, causing a secondary shift of the AD curve.*** We measure these multiplier effects at the initial price level of P_0. With a marginal propensity to consume of 0.75, we've seen that induced consumption declines by $300 billion when autonomous investment declines by $100 billion. In Figure 10.6 this is illustrated by the *second* shift of the aggregate demand curve, from AD_1 to AD_2. Notice that the horizontal distance between AD_1 and AD_2 is $300 billion.

Price and Output Effects

Although aggregate demand has fallen (shifted) by $400 billion, real output doesn't necessarily drop that much. ***The impact of a shift in aggregate demand is reflected in both output and price changes.*** This is evident in Figure 10.7, which is a close-up view of Figure 10.6. When AD shifts from AD_0 to AD_2 the macro equilibrium moved down the sloped AS curve to point *c*. At point *c* the new equilibrium output is Q_E and the new price level is P_E.

Recessionary GDP Gap. As long as the aggregate supply curve is upward-sloping, the shock of any AD shift will be spread across output and prices. In Figure 10.7, the net effect on real output is shown as the real GDP gap. ***The recessionary GDP gap equals the difference between equilibrium real GDP (Q_E) and full-employment real GDP (Q_F).*** It

recessionary GDP gap: The amount by which equilibrium GDP falls short of full-employment GDP.

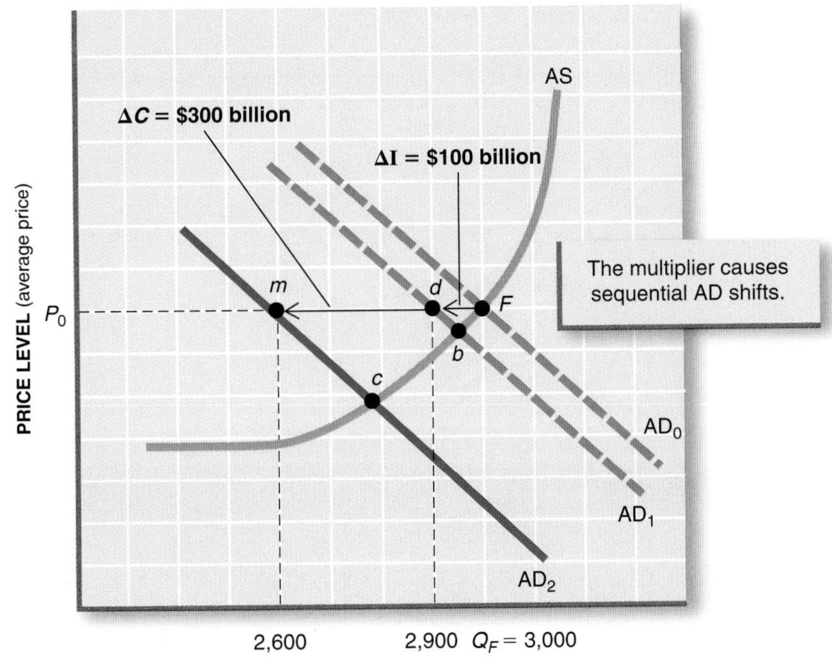

FIGURE 10.6
Multiplier Effects

A decline in investment spending reduces household income, setting off negative multiplier effects. Hence, the *initial* shift of AD_0 to AD_1 is followed by a *second* shift from AD_1 to AD_2. The second shift represents reduced consumption.

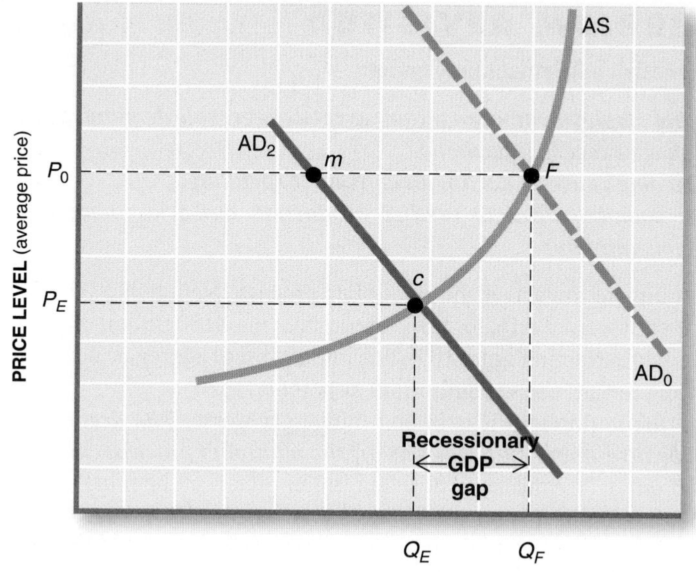

FIGURE 10.7
Recessionary GDP Gap

The real GDP gap is the difference between equilibrium GDP (Q_E) and full-employment GDP (Q_F). It represents the lost output due to a recession.

cyclical unemployment: Unemployment attributable to a lack of job vacancies, that is, to an inadequate level of aggregate demand.

represents the amount by which the economy is underproducing during a recession. As we noted in Chapter 9, this is a classic case of **cyclical unemployment.**

Short-Run Inflation-Unemployment Trade-Offs

Figure 10.7 not only illustrates how much output declines when AD falls but also provides an important clue about the difficulty of restoring full employment. Suppose the recessionary GDP gap were $200 billion, as illustrated in Figure 10.8. How much more AD would we need to get back to full employment?

Upward-Sloping AS. Suppose aggregate demand at the equilibrium price level (P_E) were to increase by exactly $200 billion (including multiplier effects), as illustrated by the shift to AD_3. Would that get us back to full-employment output? Not according to Figure 10.8. ***When AD increases, both output and prices go up.*** Because the AS curve is upward-sloping, the $200 billion shift from AD_2 to AD_3 moves the new macro

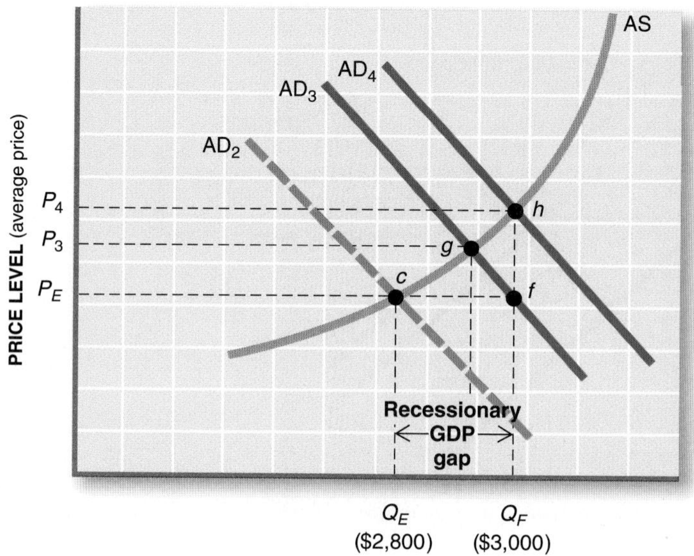

FIGURE 10.8
The Unemployment-Inflation Trade-Off

If the short-run AS curve is upward-sloping, an AD increase will raise output *and* prices. If AD increases by the amount of the recessionary GDP gap only (AD_2 to AD_3), full employment (Q_F) won't be reached. Macro equilibrium moves to point *g*, not point *f*.

equilibrium to point *g* rather than point *f.* We'd like to get to point *f* with full employment and price stability. But as demand picks up, producers are likely to raise prices. This leads us up the AS curve to point *g*. At point *g*, we're still short of full employment and have experienced a bit of inflation (an increased price level). ***So long as the short-run AS is upward-sloping, there's a trade-off between unemployment and inflation.*** We can get lower rates of unemployment (more real output) only if we accept some inflation.

"Full" vs. "Natural" Unemployment. The short-term trade-off between unemployment and inflation is the basis for the definition of "full" employment. We don't define full employment as *zero* unemployment; we define it as the rate of unemployment *consistent with price stability.* As noted in Chapter 6, **full employment** is typically defined as a 4 to 6 percent rate of unemployment. What the upward-sloping AS curve tells us is that ***the closer the economy gets to capacity output, the greater the risk of inflation.*** To get back to full employment in Figure 10.8, aggregate demand would have to increase to AD_4, with the price level rising to P_4.

full employment: The lowest rate of unemployment compatible with price stability; variously estimated at between 4 and 6 percent unemployment.

Not everyone accepts this notion of full employment. As we saw in Chapter 8, neoclassical and monetarist economists prefer to focus on *long*-run outcomes. In their view, the long-run AS curve is vertical (see Figure 8.12). In that long-run context, there's no unemployment-inflation trade-off: An AD shift doesn't change the "natural" (institutional) rate of unemployment but does alter the price level. We'll examine this argument in Chapters 16 and 17.

ADJUSTMENT TO AN INFLATIONARY GDP GAP

As we've observed, ***a sudden shift in aggregate demand can have a cumulative effect on macro outcomes*** that's larger than the initial imbalance. This multiplier process works both ways: Just as a *decrease* in investment (or any other AD component) can send the economy into a recessionary tailspin, an *increase* in investment might initiate an inflationary spiral.

Figure 10.9 illustrates the consequences of a sudden jump in investment spending. We

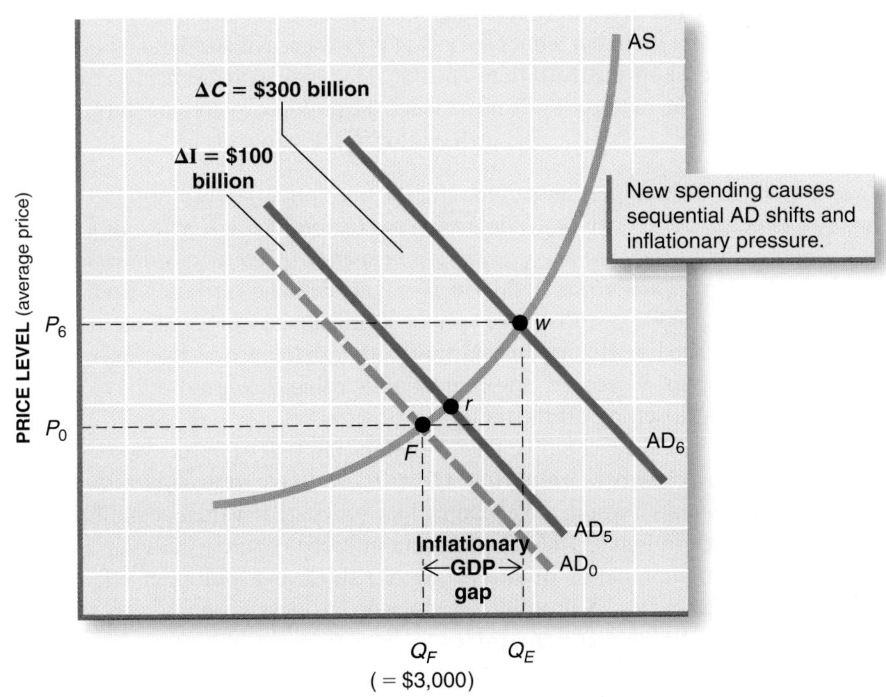

FIGURE 10.9
Demand-Pull Inflation

An increase in investment or other autonomous spending sets off multiplier effects shifting AD to the right. AD shifts to the right *twice,* first (AD_0 to AD_5) because of increased investment, then (AD_5 to AD_6) because of increased consumption. The increased AD moves the economy up the short-run AS curve, causing some inflation. How much inflation results depends on the slope of the AS curve.

start out again in the happy equilibrium (point F), where full employment (Q_F) and price stability (P_0) prevail. Initial spending consists of

C = \$2,350 billion G = \$150 billion

I = \$400 billion $X - M$ = \$100 billion

Increased Investment

Then investors suddenly decide to step up the rate of investment. Perhaps their expectations for future sales have risen. Maybe new technology has become available that compels firms to modernize their facilities. Whatever the reason, investors decide to raise the level of investment from \$400 billion to \$500 billion at the current price level (P_0). This change in investment spending shifts the aggregate demand curve from AD_0 to AD_5 (a horizontal shift of \$100 billion).

Inventory Depletion. One of the first things you'll notice when AD shifts like this is that available inventories shrink. Investors can step up their *spending* more quickly than firms can increase their *production.* A lot of the increased investment demand will have to be satisfied from existing inventory. The decline in inventory is a signal to producers that it might be a good time to raise prices a bit. Thus, ***inventory depletion is a warning sign of impending inflation.*** As the economy moves up from point F to point r in Figure 10.9, that inflation starts to become visible.

Household Incomes

Whether or not prices start rising quickly, household incomes will get a boost from the increased investment. Producers will step up the rate of output to rebuild inventories and supply more investment goods (equipment and structures). To do so, they'll hire more workers or extend working hours. The end result for workers will be fatter paychecks.

Induced Consumption

What will households do with these heftier paychecks? By now, you know what the consumer response will be. The marginal propensity to consume prompts an increase in consumer spending. Eventually, consumer spending increases by a *multiple* of the income change. In this case, the consumption increase is \$300 billion (see Table 10.1).

Figure 10.9 illustrates the secondary shift of AD caused by multiplier-induced consumption. Notice how the AD curve shifts a second time, from AD_5 to AD_6.

A New Equilibrium

demand-pull inflation: An increase in the price level initiated by excessive aggregate demand.

The ultimate impact of the investment surge is reflected in the new equilibrium at point w. As before, the shift of AD has affected both real output and prices. Real output does increase beyond the full-employment level, but it does so only at the expense of accelerating inflation. This is a classic case of **demand-pull inflation.** The initial increase in investment was enough to kindle a little inflation. The multiplier effect worsened the problem by forcing the economy further along the ever-steeper AS curve. The **inflationary GDP gap** ends up as $Q_E - Q_F$.

Booms and Busts

inflationary GDP gap: The amount by which equilibrium GDP exceeds full-employment GDP.

The Keynesian analysis of leakages, injections, and the multiplier paints a fairly grim picture of the prospects for macro stability. ***The basic conclusion of the Keynesian analysis is that the economy is vulnerable to abrupt changes in spending behavior and won't self-adjust to a desired macro equilibrium.*** A shift in aggregate demand can come from almost anywhere. The September 2001 terrorist attack on the World Trade Center shook both consumer and investor confidence. Businesses starting cutting back production even *before* inventories started piling up. Worsened *expectations* rather than rising inventories caused investment demand to shift, setting off the multiplier process.

When the aggregate demand curve shifts, macro equilibrium will be upset. Moreover, ***the responses of market participants to an abrupt AD shift are likely to worsen rather than improve market outcomes.*** As a result, the economy may gravitate toward an equilibrium of stagnant recession (point c in Figure 10.6) or persistent inflation (point w in Figure 10.9).

As Keynes saw it, the combination of alternating AD shifts and multiplier effects also causes recurring business cycles. A drop in consumer or business spending can set off a recessionary spiral of declining GDP and prices. A later increase in either consumer or business spending can set the ball rolling in the other direction. This may result in a series of economic booms and busts.

THE ECONOMY TOMORROW

MAINTAINING CONSUMER CONFIDENCE

This chapter emphasized how a sudden change in investment might set off the multiplier process. Investors aren't the only potential culprits, however. A sudden change in government spending or exports could just as easily start the multiplier ball rolling. In fact, the whole process could originate with a change in *consumer* spending.

Consumer Confidence. Recall the two components of consumption: *autonomous* consumption and *induced* consumption. These two components may be expressed as

$$C = a + bY$$

We've seen that autonomous consumption is influenced by *non*income factors, including consumer confidence. What's more, consumer confidence can change abruptly, as Figure 10.10 confirms. When it does, the value of a in the consumption function will change and the consumption function itself will shift. A change in consumer confidence might also change the marginal propensity to consume, the b in the equation. According to a recent World Bank study, every 1 percent change in consumer confidence alters autonomous consumer spending by $1.1 billion.

The reverberation of a change in consumer confidence will cause *two* shifts of the AD curve. The first shift will be due to the effect of changed consumer confidence on *autonomous* consumption. The second shift will result from the multiplier effects on *induced*

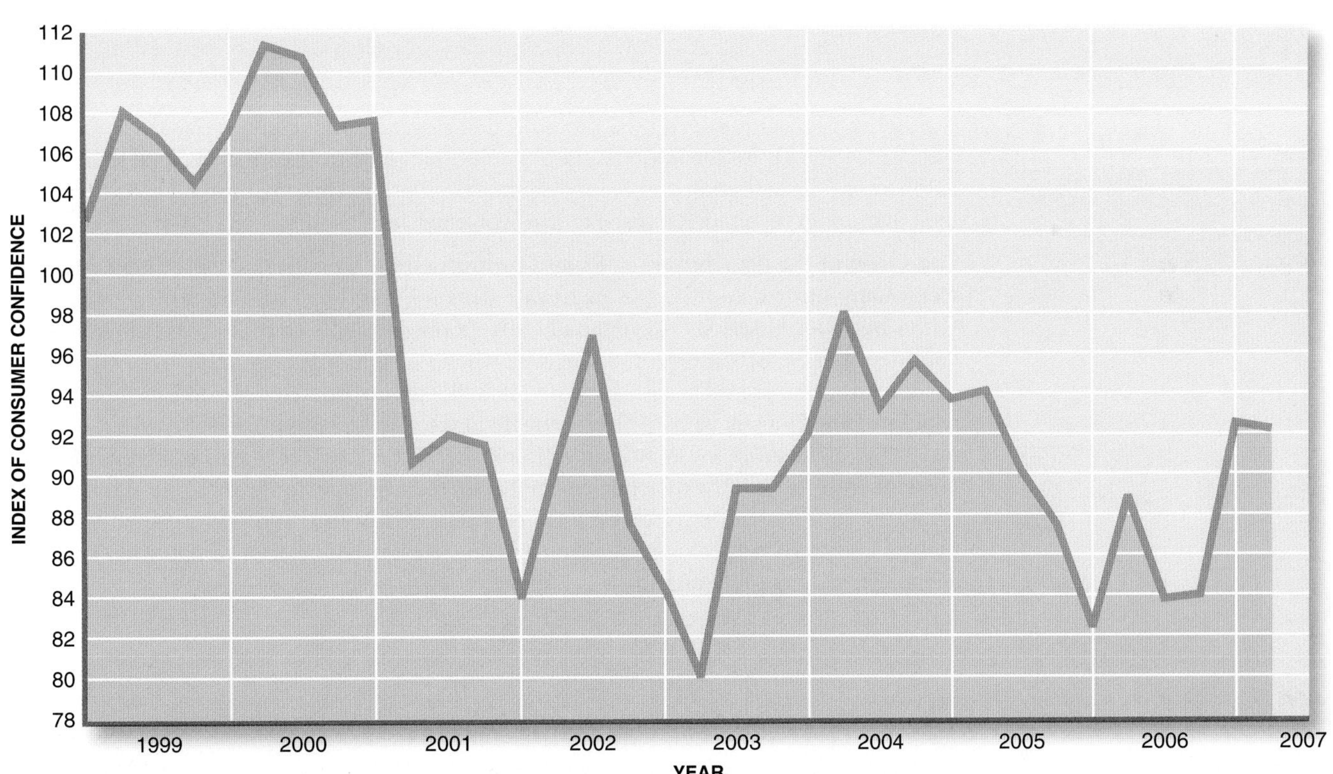

FIGURE 10.10
Consumer Confidence

Consumer confidence is affected by various financial, political, and international events. Changes in consumer confidence affect consumer behavior and thereby shift the AD curve.

Source: University of Michigan

WORLD VIEW

Thrift Shift—The More the Japanese Save for a Rainy Day, the Gloomier It Gets

Stuffing Yen into the Drawer

A decade ago, when Japan was considered economically mighty and the U.S. was struggling, many economists agreed that a big reason for the disparity was savings: The thrifty Japanese had plenty to invest in their future, the wanton Americans too little.

Today, the average Japanese family puts away more than 13 percent of its income, the average American family 4 percent. Yet Japan is in the tank while the U.S. prospers.

Is saving no longer an economic virtue and profligacy no longer a vice? Did Benjamin Franklin get it all wrong? Maybe not—but it isn't as simple as Franklin's Poor Richard's Almanac made it seem:

An economy can save too much.

Japan is the first major developed country since World War II to confront the "paradox of thrift," the condition John Maynard Keynes worried about, where bad times lead individuals to save more, suppressing overall demand and making a country even worse off.

But these days, the pressing savings crisis is in Tokyo. Interest rates on bank deposits run below 1 percent, and still "households are saving too much," says Kengo Inoue, a Bank of Japan economist. "That's depressing demand and, over time, corporate investment." That, in turn, has become a drag on all of Asia.

So the Japanese government nudges its citizens to live it up. The Finance Ministry, concerned that families would simply tuck away a recent $500-a-household income-tax cut, launched a media blitz to advise people on how to spend the money.

—Jacob M. Schlesinger and David P. Hamilton

Source: *The Wall Street Journal,* July 2, 1998. WALL STREET JOURNAL.

Analysis: When Japanese consumers became more pessimistic about their economy, they started saving more and spending less. This shifted AD leftward and deepened the recession. Government officials urged them to spend more.

webnote

For data on consumer confidence visit the University of Michigan at www.sca.isr.umich.edu

consumption. This is exactly the kind of dilemma that prolonged the Japanese recession (see World View). As the outlook got gloomier, Japanese households decided to *decrease* autonomous consumption and reduce the marginal propensity to consume. Unfortunately, their attempt to save more and spend less worsened Japan's recession.

The Official View: Always a Rosy Outlook. Because consumer spending vastly outweighs any other component of aggregate demand, the threat of abrupt changes in consumer behavior is serious. Recognizing this, public officials strive to maintain consumer confidence in the economy tomorrow, even when such confidence might not be warranted. That's what Japanese officials were doing in 1998, described in the World View. That's also why President Hoover, bank officials, and major brokerage houses tried to assure the public in 1929 that the outlook was still rosy. (Look back at the first few pages of Chapter 8.) The "rosy outlook" is still the official perspective on the economy tomorrow. The White House is always upbeat about prospects for the economy. If it weren't—if it were even to hint at the possibility of a recession—consumer and investor confidence might wilt. Then the economy might quickly turn ugly.

SUMMARY

- The circular flow of income has offsetting leakages (consumer saving, taxes, business saving, imports) and injections (autonomous consumption, investment, government spending, exports). LO1
- When desired injections equal leakage, the economy is in equilibrium. LO3
- An imbalance of injections and leakages will cause the economy to expand or contract. An imbalance at full-employment GDP will cause cyclical unemployment or demand-pull inflation. How serious these problems become depends on how the market responds to the initial imbalance. LO3

- Classical economists believed (changing) interest rates and price levels would equalize injections and leakages (especially consumer saving and investment), restoring full-employment equilibrium. LO1, LO3
- Keynes showed that spending imbalances might actually *worsen* if consumer and investor expectations changed. LO2
- An abrupt change in autonomous spending (injections) shifts the AD curve, setting off a sequential multiplier process (further AD shifts) that magnifies changes in equilibrium GDP. LO2
- The multiplier itself is equal to 1/(1 − MPC). It indicates the cumulative change in demand that follows an initial (autonomous) disruption of spending flows. LO2
- As long as the short-run aggregate supply curve slopes upward, AD shifts will affect both real output and prices. LO2
- The recessionary GDP gap measures the amount by which equilibrium GDP falls short of full-employment GDP. LO3
- Sudden changes in consumer confidence would destabilize the economy. To avoid this, policymakers always maintain a rosy outlook. LO2, LO3

Key Terms

aggregate demand
full-employment GDP
leakage
gross business saving
injection
equilibrium GDP
marginal propensity to consume (MPC)
multiplier
recessionary GDP gap
cyclical unemployment
full employment
demand-pull inflation
inflationary GDP gap

Questions for Discussion

1. How might declining prices affect a firm's decision to borrow and invest? LO3
2. Why wouldn't investment and saving flows at full employment always be equal? LO1
3. When unwanted inventories pile up in retail stores, how is production affected? What are the steps in this process? LO3
4. How can equilibrium output exceed full-employment output (as in Figure 10.9)? LO3
5. How might the airline industry job losses described in the News feature on page 200 affect incomes in the clothing and travel industries? LO2
6. Why would Asian economies stall when the U.S. economy slumps (World View, page 202)? How could the Asian economies self-adjust? Is that likely? LO3
7. What forces might turn an economic bust into an economic boom? What forces might put an end to the boom? LO3
8. What might trigger an abrupt decline in consumer spending? LO1, LO3
9. What might get the international multiplier effect (World View, page 202) moving in the right direction? LO2
10. Will the price level always rise when AD increases? Why or why not? LO2

problems The Student Problem Set at the back of this book contains numerical and graphing problems for this chapter.

web activities to accompany this chapter can be found on the Online Learning Center: **http://www.mhhe.com/economics/schiller11e**

Fiscal Policy Tools

The government's tax and spending activities influence economic outcomes. Keynesian theory emphasizes the market's lack of self-adjustment, particularly in recessions. If the market doesn't self-adjust, then the government may have to intervene. Specifically, the government may have to use its tax and spending power (fiscal policy) to stabilize the macro economy at its full-employment price-stability equilibrium. Chapters 11 and 12 look closely at the policy goals, strategies, and tools of fiscal policy.

Fiscal Policy

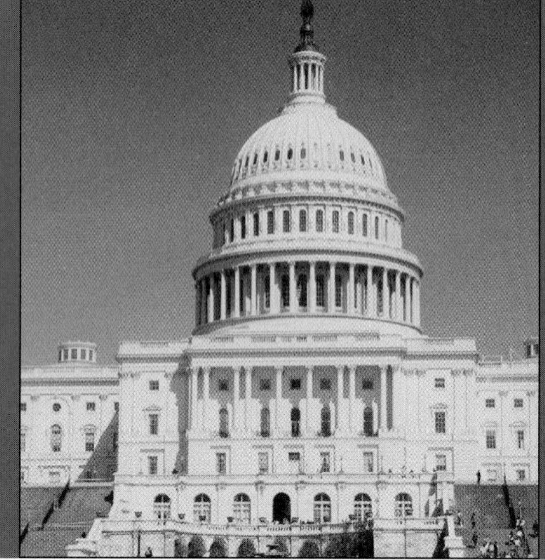

LEARNING OBJECTIVES

After reading this chapter, you should know:

LO1. What the AD shortfall and AD excess measure.

LO2. The tools of fiscal policy.

LO3. How fiscal stimulus or restraint affects macro outcomes.

The Keynesian theory of macro instability is practically a mandate for government intervention. From a Keynesian perspective, too little aggregate demand causes unemployment; too much aggregate demand causes inflation. Since the market itself won't correct these imbalances, the federal government must. Keynes concluded that the government must intervene to manage the level of aggregate demand. This implies increasing aggregate demand when it's deficient and decreasing aggregate demand when it's excessive.

This chapter examines some tools the federal government can use to alter macroeconomic outcomes. The questions we confront are

- **Can government spending and tax policies help ensure full employment?**
- **What policy actions will help fight inflation?**
- **What are the risks of government intervention?**

As we'll see, the government's tax and spending activities affect not only the *level* of output and prices but the *mix* of output as well.

TAXES AND SPENDING

Article I of the U.S. Constitution empowers Congress "to lay and collect taxes, duties, imposts and excises, to pay the debts and provide for the common defense and general welfare of the United States." Up until 1915, however, the federal government collected few taxes and spent little. In 1902, the federal government employed fewer than 350,000 people and spent a mere $650 million. Today, the federal government employs over 4 million people and spends roughly $3 trillion a year.

Government Revenue

The tremendous expansion of the federal government started with the Sixteenth Amendment to the U.S. Constitution (1913), which extended the government's taxing power to *incomes.* Prior to that, most government revenue came from taxes on imports, whiskey, and tobacco. Once the federal government got the power to tax incomes, it had the revenue base to finance increased expenditure.

Today, the federal government collects nearly $3 trillion a year in tax revenues. Nearly half of that revenue comes from individual income taxes (see Figure 4.6). Social Security payroll taxes are the second-largest revenue source, followed at a distance by corporate income taxes. The customs, whiskey, and tobacco taxes on which the federal government depended in 1902 now count for very little.

Government Expenditure

In 1902, federal government expenditures mirrored tax revenues: Both were very small. Today, things are very different. The federal government now spends all of its much larger tax revenues—and more. Uncle Sam even borrows additional funds to pay for federal spending. In Chapter 12 we look at the implications of the budget deficits that help finance federal spending. In this chapter we focus on how government spending *directly* affects **aggregate demand.**

aggregate demand: The total quantity of output demanded at alternative price levels in a given time period, *ceteris paribus.*

Purchases vs. Transfers. To understand how government spending affects aggregate demand, we must again distinguish between government *purchases* and *income transfers.* Government spending on defense, highways, and health care entail the purchase of goods and services in product markets; they're part of aggregate demand. By contrast, the government doesn't buy anything when it mails out Social Security checks. Those checks simply transfer income from taxpayers to retired workers. **Income transfers** don't become part of aggregate demand until the transfer recipients decide to spend that income.

income transfers: Payments to individuals for which no current goods or services are exchanged, such as Social Security, welfare, unemployment benefits.

As we observed in Chapter 4, less than half of all federal government spending entails the purchase of goods and services. The rest of federal spending is either an income transfer or an interest payment on the national debt.

Fiscal Policy

The federal government's tax and spending powers give it a great deal of influence over aggregate demand. ***The government can alter aggregate demand by***

- ***Purchasing more or fewer goods and services.***
- ***Raising or lowering taxes.***
- ***Changing the level of income transfers.***

Fiscal policy entails the use of these various budget levers to influence macroeconomic outcomes. ***From a macro perspective, the federal budget is a tool that can shift aggregate demand and thereby alter macroeconomic outcomes.*** Figure 11.1 puts this tool into the framework of the basic AS/AD model.

fiscal policy: The use of government taxes and spending to alter macroeconomic outcomes.

Although fiscal policy can be used to pursue any of our economic goals, we begin our study by exploring its potential to ensure full employment. We then look at its impact on inflation. Along the way we also observe the potential of fiscal policy to alter the mix of output and the distribution of income.

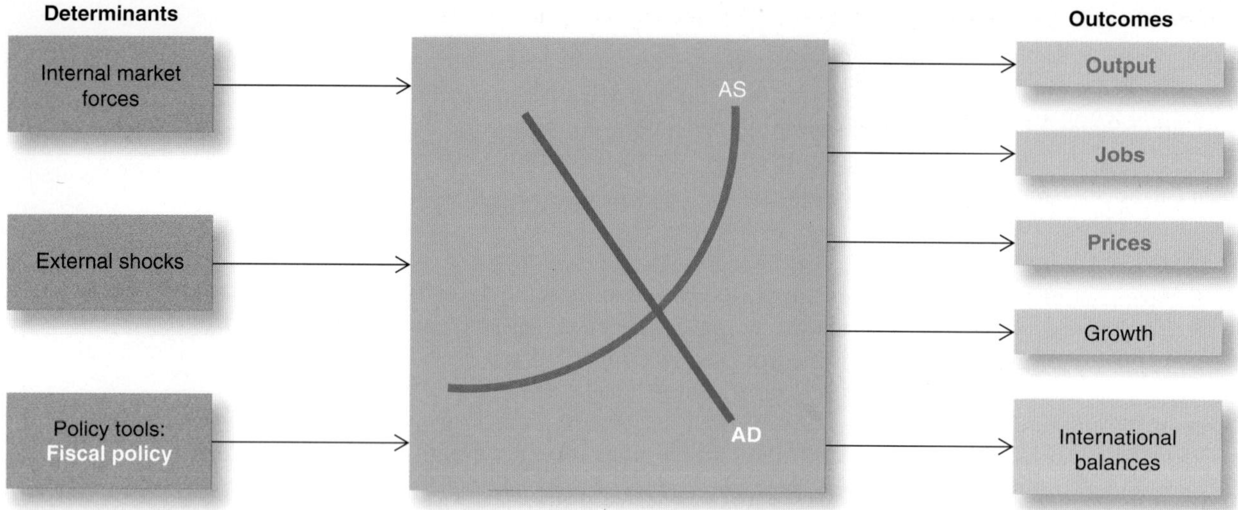

FIGURE 11.1
Fiscal Policy

Fiscal policy refers to the use of the government tax and spending powers to alter macro outcomes. Fiscal policy works principally through shifts of the aggregate demand curve.

FISCAL STIMULUS

equilibrium (macro): The combination of price level and real output that is compatible with both aggregate demand and aggregate supply.

The basic premise of fiscal policy is that the market's short-run macro equilibrium may not be a desirable one. This is clearly the case in Figure 11.2. **Macro equilibrium** occurs at Q_E, where $5.6 trillion of output is being produced. Full-employment GDP occurs at Q_F, where the real value of output is $6 trillion. Accordingly, the economy depicted in Figure 11.2 confronts a **recessionary GDP gap** of $400 billion.

Keynesian Strategy

recessionary GDP gap: The amount by which equilibrium GDP falls short of full-employment GDP.

The Keynesian model of the adjustment process helps us not only understand how an economy can get into such trouble but also see how it might get out. Keynes emphasized how the aggregate demand curve *shifts* with changes in spending behavior. He also emphasized how new injections of spending into the circular flow multiply into much larger changes in total spending. From a Keynesian perspective, then, the way out of recession is obvious:

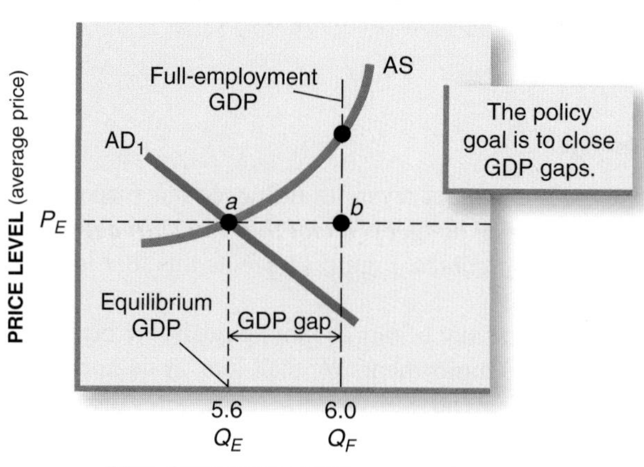

FIGURE 11.2
The Policy Goal

If the economy is in a recessionary equilibrium like point *a*, the policy goal is to increase output to full employment (Q_F). Keynes urged the government to use its tax and spending powers to shift the AD curve rightward.

Get someone to spend more on goods and services. Should desired spending increase, the aggregate demand curve would *shift* to the right, leading the economy out of recession. That additional spending impetus could come from increased government purchases or from tax cuts that induce increased consumption or investment. Such a **fiscal stimulus** might propel the economy out of recession.

fiscal stimulus: Tax cuts or spending hikes intended to increase (shift) aggregate demand.

Although the general strategy for Keynesian fiscal policy is clear, the scope of desired intervention isn't so evident. Two strategic policy questions must be addressed:

- By how much do we want to shift the AD curve to the right?
- How can we induce the desired shift?

The Fiscal Target

At first glance, the size of the desired AD shift might seem obvious. If the GDP gap is $400 billion, why not just increase aggregate demand by that amount?

The Naive Keynesian Model. Keynes thought that policy might just work. The intent of the expansionary fiscal policy is to achieve full employment. In Figure 11.3, this goal would be attained at point *b*. When the AD curve shifts rightward by $400 billion, the new AD_2 curve in fact passes through point *b*, creating the possibility of achieving our full-employment goal.

Will the economy move so easily from point *a* to point *b*? Only under very special conditions. The economy would move from point *a* to point *b* in Figure 11.3 only if the **aggregate supply** curve were horizontal. In other words, we'd achieve full employment at the current price level (P_E) with the shift to AD_2 only if prices didn't rise when the economy expanded. This is the expectation of the naive Keynesian model. In fairness to Keynes, we must recall that he developed this approach during the Great Depression, when prices were *falling*. No one was worried that prices would rise if demand increased.

aggregate supply: The total quantity of output producers are willing and able to supply at alternative price levels in a given time period, *ceteris paribus*.

Price-Level Changes. Even in today's economy, prices may not rise every time aggregate demand increases. Over some ranges of real output, the AS curve may actually be horizontal. Eventually, however, we expect the AS curve to slope upward. When it does, any increase in aggregate demand affects both real output *and* prices. In those circumstances, an increase in aggregate demand doesn't translate dollar-for-dollar into increased real GDP.

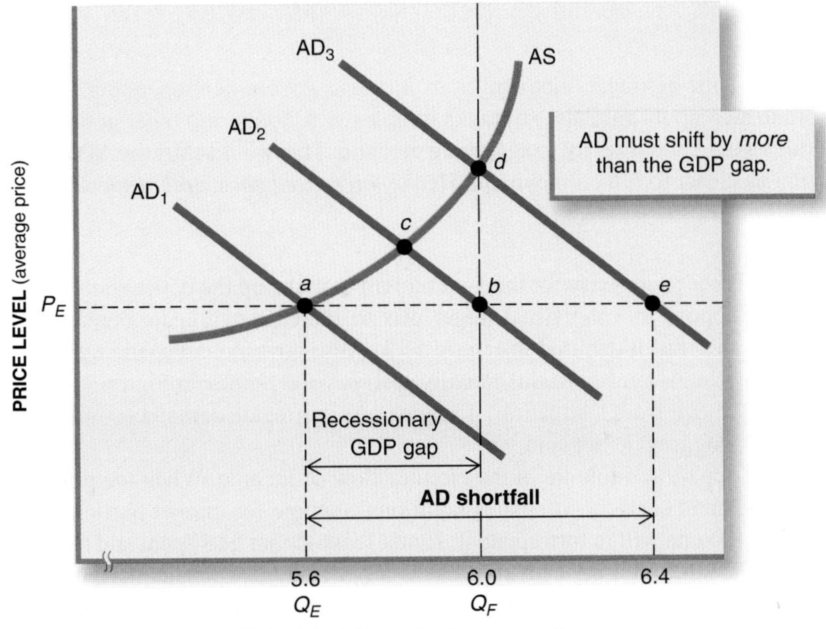

FIGURE 11.3
The AD Shortfall

If aggregate demand increased by the amount of the recessionary GDP gap, we would get a shift from AD_1 to AD_2. The new equilibrium would occur at point *c*, leaving the economy short of full employment (Q_F). (Some of the increased demand pushes up prices instead of output.)

To reach full-employment equilibrium (point *d*), the AD curve must shift to AD_3, thereby eliminating the entire AD shortfall. The AD shortfall—the horizontal distance between point *a* and point *e*—is the fiscal policy target for achieving full employment.

Instead, ***when the AD curve shifts to the right, the economy moves up the aggregate supply (AS) curve, not horizontally to the right. As a result both real output and the price level change.***

Figure 11.3 illustrates the consequences of the upward-sloping aggregate supply curve. Suppose we actually increased aggregate demand by $400 billion, an amount equal to the initial GDP gap. When the aggregate demand curve shifts from AD_1 to AD_2, the economy moves to the macro equilibrium at point *c,* not to point *b.* As demand picks up, we expect cost pressures to increase, pushing the price level up the upward-sloping AS curve. At point *c*, the AS and AD_2 curves intersect, establishing a new equilibrium. At that equilibrium, the price level is higher than it was initially (P_E). Real output is higher as well. But at point *c* we are still short of the full-employment target (Q_F). Hence, the naive Keynesian policy fails to achieve full employment. To do better, we must recognize that ***shifting (increasing) aggregate demand by the amount of the GDP gap will achieve full employment only if the price level doesn't rise.***

The AD Shortfall. Although the naive Keynesian approach doesn't work, we needn't forsake fiscal policy. Figure 11.3 simply tells us that the naive Keynesian policy prescription (increasing AD by the amount of the GDP gap) probably won't cure all our unemployment ills. It also suggests, however, that a *larger* dose of fiscal stimulus might just work. ***So long as the AS curve slopes upward, we must increase aggregate demand by more than the size of the recessionary GDP gap in order to achieve full employment.***

AD shortfall: The amount of additional aggregate demand needed to achieve full employment after allowing for price-level changes.

Figure 11.3 illustrates this new policy target. The **AD shortfall** is the amount of additional aggregate demand needed to achieve full employment *after allowing for price-level changes.* Notice in Figure 11.3 that full employment (Q_F) is achieved only when the AD curve intersects the AS curve at point *d.* To get there, the aggregate demand curve must shift from AD_1 all the way to AD_3. That third aggregate demand curve passes through point *e* as well. Hence, aggregate demand must increase until it passes through point *e.* This ***horizontal distance between point* a *and point* e *in Figure 11.3 measures the AD shortfall.*** Aggregate demand must increase (shift) by the amount of the AD shortfall in order to achieve full employment. Thus, ***the AD shortfall is the fiscal target.*** In Figure 11.3, the AD shortfall amounts to $800 billion ($0.8 trillion). That's how much *additional* aggregate demand is required to reach full employment (Q_F).

Were we to increase AD by enough to attain full employment, it's apparent in Figure 11.3 that prices would increase as well. We'll examine this dilemma later; for the time being we focus on the policy options for increasing aggregate demand by the desired amount.

More Government Spending

The simplest way to shift aggregate demand is to increase government spending. If the government were to step up its purchases of tanks, highways, schools, and other goods, the increased spending would add directly to aggregate demand. This would shift the AD curve rightward, moving us closer to full employment. Hence, ***increased government spending is a form of fiscal stimulus.***

Multiplier Effects. It isn't necessary for the government to make up the entire shortfall in aggregate demand. Suppose that the fiscal target was to increase aggregate demand by $800 billion, the AD shortfall illustrated in Figure 11.3. Were government spending to increase by that amount, the AD curve would actually shift *beyond* point *e* in Figure 11.3. In that case we'd quickly move from a situation of *inadequate* aggregate demand (point *a*) to a situation of *excessive* aggregate demand.

The origins of this apparent riddle lie in the circular flow of income. When the government buys more goods and services, it creates additional income for market participants. The recipients of this income will in turn spend it. Hence, each dollar gets spent and respent many times. This is the multiplier adjustment process we encountered in Chapter 10. As a result of this process, ***every dollar of new government spending has a multiplied impact on aggregate demand.***

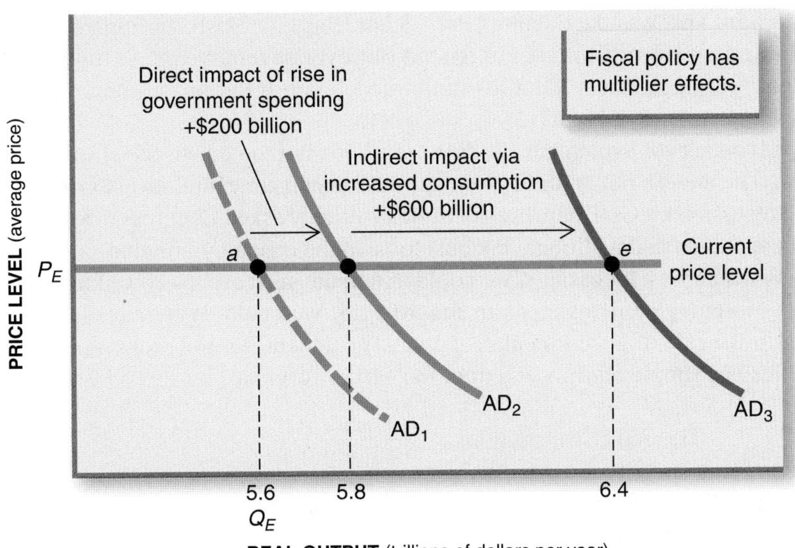

FIGURE 11.4
Multiplier Effects

Fiscal stimulus will set off the multiplier process. As a result of this, aggregate demand will increase (shift) in two distinct steps: (1) the initial fiscal stimulus (AD_1 to AD_2) and (2) induced changes in consumption (AD_2 to AD_3). In this case, a $200 billion increase in government spending causes an $800 billion increase in aggregate demand at the *existing* price level.

How much "bang" the economy gets for each government "buck" depends on the value of the **multiplier.** Specifically,

$$\text{Total change in spending} = \text{multiplier} \times \text{new spending injection}$$

The multiplier adds a lot of punch to fiscal policy. Suppose that households have a **marginal propensity to consume** equal to 0.75. In this case, the multiplier would have a value of 4 and each dollar of new government expenditure would increase aggregate demand by $4.

Figure 11.4 illustrates that leveraged impact of government spending. Aggregate demand shifts from AD_1 to AD_2 when the government buys an additional $200 billion of output. Multiplier effects then increase consumption spending by $600 billion more. This additional consumption shifts aggregate demand further, to AD_3. Thus, ***the impact of fiscal stimulus on aggregate demand includes both the new government spending and all subsequent increases in consumer spending triggered by multiplier effects.*** In Figure 11.4, the shift from AD_1 to AD_3 includes

AD_1 to AD_2: Shift due to $200 billion injection of new government spending.
AD_2 to AD_3: Shift due to multiplier-induced increase in consumption ($600 billion).

As a result of these initial and multiplier-induced shifts, aggregate demand at the current price level (P_E) increases by $800 billion. Thus,

$$\text{Cumulative increase (horizontal shift) in AD} = \text{new spending injection (fiscal stimulus)} + \text{induced increase in consumption}$$

$$= \text{multiplier} \times \text{fiscal stimulus (new spending injection)}$$

The second equation is identical to the first but expressed in the terminology of fiscal policy. The "fiscal stimulus" is the "new spending injection" that sets the multiplier process in motion.

multiplier: The multiple by which an initial change in aggregate spending will alter total expenditure after an infinite number of spending cycles; 1/(1 − MPC).

marginal propensity to consume (MPC): The fraction of each additional (marginal) dollar of disposable income spent on consumption; the change in consumption divided by the change in disposable income.

The Desired Stimulus. Multiplier effects make changes in government spending a powerful policy lever. The multiplier also increases the risk of error, however. Whereas too little fiscal stimulus may leave the economy in a recession, too much can rapidly lead to excessive spending and inflation. This was the dilemma President George W. Bush confronted in his first year. He wanted a $1.6 trillion tax cut spread out over several years. Critics worried, however, that too much fiscal stimulus might accelerate inflation. A compromise of $1.35 trillion was struck in early 2001.

After the terrorist attacks of September 11, 2001, too *little,* not too much, fiscal stimulus was a greater risk. The attacks put an immediate damper on consumer and investor spending, widening the recessionary GDP gap. President Bush quickly asked Congress to approve more government spending and additional tax cuts to keep the economy growing.

Policy decisions would be a lot easier if we could anticipate such events. If we knew the exact dimensions of aggregate demand, as in Figure 11.3, we could easily calculate the required increase in the rate of government spending. The general formula for computing the *desired* stimulus is a simple rearrangement of the earlier formula:

$$\text{Desired fiscal stimulus} = \frac{\text{AD shortfall}}{\text{the multiplier}}$$

In the economy in Figure 11.3, we assumed the policy goal was to increase aggregate demand by the amount of the AD shortfall ($800 billion). Accordingly, we conclude that

$$\text{Desired fiscal stimulus} = \frac{\$800 \text{ billion}}{4}$$

$$= \$200 \text{ billion}$$

To see what happened to real GDP in South Korea after the 2001 fiscal stimulus, check out GDP data at www.koreaeconomy.org

In other words, a $200 billion increase in government spending at the current price level would be enough fiscal stimulus to close the $800 billion AD shortfall and achieve full employment.

In practice, we rarely know the exact size of the shortfall in aggregate demand. The multiplier is also harder to calculate when taxes and imports enter the picture. Nevertheless, the foregoing formula does provide a useful rule of thumb for determining how much fiscal stimulus is needed to achieve any desired increase in aggregate demand. Such calculations helped the South Korean government decide how much fiscal stimulus was needed in 2001 to keep its economy out of recession (see World View).

Tax Cuts

Although injections of government spending can close a GDP gap, increased government purchases aren't the only way to get there. The increased demand required to raise output and employment levels from Q_E to Q_F could emerge from increases in autonomous consumption or investment as well as from increased government spending. It could also come

WORLD VIEW

Seoul Plans Spending to Boost Economy

South Korea's finance minister, Jin Nyum, said the government, state-run companies and funds would increase third-quarter spending on infrastructure and other projects by 4.3 trillion won ($3.35 billion) to a total 30.3 trillion won, in a move to bolster an economy that has been hurt by declining exports. He spoke after President Kim Dae Jung met with economic ministers. Among planned steps to boost the economy are a cut in interest rates on loans to companies that participate in state projects and increased financial support to exporters. The government is also considering a tax cut, Mr. Jin said.

Analysis: Fear of a pending decline in aggregate demand prompted South Korea's government to increase government spending on roads, bridges, and telecom networks. The government hoped such a fiscal stimulus would offset a decline in export sales and avert recession.

IN THE NEWS 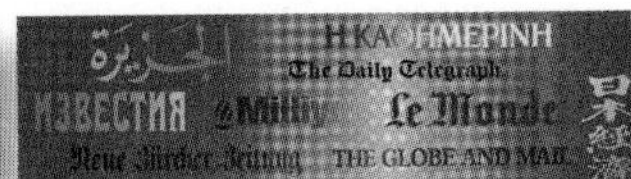  

Spending Propels Growth

Fueled by a surge in consumer spending, the U.S. economy took off in the July–September period, with growth running perhaps as high as a 7 percent annual rate, a number of economists said yesterday.

Such predictions got a boost from a Commerce Department report yesterday that retail sales grew at a 12.2 percent annual rate in the third quarter, despite a 0.2 percent decline last month. Some analysts said the federal personal income tax cut that took effect July 1 was partially responsible for the jump in spending.

"You give consumers a tax cut and they'll spend it," said Ken Mayland of ClearView Economics in Cleveland. "That's the way America works."

—John M. Berry

Source: *The Washington Post,* October 16, 2003.

Analysis: Tax cuts increase disposable incomes. Typically, consumers use most of this increased income to buy more products, thereby shifting AD rightward.

from abroad, in the form of increased demand for our exports. In other words, any "Big Spender" would help, whether from the public sector or the private sector. Of course, the reason we're initially at Q_E instead of Q_F in Figure 11.3 is that consumers, investors, and export buyers have chosen *not* to spend as much as required for full employment.

Consumer and investor decisions are subject to change. Moreover, fiscal policy can encourage such changes. Congress not only buys goods and services but also levies taxes. By lowering taxes, the government increases the **disposable income** of the private sector. This was the objective of the early Bush tax cuts, which gave all tax payers a rebate of \$300–600 in the summer of 2001. By putting \$38 billion more after-tax income into the hands of consumers, Congress hoped to stimulate (shift) the consumption component of aggregate demand.

disposable income: After-tax income of consumers; personal income less personal taxes.

Taxes and Consumption. A tax cut directly increases the disposable income of consumers. The question here, however, is how a tax cut affects *spending.* By how much will consumption increase for every dollar of tax cuts?

The answer lies in the marginal propensity to consume. Consumers won't spend every dollar of tax cuts; they'll *save* some of the cut and spend the rest. The MPC tells us how the tax-cut dollar will be split between saving and spending. If the MPC is 0.75, consumers will spend \$0.75 out of every tax-cut \$1.00. In other words,

$$\text{Initial increase in consumption} = \text{MPC} \times \text{tax cut}$$

If taxes were cut by \$200 billion, the resulting spree would amount to

$$\begin{aligned}\text{Initial increase in consumption} &= 0.75 \times \$200 \text{ billion}\\ &= \$150 \text{ billion}\end{aligned}$$

Hence, ***the effect of a tax cut that increases disposable incomes is to stimulate consumer spending.*** A tax cut therefore shifts the aggregate demand curve to the right. This chain of events is what the accompanying News calls "the way America works."

The initial consumption spree induced by a tax cut starts the multiplier process in motion. The new consumer spending creates additional income for producers and workers, who will then use the additional income to increase their own consumption. This will propel us along the multiplier path already depicted in Figure 11.4. The cumulative change in total spending will be

$$\frac{\text{Cumulative change}}{\text{in spending}} = \text{multiplier} \times \frac{\text{initial change}}{\text{in consumption}}$$

In this case, the cumulative change is

$$\text{Cumulative change in spending} = \frac{1}{1 - \text{MPC}} \times \$150 \text{ billion}$$
$$= 4 \times \$150 \text{ billion}$$
$$= \$600 \text{ billion}$$

Here again we see that the multiplier increases the impact on aggregate demand of a fiscal policy stimulus. There's an important difference here, though. When we increased government spending by $200 billion, aggregate demand increased by $800 billion. When we cut taxes by $200 billion, however, aggregate demand increases by only $600 billion. Hence, ***a tax cut contains less fiscal stimulus than an increase in government spending of the same size.***

The lesser stimulative power of tax cuts is explained by consumer saving. Only part of a tax cut gets spent. Consumers save the rest. This is evident in Figure 11.5, which illustrates the successive rounds of the multiplier process. Notice that the tax cut is used to increase both consumption and saving, according to the MPC. Only that part of the tax cut that's used for consumption enters the circular flow as a spending injection. Hence, ***the initial spending injection is less than the size of the tax cuts.*** By contrast, every dollar of government purchases goes directly into the circular flow. Accordingly, tax cuts are less powerful than government purchases because the initial *spending* injection is smaller.

This doesn't mean we can't close the AD shortfall with a tax cut. It simply means that the desired tax cut must be larger than the required stimulus. It remains true that

$$\text{Desired fiscal stimulus} = \frac{\text{AD shortfall}}{\text{the multiplier}}$$

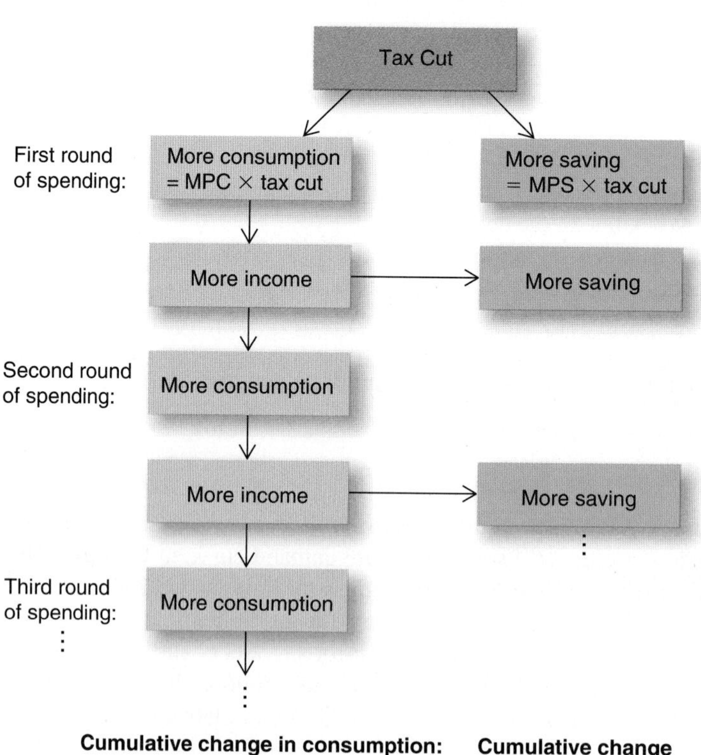

FIGURE 11.5
The Tax Cut Multiplier

Only part of a tax cut is used to increase consumption; the remainder is saved. Accordingly, the initial spending injection is less than the tax cut. This makes tax cuts less stimulative than government purchases of the same size. The multiplier still goes to work on that new consumer spending, however.

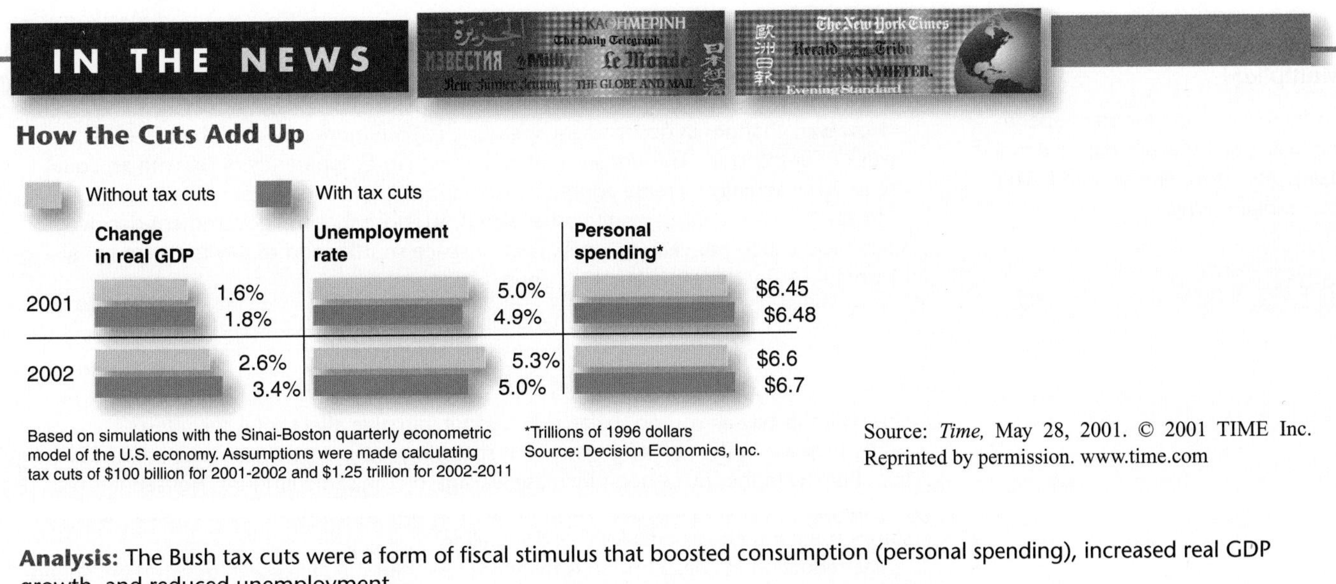

Source: *Time,* May 28, 2001. © 2001 TIME Inc. Reprinted by permission. www.time.com

Analysis: The Bush tax cuts were a form of fiscal stimulus that boosted consumption (personal spending), increased real GDP growth, and reduced unemployment.

But now we're using a consumption shift as the fiscal stimulus rather than increased government spending. Hence, we have to allow for the fact that the initial surge in consumption (the fiscal stimulus) will be *less* than the tax cut. Specifically,

$$\text{Initial consumption injection} = \text{MPC} \times \text{tax cut}$$

Hence, if we want to use a consumer tax cut to close a GDP gap, we have

$$\text{Desired tax cut} = \frac{\text{desired fiscal stimulus}}{\text{MPC}}$$

In the economy in Figure 11.3, we assumed that the desired stimulus is $200 billion and the MPC equals 0.75. Hence, the desired tax cut is

$$\text{Desired tax cut} = \frac{\$200 \text{ billion}}{0.75} = \$267 \text{ billion}$$

By cutting taxes $267 billion, we directly increase disposable income by the same amount. Consumers then increase their rate of spending $200 billion (0.75 × $267 billion); they save the remaining $67 billion. As the added spending enters the circular flow, it starts the multiplier process, ultimately increasing aggregate demand by $800 billion per year.

This comparison of government purchases and tax cuts clearly reveals their respective power. What we've demonstrated is that ***a dollar of tax cuts is less stimulative than a dollar of government purchases.*** This doesn't mean that tax cuts are undesirable, just that they need to be larger than the desired injection of spending. The nearby News shows that the 2001 tax cut boosted both consumer spending and, as a result, real GDP growth.

The different effects of tax cuts and increased government spending have an important implication for government budgets. Because some of the power of a tax cut "leaks" into saving, tax increases don't "offset" government spending of equal value. This unexpected result is described in Table 11.1.

webnote

Different views of how the Bush tax cuts might affect spending, employment, and real GDP are available from the Heritage Foundation at www.heritage.org/research/taxes/issues2004.cfm and the Brookings Institution at www.brookings.edu/comm/policybriefs/pb101.htm

Taxes and Investment. A tax cut may also be an effective mechanism for increasing *investment* spending. As we observed in Chapter 9, investment decisions are guided by expectations of future profit. If a cut in corporate taxes raises potential after-tax profits, it should encourage additional investment. Once additional investment spending enters the circular flow, it, too, has a multiplier effect.

TABLE 11.1
The Balanced Budget Multiplier

An increase in government spending paid for by a tax cut of equal size shifts aggregate demand. This box explains why.

Many taxpayers and politicians demand that any new government spending be balanced with new taxes. Such balancing at the margin, it's asserted, will keep the budget deficit from rising, while avoiding further economic stimulus.

However, changes in government spending (*G*) are more powerful than changes in taxes (*T*) or transfers. This implies that an increase in *G* apparently offset with an equal rise in *T* will actually increase aggregate demand.

To see how this curious result comes about, suppose that the government decided to spend $50 billion per year on a new fleet of space shuttles and to pay for them by raising income taxes by the same amount. Thus

$$\begin{aligned} \text{Change in } G &= +\$50 \text{ billion per year} \\ \text{Change in } T &= +\$50 \text{ billion per year} \\ \text{Change in budget balance} &= 0 \end{aligned}$$

How will this pay-as-you-go (balanced) budget initiative affect total spending?

The increase in the rate of government spending represents a new injection of $50 billion. But the higher taxes don't increase leakage by the same amount. Households will pay taxes by reducing *both* consumption and saving. The initial reduction in annual consumer spending equals only MPC × $50 billion.

The reduction in consumption is therefore less than the increase in government spending, implying a net increase in *aggregate* spending. The *initial* change in aggregate demand brought about by this balanced budget expenditure is

$$\begin{aligned} \text{Initial increase in government spending} &= \$50 \text{ billion} \\ \text{less Initial reduction in consumer spending} &= \underline{\text{MPC} \times \$50 \text{ billion}} \\ \text{Net initial change in total spending} &= (1 - \text{MPC})\$50 \text{ billion} \end{aligned}$$

Like any other changes in the rate of spending, this initial increase in aggregate spending will start a multiplier process in motion. The *cumulative* change in expenditure will be much larger, as indicated by the multiplier. In this case, the cumulative (ultimate) change in total spending is

$$\begin{array}{c} \text{The multiplier} \times \text{initial change in spending per year} = \text{cumulative change in total spending} \\ \dfrac{1}{1 - \text{MPC}} \times (1 - \text{MPC})\$50 \text{ billion} = \$50 \text{ billion} \end{array}$$

Thus, the balanced budget multiplier is equal to 1. In this case, a $50 billion increase in annual government expenditure combined with an equivalent increase in taxes increases aggregate demand by $50 billion per year.

webnote

To follow the ups and downs of Federal income tax as a percentage of GDP, go to the Congressional Budget Office at www.cbo.gov and choose "Historical Budget Data."

Tax cuts designed to stimulate consumption (*C*) and investment (*I*) have been used frequently. In 1963, President John F. Kennedy announced his intention to reduce taxes in order to stimulate the economy, citing that the marginal propensity to consume for the average U.S. family at that time appeared to be exceptionally high.

The second-largest tax cut in history was initiated by President Ronald Reagan. In 1981, Congress cut personal taxes $250 billion over a 3-year period and cut business taxes another $70 billion. The resulting increase in disposable income stimulated consumer spending and helped push the economy out of the 1981–82 recession. When the economy slowed down at the end of the 1980s, President George H. Bush proposed to cut the capital gains tax, hoping to stimulate investment. President Clinton also embraced the notion of tax incentives for investment. He favored a tax credit for new investments in plant and equipment to increase the level of investment and set off multiplier effects for many years.

President George W. Bush pulled out all the tax-cut stops. Immediately upon taking office in 2001, he convinced Congress to pass a $1.35 trillion tax cut for consumers, spread over several years. He followed that up with business tax cuts in 2002 and 2003. The cumulative impact of these tax cuts shifted AD significantly to the right and accelerated recovery from the 2001 recession.

Increased Transfers

A third fiscal policy option for stimulating the economy is to increase transfer payments. If Social Security recipients, welfare recipients, unemployment insurance beneficiaries, and veterans get larger benefit checks, they'll have more disposable income to spend. The resulting increase in consumption will boost aggregate demand.

Increased transfer payments don't, however, increase injections dollar-for-dollar. Here again, we have to recognize that consumers will save some of their additional transfer payments; only part (MPC) of the additional income will be injected into the spending stream. Hence, ***the initial fiscal stimulus (AD shift) of increased transfer payments is***

$$\text{Initial fiscal stimulus (injection)} = \text{MPC} \times \text{increase in transfer payments.}$$

This initial stimulus sets the multiplier in motion, shifting the aggregate demand curve further to the right.

FISCAL RESTRAINT

The objective of fiscal policy isn't always to increase aggregate demand. At times the economy is already expanding too fast and **fiscal restraint** is more appropriate. In these circumstances, policymakers are likely to be focused on inflation, not unemployment. Their objective will be to *reduce* aggregate demand, not to stimulate it.

fiscal restraint: Tax hikes or spending cuts intended to reduce (shift) aggregate demand.

The means available to the federal government for restraining aggregate demand emerge again from both sides of the budget. The difference here is that we use the budget tools in reverse. We now want to reduce government spending, increase taxes, or decrease transfer payments.

The Fiscal Target

As before, our first task is to determine how much we want aggregate demand to fall. To determine this, we must consult Figure 11.6. The initial equilibrium in this case occurs at point E_1, where the AS and AD_1 curves intersect. At that equilibrium the unemployment rate falls below the rate consistent with full employment (Q_F) and we produce the output Q_1. The resulting strains on production push the price level to P_E, higher than we're willing to accept. Our goal is to maintain the price level at P_F, which is consistent with our notion of full employment *and* price stability.

In this case, we have an **inflationary GDP gap**—that is, equilibrium GDP exceeds full-employment GDP by the amount $Q_1 - Q_F$, or \$200 billion. If we want to restore price stability (P_F), however, we need to reduce aggregate demand by *more* than this GDP gap.

inflationary GDP gap: The amount by which equilibrium GDP exceeds full-employment GDP.

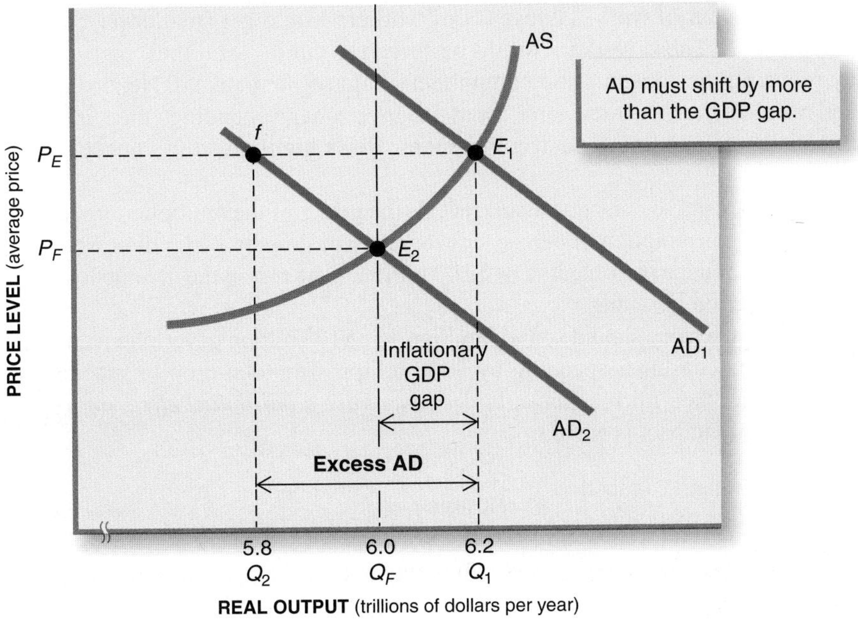

FIGURE 11.6
Excess Aggregate Demand

Too much aggregate demand (AD_1) causes the price level to rise (P_E) above its desired level (P_F). To restore price stability, the AD curve must shift leftward by the entire amount of the excess AD (here shown as $Q_1 - Q_2$). In this case, the excess AD amounts to \$400 billion. If AD shifts by that much (from AD_1 to AD_2), the excess AD is eliminated and equilibrium moves from E_1 to E_2.

AD excess: The amount by which aggregate demand must be reduced to achieve full-employment equilibrium after allowing for price-level changes.

The **AD excess** takes into account potential changes in the price level. Observe that ***the AD excess exceeds the inflationary GDP gap.*** In Figure 11.6, the AD excess equals the horizontal distance from E_1 to point *f*, which amounts to \$400 billion. This excess aggregate demand is our fiscal policy target. To restore price stability, we must shift the AD curve leftward until it passes through point *f*. The AD_2 curve does this. The shift to AD_2 moves the economy to a new equilibrium at E_2. At E_2 we have less output but also a lower price level (less inflation).

Knowing the dimensions of excess aggregate demand, we can compute the desired fiscal restraint as

$$\text{Desired fiscal restraint} = \frac{\text{excess AD}}{\text{the multiplier}}$$

In other words, first we determine how far we want to shift the AD curve to the left, that is, the AD excess. Then we compute how much government spending or taxes must be changed to achieve the desired shift, taking into account multiplier effects.

Budget Cuts

The first option to consider is budget cuts. By how much should we reduce government expenditure on goods and services? The answer is simple in this case: We first calculate the desired fiscal restraint, as computed above. Then we cut government expenditure by that amount.

The GDP gap in Figure 11.6 amounts to \$200 billion ($Q_1 - Q_F$). If aggregate demand is reduced by that amount, however, some of the restraint will be dissipated in price-level reductions. To bring *equilibrium* GDP down to the full-employment (Q_F) level, even more of a spending reduction is needed. In this case, the excess AD amounts to \$400 billion.

Budget cuts of less than \$400 billion will achieve the desired reduction in aggregate demand. If we assume a marginal propensity to consume of 0.75, the multiplier equals 4. In these circumstances, the desired fiscal restraint is

$$\begin{aligned}\text{Desired fiscal restraint} &= \frac{\text{excess AD}}{\text{the multiplier}}\\ &= \frac{\$400\text{ billion}}{4}\\ &= \$100\text{ billion}\end{aligned}$$

What would happen to aggregate demand if the federal government cut that much spending out of, say, the defense budget? Such a military cutback would throw a lot of aerospace employees out of work. Thousands of workers would get smaller paychecks, or perhaps none at all. These workers would be forced to cut back on their own spending, thereby reducing the consumption component of aggregate demand. Hence, aggregate demand would take two hits: first a cut in government spending, then induced cutbacks in consumer spending. The accompanying News highlights the impact of this multiplier process.

The marginal propensity to consume again reveals the power of the multiplier process. If the MPC is 0.75, the consumption of aerospace workers will drop by \$75 billion when the government cutbacks reduce their income by \$100 billion. (The rest of the income loss will be covered by a reduction in saving.)

From this point on the story should sound familiar. The \$100 billion government cutback will ultimately reduce consumer spending by \$300 billion. The total drop in spending is thus \$400 billion. Like their mirror image, ***budget cuts have a multiplied effect on aggregate demand.*** The total impact is equal to

$$\text{Cumulative reduction in spending} = \text{multiplier} \times \text{initial budget cut (fiscal restraint)}$$

This cumulative reduction in spending would eliminate excess aggregate demand. We conclude, then, that ***the budget cuts should equal the size of the desired fiscal restraint.***

IN THE NEWS 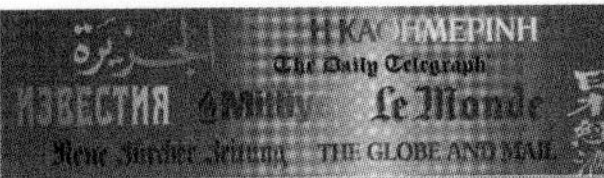  

Economy Is Already Feeling the Impact of Federal Government's Spending Cuts

WASHINGTON—Skeptical about the federal government's pledge to tighten its belt? Consider this: It already has, and that's one reason the economy is so sluggish.

Federal purchases of goods and services dropped 3.3 percent in 1992, the first decline in three years and the largest in almost 20. Behind the decline were huge defense cutbacks: These purchases tumbled more than 6.0 percent during the year. . . .

The economy has felt the pinch. Kurl Karl of the WEFA Group, economic consultants based in suburban Philadelphia, estimates that cuts in purchases by the federal government knocked as much as 0.5 percentage point off the gross domestic product last year, costing roughly 400,000 jobs, and will probably do the same in 1993.

"Government cuts in defense spending have definitely been a drag" on the economy, says Jim O'Sullivan, economist with Morgan Guaranty in New York.

—Lucinda Harper

Source: *The Wall Street Journal,* August 18, 1993.

Analysis: Reductions in governmental spending on goods and services directly decrease aggregate demand. Multiplier effects induce additional cutbacks in consumption, further reducing aggregate demand.

Tax Hikes

Tax increases can also be used to shift the AD curve to the left. The direct effect of a tax increase is a reduction in disposable income. People will pay the higher taxes by reducing their consumption *and* saving less. Only the reduced consumption results in less aggregate demand. As consumers tighten their belts, they set off the multiplier process, leading again to a much larger, cumulative shift of aggregate demand.

Because people pay higher tax bills by reducing both consumption and saving (by MPC and MPS, respectively), ***taxes must be increased more than a dollar to get a dollar of fiscal restraint.*** This leads us to the following guideline:

$$\text{Desired increase in taxes} = \frac{\text{desired fiscal restraint}}{\text{MPC}}$$

In other words, changes in taxes must always be larger than the desired change in leakages or injections. How much larger depends on the marginal propensity to consume. In this case

$$\text{Desired fiscal restraint} = \frac{\text{excess AD}}{\text{the multiplier}} = \frac{\$400 \text{ billion}}{4} = \$100 \text{ billion}$$

Therefore, the appropriate tax increase is

$$\text{Desired tax hike} = \frac{\text{desired fiscal restraint}}{\text{the multiplier}} = \frac{\$100 \text{ billion}}{\text{MPC}} = \frac{\$100 \text{ billion}}{0.75} = \$133 \text{ billion}$$

Were taxes increased by this amount, consumers would reduce their consumption by \$100 billion (= 0.75 × \$133 billion). This cutback in consumption would set off the multiplier, leading to a cumulative reduction in spending of $400 billion. In Figure 11.6, aggregate demand would shift from AD_1 to AD_3.

Tax increases have been used to "cool" the economy on several occasions. In 1968, for example, the economy was rapidly approaching full employment and Vietnam War expenditures were helping to drive up prices. Congress responded by imposing a 10 percent surtax (temporary additional tax) on income, which took more than $10 billion in purchasing power away from consumers. Resultant multiplier effects reduced spending in 1969 over $20 billion and thus helped restrain price pressures.

In 1982 there was great concern that the 1981 tax cuts had been excessive and that inflation was emerging. To reduce that inflationary pressure, Congress withdrew some of its earlier tax cuts, especially those designed to increase investment spending. The net effect of the Tax Equity and Fiscal Responsibility Act of 1982 was to increase taxes roughly $90 billion for the years 1983 to 1985. This shifted aggregate demand leftward, thus reducing price-level pressures.

Reduced Transfers

The third option for fiscal restraint is to reduce transfer payments. ***A cut in transfer payments works like a tax hike, reducing the disposable income of transfer recipients.*** With less income, consumers spend less, as reflected in the MPC. The appropriate size of the transfer cut can be computed exactly as the desired tax increase in the preceding formula.

Although transfer cuts have the same fiscal impact as a tax hike, they're seldom used. An outright cut in transfer payments has a direct and very visible impact on recipients, including the aged, the poor, the unemployed, and the disabled. Hence, this policy option smacks of "balancing the budget on the backs of the poor." In practice, *absolute* cuts in transfer payments are rarely proposed. Instead, this lever is sometimes used to reduce the rate of increase in transfer benefits. Then only *future* benefits are reduced, and not so visibly.

FISCAL GUIDELINES

A Primer: Simple Rules

The essence of fiscal policy entails deliberate shifting of the aggregate demand curve. The steps required to formulate fiscal policy are straightforward:

- ***Specify the amount of the desired AD shift*** (excess AD or AD shortfall).
- ***Select the policy tools needed to induce the desired shift.***

As we've seen, the fiscal policy toolbox contains a variety of tools for managing aggregate demand. When the economy is in a slump, the government can stimulate the economy with more government purchases, tax cuts, or an increase in transfer payments. When the economy is overheated, the government can reduce inflationary pressures by reducing government purchases, raising taxes, and cutting transfer payments. Table 11.2 summarizes the policy options and the desired use of each. As confusing as this list of options might at first appear, the guidelines are pretty simple. To use them all one needs to know is the size of the AD shortfall or excess and the marginal prosperity to consume.

A Warning: Crowding Out

The fiscal policy guidelines in Table 11.2 are a useful guide. However, they neglect a critical dimension of fiscal policy. Notice that we haven't said anything about how the government is going to *finance* its expenditures. Suppose the government wanted to stimulate the economy with a $50 billion increase in federal purchases. How would it pay for those purchases? If the government raised taxes for this purpose, the fiscal stimulus would be largely offset by resultant declines in consumption and investment. If, instead, the government *borrows* the money from the private sector, less credit may be available to finance consumption and investment, again creating an offsetting reduction in private demand. In either case, government spending may "crowd out" some private expenditure. If this happens, some of the intended fiscal stimulus may be offset by the **crowding out** of private expenditure. We examine this possibility further in Chapter 12 when we look at the budget deficits that help finance fiscal policy.

crowding out: A reduction in private-sector borrowing (and spending) caused by increased government borrowing.

TABLE 11.2
Fiscal Policy Primer

The goal of fiscal policy is to eliminate GDP gaps by shifting the AD curve rightward (to reduce unemployment) or leftward (to curb inflation). The desired shifts may be measured by the AD shortfall or the AD excess. In either case the desired fiscal initiative is equal to the desired shift divided by the multiplier. Once the size of the desired stimulus or restraint is known, the size of the appropriate policy response is easily calculated.

Macro Problem: Weak Economy (unemployment)
Policy Strategy: Fiscal Stimulus (rightward AD shift)

$$\text{Desired fiscal stimulus} = \frac{\text{AD shortfall}}{\text{the multiplier}}$$

Policy Tools	Amount
• Increase government purchases	desired fiscal stimulus
• Cut taxes	$\frac{\text{desired fiscal stimulus}}{\text{MPC}}$
• Increase transfers	$\frac{\text{desired fiscal stimulus}}{\text{MPC}}$

Macro Problem: Overheated Economy (inflation)
Policy Strategy: Fiscal Restraint (leftward AD shift)

$$\text{Desired fiscal restraint} = \frac{\text{excess AD}}{\text{the multiplier}}$$

Policy Tools	Amount
• Reduce government purchases	desired fiscal restraint
• Increase taxes	$\frac{\text{desired fiscal restraint}}{\text{MPC}}$
• Reduce transfer payments	$\frac{\text{desired fiscal restraint}}{\text{MPC}}$

Time Lags

Another limitation on fiscal policy is *time.* In the real world it takes time to recognize that the economy is in trouble. A blip in the unemployment or inflation rate may not signal a trend. Before intervening, we may want to be more certain that a recessionary or inflationary GDP gap is emerging. Then it will take time to develop a policy strategy and to get Congress to pass it. Once it's implemented, we'll have to wait for the many steps in the multiplier process to unfold. In the best of circumstances, the fiscal policy rescue may not arrive for quite a while. In the meantime, the very nature of our macro problems could change if the economy is hit with other internal or external shocks.

Pork Barrel Politics

Before putting too much faith in fiscal policy, we should also remember who designs and implements tax and spending initiatives: the U.S. Congress. Once a tax or spending plan arrives at the Capitol, politics take over. However urgent fiscal restraint might be, members of Congress are reluctant to sacrifice any spending projects in their own districts. And if taxes are to be cut, they want *their* constituents to get the biggest tax savings. And no one in Congress wants a tax hike or spending cut *before* the election. This kind of pork barrel politics can alter the content and timing of fiscal policy. We'll examine the *politics* of fiscal policy further in Chapters 12 and 19.

webnote

To review the latest budget data, go to the Congressional Budget Office at www.cbo.gov. CNN (www.cnn.com) is a good source for budget news.

THE ECONOMY TOMORROW

THE CONCERN FOR CONTENT

The guidelines for fiscal policy don't say anything about how the government spends its revenue or whom it taxes. The important thing is that the right amount of spending take place at the right time. In other words, insofar as our stabilization objectives are concerned, the content of total spending is of secondary interest; the level of spending is the only thing that counts.

The "Second Crisis." But it does matter, of course, whether federal expenditures are devoted to military hardware, urban transit systems, or tennis courts. Our economic goals include not only full employment and price stability but also a desirable mix of output, an equitable distribution of income, and adequate economic growth. These other goals are directly affected by the content of total spending. The relative emphasis on, and sometimes exclusive concern for, stabilization objectives—to the neglect of related GDP content—has been designated by Joan Robinson as the "second crisis of economic theory." She explains:

> The first crisis arose from the breakdown of a theory which could not account for the *level* of employment. The second crisis arises from a theory that cannot account for the *content* of employment.
>
> Keynes was arguing against the dominant orthodoxy which held that government expenditure could not increase employment. He had to prove, first of all, that it could. He had to show that an increase in investment will increase consumption—that more wages will be spent on more beer and boots whether the investment is useful or not. He had to show that the secondary increase in real income [the multiplier effect] is quite independent of the object of the primary outlay. Pay men to dig holes in the ground and fill them up again if you cannot do anything else.
>
> There was an enormous orthodox resistance to this idea. The whole weight of the argument had to be on this one obvious point.
>
> The war was a sharp lesson in Keynesism. Orthodoxy could not stand up any longer. Government accepted the responsibility to maintain a high and stable level of employment. Then economists took over Keynes and erected the new orthodoxy. Once the point had been established the question should have changed. Now that we all agree that government expenditure can maintain employment, we should argue about what the expenditure should be for. Keynes did not *want* anyone to dig holes and fill them.[1]

webnote

For a liberal viewpoint of the content of federal spending, go to the Center on Budget and Policy Priorities at www.cbpp.org. For a conservative perspective, go to the National Center for Policy Analysis at www.ncpa.org

The alternatives to paying people for digging and filling holes in the ground are virtually endless. With $3 trillion to spend each year, the federal government has great influence not only on short-run prices and employment but also on the mix of output, the distribution of income, and the prospects for long-run growth. In other words, fiscal policy helps shape the dimensions of the economy tomorrow.

Public vs. Private Spending. One of the most debated issues in fiscal policy is the balance between the public and private sectors. Critics of Keynesian theory object to its apparent endorsement of government growth. They fear that using government spending to stabilize the economy will lead to an ever-larger public sector. They attribute the growth of the government's GDP share (from 10 percent in 1930 to 19 percent today) to the big-government bias of Keynesian fiscal policy.

In principle, this big-government bias doesn't exist. Keynes never said government spending was the only lever of fiscal policy. Even in 1934 he advised President Roosevelt to pursue only *temporary* increases in government spending. As we've seen, tax policy can be used to alter consumer and investor spending as well. Hence, fiscal policy can just as easily focus on changing the level of *private*-sector spending as on changing *public*-sector spending. In 1934, however, business confidence was so low that tax-induced increases in investment seemed unlikely. In less desperate times, the choice of which fiscal tool to use is a political decision, not a Keynesian mandate. President Clinton favored increased government spending to stimulate the economy, whereas President George W. Bush favored tax cuts to bolster private spending.

Output Mixes within Each Sector. In addition to choosing whether to increase public or private spending, fiscal policy must also consider the specific content of spending within each sector. Suppose we determine that stimulation of the private sector is preferable to additional government spending as a means of promoting full employment. We still have many choices. We could, for example, cut corporate taxes, cut individual taxes, reduce

[1]From "The Second Crisis of Economic Theory," by Joan Robinson, *American Economic Review,* May 1972, p. 6. Used by permission of American Economic Association.

excise taxes, or increase Social Security benefits. Each alternative implies a different mix of consumption and investment and a different distribution of income. Congressional Democrats, for example, characterized President George W. Bush's original 2001 tax-cut plan as a "fat cat's tax break." They objected that too much of the tax cuts went to high-income taxpayers. They wanted a smaller tax cut for the rich, more tax relief for the poor, and more government spending on social programs. After months of negotiation, they got a compromise that altered both the mix of output and the distribution of income a bit more to their liking. They got even a more satisfying mix of output after they gained control of Congress in 2006.

SUMMARY

- The economy's short-run macro equilibrium may not coincide with full employment and price stability. Keynes advocated government intervention to shift the AD curve to a more desirable equilibrium. LO1
- Fiscal policy refers to the use of the government's tax and spending powers to achieve desired macro outcomes. The tools of fiscal stimulus include increasing government purchases, reducing taxes, and raising income transfers. LO2
- Fiscal restraint may originate in reductions in government purchases, increases in taxes, or cuts in income transfers. LO2
- Government purchases add directly to aggregate demand; taxes and transfers have an indirect effect by inducing changes in consumption and investment. This makes changes in government spending more powerful per dollar than changes in taxes or transfers. LO3
- Fiscal policy initiatives have a multiplied impact on total spending and output. An increase in government spending, for example, will result in more disposable income, which will be used to finance further consumer spending. LO3
- The objective of fiscal policy is to close GDP gaps. To do this, the aggregate demand curve must shift by *more* than the size of the GDP gap to compensate for changing price levels. The desired shift is equal to the AD shortfall (or excess). LO3
- Because of multiplier effects, the desired fiscal stimulus or restraint is always less than the size of the AD shortfall or excess. LO1
- Changes in government spending and taxes alter the content of GDP and thus influence what to produce. Fiscal policy affects the relative size of the public and private sectors as well as the mix of output in each sector. LO3

Key Terms

aggregate demand
income transfers
fiscal policy
equilibrium (macro)
recessionary GDP gap
fiscal stimulus
aggregate supply
AD shortfall
multiplier
marginal propensity to consume (MPC)
disposable income
fiscal restraint
inflationary GDP gap
AD excess
crowding out

Questions for Discussion

1. How can you tell if the economy is in equilibrium? How could you estimate the GDP gap? LO1
2. Will an extra $20 billion per year spent on housing have the same impact on the economy as an extra $20 billion spent on interstate highways? Explain. LO3
3. What happens to aggregate demand when transfer payments and the taxes to pay them both rise? LO3
4. Why are the AD shortfall and AD excess larger than their respective GDP gaps? Are they ever the same size? LO1
5. Will consumers always spend the same percentage of any tax cut? Why might they spend more or less than usual? LO2

6. How does the slope of the AS curve affect the size of the AD shortfall? If the AS curve were horizontal, how large would the AD shortfall be in Figure 11.3? LO1
7. According to the World View on page 218, what prompted South Korea's fiscal stimulus in 2001? Had the government not intervened, what might have happened? LO1
8. How quickly should Congress act to remedy an AD excess or shortfall? What are the risks of quick fiscal policy responses? LO2, LO3
9. Why do critics charge that fiscal policy has a "big-government bias"? LO2
10. When the Democrats took control of the Congress in 2007, they proposed more government spending paid for with higher taxes on "the rich." What impact would those options have on macro equilibrium? LO3

problems The Student Problem Set at the back of this book contains numerical and graphing problems for this chapter.

web activities to accompany this chapter can be found on the Online Learning Center: **http://www.mhhe.com/economics/schiller11e**

12 Deficits, Surpluses, and Debt

LEARNING OBJECTIVES

After reading this chapter, you should know:

LO1. The difference between cyclical and structural deficits.

LO2. How "crowding out" works.

LO3. Who bears the burden of the national debt.

President George W. Bush's string of massive tax cuts (2001–3) were the centerpiece of his fiscal policy. Although those cuts provided timely fiscal stimulus, they were a mixed macro blessing. First of all, critics charged that the tax *cuts* were excessively skewed toward the rich. Democrats also pointed out that increased government spending on infrastructure and social programs would have provided even more fiscal stimulus and maybe a more desirable mix of output. Finally, a slew of Democrats and Republicans alike expressed alarm about the huge budget deficits that accompanied the tax cuts. Professor Laura Tyson, President Clinton's former economic adviser, went so far as to proclaim that those tax-cut deficits were "sapping America's strength" (see News on next page). As she saw it, the Bush tax cuts would ultimately hurt, not help, the U.S. economy.

How can this be?! Didn't we just show how tax cuts shift aggregate demand rightward, propelling the economy toward full employment? Why would anyone have misgivings about such beneficial intervention?

The core critique of fiscal stimulus focuses on the *budget* consequences of government pump-priming. Fiscal stimulus entails either tax cuts or increased government spending. Either option increases the size of the government's budget deficit. Hence, we need to ask how fiscal stimulus is *financed* before we close the books on fiscal policy. We start with these questions:

- **How do deficits arise?**
- **What harm, if any, do deficits cause?**
- **Who will pay off the accumulated national debt?**

As we'll see, the answers to these questions add an important dimension to fiscal policy debates.

IN THE NEWS 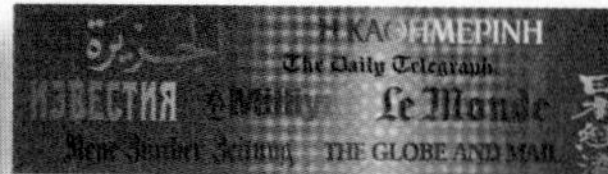 

The Bush Tax Cuts Are Sapping America's Strength

When George W. Bush became President, the federal government enjoyed a projected 10-year budget surplus of $5.6 trillion. Today, less than three years later, Washington confronts sizable annual budget deficits regardless of the cyclical ups and downs of the economy. A growing number of private forecasters now predict a 10-year deficit of around $4 trillion—$6.7 trillion excluding the Social Security surplus. Government debt and interest payments are slated to double as a share of the economy over the next decade, crowding out private investment and government spending on anything else. . . .

The Administration argues that its tax cuts are necessary to stimulate growth in a sluggish economy. But this argument is specious. The economy may have needed a temporary infusion of additional demand during the past three years. But . . . these cuts are likely to reduce the economy's long-term growth. Why? Any positive business-investment incentives from lower taxes will be outweighed by the curtailing of national saving and investment caused by mammoth budget deficits. To the extent that larger deficits diminish domestic saving, they eat into productive investment. To the extent that larger deficits are funded by borrowing from the rest of the world, they raise the nation's foreign debt and drive future income into servicing this debt. Contrary to the claims of Administration ideologues, larger deficits mean lower future living standards.

—Laura D'Andrea Tyson

Source: *BusinessWeek,* August 11, 2003. Reprinted by permission. Copyright 2003 by The McGraw-Hill Companies.

Analysis: Tax cuts reduce tax revenues and thereby enlarge the government's budget deficit. Larger deficits, in turn, may create new macro problems.

BUDGET EFFECTS OF FISCAL POLICY

fiscal policy: The use of government taxes and spending to alter macroeconomic outcomes.

Keynesian theory highlights the potential of **fiscal policy** to solve our macro problems. The guidelines are simple. Use fiscal stimulus—stepped-up government spending, tax cuts, increased transfers—to eliminate unemployment. Use fiscal restraint—less spending, tax hikes, reduced transfers—to keep inflation under control. From this perspective, the federal budget is a key policy tool for controlling the economy.

Budget Surpluses and Deficits

deficit spending: The use of borrowed funds to finance government expenditures that exceed tax revenues.

budget deficit: Amount by which government spending exceeds government revenue in a given time period.

Use of the budget to stabilize the economy implies that federal expenditures and receipts won't always be equal. In a recession, for example, the government has sound reasons both to cut taxes and to increase its own spending. By reducing tax revenues and increasing expenditures simultaneously, however, the federal government will throw its budget out of balance. This practice is called **deficit spending,** a situation in which the government borrows funds to pay for spending that exceeds tax revenues. The size of the resulting **budget deficit** is equal to the difference between expenditures and receipts:

Budget deficit = government spending − tax revenues > 0

As Table 12.1 shows, the federal government had a huge budget deficit in 2004. In that year the government spent $2.3 trillion but had revenues of just less than $1.9 trillion, leaving a budget deficit of over $400 billion.

TABLE 12.1
Budget Deficits and Surpluses

Budget deficits arise when government outlays (spending) exceed revenues (receipts). When revenues exceed outlays, a budget surplus exists.

Budget Totals (in billions of dollars)	2000	2001	2002	2003	2004	2005	2006
Revenues	2,025	1,991	1,853	1,782	1,880	2,154	2,407
Outlays	−1,789	−1,863	−2,011	−2,160	−2,293	−2472	−2,654
Surplus (deficit)	236	128	(158)	(378)	(413)	(318)	(247)

Source: Congressional Budget Office.

As Figure 12.1 illustrates, the 2004 deficit was the largest one in over 30 years—by a long shot. The figure also reveals, however, that budget deficits have been common. In fact, the few years (1969, 1998–2001) in which the government ran a **budget surplus** were a rare departure from the historical pattern.

budget surplus: An excess of government revenues over government expenditures in a given time period.

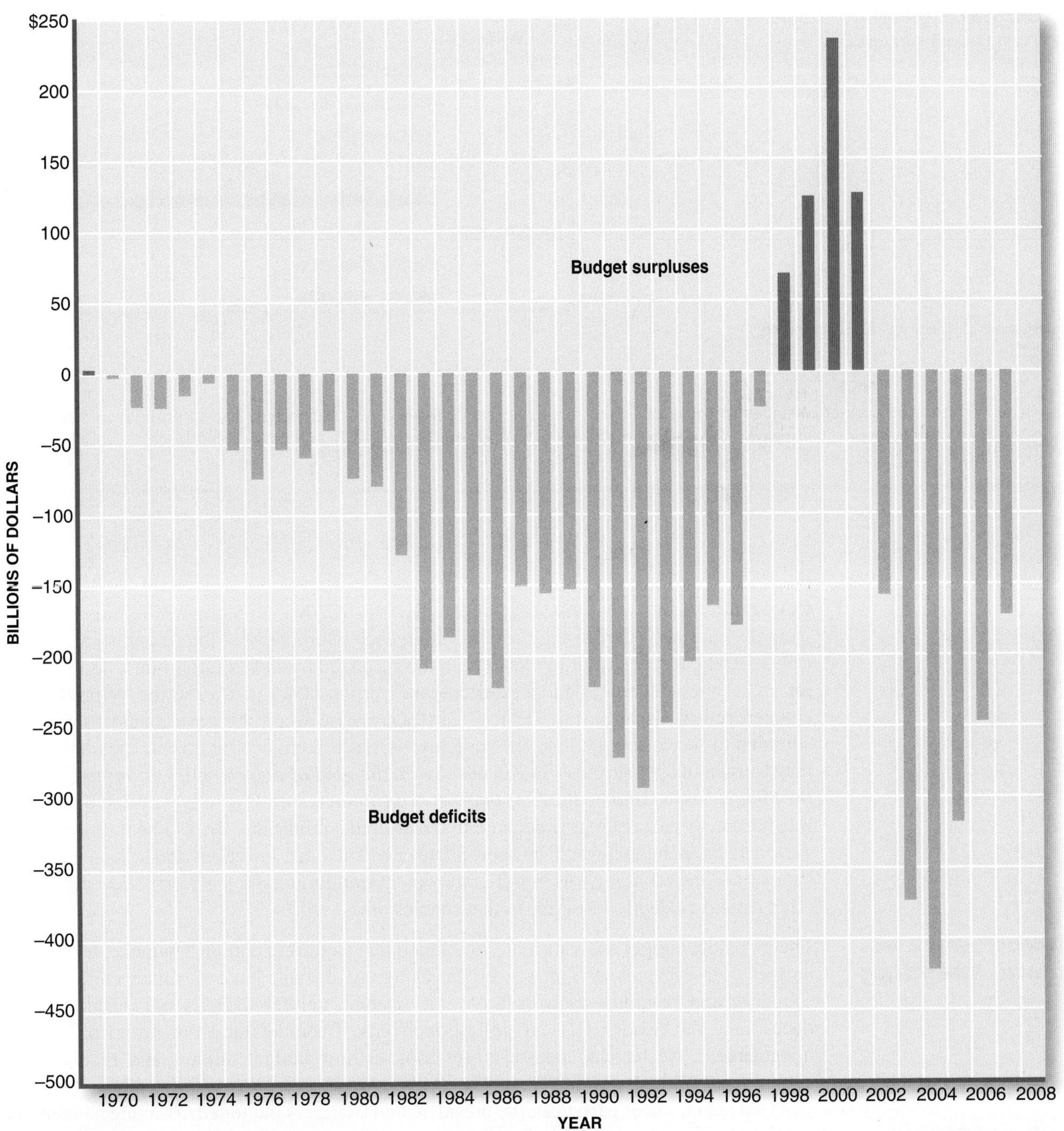

FIGURE 12.1
A String of Deficits

Budget deficits are overwhelmingly the rule, not the exception. A budget surplus was achieved in only 4 years (1998–2001) since 1970. Deficits result from both cyclical slowdowns and discretionary policies.

Source: Congressional Budget Office.

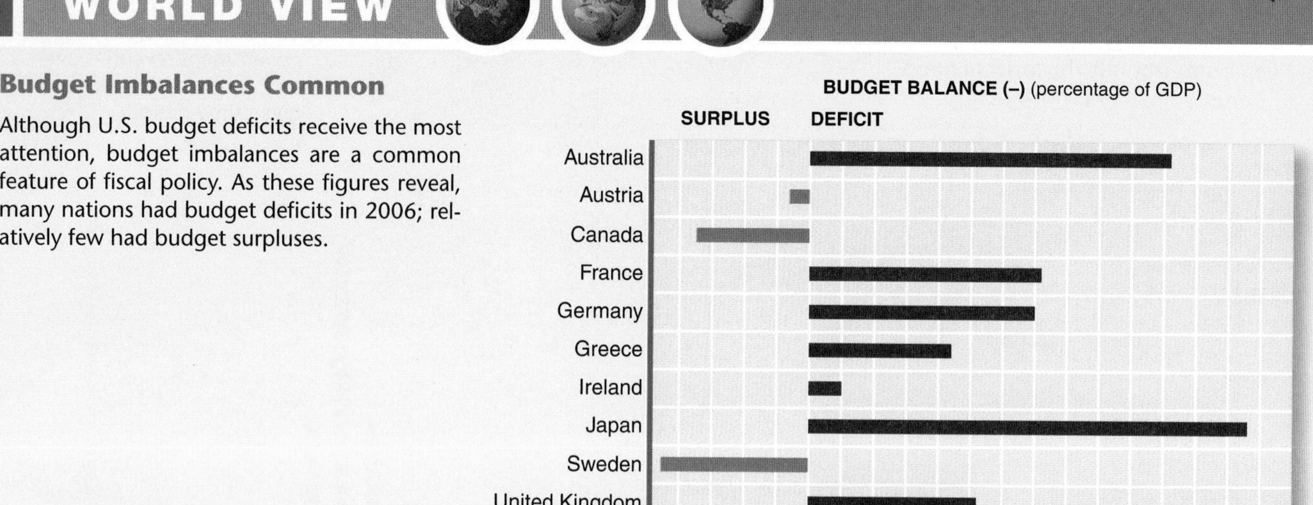

Budget Imbalances Common

Although U.S. budget deficits receive the most attention, budget imbalances are a common feature of fiscal policy. As these figures reveal, many nations had budget deficits in 2006; relatively few had budget surpluses.

Source: International Monetary Fund. www.imf.org

Analysis: To compare U.S. budget balances to those of other industrialized countries, we must adjust for differences in size by computing the *ratio* of deficits or surpluses to GDP. By this measure, U.S. budget imbalances haven't been that large.

Keynesian View. What made the budget deficits of 2003–5 so remarkable was not only their absolute size but also their sudden emergence after a brief string of budget surpluses (1998–2001). Keynes wouldn't have been too surprised by such a turnaround, however. As far as he was concerned, budget deficits and surpluses are just a routine by-product of countercyclical fiscal policy. Deficits can easily arise when the government uses fiscal stimulus to increase aggregate demand, just as fiscal restraint (tax hikes; spending cuts) may cause a budget surplus. As Keynes saw it, ***the goal of macro policy is not to balance the budget but to balance the economy (at full employment).*** If a budget deficit or surplus was needed to shift aggregate demand to the desired equilibrium, then so be it. In Keynes's view, a balanced budget would be appropriate only if all other injections and leakages were in balance and the economy was in full-employment equilibrium. As the World View confirms, other nations evidently subscribe to that conclusion as well.

Discretionary vs. Automatic Spending

Theory aside, budget analysts have concluded that Congress couldn't balance the federal budget every year even if it wanted to. Congress doesn't have as much control over spending and revenues as people assume. Hence, neither deficits nor surpluses are necessarily the result of fiscal policy decisions. To understand the limits of budget management, we have to take a closer look at how budget outlays and receipts are actually determined.

fiscal year (FY): The 12-month period used for accounting purposes; begins October 1 for the federal government.

At the beginning of each year, the president and Congress put together a budget blueprint for the next **fiscal year (FY).** They don't start from scratch, however. Most budget line items reflect commitments made in earlier years. In FY 2008, for example, the federal budget included $586 billion in Social Security benefits. The FY 2008 budget also provided for $79 billion in veterans benefits, $253 billion for interest payments on the national debt, and many billions more for completion of projects begun in previous years. Short of repudiating all prior commitments, there's little that Congress or the president can do to alter these expenditures in any given year. ***To a large extent, current revenues and expenditures are the result of decisions made in prior years.*** In this sense, much of each year's budget is considered "*uncontrollable.*"

At present, uncontrollables account for roughly 80 percent of the federal budget. This leaves only 20 percent for **discretionary fiscal spending**—that is, spending decisions not "locked in" by prior legislative commitments. In recent years, rising interest payments and increasing entitlements (Social Security, Medicare, civil service pensions, etc.) have reduced the discretionary share of the budget even further. This doesn't mean that discretionary fiscal policy is no longer important; it simply means that the potential for *changing* budget outlays in any year is much smaller than it might first appear. Yet, the ability to *change* tax or spending levels is the force behind Keynesian fiscal policy. Recall that deliberate changes in government spending or taxes are the essence of **fiscal restraint** and **fiscal stimulus.** If most of the budget is uncontrollable, those policy tools are less effective.

discretionary fiscal spending: Those elements of the federal budget not determined by past legislative or executive commitments.

fiscal restraint: Tax hikes or spending cuts intended to reduce (shift) aggregate demand.

fiscal stimulus: Tax cuts or spending hikes intended to increase (shift) aggregate demand.

Automatic Stabilizers. Most of the uncontrollable line items in the federal budget have another characteristic that directly affects budget deficits: Their value *changes* with economic conditions. Consider unemployment insurance benefits. The unemployment insurance program, established in 1935, provides that persons who lose their jobs will receive some income (an average of $280 per week) from the government. The law establishes the *entitlement* to unemployment benefits but not the amount to be spent in any year. Each year's expenditure depends on how many workers lose their jobs and qualify for benefits. In 2002, for example, outlays for unemployment benefits increased by $17 billion. That increase in federal spending wasn't the result of any new policy decisions. Spending went up simply because more workers lost their jobs in the 2001 recession. The spending increase was *automatic,* not *discretionary.*

Welfare benefits also increased by $5 billion in 2002. This increase in spending also occurred automatically in response to worsened economic conditions. As more people lost jobs and used up their savings, they turned to welfare for help. They were *entitled* to welfare benefits according to eligibility rules already written; no new congressional or executive action was required to approve this increase in government spending.

Notice that ***outlays for unemployment compensation and welfare benefits increase when the economy goes into recession.*** This is exactly the kind of fiscal policy that Keynes advocated. The increase in **income transfers** helps offset the income losses due to recession. These increased transfers therefore act as **automatic stabilizers**—injecting new spending into the circular flow during economic contractions. Conversely, transfer payments *decline* when the economy is *expanding* and fewer people qualify for unemployment or welfare benefits. Hence, no one has to pull the fiscal policy lever to inject more or less entitlement spending into the circular flow; much of it happens automatically.

income transfers: Payments to individuals for which no current goods or services are exchanged, such as Social Security, welfare, unemployment benefits.

Automatic stabilizers also exist on the revenue side of the federal budget. Income taxes are an important stabilizer because they move up and down with the value of spending and output. As we've observed, if household incomes increase, a jump in consumer spending is likely to follow. The resultant multiplier effects might create some demand-pull inflation. The tax code lessens this inflationary pressure. When you get more income, you have to pay more taxes. Hence, income taxes siphon off some of the increased purchasing power that might have found its way to product markets. Progressive income taxes are particularly effective stabilizers, as they siphon off increasing proportions of purchasing power when incomes are rising and decreasing proportions when aggregate demand and output are falling.

automatic stabilizer: Federal expenditure or revenue item that automatically responds countercyclically to changes in national income, like unemployment benefits, income taxes.

Cyclical Deficits

Automatic stabilizers imply that policymakers don't have total control of each year's budget. In reality, ***the size of the federal deficit or surplus is sensitive to expansion and contraction of the macro economy.***

Table 12.2 shows just how sensitive the budget is to cyclical forces. When the GDP growth rate falls by 1 percent, tax revenues decline by $38 billion. As the economy slows, people also turn to the government for additional income support: Unemployment benefits and other transfer payments increase by $2 billion. As a consequence, the budget deficit

TABLE 12.2
The Budget Impact of Cyclical Forces (in 2007 dollars)

Changes in economic conditions alter federal revenue and spending. When GDP growth slows, tax revenues decline and income transfers increase. This widens the budget deficit.

Higher rates of inflation increase both outlays and revenues but not equally.

The cyclical balance reflects these budget impacts.

- ***Changes in Real GDP Growth***

When the GDP growth rate decreases by one percentage point:

1. Government spending (*G*) automatically increases for:
   Unemployment insurance benefits
   Food stamps
   Welfare benefits
   Social Security benefits
   Medicaid
   Total increase in outlays: +$2 billion
2. Government tax revenues (*T*) automatically decline for:
   Individual income taxes
   Corporate income taxes
   Social Security payroll taxes:
   Total decline in revenues: −$38 billion
3. **The deficit increases by $40 billion**

- ***Changes in Inflation***

When the inflation rate increases by one percentage point:

1. Government spending (*G*) automatically increases for:
   Indexed retirement and Social Security benefits
   Higher interest payments
   Total increase in outlays: +$40 billion
2. Government tax revenues (*T*) automatically increase for:
   Corporate income taxes
   Social Security payroll taxes
   Total increase in revenues: +$45 billion
3. **The deficit shrinks by $5 billion**

Source: Congressional Budget Office (first year effects).

increases by $40 billion. This is exactly what happened in FY 2002: The recession that began in March 2001 shrank the budget surplus by roughly $30 billion.

Inflation also affects the budget. Because Social Security benefits are automatically adjusted to inflation, federal outlays increase as the price level rises. This added expenditure is offset, however, by inflation-swollen tax receipts. Both Social Security payroll taxes and corporate profit taxes rise automatically with inflation. These offsetting expenditure and revenue effects almost cancel each other out: Table 12.2 shows that a one-point increase in the inflation rate *shrinks* the budget deficit by only $5 billion.

The most important implication of Table 12.2 is that neither the president nor the Congress has complete control of the federal deficit. ***Actual budget deficits and surpluses may arise from economic conditions as well as policy.*** Perhaps no one learned this better than President Reagan. In 1980 he campaigned on a promise to balance the budget. The 1981–82 recession, however, caused the actual deficit to soar. The president later had to admit that actual deficits aren't solely the product of big spenders in Washington.

President George H. Bush explained the persistence of huge deficits during his presidency on the same basis. During the recession of 1990–91, the nation's unemployment rate jumped by more than two percentage points. That setback alone added roughly $84 billion to the federal deficit.

President Clinton had more luck with the deficit. Although he increased discretionary spending in his first 2 years, the annual budget deficit *shrank* by over $90 billion between 1993 and 1995. Most of the deficit reduction was due to automatic stabilizers that kicked in as GDP growth accelerated and the unemployment rate fell. As the economy continued to grow sharply, the unemployment rate fell to 4 percent. That surge in the economy increased tax revenues, reduced income transfers, and propelled the 1998 budget into surplus. It was primarily the economy, not the president or the Congress, that produced the first budget surplus in a generation.

Fiscal Year	Budget Balance	=	Cyclical Component	+	Structural Component
2000	+236		+131		+105
2001	+128		+23		+105
2002	−158		−32		−126
2003	−378		−102		−276
2004	−413		−127		−286
2005	−318		−81		−237
2006	−248		−6		−242

Source: Congressional Budget Office.

TABLE 12.3
Cyclical vs. Structural Budget Balances (in billions of dollars)

The budget balance includes both cyclical and structural components. Changes in the structural component result from policy changes; changes in the cyclical component result from changes in the economy. Between FY 2000 and FY 2001 the structural surplus was unchanged (at $105 billion), implying zero policy intervention. The cyclical surplus shrank by $108 billion, however, as the economy fell into a recession. As a result, the federal surplus was cut nearly in half.

That part of the federal deficit attributable to cyclical disturbances (unemployment and inflation) is referred to as the **cyclical deficit.** As we've observed,

- ***The cyclical deficit widens when GDP growth slows or inflation decreases.***
- ***The cyclical deficit shrinks when GDP growth accelerates or inflation increases.***

cyclical deficit: That portion of the budget balance attributable to short-run changes in economic conditions.

If observed budget balances don't necessarily reflect fiscal policy decisions, how are we to know whether fiscal policy is stimulative or restrictive? Clearly, some other indicator is needed.

Structural Deficits

To isolate the effects of fiscal policy, economists break down the actual budget balance into *cyclical* and *structural* components:

$$\text{Total budget balance} = \text{cyclical balance} + \text{structural balance}$$

The cyclical portion of the budget balance reflects the impact of the business cycle on federal tax revenues and spending. The **structural deficit** reflects fiscal policy decisions. Rather than comparing actual outlays to actual receipts, the structural deficit compares the outlays and receipts that would occur if the economy were at full employment.[1] This technique eliminates budget distortions caused by cyclical conditions. Any remaining changes in spending or outlays must be due to policy decisions. Hence, ***part of the deficit arises from cyclical changes in the economy; the rest is the result of discretionary fiscal policy.***

structural deficit: Federal revenues at full employment minus expenditures at full employment under prevailing fiscal policy.

Table 12.3 shows how the total, cyclical, and structural balances have behaved in recent years. Consider what happened to the federal budget in 2000–2001. In 2000 the federal surplus was $236 billion. In 2001 the surplus shrunk to $128 billion. The shrinking surplus suggests that the government was trying to stimulate economic activity with expansionary fiscal policies (tax cuts, spending hikes). But this wasn't the case. The primary reason for the smaller 2001 surplus was an abrupt halt in GDP growth. As the economy slipped into recession, the *cyclical* component shifted from a *surplus* of $131 billion in 2000 to only $23 billion in 2001. This $108 billion swing in the cyclical budget accounted for all the decrease in the total budget surplus. By contrast, the *structural* surplus was *unchanged* (at $105 billion), reflecting the absence of *discretionary* fiscal stimulus.

webnote

For more historical data on cyclical and structural deficits, visit the U.S. Congressional Budget Office Web site at www.cbo.gov and look for "Historical Budget Data."

By distinguishing between the structural budget and the actual budget, we can evaluate fiscal policy more accurately. Only changes in the structural deficit are relevant. In fact,

[1]The structural deficit is also referred to as the "full-employment," "high-employment," or "standardized" deficit.

IN THE NEWS

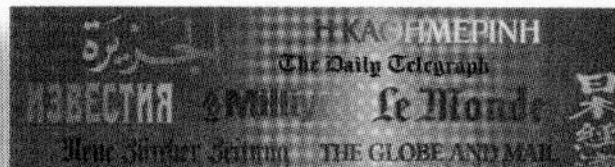

Fiscal Policy in the Great Depression

In 1931 President Herbert Hoover observed, "Business depressions have been recurrent in the life of our country and are but transitory." Rather than proposing fiscal stimulus, Hoover complained that expansion of public-works programs had unbalanced the federal budget. In 1932 he proposed *cut-backs* in government spending and *higher* taxes. In his view, the "unquestioned balancing of the federal budget . . . is the first necessity of national stability and is the foundation of further recovery."

Franklin Roosevelt shared this view of fiscal policy. He criticized Hoover for not balancing the budget, and in 1933, warned Congress that "all public works must be considered from the point of view of the ability of the government treasury to pay for them."

As the accompanying figure shows, the budget deficit persisted throughout the Great Depression. But these deficits were the result of a declining economy, not stimulative fiscal policy. The structural deficit actually *decreased* from 1931 to 1933 (see figure), thereby restraining aggregate spending at a time when producers were desperate for increasing sales. Only when the structural deficit was expanded tremendously by spending during World War II did fiscal policy have a decidedly positive effect. Federal defense expenditures jumped from \$2.2 billion in 1940 to \$87.4 billion in 1944!

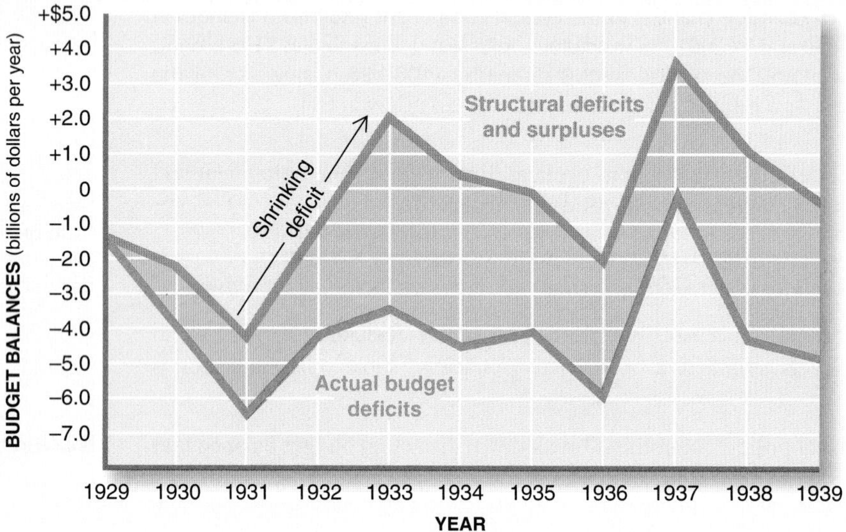

Source: Adapted from E. Cary Brown, "Fiscal Policy in the Thirties: A Reappraisal," *American Economic Review,* December 1956. Table 1. Used by permission of The American Economic Association.

Analysis: From 1931 to 1933, the structural deficit decreased from \$4.5 billion to a \$2 billion *surplus.* This fiscal restraint reduced aggregate demand and deepened the Great Depression.

only changes in the structural budget balance measure the thrust of fiscal policy. By this measure we categorize fiscal policy in the following ways:

- ***Fiscal stimulus is measured by the increase in the structural deficit*** (or shrinkage in the structural surplus).
- ***Fiscal restraint is gauged by the decrease in the structural deficit*** (or increase in the structural surplus).

According to this measure, fiscal policy was actually restrictive during the Great Depression, when fiscal stimulus was desperately needed (see News). Both Presidents Hoover and Roosevelt thought the government should rein in its spending when tax revenues declined, so as to keep the federal budget balanced. It took years of economic devastation before the fiscal policy lever was reversed. Also notice in Table 12.3 the abrupt shift from structural surplus (+\$105) in 2001 to structural deficit (−\$126) in 2002. This \$231 billion swing in the structural balance reflects the fiscal stimulus of the initial Bush tax cuts and stepped-up defense spending.

ECONOMIC EFFECTS OF DEFICITS

No matter what the origins of budget deficits, most people are alarmed by them. Should they be? What are the *consequences* of budget deficits?

Crowding Out

We've already encountered one potential consequence of deficit financing: ***If the government borrows funds to finance deficits, the availability of funds for private-sector spending may be reduced.*** This is the **crowding-out** problem first noted in Chapter 11. If crowding out occurs, the increase in government expenditure will be at least partially offset by reductions in consumption and investment.

crowding out: A reduction in private-sector borrowing (and spending) caused by increased government borrowing.

If the economy were operating at full employment, crowding out would be inevitable. At full employment, we'd be on the production possibilities curve, using all available resources. As Figure 12.2 reminds us, additional government purchases can occur only if private-sector purchases are reduced. In real terms, ***crowding out implies less private-sector output.***

Crowding out is complete only if the economy is at full employment. If the economy is in recession. it's possible to get more public-sector output (like highways, schools, defense) without cutbacks in private-sector output. This possibility is illustrated by the move from point *c* to point *b* in Figure 12.2.

Tax cuts have crowding-out effects as well. The purpose of the 2001 tax cuts was to stimulate consumer spending. As the economy approaches full employment, however, how can more consumer output be produced? At the production possibilities limit, the added consumption will force cutbacks in either investment or government services. This was the outcome Professor Tyson feared would eventually "sap America's strength" (see News, page 232).

What Figure 12.2 emphasizes is that ***the risk of crowding out is greater the closer the economy is to full employment.*** This implies that deficits are less appropriate at high levels of employment but more appropriate at low levels of employment.

Opportunity Cost

Even if crowding out does occur, that doesn't mean that deficits are necessarily too big. Crowding out simply reminds us that there's an **opportunity cost** to government spending. We still have to decide whether the private-sector output crowded out by government expenditure is more or less desirable than the increased public-sector output.

opportunity cost: The most desired goods or services that are forgone in order to obtain something else.

President Clinton defended government expenditure on education, training, and infrastructure as public "investment." He believed that any resulting crowding out of private-sector expenditure wasn't necessarily an unwelcome trade-off. Public investments in

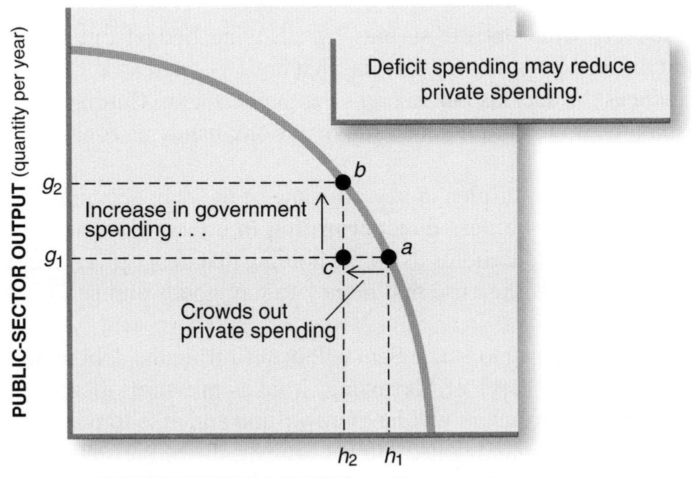

FIGURE 12.2
Crowding Out

If the economy is fully employed, an increase in public-sector expenditure (output) will reduce private-sector expenditure (output). In this case a deficit-financed increase in government expenditure moves the economy from point *a* to point *b*. In the process the quantity $h_1 - h_2$ of private-sector output is crowded out to make room for the increase in public-sector output (from g_1 to g_2). If the economy started at point *c*, however, with unemployed resources, crowding out need not occur.

education, health care, and transportation systems might even accelerate long-term economic growth.

President George W. Bush saw things differently. He preferred a mix of output that included less public-sector output and more private-sector output. Accordingly, he didn't regard any resulting crowding out of government spending as a real loss.

Interest-Rate Movements

Although the production possibilities curve illustrates the inevitability of crowding out at full employment, it doesn't explain *how* the crowding out occurs. Typically, the mechanism that enforces crowding out is the rate of interest. When the government borrows more funds to finance larger deficits, it puts pressure on financial markets. That added pressure may cause interest rates to rise. If they do, households will be less eager to borrow more money to buy cars, houses, and other debt-financed products. Businesses, too, will be more hesitant to borrow and invest. Hence, ***rising interest rates are both a symptom and a cause of crowding out.***

Rising interests may also crowd out *government* spending in the wake of tax cuts. As interest rates rise, government borrowing costs rise as well. According to the Congressional Budget Office, a one-point rise in interest rates increases Uncle Sam's debt expenses by over $100 billion over 4 years. These higher interest costs leave less room in government budgets for financing new projects.

How much interest rates rise again depends on how close the economy is to its productive capacity. If there is lots of excess capacity, interest-rate–induced crowding out isn't very likely. As capacity is approached, however, interest rates and crowding out are both likely to increase.

ECONOMIC EFFECTS OF SURPLUSES

Although budget deficits are clearly the norm, we might at least ponder the economic effects of budget *surpluses.* Essentially, they are the mirror image of those for deficits.

Crowding In

When the government takes in more revenue than it spends, it adds to leakage in the circular flow. But Uncle Sam doesn't hide the surplus under a mattress. And the sums involved (such as $236 billion in FY 2000) are too large to put in a bank. Were the government to buy corporate stock with the budget surplus, it would effectively be nationalizing private enterprises. So where does the surplus go?

There are really only four potential uses for a budget surplus, namely,

- ***Spend it on goods and services.***
- ***Cut taxes.***
- ***Increase income transfers.***
- ***Pay off old debt ("save it").***

The first three options effectively wipe out the surplus by changing budget outlays or receipts. There are important differences here, though. The first option—increased government spending—not only reduces the surplus but enlarges the public sector. Cutting taxes or increasing income transfers, by contrast, puts the money into the hands of consumers and enlarges the private sector.

crowding in: An increase in private-sector borrowing (and spending) caused by decreased government borrowing.

The fourth budget option is to use the surplus to pay off some of the debt accumulated from earlier deficits. This has a similar but less direct **crowding-in** effect. If Uncle Sam pays off some of his accumulated debt, households that were holding that debt (government bonds) will end up with more money. If they use that money to buy goods and services, then private-sector output will expand.

Even people who haven't lent any money to Uncle Sam will benefit from the debt reduction. When the government reduces its level of borrowing, it takes pressure off market interest rates. As interest rates drop, consumers will be more willing and able to purchase big-ticket items such as cars, appliances, and houses, thus changing the mix of output in favor of private-sector production.

Cyclical Sensitivity

Like crowding out, the extent of crowding in depends on the state of the economy. In a recession, a surplus-induced decline in interest rates isn't likely to stimulate much spending. If consumer and investor confidence are low, even a surplus-financed tax cut might not lift private-sector spending much. This was clearly the case in 2001. Taxpayers were slow to spend their tax-rebate checks and businesses were initially unpersuaded by low interest rates to increase their investment spending.

THE ACCUMULATION OF DEBT

Because the U.S. government has had more years of budget deficits than budget surpluses, Uncle Sam has accumulated a large **national debt.** In fact, the United States started out in debt. The Continental Congress needed to borrow money in 1777 to continue fighting the Revolutionary War. The Congress tried to raise tax revenues and even printed new money (the Continental dollar) in order to buy needed food, tents, guns, and ammunition. But by the winter of 1777, these mechanisms for financing the war were failing. To acquire needed supplies, the Continental Congress plunged the new nation into debt.

national debt: Accumulated debt of the federal government.

Debt Creation

As with today's deficits, the Continental Congress acknowledged its loans by issuing bonds. Today the U.S. Treasury is the fiscal agent of the U.S. government. The Treasury collects tax revenues, signs checks for federal spending, and—when necessary—borrows funds to cover budget deficits. When the Treasury borrows funds, it issues **Treasury bonds;** these are IOUs of the federal government. People buy bonds—lend money to the U.S. Treasury—because bonds pay interest and are a very safe haven for idle funds.

The total stock of all outstanding bonds represents the national debt. It's equal to the sum total of our accumulated deficits, less net repayments in years when a budget surplus existed. In other words, ***the national debt is a stock of IOUs created by annual deficit flows.*** Whenever there's a budget deficit, the national debt increases. In years when a budget surplus exists, the national debt can be pared down.

Treasury bonds: Promissory notes (IOUs) issued by the U.S. Treasury.

Early History, 1776–1900

The United States began accumulating debt as soon as independence was declared. By 1783, the United States had borrowed over $8 million from France and $250,000 from Spain. Most of these funds were secretly obtained to help finance the Revolutionary War.

During the period 1790–1812, the United States often incurred debt but typically repaid it quickly. The War of 1812, however, caused a massive increase in the national debt. With neither a standing army nor an adequate source of tax revenues to acquire one, the U.S. government had to borrow money to repel the British. By 1816, the national debt was over $129 million. Although that figure seems tiny by today's standards, it amounted to 13 percent of national income in 1816.

1835–1836: Debt-Free! After the War of 1812, the U.S. government used recurrent budget surpluses to repay its debt. These surpluses were so frequent that the U.S. government was completely out of debt by 1835. In 1835 and again in 1836, the government had neither national debt nor a budget deficit. The dilemma in those years was how to use the budget *surplus!* Since there was no accumulated debt, the option of using the surplus to reduce the debt didn't exist. In the end, Congress decided simply to distribute the surplus funds to the states. That was the last time the U.S. government was completely out of debt.

The Mexican-American War (1846–48) necessitated a sudden increase in federal spending. The deficits incurred to fight that war caused a fourfold increase in the debt. That debt was pared down the following decade. Then the Civil War (1861–65) broke out, and both sides needed debt financing. By the end of the Civil War, the North owed over $2.6 billion, or approximately half its national income. The South depended more heavily on newly printed Confederate currency to finance its side of the Civil War, relying on bond issues for only one-third of its financial needs. When the South lost, however, neither Confederate currency nor Confederate bonds had any value.[2]

Twentieth Century

The Spanish-American War (1898) also increased the national debt. But all prior debt was dwarfed by World War I, which increased the national debt from 3 percent of national income in 1917 to 41 percent at the war's end.

The national debt declined during the 1920s because the federal government was consistently spending less revenue than it took in. Budget surpluses disappeared quickly when the economy fell into the Great Depression, however, and the cyclical deficit widened (see News, page 238).

World War II. The most explosive jump in the national debt occurred during World War II, when the government had to mobilize all available resources. Rather than raise taxes to the fullest, the U.S. government restricted the availability of consumer goods. With consumer goods rationed, consumers had little choice but to increase their saving. Uncle Sam encouraged people to lend their idle funds to the U.S. Treasury by buying U.S. war bonds. The resulting bond purchases raised the national debt from 45 percent of GDP in 1940 to over 125 percent of GDP in 1946 (see Figure 12.3).

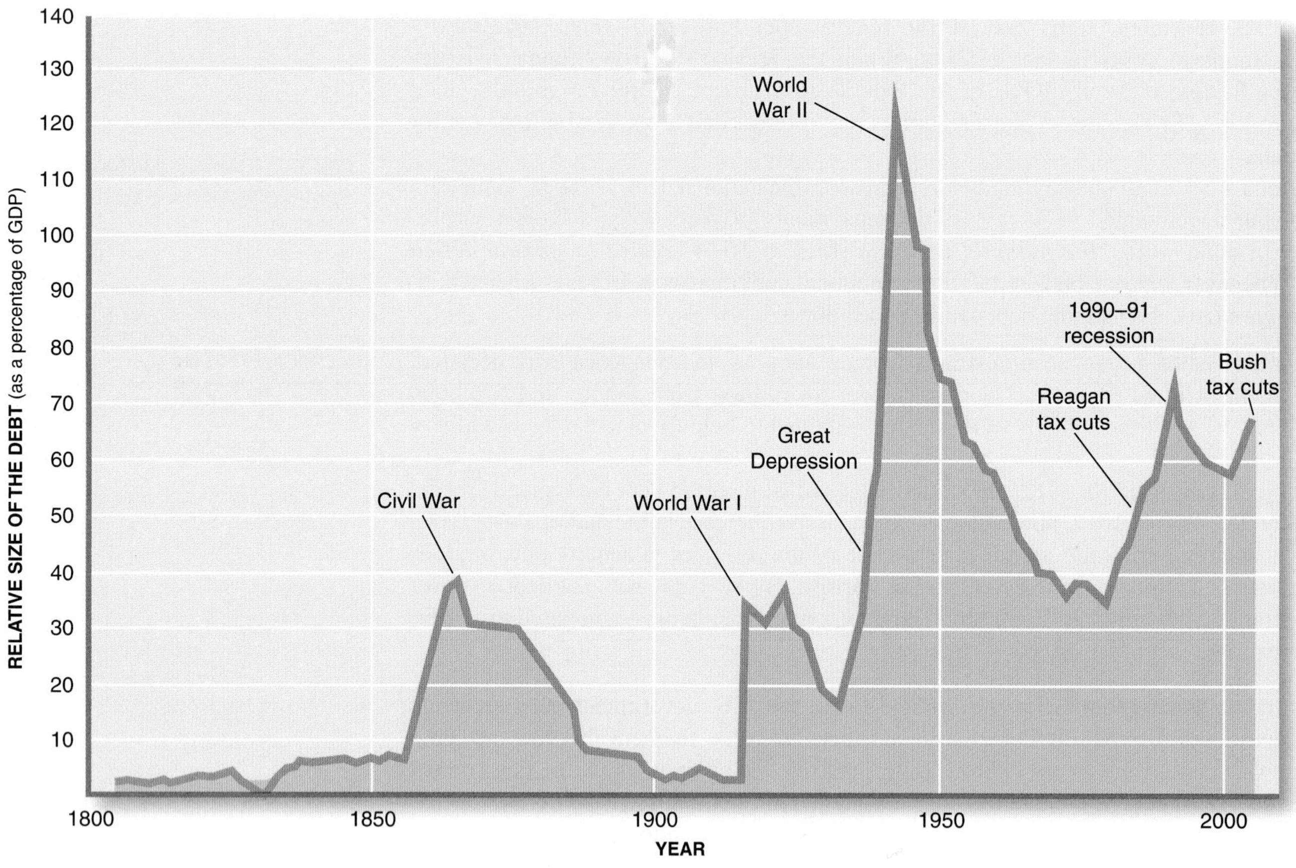

FIGURE 12.3
Historical View of the Debt/GDP Ratio

From 1790 to 1917, the national debt exceeded 10 percent of GDP only during the Civil War years. After 1917, however, the debt ratio grew sharply. World War I, the Great Depression, and World War II all caused major increases in the debt ratio. The tax cuts of 1981–84 and 2001–5 and the recessions of 1990–91 and 2001 caused further increases in the debt/GDP ratio.

Source: Office of Management and Budget.

[2]In anticipation of this situation, European leaders had forced the South to guarantee most of its loans with cotton. When the South was unable to repay its debts, these creditors could sell the cotton they had held as collateral. But most holders of Confederate bonds or currency received nothing.

The 1980s. During the 1980s, the national debt jumped again—by nearly $2 *trillion*. This 10-year increase in the debt exceeded all the net debt accumulation since the country was founded. This time, however, the debt increase wasn't war-related. Instead, the debt explosion of the 1980s originated in recessions (1980–82 and 1990–91), massive tax cuts (1981–84), and increased defense spending. The recessions caused big jumps in the cyclical deficit while the Reagan tax cuts and military buildup caused the structural deficit to jump fourfold in only 4 years (1982–86).

The 1990s. The early 1990s continued the same trend. Discretionary federal spending increased sharply in the first 2 years of the George H. Bush administration. The federal government was also forced to bail out hundreds of failed savings and loan associations. Although taxes were raised a bit and military spending was cut back, the structural deficit was little changed. Then the recession of 1990–91 killed any chance of achieving smaller deficits. In only 4 years (1988–92) the national debt increased by another $1 trillion.

In 1993, the Clinton administration persuaded Congress to raise taxes, thereby reducing the structural deficit. Continuing recovery from the 1990–91 recession also reduced the cyclical deficit. Nevertheless, the budget deficits of 1993–96 pushed the national debt to over $5 trillion.

webnote

The U.S. National Debt Clock tracks the debt. To see it, visit www.brillig.com/debt_clock or www.treasurydirect.gov/NP/BPDLogin?application=np

2000–. After a couple of years of budget surplus, the accumulated debt still exceeded $5.6 trillion in 2002. Then the Bush tax cuts and the defense buildup kicked in. As the structural deficit soared (Table 12.4) the national debt surged again. By 2007 the debt approached $9 trillion, which works out to nearly $30,000 of debt for every U.S. citizen.

WHO OWNS THE DEBT?

To the average citizen, the accumulated national debt is both incomprehensible and frightening. Who can understand debts that are measured in *trillions* of dollars? Who can ever be expected to pay them?

Liabilities = Assets

The first thing to note about the national debt is that it represents not only a liability but an asset as well. When the U.S. Treasury borrows money, it issues bonds. Those bonds are a **liability** for the federal government since it must later repay the borrowed funds. But those same bonds are an **asset** to the people who hold them. Bondholders have a claim to future repayment. They can even convert that claim into cash by selling their bonds in the bond market. Therefore, ***national debt creates as much wealth (for bondholders) as liabilities (for the U.S. Treasury).*** Neither money nor any other form of wealth disappears when the government borrows money.

liability: An obligation to make future payment; debt.

asset: Anything having exchange value in the marketplace; wealth.

Year	Total Debt Outstanding (millions of dollars)	Year	Total Debt Outstanding (millions of dollars)
1791	75	1920	24,299
1800	83	1930	16,185
1810	53	1940	42,967
1816	127	1945	258,682
1820	91	1960	286,331
1835	0	1970	370,919
1850	63	1980	914,300
1865	2,678	1985	1,827,500
1890	1,122	1990	3,163,000
1900	1,263	1995	5,076,000
1915	1,191	2000	5,629,000
		2007	8,900,000

Source: Office of Management and Budget.

TABLE 12.4
The National Debt

It took nearly a century for the national debt to reach $1 trillion. Then the debt tripled in a mere decade. The accumulated debt now totals $9 trillion.

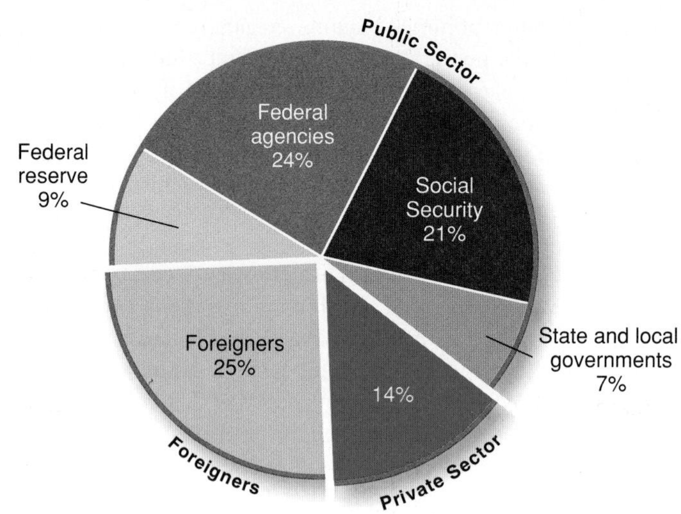

FIGURE 12.4
Debt Ownership

The bonds that create the national debt represent wealth that's owned by bondholders. Half of that wealth is held by the U.S. government itself. The private sector in the United States holds only 14 percent of the debt, and foreigners own about 25 percent.

Source: U.S. Treasury Department (2007 data).

The fact that total bond assets equal total bond liabilities is of little consolation to taxpayers confronted with $9 trillion of national debt and worry when, if ever, they'll be able to repay it. The fear that either the U.S. government or its taxpayers will be "bankrupted" by the national debt always lurks in the shadows. How legitimate is that fear?

Ownership of the Debt

Figure 12.4 shows who owns the bonds the U.S. Treasury has issued. The largest bondholder is the U.S. government itself: ***Federal agencies hold roughly 50 percent of all outstanding Treasury bonds.*** The Federal Reserve System, an independent agency of the U.S. government, acquires Treasury bonds in its conduct of monetary policy (see Chapters 14 and 15). Other agencies of the U.S. government also purchase bonds. The Social Security Administration, for example, maintains a trust fund balance to cover any shortfall between monthly payroll tax receipts and retirement benefits. Most of that balance is held in the form of interest-bearing Treasury bonds. Thus, one arm of the federal government (the U.S. Treasury) owes another arm (the U.S. Social Security Administration) a significant part of the national debt. Because Social Security has been accumulating huge annual reserves in recent years, it's now the largest single holder of the national debt.

State and local governments hold another 7 percent of the national debt. This debt, too, arises when state and local governments use their own budget surpluses to purchase interest-bearing Treasury bonds.

The private sector owns only about 14 percent of the national debt. This private wealth is in the form of familiar U.S. savings bonds or other types of Treasury bonds. Much of this private wealth is held *indirectly* by banks, insurance companies, money-market funds, corporations, and other institutions. All this wealth is ultimately owned by the people who have deposits at the bank or in money market funds, who own stock in corporations, or who are insured by companies that hold Treasury bonds. Thus, ***U.S. households hold only 14 percent of the national debt, either directly or indirectly.***

internal debt: U.S. government debt (Treasury bonds) held by U.S. households and institutions.

All the debt held by U.S. households, institutions, and government entities is referred to as **internal debt**. As Figure 12.4 illustrates, 75 percent of the national debt is internal. In other words, we owe most of the national debt to ourselves.

external debt: U.S. government debt (Treasury bonds) held by foreign households and institutions.

The remaining 25 percent of the national debt is held by foreign banks, corporations, households, and governments. U.S. Treasury bonds are attractive to global participants because of their relative security, the interest they pay, and the general acceptability of dollar-denominated assets in world trade. Bonds held by foreign households and institutions are referred to as **external debt.**

BURDEN OF THE DEBT

refinancing: The issuance of new debt in payment of debt issued earlier.

It may be comforting to know that most of our national debt is owned internally, and much of it by the government itself. Figure 12.4 won't still the fears of most taxpayers, however, especially those who don't hold any Treasury bonds. From their perspective, the total debt still looks frightening.

Refinancing

How much of a "burden" the debt really represents isn't so evident. For nearly 30 years (1970–97), the federal government kept piling up more debt without apparent economic damage. As we saw earlier (Figure 12.3), deficits and debt stretched out over even longer periods in earlier decades.

How was the government able to pile debt upon debt? Quite simple: As debts have become due, the federal government has simply borrowed new funds to pay them off. New bonds have been issued to replace old bonds. This **refinancing** of the debt is a routine feature of the U.S. Treasury's debt management.

The ability of the U.S. Treasury to refinance its debt raises an intriguing question. What if the debt could be eternally refinanced? What if no one *ever* demanded to be paid off more than others were willing to lend Uncle Sam? Then the national debt would truly grow forever.

Two things are worrisome about this scenario. First, eternal refinancing seems like a chain letter that promises to make everyone rich. In this case, the chain requires that people hold ever-larger portions of their wealth in the form of Treasury bonds. People worry that the chain will be broken and that they'll be forced to repay all the outstanding debt. Parents worry that the scheme might break down in the next generation, unfairly burdening their own children or grandchildren (see cartoon).

"What's this I hear about you adults mortgaging my future?"

Permission by Dave Carpenter.

Analysis: The fear that present generations are passing the debt burden to future generations is exaggerated.

Aside from its seeming implausibility, the notion of eternal refinancing seems to defy a basic maxim of economics, namely, that "there ain't no free lunch." Eternal refinancing makes it look as though government borrowing has no cost, as though federal spending financed by the national debt is really a free lunch.

There are two flaws in this way of thinking. The first relates to the interest charges that accompany debt. The second, and more important, oversight relates to the real economic costs of government activity.

Debt Service

debt service: The interest required to be paid each year on outstanding debt.

With $9 trillion in accumulated debt, the U.S. government must make enormous interest payments every year. **Debt service** refers to these annual interest payments. In FY 2007, the U.S. Treasury paid over $230 billion in interest charges. These interest payments force the government to reduce outlays for other purposes or to finance a larger budget each year. In this respect, ***interest payments restrict the government's ability to balance the budget or fund other public-sector activities.***

Although the debt-servicing requirements may pinch Uncle Sam's spending purse, the real economic consequences of interest payments are less evident. Who gets the interest payments? What economic resources are absorbed by those payments?

As noted, most of the nation's outstanding debt is internal—that is, owned by domestic households and institutions. Therefore, most interest payments are made to people and institutions within the United States. ***Most debt servicing is simply a redistribution of income from taxpayers to bondholders.*** In many cases, the taxpayer and bondholder are the same person. In all cases, however, the income that leaks from the circular flow in the form of taxes to pay for debt servicing returns to the circular flow as interest payments. Total income is unchanged. Thus, debt servicing may not have any direct effect on the level of aggregate demand.

webnote

Find out about the U.S. Treasury government bills, notes, and bonds at www.treasurydirect.gov/instit/annceresult/press/press.htm

Debt servicing also has little impact on the real resources of the economy. The collection of additional taxes and the processing of interest payments require the use of some land, labor, and capital. But the value of the resources used for the processing of debt service is trivial—a tiny fraction of the interest payments themselves. This means that ***interest payments themselves have virtually no direct opportunity cost.*** The amount of goods and services available for other purposes is virtually unchanged as a result of debt servicing.

Opportunity Costs

If debt servicing absorbs few economic resources, can we conclude that the national debt really does represent a free lunch? Unfortunately not. But the concept of opportunity cost does provide a major clue about the true burden of the debt and who bears it.

Opportunity costs are incurred only when real resources (factors of production) are used. The amount of that cost is measured by the other goods and services that could have been produced with those resources, but weren't. As noted earlier, the *process* of debt servicing absorbs few resources and so has negligible opportunity cost. To understand the true burden of the national debt, we have to look at what that debt financed. ***The true burden of the debt is the opportunity cost of the activities financed by the debt.*** To assess that burden, we need to ask what the government did with the borrowed funds.

Government Purchases. Suppose Congress decides to upgrade our naval forces and borrows $10 billion for that purpose. What's the opportunity cost of that decision? The economic cost of the fleet upgrade is measured by the goods and services forgone in order to build more ships. The labor, land, and capital used to upgrade the fleet can't be used to produce something else. We give up the opportunity to produce another $10 billion worth of private goods and services when Congress upgrades the fleet.

The economic cost of the naval buildup is unaffected by the method of government finance. Whether the government borrows $10 billion or increases taxes by that amount, the forgone civilian output will still be $10 billion. ***The opportunity cost of government purchases is the true burden of government activity, however financed.*** The decision to finance such activity with debt rather than taxes doesn't materially alter that cost.

Transfer Payments. Suppose the government uses debt financing to pay for increased transfer payments rather than the purchase of real goods and services. What would be the burden of debt in this case?

Note first that transfer payments entail few real costs. Income transfers entail a redistribution of income from the taxpayer to the transfer recipient. The only direct costs of those transfer payments are the land, labor, and capital involved in the administrative process of making that transfer. Those direct costs are so trivial that they can be ignored. Whatever changes in output or prices occur because of transfer payments result from *indirect* behavioral responses. If taxpayers or transfer recipients respond to transfers by working, saving, or investing less, the economy may suffer. These important *indirect* effects must be distinguished from the *direct* cost of the transfers, which are minimal. As a result, the amount of income transferred isn't a meaningful measure of economic burden. Hence, the debt that originated in deficit-financed income transfers can't be viewed as a unique "burden" either.

The Real Trade-Offs

Although the national debt poses no special burden to the economy, the transactions it finances have a substantial impact on the basic questions of WHAT, HOW, and FOR WHOM to produce. The mix of output is influenced by how much deficit spending the government undertakes. The funds obtained by borrowing allow the federal government to bid for scarce resources. Private investors and consumers will have less access to loanable funds and be less able to acquire incomes or goods. The larger the deficit, the more the private sector gets squeezed. Hence, deficit financing allows the government to obtain more resources and change the mix of output. In general, ***deficit financing tends to change the mix of output in the direction of more public-sector goods.***

As noted earlier, the deficits of the 1980s helped finance a substantial military buildup. The same result could have been financed with higher taxes. Taxes are more visible and always unpopular, however. By borrowing rather than taxing, the federal government's claim on scarce resources is less apparent. Either financing method allows the public sector to expand at the expense of the private sector. This resource reallocation reveals the true burden of the debt: ***The burden of the debt is really the opportunity cost (crowding out) of deficit-financed government activity.*** How large that burden is depends on how many unemployed resources are available and the behavioral responses of consumers and investors to increased government activity.

Notice also *when* that cost is incurred. If the military is upgraded this year, then the opportunity cost is incurred this year. It's only while resources are actually being used by the military that we give up the opportunity to use them elsewhere. Opportunity costs are incurred at the time a government activity takes place, not when the resultant debt is paid. In other words, ***the primary burden of the debt is incurred when the debt-financed activity takes place.***

If the entire military buildup is completed this year, what costs are borne next year? None. The land, labor, and capital available next year can be used for whatever purposes are then desired. Once the military buildup is completed, no further resources are allocated to that purpose. The real costs of government projects can't be postponed until a later year. In other words, the real burden of the debt can't be passed on to future generations. On the contrary, future generations will benefit from the sacrifices made today to build ships, parks, highways, dams, and other public-sector projects. Future taxpayers will be able to *use* these projects without incurring the opportunity costs of their construction.

Economic Growth. Although future generations may benefit from current government spending, they may also be adversely affected by today's opportunity costs. Of particular concern is the possibility that government deficits might crowd out private investment. Investment is essential to enlarging our production possibilities and attaining higher living standards in the future. If federal deficits and debt-servicing requirements crowd our private investment, the rate of economic growth will slow, leaving future generations with less productive capacity than they would otherwise have. Thus, ***if debt-financed government spending crowds out private investment, future generations will bear some of the debt burden.*** Their burden will take the form of smaller-than-anticipated productive capacity. This is the kind of cost professor Tyson worried about (see News, page 232).

There's no certainty that such crowding out will occur. Also, any reduction in private investment may be offset by public works (such as highways, schools, defense systems) that benefit future generations. So future generations may not suffer a net loss in welfare even if the national debt slows private investment and economic growth. From this perspective, ***the whole debate about the burden of the debt is really an argument over the* optimal mix of output.** If we permit more deficit spending, we're promoting more public-sector activity. On the other hand, limits on deficit financing curtail growth of the public sector. Battles over deficits and debts are a proxy for the more fundamental issue of private versus public spending.

optimal mix of output: The most desirable combination of output attainable with existing resources, technology, and social values.

Repayment. All this sounds a little too neat. Won't future generations have to pay interest on the debts we incur today? And might they even have to pay off some of the debt?

We've already observed that the collection of taxes and processing of interest payments absorb relatively few resources. Hence, the mechanisms of repayment entail little burden.

Notice also who *receives* future interest payments. When we die, we leave behind not only the national debt but also the bonds that represent ownership of that debt. Hence, future grandchildren will be both taxpayers *and* bondholders. If interest payments are made 30 years from today, only people who are alive and holding bonds at that time will receive interest payments. ***Future interest payments entail a redistribution of income among taxpayers and bondholders living in the future.***

The same kind of redistribution occurs if and when our grandchildren decide to pay off the debt. Tax revenues will be used to pay off the debt. The debt payments will go to people then holding Treasury bonds. The entire redistribution will occur among people living in the future.

EXTERNAL DEBT

The nature of opportunity costs makes it difficult but not impossible to pass the debt burden on to future generations. The exception is the case of external debt.

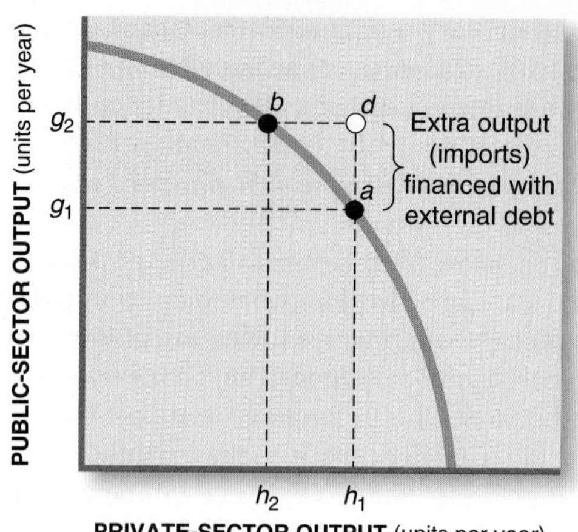

FIGURE 12.5
External Financing

A closed economy must forsake some private-sector output in order to increase public-sector output (see Figure 12.2). External financing temporarily eliminates that opportunity cost. Instead of having to move from *a* to *b,* external borrowing allows us to move from *a* to *d.* At point *d* we have more public output and no less private output.

No Crowding Out

When we borrow funds from abroad, we increase our ability to consume, invest, and finance government activity. In effect, other nations are lending us the income necessary to *import* more goods. If we can buy imports with borrowed funds (without offsetting exports), our real income will exceed our production possibilities. As Figure 12.5 illustrates, external borrowing allows us to enjoy a mix of output that lies *outside* our production possibilities curve. Specifically, ***external financing allows us to get more public-sector goods without cutting back on private-sector production (or vice versa).*** When we use external debt to finance government spending, we move from point *a* to point *d* in Figure 12.5. Imported goods and services eliminate the need to cut back on private-sector activity, a cutback that would otherwise force us to point *b.* External financing eliminates this opportunity cost. The move from point *a* to point *d* reflects the additional imports financed by external debt.

The imports needn't be public-sector goods. A tax cut at point *b* might increase consumption and imports by $h_1 - h_2$, moving the economy to point *d.* At *d* we have *more* consumption and *no less* government activity.

External financing appears to offer the proverbial free lunch. It would be a free lunch if foreign lenders were willing to accumulate U.S. Treasury bonds forever. They would then own stacks of paper (Treasury bonds), and we'd consume some of their output (our imports) each year. ***As long as outsiders are willing to hold U.S. bonds, external financing imposes no real cost.*** No goods or services are given up to pay for the additional output received.

Repayment

Foreign investors may not be willing to hold U.S. bonds indefinitely. At some point they'll want to collect their bills. To do this, they'll cash in (sell) their bonds, then use the proceeds to buy U.S. goods and services. When this happens, the United States will be *exporting* goods and services to pay off its debts. Recall that the external debt was used to acquire imported goods and services. Hence, ***external debt must be repaid with exports of real goods and services.***

DEFICIT AND DEBT LIMITS

Although external and internal debts pose very different problems, most policy discussions overlook these distinctions. In policy debates, the aggregate size of the national debt is usually the only concern. The key policy questions are whether and how to limit or reduce the national debt.

Deficit Ceilings

deficit ceiling: An explicit, legislated limitation on the size of the budget deficit.

The only way to stop the growth of the national debt is to eliminate the budget deficits that create debt. The first step in debt reduction, therefore, is a balanced annual budget. A balanced budget will at least stop the debt from growing further. **Deficit ceilings** are explicit limitations on the size of the annual budget deficit. A deficit ceiling of zero compels a balanced budget.

The Balanced Budget and Emergency Deficit Control Act of 1985—popularly referred to as the Gramm-Rudman-Hollings Act—was the first explicit attempt to force the federal budget into balance. The essence of the Gramm-Rudman Act was simple:

- First, it set a lower ceiling on each year's deficit, until budget balance was achieved.
- Second, it called for automatic cutbacks in spending if Congress failed to keep the deficit below the ceiling.

The original Gramm-Rudman law required Congress to pare the deficit from over $200 billion in FY 1985 to zero (a balanced budget) by 1991. But Congress wasn't willing to cut spending and increase taxes enough to meet those targets. And the Supreme Court declared that the "automatic" mechanism for spending cuts was unconstitutional.

In 1990, President George H. Bush and the Congress developed a new set of rules for reducing the deficit. They first acknowledged that they lacked total control of the deficit. At best, Congress could close the *structural* deficit by limiting discretionary spending or raising taxes. The Budget Enforcement Act (BEA) of 1990 laid out a plan for doing exactly this. The BEA set separate limits on defense spending, discretionary domestic spending, and international spending. It also required that any new spending initiative be offset with increased taxes or cutbacks in other programs.

webnote

For a discussion of deficits and deficit-reduction efforts, visit the U.S. Congressional Budget Office at www.cbo.gov

The Budget Enforcement Act was successful in reducing the structural deficit somewhat. But the political pain associated with spending cuts and higher taxes was too great for elected officials to bear. President George H. Bush's reelection bid was damaged by his willingness to raise taxes. And Democrats took heat for reducing the growth of social programs. Soon thereafter, legislated deficit ceilings proved to be more political ornaments than binding budget mandates.

Debt Ceilings

Explicit **debt ceilings** are another mechanism for forcing Congress to adopt specific fiscal policies. A debt ceiling can be used either to stop the accumulation of debt or to force the federal government to start *reducing* the accumulated national debt. In effect, debt ceilings are a backdoor approach to deficit reduction. ***Like deficit ceilings, debt ceilings are really just political mechanisms for forging compromises on how best to use budget surpluses or deficits.***

debt ceiling: An explicit, legislated limit on the amount of outstanding national debt.

THE ECONOMY TOMORROW

DIPPING INTO SOCIAL SECURITY

The Social Security Trust Fund has been a major source of funding for the federal government for over 20 years. Since 1985, the Trust Fund has collected more payroll (FICA) taxes each year than it has paid out in retirement benefits. As we noted already, all of those surpluses have been "invested" in Treasury securities, making the Social Security Trust Fund the U.S. Treasury's largest creditor. The Trust Fund now holds nearly $2 trillion of Treasury securities and is still accumulating more. Between 2007 and 2014, the Trust Fund will acquire another $2 trillion in Treasury securities.

Aging Baby Boomers. The persistent surpluses in the Social Security Trust Fund are largely the result of aging Baby Boomers. In the 15 years after World War II ended, birthrates soared. These Baby Boomers are now in their peak earning years (45–60) and paying lots of payroll taxes. This keeps the Social Security Trust Fund flush with cash.

As we peer into the economy tomorrow, however, the fiscal outlook is not so bright. The Baby Boomers are fast approaching retirement age. When they do retire, the Baby Boomers will throw the budget of the Social Security Trust Fund out of whack. Today, there are 3 active (tax-paying) workers for every retiree. By 2015, that worker-retiree ratio will slip to 2.7. By 2030, there'll be only 2 workers for every retiree (see Table 12.5). By then, the Trust Fund payroll-tax collections will be a lot smaller than the benefit promises made to

TABLE 12.5
Changing Worker-Retiree Ratios

Fifty years ago there were over 16 tax-paying workers for every retiree. Today there are only 3, and the ratio slips further when the Baby Boomers start retiring. This demographic change will convert Social Security surpluses into deficits, causing future budget problems.

Year	Workers per Beneficiary	Year	Workers per Beneficiary
1950	16.5	2000	3.4
1960	5.1	2015	2.7
1970	3.7	2030	2.0

Source: U.S. Social Security Administration.

retired Baby Boomers. When that happens, a primary source of government financing will disappear.

Social Security Deficits. In fact, the Trust Fund balance shifts from annual surpluses to annual deficits as soon as 2014. After that, Social Security will be able to pay promised benefits only if (1) the U.S. Treasury pays all interest due on bonds held by the Trust Fund and, ultimately, (2) the U.S. Treasury redeems the $4 trillion-plus of bonds the Trust Fund will then be holding. This is what scares aging Baby Boomers (and should worry you!).

The Baby Boomers wonder where the Treasury is going to get the funds needed to repay the Social Security Trust Fund. There really aren't many options. ***To pay back Social Security loans, the Congress will have to raise future taxes significantly, make substantial cuts in other (non–Social Security) programs or sharply increase budget deficits.*** None of these options is attractive. Worse yet, the budget squeeze created by the Social Security payback will severely limit the potential for discretionary fiscal policy.

When GDP growth slows in the economy tomorrow, it will be increasingly difficult to cut taxes or increase government spending while the U.S. Treasury is scurrying to repay Social Security Trust Fund loans. Aging Baby Boomers worry that Congress might instead cut their promised retirement benefits.

SUMMARY

- Budget imbalances result from both discretionary fiscal policy (structural deficits and surpluses) and cyclical changes in the economy (cyclical deficits and surpluses). LO1
- Fiscal restraint is measured by the reduction in the structural deficit; fiscal stimulus occurs when the structural deficit increases. LO1
- Automatic stabilizers increase federal spending and reduce tax revenues during recessions. When the economy expands, they have the reverse effect, thereby shrinking the cyclical deficit. LO1
- Deficit financing of government expenditure may crowd out private investment and consumption. The risk of crowding out increases as the economy approaches full employment. If investment becomes the opportunity cost of increased government spending or consumer tax cuts, economic growth may slow. LO2
- Crowding in refers to the increase in private-sector outputmade possible by a decline in government borrowing. LO2
- Each year's deficit adds to the national debt. The national debt grew sporadically until World War II and then skyrocketed. Tax cuts, recessions, and increased government spending since 1980 have increased the national debt to over $9 trillion. LO1
- Budget surpluses may be used to finance tax cuts or more government spending, or used to reduce accumulated national debt. LO2
- Every dollar of national debt represents a dollar of assets to the people who hold U.S. Treasury bonds. Most U.S. bonds are held by government agencies, U.S. households, and U.S. banks, insurance companies, and other institutions. LO3
- The real burden of the debt is the opportunity cost of the activities financed by the debt. That cost is borne at the time the deficit-financed activity takes place. The benefits of debt-financed activity may extend into the future. LO3

- External debt permits the public sector to expand without reducing private-sector output. External debt also makes it possible to shift some of the real debt burden on to future generations. LO3
- Deficit and debt ceilings are largely symbolic efforts to force consideration of real trade-offs, to restrain government spending, and to change the mix of output. LO3
- The coming retirement of the Baby Boomers (born 1946–60) will transform Social Security surpluses into deficits, imposing severe constraints on future fiscal policy. LO1

Key Terms

fiscal policy
deficit spending
budget deficit
budget surplus
fiscal year (FY)
discretionary fiscal spending
fiscal restraint
fiscal stimulus
income transfers
automatic stabilizer
cyclical deficit
structural deficit
crowding out
opportunity cost
crowding in
national debt
Treasury bonds
liability
asset
internal debt
external debt
refinancing
debt service
optimal mix of output
deficit ceiling
debt ceiling

Questions for Discussion

1. Who paid for the Revolutionary War? Did the deficit financing initiated by the Continental Congress pass the cost of the war on to future generations? LO3
2. In what ways do future generations benefit from this generation's deficit spending? Cite three examples LO3
3. What's considered "too much" debt or "too large" a deficit? Are you able to provide any guidelines for deficit or debt ceilings? LO2
4. If deficit spending "crowds out" some private investment, could future generations be worse off? If external financing eliminates crowding out, are future generations thereby protected? LO2
5. If tax cuts crowd out government spending, is the economy worse off? (See News, page 232.) LO2
6. A constitutional amendment has been proposed that would require Congress to balance the budget each year. Is it possible to balance the budget each year? Is it desirable? LO1
7. What should the government do with a budget surplus? LO1
8. By how much did defense spending increase in 1940 to 1944? (See back endpapers of this book.) What was crowded out? LO2
9. How long would it take to pay off the national debt? How would the economy be affected? LO3
10. Which of the following options do you favor for resolving future Social Security deficits? What are the advantages and disadvantages of each option? (a) cutting Social Security benefits, (b) raising payroll taxes, (c) cutting non–Social Security programs, and (d) raising income taxes LO1

problems The Student Problem Set at the back of this book contains numerical and graphing problems for this chapter.

web activities to accompany this chapter can be found on the Online Learning Center: **http://www.mhhe.com/economics/schiller11e**

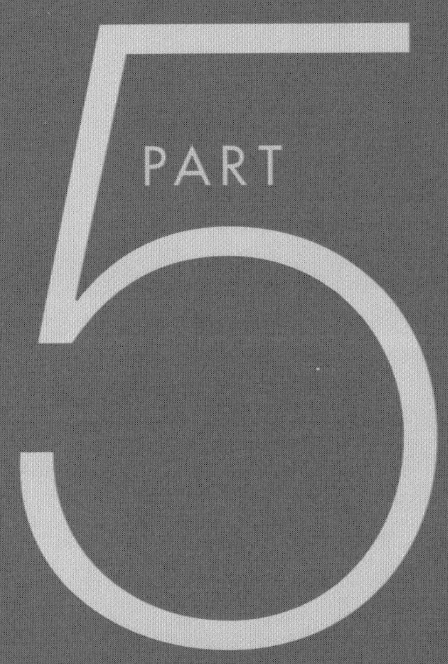

PART

Monetary Policy Options

Monetary policy tries to alter macro outcomes by managing the amount of money available in the economy. By changing the money supply and/or interest rates, monetary policy seeks to shift the aggregate demand curve in the desired direction. Chapters 13 through 15 illustrate how this policy tool works.

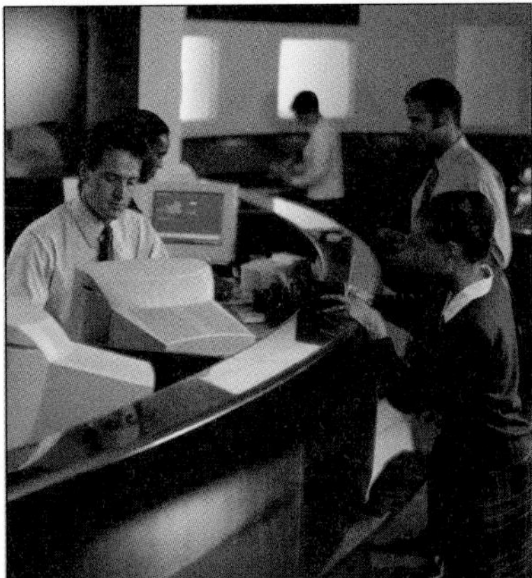

Money and Banks

13

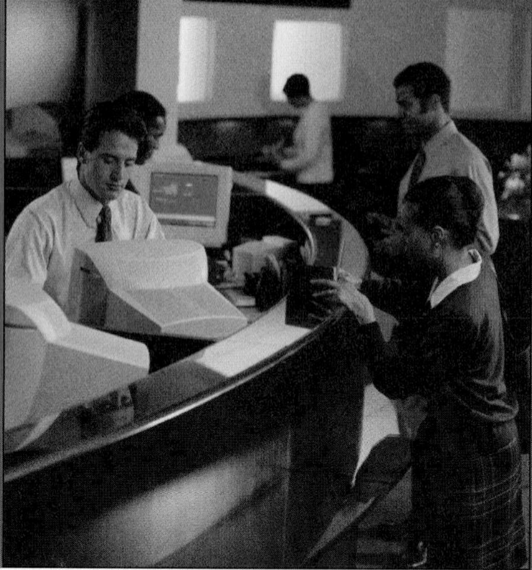

LEARNING OBJECTIVES

After reading this chapter, you should know:

LO1. What money is.

LO2. How banks create money.

LO3. How the money multiplier works.

Sophocles, the ancient Greek playwright, had very strong opinions about the role of money. As he saw it, "Of evils upon earth, the worst is money. It is money that sacks cities, and drives men forth from hearth and home; warps and seduces native intelligence, and breeds a habit of dishonesty."

In modern times, people may still be seduced by the lure of money and fashion their lives around its pursuit. Nevertheless, it's hard to imagine an economy functioning without money. Money affects not only morals and ideals but also the way an economy works.

This and the following two chapters examine the role of money in the economy today. We begin with a very simple question:

- **What is money?**

As we'll discover, money isn't exactly what you might think it is. There's a lot more money in the economy than there is cash. And there's a lot more income around than money. So money is something quite different from either cash or income. Once we've established the characteristics of money, we go on to ask:

- **How is money created?**
- **What role do banks play in the circular flow of income and spending?**

In Chapter 14 we look at how the Federal Reserve System controls the amount of money created. In Chapter 15 we look at the implications for monetary policy, another tool in our macro policy tool box.

WORLD VIEW

The Cashless Society

Bartering Chokes Russian Economy

NARO-FOMINSK, RUSSIA—Natalya Karpova, a supervisor at a fabric factory here on the outskirts of Moscow, heard good news a couple of weeks ago. Three carloads of concrete utility poles had arrived at the train station.

This was a matter of utmost importance to Karpova, because her factory was a year behind on its electric bill and had no cash on hand. The electric company agreed to accept utility poles instead, but how to pay for utility poles with no rubles?

Simple. First, her factory shipped fabric 200 miles to a sewing factory in Nizhny Novgorod. In exchange for the fabric, that factory sewed shirts for the security guards who work at a nearby automobile manufacturer. In exchange for the shirts, the auto factory shipped a car and truck to a concrete plant. In exchange for the vehicles, the concrete plant delivered the poles to the electric company.

Thus did the Narfomsholk fabric factory pay for the power to run its dye machines.

But only for a while. "Now they want a steam shovel," said Karpova, with a little sigh.

This is how Karpova's factory and much of Russia's industry survives these days: barter. By some estimates, it accounts for almost three-fourths of all transactions.

Barter is poisoning the development of capitalism in Russia because it consumes huge amounts of time that would be better spent producing goods.

Many workers have no expectation of a real paycheck. Unpaid wages now amount to an estimated $11 billion. Instead of money, the workers are stuck with whatever the factory or farm is handing out, usually what it produces. The practice is so common now that only the more bizarre substitutes for wages draw notice, such as bras or coffins.

—Sharon LaFraniere

Source: *Washington Post,* September 3, 1998. www.washingtonpost.com

Analysis: When the Russian ruble lost its value, people would no longer accept it in payment. Market transactions had to be bartered, a clumsy and inefficient process.

WHAT IS "MONEY"?

To appreciate the significance of money for a modern economy, imagine for a moment that there were no such thing as money. How would you get something for breakfast? If you wanted eggs for breakfast, you'd have to tend your own chickens or go see Farmer Brown. But how would you pay Farmer Brown for his eggs? Without money, you'd have to offer him some goods or services that he could use. In other words, you'd have to engage in primitive **barter**—the direct exchange of one good for another—in order to get eggs for breakfast. You'd get those eggs only if Farmer Brown happened to want the particular goods or services you had to offer.

> **barter:** The direct exchange of one good for another, without the use of money.

The use of money greatly simplifies market transactions. It's a lot easier to exchange money for eggs at the supermarket than to go into the country and barter with farmers every time you crave some eggs. Our ability to use money in market transactions, however, depends on the grocer's willingness to accept money as a *medium of exchange.* The grocer sells eggs for money only because he can use the same money to pay his help and buy the goods he himself desires. He too can exchange money for goods and services.

Without money, the process of acquiring goods and services would be much more difficult and time-consuming. This was evident when the value of the Russian ruble plummeted. Trading goods for Farmer Brown's eggs seems simple compared to the complicated barter deals Russian factories had to negotiate when paper money was no longer accepted (see World View). And Russian workers certainly would've preferred to be paid in cash rather than in bras and coffins.

THE MONEY SUPPLY

Many Types of Money

Although markets can't function well without money, they can get along without *dollars.* In the early days of colonial America, there were no U.S. dollars; a lot of business was conducted with Spanish and Portuguese gold coins. Later, people used Indian wampum, then tobacco, grain, fish, and furs as mediums of exchange. Throughout the colonies, gunpowder and bullets were frequently used for small change. These forms of money weren't as convenient as U.S. dollars, but they did the job.

webnote

For a brief history of coins and to learn how coins are made, visit the U.S. mint at www.usmint.gov

This historical perspective on money highlights its essential characteristics. ***Anything that serves all the following purposes can be thought of as money:***

- ***Medium of exchange:*** is accepted as payment for goods and services (and debts).
- ***Store of value:*** can be held for future purchases.
- ***Standard of value:*** serves as a yardstick for measuring the prices of goods and services.

All the items used during the colonial days satisfied these conditions and were thus properly regarded as money.

After the colonies became an independent nation, the U.S. Constitution prohibited the federal government from issuing paper money. Money was instead issued by state-chartered banks. Between 1789 and 1865, over 30,000 different paper bills were issued by 1,600 banks in 34 states. People often preferred to get paid in gold, silver, or other commodities rather than in one of these uncertain currencies.

The first paper money the federal government issued consisted of $10 million worth of "greenbacks," printed in 1861 to finance the Civil War. The National Banking Act of 1863 gave the federal government permanent authority to issue money.

Modern Concepts

The "greenbacks" we carry around today aren't the only form of "money" we use. Most people realize this when they offer to pay for goods with a check rather than cash. People do distinguish between "cash" and "money," and for good reason. The "money" you have in a checking account can be used to buy goods and services or to pay debts, or it can be retained for future use. In these respects, your checking account balance is as much a part of your "money" as are the coins and dollars in your pocket or purse. You can access your balance by writing a check or using an ATM or debit card. Checks are more convenient than cash because they eliminate trips to the bank. Checks are also safer: Lost or stolen cash is gone forever; checkbooks and credit cards are easily replaced at little or no cost. We might use checks even more frequently if everyone accepted them.

There's nothing unique about cash, then, insofar as the market is concerned. ***Checking accounts can and do perform the same market functions as cash.*** Accordingly, we must include checking account balances in our concept of **money.** The essence of money isn't its taste, color, or feel but, rather, its ability to purchase goods and services.

money: Anything generally accepted as a medium of exchange.

Credit cards are another popular medium of exchange. People use credit cards for about one-third of all purchases over $100. This use is not sufficient, however, to qualify credit cards as a form of "money." Credit card balances must be paid by check or cash. The same holds true for balances in online electronic credit accounts ("e-cash"). Electronic purchases on the Internet or online services are ultimately paid by withdrawals from a bank account (by check or computer). Online payment mechanisms and credit cards are a payment *service,* not a final form of payment (credit card companies charge fees and interest for this service). The cards themselves are not a store of value, in contrast to cash or bank account balances.

The Diversity of Bank Accounts. To determine how much money is available to purchase goods and services, we need to count up all our coins and currency—as well as our bank account balances. This effort is complicated by the variety of bank accounts people have. In addition to simple no-interest checking accounts at full-service banks, people have bank accounts that pay interest, offer automatic transfers, require minimum holding periods, offer overdraft protection, or limit the number of checks that can be written. People also have "bank" accounts in credit unions, brokerage houses, and other nontraditional financial institutions.

Although all bank account balances can be spent, they're not all used the same way. People use regular checking accounts all the time to pay bills or make purchases. But consumers can't write checks on most savings accounts. And few people want to cash in a certificate of deposit just to go to the movies. Hence, ***some bank accounts are better substitutes for cash than others.***

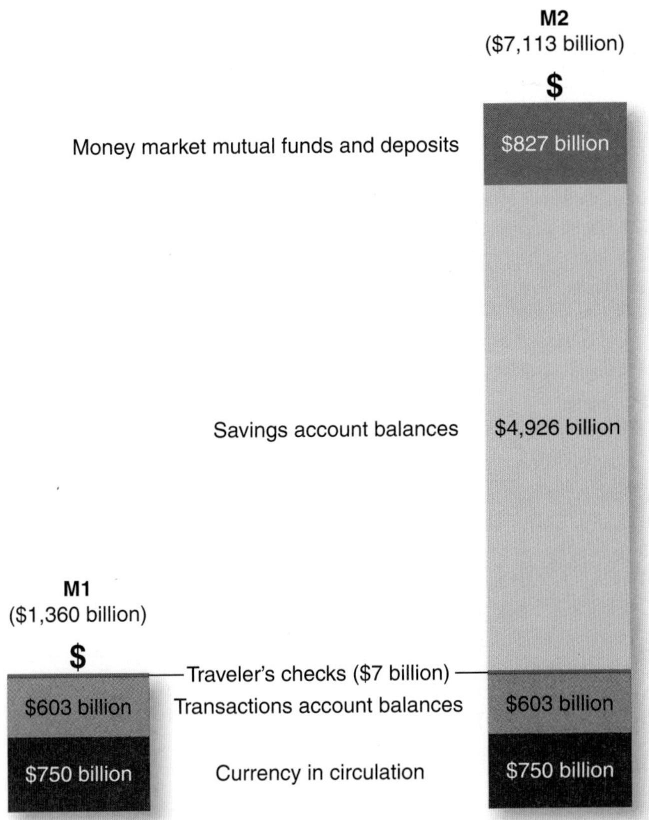

FIGURE 13.1
Composition of the Money Supply

Cash is only a part of the money supply. People also have easy access to transactions account balances and various savings account balances that are counted in measures of the money supply (M1 and M2). Because people hold so much money in money market mutual funds and savings (time-deposit) accounts, M2 is five times larger than M1.

Source: Federal Reserve (February 2007 data).

M1: Cash and Transactions Accounts

Several different measures of money have been developed to accommodate the diversity of bank accounts and other payment mechanisms. The narrowest definition of the **money supply** is designated **M1,** ***which includes***

- ***Currency in circulation.***
- ***Transactions account balances.***
- ***Traveler's checks.***

money supply: (M1) Currency held by the public, plus balances in transactions accounts.

As Figure 13.1 indicates, the second largest component of this basic money supply (M1) is **transactions account** balances, which are the balances in bank accounts that are readily accessed by check. Most people refer to these simply as "checking accounts." The term "transactions account" is broader, however, including NOW accounts, ATS accounts, credit union share drafts, and demand deposits at mutual savings banks. ***The distinguishing feature of all transactions accounts is that they permit direct payment to a third party (by check or debit card),*** without requiring a trip to the bank to make a special withdrawal. Because of this feature, transactions accounts are the readiest substitutes for cash in market transactions. Traveler's checks issued by nonbank firms such as American Express can also be used directly in market transactions, just like good old-fashioned cash.

transactions account: A bank account that permits direct payment to a third party, for example, with a check.

M2: M1 + Savings Accounts, etc.

Transactions accounts aren't the only substitute for cash. People can and do dip into savings accounts on occasion. People sometimes even cash in their certificates of deposit in order to buy something, despite the interest penalty associated with early withdrawal. And banks have made it easy to transfer funds from one type of account to another. Savings accounts can be transformed into transactions accounts with a phone call or computer instruction. As a result, ***savings account balances are almost as good a substitute for cash as transactions account balances.***

Another popular way of holding money is to buy shares of money market mutual funds. Deposits into money market mutual funds are pooled and used to purchase interest-bearing securities such as Treasury bills. The interest rates paid on these funds are typically higher

Everything you want to know about currency can be found at www.frbatlanta.org/publica/brochure/fundfac/money.htm

TABLE 13.1
Alternative Measures of the Money Supply

Measures of the money supply are intended to gauge the extent of purchasing power held by consumers. But the extent of purchasing power depends on how accessible assets are and how often people use them. The various money supply measures reflect variations in the liquidity and accessibility of assets.

Measure	Components
M1	Currency in circulation outside of bank vaults Demand deposits at commercial banks NOW and ATS accounts Credit union share drafts Demand deposits at mutual savings banks Traveler's checks (nonbank)
M2	M1 plus: Savings accounts Time deposits of less than $100,000 Money market mutual funds
M3	M2 plus: Time deposits larger than $100,000 Repurchase agreements Overnight Eurodollars
L	M3 plus other liquid assets, for example: Treasury bills U.S. savings bonds Bankers' acceptances Term Eurodollars Commercial paper

than those paid by banks. Moreover, the deposits made into the funds can often be withdrawn immediately, just like those in transactions accounts. When interest rates are high, deposits move out of regular transactions accounts into money market mutual funds in order to earn a higher return.

M2 money supply: M1 plus balances in most savings accounts and money market mutual funds.

Additional measures of the money supply have been constructed to account for the possibility of using savings account balances, money market mutual funds, and various other deposits to finance everyday spending. The most widely watched money measure is **M2,** which includes all of M1 *plus* balances in savings accounts, money market mutual funds, and some CDs ("time deposits"). As Figure 13.1 shows, M2 is nearly five times as large as M1. Table 13.1 summarizes the content of these and two other measures of money.

aggregate demand: The total quantity of output demanded at alternative price levels in a given time period, *ceteris paribus.*

Our concern about the specific nature of money stems from our broader interest in **aggregate demand.** What we want to know is how much purchasing power consumers have, since this will affect their ability to purchase goods and services. What we've observed, however, is that money isn't so easily defined. How much spending power people have depends not only on the number of coins in their pockets but also on their willingness to write checks, make trips to the bank, or convert other assets into cash.

In an increasingly complex financial system, the core concept of "money" isn't easy to pin down. Nevertheless, the official measures of the money supply (particularly M1 and M2) are fairly reliable benchmarks for gauging how much purchasing power market participants have.

CREATION OF MONEY

Once we've decided what money is, we still have to explain where it comes from. Part of the explanation is simple. Currency must be printed. Some nations use private printers for this purpose, but all U.S. currency is printed by the Bureau of Engraving and Printing in Washington, D.C. Coins come from the U.S. mints located in Philadelphia and Denver. As we observed in Figure 13.1, however, currency is a small fraction of our total money supply. So we need to look elsewhere for the origins of most money. Specifically, where do all the transactions accounts come from? How do people acquire transactions deposits? How does

BANK
DIRECT DEPOSIT DEPT.
YOU SEE, WITH DIRECT DEPOSIT OF YOUR PAYCHECK WE COMPLETELY DO AWAY WITH THE ILLUSION THAT YOU ACTUALLY EVER SEE ANY OF YOUR MONEY.

Analysis: People see very little of their money—most deposits and loans are computer entries in the banking system.

the total amount of such deposits—and therefore the money supply of the economy—change?

Deposit Creation

Most people assume that all transactions account balances come from cash deposits. But this isn't the case. Direct deposits of paychecks, for example, are carried out by computer, not by the movement of cash (see cartoon). Moreover, the employer who issues the paycheck probably didn't make any cash deposits. It's more likely that she covered those paychecks with customers' checks that she deposited or with loans granted by the bank itself.

The ability of banks to lend money opens up a whole new set of possibilities for creating money. ***When a bank lends someone money, it simply credits that individual's bank account.*** The money appears in an account just as it would with a cash deposit. And the owner of the account is free to spend that money as with any positive balance. Hence, ***in making a loan, a bank effectively creates money because transactions account balances are counted as part of the money supply.***

To understand the origins of our money supply, then, we must recognize two basic principles:

- Transactions account balances are a large portion of the money supply.
- Banks can create transactions account balances by making loans.

The following two sections examine this process of **deposit creation** more closely. We determine how banks actually create deposits and what forces might limit the process of deposit creation.

deposit creation: The creation of transactions deposits by bank lending.

Bank Regulation. Banks' deposit-creation activities are regulated by the government. The most important agency in this regard is the Federal Reserve System. "The Fed" puts limits on the amount of bank lending, thereby controlling the basic money supply. We'll discuss the structure and functions of the Fed in the next chapter; here we focus on the process of deposit creation itself.

A Monopoly Bank

Table 13.2 documents that there are thousands of banks, of various sorts, in the United States. To understand how banks create money, however, we'll make life simple. We'll assume for the moment that there's only one bank in town, University Bank. Imagine also that you've been saving some of your income by putting loose change into a piggy bank. Now, after months of saving, you break the bank and discover that your thrift has yielded $100. You immediately deposit this money in a new checking account at University Bank. How will this deposit affect the money supply?

Your initial deposit will have no immediate effect on the money supply. The coins in your piggy bank were already counted as part of the money supply (M1 and M2) because they represented cash held by the public. ***When you deposit cash or coins in a bank, you're only changing the composition of the money supply, not its size.*** The public (you) now holds

TABLE 13.2
What Is a Bank?

The essential functions of a bank are to

- Accept deposits
- Offer drafts (check writing privileges)
- Make loans

In the United States, roughly 19,000 depository institutions fulfill these functions. These "banks" are typically classified into four general categories, even though most banks (and many other financial institutions) now offer similar services.

Type of Bank	Characteristics
Commercial banks	The 7,500 commercial banks in the United States provide a full range of banking services, including savings ("time") and checking accounts and loans for all purposes. They hold nearly all demand deposits and nearly half of total savings deposits.
Savings and loan associations	Begun in 1831 as a mechanism for pooling the savings of a neighborhood in order to provide funds for home purchases, which is still the basic function of such banks. The nearly 500 S&Ls channel virtually all their savings deposits into home mortgages.
Mutual savings banks	Originally intended to serve very small savers (like the Boston Five Cents Savings Bank). They now use their deposits for a wider variety of purposes, including investment bonds and blue-chip stocks. Almost all the 800 or so mutual savings banks are located in only five states: New York, Massachusetts, Connecticut, Pennsylvania, and New Jersey.
Credit unions	Cooperative societies formed by individuals bound together by some common tie, such as a common employer or labor union. Credit union members hold savings accounts and enjoy access to the pooled savings of all members. Most credit union loans are for consumer purchases. Although there are close to 10,000 credit unions in the United States, they hold less than 5 percent of total savings deposits.

$100 less of coins but $100 more of transactions deposits. Accordingly, no money is created by the demise of your piggy bank (the initial deposit). This accounting outcome is reflected in the following "T-account" of University Bank and the composition of the money supply:

University Bank

Assets	Liabilities
+$100 in coins	+$100 in deposits

Money Supply

Cash held by the public	−$100
Transactions deposits at bank	+$100
Change in M	0

The T-account shows that your coins are now held by University Bank. In exchange, the bank has credited your checking account $100. This balance is a liability for the bank since it must allow you to withdraw the deposit on demand.

The total money supply is unaffected by your cash deposit because two components of the money supply change in opposite directions (i.e., less cash, more bank deposits). This initial deposit is just the beginning of the money creation process, however. Banks aren't in business for your convenience; they're in business to earn a profit. To earn a profit on your deposit, University Bank will have to put your money to work. This means using your deposit as the basis for making a loan to someone who's willing to pay the bank interest for use of money. If the function of banks was merely to store money, they wouldn't pay interest on their accounts or offer free checking services. Instead, you'd have to pay them for these services. Banks pay you interest and offer free (or inexpensive) checking because they can use your money to make loans that earn interest.

The Initial Loan. Typically, a bank doesn't have much difficulty finding someone who wants to borrow money. Someone is always eager to borrow money. The question is: How much money can a bank lend? Can it lend your entire deposit? Or must University Bank keep some of your coins in reserve, in case you want to withdraw them? The answer will surprise you.

Suppose University Bank decided to lend the entire $100 to Campus Radio. Campus Radio wants to buy a new antenna but doesn't have any money in its own checking account. To acquire the antenna, Campus Radio must take out a loan.

When University Bank agrees to lend Campus Radio $100, it does so by crediting the account of Campus Radio. Instead of giving Campus Radio $100 cash, University Bank simply adds an electronic $100 to Campus Radio's checking account balance. That is, the loan is made with a simple bookkeeping entry as follows:

University Bank

Assets	Liabilities
$100 in coins	$100 your account balance
$100 in loans	$100 Campus Radio account

Money Supply

Cash held by the public	no change
Transactions deposits at bank	+$100
Change in M	+$100

This simple bookkeeping procedure is the key to creating money. When University Bank lends $100 to the Campus Radio account, it "creates" money. Keep in mind that transactions deposits are counted as part of the money supply. Once the $100 loan is credited to its account, Campus Radio can use this new money to purchase its desired antenna, without worrying that its check will bounce.

Or can it? Once University Bank grants a loan to Campus Radio, both you and Campus Radio have $100 in your checking accounts to spend. But the bank is holding only $100 of **reserves** (your coins). In other words, the increased account balance obtained by Campus Radio doesn't limit your ability to write checks. There's been a net *increase* in the value of transactions deposits but no increase in bank reserves.

bank reserves: Assets held by a bank to fulfill its deposit obligations.

Secondary Deposits. What happens if Campus Radio actually spends the $100 on a new antenna? Won't this "use up all" the reserves held by the bank, endangering your check writing privileges? The answer is no.

Consider what happens when Atlas Antenna receives the check from Campus Radio. What will Atlas do with the check? Atlas could go to University Bank and exchange the check for $100 of cash (your coins). But Atlas may prefer to deposit the check in its own checking account at University Bank (still the only bank in town). This way, Atlas not only avoids the necessity of going to the bank (it can deposit the check by mail) but also keeps its money in a safe place. Should Atlas later want to spend the money, it can simply write a check. In the meantime, the bank continues to hold its entire reserves (your coins), and both you and Atlas have $100 to spend.

Fractional Reserves. Notice what's happened here. The money supply has increased by $100 as a result of deposit creation (the loan to Campus Radio). Moreover, the bank has been able to support $200 of transaction deposits (your account and either the Campus Radio or Atlas account) with only $100 of reserves (your coins). In other words, ***bank reserves are only a fraction of total deposits.*** In this case, University Bank's reserves (your $100 in coins) are only 50 percent of total deposits. Thus the bank's **reserve ratio** is 50 percent—that is,

reserve ratio: The ratio of a bank's reserves to its total transactions deposits.

$$\text{Reserve ratio} = \frac{\text{bank reserves}}{\text{total deposits}}$$

The ability of University Bank to hold reserves that are only a fraction of total deposits results from two facts: (1) people use checks for most transactions, and (2) there's no other bank. Accordingly, reserves are rarely withdrawn from this monopoly bank. In fact, if people *never* withdrew their deposits and *all* transactions accounts were held at University Bank, University Bank wouldn't need *any* reserves. In this most unusual case, University

Bank could make as many loans as it wanted. Every loan it made would increase the supply of money.

In reality, many banks are available, and people both withdraw cash from their accounts and write checks to people who have accounts in other banks. In addition, bank lending practices are regulated by the Federal Reserve System. ***The Federal Reserve System requires banks to maintain some minimum reserve ratio.*** This reserve requirement directly limits banks' ability to grant new loans.

Required Reserves. The potential impact of Federal Reserve requirements on bank lending can be readily seen. Suppose that the Federal Reserve imposed a minimum reserve requirement of 75 percent on University Bank. Such a requirement would prohibit University Bank from lending $100 to Campus Radio. That loan would result in $200 of deposits, supported by only $100 of reserves. The actual ratio of reserves to deposits would be 50 percent ($100 of reserves ÷ $200 of deposits), which would violate the Fed's assumed 75 percent reserve requirement. A 75 percent reserve requirement means that University Bank must hold **required reserves** equal to 75 percent of *total* deposits, including those created through loans.

required reserves: The minimum amount of reserves a bank is required to hold; equal to required reserve ratio times transactions deposits.

The bank's dilemma is evident in the following equation:

$$\text{Required reserves} = \text{required reserve ratio} \times \text{total deposits}$$

To support $200 of total deposits, University Bank would need to satisfy this equation:

$$\text{Required reserves} = 0.75 \times \$200 = \$150$$

But the bank has only $100 of reserves (your coins) and so would violate the reserve requirement if it increased total deposits to $200 by lending $100 to Campus Radio.

University Bank can still issue a loan to Campus Radio. But the loan must be less than $100 in order to keep the bank within the limits of the required reserve formula. Thus, ***a minimum reserve requirement directly limits deposit-creation (lending) possibilities.*** It's still true, however, as we'll now illustrate, that the banking system, taken as a whole, can create multiple loans (money) from a single deposit.

A Multibank World

Table 13.3 illustrates the process of deposit creation in a multibank world with a required reserve ratio. In this case, we assume that legally required reserves must equal at least 20 percent of transactions deposits. Now when you deposit $100 in your checking account, University Bank must hold at least $20 as required reserves.[1]

Excess Reserves. The remaining $80 the bank obtains from your deposit is regarded as **excess reserves.** These reserves are "excess" because your bank is *required* to hold in reserve only $20 (equal to 20 percent of your initial $100 deposit):

excess reserves: Bank reserves in excess of required reserves.

$$\text{Excess reserves} = \text{total reserves} - \text{required reserves}$$

The $80 of excess reserves aren't required and may be used to support additional loans. Hence, the bank can now lend $80. In view of the fact that banks earn profits (interest) by making loans, we assume that University Bank will try to use these excess reserves as soon as possible.

To keep track of the changes in reserves, deposit balances, and loans that occur in a multibank world we'll have to do some bookkeeping. For this purpose we'll again use the same balance sheet, or "T-account," that banks themselves use. On the left side of the balance sheet, a bank lists all its assets. *Assets* are things the bank owns or are owed by others,

webnote

Find the most recent data on total bank reserves, borrowed reserves, excess reserves, and required reserves at the U.S. Federal Reserve: www.Federalreserve.gov/releases. Click on "Aggregate Reserves of Depository Institutions."

[1] The reserves themselves may be held in the form of cash in the bank's vault but are usually held as credits with one of the regional Federal Reserve banks.

Step 1: You deposit cash at University Bank. The deposit creates $100 of reserves, $20 of which are designated as required reserves.

University Bank				Banking System	
Assets		Liabilities		Change in Transactions Deposits	Change in M
Required reserves	$ 20	Your deposit	$100	+$100	$0
Excess reserves	80				
Total	$100		100		

Step 2: The bank uses its excess reserves ($80) to make a loan to Campus Radio. Total deposits now equal $180. The money supply has increased.

University Bank				Banking System	
Assets		Liabilities		Δ Deposits	Δ M
Required reserves	$ 36	Your account	$100	+$80	+$80
Excess reserves	64	Campus Radio account	80		
Loans	80				
Total	$180	Total	$180		

Step 3: Campus Radio buys an antenna. This depletes Campus Radio's account but increases Atlas's balance. Eternal Savings gets $80 of reserves when the Campus Radio check clears.

University Bank				Eternal Savings				Banking System	
Assets		Liabilities		Assets		Liabilities		Δ Deposits	Δ M
Required reserves	$ 20	Your account	$100	Required reserves	$16	Atlas Antenna account	$80	$0	$0
Excess reserves	0	Campus Radio account	0	Excess reserves	64				
Loan	80								
Total	$100	Total	$100	Total	$80	Total	$80		

Step 4: Eternal Savings lends money to Herman's Hardware. Deposits, loans, and M all increase by $64.

University Bank				Eternal Savings				Banking System	
Assets		Liabilities		Assets		Liabilities		Change in Transaction Deposits	Change in M
Required reserves	$ 20	Your account	$100	Required reserves	$28.80	Atlas Antenna account	$ 80	+$64	+$64
Excess reserves	0	Campus Radio account	0	Excess reserves	51.20	Herman's Hardware account	64		
Loan	80			Loans	64				
Total	$100	Total	$100		$ 144		$144		
⋮	⋮	⋮		⋮		⋮	⋮	⋮	⋮
***n*th step:** Some bank lends $1.00								+1	+1

Cumulative Change in Banking System		
Bank Reserves	Transactions Deposits	Money Supply
+$100	+$500	+$400

TABLE 13.3
Deposit Creation

Excess reserves (step 1) are the basis of bank loans. When a bank uses its excess reserves to make a loan, it creates a deposit (step 2). When the loan is spent, a deposit will be made somewhere else (step 3). This new deposit creates additional excess reserves (step 3) that can be used for further loans (step 4, etc.). The process of deposit creation continues until the money supply has increased by a multiple of the initial deposit.

including cash held in a bank's vaults, IOUs (loan obligations) from bank customers, reserve credits at the Federal Reserve (essentially the bank's own deposits at the central bank), and securities (bonds) the bank has purchased.

On the right side of the balance sheet a bank lists all its liabilities. *Liabilities* are things the bank owes to others. The largest liability is represented by the deposits of bank customers. The bank owes these deposits to its customers and must return them "on demand."

Table 13.3 also shows the use of balance sheets. Notice how the balance of University Bank looks immediately after it receives your initial deposit (step 1, Table 13.3). Your deposit of coins is entered on *both* sides of University's balance sheet. On the left-hand side, your deposit is regarded as an asset, because your piggy bank's coins have an immediate market value and can be used to pay off the bank's liabilities. The coins now appear as *reserves.* The reserves these coins represent are further divided into required reserves ($20, or 20 percent of your deposit) and excess reserves ($80).

On the right-hand side of the balance sheet, the bank reminds itself that it has an obligation (liability) to return your deposit when you so demand. Thus, the bank's accounts balance, with assets and liabilities being equal. In fact, ***a bank's books must always balance because all the bank's assets must belong to someone (its depositors or its owners).***

University Bank wants to do more than balance its books, however; it wants to earn profits. To do so, it will have to make loans—that is, put its excess reserves to work. Suppose that it lends $80 to Campus Radio.[2] As step 2 in Table 13.3 illustrates, this loan alters both sides of University Bank's balance sheet. On the right-hand side, the bank creates a new transactions deposit for (credits the account of) Campus Radio; this item represents an additional liability (promise to pay). On the left-hand side of the balance sheet, two things happen. First, the bank notes that Campus Radio owes it $80 ("loans"). Second, the bank recognizes that it's now required to hold $36 in *required* reserves, in accordance with its higher level of transactions deposits ($180). (Recall we're assuming that required reserves are 20 percent of total transactions deposits.) Since its total reserves are still $100, $64 is left as *excess* reserves. Note again that ***excess reserves are reserves a bank isn't required to hold.***

Changes in the Money Supply. Before examining further changes in the balance sheet of University Bank, consider again what's happened to the economy's money supply during these first two steps. In the first step, you deposited $100 of cash in your checking account. This initial transaction didn't change the value of the money supply. Only the composition of the money supply (M1 or M2) was affected ($100 less cash held by the public, $100 more in transactions accounts).

Not until step 2—when the bank makes a loan—does all the excitement begin. In making a loan, the bank automatically increases the total money supply by $80. Why? Because someone (Campus Radio) now has more money (a transactions deposit) than it did before, *and no one else has any less.* And Campus Radio can use its money to buy goods and services, just like anybody else.

This second step is the heart of money creation. Money effectively appears out of thin air when a bank makes a loan. To understand how this works, you have to keep reminding yourself that money is more than the coins and currency we carry around. Transactions deposits are money too. Hence, ***the creation of transactions deposits via new loans is the same thing as creating money.***

More Deposit Creation. Suppose again that Campus Radio actually uses its $80 loan to buy an antenna. The rest of Table 13.3 illustrates how this additional transaction leads to further changes in balance sheets and the money supply.

In step 3, we see that when Campus Radio buys the $80 antenna, the balance in its checking account at University Bank drops to zero because it has spent all its money. As University Bank's liabilities fall (from $180 to $100), so does the level of its required reserves

[2]Because of the Fed's assumed minimum reserve requirement (20 percent), University Bank can now lend only $80 rather than $100, as before.

(from $36 to $20). (Note that required reserves are still 20 percent of its remaining transactions deposits.) But University Bank's excess reserves have disappeared completely! This disappearance reflects the fact that Atlas Antenna keeps *its* transactions account at another bank (Eternal Savings). When Atlas deposits the check it received from Campus Radio, Eternal Savings does two things: First it credits Atlas's account by $80. Second, it goes to University Bank to get the reserves that support the deposit.[3] The reserves later appear on the balance sheet of Eternal Savings as both required ($16) and excess ($64) reserves.

Observe that the money supply hasn't changed during step 3. The increase in the value of Atlas Antenna's transactions account balance exactly offsets the drop in the value of Campus Radio's transactions account. Ownership of the money supply is the only thing that has changed.

In step 4, Eternal Savings takes advantage of its newly acquired excess reserves by making a loan to Herman's Hardware. As before, the loan itself has two primary effects. First, it creates a transactions deposit of $64 for Herman's Hardware and thereby increases the money supply by the same amount. Second, it increases the required level of reserves at Eternal Savings. (To how much? Why?)

THE MONEY MULTIPLIER

By now it's perhaps obvious that the process of deposit creation won't come to an end quickly. On the contrary, it can continue indefinitely, just like the income multiplier process in Chapter 10. Indeed, people often refer to deposit creation as the money multiplier process, with the **money multiplier** expressed as the reciprocal of the required reserve ratio.[4] That is,

$$\text{Money multiplier} = \frac{1}{\text{required reserve ratio}}$$

money multiplier: The number of deposit (loan) dollars that the banking system can create from $1 of excess reserves; equal to 1 ÷ required reserve ratio.

Figure 13.2 illustrates the money multiplier process. When a new deposit enters the banking system, it creates both excess and required reserves. The required reserves represent

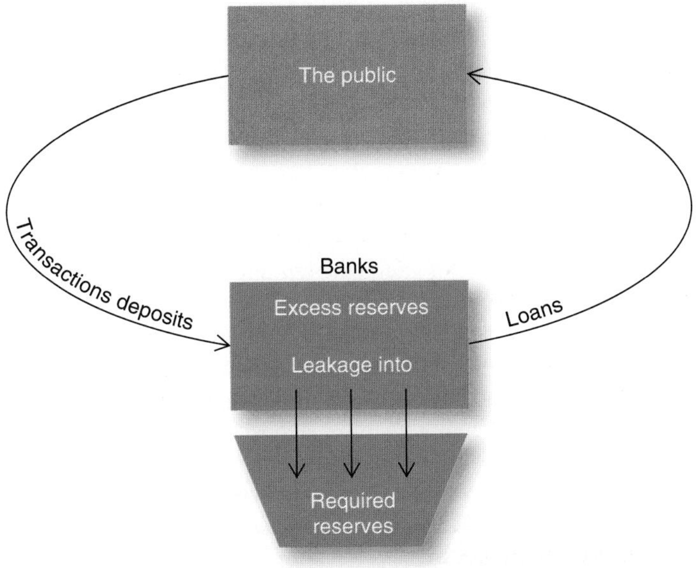

FIGURE 13.2
The Money Multiplier Process

Part of every new bank deposit leaks into required reserves. The rest—excess reserves—can be used to make loans. These loans, in turn, become deposits elsewhere. The process of money creation continues until all available reserves become required reserves.

[3]In actuality, banks rarely "go" anywhere; such interbank reserve movements are handled by bank clearing houses and regional Federal Reserve banks. The effect is the same, however. The nature and use of bank reserves are discussed more fully in Chapter 14.

[4]The money multiplier ($1/r$) is the sum of the infinite geometric progression $1 + (1 - r) + (1 - r)^2 + (1 - r)^3 + \cdots + (1 - r)^\infty$.

leakage from the flow of money since they can't be used to create new loans. Excess reserves, on the other hand, can be used for new loans. Once those loans are made, they typically become transactions deposits elsewhere in the banking system. Then some additional leakage into required reserves occurs, and further loans are made. The process continues until all excess reserves have leaked into required reserves. Once excess reserves have completely disappeared, the total value of new loans will equal initial excess reserves multiplied by the money multiplier.

The potential of the money multiplier to create loans is summarized by the equation

$$\text{Excess reserves of banking system} \times \text{money multiplier} = \text{potential deposit creation}$$

Notice how the money multiplier worked in our previous example. The value of the money multiplier was equal to 5, since we assumed that the required reserve ratio was 0.20. Moreover, the initial level of excess reserves was \$80, as a consequence of your original deposit (step 1). According to the money multiplier, then, the deposit-creation potential of the banking system was

$$\underset{(\$80)}{\text{Excess reserves}} \times \underset{(5)}{\text{money multiplier}} = \text{potential deposit creation } (\$400)$$

When all the banks fully utilized their excess reserves at each step of the money multiplier process, the ultimate increase in the money supply was in fact \$400 (see the last row in Table 13.3).

Excess Reserves as Lending Power

While you're struggling through Table 13.3, notice the critical role that excess reserves play in the process of deposit creation. A bank can make additional loans only if it has excess reserves. Without excess reserves, all of a bank's reserves are required, and no further liabilities (transactions deposits) can be created with new loans. On the other hand, a bank with excess reserves can make additional loans. In fact,

- ***Each bank may lend an amount equal to its excess reserves and no more.***

As such loans enter the circular flow and become deposits elsewhere, they create new excess reserves and further lending capacity. As a consequence,

- ***The entire banking system can increase the volume of loans by the amount of excess reserves multiplied by the money multiplier.***

By keeping track of excess reserves, then, we can gauge the lending capacity of any bank or, with the aid of the money multiplier, the entire banking system.

Table 13.4 summarizes the entire money multiplier process. In this case, we assume that all banks are initially "loaned up"—that is, without any excess reserves. The money multiplier process begins when someone deposits \$100 in cash into a transactions account at Bank A. If the required reserve ratio is 20 percent, this initial deposit creates \$80 of excess reserves at Bank A while adding \$100 to total transactions deposits.

If Bank A uses its newly acquired excess reserves to make a loan that ultimately ends up in Bank B, two things happen: Bank B acquires \$64 in excess reserves (0.80 × \$80), and total transactions deposits increase by another \$80.

The money multiplier process continues with a series of loans and deposits. When the twenty-sixth loan is made (by bank Z), total loans grow by only \$0.30 and transactions deposits by an equal amount. Should the process continue further, the *cumulative* change in loans will ultimately equal \$400, that is, the money multiplier times initial excess reserves. The money supply will increase by the same amount.

Required reserves = 0.20	Change in Transactions Deposits	Change in Total Reserves	Change in Required Reserves	Change in Excess Reserves	Change in Lending Capacity
If $100 in cash is deposited in Bank A, Bank A acquires	$100.00	$100.00	$20.00	$80.00	$80.00
If loan made and deposited elsewhere, Bank B acquires	80.00	80.00	16.00	64.00	64.00
If loan made and deposited elsewhere, Bank C acquires	64.00	64.00	12.80	51.20	51.20
If loan made and deposited elsewhere, Bank D acquires	51.20	51.20	10.24	40.96	40.96
If loan made and deposited elsewhere, Bank E acquires	40.96	40.96	8.19	32.77	32.77
If loan made and deposited elsewhere, Bank F acquires	32.77	32.77	6.55	26.27	26.22
If loan made and deposited elsewhere, Bank G acquires	26.22	26.22	5.24	20.98	20.98
. . .					
If loan made and deposited elsewhere, Bank Z acquires	0.38	0.38	0.08	0.30	0.30
Cumulative, through Bank Z	$498.80	$100.00	$99.76	$0.24	$398.80
	. . .	. . .	. . .	. . .	. . .
And if the process continues indefinitely	$500.00	$100.00	$100.00	$0.00	$400.00

Note: A $100 cash deposit creates $400 of new lending capacity when the required reserve ratio is 0.20. Initial excess reserves are $80 (= $100 deposit − $20 required reserves). The money multiplier is 5 (= 1 ÷ 0.20). New lending potential equals $400 (= $80 excess reserves × 5).

TABLE 13.4
The Money Multiplier at Work

The process of deposit creation continues as money passes through different banks in the form of multiple deposits and loans. At each step, excess reserves and new loans are created. The lending capacity of this system equals the money multiplier times excess reserves. In this case, initial excess reserves of $80 create the possibility of $400 of new loans when the reserve ratio is 0.20 (20 percent).

BANKS AND THE CIRCULAR FLOW

The bookkeeping details of bank deposits and loans are rarely exciting and often confusing. But they do demonstrate convincingly that banks can create money. In that capacity, ***banks perform two essential functions for the macro economy:***

- ***Banks transfer money from savers to spenders by lending funds (reserves) held on deposit.***
- ***The banking system creates additional money by making loans in excess of total reserves.***

In performing these two functions, banks change the size of the money supply—that is, the amount of purchasing power available for buying goods and services. Market participants may respond to these changes in the money supply by altering their spending behavior and shifting the aggregate demand curve.

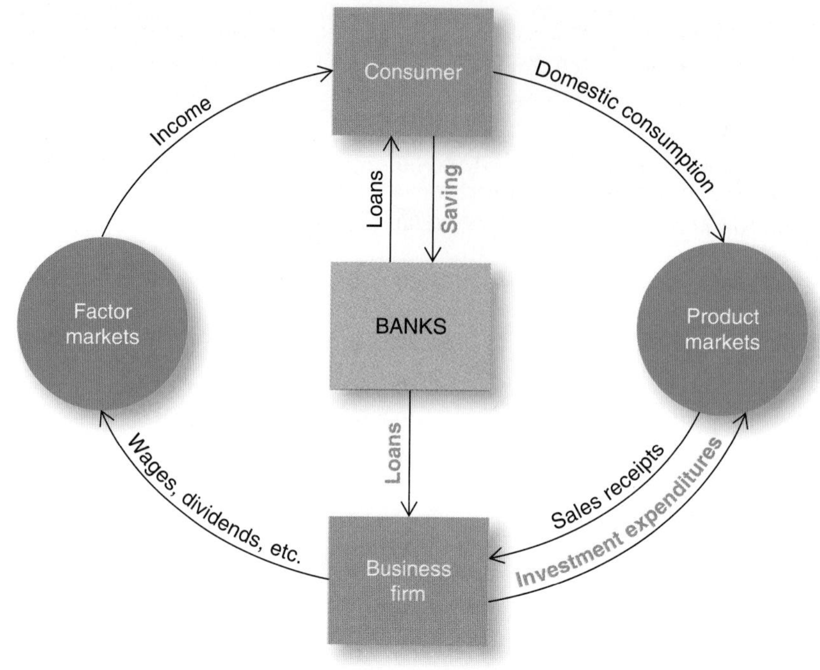

FIGURE 13.3
Banks in the Circular Flow

Banks help transfer income from savers to spenders by using their deposits to make loans to business firms and consumers who want to spend more money than they have. By lending money, banks help maintain any desired rate of aggregate demand.

Figure 13.3 is a simplified perspective on the role of banks in the circular flow. As before, income flows from product markets through business firms to factor markets and returns to consumers in the form of disposable income. Consumers spend most of their income but also save (don't spend) some of it.

Financing Injections

The leakage represented by consumer saving is a potential source of stabilization problems, particularly unemployment. If additional spending by business firms, foreigners, or governments doesn't compensate for consumer saving at full employment, a recessionary GDP gap will emerge, creating unemployment (see Chapters 9 and 10). Our interest here is in the role the banking system can play in encouraging such additional spending.

Suppose for the moment that *all* consumer saving was deposited in piggy banks rather than depository institutions (banks) and that no one used checks. Under these circumstances, banks couldn't transfer money from savers to spenders by holding deposits and making loans.

In reality, a substantial portion of consumer saving *is* deposited in banks. These and other bank deposits can be used as the basis of loans, thereby returning purchasing power to the circular flow. In fact, the primary economic function of banks isn't to store money but to transfer purchasing power from savers to spenders. They do so by lending money to businesses for new plant and equipment, to consumers for new homes or cars, and to government entities that desire greater purchasing power. Moreover, because the banking system can make *multiple* loans from available reserves, banks don't have to receive all consumer saving in order to carry out their function. On the contrary, ***the banking system can create any desired level of money supply if allowed to expand or reduce loan activity at will.***

Constraints on Deposit Creation

There are three major constraints on the deposit creation of the banking system.

Deposits. The first constraint is the willingness of consumers and businesses to continue using and accepting checks rather than cash in the marketplace. If people preferred to hold cash rather than checkbooks, banks wouldn't be able to acquire or maintain the reserves that are the foundation of bank lending activity.

Borrowers. The second constraint on deposit creation is the willingness of consumers, businesses, and governments to borrow the money that banks make available. The chain of events we've observed in deposit creation depends on the willingness of Campus Radio to borrow $80, of Herman's Hardware to borrow $64, and so on. If no one wanted to borrow any money, deposit creation would never begin. By the same reasoning, if all excess reserves aren't borrowed (lent), deposit creation won't live up to its theoretical potential.

Regulation. The third major constraint on deposit creation is the Federal Reserve System. As we've observed, the Fed may limit deposit creation by imposing reserve requirements. These and other tools of monetary policy are discussed in Chapter 14.

THE ECONOMY TOMORROW

WHEN BANKS FAIL

The power of banks to create money originates in the *fractional reserve* system. As we've observed, a bank holds reserves that are a small fraction of its liabilities, implying that ***no bank could pay off its customers if they all sought to withdraw their deposits at one time.***

Bank Panics. In earlier times, banks did experience occasional "runs" when depositors would rush to withdraw their funds. Such depositor runs usually began when word spread that a particular bank was running low on cash and might close. Depositor runs became self-fulfilling confirmation of a bank's insolvency. The resulting bank closing wiped out customer deposits, curtailed bank lending, and often pushed the economy into recession. This is what happened in Argentina in 2001–2003 (see World View).

During the Great Depression there was widespread fear that the U.S. banking system would collapse. Borrowers weren't able to repay their loans and depositors were withdrawing more cash. As their reserves dwindled, banks' ability to create money evaporated. Suddenly, a chunk of money (bank deposits and loans) just disappeared. With little cash coming in and a lot of cash flowing out, banks quickly ran out of cash reserves and had to shut their doors. Between 1930 and 1933, over 9,000 banks failed. To prevent total collapse of the banking system, newly elected president Franklin Roosevelt declared a "bank holiday" that closed all the nation's banks for 1 week.

WORLD VIEW

Argentines Lose Confidence in Banks

BUENOS AIRES—"I should have known better than to trust a bank," sneered Laura Alonso, 62, a retired waitress who walked out of a Bank-Boston branch Friday with a wad of pesos stuffed in her bra.

As Alonso has regularly done since a partial limit on withdrawals was imposed here in December, she withdrew her monthly maximum and prepared to rush the cash to the only savings institution she still trusts: her mattress. . . .

With deposits continuing to flow out and confidence at a low point, analysts say it could take months or even years for banks to begin major new lending. That delay could seriously extend a credit crunch here and hamper economic recovery. . . .

"The huge confidence problem with banks is worsening the crisis," said Carina Espino, an analyst with Standard & Poor's in Buenos Aires. "Money is merely being withdrawn, not deposited. So the question is, with no new deposits, where will new lending come from?"

—Anthony Faiola

Source: *Washington Post,* March 8, 2002, p. A22.

Analysis: If consumers won't keep their money in banks, the banking system can't make the loans needed to increase aggregate demand.

Deposit Insurance. Congress used that opportunity to create a deposit insurance that would protect customer deposits. The Federal Deposit Insurance Corporation (FDIC) and the Federal Savings and Loan Insurance Corporation (FSLIC) were created in 1933 and 1934 to ensure depositors that they'd get their money back even if their bank failed. The guarantee of insured deposits eliminated the motivation for deposit runs. If a bank closed, the federal government would step in and repay deposits.

The S&L Crisis. Federal deposit insurance greatly increased public confidence in the banking system. It didn't, however, ward off bank failures. In some respects, deposit insurance even *contributed* to bank failures. By insuring deposits, the federal government eliminated a major risk for bank customers. Depositors no longer had to concern themselves with the soundness of a bank's lending practices; their deposits were insured. This created the opportunity for bank owners to engage in riskier loans that had greater profit potential.

During the 1970s, accelerating inflation pushed interest rates up. To attract deposits, banks had to offer higher rates of interest on customer deposits. Many of their loans, however, were already set at lower interest rates. This was particularly true for savings and loan associations (S&Ls), which traditionally lent most of their funds in long-term home mortgages. Suddenly, they were stuck earning low interest rates on long-term mortgages while paying high interest rates on short-term deposits. This was a recipe for failure.

The woes of the S&Ls were exacerbated by increased competition from new financial institutions (like money market mutual funds) that enticed deposits away from S&Ls. Sharp downturns in oil prices and real estate also weakened borrowers' ability to repay their loans. These and other forces caused more than half the S&Ls that existed in 1970 to disappear by 1990. In 1988, more banks failed (200) than in any year since the Great Depression. The 1990–91 recession pushed still more banks into insolvency.

Bank Bailouts. The FSLIC and FDIC averted bank panics by paying off depositors in failed banks. So many S&Ls failed, however, that the FSLIC itself ran out of funds. Congress had to appropriate ever larger sums of money to bail out the banks. In 1992 alone, over $60 billion was spent on bank bailouts.

When the federal government steps in to pay insured deposits, it also assumes control of a failing bank. The government then tries to arrange a merger or acquisition with a stronger bank. In the process, the federal government acquires some or all of the outstanding loans of the failed bank. The Resolution Trust Corporation (RTC) was created in 1989 to manage these loans. The RTC tried to collect outstanding loans or sell the properties (such as office buildings, shopping centers, homes) that were financed with those loans. Part of the huge outlays for bank bailouts in the early 1990s were offset by the proceeds from these RTC property sales.

Banks will continue to compete for deposits and loans in the economy tomorrow. They'll have the advantage of deposit insurance—provided by the FDIC and the renamed Savings Association Insurance Fund (SAIF)—in attracting new funds. Congress, however, has set more stringent requirements on the types of loans and investments banks can make. It has also forced bank owners to put more of their own funds at risk. The intent of these changes is to improve the financial stability of banks while assuring the public that their deposits are safe in the economy tomorrow—even in banks with only fractional reserves.

SUMMARY

- In a market economy, money serves a critical function in facilitating exchanges and specialization, thus permitting increased output. *Money* refers to any medium that's generally accepted in exchange. LO1
- Because people use bank account balances to buy goods and services, such balances are also regarded as money. The money supply M1 includes cash plus transactions account (checkable) deposits. M2 adds savings account balances and other deposits to form a broader measure of the money supply. LO1
- Banks have the power to create money by making loans. In making loans, banks create new transactions deposits, which become part of the money supply. LO2

- Banks' ability to make loans—create money—depends on their reserves. Only if a bank has excess reserves—reserves greater than those required by federal regulation—can it make new loans. LO2
- As loans are spent, they create deposits elsewhere, making it possible for other banks to make additional loans. The money multiplier (1 ÷ required reserve ratio) indicates the total value of deposits that can be created by the banking system from excess reserves. LO3
- The role of banks in creating money includes the transfer of money from savers to spenders as well as deposit creation in excess of deposit balances. Taken together, these two functions give banks direct control over the amount of purchasing power available in the marketplace. LO2
- The deposit-creation potential of the banking system is limited by government regulation. It's also limited by the willingness of market participants to hold deposits or borrow money. LO3
- When banks fail, the federal government (FDIC or SAIF) guarantees to pay deposits. To reduce bank failures, bank owners are now required to put more of their own assets at risk. LO2

Key Terms

barter
money
money supply (M1, M2)
transactions account
aggregate demand
deposit creation
bank reserves
reserve ratio
required reserves
excess reserves
money multiplier

Questions for Discussion

1. Why are checking account balances, but not credit cards, regarded as "money"? LO1
2. How are an economy's production possibilities affected when workers are paid in bras and coffins rather than cash? (See World View, page 255, about bartering in Russia.) LO1
3. What percentage of your monthly bills do you pay with (*a*) cash, (*b*) check, (*c*) credit card, and (*d*) automatic transfers. How do you pay off the credit card balance? How does your use of cash compare with the composition of the money supply (Figure 13.1)? LO1
4. If you can purchase airline tickets with online computer services, should your electronic account be counted in the money supply? Explain. LO1
5. Does the fact that your bank keeps only a fraction of your account balance in reserve make you uncomfortable? Why don't people rush to the bank and retrieve their money? What would happen if they did? LO2
6. If people never withdrew cash from banks, how much money could the banking system potentially create? Could this really happen? What might limit deposit creation in this case? LO3
7. If all banks heeded Shakespeare's admonition "Neither a borrower nor a lender be," what would happen to the circular flow? LO2
8. How does federal deposit insurance encourage greater risk-taking by banks? Could the banking system function without government deposit insurance? How? LO2
9. How did the banking crisis in Argentina (World View, page 269) affect that nation's GDP growth prospects? LO3

problems The Student Problem Set at the back of this book contains numerical and graphing problems for this chapter.

web activities to accompany this chapter can be found on the Online Learning Center: **http://www.mhhe.com/economics/schiller11e**

The Federal Reserve System

14

LEARNING OBJECTIVES

After reading this chapter, you should know:

L01. How the Federal Reserve is organized.

L02. The Fed's major policy tools.

L03. How open market operations work.

We've seen how money is created with bank loans. We've also gotten a few clues about how the government limits money creation and thus aggregate demand. This chapter examines the mechanics of government control more closely. The basic issues addressed are

- **How does the government control the amount of money in the economy?**
- **Which government agency is responsible for exercising this control?**
- **How are banks and bond markets affected by the government's policies?**

Most people have a ready answer for the first question. The popular view is that the government controls the amount of money in the economy by printing more or fewer dollar bills. But we've already observed that the concept of "money" isn't so simple. In Chapter 13 we demonstrated that banks, not the printing presses, create most of our money. In making loans, banks create transactions deposits that are counted as part of the money supply.

Because bank lending activities are the primary source of money, the ***government must regulate bank lending if it wants to control the amount of money in the economy.*** That's exactly what the Federal Reserve System does. The Federal Reserve System—the "Fed"—not only limits the volume of loans that the banking system can make from available reserves; it can also alter the amount of reserves banks hold.

The Federal Reserve System's control over the supply of money is the key mechanism of **monetary policy.** The potential of this policy lever to alter macro outcomes (unemployment, inflation, etc.) is examined in Chapter 15. For the time being, however, we focus on the *tools* of monetary policy.

STRUCTURE OF THE FED

monetary policy: The use of money and credit controls to influence macroeconomic outcomes.

In the absence of any government regulation, the supply of money would be determined by individual banks. Moreover, individual depositors would bear all the risks of bank failures. In fact, this is the way the banking system operated until 1914. The money supply was subject to abrupt changes, and consumers frequently lost their savings in recurrent bank failures.

A series of bank failures resulted in a severe financial panic in 1907. Millions of depositors lost their savings, and the economy was thrown into a tailspin. In the wake of this panic, a National Monetary Commission was established to examine ways of restructuring the banking system. The mandate of the commission was to find ways to avert recurrent financial crises. After 5 years of study, the commission recommended the creation of a Federal Reserve System. Congress accepted the commission's recommendations, and President Wilson signed the Federal Reserve Act in December 1913.

Federal Reserve Banks

The core of the Federal Reserve System consists of 12 Federal Reserve banks. Each bank acts as a central banker for the private banks in its region. In this role, the regional Fed banks perform the following services:

- ***Clearing checks between private banks.*** Suppose the Bank of America in San Francisco receives a deposit from one of its customers in the form of a share draft written on the New York State Employees Credit Union. The Bank of America doesn't have to go to New York to collect the cash or other reserves that support that draft. Instead, the Bank of America can deposit the draft (check) at its account with the Federal Reserve Bank of San Francisco. The Fed then collects from the credit union. This vital clearinghouse service saves the Bank of America and other private banks a great deal of time and expense in processing the 40 *billion* checks that are written every year. (The Fed employs 5,000 people for this processing activity.)
- ***Holding bank reserves.*** Notice that the Fed's clearinghouse service was facilitated by the fact that the Bank of America and the New York Employees Credit Union had their own accounts at the Fed. As we noted in Chapter 13, banks are *required* to hold some minimum fraction of their deposits in reserve. Only a small amount of reserves is held as cash in a bank's vaults. The rest is held in reserve accounts at the regional Federal Reserve banks. These accounts not only provide greater security and convenience for bank reserves but also enable the Fed to monitor the actual level of bank reserves.
- ***Providing currency.*** Before every major holiday there's a great demand for cash. People want some pocket money during holidays and know that it's difficult to cash checks on weekends or holidays, especially if they're going out of town. So they load up on cash at their bank or ATMs. After the holiday is over, most of this cash is returned to the banks, typically by the stores, gas stations, and restaurants that benefited from holiday spending. Because banks hold very little cash in their vaults, they turn to the Fed to meet these sporadic cash demands. A private bank can simply call the regional Federal Reserve bank and order a supply of cash, to be delivered (by armored truck) before a weekend or holiday. The cash will be deducted from the bank's own account at the Fed. When all the cash comes back in after the holiday, the bank can reverse the process, sending the unneeded cash back to the Fed.
- ***Providing loans.*** The Federal Reserve banks may also loan reserves to private banks. This practice, called "discounting," is examined more closely in a moment.

The Board of Governors

At the top of the Federal Reserve System's organization chart (Figure 14.1) is the Board of Governors, which is responsible for setting monetary policy. The Board, located in Washington, D.C., consists of seven members ("governors"), appointed by the president of the United States and confirmed by the U.S. Senate. Board members are appointed for 14-year terms and can't be reappointed. Their exceptionally long appointments give the Fed governors a measure of political independence. They're not beholden to any elected official and will hold office longer than any president.

FIGURE 14.1
Structure of the Federal Reserve System

The Fed's broad policies are determined by the seven-member Board of Governors. The 12 Federal Reserve banks provide central banking services to individual banks in their respective regions. The Federal Open Market Committee directs Federal Reserve transactions in the money market. Various committees offer formal and informal advice to the Board of Governors.

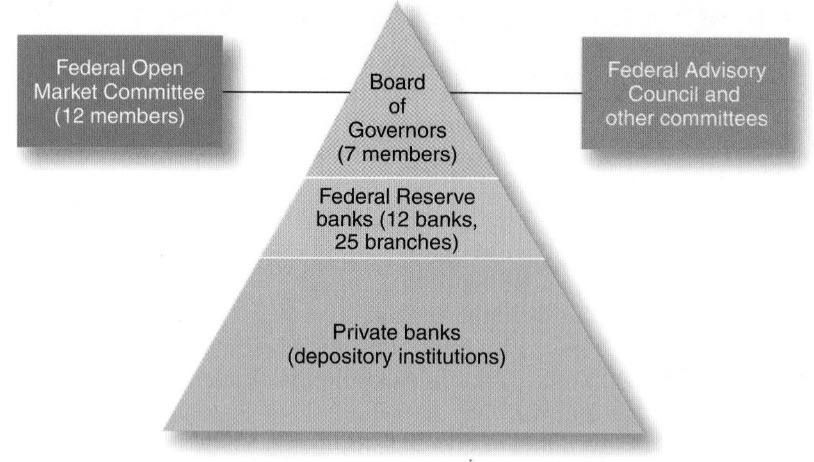

webnote

Who runs the Fed? Read profiles of the governors at www.federalreserve.gov/bios

The intent of the Fed's independence is to keep control of the nation's money supply beyond the immediate reach of politicians (especially members of Congress, elected for 2-year terms). The designers of the Fed system feared that political control of monetary policy would cause wild swings in the money supply and macro instability. Critics argue, however, that the Fed's independence makes it unresponsive to the majority will.

The president selects one of the governors to serve as chairman of the Board for 4 years. The current chairman, Ben Bernanke, was appointed by President Bush in January 2006. Previously he had been an economics professor at Princeton University and had served as chair of Bush's Council of Economic Advisers. Chairman Bernanke is the primary spokesperson for Fed policy and reports to Congress every 6 months on the conduct of monetary policy.

The Federal Open Market Committee (FOMC)

A key arm of the Board is the Federal Open Market Committee (FOMC), which is responsible for the Fed's daily activity in financial markets. The FOMC plays a critical role in setting short-term interest rates and the level of reserves held by private banks. The membership of the FOMC includes all seven governors and 5 of the 12 regional Reserve bank presidents. The FOMC meets in Washington, D.C., every 4 or 5 weeks throughout the year to review the economy's performance. It decides whether the economy is growing fast enough (or too fast) and then adjusts monetary policy as needed.

MONETARY TOOLS

money supply (M1): Currency held by the public, plus balances in transactions accounts.

M2 money supply: M1 plus balances in most savings accounts and money market mutual funds.

Our immediate interest isn't in the structure of the Federal Reserve but the way the Fed is able to alter the **money supply.** The Fed's control of the money supply is exercised by use of three policy instruments:

- Reserve requirements
- Discount rates
- Open market operations

Reserve Requirements

required reserves: The minimum amount of reserves a bank is required to hold; equal to required reserve ratio times transactions deposits.

The Fed's first policy tool focuses on reserve requirements. As noted in Chapter 13, the Fed requires private banks to keep some stated fraction of their deposits "in reserve." These **required reserves** are held either in the form of actual vault cash or, more commonly, as credits (deposits) in the bank's "reserve account" at a regional Federal Reserve bank. ***By changing the reserve requirements, the Fed can directly alter the lending capacity of the banking system.***

Recall that the banking system's ability to make additional loans—create deposits—is determined by two factors: (1) the amount of excess reserves banks hold and (2) the money multiplier. Both factors are directly influenced by the Fed's required reserve ratio.

Computing Excess Reserves. Suppose, for example, that banks hold \$100 billion of deposits and total reserves of \$30 billion. Assume too that the minimum reserve requirement is 20 percent. Under these circumstances, banks are holding more reserves than they have to. Recall that

$$\text{Required reserves} = \text{Required reserve ratio} \times \text{total deposits}$$

so, in this case

$$\begin{aligned}\text{Required reserves} &= 0.20 \times \$100 \text{ billion} \\ &= \$20 \text{ billion}\end{aligned}$$

Banks are *required* to hold \$20 billion in reserve to meet Federal Reserve regulations. They're actually holding \$30 billion, however. The \$10 billion difference between actual and required reserves is **excess reserves**—that is,

$$\text{Excess reserves} = \text{total reserves} - \text{required reserves}$$

excess reserves: Bank reserves in excess of required reserves

The existence of excess reserves implies that banks aren't fully utilizing their lending powers. With \$10 billion of excess reserves and the help of the **money multiplier** the banks *could* lend an additional \$50 billion.

money multiplier: The number of deposit (loan) dollars that the banking system can create from \$1 of excess reserves; equal to 1 ÷ required reserve ratio.

The potential for additional loans is calculated as

$$\text{Available lending capacity of banking system} = \text{excess reserves} \times \text{money multiplier}$$

or, in this case,

$$\$10 \text{ billion} \times \frac{1}{0.20} = \$50 \text{ billion of unused lending capacity}$$

That is, the banking system could create another \$50 billion of money (transactions account balances) without any additional reserves.

A simple way to confirm this—and thereby check your arithmetic—is to note what would happen to total deposits if the banks actually made further loans. Total deposits would increase to \$150 billion in this case (the initial \$100 billion plus the new \$50 billion), an amount that could be supported with \$30 billion in reserves (20 percent of \$150 billion).

Soaking Up Excess Reserves. But what if the Fed doesn't want the money supply to increase this much? Maybe prices are rising and the Fed wants to restrain rather than stimulate total spending in the economy. Under such circumstances, the Fed would want to restrict the availability of credit (loans). Does it have the power to do so? Can the Fed reduce the lending capacity of the banking system?

The answer to both questions is clearly yes. ***By raising the required reserve ratio, the Fed can immediately reduce the lending capacity of the banking system.***

Table 14.1 summarizes the impact of an increase in the required reserve ratio. In this case, the required reserve ratio is increased from 20 to 25 percent. Notice that this change

TABLE 14.1
The Impact of an Increased Reserve Requirement

	Required Reserve Ratio	
	20 Percent	25 Percent
1. Total deposits	\$100 billion	\$100 billion
2. Total reserves	30 billion	30 billion
3. Required reserves	20 billion	25 billion
4. Excess reserves	10 billion	5 billion
5. Money multiplier	5	4
6. Unused lending capacity	\$ 50 billion	\$ 20 billion

An increase in the required reserve ratio reduces both excess reserves (row 4) and the money multiplier (row 5). As a consequence, changes in the reserve requirement have a substantial impact on the lending capacity of the banking system (row 6).

IN THE NEWS

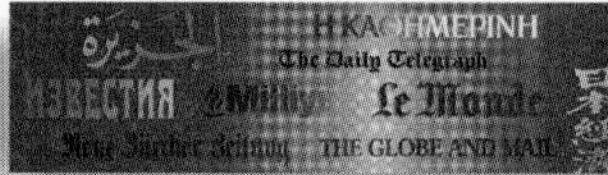

Fed Cuts Deposit-Reserve Requirements

Reduction Is the Latest Bid to Bolster Bank Profits and Encourage Lending

WASHINGTON—The Federal Reserve Board, in another attempt to shore up bank profits so bankers will be more willing to lend, reduced the fraction of deposits that must be held as reserves.

The Fed cut to 10 percent from 12 percent the percentage of checking account deposits that banks are required to hold as reserves. Because reserves must be in cash or in accounts that don't pay any interest, the change will add between $300 million and $600 million to bank industry profits.

—David Wessel

Source: *The Walll Street Journal,* February 19, 1992. WALL STREET JOURNAL.

Analysis: A reduction in the reserve requirement transforms some of the banking system's required reserves into excess reserves, thus increasing potential lending activity and profits. It also increases the size of the money multiplier.

in the reserve requirement has no effect on the amount of deposits in the banking system (row 1, Table 14.1) or the amount of total reserves (row 2). They remain at $100 billion and $30 billion, respectively. What the increased reserve requirement does affect is the way those reserves can be used. Before the increase, only $20 billion in reserves were *required,* leaving $10 billion of *excess* reserves. Now, however, banks are required to hold $25 billion (0.25 × $100 billion) in reserves, leaving them with only $5 billion in excess reserves. Thus an increase in the reserve requirement immediately reduces excess reserves, as illustrated in row 4, Table 14.1.

There's also a second effect. Notice what happens to the money multiplier (1 ÷ reserve ratio). Previously it was 5(= 1 ÷ 0.20); now it's only 4(= 1 ÷ 0.25). Consequently, a higher reserve requirement not only reduces excess reserves but diminishes their lending power as well.

A change in the reserve requirement, therefore, hits banks with a triple whammy. ***A change in the reserve requirement causes a change in***

- ***Excess reserves.***
- ***The money multiplier.***
- ***The lending capacity of the banking system.***

These changes lead to a sharp reduction in bank lending power. Whereas the banking system initially had the power to increase the volume of loans by $50 billion ($10 billion of excess reserves × 5), it now has only $20 billion ($5 million × 4) of unused lending capacity, as noted in the last row in Table 14.1.

Changes in reserve requirements are a powerful tool for altering the lending capacity of the banking system. The Fed uses this tool sparingly, so as not to cause abrupt changes in the money supply and severe disruptions of banking activity. From 1970 to 1980, for example, reserve requirements were changed only twice, and then by only half a percentage point each time (for example, from 12.0 to 12.5 percent). The Fed last cut the reserve requirement from 12 to 10 percent in 1992 to increase bank profits and encourage more lending (see News). Smaller banks have a lower reserve requirement (3 percent), which gives them a competitive advantage.

The Discount Rate

Banks have a tremendous incentive to maintain their reserves at or close to the minimum established by the Fed. Bank reserves held at the Fed earn no interest, but loans and bonds do. Hence, a profit-maximizing bank seeks to keep its excess reserves as low as possible, preferring to put its reserves to work. In fact, banks have demonstrated an uncanny ability to keep their reserves

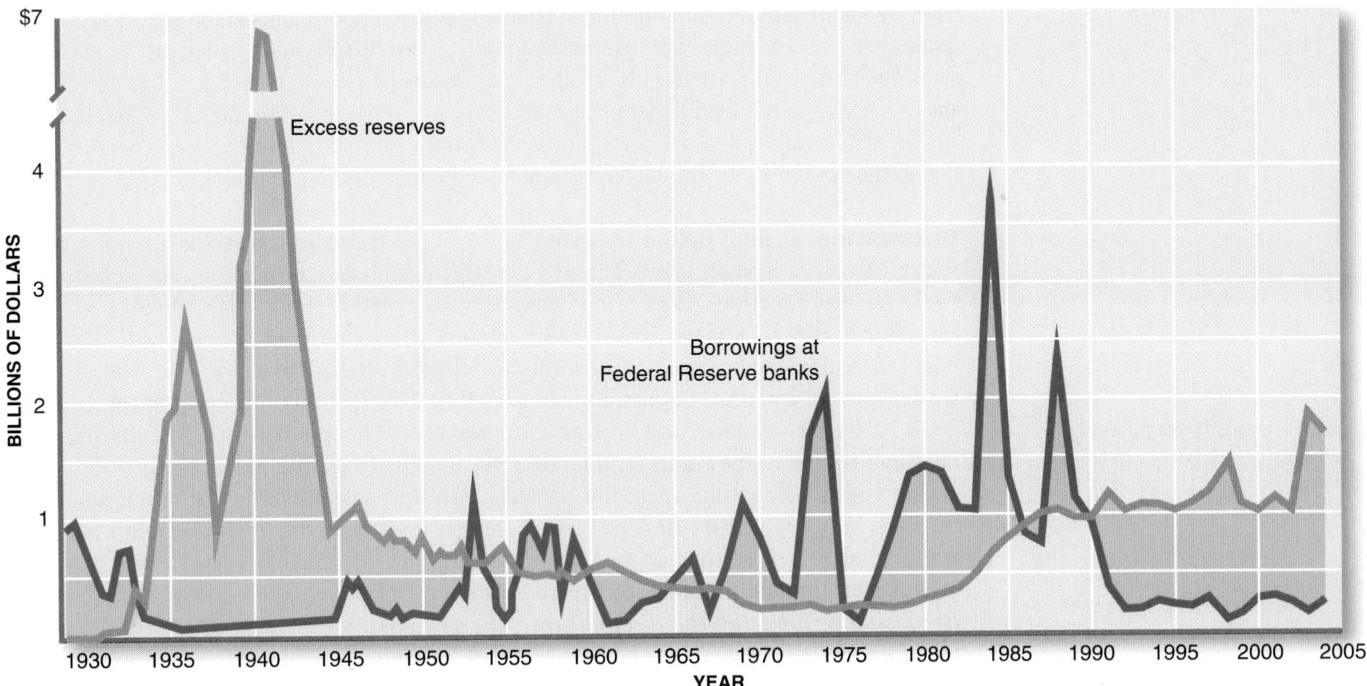

FIGURE 14.2
Excess Reserves and Borrowings

Excess reserves represent unused lending capacity. Hence, banks strive to keep excess reserves at a minimum. One exception to this practice occurred in the Great Depression, when banks were hesitant to make any loans. In trying to minimize excess reserves, banks occasionally fall short of required reserves. At such times they may borrow from other banks (the federal funds market), or they may borrow reserves from the Fed. Borrowing from the Fed is called "discounting."

close to the minimum federal requirement. As Figure 14.2 illustrates, the only time banks held huge excess reserves was in the Great Depression of the 1930s. The banks didn't want to make any more loans and were fearful of panicky customers withdrawing their deposits.

Because banks continually seek to keep excess reserves at a minimum, they run the risk of falling below reserve requirements. A large borrower may be a little slow in repaying a loan, or the rate of deposit withdrawals and transfers may exceed expectations. At such times, a bank may find that it doesn't have enough reserves to satisfy Fed requirements.

Banks could ensure continual compliance with reserve requirements by maintaining large amounts of excess reserves. But that's an unprofitable procedure, and a profit-maximizing bank will seek other alternatives.

webnote

The St. Louis Fed bank tracks bank reserves and borrowings; to update Figure 14.2, go to http://research.stlouisfed.org/fred2/categories/122

The Federal Funds Market. A bank that finds itself short of reserves can turn to other banks for help. If a reserve-poor bank can borrow some reserves from a reserve-rich bank, it may be able to bridge its temporary deficit and satisfy the Fed. ***Reserves borrowed by one bank from another are referred to as "federal funds" and are lent for short periods, usually overnight.*** Although trips to the federal funds market—via telephone and computer—will usually satisfy Federal Reserve requirements, such trips aren't free. The lending bank will charge interest (the **federal funds rate**) on its interbank loan.[1] The use of the federal funds market to satisfy Federal Reserve requirements also depends on other banks having excess reserves to lend.

federal funds rate: The interest rate for interbank reserve loans.

[1]An overnight loan of $1 million at 6 percent interest (per year) costs $165 in interest charges plus any service fees that might be added. Banks make multimillion-dollar loans in the federal funds market.

Sale of Securities. Another option available to reserve-poor banks is the sale of securities. Banks use some of their excess reserves to buy government bonds, which pay interest. If a bank needs more reserves to satisfy federal regulations, it can sell these securities and deposit the proceeds at a regional Federal Reserve bank. Its reserve position thereby increases. This option also involves distinct costs, however, both in forgone interest-earning opportunities and in the possibility of capital losses when the bond is offered for quick sale.

Discounting. A third option for avoiding a reserve shortage lies in the structure of the Federal Reserve System itself. The Fed not only establishes certain rules of behavior for banks but also functions as a central bank, or banker's bank. Banks maintain accounts with the regional Federal Reserve banks, much the way you and I maintain accounts with a local bank. Individual banks deposit and withdraw "reserve credits" from these accounts, just as we deposit and withdraw dollars. Should a bank find itself short of reserves, it can go to the Fed's "discount window" and borrow some reserves. This process is called **discounting.** Discounting means the Fed is lending reserves directly to private banks.[2]

discounting: Federal Reserve lending of reserves to private banks.

The Fed's discounting operation provides private banks with an important source of reserves, but not without cost. The Fed too charges interest on the reserves it lends to banks, a rate of interest referred to as the **discount rate.**

discount rate: The rate of interest the Federal Reserve charges for lending reserves to private banks.

The discount window is a mechanism for directly influencing the size of bank reserves. ***By raising or lowering the discount rate, the Fed changes the cost of money for banks and therewith the incentive to borrow reserves.*** At high discount rates, borrowing from the Fed is expensive. High discount rates also signal the Fed's desire to restrain the money supply and an accompanying reluctance to lend reserves. Low discount rates, on the other hand, make it profitable to acquire additional reserves and exploit one's lending capacity to the fullest. Low discount rates also indicate the Fed's willingness to support credit expansion. The accompanying News tells how the Fed reduced both the federal funds rate and the discount rate in August 2001 to encourage more borrowing and spending. After the September 11 attacks on the World Trade Center and Pentagon, the Fed reduced both rates again, and quite sharply.

Open Market Operations

Reserve requirements and discount window operations are important tools of monetary policy. But they don't come close to open market operations in day-to-day impact on the money supply. ***Open market operations are the principal mechanism for directly altering the reserves of the banking system.*** Since reserves are the lifeblood of the banking system, open market operations are of immediate and critical interest to private banks and the larger economy.

Portfolio Decisions. To appreciate the impact of open market operations, you have to think about the alternative uses for idle funds. All of us have some idle funds, even if they amount to just a few dollars in our pocket or a minimal balance in our checking account. Other consumers and corporations have great amounts of idle funds, even millions of dollars at any time. Here we're concerned with what people decide to do with such funds.

People (and corporations) don't hold all their idle funds in transactions accounts or cash. Idle funds are also used to purchase stocks, build up savings account balances, and purchase bonds. These alternative uses of idle funds are attractive because they promise some additional income in the form of interest, dividends, or capital appreciation, such as higher stock prices. Deciding where to place idle funds is referred to as the **portfolio decision.**

portfolio decision: The choice of how (where) to hold idle funds.

Hold Money or Bonds? The Fed's ***open market operations focus on one of the portfolio choices people make: whether to deposit idle funds in bank accounts or purchase government bonds.*** The Fed attempts to influence this choice by making bonds more or less attractive,

[2]In the past banks had to present loan notes to the Fed in order to borrow reserves. The Fed "discounted" the notes by lending an amount equal to only a fraction of their face value. Although banks no longer have to present loans as collateral, the term "discounting" endures.

IN THE NEWS

Fed Again Reduces Key Rate

Federal Reserve officials, concerned about the uncertain outlook for the U.S. economy amid a global slowdown in growth, lowered their target for short-term interest rates yesterday for a seventh time this year and left the door open for more cuts if needed.

In announcing its decision, the Fed's top policymaking group, the Federal Open Market Committee, noted that U.S. consumer spending has held up recently "but business profits and capital spending continue to weaken and growth abroad is slowing, weighing on the U.S. economy."

The committee lowered the central bank's target for the federal funds rate, the interest rate financial institutions charge one another on overnight loans, by another quarter of a percentage point, to 3.5 percent. The key rate, which influences many other interest rates, including banks' prime lending rate, is now 3 percentage points lower than it was Jan. 1. . . .

In a separate but related action, the Federal Reserve Board reduced the central bank's largely symbolic discount rate, the interest rate financial institutions pay when they borrow money from one of the 12 regional Federal Reserve banks, to 3 percent from 3.25 percent.

—John M. Berry

Source: *Washington Post,* August 22, 2001. www.thewashingtonpost.com

Analysis: By reducing the federal funds and discount rates, the Fed encourages banks to borrow reserves and make more loans. Lower interest rates also encourage businesses and consumers to borrow and spend more.

as circumstances warrant. The Fed's goal is to encourage people to move funds from banks to bond markets or vice versa. In the process, reserves either enter or leave the banking system, thereby altering the lending capacity of banks.

Figure 14.3 depicts the general nature of the Fed's open market operations. As we first observed in Chapter 13 (Figure 13.2), the process of deposit creation begins when people deposit money in the banking system. But people may also hold their assets in the form of bonds. The Fed's objective is to alter this portfolio decision by buying or selling bonds. ***When the Fed buys bonds from the public, it increases the flow of deposits (reserves) to the banking system. Bond sales by the Fed reduce the inflow.***

The Bond Market. To understand how open market operations work, let's look closer at the bond market. Not all of us buy and sell bonds, but a lot of consumers and corporations do: Daily volume in bond markets is nearly $1 *trillion.* What's being exchanged in this market, and what factors influence decisions to buy or sell?

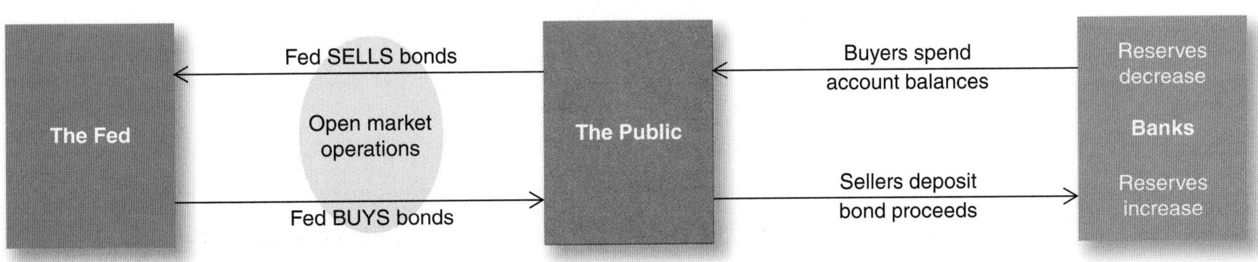

FIGURE 14.3
Open Market Operations

People may hold assets in the form of bank deposits (money) or bonds. When the Fed buys bonds from the public, it increases the flow of deposits (and reserves) to the banks. When the Fed sells bonds, it diminishes the flow of deposits and therewith the banks' capacity to lend (create money).

In our discussion thus far, we've portrayed banks as intermediaries between savers and spenders. Banks aren't the only mechanism available for transferring purchasing power from nonspenders to spenders. Funds are lent and borrowed in bond markets as well. In this case, a corporation may borrow money directly from consumers or other institutions. When it does so, it issues a bond as proof of its promise to repay the loan. A **bond** is simply a piece of paper certifying that someone has borrowed money and promises to pay it back at some future date. In other words, a bond is nothing more than an IOU. In the case of bond markets, however, the IOU is typically signed by a giant corporation or a government agency rather than a friend. It's therefore more widely accepted by lenders.

bond: A certificate acknowledging a debt and the amount of interest to be paid each year until repayment; an IOU.

Because most corporations and government agencies that borrow money in the bond market are well known and able to repay their debts, their bonds are actively traded. If I lend $1,000 to General Motors on a 10-year bond, for example, I don't have to wait 10 years to get my money back; I can resell the bond to someone else at any time. If I do, that person will collect the face value of the bond (plus interest) from GM when it's due. The actual purchase and sale of bonds take place in the bond market. Although a good deal of the action occurs on Wall Street in New York, the bond market has no unique location. Like other markets we've discussed, the bond market exists whenever and however (electronically) bond buyers and sellers get together.

Bond Yields. People buy bonds because bonds pay interest. If you buy a General Motors bond, GM is obliged to pay you interest during the period of the loan. For example, an 8 percent 2025 GM bond in the amount of $1,000 states that GM will pay the bondholder $80 interest annually (8 percent of $1,000) until 2025. At that point GM will repay the initial $1,000 loan (the "principal").

yield: The rate of return on a bond; the annual interest payment divided by the bond's price.

The current **yield** paid on a bond depends on the promised interest rate (8 percent in this case) and the actual purchase price of the bond. Specifically,

$$\text{Yield} = \frac{\text{annual interest payment}}{\text{price paid for bond}}$$

If you pay $1,000 for the bond, then the current yield is

$$\text{Yield} = \frac{\$80}{\$1{,}000} = 0.08, \text{ or } 8\%$$

which is the same as the interest rate printed on the face of the bond. But what if you pay only $900 for the bond? In this case, the interest rate paid by GM remains at 8 percent, but the *yield* jumps to

$$\text{Yield} = \frac{\$80}{\$900} = 0.089, \text{ or } 8.9\%$$

Buying a $1,000 bond for only $900 might seem like too good a bargain to be true. But bonds are often bought and sold at prices other than their face value (see News on the next page). In fact, ***a principal objective of Federal Reserve open market activity is to alter the price of bonds, and therewith their yields.*** By doing so, the Fed makes bonds a more or less attractive alternative to holding money.

Open Market Activity. The basic premise of open market activity is that participants in the bond market will respond to changes in bond prices and yields. As we've observed, ***the less you pay for a bond, the higher its yield.*** Accordingly, the Fed can induce people to *buy* bonds by offering to sell them at a lower price (e.g., a $1,000, 8 percent bond for only $900). Similarly, the Fed can induce people to *sell* bonds by offering to buy them at higher prices. In either case, the Fed hopes to move reserves into or out of the banking system. In other words, **open market operations** entail the purchase and sale of government securities (bonds) for the purpose of altering the flow of reserves into and out of the banking system.

open market operations: Federal Reserve purchases and sales of government bonds for the purpose of altering bank reserves.

IN THE NEWS

Zero-Coupon Bonds

Conventional bonds make interest payments each year, often quarterly. However, some bonds pay no current interest. Because so-called zero-coupon bonds make no interest payments, they have a *current* yield of zero. In effect, a zero-coupon bond accumulates interest payments, paying them all at once when the bond comes due. The *yield* to *maturity* on such bonds is implied by the difference between the purchase price and the face value of the bond. A $1,000 "zero" due in 10 years, for example, might cost only $400 today. You lend $400 now and get back $1,000 in 10 years. The implied yield to maturity is approximately 9 percent.

Analysis: The yield (return) on a bond depends not only on annual interest payments but also on the difference between the price paid for the bond and its face (payoff) value.

Open Market Purchases. Suppose the Fed's goal is to increase the money supply. It's strategy is to provide the banking system with additional reserves. To do so, it must persuade people to deposit a larger share of their financial assets in banks and hold less in other forms, particularly government bonds. The tool for doing this is bond prices. ***If the Fed offers to pay a higher price for bonds ("bids up bonds"), it will effectively lower bond yields and market interest rates.*** The higher prices and lower yields will reduce the attractiveness of holding bonds. If the price offered by the Fed is high enough, people will sell some of their bonds to the Fed and deposit the proceeds of the sale in their bank accounts. This influx of money into bank accounts will directly increase bank reserves. Bingo, goal achieved.

Figure 14.4 illustrates the dynamics of open market operations in more detail. When the Fed buys a bond from the public, it pays with a check written on itself (step 1 in Figure 14.4). What will the bond seller do with the check? There really aren't any options. If the seller wants to use the proceeds of the bond sale, he or she will have to deposit the Fed check at a bank (step 2 in the figure). The bank, in turn, deposits the check at a regional Federal Reserve bank, in exchange for a reserve credit (step 3). The bank's reserves are directly increased by the amount of the check. Thus, ***by buying bonds, the Fed increases bank reserves.*** These reserves can be used to expand the money supply still further, as banks put their newly acquired reserves to work making loans.

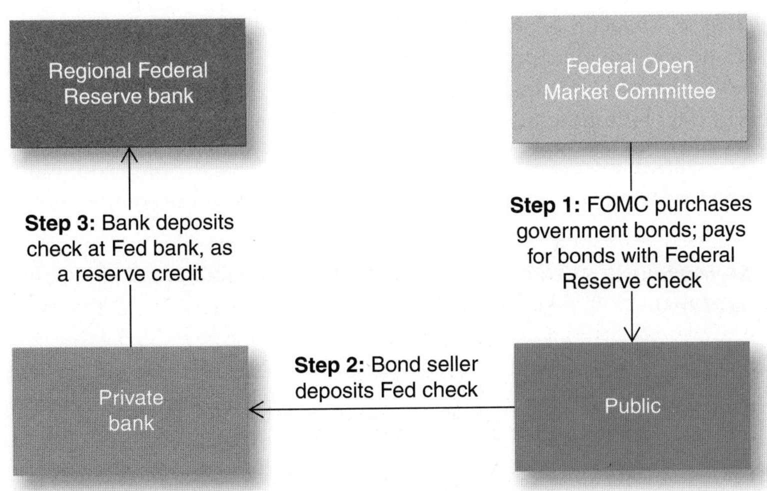

FIGURE 14.4
An Open Market Purchase

The Fed can increase bank reserves by buying bonds from the public. The Fed check used to buy bonds (step 1) gets deposited in a private bank (step 2). The bank returns the check to the Fed (step 3), thereby obtaining additional reserves. To decrease bank reserves, the Fed would sell bonds, thus reversing the flow of reserves.

Open Market Sales. Should the Fed desire to slow the growth in the money supply, it can reverse the whole process. Instead of offering to *buy* bonds, the Fed in this case will try to *sell* bonds. If the Fed "bids bonds down" (offers to sell them at low prices), bond yields will rise. In response, individuals, corporations, and government agencies will convert some of their transactions deposits into bonds. When they do so, they write a check, paying the Fed for the bonds.[3] The Fed then returns the check to the depositor's bank, taking payment through a reduction in the bank's reserve account. The reserves of the banking system are thereby diminished, as is the capacity to make loans. Thus, ***by selling bonds, the Fed reduces bank reserves.***

The Fed Funds Rate

A market signal of these changing reserve flows is provided by the federal funds rate. Recall that "fed funds" are excess reserves traded among banks. If the Fed pumps more reserves into the banking system (by buying bonds), the interest rate charged for overnight reserve loans—the federal funds rate—will decline. Conversely, if the Fed is reducing bank reserves (by selling bonds), the federal funds rate will increase. Hence, the federal funds rate is a highly visible signal of Federal Reserve open market operations. When Alan Greenspan reduced the federal funds rate *11 times* in 2001, the Fed was underscoring the urgency of monetary stimulus to combat the recession and the aftereffects of the September 11 terrorist attacks.

webnote

How has the federal funds rate changed in the past 8 weeks? What does it signal about Federal Reserve activity? For data on the fed funds rate visit the Fed's Web site at www.federalreserve.gov

Beginning in June 2004 the Fed used this same tool to *reduce* lending activity. In fact, the Fed completely reversed course and raised the fed funds rate *17 times* between June 2004 and June 2006.

When the Fed announces a change in the federal funds rate, it always refers to the "target" rate. The Fed doesn't actually *set* the fed funds rate. It only establishes a desired "target" rate. The Fed raises the target rate and seeks to hit it by selling more bonds in the market.

Volume of Activity. To appreciate the significance of open market operations, you need a sense of the magnitudes involved. As we noted earlier, the volume of trading in U.S. bond markets is nearly $1 *trillion* a day. The Fed alone owned over $600 billion worth of government securities at the beginning of 2007 and bought or sold enormous sums daily. Thus, open market operations involve tremendous amounts of money and, by implication, potential bank reserves. Each $1 of reserves represents something like $10 of potential lending capacity (via the money multiplier). Thus, open market operations can have a profound impact on the money supply.

INCREASING THE MONEY SUPPLY

The three major tools of monetary policy are reserve requirements, discount rates, and open market operations. The Fed can use these tools individually or in combination to change the money supply. This section illustrates the use of each tool to attain a specific policy goal.

Suppose the policy goal is to increase the money supply from an assumed level of $340 billion to $400 billion. In surveying the nation's banks, the Fed discovers the facts shown in Table 14.2. On the basis of the facts presented in Table 14.2, it's evident that

- The banking system is "loaned up." Because excess reserves are zero (see row 5 in Table 14.2), there's no additional lending capacity.
- The required reserve ratio must be equal to 25 percent, because this is the current ratio of required reserves ($60 billion) to total deposits ($240 billion).

Accordingly, if the Fed wants to increase the money supply, it will have to pump additional reserves into the banking system or lower the reserve requirement. ***To increase the money supply the Fed can***

- ***Lower reserve requirements.***
- ***Reduce the discount rate.***
- ***Buy bonds.***

[3]In actuality, the Fed deals directly with only 36 "primary" bond dealers. These intermediaries then trade with each other, "secondary" dealers, financial institutions, and individuals. These additional steps don't significantly alter the flow of funds depicted here. Using electronic transactions rather than paper checks doesn't alter the flow of funds either.

Item	Amount
1. Cash held by public	$100 billion
2. Transactions deposits	240 billion
3. Total money supply (M1)	$340 billion
4. Required reserves	$ 60 billion
5. Excess reserves	0
6. Total reserves of banks	$ 60 billion
7. U.S. bonds held by public	$460 billion
8. Discount rate	7%

TABLE 14.2
How to Increase the Money Supply

The accompanying data depict a banking system that has $340 billion of money (M1) and no further lending capacity (excess reserves = 0). To enlarge M1 to $400 billion, the Fed can (1) lower the required reserve ratio, (2) reduce the discount rate, or (3) buy bonds held by the public.

Lowering Reserve Requirements

Lowering the reserve requirements is an expedient way of increasing the lending capacity of the banking system. But by how much should the reserve requirement be reduced?

Recall that the Fed's goal is to increase the money supply from $340 billion to $400 billion, an increase of $60 billion. If the public isn't willing to hold any additional cash, this entire increase in money supply will have to take the form of added transactions deposits. In other words, total deposits will have to increase from $240 billion to $300 billion. These additional deposits will have to be *created* by the banks, in the form of new loans to consumers or business firms.

If the banking system is going to support $300 billion in transactions deposits with its *existing* reserves, the reserve requirement will have to be reduced from 25 percent; thus,

$$\frac{\text{Total reserves}}{\text{Desired level of deposits}} = \frac{\$60 \text{ billion}}{\$300 \text{ billion}} = 0.20$$

At the moment the Fed lowers the minimum reserve ratio to 0.20, *total* reserves won't change. The bank's potential lending power will change, however. Required reserves will drop to $48 billion (0.20 × $240 billion), and excess reserves will jump from zero to $12 billion. These new excess reserves imply an additional lending capacity:

$$\underset{(\$12 \text{ billion})}{\text{Excess reserves}} \times \underset{(5)}{\text{money multiplier}} = \underset{(\$60 \text{ billion})}{\text{unused lending capacity}}$$

If the banks succeed in putting all this new lending power to work—actually make $60 billion in new loans—the Fed's objective of increasing the money supply will be attained.

Lowering the Discount Rate

The second monetary tool available to the Fed is the discount rate. We assumed it was 7 percent initially (see row 8 in Table 14.2). If the Fed lowers this rate, it will become cheaper for banks to borrow reserves from the Fed. The banks will be more willing to borrow (cheaper) reserves so long as they can make additional loans to their own customers at higher interest rates. The profitability of discounting depends on the *difference* between the discount rate and the interest rate the bank charges its loan customers. The Fed increases this difference when it lowers the discount rate.

There's no way to calculate the appropriate discount rate without more detailed knowledge of the banking system's willingness to borrow reserves from the Fed. Nevertheless, we can determine how much reserves the banks *must* borrow if the Fed's money supply target is to be attained. The Fed's objective is to increase transactions deposits by $60 billion. If these deposits are to be created by the banks—and the reserve requirement is unchanged at 0.25—the banks will have to borrow an additional $15 billion of reserves ($60 billion divided by 4, the money multiplier).

Buying Bonds

The Fed can also get additional reserves into the banking system by buying U.S. bonds in the open market. As row 7 in Table 14.2 indicates, the public holds $460 billion in U.S. bonds, none of which are counted as part of the money supply. If the Fed can persuade people to sell some of these bonds, bank reserves will surely rise.

webnote

For an inside view of how the Fed uses its policy tools, visit www.federalreserveeducation.org

To achieve its money supply target, the Fed will offer to buy $15 billion of U.S. bonds. It will pay for these bonds with checks written on its own account at the Fed. The people who sold the bonds will deposit these checks in their own transactions accounts. As they do so, they'll directly increase bank deposits and reserves by $15 billion.

Is $15 billion of open market purchases enough? Yes. The $15 billion is a direct addition to transactions deposits, and therefore to the money supply. The additional deposits bring in $15 billion of reserves, only $3.75 billion of which is required (0.25 × $15 billion). Hence, the new deposits bring in $11.25 billion of excess reserves, which themselves create an additional lending capacity:

$$\underset{(\$11.25\text{ billion})}{\text{Excess reserves}} \times \underset{(4)}{\text{money multiplier}} = \underset{(\$45\text{ billion})}{\text{unused lending capacity}}$$

Thus, the $15 billion of open market purchases will eventually lead to a $60 billion increase in M1 as a consequence of both direct deposits ($15 billion) and subsequent loan activity ($45 billion).

Federal Funds Rate. When the Fed starts bidding up bonds, bond yields and market interest rates will start falling. So will the federal funds rate. This will give individual banks an incentive to borrow any excess reserves available, thereby accelerating deposit (loan) creation.

DECREASING THE MONEY SUPPLY

All the tools used to increase the money supply can also be used to decrease it. ***To reduce the money supply, the Fed can***

- ***Raise reserve requirements.***
- ***Increase the discount rate.***
- ***Sell bonds.***

On a week-to-week basis the Fed does occasionally seek to reduce the total amount of cash and transactions deposits held by the public. These are minor adjustments, however, to broader policies. A growing economy needs a steadily increasing supply of money to finance market exchanges. Hence, the Fed rarely seeks an outright reduction in the size of the money supply. What it does do is regulate the *rate of growth* in the money supply. When the Fed wants to slow the rate of consumer and investor spending, it restrains the *growth* of money and credit. Although many people talk about "reducing" the money supply, they're really talking about slowing its rate of growth. More immediately, they expect to see *rising* interest rates. To slow economic growth (and potential price inflation) China pursued this sort of monetary restraint in 2007 (see World View).

WORLD VIEW

China Sets Measures to Combat Inflation

China announced measures aimed at offsetting inflation risks associated with its surging economy and stemming the flow of money into the country the growth has encouraged.

. . . the People's Bank of China, the central bank, said it would tighten credit with its fourth increase in the reserve requirement in less than a year, a technical move meant to soak up money in the financial system and crimp bank lending. The reserve requirement is the percentage of deposits commercial banks must keep with the central bank rather than lend. The latest 0.5 percentage-point increase, effective Jan. 15, will put the ratio at 9.5%.

Source: *The Wall Street Journal,* January 6–7, 2007, p. A3.

Analysis: Central banks raise interest rates and slow money-supply growth when they sense inflationary pressures.

THE ECONOMY TOMORROW

IS THE FED LOSING CONTROL?

The policy tools at the Fed's disposal imply tight control of the nation's money supply. By altering reserve requirements, discount rates, or open market purchases, the Fed apparently has the ability to increase or decrease the money supply at will. But the Fed's control is far from complete. The nature of "money," as well as our notion of what a "bank" is, keeps changing. As a result, the Fed has to run pretty fast just to stay in place.

Monetary Control Act. Before 1980, the Fed's control of the money supply wasn't only incomplete but actually weakening. The Fed didn't have authority over all banks. Only one-third of all commercial banks were members of the Federal Reserve System and subject to its regulations. All savings and loan associations and other savings banks remained outside the Federal Reserve System. These banks were subject to regulations of state banking commissions and other federal agencies but not to Federal Reserve requirements. As a consequence, a substantial quantity of money and near-money lay beyond the control of the Fed.

To increase the Fed's control of the money supply, Congress passed the Depository Institutions Deregulation and Monetary Control Act of 1980. Commonly referred to simply as the Monetary Control Act, that legislation subjected *all* commercial banks, S&Ls, savings banks, and most credit unions to Fed regulation. All depository institutions now have to satisfy Fed reserve requirements. All depository institutions also enjoy access to the Fed's discount window. These reforms (phased in over a period of 7 years) obliterated the distinction between member and nonmember banks and greatly strengthened the Fed's control of the banking system.

Decline of Traditional Banks. Ironically, ***as the Fed's control of the banks was increasing, the banks themselves were declining in importance.*** Banks are part of a larger financial services industry that provides deposit, credit, and payment services. Many of these services are provided by financial institutions other than banks. These nonbank financial institutions have grown in importance while traditional banks have declined in number and importance.

Accepting and holding deposits is a core bank function. Consumers can also place idle funds in money market mutual funds (MMMF), however. MMMFs typically pay higher interest rates than traditional bank accounts and also permit limited check writing privileges. They thus serve as a potential substitute for traditional banks. Many brokerage houses also offer to hold idle cash in interest-earning accounts for their stock and bond customers.

Nonbanks are also competing against banks for loan business; 30 percent of all consumer loans are now made through credit cards. Banks themselves were once the primary source of credit cards. Now corporate giants like AT&T, GM, Sears, and American Airlines offer nonbank credit cards. Large corporations also offer loans to consumers who want to buy their products and even extend loans to unaffiliated businesses.

Insurance companies and pension funds also use their vast financial resources to make loans. The Teachers Insurance and Annuity Association (TIAA)—the pension fund for college professors—has lent over $10 billion directly to corporations. Many insurance companies provide long-term loans for commercial real estate.

Global Finance. Foreign banks, corporations, and pension funds may also extend credit to American businesses. They may also hold deposits of U.S. dollars abroad (for example, Eurodollars). As the accompanying World View illustrates, money—even terrorists' money—travels easily across national borders.

All this credit and deposit activity by global and nonbank institutions competes with traditional banks. And the nonbanks are winning the competition. In the past 20 years, the share of all financial institution assets held by banks has dropped from 37 percent to 27 percent, which means that banks are less important than they once were. This has made control of the money supply increasingly difficult.

WORLD VIEW

Fighting Terror/Targeting Funds; Laws May Not Stop Flow of Terror Funds

Congress is expected to approve legislation as early as today aimed at crippling the ability of terrorists to send money around the world. But law enforcement officials say that the increased globalization of electronic money transfer systems has made it easier than ever to move cash and avoid detection. . . .

The question, money laundering specialists say, is whether any unilateral action Congress takes can do much to stop the flow of dirty money across the world's borders. "The technology is changing all the time that makes it easier to transfer funds anonymously and to send money through five or six countries in one day," said William Schroeder, former director of the FBI's legal forfeiture division. "That makes it extremely difficult to connect people with money, to locate a money trail and follow it from person to person. . ."

Security cameras in Portland, Maine, captured pictures of suspected terrorists Muhammad Atta and Abdulaziz Alomari visiting two different ATMs on Sept. 10. Bank cash machines hardly qualify as cutting edge, but ATMs help criminals, according to the Treasury Department's Financial Crimes Enforcement Network, by allowing them "to wire funds into accounts in the United States from other nations and almost instantaneously and virtually anonymously to withdraw those funds."

Last year, federal prosecutors revealed that a husband-and-wife team with little more than a laptop computer and a license for what turned out to be a shell bank in Russia laundered more than $7 billion between 1996 and 1998. Using wire transfer software from the Bank of New York, the couple allegedly worked with the Russian mafia to send money from Moscow to New York to a series of offshore banks without tipping off regulators.

"If you know what you're doing, you can send money from the US to Spain to Cyprus to the Cayman Islands to Peru in a matter of minutes," said Schroeder.

—Scott Bernard Nelson

Source: *Boston Globe,* October 24, 2001. Copyright 2001 by Globe Newspaper Co. (MA). Reprinted with permission.

Analysis: Nearly two-thirds of all U.S. currency circulates outside the United States, and over $1.5 trillion is transmitted by bank wire every day. This globalization of money makes it hard not only to track terrorists' money but also to control the domestic money supply.

Focus on Fed Funds Rate, Not Money Supply. Because of the difficulties in managing an increasingly globalized and electronic flow of funds, the Fed has shifted away from money-supply targets to interest rate targets. Although changes in the money supply and in interest rates are intrinsically related, interest rates are easier and faster to track. The Fed also has the financial power to change short-term interest rates through its massive open market operations. If it chooses, the Fed can also offset abrupt changes in the flow of funds across national borders that might otherwise disrupt domestic interest rates. Last, but not least, the Fed recognizes that interest rates, not more obscure data on the money-supply or bank reserves, are the immediate concern in investment and big-ticket consumption decisions. As a result, the Fed will continue to use the federal funds rate as its primary barometer of monetary policy in the economy tomorrow.

SUMMARY

- The Federal Reserve System controls the nation's money supply by regulating the loan activity (deposit creation) of private banks (depository institutions). LO2
- The core of the Federal Reserve System is the 12 regional Federal Reserve banks, which provide check-clearance, reserve deposit, and loan ("discounting") services to individual banks. Private banks are required to maintain minimum reserves on deposit at the regional Federal Reserve banks. LO1
- The general policies of the Fed are set by its Board of Governors. The Board's chair is selected by the U.S. president and confirmed by the Senate. The chair serves as the chief spokesperson for monetary policy. The Fed's policy strategy is implemented by the Federal Open Market Committee (FOMC), which directs open market sales and purchase of U.S. bonds. LO1
- The Fed has three basic tools for changing the money supply. By altering the reserve requirement, the Fed

can immediately change both the quantity of excess reserves in the banking system and the money multiplier, which limits banks' lending capacity. By altering discount rates (the rate of interest charged by the Fed for reserve borrowing), the Fed can also influence the amount of reserves maintained by banks. Finally, and most important, the Fed can increase or decrease the reserves of the banking system by buying or selling government bonds, that is, by engaging in open market operations. LO2

- When the Fed buys bonds, it causes an increase in bank reserves (and lending capacity). When the Fed sells bonds, it induces a reduction in reserves (and lending capacity). LO3
- The federal funds (interest) rate is a market signal of Fed open market activity and intentions. LO2
- In the 1980s, the Fed gained greater control of the banking system. Global and nonbank institutions such as pension funds, insurance companies, and nonbank credit services have grown in importance, however, making control of the money supply more difficult. LO2

Key Terms

monetary policy
money supply (M1, M2)
required reserves
excess reserves
money multiplier
federal funds rate
discounting
discount rate
portfolio decision
bond
yield
open market operations

Questions for Discussion

1. Why do banks want to maintain as little excess reserves as possible? Under what circumstances might banks want to hold excess reserves? (*Hint:* See Figure 14.2.) LO2
2. Why do people hold bonds rather than larger savings account or checking account balances? Under what circumstances might they change their portfolios, moving their funds out of bonds and into bank accounts? LO3
3. What is the current price and yield of 10-year U.S. Treasury bonds? Of General Motors bonds? (Check the financial section of your daily newspaper.) What accounts for the difference? LO3
4. Why did China raise reserve requirements in 2007? How did they expect consumers and businesses to respond? (See World View, page 284.) LO2
5. Why might the Fed want to decrease the money supply? LO2
6. Why would a zero-coupon bond (see News, page 281) have a lower price than a bond paying annual interest? LO3
7. In 2000–2001, bond yields in Japan fell to less than 1.5 percent as the Bank of Japan bid up bond prices. Yet, relatively few people moved their assets out of bonds into banks. How might this failure of open market operations be explained? LO3
8. In 2001, the Fed reduced both the discount and federal fund rates dramatically. But bank loan volume didn't increase. What considerations might have constrained the market's response to Fed policy? LO2
9. If bondholders expect the Fed to raise interest rates, what action might they take? How would this affect the Fed's goal? LO3

problems The Student Problem Set at the back of this book contains numerical and graphing problems for this chapter.

web activities to accompany this chapter can be found on the Online Learning Center: **http://www.mhhe.com/economics/schiller11e**

Monetary Policy

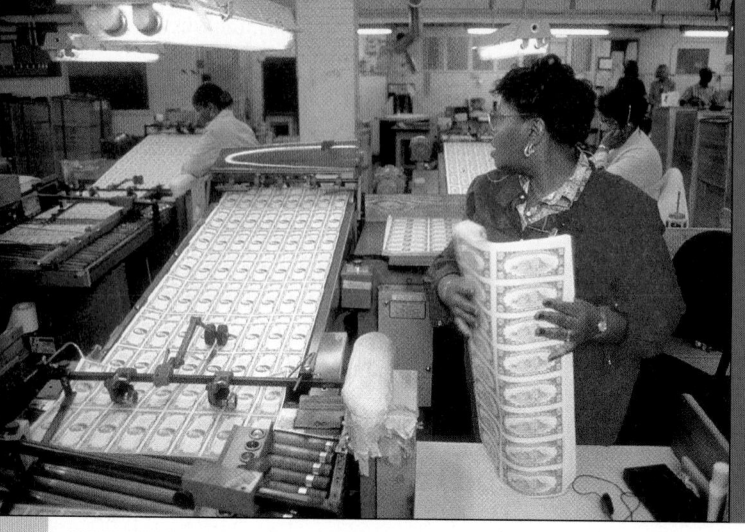

LEARNING OBJECTIVES

After reading this chapter, you should know:

LO1. How monetary policy affects macro outcomes.

LO2. The constraints on monetary-policy impact.

LO3. The differences between Keynesian and monetarist monetary theories.

So what if the Federal Reserve System controls the nation's money supply? Why is this significant? Does it matter how much money is available?

Vladimir Lenin thought so. The first communist leader of the Soviet Union once remarked that the best way to destroy a society is to destroy its money. If a society's money became valueless, it would no longer be accepted in exchange for goods and services in product markets. People would have to resort to barter, and the economy's efficiency would be severely impaired. Adolf Hitler tried unsuccessfully to use this weapon against Great Britain during World War II. His plan was to counterfeit British currency, then drop it from planes flying over England. He believed that the sudden increase in the quantity of money, together with its suspect origins, would render the British pound valueless.

Even in peacetime, the quantity of money in circulation influences its value in the marketplace. Moreover, interest rates and access to credit (bank loans) are basic determinants of spending behavior. Consequently, control over the money supply implies an ability to alter macroeconomic outcomes.

But how much influence does the money supply have on macro performance? Specifically,

- **What's the relationship between the money supply, interest rates, and aggregate demand?**
- **How can the Fed use its control of the money supply or interest rates to alter macro outcomes?**
- **How effective is monetary policy, compared to fiscal policy?**

Economists offer very different answers to these questions. Some argue that changes in the money supply directly affect macro outcomes; others argue that the effects of such changes are indirect and less certain.

Paralleling these arguments about *how* **monetary policy** works are debates over the relative effectiveness of monetary and fiscal policy. Some economists argue that monetary policy is more effective than fiscal policy; others contend the reverse is true. This chapter examines these different views of money and assesses their implications for macro policy.

THE MONEY MARKET

The best place to learn how monetary policy works is the money *market.* You must abandon any mystical notions you may harbor about money and view it like any other commodity that's traded in the marketplace. Like other goods, there's a supply of money and a demand for money. Together they determine the "price" of money, or the **interest rate.**

monetary policy: The use of money and credit controls to influence macroeconomic outcomes.

interest rate: The price paid for the use of money.

At first glance, it may appear strange to call interest rates the price of money. But when you borrow money, the "price" you pay is measured by the interest rate you're charged. When interest rates are high, money is "expensive." When interest rates are low, money is "cheap."

Money Balances

Even people who don't borrow must contend with the price of money. Money, as we've seen, comes in many different forms. A common characteristic of all money is that it can be held as a store of value. People hold cash and maintain positive bank balances for this purpose. Most of the money in our common measures of **money supply (M1, M2)** is in the form of bank balances. There's an opportunity cost associated with such money balances, however. Money held in transactions accounts earns little or no interest. Money held in savings accounts and money market mutual funds does earn interest but usually at relatively low rates. By contrast, money used to buy bonds or stocks or to make loans is likely to earn a higher interest rate of return.

money supply (M1): Currency held by the public, plus balance in transactions accounts.

money supply (M2): M1 plus balances in most savings accounts and money market mutual funds.

The Price of Money. The nature of the "price" of money should be apparent: People who hold *cash* are forgoing an opportunity to earn interest. So are people who hold money in checking accounts that pay no interest. In either case, ***forgone interest is the opportunity cost (price) of money people choose to hold.*** How high is that price? It's equal to the market rate of interest.

Money held in interest-paying bank accounts does earn some interest. In this case, the opportunity cost of holding money is the *difference* between the prevailing rate of interest and the rate paid on deposit balances. As is the case with cash and regular checking accounts, opportunity cost is measured by the forgone interest.

The Demand for Money

Once we recognize that money does have a price, we can easily formulate a demand for money. As is the case with all goods, the **demand for money** is a schedule (or curve) showing the quantity of money demanded at alternative prices (interest rates).

demand for money: The Quantities of money people are willing and able to hold at alternative interest rates, *ceteris paribus.*

The decision to hold (demand) money balances is the kind of **portfolio decision** we examined in Chapter 14. While at first glance it might seem irrational to hold money balances that pay little or no interest, there are many good reasons for doing so.

portfolio decision: The choice of how (where) to hold idle funds.

Transactions Demand. Even people who've mastered the principles of economics hold money. They do so because they want to buy goods and services. In order to transact business in product or factor markets, we need money in the form of either cash or a positive bank account balance. Debit cards and ATM cards don't work unless there's money in the bank. Payment by e-cash also requires a supporting bank balance. Even when we use credit cards, we're only postponing the date of payment by a few weeks or so. Some merchants won't even accept credit cards, especially for small purchases. Accordingly, we recognize the existence of a basic **transactions demand for money.**

transactions demand for money: Money held for the purpose of making everyday market purchases.

Precautionary Demand. Another reason people hold money is their fear of the proverbial rainy day. A sudden emergency may require money purchases over and above normal transactions needs. Such needs may arise when the banks are closed or in a community where one's checks aren't accepted. Also, future income is uncertain and may diminish unexpectedly. Therefore, people hold a bit more money (cash or bank account balances) than they anticipate spending. This **precautionary demand for money** is the extra money being held as a safeguard against the unexpected.

precautionary demand for money: Money held for unexpected market transactions or for emergencies.

Speculative Demand. People also hold money for speculative purposes. Suppose you were interested in buying stocks or bonds but hadn't yet picked the right ones or regarded their present prices as too high. In such circumstances, you might want to hold some money so that you could later buy a "hot" stock or bond at a price you think attractive. Thus, you'd be holding money in the hope that a better financial opportunity would later appear. In this sense, you'd be *speculating* with your money, forgoing present opportunities to earn interest in the hope of hitting a real jackpot later. These money balances represent a **speculative demand for money.**

speculative demand for money: Money held for speculative purposes, for later financial opportunities.

The Market Demand Curve. These three motivations for holding money combine to create a *market demand* for money. The question is, what shape does this demand curve take? Does the quantity of money demanded decrease sharply as the rate of interest rises? Or do people tend to hold the same amount of money, regardless of its price?

People do cut down on their money balances when interest rates rise. At such times, the opportunity cost of holding money is simply too high. This explains why so many people move their money out of transactions deposits (M1) and into money market mutual funds (M2) when interest rates are extraordinarily high (for example, in 1980–82). Corporations are even more careful about managing their money when interest rates rise. Better money management requires watching checking account balances more closely and even making more frequent trips to the bank, but the opportunity costs are worth it.

Figure 15.1 illustrates the total market demand for money. Like nearly all demand curves, the market demand curve for money slopes downward. The downward slope indicates that ***the quantity of money people are willing and able to hold (demand) increases as interest rates fall* (ceteris paribus).**

Equilibrium

Once a money demand curve and a money supply curve are available, the action in money markets is easy to follow. Figure 15.1 summarizes this action. The money demand curve in Figure 15.1 reflects existing demands for holding money. The money supply curve is drawn at an arbitrary level of g_1. In practice, its position depends on Federal Reserve policy (Chapter 14), the lending behavior of private banks, and the willingness of consumers and investors to borrow money.

The intersection of the money demand and money supply curves (E_1) establishes an **equilibrium rate of interest.** Only at this interest rate is the quantity of money supplied equal to the quantity demanded. In this case, we observe that an interest rate of 7 percent equates the desires of suppliers and demanders.

equilibrium rate of interest: The interest rate at which the quantity of money demanded in a given time period equals the quantity of money supplied.

At any rate of interest other than 7 percent, the quantity of money demanded wouldn't equal the quantity supplied. Look at the imbalance that exists, for example, when the interest rate is 9 percent. At that rate, the quantity of money supplied (g_1 in Figure 15.1) exceeds the quantity demanded (g_2). All the money (g_1) must be held by someone, of course. But the demand curve indicates that people aren't *willing* to hold so much money at that interest rate (9 percent). People will adjust their portfolios by moving money out of cash and bank accounts into bonds or other assets that offer higher returns. This will tend to lower interest rates (recall

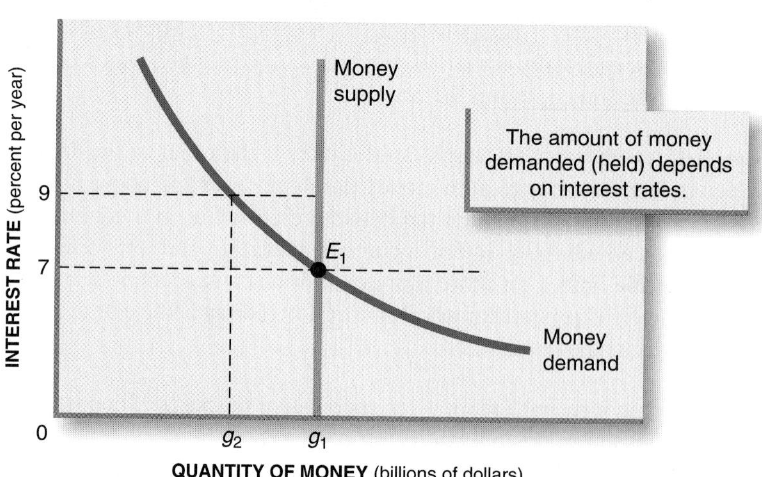

FIGURE 15.1
Money Market Equilibrium

All points on the money demand curve represent the quantity of money people are willing to hold at a specific interest rate. The equilibrium interest rate occurs at the intersection (E_1) of the money supply and money demand curves. At that rate of interest, people are willing to hold as much money as is available. At any other interest rate (for example, 9 percent), the quantity of money people are *willing* to hold won't equal the quantity available, and people will adjust their portfolios.

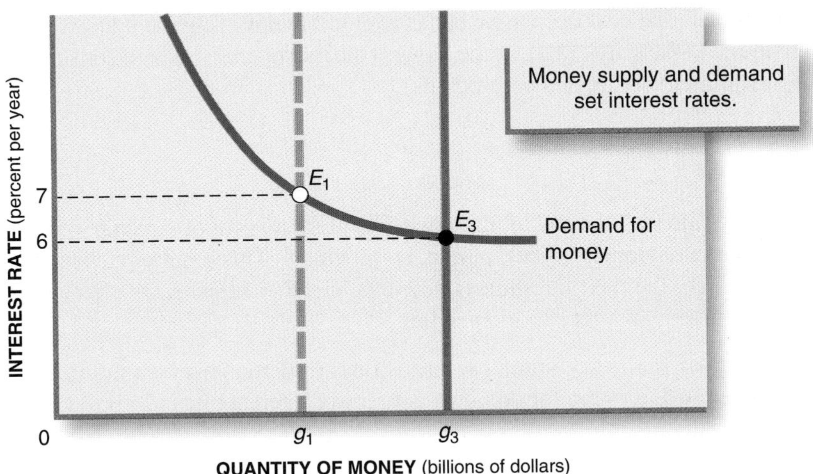

FIGURE 15.2
Changing the Rate of Interest

Changes in the money supply alter the equilibrium rate of interest. In this case, an increase in the money supply (from g_1 to g_3) lowers the equilibrium rate of interest (from 7 percent to 6 percent).

that buying bonds tends to lower their yields). As interest rates drop, people are willing to hold more money. Ultimately we get to E_1, where the quantity of money demanded equals the quantity supplied. At that equilibrium, people are content with their portfolio choices.

Changing Interest Rates

The equilibrium rate of interest is subject to change. As we saw in Chapter 14, the Federal Reserve System can alter the money supply through changes in reserve requirements, changes in the discount rate, or open market operations. By implication, then, ***the Fed can alter the equilibrium rate of interest.***

Figure 15.2 illustrates the potential impact of monetary policy on the equilibrium rate of interest. Assume that the money supply is initially at g_1 and the equilibrium interest rate is 7 percent. The Fed then increases the money supply to g_3 by lowering the reserve requirement, reducing the discount rate, or, most likely, purchasing additional bonds in the open market. This expansionary monetary policy brings about a new equilibrium, at E_3. At this intersection, the market rate of interest is only 6 percent. Hence, by increasing the money supply, the Fed tends to lower the equilibrium rate of interest. To put the matter differently, people are *willing* to hold larger money balances only at lower interest rates.

Were the Fed to reverse its policy and reduce the money supply, interest rates would rise. You can see this result in Figure 15.2 by observing the change in the rate of interest that occurs when the money supply *shrinks* from g_3 to g_1.

Federal Funds Rate. As we noted in Chapter 14, the most visible market signal of the Fed's activity is the **federal funds rate.** When the Fed injects or withdraws reserves from the banking system (via open market operations), the interest rate on interbank loans is most directly affected. Any change in the federal funds rate, moreover, is likely to affect a whole hierarchy of interest rates (see Table 15.1). ***The federal funds rate reflects the cost***

federal funds rate: The interest rate for interbank reserve loans.

Interest Rate	Type of Loan	Rate
Federal funds rate	Interbank reserves, overnight	5.25%
Discount rate	Reserves lent to banks by Fed	6.25
Prime rate	Bank loans to blue-chip corporations	8.25
Mortgage rate	Loans for house purchases; up to 30 years	6.06
Auto loan	Financing of auto purchase	6.45
Consumer installment credit	Loans for general purposes	12.49
Credit cards	Financing of unpaid credit card purchases	15.09

Source: Federal Reserve.

TABLE 15.1
The Hierarchy of Interest Rates

Interest rates reflect the risks and duration of loans. Because risks and loan terms vary greatly, dozens of different interest rates are available. Here are a few of the more common rates as of March 2007.

of funds for banks. When that cost decreases, banks respond by lowering the interest rates *they* charge to businesses (the prime rate), home buyers (the mortgage rate), and consumers (e.g., auto loans, installment credit, and credit cards).

INTEREST RATES AND SPENDING

A change in the interest rate isn't the end of this story. The ultimate goal of monetary policy is to alter macroeconomic outcomes: prices, output, employment. This requires a change in aggregate demand. Hence, the next question is how changes in interest rates affect consumer, investor, government, and net export spending.

Monetary Stimulus

aggregate demand: The total quantity of output demanded at alternative price levels in a given time period, *ceteris paribus.*

Consider first a policy of monetary stimulus. The strategy of monetary stimulus is to increase **aggregate demand.** A tactic for doing so is to lower interest rates.

Investment. Will lower interest rates encourage spending? In Chapter 9 we observed that investment decisions are sensitive to the rate of interest. Specifically, we demonstrated that lower rates of interest reduce the cost of buying plant and equipment, making capital investment more profitable. Lower interest rates also reduce the opportunity cost of holding inventories. Accordingly, a lower rate of interest should result in a higher rate of desired investment spending, as shown by the movement down the investment-demand curve in step 2 of Figure 15.3.

webnote

Compare the interest rates in Table 15.1 with today's rates at www.stls.frb.org

Aggregate Demand. The increased investment brought about by lower interest rates represents an injection of new spending into the circular flow. That jump in spending will kick off multiplier effects and result in an even larger increase in aggregate demand. Step 3 in Figure 15.3 illustrates this increase by the rightward *shift* of the AD curve. Market participants, encouraged by lower interest rates, are now willing to buy more output at the prevailing price level.

Consumers too may change their behavior when interest rates fall. As interest rates fall, mortgage payments decline. Monthly payments on home equity and credit card balances may also decline. These lower interest changes free up billions of consumer dollars. This increased net cash flow and lower interest rates may encourage consumers to buy new cars,

Step 1: An increase in the money supply lowers the rate of interest.

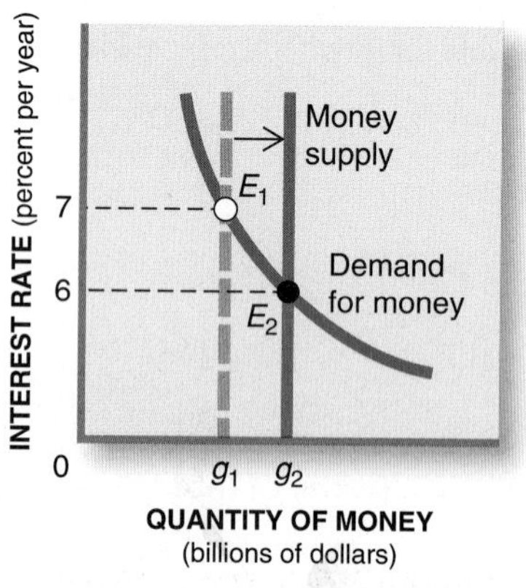

Step 2: Lower interest rates stimulate investment.

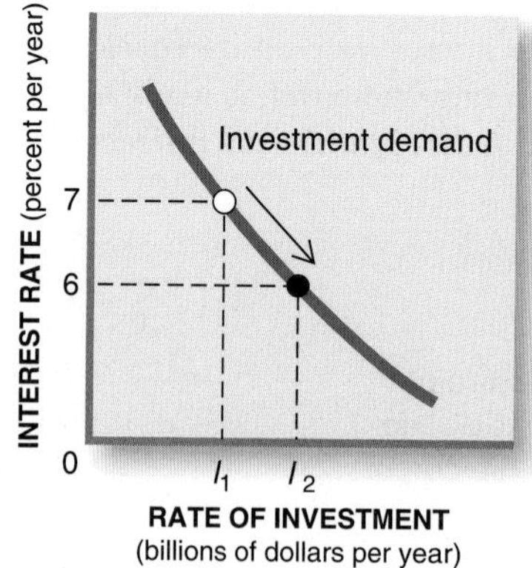

Step 3: More investment increases aggregate demand (including multiplier effects).

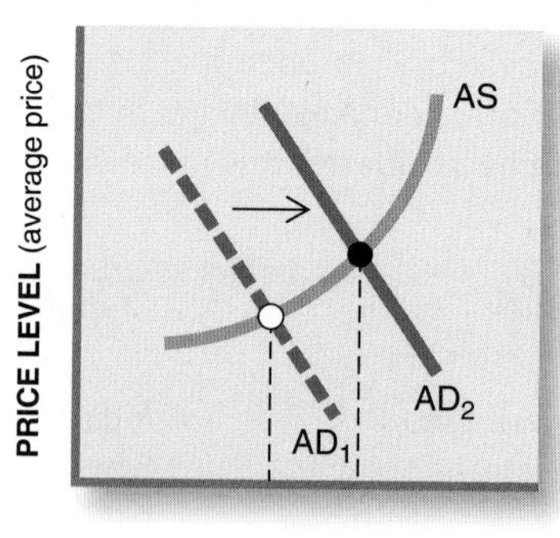

FIGURE 15.3
Monetary Stimulus

An increase in the money supply may reduce interest rates and encourage more investment. The increase in investment will trigger multiplier effects that increase aggregate demand by an even larger amount.

IN THE NEWS

More People Refinance to Wring Cash Out of Their Homes

McLEAN, Va.—Jay and Sharon Sebastian refinanced the mortgage on their 30-year-old home this month for the second time in less than a year. And, like millions of others, they took out some cold, hard cash that soon will be spent.

Not only did they reduce their 30-year fixed interest rate from 6⅝% to 6%, they upped the mortgage on their four-bedroom, three-bath home in this Washington, D.C., suburb to $300,000 from the previous $275,000 balance. The bank cut them a check for $25,000, which they're using to remodel their outdated kitchen with granite countertops, hardwood floors and stainless steel appliances.

"The check is going in the mail today for the (remodeling) deposit, so it's going right back into the economy," says Jay, a 40-year-old software development manager.

Luckily for the economy, many homeowners are doing the same thing.

Most Take Extra Cash

As mortgage rates hover near record lows, nearly two-thirds of the millions of Americans who are refinancing their homes are doing "cash-outs"—when homeowners increase their mortgage amounts based on the appreciation of their homes and pocket the difference. . . .

The extra cash, along with lower monthly mortgage payments from a raft of refinancings, is acting as a key source of spending as the U.S. economy struggles to stay on its feet, many economists say. . . .

An estimated $140 billion was cashed out last year. That helped boost consumer spending in a year that saw a recession, a falling stock market and the Sept. 11 attacks. . . .

The benefit to the economy doesn't stop at the first sale. If the Sebastians' contractor decides to use his cut to take his family on a trip to Disney World, which then hires a new person to play a dwarf and that person buys a new stereo, the economy has benefited three more times.

—Barbara Hagenbaugh

Analysis: Lower interest rates encourage market participants to borrow and spend more money. This shifts the AD curve rightward, setting off multiplier effects.

appliances, or other big-ticket items (see News). State and local governments may also conclude that lower interest rates increase the desirability of bond-financed public works. All such responses would add to aggregate demand.

From this perspective, ***the Fed's goal of stimulating the economy is achieved in three distinct steps:***

- ***An increase in the money supply.***
- ***A reduction in interest rates.***
- ***An increase in aggregate demand.***

Quantitative Impact. Just how much stimulus can monetary policy create? According to former Fed Chairman Alan Greenspan, the impact of monetary policy can be impressive:

Greenspan's policy guide:	1/10 point reduction in long-term interest rate	=	$10 billion fiscal stimulus

By this rule of thumb, a full-point reduction in long-term interest rates would increase aggregate demand just as much as a $100 billion injection of new government spending. This kind of stimulus was evident in 2002–3: low interest rates prompted a consumer-driven spending spree (see News). This injection of new spending shifted the AD curve rightward, propelling the economy out of recession.

Monetary Restraint

Like fiscal policy, monetary policy is a two-edged sword, at times seeking to increase aggregate demand and at other times trying to restrain it. When inflation threatens, the goal of monetary policy is to reduce the rate of total spending, which puts the Fed in the position of "leaning against the wind." If successful, the resulting reduction in spending will keep aggregate demand from increasing inflationary pressures.

IN THE NEWS

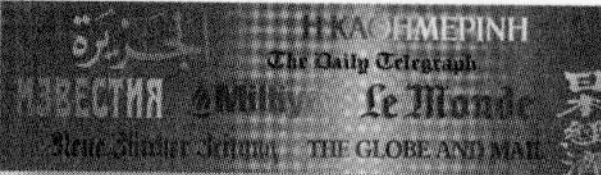

Fed Shifts Focus from Job Growth to Rising Prices

WASHINGTON—An unexpected quickening in the pace of price increases in the past two months is challenging the Federal Reserve's plan to raise short-term interest rates only slowly from today's 46-year lows.

The recent shift in prices is at odds with Fed officials' forecast that the combination of unemployment, unused industrial capacity and rapid growth in productivity would keep inflation very low for another year or two.

Fed officials, though not ready to abandon the forecast, acknowledge that their primary concern has shifted in the past few months from sluggish job growth to rising prices. If inflation moves higher in coming months, they are likely to reexamine their public assessment, made earlier this month, that rates will rise "at a pace that is likely to be measured."

"The flareup in inflation in the first quarter is a matter for concern," Fed Governor Ben Bernanke said yesterday in a speech in Seattle. "The inflation data bear close watching." . . .

The Fed is almost certain to raise its target for the federal-funds rate, charged on overnight loans between banks, from 1% at its late June meeting. Markets are assuming the rate will then rise rapidly to about 2% by the end of the year. . . .

—Greg Ip

Source: *The Wall Street Journal,* May 21, 2004.

Analysis: When inflationary pressures build up, monetary restraint is appropriate. Higher interest rates may slow spending and restrain aggregate demand.

Higher Interest Rates. The mechanics of monetary policy designed to combat inflation are similar to those used to fight unemployment; only the direction is reversed. In this case, we seek to discourage spending by increasing the rate of interest. The Fed can push interest rates up by selling bonds, increasing the discount rate, or increasing the reserve requirement. All these actions reduce the money supply and help establish a new and higher equilibrium rate of interest.

The ultimate objective of a restrictive monetary policy is to reduce aggregate demand. For monetary restraint to succeed, spending behavior must be responsive to interest rates.

webnote

For an official explanation of monetary policy, with links to relevant data, visit the Minneapolis Fed at http://woodrow.mpls.frb.fed.us/info/policy

Reduced Aggregate Demand. Figure 15.3 showed the impact of interest rates on investment and aggregate demand. If the interest rate rises from 6 to 7 percent, investment declines from I_2 to I_1 and the AD curve shifts *leftward.* At higher rates of interest, many marginal investments will no longer be profitable. Likewise, many consumers will decide that they can't afford the higher monthly payments associated with increased interest rates; purchases of homes, cars, and household appliances will be postponed. State and local governments may also decide to cancel or postpone bond-financed projects. Thus, ***monetary restraint is achieved with***

- ***A decrease in the money supply.***
- ***An increase in interest rates.***
- ***A decrease in aggregate demand.***

The resulting leftward shift of the AD curve lessens inflationary pressures.

Ironically, the monetary stimulus of 2001–2 was so effective that the Fed started worrying about inflation in mid-2004 (see News). In June 2004, monetary policy switched to restraint, not stimulus. Over the next 2 years the Fed raised the federal-funds target rate 17 times.

POLICY CONSTRAINTS

The mechanics of monetary policy are simple enough. They won't always work as well as we might hope, however. Several constraints can limit the Fed's ability to alter the money supply, interest rates, or aggregate demand.

Constraints on Monetary Stimulus

Short- vs. Long-Term Rates. One of the most visible constraints on monetary policy is the distinction between short-term interest rates and long-term interest rates. Greenspan's policy guide (page 293) focuses on changes in *long-term* rates like mortgages and installment loans. Yet, the Fed's open market operations have the most direct effect on *short-term* rates (e.g., the overnight federal funds rate). As a consequence, ***the success of Fed intervention depends in part on how well changes in long-term interest rates mirror changes in short-term interest rates.***

In 2001, the Fed reduced the federal funds rate by three full percentage points between January and September, the biggest reduction in short-term rates since 1994. Long-term rates fell much less, however. The interest rate on 30-year mortgages, for example, fell less than half a percentage point in the first few months of monetary stimulus.

The same thing happened when the Fed reversed direction in 2004–6. The *short*-run fed funds rate was ratcheted up from 1.0 to 5.25 percent during that period. But *long*-term rates (e.g., 10-year Treasury bonds and home mortgages) rose only modestly. Fed Chairman Alan Greenspan characterized these discrepant trends as a "conundrum."

Reluctant Lenders. There are several reasons why long-term rates might not closely mirror cuts in short-term rates. The first potential constraint is the willingness of private banks to increase their lending activity. The Fed can reduce the cost of funds to the banking system; the Fed can even reduce reserve requirements. But the money supply won't increase unless banks lend more money.

If the banks instead choose to accumulate excess reserves, the money supply won't increase as much as intended. We saw this happen in the Great Depression (Figure 14.2). This happened again in 2001, when the Fed was trying to stimulate the economy but banks were reluctant to increase their loan activity (see News). Banks were trying to shore up their own equity and were wary of making any new loans that might not get repaid in a weak economy. In such cases, long-term rates stay relatively high even when short-term rates are falling.

IN THE NEWS

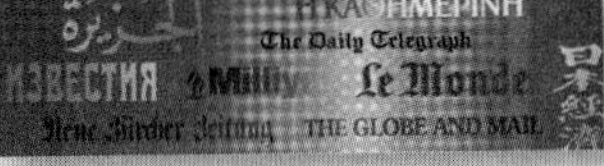

Uneasy Banks May Tighten Loans, Stunt Recovery

Institutions Seeing More Write-Offs, Delinquencies

A rising tide of bad commercial loans could make banks more reluctant to lend and blunt the impact of the Federal Reserve's latest interest rate cut.

Banks earned a record $19.9 billion in the first quarter, but the proportion of commercial loans 90 days or more past due increased to 1.8 percent—a seven year high, according to a report released Wednesday by the Federal Deposit Insurance Corp.

In the same period, banks wrote off $7 billion in bad loans, up 38 percent from a year earlier.

The combination of higher write-offs and delinquent loans is worrisome, experts say. . . .

Banks will have to set aside more money as a reserve against loan losses, which will hurt their earnings.

More worrisome: Banks tend to reduce lending when write-offs rise. Even though the Fed's rate cuts could spur loan demand from corporate borrowers, companies could find loans harder to get, which could slow an economic recovery.

Last week, Fed Chief Alan Greenspan noted in a speech the increase in problem loans and urged banks not to choke off credit to healthy borrowers.

But about half of all banks have tightened their commercial loan standards this year, according to a survey released Wednesday by the Comptroller of the Currency, which regulates national banks. The most frequently cited reason was the economic outlook.

—Christine Dugas

Source: *USA Today,* June 23, 2001.

Analysis: If banks are reluctant to make new loans in an depressed economy, new bank reserves created by the Fed won't bolster more spending.

Liquidity Trap. There are circumstances in which even *short-term* rates may not fall when the Fed wants them to. The possibility that interest rates may not respond to changes in the money supply is illustrated by the "liquidity trap." When interest rates are low, the opportunity cost of holding money is cheap. At such times people may decide to hold all the money they can get, waiting for income-earning opportunities to improve. Bond prices, for example, may be high and their yields low. Buying bonds at such times entails the risk of capital losses (when bond prices fall) and little reward (since yields are low). Accordingly, market participants may decide just to hold any additional money the Fed supplies. At this juncture—a phenomenon Keynes called the **liquidity trap**—further expansion of the money supply has no effect on the rate of interest. The horizontal section of the money demand curve in Figure 15.4*a* portrays this situation.

liquidity trap: The portion of the money demand curve that is horizontal; people are willing to hold unlimited amounts of money at some (low) interest rate.

What happens to interest rates when the initial equilibrium falls into this trap? Nothing at all. Notice that the equilibrium rate of interest doesn't fall when the money supply is increased from g_1 to g_2 (Figure 15.4*a*). People are willing to hold all that additional money without a reduction in the rate of interest.

Low Expectations. Even if both short- and long-term interest rates do fall, we've no assurance that aggregate demand will increase as expected. Keynes put great emphasis on *expectations.* Recall that investment decisions are motivated not only by interest rates but by expectations as well. During a recession—when unemployment is high and the rate of spending low—corporations have little incentive to expand production capacity. With little expectation of future profit, investors are likely to be unimpressed by "cheap money" (low interest rates) and may decline to use the lending capacity that banks make available.

Investment demand that's slow to respond to the stimulus of cheap money is said to be *inelastic* because it won't expand. Consumers too are reluctant to borrow when current and future income prospects are uncertain or distinctly unfavorable. Accordingly, even if the

(*a*) A liquidity trap can stop interest rates from falling.

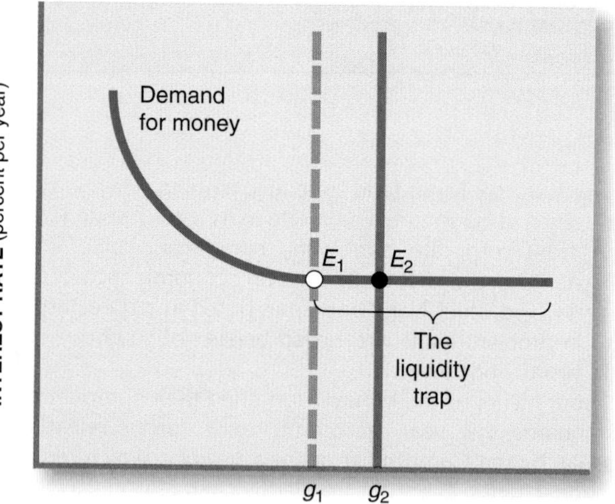

(*b*) Inelastic investment demand can also impede monetary policy.

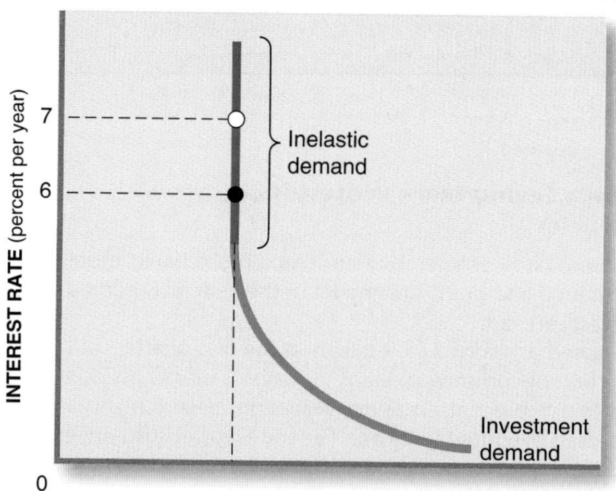

FIGURE 15.4
Constraints on Monetary Stimulus

(*a*) Liquidity Trap If people are willing to hold unlimited amounts of money at the prevailing interest rate, increases in the money supply won't push interest rates lower. A liquidity trap—the horizontal segment of the money demand curve—prevents interest rates from falling.

(*b*) Inelastic Demand A lower interest rate won't always stimulate investment. If investors have unfavorable expectations for future sales, small reductions in interest rates may not alter their investment decisions. Here the rate of investment remains constant when the interest rate drops from 7 to 6 percent. This kind of situation blocks the second step in the Keynesian approach to monetary policy (see Figure 15.3*b*).

IN THE NEWS  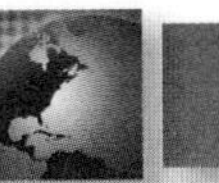 

Vicious Cycle

Despite Rate Cuts, Mood in Boardrooms Is Darkening Further

Washington—Despite Wall Street's widespread hopes for an economic recovery in the second half of 2001, America's business leaders have adopted a decidedly gloomier view.

At companies across the nation, sales and earnings continue to fall below already-lowered expectations. Federal Reserve officials attempted to drive away that storm cloud yesterday by cutting interest rates by a quarter percentage point, their sixth rate cut in as many months. . . .

Fed officials, citing the risks of "economic weakness in the foreseeable future," sent a clear signal that they were poised to keep easing credit conditions through the summer.

The nation's businesses, meanwhile, have dealt with those same uncertainties by cutting spending, closing facilities and laying off workers—actions that, in turn, further dim the prospects for an imminent turnaround and complicate the Fed's job of keeping the economy out of the ditch. . . .

—Greg Ip

Source: *The Wall Street Journal,* June 28, 2001.

Analysis: Interest rate cuts are supposed to stimulate investment and consumption. But gloomy expectations may deter people from borrowing and spending.

Fed is successful in lowering interest rates, there's no assurance that lower interest rates will stimulate borrowing and spending. Such a reluctance to spend was evident early in 2001, even before the September 11 terrorist attacks. Although the Fed managed to push interest rates down to 20-year lows, investors and consumers preferred to pay off old debts rather than incur new ones (see News). The September 11 attacks made people even more reluctant to borrow and spend.

Monetary stimulus was even less effective in Japan in 1999–2001. When the Japanese central bank cut the discount rate from an extraordinary low ½ percent to an unheard of ¼ percent, no one responded. In the lengthening recession Japanese consumers were trying to save more of their money and producer expectations were glum. So even *really* cheap loans didn't budge the aggregate demand curve.

The vertical portion of the investment demand curve in Figure 15.4*b* illustrates the possibility that investment spending may not respond to changes in the rate of interest. Notice that a reduction in the rate of interest from 7 percent to 6 percent doesn't increase investment spending. In this case, businesses are simply unwilling to invest any more funds. As a consequence, aggregate spending doesn't rise. The Fed's policy objective remains unfulfilled, even though the Fed has successfully lowered the rate of interest. Recall that the investment demand curve may also *shift* if expectations change. If expectations worsened, the investment demand curve would shift to the left and might result in even *less* investment at 6 percent interest (see Figure 15.4*b*).

Time Lags. Even when expectations are good, businesses won't respond *instantly* to changes in interest rates. Lower interest rates make investments more profitable. But it still takes time to develop and implement new investments. Hence, ***there is always a time lag between interest-rate changes and investment responses.***

The same is true for consumers. Consumers don't rush out the door to refinance their homes or buy new ones the day the Fed reduces interest rates. They might start *thinking* about new financing, but aren't likely to *do* anything for a while. As the News on the next page suggests, it may take 6–12 months before market behavior responds to monetary policy. It took at least that long before investors and consumers responded to the monetary stimulus of 2001–2.

IN THE NEWS

Lag Time Is a Variable to Watch in Fed Rate Cut

NEW YORK—Here is a New Economy paradox: Thanks to the increasingly free flow of information, it takes less time than ever for companies and individuals to adjust to changes in the economy. Yet shifts in monetary policy, while perhaps having a faster impact than in the past, can still take between six and 12 months to make their presence really felt.

"We're not going to see growth any stronger tomorrow than it was yesterday," says Bruce Steinberg, chief economist at Merrill Lynch & Co. In fact, he says, "It is going to be the second half of the year at the soonest," before the economy feels the full impact of the half percentage-point decline in interest rates that the Federal Reserve pushed through on Wednesday.

Why such a long lag? Economists say that makets and information may be traveling at supercharged speeds, but simple decisions about how to invest in stocks, whether to buy a new home and when's the right time to upgrade business equipment, travel at very human speeds—and can take months to play out.

—Jon E. Hilsenrath

Source: *The Wall Street Journal,* January 5, 2000.

Analysis: It takes time for consumers and businesses to develop and implement new loan and expenditure decisions. This creates a time lag for monetary-policy effects.

Limits on Monetary Restraint

Expectations. Time lags and expectations could also limit the effectiveness of monetary restraint. In pursuit of "tight" money, the Fed could drain bank reserves and force interest rates higher. Yet market participants might continue to borrow and spend if high expectations for rising sales and profits overwhelm high interest rates in investment decisions. Consumers too might believe that future incomes will be sufficient to cover larger debts and higher interest charges. Both groups might foresee accelerating inflation that would make even high interest rates look cheap in the future. This was apparently the case in Britain in 2004, as the World View below documents.

Global Money. Market participants might also tap global sources of money. If money gets too tight in domestic markets, business may borrow funds from foreign banks or institutions. GM, Disney, ExxonMobil, and other multinational corporations can borrow funds

WORLD VIEW

Rising Rates Haven't Thwarted Consumers

THE BANK OF ENGLAND continued its tightening of monetary policy on June 10. And with the British economy still expanding at a decent clip, more hikes are on the way.

As expected by most economists, the BOE raised its lending rate by a quarter-point, to 4.5%. It was the fourth bump up since November, 2003. In explaining the move, the BOE's statement pointed to above-trend output growth, strong household, business, and public spending, as well as a labor market that "has tightened further." . . .

The BOE is the first of the world's major central banks to raise rates, but the moves have done little to curb borrowing, especially by consumers. Home buying remains robust. . . .

The easy access to credit and the strong labor markets are boosting consumer spending.

Source: *BusinessWeek,* June 28, 2004.

Analysis: Strong expectations and rising incomes may fuel continued spending even when interest rates are rising.

from foreign subsidiaries, banks, and even bond markets. As we saw in Chapter 14, market participants can also secure funds from nonbank sources in the United States. These nonbank and global lenders make it harder for the Fed to restrain aggregate demand.

How Effective? In view of all these constraints on monetary policies, some observers have concluded that monetary policy is an undependable policy lever. Keynes, for example, emphasized that monetary policy wouldn't be very effective in ending a deep recession. He believed that the combination of reluctant bankers, the liquidity trap, and low expectations would render monetary stimulus ineffective. Using monetary policy to stimulate the economy in such circumstances would be akin to "pushing on a string." Alan Greenspan came to much the same conclusion in September 1992 when he said that further Fed stimulus would be ineffective in accelerating a recovery from the 1990–91 recession. He believed, however, that earlier cuts in interest rates would help stimulate spending once banks, investors, and consumers gained confidence in the economic outlook. The same kind of problem existed in 2001: The Fed's actions to reduce interest rates (11 times in as many months!) weren't enough to propel the economy forward in 2001–2. Market participants had to recover their confidence in the future before they would start spending "cheap" money. When that happened, the market response was strong (see News, page 293).

The limitations on monetary restraint aren't considered as serious. The Fed has the power to reduce the money supply. If the money supply shrinks far enough, the rate of spending will have to slow down.

THE MONETARIST PERSPECTIVE

The Keynesian view of money emphasizes the role of interest rates in fulfilling the goals of monetary policy. ***In the Keynesian model, changes in the money supply affect macro outcomes primarily through changes in interest rates.*** The three-step sequence of (1) money supply change, (2) interest rate movement, and (3) aggregate demand shift makes monetary policy subject to several potential uncertainties. As we've seen, the economy doesn't always respond as expected to Fed policy.

An alternative view of monetary policy seizes on those occasional failures to offer another explanation of how the money supply affects macro outcomes. The so-called monetarist school dismisses changes in short-term interest rates (e.g., the federal funds rate) as unpredictable and ineffective. They don't think real output levels are affected by monetary stimulus. As they see it, only the price level is affected by Fed policy, and then only by changes in the money supply. Monetarists conclude that monetary policy isn't an effective tool for fighting short-run business cycles, but it is a powerful tool for managing inflation.

The Equation of Exchange

Monetarists assert that the potential of monetary policy can be expressed in a simple equation called the **equation of exchange,** written as

$$MV = PQ$$

where M refers to the quantity of money in circulation and V to its **velocity** of circulation. Total spending in the economy is equal to the average price (P) of goods times the quantity (Q) of goods sold in a period. This spending is financed by the supply of money (M) times the velocity of its circulation (V).

equation of exchange: Money supply (M) times velocity of circulation (V) equals level of aggregate spending ($P \times Q$).

income velocity of money (V): The number of times per year, on average, a dollar is used to purchase final goods and services; $PQ \div M$.

Suppose, for example, that only two participants are in the market and that the money supply consists of one crisp $20 bill. What's the limit to total spending in this case? If you answer "$20," you haven't yet grasped the nature of the circular flow. Suppose I begin the circular flow by spending $20 on eggs, bacon, and a gallon of milk. The money I spend ends up in Farmer Brown's pocket because he is the only other market participant. Once in possession of the money, Farmer Brown may decide to satisfy his long-smoldering desire to learn something about economics and buy one of my books. If he acts on that decision, the \$20 will return to me. At that point, both Farmer Brown and I have sold \$20 worth of goods. Hence, \$40 of total spending has been financed with one \$20 bill.

As long as we keep using this \$20 bill to buy goods and services from each other, we can continue to do business. Moreover, the faster we pass the money from hand to hand during any period of time, the greater the value of sales each of us can register. If the money is passed from hand to hand eight times, then I'll be able to sell \$80 worth of textbooks and Farmer Brown will be able to sell \$80 worth of produce during that period, for a total nominal output of \$160. ***The quantity of money in circulation and the velocity with which it travels (changes hands) in product markets will always be equal to the value of total spending and income (nominal GDP).*** The relationship is summarized as

$$M \times V = P \times Q$$

In this case, the *equation of exchange* confirms that

$$\$20 \times 8 = \$160$$

The value of total sales for the year is \$160.

Monetarists use the equation of exchange to simplify the explanation of how monetary policy works. There's no need, they argue, to follow the effects of changes in M through the money markets to interest rates and further to changes in total spending. The basic consequences of monetary policy are evident in the equation of exchange. The two sides of the equation of exchange must always be in balance. Hence, we can be absolutely certain that ***if* M *increases, prices* (P) *or output* (Q) *must rise, or* V *must fall.***

The equation of exchange is an incontestable statement of how the money supply is related to macro outcomes. The equation itself, however, says nothing about *which* variables will respond to a change in the money supply. The *goal* of monetary policy is to change the macro outcomes on the right side of the equation. It's *possible,* however, that a change in M might be offset with a reverse change in V, leaving P and Q unaffected. Or it could happen that the *wrong* macro outcome is affected. Prices (P) might rise, for example, when we're trying to increase real output (Q).

Stable Velocity

Monetarists add some important assumptions to transform the equation of exchange from a simple identity to a behavioral *model* of macro performance. The first assumption is that the velocity of money (V) is stable. How fast people use their money balances depends on the institutional structure of money markets and people's habits. Neither the structure of money markets nor people's habits are likely to change in the short run. Accordingly, a short-run increase in M won't be offset by a reduction in V. Instead, the impact of an increased money supply will be transmitted to the right-hand side of the equation of exchange, which means that ***total spending must rise if the money supply* (M) *grows and* V *is stable.***

Money Supply Focus

From a monetarist perspective, there's no need to trace the impacts of monetary policy through interest rate movements. The focus on interest rates is a uniquely Keynesian perspective. Monetarists claim that interest rate movements are secondary to the major thrust of monetary policy. ***As monetarists see it, changes in the money supply must alter total spending, regardless of how interest rates move.***

A monetarist perspective leads to a whole different strategy for the Fed. Because interest rates aren't part of the monetarist explanation of how monetary policy works, the Fed shouldn't try to manipulate interest rates; instead, it should focus on the money supply itself. Monetarists also argue that the Fed can't really control interest rates well since they depend on both the supply of and the demand for money. What the Fed *can* control is the supply of money, and the equation of exchange clearly shows that money matters.

"Natural" Unemployment

Some monetarists add yet another perspective to the equation of exchange. They assert that not only V but Q as well is stable. If this is true, then changes in the money supply (M) would affect only prices (P).

The Dropouts—Used by permission of Howard Post.

Analysis: If the money supply shrinks (or its growth rate slows), price levels will rise less quickly.

What does it mean for Q to be stable? The argument here is that the quantity of goods produced is primarily dependent on production capacity, labor market efficiency, and other "structural" forces. These structural forces establish a **"natural" rate of unemployment** that's fairly immune to short-run policy intervention. This is the *long-run* aggregate supply curve we first encountered in Chapter 8. From this perspective, there's no reason for producers to depart from this "natural" rate of output when the money supply increases. Producers are smart enough to know that both prices and costs will rise when spending increases. Hence, rising prices won't create any new profit incentives for increasing output. Firms will just continue producing at the "natural" rate with higher (nominal) prices and costs. As a result, increases in aggregate spending—whether financed by more M or faster V—aren't likely to alter real output levels. Q will stay constant.

natural rate of unemployment: long-term rate of unemployment determined by structural forces in labor and product markets.

If the quantity of real output is in fact stable, then P is the only thing that can change. Thus, ***the most extreme monetarist perspective concludes that changes in the money supply affect prices only.*** As the "simple economics" in the accompanying cartoon suggests, a decrease in M should directly reduce the price level. When *M increases,* total spending rises, but the higher nominal value of spending is completely absorbed by higher prices. In this view, monetary policy affects only the rate of inflation. This is the kind of money-driven inflation that bedeviled George Washington's army (see News on next page).

Figure 15.5 illustrates the extreme monetarist argument in the context of aggregate supply and demand. The assertion that real output is fixed at the natural rate of unemployment is reflected in the vertical aggregate supply curve. With real output stuck at Q^*, any increase in aggregate demand directly raises the price level.

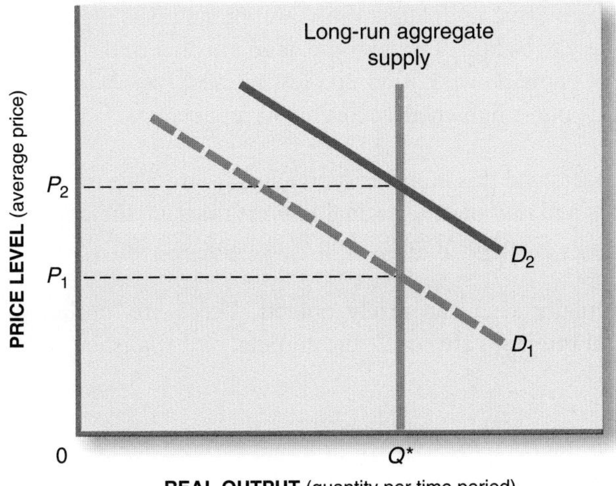

FIGURE 15.5
The Monetarist View

Monetarists argue that the rate of real output is set by structural factors. Furthermore, firms aren't likely to be fooled into producing more just because prices are rising if costs are rising just as much. Hence, long-run aggregate supply remains at the "natural" level Q^*. Any monetary-induced increases in aggregate demand, therefore, raise the price level (inflation) but not output.

IN THE NEWS

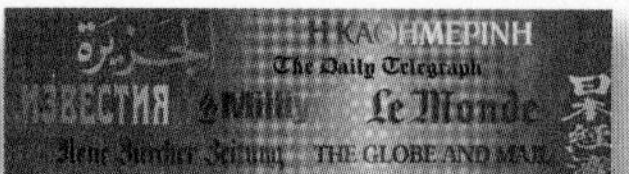

"Not Worth a Continental": The U.S. Experience with Hyperinflation

The government of the United States had no means to pay for the Revolutionary War. Specifically, the federal government had no power to levy taxes that might transfer resources from the private sector to the public sector. Instead, it could only request the states to levy taxes of their own and contribute them to the war effort. The states were not very responsive, however: state contributions accounted for only 6 percent of federal revenues during the war years.

To pay for needed weapons and soldiers, the federal government had only two other options, either (1) borrow money or (2) create new money. When loans proved to be inadequate, the Continental Congress started issuing new paper money—the "Continental" dollar—in 1775. By the end of 1779, Congress had authorized issuance of over $250 million in Continental dollars.

At first the paper money enabled George Washington's troops to acquire needed supplies, ammunition, and volunteers. But soon the flood of paper money inundated product markets. Wholesale prices of key commodities skyrocketed. Commodity prices *doubled* in 1776, in 1777, and again in 1778. Then prices increased *tenfold* in the next two years.

Many farmers and storekeepers refused to sell goods to the army in exchange for Continental dollars. Rapid inflation had taught them that the paper money George Washington's troops offered was nearly worthless. The expression "not worth a Continental" became a popular reference to things of little value.

The states tried price controls and even empowered themselves to seize needed war supplies. But nothing could stop the inflation fueled by the explosive increase in the money supply. Fortunately, the war ended before the economy collapsed. After the war, the U.S. Congress established a new form of money, and in 1787 it empowered the federal government to levy taxes and mint gold and silver coins.

—Sidney Ratner, James H. Soltow, and Richard Sylla

Source: *The Evolution of the American Economy,* 2nd ed. (1993).

Analysis: Rapid expansion of the money supply will push the price level up. As inflation accelerates, money becomes less valuable.

Monetarist Policies

At first glance, the monetarist argument looks pretty slick. Keynesians worry about how the money supply affects interest rates, how interest rates affect spending, and how spending affects output. By contrast, monetarists point to a simple equation ($MV = PQ$) that produces straightforward responses to monetary policy.

There are fundamental differences between the two schools here, not only about how the economy works but also about how successful macro policy might be. To appreciate those differences, consider monetarist responses to inflationary and recessionary gaps.

Fighting Inflation. Consider again the options for fighting inflation. The policy goal is to reduce aggregate demand. From a Keynesian perspective, the way to achieve this reduction is to shrink the money supply and drive up interest rates. But monetarists argue that nominal interest rates are already likely to be high. Furthermore, if an effective anti-inflation policy is adopted, interest rates will come *down,* not go up. Yes, interest rates will come *down,* not go up, when the money supply is tightened, according to monetarists.

Real vs. Nominal Interest. To understand this monetarist conclusion, we have to distinguish between *nominal* interest rates and *real* ones. Nominal interest rates are the ones we actually see and pay. When a bank pays 5½ percent interest on your bank account, it's quoting (and paying) a nominal rate.

real interest rate: The nominal rate of interest minus anticipated inflation rate.

Real interest rates are never actually seen and rarely quoted. These are "inflation-adjusted" rates. Specifically, the **real interest rate** equals the nominal rate *minus* the anticipated rate of inflation; that is,

$$\begin{matrix}\text{Real} \\ \text{interest} \\ \text{rate}\end{matrix} = \begin{matrix}\text{nominal} \\ \text{interest} \\ \text{rate}\end{matrix} - \begin{matrix}\text{anticipated} \\ \text{inflation} \\ \text{rate}\end{matrix}$$

Recall what inflation does to the purchasing power of the dollar: As inflation continues, each dollar purchases fewer goods and services. As a consequence, dollars borrowed today are of less real value when they're paid back later. The real rate of interest reflects this inflation adjustment.

Suppose you lend someone $100 at the beginning of the year, at 8 percent interest. You expect to get more back at the end of the year than you start with. That "more" you expect refers to *real* goods and services, not just dollar bills. Specifically, you anticipate that when the loan is repaid with interest at the end of the year, you'll be able to buy more goods and services than you could at the beginning. This expectation of a *real* gain is at least part of the reason for making a loan.

Your expected gain won't materialize, however, if all prices rise by 8 percent during the year. If the inflation rate is 8 percent, you'll discover that $108 buys you no more at the end of the year than $100 would have bought you at the beginning. Hence, you'd have given up the use of your money for an entire year without any real compensation. In such circumstances, the *real* rate of interest turns out to be zero; that is,

$$\begin{array}{c} \text{Real} \\ \text{interest} \\ \text{rate} \end{array} = \begin{array}{c} 8\%\ \text{nominal} \\ \text{interest} \\ \text{rate} \end{array} - \begin{array}{c} 8\%\ \text{inflation} \\ \text{rate} \end{array}$$

$$= 0\%$$

The nominal rate of interest, then, really has two components: (1) the real rate of interest, and (2) an inflation adjustment. If the real rate of interest was 4 percent and an inflation rate of 9 percent was expected, the nominal rate of interest would be 13 percent. If inflationary expectations *declined,* the *nominal* interest rate would *fall.* This is evident in the rearranged formula:

$$\begin{array}{c} \text{Nominal} \\ \text{interest rate} \end{array} = \begin{array}{c} \text{real} \\ \text{interest rate} \end{array} + \begin{array}{c} \text{anticipated rate} \\ \text{of inflation} \end{array}$$

If the real interest rate is 4 percent and anticipated inflation falls from 9 to 6 percent, the nominal interest rate would decline from 13 to 10 percent.

A central assumption of the monetarist perspective is that the real rate of interest is fairly stable. This is a critical point. ***If the real rate of interest is stable, then changes in the nominal interest rate reflect only changes in anticipated inflation.*** From this perspective, high nominal rates of interest are a symptom of inflation, not a cure. Indeed, high nominal rates may even look cheap if inflationary expectations are worsening faster than interest rates are rising. This was the case in Zimbabwe in 2007, when the nominal interest rate rose above 400 percent (see World View, page 139).

Consider the implications of all this for monetary policy. Suppose we want to close an inflationary GDP gap. Monetarists and Keynesians alike agree that a reduced money supply (M) will deflate total spending. But Keynesians rely on a "quick fix" of *higher* interest rates to slow consumption and investment spending. Monetarists, by contrast, assert that nominal interest rates will *fall* if the Fed tightens the money supply. Once market participants are convinced that the Fed is going to reduce money supply growth, inflationary expectations diminish. When inflationary expectations diminish, nominal interest rates will begin to fall.

webnote

To get a global view of how interest rates and inflation move together, visit Australia (their central bank) at www.rba.gov.au

Short- vs. Long-Term Rates (again). The monetarist argument helps resolve the "conundrum" that puzzled former Fed Chairman Alan Greenspan, that is, the contradictory movements of short-term and long-term interest rates. As we observed earlier, short-run rates (like the federal funds rate) are very responsive to Fed intervention. But long-term rates are much slower to respond. This suggests that banks and borrowers look beyond current economic conditions in making long-term financial commitments.

If the Fed is reducing money-supply growth, short-term rates may rise quickly. But long-term rates won't increase unless market participants expect inflation to worsen. Given the pivotal role of long-term rates in investment decisions, the Fed may have to stall GDP growth—even spark a recession—to restrain aggregate demand enough to stop prices from rising. Rather than take such risks, ***monetarists advocate steady and predictable changes in the money supply.*** Such a policy, they believe, would reduce uncertainties and thus stabilize both long-term interest rates and GDP growth.

Fighting Unemployment. The link between anticipated inflation and nominal interest rates also constrains expansionary monetary policy. The Keynesian cure for a recession is to expand M and lower interest rates. But monetarists fear that an increase in M will lead—via the equation of exchange—to higher P. If everyone believed this would happen, then an unexpectedly large increase in M would immediately raise people's inflationary expectations. Even if short-term interest rates fell, long-term interest rates might actually rise. This would defeat the purpose of monetary stimulus.

From a monetarist perspective, expansionary monetary policies aren't likely to lead us out of a recession. On the contrary, such policies might heap inflation problems on top of our unemployment woes. All monetary policy should do, say the monetarists, is ensure a stable and predictable rate of growth in the money supply. Then people could concentrate on real production decisions without worrying so much about fluctuating prices.

THE CONCERN FOR CONTENT

Monetary policy, like fiscal policy, can affect more than just the *level* of total spending. We must give some consideration to the impact of Federal Reserve actions on the *content* of the GDP if we're going to be responsive to the "second crisis" of economic theory.[1]

The Mix of Output

Both Keynesians and monetarists agree that monetary policy will affect nominal interest rates. When interest rates change, not all spending decisions will be affected equally. High interest rates don't deter consumers from buying pizzas, but they do deter purchases of homes, cars, and other big-ticket items typically financed with loans. Hence, the housing and auto industries bear a disproportionate burden of restrictive monetary policy. Accordingly, when the Fed pursues a policy of tight money—high interest rates and limited lending capacity—it not only restrains total spending but reduces the share of housing and autos in that spending. Utility industries, public works projects, and state and local finances are also disproportionately impacted by monetary policy.

In addition to altering the content of demand and output, monetary policy affects the competitive structure of the market. When money is tight, banks must ration available credit among loan applicants. Large and powerful corporations aren't likely to run out of credit because banks will be hesitant to incur their displeasure and lose their business. Thus, General Motors and IBM stand a much better chance of obtaining tight money than does the corner grocery store. Moreover, if bank lending capacity becomes too small, GM and IBM can always resort to the bond market and borrow money directly from the public. Small businesses seldom have such an alternative.

Income Redistribution

Monetary policy also affects the distribution of income. When interest rates fall, borrowers pay smaller interest charges. On the other hand, lenders get smaller interest payments. Hence, a lower interest rate redistributes income from lenders to borrowers. When interest rates declined sharply in 2001–4, homeowners refinanced their mortgages and saved billions of dollars in interest payments (News, page 293). The decline in interest rates, however, *reduced* the income of retired persons, who depend heavily on interest payments from certificates of deposit, bonds, and other assets.

[1]See the quotation from Joan Robinson in Chapter 11, calling attention to the exclusive focus of economists on the *level* of economic activity (the "first crisis"), to the neglect of content (the "second crisis").

THE ECONOMY TOMORROW

WHICH LEVER TO PULL?

Our success in managing the macro economy of tomorrow depends on pulling the right policy levers at the right time. But which levers should be pulled? Keynesians and monetarists offer very different prescriptions for treating an ailing economy. Can we distill some usable policy guidelines from this discussion for policy decisions in the economy tomorrow?

The Policy Tools. The equation of exchange is a convenient summary of the differences between Keynesian and monetarist perspectives. There's no disagreement about the equation itself: Aggregate spending ($M \times V$) *must* equal the value of total sales ($P \times Q$). ***What Keynesians and monetarists argue about is which of the policy tools—M or V—is likely to be effective in altering aggregate spending.***

- ***Monetarists*** point to changes in the money supply (M) as the principal lever of macroeconomic policy. They assume V is reasonably stable.
- ***Keynesian*** fiscal policy *must* rely on changes in the velocity of money (V) because tax and expenditure policies have no direct impact on the money supply.

Crowding Out. The extreme monetarist position that *only* money matters is based on the assumption that the velocity of money (V) is constant. ***If V is constant, changes in total spending can come about only through changes in the money supply.*** There are no other policy tools on the left side of the equation of exchange.

Think about an increase in government spending designed to stimulate the economy. How does the government pay for this fiscal policy stimulus? Monetarists argue that there are only two ways to pay for this increased expenditure (G): The government must either raise additional taxes or borrow more money. If the government raises taxes, the disposable income of consumers will be reduced, and private spending will fall. On the other hand, if the government borrows more money to pay for its expenditures, there will be less money available for loans to private consumers and investors. In either case, more government spending (G) implies less private spending (C or I). Thus, *increased* G effectively **"crowds out"** some C or I, leaving total spending unchanged. From this viewpoint, fiscal policy is ineffective; it can't even shift the aggregate demand curve. At best, fiscal policy can change the composition of demand and thus the mix of output. Only changes in M (monetary policy) can shift the aggregate demand curve.

crowding out: A reduction in private-sector borrowing (and spending) caused by increased government borrowing.

Milton Friedman, formerly of the University of Chicago, championed the monetarist view with this argument:

> I believe that the state of the government budget matters; matters a great deal—for some things. The state of the government budget determines what fraction of the nation's income is spent through the government and what fraction is spent by individuals privately. The state of the government budget determines what the level of our taxes is, how much of our income we turn over to the government. The state of the government budget has a considerable effect on interest rates. If the federal government runs a large deficit, that means the government has to borrow in the market, which raises the demand for loanable funds and so tends to raise interest rates.
>
> If the government budget shifts to a surplus, that adds to the supply of loanable funds, which tends to lower interest rates. It was no surprise to those of us who stress money that enactment of the surtax was followed by a decline in interest rates. That's precisely what we had predicted and what our analysis leads us to predict. But—and I come to the main point—in my opinion, the state of the budget by itself has no significant effect on the course of nominal income, on inflation, on deflation, or on cyclical fluctuations.[2]

[2]Milton Friedman and Walter W. Heller, *Monetary vs. Fiscal Policy* (New York: Norton, 1969), pp. 50–51.

Keynesians reply that the alleged constant velocity of money is a monetarist's pipe dream. Some even argue that the velocity of money is so volatile that changes in *V* can completely offset changes in *M,* leaving us with the proposition that money doesn't matter.

The liquidity trap illustrates the potential for *V* to change. Keynes argued that people tend to accumulate money balances—slow their rate of spending—during recessions. A slowdown in spending implies a reduction in the velocity of money. Indeed, in the extreme case of the liquidity trap, the velocity of money falls toward zero. Under these circumstances, changes in *M* (monetary policy) won't influence total spending. The velocity of money falls as rapidly as *M* increases. On the other hand, increased government spending (fiscal policy) can stimulate aggregate spending by putting idle money balances to work (thereby increasing *V*). Changes in fiscal policy will also influence consumer and investor expectations, and thereby further alter the rate of aggregate spending.

How Fiscal Policy Works: Two Views. Tables 15.2 and 15.3 summarize these different perspectives on fiscal and monetary policy. The first table evaluates fiscal policy from both Keynesian and monetarist viewpoints. The central issue is whether and how a change in government spending (*G*) or taxes (*T*) will alter macroeconomic outcomes. Keynesians assert that aggregate demand will be affected as the velocity of money (*V*) changes. Monetarists say no, because they anticipate an unchanged *V.*

If aggregate demand isn't affected by a change in *G* or *T,* then fiscal policy won't affect prices (*P*) or real output (*Q*). Thus, monetarists conclude that fiscal policy isn't a viable tool for combating either inflation or unemployment. By contrast, Keynesians believe *V will* change and that output and prices will respond accordingly.

Insofar as interest rates are concerned, monetarists recognize that nominal interest rates will be affected (read Friedman's quote again) but *real* rates won't be. Real interest rates depend on real output and growth, both of which are seen as immune to fiscal policy. Keynesians see less impact on nominal interest rates and more on real interest rates.

What all this boils down to is this: Fiscal policy, by itself, will be effective only if it can alter the velocity of money. ***How well fiscal policy works depends on how much the velocity of money can be changed by government tax and spending decisions.***

How Monetary Policy Works: Two Views. Table 15.3 offers a similar summary of monetary policy. This time the positions of monetarists and Keynesians are reversed, or nearly so. Monetarists say a change in *M* must alter total spending ($P \times Q$) because *V* is stable. Keynesians assert that *V* may vary, so they aren't convinced that monetary policy

TABLE 15.2
How Fiscal Policy Matters: Monetarist vs. Keynesian Views

Monetarists and Keynesians have very different views on the impact of fiscal policy. Monetarists assert that changes in government spending (*G*) and taxes (*T*) don't alter the velocity of money (*V*). As a result, fiscal policy alone can't alter total spending. Keynesians reject this view, arguing that *V* is changeable. They claim that tax cuts and increased government spending increase the velocity of money and so alter total spending.

Do Changes in *G* or *T* Affect:	Monetarist View	Keynesian View
1. Aggregate demand?	No (stable *V* causes crowding out)	Yes (*V* changes)
2. Prices?	No (aggregate demand not affected)	Maybe (if at capacity)
3. Real output?	No (aggregate demand not affected)	Yes (output responds to demand)
4. Nominal interest rates?	Yes (crowding out)	Maybe (may alter demand for money)
5. Real interest rates?	No (determined by real growth)	Yes (real growth and expectations may vary)

Do Changes in M Affect:	Monetarist View	Keynesian View
1. Aggregate demand?	Yes (V stable)	Maybe (V may change)
2. Prices?	Yes (V and Q stable)	Maybe (V and Q may change)
3. Real output?	No (rate of unemployment determined by structural forces)	Maybe (output responds to demand)
4. Nominal interest rates?	Yes (but direction unknown)	Maybe (liquidity trap)
5. Real interest rates?	No (depends on real growth)	Maybe (real growth may vary)

TABLE 15.3
How Money Matters: Monetarist vs. Keynesian Views

Because monetarists believe that V is stable, they assert that changes in the money supply (M) must alter total spending. But all the monetary impact is reflected in prices and nominal interest rates; *real* output and interest rates are unaffected.

Keynesians think that V is variable and thus that changes in M might *not* alter total spending. If monetary policy does alter aggregate spending, however, Keynesians expect all outcomes to be affected.

will always work. The heart of the controversy is again the velocity of money. Monetary policy works as long as V is stable, or at least predictable. ***How well monetary policy works depends on how stable or predictable* V *is.***

Once the central role of velocity is understood, everything else falls into place. Monetarists assert that prices but not output will be directly affected by a change in M because the right-hand side of the equation of exchange contains only two variables (P and Q), and one of them (Q) is assumed unaffected by monetary policy. Keynesians, by contrast, aren't so sure prices will be affected by M or that real output won't be. It all depends on V and the responsiveness of P and Q to changes in aggregate spending.

Finally, monetarists predict that nominal interest rates will respond to changes in M, although they're not sure in what direction. It depends on how inflationary expectations adapt to changes in the money supply. Keynesian economists aren't so sure nominal interest rates will change but are sure about the direction if they do.

Is Velocity Stable? Tables 15.2 and 15.3 highlight the velocity of money as a critical determinant of policy impact. The critical question appears to be whether V is stable. Why hasn't someone answered this simple question and resolved the debate over fiscal versus monetary policy?

Long-Run Stability. The velocity of money (V) turns out, in fact, to be quite stable over long periods of time. Over the past 30 years the velocity of money (M2) has averaged about 1.64, as Figure 15.6 illustrates. Moreover, the range of velocity has been fairly narrow, extending from a low of 1.56 in 1987 to a high of 2.05 in 1997. Monetarists conclude that the historical pattern justifies the assumption of a stable V.

Short-Run Instability. Keynesians reply that monetarists are farsighted and so fail to see significant short-run variations in V. The difference between a velocity of 1.56 and velocity of 2.05 translates into hundreds of billions of dollars in aggregate demand. Moreover, there's a pattern to short-run variations in V: Velocity tends to decline in recessions (see Figure 15.6). These are precisely the situations in which fiscal stimulus (increasing V) would be appropriate.

Money Supply Targets The differing views of Keynesians and monetarists clearly lead to different conclusions about which policy lever to pull.

Monetarist Advice. The monetarists' policy advice to the Fed is straightforward. ***Monetarists favor fixed money supply targets.*** They believe that V is stable in the long run and unpredictable in the short run. Hence, the safest course of action is to focus on M. All the Fed has to do is announce its intention to increase the money supply by some fixed amount

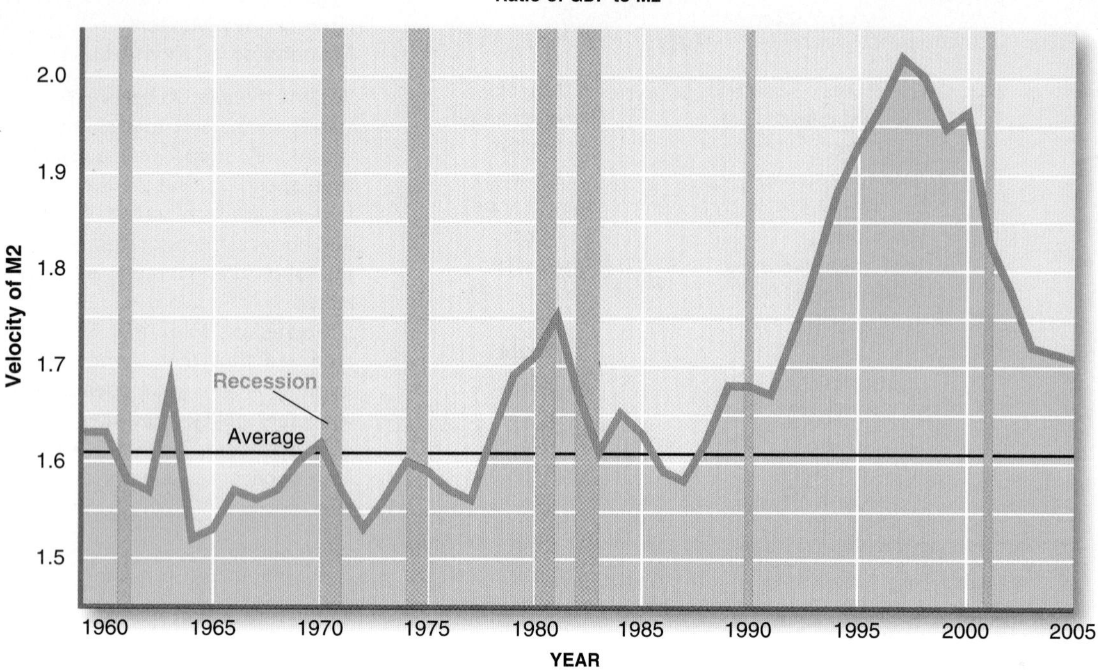

FIGURE 15.6
The Velocity of M2

The velocity of money (the ratio of GDP to M2) averages about 1.64. However, *V* appears to decline in recessions. Keynes urged the use of fiscal stimulus to boost *V*. Monetarists caution that short-run changes in *V* are too unpredictable.

Source: Federal Reserve.

(such as 3 percent per year), then use its central banking powers to hit that money growth target. After rock-bottom interest rates failed to ignite the Japanese economy, the Bank of Japan decided to adopt the monetarist approach in 2001 (see World View).

Interest Rate Targets. Keynesian Advice. ***Keynesians reject fixed money supply targets,*** favoring more flexibility in control of the money supply. In their view, a fixed money supply target would render monetary policy useless in combating cyclical swings of the economy. Keynesians prefer the risks of occasional policy errors to the straitjacket of a fixed money supply target. ***Keynesians advocate targeting interest rates, not the money supply.*** Keynesians also advocate liberal use of the fiscal policy lever.

Inflation Targeting. In the past, the Fed has tried both monetarist and Keynesian strategies for managing aggregate demand, depending on the needs of the economy and the convictions of the Fed chairman. The current chairman, Ben Bernanke, isn't committed to either the monetarist or Keynesian perspective. Instead, he tries to walk a thin line between these perspectives. Like his predecessors, Bernanke believes that price stability is the Fed's primary goal. So long as inflation stays below a certain benchmark, there is no reason for the Fed to adjust its policy levers—autopilot will do just fine. When inflation rises above the inflation "target" (currently, 2–3 percent), however, the Fed must mobilize its policy tools.

inflation targeting: The use of an inflation ceiling ("target") to signal the need for monetary-policy adjustments.

What market participants like about this **inflation targeting** strategy is that it appears to offer greater predictability about whether and how the Fed will act. Critics point out, though, that *future* inflation, not *past* inflation is the central policy concern. Because today's price movements may or may not be precursors of future inflation, the decision to pull monetary levers is still a judgment call. Former Chairman Alan Greenspan recognized this when he said, "The Federal Reserve specializes in precision guesswork." As Fed Chairman Bernanke peers into the economy tomorrow, he will certainly need that same skill.

WORLD VIEW

Deflation Still Haunts the Bank of Japan

Critics Say Pledge to Raise a Money-Supply Target Hasn't Produced Results

TOKYO—The Japanese central bank, which had raised hopes it would try to reflate the nation's weak economy, again faces mounting criticism that it is failing to fight the demon of deflation.

The Bank of Japan said in March it would start aiming for a higher money supply, departing from the ordinary practice of targeting a key interest rate, to ease the price declines hammering Japanese companies. . . .

In March, the bank unveiled a policy dubbed "quantitative easing," saying it would begin targeting increases in a part of the money supply—the reserve funds that private-sector banks keep at the Bank of Japan—starting with a boost to five trillion yen ($40.48 billion) from four trillion yen. The bank also said it would increase its outright purchases of long-term Japanese government bonds if necessary to top up the money supply.

—Michael Williams

Source: *The Wall Street Journal,* August 9, 2001.

Analysis: When low (near zero) interest rates failed to spark an economy recovery, the Bank of Japan focused on increases in the money supply. Their goal was to keep the price level (*P*) from falling.

SUMMARY

- The essence of monetary policy lies in the Federal Reserve's control over the money supply. By altering the money supply, the Fed can determine the amount of purchasing power available. LO1
- There are sharp disagreements about how monetary policy works. Keynesians argue that monetary policy works indirectly, through its effects on interest rates and spending. Monetarists assert that monetary policy has more direct and more certain impacts, particularly on price levels. LO3
- In the Keynesian view, the demand for money is important. This demand reflects desires to hold money (in cash or bank balances) for transactions, precautionary, and speculative purposes. The interaction of money supply and money demand determines the equilibrium rate of interest. LO1
- From a Keynesian perspective, the impact of monetary policy on the economy occurs in three distinct steps: (1) changes in the money supply alter interest rates; (2) changes in interest rates alter the rate of expenditure; and (3) the change in desired expenditure alters (shifts) aggregate demand. LO1
- For Keynesian monetary policy to be fully effective, interest rates must be responsive to changes in the money supply, and spending must be responsive to changes in interest rates. Neither condition is assured. In a liquidity trap, people are willing to hold unlimited amounts of money at some low rate of interest. The interest rate won't fall below this level as the money supply increases. Also, investor expectations of sales and profits may override interest rate considerations in the investment decision. LO2
- Fed policy has the most direct impact on short-term interest rates, particularly the overnight federal funds rate. Long-term rates are less responsive to open market operations. LO2
- The monetarist school emphasizes long-term linkages. Using the equation of exchange ($MV = PQ$) as a base, monetarists assert that the velocity of money (V) is stable, so that changes in M must influence ($P \times Q$). Monetarists focus on the money supply; Keynesians, on interest rates. LO3
- Some monetarists also argue that the level of real output (Q) is set by structural forces, as illustrated by the vertical, long-run aggregate supply curve. Q is therefore insensitive to changes in aggregate spending. If both V and Q are constant, changes in M directly affect P. LO1
- Monetary policy attempts to influence total expenditure by changing M and will be fully effective only if V is constant. Fiscal policy attempts to influence total expenditure by changing V and will be fully effective only if M doesn't change in the opposite direction. The controversy over the effectiveness of fiscal versus monetary policy depends on whether the velocity of money (V) is stable or instead is subject to policy influence. LO3
- The velocity of money is more stable over long periods of time than over short periods. Keynesians conclude that this makes fiscal policy more powerful in the short run. Monetarists conclude that the unpredictability of short-run velocity makes any short-run policy risky. LO3
- Inflation targeting signals Fed intervention when inflation rises above a policy-set ceiling ("target"), currently 2–3 percent. LO1

Key Terms

monetary policy
interest rate
money supply (M1, M2)
demand for money
portfolio decision
transactions demand for money
precautionary demand for money
speculative demand for money
equilibrium rate of interest
federal funds rate
aggregate demand
liquidity trap
equation of exchange
income velocity of money (*V*)
natural rate of unemployment
real interest rate
crowding out
inflation targeting

Questions for Discussion

1. What proportions of your money balance are held for transactions, precautionary, and speculative purposes? Can you think of any other purposes for holding money? LO1
2. Why do high interest rates so adversely affect the demand for housing and yet have so little influence on the demand for pizzas? LO1
3. If the Federal Reserve banks mailed everyone a brand-new $100 bill, what would happen to prices, output, and income? Illustrate your answer by using the equation of exchange. LO1
4. Can there be any inflation without an increase in the money supply? How? LO3
5. How might the existence of multiplier effects increase the risk of inflation when interest rates are cut? LO1
6. When prices started doubling (see News, page 302), why didn't the Continental Congress print even *more* money so Washington's army could continue to buy supplies? What brings an end to such "inflation financing"? LO3
7. Could long-term interest rates rise when short-term rates are falling? What would cause such a pattern? LO3
8. In the News on page 293, what starts the multiplier process? When will it stop? LO1
9. Why were banks reluctant to use their lending capacity in 2001? (See News, page 295.) What did they do with their increased reserves? LO2
10. How did the Bank of Japan hope to increase the money supply in 2001? (See World View, page 309.) If *M* did increase, would the economy necessarily recover? LO2
11. Does inflation targeting resolve uncertainties about Fed policy? LO1

problems The Student Problem Set at the back of this book contains numerical and graphing problems for this chapter.

web activities to accompany this chapter can be found on the Online Learning Center:
http://www.mhhe.com/economics/schiller11e

Supply-Side Options

Fiscal and monetary policies attempt to alter macro outcomes by managing aggregate demand. Supply-side policies focus instead on possibilities for shifting the aggregate *supply* curve. In the short run, any increase in aggregate supply promotes more output and less inflation. Supply-siders also emphasize how rightward shifts of aggregate supply are critical to long-run economic growth. Chapter 16 focuses on short-run supply-side options; Chapter 17 takes the long-run view.

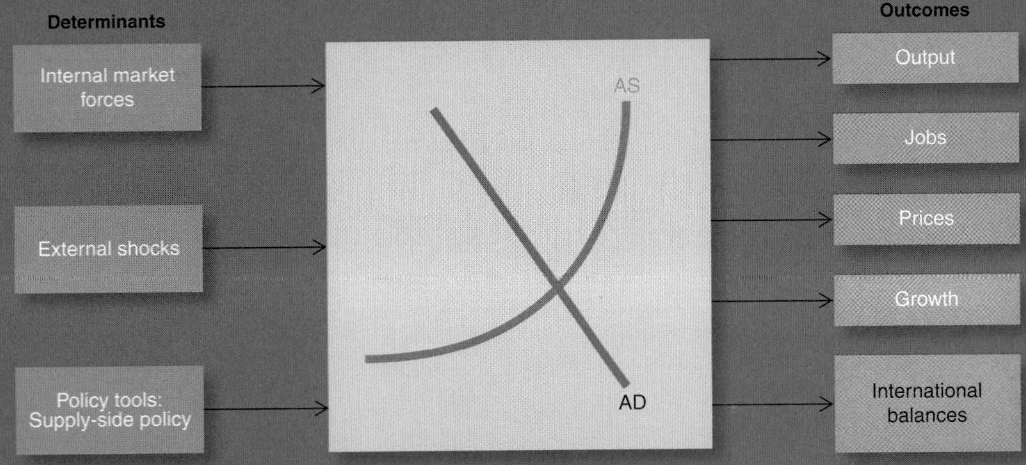

Supply-Side Policy: Short-Run Options

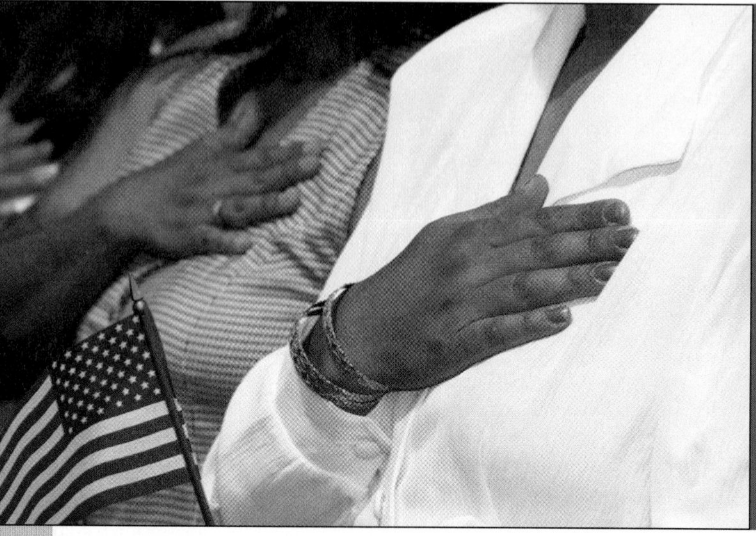

LEARNING OBJECTIVES

After reading this chapter, you should know:

LO1. Why the short-run AS curve slopes upward.

LO2. How an unemployment-inflation trade-off arises.

LO3. The tools of supply-side policy.

Fiscal and monetary policies focus on the *demand* side of the macro economy. The basic premise of both approaches is that macro goals can be achieved by shifting the aggregate demand curve. The aggregate demand curve isn't the only game in town, however; there's an aggregate supply curve as well. Why not focus instead on possibilities for shifting the aggregate *supply* curve?

Any policies that alter the willingness or ability to supply goods at various price levels will shift the aggregate supply curve. This chapter identifies some of those policy options and examines how they affect macro outcomes. The focus is on two questions:

- **How does the aggregate supply curve affect macro outcomes?**
- **How can the aggregate supply curve be shifted?**

As we'll see, the aggregate supply curve plays a critical role in determining how difficult it is to achieve the goals of full employment and price stability.

AGGREGATE SUPPLY

The impetus for examining the supply side of the macro economy sprang up in the stagflation of the 1970s. **Stagflation** occurs when both unemployment *and* inflation increase at the same time. From 1973 to 1974, for example, consumer price inflation surged from 8.7 to 12.3 percent. At the same time, the unemployment rate jumped from 4.9 to 5.6 percent. How could this happen? ***No shift of the aggregate demand curve can increase inflation and unemployment at the same time.*** If aggregate demand increases (shifts right), the price level may rise but unemployment should decline with increased output. If aggregate demand decreases (shifts left), inflation should subside but unemployment increase. In other words, most demand-side theories predict that inflation and unemployment move in *opposite* directions in the short run. When this didn't happen, an alternative explanation was sought. The explanation was found on the supply side of the macro economy. Two critical clues were (1) the shape of the **aggregate supply** curve and (2) potential AS shifts.

stagflation: The simultaneous occurrence of substantial unemployment and inflation.

aggregate supply: The total quantity of output producers are willing and able to supply at alternative price levels in a given time period, *ceteris paribus.*

SHAPE OF THE AS CURVE

As we've seen, the basic short-run objective of fiscal and monetary policy is to attain full employment and price stability. The strategy is to shift the aggregate demand curve to a more favorable position. Now the question turns to the *response* of producers to an aggregate demand shift. Will they increase real output? Raise prices? Or some combination of both?

The answer depends on the shape of the aggregate supply curve: ***The response of producers to an AD shift is expressed in the slope and position of the aggregate supply curve.*** Until now we've used a generally upward-sloping AS curve to depict aggregate supply. Now we'll consider a range of different supply responses.

Three Views of AS

Figure 16.1 illustrates three very different supply behaviors.

Keynesian AS. Part (*a*) depicts what we've called the "naive" Keynesian view. Recall that Keynes was primarily concerned with the problem of unemployment. He didn't think there was much risk of inflation in the depths of a recession. He expected producers to increase output, not prices, when aggregate demand expanded. This expectation is illustrated by a *horizontal* AS curve. When fiscal or monetary stimulus shifts the AD curve rightward, output (Q) rises but not the price level (P). Only when capacity (Q^*) is reached do prices start rising abruptly.

Monetarist AS. The monetarist view of supply behavior is very different. In the most extreme monetarist view, real output remains at its "natural" rate, regardless of fiscal or monetary interventions. Rising prices don't entice producers to increase output because costs are likely to rise just as fast. They instead make output decisions based on more fundamental factors like technology and market size. The AS curve is *vertical* because output doesn't respond to changing price levels. (This is the long-run AS curve we first encountered in Chapter 8.) With a vertical AS curve, only prices can respond to a shift in aggregate demand. In Figure 16.1*b,* the AS curve is anchored at the natural rate of unemployment Q_N. When aggregate demand increases from AD_4 to AD_5, the price level (P) rises, but output (Q) is unchanged.

Hybrid AS. Figure 16.1*c* blends these Keynesian and monetarist perspectives into a hybrid AS curve. At low rates of output, the curve is nearly horizontal; at high rates of output, the AS curve becomes nearly vertical. In the broad middle of the AS curve, the curve slopes gently upward. In this area, shifts of aggregate demand affect *both* prices and output. The message of this hybrid AS curve is that the outcomes of fiscal and monetary policy depend on how close the economy is to full employment. ***The closer we are to capacity, the greater the risk that fiscal or monetary stimulus will spill over into price inflation.***

FIGURE 16.1
Contrasting Views of Aggregate Supply

(*a*) Keynesian AS In the simple Keynesian model, the rate of output responds fully and automatically to increases in demand until full employment (Q^*) is reached. If demand increases from AD_1 to AD_2, equilibrium GDP will expand from Q_1 to Q^*, without any inflation. Inflation becomes a problem only if demand increases beyond capacity—to AD_3, for example.

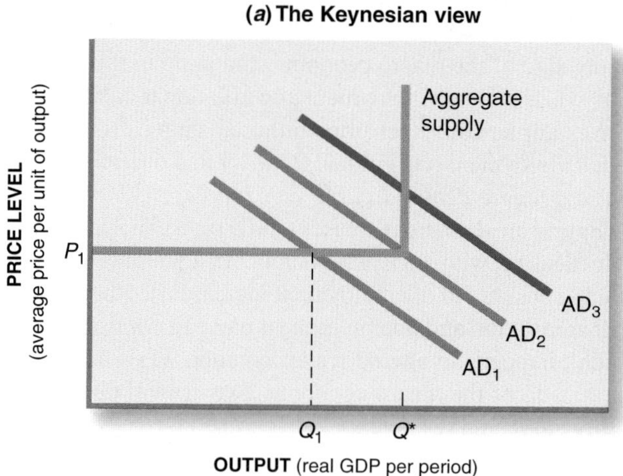

(*b*) Monetarist AS Monetarists assert that changes in the money supply affect prices but not output. They regard aggregate supply as a fixed quantum, at the long-run, natural rate of unemployment (here noted as Q_N). Accordingly, a shift of demand (from AD_4 to AD_5) can affect only the price level (from P_4 to P_5).

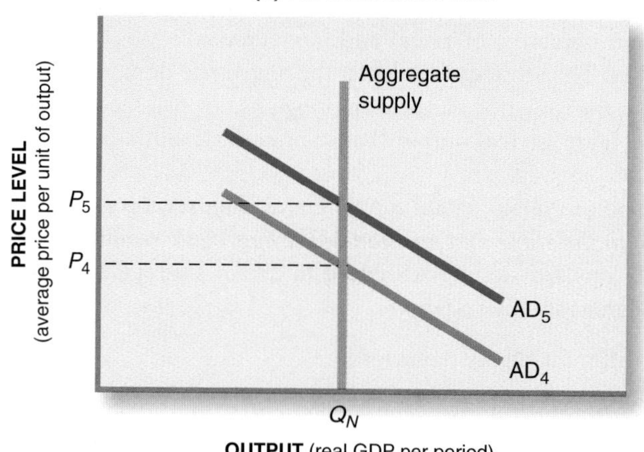

(*c*) Hybrid AS The consensus view incorporates Keynesian and monetarist perspectives but emphasizes the upward slope that dominates the middle of the AS curve. When demand increases, both price levels and the rate of output increase. Hence, the slope and position of the AS curve limit the effectiveness of fiscal and monetary policies.

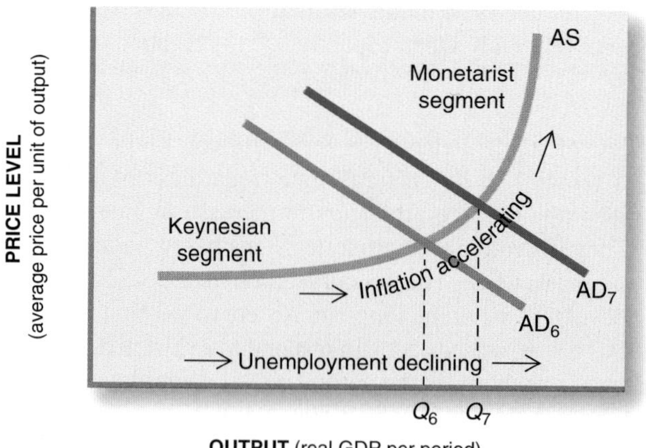

The Inflation-Unemployment Trade-Off

Because Figure 16.1*c* allows for varying output/price responses at different levels of economic activity, that AS curve is regarded as the most realistic for short-run outcomes. However, the upward-sloping section of the AS curve in Figure 16.1*c* has some disturbing implications. Because both prices and output respond to demand-side shifts, the economy can't reduce both unemployment and inflation at the same time—at least not with fiscal

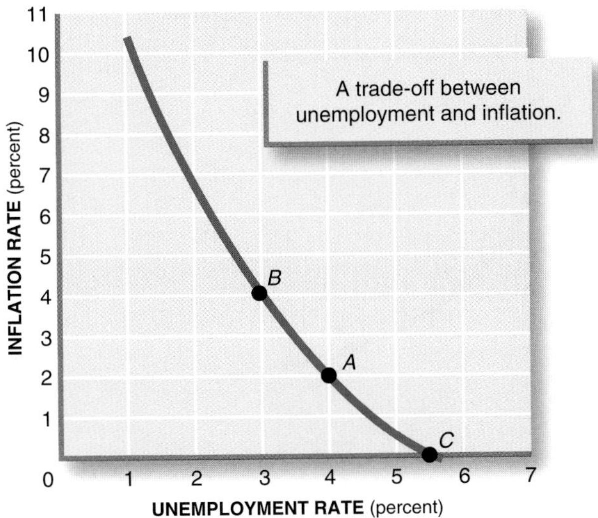

FIGURE 16.2
The Phillips Curve

The Phillips curve illustrates a trade-off between full employment and price stability. In the 1960s it appeared that efforts to reduce unemployment rates below 5.5 percent (point *C*) led to increasing rates of inflation (points *A* and *B*). Inflation threatened to reach unacceptable heights long before everyone was employed.

and monetary policies. To see why this is the case, consider the simple geometry of policy stimulus and restraint.

Demand Stimulus. Monetary and fiscal stimulus shift the aggregate demand curve rightward. This demand-side effect is evident in all three graphs in Figure 16.1. However, ***all rightward shifts of the aggregate demand curve increase both prices and output if the aggregate supply curve is upward-sloping.*** This implies that fiscal and monetary efforts to reduce unemployment will also cause some inflation.

Demand Restraint. Monetary and fiscal restraint shift the aggregate demand curve leftward. ***If the aggregate supply curve is upward-sloping, leftward shifts of the aggregate demand curve cause both prices and output to fall.*** Therefore, fiscal and monetary efforts to reduce inflation will also increase unemployment.

The Phillips Curve. The message of the upward-sloping aggregate supply curve is clear: ***Demand-side policies alone can never succeed completely; they'll always cause some unwanted inflation or unemployment.***

Our macro track record provides ample evidence of this dilemma. Consider, for example, our experience with unemployment and inflation during the 1960s, as shown in Figure 16.2. This figure shows a **Phillips curve,** indicating that prices (*P*) generally started rising before the objective of expanded output (*Q*) had been completely attained. Inflation struck before full employment was reached.

Phillips curve: A historical (inverse) relationship between the rate of unemployment and the rate of inflation; commonly expresses a trade-off between the two.

The Phillips curve was developed by a New Zealand economist, Alban W. Phillips, to summarize the relationship between unemployment and inflation in England for the years 1826–1957.[1] The Phillips curve was raised from the status of an obscure graph to that of a policy issue by the discovery that the same kind of relationship apparently existed in other countries and at other times. Paul Samuelson and Robert Solow of the Massachusetts Institute of Technology were among the first to observe that the Phillips curve was a reasonable description of U.S. economic performance for the years 1900–1960. For the post–World War II years in particular, Samuelson and Solow noted that an unemployment rate of 4 percent was likely to be accompanied by an inflation rate of approximately 2 percent. This

[1]A. W. Phillips. "The Relationship between Unemployment and the Rate of Change of Money Wage Rates in the United Kingdom, 1826–1957," *Economica* (November 1958). Phillips's paper studied the relationship between unemployment and *wage* changes rather than *price* changes; most later formulations (and public policy) focus on prices.

(*a*) Increases in aggregate demand cause . . .

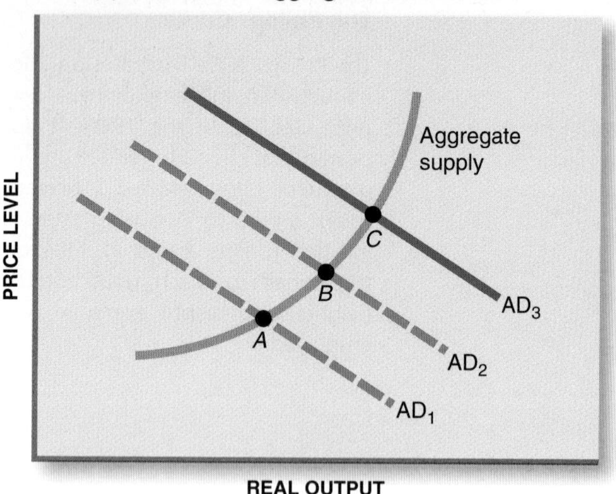

(*b*) A trade-off between unemployment and inflation.

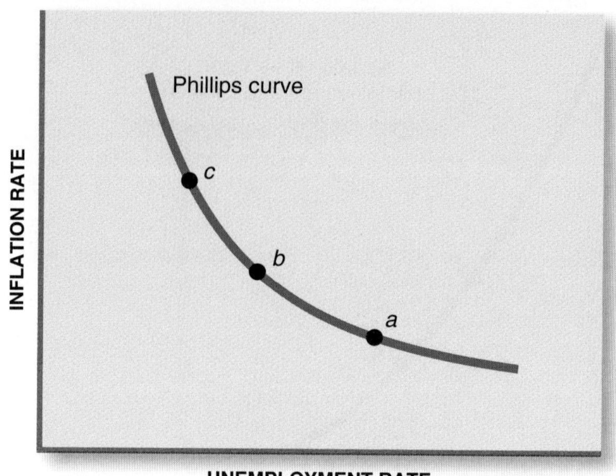

FIGURE 16.3
The Phillips Curve Trade-Off

If the aggregate supply curve slopes upward, increases in aggregate demand always cause both prices and output to rise. Thus, higher inflation becomes a cost of achieving lower unemployment. In (*a*), increased demand moves the economy from point *A* to point *B*. At *B*, unemployment is lower, but prices are higher. This trade-off is illustrated on the Phillips curve in (*b*). Each point on the Phillips curve represents a different AS/AD equilibrium from the graph on the left.

relationship is expressed by point *A* in Figure 16.2. By contrast, lower rates of unemployment were associated with higher rates of inflation, as at point *B*. Alternatively, complete price stability appeared attainable only at the cost of an unemployment rate of 5.5 percent (point *C*). A seesaw kind of relationship existed between inflation and unemployment: When one went up, the other fell.

The trade-off between unemployment and inflation originates in the upward-sloping AS curve. Figure 16.3*a* illustrates this point. Suppose the economy is initially at equilibrium *A*, with fairly stable prices but low output. When aggregate demand expands to AD_2, prices rise along with output, so we end up with higher inflation but less unemployment. This is also shown in Figure 16.3*b* by the move from point *a* to point *b* on the Phillips curve. The move from point *a* to point *b* indicates a decline in unemployment (more output) but an increase in inflation (higher price level). If demand is increased further, to AD_3, a still lower unemployment rate is achieved but at the cost of higher inflation (point *c*).

SHIFTS OF THE AS CURVE

The unemployment-inflation trade-off implied by the upward-sloping AS curve is not etched in stone. Many economists argue that the economy can attain lower levels of unemployment *without* higher inflation. This certainly appeared to be the case in the 1990s: Unemployment rates fell sharply from 1992 to 2000 without any increase in inflation. How could this have happened? There's no AD shift in any of part of Figure 16.3 that would reduce both unemployment *and* inflation.

Rightward AS Shifts: All Good News

Only a rightward shift of the AS curve can reduce unemployment and inflation at the same time. When aggregate supply increases from AS_1 to AS_2 in Figure 16.4, macro equilibrium moves from E_1 to E_2. At E_2 real output is higher, so the unemployment rate must be lower. At E_2 the price level is also lower, indicating reduced inflation. Hence, a rightward shift of the AS curve offers the best of two worlds—something aggregate *demand* shifts (Figure 16.1) can't do.

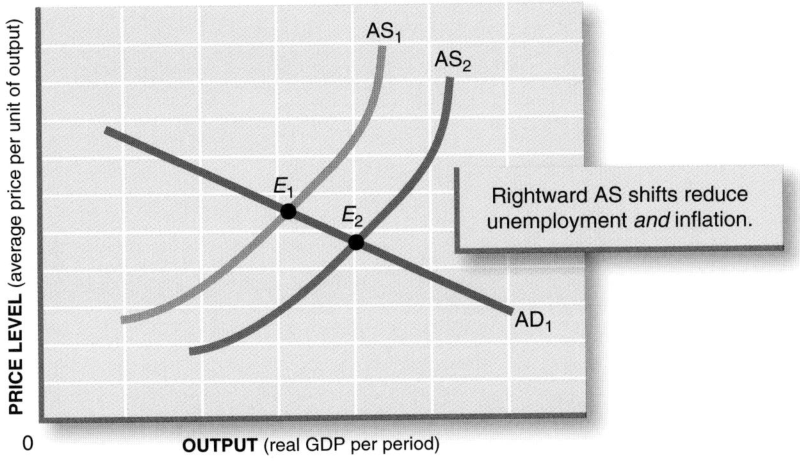

FIGURE 16.4
Shifts of Aggregate Supply

A rightward AS shift (AS_1 to AS_2) reduces both unemployment and inflation. A leftward shift has the opposite effect, creating stagflation.

Phillips Curve Shift. As we saw in Figure 16.3, the Phillips curve is a direct by-product of the AS curve. Accordingly, ***When the AS curve shifts, the Phillips curve shifts as well.*** As Figure 16.5 illustrates, the Phillips curve shifts to the left, the opposite of the AS shift in Figure 16.4. No new information is conveyed here. The Phillips curve simply focuses more directly on the implied change in the unemployment-inflation trade-off. ***When the Phillips curve shifts to the left, the unemployment-inflation trade-off eases.***

The Misery Index. To keep track of simultaneous changes in unemployment and inflation, Arthur Okun developed the "misery index"—a simple sum of the inflation and unemployment rates. As the News feature on the next page illustrates, macro misery diminished substantially during the first Reagan administration (1981–84). President Clinton also benefited from a leftward shift of the Phillips curve through 1998, but saw the misery index climb in 1999–2000. President George W. Bush experienced a sharp increase in the misery index during the recession of 2001. The misery index didn't recede until 2004, when strong output growth reduced the unemployment rate.

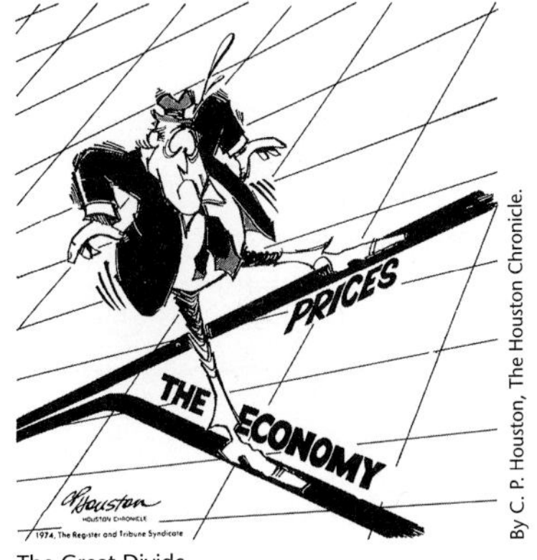

The Great Divide

Analysis: Leftward shifts of the aggregate supply curve push price levels up and output down. The remedy for such stagflation is a rightward shift of aggregate supply.

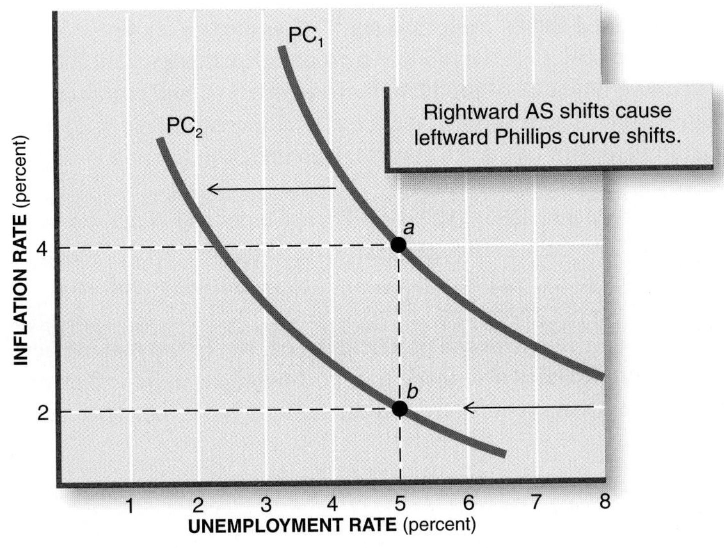

FIGURE 16.5
A Phillips Curve Shift

If the Phillips curve shifts leftward, the short-run unemployment inflation trade-off eases. With PC_1, 5 percent unemployment ignites 4 percent inflation (point *a*). With PC_2, 5 percent unemployment causes only 2 percent inflation (point *b*).

IN THE NEWS

The Misery Index

Unemployment is a problem and so is inflation. Being burdened with both problems at the same time is real misery.

The late Arthur Okun proposed measuring the extent of misery by adding together the inflation and unemployment rates. He called the sum of the two rates the "discomfort index". Political pundits quickly renamed it the "misery index".

In essence, the misery index is a measure of stagflation—the simultaneous occurrence of inflation and unemployment. In 1980, the misery index peaked at 19.6 percent as a result of high inflation (12.5 percent) as well as high unemployment (7.1 percent). Stagflation—and the misery it causes—has since receded markedly.

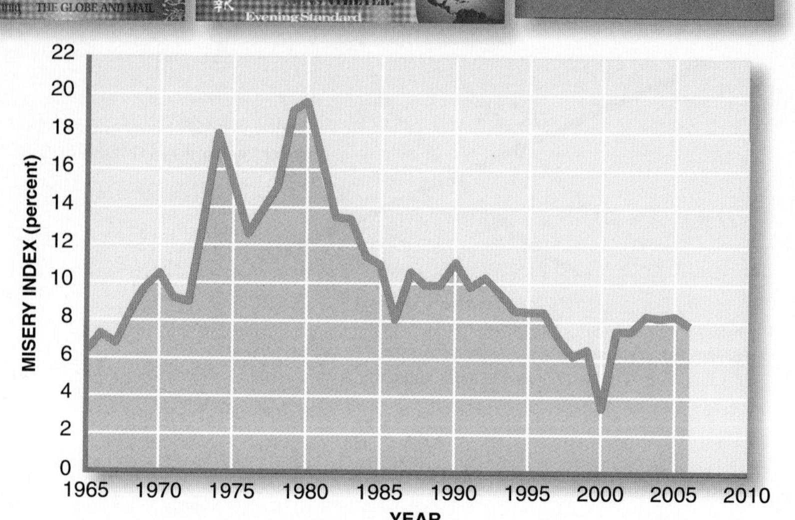

Source: *Economic Report of the President, 2007.*

Analysis: Stagflation refers to the simultaneous occurrence of inflation and unemployment. The "misery index" combines both problems into a single measure of macro performance.

Leftward AS Shifts: All Bad News

Whereas rightward AS shifts appear to be a dream come true, leftward AS shifts are a real nightmare. Imagine in Figure 16.4 that the AS shift is reversed, that is, from AS_2 to AS_1. What would happen? Output would decrease and prices would rise, exactly the kind of dilemma depicted in the previous cartoon. In other words, nothing would go in the right direction. This would be rampant stagflation.

webnote

To update the misery index, retrieve data on unemployment and inflation from the U.S. Bureau of Labor Statistics at www.bls.gov

A natural disaster can trigger a leftward shift of the AS curve, especially in smaller nations. When a tsunami washed over nations in the Indian Ocean in December 2004, over 200,000 people were killed. In Sri Lanka, 80 percent of the fishing fleet was destroyed, along with port facilities, railroads, highways, and communications systems. The huge loss of human and physical capital reduced Sri Lanka's production possibilities. This was reflected in a leftward shift of the AS curve.

In an economy as large as United States', leftward shifts of aggregate supply are less dramatic. But Mother Nature can still push the AS curve around. Hurricanes Katrina and Rita, for example, destroyed vast amounts of production, transportation, and communications infrastructure in August 2005. The resulting delays and cost increases (see following News) were reflected in a leftward shift of the AS curve and an uptick in the misery index in 2005 (see News above).

The September 11, 2001, terrorist attacks on the World Trade Center and Pentagon were another form of external shock. The attacks directly destroyed some production capacity (office space, telecommunications links, and transportation links). But they took an even greater toll on the *willingness* to supply goods and services. In the aftermath of the attacks businesses, perceiving new risks to investment and production, held back from making new commitments. Increased security measures also made transporting goods more expensive. All of these responses shifted the AS curve leftward and the Phillips curve rightward, adding to macro misery.

Policy Tools

From the supply side of macro markets, the appropriate response to negative external shocks is clear: Shift the AS curve rightward. As the foregoing graphs have demonstrated, ***rightward***

IN THE NEWS

Hurricane Damage to Gulf Ports Delays Deliveries, Raises Costs

The damage to important Gulf Coast ports and waterways from Hurricanes Katrina and Rita is delaying deliveries, sharply boosting shipping costs and will complicate rebuilding efforts in areas devastated by the storms.

The rising costs could put more downward pressure on growth, particularly for industries dependent on key products that typically flow through the region. Bringing imported steel through substitute ports could add to the prices paid by U.S. manufacturers, said John Martin, president of Martin Associates, a maritime-transportation consulting firm in Lancaster, Pa. The rising cost of forest products like lumber could add to the mounting price tag for rebuilding the region, while grain companies could see their exports become less competitive.

Ports from Houston to Mobile, Ala., that handle more than a third of U.S. cargo by tonnage were battered by the hurricanes, along with nearby shipping terminals, warehouses, navigation channels, roads and rail lines. . . .

Barge-tariff rates—the rates paid by grain companies for transportation outside longer-term shipping contracts—to move grain from St. Louis to New Orleans for export have soared by 60% to 100% since Katrina hit.

—Daniel Machalaba

Source: *The Wall Street Journal,* October 3, 2005, p. A8.

Analysis: A natural disaster that destroys both human and physical capital shifts the aggregate supply curve to the left, reducing output and raising price levels.

shifts of the aggregate supply curve always generate desirable macro outcomes. The next question, of course, is how to shift the aggregate supply curve in the desired (rightward) direction. Supply-side economists look for clues among the forces that influence the supply-side response to changes in demand. Among those forces, the following policy options have been emphasized:

- Tax incentives for saving, investment, and work.
- Human capital investment.
- Deregulation.
- Trade liberalization.
- Infrastructure development.

All these policies have the potential to change supply decisions *independently* of any changes in aggregate demand. If they're effective, they'll result in a rightward shift of the AS curve and an *improved* trade-off between unemployment and inflation.

TAX INCENTIVES

The most renowned supply-side policy option for improving the unemployment-inflation trade-off was the "supply-side" tax cuts of the early 1980s. Tax cuts are of course a staple of Keynesian economics. But tax cuts take on a whole new role on the supply side of the economy. ***In Keynesian economics, tax cuts are used to increase aggregate demand.*** By putting more disposable income in the hands of consumers, Keynesian economists seek to increase expenditure on goods and services. Output is expected to increase in response. From a Keynesian perspective, the form of the tax cut is not very important, as long as disposable income increases.

The supply side of the economy encourages a different view of taxes. ***Taxes not only alter disposable income but also affect the incentives to work and produce.*** High tax rates destroy the incentives to work and produce, so they end up reducing total output. Low tax rates, by contrast, allow people to keep more of what they earn and so stimulate greater output. ***The direct effects of taxes on the supply of goods are the concern of supply-side***

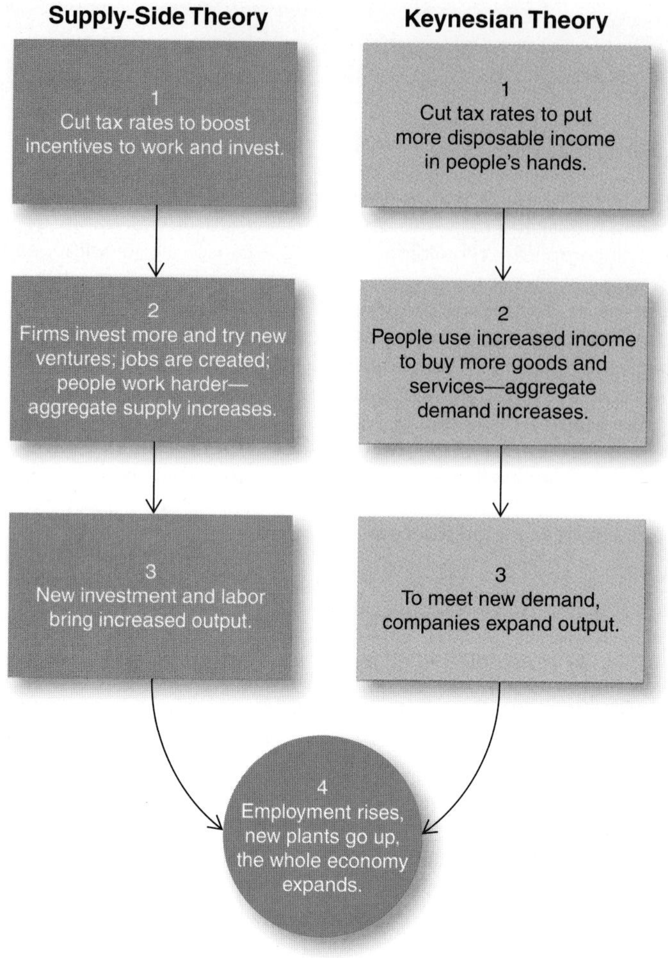
Supply-Side Theory
Keynesian Theory
1
Cut tax rates to boost incentives to work and invest.
1
Cut tax rates to put more disposable income in people's hands.
2
Firms invest more and try new ventures; jobs are created; people work harder—aggregate supply increases.
2
People use increased income to buy more goods and services—aggregate demand increases.
3
New investment and labor bring increased output.
3
To meet new demand, companies expand output.
4
Employment rises, new plants go up, the whole economy expands.

FIGURE 16.6
Two Theories for Getting the Economy Moving

Keynesians and supply-siders both advocate cutting taxes to reduce unemployment. But they have very different views on the kind of tax cuts required and the impact of any cuts enacted.

economists. Figure 16.6 shows the difference between demand-side and supply-side perspectives on tax policy.

Marginal Tax Rates

marginal tax rate: The tax rate imposed on the last (marginal) dollar of income.

Supply-side theory places special emphasis on *marginal* tax rates. The **marginal tax rate** is the tax rate imposed on the last (marginal) dollar of income received. In our progressive income tax system, marginal tax rates increase as more income is received. Uncle Sam takes a larger share out of each additional dollar earned. In 2007, the highest marginal tax rate on personal income was 35 percent. That top tax rate was far below the 91 percent rate that existed in 1944, but it was also a lot higher than the 12 percent tax rate imposed in 1914 (see Figure 16.7).

In view of the wild history of tax rates, one might wonder whether the rate selected matters. Specifically, does the marginal tax rate affect supply decisions? Will people work and invest as much when the marginal tax rate is 91 percent as when it is only 12 percent? Doesn't seem likely, does it.

Labor Supply. The marginal tax rate directly changes the financial incentive to *increase* one's work. ***If the marginal tax rate is high, there's less incentive to work more***—Uncle Sam will get most of the added income. Confronted with high marginal tax rates, workers may choose to stay home rather than work an extra shift. Families may decide that it doesn't pay to send both parents into the labor market. When marginal tax rates are low, by contrast, those extra work activities generate bigger increases in disposable income.

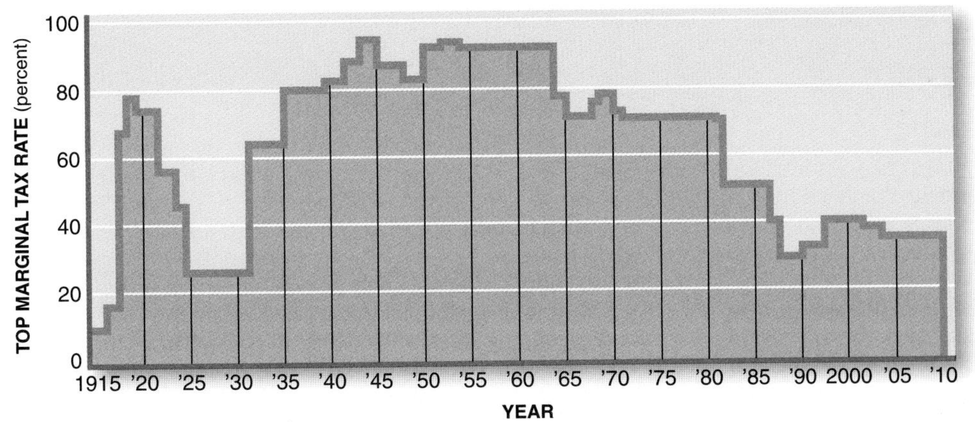

FIGURE 16.7
Changes in Marginal Tax Rates since 1915

The top marginal tax rate on income has varied from a low of 12 percent in 1914 to a high of 91 percent in 1944. Supply-side theory emphasizes how these varying tax rates affect work, investment, and production decisions, that is, aggregate supply.

Entrepreneurship. Marginal tax rates affect not only labor-supply decisions but also decisions on whether to start or expand a business. Most small businesses are organized as sole proprietorships or partnerships and subject to *personal,* not *corporate,* tax rates. Hence, a decline in personal tax rates will affect the risk/reward balance for potential entrepreneurs. Columbia Business School professors William Gentry and Glenn Huber have demonstrated that progressive marginal tax rates discourage entry into self-employment. Syracuse professor Douglas Holtz-Eakin and Princeton economist Harvey Rosen have shown that the growth rate, investment, and employment of small businesses are also affected by marginal tax rates. As Holtz-Eakin concluded, "taxes matter."

Investment. Taxes matter for corporations too. Corporate entities account for nearly 90 percent of business output and 84 percent of business assets. Like small proprietorships, corporations, too, are motivated by *after*-tax profits. Hence, corporate **investment** decisions will be affected by corporate tax rates. If Uncle Sam imposes a high tax rate on corporate profits, the payoff to investors will be diminished. Potential investors may decide to consume their income or to purchase tax-free bonds rather than invest in plant and equipment. If that happens, total investment will decline and output will suffer. Accordingly, ***if high tax rates discourage investment, aggregate supply will be constrained.***

investment: Expenditures on (production of) new plant, equipment, and structures (capital) in a given time period, plus changes in business inventories.

Tax-Induced Supply Shifts

If tax rates affect supply decisions, then *changes* in tax rates will shift aggregate supply. Specifically, supply-siders conclude that ***a reduction in marginal tax rates will shift the aggregate supply curve to the right.*** The increased supply will come from three sources: more work effort, more entrepreneurship, and more investment. This increased willingness to produce will reduce the rate of unemployment. The additional output will also help reduce inflationary pressures. Thus we end up with less unemployment *and* less inflation.

From a supply-side perspective, the form of the tax cut is critical. For example, **tax rebates** are a one-time windfall to consumers and have no effect on marginal tax rates. As a consequence, disposable income rises, but not the incentives for work or production. Rebates directly affect only the demand side of the economy.

tax rebate: A lump-sum refund of taxes paid.

To stimulate aggregate *supply,* tax *rates* must be reduced, particularly at the margin. These cuts can take the form of reductions in personal income tax rates or reductions in the marginal tax rates imposed on businesses. In either case, the lower tax rates will give people a greater incentive to work, invest, and produce. This was the motivation for the Reagan tax cuts of 1981–84. Shifting the aggregate supply curve rightward was also the goal of President George W. Bush's 2001 proposal to cut the top marginal tax rate from 39.6 percent to 33 percent. Congress ultimately adopted a package of supply-side and demand-side

IN THE NEWS

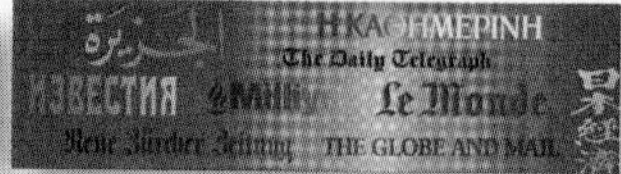

Congress Passes Tax Cut Package

The House and Senate gave final approval to a far-reaching package of tax breaks yesterday, handing President Bush a major victory on his top legislative priority at the close of a tumultuous week in which he and the Republicans lost control of the Senate.

The tax cut, the largest approved by Congress in two decades, provides for millions of refund checks of up to $600 apiece to be mailed to Americans this summer, and grants reductions in most tax rates, tax relief for married couples and parents of young children, and a repeal of the estate tax, though not until 2010.

All of these were priorities set out by the president, who welcomed the tax bill's passage after returning to the White House from Camp David. The plan "cuts income taxes for everyone who pays them. Nothing could be more profound, and nothing could be more fair," Bush said. . . .

The concept of issuing checks to provide immediate tax relief—and help stimulate the economy—was not in Bush's original plan and had not been included in either the House or Senate versions of the legislation; the House and Senate proposals had instead called for adjusting taxpayers' withholding tables.

But the administration, confronting claims from economists that adjusting the withholding tables would not provide a big enough economic boost and charges from Democrats that the tax cut was geared for the wealthy, pressed for including the refund checks in the final tax deal. . . .

The tax bill reduces the top rate from 39.6 percent to 35 percent by 2006, while the president had sought a 33 percent rate.

—Glenn Kessler and Juliet Eilperin

Source: *The Washington Post,* May 27, 2001. www.washingtonpost.com

Analysis: Tax cuts can focus on demand-side or supply-side incentives. The 2001 tax-cut package included both: tax rebates to stimulate demand and reductions in marginal tax rates to stimulate supply.

incentives (see News above). On the supply side it phased in a cut in the top marginal tax rate to 35 percent. To shift aggregate demand, Congress also authorized $38 billion of tax rebates in 2001.

Table 16.1 illustrates the distinction between Keynesian and supply-side tax cuts. Under both tax systems (A and B), a person earning $200 pays $80 in taxes before the tax cut and $60 after the tax cut. But under system A, the marginal tax rate is always 50 percent, which means that Uncle Sam is getting half of every dollar earned above $100. By contrast, system B imposes a marginal tax rate of only 30 percent—$0.30 of every dollar above $100 goes to the government. Under system B, people have a greater incentive to earn *more* than $100. Although both systems raise the same amount of taxes, system B offers greater incentives to work extra hours and produce more output.

Tax Elasticity of Supply

All economists agree that tax rates influence people's decisions to work, invest, and produce. But the policy-relevant question is, *how much* influence do taxes have? Do reductions in the marginal tax rate shift the aggregate supply curve far to the right? Or are the resultant shifts quite small?

tax elasticity of supply: The percentage change in quantity supplied divided by the percentage change in tax rates.

The response of labor and capital to a change in tax rates is summarized by the **tax elasticity of supply.** Like other elasticities, this one measures the proportional response of supplies to a change in price (in this case, a tax *rate*). Specifically, the tax elasticity of supply is the percentage change in quantity supplied divided by the percentage in tax rates, that is,

$$\text{Tax elasticity of supply} = \frac{\%\text{ change in quantity supplied}}{\%\text{ change in tax rate}}$$

Normally we expect quantity supplied to go up when tax rates go down. Elasticity (E) is therefore negative, although it's usually expressed in absolute terms (without the minus sign). The (absolute) value of E must be greater than zero, since we expect *some* response to a tax cut. The policy issue boils down to the question of how large E actually is.

Initial Alternatives					
			Tax Rate		
Tax System	Initial Tax Schedule	Tax on Income of $200	Average	Marginal	Disposable Income
A	$30 + 50% of income over $100	$80	40%	50%	$120
B	$50 + 30% of income over $100	$80	40%	30%	$120

TABLE 16.1
Average vs. Marginal Tax Rates

The same amount of taxes can be raised via two very different systems. Here a person earning $200 pays $80 in taxes under either system (A or B). Thus, the *average* tax rate (total tax ÷ total income) is the same in both cases ($80 ÷ $200 = 40%). The *marginal* tax rates are very different, however. System A has a high marginal rate (50%), whereas system B has a low marginal tax rate (30%). System B provides a greater incentive for people to earn over $100.

Alternative Forms of Tax Cut					
			Tax Rate		
Tax System	Revised Tax Schedule	Tax on Income of $200	Average	Marginal	Disposable Income
A	$10 + 50% of income over $100	$60	30%	50%	$140
B	$30 + 30% of income over $100	$60	30%	30%	$140

The average tax rate could be cut to 30 percent under either system. Under both systems, the revised tax would be $60 and disposable income would be increased to $140. Keynesians would be happy with either form of tax cut. But supply-siders would favor system B because the lower marginal tax rate gives people more incentive to earn higher incomes.

If the tax elasticity of supply were large enough, a tax cut might actually *increase* tax revenues. Suppose the tax elasticity were equal to 1.5. In that case a tax cut of 10 percent would cause output supplied to increase by 15 percent (= 1.5 × 10%). Such a large increase in the tax base (income) would result in *more* taxes being paid even though the tax *rate* was reduced. One of President Reagan's economic advisers, Arthur Laffer, actually thought such an outcome was possible. He predicted that tax revenues would *increase* after the Reagan supply-side tax cuts were made. In reality, the tax elasticity of supply turned out to be much smaller (around 0.15) and tax revenues fell substantially. The aggregate supply curve *did* shift to the right, but not very far, when marginal tax rates were cut.

The evidently low tax elasticity of supply helped President Clinton convince Congress to *increase* marginal tax rates in 1993. Although opponents objected that higher tax rates would reduce work and investment, the Clinton administration pointed out that any leftward shift of aggregate supply was likely to be small. President George W. Bush reversed that shift with the 2001–4 marginal tax-rate cuts. According to a 2006 study by the Congressional Research Service, those tax-rate cuts elicited a 0.20 tax elasticity of supply.

Savings Incentives

Supply-side economists emphasize the importance of *long-run* responses to changed tax incentives. On the demand side, an increase in income translates very quickly into increased spending. On the supply side, things don't happen so fast. It takes time to construct new plants and equipment. People are also slow to respond to new work and investment incentives. Hence, the full benefits of supply-side tax cuts—or the damage done by tax hikes—won't be immediately visible.

Of particular concern to supply-side economists is the rate of saving in the economy. Demand-side economists emphasize spending and tend to treat **saving** as a leakage problem. Supply-siders, by contrast, emphasize the importance of saving for financing investment

saving: That part of disposable income not spent on current consumption; disposable income less consumption.

Analysis: In the short run, consumer saving may reduce aggregate demand. However, saving also finances increased investment, which is essential to long-run growth.

and economic growth. At full employment, a greater volume of investment is possible only if the rate of consumption is cut back. In other words, additional investment requires additional saving. Hence, ***supply-side economists favor tax incentives that encourage saving as well as greater tax incentives for investment.*** This kind of perspective contrasts sharply with the Keynesian emphasis on stimulating consumption, as the accompanying cartoon emphasizes.

Investment Incentives

An alternative lever for shifting aggregate supply is to offer tax incentives for investment. The 1981 tax cuts focused on *personal* income tax rates. By contrast, President George H. Bush advocated cutting capital gains taxes. These are taxes levied on the increase in the value of property, such as land, buildings, and corporate stock, when it's sold. Lower capital gains taxes, Bush argued, would encourage people to start businesses or invest in them.

President Clinton also emphasized the need for investment incentives. His very first proposal for stimulating the economy was a temporary investment tax credit. People who invested in new plant and equipment would receive a tax credit equal to 10 percent of their investment. In effect, Uncle Sam would pay for part of any new investment by collecting less taxes. Because the credit is available only to those who make new investments, it's a particularly efficient lever for shifting the aggregate supply curve. President Clinton withdrew the investment-credit proposal, however, when he decided that deficit reduction was a higher priority.

President George W. Bush pulled this supply-side lever more firmly. After securing the huge *personal* tax cuts in 2001, Bush sought *business* tax cuts. In 2002 Congress approved larger capital expensing, which reduced the after-tax cost of new investments. In 2003, tax rates on dividends and capital gains were reduced, making investment still more profitable.

webnote

The U.S. Bureau of Economic Analysis (BEA) maintains quarterly data on the personal saving rate of U.S. households. See "Overview of the U.S. Economy" at www.bea.gov/newsreleases/glance.htm

webnote

Find out *ways* to save taxes at www.irs.gov. Click on "Information for Individuals."

HUMAN CAPITAL INVESTMENT

A nation's ability to supply goods and services depends on its *human* capital as well as its *physical* capital. If the size of the labor force increased, more output could be produced in any given price level. Similarly, if the *quality* of the workforce were to increase, more output could be supplied at any given price level. In other words, increases in **human capital**—the skills and knowledge of the workforce—add to the nation's potential output.

human capital: The knowledge and skills possessed by the workforce.

Structural Unemployment

A mismatch between the skills of the workforce and the requirements of new jobs is a major cause of the unemployment-inflation trade-off. When aggregate demand increases, employers want to hire more workers. But the available (unemployed) workers may not have the skills employers require. This is the essence of **structural unemployment.** The consequence is that employers can't increase output as fast as they'd like to. Prices, rather than output, increase.

structural unemployment: Unemployment caused by a mismatch between the skills (or location) of job seekers and the requirements (or location) of available jobs.

The larger the skills gap between unemployed workers and the requirements of emerging jobs, the worse will be the Phillips curve trade-off. To improve the trade-off, the skills gap must be reduced. This is another supply-side imperative. ***Investments in human capital reduce structural unemployment and shift the aggregate supply curve rightward.***

Worker Training

The tax code is a policy tool for increasing human capital investment as well as physical capital investment. In this case tax credits are made available to employers who offer more worker training. Such credits reduce the employer's after-tax cost of training.

President Clinton proposed even stronger incentives for employer-based training. He wanted to *require* employers to spend at least 1.5 percent of their total payroll costs on training activities. Those employers who didn't provide training activities directly would have to pay an equivalent sum into a public training fund. This "play-or-pay" approach would force employers to invest in the human capital of their employees.

Although the "play-or-pay" concept is intriguing, it might actually shift the aggregate supply curve the *wrong* way. The *costs* of employing workers would rise in the short run as employers shelled out more money for training or taxes. Hence, the aggregate supply curve would shift *leftward* in the short run, worsening the unemployment-inflation trade-off. Only later might AS shift rightward, and then only to the extent that training actually improved **labor productivity.**

labor productivity: Amount of output produced by a worker in a given period of time; output per hour.

Education Spending

Another way to increase human capital is to expand and improve the efficacy of the education system. President George H. Bush encouraged local school systems to become more competitive. He suggested they experiment with vouchers that would allow students to attend the school of their choice. Schools would then have to offer services that attracted voucher-carrying students. Those schools that didn't compete successfully wouldn't have enough funds (vouchers) to continue.

President Clinton advocated a more conventional approach. He urged Congress to allocate more funds to the school system, particularly programs for preschoolers, like Head Start, and for disadvantaged youth. He acknowledged that vouchers might increase school quality but wanted to limit their use to public schools.

President George W. Bush characterized himself as the "education President." He increased federal spending on education and improved tax incentives for college-savings accounts and tuition payments. His No Child Left Behind program also increased school accountability for human capital development. None of these tools generate a quick AS-curve shift. Rather, any improvements in labor productivity are likely to emerge many years later.

Affirmative Action

Lack of skills and experience aren't the only reasons it's sometimes hard to find the "right" workers. The mismatch between employed workers and jobs is often less a matter of skills than of race, gender, or age. In other words, discrimination can create an artificial barrier between job seekers and available job openings.

If discrimination tends to shift the aggregate supply curve leftward, then reducing discriminatory barriers should shift it to the right. Equal opportunity programs are thus a natural extension of a supply-side approach to macro policy. However, critics are also quick to point out the risks inherent in government regulation of hiring decisions. From a supply-side perspective, laws that forbid discrimination are welcome and should be enforced. But aggressive affirmative action programs that require employers to hire specific numbers of women or minority workers limit productive capabilities and can lead to excessive costs.

Transfer Payments

Welfare programs also discourage workers from taking available jobs. Unemployment and welfare benefits provide a source of income when a person isn't working. Although these

transfer payments: Payments to individuals for which no current goods or services are exchanged, like Social Security, welfare, unemployment benefits.

transfer payments are motivated by humanitarian goals, they also inhibit labor supply. Transfer recipients must give up some or all of their welfare payments when they take a job, which makes working less attractive and therefore reduces the number of available workers. The net result is a leftward shift of the aggregate supply curve.

In 1996, Congress reformed the nation's core welfare program. The supply-side emphasis of that reform was manifest in the very title of the reform legislation: the Personal Responsibility and Work Opportunity Act. Congress set time limits on how long people can draw welfare benefits. The act also required recipients to engage in job-related activities like job search and training while still receiving benefits.

The 1996 reforms had a dramatic effect on recipient behavior. Nationally, over 5 million adults left welfare between 1996 and 2001. Over half of these ex-welfare recipients entered the labor force, thereby shifting the AS curve rightward.

Recognizing that income transfers reduce aggregate supply doesn't force us to eliminate all welfare programs. Welfare programs are also intended to serve important social needs. The AS/AD framework reminds us, however, that the structure of such programs will affect aggregate supply. With over 60 million Americans receiving income transfers, the effect on aggregate supply can be significant.

DEREGULATION

Government intervention affects the shape and position of the aggregate supply curve in other ways. The government intervenes directly in supply decisions by *regulating* employment and output behavior. In general, such regulations limit the flexibility of producers to respond to changes in demand. Government regulation also tends to raise production costs. The higher costs result not only from required changes in the production process but also from the expense of monitoring government regulations and filling out endless government forms. Thomas Hopkins, a Rochester Institute of Technology economist, estimates that the total costs of regulation exceed $700 billion a year. These added costs of production shift the aggregate supply curve to the left.

Factor Markets

Government intervention in factor markets increases the cost of supplying goods and services in many ways.

Minimum Wages. Minimum wage laws are one of the most familiar forms of factor-market regulation. The Fair Labor Standards Act of 1938 required employers to pay workers a minimum of 25 cents per hour. Over time, Congress has increased the coverage of that act and the minimum wage itself repeatedly.

The goal of the minimum wage law is to ensure workers a decent standard of living. But the law has other effects as well. By prohibiting employers from using lower-paid workers, it limits the ability of employers to hire additional workers. Teenagers, for example, may not have enough skills or experience to merit the federal minimum wage. Employers may have to rely on more expensive workers rather than hire unemployed teenagers.

Here again the issue is not whether minimum wage laws serve any social purposes but how they affect macro outcomes. By shifting the aggregate supply curve leftward, minimum wage laws make it more difficult to achieve full employment with stable prices.

Mandatory Benefits. Government-directed fringe benefits have the same kind of effect on aggregate supply. One of the first bills President Clinton signed into law was the Family and Medical Leave Act, which requires all businesses with 50 or more employees to grant leaves of absence for up to 12 weeks. The employer must continue to pay health benefits during such absences and must also incur the costs of recruiting and training temporary replacements. The General Accounting Office estimated this would add nearly $700 million per year to payroll costs. These added payroll costs add to the costs of production, making producers less willing to supply output at any given price level.

Occupational Health and Safety. Government regulation of factor markets extends beyond wages and benefits. The government also sets standards for workplace safety and health. The Occupational Safety and Health Administration (OSHA), for example, issued new rules in November 2000 to reduce ergonomic injuries at work. The rules would have required employers to redesign workplaces (assembly lines, computer workstations) to accommodate individual workers. The rules would have also required employers to pay higher health care costs and grant more injury-related leave. OSHA itself estimated that the new regulations would cost employers $4.5 billion a year. Employers said the ergonomics regulations would cost *far* more that—up to $125 billion a year. Concern over the implied upward shift of aggregate supply prompted Congress to rescind the new ergonomics rules in early 2001, before they took effect.

Product Markets

The government's regulation of factor markets tends to raise production costs and inhibit supply. The same is true of regulations imposed directly on product markets, as the following examples illustrate.

Transportation Costs. At the federal level, various agencies regulate the output and prices of transportation services. Until 1984, the Civil Aeronautics Board (CAB) determined which routes airlines could fly and how much they could charge. The Interstate Commerce Commission (ICC) has had the same kind of power over trucking, interstate bus lines, and railroads. The routes, services, and prices for ships (in U.S. coastal waters and foreign commerce) have been established by the Federal Maritime Commission. In all these cases, the regulations constrained the ability of producers to respond to increases in demand. The rate of output was kept too low and prices too high.

Similar problems continue to inflate intrastate trucking costs. All but eight states limit the routes, the loads, and the prices of intrastate trucking companies. These regulations promote inefficient transportation and protect producer profits. The net cost to the economy is at least $8 billion, or about $128 a year for a family of four.

Many cities and counties also limit the number of taxicabs and regulate their prices. The net effect of such regulation is to limit competition and drive up the cost of transportation.

webnote

The Cato Institute, a conservative Washington, D.C., think tank, publishes lots of studies on regulatory costs; visit www.cato.org/research/reglt-st.html

Food and Drug Standards. The Food and Drug Administration (FDA) has a broad mandate to protect consumers from dangerous products. In fulfilling this responsibility, the FDA sets health standards for the content of specific foods. The FDA also sets standards for the testing of new drugs and evaluates the test results.

The goal of FDA regulation is to minimize health risks to consumers. Like all regulation, however, the FDA standards entail real costs. The tests required for new drugs are expensive and time-consuming. Getting a new drug approved for sale can take years of effort and require a huge investment. The net results are that (1) fewer new drugs are brought to market and (2) those that do reach the market are more expensive than they would have been in the absence of regulation. In other words, the aggregate supply of goods is shifted to the left.

webnote

For the EPA's assessment of how its own regulations affect the U.S. economy, go to www.epa.gov and click on "Browse EPA Topics," then choose "Economics."

Other examples of government regulation are commonplace. The Environmental Protection Agency (EPA) regulates auto emissions, the discharge of industrial wastes, and water pollution. The U.S. Congress restricts foreign imports and raises their prices. The Federal Trade Commission (FTC) limits firms' freedom to increase their output or advertise their products.

Reducing Costs

Many—perhaps most—of these regulatory activities are beneficial. In fact, all were originally designed to serve specific public purposes. As a result of such regulation, we get safer drugs, cleaner air, and less deceptive advertising. We must also consider the costs involved, however. All regulatory activities impose direct and indirect costs. These costs must be compared to the benefits received. ***The basic contention of supply-side economists is that regulatory costs are now too high.*** To improve our economic performance, they assert, we must *deregulate* the production process, thereby shifting the aggregate supply curve to the right again.

EASING TRADE BARRIERS

Government regulation of international trade also influences the shape and position of aggregate supply. Trade flows affect both factor and product markets.

Factor Markets

In factor markets, U.S. producers buy raw materials, equipment parts, and components from foreign suppliers. Tariffs (taxes on imported goods) make such inputs more expensive, thereby increasing the cost of U.S. production. Regulations or quotas that make foreign inputs less accessible or more expensive similarly constrain the U.S. aggregate supply curve. The quota on imported sugar, for example, increases the cost of U.S.-produced soda, cookies, and candy. Just that one trade barrier has cost U.S. consumers over $2 billion in higher prices.

Product Markets

The same kind of trade barriers affect product markets directly. With completely unrestricted ("free") trade, foreign producers would be readily available to supply products to U.S. consumers. If U.S. producers were approaching capacity or incurring escalating cost pressures, foreign suppliers would act as a safety valve. By increasing the quantity of output available at any given price level, foreign suppliers help flatten out the aggregate supply curve.

Despite the success of the North American Free Trade Agreement (NAFTA) and the World Trade Organization (WTO) in reducing trade barriers, half of all U.S. imports are still subject to tariffs. Nontariff barriers (regulation, quotas, and so forth) also still constrain aggregate supply. This was evident in the multiyear battle over Mexican trucking. Although NAFTA authorized Mexican trucking companies to compete freely in the United States by 2000, U.S. labor unions (Teamsters) and trucking companies vigorously protested their entry, delaying the implied reduction in transportation costs for 7 years.

Immigration

Another global supply-side policy lever is immigration policy. Skill shortages in U.S. labor markets can be overcome with education and training. But even faster relief is available in the vast pool of foreign workers. In 2000, Congress increased the quota for software engineers and other high-tech workers by 70 percent, to 195,000 workers. The intent was to relieve the skill shortage in high-tech industries and with it, the cost pressures that were increasing the slope of the aggregate supply curve. Temporary visas for farm workers also help avert cost-push inflation in the farm sector. By regulating the flow of immigrant workers, Congress has the potential to alter the shape and position of the short-run AS curve.

INFRASTRUCTURE DEVELOPMENT

infrastructure: The transportation, communications, education, judicial, and other institutional systems that facilitate market exchanges.

Another way to reduce the costs of supplying goods and services is to improve the nation's **infrastructure,** that is, the transportation, communications, judicial, and other systems that bind the pieces of the economy into a coherent whole. The interstate highway system, for example, enlarged the market for producers looking for new sales opportunities. Improved air traffic controls and larger airports have also made international markets and factors of production readily accessible. Without interstate highways and international airports, the process of supplying goods and services would be more localized and much more expensive.

It's easy to take infrastructure for granted until you have to make do without it. In recent years, U.S. producers have rushed into China, Russia, and eastern Europe looking for new profit opportunities. What they discovered is that even simple communication is difficult where Internet access and even telephones are often scarce. Outside the major cities business facilities and accommodations are often equally scarce. There are few established clearinghouses for marketing information, and labor markets are fragmented and localized. Getting started sometimes requires doing everything from scratch.

Although the United States has a highly developed infrastructure, it too could be improved. There are roads and bridges to repair, more airports to be built, faster rail systems to construct, and space-age telecommunications networks to install. Spending on this kind of infrastructure will not only increase aggregate demand (fiscal stimulus) but also shift aggregate supply.

"*I blame government, labor, business, and my ex-wife.*"

Analysis: Because so many factors affect aggregate supply, it's hard to single out any one AS shift factor as decisive.

EXPECTATIONS

Last, but not least, we must again take expectations into account. Expectations play a crucial role not only in consumer expenditure decisions but in production and investment decisions as well. Hence, expectations will influence the shape of the short-run aggregate supply curve—the *willingness* and ability to supply output at various prices. If producers expect more "business-friendly" government policies they will be more willing to invest in new plant, equipment, and software. By contrast, the prospect of increasing government regulation or higher taxes deters investors from expanding production capacity. ***Because investment is always a bet on future economic conditions, expectations directly affect the shape of the AS curve.***

THE ECONOMY TOMORROW

REBUILDING AMERICA

The output of the U.S. economy depends not only on *private* investment but on *public* investment as well. The infrastructure of transportation, communications, and environmental systems all affects the nation's production possibilities. As we look to the future, we have to wonder whether that infrastructure will satisfy the needs of the economy tomorrow. If it doesn't, it will become increasingly difficult and costly to increase output. Inadequate infrastructure would not only worsen short-term macro outcomes but also impair our ability to compete in world markets.

Declining Infrastructure Investment. The United States has over $2 trillion worth of public, nonmilitary infrastructure, including highways, bridges, sewage systems, buildings, hospitals, and schools. Like private capital (business plant, equipment, and structures), this *public* capital contributes to our production possibilities.

Investment in public infrastructure slowed down in the 1970s and 1980s. The rate of infrastructure investment peaked at around 3.5 percent of GDP in the mid-1960s. It then declined steadily to a low of about 0.5 percent of GDP in the early 1980s. As a result of this decline in spending, the United States has barely been able to *maintain* existing infrastructure, much less *expand* it. Studies by Alan Aschauer and others suggest that ***declining infrastructure investment has reduced actual and potential output.*** In other words, crumbling infrastructure has shifted the aggregate supply curve leftward.

Not everyone agrees that the nation's infrastructure is actually crumbling. Accident rates on the roads, rails, and in the air have been declining. Moreover, the quality of interstate roads—including the 155,000-mile national highway system—has improved significantly since 1980. But everyone agrees that ***the transportation system isn't keeping up with a growing economy.*** Highway traffic is increasing at 2.5 percent a year, while airline passenger traffic is rising at closer to 4 percent a year. To accommodate this growth, we need more and better transportation systems.

The Cost of Delay. The failure to expand the infrastructure could prove costly. The U.S. Department of Transportation estimates that people now spend nearly 3.5 *billion* hours a year in traffic delays. If the nation's highways don't improve, those delays will skyrocket to more than 4 *billion* hours a year a decade from now. That's a lot of labor resources to leave idle. Moreover, cars stuck on congested highways waste a lot of gasoline: nearly 4 billion gallons a year.

Delays in air travel impose similar costs. The Federal Aviation Administration says air travel delays increase airline operating costs by over $2 billion a year and idle over $3 billion worth of passenger time. That time imposes a high opportunity cost in forgone business transactions and shortened vacations. Ultimately, all these costs are reflected in lower productivity, reduced output, and higher prices.

The Rebuilding Process. To alleviate these constraints on aggregate supply, Congress voted to accelerate infrastructure spending. The Transportation Equity Act of 2000 raised federal spending to over $600 billion in this decade. Among the public investments:

- ***Highways:*** Highway construction and rehabilitation.
- ***Air traffic control:*** Modernization of the air traffic control system.
- ***Weather service:*** Modernization of the weather service (new satellites, a supercomputer).
- ***Maglev trains:*** Research on magnetically levitated ("maglev") trains that can travel at 300 miles per hour and are environmentally clean.
- ***Smart cars and highways:*** Research and testing of cars and highways outfitted with radar, monitors, and computers to reduce congestion and accidents.

Other legislation authorized more spending on sewage systems, access to space (for example, the space shuttle), modernization of the postal service, and construction of more hospitals, prisons, and other buildings. These infrastructure improvements increase aggregate supply, improving both short- and long-run economic outcomes. In the process, they create more potential for economic growth without inflation in the economy tomorrow.

SUMMARY

- Fiscal and monetary policies seek to attain full employment and price stability by altering the level of aggregate demand. Their success depends on microeconomic responses, as reflected in the price and output decisions of market participants. LO1
- The market's response to shifts in aggregate demand is reflected in the shape and position of the aggregate supply curve. If the AS curve slopes upward, a trade-off between unemployment and inflation exists. The Phillips curve illustrates the trade-off. LO2
- If the AS curve shifts to the left, the trade-off between unemployment and inflation worsens. Stagflation—a combination of substantial inflation and unemployment—results. This is illustrated by rightward shifts of the Phillips curve. LO2
- Supply-side policies attempt to alter price and output decisions directly. If successful, they'll shift the aggregate supply curve to the right. A rightward AS shift implies less inflation *and* less unemployment. LO3
- Marginal tax rates are a major concern of supply-side economists. High tax rates discourage extra work, investment, and saving. A reduction in marginal tax rates should shift aggregate supply to the right. LO3
- The tax elasticity of supply measures the response of quantity supplied to changes in tax rates. Empirical evidence suggests that tax elasticity is low and that short-run shifts of the aggregate supply curve are therefore small. LO3
- Investments in human capital increase productivity and therefore shift aggregate supply also. Workers' training and education enhancement are policy tools. LO3
- Government regulation often raises the cost of production and limits output. Deregulation is intended to reduce costly restrictions on price and output behavior, thereby shifting the AS curve to the right. LO3

- Public infrastructure is part of the economy's capital resources. Investments in infrastructure (such as transportation systems) facilitate market exchanges and expand production possibilities. LO3
- Trade barriers shift the AS curve leftward by raising the cost of imported inputs and the price of imported products. Lowering trade barriers increases aggregate supply. LO3

Key Terms

stagflation
aggregate supply
Phillips curve
marginal tax rate
investment
tax rebate
tax elasticity of supply
saving
human capital
structural unemployment
labor productivity
transfer payments
infrastructure

Questions for Discussion

1. Why might prices rise when aggregate demand increases? What factors might influence the extent of price inflation? LO1
2. What were the unemployment and inflation rates last year? Where would they lie on Figure 16.5? Can you explain the implied shift from curve PC_2? LO2
3. Why would a Gulf Coast hurricane have *national* impact on aggregate supply? (News, page 319). LO1
4. Which of the following groups are likely to have the highest tax elasticity of labor supply? (*a*) college students, (*b*) single parents, (*c*) primary earners in two-parent families, and (*d*) secondary earners in two-parent families. Why are there differences? LO3
5. How is the aggregate supply curve affected by (*a*) minimum wage laws, and (*b*) Social Security payroll taxes and retirement benefits? LO3
6. OSHA predicted that its proposed ergonomics rules (text, page 327) would have cut repetitive-stress injuries by 50 percent. Was Congress correct in repealing those rules? LO1
7. If all workplace-safety regulations both (*a*) improve workers well-being and (*b*) raise production costs, how should the line between "good" regulations and "bad" regulations be drawn? LO3
8. How do each of the following infrastructure items affect aggregate supply? (*a*) highways, (*b*) schools, (*c*) sewage systems, and (*d*) courts and prisons. LO3
9. How would the volume and timing of capital investments be affected by (*a*) a permanent cut in the capital-gains tax, and (*b*) a temporary 10-percent tax credit? LO3
10. Why would Democrats oppose a capital-gains tax cut that might invigorate a stalled economy? LO3
11. In the cartoon on page 324, which "expert" is the supply-sider? LO3

problems The Student Problem Set at the back of this book contains numerical and graphing problems for this chapter.

web activities to accompany this chapter can be found on the Online Learning Center: **http://www.mhhe.com/economics/schiller11e**

Growth and Productivity: Long-Run Possibilities

LEARNING OBJECTIVES

After reading this chapter, you should know:

LO1. The principal sources of economic growth.

LO2. Policy tools for accelerating growth.

LO3. The pros and cons of continued growth.

Economic growth is the fundamental determinant of the long-run success of any nation, the basic source of rising living standards, and the key to meeting the needs and desires of the American people.

—*Economic Report of the President, 1992*

Imagine a world with no fax machines, no cell phones, no satellite TV, and no digital sound. Such a world actually existed—and only 30 years ago! At the time, personal computers were still on the drawing board, and laptops weren't even envisioned. Web sites were a place where spiders gathered, not locations in the Internet. Home video hadn't been seen, and no one had yet popped any microwave popcorn. Biotechnology hadn't yet produced any blockbuster drugs, and people wore the same pair of athletic shoes for a wide variety of sports.

New products are evidence of economic progress. Over time, we produce not only *more* goods and services but also *new* and *better* goods and services. In the process, we get richer: Our material living standards rise.

Rising living standards aren't inevitable, however. According to World Bank estimates, almost 3 *billion* people—nearly half the world's population—continue to live in abject poverty (with incomes of less than $2 per day). Worse still, living standards in many of the poorest countries have *fallen* in the last decade. Living standards also fell in eastern Europe when communism collapsed and a painful transition to market economies began.

This chapter takes a longer-term view of economic performance. Chapters 8 to 16 were concerned with the business cycle—that is, *short-run* variations in output and prices. This chapter looks at the prospects for *long-run* growth and considers three questions:

- **How important is economic growth?**
- **How does an economy grow?**
- **Is continued economic growth possible? Is it desirable?**

We develop answers to these questions by first examining the nature of economic growth and then examining its sources and potential limits.

THE NATURE OF GROWTH

Economic growth refers to increases in the output of goods and services. But there are two distinct ways in which output increases, and they have very different implications for our economic welfare.

Short-Run Changes in Capacity Utilization

The easiest kind of growth comes from increased use of our productive capabilities. In any given year there's a limit to an economy's potential output. This limit is determined by the quantity of resources available and our technological know-how. We've illustrated these short-run limits with a **production possibilities** curve, as in Figure 17.1*a*. By using all our available resources and our best expertise, we can produce any combination of goods and services on the production possibilities curve.

production possibilities: The alternative combinations of final goods and services that could be produced in a given time period with all available resources and technology.

We don't always take full advantage of our productive capacity. The economy often produces a mix of output that lies *inside* our production possibilities, like point *A* in Figure 17.1*a*. When this happens, a major *short-run* goal of macro policy is to achieve full employment—to move us from point *A* to some point on the production possibilities curve (such as point *B*). In the process, we produce more output.

Long-Run Changes in Capacity

Once we're fully utilizing our productive capacity, further increases in output are attainable only if we *expand* that capacity. To do so we have to *shift* the production possibilities curve outward as in Figure 17.1*b*. Such shifts imply an increase in *potential* GDP—that is, our productive capacity.

Over time, increases in capacity are critical. Short-run increases in the utilization of existing capacity can generate only modest increases in output. Even high unemployment rates, such as 7 percent, leave little room for increased output. ***To achieve large and lasting increases in output we must push our production possibilities outward.*** For this reason, economists often define **economic growth** in terms of changes in *potential* GDP.

economic growth: An increase in output (real GDP); an expansion of production possibilities.

The unique character of economic growth can also be illustrated with aggregate supply and demand curves. Figure 17.2 depicts both a sloped, *short-run* AS curve and a vertical, *long-run*

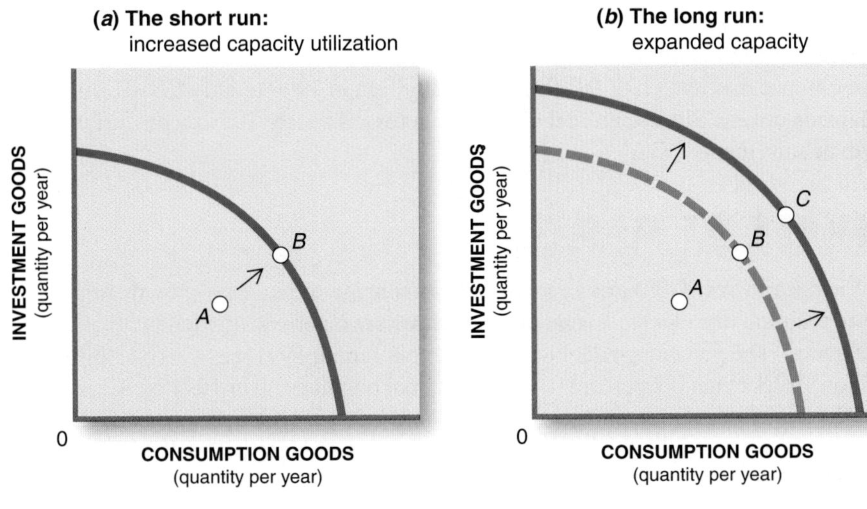

FIGURE 17.1
Two Types of Growth

Increases in output result from increased use of existing capacity or from increases in that capacity itself. In part *a* the mix of output at point *A* doesn't make full use of production possibilities. We can get additional output by employing more of our available resources or using them more efficiently. This is illustrated by point *B* (or any other point on the curve).

Once we're on the production possibilities curve, we can get more output only by *increasing* our productive capacity. This is illustrated by the outward *shift* of the production possibilities curve in part *b*.

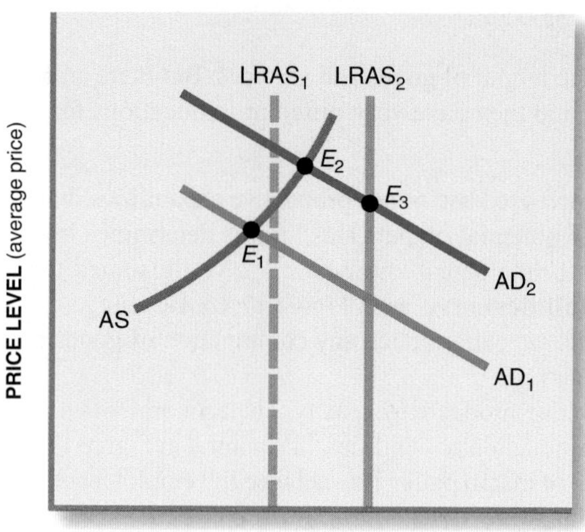

FIGURE 17.2
Shifts of Long-Run Supply

Macro stabilization policies try to shift the aggregate demand curve (e.g., from AD$_1$ to AD$_2$) to achieve greater output and employment. The vertical long-run AS curve implies that these efforts will have no lasting impact on the natural rate of output, however. To achieve economic growth, the long-run aggregate supply curve must be shifted to the right (e.g., from LRAS$_1$ to LRAS$_2$).

AS curve. In the short run, macro stabilization policies try to shift the AD curve to a more desirable price-output equilibrium. Such demand-side policies are unlikely to change the country's long-run capacity to produce, however. At best they move the macro equilibrium to a more desirable point on the *short-run* AS curve (for example, from E_1 to E_2 in Figure 17.2).

Our productive capacity may increase nevertheless. If it does, the "natural" long-run AS curve will also shift. In this framework, ***economic growth implies a rightward shift of the long-run aggregate supply curve.*** Should that occur, the economy will be able to produce still more output with less inflationary pressure (e.g., as at E_3 in Figure 17.2).

Nominal vs. Real GDP

real GDP: The value of final output produced in a given period, adjusted for changing prices.

base period: The time period used for comparative analysis; the basis for indexing, e.g., of price changes.

Notice we refer to *real* GDP, not *nominal* GDP, in our concept of economic growth. Nominal GDP can rise even when the quantity of goods and services falls, as was the case in 1991. The total quantity of goods and services produced in 1991 was less than the quantity produced in 1990. Nevertheless, prices rose enough in 1991 to keep nominal GDP growing.

Real GDP refers to the actual quantity of goods and services produced. Real GDP avoids the distortions of inflation by adjusting for changing prices. By using 2000 prices as a **base period,** we observe that real GDP fell from $7,113 billion in 1990 to only $7,101 billion in 1991 (see inside cover). Since then real GDP has increased nearly 70 percent—an impressive growth achievement.

MEASURES OF GROWTH

The Growth Rate

growth rate: Percentage change in real output from one period to another.

webnote

The U.S. Bureau of Economic Analysis (BEA) maintains quarterly data on real GDP growth in its "overview of the U.S. economy" at www.bea.gov/newsreleases/glance.htm

Typically, changes in real GDP are expressed in percentage terms, as a growth *rate.* The **growth rate** is simply the change in real output between two periods divided by total output in the base period. The percentage decline in real output during 1991 was thus $12 billion ÷ $7,113 billion, or less than 0.2 percent. By contrast, real output grew in 1992 by 3.3 percent.

Figure 17.3 illustrates the recent growth experience of the U.S. economy. In the 1960s, real GDP grew by an average of 4.1 percent per year. Economic growth slowed to only 2.8 percent in the 1970s, however, with actual output declines in 3 years. The steep recession of 1982, as seen in Figure 17.3, reduced GDP growth in the 1980s to an even lower rate: 2.5 percent per year. The 1990s started out even worse, with negligible growth in 1990 and a recession in 1991. The economy performed a lot better after that, however. From 1997 to 2000, real GDP grew by more than 4.5 percent a year. That acceleration of the growth rate was so impressive that observers began to talk about a "New Economy," in which faster growth would be the norm (see News on next page).

The notion of a fast-growth New Economy was badly shaken in 2001. In the first quarter of 2001, GDP fell by 0.2 percent and then by 0.6 percent in the second quarter. In the third quarter (which included the Sept. 11 terrorist attacks), real GDP again declined by 1.3

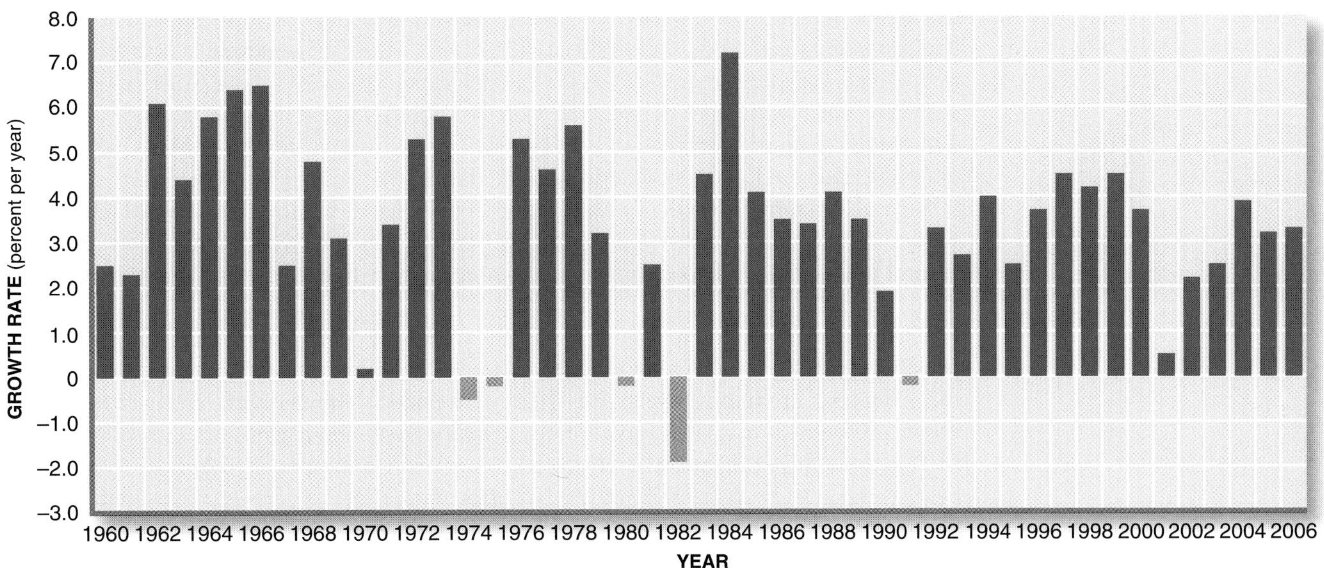

FIGURE 17.3
Recent U.S. Growth Rates

Total output typically increases from one year to another. The focus of policy is on the growth *rate,* that is, how fast real GDP increases from one year to the next. Annual growth rates since 1960 have ranged from a high of 7.2 percent (1984) to a low of *minus* 1.9 percent (1982).

Source: *Economic Report of the President, 2007.*

percent. Analysts fretted over whether the economy would ever get back on the "fast track" of 3.5–4.0 percent growth or would instead be saddled with years of more sluggish growth (2.0–2.5 pe rcent)—or worse.

The Exponential Process. At first blush, all the anxiety about growth rates seems a bit overblown. Indeed, the whole subject of economic growth looks rather dull when you discover that "big" gains in economic growth are measured in fractions of a percent. However,

IN THE NEWS

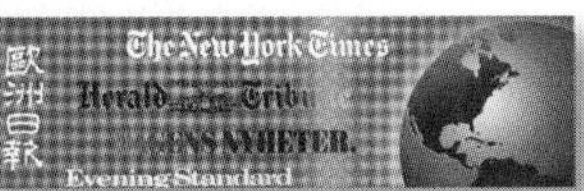

The New Economy

The U.S. economy today displays several exceptional features. The first is its strong rate of productivity growth. . . . A second is its unusually low levels of both inflation and unemployment. . . . A third is the disappearance of Federal budget deficits. . . . A fourth is the strength of the U.S. economy's performance relative to other industrial economies. . . . These developments reveal profound changes in economic trends that justify the term "New Economy."

Three interrelated factors lie behind these extraordinary economic gains: technological innovation, organizational changes in business, and public policy. . . . The interactions among these three factors have created a virtuous cycle in which developments in one area reinforce and stimulate developments in another. The result is an economic system in which the whole is greater than the sum of the parts. . . .

This Report defines the New Economy by the extraordinary gains in performance—including rapid productivity growth, rising incomes, low unemployment, and moderate inflation—that have resulted from this combination of virtually reinforcing advances in technologies, business practices, and economic policies.

Source: *Economic Report of the President, 2001,* pp. 22–23.

Analysis: The successes of the late 1990s spawned the hope of continuing rapid gains in productivity and GDP growth—a "new" economy. The recession of 2001, coupled with widespread "dot.com" failures, shed doubt on this concept.

webnote

Find growth rates of various countries from the World Bank at www.worldbank.org/data. Click on "Data by Topic," then choose "Macroeconomics and Growth." Under "Economic Growth and Structure," click on "Growth of Output."

this initial impression isn't fair. First, even 1 year's "low" growth implies lost output. If we had just *maintained* output in 1991 at its 1990 level—that is, "achieved" a *zero* growth rate rather than a 0.2 percent decline—we would have had $12 billion more worth of goods and services, which works out to over $40 worth of goods and services per person. In today's $14 trillion economy, each 1 percent of GDP growth translates into almost $500 more output per person. Lots of people would like that extra output.

Second, economic growth is a *continuing* process. Gains made in one year accumulate in future years. It's like interest you earn at the bank: If you leave your money in the bank for several years, you begin to earn interest on your interest. Eventually you accumulate a nice little bankroll.

The process of economic growth works the same way. Each little shift of the production possibilities curve broadens the base for future GDP. As shifts accumulate over many years, the economy's productive capacity is greatly expanded. Ultimately we discover that those "little" differences in annual growth rates generate tremendous gains in GDP.

This cumulative process, whereby interest or growth is compounded from one year to the next, is called an "exponential process." At growth rates of 2.5 percent, GDP doubles in 28 years. With 3.5 percent growth, GDP doubles in only 20 years. In a single generation the *difference* between 2.5 percent growth and 3.5 percent growth amounts to nearly $10 trillion of output a year. That *difference* is roughly two-thirds of this year's total output. From this longer-term perspective, the difference between 2.5 percent and 3.5 percent growth begins to look very meaningful.

GDP per Capita: A Measure of Living Standards

GDP per capita: Total GDP divided by total population; average GDP.

The exponential process looks even more meaningful when we translate it into *per capita* terms. We can do so by looking at GDP *per capita* rather than total GDP. **GDP per capita** is simply total output divided by total population. In 2006, the total output of the U.S. economy was $13 trillion. Since there were 300 million of us to share that output, GDP per capita was

$$\frac{\text{GDP per capita}}{(2006)} = \frac{\$13 \text{ trillion of output}}{300 \text{ million people}} = \$43{,}333$$

This does not mean that every man, woman, and child in the United States received $43,333 worth of goods and services in 2006; it simply indicates how much output was potentially available to the "average" person. GDP per capita is often used as a basic measure of our standard of living.

Growth in GDP per capita is attained only when the growth of output exceeds population growth. In the United States, this condition is usually achieved. Even when *total* GDP growth slowed in the 1970s and 1980s, *per capita* GDP kept rising because the U.S. population was growing by only 1 percent a year. Hence, even relatively slow economic growth of 2.5 percent a year was enough to keep raising living standards.

The developing nations of the Third World aren't so fortunate. Many of these countries bear both slower *economic* growth and faster *population* growth. They have a difficult time *maintaining* living standards, much less increasing them. Madagascar, for example, is one of the poorest countries in the world, with GDP per capita of roughly $900. Yet its population continues to grow rapidly (2.8 percent per year), putting constant pressure on living standards. In recent years, Madagascar's GDP grew at a slower rate of only 2.0 percent. As a consequence, GDP per capita *declined* nearly 0.8 percent per year. As we'll see in Chapter 37, many other poor nations are in similarly dire straits.

By comparison with these countries, the United States has been most fortunate. Our GDP per capita has more than doubled since 1980s, despite several recessions. This means that the average person today has twice as many goods and services as the average person had a generation ago.

What about the future? Will we continue to enjoy substantial gains in living standards? Many Americans harbor great doubts. A 2005 poll revealed that 40 percent of adults believe their children's living standards will be no higher than today's. That would happen only if population growth outstrips or equals GDP growth. That seems most unlikely. Table 17.1 displays more optimistic scenarios in which GDP continues to grow faster than the popula-

Net Growth Rate (%)	Doubling Time (years)
0.0%	Never
0.5	140 years
1.0	70
1.5	47
2.0	35
2.5	30
3.0	24
3.5	20
4.0	18

TABLE 17.1
The Rule of 72

Small differences in annual growth rates cumulate into large differences in GDP. Shown here are the number of years it would take to double GDP per capita at various net growth rates. *"Net" growth* refers to the GDP growth rate minus the population growth rate.

Doubling times can be approximated by the "rule of 72." Seventy-two divided by the growth rate equals the number of years it takes to double.

tion. If GDP *per capita* continues to grow at 2 percent per year—as it did in the 1990s—it will take 35 years to double our standard of living. If GDP per capita grows just half a percent faster, say, by 2.5 percent per year, our standard of living will double in only 30 years.

GDP per Worker: A Measure of Productivity

The potential increases in living standards depicted in Table 17.1 won't occur automatically. Someone is going to have to produce more output if we want GDP per capita to rise. One reason our living standard rose in the 1980s is that the labor force grew faster than the population. Those in the World War II baby boom had reached maturity and were entering the **labor force** in droves. At the same time, more women took jobs outside the home, a trend that continued into the 1990s (see Figure 6.2). As a consequence, the **employment rate** increased significantly, as Figure 17.4 shows. With the number of workers growing faster than the population, GDP per capita was sure to rise.

labor force: All persons over age 16 who are either working for pay or actively seeking paid employment.

employment rate: The percentage of the adult population that is employed.

The employment rate can't increase forever. At the limit, everyone would be in the labor market, and no further workers could be found. Further increases in GDP per capita could only come from increases in output *per worker.*

The most common measure of **productivity** is output per labor-hour, which is simply the ratio of total output to the number of hours worked. As noted earlier, total GDP in 2006 was

productivity: Output per unit of input, for example, output per labor-hour.

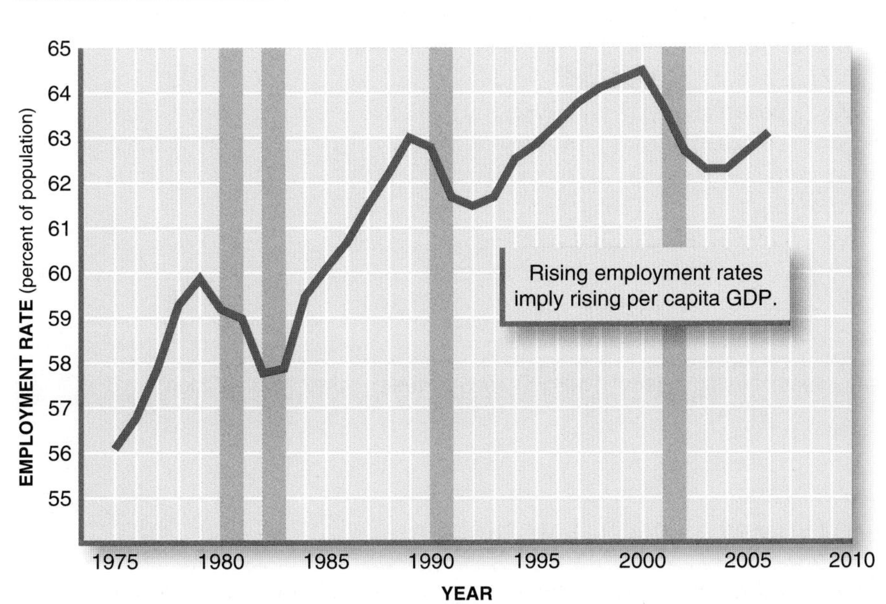

FIGURE 17.4
A Rising Employment Rate

The entry of Baby Boomers (born 1946–60) into the labor force and increased labor-force attachment of women caused the ratio of workers to total population (the employment rate) to rise from 1975 to 2000. This boosted per capita GDP.

webnote

The U.S. Bureau of Labor Statistics (BLS) maintains quarterly data on labor productivity at www.bls.gov/data

approximately \$13 trillion. In that same year the labor force was employed for a total of 254 billion hours. Hence, the average worker's productivity was

$$\text{Labor productivity} = \frac{\text{total output}}{\text{total labor-hours}} = \frac{\$13 \text{ trillion}}{254 \text{ billion hours}} = \$51 \text{ per hour}$$

The increase in our GDP per capita in recent decades is directly related to the higher productivity of the average U.S. worker. The average worker today produces twice as many goods and services as the average worker did in 1980.

The Productivity Turnaround. For economic growth to continue, the productivity of the average U.S. worker must rise still further. Will it? As Figure 17.5 reveals, productivity grew at an average pace of 1.4 percent from 1973 to 1995. Along the way, however, there were many years (e.g., 1978–84) in which productivity advances slowed to a snail's pace. This productivity slowdown constrained GDP growth.

After 1995, productivity advances accelerated sharply, as seen in Figure 17.5. This productivity jump was so impressive that it raised hopes for a "New Economy" (see News, page 335), in which technological breakthroughs, better management, and enlightened public policy would keep both productivity and GDP growing at faster rates.

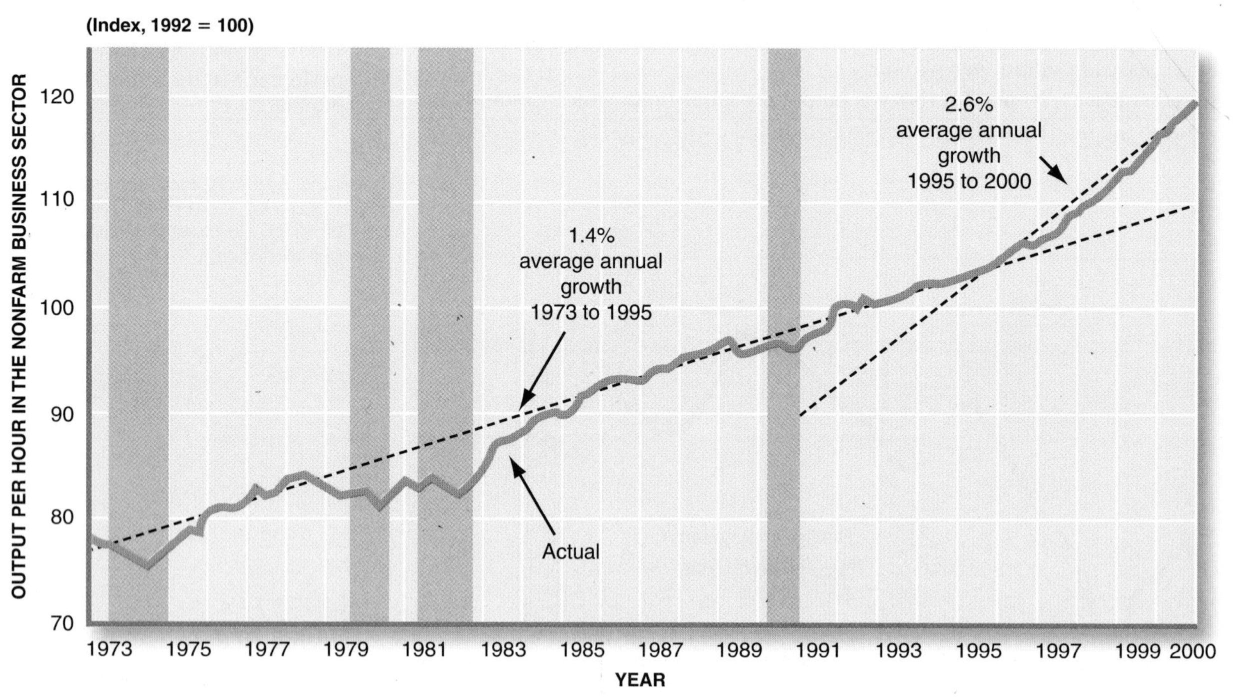

FIGURE 17.5
Productivity Gains

Increasing productivity (output per worker) is the critical factor in raising per capita GDP over time. Productivity advances slowed in 1978–84 but accelerated sharply in 1995–2000.

Note: Shaded areas indicate recessions.

Source: *U.S. Department of Commerce.*

SOURCES OF GROWTH

The arithmetic of economic growth is simple. Future output growth depends on two factors:

$$\text{Growth rate of total output} = \text{growth rate of labor force} + \text{growth rate of productivity}$$

Accordingly, how fast GDP increases in the future depends on how fast the labor force grows and how fast productivity advances. Since the long-run growth of the labor force has stabilized at around 1.1 percent, the real uncertainty about future economic growth originates in the unpredictability of productivity advances. Will output per worker increase at the snail's pace of only 1 percent a year or at much faster rates of 2, 3, or even 4 percent per year?

To assess the potential for U.S. productivity gains, we need to examine the sources of productivity improvement. ***The sources of productivity gains include***

- ***Higher skills***—an increase in labor skills.
- ***More capital***—an increase in the ratio of capital to labor.
- ***Technological advance***—the development and use of better capital equipment and products.
- ***Improved management***—better use of available resources in the production process.

Human-Capital Investment

Continuing advances in education and skills training have greatly increased the quality of U.S. labor. In 1950, less than 8 percent of all U.S. workers had completed college. Today, nearly 30 percent of the workforce has completed 4 years of college. There has also been a substantial increase in vocational training, both in the public sector and by private firms.

In the 1970s, these improvements in the quality of individual workers were offset by a change in the composition of the labor force. As we observed in Chapters 6 and 16, the proportion of teenagers and women in the labor force grew tremendously in the 1960s and 1970s. These Baby Boomers and their mothers contributed to higher output. Because teenagers and women (re)entering the labor market generally have less job experience than adult men, however, *average* productivity fell.

This phenomenon reversed itself in the 1990s, as the Baby Boomers reached their prime working years. The increased productivity of the workforce is not a reflection of the aging process itself. Rather, the gains in productivity reflect the greater **human-capital** investment associated with more schooling and more on-the-job learning.

human capital: The knowledge and skills possessed by the workforce.

Physical-Capital Investment

The knowledge and skills a worker brings to the job don't completely determine his or her productivity. A worker with no tools, no computers, and no machinery won't produce much even if she has a Ph.D. Similarly, a worker with outmoded equipment won't produce as much as an equally capable worker equipped with the newest machines and the best technology. From this perspective, ***a primary determinant of labor productivity is the rate of capital investment.*** In other words, improvements in output per *worker* depend in large part on increases in the quantity and quality of *capital* equipment (see World View).

The efforts of the average U.S. worker are presently augmented with over $100,000 of invested capital. This huge capital endowment is a prime source of high productivity. To *increase* productivity, however, the quality and quantity of capital available to the average worker must continue to increase. That requires capital spending to increase faster than the labor force. With the labor force growing at 1.1 percent a year, that's not a hard standard to beat. How *much* faster capital investment grows is nevertheless a decisive factor in productivity gains. In the 1980s, investment growth was slow and erratic. In the 1990s, however, capital investment accelerated markedly. Investment in information technology (computers, software, and telecommunications equipment) was exceedingly robust, reaching growth rates as high as 25 percent. In the process, workers got "smarter," communications improved, and productivity jumped. The Council of Economic Advisers credited this boom in information-technology investment with nearly one-third of *all* the 1995–99 GDP growth.

Saving and Investment Rates. The dependence of productivity gains on capital investment puts a new perspective on consumption and saving. In the short run, the primary

WORLD VIEW

High Investment = Fast Growth

Investment in new plant and equipment is essential for economic growth. In general, countries that allocate a larger share of output to investment will grow more rapidly. In recent years, China has had one of the world's fastest GDP growth rates and one of the highest investment rates.

Country	Gross Investment as Percentage of GDP	Growth Rate of GDP (average, 2000–2005)
Azerbaijan	55	12.7
China	39	9.6
Latvia	33	7.9
India	24	6.9
United States	18	2.8
Uruguay	13	1.0

Source: World Bank. Used with permission by the International Bank for Reconstruction and Development/The World Bank.

Analysis: Investment increases production possibilities. Countries that devote a larger share of output to investment tend to grow faster.

concern of macroeconomic policy is to balance aggregate demand and aggregate supply. In this context, savings are a form of leakage that requires offsetting injections of investment or government spending. From the longer-run perspective of economic growth, saving and investment take on added importance. ***Savings aren't just a form of leakage but a basic source of investment financing.*** If we use all our resources to produce consumer, export, and public-sector goods, there won't be any investment. In that case, we might not face a short-run stabilization problem—our productive capacity might be fully utilized—but we'd confront a long-run *growth* problem. Indeed, if we consumed our entire output, our productive capacity would actually shrink since we wouldn't even be replacing worn-out plant and equipment. We must have at least enough savings to finance **net investment.**

net investment: Gross investment less depreciation.

Household and Business Saving. Household saving rates in the United States have been notoriously low and falling since the early 1980s. In 2000 and again in 2006, U.S. households actually *dis*saved—spending more on consumption than their disposable incomes. Despite the meager flow of household saving, investment growth actually accelerated in the late 1990s. Virtually all of that investment was financed with *business saving* and *foreign investment.* The retained earnings and depreciation allowances that create business savings generated a huge cash flow for investment in the 1990s.

Foreign Investment. In addition to this business-saving flow, foreign investors poured money into U.S. plant, equipment, software, and financial assets. These two income flows more than compensated for the virtual absence of household saving. Many people worry, though, that foreign investments may get diverted elsewhere and that business saving will drop when profits diminish. Then continued investment growth will be more dependent on a flow of funds from household saving.

Management Training

The accumulation of more and better capital equipment does not itself guarantee higher productivity or faster GDP growth. The human factor is still critical: How well resources are organized and managed will affect the rate of growth. Hence, entrepreneurship and the quality of continuing management are also major determinants of economic growth.

It's difficult to characterize differences in management techniques or to measure their effectiveness. However, much attention has been focused in recent years on the alleged shortsightedness of U.S. managers. U.S. firms, it is said, focus too narrowly on short-run profits, neglecting long-term productivity. There is little evidence of such a failure, however. The spreading use of stock options in management ranks ties executives' compensation to multiyear performance. Moreover, productivity trends in the United States have not only accelerated in recent years but also have consistently surpassed productivity gains in other industrial nations (see World View). To maintain that advantage, U.S. corporations spend billions of dollars each year on continuing management training. Accordingly, the charge of shortsightedness is better regarded as a precautionary warning than an established fact.

Research and Development

A fourth and vital source of productivity advance is research and development (R&D), a broad concept that includes scientific research, product development, innovations in production techniques, and the development of management improvements. R&D activity may be a specific, identifiable activity such as in a research lab, or it may be part of the process of learning by doing. In either case, the insights developed from R&D generally lead to new products and cheaper ways of producing them. Over time, R&D is credited

WORLD VIEW

U.S. Workers Compete Well

U.S. workers are the most productive in the world, producing close to $80,000 of output per year. In manufacturing, the U.S. productivity lead continues to widen. Among the 15 industrial nations tracked by the Bureau of Labor Statistics, only two had faster productivity growth than the United States since 2000.

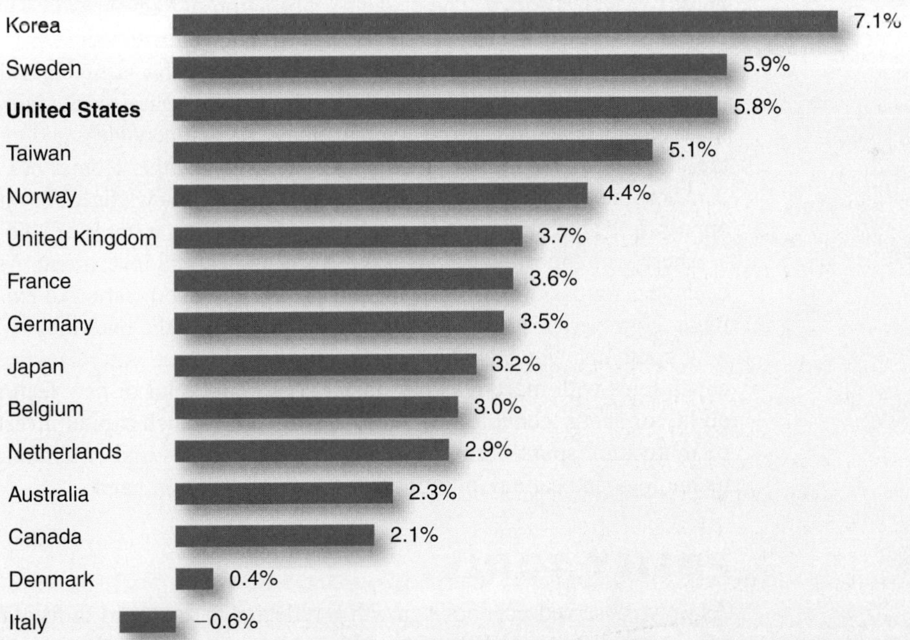

Source: U.S. Bureau of Labor Statistics.

Analysis: U.S. productivity gains are among the fastest of industrial nations. These gains are fueled by research and development and investment spending.

IN THE NEWS

Intel Reveals Major Chip-Design Advance

Intel announced yesterday that it had mastered a new design that makes computing more powerful, less expensive and so much more efficient that mobile devices like cellphones may soon accomplish tasks reserved until recently for desktop computers and other equipment with larger processors. . . .

These advances are the latest in a series of fundamental improvements in chip design that have long driven the technology revolution. According to the tenet known as Moore's Law, named for Intel co-founder Gordon E. Moore, progress in building chips doubles the power of computer processors about every 18 months.

But this axiom is more a historical observation and than a guarantee, and engineers had recently become increasingly skeptical about whether the rate of process could be maintained. Intel's announcement signaled that the pace could continue for the time being.

—Alan Sipress

Source: *Washington Post,* January 28, 2007, p. A 10. © **2007, The Washington Post, excerpted with permission.**

Analysis: A steady stream of inventions and innovations advances worker productivity, raising the potential for continued economic growth.

webnote

The National Science Foundation tracks R&D spending. Visit www.nsf.gov and click on "Science Statistics."

with the greatest contributions to economic growth. In his study of U.S. growth during the period 1929–82, Edward Denison concluded that 26 percent of *total* growth was due to "advances in knowledge." Gordon Moore, the co-founder of Intel, doesn't see an end to research-based productivity advance. His "Moore's Law" predicts a *doubling* of computer power every 18 months. As the accompanying News suggests, he may not be wrong.

New Growth Theory. The evident contribution of "advances in knowledge" to economic growth has spawned a new perspective called "new growth theory." "Old growth theory," it is said, emphasized the importance of bricks and mortar, that is, saving and investing in new plant and equipment. By contrast, "new" growth theory emphasizes the importance of investing in ideas. Paul Romer, a Stanford economist, asserts that new ideas and the spread of knowledge are the primary engines of growth. Unfortunately, neither Romer nor anyone else is exactly sure how one spawns new ideas or best disseminates knowledge. The only evident policy lever appears to be the support of research and development, a staple of "old" growth theory.

There's an important link between R&D and capital investment. As noted earlier, part of each year's gross investment compensates for the depreciation of existing plant and equipment. However, new machines are rarely identical to the ones they replace. When you get a new computer, you're not just *replacing* an old one; you're *upgrading* your computing capabilities with more memory, faster speed, and a lot of new features. Indeed, the availability of *better* technology is often the motive for such capital investment. The same kind of motivation spurs businesses to upgrade machines and structures. Hence, advances in technology and capital investment typically go hand in hand.

POLICY TOOLS

As we've observed, economic growth is reflected in rightward shifts of the long-run aggregate supply curve (Figure 17.2). It should not surprise you, then, that growth policy makes liberal use of the tools in the supply-side toolbox (Chapter 16). The challenge for growth policy is to select those tools that will give the economy *long*-run increases in productive capacity.

Increasing Human-Capital Investment

Since *workers* are the ultimate source of output and productivity growth, the first place to look for growth-accelerating tools is in the area of human-capital development.

Governments at all levels already play a tremendous role in human-capital development by building, operating, and subsidizing schools. The quantity and quality of continuing investments in America's schools will have a major effect on future productivity. Government policy

WORLD VIEW

Work Visas Are Allowing Washington to Sidestep Immigration Reform

The inscription on the Statue of Liberty is quietly being rewritten: "Give me your tired, your poor, your huddled masses yearning to breathe free; I'll also take your skilled employees under the temporary visa program, H-1B."

The H-1B visa was established in 1990 to permit foreigners with a college degree or higher to work in the United States for a renewable three-year term for employers who petition on their behalf. . . . Demand for H-1B visas by employers is high, particularly among high-technology companies. . . .

In addition to workers with H-1B visas, hundreds of thousands of other foreigners are admitted to work temporarily in the United States under visa categories covering intracompany transfers, individuals with extraordinary ability, registered nurses and workers in nonprofit religious organizations. A fast-growing category is the Nafta TN visa, which offers an unlimited number of temporary visas for professional workers from Canada and soon Mexico.

In a new book, "Heaven's Door," George Borjas, a Harvard economist, proposes that the United States adopt a Canadian-style point system, in which applicants for visas are assigned points on the basis of characteristics like their ability to speak English, work-force skills, family ties, refugee status and ethnic diversity. Those whose total points exceed a certain threshold would be admitted.

—Alan B. Krueger

The New York Times

Source: *The New York Times*, May 25, 2000. Copyright © 2000 The New York Times Company. Reprinted with permission. www.nytimes.com

Analysis: Immigrant flows affect a nation's stock of human capital. Can or should immigrants be selected on the basis of human-capital traits?

also plays an *indirect* role in schooling decisions by offering subsidized loans for college and vocational education.

Immigration policy is also a determinant of the nation's stock of human capital. At least 1 million immigrants enter the United States every year. Most of the *legal* immigrants are relatives of people already living in the United States as permanent residents (with green cards) or naturalized citizens. In addition to these *family-based* visas, the United States also grants a much smaller number of *employment-based* visas. The H-1B program offers temporary (3-year) visas to highly skilled foreigners who want to work in U.S. firms. By admitting highly skilled workers, the United States gains valuable human capital and relieves some structural unemployment. Only 65,000 H-1B visas are available each year, however—a tiny percent of the U.S. labor force. Temporary visas for agricultural (H-2A) and other less-skilled workers (H-2B) are smaller still. To accelerate our productivity and GDP growth, observers urge us to expand these programs, particularly along the lines of Canada's explicit skill preferences (see World View).

webnote

The U.S. Immigration and Naturalization Service (INS) maintains a profile of immigrants, including their occupational skills. Visit www.uscis.gov

Increasing Physical-Capital Investment

As in the case of human capital, the possibilities for increasing physical-capital investment are also many and diverse.

Investment Incentives. The tax code is a mechanism for stimulating investment. Faster depreciation schedules, tax credits for new investments, and lower business tax rates all encourage increased investment in physical capital. The 2002 and 2003 tax cuts were designed for this very purpose.

webnote

See if you would qualify for Canadian immigration by completing the self-assessment worksheet provided by Canada's Department of Citizenship and Immigration at www.cic.gc.ca/english

Savings Incentives. In principle, the government can also deepen the savings pool that finances investment. Here again, the tax code offers some policy levers. Tax preferences for Individual Retirement Accounts and other pension savings may increase the marginal propensity to save or at least redirect savings flows to longer-term investments. The Bush 2001 tax package (Chapter 11) included not only a *short-run* fiscal stimulus (e.g., tax rebates) but also enhanced incentives for *long-term* savings (retirement and college savings accounts).

Infrastructure Development. The government also directly affects the level of physical capital through its public works spending. As we observed in Chapter 16, the $2 trillion already invested in bridges, highways, airports, sewer systems, and other infrastructure is an important part of America's capital stock. In 2004, Congress passed a new Highway bill that authorizes nearly $300 billion in infrastructure spending. Investments of that sort reduce transportation and commuting costs, making more resources available for production.

Fiscal Responsibility. In addition to these many supply-side interventions, the government's *macro* policies also affect the rate of investment and growth. Of particular interest in this regard is the federal government's budget balance. As we've seen, budget deficits may be a useful mechanism for attaining short-run macro stability. Those same deficits, however, may have negative long-run effects. If Uncle Sam borrows more funds from the national savings pool, other borrowers may end up with less. As we saw in Chapter 12, there's no guarantee that federal deficits will result in the **crowding out** of private investment. Let's recognize the risk of such an outcome, however. Hence, ***fiscal and monetary policies must be evaluated in terms of their impact not only on (short-run) aggregate demand but also on long-run aggregate supply.***

crowding out: A reduction in private-sector borrowing (and spending) caused by increased government borrowing.

In this regard, the transformation of federal budget deficits to budget surpluses after 1997 facilitated the **crowding in** of private investment. After 1997, more funds were available to private investors and at lower interest rates. This surely contributed to the accelerated growth of capital investment in 1996–2000. Since then, budget balances have swung sharply into the red (see Figure 12.1).

crowding in: An increase in private-sector borrowing (and spending) caused by decreased government borrowing.

Maintaining Stable Expectations

The position of the long-run AS curve also depends on a broader assessment of the economic outlook. Expectations are a critical factor in both consumption and investment behavior. People who expect to lose their job next year are unlikely to buy a new car or house this year. Likewise, if investors expect interest rates to jump next year, they may be less willing to initiate long-run capital projects.

A sense of political and economic stability is critical to any long-run current trend. Within that context, however, specific perceptions of government policy may also alter investment plans. Investors may look to the Fed for a sense of monetary stability. They may be looking for a greater commitment to long-run price stability than to short-run adjustments of aggregate demand. In the fiscal policy area the same kind of commitment to long-run fiscal discipline rather than to short-run stimulus may be sought. Such possibilities imply that macro policy must be sensitive to long-run expectations.

Institutional Context

Last, but not least, the prospects for economic growth depend on the institutional context of a nation's economy. We first encountered this proposition in Chapter 1. In the World View on page 15, nations were ranked on the basis of an Index of Freedom. Studies have shown how greater economic freedom—secure property rights, open trade, lower taxes, less regulation—typically fosters faster growth. In less regulated economies there's more scope for entrepreneurship and more opportunity to invest. Recognizing this, nations around the world, from India to China, to Russia, to Latin America, have deregulated industries, privatized state enterprises, and promoted more open trade and investment.

THE ECONOMY TOMORROW

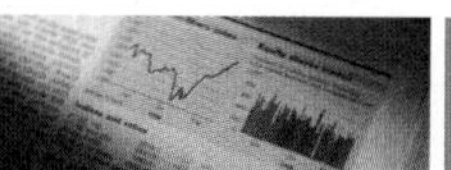

LIMITLESS GROWTH?

Suppose we pulled all the right policy levers and were able to keep the economy on a fast-paced growth track. Could the economy keep growing forever? Wouldn't we use up all available resources and ruin the environment in the process? How much long-term growth is really possible—or even desirable?

The Malthusian Formula for Destruction. The prospect of an eventual limit to economic growth originated in the eighteenth-century warnings of the Reverend Thomas

Malthus. Malthus argued that continued economic growth was impossible because food production couldn't keep pace with population growth. His dire projections earned the economics profession its characterization as the "dismal science."

When Malthus first issued his warnings, in 1798, the population of England (including Wales) was about 9 million. Annual production of barley, oats, and related grains was approximately 162 million bushels, and wheat production was around 50 million bushels, just about enough to feed the English population (a little had to be imported from other countries). Although the relationship between food and population was satisfactory in 1798, Malthus reasoned that starvation was not far off. First of all, he observed that "population, when unchecked, goes on doubling itself every 25 years, or increases in a geometrical ratio."[1] Thus, he foresaw the English population increasing to 36 million people by 1850, 144 million by 1900, and more than 1 billion by 1975, unless some social or natural restraints were imposed on population growth.

Limits to Food Production. One natural population check that Malthus foresaw was a scarcity of food. England had only a limited amount of land available for cultivation and was already farming the most fertile tracts. Before long, all available land would be in use and only improvements in agricultural productivity (output per acre) could increase food supplies. Some productivity increases were possible, Malthus concluded, but "the means of subsistence, under circumstances the most favorable to human industry, could not possibly be made to increase faster than in an arithmetical ratio."[2]

With population increasing at a *geometric* rate and food supplies at an *arithmetic* rate, the eventual outcome is evident. Figure 17.6 illustrates how the difference between a **geometric growth** path and an **arithmetic growth** path ultimately leads to starvation. As Malthus calculated it, per capita wheat output would decline from 5.5 bushels in 1800 to only 1.7 bushels in 1900 (Figure 17.5*b*). This wasn't enough food to feed the English people. According to Malthus's projections, either England died off about 100 years ago or it has been maintained at the brink of starvation for more than a century only by recurrent plagues, wars, or the kind of "moral restraint" that's commonly associated with Victorian preachments.

geometric growth: An increase in quantity by a constant proportion each year.

arithmetic growth: An increase in quantity by a constant amount each year.

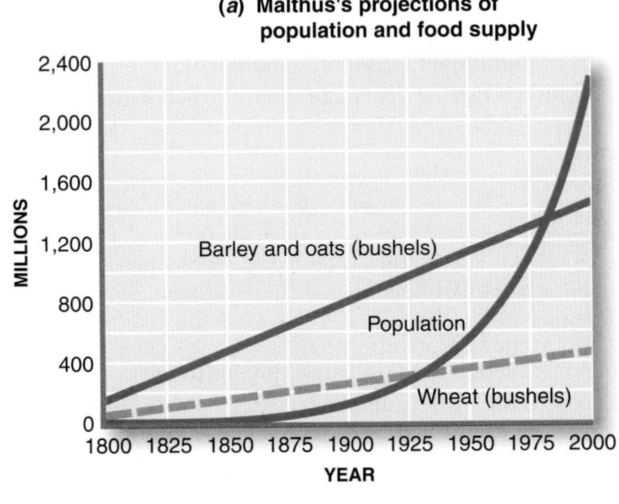

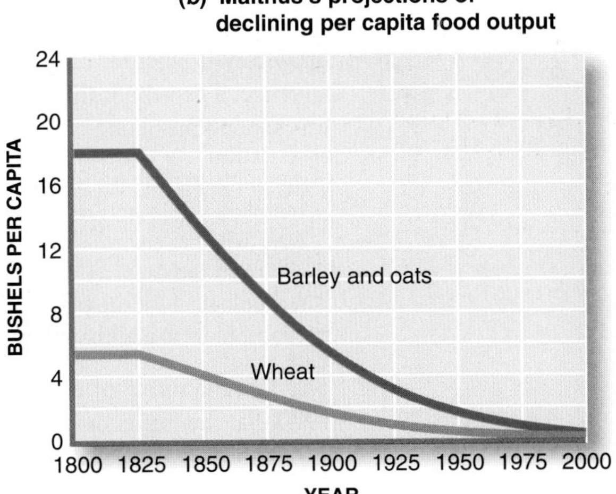

FIGURE 17.6
The Malthusian Doomsday

By projecting the growth rates of population and food output into the future, Malthus foresaw England's doomsday. At that time, the amount of available food per capita would be too small to sustain human life. Fortunately, Malthus overestimated population growth and underestimated productivity growth.

Source: Mathus's arithmetic applied to actual data for 1800 (see text).

[1]Thomas Malthus, *An Essay on the Principle of Population* (1798; reprint ed., Homewood, IL: Richard D. Irwin, 1963), p. 4.
[2]Ibid., p. 5.

Malthus's logic was impeccable. As long as population increased at a geometric rate while output increased at an arithmetic rate, England's doomsday was as certain as two plus two equals four. Malthus's error was not in his logic but in his empirical assumptions. He didn't know how fast output would increase over time, any more than we know whether people will be wearing electronic wings in the year 2203. He had to make an educated guess about future productivity trends. He based his estimates on his own experiences at the very beginning of the Industrial Revolution. As it turned out (fortunately), he had no knowledge of the innovations that would change the world, and he grossly underestimated the rate at which productivity would increase. ***Output, including agricultural products, has increased at a geometric rate, not at the much slower arithmetic rate foreseen by Malthus.*** As we observed earlier, U.S. output has grown at a long-term rate of roughly 3 percent a year. This *geometric* growth has doubled output every 25 years or so. That rate of economic growth is more than enough to raise living standards for a population growing by only 1 percent a year.

Resource Constraints. As Yale historian Paul Kennedy has suggested, maybe Malthus's doomsday predictions were just premature, not wrong. Maybe growth will come to a screeching halt when we run out of arable land, water, oil, or some other vital resource.

Malthus focused on arable land as the ultimate resource constraint. Other doomsday prophets have focused on the supply of whale oil, coal, oil, potatoes, and other "essential" resources. All such predictions ignore the role of markets in both promoting more efficient uses of scarce resources and finding substitutes for them. If, for example, the world were really running out of oil, what would happen to oil prices? Oil prices would rise substantially, prompting consumers to use oil more efficiently and prompting producers to develop alternative fuel sources.

If productivity and the availability of substitutes increase fast enough, the price of "scarce" resources might actually fall rather than rise. This possibility prompted a famous "Doomsday bet" between University of Maryland business professor Julian Simon and Stanford ecologist Paul Ehrlich. In 1980, Paul Ehrlich identified five metals that he predicted would become so scarce as to slow economic growth. Simon wagered that the price of those metals would actually *decline* over the ensuing decade as productivity and available substitutes increased. In 1990, their prices had fallen, and Ehrlich paid Simon for the bet.

Environmental Destruction. The market's ability to circumvent resource constraints would seem to augur well for our future. Doomsayers warn, though, that other limits to growth will emerge, even in a world of "unlimited" resources and unending productivity advance. The villain this time is pollution. Over 20 years ago, Paul Ehrlich warned about this second problem:

> Attempts to increase food production further will tend to accelerate the deterioration of our environment, which in turn will eventually *reduce* the capacity of the Earth to produce food. It is not clear whether environmental decay has now gone so far as to be essentially irreversible; it is possible that the capacity of the planet to support human life has been permanently impaired. Such technological "successes" as automobiles, pesticides, and inorganic nitrogen fertilizers are major contributors to environmental deterioration.[3]

The "inevitability" of environmental destruction led G. Evelyn Hutchinson to conclude in 1970 that the limits of habitable existence on Earth would be measured "in decades." [4]

It's not difficult for anyone with the basic five senses to comprehend the pollution problem. Pollution is as close these days as the air we breathe. Moreover, we can't fail to observe a distinct tendency for pollution levels to rise along with GDP and population expansion. If one projects such pollution trends into the future, things are bound to look pretty ugly.

Although pollution is universally acknowledged to be an important and annoying problem, we can't assume that the *rate* of pollution will continue unabated. On the contrary, the

[3]Paul R. Ehrlich and Anne H. Ehrlich, *Population, Resources, Environment: Issues in Human Ecology,* 2nd ed. (San Francisco: W. H. Freeman, 1972), p. 442.

[4]Evelyn Hutchinson, "The Biosphere," *Scientific American,* September 1970, p. 53: Dennis L. Meadows et al., *The Limits to Growth* (New York: Universe Books, 1972), Chapter 4.

growing awareness of the pollution problem has prompted to significant abatement efforts. The Environmental Protection Agency (EPA), for example, is unquestionably a force working for cleaner air and water. Indeed, active policies to curb pollution are as familiar as auto-exhaust controls, DDT bans, and tradable CO_2 and SO_2 permits. A computer programmed 10 or 20 years ago to project present pollution levels wouldn't have foreseen these abatement efforts and would thus have overestimated current pollution levels.

This isn't to say that we have in any final way "solved" the pollution problem or that we're even doing the best job we possibly can. It simply says that geometric increases in pollution aren't inevitable. There's simply no compelling reason why we have to continue polluting the environment; if we stop, another doomsday can be averted.

The Possibility of Growth. The misplaced focus on doomsday scenarios has a distinct opportunity cost. As Robert Solow summed up the issue:

> My real complaint about the Doomsday school [is that] it diverts attention from the really important things that can actually be done, step by step, to make things better. The end of the world *is* at hand—the earth, if you take the long view, will fall into the sun in a few billion years anyway, unless some other disaster happens first. In the meantime, I think we'd be better off passing a strong sulfur-emissions tax, or getting some Highway Trust Fund money allocated to mass transit, or building a humane and decent floor under family incomes, or overriding President Nixon's veto of a strong Water Quality Act, or reforming the tax system, or fending off starvation in Bengal—instead of worrying about the generalized "predicament of mankind."[5]

Karl Marx expressed these same thoughts nearly a century earlier. Marx chastised "the contemptible Malthus" for turning the attention of the working class away from what he regarded as the immediate problem of capitalist exploitation to some distant and ill-founded anxiety about "natural" disaster.[6]

The Desirability of Growth. Let's concede, then, that continued, perhaps even "limitless" growth is *possible.* Can we also agree that it's *desirable?* Those of us who commute on congested highways, worry about global warming, breathe foul air, and can't find a secluded camping site may raise a loud chorus of nos. But before reaching a conclusion let's at least determine what it is people don't like about the prospect of continued growth. Is it really economic growth per se that people object to, or instead the specific ways GDP has grown in the past?

"And so, extrapolating from the best figures available, we see that current trends, unless dramatically reversed, will inevitably lead to a situation in which the sky will fall."

Analysis: Most doomsday predictions fail to recognize the possibilities for behavioral change—or the role of market incentives in encouraging it.

[5]Robert M. Solow. "Is the End of the World at Hand?" *Challenge,* March 1973, p. 50.
[6]Cited by John Maddox in *The Doomsday Syndrome* (New York: McGraw-Hill, 1972), pp. 40 and 45.

First of all, let's distinguish very clearly between economic growth and population growth. Congested neighborhoods, dining halls, and highways are the consequence of too many people, not of too many goods and services. Indeed, if we had *more* goods and services—if we had more houses and transit systems—much of the population congestion we now experience might be relieved. Maybe if we had enough resources to meet our existing demands *and* to build a solar-generated "new town" in the middle of Montana, people might move out of the crowded neighborhoods of Chicago and St. Louis. Well, probably not, but at least one thing is certain; with fewer goods and services, more people will have to share any given quantity of output.

Which brings us back to the really essential measure of growth, GDP per capita. Are there any serious grounds for desiring *less* GDP per capita, a reduced standard of living? And don't say yes just because you think we already have too many cars on our roads or calories in our bellies. That argument refers to the *mix* of output again and doesn't answer the question of whether we want *any* more goods or services per person. Increasing GDP per capita can take a million forms, including the educational services you're now consuming. The rejection of economic growth per se implies that none of those forms is desirable in the economy tomorrow.

SUMMARY

- Economic growth refers to increases in real GDP. Short-run growth may result from increases in capacity utilization (like less unemployment). In the long run, however, growth requires increases in capacity itself—rightward shifts on the long-run aggregate supply curve. LO1
- GDP per capita is a basic measure of living standards. GDP per worker is a basic measure of productivity. LO1
- The rate of economic growth is set by the growth rate of the labor force *plus* the growth rate of output per worker (productivity). Over time, increases in productivity have been the primary cause of rising living standards. LO1
- Productivity gains come from many sources, including better labor quality, increased capital investment, research and development, improved management, and supportive government policies. LO2
- Supply-side policies increase both the short- and long-run capacity to produce. Monetary and fiscal policies may also affect capital investment and thus the rate of economic growth. LO2
- Productivity growth accelerated in 1995–2000 due to fast investment growth, especially in information technology. Sustaining rapid productivity gains is the critical challenge for long-run GDP growth. LO1
- Recent U.S. investment growth has been financed with business saving and foreign investment. U.S. households save very little. LO1
- The argument that there are identifiable and imminent limits to growth—perhaps even a cataclysmic dooms-day—are founded on one of two concerns: (1) the depletion of resources and (2) pollution of the ecosystem. LO3
- The flaw in doomsday arguments is that they regard existing patterns of resource use or pollution as unalterable. They consistently underestimate the possibilities for technological advance or market adaptation. LO3
- Continued economic growth is desirable as long as it brings a higher standard of living for people and an increased ability to produce and consume socially desirable goods and services. LO3

Key Terms

production possibilities
economic growth
real GDP
base period
growth rate
GDP per capita
labor force
employment rate
productivity
human capital
net investment
crowding out
crowding in
geometric growth
arithmetic growth

Questions for Discussion

1. In what specific ways (if any) does a college education increase a worker's productivity? LO1
2. Why do productivity gains slow down in recessions? (See Figure 17.5.) LO1

3. Why don't we consume all our current output instead of sacrificing some present consumption for investment ? LO1
4. Should we grant immigration rights based on potential contributions to economic growth as Canada does? (See World View, page 343.) LO2
5. How would a growing federal budget surplus affect the prospects for long-run economic growth? Why might a growing surplus *not* be desirable? LO2
6. Should fiscal policy encourage more consumption or more saving? Does it matter? LO2
7. In 1866, Stanley Jevons predicted that economic growth would come to a halt when England ran out of coal, a doomsday that he reckoned would occur in the mid-1970s. How did we avert that projection? Will we avert an "oil crisis" in the same way? LO3
8. Fertility rates in the United States have dropped so low that we're approaching zero population growth, a condition that France has maintained for decades. How will this affect our economic growth? Our standard of living? LO1
9. Is limitless growth really possible? What forces do you think will be most important in slowing or halting economic growth? LO3
10. Why do some nations grow and prosper while others stagnate? LO1

problems The Student Problem Set at the back of this book contains numerical and graphing problems for this chapter.

web activities to accompany this chapter can be found on the Online Learning Center: **http://www.mhhe.com/economics/schiller11e**

PART 7 Policy Constraints

Macro theories often provide conflicting advice about whether and how the government ought to intervene. To make matters worse, the information needed to make a decision is typically incomplete. Politics muddies the waters too by changing priorities and restricting the use of policy tools. Finally, there's the inescapable reality that everything changes at once—there's no *ceteris paribus* in the real world. Chapters 18 and 19 consider these constraints on policy development and implementation. Chapter 18 assesses how global markets limit domestic policy choices. Chapter 19 surveys the entire panoply of real-world factors that infringe on macroeconomic policy decisions.

Global Macro

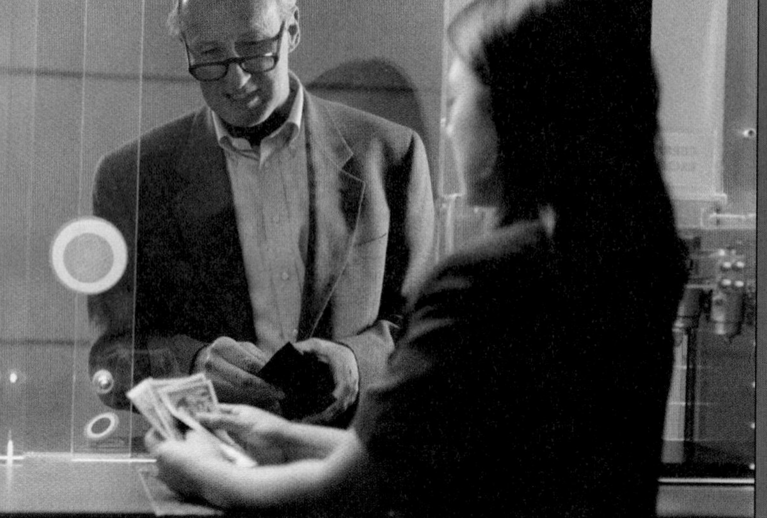

LEARNING OBJECTIVES

After reading this chapter, you should know:

LO1. The difference between "open" and "closed" economy multipliers.

LO2. How trade flows are affected by fiscal policy.

LO3. How global capital flows constrain monetary policy.

In this global economy there is no such thing as a purely domestic policy.
—President Bill Clinton
American University, February 26, 1993

Two years after making that statement, President Clinton got a crash course in global macroeconomics. The Mexican economy took a nosedive in 1995: Unemployment rose, prices skyrocketed, and the value of the Mexican peso plunged. President Clinton and his economic advisers quickly realized that this turn of events wasn't simply a Mexican problem. Mexico is one of America's largest export markets. If the Mexican economy sinks into a recession, Mexican consumers and businesses won't be able to buy so many U.S.-made goods. The U.S. economy would suffer export losses and related job losses.

The financial markets of Mexico and the United States are also linked. When the peso collapsed, many Mexicans rushed to convert their currency into U.S. dollars. As they moved assets into American banks, U.S. bank reserves increased. This capital inflow made the Fed's job of controlling the money supply that much more difficult.

There was no way the United States could seal off its economy from the Mexican crisis. So long as resources, goods, and money can move across national borders, countries are economically interdependent. Ironically, the 1993 North American Free Trade Agreement (NAFTA) had increased the interdependence between Mexico and the United States. Therefore, helping Mexico was also a way of helping the United States avert economic damage. This realization helped convince President Clinton to "bail out" Mexico with a multibillion-dollar loan. The U.S. Federal Reserve also helped control disruptions in currency flows and values.

The global economy got an even greater jolt when terrorists destroyed the World Trade Center in September 2001. The economic shock disrupted not only U.S. markets but global ones as well. As the accompanying World View relates, nations around the world worried that the economic shock to the U.S. economy would destabilize their economies too. If U.S. consumers and businesses curtailed their spending, export sales of other nations would decline. A *global* crisis, not just an *American* crisis, would ensue. Mindful of that possibility, the world's leaders quickly worked out a coordinated policy response.

This chapter explores this global interdependence. Of particular concern are the following questions:

- **How does the U.S. economy interact with the rest of the world?**
- **How does the rest of the world affect U.S. macro outcomes?**
- **How does global interdependence limit macro policy options?**

As we'll see, international transactions significantly affect U.S. economic performance and policy.

WORLD VIEW

Tragedy Dashes Hopes for Europe's Economy

The economic fallout doesn't stop at the U.S. border.

In the aftermath of last week's terror strikes, European companies say the uncertainty over what happens next will weigh on an already weak European economy for weeks, even months.

Economies around the world—including Japan, which has been struggling for years—had all been hoping to avoid recession this year, based on the prospect of the U.S. economy recovering. Those hopes are now gone.

Unease spells trouble for any economy: Businesses delay big orders; potential merger partners put their deal talks on ice; companies hold off on expansion plans; and consumers save rather than buy. "People won't be ordering big machines for a couple of million marks right now," said Diether Klingelnberg, whose company in Hueckeswagen, Germany, makes machine parts for the airline industry, among other sectors. "People want to wait and see what will happen."...

Baudouin Velge, chief economist of the Belgian Federation of Employers, a trade group representing 30,000 Belgian companies, figures, "The American economy will be hit by this for another six months," which delays the main boost Europe was counting on for its own recovery. The U.S. buys 22 percent of Europe's exports. Economists estimate a percentage-point drop in U.S. economic growth translates into a half-percentage point decline in European growth.

—Christopher Rhoads and G. Thomas Sims

Analysis: The flow of goods, labor, and money across national borders makes countries economically interdependent. A shock to the U.S. economy disrupts foreign economies as well, and vice versa.

INTERNATIONAL TRADE

Japanese cars are the most visible reminders of America's global interdependence. American consumers purchase over 1 million cars from Japan each year and buy another million or so Toyotas, Nissans, Hondas, Mazdas, and Subarus produced in the United States. On the other side of the Pacific Ocean, Japanese autoworkers are apt to wear Levis, sip Coca-Cola, and grab a quick meal at McDonald's.

The motivations for international trade are explained at length in Chapter 35. Also discussed in Chapter 35 are the *microeconomic* demands for greater protection from "unfair" imports. What concerns us here is how such trade affects our domestic *macro* performance. Does trade help or hinder our efforts to attain full employment, price stability, and economic growth?

imports: Goods and services purchased from international sources.

leakage: Income not spent directly on domestic output but instead diverted from the circular flow, such as saving, imports, taxes.

Imports as Leakage

We first noticed in Chapter 9 that **imports** are a source of **leakage** in the circular flow. The income that U.S. consumers spend on Japanese cars *could* be spent in America. When that income instead leaks out of the circular flow, it limits domestic spending and related **multiplier** effects.

The basic macro model can be expanded easily to include this additional leakage. In a **closed economy** (one that doesn't trade), total income and domestic spending are always equal—that is,

$$\text{Closed economy: } C + I + G = Y$$

When some goods are sold as exports and others can be purchased from abroad, however, this equality no longer holds. In an **open economy,** we have to take account of imports and exports: that is,

$$\text{Open economy: } C + I + G + X = Y + M$$

where X refers to exports and M to imports. ***In an open economy, the combined spending of consumers, investors, and the government may not equal domestic output.*** Total spending is augmented by the demand for exports, and the supply of goods is increased by imports.

multiplier: The multiple by which an initial change in aggregate spending will alter total expenditure after an infinite number of spending cycles.

closed economy: A nation that doesn't engage in international trade.

open economy: A nation that engages in international trade.

marginal propensity to import (MPM): The fraction of each additional (marginal) dollar of disposable income spent on imports.

marginal propensity to save (MPS): The fraction of each additional (marginal) dollar of disposable income not spent on consumption; 1 − MPC.

Although imported goods may be desired, their availability complicates macro policy. Increases in aggregate spending are supposed to boost domestic output and employment. With imports, however, the link between spending and output is weakened. ***Part of any increase in income will be spent on imports.*** This fraction is called the **marginal propensity to import (MPM)**. Like its cousin, the **marginal propensity to save (MPS)**, the marginal propensity to import

- Reduces the initial impact on domestic demand of any income change.
- Reduces the size of the multiplier.

Reduced Multiplier Effects. Table 18.1 illustrates the impact of imports on the Keynesian multiplier process. The process starts with an increase of $10 billion in new government spending. This injection directly adds $10 billion to consumer income (assuming an economy with no income taxes).

The successive panels of Table 18.1 illustrate the sequence of events that follows. In the closed economy, consumers have only two uses for their income: to spend it on domestic consumption (B1) or to save it (B2). We assume here the marginal propensity to save is 0.10. Hence consumers save $1 billion and spend the remaining $9 billion on domestic consumption.

In an open economy, consumers have an additional choice. They may spend their income on domestic goods (B1), save it (B2), *or* spend it on imported goods (B3). In Table 18.1 we assume that the marginal propensity to import is 0.10. Hence, consumers use their additional $10 billion of income the following way:

$8 billion spent on domestic consumption.
$1 billion saved.
$1 billion spent on imports.

In the open economy, only $8 billion rather than $9 billion is initially spent on domestic consumption. Thus, ***imports reduce the initial spending impact of added income.***

Import leakage continues through every round of the circular flow. As a consequence, ***imports also reduce the value of the multiplier.*** In this case, the multiplier is reduced from 10 to 5.

TABLE 18.1
Imports as Leakage

Import leakage reduces the initial spending impact of changes in consumer income. Continuing import leakage reduces the size of the multiplier as well.

In this case, the ultimate impact of added government spending is cut in half by import leakage: Aggregate demand increases by $50 billion in the open economy, rather than $100 billion (as in the closed economy) in response to a $10 billion increase in government spending.

Action	Cumulative Change in Aggregate Demand: Closed Economy	Cumulative Change in Aggregate Demand: Open Economy
A. Government spends additional $10 billion	+$10 billion	+$10 billion
B. Consumers use added $10 billion of income for:		
1. Domestic consumption	+$9 billion	+$8 billion
2. Saving (MPS = 0.1)	($1 billion)	($1 billion)
3. Imports (MPM = 0.1)	0	($1 billion)
C. Multiplier	$\frac{1}{\text{MPS}} = 10$	$\frac{1}{\text{MPS} + \text{MPM}} = 5$
D. Additional multiplier-induced consumption = C × B1	+$90 billion	+$40 billion
E. Cumulative change = A + D	+$100 billion	+$50 billion

To see how this change in the multiplier comes about, note that ***the value of the multiplier depends on the extent of leakage.*** The most general form of the multiplier is

$$\text{Generalized multiplier} = \frac{1}{\text{leakage fraction}}$$

In a closed (no trade) and private (no taxes) economy, the multiplier takes the familiar Keynesian form:

$$\begin{array}{c}\text{Closed economy}\\ \text{multiplier}\\ \text{(without taxes)}\end{array} = \frac{1}{\text{MPS}}$$

In this case, consumer saving is the only form of leakage. Therefore, the marginal propensity to save (MPS) is the entire leakage fraction. In Table 18.1 the closed-economy multiplier is equal to 10 (see panel C).

Once we open the economy to trade, we have to contend with additional leakage. In an open economy, leakage results from the MPS *and* the MPM. Thus, the generalized multiplier becomes:

$$\begin{array}{c}\text{Open economy}\\ \text{multiplier}\\ \text{(without taxes)}\end{array} = \frac{1}{\text{MPS} + \text{MPM}}$$

Imports act just like saving leakage, decreasing the multiplier bang of each autonomous buck. In Table 18.1 (panel C),

$$\text{Open economy multiplier} = \frac{1}{\text{MPS} + \text{MPM}} = \frac{1}{0.1 + 0.1} = \frac{1}{0.2} = 5$$

The consequences of these different multipliers are striking. Panel D shows that additional consumption of $90 billion is induced in the closed economy. By comparison, the open economy generates only $40 billion of additional consumption.

The last panel of Table 18.1 summarizes the consequences for aggregate demand. The cumulative increase in aggregate demand is

$$\begin{array}{c}\text{Cumulative change}\\ \text{in aggregate demand}\end{array} = \begin{array}{c}\text{initial change}\\ \text{in spending}\end{array} \times \begin{array}{c}\text{income}\\ \text{multiplier}\end{array}$$

In this example, the initial injection of spending is the $10 billion spent by the government. In the closed economy, this injection leads to a $100 billion increase in aggregate demand (panel E). In the open economy, the same injection increases aggregate demand—only $50 billion!

This end result is also illustrated in Figure 18.1, which shows how imports limit the shift of aggregate demand. The smaller shift that occurs in the open economy results in a smaller increase in equilibrium real GDP. In this sense ***imports, by increasing leakage, reduce the impact of fiscal stimulus.*** Notice in Figure 18.1 the much larger induced consumption in the closed economy. The fiscal stimulus shifts aggregate demand to AD_4 in the closed economy but only to AD_3 in the open economy. The end result is less of an increase in domestic output (and less inflationary pressure as well).

Global Stabilizer. The import leakage that reduces the effectiveness of fiscal stimulus can also act as an automatic stabilizer. This was particularly evident in early 2001. The slowdown in U.S. aggregate demand was heavily concentrated in high-tech sectors that are highly dependent on imported equipment and components, that is, industries with a very high marginal propensity to import. Hence, foreign producers absorbed a large share of the pain caused by the U.S. slowdown (see World View on next page). In the absence of that safety valve, the U.S. economy would have suffered larger multiplier effects and a more severe slowdown.

FIGURE 18.1
Imports Reduce Multiplier Effects

The amount of additional demand created by a fiscal stimulus depends on the marginal propensity to import. In a closed economy (MPM = 0) aggregate demand increases from AD_1 to AD_4. In an open economy (MPM > 0) imports limit spending on domestic goods, shifting aggregate demand only to AD_3.

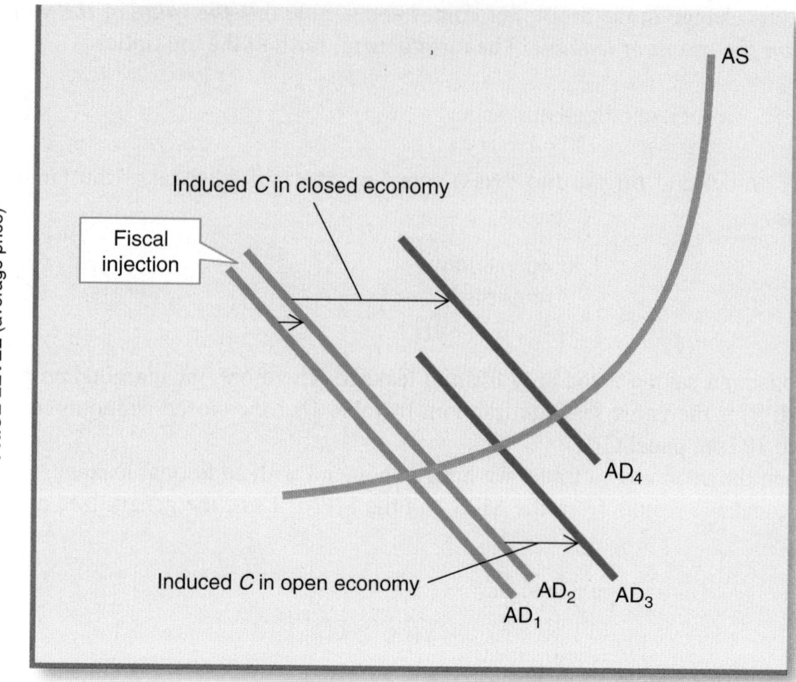

U.S. Growth Slows—and Foreign Economies Feel the Pain

But the Falloff in American Imports Is Limiting U.S. Weakness

If you want a vivid illustration of America's role in the global slowdown, consider that the U.S. buys up nearly one-fourth of the rest of the world's exports. And the growth rate of the volume of goods coming into the U.S. has swung from a 17 percent annual pace last autumn to a −5 percent pace currently. No wonder many economies abroad are struggling.

To an important extent, though, the rest of the world's pain is America's gain. True, the growing weakness in exports has been a considerable drag on the ailing manufacturing sector. But the dropoff in imports is acting like a shock absorber, because much of the fallout from weaker demand is being felt by foreign producers, not the U.S. economy. . . .

In this particular slowdown, the stabilizing influence of falling imports is especially large. That's because the slump is concentrated in business-sector cuts in capital spending and inventories, mainly for tech-equipment. About 36 percent of U.S. dollar outlays for capital goods goes to imports. For tech gear alone, imports account for about 16 percent. That means foreign companies—and countries—are absorbing a large share of the burden of dealing with U.S. corporate cutbacks. One case in point: Singapore is in recession mostly because its shipments to the U.S. of semiconductors and other tech components have plunged dramatically.

—James C. Cooper and Kathleen Madigan

Source: *BusinessWeek,* August 6, 2001. © 2001 The McGraw-Hill Companies, Inc. Reprinted with permission. www.businessweek.com

Analysis: Imports act as an automatic stabilizer by (1) absorbing some of lost sales in an economic downturn and (2) adding to aggregate supply as domestic capacity is approached.

Exports as Injections

International trade is a two-way street. Whereas we import goods and services from the rest of the world, other countries buy our **exports**. Thus, ***export sales inject spending into our circular flow at the same time that imports cause leakage from it.***

Any changes in exports are regarded as autonomous, since export sales depend primarily on the income and spending behavior of foreigners. Hence, ***a change in export demand causes a shift of the aggregate demand curve.*** Like any other injection, an increase in export demand would set off a chain of multiplier effects. In other words, small changes in exports generate larger (multiplied) shifts of aggregate demand. This was a distinct risk for the U.S. economy in the 1997–98 Asian crisis: A reduction in American exports to Asia could have snowballed into very large job losses. When Japan fell into another recession in early 2001, U.S. exporters again lost sales and laid off workers. On the other hand, strong economic growth in China, India, and other nations increases demand for U.S. exports, shifting the AD curve rightward.

exports: Goods and services sold to foreign buyers.

TRADE IMBALANCES

With exports adding to aggregate spending, and imports subtracting from the circular flow, the net impact of international trade on the domestic economy comes down to a question of balance. ***The impact of trade on domestic AD depends on changes in the difference between exports (injections) and imports (leakages).*** If exports and imports were exactly equal, there would be no net stimulus or leakage from the rest of the world.

A convenient way of emphasizing the offsetting effects of exports and imports is to rearrange the income identity to

$$C + I + G + (X - M) = Y$$

where $(X - M)$ equals **net exports.**

net exports: The value of exports minus the value of imports: $(X - M)$.

If exports and imports were always equal, the term $(X - M)$ would disappear and we could focus on domestic spending behavior. But why would we expect imports and exports to be equal? We now know that even *domestic* injections such as investment aren't likely to equal domestic leakages like saving. Indeed, the short-run macro stability problem arises because investment and saving decisions are made by different people and for very different reasons. There's no *a priori* reason to expect those outcomes to be identical.

The same problem affects international trade. Foreign decisions about how much to spend on American exports are made outside U.S. borders. Decisions in the United States about how much to spend on imports are made by American consumers, investors, and government agencies. Because these sets of shoppers are so isolated from one another, it seems unlikely that exports will ever equal imports. Instead, we have to expect a trade imbalance.

trade surplus: The amount by which the value of exports exceeds the value of imports in a given time period (positive net exports).

There are specific terms for characterizing trade imbalances. A U.S. **trade surplus** exists when America is exporting more goods and services than it's importing—that is, when net exports $(X - M)$ are positive. When U.S. net exports are negative, imports exceed exports and the United States has a **trade deficit.** In 2006 the United States had a trade deficit of $765 billion. That deficit implies that U.S. consumers, investors, and government agencies were buying $765 billion more output in 2006 than American factories and offices were producing.

trade deficit: The amount by which the value of imports exceeds the value of exports in a given time period (negative net exports).

Macro Effects

A trade deficit isn't all bad. After all, when imports exceed exports, we end up consuming more than we're producing. In effect, ***a trade deficit permits domestic living standards to exceed domestic output.*** It's almost like getting something for nothing—the proverbial free lunch. A trade deficit can also be an important safety valve for rising inflation pressures. In 2006, the U.S. economy was growing nicely and signs of demand-pull inflation were emerging (since June 2004 the Fed had been raising interest rates). The ready availability of imported inputs and products helped keep inflation in check.

Trade deficits aren't always so beneficial. A trade deficit represents net leakage. That leakage may frustrate attempts to attain full employment. As we observed (Figure 18.1),

webnote

To track changes in the U.S. trade balance, see the import and export data in "Balance of Payments" at the Bureau of Economic Analysis: www.bea.gov

crowding out: A reduction in private-sector borrowing (and spending) caused by increased government borrowing.

import leakage necessitates a larger fiscal injection to reach any particular spending goal. Larger injections may not be possible, especially if *budget* deficit concerns limit fiscal-policy initiatives.

Crowding Out Net Exports. One reason people worry about budget deficits is that increased government spending may supplant private investment and consumption. This is the **crowding out** problem we first encountered in Chapter 12. It takes on a new dimension in an open economy. In an open economy, increased government purchases need not reduce private-sector spending—even at full employment! Increased imports can satisfy the increase in aggregate demand. Thus, in an open economy ***an increase in imports can reduce domestic crowding out.***

The elbow room provided by imports relieves some of the worries about federal *budget* deficits. New concerns arise, however, about *trade* deficits. As imports increase, our net export position deteriorates. Hence, ***in an open economy fiscal stimulus tends to crowd out net exports by boosting imports.*** Indeed, any fiscal stimulus intended to boost domestic output will *worsen* the trade deficit. Consumers will spend some fraction of their additional income—the marginal propensity to import (MPM)—on imports. These added imports will widen the trade gap. Thus, ***the objective of reducing the trade deficit may conflict with the goal of attaining full employment.***

A trade surplus can create similar problems. The additional spending implied by positive net exports may fuel inflationary pressures. If the economy is overheating, the policy objective is to restrain aggregate spending. But fiscal and monetary restraints don't directly affect the incomes, expectations, or tastes of foreign consumers. Foreign spending on U.S. goods may continue unabated, even as domestic monetary and fiscal restraint squeezes domestic consumers and investors. Indeed, domestic monetary and fiscal restraint will have to be harder, just to offset continuing export demand.

Worse yet, the trade surplus may grow in response to restrictive macro policies. Domestic consumers, squeezed by monetary and fiscal restraint, will reduce purchases of imported goods. On the other hand, if fiscal and monetary restraint reduces domestic inflation, foreigners may increase their export purchases. Here again, ***trade goals and domestic macro goals may conflict.***

Foreign Perspectives

Who cares if our trade balance worsens? Why don't we just focus on our domestic macro equilibrium and ignore any trade imbalances that result? If we ignored trade imbalances, we wouldn't have a goal conflict and could achieve our domestic policy goals.

Unfortunately, our trading partners may not be content to ignore our trade imbalances. ***If the United States has a trade deficit, other countries must have a trade surplus.*** This is simple arithmetic. Its implications are potentially worrisome, however. The rest of the world might not be happy about shipping us more output than they're getting in return. In real economic terms, they'd be picking up the tab for our "free lunch." Their exports would be financing a higher standard of living for us than our output alone permitted. At the same time, their living standards would be less than their own output made possible. These disparities could cause tension. In addition, foreign nations might also be concerned about inflationary pressures of their own and so resist additional demand for their exports (our imports).

The whole notion of macro equilibrium gets much more complicated when we adopt these global views. From a global perspective, ***we can't focus exclusively on domestic macro goals and ignore international repercussions.*** If our trade balance upsets other economies, foreign nations may respond with their own macro and trade initiatives. These responses, in turn, would affect America's trade flows and so alter domestic outcomes. A *global* macro equilibrium would be attained only when no trading partner had reason to change macro or trade policy.

A Policy Constraint

From a macro perspective, our basic objective in both an open and a closed economy remains the same: to find the optimal balance of aggregate demand and aggregate supply. Trade flows may help or hinder this effort, depending on the timing, size, and source of the

Oil Shocks

In 1973, in 1979, in 2000, 2004, and again in 2006, the Organization of Petroleum Exporting Countries (OPEC) sharply increased crude oil prices. The price of oil quadrupled in 1973 and doubled again in 1979. In 2006, the price of oil jumped to nearly $80 per barrel. The resulting "shock" to macro equilibrium caused both higher unemployment and more inflation in oil-importing nations.

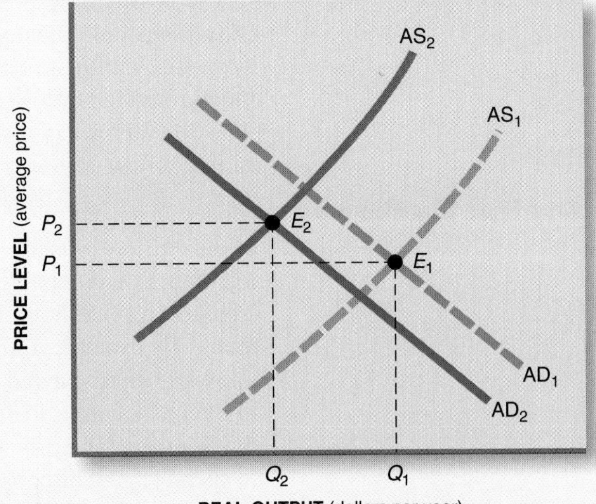

Inflationary Impact

An increase in the price of oil sets the stage for cost-push inflation. Industries using oil to fuel their machines or heat their furnaces are hit with an increase in production costs. These higher costs shift the aggregate *supply* curve to the left, as in the accompanying figure (AS_1 to AS_2). The end result is more inflation.

Decreased Consumption

Although the most visible effect of oil shocks is inflation, the greatest threat often lies on the demand side of product and factor markets. OPEC price boosts force consumers to spend more of their income on foreign oil imports. In 2006, the jump in oil prices raised fuel costs for U.S. households by over $800 per year. This sudden increase in import leakage left consumers with less income to spend on domestic output. Thus, the aggregate *demand* curve shifted to the left, as from AD_1 to AD_2.

Analysis: Abrupt changes in the price or availability of imported goods will alter domestic output and spending. Such external shocks can worsen domestic inflation and unemployment.

trade imbalance. Sudden *changes* in trade flows can create an external shock that upsets macro policy goals (see World View on "oil shocks"). All we know for certain is

- Imports and exports alter the levels of aggregate demand and aggregate supply.
- Trade flows may help or hinder domestic macro policy in attaining its objectives.
- Macro policy decisions need to take account of international trade repercussions.

Thus, international trade adds an important new wrinkle to macro policy decision making.

INTERNATIONAL FINANCE

Our global interactions with the rest of the world are further complicated by international money flows. Money flows across international borders as easily as goods and services. In fact, money *must* move across borders to pay for imports and exports. In addition, people move money across borders to get bigger profits, higher interest rates, or more security. Like trade in goods and services, these international money flows alter macro outcomes and complicate macro decision making.

Capital Inflows

In 2006, nearly $2 trillion of foreign capital flowed into the United States. A lot of this capital inflow was used to purchase U.S. bonds. The Treasury bonds were attractive to international investors for two reasons. First, real interest rates in the U.S. economy were relatively high, making them a more attractive investment than foreign bonds. Second, the U.S. economy looked more prosperous and more politically stable than many other places, making Treasury bonds appear more secure. Corporate bonds, stocks, and other U.S. investments also looked attractive in early 2006, for much the same reasons. So people and institutions around the world moved some of their funds into U.S. markets, creating a tremendous capital inflow.

The profits of U.S. corporations operating abroad added to that capital inflow. When U.S. firms build plants abroad, they anticipate earning profits they can bring home. Over time, U.S. multinational firms have accumulated a sizable share of world markets, giving them a regular inflow of international profits. McDonald's, for example, operates more than 30,000 restaurants in 119 countries. Profits from its foreign outlets add to America's capital inflow.

Capital Outflows

Money flows out of the United States to the rest of the world for the same purposes. Most of the outflow is used to pay for U.S. imports (including foreign travel by U.S. citizens). In addition, U.S. companies investing in foreign countries need to buy foreign land, labor, and capital. And U.S. households and institutions may be attracted to overseas *financial* investments, for example, foreign bonds or stocks. Some people simply want to keep their money in Swiss banks to avoid scrutiny or evade taxes. Finally, the U.S. government spends money in foreign countries to maintain American defenses, operate embassies, encourage economic development, and provide emergency relief. The war in Iraq required the U.S. government to spend tens of billions of dollars on foreign goods and services. All these activities cause a dollar outflow.

Part of the dollar outflow is also prompted by foreign investors and institutions. As interest and profits accumulate on their U.S.-based investments, foreign investors may want to retrieve some of their assets. Those repatriated interest and profit payments are part of the capital *outflows.* If the relative attractiveness of investments in the United States diminishes, even more foreign capital will flow out. When the U.S. stock market crashed in 2000–2001, many foreign investors took their money and ran.

CAPITAL IMBALANCES

capital deficit: The amount by which the capital outflow exceeds the capital inflow in a given time period.

capital surplus: The amount by which the capital inflow exceeds the capital outflow in a given time period.

Like trade flows, capital flows won't always be balanced. At times, the outflow of dollars will exceed the inflow, and the United States will experience a **capital deficit.** At other times, the balance may be reversed, leaving the United States with a **capital surplus.** In 2006, the United States had a capital surplus of nearly $700 billion.

The huge capital surplus of 2006 is directly related to the huge trade deficit in that same year. When we import more than we export, we're effectively buying foreign goods and services on credit. The bulk of that credit is derived from the net inflow of foreign capital. The net inflow of money prompted by foreign investors creates a pool of funds that can be used to purchase foreign goods and services. If the capital inflow were smaller, our ability to purchase imports would be less, too. The reverse of this is true as well. If Americans weren't buying so many imports, foreigners wouldn't have as many dollars to invest in U.S. banks, corporations, and property. Thus, ***capital imbalances are directly related to trade imbalances.***

Macro Effects

Capital imbalances are a problem for monetary policy. The essence of monetary policy is control of the money supply. When money is able to move across international borders at will, control of the money supply becomes more difficult.

Suppose inflationary forces are building and the Fed wants to reduce money supply growth. To do so, it might engage in open market operations, with the objective of net selling. By selling bonds, the Fed wants to draw reserves out of the banking system and thereby slow money supply growth. The bond sales will also tend to raise interest rates and thus dampen both consumer and investor spending. This now-familiar sequence of events is illustrated on the left side of Figure 18.2.

The figure also illustrates how an open economy complicates monetary policy. The higher interest rates caused by the Fed's bond sales attract foreign investors. As the return on U.S. bonds increases, the inflow of foreign capital will accelerate. This will frustrate the Fed's goal of reducing money supply growth and tend to put downward pressure on domestic

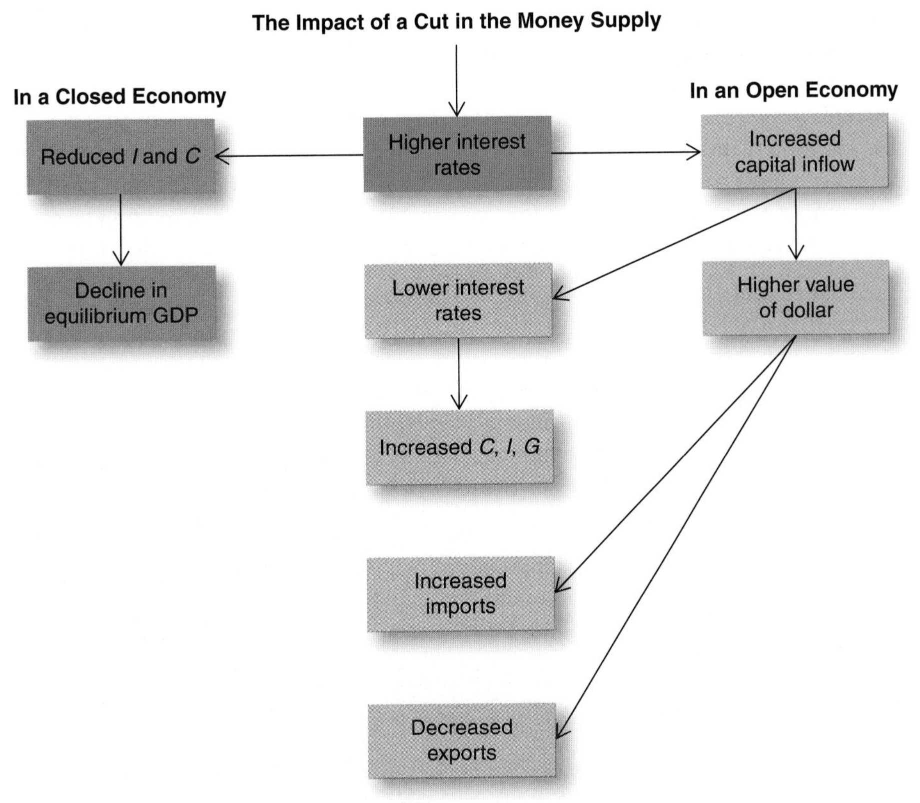

FIGURE 18.2
International Constraints on Monetary Policy

A reduction in the money supply is intended to reduce consumption and investment spending and thereby relieve inflationary pressures. If the money supply reduction increases domestic interest rates, however, it may trigger additional capital inflow. That increased capital inflow will frustrate monetary policy by increasing the money supply and holding down interest rates. The capital inflow will also tend to increase the value of the U.S. dollar and so widen the trade deficit.

interest rates. The Fed will have to work harder (e.g., sell more bonds) to achieve any desired money supply target.

Exchange Rates

An important feature of Figure 18.2 is the box marked "higher value of dollar." When we purchase goods and services from foreign countries, we must exchange our dollars for foreign currency. The Japanese workers who make Toyotas, for example, are paid in yen. Their willingness to supply cars is based on how many yen, not dollars, they'll receive. Thus, we must first exchange dollars for yen before we can import Toyotas. When you travel abroad, you do these exchanges yourself, typically at banks, hotels, or foreign-exchange offices. When you stay at home and buy imported goods, someone else handles the exchange for you.

Whether you or some middleperson does the exchange is irrelevant. What matters is how many yen you get for your dollars. The more yen you get, the more Toyotas and other Japanese goods you're able to buy. In other words, ***if the dollar's value in the world markets is high, imports are cheap.***

The dollar's value in international trade is reflected in the **exchange rate.** The exchange rate is simply the price (value) of one currency, measured in terms of another. The exchange rate prevailing at any time reflects the interplay of trade and capital flows and all their determinants. (Foreign exchange markets are examined in Chapter 36.) What matters here is that exchange rates *change,* often in response to monetary and fiscal policy.

> exchange rate: The price of one country's currency expressed in terms of another's; the domestic price of a foreign currency.

In Figure 18.2. restrictive monetary policy causes domestic interest rates to rise. These higher interest rates make U.S. bonds more attractive and so increase capital inflow from the rest of the world. To buy Treasury bonds, however, foreign investors need dollars. As they clamor to exchange their yen, euros, and pounds for dollars, the value (price) of the dollar will increase. A higher dollar means that you can get more yen for every dollar. Imports thus become cheaper, and so Americans buy more of them. On the other hand, a stronger (more expensive) dollar makes U.S. exports costlier for foreign consumers, and so they buy fewer American products. The end result is a widening trade gap.

Similar global obstacles can impede policies of monetary stimulus. Suppose the Fed cut interest rates to stimulate aggregate demand. Those lower interest rates might start a capital outflow, as global investors sought higher returns elsewhere. This accelerated outflow would reduce the value of the dollar, making imports more expensive. The implied upward shift of aggregate supply would frustrate efforts to accelerate real GDP growth. The capital outflow would also make it harder to reduce interest rates.

Capital Flows—Another Policy Constraint

International capital flows add yet another complication to macro policy. The very existence of international capital flows weakens the Fed's ability to control the money supply. These global linkages were a significant policy constraint in 2001: The weakening U.S. dollar kept the Fed from offering more monetary stimulus. Lower interest rates would have boosted U.S. aggregate demand but also weakened the U.S. dollar further. We conclude, then, that global money links create another policy headache: In addition to all our other macro worries, we now have to be concerned about

- The flow of capital into and out of the country.
- The effect of capital imbalances on domestic macro performance.
- How macro policy will affect international capital flows, exchange rates, and trade balances.

PRODUCTIVITY AND COMPETITIVENESS

The global dimensions of the economy add a whole new layer of complexity to macro policy. One might reasonably wonder whether international trade and finance is really worth all the trouble. Couldn't we get along just as well without the rest of the world?

Specialization

Perhaps. But we wouldn't be able to drink much coffee. Or spend summer vacations in Europe. Or buy Japanese cars and Mexican beer.

To decide whether international trade and finance are worth all the trouble, we have to consider how international exchanges affect our standard of living. One obvious advantage of trade is that it gives us access to goods and services we don't or can't produce at home, such as coffee, vacations abroad, bananas, and Italian shoes. These ***imported goods and services broaden our consumption possibilities.***

Most of the goods and services we import *could* be produced at home. Cars and shoes are made in America as well as abroad, as is a small quantity of coffee and bananas (in Hawaii). Even more coffee and bananas *could* be produced in the United States if we invested enough in greenhouses that duplicated tropical conditions. Homegrown coffee and bananas would turn out to be terribly expensive, however, so we're better off importing them. This leaves domestic resources available for the production of other goods that we can more easily grow (corn), manufacture (airplanes), or build (houses). In other words, we're better off *specializing* in the production of things we do relatively well and *trading* with other nations for the rest of the goods and services we desire. This is the principle of **comparative advantage** we first encountered in Chapter 2. In essence, it recommends that we produce what we do best and trade with other nations for goods they produce best. ***Specialization among countries increases world efficiency and output, making all nations richer.***

comparative advantage: The ability of a country to produce a specific good at a lower opportunity cost than its trading partners.

Chapter 35 demonstrates the benefits of international specialization (the theory of comparative advantage). At this juncture we may note that the same principles that motivate *individuals* to specialize and then exchange their goods and services also motivate *nations* to specialize and then exchange their goods and services in international trade. In both cases, **productivity** and total output increase.

productivity: Output per unit of input, for example, output per labor-hour.

Competitiveness

The increased output and productivity that specialization makes possible aren't the only benefits of international trade. ***Trade stimulates improvements in productivity.*** The presence of foreign producers keeps domestic producers on their toes. To compete in international markets, domestic producers must reduce costs and increase efficiency.

In recent years, America's huge trade deficits have provoked questions about the competitiveness of U.S. producers. The excess of imports over exports suggests to many people that America isn't producing goods of the quality and value that consumers demand. Productivity may have lagged in some U.S. industries. And other nations inevitably become more efficient in producing certain goods and services. But the trade gap isn't a general indictment of U.S. competitiveness.

As we've observed, international trade and capital flows are interrelated, and both are directly influenced by exchange rates. In the early 1980s, the relative attractiveness of America's capital markets led to a surge of capital inflows and a higher exchange rate for the U.S. dollar. Between 1981 and 1985, the world value of the U.S. dollar rose by 50 percent, which made all American goods more expensive in international markets. To *maintain* their prices in international markets, U.S. producers would have had to cut costs enough to offset that increase in the dollar's value. Although American productivity increased faster than foreign productivity in those years, few U.S. producers could stay ahead of the rising dollar. The resulting increase in the trade deficit was a product of the rising dollar, not of a decline in U.S. productivity. The same thing happened again during the period 1996–99, when the value of the dollar and the trade deficit both jumped. The same sequence was repeated in 2001.

Although a trade gap isn't necessarily evidence of declining competitiveness, it does draw policy attention to productivity issues. Productivity improvements are essential to economic growth and rising living standards. If a trade gap stimulates fiscal, monetary, and supply-side policies that foster productivity advances, then the economy may be better off as a result. By the same token, trade gaps remind us that policies that restrain productivity improvements (research, innovation, and investment) also have international consequences.

webnote

The U.S. Bureau of Labor Statistics (BLS) assembles international comparisons of manufacturing productivity (also published in the *Monthly Labor Review*); visit www.bls.gov/fls

GLOBAL COORDINATION

As all countries begin to acknowledge the international dimensions of their economies, the desire for coordination grows. The coordination is pursued both through formal institutions and informal "understandings" among the major industrialized nations.

IMF

The most visible institution for global coordination is the International Monetary Fund (IMF). The IMF is sort of a bankers' United Nations. All nations contribute funds to the IMF, which then uses those funds to assist nations whose currency is in trouble. When Thailand devalued its currency (the baht) in July 1997, for example, the currencies of other Asian nations also plunged. This Asian crisis threatened U.S. exports as well as those of other nations. There was a distinct threat that the "Asian flu" would become a global contagion. To keep the Asian flu from spreading, the IMF lent more than $100 billion to Thailand, Korea, Indonesia, and other Asian nations. The IMF also loaned Brazil over $40 billion in 1998–99 and Argentina $22 billion in 2001 to avoid a "Latin flu" from spreading to other South American nations and the global economy.

Although the IMF often provides global "first aid," IMF assistance typically comes with strings attached. The IMF often insists that a debtor nation alter its domestic monetary fiscal or trade policies as a condition of an IMF bailout. Such intrusions into domestic macro policy are often resented, especially when they entail high political costs in the debtor nation (as in Argentina in 2001–2).

webnote

For a summary of IMF activities and recent bailouts, visit www.imf.org

Group of Eight

The eight largest industrial countries (the United States, Japan, Canada, Germany, France, Italy, Great Britain, and Russia) attain a less formal mode of global coordination. The finance economic ministers of these nations meet periodically to assess the global outlook and coordinate macro policy. Although the Group of Eight (the G-8) has no formal apparatus for joint actions, any informal agreements it reaches can have a substantial effect on global trade and capital flow. Reaching agreement isn't always easy, however. In mid-2001,

WORLD VIEW 

Global Markets Await Action by U.S. Fed

Other Central Banks Will Face Pressure to Follow Suit on Rates; Borrowing Costs to Feel Impact

It is the quarter point heard 'round the world—and the trigger hasn't even been pulled yet.

As the Federal Reserve prepares to increase interest rates today, other central bankers will face pressure to follow suit, raising borrowing costs for corporations and governments worldwide . . .

The European Central Bank, overseeing a still-fragile economic recovery, is resisting the Fed's powerful pull. The economies of the dozen nations that use the euro are expected to expand a measly 1.8% this year, well below the global average forecast of 4.5%. At the ECB's monthly meeting tomorrow, policy makers likely will leave their key rate at 2%, where it has been since they cut rates a little more than a year ago. At a subsequent news conference, bank President Jean-Claude Trichet probably will try to tamp down suggestions that the ECB will be compelled to follow the Fed. . . .

Emerging bond and stock markets look even more vulnerable. Rising U.S. rates make the more volatile developing countries less attractive and put additional pressure on their economies when borrowing rates go higher.

—Craig Karmin in New York, Michael R. Sesit in Paris and Martin Fackler in Tokyo

Source: *The Wall Street Journal* June 30, 2004, p. C1.

Analysis: Global coordination of economic policies is limited by the different priorities of individual nations. In the absence of coordination, policy success is more difficult.

the Federal Reserve's attempts to stimulate the U.S. economy were frustrated by higher interest rates in Europe. Despite Fed pleas for greater monetary stimulus, the European Central Bank kept interest rates relatively high. In 2004, the monetary policy positions were reversed. The Fed wanted to *raise* interest rates to contain inflationary pressures, but the European Central Bank was still trying to stimulate economic growth with low interest rates (see World View).

Global interests will never fully displace national policy priorities. However, even limited global coordination helps smooth out some of the rough spots of macro performance in an increasingly interdependent world.

THE ECONOMY TOMORROW

A GLOBAL CURRENCY?

The Euro. On January 1, 1999, 11 European nations adopted a simple currency, the *euro.* That wasn't an easy or quick policy decision. The quest for a common European currency began in the Middle Ages. The latest push for the euro began over 40 years ago. In view of this history, one has to wonder why a single European currency was sought and why it took so long to attain.

The allure of a common currency is that it facilitates trade and capital flows across national borders. A common currency eliminates the uncertainties and added costs of diverse currencies. European businesses spent nearly $13 billion a year just on currency conversions. Exchange rate fluctuation also impeded cross-border business transactions, which is why the U.S. Congress created a national currency to replace the hundreds of state and private bank currencies that existed prior to 1863.

Macro Coordination. There's a huge difference, however, between creating a common *national* currency (the U.S. dollar) and a common *cross-national* currency like the euro. The 50 states that make up the United States share a common set of laws, monetary institutions, and government. The nations of the European Union (EU) don't even share a common language, much less governmental authority. Accordingly, in creating a common currency, they agreed to submerge some national interests to broader European goals.

webnote

Information on the euro and economic conditions in Euroland is posted at http://europa.eu/index_en.htm

To maintain a common currency, nations must maintain common macro policies. Germany, for example, has been particularly vigilant about inflation, while Italy has given higher priority to reducing unemployment. As a result, German monetary policy tended to be tighter (more restrictive) than Italian monetary policy. When they adopted a common currency, Germany, Italy, and the other nine original EU members had to find a middle ground for monetary policy.

The nations of the European Monetary Union went way beyond monetary coordination. After a 3-year trial period, they turned over monetary-policy control to a single, common central bank, the European Central Bank (ECF). The ECF now operates like the U.S. Federal Reserve, setting interest rates and managing the money supply for the 13 members of the European Monetary Union.

The nations of the EMU were convinced that the benefits of economic integration outweighed the costs of reduced policy discretion. Other nations balked at that trade-off, however. England, Sweden, Denmark, and Switzerland opted to keep their own national currencies and national control over monetary policy. To reap more benefits from global markets, however, these and other European nations try to coordinate monetary and trade policies.

The 200-plus nations of the world aren't about to adopt a single currency, much less forsake the tools of monetary policy. To facilitate trade, however, most nations use "hard" currencies—the U.S. dollar, the euro, yen, or the Swiss franc—as benchmarks of value. Goods exported from Morocco, for example, are typically priced in both diran and euros. Brazilian coffee is priced in both reals and U.S. dollars. This practice reduces some of the risks associated with fluctuating exchange rates and thereby facilitates more trade. As trade expands, incomes grow and the nations of the world become more integrated in the economy tomorrow.

SUMMARY

- The United States exports about 11 percent of total output and imports an even larger percentage. This international trade ties our macro performance to that of the rest of the world. LO1
- Imports represent leakage from the circular flow and so tend to reduce equilibrium GDP. The marginal propensity to import also diminishes the multiplier impact of fiscal and monetary policies. LO2
- Exports represent added spending on domestic output and so tend to increase equilibrium GDP. This added demand may conflict with restrictive macro policy objectives. LO1
- Trade imbalances occur when exports and imports are unequal. Trade deficits imply that we're consuming more output than we're producing. Trade surpluses indicate the opposite. LO1
- Fiscal stimulus increases imports and crowds out net exports. The resulting increase in the trade deficit may constrain policy options. LO2
- Capital imbalances occur when capital inflows don't equal capital outflows. Capital surpluses help finance trade deficits but may also conflict with macro policy goals at home or abroad. LO3
- International trade and capital flows place additional constraints on macro policy. Macro policy must both anticipate and respond to changes in trade and capital flows. LO3
- The benefits of international trade and capital markets are the broadening of consumption possibilities and the enhanced productivity they promote. Productivity advances arise from specialization in production and from the competitive pressure of foreign producers and markets. LO1
- In adopting a common currency, EU nations have broadened markets and accelerated productivity and growth. To maintain that currency, they have had to submerge some national priorities. LO3

Key Terms

imports
leakage
multiplier
closed economy
open economy
marginal propensity to import (MPM)
marginal propensity to save (MPS)
exports
net exports
trade surplus
trade deficit
crowding out
capital deficit
capital surplus
exchange rate
comparative advantage
productivity

Questions for Discussion

1. What is the "shock absorber" referred to in the World View on page 356? How does it work? LO1
2. How is the U.S. economy affected by (*a*) a recession in Mexico, (*b*) stimulative monetary policies in Mexico, and (*c*) a drop in the value of the peso? LO1
3. Suppose investors in other countries increased their purchases of U.S. corporate stock. How would this influx of capital affect the U.S. economy? LO3
4. Why is it unrealistic to expect trade flows to be balanced? LO1
5. Farmers in the United States export about one-third of their major crops. What would happen to U.S. farmers if foreign consumers stopped buying American food? What would happen to our macro equilibrium? LO1
6. Japan imports most of the raw materials it uses in the production of finished goods. If global raw-material prices rose sharply, how would Japan's economy be affected? Would Japanese exports be affected? LO1
7. How would a tax cut in the United States affect international capital and trade flows? LO2
8. Why would the European Central Bank (ECB) need to be prodded into raising interest rates (see World View, page 364)? What held the ECB back? LO3
9. Who gains and who loses when the global value of the U.S. dollar rises? LO1
10. Would a higher marginal propensity to import help or hinder domestic macro policy? LO2
11. What does England gain from maintaining its own non-euro currency? What does it lose? LO3

problems The Student Problem Set at the back of this book contains numerical and graphing problems for this chapter.

web activities to accompany this chapter can be found on the Online Learning Center: **http://www.mhhe.com/economics/schiller11e**

19 Theory versus Reality

LEARNING OBJECTIVES

After reading this chapter, you should know:

LO1. The tools of macro policy.

LO2. How macro tools should work.

LO3. The constraints on policy effectiveness.

There is no one solution. It isn't just a question of the budget. It isn't just the question of inflationary labor rates. It isn't just the question of sticky prices. It isn't just the question of what the Government does to keep prices up or to make regulations that tend to be inflationary. It isn't just the weather or just the drought.

It is all these things. The interaction of these various factors is what is so terribly difficult for us to understand and, of course, what is so terribly difficult for us to deal with.

—Former Secretary of the Treasury W. Michael Blumenthal

Macroeconomic theory is supposed to explain the business cycle and show policymakers how to control it. But something is obviously wrong. Despite our relative prosperity, we haven't consistently achieved the goals of full employment, price stability, and vigorous economic growth. All too often, either unemployment or inflation surges or economic growth slows down. No matter how hard we try to eliminate it, the business cycle seems to persist.

What accounts for this gap between the promises of economic theory and the reality of economic performance? Are the theories inadequate? Or is sound economic advice being ignored?

Many people blame the economists. They point to the conflicting advice of Keynesians, monetarists, and supply-siders and wonder what theory is supposed to be followed. If economists themselves can't agree, it is asked, why should anyone else listen to them?

Not surprisingly, economists see things a bit differently. First, they point out, the **business cycle** isn't as bad as it used to be. Since World War II, the economy has had many ups and downs, but none as severe as the Great Depression or earlier catastrophes. Second, economists complain that "politics" often takes precedence over good economic advice. Politicians are reluctant, for example, to raise taxes, cut spending, or slow money growth in order to control inflation. Their concern is winning the next election, not solving the country's economic problems.

When President Jimmy Carter was in office, he anguished over another problem: the complexity of economic decision making. In the real world, neither theory nor politics can keep up with all our economic goals. As President Carter observed: "We cannot concentrate just on inflation or just on unemployment or just on deficits in the federal budget or our international payments. Nor can we act in isolation from other countries. We must deal with all of these problems simultaneously and on a worldwide basis."

No president learned this lesson faster or more forcefully than George W. Bush. Just as he was putting the final touches on a bipartisan consensus on taxes, spending, and debt reduction, terrorists destroyed the World Trade Center and damaged the Pentagon. In response to those attacks, all major economic policy decisions had to be revised.

As if the burdens of a continuously changing world weren't enough, the president must also contend with sharply differing economic theories and advice, a slow and frequently hostile Congress, a massive and often unresponsive bureaucracy, and a complete lack of knowledge about the future.

business cycle: Alternating periods of economic growth and contraction.

This chapter confronts these and other frustrations of the real world head on. In so doing, we provide answers to the following questions:

- **What's the ideal "package" of macro policies?**
- **How well does our macro performance live up to the promises of that package?**
- **What kinds of obstacles prevent us from doing better?**

The answers to these questions may shed some light on a broader concern that has long troubled students and policymakers alike, namely, "If economists are so smart, why is the economy always in such a mess?"

webnote

The Library of Congress maintains a summary of recent congressional tax legislation at http:// thomas.loc.gov. Go to "Bills, Resolutions," then "Bill Summary, Status." Enter "taxes."

POLICY TOOLS

Table 19.1 summarizes the macroeconomic tools available to policymakers. Although this list is brief, we hardly need a reminder at this point of how powerful each instrument can be. Every one of these major policy instruments can significantly change our answers to the basic economic questions of WHAT, HOW, and FOR WHOM to produce.

Fiscal Policy

fiscal policy: The use of government taxes and spending to alter macroeconomic outcomes.

The basic tools of **fiscal policy** are contained in the federal budget. Tax cuts are supposed to increase aggregate demand by putting more income in the hands of consumers and businesses. Tax increases are intended to curtail spending and reduce inflationary pressures. Table 19.2 summarizes some of the major tax changes of recent years.

The expenditure side of the federal budget is another fiscal policy tool. From a Keynesian perspective, increases in government spending raise aggregate demand and so encourage more production. A slowdown in government spending is supposed to restrain aggregate demand and lessen inflationary pressures.

automatic stabilizer: Federal expenditure or revenue item that automatically responds countercyclically to changes in national income—such as unemployment benefits and income taxes.

structural deficit: Federal revenues at full employment minus expenditures at full employment under prevailing fiscal policy.

fiscal stimulus: Tax cuts or spending hikes intended to increase (shift) aggregate demand.

fiscal restraint: Tax hikes or spending cuts intended to reduce (shift) aggregate demand.

Who Makes Fiscal Policy? As we first observed in Chapter 11, changes in taxes and government spending originate both in economic events and explicit policy decisions. When the economy slows, tax revenues decline, and government spending increases automatically. Conversely, when real GDP grows, tax revenues automatically rise, and government transfer payments decline. These **automatic stabilizers** are a basic countercyclical feature of the federal budget. They don't represent active fiscal policy. On the contrary, ***fiscal policy refers to deliberate changes in tax or spending legislation.*** These changes can be made only by the U.S. Congress. Every year the president proposes specific budget and tax changes, negotiates with Congress, then accepts or vetoes specific acts that Congress has passed. The resulting policy decisions represent "discretionary" fiscal policy. Those policy decisions expand or shrink the **structural deficit** and thus give the economy a shot of **fiscal stimulus** or **fiscal restraint**.

TABLE 19.1
The Policy Tools

Economic policymakers have access to a variety of policy instruments. The challenge is to choose the right tools at the right time.

Type of Policy	Policy Tools
Fiscal	Tax cuts and increases
	Changes in government spending
Monetary	Open market operations
	Reserve requirements
	Discount rates
Supply-side	Tax incentives for investment and saving
	Deregulation
	Human-capital investment
	Infrastructure development
	Free trade
	Immigration

TABLE 19.2
Fiscal Policy Milestones

1986	Tax Reform Act	Major reduction in tax rates coupled with broadening of tax base
1990	Budget Enforcement Act	Limits set on discretionary spending; pay-as-you-go financing required
1993	Clinton "New Direction"	Tax increases and spending cuts to achieve $300 billion deficit reduction
1994	Contract with America	Republican-led Congress cuts spending, sets 7-year target for balanced budget
1997	Balanced Budget Act, Taxpayer Relief Act	Package of tax cuts and spending cuts to balance budget by 2002
2001	Economic Growth and Tax Relief Act	Eight-year, $1.35 trillion in personal tax cuts
2002	Job Creation and Worker Assistance Act	Business investment tax cuts
2003	Jobs and Growth Tax Relief Act	Cuts in dividend and capital-gains taxes
2004	Working Families Tax Tax Relief Act	Extends 2001–3 tax cuts until 2008–10

Monetary Policy

The policy arsenal in Table 19.1 also contains monetary tools. Tools of **monetary policy** include open market operations, discount rate changes, and reserve requirements.

monetary policy: The use of money and credit controls to influence macroeconomic outcomes.

As we saw in Chapter 15, there are disagreements over how these monetary tools should be used. Keynesians believe that interest rates are the critical policy lever. In their view, the money supply should be expanded or curtailed in order to achieve whatever interest rate is needed to shift aggregate demand. Monetarists, on the other hand, contend that the money supply itself is the critical policy tool and that it should be expanded at a steady and predictable rate. This policy, they believe, will ensure price stability and a **natural rate of unemployment.**

natural rate of unemployment: Long-term rate of unemployment determined by structural forces in labor and product markets.

Who Makes Monetary Policy? Actual monetary policy decisions are made by the Federal Reserve's Board of Governors. Twice a year the Fed provides Congress with a broad overview of the economic outlook and monetary objectives. The Fed's assessment of the economy is updated at meetings of the Federal Open Market Committee (FOMC). The FOMC decides which monetary policy levers to pull.

Table 19.3 depicts milestones in recent monetary policy. Of particular interest is the October 1979 decision to adopt a pure monetarist approach. This involved an exclusive focus on the money supply, without regard for interest rates. After interest rates soared and the economy appeared on the brink of a depression, the Fed abandoned the monetarist approach and again began keeping an eye on both interest rates (the Keynesian focus) and the money supply.

Monetarists contend that the Fed never fully embraced their policy. The money supply grew at a very uneven pace in 1980, they argue, not at the steady, predictable rate that they demanded. Nevertheless, the policy shifts of 1979 and 1982 were distinctive and had dramatic effects.

A quick review of Table 19.3 reveals that such monetary policy reversals have been quite frequent. There were U-turns in monetary policy between 1982 and 1983, 1989 and 1991, 1998 and 1999, 2000 and 2001, and again between 2003 and 2004.

supply-side policy: The use of tax incentives, (de)regulation, and other mechanisms to increase the ability and willingness to produce goods and services.

Supply-Side Policy

Supply-side theory offers the third major set of policy tools. The focus of **supply-side policy** is to provide incentives to work, invest, and produce. Of particular concern are high tax rates and regulations that reduce supply incentives. Supply-siders argue that marginal tax rates and government regulation must be reduced in order to get more output without added inflation.

In the 1980s tax rates were reduced dramatically. The maximum marginal tax rate on individuals was cut from 70 to 50 percent in 1981, and then still further, to 28 percent, in

TABLE 19.3
Monetary Policy Milestones

October 1979	Fed adopts monetarist approach, focusing exclusively on money supply; interest rates soar
July 1982	Deep into recession, Fed votes to ease monetary restraint
October 1982	Fed abandons pure monetarist approach and expands money supply rapidly
May 1983	Fed reverses policy and begins slowing money supply growth
1985	Fed increases money supply with discount-rate cuts and open market purchases
1987	Fed abandons money supply targets as policy guides; money supply growth decreases; discount rate increased
1989	Greenspan announces goal of "zero inflation," tightens policy
1991	Deep in recession, the Fed begins to ease monetary restraint
1994	Fed slows M2 growth to 1 percent; raises federal funds rate by three percentage points as economy nears full employment
1995	Greenspan trumpets "soft landing" and eases monetary restraint
1998	Fed cuts interest rates to cushion U.S. from Asian crisis
1999–2000	Fed raises interest rates six times
2001–2003	Fed cuts interest rates 13 times
2004–2006	Fed raises fed funds rate 17 times

1987. The 1980s also witnessed major milestones in the deregulation of airlines, trucking, telephone service, and other industries (see Table 19.4 on the next page).

Some of the momentum toward less regulation was reversed during the 1990s. New regulatory costs on business were created by the Americans with Disabilities Act, the 1990 amendments to the Clean Air Act, and the Family Leave Act of 1993. All three laws provide important benefits to workers or the environment. At the same time, however, they also make supplying goods and services more expensive.

The Clinton administration broadened supply-side efforts to include infrastructure development and increased investment in human capital (through education and skill training programs). These activities increase the capacity to produce and so shift the aggregate supply curve rightward. The Clinton administration also toughened environmental regulation, however, and sought legislation that would require employers to provide more training and fringe benefits (like health insurance), initiatives that shift the aggregate supply curve leftward. George W. Bush sought to reduce such regulations. He also succeeded in reducing marginal tax rates on both labor and capital.

Who Makes Supply-Side Policy? Because tax rates are a basic tool of supply-side policy, fiscal and supply-side policies are often intertwined. When Congress changes the tax laws, it almost always alters marginal tax rates and thus changes production incentives. Notice, for example, that tax legislation appears in Table 19.4 as well as in Table 19.2. The Taxpayer Relief Act of 1997 not only changed total tax revenues (fiscal policy) but also restructured production and investment incentives (supply-side policy). The 2001–3 tax cuts also had both demand-side and supply-side provisions.

Supply-side and fiscal policies also interact on the outlay side of the budget. The Transportation Equity Act of 2000, for example, authorized accelerated public works spending (fiscal stimulus) on intrastructure development (increase in supply capacity). President Clinton's Rebuild America program also affected both aggregate demand and aggregate supply. ***Deciding whether to increase spending is a fiscal policy decision; deciding how to spend available funds may entail supply-side policy.***

TABLE 19.4
Supply-Side Milestones

1990	Social Security Act amendments	Increased payroll tax to 7.65 percent
1990	Americans with Disabilities Act	Required employers to provide greater access for disabled individuals
1990	Immigration Act	Increased immigration, especially for highly skilled workers
1990	Clean Air Act amendments	Increased pollution controls
1993	Rebuild America Program	Increased spending on infrastructure and human-capital investment
	Family Leave Act	Required employers to provide unpaid leaves of absence for workers
	NAFTA	Lowered North American trade barriers
1994	GATT renewed	Lowered world trade barriers
1996	Telecommunications Act	Permitted greater competition in cable and telephone industries
1996	Personal Responsibility and Work Opportunity Act	Required more welfare recipients to work
1997	Taxpayer Relief Act	Created tuition tax credits, cut capital gains tax
1998	Workforce Investment Act	Increased funds for skills training
2000	Transportation Equity Act	Provided new funding for highways, rails
2001	Economic Growth and Tax Relief Act	Increased savings incentives; reduced marginal tax rates
2002	Job Creation and Worker Assistance Act	Provided more tax incentives for investment
2003	Jobs and Growth Tax Relief Act	Reduced taxes on capital gains and dividends
2007	Minimum wage hike	Raised from $5.15 to $7.15 in 2009

Regulatory policy is also fashioned by Congress. The president and executive agencies play a critical role in this supply-side area in the day-to-day decisions on how to interpret and enforce regulatory policies.

IDEALIZED USES

These fiscal, monetary, and supply-side tools are potentially powerful levers for controlling the economy. In principle, they can cure the excesses of the business cycle and promote faster economic growth. To see how, let's review their use in three distinct macroeconomic settings.

Case 1: Recession

When output and employment levels fall far short of the economy's full-employment potential, the mandate for public policy is clear. Aggregate demand must be increased so that producers can sell more goods, hire more workers, and move the economy toward its productive capacity. At such times the most urgent need is to get people back to work and close the **recessionary GDP gap.**

recessionary GDP gap: The amount by which equilibrium GDP falls short of full-employment GDP.

How can the government end a recession? Keynesians emphasize the need to increase aggregate demand by cutting taxes or boosting government spending. The resulting stimulus will set off a **multiplier** reaction. If the initial stimulus and multiplier are large enough, the recessionary GDP gap can be closed, propelling the economy to full employment.

multiplier: The multiple by which an initial change in aggregate spending will alter total expenditure after an infinite number of spending cycles; $1/(1 - MPC)$.

Modern Keynesians acknowledge that monetary policy might also help. Specifically, increases in the money supply may lower interest rates and thus give investment spending a further boost. To give the economy a really powerful stimulus, we might want to pull all these

Analysis: When the economy is flat on its back, it may need both monetary and fiscal stimulus.

policy levers at the same time. That's what the government did in early 2001—using tax cuts, lower interest rates, and increased spending to jump start the economy (see cartoon).

Monetarists would proceed differently. First, they see no point in toying with the federal budget. In the pure monetarist model, changes in taxes or government spending may alter the mix of output but not its level. So long as the **velocity of money (V)** is constant, fiscal policy doesn't matter. In this view, the appropriate policy response to a recession is patience. As sales and output slow, interest rates will decline, and new investment will be stimulated.

velocity of money (V): The number of times per year, on average, that a dollar is used to purchase final goods and services; $PQ \div M$.

Supply-siders emphasize the need to improve production incentives. They urge cuts in marginal tax rates on investment and labor. They also look for ways to reduce government regulation. Finally, they urge that any increase in government spending (fiscal stimulus) focus on long-run capacity expansion such as infrastructure development.

Case 2: Inflation

An overheated economy provides as clear a policy mandate as does a sluggish one. In this case, the immediate goal is to restrain aggregate demand until the rate of total expenditure is compatible with the productive capacity of the economy. This entails shifting the aggregate demand curve to the left in order to close the **inflationary GDP gap.** Keynesians would do this by raising taxes and cutting government spending. Keynesians would also see the desirability of increasing interest rates to curb investment spending.

inflationary GDP gap: The amount by which equilibrium GDP exceeds full-employment GDP.

Monetarists would simply cut the money supply. In their view, the short-run aggregate supply curve is unknown and unstable. The only predictable response is reflected in the vertical, long-run aggregate supply curve. According to this view, changes in the money supply alter prices, not output. Inflation is seen simply as "too much money chasing too few goods." Monetarists would turn off the money spigot. The Fed's job in this situation isn't only to reduce money supply growth but to convince market participants that a more cautious monetary policy will be continued. This was the intent of Chairman Greenspan's 1989 public commitment to zero inflation (Table 19.3).

Supply-siders would point out that inflation implies both "too much money" *and* "not enough goods." They'd look at the supply side of the market for ways to expand productive capacity. In a highly inflationary setting, they'd propose more incentives to save. The additional savings would automatically reduce consumption while creating a larger pool of investable funds. Supply-siders would also cut taxes and regulations that raise production costs and lower import barriers that keep out cheaper foreign goods.

Case 3: Stagflation

Although serious inflations and recessions provide clear mandates for economic policy, there's a vast gray area between these extremes. Occasionally, the economy suffers from both inflation and unemployment at the same time, a condition called **stagflation.** In 1980, for example, the unemployment rate (7.1 percent) and the inflation rate (12.5 percent) were both too high. With an upward-sloping aggregate supply curve, the easy policy options were foreclosed. If aggregate demand were stimulated to reduce unemployment, the resultant pressure on prices might fuel the existing inflation. And if fiscal and monetary restraints were used to reduce inflationary pressures, unemployment might worsen. In such a situation, there are no simple solutions.

stagflation: The simultaneous occurrence of substantial unemployment and inflation.

Knowing the causes of stagflation will help achieve the desired balance. If prices are rising before full employment is reached, some degree of structural unemployment is likely. An appropriate policy response might include more vocational training in skill-shortage areas as well as a redirection of aggregate demand toward labor-surplus sectors.

High tax rates or costly regulations might also contribute to stagflation. If either constraint exists, high prices (inflation) may not be a sufficient incentive for increased output. In this case, reductions in tax rates and regulation might help reduce both unemployment and inflation, which is the basic strategy of supply-side policies.

Stagflation may also arise from a temporary contraction of aggregate supply that both reduces output and drives up prices. In this case, neither structural unemployment nor excessive demand is the culprit. Rather, an "external shock" (such as a natural disaster or a terrorist attack) or an abrupt change in world trade (such as an oil embargo) is likely to be the cause of the policy dilemma. Accordingly, none of our familiar policy tools is likely to provide a complete "cure." In most cases, the economy simply has to adjust to a temporary setback.

Fine-Tuning

The apparently inexhaustible potential of public policy to alter the economy's performance has often generated optimistic expectations about the efficacy of fiscal, monetary, and supply-side tools. In the early 1960s, such optimism pervaded even the highest levels of government. Those were the days when prices were relatively stable, unemployment rates were falling, the economy was growing rapidly, and preparations were being made for the first trip into space. The potential of economic policy looked great indeed. It was also during the 1960s that a lot of people (mostly economists) spoke of the potential for **fine-tuning,** or altering economic outcomes to fit very exacting specifications. Flexible responses to changing market conditions, it was argued, could ensure fulfillment of our economic goals. The prescription was simple: When unemployment is the problem, simply give the economy a jolt of fiscal or monetary stimulus; when inflation is worrisome, simply tap on the fiscal or monetary brakes. To fulfill our goals for content and distribution, simply pick the right target for stimulus or restraint. With a little attention and experience, the right speed could be found and the economy guided successfully down the road to prosperity. As the economic expansion of the 1990s stretched into the record books, the same kind of economic mastery was claimed. More than a few prominent economists claimed the business cycle was dead.

fine-tuning: Adjustments in economic policy designed to counteract small changes in economic outcomes; continuous responses to changing economic conditions.

THE ECONOMIC RECORD

The economy's track record doesn't live up to these high expectations. To be sure, the economy has continued to grow and we've attained an impressive standard of living. We can't lose sight of the fact that our per capita income greatly exceeds the realities and even the expectations in most other countries of the world. Nevertheless, we must also recognize that our economic history is punctuated by periods of recession, high unemployment, inflation, and recurring concern for the distribution of income and mix of output.

Analysis: There are different theories about when and how the government should "fix" the economy. Policymakers must decide which advice to follow in specific situations.

The graphs in Figure 19.1 provide a quick summary of the gap between the theory and reality of economic policy. The Employment Act of 1946 committed the federal government to macro stability. It's evident that we haven't kept that commitment. In the 1970s we rarely came close. Although we approached all three goals in the mid-1980s, our achievements were short-lived. Economic growth ground to a halt in 1989, and the economy slipped into yet another recession in 1990. Although inflation stayed low, unemployment rates jumped.

The economy performed very well again from 1992 until early 2000. After that, however, growth came to an abrupt halt again. With the economy teetering on recession, the

FIGURE 19.1
The Economic Record

The Full Employment and Balanced Growth Act of 1978 established specific goals for unemployment (4 percent), inflation (3 percent), and economic growth (4 percent). We've rarely attained those goals, however, as these graphs illustrate. Measurement, design, and policy implementation problems help explain these shortcomings.

Source: *Economic Report of the President, 2007.*

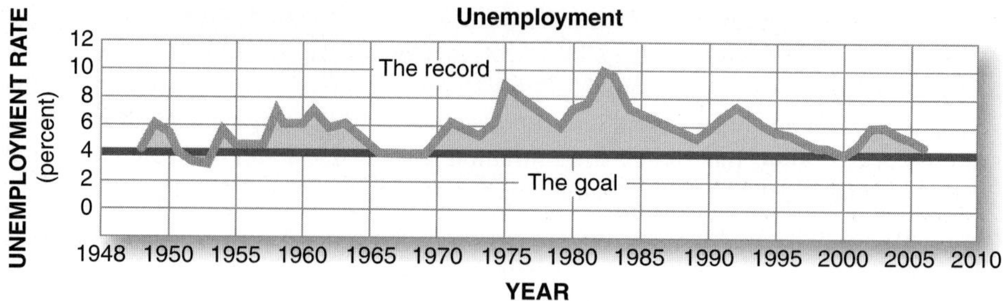

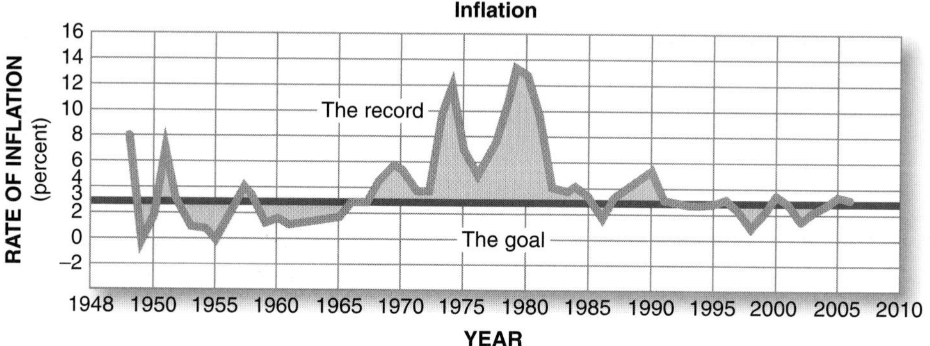

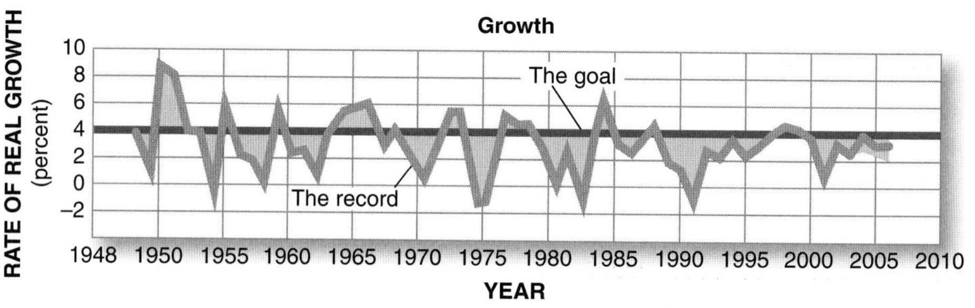

unemployment rate started rising in mid-2000. Some of the people who had proclaimed the business cycle to be dead were out of work. Then the economy was hit by the external shock of a terrorist attack that suspended economic activity and shook investor and consumer confidence. It took 2 years to get unemployment rates back down into the "full-employment" range (4–6 percent).

growth recession: A period during which real GDP grows, but at a rate below the long-term trend of 3 percent.

Looking back over the entire postwar period, the record includes 9 years of outright recession (actual declines in output) and another 20 years of **growth recession** (growth of less than 3 percent). Moreover, the distribution of income in 2006 looked worse than that of 1946, and more than 35 million people were still officially counted as poor in the later year.

Despite many setbacks, recent economic performance of the United States has been better than that of other Western nations. Other economies haven't grown as fast as the U.S. nor reduced unemployment as much. But, as the World View on the next page shows, some countries did a better job of restraining prices.

When one looks at the specific policy initiatives of various administrations, the gap between theory and practice is even larger. The Fed's decision to reduce the money supply on repeated occasions during the Great Depression was colossally perverse. Only slightly less so was the Fed's decision to expand the money supply rapidly in 1978, despite evidence that inflationary pressures were already building up. During 1980–81 and again in 1989–90, the Fed slowed money supply growth much more and far longer than was justified. As a consequence, the economy suffered two consecutive recessions in the early 1980s and another one in the early 1990s. Pretty much the same sequence occured in 1999–2001.

WORLD VIEW

Comparative Macro Performance

The performance of the U.S. economy in the 2000s was better than most developed economies. Japan had the greatest success in restraining inflation (*minus* 0.6 percent) but suffered from sluggish growth (1.8 percent per year). The United States grew faster and also experienced less unemployment than most European countries.

Performance (annual average percentage)	U.S.	Japan	Germany	United Kingdom	France	Canada
Real growth	2.7	1.8	1.2	2.7	1.9	3.0
Inflation	2.3	−0.6	1.7	2.6	1.9	2.3
Unemployment	5.1	5.0	9.2	5.0	9.3	6.5

Source: International Monetary Fund. www.imf.org

Analysis: Macroeconomic performance varies a lot, both over time and across countries. In the 2000s, U.S. economic performance was above average on most measures.

On the fiscal side of the ledger, we must recall President Roosevelt's timid efforts to expand aggregate demand during the Great Depression. Also worth remembering is President Johnson's refusal to pay for the Vietnam War by either raising taxes or cutting nonmilitary expenditures. The resulting strain on the economy's capacity kindled inflationary pressures that lasted for years. For his part, President Carter increased labor costs (higher payroll taxes and minimum wages), farm prices, and government spending at a time when inflation was a foremost policy concern. President Reagan made his share of mistakes too, including the pursuit of deep budget cuts in the early stages of a recession. President George H. Bush ignored the recession for an entire year, believing that "self-adjustment" would ensure recovery. That mistake cost him his job.

President Clinton pushed through a tax increase in 1993 that helped subdue the recovery from the 1990–91 recession. He also caused the aggregate supply curve to shift upward by forcing employers to pay higher labor costs. President George W. Bush cut taxes and regulation to shift both aggregate supply and aggregate demand in the right direction. But his insistence on cutting the growth of federal spending in the midst of the 2001 recession was ill-timed (and ultimately reversed). Later he balked at using tax increases to help pay for the Iraq war, forcing the Fed to assume the entire burden of AD restraint.

WHY THINGS DON'T ALWAYS WORK

There's plenty of blame to go around for all the blemishes on our economic record. Some people blame the Fed, others blame Congress, still others blame China or Mexico. Some forces, however, constrain economic policy even when no one is specifically to blame. In this regard, we can distinguish ***four obstacles to policy success:***

- ***Goal conflicts***
- ***Measurement problems***
- ***Design problems***
- ***Implementation problems***

Goal Conflicts

The first factor to take note of is potential conflicts in policy priorities. President Clinton had to confront this problem his first day in office. He had pledged to create new jobs by

IN THE NEWS   

Deficit-Cutting Wilts in Heat from Voters

Entitlements Remain Mostly Off-Limits

In April, Sen. Pete V. Domenici (R-N.M.) suggested a plan for digging out of the massive federal deficit. His idea seemed modest on its face but was revolutionary by Washington standards.

Domenici proposed capping cost-of-living increases in entitlement programs, the automatic spending engines such as Medicaid, Medicare and federal retirement that are exempt from annual congressional review. . . .

Even before his proposal took shape, more than 3,000 New Mexico constituents sent him identical postcards opposing any effort to cap entitlement programs.

The National Council of Senior Citizens dubbed the plan "the most outrageous attack on the elderly we have seen in years." The Veterans of Foreign Wars expressed "shock and outrage." Milk producers accused Domenici of trying to balance the budget "on the back of farmers."

That was enough for the Senate, which voted 69 to 28 to reject the proposal.

—Eric Pianin

Source: *The Washington Post,* August 4, 1992. www.washingtonpost.com

Analysis: Changes in economic policy inevitably alter incomes and stir political opposition. Cuts in government spending are particularly difficult to enact.

increasing public infrastructure spending and offering a middle-class tax cut. He had also promised to reduce the deficit, however. This created a clear goal conflict. In the end, President Clinton had to settle for a smaller increase in infrastructure spending and a tax *increase.* President George W. Bush confronted similar problems. In the 2000 presidential campaign he had promised a big increase in federal spending on education. By the time he took office, however, the federal budget surplus was rapidly shrinking, and the goal of preserving the non–Social Security ("on budget") surplus took precedence. The conflict between spending priorities and budget balancing became much more intense when President Bush decided to attack Iraq.

These and other goal conflicts have their roots in the short-run trade-off between unemployment and inflation. Should we try to cure inflation, unemployment, or just a bit of both? Answers are likely to vary. Unemployed people put the highest priority on attaining full employment. Labor unions press for faster economic growth. Bankers, creditors, and people on fixed incomes demand an end to inflation.

This goal conflict is often institutionalized in the decision-making process. The Fed is traditionally viewed as the guardian of price stability. The president and Congress worry more about people's jobs and government programs, so they are less willing to raise taxes or cut spending.

Distributional goals may also conflict with macro objectives. Anti-inflationary policies may require cutbacks in programs for the poor, the elderly, or needy students. These cutbacks may be politically impossible (see News). Likewise, tight-money policies may be viewed as too great a burden for small businesses, home builders, and auto manufacturers.

Although the policy tools in Table 19.1 are powerful, they can't grant all our wishes. Since we still live in a world of scarce resources, ***all policy decisions entail opportunity costs,*** which means that we'll always be confronted with trade-offs. The best we can hope for is a set of compromises that yields *optimal* outcomes, not ideal ones.

Measurement Problems

One reason firefighters are pretty successful in putting out fires before entire cities burn down is that fires are highly visible phenomena. But such visibility isn't characteristic of economic problems. An increase in the unemployment rate from 5 to 6 percent, for example, isn't the kind of thing you notice while crossing the street. Unless you work in the unemployment insurance office or lose your own job, the increase in unemployment isn't likely to attract your attention. The same is true of prices; small increases in product prices

IN THE NEWS

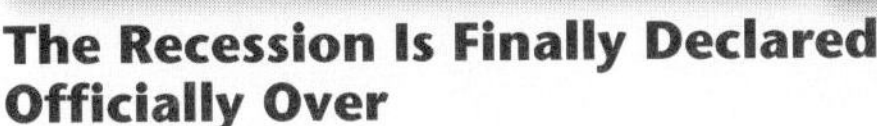

The Recession Is Finally Declared Officially Over

The National Bureau of Economic Research said the U.S. economic recession that began in March 2001 ended eight months later, not long after the Sept. 11 terrorist attacks.

Most economists concluded more than a year ago that the recession ended in late 2001. But yesterday's declaration by the NBER—a private, nonprofit economic research group that is considered the official arbiter of recession timing—came after a lengthy internal debate over whether there can be an economic recovery if the labor market continues to contract. The bureau's answer: a decisive yes. . . .

The NBER committee is notoriously slow in making its declarations on the timing of the business cycle. Still, the 20 months it waited to declare the recession's end was slightly shorter than the 21 months it took to declare the end of the 1990–91 recession. That, too, was a so-called jobless recovery, though the job losses weren't as severe as they have been lately.

—Jon E. Hilsenrath

Analysis: In the absence of timely information, today's policy decisions are inevitably based on yesterday's perceptions.

aren't likely to ring many alarms. Hence, both inflation and unemployment may worsen considerably before anyone takes serious notice. Were we as slow and ill-equipped to notice fires, whole neighborhoods would burn before someone rang the alarm.

Measurement problems are a very basic policy constraint. To formulate appropriate economic policy, we must first determine the nature of our problems. To do so, we must measure employment changes, output changes, price changes, and other macro outcomes. The old adage that governments are willing and able to solve only those problems they can measure is relevant here. Indeed, before the Great Depression, a fundamental constraint on public policy was the lack of statistics on what was happening in the economy. One lasting benefit of that experience is that we now try to keep informed on changing economic conditions. The information at hand, however, is always dated and incomplete. ***At best, we know what was happening in the economy last month or last week.*** The processes of data collection, assembly, and presentation take time, even in this age of high-speed computers. The average recession lasts about 11 months, but official data generally don't even confirm the existence of a recession until 8 months after a downturn starts! As the accompanying News reveals, the 2001 recession ended nearly 2 years before researchers confirmed its demise!

Forecasts. In an ideal world, policymakers wouldn't just *respond* to economic problems but would also *anticipate* their occurrence. If an inflationary GDP gap is emerging, for example, we want to take immediate action to keep aggregate spending from increasing. That is, the successful firefighter not only responds to a fire but also looks for hazards that might start one.

Unfortunately, economic policymakers are again at a disadvantage. Their knowledge of future problems is even worse than their knowledge of current problems. ***In designing policy, policymakers must depend on economic forecasts,*** that is, informed guesses about what the economy will look like in future periods.

Macro Models. Those guesses are often based on complex computer models of how the economy works. These models—referred to as *econometric macro models*—are mathematical summaries of the economy's performance. The models try to identify the key determinants of macro performance and then show what happens to macro outcomes when they change. As the News on the next page suggests, the apparent precision of such computer models may disguise "a black art."

IN THE NEWS

Tough Calls in Economic Forecasting

Seers Often Peer into Cracked Crystal Balls

In presenting his annual economic outlook last Thursday, the chairman of President Clinton's Council of Economic Advisers was having nothing to do with all the recession talk going around.

"Let me be clear," Martin Baily said, "we don't think that we're going into recession."

The same message was delivered the next day by Clinton in a Rose Garden economic valedictory. Citing the predictions of 50 private forecasters known as the Blue Chip Consensus—"the experts who make a living doing this," as he put it—Clinton assured Americans that the economy would continue to grow this year at an annual rate of 2 percent to 3 percent.

What the president and his adviser failed to mention was that "the experts" have not predicted any of the nine recessions since the end of World War II. . . .

Allen Sinai of Decision Economics, a respected private forecaster, agreed. "Its probably only fair for forecasters to admit at times like this that we're simply not well equipped to predict turning points," he said. "A recession, by its nature, is a speculative call."

On first blush, such humility may seem at odds with the aura surrounding the modern day forecaster. Using high-speed computers and sophisticated models of the U.S. economy, they constantly revise their two-year predictions for everything from unemployment to business investment to long-term interest rates, expressed numerically to the first decimal point.

But according to the forecasters themselves, what may appear to be a precise science is a black art, one that is constantly confounded by the changing structure of the economy and the refusal of investors, consumers and business executives to behave as rationally and predictably in real life as they do in the economic models.

"The reason we have trouble calling recessions is that all recessions are anomalies," said Joel Prakken, president of Macroeconomic Advisers of St. Louis, one of the nation's leading forecasting firms.

—Steven Pearlstein

Source: *The Washington Post,* January 15, 2001. www.washingtonpost.com

Analysis: Even the most sophisticated computer models rely on basic assumptions about consumer and investor behavior. If the assumptions are wrong, the forecasts will likely be wrong as well (as they were in early 2001).

An economist "feeds" the computer two essential inputs. One is a quantitative model of how the economy allegedly works. A Keynesian model, for example, includes equations that show multiplier spending responses to tax cuts. A monetarist model shows that tax cuts raise interest rates, not total spending ("crowding out"), and a supply-side model stipulates labor-supply and production responses. The computer can't tell which theory is right; it just predicts what it's programmed to see. In other words, the computer sees the world through the eyes of its economic master.

webnote

For an overview of the forecasting model the Congressional Budget Office uses, visit www.cbo.gov

The second essential input in a computer forecast is the assumed values for critical variables. A Keynesian model, for example, must specify how large a multiplier to expect. All the computer does is carry out the required mathematical routines, once it's told that the multiplier is relevant and what its value is. It can't discern the true multiplier any better than it can pick the right theory.

Given the dependence of computers on the theories and perceptions of their economic masters, it's not surprising that computer forecasts often differ greatly. It's also not surprising that they're often wrong. Even policymakers who are familiar with both economic theory and computer models can make some pretty bad calls. In January 1990, Fed chairman Alan Greenspan assured Congress that the risk of a recession was as low as 20 percent. Although he said he "wouldn't bet the ranch" on such a low probability, he was confident that the odds of a recession were below 50 percent. Five months after his testimony, the 1990–91 recession began.

The Council of Economic Advisers has made similar blunders. As the previous News reveals, the CEA was forecasting 2–3 percent growth just as the economy was falling into the 2001 recession.

Leading Indicators. Given the complexity of macro models, many people prefer to use simpler tools for divining the future. One of the most popular is the Index of Leading Economic Indicators. As noted in Chapter 9 (see Table 9.2), the Leading Indicators are things we can observe today that are logically linked to future production (e.g., orders for new equipment). Unfortunately, the logical sequence of events doesn't always unfold as anticipated. All too often, the links in the chain of Leading Indicators are broken by changing expectations and unanticipated events.

Crystal Balls. In view of the fragile foundations and spotty record of computer and index-based forecasts, many people shun them altogether, preferring to use their own "crystal balls." The Foundation for the Study of Cycles has identified 4,000 different crystal balls that people use to gauge the health of the economy, including the ratio of used-car to new-car sales (it rises in recession); the number of divorce petitions (it rises in bad times); animal population cycles (they peak just before economic downturns); and even the optimism/pessimism content of popular music (a reflection of consumer confidence). Corporate executives claim that such crystal balls are as valuable as professional economic forecasts. In a Gallup survey of CEOs, most respondents said economists' forecasts had little or no influence on company plans or policies. The head of one large company said, "I go out of my way to ignore them." The general public apparently shares this view, giving higher marks to the forecasts of sportswriters and weather forecasters than to those of economists.

webnote

The Dismal Sciences company assembles economic forecasts and a broad array of economic statistics, along with user-friendly commentary. You can visit the company at www.dismal.com

Economic forecasters defend themselves in two ways. First, they note that economic policy decisions are inevitably based on anticipated changes in the economy's performance. The decision to stimulate or restrain the economy can't be made by a flip of a coin; *someone* must try to foresee the future course of the economy. Second, forecasters claim that their quantitative approach is the only honest one. Because forecasting models require specific behavioral assumptions and estimates, they force people to spell out their versions of the future. Less rigorous ("gut feeling") approaches are too ambiguous and often inconsistent.

These are valid arguments. Still, one must be careful to distinguish the precision of computers from the inevitable uncertainties of their spoon-fed models. The basic law of the computer is GIGO: garbage in, garbage out. If the underlying models and assumptions are no good, the computer's forecasts won't be any better.

Policy and Forecasts. The task of forecasting the economic future is made still more complex by the interdependency of forecasts, policy decisions, and economic outcomes (see Figure 19.2). First, a forecast is made, based on current economic conditions, likely disturbances to the economy, and anticipated economic policy. These forecasts are then

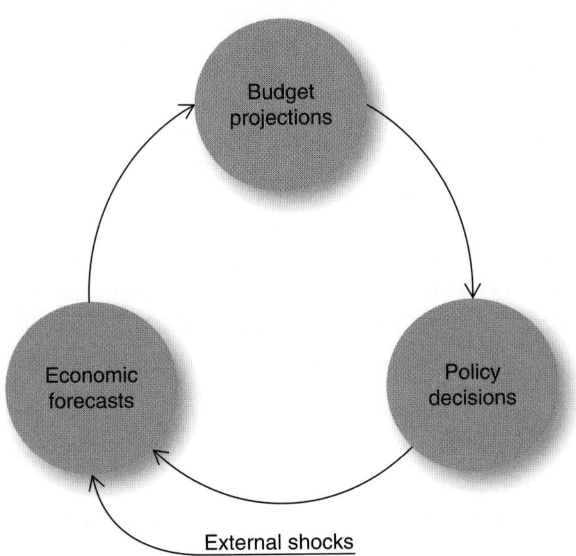

FIGURE 19.2
The Mutual Dependence of Forecasts and Policy

Because tax revenues and government spending are sensitive to economic conditions, budget projections must rely on economic forecasts. The budget projections may alter policy decisions, however, and so change the basis for the initial forecasts. This interdependence among macro forecasts, budget projections, and policy decisions is virtually inevitable.

used to project likely budget deficits and other policy variables. Congress and the president react to these projections by revising fiscal, monetary, or supply-side policies. These changes, in turn, alter the basis for the initial forecasts.

This interdependence among forecasts, budget projections, and policy decisions was superbly illustrated in the early months of the George W. Bush presidency. At the beginning of 2001, both the White House and the Congress were forecasting enormous budget surpluses. The central policy debate focused on what to do with those surpluses. The Democrats wanted to spend the surplus; the Republicans wanted to give it back to households with larger tax cuts. As the debate dragged on, however, the weakening economy shrunk the surplus. In August 2001, the Congressional Budget Office (CBO) announced that the "on-budget" (non–Social Security) surplus it had forecast just 7 months earlier had vanished. This forced both political parties to change their policy proposals. Protecting the vanishing surplus became the political priority. Spending proposals were scaled back, as were hopes of debt repayment.

External Shocks. The CBO's forecasts of budget surpluses were already far wrong *before* the September 11, 2001, terrorist attack on the World Trade Center. That attack created an external shock that caused everyone to revise their economic forecasts. In the immediate aftermath of the attack, financial markets closed, air travel was suspended, sports events and concerts were canceled, businesses closed, and consumers stayed away from shopping malls. The economic setback reduced tax revenues, increased federal outlays, and widened the federal deficit. Hurricanes Katrina and Rita had similar, though smaller, impacts (see News, page 318).

The very nature of external *shocks* is that they are *unanticipated.* Hence, even if we knew enough about the economy to forecast "shockless" outcomes perfectly, an external shock could always disrupt the economy and ruin our forecasts. In reality, forecasting methods aren't even good enough to predict the behavior of a "shockless" economy with precision.

As the accompanying News reveals, the CBO's forecasting errors in 2001 and 2005 were not an exception; they were the norm. When policymakers rely on such forecasts, they are likely to fail all too often.

Design Problems

Assume for the moment that we somehow are able to get a reliable forecast of where the economy is headed. The outlook, let's suppose, is bad. Now we're in the driver's seat to steer the economy past looming dangers. We need to chart our course—to design an economic plan. What action should we take? Which theory of macro behavior should guide us? How will the marketplace respond to any specific action we take?

IN THE NEWS

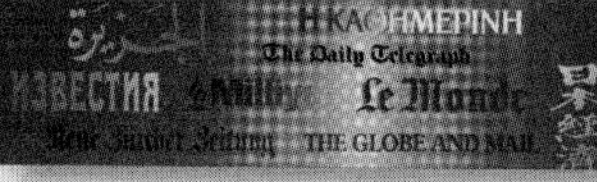

CBO's Flawed Forecasts

Every year the Congressional Budget Office (CBO) forecasts the federal budget balance for the next five years. Those forecasts are rarely accurate. The typical CBO forecasting error for the *current* fiscal year amounts to 0.5 percent of GDP, or about $70 billion. Moreover, the errors widen for future years: For the *fifth* year out, CBO's forecasts typically miss the actual budget balance by a startling 3 percent of GDP. This implies that CBO's January 2007 forecast of the 2012 budget balance (a $54 billion deficit) may be off the mark by $400 billion!

Since 1981, CBO has both over- and underestimated federal budget balances. There has been a slightly pessimistic bias, however, especially in the boom years of 1992–2000 and 2003–2007. Forecasts from the president's Office of Management and Budget (OMB) haven't been any better.

Source: Congressional Budget Office, *The Budget and Economic Outlook, Fiscal Years 2008–2017.* January 2007.

Analysis: The economic and budget forecasts that guide policy decisions are often flawed. This reduces the chances of policy success.

Suppose, for example, that we adopt a Keynesian approach to ending a recession. Specifically, we cut income taxes to stimulate consumer spending. How do we know that consumers will respond as anticipated? In 1998, Japanese households used their tax cut to increase *savings* rather than consumption. In 2001, U.S. households were also slow to spend their tax rebates. When consumers don't respond as anticipated, the intended fiscal stimulus doesn't materialize. Such behavioral responses frustrate even the best-intentioned policy. The successful policymaker needs a very good crystal ball, one that will also foretell how market participants are going to respond to any specific actions taken.

webnote

For the latest CBO and Office of Management and Budget (OMB) macro forecasts, visit www.cbo.gov and click on "Economic Projections."

Implementation Problems

Measurement and design problems can break the spirit of even the best policymaker (or the policymaker's economic advisers). Yet measurement and design problems are only part of the story. A good idea is of little value unless someone puts it to use. Accordingly, to understand fully why things go wrong, we must also consider the difficulties of *implementing* a well-designed policy.

Congressional Deliberations. Suppose that the president and his Council of Economic Advisers (perhaps in conjunction with the National Economic Council, the secretary of the Treasury, and the director of the Office of Management and Budget) decide that aggregate demand is slowing. A tax cut, they believe, is necessary to stimulate demand for goods and services. Can they simply go ahead and cut tax rates? No, because only the Congress can legislate tax changes. Once the president decides on the appropriate policy, he must ask Congress for authority to take the required action, which means a delay in implementing policy or possibly no policy at all.

At the very least, the president must convince Congress of the wisdom of his proposed policy. The tax proposal must work its way through separate committees of both the House of Representatives and the Senate, get on the congressional calendar, and be approved in each chamber. If there are important differences in Senate and House versions of the tax-cut legislation, they must be compromised in a joint conference. The modified proposal must then be returned to each chamber for approval.

The same kind of process applies to the outlay side of the budget. Once the president has submitted his budget proposals (in January), Congress reviews them, then sets its own spending goals. After that, the budget is broken down into 13 different categories, and a separate appropriations bill is written for each one. These bills spell out in detail how much can be spent and for what purposes. Once Congress passes them, they go to the president for acceptance or veto.

Budget legislation requires Congress to finish these deliberations by October 1 (the beginning of the federal fiscal year), but Congress rarely meets this deadline. In most years, the budget debate continues well into the fiscal year. In some years, the budget debate isn't resolved until the fiscal year is nearly over! The final budget legislation is typically more than 1,000 pages long and so complex that few people understand all its dimensions.

Time Lags. This description of congressional activity isn't an outline for a civics course; rather, it's an important explanation of why economic policy isn't fully effective. ***Even if the right policy is formulated to solve an emerging economic problem, there's no assurance that it will be implemented. And if it's implemented, there's no assurance that it will take effect at the right time.*** One of the most frightening prospects for economic policy is that a policy design intended to serve a specific problem will be implemented much later, when economic conditions have changed. This isn't a remote danger. According to Christina Romer and Paul Romer, the Fed doesn't pull the monetary-stimulus lever until a recession is under way, and Congress is even slower in responding to an economic downturn. Indeed, a U.S. Treasury Department study concluded that almost every postwar fiscal stimulus package was enacted well after the end of the recession it was intended to cure!

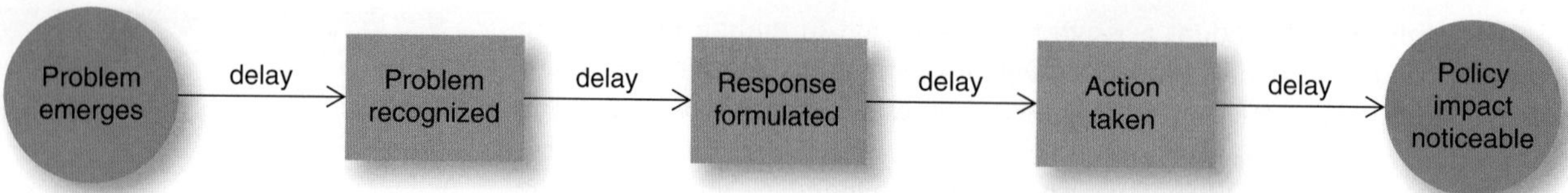

FIGURE 19.3
Policy Response: A Series of Time Lags

Even the best-intentioned economic policy can be frustrated by time lags. It takes time for a problem to be recognized, time to formulate a policy response, and still more time to implement that policy. By the time the policy begins to affect the economy, the underlying problem may have changed.

Figure 19.3 is a schematic view of why macro policies don't always work as intended. There are always delays between the time a problem emerges and the time it's recognized. There are additional delays between recognition and response design, between design and implementation, and finally between implementation and impact. Not only may mistakes be made at each juncture, but even correct decisions may be overcome by changing economic conditions.

Politics vs. Economics. Politics often contributes to delayed and ill-designed policy interventions. Especially noteworthy in this regard is the potential conflict of economic policy with political objectives. The president and Congress are always reluctant to impose fiscal restraints (tax increases or budget cutbacks) in election years, regardless of economic circumstances. As the cartoon below emphasizes, fiscal restraint is never popular.

The tendency of Congress to hold fiscal policy hostage to electoral concerns has created a pattern of short-run stops and starts—a kind of policy-induced business cycle. Indeed, some argue that the business cycle has been replaced with the political cycle: The economy is stimulated in the year of an election and then restrained in the postelection year. The conflict between the urgent need to get reelected and the necessity to manage the economy results in a seesaw kind of instability.

> **webnote**
>
> Senator John McCain maintains a list of political "pork" spending at http://mccain.senate.gov/index.cfm?fuseaction=NewsCenter.Pork

Even when the need for fiscal *stimulus* seems urgent—like after the September 11 terrorist attacks—politics can slow and distort the policy response. Two months after the attacks Republican and Democrat lawmakers were still far apart on how much fiscal stimulus to provide and what form the stimulus should take (see News). Critics feared that by the time Congress acted, the stimulus would be too late and possibly excessive. Similar political stalemates about who should deliver emergency aid and to whom slowed the fiscal response to Hurricane Katrina.

SHOE JEFF MacNELLY

Analysis: Budget cuts are not popular with voters—even when economic conditions warrant fiscal restraint.

In theory, the political independence of the Fed's Board of Governors provides some protection from ill-advised but politically advantageous policy initiatives. In practice, however, the Fed's relative obscurity and independence may backfire. The president and the Congress know that if they don't take effective action against inflation—by raising taxes or cutting government spending—the Fed can and will take stronger action to restrain aggregate demand. This is a classic case of having one's cake and eating it too. Elected officials win votes for not raising taxes or cutting some constituent's favorite spending program. They then take credit for any reduction in the rate of inflation brought about by Federal Reserve policies. To top it off, Congress and the president can also blame the Fed for driving up interest rates or starting a recession if monetary policy becomes too restrictive!

Finally, we must recognize that policy design is obstructed by a certain attention deficit (see cartoon below). Neither people on the street nor elected public officials focus constantly on economic goals and activities. Even students enrolled in economics courses have a hard time keeping their minds on the economy and its problems. The executive and legislative branches of government, for their part, are likely to focus on economic concerns only when economic problems become serious or voters demand action. Otherwise, policymakers are apt to be complacent about economic policy as long as economic performance is within a tolerable range of desired outcomes.

AMERICA'S PROBLEM:

Mike Thompson; Copley News Service.

Analysis: Economic problems often don't arouse public or policy interest until they become severe.

IN THE NEWS

Stimulus Package Stalled over Tax Breaks, Spending

WASHINGTON—A multibilliondollar economic stimulus package aimed at energizing the faltering economy, helping the unemployed and giving low-income workers a tax rebate faces a stalemate in a deeply divided Senate this week.

Democrats and Republicans said Tuesday that bipartisan negotiations are needed if Congress is to find agreement on a bill that President Bush wants passed by the end of the month. But the two parties remain so far apart that they are only talking about talking, not actually working out a solution.

Democrats lack the votes to pass their $66.4 billion tax package and an additional $20 billion in domestic security spending that they want to attach. Republicans don't have enough votes for their alternative, either.

The problem for both sides: Passing anything in the Senate, controlled 50-49 by Democrats with one independent, requires consensus. Either side can invoke Senate rules that set a 60-vote hurdle, rather than a simple majority, for passage.

How does either side get there? "That's a good question," Sen. Daschle said. "Neither side has 60 votes at this point. So we know we've got to work together . . . ".

Adding to the disarray is a dispute over the Democrats' proposal to spend $20 billion more on homeland security, which Bush vowed to veto last week. Republicans say Democrats have simply dusted off old wish lists for public works and pork-barrel projects. And they say Democrats have even more spending cloaked in their tax bill, including $6 billion in farm aid that provides subsidies to bison ranchers.

"I thought this was going to be a stimulus package instead of a pork package," [Sen.] Lott said.

—William M. Welch

Source: *USA Today,* November 14, 2001. www.usatoday.com

Analysis: Political disputes over the size and content of budget initiatives can slow and distort economic policy responses.

THE ECONOMY TOMORROW

HANDS ON OR HANDS OFF?

In view of the goal conflicts and the measurement, design, and implementation problems that policymakers confront, it's less surprising that things sometimes go wrong than that things so often work out right. The maze of obstacles through which theory must pass before it becomes policy explains many economic disappointments. On this basis alone, we may conclude that ***consistent fine-tuning of the economy isn't compatible with either our design capabilities or our decision-making procedures.*** We have exhibited a strong capability to avoid major economic disruptions in the last four decades. We haven't, however, been able to make all the minor adjustments necessary to fulfill our goals completely. As Arthur Burns, former chairman of the Fed's Board of Governors, said:

> There has been much loose talk of "fine tuning" when the state of knowledge permits us to predict only within a fairly broad level the course of economic development and the results of policy actions.[1]

Hands Off. Some critics of economic policy take this argument a few steps further. If fine-tuning isn't really possible, they say, we should abandon discretionary policies altogether and follow fixed rules for fiscal and monetary intervention.

As we saw in Chapter 15, pure monetarism would require the Fed to increase the money supply at a constant rate. Critics of fiscal policy would require the government to maintain balanced budgets, or at least to offset deficits in sluggish years with surpluses in years of high growth. Such rules would prevent policymakers from over- or understimulating the economy. Such rules would also add a dose of certainty to the economic outlook.

[1]*Newsweek,* August 27, 1973, p. 4.

Milton Friedman was one of the most persistent advocates of fixed policy rules. With discretionary authority, Friedman argued:

> the wrong decision is likely to be made in a large fraction of cases because the decision-makers are examining only a limited area and not taking into account the cumulative consequences of the policy as a whole. On the other hand, if a general rule is adopted for a group of cases as a bundle, the existence of that rule has favorable effects on people's attitudes and beliefs and expectations that would not follow even from the discretionary adoption of precisely the same policy on a series of separate occasions.[2]

The case for a hands-off policy stance is based on practical, not theoretical, arguments. ***Everyone agrees that flexible, discretionary policies* could *result in better economic performance. But Friedman and others argue that the practical requirements of monetary and fiscal management are too demanding and thus prone to failure.*** Moreover, required policies may be compromised by political pressures.

New Classical Economics. Monetarist critiques of discretionary policy are echoed by a new perspective referred to as new classical economics (NCE). Classical economists saw no need for discretionary macro policy. In their view, the private sector is inherently stable and government intervention serves no purpose. New classical economics reaches the same conclusion. As Robert Barro, a proponent of NCE, put it: "It is best for the government to provide a stable environment, and then mainly stay out of the way."[3] Barro and other NCE economists based this laissez-faire conclusion on the intriguing notion of **rational expectations.** This notion contends that people make decisions on the basis of all available information, including the *future* effects of *current* government policy.

rational expectations: Hypothesis that people's spending decisions are based on all available information, including the anticipated effects of government intervention.

Suppose, for example, that the Fed decided to increase the money supply in order to boost output. If people had rational expectations, they'd anticipate that this money supply growth will fuel inflation. To protect themselves, they'd immediately demand higher prices and wages. As a result, the stimulative monetary policy would fail to boost real output. (Monetarists reach the same conclusion but for different reasons; for monetarists, the countervailing forces are technological and institutional rather than rational expectations.)

Discretionary fiscal policy could be equally ineffective. Suppose Congress accelerated government spending in an effort to boost aggregate demand. Monetarists contend that the accompanying increase in the deficit would push interest rates up and crowd out private investment and consumption. New classical economists again reach the same conclusion via a different route. They contend that people with rational expectations would anticipate that a larger deficit now will necessitate tax increases in later years. To prepare for later tax bills, consumers will reduce spending now, thereby saving more. This "rational" reduction in consumption will offset the increased government expenditure, thus rendering fiscal policy ineffective.

If the new classical economists are right, then the only policy that works is one that surprises people—one that consumers and investors don't anticipate. But a policy based on surprises isn't very practical. Accordingly, new classical economists conclude that minimal policy intervention is best. This conclusion provides yet another guideline for policy decisions. See Table 19.5 for a roster of competing theories.

Hands On. ***Proponents of a hands-on policy strategy acknowledge the possibility of occasional blunders. They emphasize, however, the greater risks of doing nothing when the economy is faltering.*** Some proponents of the quick fix even turn the new classical economics argument on its head. Even the wrong policy, they argue, might be better than doing nothing if enough market participants believed that *change* implied *progress.* They cite the jump in consumer confidence that followed the election of Bill Clinton, who had emphasized the need for a *change* in policy but hadn't spelled out the details of that change.

[2]Milton Friedman, *Capitalism and Freedom* (Chicago: University of Chicago Press, 1962), p. 53.
[3]Robert Barro, "Don't Fool with Money, Cut Taxes," *The Wall Street Journal,* November 21, 1991, p. A14.

TABLE 19.5
Who's on First? Labeling Economists

It's sometimes hard to tell who's on what side in economic debates. Although some economists are proud to wear the colors of monetarists, Keynesians, or other teams, many economists shun such allegiances. Indeed, economists are often accused of playing on one team one day and on another team the next, making it hard to tell which team is at bat. To simplify matters, this guide may be used for quick identification of the players. Closer observation is advised, however, before choosing up teams.

Keynesians	Keynesians believe that the private sector is inherently unstable and prone to stagnate at low levels of output and employment. They want the government to manage aggregate demand with changes in taxes and government's spending.
Modern ("neo") Keynesians	Post–World War II followers of Keynes worry about inflation as well as recession. They urge budgetary restraint to cool an overheated economy. They also use monetary policy to change interest rates.
Monetarists	The money supply is their only heavy hitter. By changing the money supply, they can raise or lower the price level. Pure monetarists shun active policy, believing that it destabilizes the otherwise stable private sector. Output and employment gravitate to their natural levels.
Supply-siders	Incentives to work, invest, and produce are the key to their plays. Cuts in marginal tax rates and government regulation are used to expand production capacity, thereby increasing output and reducing inflationary pressures.
New classical economists	They say fine-tuning won't work because once the private sector realizes what the government is doing, it will act to offset it. They also question the credibility of quick-fix promises. They favor steady, predictable policies.
Marxists	Marxists contend that the failures of the economy are inherent in its capitalist structure. The owners of capital won't strive for full employment or a more equitable income distribution. Workers, without any capital, have little incentive to excel. This team proposes starting a new game, with entirely different rules.

The surge in confidence itself stimulated consumer purchases, even before President Clinton took office. The same kind of response occurred after the September 11, 2001, terrorist attacks. Consumers were dazed and insecure. There was a serious risk that they would curtail spending if the government didn't *do something.* Details aside, they just wanted reassurance that someone was taking charge of events. Quick responses by the Fed (increasing the money supply), the Congress (authorizing more spending), and President Bush (mobilizing security and military forces) kept consumer confidence from plunging.

Just doing *something* isn't the purpose of a hands-on policy, of course. Policy activists believe that we have enough knowledge about how the economy works to pull the right policy levers most of the time. They also point to the historical record. Our economic track record may not be perfect, but the historical record of prices, employment, and growth has improved since active fiscal and monetary policies were adopted. Without flexibility in the money supply and the budget, they argue, the economy would be less stable and our economic goals would remain unfulfilled.

The historical evidence for discretionary policy is ambiguous. Victor Zarnowitz showed that the U.S. economy has been much more stable since 1946 than it was in earlier periods (1875–1918 and 1919–1945). Recessions have gotten shorter and economic expansions longer. But a variety of factors—including a shift from manufacturing to services, a larger government sector, and automatic stabilizers—has contributed to this improved macro performance. The contribution of discretionary macro policy is less clear. It's easy to observe what actually happened but almost impossible to determine what would have occurred in other circumstances.

Finally, one must contend with the difficulties inherent in adhering to any fixed rules. How is the Fed, for example, supposed to maintain a steady rate of growth in the money supply? As we observed in Chapter 13, people move their funds back and forth between different kinds of "money." Also, the demand for money is subject to unpredictable shifts. To maintain a steady rate of growth in M2 or any other measure of money would require superhuman foresight and responses. As former Fed Chairman Paul Volcker told Congress, it would be "exceedingly dangerous and in fact practically impossible to eliminate substantial elements of discretion in the conduct of Federal Reserve policy."

The same is true of fiscal policy. Government spending and taxes are directly influenced by changes in unemployment, inflation, interest rates, and growth. These automatic stabilizers make it virtually impossible to maintain any fixed rule for budget balancing. Moreover, if we eliminated the automatic stabilizers, we'd risk greater instability.

Modest Expectations. The clamor for fixed policy rules is more a rebuke of past policy than a viable policy alternative. We really have no choice but to pursue discretionary policies. Recognition of measurement, design, and implementation problems is important for an understanding of the way the economy functions. Even though it's impossible to reach all our goals, we can't abandon conscientious attempts to get as close as possible to goal fulfillment. If public policy can create a few more jobs, a better mix of output, a little more growth and price stability, or an improved distribution of income in the economy tomorrow, those initiatives are worthwhile.

SUMMARY

- The government possesses an array of macro policy tools, each of which can significantly alter economic outcomes. To end a recession, we can cut taxes, expand the money supply, or increase government spending. To curb inflation, we can reverse each of these policy tools. To overcome stagflation, we can combine fiscal and monetary levers with improved supply-side incentives. LO1, LO2
- Although the potential of economic theory seems impressive, the economic record doesn't look as good. Persistent unemployment, recurring economic slowdowns, and nagging inflation suggest that the realities of policymaking are more difficult than theory implies. LO3
- To some extent, the failures of economic policy are a reflection of scarce resources and competing goals. Even when consensus exists, however, serious obstacles to effective economic policy remain. These obstacles include
  - (*a*) Measurement problems. Our knowledge of economic performance is always dated and incomplete.
  - (*b*) Design problems. We don't know exactly how the economy will respond to specific policies.
  - (*c*) Implementation problems. It takes time for Congress and the president to agree on an appropriate plan of action. Moreover, political needs may take precedence over economic needs.

  For all these reasons, discretionary policy rarely lives up to its theoretical potential. LO3
- Monetarists and new classical economists favor rules rather than discretionary macro policies. They argue that discretionary policies are unlikely to work and risk being wrong. Critics respond that discretionary policies are needed to cope with ever-changing economic circumstances. LO3

Key Terms

business cycle
fiscal policy
automatic stabilizer
structural deficit
fiscal stimulus
fiscal restraint
monetary policy
natural rate of unemployment
supply-side policy
recessionary GDP gap
multiplier
velocity of money (V)
inflationary GDP gap
stagflation
fine-tuning
growth recession
rational expectations

Questions for Discussion

1. What policies would Keynesian, monetarists, and supply-siders advocate for (*a*) restraining inflation and (*b*) reducing unemployment? LO1
2. Why do policymakers respond so slowly to economic problems? LO3
3. If policymakers have instant data on the economy's performance, should they respond immediately? Why or why not? LO3
4. Suppose it's an election year and aggregate demand is growing so fast that it threatens to set off an inflationary movement. Why might Congress and the president hesitate to cut back on government spending or raise taxes, as economic theory suggests is appropriate? LO3
5. In his fiscal 2002 budget, President Bush proposed increases in defense spending while arguing for cutbacks in total spending. Should military spending be subject to macroeconomic constraints? What programs should be expanded or contracted to bring about needed changes in the budget? Is this feasible? LO2
6. Prior to assuming office, President-elect Clinton pledged to propose a tax credit for new investment during the first months of his administration. How might such an announcement affect the timing of investment decisions? LO3
7. Suppose the government proposes to cut taxes while maintaining the current level of government expenditures. To finance this deficit, it may either (*a*) sell bonds to the public or (*b*) print new money (via Federal Reserve cooperation). What are the likely effects of each of these alternatives on each of the following? Would Keynesians, monetarists, and supply-siders give the same answers? LO2
   (*a*) Interest rates
   (*b*) Consumer spending
   (*c*) Business investment
   (*d*) Aggregate demand
8. Suppose the economy is slumping into recession and needs a fiscal policy boost. Voters, however, are opposed to larger federal deficits. What should policymakers do? LO2
9. How were each of the following affected by the 2001 terrorist attack on the World Trade Center? LO2
   (*a*) Federal tax revenues
   (*b*) Federal spending
   (*c*) U.S. imports
   (*d*) Short-run GDP growth
   (*e*) Long-run GDP growth

problems The Student Problem Set at the back of this book contains numerical and graphing problems for this chapter.

web activities to accompany this chapter can be found on the Online Learning Center: **http://www.mhhe.com/economics/schiller11e**

PART

Product Markets: The Basics

The prices and products we see every day emerge from decisions made by millions of individual consumers and firms. A primary objective of microeconomic theory is to explain how those decisions are made. How high a price are consumers willing to pay for the products they want? Which products will consumers actually purchase—and in what quantities? We explore these dimensions of consumer *demand* in Chapter 20. We move to the *supply* side in Chapter 21, examining the costs that businesses incur in producing the products consumers demand.

Consumer Demand

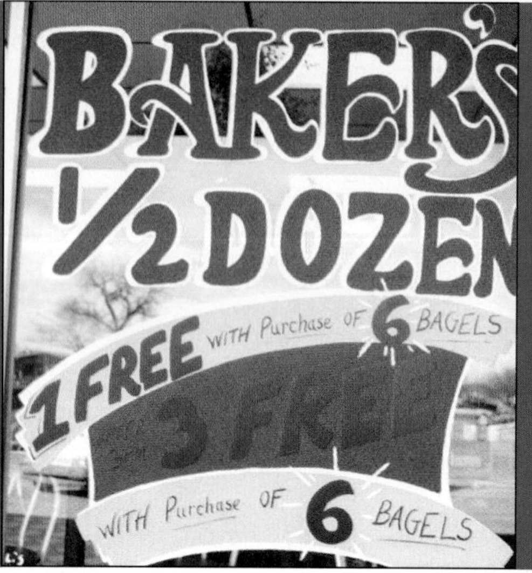

LEARNING OBJECTIVES

After reading this chapter, you should know:

LO1. The basis for the law of demand.

LO2. What price and income elasticities of demand measure.

LO3. How consumers maximize utility.

Steve Jobs knew he had a winner with the iPhone. Every time Apple added a feature to the iPod, sales picked up. Now Jobs had a product that combined cell phone services with wireless computing and audio and video download capabilities—all accessible on a touch screen. It was sure to be a hit. The only sticky question was *price*. What price should Apple put on its new iPhone? Its goal was to sell 10 million iPhones in the first 2 years of production. If it set the price low enough, it could surely do that. But Apple didn't want to give away the iPhone—it wanted to make a nice profit. Yet, if it set the price *too* high, sales would fall short of its sales target. What price should it charge? Apple's pricing committee had to know how many iPhones consumers would buy at different prices. In other words, they had to know the dimensions of *consumer demand*. After considerable deliberation, they set the initial price at $499 for the 4-GB iPhone, launched in January 2007.

Apple's iPhone pricing dilemma underscores the importance of *prices* in determining consumer behavior. Consumers "want," "need," and "just have to have" a vast array of goods and services. When decision time comes, however, product *prices* often dictate what consumers will actually buy. As we observed in Chapter 3, the quantity of a product *demanded* depends on its price.

This chapter takes a closer look at how product prices affect consumer decisions. We focus on three related questions:

- **How do we decide how much of any good to buy?**
- **How does a change in a product's price affect the quantity we purchase or the amount of money we spend on it?**
- **Why do we buy certain products but not others?**

The law of demand (first encountered in Chapter 3) gives us some clues for answering these questions. But we need to look beyond that law to fashion more complete answers. We need to know what forces give demand curves their downward-sloping shape. We also need to know more about how to *use* demand curves to predict consumer behavior.

DETERMINANTS OF DEMAND

In seeking explanations for consumer behavior, we have to recognize that the field of economics doesn't have all the answers. But it does offer a unique perspective that sets it apart from other fields of study.

The Sociopsychiatric Explanation

Consider first the explanations of consumer behavior offered by other fields of study. Psychiatrists and psychologists have had a virtual field day formulating such explanations. Freud was among the first to describe us humans as bundles of subconscious (and unconscious) fears, complexes, and anxieties. From a Freudian perspective, we strive for ever higher levels of consumption to satisfy basic drives for security, sex, and ego gratifications. Like the most primitive of people, we clothe and adorn ourselves in ways that assert our identity and worth. We eat and smoke too much because we need the oral gratifications and security associated with mother's breast. Oversized homes and cars give us a source of warmth and security remembered from the womb. On the other hand, we often buy and consume some things we expressly don't desire, just to assert our rebellious feelings against our parents (or parent substitutes). In Freud's view, it's the constant interplay of these id, ego, and superego drives that motivates us to buy, buy, buy.

Sociologists offer additional explanations for our consumption behavior. They observe our yearning to stand above the crowd, to receive recognition from the masses. For people with exceptional talents, such recognition may come easily. But for the ordinary person, recognition may depend on conspicuous consumption. A sleek car, a newer fashion, a more exotic vacation become expressions of identity that provoke recognition, even social acceptance. We strive for ever higher levels of consumption—not just to keep up with the Joneses but to surpass them.

Not *all* consumption is motivated by ego or status concerns. Some food is consumed for the sake of self-preservation, some clothing worn for warmth, and some housing built for shelter. The typical U.S. consumer has more than enough income to satisfy these basic needs, however. In today's economy, most consumers also have *discretionary* income that can be used to satisfy psychological or sociological longings. Single women are able to spend a lot of money on clothes and pets, and men spend freely on entertainment, food, and drink (see News). Teenagers show off their affluence in purchases of electronic goods, cars, and clothes (see Figure 20.1).

webnote

Each year the Bureau of Labor does another consumer expenditure survey. For the most recent data, visit www.bls.gov and first click on "Demographics" and then "Consumer Spending"

IN THE NEWS

Men vs. Women: How They Spend

Are men really different from women? If spending habits are any clue, males do differ from females. That's the conclusion one would draw from the latest Bureau of Labor Statistics (BLS) survey of consumer expenditure. Here's what BLS found out about the spending habits of young (under age 25) men and women who are living on their own:

Common Traits

- Young men have slightly more income to spend ($18,189 per year) than do young women ($15,421). Both sexes go deep into debt, however, by spending $4,000–$5,000 more than their incomes.
- Neither sex spends much on charity, reading, or health care.

Distinctive Traits

- Young men spend 15 percent more at fast-food outlets, restaurants, and carryouts.
- Men spend 70 percent more on alcoholic beverages and smoking.
- Men spend almost twice as much as women do on television and stereo equipment.
- Young women spend twice as much money on clothing, personal care items and their pets.

Source: U.S. Bureau of Labor Statistics, 2004–2005, Consumer Expenditure Survey. www.bls.gov

Analysis: Consumer patterns vary by gender, age, and other characteristics. Economists try to isolate the common influences on consumer behavior.

FIGURE 20.1
Affluent Teenagers

Teenagers spend over $200 billion a year. Much of this spending is for cars, stereos, and other durables. The percentage of U.S. teenagers owning certain items is shown here.

Source: Teenage Research Unlimited (2006 data).

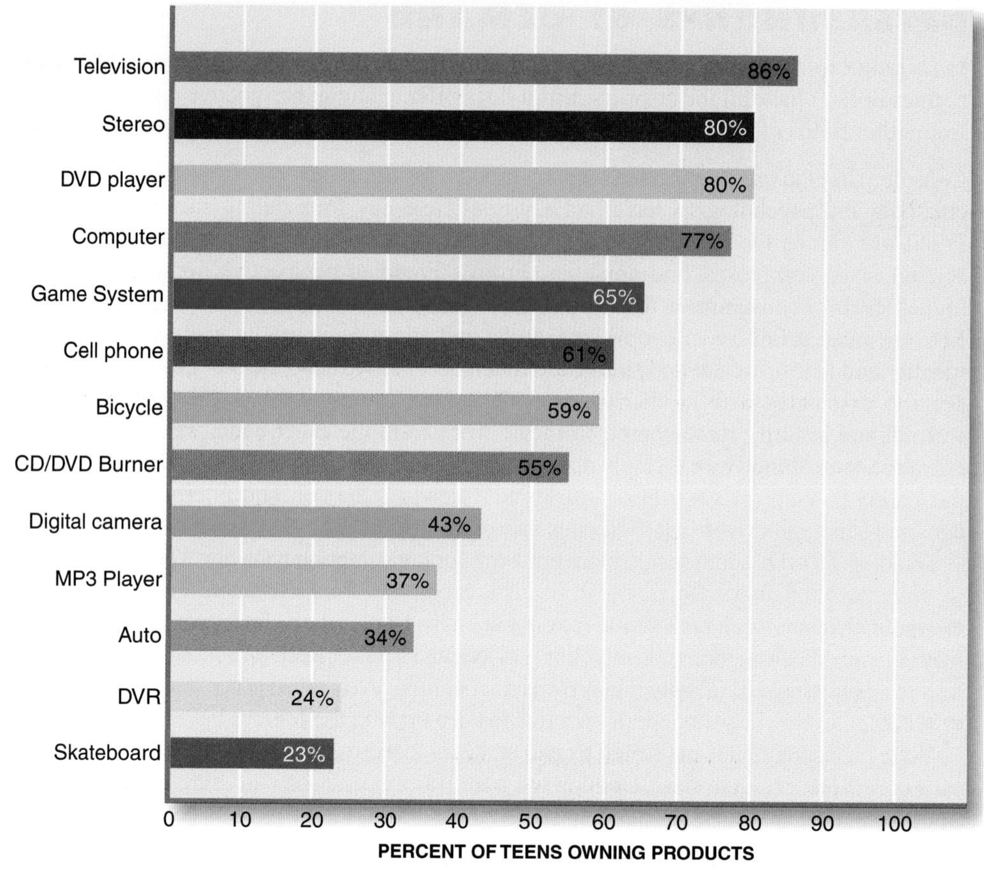

The Economic Explanation

Although psychiatrists and sociologists offer intriguing explanations for our consumption patterns, their explanations fall a bit short. Sociopsychiatric theories tell us why teenagers, men, and women *desire* certain goods and services. But they don't explain which goods will actually be *purchased.* Desire is only the first step in the consumption process. To acquire goods and services, one must be willing and able to *pay* for one's wants. Producers won't give you their goods just to satisfy your Freudian desires. They want money in exchange for their goods. Hence, ***prices and income are just as relevant to consumption decisions as are more basic desires and preferences.***

demand: The willingness and ability to buy specific quantities of a good at alternative prices in a given time period, *ceteris paribus.*

In explaining consumer behavior, economists focus on the *demand* for goods and services. As we observed in Chapter 3, **demand** entails the *willingness and ability to pay* for goods and services. To say that someone *demands* a particular good means that he or she will offer to *buy* it at some price(s). ***An individual's demand for a specific product is determined by these four factors:***

- ***Tastes*** (desire for this and other goods).
- ***Income*** (of the consumer).
- ***Expectations*** (for income, prices, tastes).
- ***Other goods*** (their availability and prices).

Note again that desire (tastes) is only one determinant of demand. Other determinants of demand (income, expectations, and other goods) also influence whether a person will be willing and able to buy a certain good at a specific price.

The remainder of this chapter examines these determinants of demand. The objective is not only to explain consumer behavior but also to predict how consumption patterns change in response to *changes* in the price of a good or to *changes* in underlying tastes, income, prices or availability of other goods, or expectations.

THE DEMAND CURVE

Utility Theory

The starting point for an economic analysis of demand is quite simple. Economists accept consumer tastes as the outcome of sociopsychiatric and cultural influences. They don't look beneath the surface to see how those tastes originated. Economists want to know only how those tastes (desires) affect consumption decisions.

The first observation economists make is that the more pleasure a product gives us, the higher the price we'd be willing to pay for it. If the oral sensation of buttered popcorn at the movies really turns you on, you're likely to be willing to pay dearly for it. If, on the other hand, you have no great taste or desire for popcorn, the theater might have to give it away before you'd eat it.

Total vs. Marginal Utility. Economists use the term **utility** to refer to the expected pleasure, or satisfaction, obtained from goods and services. We also make an important distinction between total utility and marginal utility. **Total utility** refers to the amount of satisfaction obtained from your *entire* consumption of a product. By contrast, **marginal utility** refers to the amount of satisfaction you get from consuming the *last* (i.e., "marginal") unit of a product. More generally, note that

utility: The pleasure or satisfaction obtained from a good or service.

total utility: The amount of satisfaction obtained from entire consumption of a product.

$$\text{Marginal utility} = \frac{\text{change in total utility}}{\text{change in quantity}}$$

marginal utility: The change in total utility obtained by consuming one additional (marginal) unit of a good or service.

Diminishing Marginal Utility. The concepts of total and marginal utility explain not only why we buy popcorn at the movies but also why we stop eating it at some point. Even people who love popcorn (i.e., derive great *total* utility from it) don't eat endless quantities of it. Why not? Presumably because the thrill diminishes with each mouthful. The first box of popcorn may bring sensual gratification, but the second or third box is likely to bring a stomachache. We express this change in perceptions by noting that the *marginal* utility of the first box of popcorn is higher than the additional or *marginal* utility derived from the second box.

The behavior of popcorn connoisseurs isn't abnormal. As a rule, the amount of additional utility we obtain from a product declines as we continue to consume it. The third slice of pizza isn't as desirable as the first, the sixth beer not as satisfying as the fifth, and so forth. Indeed, this phenomenon of diminishing marginal utility is so nearly universal that economists have fashioned a law around it. This **law of diminishing marginal utility** states that each successive unit of a good consumed yields less *additional* utility.

law of diminishing marginal utility: The marginal utility of a good declines as more of it is consumed in a given time period.

The law of diminishing marginal utility does *not* say that we won't like the second box of popcorn, the third pizza slice, or the sixth beer; it just says we won't like them as much as the ones we've already consumed. Time is also important here: If the first box of popcorn was eaten last year, the second box may now taste just as good. The law of diminishing marginal utility applies to short time periods.

Figure 20.2 on the next page illustrates how utility changes with the level of consumption. Notice that total utility continues to rise as we consume the first five boxes (ugh!) of popcorn. But total utility increases by smaller and smaller increments. Each successive step of the total utility curve in Figure 20.2 is a little smaller.

The height of each step of the total utility curve in Figure 20.2 represents *marginal* utility—the increments to total utility. *Marginal* utility is clearly diminishing. Nevertheless, because marginal utility is still *positive,* total utility is increasing. ***As long as marginal utility is positive, total utility must be increasing*** (note that the total utility curve is still rising for the fifth box of popcorn).

The situation changes with the sixth box of popcorn. According to Figure 20.2, the good sensations associated with popcorn consumption are completely forgotten by the time the sixth box arrives. Nausea and stomach cramps take over. Indeed, the sixth box is absolutely *distasteful,* as reflected in the downturn of *total* utility and the *negative* value for marginal utility. We were happier—in possession of more total utility—with only five boxes of popcorn. The sixth box—yielding *negative* marginal utility—reduces total satisfaction. This is the kind of sensation you'd probably experience if you ate six hamburgers (see cartoon).

webnote

Do Americans have a taste for Jumbo Jacks? Go to facts at www.jackinthebox.com

Not every good ultimately reaches negative marginal utility. Yet the more general principle of diminishing marginal utility is experienced daily. That is, ***eventually additional quantities of a good yield increasingly smaller increments of satisfaction.***

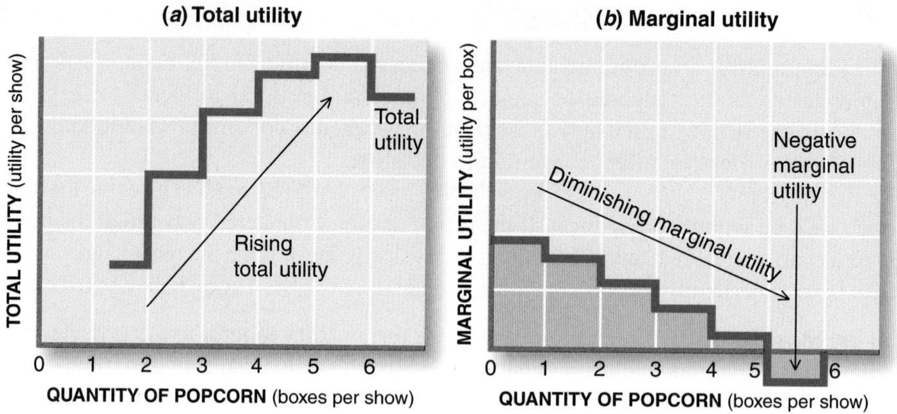

FIGURE 20.2
Total vs. Marginal Utility

The *total* utility derived from consuming a product comes from the *marginal* utilities of each successive unit. The total utility curve shows how each of the first five boxes of popcorn contributes to total utility. Note that each successive step is smaller. This reflects the law of diminishing marginal utility.

The sixth box of popcorn causes the total-utility steps to descend; the sixth box actually *reduces* total utility. This means that the sixth box has *negative* marginal utility.

The marginal utility curve (*b*) shows the change in total utility with each additional unit. It's derived from the total utility curve. Marginal utility here is positive but diminishing for the first five boxes.

Price and Quantity

Marginal utility is essentially a measure of how much we desire particular goods, our *taste.* But which ones will we buy? Clearly, we don't always buy the products we most desire. *Price* is often a problem. All too often we have to settle for goods that yield less marginal utility simply because they are available at a lower price. This explains why most people don't drive Porsches. Our desire ("taste") for a Porsche may be great, but its price is even greater. The challenge for most of us is to somehow reconcile our tastes with our bank balances.

Analysis: No matter how much we like a product, marginal utility is likely to diminish as we consume more of it. If marginal utility becomes *negative* (as here), total satisfaction will decrease.

In deciding whether to buy something, our immediate focus is typically on a single variable, namely *price.* Assume for the moment that a person's tastes, incomes, and expectations are set in stone, and that the prices of other goods are set as well. This is the ***ceteris paribus*** assumption we first encountered in Chapter 1. It doesn't mean that other influences on consumer behavior are unimportant. Rather, *ceteris paribus* simply allows us to focus on one variable at a time. In this case, we are focusing on price. What we want to know is how high a price a consumer is willing to pay for another unit of a product. This is the question Steve Jobs had to confront when Apple launched the iPhone.

ceteris paribus: The assumption of nothing else changing.

The concepts of marginal utility and *ceteris paribus* enable us to answer this question. The more marginal utility a product delivers, the more a consumer will be willing to pay for it. We also noted that marginal utility *diminishes* as increasing quantities of a product are consumed, suggesting that consumers are willing to pay progressively *less* for additional quantities of a product. The moviegoer willing to pay 50 cents for that first mouthwatering ounce of buttered popcorn may not be willing to pay so much for a second or third ounce. The same is true for a second pizza, the sixth beer, and so forth. ***With given income, tastes, expectations, and prices of other goods and services, people are willing to buy additional quantities of a good only if its price falls.*** In other words, as the marginal utility of a good diminishes, so does our willingness to pay. This **law of demand** is illustrated in Figure 20.3 with the downward-sloping **demand curve.**

The law of demand and the law of diminishing marginal utility tell us nothing about why we crave popcorn or why our cravings subside. Those explanations are reserved for psychiatrists, sociologists, and physiologists. The laws of economics simply describe our market behavior.

law of demand: The quantity of a good demanded in a given time period increases as its price falls, *ceteris paribus.*

demand curve: A curve describing the quantities of a good a consumer is willing and able to buy at alternative prices in a given period, *ceteris paribus.*

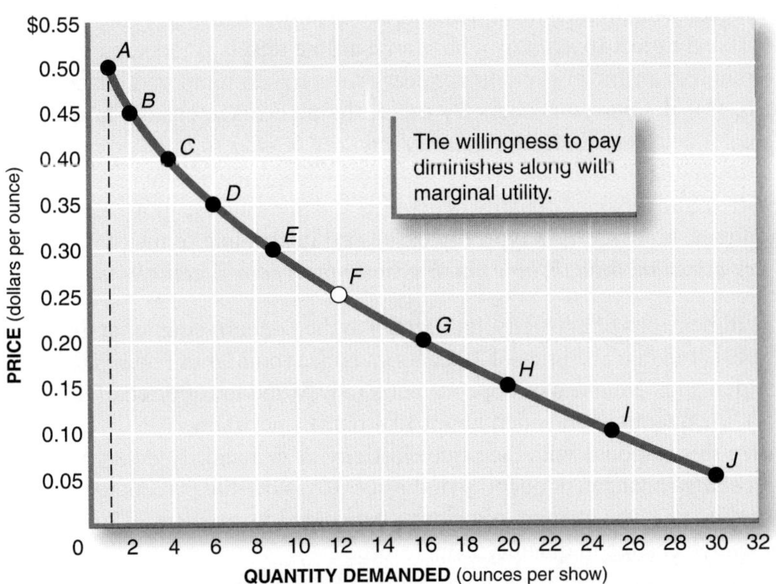

	Price (per ounce)	Quantity Demanded (ounces per show)
A	$0.50	1
B	0.45	2
C	0.40	4
D	0.35	6
E	0.30	9
F	0.25	12
G	0.20	16
H	0.15	20
I	0.10	25
J	0.05	30

FIGURE 20.3
An Individual's Demand Schedule and Curve

Consumers are generally willing to buy larger quantities of a good at lower prices. This demand schedule illustrates the specific quantities demanded at alternative prices. If popcorn sold for 25 cents per ounce, this consumer would buy 12 ounces per show (row *F*). At higher prices, less popcorn would be purchased.

A downward-sloping demand curve expresses the law of demand: The quantity of a good demanded increases as its price falls. Notice that points *A* through *J* on the curve correspond to the rows of the demand schedule.

PRICE ELASTICITY

The theory of demand helps explain consumer behavior. But it's not terribly helpful to the theater owner who's actually worried about popcorn sales. The general observation that popcorn sales decline when prices increase would be of little use. What the theater owner wants to know is *by how much* the quantity demanded would fall if the price were raised. Steve Jobs wanted to know the same thing about the demand for iPhones.

The central question in all these decisions is the response of quantity demanded to a change in price. ***The response of consumers to a change in price is measured by the price elasticity of demand.*** Specifically, the **price elasticity of demand** refers to the percentage change in quantity demanded divided by the percentage change in price—that is,

price elasticity of demand: The percentage change in quantity demanded divided by the percentage change in price.

$$\text{Price elasticity } (E) = \frac{\text{\% change in quantity demanded}}{\text{\% change in price}}$$

What would the value of price elasticity be if air travel didn't change at all when airfares were cut by 5 percent? In that case the price elasticity of demand would be

$$E = \frac{\text{\% change in quantity demanded}}{\text{\% change in price}}$$

$$= \frac{0}{5} = 0$$

But is this realistic? According to the law of demand, the quantity demanded goes up when price goes down. So we'd expect *somebody* to buy more airline tickets if fares fell by 5 percent. In a large market like air travel, we don't expect *everybody* to jump on a plane when airfares are reduced. But if *some* consumers fly more, the percentage change in quantity demanded will be larger than zero. Indeed, ***the law of demand implies that the price elasticity of demand will always be greater than zero.*** Technically, the price elasticity of demand (E) would be a negative number since quantity demanded and price always move in opposite directions. For simplicity, however, E is typically expressed in absolute terms (without the minus sign). ***The key question, then, is how much greater than zero* E *actually is.***

Computing Price Elasticity

To get a feel for the dimensions of elasticity, let's return to the popcorn counter at the movies. We've already observed that at a price of 45 cents an ounce (point B in Figure 20.3), the average moviegoer demands 2 ounces of popcorn per show. At the lower price of 40 cents per ounce (point C), the quantity demanded jumps to 4 ounces per show.

We can summarize this response with the price elasticity of demand. To do so, we have to calculate the *percentage* changes in quantity and price. Consider the percentage change in quantity first. In this case, the change in quantity demanded is 4 ounces − 2 ounces = 2 ounces. The *percentage* change in quantity is therefore

$$\text{\% change in quantity} = \frac{2}{q}$$

The problem is to transform the denominator q into a number. Should we use the quantity of popcorn purchased *before* the price reduction, that is, $q_1 = 2$? Or should we use the quantity purchased *after* the price reduction, that is, $q_2 = 4$? The choice of denominator will have a big impact on the computed percentage change. To ensure consistency, economists prefer to use the *average* quantity in the denominator.[1] The average quantity is simply

$$\text{Average quantity} = \frac{q_1 + q_2}{2} = \frac{2 + 4}{2} = 3 \text{ ounces}$$

[1]This procedure is referred to as the *arc* (midpoint) elasticity of demand. If a single quantity (price) is used in the denominator, we refer to the *point* elasticity of demand.

We can now complete the calculation of the percentage change in quantity demanded. It is

$$\frac{\%\text{ change in}}{\text{quantity demanded}} = \frac{\text{change in quantity}}{\text{average quantity}} = \frac{q_2 - q_1}{\frac{q_1 + q_2}{2}} = \frac{2}{3} = 0.667$$

Popcorn sales increased by an average of 67 percent when the price of popcorn was reduced from 45 cents to 40 cents per ounce.

The computation of the percentage change in price is similar. We first note that the price of popcorn fell by 5 cents (45¢ − 40¢) when we move from point *B* to point *C* on the demand curve (Figure 20.3). We then compute the *average* price of popcorn in this range of the demand curve as

$$\text{Average price of popcorn} = \frac{p_1 + p_2}{2} = \frac{45 + 40}{2} = 42.5 \text{ cents}$$

This average is our denominator in calculating the percentage price change. Using these numbers, we see that the absolute value of the percentage change is

$$\%\text{ change in price} = \frac{\text{change in price}}{\text{average price}} = \frac{p_2 - p_1}{\frac{p_1 + p_2}{2}} = \frac{5}{42.5} = 0.118$$

The price of popcorn fell by 11.8 percent.

Now we have all the information required to compute the price elasticity of demand. In this case,

$$E = \frac{\%\text{ change in quantity demanded}}{\%\text{ change in price}} = \frac{0.667}{0.118} = 5.65$$

What we get from all these calculations is a very useful number. It says that the consumer response to a price reduction will be extremely large. Specifically, the quantity of popcorn consumed will increase 5.65 times as fast as price falls. A 1 percent reduction in price brings about a 5.65 percent increase in purchases. The theater manager can therefore boost popcorn sales greatly by lowering price a little.

Elastic vs. Inelastic Demand. We characterize the demand for various goods in one of three ways: *elastic, inelastic,* or *unitary elastic.* If **E *is larger than 1, demand is elastic.*** Consumer response is large relative to the change in price.

If *E* is less than 1, we say demand is inelastic. ***If demand is inelastic (E < 1), consumers aren't very responsive to price changes.***

If *E* is equal to 1, demand is *unitary* elastic. In this case, the percentage change in quantity demanded is exactly equal to the percentage change in price.

Consider the case of smoking. Many smokers claim they'd "pay anything" for a cigarette after they've run out. But would they? Would they continue to smoke just as many cigarettes if prices doubled or tripled? If so, the demand curve would be vertical (as in Figure 20.4*b* on the next page) rather than downward-sloping. Research suggests this is not the case: Higher cigarette prices *do* curb smoking. There is at least *some* elasticity in the demand for cigarettes. But the elasticity of demand is low; Table 20.1 indicates that the price elasticity of cigarette demand is only 0.4.

Although the average adult smoker is not very responsive to changes in cigarette prices, teen smokers apparently are. As the News on page 399 indicates, teen smoking drops by almost 7 percent when cigarette prices increase by 10 percent. Thus, the price elasticity of

webnote

The American Cancer Society stages a Great American Smokeout every November. The society's goal is to help people, particularly teenagers, stop smoking. For statistics on smoking trends, visit www.cancer.org/docroot/PED/PED_10_4_Great_American_Smokeout.asp

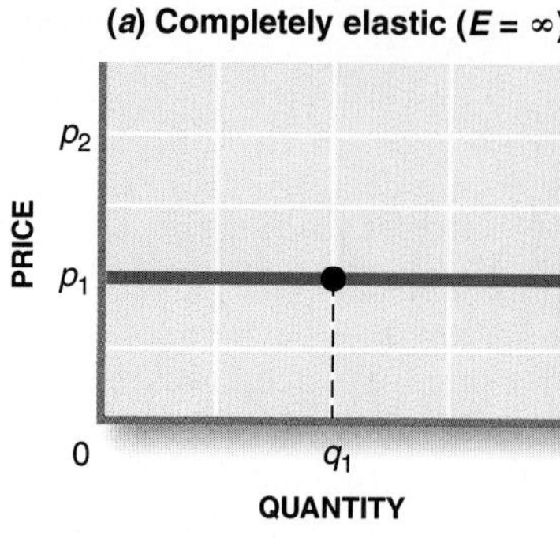

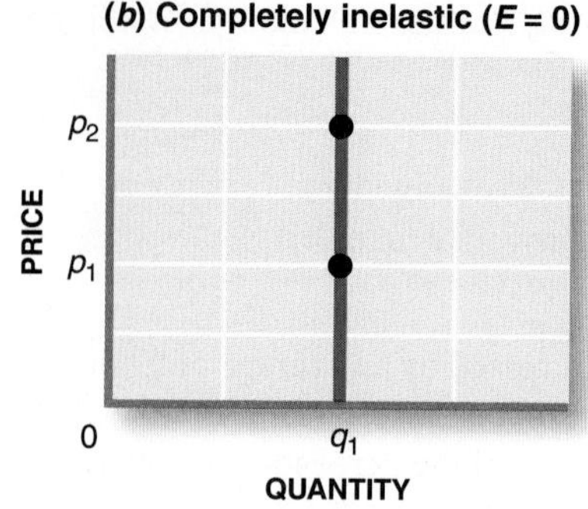

FIGURE 20.4
Extremes of Elasticity

If demand were perfectly elastic ($E = \infty$), the demand curve would be *horizontal.* In that case, any increase in price (e.g., p_1 to p_2) would cause quantity demanded to fall to zero.

A *vertical* demand curve implies that an increase in price won't affect the quantity demanded. In this situation of completely *in*elastic ($E = 0$) demand, consumers are willing to pay *any* price to get the quantity q_1.

In reality, elasticities of demand for goods and services lie between these two extremes (obeying the law of demand).

---

teen demand for smoking is

$$E = \frac{\text{percent drop in quantity demanded}}{\text{percent increase in price}} = \frac{7\%}{10\%} = 0.7$$

Hence, higher cigarette prices can be an effective policy tool for curbing teen smoking. The drop in teen smoking after prices jumped in 1998 (see News) confirms this expectation.

TABLE 20.1
Elasticity Estimates

Price elasticities vary greatly. When the price of gasoline increases, consumers reduce their consumption only slightly. When the price of fish increases, however, consumers cut back their consumption substantially. These differences reflect the availability of immediate substitutes, the prices of the goods, and the amount of time available for changing behavior.

Product	Price Elasticity
Relatively elastic ($E > 1$)	
Airline travel, long run	2.4
Restaurant meals	2.3
Fresh fish	2.2
New cars, short run	1.2–1.5
Unitary elastic ($E = 1$)	
Private education	1.1
Radios and televisions	1.2
Shoes	0.9
Movies	0.9
Relatively inelastic ($E < 1$)	
Cigarettes	0.4
Coffee	0.3
Gasoline, short run	0.2
Electricity (in homes)	0.1
Long-distance phone calls	0.1

Source: Compiled from Hendrick S. Houthakker and Lester D. Taylor, *Consumer Demand in the United States,* 1929–1970 (Cambridge: Harvard University Press, 1966); F. W. Bell, "The Pope and Price of Fish," *American Economic Review,* December 1968; Herbert Scarf and John Shoven, *Applied General Equilibrium Analysis* (New York: Cambridge University Press, 1984); and Michael Ward, "Product Substitutability and Competition in Long-Distance Telecommunications," *Economic Inquiry,* October 1999.

IN THE NEWS

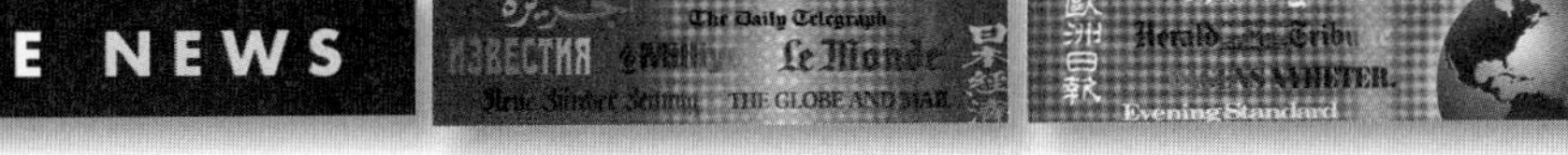
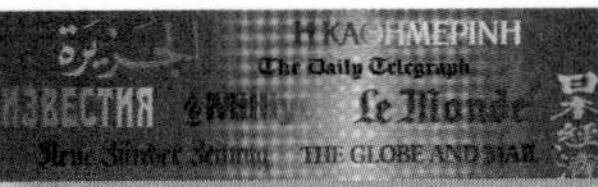

Dramatic Rise in Teenage Smoking

Smoking among youths in the United States rose precipitously starting in 1992 after declining for the previous 15 years. By 1997, the proportion of teenage smokers had risen by one-third from its 1991 trough.

A prominent explanation for the rise in youth smoking over the 1990s was a sharp decline in cigarette prices in the early 1990s, caused by a price war between the tobacco companies. Gruber and Zinman find that young people are very sensitive to the price of cigarettes in their smoking decisions. The authors estimate that for every 10 percent decline in the price, youth smoking rises by almost 7 percent, a much stronger price sensitivity than is typically found for adult smokers. As a result, the price decline of the early 1990s can explain about a quarter of the smoking rise from 1992 through 1997. Similarly, the significant decline in youth smoking observed in 1998 is at least partially explainable by the first steep rise in cigarette prices since the early 1990s. The authors also find that black youths and those with less-educated parents are much more responsive to changes in cigarette prices than are white teens and those with more-educated parents.

However, price does not appear to be an important determinant of smoking by younger teens. This may be because they are more experimental smokers.

Source: National Bureau of Economic Research, *NBER Digest,* October 2000. www.nber.org/digest

Analysis: The effectiveness of higher cigarette prices in curbing teen smoking depends on the price elasticity of demand.

According to Table 20.1, the demand for airline travel is even more price-elastic. Whenever a fare cut is announced, the airlines get swamped with telephone inquiries. If fares are discounted by 25 percent, the number of passengers may increase by as much as 60 percent. As Table 20.1 shows, the elasticity of airline demand is 2.4, meaning that the percentage change in quantity demanded (60 percent) will be 2.4 times larger than the price cut (25 percent).

Determinants of Elasticity

Why are consumers price-sensitive ($E > 1$) with some goods and not ($E < 1$) with others? To answer that, we must go back to the demand curve itself. The elasticity of demand is computed between points on a given demand curve. Hence, ***the price elasticity of demand is influenced by all the determinants of demand.*** Four factors are particularly worth noting.

Necessities vs. Luxuries. Some goods are so critical to our everyday life that we regard them as "necessities". A hair brush, toothpaste, and perhaps textbooks might fall into this category. Our "taste" for such goods is so strong that we can't imagine getting along without them. As a result, we don't change our consumption of "necessities" very much when the price increases; ***demand for necessities is relatively inelastic.***

A "luxury" good, by contrast, is something we'd *like* to have but aren't likely to buy unless our income jumps or the price declines sharply, such as vacation travel, new cars, and iPhones. We want them but can get by without them. That is, ***demand for luxury goods is relatively elastic.***

Availability of Substitutes. Our notion of which goods are necessities is also influenced by the availability of substitute goods. The high elasticity of demand for fish (Table 20.1) reflects the fact that consumers can always eat chicken, beef, or pork if fish prices rise. On the other hand, most bleary-eyed coffee drinkers can't imagine any other product that could substitute for a cup of coffee. As a consequence, when coffee prices rise, consumers don't reduce their purchases very much at all. Likewise, the low elasticity of demand for gasoline reflects the fact that most cars can't run on alternative fuels. In general, ***the greater the availability of substitutes, the higher the price elasticity of demand.*** This is a principle that New York City learned when it raised the price of cigarettes in 2002. As the News explains, smugglers quickly supplied a substitute good and legal sales of cigarettes declined drastically in New York City.

Relative Price (to income). Another important determinant of elasticity is the price of the good in relation to a consumer's income. Airline travel and new cars are quite expensive, so even a small percentage change in their prices can have a big impact on a consumer's

IN THE NEWS

New York City's Costly Smokes

New York City has the nation's costliest smokes. NYC Mayor Michael Bloomberg raised the city's excise tax from 8 cents a pack to $1.50 effective July 2002. Together with state and federal taxes, that raised the retail price of smokes in NYC to nearly $8 a pack.

Mayor Bloomberg expected the city to reap a tax bonanza from the 350 million packs of cigarettes sold annually in NYC. What he got instead was a lesson in elasticity. NYC smokers can buy cigarettes for a lot less money outside the city limits. Or they can stay home and buy cigarettes on the Internet from (untaxed) Indian reservations, delivered by UPS. They can also buy cigarettes smuggled in from low-tax states like Kentucky, Virginia, and North Carolina. What matters isn't the price elasticity of demand for cigarettes in general (around 0.4), but the elasticity of demand for *NYC-taxed* cigarettes. That turned out to be quite high. Unit sales of NYC cigarettes plummeted by 44 percent after the "Bloomberg tax" was imposed.

Source: *"NewsFlash," Economy Today,* October 2002.

Analysis: If demand is price-elastic, a price increase will lead to a disproportionate drop in unit sales. In this case, the ready availability of substitutes (cigarettes from other jurisdictions) made demand highly price-elastic.

budget (and consumption decisions). The demand for such big-ticket items tends to be elastic. By contrast, coffee is so cheap that even a large *percentage* change in price doesn't affect consumer behavior very much.

Because the relative price of a good affects price elasticity, the value of E_1 *changes* along a given demand curve. At current prices the elasticity of demand for coffee is low. How would consumers behave, however, if coffee cost $5 a cup? Some people would still consume coffee. At such higher prices, however, the quantity demanded would be much more sensitive to price changes. Accordingly, when we observe, as in Table 20.1, that the demand for coffee is price-inelastic, that observation applies only to the current range of prices. Were coffee prices dramatically higher, the price elasticity of demand would be higher as well. As a rule, ***the price elasticity of demand declines as price moves down the demand curve.***

Time. Finally, time affects the price elasticity of demand. Car owners can't switch to electric autos every time the price of gasoline goes up. In the short run, the elasticity of demand

IN THE NEWS

Professor Becker Corrects President's Math

President Clinton has seized upon the cigarette excise tax as an expedient and politically correct means of increasing federal revenue. In 1994, the federal government took in $12 billion from the present 24-cents-per-pack tax. If the tax were quadrupled to $1 a pack, Clinton figures tax revenues would increase by more than $50 billion over three years. Those added revenues would help finance the health-care reforms the President so dearly wants.

Professor Gary Becker, a Nobel Prize–winning economist at the University of Chicago, says Clinton's math is wrong. The White House assumed that cigarette sales would drop by 4 percent for every 10 percent increase in price. Professor Becker says that reflects only the first-year response to higher prices, not the full adjustment of smokers' behavior. Over a three-year period, cigarette consumption is likely to decline by 8 percent for every 10 percent increase in price—twice as much as Clinton assumed. As a result, the $1-a-pack tax will bring in much less revenue than President Clinton projected.

Source: *BusinessWeek,* August 15, 1994. www.businessweek.com

Analysis: It takes time for people to adjust their behavior to changed prices. Hence, the short-run price elasticity of demand is lower than the long-run elasticity.

for gasoline is quite low. With more time to adjust, however, consumers can buy more fuel-efficient cars, relocate their homes or jobs, and even switch fuels. As a consequence, ***the long-run price elasticity of demand is higher than the short-run elasticity.*** Nobel Prize–winning economist Gary Becker used the distinction between long-run and short-run elasticities to explain why a proposed increase in cigarette excise taxes wouldn't generate nearly as much revenue as President Clinton expected (see previous News).

PRICE ELASTICITY AND TOTAL REVENUE

The concept of price elasticity refutes the popular misconception that producers charge the "highest price possible." Were that true, Steve Jobs would have priced the initial iPhone at $8,996. Except in the very rare case of completely inelastic demand, this notion makes no sense. Indeed, higher prices not only reduce unit sales, but may actually reduce total sales revenue as well.

The **total revenue** of a seller is the amount of money received from product sales. It is determined by the quantity of the product sold and the price at which it is sold:

total revenue: The price of a product multiplied by the quantity sold in a given time period.

$$\text{Total revenue} = \text{price} \times \text{quantity sold}$$

In the movie theater example, if the price of popcorn is 40 cents per ounce and only 4 ounces are sold, total revenue equals $1.60 per show. This revenue is illustrated by the shaded rectangle in Figure 20.5. (The area of a rectangle is equal to its height [p] times its width [q].)

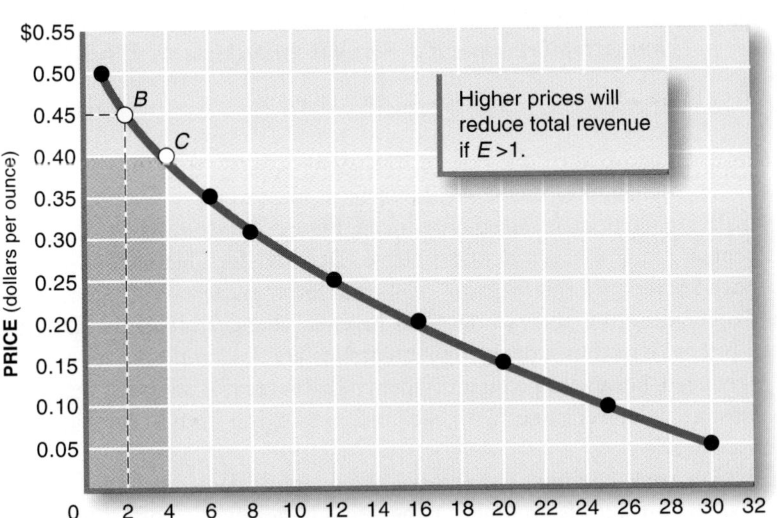

	Price	×	Quantity Demanded	=	Total Revenue
A	50¢		1		$0.50
B	45		2		0.90
C	40		4		1.60
D	35		6		2.10
E	30		8		2.40
F	25		12		3.00
G	20		16		3.20
H	15		20		3.00
I	10		25		2.50
J	5		30		1.50

FIGURE 20.5
Elasticity and Total Revenue

Total revenue is equal to the price of the product times the quantity sold. It is illustrated by the area of the rectangle formed by $p \times q$.

The shaded rectangle illustrates total revenue ($1.60) at a price of 40 cents and a quantity demanded of 4 ounces. When price is increased to 45 cents (point *B*), the rectangle and total revenue shrink (see dashed lines) because demand is relatively elastic in that price range. Price hikes increase total revenue only if demand is inelastic.

TABLE 20.2
Price Elasticity of Demand and Total Revenue

The impact of higher prices on total revenue depends on the price elasticity of demand. Higher prices result in higher total revenue only if demand is inelastic. If demand is elastic, *lower* prices result in *higher* revenues.

If Demand is	Effect on Total Revenue of	
	Price Increase	Price Reduction
Elastic ($E > 1$)	Decrease	Increase
Inelastic ($E < 1$)	Increase	Decrease
Unitary elastic ($E = 1$)	No change	No change

Now consider what happens to total revenue when the price of popcorn is increased. From the law of demand, we know that an increase in price will lead to a decrease in quantity demanded. But what about total revenue? The change in total revenue depends on *how much* quantity demanded falls when price goes up.

Suppose we raise popcorn prices again, from 40 cents back to 45 cents. What happens to total revenue? At 40 cents per box, 4 ounces are sold (see Figure 20.5) and total revenue equals $1.60. If we increase the price to 45 cents, only 2 ounces are sold and total revenue drops to 90 cents. In this case, an *increase* in price leads to a *decrease* in total revenue. This new and smaller total revenue is illustrated by the dashed rectangle in Figure 20.5.

Price increases don't always lower total revenue. If consumer demand was relatively *inelastic* ($E < 1$), a price increase would lead to *higher* total revenue. Thus, we conclude that

- ***A price hike increases total revenue only if demand is inelastic* (E < 1).**
- ***A price hike reduces total revenue if demand is elastic* (E > 1).**
- ***A price hike does not change total revenue if demand is unitary-elastic* E = 1.**

Table 20.2 summarizes these and other responses to price changes.

Changing Value of *E*. Once we know the price elasticity of demand, we can predict how consumers will respond to changing prices. We can also predict what will happen to the total revenue of the seller when price is raised or reduced. Figure 20.6 shows how elasticity and total revenue change along a given demand curve. Demand for cigarettes is *elastic* ($E > 1$) at prices above $6 per pack but *inelastic* ($E < 1$) at lower prices.

The bottom half of Figure 20.6 shows how total revenue changes along the demand curve. At very high prices (e.g., $14 a pack), few cigarettes are sold and total revenue is low. As the price is reduced, however, the quantity demanded increases so much that total revenue *increases,* despite the lower price. With each price reduction from $14 down to $6 total revenue increases.

Price cuts below $6 a pack continue to increase the quantity demanded (the law of demand). The increase in unit sales is no longer large enough, however, to offset the price reductions. Total revenue starts falling after price drops below $6 per pack. The lesson to remember here is that ***the impact of a price change on total revenue depends on the (changing) price elasticity of demand.***

OTHER ELASTICITIES

The price elasticity of demand tells us how consumers will respond to a change in the price of a good under the assumption of *ceteris paribus.* But other factors do change, and consumption behavior may respond to those changes as well.

Shifts vs. Movements

We recognized this problem in Chapter 3 when we first distinguished *movements* along a demand curve from *shifts* of the demand curve. A movement along an unchanged demand curve represents consumer response to a change in the *price* of that specific good. The magnitude of that movement is expressed in the price elasticity of demand.

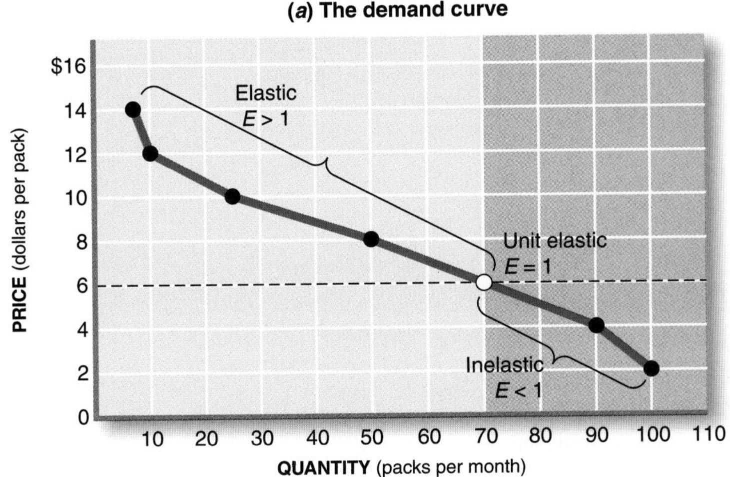

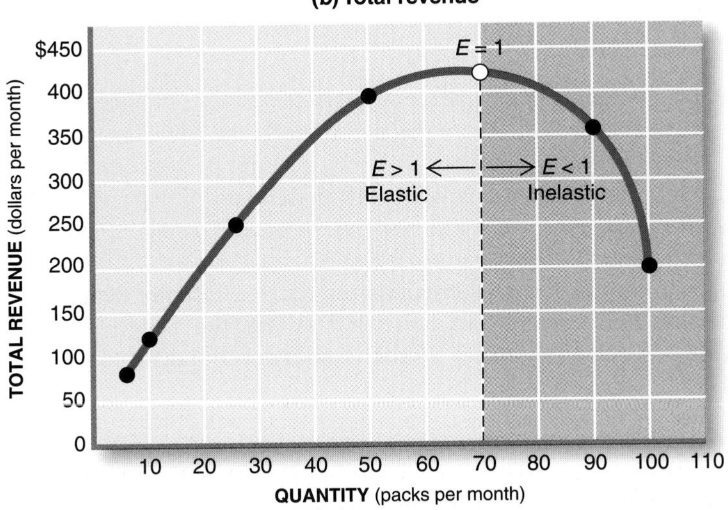

Price of Cigarettes	×	Quantity Demanded	=	Total Revenue	
$2		100		$200	Low elasticity; $E < 1$ (total revenue rises when price increases)
4		90		360	
6		70		420	
8		50		400	High elasticity; $E > 1$ (total revenue falls when price increases)
10		25		250	
12		10		120	
14		6		84	

FIGURE 20.6
Price Elasticity Changes along a Demand Curve

The concept of price elasticity can be used to determine whether people will spend more money on cigarettes when price rises. The answer to this question is yes and no, depending on how high the price goes.

Notice in the table and the graphs that total revenue rises when the price of cigarettes increases from \$2 to \$4 a pack and again to \$6. At low prices, the demand for cigarettes appears relatively inelastic: Price and total revenue move in the same direction.

As the price of cigarettes continues to increase, however, total revenue starts to fall. As the price is increased from \$6 to \$8 a pack, total revenue drops. At higher prices, the demand for cigarettes is relatively elastic: Price and total revenue move in *opposite* directions. Hence, the price elasticity of demand depends on where one is on the demand curve.

When the underlying determinants of demand change, the entire demand curve shifts. These shifts also alter consumer behavior. The *price* elasticity of demand is of no use in gauging these behavioral responses, since it refers to price changes (movements along a constant demand curve) for that good only.

Income Elasticity

A change in any determinant of demand will shift the demand curve. Suppose consumer incomes were to increase. How would popcorn consumption be affected? Figure 20.7

FIGURE 20.7
Income Elasticity

If income changes, the demand curve *shifts*. In this case, an increase in income enables consumers to buy more popcorn at every price. At a price of 25 cents, the quantity demanded increases from 12 ounces (point *F*) to 16 ounces (point *N*). The *income elasticity of demand* measures this response of demand to a change in income.

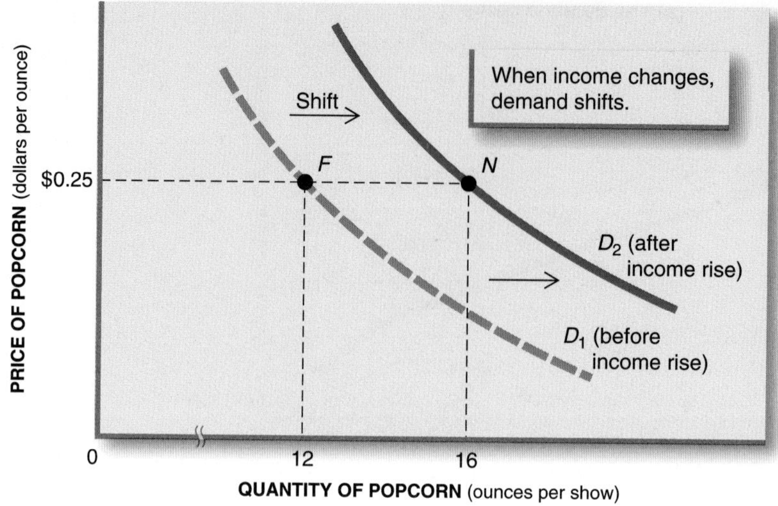

provides an answer. Before the change in income, consumers demanded 12 ounces of popcorn at a price of 25 cents per ounce. With more income to spend, the new demand curve (D_2) suggests that consumers will now purchase a greater quantity of popcorn at every price. The increase in income has caused a rightward **shift in demand.** If popcorn continues to sell for 25 cents per ounce, consumers will now buy 16 ounces per show (point *N*) rather than only 12 ounces (point *F*).

shift in demand: A change in the quantity demanded at any (every) given price.

It appears that changes in income have a substantial impact on consumer demand for popcorn. The graph in Figure 20.7 doesn't tell us, however, how large the change in income was. Will a *small* increase in income cause such a shift, or does popcorn demand increase only when moviegoers have a *lot* more money to spend?

Figure 20.7 doesn't answer these questions. But a little math will. Specifically, the **income elasticity of demand** relates the *percentage* change in quantity demanded to the *percentage* change in income—that is,

income elasticity of demand: Percentage change in quantity demanded divided by percentage change in income.

$$\text{Income elasticity of demand} = \frac{\text{\% change in quantity demanded (at given price)}}{\text{\% change in income}}$$

The similarity to the price elasticity of demand is apparent. In this case, however, the denominator is *income* (a determinant of demand), not *price.*

Computing Income Elasticity. As was the case with price elasticity, we compute income elasticity with *average* values for the changes in quantity and income. Suppose that the shift in popcorn demand illustrated in Figure 20.7 occurred when income increased from \$110 per week to \$120 per week. We would then compute

$$\text{Income elasticity} = \frac{\dfrac{\text{change in quantity demanded}}{\text{average quantity}}}{\dfrac{\text{change in income}}{\text{average income}}}$$

$$= \frac{\dfrac{16 \text{ ounces} - 12 \text{ ounces}}{14 \text{ ounces}}}{\dfrac{\$120 - \$110}{\$115}}$$

$$= \frac{4}{14} \div \frac{10}{115}$$

$$= \frac{0.286}{0.087} = 3.29$$

Popcorn purchases are very sensitive to changes in income. When incomes rise by 8.7 percent, popcorn sales increase by a whopping 28.6 percent (that is, 8.7% × 3.29). The computed elasticity of 3.29 summarizes this relationship.

Normal vs. Inferior Goods. Demand and income don't always move in the same direction. Popcorn is a **normal good** because consumers buy more of it when their incomes rise. People actually buy *less* of some goods, however, when they have more income. With low incomes, people buy discount clothes, used textbooks, and cheap beer, and they eat at home. With more money to spend, they switch to designer clothes, new books, premium beers, and restaurant meals (see News). The former items are called **inferior goods** because the quantity demanded *falls* when income *rises.* Similarly, when incomes *decline,* people demand *more* spaghetti and the services of credit agencies and pawnbrokers. ***For inferior goods, the income elasticity of demand is negative: for normal goods, it is positive.***

normal good: Good for which demand increases when income rises.

inferior good: Good for which demand decreases when income rises.

Cross-Price Elasticity

Changes in income are only one of the forces that shift demand curves. If popcorn were the only snack offered in movie theaters, people would undoubtedly eat more of it. In reality, people have other choices: candy, soda, ice cream, and more. Thus, the decision to buy popcorn depends not only on *its* price but also on the price and availability of other goods.

Suppose for the moment that the prices of these other goods were to fall. Imagine that candy bars were put on sale for a quarter, rather than the usual dollar. Would this price reduction on candy affect the consumption of popcorn?

IN THE NEWS

Stung by the Economy, Americans Lose Their Appetite for Dining Out

Restaurants' Sales Growth Slows as Consumers, Corporations Limit Nonessential Spending

Robin Gomes put her family on a budget last month, and that was bad news for restaurateurs.

Ms. Gomes, a 33-year-old home-loan coordinator in San Ramon, Calif., used to dine out with her husband and two children four times a week, dropping $50 to $60 a meal. Under the new budget, restaurant meals have been cut to once a week.

Far from being an isolated example, the Gomes family is part of a growing throng of stay-at-homes. As the shaky economy gives more consumers the jitters, the $258 billion restaurant and bar industry is grappling with its biggest slowdown in a decade. . . .

Growth in sales at restaurants and bars has declined steadily. For the 12 months ending this past Jan. 31, sales were 4.4 percent higher than the comparable year-earlier figure, according to figures from Technomic Inc., a Chicago food-consulting group, and the U.S. Census Bureau. But for the 12 months ending July 31, sales were only 2.4 percent above the prior 12-month period. Though sales are still above last year's, 2001 is shaping up to have the slowest growth since the 1991 recession, when sales dropped 1.2 percent. . . .

Upscale restaurants that thrived on corporate largesse are taking a big hit. Morton's Restaurant Group Inc., a chain of 61 steakhouses, saw same-store sales decline 9.6 percent in the second quarter.

—Shirley Leung

Source: *The Wall Street Journal,* August 22, 2001.

Analysis: Changes in income shift consumer demand curves. People buy fewer *normal* goods and more *inferior* goods when incomes decline.

FIGURE 20.8
Substitutes and Complements

The curve D_1 represents the initial demand for popcorn, given the prices of other goods. Other prices may change, however. If a reduction in the price of another good (candy) causes a *reduction* in the demand for this good (popcorn), the two goods are *substitutes.* Popcorn demand shifts to the left (to D_2) when the price of a *substitute good* falls.

If a reduction in the price of another good (e.g., Pepsi) leads to an *increase* in the demand for this good (popcorn), the two goods are *complements.* Popcorn demand shifts to the right (to D_3) when the price of a *complementary good* falls.

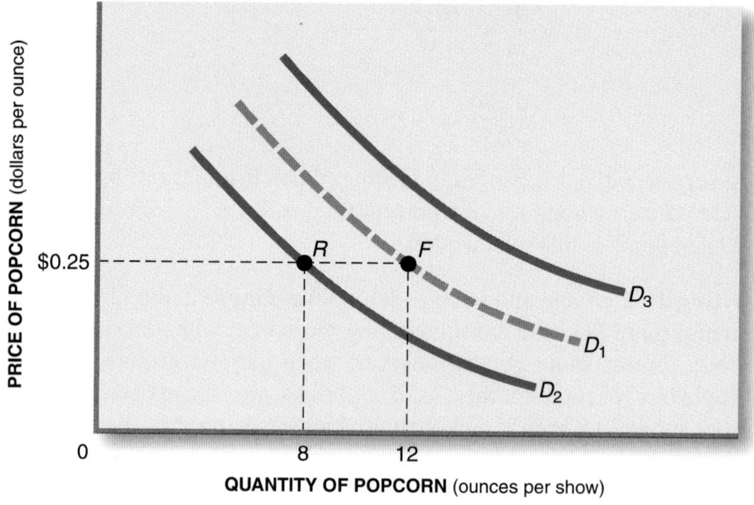

According to Figure 20.8, the demand for popcorn might *decrease* if the price of candy fell. The leftward shift of the demand curve from D_1 to D_2 tells us that consumers now demand less popcorn at every price. At 25 cents per ounce, consumers now demand only 8 ounces of popcorn (point *R*) rather than the previous 12 ounces (point *F*). In other words, a decline in the price of *candy* has caused a reduction in the demand for *popcorn.* We conclude that candy and popcorn are **substitute goods**—when the price of one declines, demand for the other falls.

substitute goods: Goods that substitute for each other; when the price of good *X* rises, the demand for good *Y* increases, *ceteris paribus.*

Popcorn sales would follow a very different path if the price of soda fell. People like to wash down their popcorn with soda. When soda prices fall, moviegoers actually buy *more* popcorn. Here again, ***a change in the price of one good affects the demand for another good.*** In this case, however, we're dealing with **complementary goods,** since a decline in the price of one good causes an increase in the demand for the other good.

complementary goods: Goods frequently consumed in combination; when the price of good *X* rises, the demand for good *Y* falls, *ceteris paribus.*

The distinction between substitute goods and complementary goods is illustrated in Figure 20.8. Note that ***in the case of substitute goods the price of one good and the demand for the other move in the same direction.*** (A *decrease* in candy prices causes a *decrease* in popcorn demand.) Likewise, as the price of music downloads *declined,* the demand for CD burners (a complementary good) *increased* but the demand for pre-recorded music CDs (substitute goods) *declined* (see News).

In the case of complementary goods (e.g., Pepsi and popcorn, cream and coffee), the price of one good and the demand for the other move in opposite directions. This helps explain why U.S. consumers bought more cars in 1998–99 when gasoline prices were falling and fewer SUVs in 2006 when gasoline prices were rising. The concept of complementary goods also explains why the demand for computer software increases when the price of computer hardware drops.

Calculating Cross-Price Elasticity. The mathematical relationship between the price of one good and demand for another is summarized in yet another elasticity concept. The **cross-price elasticity of demand** is the *percentage* change in the quantity demanded on one good divided by the *percentage* change in the price of *another* good—that is,

cross-price elasticity of demand: Percentage change in the quantity demanded of *X* divided by percentage change in price of *Y.*

$$\text{Cross-price elasticity of demand} = \frac{\%\text{ change in quantity demanded of good } X \text{ (at given price)}}{\%\text{ change in price of good } Y}$$

What has changed here is the denominator again. Now the denominator refers to a change in the price of *another* good rather than the *same* good.

IN THE NEWS

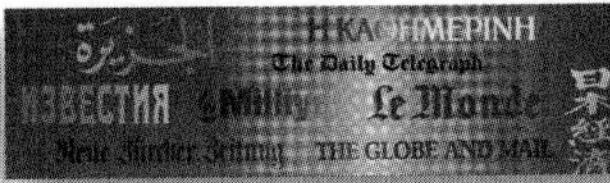

Album Sales Slump As Downloads Rise

As music-buying habits increasingly shift toward digital downloads, the industry experienced dramatic ups and downs in its 2005 sales results.

Down:

- Total album sales, falling from 666.7 million in 2004 to 618.9 million, according to Nielsen SoundScan, a drop of 7.2% after a 1.5% gain over 2003's sales total.
- CD sales (95% of total album sales), off even more dramatically, from 651.1 million to 598.9 million (down 8.0%).

Up:

- Digital track downloads, rising from 150% to 352.7 million.
- Digital album downloads, climbing 194% to 16.2 million from 5.5 million.
- Internet album sales, up 11%, accounting for nearly 25 million sales.
- Overall music purchases (encompassing albums, singles, music video and digital downloads), which were up 22.7% over 2004 and passed 1 billion units for the first time.

—Ken Barnes

By the numbers

After a one-year gain, CD sales dropped again in 2005, by 8.0%. They're now 15.5% below 2000's record level. Digital track downloads continued to explode in 2005, rising 150% over 2004.

	CD sales	Digital tracks
2005	598.9	352.7
2004	651.1	140.9
2003	635.8	19.2*
2002	649.5	
2001	712.0	
2000	730.0	

Figures in millions of units.

Source: Nielsen SoundScan, which tracked digital downloads for only the second half of 2003*.

Source: *USA Today,* January 5, 2006, p. D1. Reprinted with permission.

Analysis: Music downloads and pre-recorded CDs are *substitute goods.* As the price of downloads falls, demand for music CDs declines. Music downloads and CD burners, on the other hand, are *complementary goods.*

The cross-price elasticity of demand makes it easy to distinguish substitute and complementary goods. ***If the cross-price elasticity is positive, the two goods are substitutes; if the cross-price elasticity is negative, the two goods are complements.*** Pepsi and popcorn are complements because a fall (−) in the price of one leads to an increase (+) in the demand for the other; in other words, the cross-price elasticity is negative.

CHOOSING AMONG PRODUCTS

Our analysis of demand thus far has focused on the decision to buy a single product, at varying prices. Actual consumer behavior is multidimensional, however, and therefore more complex. When we go shopping, our concern isn't limited to how much of one good to buy. Rather, we must decide *which* of many available goods to buy at their respective prices.

The presence of so many goods complicates consumption decisions. Our basic objective remains the same, however: We want to get as much satisfaction as possible from our available income. In striving for that objective, we have to recognize that the purchase of any single good means giving up the opportunity to buy more of other goods. In other words, consuming popcorn (or any other good) entails distinct **opportunity costs.**

opportunity cost: The most desired goods or services that are forgone in order to obtain something else.

Marginal Utility vs. Price

The economic explanation for consumer choice builds on the theory of marginal utility and the law of demand. Suppose you have a $10 gift card for music and video-game downloads. The first proposition of consumer choice says you'll prefer the download that gives you the most satisfaction. Hardly a revolutionary proposition.

The second postulate of consumer choice takes into account market prices. Suppose you *prefer* a video game, but music downloads are cheaper. Under these circumstances, your budget may win out over your desires. There's nothing irrational about downloading a song instead of a more desirable video game when you have only a limited amount of income to spend. On the contrary, ***rational behavior requires one to compare the anticipated utility of each expenditure with its price.*** The smart thing to do, then, is to choose those products that promise to provide the most pleasure for the amount of income available.

Suppose your desire for a video game is *twice* as great as your desire to hear a tune. In economic terms, this means that the marginal utility of the first video game is two times that of the first music download. Which one should you download? Before hitting buttons on the keyboard, you'd better look at relative prices. What if a game costs $3 and a song costs only $1? In this case, you must pay *three* times as much for a video game that gives only *twice* as much pleasure. This isn't a good deal. You could get more utility *per dollar* by downloading music.

The same kind of principle explains why some rich people drive a Ford rather than a shiny new Mercedes. The marginal utility (MU) of driving a Mercedes is substantially higher than the MU of driving a Ford. A nice Mercedes, however, costs about three times as much as a basic Ford. A rich person who drives a Ford must feel that driving a Mercedes is not three times as satisfying as driving a Ford. For such people, a Ford yields more *marginal utility per dollar spent.*

The key to utility maximization, then, isn't simply to buy the things you like best. Instead, you must compare goods on the basis of their marginal utility *and* price. ***To maximize utility, the consumer should choose the good that delivers the most marginal utility per dollar.***

Utility Maximization

This basic principle of consumer choice is easily illustrated. Think about spending that $10 gift card on music or game downloads, the only available choices. Your goal, as always, is to get as much pleasure as possible from this limited income. That is, you want to maximize the *total* utility attainable from the expenditure of your income. The question is how to do it. What combination of songs and games will maximize the utility you get from $10?

We've already assumed that the marginal utility (MU) of the first game is two times higher than the MU of the first song. This is reflected in the second row of Table 20.3. The MU of the first video game has been set arbitrarily at 20 utils (units of utility). We don't need to know whether 20 utils is a real thrill or just a bit of amusement. Indeed, the concept of "utils" has little meaning by itself; it's only a useful basis for comparison. In this case,

TABLE 20.3
Maximizing Utility

Q: How can you get the most satisfaction (utility) from $10 if you must choose between downloading songs at $1 apiece or video games at $3 apiece?
A: By playing two games and playing four songs. See text for explanation.

	Amount of Utility (in units of utility, or utils)			
	From Music Downloads		From Game Downloads	
Quantity Consumed	Total	Marginal	Total	Marginal
0	0		0	
		10		20
1	10		20	
		9		18
2	19		38	
		8		16
3	27		54	
		6		12
4	33		66	
		5		6
5	37		72	
		4		1
6	41		73	
		3		
7	44			
		2		
8	46			
		1		
9	47			
		0		
10	47			

we want to compare the MU of the first game with the MU of the first song. Hence, we set the MU of the first game at 20 utils and the MU of the first song at 10 utils. The first game download is twice as satisfying as the first music download:

$$\text{MU game} = 2\text{MU song}$$

The remainder of Table 20.3 indicates how marginal utility diminishes with increasing consumption of a product. Look at what happens to the sound of music. The marginal utility of the first song is 10; but the MU of the second song is only 9 utils. The third song generates even less MU (= 8). You started with your favorite song; now you're working down your hits list. By the time you get to a sixth song, music downloads aren't raising your spirits much (MU = 4). By the tenth song, you're tired of music (MU = 0).

Game downloads also conform to the law of diminishing marginal utility. You start with your favorite game (MU = 20), seeking a high score. The second game is fun, too, though not quite as much (MU = 18). As you keep playing, frustration rises and marginal utility diminishes. By the time you play a sixth game your nerves are just about shot; the sixth game gives you only 1 util of marginal utility.

With these psychological insights to guide us, we can now determine how best to spend $10. What we're looking for is the combination of songs and video games that *maximizes* the total utility attainable from an expenditure of $10. We call this combination **optimal consumption**—that is, the mix of goods that yields the most utility for the available income.

optimal consumption: The mix of consumer purchases that maximizes the utility attainable from available income.

We can start looking for the optimal mix of consumer purchases by assessing the utility of spending the entire $10 on video games. At $3 per play, we could buy three games. This would give us *total* utility of 54 utils (see Table 20.3). Plus, we'd have enough change to download one song (MU = 10), for a grand utility total of 64 utils.

Alternatively, you could also spend the entire gift card on music downloads. With $10 to spend, you could buy 10 songs. However, this would generate only 47 utils of total utility. Hence, if you were forced to choose between *only* downloading songs or *only* playing video games, you'd pick the games.

Fortunately, we don't have to make such extreme choices. In reality, we can buy a *combination* of songs and video games. This complicates our decision making (with more choices) but permits us to attain higher levels of total satisfaction.

To reach the peak of satisfaction, consider spending your $10 in $3 dollar increments. How should you spend the first $3? If you spend it on one game, you'll get 20 utils of satisfaction. On the other hand, $3 will buy your first three music downloads. The first song has an MU of 10 and the second song adds another 9 utils to your happiness. The third song brings in another 8 utils. Hence, by spending the $3 on songs, you reap 27 utils of total utility. This is superior to the pleasure of a first game and it's therefore your first purchase.

Having downloaded three songs, you now can spend the second $3. How should it be spent? Your choice now is that first game or a fourth, fifth, and sixth song. That first unplayed game still promises 20 utils of real pleasure. By constrast, the MU of a fourth song is 6 utils. And the MU of a fifth song is only 5 utils. Together, then, the fourth, fifth, and sixth songs will increase your total utility by 15 utils, whereas a first game will give you 20 utils. You should spend the second $3 on a game download.

The decision on how to spend the remaining four dollars is made the same way. The final choice is to purchase either a second game (MU = 18) or the fourth, fifth, and sixth songs (MU = 15). The second game offers more marginal utility and is thus the correct decision.

After working your way through these calculations, you'll end up downloading two games and four songs. Was it worth it? Do you end up with more total utility than you could have gotten from any other combination? The answer is yes. The *total* utility of two games (38 utils) and four songs (33 utils) is 71 units of utility. This is significantly better than the alternatives of spending your $10 on songs alone (total utility = 47) or three games and a song (total utility = 64). In fact, the combination of two games and four songs is the *best* one you can find. Because this combination maximizes the total utility of your income ($10), it represents *optimal consumption.*

Utility-Maximizing Rule

Optimal consumption refers to the mix of output that maximizes total utility for the limited amount of income you have to spend. The basic approach to utility maximization is to purchase the good next that delivers the most *marginal utility per dollar.* Marginal utility per dollar is simply the MU of the good divided by its price: MU ÷ *P.*

From Table 20.3 we know that a first game has an MU of 20 and a price of $3. It thus delivers a marginal utility per dollar of

$$\frac{MU_{\text{first game}}}{P_{\text{game}}} = \frac{20}{\$3} = 6.33 \text{ utils per dollar}$$

On the other hand, the first song has a marginal utility of 10 and a price of $1. It offers a marginal utility per dollar of

$$\frac{MU_{\text{first song}}}{P_{\text{song}}} = \frac{10}{\$1} = 10 \text{ utils per dollar}$$

From this perspective, the first song is a better deal than the first game and should be purchased.

Optimal consumption implies that the utility-maximizing combination of goods has been found. If this is true, you can't increase your total utility by trading one good for another. All goods included in the optimal consumption mix yield the *same* marginal utility per dollar. We know we've reached maximum utility when we've satisfied the following rule:

$$\text{Utility-maximizing rule: } \frac{MU_x}{P_x} = \frac{MU_y}{P_y}$$

where *x* and *y* represent any two goods included in our consumption.

Rational consumer choice thus depends on comparisons of marginal utilities and prices. If a dollar spent on product *X* yields more marginal utility than a dollar spent on product *Y,* we should buy product *X.* To use this principle, of course, we have to know the amounts of utility obtainable from various goods and be able to perform a little arithmetic. By doing so, however, we can get the greatest satisfaction from our limited income.

Equilibrium Outcomes

All these graphs and equations make consumer choice look dull and mechanical. Economic theory seems to suggest that consumers walk through shopping malls with marginal-utility tables and hand-held computers. In reality, no one does this—not even your economics instructor. Yet, economic theory is pretty successful in predicting consumer decisions. Consumers don't always buy the optimal mix of goods and services with their limited income. But after some trial and error, consumers adjust their behavior. What economic theory predicts is that the final choices—the *equilibrium* outcomes—will be the predicted optimal ones.

THE ECONOMY TOMORROW

CAVEAT EMPTOR

LeBron James is paid over $35 million a year to help convince us to drink Sprite and Powerade ("Flava 23"), wear Nike shoes, use Juice batteries, and chew Bubblicious gum (see News). In 2007, LeBron started pitching Microsoft's Vista operating system. Do his sponsors know something economic theory doesn't? Economists *assume* consumers know what they want and will act rationally to get the most satisfaction they can. The companies that sponsor basketball star LeBron James don't accept that assumption. They think your tastes will follow LeBron's lead.

IN THE NEWS

James Still Blowin' Up with Bubblicious Deal

LeBron James has snapped up another big endorsement deal. The Cleveland Cavaliers' rookie star signed a four-year, $5 million contract with Bubblicious bubble gum, increasing his sponsorship deals to nearly $135 million.

Like his idol, Michael Jordan, the 19-year-old James chews gum during games and occasionally blows a bubble or two—making him a natural fit for London-based Cadbury Schweppes PLC.

Bubblicious will have a James-inspired flavor, according to his agent, Aaron Goodwin. Goodwin said he's talking with four or five companies, including McDonald's and Kraft, about future projects.

James has been racking up big-money endorsement contracts with sponsors since May, when he signed a seven-year, $90 million deal with Nike—the richest initial shoe contract ever offered an athlete.

He has deals with Coca Cola/Sprite ($16 million), Juice Batteries ($8 million) and Upper Deck ($5 million). James also signed a three-year, $13 million deal with the Cavaliers in July.

Source: *The Washington Post,* February 24, 2004. Reprinted with permission of the Associated Press.

Analysis: Companies pay huge amounts for celebrity endorsements, hoping to change consumer tastes (increase demand for a specific product).

Advertisers now spend over $400 *billion* per year to change our tastes. In the United States, this spending works out to over $400 per consumer, one of the highest per capita advertising rates in the world (see World View on the next page). Some of this advertising (including product labeling) is intended to provide information about existing products or to bring new products to our attention. A great deal of advertising, however, is also designed to exploit our senses and lack of knowledge. Recognizing that we're guilt-ridden, insecure, and sex-hungry, advertisers promise exoneration, recognition, and love; all we have to do is buy the right product.

A favorite target of advertisers is our sense of insecurity. Thousands of products are marketed in ways that appeal to our need for identity. Thousands of brand images are designed to help the consumer answer the nagging question, Who am I? The answers, of course, vary. *Playboy* magazine says, I'm a virile man of the world; Marlboro cigarettes say, I'm a rugged individualist who enjoys "man-sized flavor." Sprite says, I'll be a winner if I drink the same soda LeBron James does. And I'll be able to jump 8 feet high if I wear Air Zoom shoes.

Are Wants Created? Advertising can't be blamed for all of our foolish consumption. Even members of the most primitive tribes, uncontaminated by the seductions of advertising, adorned themselves with rings, bracelets, and pendants. Furthermore, advertising has grown to massive proportions only in the past 50 years, but consumption spending has been increasing throughout recorded history. Finally, a lot of advertising simply fails to change buying decisions. Accordingly, it's a mistake to attribute the growth or content of consumption entirely to the persuasions of advertisers.

This isn't to say that advertising has necessarily made us happier. The objective of all advertising is to alter the choices we make. Just as product images are used to attract us to particular products, so are pictures of hungry, ill-clothed children used to persuade us to give money to charity. In the same way, public relations gimmicks are employed to sway our votes for public servants. In the case of consumer products, advertising seeks to increase tastes for particular goods and services and therewith our willingness to pay. ***A successful advertising campaign is one that shifts the demand curve for a specific***

Where the Pitch Is Loudest

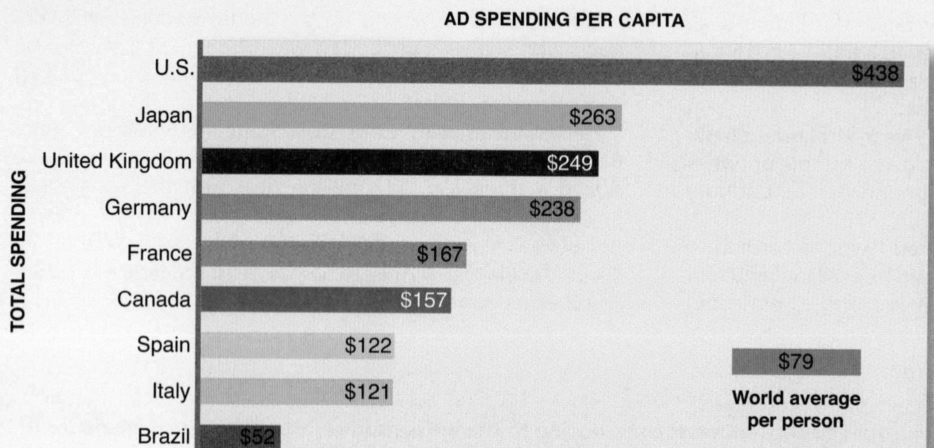

Source: *Ad Age Global,* February 2001. Reprinted with permission. Copyright Crain Communications, Inc. 2001.

Analysis: Producers advertise to change consumer tastes (preferences). At higher levels of income, advertising is likely to play a greater role in consumption decisions.

product to the right, inducing consumers to increase their purchases of a product at every price (see Figure 20.9). Advertising may also increase brand loyalty, making the demand curve less elastic (reducing consumer responses to price increases). By influencing our choices in this way, advertising will affect the consumption choices we make in the economy tomorrow. Advertising alone is unlikely to affect the total *level* of consumption, however.

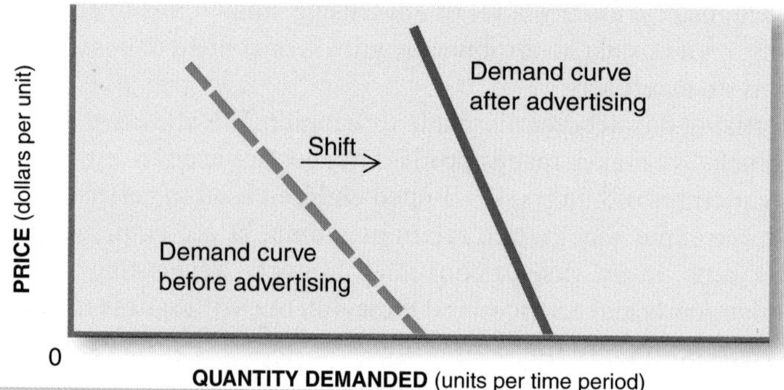

FIGURE 20.9
The Impact of Advertising on a Demand Curve

Advertising seeks to increase our taste for a particular product. If our taste (the product's perceived utility) increases, so will our willingness to buy. The resulting change in demand is reflected in a rightward shift of the demand curve, often accompanied by diminished elasticity.

SUMMARY

- Our desires for goods and services originate in the structure of personality and social dynamics and aren't explained by economic theory. Economic theory focuses on *demand*—that is, our ability and willingness to buy specific quantities of a good at various prices. LO1
- Marginal utility measures the additional satisfaction obtained from consuming one more unit of a good. The law of diminishing marginal utility says that the more of a product we consume, the smaller the increments of pleasure we tend to derive from additional units of it. This is a basis for the law of demand. LO1
- The price elasticity of demand is a numerical measure of consumer response to a change in price, *ceteris paribus*. It equals the percentage change in quantity demanded divided by the percentage change in price. Elasticity depends on the relative price of a good, the availability of substitutes, and time. LO2
- The effect of a price change on total revenue depends on price elasticity. Total revenue and price move in the *same* direction only if demand is price-inelastic ($E < 1$). LO2
- The shape and position of any particular demand curve depend on a consumer's income, tastes, expectations, and the price and availability of other goods. Should any of these factors change, the assumption of *ceteris paribus* will no longer hold, and the demand curve will *shift*. LO1
- The income elasticity of demand measures the response of demand to a change in income. If demand increases (shifts right) with income, the product is a normal good. If demand declines (shifts left) when income rises, it's an inferior good. LO2
- Cross-price elasticity measures the response of demand for one good to a change in the price of another. The cross-price elasticity of demand is positive for substitute goods and negative for complementary goods. LO2
- In choosing among alternative goods and services, a consumer compares the prices and anticipated satisfactions that they offer. To maximize utility with one's available income—to achieve an optimal mix of goods and services—one has to get the most utility for every dollar spent. To do so, one must compare the relative prices and pleasures and choose those goods which offer the most marginal utility per dollar. LO3
- Advertising seeks to change consumer tastes and thus the willingness to buy. If tastes do change, the demand curve for that product will shift. LO1

Key Terms

demand
utility
total utility
marginal utility
law of diminishing marginal utility
ceteris paribus
law of demand
demand curve
price elasticity of demand
total revenue
shift in demand
income elasticity of demand
normal good
inferior good
substitute goods
complementary goods
cross-price elasticity of demand
opportunity cost
optimal consumption

Questions for Discussion

1. What does the demand for enrollments in your college look like? What is on the axes? Is the demand price-elastic? Income-elastic? How could you find out? LO1
2. If the marginal utility of pizza never diminished, how many pizzas would you eat? LO3
3. How does total and marginal utility change as you spend more time surfing the Net? LO3
4. If the price of gasoline doubled, how would consumption of (*a*) gasoline, (*b*) cars, and (*c*) public transportation be affected? How quickly would these adjustments be made? LO2
5. Identify two goods each whose demand exhibits (*a*) high income elasticity, (*b*) low income elasticity, (*c*) high price elasticity, and (*d*) low price elasticity. What accounts for the differences in elasticity? LO2
6. Why is the demand for New York City cigarettes so much more elastic than the overall market demand for cigarettes? (See News, page 400.) LO1
7. Why are per capita advertising expenditures so high in the United States and so low in Brazil? (See World View, page 412.) LO1
8. According to the News stories on pages 399 and 400, how does the price elasticity of demand differ for teenagers and adults? Why? LO2
9. If you owned a movie theater, would you want the demand for movies to be elastic or inelastic? LO2
10. How has the Internet affected the price elasticity of demand for air travel? LO2
11. If the elasticity of demand for coffee is so low (Table 20.1), why doesn't Starbucks raise the price of coffee to $10 a cup? LO2
12. What would happen to unit sales and total revenue for this textbook if the bookstore reduced its price? LO2
13. Is the demand for iPhones price inelastic or elastic? Why? Is income elasticity high or low? LO2

problems The Student Problem Set at the back of this book contains numerical and graphing problems for this chapter.

web activities to accompany this chapter can be found on the Online Learning Center: **http://www.mhhe.com/economics/schiller11e**

APPENDIX

INDIFFERENCE CURVES

A consumer's demand for any specific product is an expression of many forces. As we've observed, the actual quantity of a product demanded by a consumer varies inversely with its price. The price-quantity relationship is determined by

- ***Tastes*** (desire for this and other goods).
- ***Income*** (of the consumer).
- ***Expectations*** (for income, prices, tastes).
- ***Other goods*** (their availability and price).

Economic theory attempts to show how each of these forces affects consumer demand. Thus far, we've used two-dimensional demand curves to illustrate the basic principles of demand. We saw that, in general, a change in the price of a good causes a movement along the demand curve, while a change in tastes, income, expectations, or other goods shifts the entire demand curve to a new position.

We haven't looked closely at the origins of demand curves, however. We assumed that a demand curve could be developed from observations of consumer behavior, such as the number of boxes of popcorn that were purchased at various prices (Figure 20.3). Likewise, we observed how the demand curve shifts in response to changes in tastes, income, expectations, or other goods (Figures 20.7 and 20.8).

It's possible, however, to derive a demand curve without actually observing consumer behavior. In theory we can identify consumer *preferences* (tastes), then use those preferences to construct a demand curve. In this case, the demand curve is developed explicitly from known preferences rather than on the basis of market observations. The end result—the demand curve—is the same, at least so long as consumers' behavior in product markets is consistent with their preferences.

Indifference curves are a mechanism for illustrating consumer tastes. We examine their construction and use in this appendix. As suggested above, indifference curves provide an explicit basis for constructing a demand curve. In addition, they are another way of viewing how consumption is affected by price, tastes, and income. Indifference curves are also a useful tool for illustrating explicitly consumer *choice*—that is, the decision to purchase one good rather than another.

Constructing an Indifference Curve

marginal utility: The change in total utility obtained by consuming one additional (marginal) unit of a good or service.

Suppose you're in an arcade and want to buy some Cokes and play video games but don't have enough money to buy enough of each. The income constraint compels you to make hard decisions. You have to consider the **marginal utility** each additional Coke or video game will provide, compare their respective prices, then make a selection. With careful introspection and good arithmetic you could select the optimal mix of Cokes and video games—that is, the combination that yields the most satisfaction (utility) for the income

Combination	Cokes	Video Games
A	1	8
B	2	5
C	3	4

TABLE 20A.1
Equally Satisfying Combinations

Different combinations of two goods may be equally satisfying. In this case we assume that the combinations *A, B,* and *C* all yield equal total utility. Hence, the consumer will be indifferent about which of the three combinations he or she receives.

available. This process of identifying your **optimal consumption** was illustrated in Table 20.3 with downloads of music and video games.

optimal consumption: The mix of consumer purchases that maximizes the utility attainable from available income.

Computing your optimal consumption is difficult because you must assess the marginal utility of each prospective purchase. In Table 20.3 we assumed that the marginal utility of the first music download was 10 utils, while the first game download had a marginal utility of 20. Then we had to specify the marginal utility of every additional music and game download. Can we really be so specific about our tastes?

Indifference curves require a bit less arithmetic. ***Instead of trying to measure the marginal utility of each prospective purchase, we now look for combinations of goods that yield equal satisfaction.*** In the arcade, this entails different combinations of Cokes and games. All we need do is determine that one particular combination of Cokes and video games is as satisfying as another. We don't have to say how many "units of pleasure" both combinations provide—it's sufficient that they're both equally satisfying.

The initial combination of 1 Coke and 8 video games is designated as a combination *A* in Table 20A.1. This combination of goods yields a certain, but unspecified, level of total utility. What we want to do now is to find another combination of Cokes and games that's just as satisfying as combination *A*. Finding other combinations of equal satisfaction isn't easy, but it's at least possible. After a lot of soul searching, we decide that 2 Cokes and 5 video games would be just as satisfying as 1 Coke and 8 games.[1] This combination is designated as *B* in Table 20A.1.

Table 20A.1 also depicts a third combination of Cokes and video games that's as satisfying as the first. Combination *C* includes 3 Cokes and 4 games, a mix of consumption assumed to yield the same total utility as 1 Coke and 8 games (combination *A*).

Notice that we haven't said anything about how much pleasure combinations *A, B,* and *C* provide. We're simply asserting that these three combinations are *equally* satisfying.

Figure 20A.1 illustrates the information about tastes that we've assembled. Points *A, B,* and *C* represent the three equally satisfying combinations of Cokes and video games we've identified. By connecting these points we create an **indifference curve.** The indifference curve illustrates all combinations of two goods that are equally satisfying. A consumer would be just as happy with any combination represented on the curve, so a choice among them would be a matter of indifference.

indifference curve: A curve depicting alternative combinations of goods that yield equal satisfaction.

An Indifference Map. Not all combinations of Cokes and video games are as satisfying as combination *A,* of course. Surely, 2 Cokes and 8 games would be preferred to only 1 Coke and 8 games. Indeed, ***any combination that provided more of one good and no less of the other would be preferred.*** Point *D* in Figure 20A.2 illustrates just one such combination. Combination *D* must yield more total utility than combination *A* because it includes one more Coke and no fewer games. A consumer wouldn't be indifferent to a choice between *A* and *D*; on the contrary, combination *D* would be preferred.

Combination *D* is also preferred to combinations *B* and *C.* How do we know? Recall that combinations *A, B,* and *C* are all equally satisfying. Hence, if combination *D* is better

[1]The utility computations used here aren't based on Table 20.3; a different set of tastes is assumed.

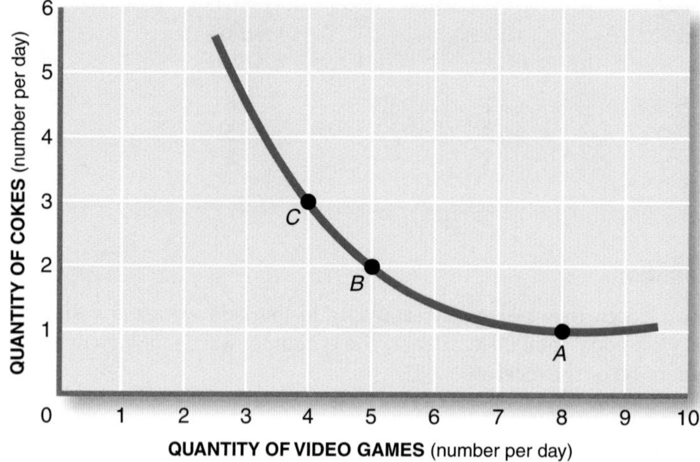

FIGURE 20A.1
An Indifference Curve

An indifference curve illustrates the various combinations of two goods that would provide equal satisfaction. The consumer is assumed to be indifferent to a choice between combinations *A, B,* and *C* (and all other points on the curve), as they all yield the same total utility.

than *A,* it must also be better than *B* and *C.* Given a choice, a consumer would select combination *D* (2 Cokes, 8 games) in preference to *any* combination depicted on indifference curve I_1.

There are also combinations that are as satisfying as *D,* of course. These possibilities are illustrated on indifference curve I_2. All these combinations are equally satisfying and must therefore be preferred to any points on indifference curve I_1. In general, ***the farther the indifference curve is from the origin, the more total utility it yields.***

The curve I_3 illustrates various combinations that are less satisfying. Combination *F,* for example, includes 3 Cokes and 3 games. This is 1 game less than the number available in combination *C.* Therefore, *F* yields less total utility than *C* and isn't preferred: A consumer would rather have combination *C* than *F.* By the same logic we used above, all points on indifference curve I_3 are less satisfying than combinations on curve I_2 or I_1.

Curves 1, 2, and 3 in Figure 20A.2 are the beginnings of an **indifference map.** An indifference map depicts all the combinations of goods that would yield various levels of satisfaction. A single indifference curve, in contrast, illustrates all combinations that provide a single (equal) level of total utility.

indifference map: The set of indifference curves that depicts all possible levels of utility attainable from various combinations of goods.

Utility Maximization

We assume that all consumers strive to maximize their utility. They want as much satisfaction as they can get. In the terminology of indifference curves, this means getting to the indifference curve that's farthest from the origin. The farther one is from the origin, the greater the total utility.

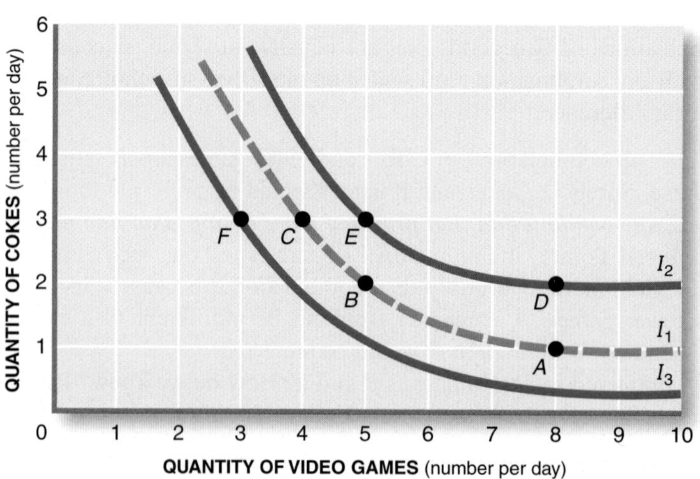

FIGURE 20A.2
An Indifference Map

All combinations of goods depicted on any given indifference curve (e.g., I_2) are equally satisfying. Other combinations are more or less satisfying, however, and thus lie on higher (I_2) or lower (I_3) indifference curves. An indifference map shows all possible levels of total utility (e.g., $I_1, I_2, I_3, \ldots, I_n$) and their respective consumption combinations.

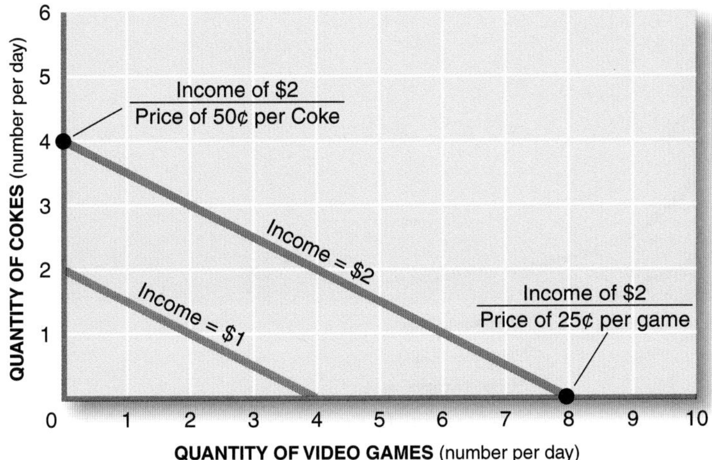

FIGURE 20A.3
The Budget Constraint

Consumption possibilities are limited by available income. The budget constraint illustrates this limitation. The end points of the budget constraint are equal to income divided by the price of each good. All points on the budget constraint represent affordable combinations of goods.

Although the goal of consumers is evident, the means of achieving it isn't so clear. Higher indifference curves aren't only more satisfying, they're also more expensive. We're confronted again with the basic conflict between preferences and prices. With a limited amount of income to spend, we can't attain infinite satisfaction (the farthest indifference curve). We have to settle for less (an indifference curve closer to the origin). The question is: How do we maximize the utility attainable with our limited income?

The Budget Constraint. For starters, we have to determine how much we have to spend. Suppose for the moment that we have only $2 to spend in the arcade and that Cokes and video games are still the only objects of our consumption desires. The price of a Coke is 50 cents; the price of a game is 25 cents. Accordingly, the maximum number of Cokes we could buy is 4 if we didn't play any video games. On the other hand, we could play as many as 8 games if we were to forsake Coke.

Figure 20A.3 depicts the limitations placed on our consumption possibilities by a finite income. The **budget constraint** illustrates all combinations of goods affordable with a given income. In this case, the outermost budget line illustrates the combinations of Cokes and video games that can be purchased with $2.

budget constraint: A line depicting all combinations of goods that are affordable with a given income and given prices.

The budget line is easily drawn. The end points of the budget constraint are found by dividing one's income by the price of the good on the corresponding axis. Thus, the outermost curve begins at 4 Cokes ($2 ÷ 50 cents) and ends at 8 games ($2 ÷ 25 cents). All the other points on the budget constraint represent other combinations of Cokes and video games that could be purchased with $2.

A smaller income is also illustrated in Figure 20A.3. If we had only $1 to spend, we could afford fewer Cokes and fewer games. Hence, a smaller income is represented by a budget constraint that lies closer to the origin.

Optimal Consumption. With a budget constraint looming before us, the limitation on utility maximization is evident. We want to reach the highest indifference curve possible. Our limited income, however, restricts our grasp. We can go only as far as our budget constraint allows. In this context, ***the objective is to reach the highest indifference curve that is compatible with our budget constraint.***

Figure 20A.4 illustrates the process of achieving optimal consumption. We start with an indifference map depicting all utility levels and product combinations. Then we impose a budget line that reflects our income. In this case, we continue to assume that Coke costs 50 cents, video games cost 25 cents, and we have $2 to spend. Hence, ***we can afford only those consumption combinations that are on or inside the budget line.***

Which particular combination of Cokes and video games maximizes the utility of our $2? It must be 2 Cokes and 4 video games, as reflected in point *M*. Notice that point *M* isn't only on the budget line but also touches indifference curve I_c. No other point on the budget

FIGURE 20A.4
Optimal Consumption

The optimal consumption combination—the one that maximizes the utility of spendable income—lies at the point where the budget line is tangent to (just touches) an indifference curve. In this case, point *M* represents the optimal mix of Cokes and video games, since no other affordable combination lies on a higher indifference curve than I_c.

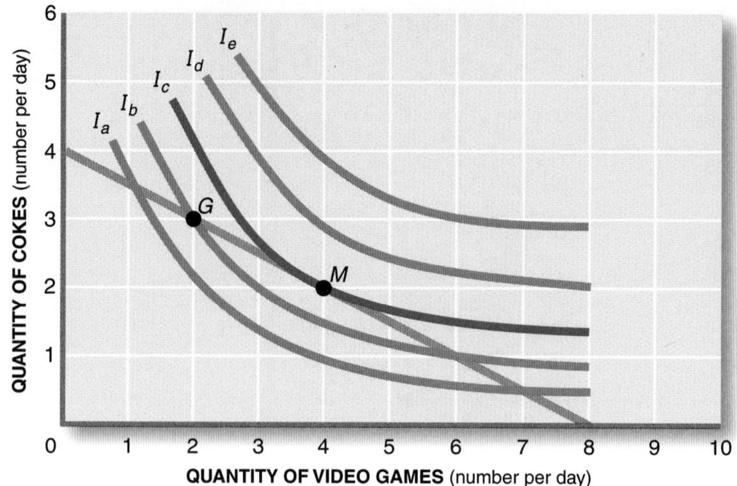

line touches I_c or any higher indifference curve. Accordingly, I_c represents the most utility we can get for \$2 and is attainable only if we consume 2 Cokes and 4 video games. Any other affordable combination yields less total utility—that is, falls on a lower indifference curve. Point *G,* for example, which offers 3 Cokes and 2 video games for \$2, lies on the indifference curve I_b. Because I_b lies closer to the origin than I_c, point *G* must be less satisfying than point *M.* We conclude, then, that ***the point of tangency between the budget constraint and an indifference curve represents optimal consumption.*** It's the combination we should buy if we want to maximize the utility of our limited income.

Marginal Utility and Price: A Digression. We earlier illustrated the utility-maximizing rule, which required a comparison of the ratios of marginal utilities to prices. Specifically, optimal consumption was represented as that combination of Cokes and video games that yielded

$$\frac{\text{MU Coke}}{P\text{ Coke}} = \frac{\text{MU games}}{P\text{ games}}$$

Does point *M* in Figure 20A.4 conform to this rule?

To answer this question, first rearrange the preceding equation as follows:

$$\frac{\text{MU Coke}}{\text{MU games}} = \frac{P\text{ Coke}}{P\text{ games}}$$

In this form, the equation says that the relative marginal utilities of Cokes and video games should equal their relative prices when consumption is optimal. In other words, if a Coke costs twice as much as a video game, then it must yield twice as much marginal utility if the consumer is to be in an optimal state. Otherwise, some substitution of Cokes for video games, or vice versa, would be desirable.

With this foundation, we can show that point *M* conforms to our earlier rule. Consider first the slope of the budget constraint, which is determined by the relative prices of Cokes and video games. In fact, ***the (absolute) slope of the budget constraint equals the relative price of the two goods.*** In Figure 20A.4 the slope equals the price of video games divided by the price of Cokes (25 cents ÷ 50 cents = ½). It tells us the rate at which video games can be exchanged for Cokes in the market. In this case, one video game is "worth" half a Coke.

The relative marginal utilities of the two goods are reflected in the slope of the indifference curve. Recall that the curve tells at what rate a consumer is willing to substitute one good for another, with no change in total utility. In fact, the slope of the indifference curve is called the **marginal rate of substitution.** It's equal to the relative marginal utilities of the two goods. Presumably one would be indifferent to a choice between 2 Cokes +

marginal rate of substitution: The rate at which a consumer is willing to exchange one good for another; the relative marginal utilities of two goods.

5 games and 3 Cokes + 4 games—as suggested in Table 20A.1—only if the third Coke were as satisfying as the fifth video game.

At the point of optimal consumption (M) in Figure 20A.4 the budget constraint is tangent to the indifference curve I_c, which means that the two curves must have the same slope at the point. In other words,

$$\frac{P\text{ games}}{P\text{ Cokes}} = \frac{\text{MU games}}{\text{MU Cokes}}$$

or alternatively,

$$\frac{\text{Rate of}}{\text{market exchange}} = \frac{\text{marginal rate}}{\text{of substitution}}$$

Both indifference curves and marginal utility comparisons lead us to the same optimal mix of consumption.

Deriving the Demand Curve

We noted at the beginning of this appendix that indifference curves not only give us an alternative path to optimal consumption but also can be used to derive a demand curve. To do this, we need to consider how the optimal consumption combination changes when the price of one good is altered. We can see what happens in Figure 20A.5.

Figure 20A.5 starts with the optimal consumption attained at point *M,* with income of \$2 and prices of 50 cents for a Coke and 25 cents for a video game. Now we're going to change the price of video games and observe how consumption changes.

Suppose that the price of a video game doubles, from 25 cents to 50 cents. This change will shift the budget constraint inward: Our income of \$2 now buys a maximum of 4 games rather than 8. Hence, the lower end point of the budget constraint moves from 8 games to 4 games. ***Whenever the price of a good changes, the budget constraint shifts.***

Only one end of the budget constraint is changed in Figure 20A.5. The budget line still begins at 4 Cokes because the price of Coke is unchanged. If only one price is changed, then only one end of the budget constraint is shifted.

Because the budget constraint has shifted inward, the combination *M* is no longer attainable. Two Cokes (at 50 cents each) and 4 games (at 50 cents each) now cost more than \$2. We're now forced to accept a lower level of total utility. According to Figure 20A.5, optimal consumption is now located at point *N.* This is the point of tangency between the new budget constraint and a lower indifference curve. At point *N* we consume 1 Coke and 3 video games.

Consider what has happened here. The price of video games has increased (from 25 cents to 50 cents), and the quantity of games demanded has decreased. This is the kind of relationship that demand curves describe. **Demand curves** indicate how the quantity demanded of a good changes in response to a change in its price, given a fixed income and all other things

demand curve: A curve describing the quantities of a good a consumer is willing and able to buy at alternative prices in a given time period, *ceteris paribus.*

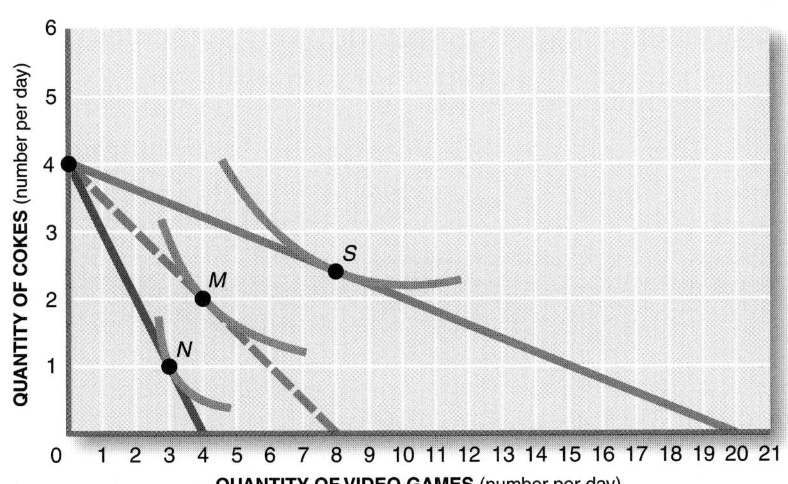

FIGURE 20A.5
Changing Prices

When the price of a good changes, the budget constraint shifts, and a new consumption combination must be sought. In this case, the price of video games is changing. When the price of games increases from 25 cents to 50 cents, the budget constraint shifts inward and optimal consumption moves from point *M* to point *N.*

FIGURE 20A.6
The Demand for Video Games

Figure 20A.5 shows how optimal consumption is altered when the price of video games changes. From that figure we can determine the quantity of video games demanded at alternative prices, *ceteris paribus.* That information is summarized here in the demand schedule (below) and the demand curve (above).

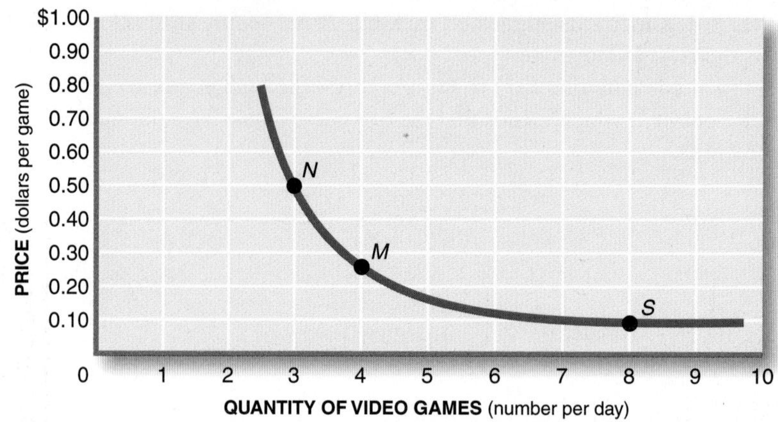

Point	Price (per game)	Quantity Demanded (games per day)
N	50 cents	3
M	25	4
S	10	8

law of demand: The quantity of a good demanded in a given time period increases as its price falls, *ceteris paribus.*

held constant. Not only does Figure 20A.5 provide the same information, it also conforms to the **law of demand:** As the price of games increases, the quantity demanded falls.

Suppose the price of video games were to fall rather than increase. Specifically, assume that the price of a game fell to 10 cents. This price reduction would shift the budget constraint farther out on the horizontal axis, since as many as 20 games could then be purchased with $2. As a result of the price reduction, we can now buy more goods and thus attain a higher level of satisfaction.

Point *S* in Figure 20A.5 indicates the optimal combination of Cokes and video games at the new video game price. At these prices, we consume 8 video games and 2.4 Cokes (we may have to share with a friend). The law of demand is again evident: When the price of video games declines, the quantity demanded increases.

The Demand Schedule and Curve. Figure 20A.6 summarizes the information we've acquired about the demand for video games. The demand schedule depicts the price-quantity relationships prevailing at optimal consumption points *N, M,* and *S* (from Figure 20A.5). The demand curve generalizes these observations to encompass other prices. What we end up with is a demand curve explicitly derived from our (assumed) knowledge of consumer tastes.

21 The Costs of Production

LEARNING OBJECTIVES

After reading this chapter, you should know:

LO1. What the production function reveals.

LO2. The law of diminishing returns.

LO3. How the various measures of cost are related.

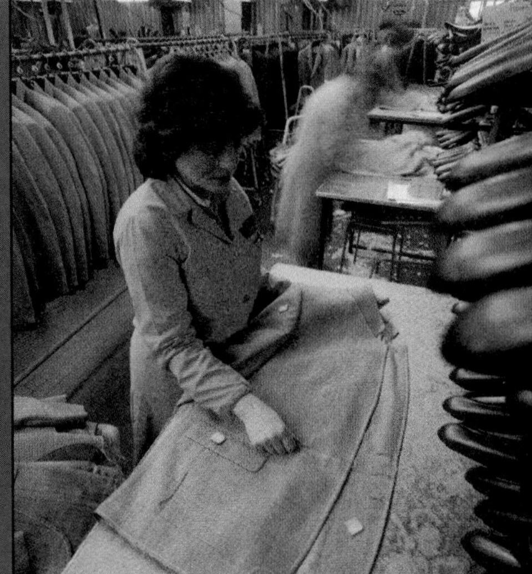

Last year U.S. consumers bought more than $2 *trillion* worth of imported goods, including Japanese cars, Italian shoes, and toys from China. As you might expect, this angers domestic producers, who frequently end up with unsold goods, half-empty factories, and unemployed workers. They rage against the "unfair" competition from abroad, asserting that producers in Korea, Brazil, and China can undersell U.S. producers because workers in these countries are paid dirt-poor wages.

But lower wages don't necessarily imply lower costs. You could pay me $2 per hour to type and still end up paying a lot for typing. Truth is, I type only about 10 words a minute, with lots of misteaks. The cost of producing goods depends not only on the price of inputs (e.g., labor) but also on how much they produce.

In this chapter we begin looking at the costs of producing the goods and services that market participants demand. We confront the following questions:

- **How much output *can* a firm produce?**
- **How do the *costs* of production vary with the rate of output?**
- **Do larger firms have a cost advantage over smaller firms?**

The answers to these questions are important not only to producers faced with foreign competition but to consumers as well. The costs of producing a good have a direct impact on the prices consumers pay.

THE PRODUCTION FUNCTION

No matter how large a business is or who owns it, all businesses confront one central fact: It costs something to produce goods. To produce corn, a farmer needs land, water, seed, equipment, and labor. To produce fillings, a dentist needs a chair, a drill, some space, and labor. Even the "production" of educational services such as this economics class requires the use of labor (your teacher), land (on which the school is built), and capital (the building, blackboard, computers). In short, unless you're producing unrefined, unpackaged air, you need **factors of production**—that is, resources that can be used to produce a good or service. These factors of production provide the basic measure of economic cost. The costs of your economics class, for example, are measured by the amounts of land, labor, and capital it requires. These are *resource* costs of production.

factors of production: Resource inputs used to produce goods and services, such as land, labor, capital, and entrepreneurship.

To assess the costs of production, we must first determine how many resources are actually needed to produce a given product. You could use a lot of resources to produce a product or use just a few. What we really want to know is how *best* to produce. What's the *smallest* amount of resources needed to produce a specific product? Or we could ask the same question from a different perspective: What's the *maximum* amount of output attainable from a given quantity of resources.

The answers to these questions are reflected in the **production function,** which tells us the maximum amount of good X producible from various combinations of factor inputs. With one chair and one drill, a dentist can fill a *maximum* of 32 cavities per day. With two chairs, a drill, and an assistant, a dentist can fill up to 55 cavities per day.

production function: A technological relationship expressing the maximum quantity of a good attainable from different combinations of factor inputs.

A production function is a technological summary of our ability to produce a particular good.[1] Table 21.1 provides a partial glimpse of one such function. In this case, the output is designer jeans, as produced by Low-Rider Jeans Corporation. The essential inputs in the production of jeans are land, labor (garment workers), and capital (a factory and sewing machines). With these inputs, Low-Rider Jeans Corporation can produce and sell hip-hugging jeans to style-conscious consumers.

Varying Input Levels

As in all production endeavors, we want to know how much output we can produce with available resources. To make things easy, we'll assume that the factory is already built, with fixed space dimensions. The only inputs we can vary are labor (the number of garment workers per day) and additional capital (the number of sewing machines we lease per day).

Capital Input (sewing machines per day)	Labor Input (workers per day)								
	0	1	2	3	4	5	6	7	8
	Jeans Output (pairs per day)								
0	0	0	0	0	0	0	0	0	0
1	0	15	34	44	48	50	51	51	47
2	0	20	46	64	72	78	81	82	80
3	0	21	50	73	83	92	99	103	103

TABLE 21.1
A Production Function

A production function tells us the maximum amount of output attainable from alternative combinations of factor inputs. This particular function tells us how many pairs of jeans we can produce in a day with a given factory and varying quantities of capital and labor. With one sewing machine, and one operator, we can produce a maximum of 15 pairs of jeans per day, as indicated in the second column of the second row. To produce more jeans, we need more labor or more capital.

[1]By contrast, the production possibilities curve discussed in Chapter 1 expresses our ability to produce various *combinations* of goods, given the use of *all* our resources. The production possibilities curve summarizes the output capacity of the entire economy. A production function describes the capacity of a single firm.

In these circumstances, the quantity of jeans we can produce depends on the amount of labor and capital we employ. ***The purpose of a production function is to tell us just how much output we can produce with varying amounts of factor inputs.*** Table 21.1 provides such information for jeans production.

Consider the simplest option, that of employing no labor or capital (the upper-left corner in Table 21.1). An empty factory can't produce any jeans; maximum output is zero per day. Even though land, capital (an empty factory), and even denim are available, some essential labor and capital inputs are missing, and jeans production is impossible.

Suppose now we employ some labor (a machine operator) but don't lease any sewing machines. Will output increase? Not according to the production function. The first row in Table 21.1 illustrates the consequences of employing labor without any capital equipment. Without sewing machines (or even needles, another form of capital), the operators can't make jeans. Maximum output remains at zero, no matter how much labor is employed in this case.

The dilemma of machine operators without sewing machines illustrates a general principle of production: ***The* productivity *of any factor of production depends on the amount of other resources available to it.*** Industrious, hardworking machine operators can't make designer jeans without sewing machines.

productivity: Output per unit of input, for example, output per labor-hour.

We can increase the productivity of garment workers by providing them with machines. The production function again tells us by *how much* jeans output could increase. Suppose we leased just one machine per day. Now the second row in Table 21.1 is the relevant one. It says jeans output will remain at zero if we lease one machine but employ no labor. If we employ one machine *and* one worker, however, the jeans will start rolling out the front door. Maximum output under these circumstances (row 2, column 2) is 15 pairs of jeans per day. Now we're in business!

The remaining columns in row 2 tell us how many additional jeans we can produce if we hire more workers, still leasing only one sewing machine. With one machine and two workers, maximum output rises to 34 pairs per day. If a third worker is hired, output could increase to 44 pairs.

Table 21.1 also indicates how production would increase with additional sewing machines (capital). By reading down any column of the table, you can see how more machines increase potential jeans output.

Efficiency

The production function summarized in Table 21.1 underscores the essential relationship between resource *inputs* and product *outputs.* It's also a basic introduction to economic costs. To produce 15 pairs of jeans per day, we need one sewing machine, an operator, a factory, and some denim. All these inputs comprise the *resource cost* of producing jeans.

Another feature of Table 21.1 is that it conveys the *maximum* output of jeans producible from particular input combinations. The standard garment worker and sewing machine, when brought together at Low-Rider Jeans Corporation, can produce *at most* 15 pairs of jeans per day. They could also produce a lot less. Indeed, a careless cutter can waste a lot of denim. A lazy or inattentive one won't keep the sewing machines humming. As many a producer has learned, actual output can fall far short of the limits described in the production function. Indeed, jeans output will reach the levels in Table 21.1 only if the jeans factory operates with relative **efficiency.** This requires getting maximum output from the resources used in the production process. ***The production function represents maximum technical efficiency—that is, the most output attainable from any given level of factor inputs.***

efficiency (technical): Maximum output of a good from the resources used in production.

We can always be inefficient, of course. This merely means getting less output than possible for the inputs we use. But this isn't a desirable situation. To a factory manager, it means less output for a given amount of input (cost). To society as a whole, inefficiency implies a waste of resources. If Low-Rider Jeans isn't producing efficiently, we're being denied some potential output. It's not only a question of having fewer jeans. We could also use the labor and capital now employed by Low-Rider Jeans to produce something else. Specifically, the **opportunity cost** of a product is measured by the most desired goods and services that could have been produced with the same resources. Hence, if jeans production isn't up to par, society is either (1) getting fewer jeans than it should for the resources

opportunity cost: The most desired goods or services that are forgone in order to obtain something else.

devoted to jeans production or (2) giving up too many other goods and services in order to get a desired quantity of jeans.

Although we can always do worse than the production function suggests, we can't do better, at least in the short run. The production function represents the *best* we can do with our current technological know-how. For the moment, at least, there's no better way to produce a specific good. As our technological and managerial capabilities increase, however, we'll attain higher levels of future productivity. These advances in our productive capability will be represented by new production functions.

Short-Run Constraints

Let's step back from the threshold of scientific advance for a moment and return to Low-Rider Jeans. Forget about possible technological breakthroughs in jeans production (e.g., electronic sewing machines or robot operators) and concentrate on the economic realities of our modest endeavor. For the present we're stuck with existing technology. In fact, all the output figures in Table 21.1 are based on the use of a specific factory. Once we've purchased or leased that factory, we've set a limit to current jeans production. When such commitments to fixed inputs (e.g., the factory) exist, we're dealing with a **short-run** production problem. If no land or capital were in place—if we could build or lease any-sized factory—we'd be dealing with a *long-run* decision.

short run: The period in which the quantity (and quality) of some inputs can't be changed.

Our short-run objective is to make the best possible use of the factory we've acquired. This entails selecting the right combination of labor and capital inputs to produce jeans. To simplify the decision, we'll limit the number of sewing machines in use. If we lease only one sewing machine, then the second row in Table 21.1 is the only one we have to consider. In this case, the single sewing machine (capital) becomes another short-run constraint on the production of jeans. With a given factory and one sewing machine, the short-run rate of output depends entirely on how many workers are hired.

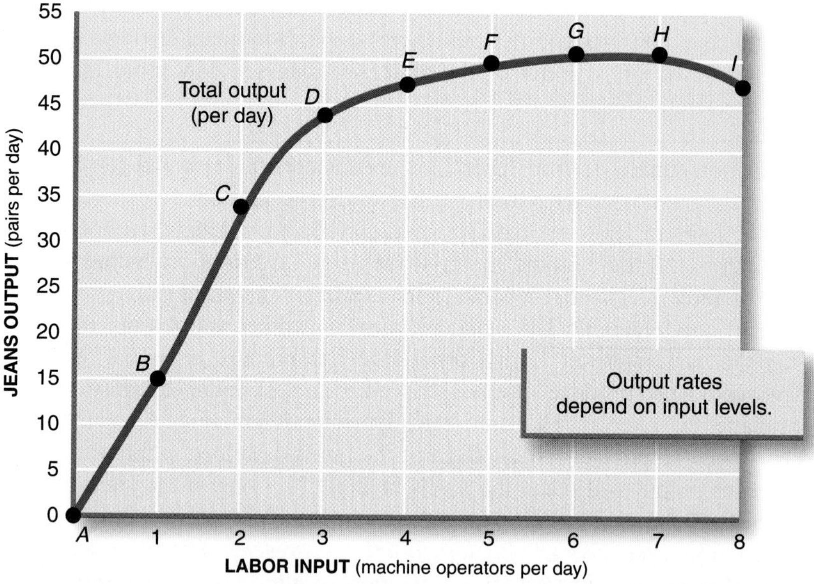

FIGURE 21.1
Short-Run Production Function

In the short run some inputs (e.g., land and capital) are fixed in quantity. Output then depends on how much of a variable input (e.g., labor) is used. The short-run production function shows how output changes when more labor is used. This figure and the table below are based on the second (one-machine) row in Table 21.1.

	A	*B*	*C*	*D*	*E*	*F*	*G*	*H*	*I*
Number of workers	0	1	2	3	4	5	6	7	8
Total output	0	15	34	44	48	50	51	51	47
Marginal physical product	—	15	19	10	4	2	1	0	−4

Figure 21.1 illustrates the short-run production function applicable to the factory with one sewing machine. As noted before, a factory with a sewing machine but no machine operators produces no jeans. This was observed in Table 21.1 (row 1, column 0) and is now illustrated by point *A* in Figure 21.1. To get any jeans output, we need to hire some labor. In this simplified example, ***labor is the variable input that determines how much output we get from our fixed inputs (land and capital).*** By placing one worker in the factory, we can produce 15 pairs of jeans per day. This possibility is represented by point *B*. The remainder of the production function shows how jeans output changes as we employ more workers in our single-machine factory.

MARGINAL PRODUCTIVITY

The short-run production function not only defines the *limit* to output but also shows how much each worker contributes to that limit. Notice again that jeans output increases from zero (point *A* in Figure 21.2) to 15 pairs (point *B*) when the first machine operator is hired. In other words, total output *increases* by 15 pairs when we employ the first worker. This increase is called the **marginal physical product (MPP)** of that first worker—that is, the *change* in total output that results from employment of one more unit of (labor) input, or

marginal physical product (MPP): The change in total output associated with one additional unit of input.

$$\text{Marginal physical product (MPP)} = \frac{\text{change in total output}}{\text{change in input quantity}}$$

With zero workers, total output was zero. With the first worker, total output increases to 15 pairs of jeans per day. The MPP of the first worker is 15 pairs of jeans.

If we employ a second operator, jeans output more than doubles, to 34 pairs per day (point *C*). The 19-pair *increase* in output represents the marginal physical product of the *second* worker.

The higher MPP of the second worker raises a question about the first. Why was the first's MPP lower? Laziness? Is the second worker faster, less distracted, or harder working?

The second worker's higher MPP isn't explained by superior talents or effort. We assume, in fact, that all "units of labor" are equal—that is, one worker is just as good as another.[2] Their different marginal products are explained by the structure of the production process,

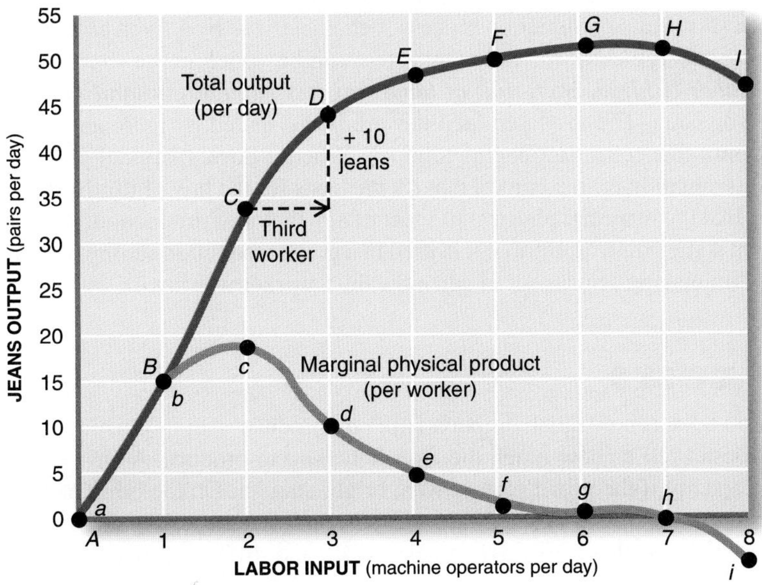

FIGURE 21.2
Marginal Physical Product (MPP)

Marginal physical product is the *change* in total output that results from employing one more unit of input. The *third* unit of labor, for example, increases *total output* from 34 (point C) to 44 (point *D*). Hence the *marginal* output of the third worker is 10 pairs of jeans (point *d*). What's the MPP of the fourth worker? What happens to *total* output when this worker is hired?

[2]In reality, garment workers do differ greatly in energy, talent, and diligence. These differences can be eliminated by measuring units of labor in *constant-quality* units. A person who works twice as hard as everyone else would count as two *quality-adjusted* units of labor.

not by their respective abilities. The first garment worker not only had to sew jeans but also to unfold bolts of denim, measure the jeans, sketch out the patterns, and cut them to approximate size. A lot of time was spent going from one task to another. Despite the worker's best efforts, this person simply couldn't do everything at once.

A second worker alleviates this situation. With two workers, less time is spent running from one task to another. While one worker is measuring and cutting, the other can continue sewing. This improved *ratio* of labor to other factors of production results in the large jump in total output. The second worker's superior MPP isn't unique to this person: It would have occurred even if we'd hired the workers in the reverse order.

Diminishing Marginal Returns

Unfortunately, total output won't keep rising so sharply if still more workers are hired. Look what happens when a third worker is hired. Total jeans production continues to increase. But the increase from point C to point D in Figure 21.2 is only 10 pairs per day. Hence, the third worker's MPP (10 pairs) is *less* than that of the second (19 pairs). Marginal physical product is *diminishing.* This concept is illustrated by point d in Figure 21.2.

What accounts for this decline in MPP? The answer lies in the ratio of labor to other factors of production. A third worker begins to crowd our facilities. We still have only one sewing machine. Two people can't sew at the same time. As a result, some time is wasted as the operators wait for their turns at the machine. Even if they split up the various jobs, there will still be some "downtime," since measuring and cutting aren't as time-consuming as sewing. Consequently, we can't make full use of a third worker. The relative scarcity of other inputs (capital and land) constrains the third worker's marginal physical product.

Resource constraints are even more evident when a fourth worker is hired. Total output increases again, but the increase this time is very small. With three workers, we got 44 pairs of jeans per day (point D); with four workers, we get a maximum of 48 pairs (point E). Thus the fourth worker's MPP is only 4 pairs of jeans. There simply aren't enough machines to make productive use of so much labor.

If a seventh worker is hired, the operators get in one another's way, argue, and waste denim. Notice in Figure 21.1 that total output doesn't increase at all when a seventh worker is hired (point H). The MPP of the seventh worker is zero (point h). Were an eighth worker hired, total output would actually *decline,* from 51 pairs (point H) to 47 pairs (point I). The eighth worker has a *negative* MPP (point i in Figure 21.2).

Law of Diminishing Returns. The problems of crowded facilities apply to most production processes. In the short run, a production process is characterized by a fixed amount of available land and capital. Typically, the only factor that can be varied in the short run is labor. Yet, ***as more labor is hired, each unit of labor has less capital and land to work with.*** This is simple division: The available facilities are being shared by more and more workers. At some point, this constraint begins to pinch. When it does, marginal physical product declines. This situation is so common that it's the basis for the **law of diminishing returns,** which says that the marginal physical product of any factor of production, such as labor, will diminish at some point, as more of it is used in a given production setting. Notice in Figure 21.2 how diminishing returns set in when the third worker was hired.

law of diminishing returns: The marginal physical product of a variable input declines as more of it is employed with a given quantity of other (fixed) inputs.

RESOURCE COSTS

A production function tells us how much output a firm *can* produce with its existing plant and equipment. It doesn't tell us how much the firm will *want* to produce. A firm *might* want to produce at capacity if the profit picture were bright enough. On the other hand, a firm might not produce *any* output if costs always exceeded sales revenue. The most desirable rate of output is the one that maximizes total **profit**—the difference between total revenue and total costs.

profit: The difference between total revenue and total cost.

The production function therefore is just a starting point for supply decisions. To decide how much output to produce with that function, a firm must next examine the costs of production. How fast do costs rise when output increases?

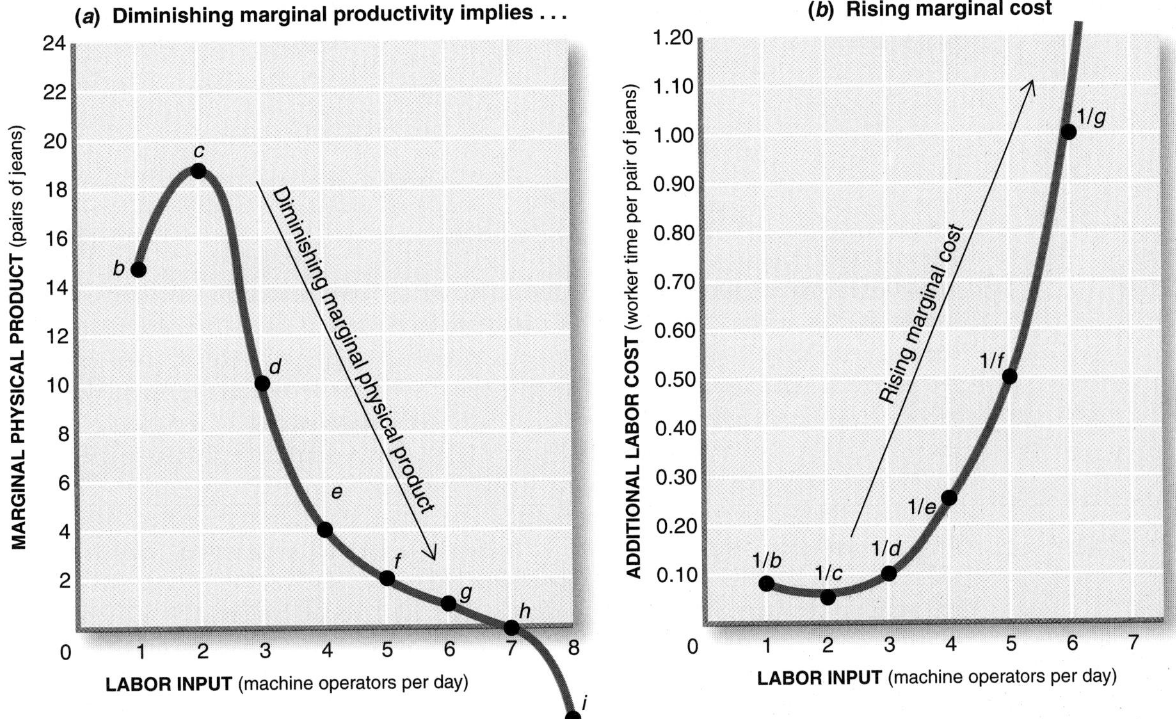

FIGURE 21.3
Falling MPP Implies Rising Marginal Cost

Marginal physical product (MPP) is the additional output obtained by employing one more unit of input. If MPP is falling, each additional unit of input is producing less additional output, which means that the input cost of each unit of output is rising. The third worker's MPP is 10 pairs (point *d* in part *a*). Therefore, the labor cost of these additional jeans is approximately 1/10 unit of labor per pair (point 1/*d* in part *b*).

The law of diminishing returns provides a clue to how fast costs rise. ***The economic cost of a product is measured by the value of the resources needed to produce it.*** What we've seen here is that those resource requirements eventually increase. Each additional sewing machine operator produces fewer and fewer jeans. In effect, then, each additional pair of jeans produced uses more and more labor.

Suppose we employ one sewing machine and one operator again, for a total output of 15 pairs of jeans per day; see point *b* in Figure 21.3*a*. Now look at production from another perspective, that of *costs*. How much labor cost are we using at point *b* to produce one pair of jeans? The answer is simple. Since one worker is producing 15 pairs of jeans, the labor input per pair of jeans must be one-fifteenth of a worker's day, that is, 0.067 unit of labor; see point 1/*b* in Figure 21.3*b*. All we're doing here is translating *output* data into related *input* (cost) data.

Marginal Resource Cost

The next question is, How do input costs change when output increases. As point *c* in Figure 21.3*a* reminds us, total output increases by 19 pairs when we hire a second worker. What's the implied labor cost of those *additional* 19 pairs? By dividing one worker by 19 pairs of jeans, we observe that the labor cost of that extra output is one-nineteenth, or 0.053 of a worker's day; see point 1/*c* in Figure 21.3*b*.

When we focus on the *additional* costs incurred from increasing production, we're talking about *marginal* costs. Specifically, **marginal cost (MC)** refers to the *increase* in total costs required to get one additional unit of output. More generally,

marginal cost (MC): The increase in total cost associated with a one-unit increase in production.

$$\text{Marginal cost (MC)} = \frac{\text{change in total cost}}{\text{change in output}}$$

In our simple case where labor is the only variable input, the marginal cost of the added jeans is

$$\text{Marginal cost} = \frac{\text{1 additional worker}}{\text{19 additional pairs}}$$

$$= 0.053 \text{ workers per pair}$$

The amount 0.053 of labor represents the *change* in total resource cost when we produce one *additional* pair of jeans.

Notice in Figure 21.3*b* that the marginal labor cost of jeans production declines when the second worker is hired. Marginal cost falls from 0.067 unit of labor (plus denim) per pair (point 1/*b* in Figure 21.3*b*) to only 0.053 unit of labor per pair (point 1/*c*). It costs less labor *per pair* to use two workers rather than only one. This is a reflection of the second worker's increased MPP. ***Whenever MPP is increasing, the marginal cost of producing a good must be falling.*** This is illustrated in Figure 21.3 by the upward move from *b* to *c* in part *a* and the corresponding downward move from 1/*b* to 1/*c* in part *b.*

Unfortunately, marginal physical product typically declines at some point. As it does, the marginal costs of production rise. In this sense, each additional pair of jeans becomes more expensive—it uses more and more labor per pair. Figure 21.3 illustrates this inverse relationship between MPP and marginal cost. The third worker has an MPP of 10 pairs, as illustrated by point *d.* The marginal labor input of these extra 10 pairs is thus 1 ÷ 10, or 0.10 unit of labor. In other words, one-tenth of a third worker's daily effort goes into each pair of jeans. This additional labor cost *per unit* is illustrated by 1/*d* in part *b* of the figure.

Note in Figure 21.3 how marginal physical product declines after point *c* and how marginal costs rise after point 1/*c*. This is no accident. ***If marginal physical product declines, marginal cost increases.*** Thus, increasing marginal cost is as common as—and the direct result of—diminishing returns. These increasing marginal costs aren't the fault of any person or factor, simply a reflection of the resource constraints found in any established production setting (i.e., existing and limited plant and equipment). In the short run, the quantity and quality of land and capital are fixed, and we can vary only their intensity of use, such as with more or fewer workers. It's in this short-run context that we keep running into diminishing marginal returns and rising marginal costs.

DOLLAR COSTS

This entire discussion of diminishing returns and marginal costs may seem a bit alien. After all, we're interested in the costs of production, and costs are typically measured in *dollars,* not such technical notions as MPP. Jeans producers need to know how many dollars it costs to keep jeans flowing; they don't want a lecture on marginal physical product.

Jeans manufacturers don't have to study marginal physical products, or even the production function. They can confine their attention to dollar costs. The dollar costs observed, however, are directly related to the underlying production function. To understand *why* costs rise—and how they might be reduced—some understanding of the production function is necessary. In this section we translate production functions into dollar costs.

Total Cost

total cost: The market value of all resources used to produce a good or service.

The **total cost** of producing a product includes the market value of all the resources used in its production. To determine this cost we simply identify all the resources used in production, determine their value, and then add up everything.

In the production of jeans, these resources included land, labor, and capital. Table 21.2 identifies these resources, their unit values, and the total dollar cost associated with their use. This table is based on an assumed output of 15 pairs of jeans per day, with the use of one worker and one sewing machine (point *B* in Figure 21.2). The rent on the factory is \$100 per day, a sewing machine rents for \$20 per day, the wages of a garment worker are \$80 per day. We'll assume Low-Rider Jeans Corporation can purchase bolts of denim for \$30 apiece, with each bolt providing enough denim for 10 pairs of jeans. In other words, one-tenth of a bolt (\$3 worth of material) is required for one pair of jeans. We'll ignore any

Resource Input	×	Unit Price	=	Total Cost
1 factory		$100 per day		$100
1 sewing machine		20 per day		20
1 operator		80 per day		80
1.5 bolts of denim		30 per bolt		45
Total cost				$245

TABLE 21.2
The Total Costs of Production (total cost of producing 15 pairs of jeans per day)

The total cost of producing a good equals the market value of all the resources used in its production. In this case, the production of 15 pairs of jeans per day requires resources worth $245.

other potential expenses. With these assumptions, the total cost of producing 15 pairs of jeans per day amounts to $245, as shown in Table 21.2.

Fixed Costs. Total costs will change of course as we alter the rate of production. But not all costs increase. In the short run, some costs don't increase at all when output is increased. These are **fixed costs,** in the sense that they don't vary with the rate of output. The factory lease is an example. Once you lease a factory, you're obligated to pay for it, whether or not you use it. The person who owns the factory wants $100 per day. Even if you produce no jeans, you still have to pay that rent. That's the essence of fixed costs.

fixed costs: Costs of production that don't change when the rate of output is altered (e.g., the cost of basic plant and equipment).

The leased sewing machine is another fixed cost. When you rent a sewing machine, you must pay the rental charge. It doesn't matter whether you use it for a few minutes or all day long—the rental charge is fixed at $20 per day.

Variable Costs. Labor costs are another story altogether. The amount of labor employed in jeans production can be varied easily. If we decide not to open the factory tomorrow, we can just tell our only worker to take the day off without pay. We'll still have to pay rent, but we can cut back on wages. On the other hand, if we want to increase daily output, we can also get additional workers easily and quickly. Labor is regarded as a **variable cost** in this line of work—that is, a cost that *varies* with the rate of output.

variable costs: Costs of production that change when the rate of output is altered (e.g., labor and material costs).

The denim itself is another variable cost. Denim not used today can be saved for tomorrow. Hence, how much we "spend" on denim today is directly related to how many jeans we produce. In this sense, the cost of denim input varies with the rate of jeans output.

Figure 21.4 illustrates how these various costs are affected by the rate of production. On the vertical axis are the costs of production, in dollars per day. Notice that the total

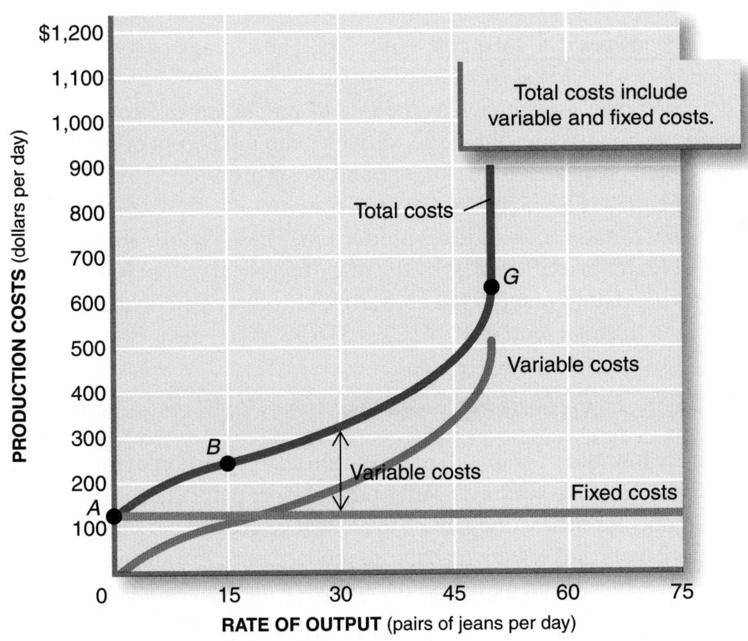

FIGURE 21.4
The Cost of Jeans Production

Total cost includes both fixed and variable costs. Fixed costs must be paid even if no output is produced (point *A*). Variable costs start at zero and increase with the rate of output. The total cost of producing 15 pairs of jeans (point *B*) includes $120 in fixed costs (rent on the factory and sewing machines) and $125 in variable costs (denim and wages). Total cost rises as output increases, because additional variable costs must be incurred.

In this example, the short-run capacity is equal to 51 pairs (point *G*). If still more inputs are employed, costs will rise but not total output.

cost of producing 15 pairs per day is still $245, as indicated by point *B*. This cost figure consists of

Dollar Cost of Producing 15 Pairs

Fixed costs:		
Factory rent	$100	
Sewing machine rent	20	
Subtotal		$120
Variable costs:		
Wages to labor	$80	
Denim	45	
Subtotal		$125
Total costs		$245

If we increase the rate of output, total costs will rise. ***How fast total costs rise depends on variable costs only,*** however, since fixed costs remain at $120 per day. (Notice the horizontal fixed-cost curve in Figure 21.4.)

With one sewing machine and one factory, there's an absolute limit to daily jeans production. According to the production function in Figure 21.1, the capacity of a factory with one machine is roughly 51 pairs of jeans per day. If we try to produce more jeans than this by hiring additional workers, our total costs will rise, but our output won't. Recall that the seventh worker had a *zero* marginal physical product (Figure 21.2). In fact, we could fill the factory with garment workers and drive total costs sky-high. But the limits of space and one sewing machine don't permit output in excess of 51 pairs per day. This limit to productive capacity is represented by point *G* on the total cost curve. Further expenditure on inputs will increase production *costs* but not *output.*

Although there's no upper limit to costs, there is a lower limit. If output is reduced to zero, total costs fall only to $120 per day, the level of fixed costs, as illustrated by point *A* in Figure 21.4. As before, ***there's no way to avoid fixed costs in the short run.*** Indeed, those fixed costs define the short run.

Average Costs

average total cost (ATC): Total cost divided by the quantity produced in a given time period.

While Figure 21.4 illustrates *total* costs of production, other measures of cost are often desired. One of the most common measures of cost is average, or per-unit, cost. **Average total cost (ATC)** is simply total cost divided by the rate of output:

$$\text{Average total cost (ATC)} = \frac{\text{total cost}}{\text{total output}}$$

At an output of 15 pairs of jeans per day, total costs are $245. The average cost of production is thus $16.33 per pair (= 245 ÷ 15) at this rate of output.

Figure 21.5 shows how average costs change as the rate of output varies. Row *J* of the cost schedule, for example, again indicates the fixed, variable, and total costs of producing 15 pairs of jeans per day. Fixed costs are still $120; variable costs are $125. Thus the total cost of producing 15 pairs per day is $245, as we saw earlier.

The rest of row *J* shows the average costs of jeans production. These figures are obtained by dividing each dollar total (columns 2, 3, and 4) by the rate of physical output (column 1). At an output rate of 15 pairs per day, **average fixed cost (AFC)** is $8 per pair, **average variable cost (AVC)** is $8.33, and *average total cost (ATC)* is $16.33. ATC, then, is simply the sum of AFC and AVC:

average fixed cost (AFC): Total fixed cost divided by the quantity produced in a given time period.

average variable cost (AVC): Total variable cost divided by the quantity produced in a given time period.

$$\text{ATC} = \text{AFC} + \text{AVC}$$

Falling AFC. At this relatively low rate of output, fixed costs are a large portion of total costs. The rent paid for the factory and sewing machines works out to $8 per pair ($120 ÷ 15). This high average fixed cost accounts for nearly one-half of total average costs. This suggests that it's quite expensive to lease a factory and sewing machine to produce only 15 pairs of jeans per day. To reduce average costs, we must make fuller use of our leased plant and equipment.

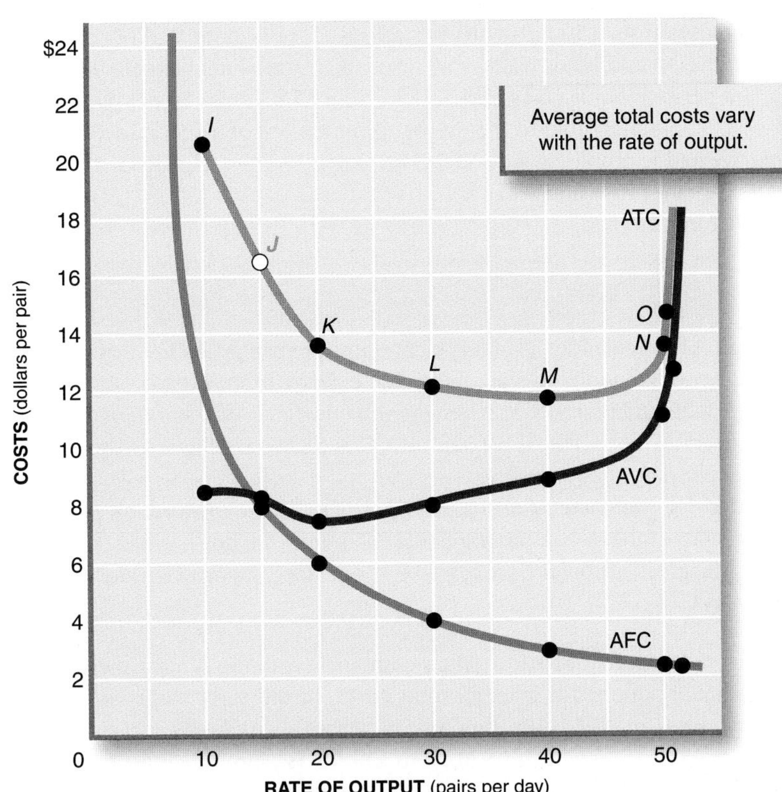

FIGURE 21.5
Average Costs

Average total cost (ATC) in column 7 equals total cost (column 4) divided by the rate of output (column 1). Since total cost includes both fixed (column 2) and variable (column 3) costs, ATC also equals AFC (column 5) plus AVC (column 6). This relationship is illustrated in the graph. The ATC of producing 15 pairs per day (point *J*) equals \$16.33—the sum of AFC (\$8) and AVC (\$8.33).

	(1) Rate of Output	(2) Fixed Costs	+	(3) Variable Costs	=	(4) Total Cost	(5) Average Fixed Cost	+	(6) Average Variable Cost	=	(7) Average Total Cost
H	0	\$120		\$ 0		\$120	—		—		—
I	10	120		85		205	\$12.00		\$ 8.50		\$20.50
J	15	120		125		245	8.00		8.33		16.33
K	20	120		150		270	6.00		7.50		13.50
L	30	120		240		360	4.00		8.00		12.00
M	40	120		350		470	3.00		8.75		11.75
N	50	120		550		670	2.40		11.00		13.40
O	51	120		633		753	2.35		12.41		14.76

Notice what happens to average costs when the rate of output is increased to 20 pairs per day (row *K* in Figure 21.5). Average fixed costs go down, to only \$6 per pair. This sharp decline in AFC results from the fact that total fixed costs (\$120) are now spread over more output. Even though our rent hasn't dropped, the *average* fixed cost of producing jeans has.

If we produce more than 20 pairs of jeans per day, AFC will continue to fall. Recall that

$$\text{AFC} = \frac{\text{total fixed cost}}{\text{total output}}$$

The numerator is fixed (at \$120 in this case). But the denominator increases as output expands. Hence, ***any increase in output will lower average fixed cost.*** This is reflected in Figure 21.5 by the constantly declining AFC curve.

As jeans output increases from 15 to 20 pairs per day, AVC falls as well. AVC includes the price of denim purchased and labor costs. The price of denim is unchanged, at $3 per pair ($30 per bolt). But per-unit *labor* costs have fallen, from $5.33 to $4.50 per pair. Thus, the reduction in AVC is completely due to the greater productivity of a second worker. To get 20 pairs of jeans, we had to employ a second worker part-time. In the process, the marginal physical product of labor rose and AVC fell.

With both AFC and AVC falling, ATC must decline as well. In this case, *average* total cost falls from $16.33 per pair to $13.50. This is reflected in row *K* in the table as well as in point *K* on the ATC curve in Figure 21.5.

Rising AVC. Although AFC continues to decline as output expands, AVC doesn't keep dropping. On the contrary, AVC tends to start rising quite early in the expansion process. Look at column 6 of the table in Figure 21.5. After an initial decline, AVC starts to increase. At an output of 20 pairs, AVC is $7.50. At 30 pairs, AVC is $8.00. By the time the rate of output reaches 51 pairs per day, AVC is $12.41.

Average variable cost rises because of diminishing returns in the production process. We discussed this concept before. As output expands, each unit of labor has less land and capital to work with. Marginal physical product falls. As it does, labor costs *per pair of jeans* rise, pushing up AVC.

U-Shaped ATC. The steady decline of AFC, when combined with the typical increase in AVC, results in a U-shaped pattern for average total costs. In the early stages of output expansion, the large declines in AFC outweigh any increases in AVC. As a result, ATC tends to fall. Notice that ATC declines from $20.50 to $11.75 as output increases from 10 to 40 pairs per day. This is also illustrated in Figure 21.5 with the downward move from point *I* to point *M*.

The battle between falling AFC and rising AVC takes an irreversible turn soon thereafter. When output is increased from 40 to 50 pairs of jeans per day, AFC continues to fall (row *N* in the table). But the decline in AFC (−60 cents) is overshadowed by the increase in AVC (+$2.25). Once rising AVC dominates, ATC starts to increase as well. ATC increases from $11.75 to $13.40 when jeans production expands from 40 to 50 pairs per day.

This and further increases in average total costs cause the ATC curve in Figure 21.5 to start rising. ***The initial dominance of falling AFC, combined with the later resurgence of rising AVC, is what gives the ATC curve its characteristic U shape.***

Minimum Average Cost. It's easy to get lost in this thicket of intertwined graphs and jumble of equations. A couple of landmarks will help guide us out, however. One of those is located at the very bottom of the U-shaped average total cost curve. Point *M* in Figure 21.5 represents *minimum* average total costs. By producing exactly 40 pairs per day, we minimize the amount of land, labor, and capital used per pair of jeans. For Low-Rider Jeans Corporation, point *M* represents least-cost production—the lowest-cost jeans. For society as a whole, point *M* also represents the lowest possible opportunity cost: At point *M,* we're minimizing the amount of resources used to produce a pair of jeans and therefore maximizing the amount of resources left over for the production of other goods and services.

As attractive as point *M* is, you shouldn't conclude that it's everyone's dream. The primary objective of producers is to maximize *profits.* This is not necessarily the same thing as minimizing average *costs.*

Marginal Cost

One final cost concept is important. Indeed, this last concept is probably the most important one for production. It's *marginal cost.* We encountered this concept in our discussion of resource costs, where we noted that marginal cost refers to the value of the resources needed to produce one more unit of a good. To produce *one* more pair of jeans, we need the denim itself and a very small amount of additional labor. These are the extra or added costs of increasing output by one pair of jeans per day. To compute the *dollar* value of these

Resources Used to Produce 16th Pair of Jeans	×	Market Value	=	Marginal Cost
0.053 unit of labor		0.053 × $80 per unit of labor		$4.24
0.1 bolt of denim		0.1 × $30 per bolt		3.00
				$7.24

TABLE 21.3
Resource Computation of Marginal Cost

Marginal cost refers to the value of the additional inputs needed to produce one more unit of output. To increase daily jeans output from 15 to 16 pairs, we need 0.053 unit of labor and one-tenth of a bolt of denim. These extra inputs cost $7.24.

marginal costs, we could determine the market price of denim and labor and then add them up. Table 21.3 provides an example. In this case, we calculate that the additional or *marginal* cost of producing a sixteenth pair of jeans is $7.24. This is how much *total* costs will increase if we decide to expand jeans output by only one pair per day (from 15 to 16).

Table 21.3 emphasizes the link between resource costs and dollar costs. However, there's a much easier way to compute marginal cost. ***Marginal cost refers to the change in total costs associated with one more unit of output.*** Accordingly, we can simply observe *total* dollar costs before and after the rate of output is increased. The difference between the two totals equals the *marginal cost* of increasing the rate of output. This technique is much easier for jeans manufacturers who don't know much about marginal resource utilization but have a sharp eye for dollar costs. It's also a lot easier for economics students, of course. But they have an obligation to understand the resource origins of marginal costs and what causes marginal costs to rise or fall. As we noted before, ***diminishing returns in production cause marginal costs to increase as the rate of output is expanded.***

Figure 21.6 shows what the marginal costs of producing jeans look like. At each output rate, marginal cost is computed as the *change* in total cost divided by the *change* in output. When output increases from 20 jeans to 30 jeans, total cost rises by $90. Dividing this change in costs by 10 (the change in output) gives us a marginal cost of $9, as illustrated by point *s*.

Notice in Figure 21.6 how the marginal cost curve slopes steeply up after 20 units of output have been produced. This rise in marginal costs reflects the law of diminishing returns. As increases in output become more difficult to achieve, they also become more expensive. Each additional pair of jeans beyond 20 requires a bit more labor than the preceding pair and thus entails rising marginal cost.

A Cost Summary

All these cost calculations can give you a real headache. They can also give you second thoughts about jumping into Low-Rider Jeans or any other business. There are tough choices to be made. A given firm can produce many different rates of output, each of which entails a distinct level of costs. ***The output decision has to be based not only on the* capacity *to produce (the production function) but also on the* costs *of production (the cost functions).*** Only those who make the right decisions will succeed in business.

The decision-making process is made a bit easier with the glossary in Table 21.4 and the generalized cost curves in Figure 21.7. As before, we're concentrating on a short-run production process, with fixed quantities of land and capital. In this case, however, we've abandoned the Low-Rider Jeans Corporation and provided hypothetical costs for an idealized production process. The purpose of these figures is to provide a more general view of how the various cost concepts relate to each other. Note that MC, ATC, AFC, and AVC can all be computed from total costs. All we need, then, are the first two columns of the table in Figure 21.7, and we can compute and graph all the rest of the cost figures.

FIGURE 21.6
Marginal Costs

Marginal cost is the change in total cost that occurs when more output is produced. MC equals $\Delta TC/\Delta q$. When diminishing returns set in, MC begins rising, as it does here after the output rate of 20 pairs per day is exceeded.

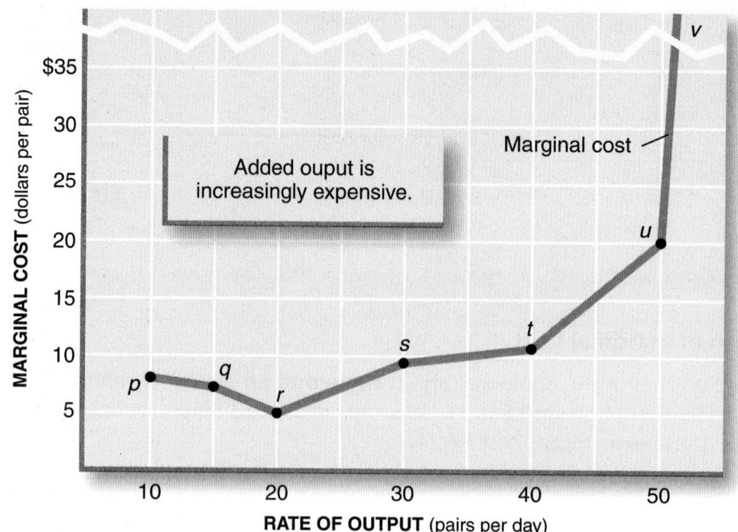

	Rate of Output	Total Cost	$\frac{\Delta TC}{\Delta q}$ = MC
	0	$120	
p	10	205	$85/10 = $8.5
q	15	245	$40/5 = $8.0
r	20	270	$25/5 = $5.0
s	30	360	$90/10 = $9.0
t	40	470	$110/10 = $11.0
u	50	670	$200/10 = $20.0
v	51	753	$83/1 = $83.0

MC-ATC Intersection. The centerpiece of Figure 21.7 is the U-shaped ATC curve. Of special significance is its relationship to marginal costs. Notice that ***the MC curve intersects the ATC curve at its lowest point*** (point *m*). This will always be the case. So long as the marginal cost of producing one more unit is less than the previous average cost, average

TABLE 21.4
A Guide to Costs

A quick reference to key measures of cost.

Total costs of production are comprised of **fixed costs** and **variable costs:**

$$TC = FC + VC$$

Dividing total costs by the quantity of output yields the **average total cost:**

$$ATC = \frac{TC}{q}$$

which also equals the sum of **average fixed cost** and **average variable cost:**

$$ATC = AFC + AVC$$

The most important measure of changes in cost is **marginal cost,** which equals the increase in total costs when an additional unit of output is produced:

$$MC = \frac{\text{change in total cost}}{\text{change in output}}$$

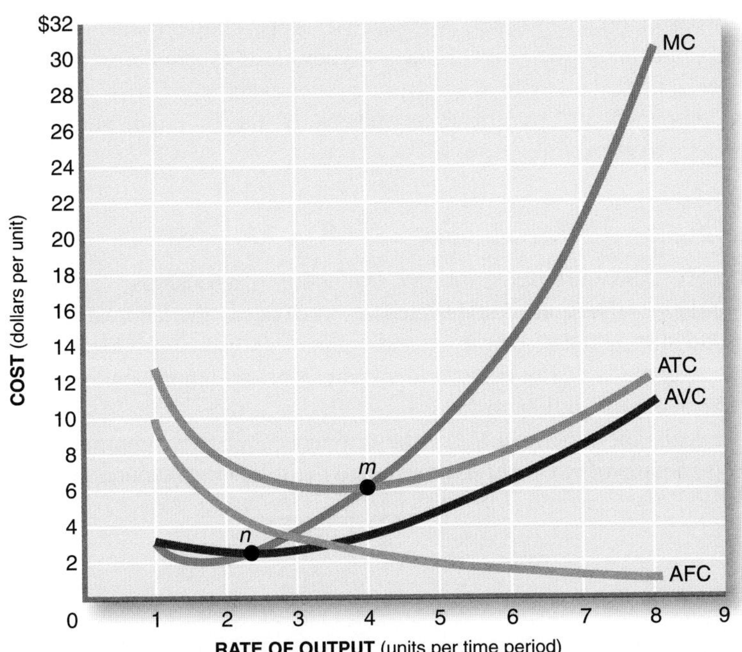

FIGURE 21.7
Basic Cost Curves

With total cost and the rate of output, all other cost concepts can be computed. The resulting cost curves have several distinct features. The AFC curve always slopes downward. The MC curve typically rises, sometimes after a brief decline. The ATC curve has a U shape. And the MC curve will always intersect both the ATC and AVC curves at their lowest points (*m* and *n*, respectively).

Rate of Output	TC	MC	ATC	AFC	AVC
0	$10.00	—	—	—	—
1	13.00	$ 3.00	$13.00	$10.00	$ 3.00
2	15.00	2.00	7.50	5.00	2.50
3	19.00	4.00	6.33	3.33	3.00
4	25.00	6.00	6.25	2.50	3.75
5	34.00	9.00	6.80	2.00	4.80
6	48.00	14.00	8.00	1.67	6.33
7	68.00	20.00	9.71	1.43	8.28
8	98.00	30.00	12.25	1.25	11.00

costs must fall. ***Thus, average total costs decline as long as the marginal cost curve lies below the average cost curve,*** as to the left of point *m* in Figure 21.7.

We already observed, however, that marginal costs rise as output expands, largely because additional workers reduce the amount of land and capital available to each worker (in the short run, the size of plant and equipment is fixed). Consequently, at some point (*m* in Figure 21.7) marginal costs will rise to the level of average costs.

As marginal costs continue to rise beyond point *m,* they begin to pull average costs up, giving the average cost curve its U shape. ***Average total costs increase whenever marginal costs exceed average costs.*** This is the case to the right of point *m,* since the marginal cost curve always lies above the average cost curve in that part of Figure 21.7.

To visualize the relationship between marginal cost and average cost, imagine computing the average height of people entering a room. If the first person who comes through the door is six feet tall, then the average height of people entering the room is six feet at that point. But what happens to average height if the second person entering the room is only three feet tall? *Average* height declines because the last (marginal) person entering the room is shorter than the previous average. Whenever the last entrant is shorter than the average, the average must fall.

The relationship between marginal costs and average costs is also similar to that between your grade in this course and your grade-point average. If your grade in economics is better (higher) than your other grades, then your overall grade-point average will rise. In other words, a high *marginal* grade will pull your *average* grade up. If you don't understand this, your grade-point average is likely to fall.

ECONOMIC VS. ACCOUNTING COSTS

The cost curves we observed here are based on *real* production relationships. The dollar costs we compute are a direct reflection of underlying resource costs: the land, labor, and capital used in the production process. Not everyone counts this way. On the contrary, accountants and businesspeople typically count dollar costs only and ignore any resource use that doesn't result in an explicit dollar cost.

Return to Low-Rider Jeans for a moment to see the difference. When we computed the dollar cost of producing 15 pairs of jeans per day, we noted the following resource inputs:

INPUTS	COST PER DAY
1 factory rent	$100
1 machine rent	20
1 machine operator	80
1.5 bolts of denim	45
Total cost	$245

explicit cost: A payment made for the use of a resource.

The total value of the resources used in the production of 15 pairs of jeans was thus $245 per day. But this figure needn't conform to *actual* dollar costs. Suppose the owners of Low-Rider Jeans decided to sew jeans. Then they wouldn't have to hire a worker or pay $80 per day in wages. **Explicit costs**—the *dollar* payments—would drop to $165 per day. The producers and their accountant would consider this a remarkable achievement. They might assert that the cost of producing jeans had fallen.

Economic Cost

An economist would draw no such conclusions. ***The essential economic question is how many resources are used in production.*** This hasn't changed. One unit of labor is still being employed at the factory; now it's simply the owner, not a hired worker. In either case, one unit of labor is not available for the production of other goods and services. Hence, society is still paying $245 for jeans, whether the owners of Low-Rider Jeans write checks in that amount or not. The only difference is that we now have an **implicit cost** rather than an explicit one. We really don't care who sews jeans—the essential point is that someone (i.e., a unit of labor) does.

implicit cost: The value of resources used, even when no direct payment is made.

The same would be true if Low-Rider Jeans owned its own factory rather than rented it. If the factory were owned rather than rented, the owners probably wouldn't write any rent checks. Hence, accounting costs would drop by $100 per day. But the factory would still be in use for jeans production and therefore unavailable for the production of other goods and services. The economic (resource) cost of producing 15 pairs of jeans would still be $245.

The distinction between an economic cost and an accounting cost is essentially one between resource and dollar costs. *Dollar cost* refers to the explicit dollar outlays made by a producer; it's the lifeblood of accountants. **Economic cost,** in contrast, refers to the *value* of *all* resources used in the production process; it's the lifeblood of economists. In other words, economists count costs as

economic cost: The value of all resources used to produce a good or service; opportunity cost.

$$\text{Economic cost} = \text{explicit costs} + \text{implicit costs}$$

As this formula suggests, ***economic and accounting costs will diverge whenever any factor of production is not paid an explicit wage (or rent, etc.).***

The Cost of Homework. These distinctions between economic and accounting costs apply also to the "production" of homework. You can pay people to write term papers for you or buy them off the Internet. At large schools you can often buy lecture notes as well. But most students do their own homework so they'll learn something and not just turn in required assignments.

Doing homework is expensive, however, even if you don't pay someone to do it. The time you spend reading this chapter is valuable. You could be doing something else if you weren't reading right now. What would you be doing? The forgone activity—the best alternative use of your time—represents the economic cost of doing homework. Even if you don't pay yourself for reading this chapter, you'll still incur that *economic* cost.

LONG-RUN COSTS

We've confined our discussion thus far to short-run production costs. ***The short run is characterized by fixed costs***—a commitment to specific plant and equipment. A factory, an office building, or some other plant and equipment have been leased or purchased: We're stuck with *fixed costs.* In the short run, our objective is to make the best use of those fixed costs by choosing the appropriate rate of production.

The long run opens up a whole new range of options. In the **long run,** we have no lease or purchase commitments. We're free to start all over again, with whatever scale of plant and equipment we desire and whatever technology is available. Quite simply, ***there are no fixed costs in the long run.*** Nor are there any commitments to existing technology. In 2004, General Motors could have built an engine plant in China of any size. But they decided to build one with a capacity of 300,000 engines (see World View). In building the plant, the company incurred a fixed cost. Once the plant was completed, GM focused on the short-run production decision of how many engines to manufacture.

long run: A period of time long enough for all inputs to be varied (no fixed costs).

Long-Run Average Costs

The opportunities available in the long run include building a plant of any desired size. Suppose we still wanted to go into the jeans business. In the long run, we could build or lease any size factory we wanted and could lease as many sewing machines as we desired. Figure 21.8 illustrates three choices: a small factory (ATC_1), a medium-sized factory (ATC_2), and a large factory (ATC_3). As we observed earlier, it's very expensive to produce lots of jeans with a small factory. The ATC curve for a small factory (ATC_1) starts to head straight up at relatively low rates of output. In the long run, we'd lease or build such a factory only if we anticipated a continuing low rate of output.

The ATC_2 curve illustrates how costs might fall if we leased or built a medium-sized factory. With a small-sized factory, ATC becomes prohibitive at an output of 50 to 60 pairs of

WORLD VIEW

GM Plans to Invest $3 Billion in China to Boost Its Presence

BEIJING—General Motors Corp. said it plans to invest more than $3 billion in China in the next three years, underscoring its bid to become a leader in the world's fastest growing auto market. . . .

The new investments are mainly for expanding its production capacity for vehicles and engines, improving its research and development center, and a new auto-financing venture it is launching this year with its main partner in China, Shanghai Automotive Industry Corp. . . .

All in all, GM expects its vehicle-assembly capacity in China to reach 1.3 million units a year by 2007 from its current 530,000 units a year.

To support its expansion, GM also plans to build a new engine plant with a production capacity of 300,000 engines a year, and a new transmission plant.

—Jane Lanhee Lee

Analysis: In the long run, a firm has no fixed costs and can select any desired plant size. Once a plant is built, leased, or purchased, a firm has fixed costs and focuses on short-run output decisions.

FIGURE 21.8
Long-Run Costs with Three Plant Size Options

Long-run cost possibilities are determined by all possible short-run options. In this case, there are three options of varying size (ATC_1, ATC_2, and ATC_3). In the long run, we'd choose the plant that yielded the lowest average cost for any desired rate of output. The solid portion of the curves (LATC) represents these choices. The smallest factory (ATC_1) is best for output levels below *a;* the largest (ATC_3), output rates in excess of *b.*

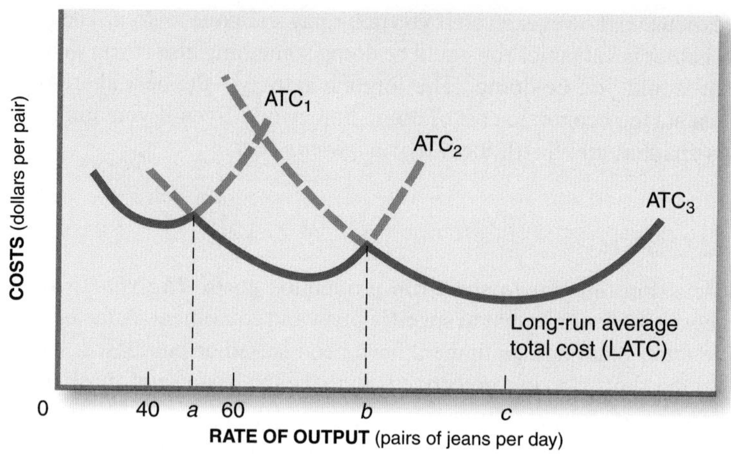

jeans per day. A medium-sized factory can produce these quantities at lower cost. Moreover, ATC continues to drop as jeans production increases in the medium-sized factory—at least for a while. Even a medium-sized factory must contend with resource constraints and therefore rising average costs: Its ATC curve is U-shaped also.

If we expected to sell really large quantities of jeans, we'd want to build or lease a large factory. Beyond the rate of output *b,* the largest factory offers the lowest average total cost. There's a risk in leasing such a large factory, of course. If our sales don't live up to our high expectations, we'll end up with very high fixed costs and thus very expensive jeans. Look at the high average cost of producing only 60 pairs of jeans per day with the large factory (ATC_3).

In choosing an appropriate factory, then, we must decide how many jeans we expect to sell. Once we know our expected output, we can select the right-sized factory. It will be the one that offers the lowest ATC for that rate of output. If we expect to sell fewer jeans than *a,* we'll choose the small factory in Figure 21.8. If we expect to sell jeans at a rate between *a* and *b,* we'll select a medium-sized factory. Beyond rate *b,* we'll want the largest factory. These choices are reflected in the solid part of the three ATC curves. The composite "curve" created by these three segments constitutes our long-run cost possibilities. ***The long-run cost curve is just a summary of our best short-run cost possibilities, using existing technology and facilities.***

We might confront more than three choices, of course. There's really no reason we couldn't build a factory to *any* desired size. In the long run, we face an infinite number of scale choices, not just three. The effect of all these choices is to smooth out the long-run cost curve. Figure 21.9 depicts the long-run curve that results. Each rate of output is most efficiently produced by some size (scale) of plant. That sized plant indicates the minimum

FIGURE 21.9
Long-Run Costs with Unlimited Options

If plants of all sizes can be built, short-run options are infinite. In this case, the LATC curve becomes a smooth U-shaped curve. Each point on the curve represents lowest-cost production for a plant size best suited to one rate of output. The long-run ATC curve has its own MC curve.

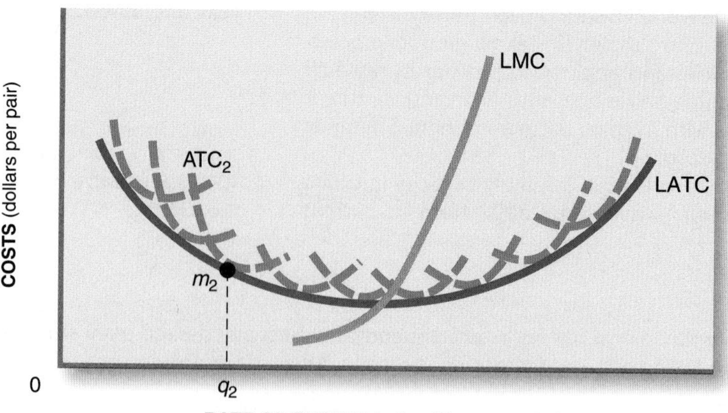

cost of producing a particular rate of output. Its corresponding short-run ATC curve provides one point on the long-run ATC curve.

Long-Run Marginal Costs

Like all average cost curves, the long-run (LATC) curve has its own marginal cost curve. The long-run marginal cost (LMC) curve isn't a composite of short-run marginal cost curves. Rather, it's computed on the basis of the costs reflected in the long-run ATC curve itself. We won't bother to compute those costs here. Note, however, that the long-run MC curve—like all MC curves—intersects its associated average cost curve at its lowest point.

ECONOMIES OF SCALE

Figure 21.8 seems to imply that a producer must choose either a small plant or a larger one. That isn't completely true. The choice is often between one large plant or *several* small ones. Suppose the desired level of output was relatively large, as at point *c* in Figure 21.8. A single small plant (ATC_1) is clearly not up to the task. But what about using several small plants rather than one large one (ATC_3)? How would costs be affected?

Notice what happens to *minimum ATC* in Figure 21.8 when the size (scale) of the factory changes. When a medium-sized factory (ATC_2) replaces a small factory (ATC_1), minimum average cost drops (the bottom of ATC_2 is below the bottom of ATC_1). This implies that a jeans producer who wants to minimize costs should build one medium-sized factory rather than try to produce the same quantity with two small ones. **Economies of scale** exist in this situation: Larger facilities reduce *minimum* average costs. Such economies of scale help explain why a single firm has come to dominate the funeral business (see News).

economies of scale: Reductions in minimum average costs that come about through increases in the size (scale) of plant and equipment.

Larger production facilities don't always result in cost reductions. Suppose a firm has the choice of producing the quantity Q_m from several small factories or from one large, centralized facility. Centralization may have three different impacts on costs; these are illustrated in Figure 21.10. In each illustration, we see the average total cost (ATC) curve for a typical small firm or plant and the ATC curve for a much larger plant producing the same product.

To learn more about the business of dying, go to www.sci-corp.com

Constant Returns. Figure 21.10*a* depicts a situation in which there's no economic advantage to centralization of manufacturing operations, because a large plant is no more efficient

IN THE NEWS

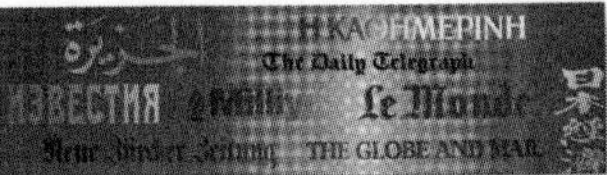

Funeral Giant Moves In on Small Rivals

Life's two certainties are death and taxes. Some day, it could be just as certain that Service Corp. International will handle your funeral.

The Houston-based company will handle one in 10 funeral services in the USA this year, or about 230,000. In just 32 years, the company has grown from a single funeral home into the world's biggest death-services provider with 2,631 funeral homes, 250 cemeteries and 137 crematoria in North America, Europe and Australia. . . .

SCI's sheer size provides big advantages over competitors. SCI is able to get cheaper prices on caskets and other products from suppliers.

Its funeral homes clustered in the same markets cut costs by sharing vehicles, personnel, services and supplies. That helps give SCI a profit of 31 cents on every dollar it takes in for a typical funeral, vs. 12 cents for the industry as a whole, SCI says.

Funeral directors "don't want to think of (death) as big business," says Betty Murray of the National Foundation of Funeral Directors. "But we're in the era of acquisitions and consolidations."

—Ron Trujillo

Source: *USA Today,* October 31, 1995. USA TODAY Copyright 1995. Reprinted with permission. www.usatoday.com

Analysis: As the size of a firm increases, it may be able to reduce the costs of doing business. Economies of scale can give a large firm a competitive advantage over smaller firms.

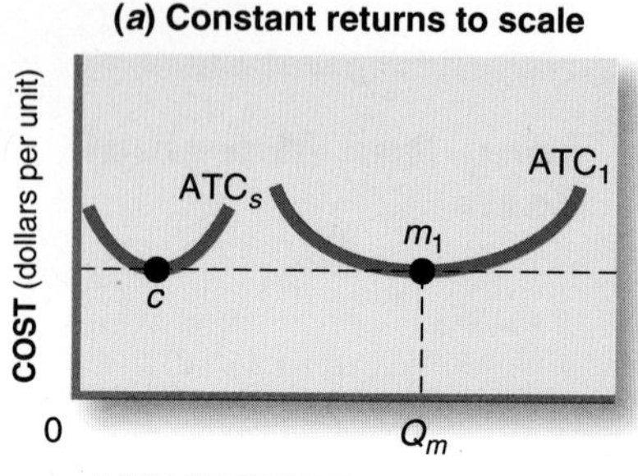

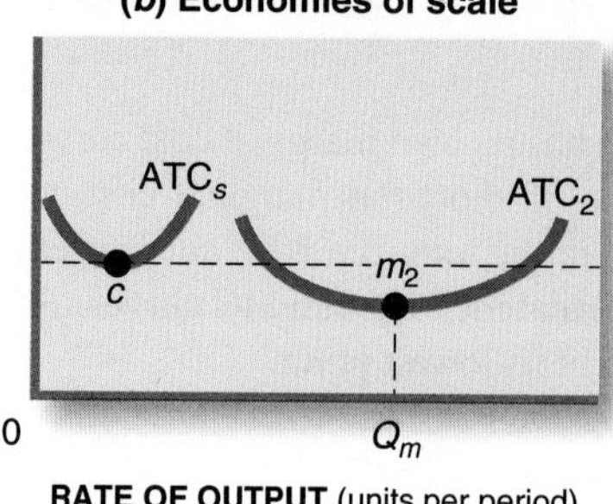

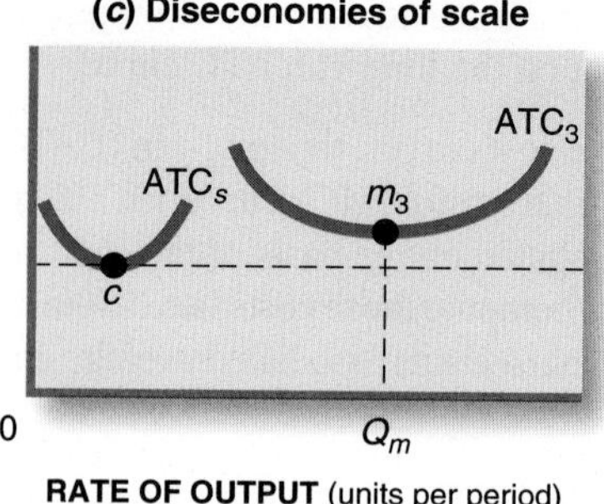

FIGURE 21.10
Economies of Scale

A lot of output (Q_m) can be produced from one large plant or many small ones. Here we contrast the average total costs associated with one small plant (ATC_s) and three large plants (ATC_1, ATC_2, and ATC_3). If a large plant attains the same *minimum* average costs (point m_1 in part *a*) as a smaller plant (point *c*), there's no advantage to large size (scale). Many small plants can produce the same output just as cheaply. However, either economies (part *b*) or diseconomies (part *c*) of scale may exist.

than a lot of small plants. The critical focus here is on the *minimum* average costs attainable for a given rate of output. Note that the lowest point on the smaller plant's ATC curve (point *c*) is no higher or lower than the lowest point on the larger firm's ATC curve (point m_1). Hence, it would be just as cheap to produce the quantity Q_m from a multitude of small plants as it would be to produce Q_m from one large plant. Thus increasing the size (or *scale*) of individual plants won't reduce minimum average costs: This is a situation of **constant returns to scale.**

constant returns to scale: Increases in plant size do not affect minimum average cost: minimum per-unit costs are identical for small plants and large plants.

Economies of Scale. Figure 21.10*b* illustrates the situation in which a larger plant can attain a lower minimum average cost than a smaller plant. That is, economies of scale (or *increasing returns to scale*) exist. This is evident from the fact that the larger firm's ATC curve falls *below* the dashed line in the graph (m_2 is less than *c*). The greater efficiency of the large factory might come from any of several sources. This is the situation of the funeral home depicted in the News feature. By centralizing core funeral services, Services Corp. International was able to reduce average costs per funeral. Larger organizations may also gain a cost advantage through specialization, by having each worker become expert in a particular skill. By contrast, a smaller establishment might have to use the same individual(s) to perform several functions, thereby reducing productivity at each task. Also, some kinds of machinery may be economical only if they're used to produce massive volumes, an opportunity only very large factories have. Finally, a large plant might acquire a persistent cost advantage through the process of learning by doing. That is, its longer experience and greater volume of output may translate into improved organization and efficiency.

Diseconomies of Scale. Even though large plants may be able to achieve greater efficiencies than smaller plants, there's no assurance that they actually will. In fact, increasing the size (scale) of a plant may actually *reduce* operating efficiency, as depicted in Figure 21.10*c*. Workers may feel alienated in a plant of massive proportions and feel little commitment to productivity. Creativity may be stifled by rigid corporate structures and off-site management. A large plant may also foster a sense of anonymity that induces workers to underperform. When these things happen, *diseconomies of scale* result. Microsoft tries to avoid such diseconomies of scale by creating autonomous cells of no more than 35 employees ("small plants") within its larger corporate structure.

In evaluating long-run options, then, we must be careful to recognize that ***efficiency and size don't necessarily go hand in hand.*** Some firms and industries may be subject to economies of scale, but others may not. Bigger isn't always better.

THE ECONOMY TOMORROW

GLOBAL COMPETITIVENESS

From 1900 to 1970, the United States regularly exported more goods and services than it imported. Since then, America has had a trade deficit nearly every year. In 2006, U.S. imports exceeded exports by more than $700 billion. To many people, such trade deficits are a symptom that the United States can no longer compete effectively in world markets.

Global competitiveness ultimately depends on the costs of production. If international competitors can produce goods more cheaply, they'll be able to undersell U.S. goods in global markets.

Cheap Foreign Labor? Cheap labor keeps costs down in many countries. The average wage in Mexico, for example, ranges from $2 to $3 an hour, compared to over $16 an hour in the United States. China's manufacturing workers make only $1 to $2 an hour. Low wages are *not,* however, a reliable measure of global competitiveness. To compete in global markets, one must produce more *output* for a given quantity of *inputs.* In other words, labor is "cheap" only if it produces a lot of output in return for the wages paid.

A worker's contribution to output is measured by *marginal physical product (MPP).* What we saw in this chapter was that ***a worker's productivity (MPP) depends on the quantity and quality of other resources in the production process.*** In this regard, U.S. workers have a tremendous advantage: They work with vast quantities of capital and state-of-the-art technology. They also come to the workplace with more education. Their high wages reflect this greater productivity.

Unit Labor Costs. A true measure of global competitiveness must take into account both factor costs (e.g., wages) and productivity. One such measure is **unit labor costs,** which indicates the labor cost of producing one unit of output. It's computed as

unit labor cost: Hourly wage rate divided by output per labor-hour.

$$\text{Unit labor cost} = \frac{\text{wage rate}}{\text{MPP}}$$

Suppose the MPP of a U.S. worker is 7 units per hour and the wage is $14 an hour. The unit labor cost would be

$$\begin{matrix}\text{Unit labor cost}\\ \text{(United States)}\end{matrix} = \frac{\$14/\text{hour}}{7\text{ units/hour}} = \begin{matrix}\$2/\text{unit}\\ \text{of output}\end{matrix}$$

By contrast, assume the average worker in Mexico has an MPP of 1 unit per hour and a wage of $3 an hour. In this case, the unit labor cost would be

$$\begin{matrix}\text{Unit labor cost}\\ \text{(Mexico)}\end{matrix} = \frac{\$3}{1} = \begin{matrix}\$3/\text{unit}\\ \text{of output}\end{matrix}$$

According to these hypothetical examples, "cheap" Mexican labor is no bargain. Mexican labor is actually *more* costly in production, despite the lower wage rate.

Productivity Advance. What these calculations illustrate is how important productivity is for global competitiveness. If we want the United States to stay competitive in global markets, U.S. productivity must increase as fast as that in other nations.

The production function introduced in this chapter helps illustrate the essence of global competitiveness in the economy tomorrow. Until now, we've regarded a firm's production function as a technological fact of life—the *best* we could do, given our state of technological and managerial knowledge. In the real world, however, the best is always getting better. Science and technology are continuously advancing. So is our knowledge of how to organize and manage our resources. These advances keep *shifting* production functions upward: More can be produced with any given quantity of inputs. In the process, the costs of production shift downward, as illustrated in Figure 21.11 by the downward shifts of the

webnote

For current data on unit labor costs and underlying wage and productivity trends, visit the U.S. Bureau of Labor Statistics at www.bls.gov

FIGURE 21.11
Improvements in Productivity Reduce Costs

Advances in technological or managerial knowledge increase our productive capability. This is reflected in upward shifts of the production function (part *a*) and downward shifts of production cost curves (part *b*).

(*a*) When the production function shifts up . . .

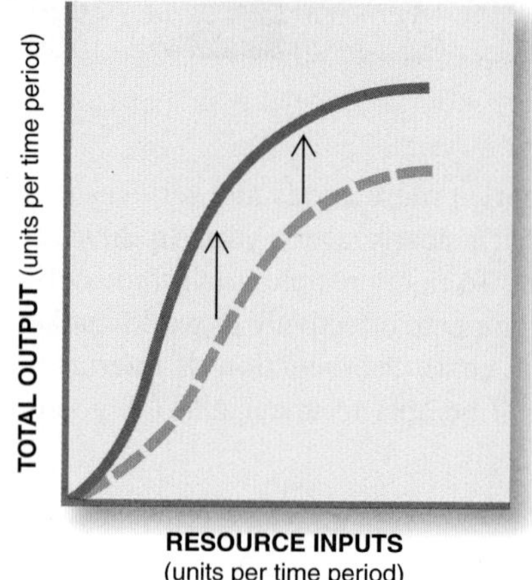

(*b*) Cost curves shift down

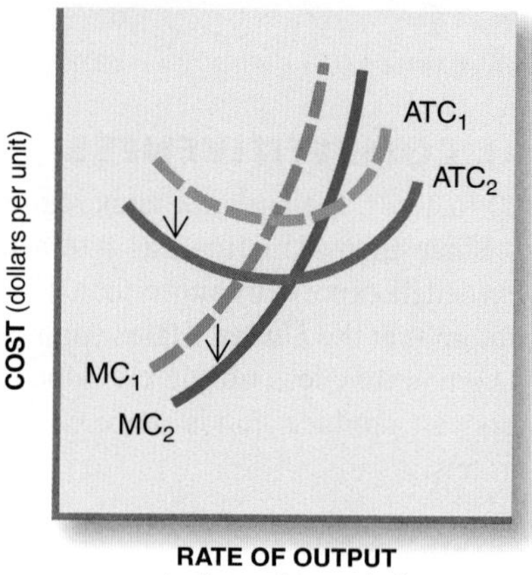

MC and ATC curves. These downward shifts imply that we can get more of the goods and services we desire with available resources. We can also compete more effectively in global markets.

Internet-driven gains. The Internet has been an important source of productivity gains in the last 10 years. Although the Internet originated over 30 years ago, its commercial potential emerged with the creation of the World Wide Web around 1990. As recently as 1995 there were only 10,000 Web sites. Now there are over 100 *million* sites. This vastly expanded spectrum of information has helped businesses cut costs in many ways. The cost of gathering information about markets and inputs has been reduced. With the reach of the Internet, firms can engage in greater specialization. Firms can also manage their inventories and supply chains much more efficiently. Transaction and communications costs are reduced as well. All of these productivity improvements are cutting U.S. production costs by $100–250 billion a

WORLD VIEW

United States Gains Cost Advantage

Productivity is increasing faster than wages in U.S. manufacturing, giving the U.S. an edge in the race for global competitiveness. In the last 10 years, the cost of producing a widget has fallen by nearly 10 percent in the U.S., but risen by nearly 17 percent in Japan. Other contenders:

Country	Change in Unit Labor Costs, 1995–2005
Italy	31.9
Denmark	24.2
Japan	16.8
United Kingdom	16.5
Canada	1.6
Korea	−9.1
United States	**−9.8**
France	−11.8
Taiwan	−26.7

Source: U.S. Bureau of Labor Statistics. www.bls.gov

Analysis: Global competitiveness depends on unit labor costs. U.S. unit labor costs have declined in the last decade or so, increasing America's competitiveness in world markets.

year. These cost savings helped U.S. businesses *reduce* unit labor costs by 0.4 percent a year in the 1990s. As the accompanying World View confirms, those gains widened the United States' lead in the ongoing race for global competitiveness. To maintain that leading position in the economy tomorrow, U.S. productivity must continue to advance at a brisk pace.

SUMMARY

- A production function indicates the maximum amount of output that can be produced with different combinations of inputs. It's a technological relationship and changes (shifts) when new technology or management techniques are discovered. LO1
- In the short run, some inputs (e.g., land and capital) are fixed in quantity. Increases in (short-run) output result from more use of variable inputs (e.g., labor). LO1
- The contribution of a variable input to total output is measured by its marginal physical product (MPP). This is the amount by which *total* output increases when one more unit of the input is employed. LO1
- The MPP of a factor tends to decline as more of it is used in a given production facility. Diminishing marginal returns result from crowding more of a variable input (e.g., labor) into a production process, reducing the amount of fixed inputs *per unit* of variable input. LO2
- Marginal cost is the increase in total cost that results when output is increased by one unit. Marginal cost increases whenever marginal physical product diminishes. LO2
- Not all costs go up when the rate of output is increased. Fixed costs such as space and equipment leases don't vary with the rate of output. Only variable costs such as labor and material go up when output is increased. LO3
- Average total cost (ATC) equals total cost divided by the quantity of output produced. ATC declines whenever marginal cost (MC) is less than average cost and rises when MC exceeds it. The MC and ATC curves intersect at minimum ATC (the bottom of the U). That intersection represents least-cost production. LO3
- The economic costs of production include the value of *all* resources used. Accounting costs typically include only those dollar costs actually paid (explicit costs). LO3
- In the long run there are no fixed costs; the size (scale) of production can be varied. The long-run ATC curve indicates the lowest cost of producing output with facilities of appropriate size. LO3
- Economies of scale refer to reductions in *minimum* average cost attained with larger plant size (scale). If minimum ATC rises with plant size, diseconomies of scale exist. LO3
- Global competitiveness and domestic living standards depend on productivity advances. Improvements in productivity shift production functions up and push cost curves down. LO1

Key Terms

factors of production
production function
productivity
efficiency
opportunity cost
short run
marginal physical product (MPP)
law of diminishing returns
profit
marginal cost (MC)
total cost
fixed costs
variable costs
average total cost (ATC)
average fixed cost (AFC)
average variable cost (AVC)
explicit cost
implicit cost
economic cost
long run
economies of scale
constant returns to scale
unit labor cost

Questions for Discussion

1. What are the production costs of your economics class? What are the fixed costs? The variable costs? What's the marginal cost of enrolling more students? LO1
2. Suppose all your friends offered to help wash your car. Would marginal physical product decline as more friends helped? Why or why not? LO2
3. How many cars *can* GM produce in China? (See World View, page 437.) How many cars will GM *want* to produce? LO1
4. Owner/operators of small gas stations rarely pay themselves an hourly wage. How does this practice affect the economic cost of dispensing gasoline? LO3
5. Corporate funeral giants have replaced small family-run funeral homes in many areas, in large part because of the lower costs they achieve. (See News, page 439.) What kind of economies of scale exist in the funeral business? Why doesn't someone build one colossal funeral home and drive costs down further? LO3

6. Are colleges subject to economies of scale or diseconomies? LO3
7. Why don't more U.S. firms move to Mexico to take advantage of low wages there? Would an *identical* plant in Mexico be as productive as its U.S. counterpart? LO1
8. How would your productivity in completing course work be measured? Has your productivity changed since you began college? What caused the productivity changes? How could you increase productivity further? LO1
9. What is the economic cost of doing this homework? LO1

problems The Student Problem Set at the back of this book contains numerical and graphing problems for this chapter.

web activities to accompany this chapter can be found on the Online Learning Center: **http://www.mhhe.com/economics/schiller11e**

PART 9

Market Structure

Market demand curves tell us what products consumers want. And production functions tell us how much it will cost producers to supply those products. What we don't yet know is how many products will actually be supplied—or at what prices. These are *behavioral decisions,* not technological facts. Chapters 22 through 26 examine these behavioral decisions. As we'll see, the *structure* of a market—the number and size of firms in it—has a profound effect on the supply of goods and services—the quantity, quality, and price of specific goods.

The Competitive Firm

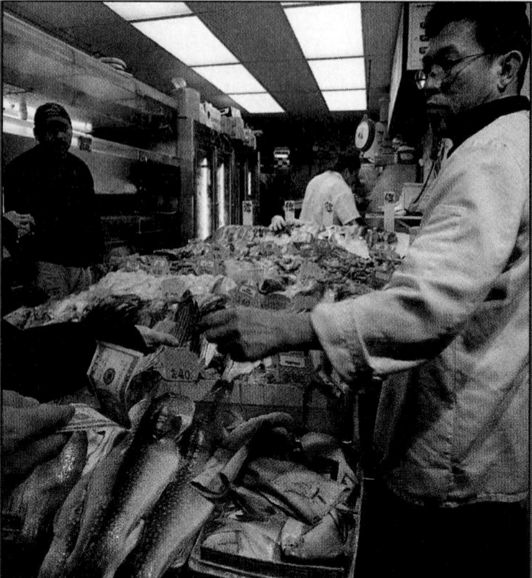

LEARNING OBJECTIVES

After reading this chapter, you should know:

LO1. What a perfectly competitive firm is.

LO2. How a competitive firm maximizes profit.

LO3. How a competitive firm's supply curve is derived.

Apple computer would love to raise the price of downloading music from its iTunes store. It isn't likely to do so, however, because too many other firms also offer digital downloads. If Apple raises its prices, customers might sign up with another company.

Your campus bookstore may be in a better position to raise prices. On most college campuses there's only one bookstore. If the campus store increases the price of books or supplies, most of its customers (you) will have little choice but to pay the higher tab.

As we discover in this and the next few chapters, the degree of competition in product markets is a major determinant of product prices, quality, and availability. Although all firms are in business to make a profit, their profit opportunities are limited by the amount of competition they face.

This chapter begins an examination of how businesses make price and production decisions. We first explore the nature of profits and how they're computed. We then observe how one type of firm—a perfectly competitive one—can *maximize* its profits by selecting the right rate of output. The following questions are at the center of this discussion:

- **What are *profits?***
- **What are the unique characteristics of competitive firms?**
- **How much output will a competitive firm produce?**

The answers to these questions will shed more light on how the *supply* of goods and services is determined in a market economy.

THE PROFIT MOTIVE

The basic incentive for producing goods and services is the expectation of profit. *Owning* plant and equipment isn't enough. To generate a current flow of income, one must *use* that plant and equipment to produce and sell goods.

profit: The difference between total revenue and total cost.

Profit is the difference between a firm's sales revenues and its total costs. It's the residual that the owners of a business receive. That profit residual may flow to the sole owner of a corner grocery store, or to the group of stockholders who collectively own a large corporation. In either case, it's the quest for profit that motivates people to own and operate a business (or a piece thereof).

Other Motivations

Profit isn't the only thing that motivates producers. Like the rest of us, producers also worry about social status and crave recognition. People who need to feel important, to control others, or to demonstrate achievement are likely candidates for running a business. Many small businesses are maintained by people who gave up 40-hour weeks, $50,000 incomes, and a sense of alienation in exchange for 80-hour weeks, $45,000 incomes, and a sense of identity and control.

In large corporations, the profit motive may lie even deeper below the surface. Stockholders of large corporations rarely visit corporate headquarters. The people who manage the corporation's day-to-day business may have little or no stock in the company. Such nonowner-managers may be more interested in their own jobs, salaries, and self-preservation than in the profits that accrue to the stockholding owners. If profits suffer, however, the corporation may start looking for new managers. The accompanying cartoon notwithstanding, the "bottom line" for virtually all businesses is the level of profits.

Is the Profit Motive Bad?

If it weren't possible to make a profit, few people would choose to supply goods and services. Yet the general public remains suspicious of the profit motive. As the News on the next page indicates, one out of four people thinks the profit motive is bad. An even higher percentage believes the profit motive results in *inferior* products at inflated prices.

As we'll see, the profit motive *can* induce business firms to pollute the environment, restrict competition, or maintain unsafe working conditions. However, ***the profit motive also encourages businesses to produce the goods and services consumers desire, at prices they're willing to pay.*** The profit motive, in fact, moves the "invisible hand" that Adam Smith said orchestrates market outcomes.

"You know what I think, folks? Improving technology isn't important. Increased profits aren't important. What's important is to be warm, decent human beings."

Analysis: The principal motivation for producing goods and services is to earn a profit. Although other goals may seem desirable, businesses that fail to earn a profit won't survive.

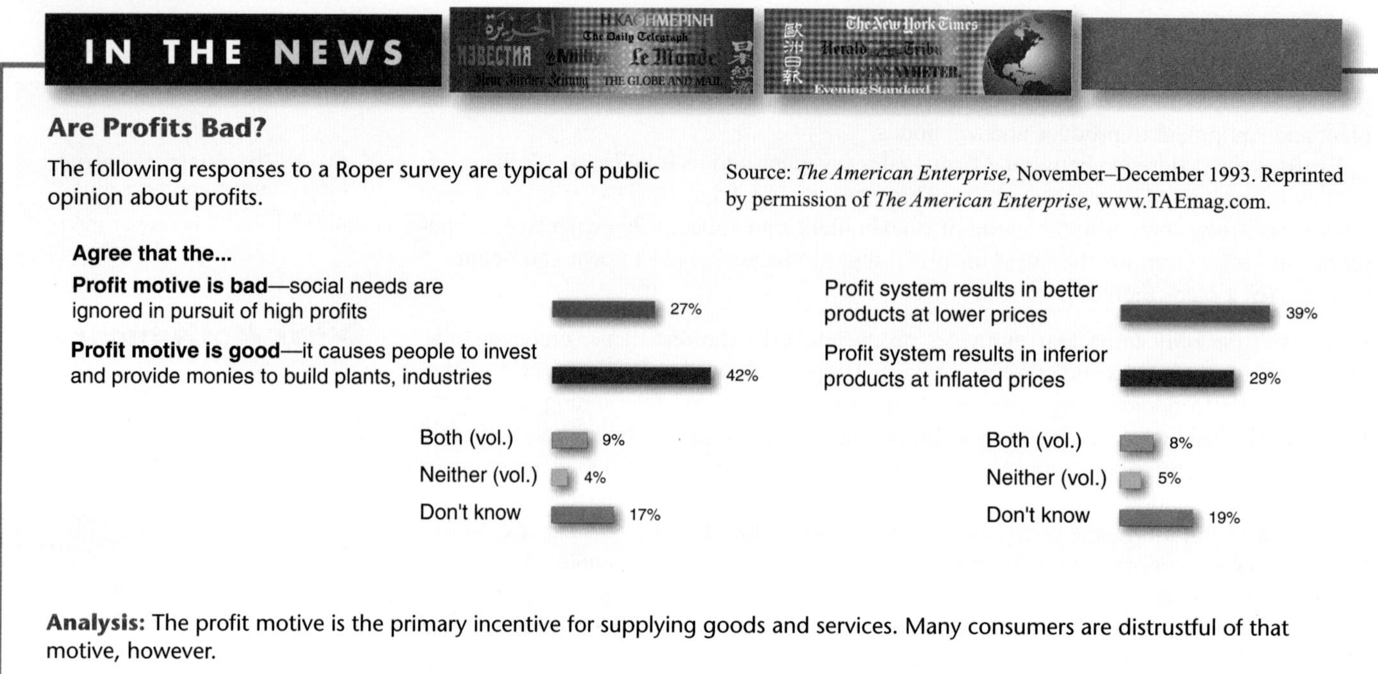

Are Profits Bad?

The following responses to a Roper survey are typical of public opinion about profits.

Source: *The American Enterprise,* November–December 1993. Reprinted by permission of *The American Enterprise,* www.TAEmag.com.

Analysis: The profit motive is the primary incentive for supplying goods and services. Many consumers are distrustful of that motive, however.

ECONOMIC VS. ACCOUNTING PROFITS

Although profits might be a necessary inducement for producers, most consumers feel that profits are too high. And that may be so in many cases. But most consumers have no idea how much profit U.S. businesses actually make. Public *perceptions* of profit are seven or eight times higher than actual profits. The typical consumer believes that 35 cents of every sales dollar goes to profits. In reality, average profit per sales dollar is closer to 5 cents.

Faulty perceptions of profits aren't confined to the general public. As surprising as it might seem, most businesses also measure their profits incorrectly.

Economic Profits

economic cost: The value of all resources used to produce a good or service; opportunity cost.

explicit costs: A payment made for the use of a resource.

implicit cost: The value of resources used, even when no direct payment is made.

economic profit: The difference between total revenues and total economic costs.

Everyone agrees that profit represents the difference between total revenues and total costs. Where people part ways is over the decision of what to include in total costs. Recall from Chapter 21 how economists compute costs. **Economic cost** refers to the value of *all* resources used in production, whether or not they receive an explicit payment. By contrast, most businesses count only **explicit costs**—that is, those they actually write checks for. They typically don't take into account the **implicit costs** of the labor or land and buildings they might own. As a result, they understate costs.

If businesses (and their accountants) understate true costs, they'll overstate true profits. Part of the accounting "profit" will really be compensation to unpaid land, labor, or capital used in the production process. ***Whenever economic costs exceed explicit costs, observed (accounting) profits will exceed true (economic) profits.*** Indeed, what appears to be an accounting profit may actually disguise an economic loss, as illustrated by Mr. Fujishige's strawberry farm once located right next to Disneyland (see News). To determine the **economic profit** of a business, we must subtract all implicit factor costs from observed accounting profits:

$$\text{Economic profit} = \text{total revenue} - \text{total economic cost}$$

$$= \text{accounting profit} - \text{implicit costs}$$

IN THE NEWS

Strawberry Fields Forever?

ANAHEIM, CALIFORNIA—Hiroshi Fujishige is a successful strawberry farmer. For over 40 years he has been earning a profit growing and selling strawberries and other produce from his 58-acre farm. Mr. Fujishige could make even more money if he stopped growing strawberries. His 58-acre strawberry patch is located across the street from Disneyland. The people from Disney have offered him $32 million just to *lease* the farm; developers have offered as much as $2 million per acre to *buy* the land. But Mr. Fujishige, who lives in a tiny house on the farm he bought 45 years ago (for $2500!) isn't selling. "I'm a farmer, and I've been farming since I got out of high school in 1941," he says. As long as he can make a profit from strawberries, he says, he'll keep growing them.

Source: *Washington Post,* March 9, 1994. © **1994, *The Washington Post.* Excerpted with permission.** www.washingtonpost.com

Analysis: Mr. Fujishige thought he was making a profit because he miscalculated costs. His *implicit* costs were enormous. When Mr. Fujishige died in 1998 his family sold the strawberry farm to Disneyland for its new California Adventure theme park.

Suppose, for example, that Table 22.1 accurately summarizes the revenues and costs associated with a local drugstore. Monthly sales revenues amount to $27,000. Explicit costs paid by the owner-manager include the cost of merchandise bought from producers for resale to consumers ($17,000), wages to the employees of the drugstore, rent and utilities paid to the landlord, and local sales and business taxes. When all these explicit costs are subtracted from total revenue, we're left with an *accounting profit* of $6,000 per month.

The owner-manager of the drugstore may be quite pleased with an accounting profit of $6,000 per month. He's working hard for this income, however. To keep his store running, the owner-manager is working 10 hours per day, 7 days a week. This adds up to 300 hours of labor per month. Were he to work this hard for someone else, his labor would be compensated explicitly—with a paycheck. Although he doesn't choose to pay himself this way, his labor still represents a real resource cost. To compute *economic* profit, we must subtract this implicit cost from the drugstore's accounting profits. Suppose the owner could earn $10 per hour in the best alternative job. Multiplying this wage rate ($10) by the number of hours he works in the drugstore (300), we see that the implicit cost of his labor is $3,000 per month.

The owner has also used his savings to purchase inventory for the store. He purchased the goods on his shelves for $120,000. If he had invested his savings in some other business, he could have earned a return of 10 percent per year. This forgone return represents a real cost. In this case, the implicit return (opportunity cost) on his capital investment amounts to $12,000 per year (10 percent × $120,000), or $1,000 per month.

TABLE 22.1
The Computation of Economic Profit

To calculate economic profit, we must take account of *all* costs of production. The economic costs of production include the implicit (opportunity) costs of the labor and capital a producer contributes to the production process. The accounting profits of a business take into account only explicit costs paid by the owner. Reported (accounting) profits will exceed economic profits whenever implicit costs are ignored.

Total (gross) revenues per month	$27,000
less explicit costs:	
Cost of merchandise sold	$17,000
Wages to cashier, stock, and delivery help	2,500
Rent and utilities	800
Taxes	700
Total explicit costs	$21,000
Accounting profit (revenue minus explicit costs)	$ 6,000
less implicit costs:	
Wages of owner-manager, 300 hours @ $10 per hour	$ 3,000
Return on inventory investment, 10% per year on $120,000	1,000
Total implicit costs	$ 4,000
Economic profit (revenue minus *all* costs)	$ 2,000

To calculate the *economic* profit this drugstore generates, we count both explicit and implicit costs. Hence, we must subtract all implicit factor payments (costs) from reported profits. The residual in this case amounts to $2,000 per month. That's the drugstore's *economic* profit.

Note that when we compute the drugstore's economic profit, we deduct the opportunity cost of the owner's capital. Specifically, we assumed that his funds would have reaped a 10 percent return somewhere else. In effect, we've assumed that a "normal" rate of return is 10 percent. This **normal profit** (the opportunity cost of capital) is an economic cost. Rather than investing in a drugstore, the owner could have earned a 10 percent return on his funds by investing in a fast-food franchise, a music store, a steel plant, or some other production activity. By choosing to invest in a drugstore instead, the owner was seeking a *higher* return on his funds—more than he could have obtained elsewhere. In other words, ***economic profits represent something over and above "normal profits."***

normal profit: The opportunity cost of capital; zero economic profit.

Our treatment of "normal" returns as an economic cost leads to a startling conclusion: On average, economic profits are zero. Only firms that reap *above-average* returns can claim economic profits. This seemingly strange perspective on profits emphasizes the opportunity costs of all economic activities. ***A productive activity reaps an economic profit only if it earns more than its opportunity cost.***

Entrepreneurship

Naturally, everyone in business wants to earn an economic profit. But relatively few people can stay ahead of the pack. To earn economic profits, a business must see opportunities that others have missed, discover new products, find new and better methods of production, or take above-average risks. In fact, economic profits are often regarded as a reward to entrepreneurship, the ability and willingness to take risks, to organize factors of production, and to produce something society desires.

Consider the local drugstore again. People in the neighborhood clearly want such a drugstore, as evidenced by its substantial sales revenue. But why should anyone go to the trouble and risk of starting and maintaining one? We noted that the owner-manager *could* earn $3,000 in wages by accepting a regular job plus $1,000 per month in returns on capital by investing in an "average" business. Why should he take on the added responsibilities and risk of owning and operating his own drugstore?

The inducement to take on the added responsibilities of owning and operating a business is the potential for economic profit, the extra income over and above normal factor payments. In the case of the drugstore owner, this extra income is the economic profit of $2,000 (Table 22.1). In the absence of such additional compensation, few people would want to make the extra effort required.

Risk

Don't forget, however, that the *potential* for profit is not a *guarantee* of profit. Quite the contrary. Substantial risks are attached to starting and operating a business. Tens of thousands of businesses fail every year, and still more suffer economic losses. From this perspective, profit also represents compensation for the risks incurred in owning or operating a business.

MARKET STRUCTURE

Not all businesses have an equal opportunity to earn an economic profit. The opportunity for profit may be limited by the *structure* of the industry in which the firm is engaged. One of the reasons Microsoft is such a profitable company is that it has long held a **monopoly** on computer operating systems. As the supplier of virtually all operating systems, Microsoft can raise software prices without losing many customers. T-shirt shops, by contrast, have to worry about all the other stores that sell similar products in the area (see News). Faced with so much competition, the owner of a T-shirt shop doesn't have the power to raise prices, or accumulate economic profits.

monopoly: A firm that produces the entire market supply of a particular good or service.

IN THE NEWS

T-Shirt Shop Owner's Lament: Too Many T-Shirt Shops

The small Texas beach resort of South Padre Island boasts white sand, blue skies (much of the time), the buoyant waters of the Gulf of Mexico and, at last count, more than 40 T-shirt shops.

And that's a problem for Shy Oogav, who owns one of those shops. "Every day you have to compete with other shops," he says. "And if you invent something new, they will copy you."

Padre Island illustrates a common condition in the T-shirt industry—unbridled, ill-advised growth. Many people believe T-shirts are the ticket to a permanent vacation—far too many people. "In the past years, everything that closed opened up again as a T-shirt shop," says Maria C. Hall, executive director of the South Padre Island Chamber of Commerce.

Mr. Oogav, a 29-year-old immigrant from Israel, came to South Padre Island on vacation six years ago, thought he had found paradise and stayed on. He subsequently got a job with one of the town's T-shirt shops, which then numbered fewer than a dozen. Now that he owns his own shop, and the competition has quadrupled, his paradise is lost. "I don't sleep at night," he says, morosely.

—Mark Pawlosky

Analysis: The ability to earn a profit depends on how many other firms offer similar products. A perfectly competitive firm, facing numerous rivals, has difficulty maintaining prices or profits.

Figure 22.1 illustrates various **market structures.** At one extreme is the monopoly structure in which only one firm produces the entire supply of the good. At the other extreme is **perfect competition.** In perfect competition a great many firms supply the same good.

market structure: The number and relative size of firms in an industry.

perfect competition: A market in which no buyer or seller has market power.

There are relatively few monopolies or perfectly competitive firms in the real world. Most of the 20 million businesses in the United States fall between these extremes. They're more accurately characterized by gradations of *imperfect* competition—markets in which competition exists, but individual firms still retain some discretionary power over prices. In a *duopoly,* two firms supply the entire market. In an *oligopoly,* like credit-card services, a handful of firms (Visa, MasterCard, American Express) dominate. In *monopolistic competition,* like fast-food restaurants, there are enough firms to ensure some competition, but not so many as to preclude some limited monopoly-type power. We examine all these market structures in later chapters, after we establish the nature of perfect competition.

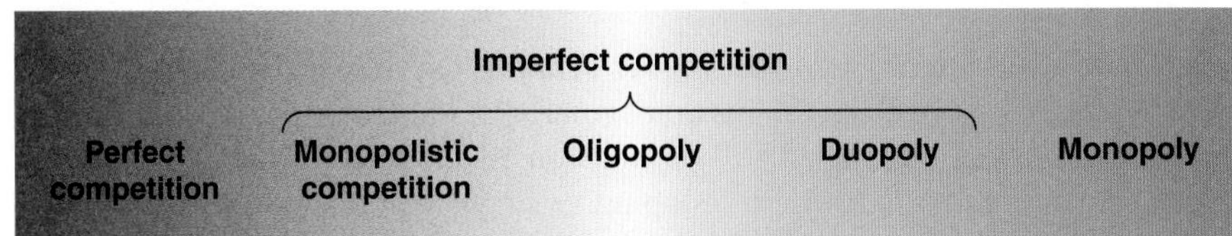

FIGURE 22.1
Market Structures

The number and relative size of firms producing a good vary across industries. Market structures range from perfect competition (a great many firms producing the same good) to monopoly (only one firm). Most real-world firms are along the continuum of *imperfect* competition. Included in that range are duopoly (two firms), oligopoly (a few firms), and monopolistic competition (many firms).

THE NATURE OF PERFECT COMPETITION

Structure

A perfectly competitive industry has several distinguishing characteristics, including

- ***Many firms***—Lots of firms are competing for consumer purchases.
- ***Identical products***—The products of the different firms are identical, or nearly so.
- ***Low-entry barriers***—It's relatively easy to get into the business.

The T-shirt business has all these traits, which is why storeowners have a hard time maintaining profits (see previous News).

Price Takers

Because they always have to contend with a lot of competition, T-shirt shops can't increase profits by raising T-shirt prices. More than 1 billion T-shirts are sold in the United States each year, by tens of thousands of retail outlets. In such a competitive industry the many individual firms that make up the industry are all *price takers:* They take the price the market sets. A competitive firm can sell all its output at the prevailing market price. If it boosts its price above that level, consumers will shop elsewhere. In this sense, a perfectly competitive firm has no **market power**—no ability to control the market price for the good it sells.

market power: The ability to alter the market price of a good or service.

At first glance, it might appear that all firms have market power. After all, who's to stop a T-shirt shop from raising prices? The important concept here, however, is *market* price, that is, the price at which goods are actually sold. If one shop raises its price to \$15 and 40 other shops sell the same T-shirts for \$10, it won't sell many shirts, and maybe none at all.

You may confront the same problem if you try to sell this book at the end of the semester. You might want to resell this textbook for \$60. But you'll discover that the bookstore won't buy it at that price. With many other students offering to sell their books, the bookstore knows it doesn't have to pay the \$60 you're asking. Because you don't have any market power, you have to accept the going price if you want to sell this book.

The same kind of powerlessness is characteristic of the small wheat farmer. Like any producer, the lone wheat farmer can increase or reduce his rate of output by making alternative production decisions. But his decision won't affect the market price of wheat.

Even the largest U.S. wheat farmers can't change the market price of wheat. The largest wheat farm produces nearly 100,000 bushels of wheat per year. But *2 billion* bushels of wheat are brought to market every year, so another 100,000 bushels simply won't be noticed. In other words, ***the output of the lone farmer is so small relative to the market supply that it has no significant effect on the total quantity or price in the market.***

A distinguishing characteristic of *powerless* firms is that, individually, they can sell all the output they produce at the prevailing market price. We call all such producers **competitive firms;** they have no independent influence on market prices. ***A perfectly competitive firm is one whose output is so small in relation to market volume that its output decisions have no perceptible impact on price.***

competitive firm: A firm without market power, with no ability to alter the market price of the goods it produces.

Market Demand Curves vs. Firm Demand Curves

It's important to distinguish between the market demand curve and the demand curve confronting a particular firm. T-shirt shops don't contradict the law of demand. The quantity of T-shirts purchased in the market still depends on T-shirt prices. That is, the *market* demand curve for T-shirts is still downward-sloping. A single T-shirt shop faces a *horizontal* demand curve only because its share of the market is so small that changes in its output don't disturb market equilibrium.

Collectively, though, individual firms do count. If all 40 of the T-shirt shops on South Padre Island (see previous News) were to increase shirt production at the same time, the market equilibrium would be disturbed. That is, a competitive market composed of individually powerless producers still sees a lot of action. The power here resides in the collective action of all the producers, however, not in the individual action of any one. Were T-shirt production to increase so abruptly, the shirts could be sold only at lower prices, in accordance with the downward-sloping nature of the *market* demand curve.

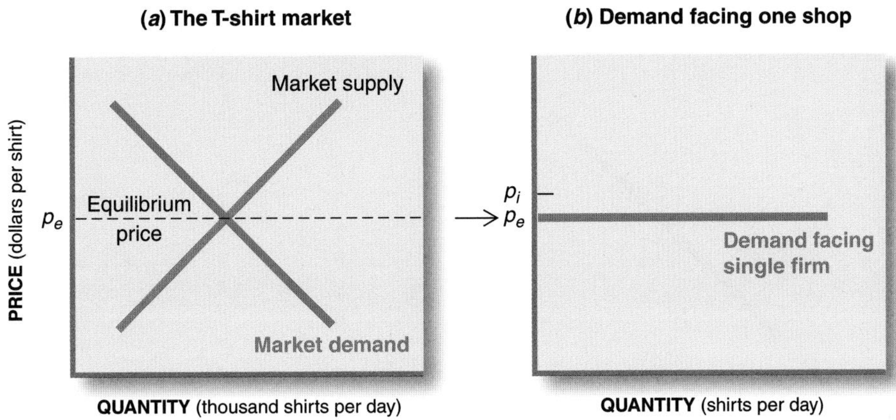

FIGURE 22.2
Market vs. Firm Demand

Consumer demand for any product is downward-sloping. The equilibrium price (p_e) of T-shirts is established by the intersection of *market* demand and *market* supply. This market-established price is the only one at which an individual shop can sell T-shirts. If the shop owner asks a higher price (e.g., p_i), no one will buy his shirts, since they can buy identical T-shirts from other shops at p_e. But he can sell all his shirts at the market-set equilibrium price. The shop owner thus confronts a horizontal demand curve for his own output. (Notice the difference in market and individual shop quantities on the horizontal axes of the two graphs.)

Figure 22.2 illustrates the distinction between the actions of a single producer and those of the market. Notice that

- ***The market demand curve for a product is always downward-sloping (law of demand).***
- ***The demand curve confronting a perfectly competitive firm is horizontal.***

THE PRODUCTION DECISION

production decision: The selection of the short-run rate of output (with existing plant and equipment).

Since a competitive firm can sell all its output at the market price, it has only one decision to make: how much to produce. Choosing a rate of output is a firm's **production decision.** Should it produce all the output it can? Or should it produce at less than capacity?

Output and Revenues

total revenue: The price of a product multiplied by the quantity sold in a given time period: $p \times q$.

In searching for the most desirable rate of output, focus on the distinction between total *revenue* and total *profit.* **Total revenue** is the price of the good multiplied by the quantity sold:

$$\text{Total revenue} = \text{price} \times \text{quantity}$$

Since a competitive firm can sell all its output at the market price (p_e), total revenue is a simple multiple of p_e. The total revenue of a T-shirt shop, for example, is the price of shirts (p_e) multiplied by the quantity sold. Figure 22.3 shows the total revenue curve that results from this multiplication. Note that ***the total revenue curve of a perfectly competitive firm is an upward-sloping straight line, with a slope equal to p_e.***

If a competitive firm wanted to maximize its total *revenue,* its production decision would be simple: It would always produce at capacity. Life isn't that simple, however; ***the firm's goal is to maximize profits, not revenues.***

Output and Costs

short run: The period in which the quantity (and quality) of some inputs can't be changed.

To maximize profits, a firm must consider how increased production will affect *costs* as well as *revenues.* How do costs vary with the rate of output?

As we observed in Chapter 21, producers are saddled with certain costs in the **short run.** A T-shirt shop has to pay the rent every month no matter how few shirts it sells. The Low-Rider Jeans Corporation in Chapter 21 had to pay the rent on its factory and lease payments

FIGURE 22.3
Total Revenue

Because a competitive firm can sell all its output at the prevailing price, its total revenue curve is linear. In this case, the market (equilibrium) price of T-shirts is assumed to be $8. Hence, a shop's total revenue is equal to $8 multiplied by quantity sold.

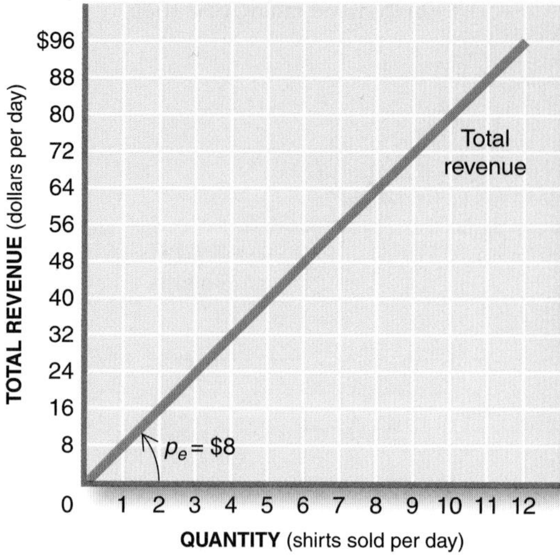

Price (per shirt)	×	Quantity (shirts per day)	=	Total revenue
$8		1		$ 8
8		2		16
8		3		24
8		4		32
8		5		40
8		6		48
8		7		56
8		8		64
8		9		72

fixed costs: Costs of production that don't change when the rate of output is altered, e.g., the cost of basic plant and equipment.

variable costs: Costs of production that change when the rate of output is altered, e.g., labor and material costs.

marginal cost (MC): The increase in total costs associated with a one-unit increase in production.

on its sewing machine. These **fixed costs** are incurred even if no output is produced. Once a firm starts producing output it incurs **variable costs** as well.

Since profits depend on the *difference* between revenues and costs, the costs of added output will determine how much profit a producer can make. Figure 22.4 illustrates a typical total cost curve. ***Total costs increase as output expands. But the rate of cost increase varies.*** Hence, the total cost curve is *not* linear. At first total costs rise slowly (notice the gradually declining slope until point *z*), then they increase more quickly (the rising slope after point *z*). This S-shaped curve reflects the *law of diminishing returns.* As we first observed in Chapter 21, **marginal costs (MC)** often decline in the early stages of production and then increase as the available plant and equipment are used more intensively. These changes in marginal cost cause *total* costs to rise slowly at first, then to pick up speed as output increases.

You may suspect by now that the road to profits is not an easy one. It entails comparing ever-changing revenues with ever-changing costs. Figure 22.5 helps simplify the problem by bringing together typical total revenue and total cost curves. Notice how total costs exceed total revenues at high rates of output (beyond point *g*). As production capacity is approached, costs tend to skyrocket, offsetting any gain in sales revenue.

FIGURE 22.4
Total Cost

Total cost increases with output. The rate of increase isn't steady, however. Typically, the rate of cost increase slows initially, then speeds up. After point *z*, diminishing returns (rising marginal costs) cause accelerating costs. These accelerating costs limit the profit potential of increased output.

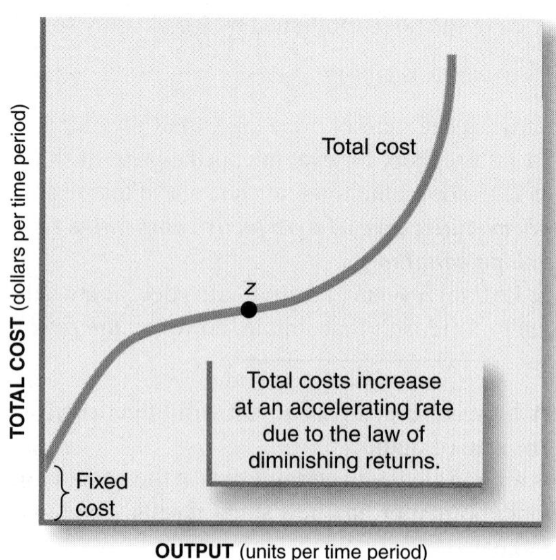

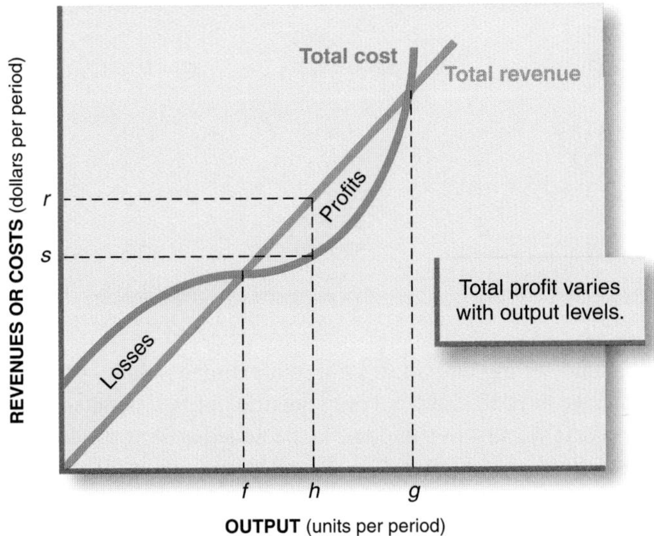

FIGURE 22.5
Total Profit

Profit is the *difference* between total revenue and total cost. It is represented as the vertical distance between the total revenue curve and the total cost curve. At output *h*, profit equals *r* minus *s*. The objective is to find that rate of output that *maximizes* profit.

Total profit in Figure 22.5 is represented by the vertical distance between the two curves. Total costs in this case exceed total revenue at low rates of output (below *f*) as well as at very high rates (above *g*). The firm is profitable only at output rates between *f* and *g*.

Although all rates of output between *f* and *g* are profitable, they aren't *equally* profitable. A quick glance at Figure 22.5 confirms that the vertical distance between total revenue and total cost varies considerably within that range. ***The primary objective of the producer is to find that one particular rate of output that maximizes total profits.*** With a ruler, one could find it in Figure 22.5 by measuring the distance between the revenue and cost curves at all rates of output. In the real world, most producers need more practical guides to profit maximization.

PROFIT-MAXIMIZING RULE

The best single rule for maximizing profits in the short run is straightforward: Never produce a unit of output that costs more than it brings in. By following this simple rule, a producer is likely to make the right production decision. We see how this rule works by looking first at the revenue side of production ("what it brings in"), then at the cost side ("what it costs").

Marginal Revenue = Price

In searching for the most profitable rate of output, we need to know what an additional unit of output will bring in—that is, how much it adds to the total revenue of the firm. In general, the contribution to total revenue of an additional unit of output is called **marginal revenue (MR).** Marginal revenue is the *change* in total revenue that occurs when output is increased by one unit; that is,

marginal revenue (MR): The change in total revenue that results from a one-unit increase in the quantity sold.

$$\text{Marginal revenue} = \frac{\text{change in total revenue}}{\text{change in output}}$$

To calculate marginal revenue, we compare the total revenues received before and after a one-unit increase in the rate of production; the *difference* between the two totals equals marginal revenue.

When the price of a product is constant, it's easy to compute marginal revenue. Suppose we're operating a catfish farm. Our product is catfish, sold at wholesale at the prevailing price of $13 per bushel. In this case, a one-unit increase in sales (one more bushel) increases total revenue by $13. As illustrated in Table 22.2, as long as the price of a product is constant, price and marginal revenue are one and the same thing. Hence, ***for perfectly competitive firms, price equals marginal revenue.***

TABLE 22.2
Total and Marginal Revenue

Marginal revenue (MR) is the *change* in total revenue associated with the sale of one more unit of output. A third bushel increases total revenue from $26 to $39; MR equals $13. If the price is constant (at $13 here), marginal revenue equals price.

Quantity Sold (bushels per day)	×	Price (per bushel)	=	Total Revenue (per day)	Marginal Revenue (per bushel)
0	×	$13	=	$ 0>	$13
1	×	13	=	13>	13
2	×	13	=	26>	13
3	×	13	=	39>	13
4	×	13	=	52>	13

Marginal Cost

Keep in mind why we're breeding and selling catfish. It's not to maximize *revenues* but to maximize *profits*. To gauge profits, we need to know not only the price of fish but also how much each bushel costs to produce. As we saw in Chapter 21, the added cost of producing one more unit of a good is its *marginal cost*. Figure 22.6 summarizes the marginal costs associated with the production of catfish.

Phillip Gould/Corbis

Analysis: Fish farmers want to maximize profits.

The production process for catfish farming is wonderfully simple. The factory is a pond; the rate of production is the number of fish harvested from the pond per day. A farmer can alter the rate of production at will, up to the breeding capacity of the pond.

Assume that the *fixed* cost of the pond is $10 per day. The fixed costs include the rental value of the pond and the cost of electricity for keeping the pond oxygenated so the fish can breathe. These fixed costs must be paid no matter how many fish the farmer harvests.

To harvest catfish from the pond, the farmer must incur additional costs. Labor is needed to net and sort the fish. The cost of labor is *variable*, depending on how much output the farmer decides to produce. If no fish are harvested, no variable costs are incurred.

The *marginal costs* of harvesting are the additional costs incurred to harvest *one* more basket of fish. Generally, we expect marginal costs to rise as the rate of production increases.

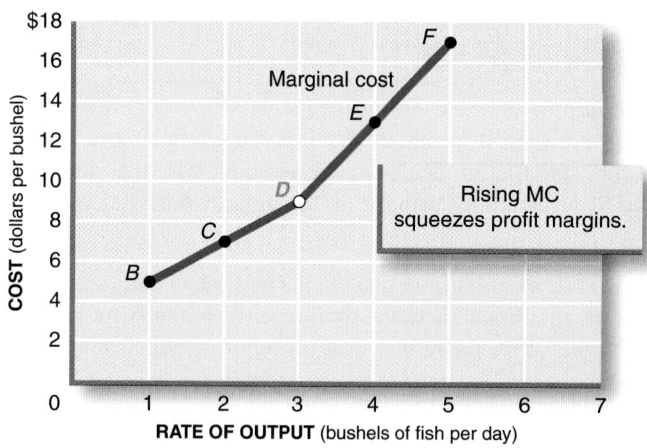

FIGURE 22.6
The Costs of Catfish Production

Marginal cost is the increase in total cost associated with a one-unit increase in production. When production expands from two to three units per day, total costs increase by $9 (from $22 to $31 per day). The marginal cost of the third bushel is therefore $9, as illustrated by point *D* in the graph.

	Rate of Output (bushels per day)	Total Cost (per day)	Marginal Cost (per day)	Average Cost (per day)
A	0	$10	—	—
B	1	15	$ 5	$15.00
C	2	22	7	11.00
D	3	31	9	10.33
E	4	44	13	11.00
F	5	61	17	12.20

The law of diminishing returns we encountered in Chapter 21 applies to catfish farming as well. As more labor is hired, each worker has less space (pond area) and capital (access to nets, sorting trays) to work with. Accordingly, it takes a little more labor time (marginal cost) to harvest each additional fish.

Figure 22.6 illustrates these marginal costs. Notice how the MC rises as the rate of output increases. At the output rate of 4 bushels per day (point *E*), marginal cost is \$13. Hence, the fourth bushel *increases* total costs by \$13. The fifth bushel is even more expensive, with a marginal cost of \$17.

Profit-Maximizing Rate of Output

We're now in a position to make a production decision. The rule about never producing anything that adds more to cost than it brings in can now be stated in more technical terms. Since price equals marginal revenue for competitive firms, we can base the production decision on a comparison of *price* and marginal cost.

MC > *p*. We don't want to produce an additional unit of output if its MC exceeds its price. If MC exceeds price, we're spending more to produce that extra unit than we're getting back: Total profits will decline if we produce it.

***p* > MC.** The opposite is true when price exceeds MC. If an extra unit brings in more revenue than it costs to produce, it is *adding* to total profit. Total profits must increase in this case. Hence, a competitive firm wants to expand the rate of production whenever price exceeds MC.

p* = MC.** Since we want to expand output when price exceeds MC and contract output if price is less than MC, the profit-maximizing rate of output is easily found. ***For perfectly competitive firms, profits are maximized at the rate of output where price equals marginal cost. The implications of this **profit-maximization rule** are summarized in Table 22.3.

profit-maximization rule: Produce at that rate of output where marginal revenue equals marginal cost.

Figure 22.7 illustrates the application of our profit-maximization rule in catfish farming. The prevailing wholesale price of catfish is \$13 a bushel. At this price we can sell all the catfish we can produce, up to our short-run capacity. The catfish can't be sold at a higher price because lots of farmers raise catfish and sell them for \$13 (see News). If we try to charge a higher price, consumers will buy their fish from other vendors. Hence, we confront a horizontal demand curve at the price of \$13.

The costs of producing catfish were examined in Figure 22.6. The key concept illustrated here is marginal cost. The MC curve slopes upward, in conventional fashion.

Figure 22.7 also depicts the total revenues, costs, and profits of alternative production rates. Study the table first. Notice that the firm loses \$10 per day if it produces no fish (row A). At zero output, total revenue is zero ($p \times q = 0$). However, the firm must still contend with fixed costs of \$10 per day. Total profit—total revenue minus total cost—is therefore *minus* \$10; the firm incurs a loss.

Row B of the table shows how this loss is reduced when 1 bushel of fish is harvested per day. The production and sale of 1 bushel per day bring in \$13 of total revenue (column 3). The total cost of producing 1 bushel per day is \$15 (column 4). Hence, the total loss at an

Price Level	Production Decision
price > MC	increase output
price = MC	maintain output (profits maximized)
price < MC	decrease output

TABLE 22.3
Short-Run Profit-Maximization Rules for Competitive Firm

The relationship between price and marginal cost dictates short-run production decisions. For competitive firms, profits are maximized at that rate of output where price = MC.

FIGURE 22.7
Maximization of Profits for a Competitive Firm

A competitive firm maximizes total profit at the output rate where MC = *p*. If MC is less than price, the firm can increase profits by producing more. If MC exceeds price, the firm should reduce output. In this case, profit maximization occurs at an output of 4 bushels per day.

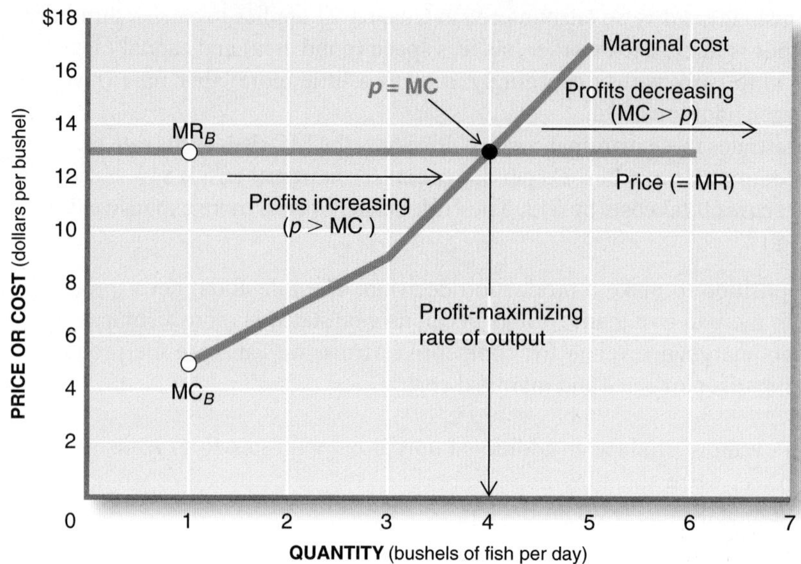

	(1) Number of Bushels (per day)	(2) Price	(3) Total Revenue	–	(4) Total Cost	=	(5) Total Profit	(6) Marginal Revenue	(7) Marginal Cost
A	0	—	—		$10		−$10	—	—
B	1	$13	$13		15		− 2	$13	$ 5
C	2	13	26		22		+ 4	13	7
D	3	13	39		31		+ 8	13	9
E	4	13	52		44		+ 8	13	13
F	5	13	65		61		+ 4	13	17

webnote

Check out the real world of catfish farming at www.aces.edu/pubs/docs/A/ANR-0273/

output rate of 1 bushel per day is $2 (column 5). This may not be what we hoped for, but it's certainly better than the $10 loss incurred at zero output.

The superiority of harvesting 1 bushel per day rather than none is also evident in columns 6 and 7 of row B. The first bushel produced has a *marginal revenue* of $13. Its *marginal cost* is only $5. Hence, it brings in more added revenue than it adds to costs. Under these circumstances—whenever price exceeds MC—output should definitely be expanded. That is one of the decision rules summarized in Table 22.3.

The excess of price over MC for the first unit of output is also illustrated by the graph in Figure 22.7. Point MR_B ($13) lies above MC_B ($5); the *difference* between these two points measures the contribution that the first bushel makes to the total profits of the firm. In this case, that contribution equals $13 − $5 = $8, and production losses are reduced by that amount when the rate of output is increased from zero to 1 bushel per day.

As long as price exceeds MC, increases in the rate of output increase total profit. Notice what happens to profits when the rate of output is increased from 1 to 2 bushels per day (row C). The price (MR) of the second bushel is $13, its MC is $7. Therefore it *adds* $6 to total profits. Instead of losing $2 per day, the firm is now making a profit of $4 per day.

The firm can make even more profits by expanding the rate of output further. The marginal revenue of the third bushel is $13; its marginal cost is $9 (row D of the table). Therefore, the third bushel makes a $4 contribution to profits.

This firm will never make huge profits. For the fourth unit of output price and MC both equal $13. It doesn't contribute to total profits, and it doesn't subtract from them. The

IN THE NEWS   

Southern Farmers Hooked on New Cash Crop

Catfish are replacing crops and dairy farming as a cash industry in much of the South, particularly in Mississippi's Delta region, where 80 percent of farm-bred catfish are grown.

Production has skyrocketed in the USA from 16 million pounds in 1975 to an expected 340 million pounds this year.

The business is growing among farmers in Alabama, Arkansas and Louisiana.

Catfish farming is similar to other agriculture, experts say. One thing is the same: It takes money to get started.

"If you have a good row-crop farmer, you have a good catfish farmer," says James Hoffman of Farm Fresh Catfish Co. in Hollandale, Miss. "But you can't take a poor row-crop farmer and make him a good catfish farmer."

Greensboro, Ala., catfish farmer Steve Hollingsworth says he spends $18,000 a week on feed for the 1 million catfish in his ponds.

"Each of the ponds has about 100,000 fish," he says. "You get about 60 cents per fish, so that's about $60,000."

The investment can be lost very quickly "if something's wrong in that pond," like an inadequate oxygen level, Hollingsworth says.

"You can be 15 minutes too late getting here, and all your fish are gone," he says.

—Mark Mayfield

Source: *USA Today,* December 5, 1989. Copyright 1989 USA TODAY. Reprinted with permission. www.usatoday.com

Analysis: People go into a competitive business like catfish farming to earn a profit. Once in business, they try to maximize total profits by equating price and marginal cost.

fourth unit of output represents the highest rate of output the firm desires. ***At the rate of output where price = MC, total profits of the firm are maximized.***[1]

Notice what happens if we expand output beyond 4 bushels per day. The price of the fifth bushel is still $13; its MC is $17. The fifth bushel adds more to costs than to revenue. If we produce that fifth bushel, total profit will decline by $4. In Figure 22.7 the MC curve lies above the price line at all output levels in excess of 4. The lesson here is clear: ***Output should not be increased if MC exceeds price.***

The correct production decision—the profit-maximizing decision—is shown in Figure 22.7 by the intersection of the price and MC curves. At this intersection, price equals MC and profits are maximized. If we produced less, we'd be giving up potential profits. If we produced more, total profits would also fall (review Table 22.3).

Adding Up Profits

To reach the right production decision, we've relied on *marginal* revenues and costs. Having found the desired rate of output, however, we may want to take a closer look at the profits we are accumulating. Figure 22.8 provides pictures of our success.

Total profits are represented in Figure 22.8*a* by the vertical distance between the total revenue and total cost curves. This is a straightforward interpretation of our definition of total profits—that is,

$$\text{Total profits} = \text{TR} - \text{TC}$$

The vertical distance between the TR and TC curves is maximized at the output of 4 bushels per day.

Our success in catfish farming can also be illustrated by *average* revenue and costs. Total profit is equal to *average* profit per unit multiplied by the number of units produced. Profit *per unit,* in turn, is equal to price *minus* average total cost—that is,

$$\text{Profit per unit} = p - \text{ATC}$$

[1]In this case, profits are the same at output levels of 3 and 4 bushels. Given the choice between the two levels, most firms will choose the higher level. By producing the extra unit of output, the firm increases its customer base. This not only denies rival firms an additional sale but also provides some additional cushion when the economy slumps. Also, corporate size may connote both prestige and power. In any case, the higher output level defines the *limit* to maximum-profit production.

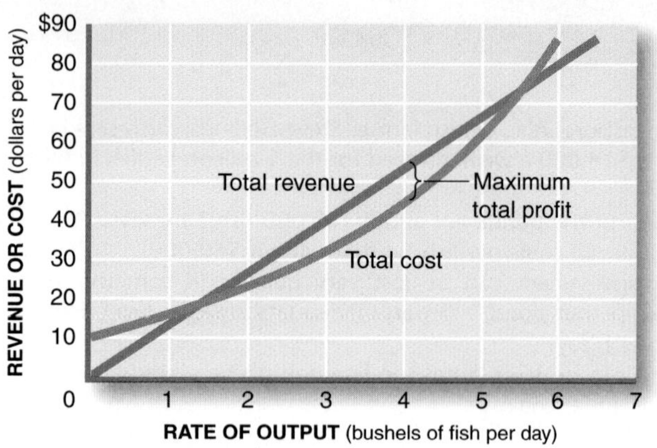

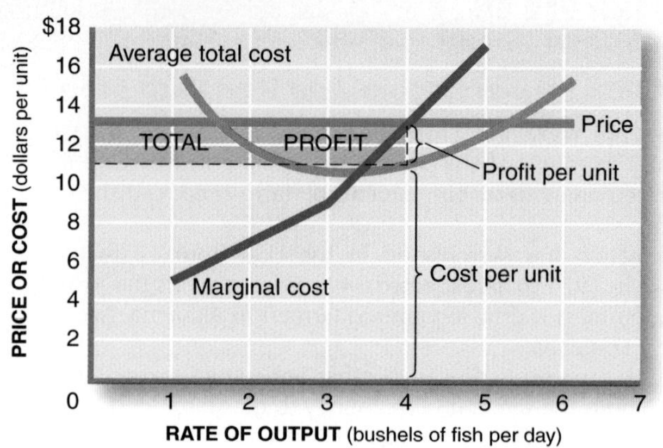

FIGURE 22.8
Alternative Views of Total Profit

Total profit can be computed as TR − TC, as in part *a*. Or it can be computed as profit *per unit* (*p* − ATC) multiplied by the quantity sold. This is illustrated in part *b* by the shaded rectangle. To find the profit-maximizing output, we could use either of these graphs or just the price and MC curves in Figure 22.7.

The price of catfish is illustrated in Figure 22.8*b* by the horizontal price line at $13. The average total cost of producing catfish is shown by the ATC curve. Like the ATC curve we encountered in Chapter 21, this one has a U shape. The *difference* between price and average cost—profit per unit—is illustrated by the vertical distance between the price and ATC curves. At 4 bushels per day, for example, profit per unit equals $13 − $11 = $2.

To compute *total* profits, we note that

$$\text{Total profits} = \text{profit per unit} \times \text{quantity}$$
$$= (p - \text{ATC}) \times q$$

In this case, the 4 bushels generate a profit of $2 each, for a *total* profit of $8 per day. *Total* profits are illustrated in Figure 22.8*b* by the shaded rectangle. (Recall that the area of a rectangle is equal to its height, the profit per unit, multiplied by its width, the quantity sold.)

Profit per unit is not only used to compute total profits but is often also of interest in its own right. Businesspeople like to cite statistics on "markups," which are a crude index to per-unit profits. However, ***the profit-maximizing producer never seeks to maximize per-unit profits. What counts is* total *profits, not the amount of profit per unit.*** This is the old $5 ice cream problem again. You might be able to maximize profit per unit if you could sell 1 cone for $5, but you would make a lot more money if you sold 100 cones at a per-unit profit of only 50 cents each.

Similarly, ***the profit-maximizing producer has no desire to produce at that rate of output where ATC is at a minimum.*** Minimum ATC does represent least-cost production. But additional units of output, even though they raise average costs, will increase total profits. This is evident in Figure 22.8; price exceeds MC for some output to the right of minimum ATC (the bottom of the U). Therefore, total profits are increasing as we increase the rate of output beyond the point of minimum average costs.

THE SHUTDOWN DECISION

The rule established for short-run profit maximization doesn't guarantee any profits. By equating price and marginal cost, the competitive producer is only assured of achieving the *optimal* output. This is the best possible rate of output for the firm, given the existing market price and the (short-run) costs of production.

But what if the best possible rate of output generates a loss? What should the producer do in this case? Keep producing output? Or shut down the factory and find something else to do?

The first instinct may be to shut down the factory to stop the flow of red ink. But this isn't necessarily the wisest course of action. It may be smarter to keep operating a money-losing operation than to shut it down.

The rationale for this seemingly ill-advised course of action resides in the fixed costs of production. ***Fixed costs must be paid even if all output ceases.*** The firm must still pay rent on the factory and equipment even if it doesn't use these inputs. That's why we call such costs "fixed."

The persistence of fixed costs casts an entirely different light on the shutdown decision. Since fixed costs will have to be paid in any case, the question becomes: Which option creates greater losses? Does the firm lose more money by continuing to operate (and incurring a loss) or by shutting down (and incurring a loss equal to fixed costs)? In these terms, the answer becomes clear: ***A firm should shut down only if the losses from continuing production exceed fixed costs.*** This happens when total revenue is less than total *variable* cost.

Price vs. AVC

The shutdown decision can be made without explicit reference to fixed costs. Figure 22.9 shows how. The relationship to focus on is between the price of a good and its average *variable* cost.

The curves in Figure 22.9 represent the short-run costs and potential demand curves for catfish. As long as the price of catfish is $13 per bushel, the typical firm will produce 4 a day, as determined by the intersection of the MC and MR (= price) curves (point *X*, in part *a*). In this case, price ($13) exceeds average *total* cost ($11) and catfish farming is profitable.

The situation wouldn't look so good, however, if the market price of catfish fell to $9. Following the rule for profit maximization, the firm would be led to point *Y* in part *b*, where MC intersects the new demand (price) curve. At this intersection, the firm would produce 3 bushels per day. But total revenues would no longer cover total costs, as can be seen from the fact that the ATC curve now lies *above* the price line. The ATC of producing 3 bushels is $10.33 (Figure 22.6); price is $9. Hence, the firm is incurring a loss of $4 per day (3 bushels at a loss of $1.33 each).

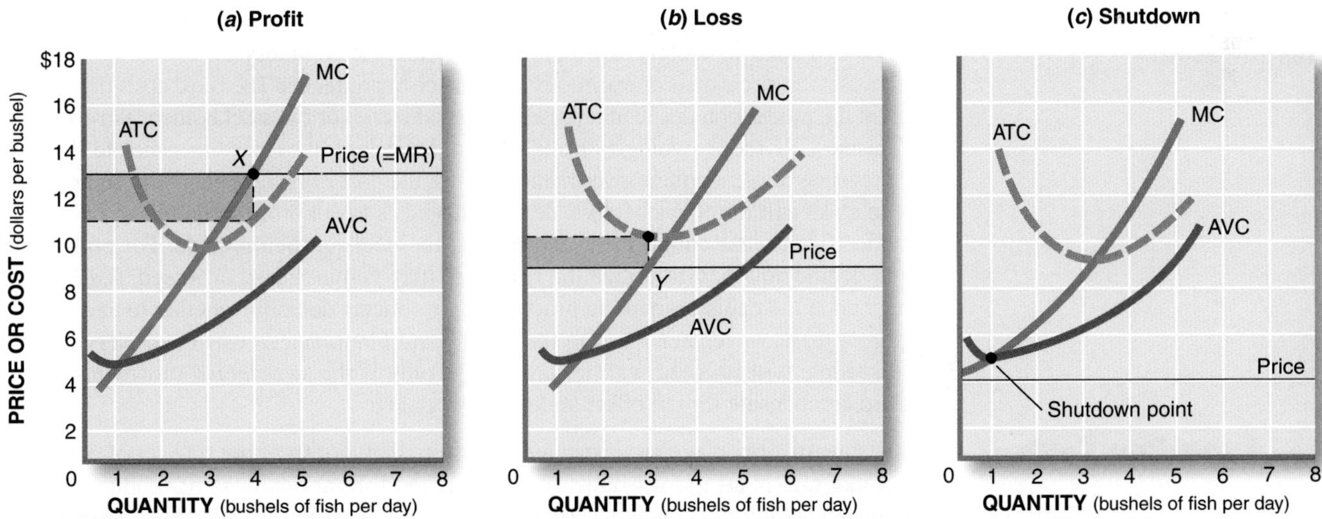

FIGURE 22.9
The Firm's Shutdown Point

A firm should cease production only if total revenue is lower than total *variable* cost. The shutdown decision may be based on a comparison of price and AVC. If the price of catfish per bushel was $13, a firm would earn a profit at point *X* in part *a*. At a price of $9, (point *Y* in part *b*), the firm is losing money (*p* is less than ATC) but is more than covering all variable costs (*p* is greater than AVC). If the price falls to $4 per bushel, as in part *c*, output should cease (*p* is less than AVC).

Should the firm stay in business under the circumstances? The answer is yes. Recall that the catfish farmer has already dug the pond and installed equipment at a (fixed) cost of $10 per day. The producer will have to pay these fixed costs whether or not the machinery is used. Stopping production would result in a loss amounting to $10 per day. Staying in business, even when catfish prices fall to $9 each, generates a loss of only $4 a day. In this case, ***where price exceeds average variable cost but not average total cost, the profit-maximization rule minimizes losses.***

The Shutdown Point

If the price of catfish falls far enough, the producer may be better off ceasing production altogether. Suppose the price of catfish fell to $4 per bushel (Figure 22.9*c*). A price this low doesn't even cover the variable cost of producing 1 bushel per day ($5). Continued production of even 1 bushel per day would imply a total loss of $11 per day ($10 of fixed costs plus $1 of variable costs). Higher rates of output would lead to still greater losses. Hence, the firm should shut down production, even though that action implies a loss of $10 per day. In all cases ***where price doesn't cover average variable costs at any rate of output, production should cease.*** Thus, the **shutdown point** occurs where price is equal to minimum average *variable* cost. Any lower price will result in losses larger than fixed costs. In Figure 22.9, the shutdown point occurs at a price of $5, where the MC and AVC curves intersect.

shutdown point: That rate of output where price equals minimum AVC.

THE INVESTMENT DECISION

When a firm shuts down, it doesn't necessarily leave (exit) the industry. General Motors still produces Cadillacs, for example, even though it idled one of its plants in 2001 (see News). ***The shutdown decision is a* short-run *response.*** It's based on the fixed costs of an established plant and the variable costs of operating it.

Ideally, a producer would never get into a money-losing business in the first place. Entry was based on an **investment decision** that the producer now regrets. ***Investment decisions are* long-run *decisions,*** however, and the firm now must pay for its bad luck or poor judgment. The investment decision entails the assumption of fixed costs (e.g., the lease of the factory); once the investment is made, the short-run production decision is designed to make the best possible use of those fixed inputs. The short-run profit-maximizing rule we've discussed applies only to this second decision; it assumes that a production unit exists. The accompanying News shows the contrast between production and investment decisions: GM *idled* its factory; Ford permanently closed its factory.

investment decision: The decision to build, buy, or lease plant and equipment; to enter or exit an industry.

long run: A period of time long enough for all inputs to be varied (no fixed costs).

The investment decision is of enormous importance to producers. The fixed costs that we've ignored in the production decision represent the producers' (or the stockholders') investment in the business. If they're going to avoid an economic loss, they have to generate at least enough revenue to recoup their investment—that is, the cost of (fixed) plant and equipment. Failure to do so will result in a net loss, despite allegiance to our profit-maximizing rule.

Whether fixed costs count, then, depends on the decision being made. For producers trying to decide how best to utilize the resources they've purchased or leased, fixed costs no longer enter the decision-making process. For producers deciding whether to enter business, sign a lease, or replace existing machinery and plant, fixed costs count very much. Businesspeople will proceed with an investment only if the *anticipated* profits are large enough to compensate for the effort and risk undertaken.

Long-Run Costs

When businesspeople make an investment decision, they confront not one set of cost figures but many. A plant not yet built can be designed for various rates of production and alternative technologies. In making long-run decisions, a producer isn't bound to one size of plant or to a particular mix of tools and machinery. In the long run, one can be flexible. In general, ***a producer will want to build, buy, or lease a plant that's the most efficient for the anticipated rate of output.*** This is the (dis)economy of scale phenomenon we discussed in the previous chapter. Once the right plant size is selected, the producer may proceed with the problem of short-run profit maximization. Once production is started, he can only hope that the investment decision was a good one and that a shutdown can be avoided.

IN THE NEWS

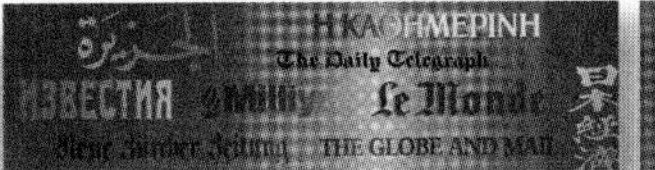

GM to Idle Cadillac Plant for Four Weeks

General Motors said Wednesday that it will idle the Lansing, Mich., Craft Center vehicle-assembly plant for four weeks beginning May 21 to cut inventories of unsold Cadillac Eldorado coupes. That will result in the temporary layoff of 300 workers, who will continue to receive 95 percent of their take-home pay.

Source: *Associated Press,* February 22, 2001. Reprinted with permission of The Associated Press.

Ford to Cut Jobs, Close Plants

Ford Motor announced a massive restructuring plan Monday . . . shedding up to 30,000 jobs and 14 factories by 2012. . . .

The automaker said Monday that it lost $1.6 billion pretax on North American auto operations last year.

The moves will reduce Ford's U.S. automaking capacity by 26%. The cuts represent 20% to 25% of Ford's North American workforce of 122,000 people.

—Chris Woodyard

Source: *USA Today,* January 24, 2006, p. 1. Reprinted with permission.

Analysis: GM's decision to idle a plant was a short-run *shutdown* decision; it is still in business. Ford, by contrast, made a long-run decision to cease operations and *exit* the industry in specific markets.

DETERMINANTS OF SUPPLY

Whether the time frame is the short run or the long run, the one central force in production decisions is the quest for profits. Producers will go into production—incur fixed costs—only if they see the potential for economic profits. Once in business, they'll expand the rate of output so long as profits are increasing. They'll shut down—cease production—when revenues don't at least cover variable costs (loss exceeds fixed costs).

Nearly anyone could make money with these principles if given complete information on costs and revenues. What renders the road to fortune less congested is the general absence of such complete information. In the real world, production decisions involve considerably more risk. People often don't know how much profit or loss they'll incur until it's too late to alter production decisions. Consequently, businesspeople are compelled to make a reasoned guess about prices and costs, then proceed. By way of summary, we can identify the major influences that will shape their short- and long-run decisions on how much output to supply to the market.

Short-Run Determinants

A competitive firm's short-run production decisions are dominated by marginal costs. Hence, the quantity of a good supplied will be affected by all forces that alter MC. Specifically, ***the determinants of a firm's supply include***

- ***The price of factor inputs.***
- ***Technology*** (the available production function).
- ***Expectations*** (for costs, sales, technology).
- ***Taxes and subsidies.***

Each determinant affects a producer's ability and willingness to supply output at any particular price.

The price of factor inputs determines how much the producer must pay for resources used in production. Technology determines how much output the producer will get from each unit of input. Expectations are critical because they express producers' perceptions of what future costs, prices, sales, and profits are likely to be. And finally, taxes and subsidies may alter costs or the amount of profit a firm gets to keep.

supply curve: A curve describing the quantities of a good a producer is willing and able to sell (produce) at alternative prices in a given time period, *ceteris paribus.*

The Short-Run Supply Curve. By using the familiar *ceteris paribus* assumption, we can isolate the effect of price on supply decisions. In other words, we can draw a short-run **supply curve** the same way we earlier constructed consumer demand curves. In this case,

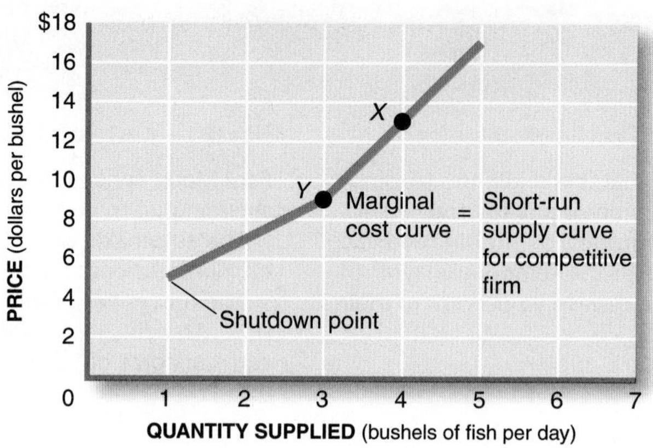

FIGURE 22.10
A Competitive Firm's Short-Run Supply Curve

For competitive firms, marginal cost defines the lowest price a firm will accept for a given quantity of output. In this sense, the marginal cost curve *is* the supply curve; it tells us how quantity supplied will respond to price. At $p = \$13$, the quantity supplied is 4; at $p = \$9$, the quantity supplied is 3.

Recall, however, that the firm will shut down if price falls below minimum average variable cost. The supply curve does not exist below minimum AVC ($5 in this case).

the forces we assume constant are input prices, technology, expectations, and taxes. The only variable we allow to change is the price of the product itself.

Figure 22.10 illustrates the response of quantity supplied to a change in price. Notice the critical role of marginal costs: ***The marginal cost curve is the short-run supply curve for a competitive firm.*** Recall our basic profit-maximization rule. A competitive producer wants to supply a good only if its price exceeds its marginal cost. Hence, marginal cost defines the lower limit for an "acceptable" price. A catfish farmer is willing and able to produce 4 bushels per day only if the price of a bushel is $13 (point X). If the price of catfish dropped to $9, the *quantity* supplied would fall to 3 (point Y). The marginal cost curve tells us what the quantity supplied would be at all other prices as well. As long as price exceeds minimum AVC (the shutdown point), the MC curve summarizes the response of a producer to price changes: It *is* the short-run supply curve of a perfectly competitive firm.

The shape of the marginal cost curve provides a basic foundation for the *law of supply.* Because marginal costs tend to rise as output expands, an increase in output makes sense only if the price of that output rises. If the price does rise, it's profitable to increase the quantity supplied.

Supply Shifts

All the forces that shape the short-run supply curve are subject to change. Factor prices change; technology changes; expectations change; and tax laws get revised. ***If any determinant of supply changes, the supply curve shifts.***

An increase in wage rates, for example, would raise the marginal cost of producing catfish. This would shift the supply curve upward, making it more expensive for producers to supply larger quantities at any given price.

An improvement in technology would have the opposite effect. By increasing productivity, new technology would lower the marginal cost of producing a good. The supply curve would shift downward.

Tax Effects

Changes in taxes will also alter supply behavior. But not all taxes have the same effect; some alter short-run supply behavior, others affect only long-run supply decisions.

Property Taxes. Property taxes are levied by local governments on land and buildings. The tax rate is typically some small fraction (e.g., 1 percent) of total value. Hence, the owner of a $10 million factory might have to pay $100,000 per year in property taxes.

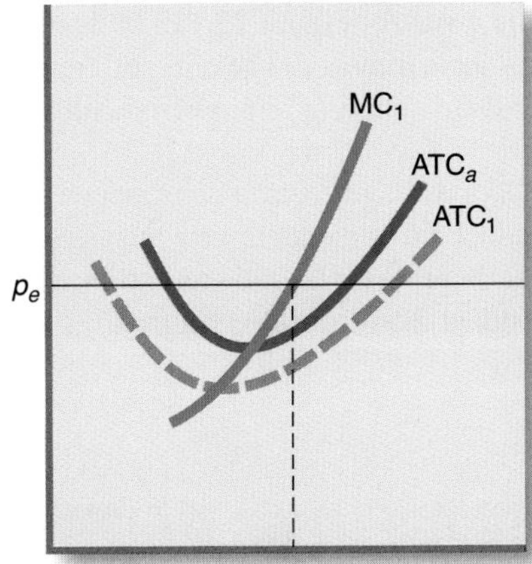

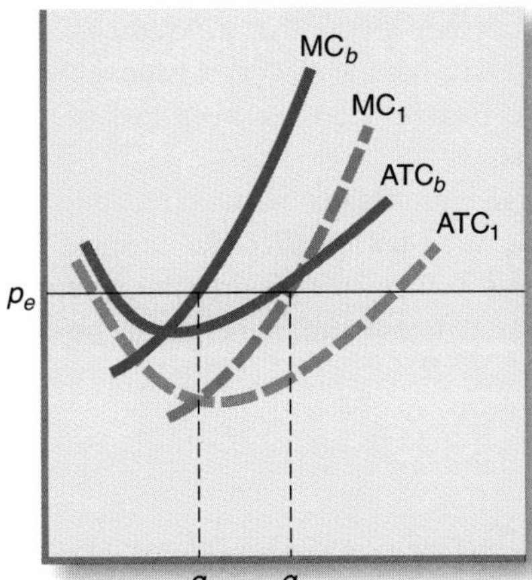

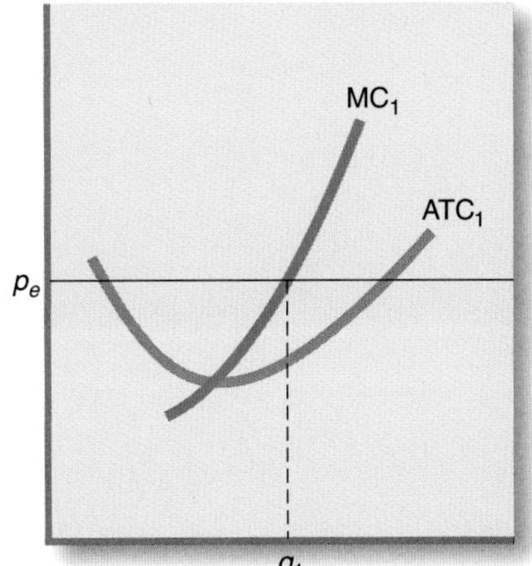

FIGURE 22.11
Impact of Taxes on Business Decisions

(*a*) Property taxes are a fixed cost for the firm. Since they don't affect marginal costs, they leave the optimal rate of output (q_1) unchanged. Property taxes raise average costs, however, and so reduce profits. Lower profits may alter investment decisions.

(*b*) Payroll taxes add directly to marginal costs and so reduce the optimal rate of output (to q_b). Payroll taxes also increase average costs and lower total and per-unit profits.

(*c*) Taxes on profits are neither a fixed cost nor a variable cost since they depend on the existence of profits. They don't affect marginal costs or price and so leave the optimal rate of output (q_1) unchanged. By reducing after-tax profits, however, such taxes lessen incentives to invest.

Property taxes have to be paid regardless of whether the factory is used. Hence, ***property taxes are a fixed cost*** for the firm. These additional fixed costs increase total costs and thus shift the average total cost (ATC) upward, as in Figure 22.11*a*.

Notice that the MC curve doesn't move when property taxes are imposed. Property taxes aren't based on the quantity of output produced. Accordingly, the production decision of the firm isn't affected by property taxes. The quantity q_1 in Figure 22.11*a* remains the optimal rate of output even after a property tax is introduced.

Although the optimal output remains at q_1, the profitability of the firm is reduced by the property tax. Profit per unit has been reduced by the upward shift of the ATC curve. If property taxes reduce profits too much, firms may move to a low-tax jurisdiction or another industry (investment decisions).

Payroll Taxes. Payroll taxes have very different effects on business decisions. Payroll taxes are levied on the wages paid by the firm. Employers must pay, for example, a 7.65 percent Social Security tax on the wages they pay (employees pay an identical amount). This tax is used to finance Social Security retirement benefits. Other payroll taxes are levied by federal and state governments to finance unemployment and disability benefits.

All payroll taxes add to the cost of hiring labor. In the absence of a tax, a worker might cost the firm $8 per hour. Once Social Security and other taxes are levied, the cost of labor increases to $8 plus the amount of tax. Hence, $8-per-hour labor might end up costing the firm $9 or more. In other words, ***payroll taxes increase marginal costs.*** This is illustrated in Figure 22.11*b* by the upward shift of the MC curve.

Notice how payroll taxes change the production decision. The new MC curve (MC_b) intersects the price line at a lower rate of output (q_b). Thus payroll taxes tend to reduce output and employment.

Profit Taxes. Taxes are also levied on the profits of a business. Such taxes are very different from either property or payroll taxes since profit taxes are paid only when profits are made. Thus they are neither a fixed cost nor a variable cost! As Figure 22.11*c* indicates, neither the MC nor the ATC curve moves when a profits tax is imposed. The only difference is that the firm now gets to keep less of its profits, instead "sharing" its profits with the government.

Although a profits tax has no direct effect on marginal or average costs, it does reduce the take-home (after-tax) profits of a business. This may reduce investments in new businesses. For this reason, many people urge the government to *reduce* corporate tax rates and so encourage increased investment. This was the objective of President Bush's 2002–3 tax cuts.

THE ECONOMY TOMORROW

INTERNET-BASED PRICE COMPETITION

Ten years ago the T-shirt shop owners on South Padre Island (see News, page 451) had to worry only about the other 40 shops at that beach resort. They worried that other shops might offer T-shirts at lower prices, forcing all the shops to cut prices. Now the level of competition is much higher. Beachgoers can now buy T-shirts at virtual shops on the Internet. Indeed, consumers can click on the Internet to find out the price of almost anything. There are even electronic shopping services that will find the lowest price for a product. Want a better deal on a car? You don't have to visit a dozen dealerships. With a few clicks, you can find the lowest price for the car you want and get directions to the appropriate dealer. In fact, you don't have to go anywhere: More and more producers will sell you their products directly over the Internet.

webnote

If you want to shop for T-shirts at a cybermall, check out www.tshirtmall.com

E-commerce intensifies competition in many ways. By allowing a consumer to shop worldwide, the Net vastly increases the number of firms in a virtual market. Even your campus bookstore now has to worry about textbook prices available at Amazon.com, Barnes and Noble, and other online booksellers.

Electronic commerce also reduces transaction costs. Retailers don't need stores or catalogs to display their products, and they can greatly reduce inventories by producing to order. This is how Dell computer supplies the $20 million of computers it sells per day online.

Electronic retailers also get a tax break. Transactions on the Net aren't subject to sales taxes. Hence, electronic retailers can offer products at lower prices without cutting profit margins, especially in high-tax states.

The evident advantages of e-commerce have made it the virtual mall of choice for many consumers. In 2006, consumers spent over $100 billion on electronic purchases. That was less than 1 percent of total consumer spending. But the trend is what counts. With Net sales more than doubling every year, e-commerce is sure to intensify price competition in the economy tomorrow.

SUMMARY

- Economic profit is the difference between total revenue and total cost. Total economic cost includes the value (opportunity cost) of *all* inputs used in the production, not just those inputs for which an explicit payment is made. LO2
- Because it must contend with many competitors, a competitive firm has no control over the price of its output. It effectively confronts a horizontal demand for its output (even though the *market* demand for the product is downward-sloping). LO1
- The short-run objective of a firm is to maximize profits from the operation of its existing facilities (fixed costs). For a competitive firm, the profit-maximizing output

occurs at the point where marginal cost equals price (marginal revenue). LO2

- A firm may incur a loss even at the optimal rate of output. It shouldn't shut down, however, so long as price exceeds average *variable* cost. If revenues at least cover variable costs, the firm's loss from production is less than fixed cost. LO2
- In the long run a producer can be flexible. There are no fixed costs and the firm may choose any-sized plant it wants. The decision to incur fixed costs (i.e., build, buy, or lease a plant) or to enter or exit an industry is an investment decision. LO2
- A competitive firm's supply curve is identical to its marginal cost curve (above the shutdown point at minimum average variable cost). In the short run, the quantity supplied will rise or fall with price. LO3
- The determinants of supply include the price of inputs, technology, taxes, and expectations. Should any of these determinants change, the firm's supply curve will shift. LO3
- Business taxes alter business behavior. Property taxes raise fixed costs; payroll taxes increase marginal costs. Profit taxes raise neither fixed costs nor marginal costs but diminish the take-home (after-tax) profits of a business. LO3
- The Internet has created virtual stores that intensify price competition. LO1

Key Terms

profit
economic cost
explicit cost
implicit cost
economic profit
normal profit
monopoly
market structure
perfect competition
market power
competitive firm
production decision
total revenue
short run
fixed costs
variable costs
marginal cost (MC)
marginal revenue (MR)
profit-maximization rule
shutdown point
investment decision
long run
supply curve

Questions for Discussion

1. What economic costs will a large corporation likely overlook when computing its "profits"? How about the owner of a family-run business or farm? LO2
2. How can the demand curve facing a firm be horizontal if the market demand curve is downward-sloping? LO1
3. How many fish should a commercial fisherman try to catch in a day? Should he catch as many as possible or return to dock before filling the boat with fish? Under what economic circumstances should he not even take the boat out? LO2
4. If a firm is incurring an economic loss, would society be better off if the firm shut down? Would the firm want to shut down? Explain. LO2
5. Why wouldn't a profit-maximizing firm want to produce at the rate of output that minimizes average total cost? LO2
6. What rate of output is appropriate for a "nonprofit" corporation (such as a hospital)? LO2
7. What costs did GM eliminate when it idled its Lansing plant (News, p. 463.) How about Ford? LO3
8. What was the opportunity cost of Mr. Fujishige's farm? (See News, page 449.) Is society better off with another Disney theme park? Explain. LO2
9. Is Apple Computer a perfectly competitive firm? Explain your answer. LO1
10. If a perfectly competitive firm raises its price above the prevailing market rate, how much of its sales might it lose? Why? Can a competitive firm ever raise its prices? If so, when? LO1

problems The Student Problem Set at the back of this book contains numerical and graphing problems for this chapter.

web activities to accompany this chapter can be found on the Online Learning Center: **http://www.mhhe.com/economics/schiller11e**

Competitive Markets

LEARNING OBJECTIVES

After reading this chapter, you should know:

LO1. The market characteristics of perfect competition.

LO2. Why economic profits approach zero in competitive markets.

LO3. How society benefits from perfect competition.

Catfish farmers in the South are very upset. During the past two decades they invested millions of dollars in converting cotton farms into breeding ponds for catfish. They now have over 150,000 acres of ponds and supply 80 percent of the nation's catfish. But profits have been scarce. Prices spiraled downward after 2000, hitting a low of 55 cents per pound in 2003. With production costs averaging 65 cents a pound, most catfish farmers lost money. With losses mounting, a lot of farmers got out of the catfish business, filling their ponds with dirt and planting cotton again. The number of U.S. catfish farms declined by half (to 1,023) in only seven years.

It wasn't supposed to happen this way. Ten years ago, catfish looked like a sure thing. But so many Southern farmers got into the business that catfish prices started falling. Then Vietnam started exporting catfish to the United States, putting still further pressure on prices (see World View on next page).

The dilemma catfish farmers found themselves in is a familiar occurrence in competitive markets. When profits look good, everybody wants to get in on the act. As more and more firms start producing the good, prices and profits tumble. This helps explain why over 200,000 new firms are formed each year and why over 50,000 others fail.

This chapter focuses on the behavior of competitive markets. We have three principal questions:

- **How are prices determined in competitive markets?**
- **How does competition affect the profits of a firm or industry?**
- **What does society gain from market competition?**

The answers to these questions will reveal how markets work when all producers are relatively small and lack market power. In subsequent chapters we emphasize how market outcomes change when markets are less competitive.

THE MARKET SUPPLY CURVE

In the previous chapter we examined the supply behavior of a perfectly competitive firm. The perfectly competitive firm is a price taker. It *responds* to the market price by producing that rate of output where marginal cost equals price.

But what about the *market* supply of catfish? We need a market supply curve to determine the **equilibrium price** the individual farmer will confront. In the previous chapter we simply drew a market supply curve arbitrarily, in order to establish a market price. Now, our objective is to find out where that **market supply** curve comes from.

Like the market supply curves we first encountered in Chapter 3, we can calculate the market supply of catfish by simple addition. All we have to do is add up the quantities each of America's 1,000 catfish farmers stands ready to supply at each price. Then we'll know the total quantity of fish to be supplied to the market at that price. Figure 23.1 illustrates this summation. Notice that ***the market supply curve is the sum of* the marginal cost *curves of all the firms.*** Hence, whatever determines the marginal cost of a typical firm will also affect industry supply. Specifically, ***the market supply of a competitive industry is determined by***

- ***The price of factor inputs.***
- ***Technology.***
- ***Expectations.***
- ***Taxes and subsidies.***
- ***The number of firms in the industry.***

equilibrium price: The price at which the quantity of a good demanded in a given time period equals the quantity supplied.

market supply: The total quantities of a good that sellers are willing and able to sell at alternative prices in a given time period, *ceteris paribus.*

marginal cost (MC): The increase in total cost associated with a one-unit increase in production.

Entry and Exit

If more firms enter an industry, the market supply curve will shift to the right. This is the problem confronting the catfish farmers in Mississippi (see World View). It's fairly inexpensive to get into the catfish business: You can start with a pond, some breeding stock, and relatively little capital equipment. These **investment decisions** shift the market supply curve to the right and drive down catfish prices. This process is illustrated in Figure 23.2*a*. Notice how the equilibrium price slides down the market demand curve from E_1 to E_2 when more firms enter the market.

If prices fall too far, entry will cease and some catfish farmers will drain their ponds and plant cotton again. As they leave (exit) the industry, the market supply curve will shift to the left.

investment decision: The decision to build, buy, or lease plant and equipment; to enter or exit an industry.

WORLD VIEW 

Whiskered Catfish Stir a New Trade Controversy

LAKE VILLAGE, ARK.—Alleamer Tyler works in quality control at Farm Fresh Catfish, a processing plant in this small Delta town on the edge of the Mississippi River. Her days are sometimes slower than in the past, because she doesn't test as many fish as she once did.

"The imports have made a huge impact," says Ms. Tyler, one of Farm Fresh's 100 employees.

Because of Vietnamese fish imports, the US catfish production has plunged in the past year. At Farm Fresh, 95,000 pounds a day were processed last year. This year, it's down to 65,000.

Mississippi leads the nation in catfish production, followed by Arkansas and Louisiana. Most US catfish are raised in the Delta, one of the most poverty-stricken areas in the country. It's a place where the loss of even a few jobs that pay $8 an hour leaves a void in the local economy.

Catfish producers say imports from Vietnam have soared from 575,000 pounds in 1998 to as much as 20 million pounds this year.

—Suzi Parker

Source: *Suzi Parker,* October 3, 2001.

Analysis: When economic profits exist in an industry, more producers try to enter. As they do, prices and economic profits decline. When losses are incurred, firms begin to exit the industry.

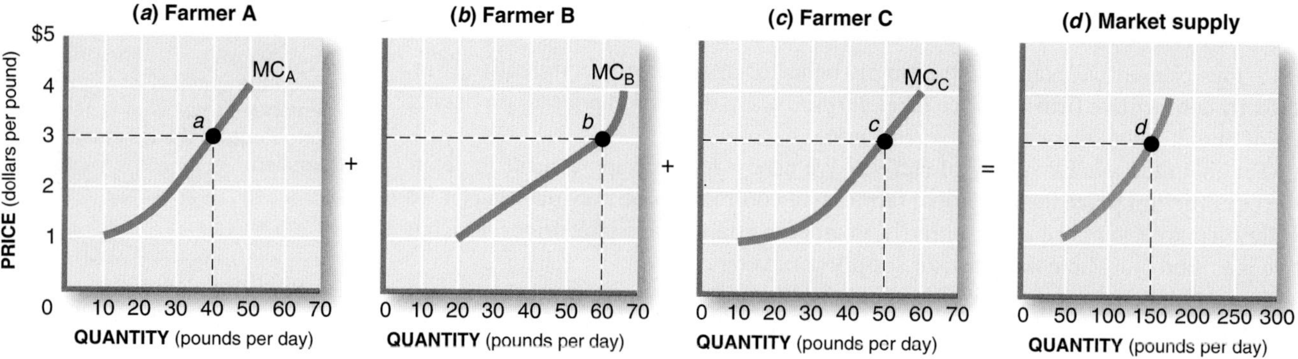

FIGURE 23.1
Competitive Market Supply

The portion of the MC curve that lies above AVC is a competitive firm's short-run supply curve. The curve MC_A tells us that Farmer A will produce 40 pounds of catfish per day if the market price is \$3 per pound.

To determine the *market* supply, we add up the quantities supplied at each price by every farmer. The total quantity supplied to the market at the price of \$3 is 150 pounds per day ($a + b + c$). Market supply depends on the number of firms and their respective marginal costs.

Tendency toward Zero Profits

economic profit: The difference between total revenues and total economic costs.

The profit motive drives these entry and exit decisions. Ten years ago catfish farming looked a whole lot more profitable than cotton farming. Farmers responded by flooding their cotton fields to create fish ponds.

The resulting shift of market supply caused the **economic profits** in catfish farming to disappear. (Notice in Figure 23.2*b* how total profits shrink when price is driven down from p_1 to p_2). Eventually the returns in catfish farming were no better than those in cotton farming. When that happened, cotton farmers stopped building fish ponds and resumed planting cotton. ***When economic profits disappear, entry ceases, and the market stabilizes.*** At that new equilibrium, catfish farmers earn only a normal (average) rate of return.

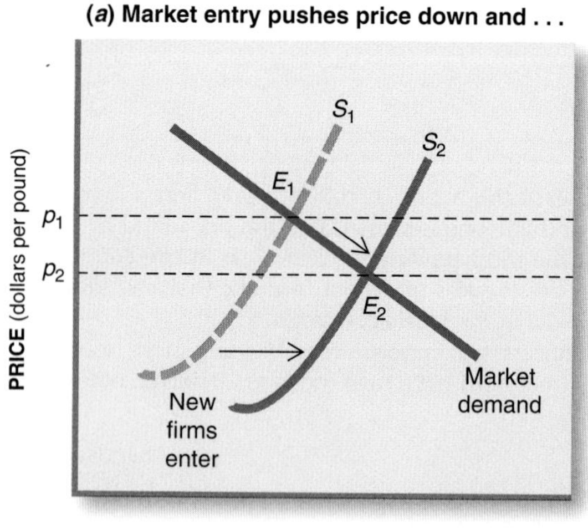

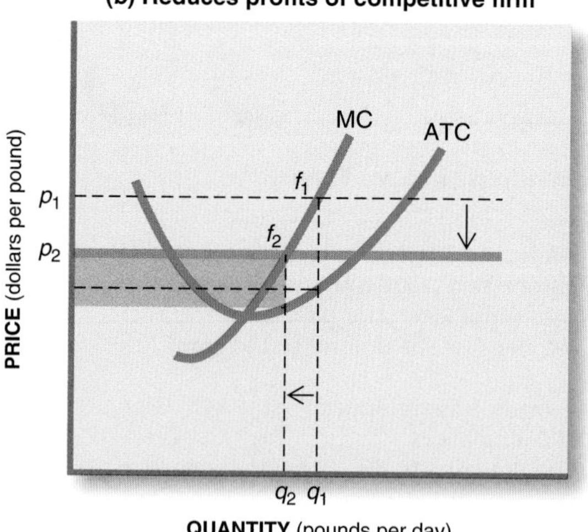

FIGURE 23.2
Market Entry

If economic profits exist in an industry, more firms will want to enter it. As they do, the market supply curve will shift to the right and cause the market price to drop from p_1 to p_2 (part *a*).

The lower market price, in turn, will reduce the output and profits of the typical firm. In part *b*, the firm's output falls from q_1 to q_2.

Catfish farmers would be happier, of course, if the price of catfish didn't decline to the point where economic profits disappear. But how are they going to prevent it? Alleamer Tyler evidently knows all about the laws of supply and demand (see the previous World View). She would dearly like to keep all those Vietnamese catfish out of this country. She also wishes those farmers in Maine would keep cranberries in their ponds rather than catfish. She would also like to get other farmers in the South to slow production a little before all the profits disappear. But Ms. Tyler is powerless to stop the forces of a **competitive market.** She can't even afford to reduce her *own* catfish production. Even though she has 200 acres of ponds, nobody would notice the resulting drop in market supplies, and catfish prices would continue to slide. The only one affected would be Ms. Tyler, who'd be denying herself the opportunity to share in the (dwindling) fortunes of the catfish market while they lasted.

competitive market: A market in which no buyer or seller has market power.

Ms. Tyler's dilemma goes a long way toward explaining why catfish farming isn't highly profitable. Whenever the profit picture looks good, everybody tries to get in on the action. This kind of pressure on prices and profits is a fundamental characteristic of competitive markets. ***As long as it's easy for existing producers to expand production or for new firms to enter an industry, economic profits won't last long.*** As we'll see shortly, this is a lesson Steve Jobs and Apple Computer have learned repeatedly.

webnote

You can track catfish output and prices and even get recipes at the Catfish Institute's Web site: www.catfishinstitute.com

Low Barriers to Entry

New producers will be able to enter a profitable industry and help drive down prices and profits as long as they don't encounter significant barriers. Such **barriers to entry** may include patents, control of essential factors of production, control of distribution outlets, well-established brand loyalty, or even governmental regulation. All such barriers make it expensive, risky, or impossible for new firms to enter an industry. In the absence of such barriers, new firms can enter an industry more readily and at less risk. Not surprisingly, firms already entrenched in a profitable industry do their best to keep out newcomers by erecting barriers to entry. Unfortunately for Ms. Tyler, there are few barriers to entering the catfish business; all you need to get started is a pond and a few fish.

barriers to entry: Obstacles, such as patents, that make it difficult or impossible for would-be producers to enter a particular market

Market Characteristics of Perfect Competition

This brief review of catfish economics illustrates a few general observations about the structure, behavior, and outcomes of a competitive market:

- ***Many firms.*** A competitive market includes a great many firms, none of which has a significant share of total output.
- ***Perfect information.*** All buyers and sellers have complete information on available supply, demand, and prices.
- ***Identical products.*** Products are homogeneous. One firm's product is the same as any other firm's product.
- ***$MC = p$.*** All competitive firms will seek to expand output until marginal cost equals price, in as much as price and marginal revenue are identical for such firms.
- ***Low barriers.*** Barriers to enter the industry are low. If economic profits are available, more firms will enter the industry.
- ***Zero economic profit.*** The tendency of production and market supplies to expand when profit is high puts heavy pressures on prices and profits in competitive industries. Economic profit will approach zero in the long run as prices are driven down to the level of average production costs.

COMPETITION AT WORK: MICROCOMPUTERS

Few markets have all the characteristics listed above. That is, ***few, if any, product markets are perfectly competitive.*** However, many industries function much like the competitive model we sketched out. In addition to catfish farming, most other agricultural product markets are characterized by highly competitive market structures, with hundreds or even thousands of producers supplying the market. Other highly competitive, and hence not very profitable, businesses are T-shirt shops, retail food, printing, clothing manufacturing and retailing, dry-cleaning establishments, beauty salons, and furniture. Online stockbroker

WORLD VIEW 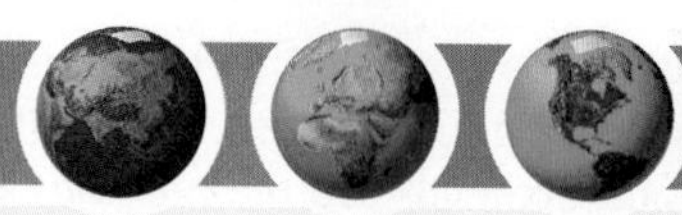

Flat Panels, Thin Margins

Rugged competition from smaller brands has made the TV sets cheaper than ever

Like just about everyone else checking out the flat-panel TVs at Best Buy in Manhattan, graphic designer Roy Gantt came in coveting a Philips, Sony, or Panasonic. But after seeing the price tags, he figured a Westinghouse might be a better buy. . . .

. . . it is just one of more than 100 flat-panel brands jamming the aisles of retailers such as Best Buy, Target, and Costco. The names on the sets range from the obscure (Sceptre, Maxent) to the recycled (Polaroid).

The free-for-all is a boon to the millions of Americans who want to trade in their bulky analog sets. . . .

For many in the industry, though, the competition is brutal. Prices for LCD sets are falling so rapidly that retailers who place orders too far in advance risk getting struck with expensive inventory. Circuit City Stores Inc. cited plummeting prices in its Feb. 8 announcement that it will shutter nearly 70 outlets. . . .

THE STAT

102

LCD television brands available in the U.S., up from 26 in 2002

Data: Pacific Media Associates

All Outsourced

Nowadays, LCD makers will sell to anyone, and the rest of the needed parts—tuners and computer chips—are available from multiple suppliers. Contract manufacturers will happily assemble all the pieces at factories in China, Mexico, or Taiwan. So the only things you need to become an instant player are strong relationships with suppliers, connections at big retailers, and a handful of engineers to design the sets.

—Pete Engardio

Source: *BusinessWeek,* February 26, 2007, p. 50.

Analysis: Competitive pressures compel producers of flat-panel TVs to keep improving the product and reducing prices. The lure of profits encourages firms to enter this expanding market even as prices drop.

services have also become highly competitive. In these markets, prices and profits are always under the threat of expanded supplies brought to market by existing or new producers.

The electronics industry offers numerous examples of how competition reduces prices and profits. Between 1972 and 1983, the price of small, hand-held calculators fell from \$200 to under \$10. The price of digital watches fell even more dramatically, from roughly \$2,000 in 1975 to under \$7 in 1990. Videocassette recorders (VCRs) that sold for \$2,000 in 1979 now sell for less than \$60. DVD players that cost \$1,500 in 1997 now sell for under \$70. Cell phones that sold for \$1,000 ten years ago are now given away. The same kind of competitive pressures have reduced the price of flat-screen TVs. New entrants keep bringing better TVs to market, while driving prices down (see World View).

The driving force behind all these price reductions and quality improvements is *competition.* Do you really believe the price of phone calls would be falling if only one firm supplied all telephone services? Do you think thousands of software writers would be toiling away right now if popular programs didn't generate enormous profits? Would Google and Dell Computer keep rolling out new products and services if other companies weren't always snapping at their heels?

Market Evolution

To appreciate how the process of competition works, we will examine the development of the personal computer industry. ***As in other industries, the market structure of the computer industry has evolved over time. It was never a monopoly, nor was it ever perfect competition.*** In its first couple of years it was dominated by only a few companies (like Apple) that were enormously successful. The high profits the early microcomputer producers obtained attracted swarms of imitators. Over 250 firms entered the microcomputer industry between 1976 and 1983 in search of high profits. The entry of so many firms transformed the industry's market structure: The industry became *more* competitive, even though not *perfectly* competitive. The increased competition pushed prices downward and improved the product.

Courtesy of Apple Computer, Inc.

Analysis: The Apple I launched the personal computer industry in 1976. Hundreds of firms entered the industry to improve on this first preassembled microcomputer.

When prices and profits tumbled, scores of companies went bankrupt. They left a legacy, however, of a vastly larger market, much improved computers, and sharply lower prices.

We'll use the early experiences of the microcomputer industry to illustrate the key behavioral features of a competitive market. As we'll see, many of these competitive features are still at work in the PC market and even more visible in the markets for Internet services, content software, digital music players, and iPhones.

Initial Conditions: The Apple I

The microcomputer industry really got started in 1977. Prior to that time, microcomputers were essentially a hobby item for engineers and programmers, who bought circuits, keyboards, monitors, and tape recorders and then assembled their own basic computers. Steve Jobs, then working at Atari, and Steven Wozniak, then working at Hewlett-Packard, were among these early computer enthusiasts. They spent their days working on large systems and their nights and weekends trying to put together small computers from mail-order parts.

Eventually, Jobs and Wozniak decided they had the capability to build commercially attractive small computers. They ordered the parts necessary for building 100 computers and set up shop in the garage of Jobs's parents. Their finished product—the Apple I—was nothing more than a circuit board with a simple, built-in operating system. This first microcomputer was packaged in a wooden box (see photo). Despite primitive characteristics, the first 100 Apple I computers sold out immediately. This quick success convinced Jobs and Wozniak to package their computers more fully—which they did by enclosing them in plastic housing—and to offer more of them for sale. Shortly thereafter, in January 1977, Apple Computer, Inc. was established.

webnote

Apple Computer, Inc.'s Web site details the development of their computer, including photos. Visit Apple at www.apple-history.com

Apple revolutionalized the market by offering a preassembled desktop computer with attractive features and an accessible price. The impact on the marketplace was much like that of Henry Ford's early Model T: Suddenly a newfangled piece of technology came into reach of the average U.S. household, and everybody, it seemed, wanted one. The first mass-produced Apple computer—called the Apple II—was just a basic keyboard with an operating system that permitted users to write their own programs. The computer had no disk drive, no monitor, and only 4K of random access memory (RAM). Consumers had to use their TV sets as screens and audiocassettes for data storage. This primitive Apple II was priced at just under $1,300 when it debuted in June 1977. Apple was producing computers at the rate of 500 per month.

Apple didn't engineer or manufacture chips or semiconductor components. Instead, it simply packaged existing components purchased from outside suppliers. Hence, it was easy for other companies to follow Apple's lead. Within a very brief time, other firms, such as Tandy

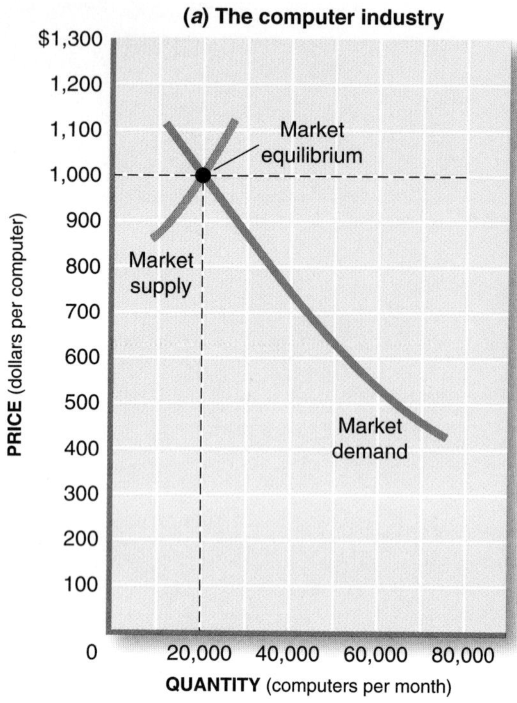

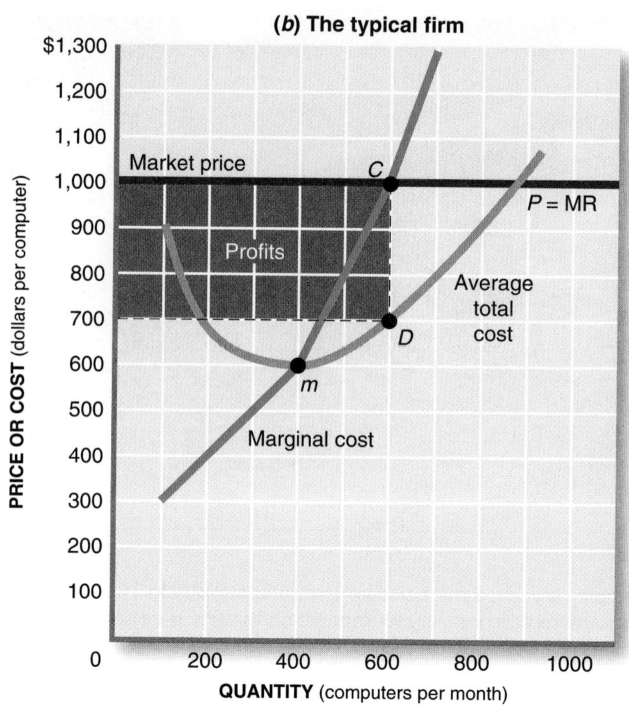

FIGURE 23.3
Initial Equilibrium in the Computer Market

(*a*) The Industry In 1978, the market price of microcomputers was $1,000. This price was established by the intersection of the market supply and demand curves.

(*b*) A Firm Each competitive producer in the market sought to produce computers at that rate (600 per month) where marginal cost equaled price (point *C*). Profit per computer was equal to price (point *C*) minus average total cost (point *D*). Total profits for the typical firm are indicated by the shaded rectangle.

(Radio Shack), also started to assemble computers. By the middle of 1978, the basic small computer was selling for $1,000, and industry sales were about 20,000 a month. Figure 23.3*a* depicts the initial (1978) equilibrium in the computer market and Figure 23.3*b* illustrates the approximate costs of production for the typical computer manufacturer at that time.

The Production Decision

production decision: The selection of the short-run rate of output (with existing plant and equipment).

The short-run goal of every producer is to find the rate of output that maximizes profits. Finding this rate entails making the best possible **production decision.** In this short-run context, ***each competitive firm seeks the rate of output at which marginal cost equals price.***

Figure 23.3*b* illustrates the cost and price curves the typical computer producer confronted in 1978. As in most lines of production, the marginal costs of computer production increased with the rate of output. Marginal costs rose in part because output could be increased in the short-run (with existing plant and equipment) only by crowding additional workers onto the assembly line. In 1978, Apple had only 10,000 square feet of manufacturing space. As more workers were hired, each worker had less capital and land to work with, and marginal physical product fell. The law of diminishing returns pushed marginal costs up.

The upward-sloping marginal cost curve intersected the price line at an output level of 600 computers per month (point *C* in Figure 23.3*b*).[1] That was the profit-maximizing rate of output (MC = *p*) for the typical manufacturer. To manufacture any more than 600 computers per month would raise marginal costs over price and reduce total profits. To manufacture any less would be to pass up an opportunity to make another buck.

[1] The marginal cost curves depicted here rise more steeply than they did in reality, but the general shape of the curves is our primary concern at this point.

Output per Month	Price	Total Revenue	Total Cost	Total Profit	Marginal Revenue*	Marginal Cost*	Average Total Cost	Profit per Unit (price minus average cost)
0	—	—	$ 60,000	−$60,000	—	—	—	—
100	$1,000	$100,000	90,000	10,000	$1,000	$ 300	$ 900	$100
200	1,000	200,000	130,000	70,000	1,000	400	650	350
300	1,000	300,000	180,000	120,000	1,000	500	600	400
400	1,000	400,000	240,000	160,000	1,000	600	600	400
500	1,000	500,000	320,000	180,000	1,000	800	640	360
600	1,000	600,000	420,000	180,000	1,000	1,000	700	300
700	1,000	700,000	546,000	154,000	1,000	1,260	780	220
800	1,000	800,000	720,000	80,000	1,000	1,740	900	100
900	1,000	900,000	919,800	−19,800	1,000	1,998	1,022	−22

*Note that output levels are calibrated in hundreds in this example; that's why we have divided the *change* in total costs and revenues from one output level to another by 100 to calculate marginal revenue and marginal cost. Very few manufacturers deal in units of 1.

TABLE 23.1
Computer Revenues, Costs, and Profits

Producers seek that rate of output where total profit is maximized. This table illustrates the output choices the typical computer producer faced in 1978. The profit-maximizing rate of output occurred at 600 computers per month. At that rate of output, marginal cost was equal to price ($1,000), and profits were $180,000 per month.

Profit Calculations

Table 23.1 shows how much *profit* a typical computer manufacturer was making in 1978. As the profit column indicates, the typical computer manufacturer could make a real killing in the computer market, reaping a monthly profit of $180,000 by producing and selling 600 microcomputers.

We could also calculate the computer manufacturers' profits by asking how much the manufacturers make on *each* computer and then multiplying that figure by total output since

$$\text{Total profit} = \text{profit per unit} \times \text{quantity sold}$$

We can compute these profits by studying the first and last columns in Table 23.1 or by using a little geometry in Figure 23.3*b*. In the figure, average costs (total costs divided by the rate of output) are portrayed by the **average total cost (ATC)** curve. At the output rate of 600 (the row in white in Table 23.1), the distance between the price line ($1,000 at point *C*) and the ATC curve ($700 at point *D*) is $300, which represents the average **profit per unit.** Multiplying this figure by the number of units sold (600 per month) will give us *total* profit per month. Total profits are represented by the shaded rectangle in Figure 23.3*b* and are equal to our earlier profit figure of $180,000 per month.

average total cost (ATC): Total cost divided by the quantity produced in a given time period.

profit per unit: Total profit divided by the quantity produced in a given time period; price minus average total cost.

The Lure of Profits

While gaping at the computer manufacturer's enormous profits, we should remind ourselves that those profits might not last long. Indeed, the more quick-witted among us already will have seen and heard enough to know they've discovered a good thing. And in fact, the kind of profits the early microcomputer manufacturers attained attracted a lot of entrepreneurial interest. ***In competitive markets, economic profits attract new entrants.*** This is what happened in the catfish industry and also in the computer industry. Within a very short time, a whole crowd of profit maximizers entered the microcomputer industry in hot pursuit of its fabulous profits. By the end of 1980, Apple had a lot of competition, including new entrants from IBM, Xerox, Digital Equipment, Casio, Sharp, and others.

Low Entry Barriers

A critical feature of the microcomputer market was its lack of entry barriers. A microcomputer is little more than a box containing a microprocessor "brain," which connects to a keyboard (to enter data), a memory (to store data), and a screen (to display data). Although the microprocessors that guide the computer are extremely sophisticated, they can be purchased on the open market. Thus, to enter the computer industry, all one needs is some space, some money to buy components, and some dexterity in putting parts together. Such ***low entry barriers permit new firms to enter competitive markets.*** According to Table 23.1, the typical producer needed only $60,000 of plant and equipment (fixed costs) to get started in the microcomputer market. Jobs and Wozniak had even less when they started making Apples in their garage.

A Shift of Market Supply

Figure 23.4 shows what happened to the computer market and the profits of the typical firm once the word got out. As more and more entrepreneurs heard how profitable computer manufacturing could be, they quickly got hold of a book on electronic circuitry, rushed to the bank, got a little financing, and set up shop. Before many months had passed, scores of new firms had started producing small computers. ***The entry of new firms shifts the market supply curve to the right.*** In Figure 23.4*a*, the supply curve shifted from S_1 to S_2. Almost as fast as a computer can calculate a profit (loss) statement, the willingness to supply increased abruptly.

But the new computer companies were in for a bit of disappointment. With so many new firms hawking microcomputers, it became increasingly difficult to make a fast buck. The downward-sloping market demand curve confirms that a greater quantity of microcomputers could be sold only if the price of computers dropped. And drop it did. The price slide began as computer manufacturers found their inventories growing and so offered price discounts to maintain sales volume. The price fell rapidly, from $1,000 in mid-1978 to $800 in early 1980.

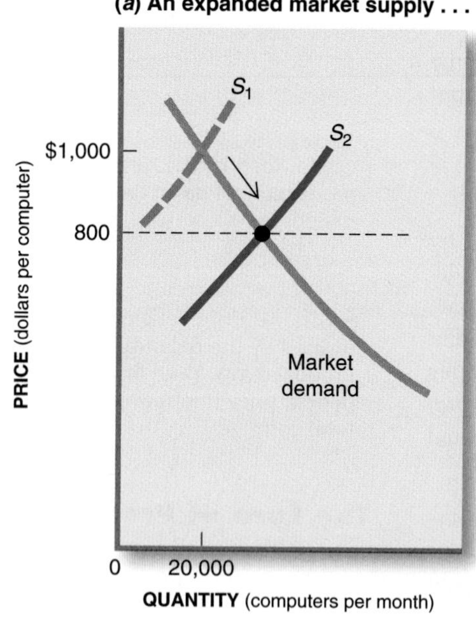

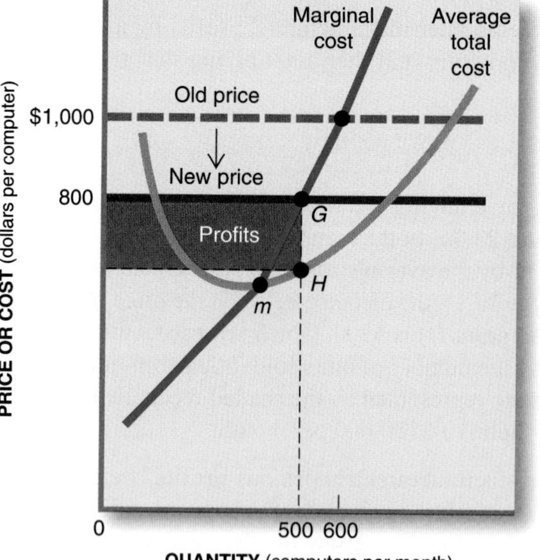

FIGURE 23.4
The Competitive Price and Profit Squeeze

***(a)* The Industry** The economic profits in the computer industry encouraged new firms to enter the industry. As they did, the market supply curve shifted from S_1 to S_2. This rightward shift of the supply curve lowered the equilibrium price of computers.

***(b)* A Firm** The lower market price, in turn, forced the typical producer to reduce output to the point where MC and price were equal again (point *G*). At this reduced rate of output, the typical firm earned less total profit than it had earned before.

The sliding market price squeezed the profits of each firm, causing the profit rectangle to shrink (compare Figure 23.3*b* to Figure 23.4*b*). The lower price also changed the production decision of the typical firm. The new price ($800) intersected the unchanged MC curve at the output rate of 500 computers per month (point *G* in Figure 23.4*b*). With average production costs of $640 (Table 23.1), the firm's total profits in 1980 were only $80,000 per month [(*P* – ATC) × 500]. Not a paltry sum, to be sure, but nothing like the fantastic fortunes pocketed earlier.

As long as an economic profit is available, it will continue to attract new entrants. Those entrepreneurs who were a little slow in absorbing the implications of Figure 23.3 eventually woke up to what was going on and tried to get in on the action, too. Even though they were a little late, they didn't want to miss the chance to cash in on the $80,000 in monthly profits still available to the typical firm. Hence, the market supply curve continued to shift, and computer prices slid further, as in Figure 23.5. This process squeezed the profits of the typical firm still more, further shrinking the profit rectangle.

As long as economic profits exist in **short-run competitive equilibrium,** that equilibrium won't last. If the rate of profit obtainable in computer production is higher than that available in other industries, new firms will enter the industry. Conversely, if the short-run equilibrium is unprofitable, firms will exit the industry. Profit-maximizing entrepreneurs have a special place in their hearts for economic profits, not computers.

short-run competitive equilibrium: p = MC.

Price and profit declines will cease when the price of computers equals the minimum average cost of production. At that price (point *m* in Figure 23.5*b*), there's no more economic profit to be squeezed out. Firms no longer have an incentive to enter the industry, and the supply curve stops shifting. This situation represents the **long-run competitive equilibrium** for the firm and for the industry. ***In long-run equilibrium, entry and exit cease, and zero economic profit (that is, normal profit) prevails*** (see Figure 23.6). Table 23.2 on the next page summarizes the profit-maximizing rules that bring about this long-run equilibrium.

long-run competitive equilibrium: p = MC = minimum ATC.

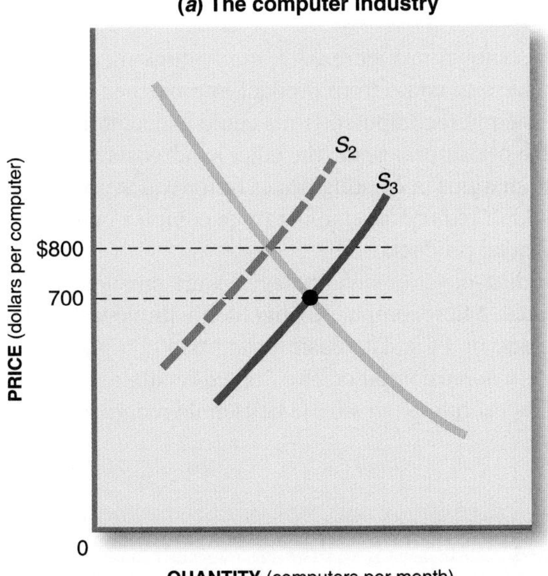

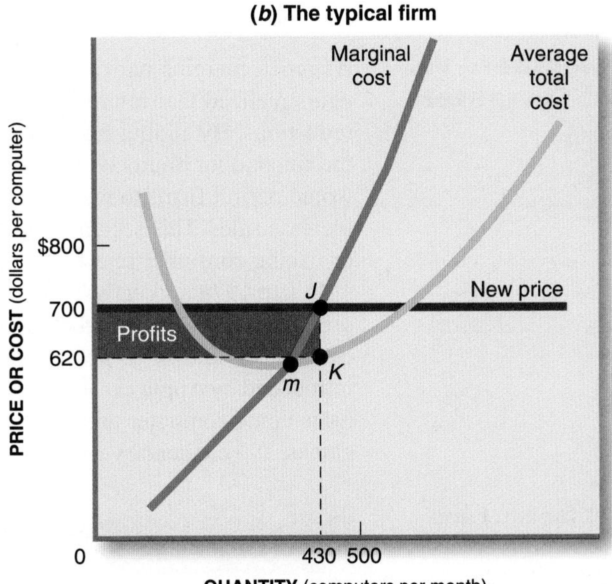

FIGURE 23.5
The Competitive Squeeze Approaching Its Limit

(*a*) The Industry Even at a price of $800 per computer, economic profits attracted still more entrepreneurs, shifting the market supply curve further (S_3). The next short-term equilibrium occurred at a price of $700 per computer.

(*b*) A Firm At this reduced market price, the typical manufacturer wanted to supply only 430 computers per month (point *J*). Total profits were much lower than they had been earlier, with fewer producers and higher prices.

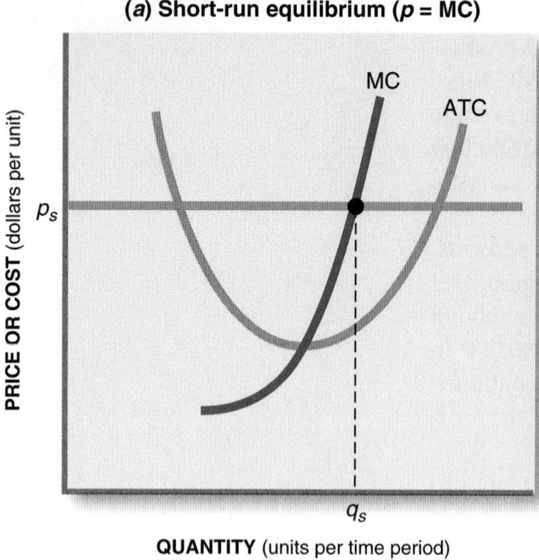

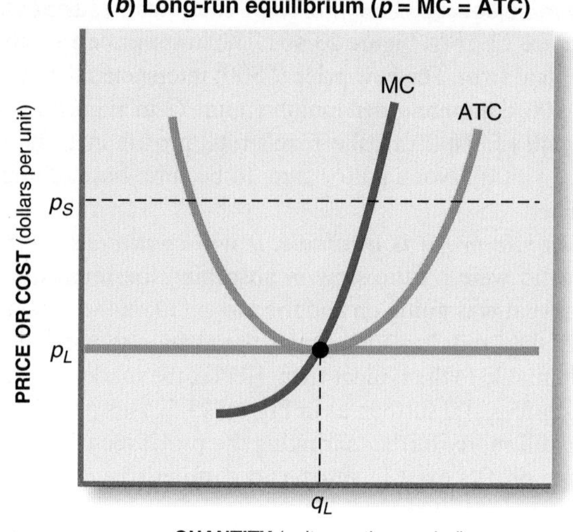

FIGURE 23.6
Short- vs. Long-run Equilibrium for the Competitive Firm

(*a*) Short-Run Competitive firms strive for the rate of output at which marginal cost (MC) equals price. When they achieve that rate of output, they are in *short-run equilibrium.* Whether profitable or not, there is no incentive to alter the rate of output produced with existing (fixed) plant and equipment; it is the *best* the firm can do in the short run.

(*b*) Long-Run If the short-run equilibrium (q_S) is profitable ($p >$ ATC), other firms will want to enter the industry. As they do, market price will fall until it reaches the level of minimum ATC. In this *long-run equilibrium* (q_L), economic profits are zero and nobody wants to enter or exit the industry.

Once a long-run equilibrium is established, it will continue until market demand shifts or technological progress reduces the cost of computer production. In fact, that's just what happened in the computer market.

Home Computers vs. Personal Computers

As profit margins narrowed to the levels shown in Figure 23.5, quick-thinking entrepreneurs realized that future profits would have to come from product improvements or cost reductions. By adding features to the basic microcomputer, firms could expect to increase the demand for microcomputers and fetch higher prices. On the other hand, cost reductions would permit firms to widen their profit margins at existing prices or to reduce prices and increase sales. This second strategy wouldn't require assembling more complex computers or risking consumer rejection of an upgraded product.

In late 1979 and early 1980, both product-development strategies were pursued. In the process, two distinct markets were created. Microcomputers upgraded with new features came to be known as *personal* computers, or PCs. The basic unadorned computer first introduced by Apple came to be known as a *home* computer. The limited capabilities of that basic home computer greatly restricted its usefulness to simple household record keeping, games, and elementary programming.

TABLE 23.2
Long-Run Rules for Entry and Exit

Firms will enter an industry if economic profits exist ($p >$ ATC). They will exit if economic losses prevail ($p <$ ATC). Entry and exit cease in long-run equilibrium with zero economic profit ($p =$ ATC). (See Table 22.4 for short-run profit-maximization rules.)

Price Level	Result for a Typical Firm	Market Response
$p >$ ATC	Profits	Enter industry (or expand capacity)
$p <$ ATC	Loss	Exit industry (or reduce capacity)
$p =$ ATC	Break even	Maintain existing capacity (no entry or exit)

Apple chose the personal computer route. It started enlarging the memory of the Apple II in late 1978 (from 4K to as much as 48K). It offered a monitor (produced by Sanyo) for the first time in May 1979. Shortly thereafter, Apple ceased making the basic Apple II and instead produced only upgraded versions (the Apple IIe, the IIc, and the III). Hundreds of other companies followed Apple's lead, touting increasingly sophisticated personal computers.

While one pack of entrepreneurs was chasing PC profits, another pack was going after the profits still available in home computers. This group chose to continue producing the basic Apple II look-alike, hoping to profit from greater efficiency, lower costs, and increasing sales.

Price Competition in Home Computers

The home computer market confronted the fiercest form of price competition. With prices continually sliding, the only way to make an extra buck was to push down the cost curve.

To reduce costs, firms sought to reduce the number of microprocessor chips installed in the computer's "brain." Fewer chips not only reduce direct materials costs, but more important, they decrease the amount of labor required for computer assembly. The key to lower manufacturing costs was more powerful chips. More powerful chips appeared when Intel, Motorola, and Texas Instruments developed 16-bit chips, doubling the computer's "brain" capabilities.

Further Supply Shifts

The impact of the improved chips on computer production costs and profits is illustrated in Figure 23.7, which takes over where Figure 23.5 left off. Recall that the market price of computers had been driven down to $700 by the beginning of 1980. At this price the typical firm maximized profits by producing 430 computers per month, as determined by the intersection of the prevailing price and MC curves (point *J* in Figure 23.7).

The only way for the firm to improve profitability at this point was to reduce costs. The new chips made such cost reductions easy. Such ***technological improvements are illustrated by a downward shift of the ATC and MC curves.*** Notice, for example, that the new technology permits 430 home computers to be produced for a lower marginal cost (about $500) than previously (point *J*).

The lower cost structure increases the profitability of computer production and stimulates a further increase in production. Note in particular that the "new MC" curve intersects the price ($700) line at an output of 600 computers per month (point *N*). By contrast, the

webnote

Find information on U.S. business failures compiled by Dun and Bradstreet at www.loc.gov/rr/business/duns/duns9.html#db9c

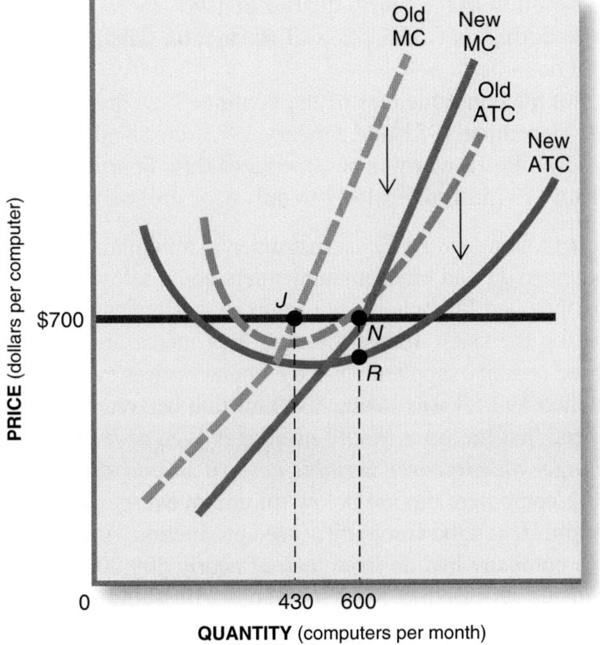

FIGURE 23.7
A Downward Shift of Costs Improves Profits and Stimulates Output

The quest for profits encouraged producers to discover cheaper ways to manufacture computers. The resulting improvements lowered costs and encouraged further increases in the rate of output. The typical computer producer increased output from point J (where p = old MC) to point *N* (where p = new MC).

TABLE 23.3
Plummeting Prices

Improved technology and fierce competition forced home computer prices down. In the span of only a few years, the price of a basic home computer fell from just under $1,000 to only $49. In the process, price fell below average variable cost, and many firms were forced to shut down.

Date		Price of Texas Instruments Model 99/4A
December	1979	$950
February	1980	700
June	1980	650
April	1981	525
December	1981	400
April	1982	249
September	1982	199
January	1983	149
September	1983	99
November	1983	49

old, higher MC curve dictated a production rate of only 430 computers per month for the typical firm (point J) at that price. Thus, existing producers suddenly had an incentive to *expand* production, and new firms had a greater incentive to *enter* the industry. The great rush into computer production was on again.

The market implications of another entrepreneurial stampede should now be obvious. As more and more firms tried to get in on the action, the market supply curve again shifted to the right. As output increased, computer prices slid further down the market demand curve.

Table 23.3 illustrates how steeply home computer prices fell after 1980. Texas Instruments (TI) was one of the largest firms producing home computers in 1980. The lower costs made possible by improved microprocessors enabled TI to sell its basic home computer for $650 in 1980. Despite modest improvements in the TI machine, TI had to reduce its price to $525 in early 1981 in order to maintain unit sales. Shortly thereafter, the additional output of new entrants and existing companies pushed market prices down still further, to around $400.

Even at $400, TI and other home computer manufacturers were making handsome profits. In the fourth quarter of 1981, total industry sales were in excess of 200,000 per month—10 times the volume sold just 3 years earlier. Profits were good, too. A single company, Atari, recorded total profits of $137 million in the fourth quarter of 1981, far more profit than Apple Computer, Inc. had made during its first 5 *years* of production. The profits of the home computer market appeared boundless.

The remainder of Table 23.3 shows the consequences of the continued competition for those "boundless" profits. Between December 1981 and January 1983, the retail price of home computers fell from $400 to $149. Profit margins became razor-thin. Fourth-quarter profits at Atari, for example, fell from $137 million in 1981 to only $1.2 million in 1983.

Shutdowns

That didn't stop the competitive process, however. At Texas Instruments, minimum *variable* costs were roughly $100 per computer, so TI and other manufacturers could afford to keep producing even at lower prices. And they had little choice but to do so, since if they didn't, other companies would quickly take up the slack. Industry output kept increasing, despite shrinking profit margins. The increased quantity supplied pushed computer prices ever lower.

By the time computer prices reached $99, TI was losing $300 million per year. In September 1983, the company recognized that the price would no longer even cover average variable costs. ***Once a firm is no longer able to cover variable costs, it should shut down production.*** When the price of home computers dipped below minimum average variable costs, TI had reached the **shutdown point,** and the company ceased production. At the time TI made the shutdown decision, the company had an inventory of nearly 500,000 unsold computers. To unload them, TI reduced its price to $49 (see Table 23.3), forcing lower prices and losses on other computer firms.

shutdown point: The rate of output where price equals minimum AVC.

IN THE NEWS

IBM to Halt PCjr Output Next Month

Computer's Sales Dried Up After Steep Price Cuts Ended Earlier This Year

NEW YORK—International Business Machines Corp. ended its up-and-down struggle to revive its PCjr home computer by announcing it would stop making the product next month.

The surprise move marks IBM's most visible product failure since its enormously successful entry into the personal-computer business four years ago. IBM announced the PCjr in late 1983 and began selling it early last year with an advertising campaign believed to exceed $40 million. IBM's efforts to make junior a hit ranged from technical changes to steep price cuts. But while aggressive IBM price cuts before Christmas increased PCjr sales substantially, sales dried up after the promotions ended in January. . . .

At the time of its introduction, the PCjr had a list of $699 or $1,269, depending on the model. The prices later were cut to $599 and $999, and the more powerful model's price dropped below the $800 level during the Christmas promotion.

—Dennis Kneale

Analysis: Competition forces firms to improve products and reduce prices. Those firms that can't keep up are forced to shut down and perhaps exit the industry.

Exits

Shortly after Texas Instruments shut down its production, it got out of the home computer business altogether. Mattel, Atari, and scores of smaller companies also withdrew from the home computer market. The exit rate between 1983 and 1985 matched the entry rate of the period 1979 to 1982.

The Personal Computer Market

The same kind of price competition that characterized the home computer market eventually hit the personal computer market too. As noted earlier, the microcomputer industry split into two segments around 1980, with most firms pursuing the upgraded personal computer market.

At first, competition in the PC market was largely confined to product improvements. Firms added more memory, faster microprocessors, better monitors, expanded operating systems, new applications software, and other features. New entrants into the market—Compaq in 1982; then Dell, AST, Gateway, and more—were the source of most product innovations.

The stampede of new firms and products into the PC market soon led to outright price competition too. As firms discovered that they couldn't sell all the PCs they were producing at prevailing prices, they were forced to offer price discounts. These discounts soon spread, and the slide down the demand curve accelerated.

Firms that couldn't keep up with the dual pace of improving technology and falling prices soon fell by the wayside. Scores of firms ceased production and withdrew from the industry once prices fell below minimum average variable cost. Even Apple, which had taken the "high road" to avoid price competition in home computers, was slowed by price competition. And IBM, which had entered the industry late, was forced to shut down its PC division after realizing that steep price cuts would be required to sell its small PCs (the "PCjr") to household users (News).

webnote

For a history of computer features, visit the Computer History Association of California at www.chac.org/chac

THE COMPETITIVE PROCESS

It is now evident that consumers reaped substantial benefits from competition in the computer market. Over 500 million home and personal computers have been sold. Along the way, technology has made personal computers 400 times faster than the first Apple IIs, with 600 times more memory. The iMac computer introduced by Apple in 1998 made the Apple I of 1976 look prehistoric (see photos). A lot of consumers have found that computers

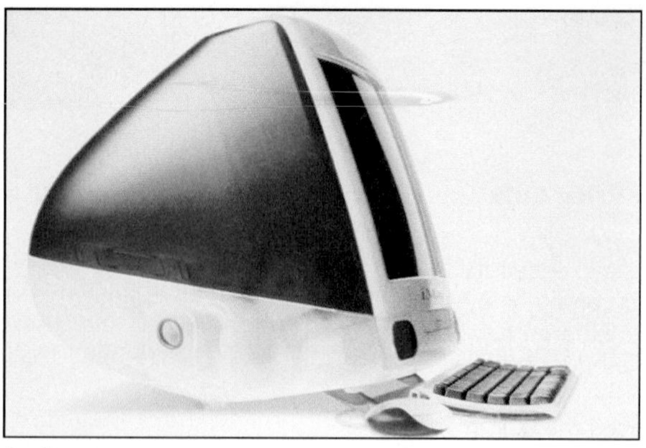
Getty Images

iMac, G3: 1998

Analysis: The evolution of personal computers from the Apple I (photo, page 473) to the latest iMac and iPhone was driven by intense competition.

Getty Images

iMac, G5: 2004

AFP/Getty Images

iPhone: 2007

are great for doing accounting chores, keeping records, writing papers, playing games, and accessing the Internet. Perhaps it's true that an abundance of inexpensive computers would have been produced in other market (or nonmarket) situations as well. But we can't ignore the fact that ***competitive market pressures were a driving force in the spectacular growth of the computer industry.*** And they still are.

Allocative Efficiency: The Right Output Mix

market mechanism: The use of market prices and sales to signal desired outputs (or resource allocations).

The squeeze on prices and profits that we've observed in the computer market is a fundamental characteristic of the competitive process. The process works as well in India (see World View) as in the United States or elsewhere. Indeed, the **market mechanism** works best under competitive pressure. The existence of economic profits is an indication that consumers place a high value on a particular product and are willing to pay a comparatively high price to get it. The high price and profits signal this information to profit-hungry entrepreneurs, who come forward to satisfy consumer demands. Thus, ***high profits in a particular industry indicate that consumers want a different mix of output*** (more of that industry's goods). The competitive squeeze on those same profits indicates that resources are being reallocated to produce that desired mix. In a competitive market, consumers get more of the goods they desire—and at a lower price.

opportunity cost: The most desired goods or services that are forgone in order to obtain something else.

The ability of competitive markets to allocate resources efficiently across industries originates in the way competitive prices are set. To attain the optimal mix of output, we must know the **opportunity cost** of producing different goods. A competitive market gives us the information necessary for making such choices. Why? Because competitive firms always strive to produce at the rate of output at which price equals marginal cost. Hence, ***the price signal the consumer gets in a competitive market is an accurate reflection of opportunity cost.*** As such, it offers a reliable basis for making choices about the mix of

WORLD VIEW

Wireless-Phone Rates in India Declining as Competition Grows

NEW DELHI—India's mobile-phone rates are expected to continue to fall as competition heats up in one of the world's fastest-growing markets.

Analysts say that even after a 60% cut in rates by two major operators this month, there are likely to be further reductions in the fiscal year ending March 31. . . .

"In terms of competitive intensity, the Indian mobile market now resembles some of the most competitive markets in the world," said Kushe Bahl, Associate Partner at McKinsey & Co. "Because of these competitive effects, prices are coming down." He said rates are set to fall farther this fiscal year, though most likely at a slower pace. During the past 10 to 12 quarters, raters have fallen on average by around 12% a quarter, Mr. Bahl said.

—Ruchira Singh

Source: *The Wall Street Journal,* September 1, 2004, p. 87.

Analysis: Competitive pressures force companies to continually improve products and cut prices.

output and attendant allocation of resources. In this sense, the **marginal cost pricing** characteristic of competitive markets permits society to answer the WHAT-to-produce question efficiently. The amount consumers are willing to pay for a good (its price) equals its opportunity cost (marginal cost).

marginal cost pricing: The offer (supply) of goods at prices equal to their marginal cost.

Production Efficiency: Minimum Average Cost

When the competitive pressure on prices is carried to the limit, we also get the right answer to the HOW-to-produce question. Competition drives costs down to their bare minimum—the hallmark of economic **efficiency.** This was illustrated by the tendency of computer prices to be driven down to the level of *minimum* average costs. Figure 23.8 summarizes this competitive process, showing how the industry moves from short-run equilibrium (point a) to long-run equilibrium (point c). Once the long-run equilibrium has been established, society is getting the most it can from its available (scarce) resources.

efficiency: Maximum output of a good from the resources used in production.

Zero Economic Profit

Competitive pressures also affect the FOR WHOM question. At the limit of long-run equilibrium, all economic profit is eliminated. This doesn't mean that producers are left empty-handed, however. The zero-profit limit is rarely, if ever, reached, because new products are continually being introduced, consumer demands change, and more efficient production processes are discovered. In fact, the competitive process creates strong pressures to pursue product and technological innovation. In a competitive market, the adage about the early bird getting the worm is particularly apt. As we observed in the computer market, the first ones to perceive and respond to the potential profitability of computer production were the ones who made the greatest profits.

Relentless Profit Squeeze

The sequence of events common to competitive markets evolves as follows:

- High prices and profits signal consumers' demand for more output.
- Economic profit attracts new suppliers.
- The market supply curve shifts to the right.
- Prices slide down the market demand curve.
- A new equilibrium is reached at which increased quantities of the desired product are produced and its price is lower. Average costs of production are at or near a minimum, much more of the product is supplied and consumed, and economic profit approaches zero.
- Throughout the process, producers experience great pressure to keep ahead of the profit squeeze by reducing costs, a pressure that frequently results in product and technological innovation.

What is essential to remember about the competitive process is that the ***potential threat of other firms expanding production or of new firms entering the industry keeps existing***

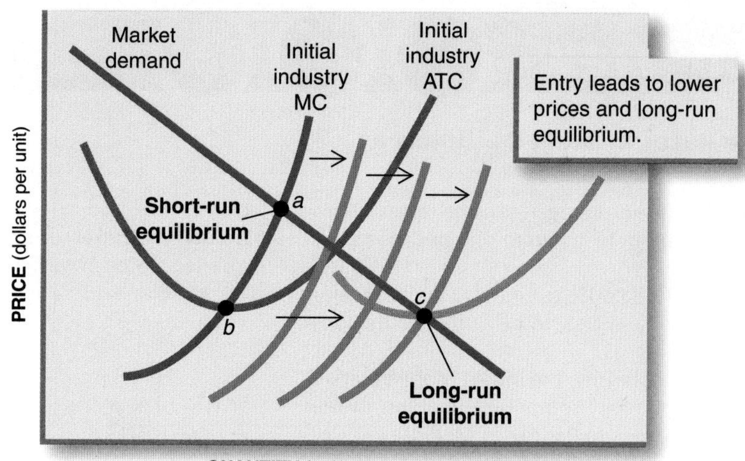

FIGURE 23.8

Summary of Competitive Process

All competitive firms seek to produce at that output where MC = *p*. Hence, a competitive *industry* will produce at that rate of output where *industry* MC (the sum of all firms' MC curves) intersects market demand (point *a*).

If economic profits exist in the industry short-run equilibrium (as they do here), more firms will enter the industry. As they do, the *industry* MC (supply) curve will shift to the right. The shifting MC curve will pull the *industry* ATC curve along with it. As the *industry* MC curve continues to shift right ward, the intersection of MC and ATC (point *b*) eventually will reach the demand curve at point *c*. At point *c*, MC still equals price, but no economic profits exist and entry (shifts) will cease. Point *c* will be the *long-term* equilibrium of the industry.

If competitive pressures reduce costs (i.e., improve technology), the supply (MC) curve will shift further to the right and *down,* reducing long-term prices even more.

Note that MC = *p* in both short- and long-run equilibrium. Notice also that equilibrium must occur on the market demand curve.

firms on their toes. Even the most successful firm can't rest on its laurels for long. To stay in the game, competitive firms must continually update technology, improve their product, and reduce costs. It is the same lesson a lot of entrepreneurs learned in the unusually fast rise and quick death of "dot.com" companies (1998–2001).

THE ECONOMY TOMORROW

$29 iPODS; $99 iPHONES?

Competition didn't end with computers or dot.com companies. Just ask Steve Jobs, the guy who started the personal computer business back in 1977. He introduced another hot consumer product in November 2001—the iPod. The iPod was the first mass-produced portable digital music player. It allowed consumers to download, store, and retrieve up to 1,000 songs. Its compact size, sleek design, and simple functionality made it an instant success: Apple was selling iPods as fast as they could be produced, piling up huge profits in the process.

So what happened? Other entrepreneurs quickly got the scent of iPod's profits. Within a matter of months, competitors were designing their own digital music players. By 2003, the "attack of the iPod clones" (see News) was in full force. Major players like Sony (MusicBox), Dell (JukeBox), Samsung (Yepp), and Creative Technology (Muvo Slim) were all bringing MP3 players to the market. Competitors were adding new features, shrinking the size, and reducing prices.

IN THE NEWS

Attack of the iPod Clones

New Players Give Apple a Run For Its Money in Portable Music; Recording Songs From the Radio

APPLE COMPUTER'S iPod portable music player is one of the best digital products of any kind ever invented. Its design is simply brilliant, and, since its debut two years ago next month, it has become an icon. Nearly 1.5 million iPods have been sold, and the slender white gadget has become the best-selling portable music player on the market, even though it is also the most expensive.

There have been other high-capacity digital music players, both before and since the iPod appeared. Most have been cheaper, but all have been inferior to the iPod, mainly because they were too big, and too clumsy to use. Meanwhile, Apple has kept improving the iPod, making it smaller and more capable.

Now, however, a new generation of would-be iPod killers is hitting the market. And, after two years of studying Apple's work, the makers of these new players are finally giving the iPod a run for its money. These products are nearly as small as the iPod, and have aped its widely admired user interface. Some have more features, and are less expensive.

—Walter S. Mossberg

Analysis: Economic profits attract entrepreneurs. As competition intensifies, products improve and prices fall.

Under these circumstances, Apple could not afford to sit back and admire its profits. Steve Jobs knew he'd have to keep running to stay ahead of the MP3-player pack. He kept improving the iPod. Within 2 years, Apple had three generations of iPods, each substantially better than the last. Memory capacity increased tenfold (to 10,000 songs), features were added, and the size shrank further. In less than 2.5 years, the iPod's price fell by 40 percent even while quality improved dramatically.

That Genius Steve Jobs

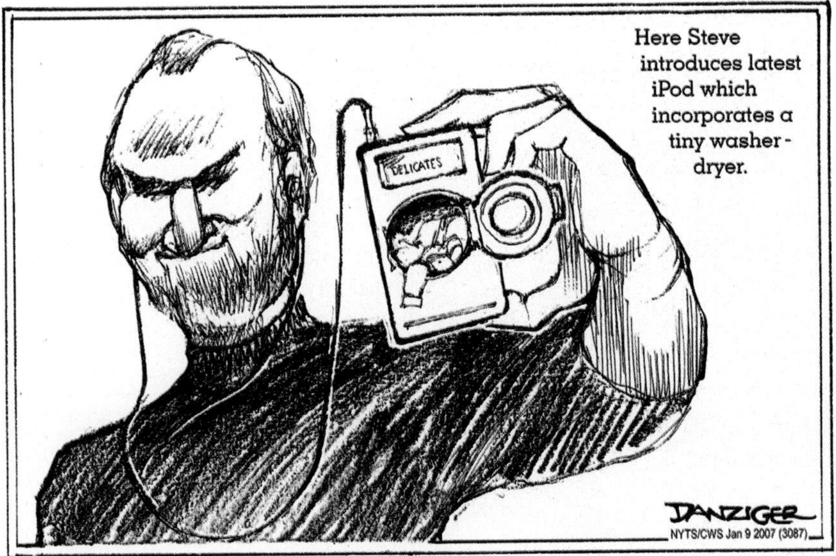

Analysis: New entrants and intense competition force producers to keep improving their products. Who knows how far this process can go?

Was that the end of the story? No way. By mid 2007 there were at least 60 iPod clones in the market, with more entrants in sight. Rivals were using flash memory chips rather than hard disks to cut costs (even though this reduces memory capacity) and prices. Microsoft launched a new MP3 player ("Zune") to interface with its Media Player software and huge music library. Sony offered a $60 digital music player to the market.

With this kind of unrelenting pressure, Apple has to keep improving the iPod and reducing its price. Apple increased iPod's memory, added video downloads of feature films, and kept dropping prices. By the time you graduate, stripped-down iPods will surely be selling for $29 or less (perhaps with washer/dryer components!—see cartoon on previous page). If that sounds preposterous, look back at the price/quality history of personal computers. The unrelenting pressure of competition is what forces producers to keep delivering better products at lower prices. Competition is not *perfect* in the MP3-player market (as we'll see), but it is still a *powerful* force. The same kind of competitive force will drive the iPhone market in the economy tomorrow.

SUMMARY

- A perfectly competitive firm has no power to alter the market price of the product it sells. The perfectly competitive firm confronts a horizontal demand curve for its own output even though the relevant *market* demand curve is negatively sloped. LO1
- Profit maximization induces the competitive firm to produce at that rate of output where marginal costs equal price. This represents the short-run equilibrium of the firm. LO1
- If short-run profits exist in a competitive industry, new firms will enter the market. The resulting shift of supply will drive market prices down the market demand curve. As prices fall, the profit of the industry and its constituent firms will be squeezed. LO2
- The limit to the competitive price and profit squeeze is reached when price is driven down to the level of minimum average total cost. At this point (long-run equilibrium) additional output and profit will be attained only if technology is improved (lowering costs) or if market demand increases. LO2
- Firms will shut down production if price falls below average variable cost. Firms will exit the industry if they foresee continued economic losses. LO2
- The most distinctive thing about competitive markets is the persistent pressure they exert on prices and profits. The threat of competition is a tremendous incentive for producers to respond quickly to consumer demands and to seek more efficient means of production. In this sense, competitive markets do best what markets are supposed to do—efficiently allocate resources. LO3

Key Terms

equilibrium price
market supply
marginal cost (MC)
investment decision
economic profit
competitive market
barriers to entry
production decision
average total cost (ATC)
profit per unit
short-run competitive equilibrium
long-run competitive equilibrium
shutdown point
market mechanism
opportunity cost
marginal cost pricing
efficiency

Questions for Discussion

1. Why would anyone want to enter a profitable industry knowing that profits would eventually be eliminated by competition? LO2
2. Why wouldn't producers necessarily want to produce output at the lowest average cost? Under what conditions would they end up doing so? LO1

3. What industries do you regard as being highly competitive? Can you identify any barriers to entry in those industries? LO1
4. Why have flat-panel TV prices fallen so much? (See World View, page 472.) LO2
5. What might cause catfish prices to rise far enough to eliminate losses in the industry? (See News, page 469.) LO2
6. As the price of computers fell, what happened to their quality? How is this possible? LO3
7. How far are mobile-phone prices likely to fall in India? (See World View, page 483.) LO3
8. Is "long-run" equilibrium permanent? What forces might dislodge it? LO2
9. What would happen to iPod sales and profits if Apple kept price and profit margins high? LO1
10. Identify two products that have either (*a*) fallen sharply in price or (*b*) gotten significantly better without price increases. How did these changes come about? LO3
11. What will drive the price of an iPhone down to $99? How long will it take? LO2

problems The Student Problem Set at the back of this book contains numerical and graphing problems for this chapter.

web activities to accompany this chapter can be found on the Online Learning Center: **http://www.mhhe.com/economics/schiller11e**

Monopoly

24

LEARNING OBJECTIVES

After reading this chapter, you should know:

LO1. How a monopolist sets price.

LO2. How monopoly and competitive outcomes differ.

LO3. The pros and cons of monopoly.

In 1908 Ford produced the Model T, the car "designed for the common man." It was cheap, reliable, and as easy to drive as the horse and buggy it was replacing. Ford sold 10,000 Model Ts in its first full year of production (1909). After that, sales more than doubled every year. In 1913, nearly 200,000 Model Ts were sold; and Ford was fast changing U.S. patterns of consumption, travel, and living standards.

During this early development of the U.S. auto industry, Henry Ford dominated the field. There were other producers, but the Ford Motor Company was the only producer of an inexpensive "motorcar for the multitudes." In this situation, Henry Ford could dictate the price and the features of his cars. When he opened his new assembly line factory at Highland Park, he abruptly raised the Model T's price by $100—an increase of 12 percent—to help pay for the new plant. Then he decided to paint all Model Ts black. When told of consumer complaints about the lack of colors, Ford advised one of his executives in 1913: "Give them any color they want so long as it's black."[1]

Henry Ford had **market power.** He could dictate what color car Americans would buy. And he could raise the price of Model Ts without fear of losing all his customers. Such power is alien to competitive firms. Competitive firms are always under pressure to reduce costs, improve quality, and cater to consumer preferences.

In this chapter we examine how market structure influences market outcomes. Specifically, we examine how a market controlled by a single producer—a monopoly—behaves. We're particularly interested in the following questions:

- **What price will a monopolist charge?**
- **How much output will the monopolist produce?**
- **Are consumers better or worse off when only one firm controls an entire market?**

[1]Charles E. Sorensen, *My Forty Years with Ford* (New York: W. W. Norton & Co., 1956), p. 127.

MARKET POWER

market power: The ability to alter the market price of a good or service.

The essence of market power is the ability to alter the price of a product. The catfish farmers in Chapter 23 had no such power. Because 2,000 farms were producing and selling the same good, each catfish producer had to act as a *price taker.* Each producer could sell all it wanted at the prevailing price but would lose all its customers if it tried to charge a higher price.

The Downward-Sloping Demand Curve

Firms that have market power *can* alter the price of their output without losing all their customers. Sales volume may drop when price is increased, but the quantity demanded won't drop to zero. In other words, ***firms with market power confront downward-sloping demand curves for their own output.***

The distinction between perfectly competitive (powerless) and imperfectly competitive (powerful) firms is illustrated again in Figure 24.1. Figure 24.1*a* re-creates the market situation that confronts a single catfish farmer. In Chapter 22, we assumed that the prevailing price of catfish was $13 a bushel and that a small, competitive firm could sell its entire output at this price. Hence, each individual firm effectively confronted a horizontal demand curve.

We also noted earlier that catfish don't violate the law of demand. As good as catfish taste, people aren't willing to buy unlimited quantities of them at $13 a bushel. To induce consumers to buy more catfish, the market price of catfish must be reduced.

This seeming contradiction between the law of demand and the situation of the competitive firm is resolved in Figure 24.1. There are *two* relevant demand curves. The one on the left, which appears to contradict the law of demand, refers to a single competitive producer. The one on the right refers to the entire *industry,* of which the competitive producer is one very tiny part. The industry or market demand curve *does* slope downward, even though individual competitive firms are able to sell their own output at the going price.

Monopoly

An industry needn't be composed of many small firms. The entire output of catfish could be produced by a single large producer. Such a firm would be a **monopoly**—a single firm that produces the entire market supply of a good.

monopoly: A firm that produces the entire market supply of a particular good or service.

The emergence of a monopoly obliterates the distinction between industry demand and the demand curve facing the firm. A monopolistic firm *is* the industry. Hence, there's only *one* demand curve to worry about, and that's the market (industry) demand curve, as illustrated in Figure 24.1*b*. This simplifies things: ***In monopoly situations, the demand curve facing the firm is identical to the market demand curve for the product.***

Price and Marginal Revenue

Although monopolies simplify the geometry, they complicate the arithmetic of **profit maximization.** The basic rule for maximizing profits is unchanged—that is, produce the rate of output where marginal revenue equals marginal cost. This rule applies to *all* firms. In a competitive industry, however, this general rule was simplified. For competitive firms,

profit-maximization rule: Produce at that rate of output where marginal revenue equals marginal cost.

(*a*) The competitive firm

PRICE (dollars per bushel)

$13

Demand facing competitive firm

0

QUANTITY (bushels of fish per day)

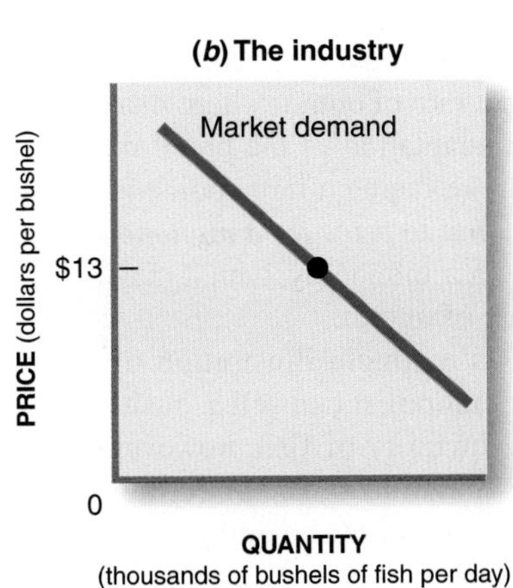

FIGURE 24.1
Firm vs. Industry Demand

A competitive firm can sell its entire output at the prevailing market price. In this sense, the firm confronts a horizontal demand curve, as in part *a*. Nevertheless, market demand for the product still slopes downward. The demand curve confronting the industry is illustrated in part *b*. Note the difference in the units of measurement (single bushels vs. thousands). A monopolist confronts the *industry* (market) demand curve.

FIGURE 24.2
Price Exceeds Marginal Revenue in Monopoly

If a firm must lower its price to sell additional output, marginal revenue is less than price. If this firm wants to increase its sales from 1 to 2 bushels per day, for example, price must be reduced from $13 to $12. The marginal revenue of the second bushel is therefore only $11. This is indicated in row *B* of the table and by point *b* on the graph.

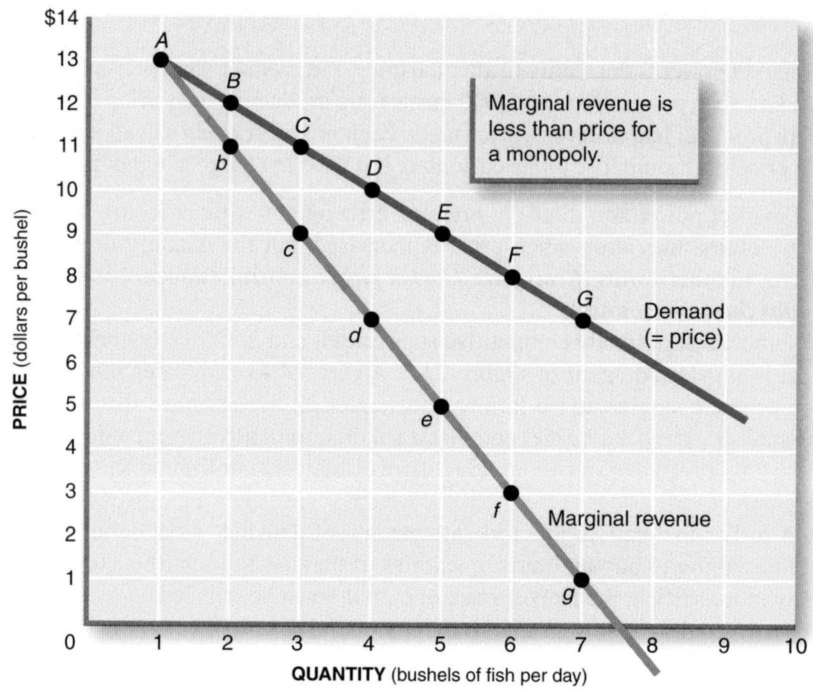

	(1) Quantity	×	(2) Price	=	(3) Total Revenue	(4) Marginal Revenue (= ΔTR ÷ Δq)
A	1		$13		$13	
					>	$11
B	2		12		24	
					>	9
C	3		11		33	
					>	7
D	4		10		40	
					>	5
E	5		9		45	

marginal revenue is equal to price. Hence, a competitive firm can maximize profits by producing at that rate of output where marginal cost equals *price.*

This special adaptation of the profit-maximizing rule doesn't work for a monopolist. The demand curve facing a monopolist is downward-sloping. Because of this, ***marginal revenue isn't equal to price for a monopolist.*** On the contrary, marginal revenue is always *less* than price in a monopoly, which makes it just a bit more difficult to find the profit-maximizing rate of output.

Figure 24.2 is a simple illustration of the relationship between price and marginal revenue. The monopolist can sell 1 bushel of fish per day at a price of $13. If he wants to sell a larger quantity of fish, however, he has to reduce his price. According to the demand curve shown here, the price must be lowered to $12 to sell 2 bushels per day. This reduction in price is shown by a movement along the demand curve from point *A* to point *B*.

How much additional revenue does the second bushel bring in? It's tempting to say that it brings in $12, since that's its price. **Marginal revenue (MR),** however, refers to the *change* in *total* revenue that results from a one-unit increase in output. More generally, we use the formula

marginal revenue (MR): The change in total revenue that results from a one-unit increase in the quantity sold.

$$\text{Marginal revenue} = \frac{\text{change in total revenue}}{\text{change in quantity sold}} = \frac{\Delta TR}{\Delta q}$$

where the delta symbol Δ denotes "change in." According to this formula, the marginal revenue of the second bushel is only $11, not the $12 price for which it was sold.

Figure 24.2 summarizes the calculations necessary for computing MR. Row *A* of the table indicates that the total revenue resulting from one sale per day is $13. To increase sales, price must be reduced. Row *B* indicates that total revenue rises to $24 per day when fish sales double. The *increase* in total revenue resulting from the added sales is thus $11. This concept is illustrated in the last column of the table and by point *b* on the marginal revenue curve.

Notice that the MR of the second bushel ($11) is *less* than its price ($12) because both bushels are being sold for $12 apiece. In effect, the firm is giving up the opportunity to sell only 1 bushel per day at $13 in order to sell a larger quantity at a lower price. In this sense, the firm is sacrificing $1 of potential revenue on the first bushel in order to increase *total* revenue. Marginal revenue measures the change in total revenue that results.

So long as the demand curve is downward-sloping, MR will always be less than price. Compare columns 2 and 4 of the table in Figure 24.2. At each rate of output in excess of 1 bushel, marginal revenue is less than price. This is also evident in the graph: ***The MR curve lies below the demand (price) curve at every point but the first.***

Profit Maximization

Although the presence of market power adds a new wrinkle, the rules of profit maximization remain the same. Now instead of looking for an intersection of marginal cost and price, we look for the intersection of marginal cost and marginal revenue. This is illustrated in Figure 24.3 by the intersection of the MR and MC curves (point *d*). Looking down from that intersection, we see that the associated rate of output is 4 bushels per day. Thus 4 bushels is the profit-maximizing rate of output.

How much should the monopolist charge for these 4 bushels? Naturally, the monopolist would like to charge a very high price. But the ability to charge a high price is limited by the demand curve. If the monopolist charges $13, consumers will buy only 1 bushel,

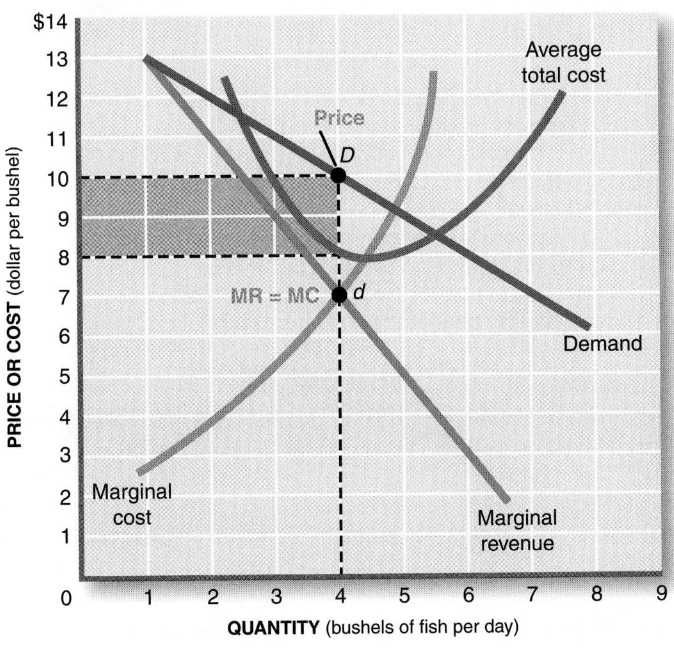

FIGURE 24.3
Profit Maximization

The most profitable rate of output is indicated by the intersection of marginal revenue and marginal cost (point *d*). This intersection (MC = MR) establishes 4 bushels as the profit maximizing rate of output. Point *D* indicates that consumers will pay $10 per bushel for this much output. Total profits equal price ($10) minus average total cost ($8), multiplied by the quantity sold (4).

leaving 3 unsold bushels of dead fish. Not a pretty picture. As the monopolist will soon learn, ***only one price is compatible with the profit-maximizing rate of output.*** In this case, the price is $10. This price is found in Figure 24.3 by moving up from the quantity 4 until reaching the demand curve at point *D*. Point *D* tells us that consumers are able and willing to buy 4 bushels of fish per day only at the price of $10 each. A monopolist who tries to charge more than $10 won't be able to sell all 4 bushels.

Figure 24.3 also illustrates the total profits of the catfish monopoly. To compute total profits we can first calculate profit per unit, that is, price minus *average* total cost. In this case, profit per unit is $2. Multiplying profit per unit by the quantity sold (4) gives us total profits of $8 per day, as illustrated by the shaded rectangle.

MARKET POWER AT WORK: THE COMPUTER MARKET REVISITED

To develop a keener appreciation for the nature of market power, we can return to the computer market of Chapter 23. This time we make some different assumptions about market structure. In particular, assume that a single firm, Universal Electronics, acquires an exclusive patent on the production of the microprocessors that function as the computer's "brain." This one firm is now in a position to deny potential competitors access to the basic ingredient of computers. The patent thus functions as a **barrier to entry,** to be erected or set aside at the will of Universal Electronics.

barriers to entry: Obstacles, such as patents, that make it difficult or impossible for would-be producers to enter a particular market.

Universal's management is familiar enough with the principles of economics (including W. C. Fields's advice about never giving a sucker an even break) to know when it's onto a good thing. It's not about to let every would-be Horatio Alger have a slice of the profit pie. Even the Russians understood this strategy during the heyday of communism. They made sure no one else could produce sable furs that could compete with their monopoly (see World View). Let's assume that Universal Electronics is equally protective of its turf and will refuse to sell or give away any rights to its patent or the chips it produces. That is, Universal Electronics sets itself up as a computer monopoly.

Let's also assume that Universal has a multitude of manufacturing plants, each of which is identical to the typical competitive firm in Chapter 23. This is an unlikely situation

WORLD VIEW

Foxy Soviets Pelt the West

Sable Monopoly Traps Hard Currency, Coats, Capitalists

LENINGRAD—Crown sable from the eastern Siberian region of Barguzin, star of the Soviet fur collection, went on sale just as a deep freeze gripped this former imperial city. . . .

Fur is one of the Soviet Union's best known consumer goods exports. It is also bait for a country eager to trap hard currency: last year, the Soviet Union earned $100 million in fur sales.

In the case of sable, the Soviet Union has something no one else has—in capitalist lingo, a monopoly.

Ivan the Terrible is said to have made the sale of live sables abroad a crime punishable by death. Peter the Great on his travels in the West is said to have carried along trunks of sable skins to use as currency.

In the best-selling novel *Gorky Park*, popular among fur traders, it was the Soviet sable monopoly that was the key to the tangled tale of murderous intrigue.

There is another story, origin and veracity unknown, that an American once traded a rare North American species to the Soviets in exchange for two live Russian sables—only to find when he got home that they had been sterilized.

—Celestine Bohlen

Source: *The Washington Post*, February 5, 1985. www.washingtonpost.com

Analysis: To ward off potential competition, a monopoly must erect barriers to entry. By not letting live sables leave the country, Russia maintained a monopoly on sable furs.

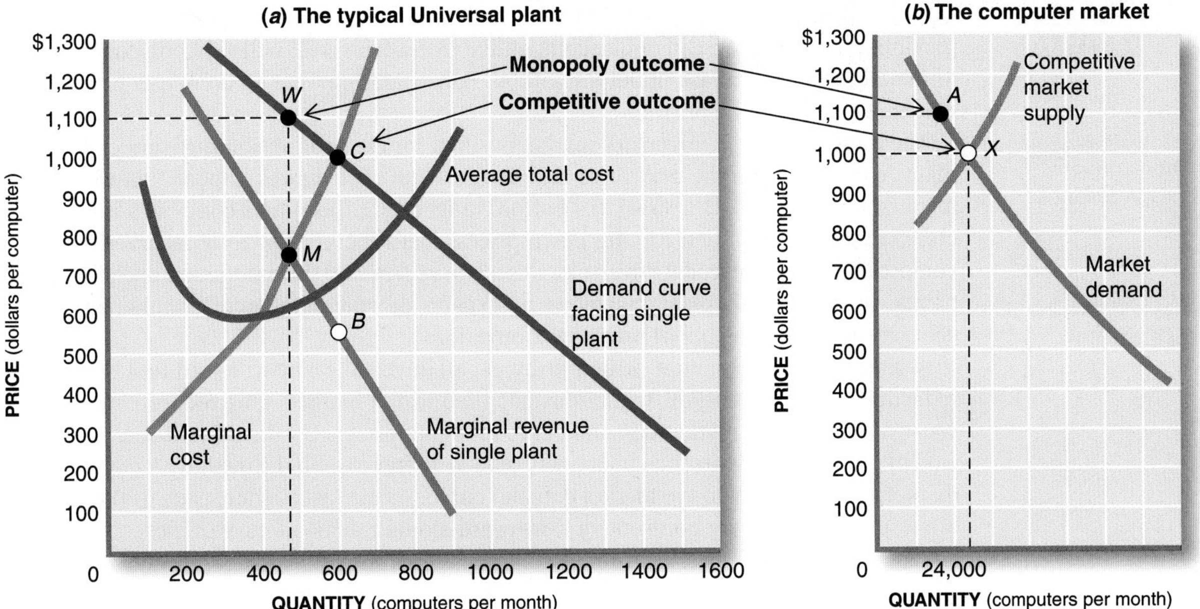

FIGURE 24.4
Initial Conditions in the Monopolized Computer Market

We assume that a monopoly firm (Universal Electronics) would confront the same costs (MC and ATC) and demand as would the competitive industry in Chapter 23. In the initial short-run equilibrium, the competitive price was $1,000 (point *C*). However, the monopolist isn't bound by the competitive market price. Instead, the monopolist must contend with downward-sloping demand and marginal revenue curves. If each monopoly plant produced where MC = $1,000 (point *C* in part *a*), marginal cost (point *C*) would exceed marginal revenue (point *B*). To maximize profits, the monopolist must find that rate of output where MC = MR (point *M* in part *a*). That rate of output can be sold at the monopoly price of $1,100 (point *W* in part *a*). Part *b* illustrates the market implications of the monopolist's production decision: A reduced quantity is sold at a higher price (point *A*).

because a monopolist would probably achieve **economies of scale** by closing at least a few plants and consolidating production in larger plants. Universal would maintain a multitude of small plants only if constant returns to scale or actual diseconomies of scale were rampant. Nevertheless, by assuming that multiple plants are maintained, we can compare monopoly behavior with competitive behavior on the basis of identical cost structures. In particular, if Universal continues to operate the many plants that once comprised the competitive home computer industry, it will confront the same short-run marginal and average cost curves already encountered in Chapter 23. Later in this chapter we relax this assumption of multiplant operations to determine whether, in the long run, a monopolist may actually lower production costs below those of a competitive industry.

economies of scale: Reductions in minimum average costs that come about through increases in the size (scale) of plant and equipment.

Figure 24.4*a* re-creates the marginal costs the typical competitive firm faced in the early stages of the microcomputer boom (from Figure 23.3 and Table 23.1). We now assume that this MC curve also expresses the costs of operating one of Universal's many (identical) plants. Thus, the extension of monopoly control is assumed to have no immediate effect on production costs.

The market demand for computers is also assumed to be unchanged. There's no reason why people should be less willing to buy computers now than they were when the market was competitive. Most consumers have no notion of how many firms produce a product. Even if they knew, there's no reason why their demand for the product would change. Thus, Figure 24.4*b* expresses an unchanged demand for computers.

Our immediate concern is to determine how Universal Electronics, as a monopolist, will respond to these unchanged demand and cost curves. Will it produce exactly as many computers as the competitive industry did? Will it sell the computers at the same price that the competitive industry did? Will it improve the product as much or as fast?

The Production Decision

production decision: The selection of the short-run rate of output (with existing plant and equipment).

Like any producer, Universal Electronics will strive to produce its output at the rate that maximizes total profits. But unlike competitive firms, Universal will explicitly take account of the fact that an increase in output will put downward pressure on computer prices. This may threaten corporate profits.

The implications of Universal's market position for the **production decision** of its many plants can be seen in the new price and marginal revenue curves imposed on each of its manufacturing plants. Universal can't afford to let each of its plants compete with the others, expanding output and driving down prices; that's the kind of folly reserved for truly competitive firms. Instead, Universal will seek to *coordinate* the production decisions of its plants, instructing all plant managers to expand or contract output simultaneously, to achieve the corporate goal of profit maximization.

A simultaneous reduction of output by each Universal plant will lead to a significant reduction in the quantity of computers supplied to the market. This reduced supply will cause a move up the market demand curve to higher prices. By the same token, an expansion of output by all Universal plants will lead to an increase in the quantity supplied to the market and a slide down the market demand curve. As a consequence, each of the monopolist's plants effectively confronts a downward-sloping demand curve. These downward-sloping demand curves are illustrated in Figure 24.4*a*.[2]

Notice that in Figure 24.4*b* the *market* demand for computers is unchanged; only the demand curve confronting each plant (firm) has changed. A competitive *industry,* like a monopoly, must obey the law of demand. But the individual firms that comprise a competitive industry all act independently, *as if* they could sell unlimited quantities at the prevailing price. That is, they all act as if they confronted a horizontal demand curve at the market price of $1,000. A competitive firm that doesn't behave in this fashion will simply lose sales to other firms. In contrast, ***a monopolist not only foresees the impact of increased production on market price but can also prevent such production increases by its separate plants.***

Marginal Revenue. The downward-sloping demand curve now confronting each Universal plant implies that marginal revenue no longer equals price. Notice that the marginal revenue curve in Figure 24.4*a* lies *below* the demand curve at every rate of output. Because marginal revenue is less than price for a monopoly, Universal's plants would no longer wish to produce up to the point where marginal cost equals price. ***Only firms that confront a horizontal demand curve (perfect competitors) equate marginal cost and price.*** Universal's plants must stick to the generic profit-maximizing rule about equating marginal revenue and marginal cost. Should the individual plant managers forget this rule, Universal's central management will fire them.

The output and price implications of Universal's monopoly position become apparent as we examine the new revenue and cost relationships. Recall that the equilibrium price of computers in the early stages of the home computer boom was $1,000. This equilibrium price is indicated in Figure 24.4*b* by the intersection of the competitive market supply curve with the market demand curve (point *X*). Each competitive *firm* produced up to the point where marginal cost (MC) equaled that price (point *C* in Figure 24.4*a*). At that point, each competitive firm was producing 600 computers a month.

Reduced Output. The emergence of Universal as a monopolist alters these production decisions. Now each Universal plant *does* have an impact on market price because its behavior is imitated simultaneously by all Universal plants. In fact, the marginal revenue associated with the 600th computer is only $575, as indicated by point *B* in Figure 24.4*a*. At this rate of output, the typical Universal plant would be operating with marginal costs ($1,000) far in excess of marginal revenues ($575). Such behavior is inconsistent with profit maximization.

[2]The demand and marginal revenue curves in Figure 24.4*a* are illustrative; they're not derived from earlier tables. As discussed above, we're assuming that the central management of Universal determines the profit-maximizing rate of output and then instructs all individual plants to produce equal shares of that output.

The enlightened Universal plant manager will soon discover that the profit-maximizing rate of output is less than 600 computers per month. In Figure 24.4*a* we see that the marginal revenue and marginal cost curves intersect at point *M*. This MR = MC intersection occurs at an output level of only 475 computers per month. Accordingly, the typical Universal plant will want to produce *fewer* computers than were produced by the typical competitive firm in the early stages of the home computer boom. Recall that individual competitive firms had no incentive to engage in such production cutbacks. They couldn't alter the market supply curve or price on their own and weren't coordinated by a central management. Thus, the first consequence of Universal's monopoly position is a reduction in the rate of industry output.

The Monopoly Price

The reduction in output at each Universal plant translates automatically into a decrease in the *quantity supplied* to the market. As consumers compete for this reduced market supply, they'll bid computer prices up. We can observe the increased prices in Figure 24.4 by looking at either the typical Universal plant or the computer market. Notice that in Figure 24.4*a* the price is determined by moving directly up from point *M* to the demand curve confronting the typical Universal plant. The demand curve always tells how much consumers are willing to pay for any given quantity. Hence, once we've determined the quantity that's going to be supplied (475 computers per month), we can look at the demand curve to determine the price ($1,100 at point *W*) that consumers will pay for these computers. That is,

- ***The intersection of the marginal revenue and marginal cost curves establishes the profit-maximizing rate of output.***
- ***The demand curve tells us how much consumers are willing to pay for that specific quantity of output.***

Figure 24.4*a* shows how Universal's monopoly position results in both reduced output and increased prices. This result is also evident in Figure 24.4*b*, where we see that a smaller quantity supplied to the market will force a move up the demand curve to the higher price of $1,100 per computer (point *A*).

Monopoly Profits

Universal's objective was and remains the maximization of profits. That it has succeeded in its effort can be confirmed by scrutinizing Figure 24.5. As you can see, the typical

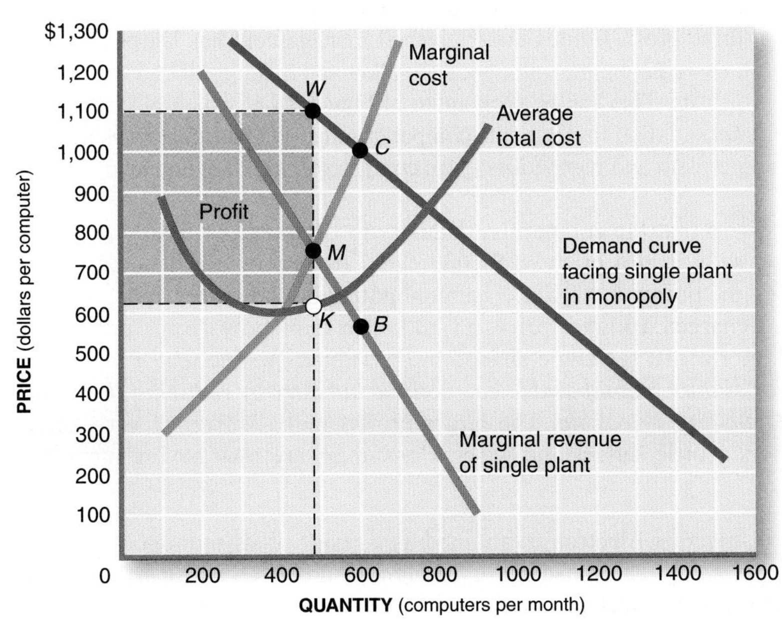

FIGURE 24.5
Monopoly Profits: The Typical Universal Plant

The profit-maximizing rate of output occurs where the marginal cost and marginal revenue curves intersect (point *M*). The demand curve indicates the price (point *W*) that consumers will pay for this output. Total profit equals price (*W*) minus average total cost (*K*) multiplied by the quantity sold (475). Total profits are represented by the shaded rectangle.

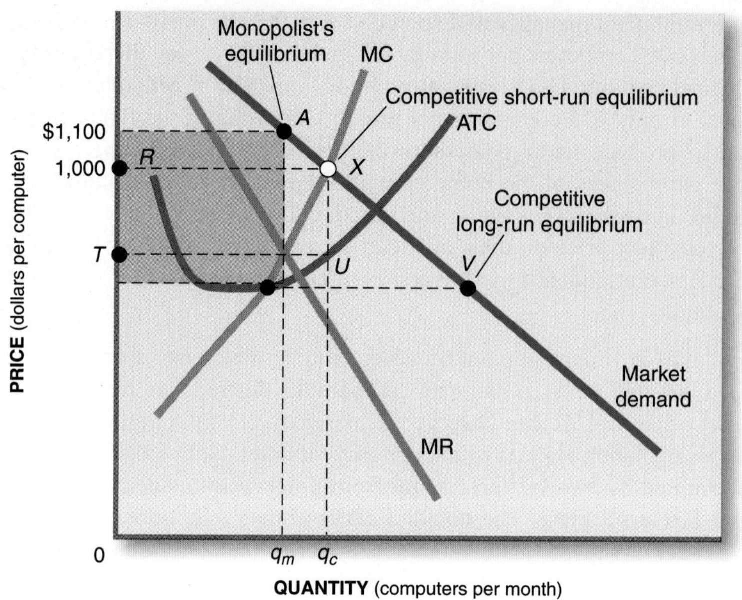

FIGURE 24.6
Monopoly Profit: The Entire Company

Total profits of the monopolist (including all plants) are illustrated by the shaded rectangle. The monopolist's total output q_m is determined by the intersection of the (industry) MR and MC curves. The price of this output is determined by the market demand curve (point *A*). In contrast, a competitive industry would produce q_c computers in the short run and sell them at a lower price (*X*) and profit per unit (*X* − *U*). Those profits would attract new entrants until long-run equilibrium (point *V*) was reached. (See Figure 23.8 for a summary of competitive market equilibrium.)

average total cost (ATC): Total cost divided by the quantity produced in a given time period.

Universal plant ends up selling 475 computers a month at a price of $1,100 each (point *W*). The **average total cost (ATC)** of production at this rate of output is only $630 (point *K*), as was detailed in Table 23.1.

As always, we can compute total profit as

$$\text{Total profit} = \text{profit per unit} \times \text{quantity sold}$$

In this case, we see that

$$\begin{aligned}\text{Total profit} &= (\$1{,}100 - \$630) \times 475 \\ &= \$223{,}250\end{aligned}$$

This figure significantly exceeds the monthly profit of $180,000 earned by the typical competitive firm in the early stages of the computer boom (see Table 23.1).

It's apparent from these profit figures that Universal management has learned its economic principles well. By reducing the output of each plant and raising prices a little, it has managed to increase profits. This can be seen again in Figure 24.6, which is an enlarged illustration of the *market* situation for the home computer industry. The figure translates the economics of our single-plant and competitive-firm comparison into the dimensions of the whole industry.

Figure 24.6 reaffirms that the competitive industry in Chapter 23 initially produces the quantity q_c and sells it at a price of $1,000 each. Its profits are denoted by the rectangle formed by the points *R, X, U, T.* The monopolist, on the other hand, produces the smaller q_m and charges a higher price, $1,100. The monopoly firm's profits are indicated by the larger profit rectangle shaded in the figure. We see that ***a monopoly receives larger profits than a comparable competitive industry by reducing the quantity supplied and pushing prices up.*** The larger profits make Universal very happy and make consumers a little sadder and wiser. Consumers are now paying more and getting less.

Barriers to Entry

The higher profits Universal Electronics attained as a result of its monopoly position aren't the end of the story. The existence of economic profit tends to bring profit-hungry entrepreneurs swarming like locusts. In the competitive computer industry in

IN THE NEWS 

Concerts Becoming a Pricier Affair; Music Industry Consolidation Has Brought Higher Ticket Fees. Some Cry Foul . . .

Members of the popular heavy-rock band Godsmack say they want to make tickets affordable for their current U.S. tour. But the economics of the concert industry may jar fans harder than the mosh pit at the band's show.

The face value of a general admission ticket to Godsmack's concert Wednesday at Verizon Wireless Amphitheater is $20. But no one attending the band's performance gets to pay that amount.

Instead, fans who purchase tickets on the phone or online are socked with a series of surcharges that boost the price to $35.60. These added costs, tacked on by distribution giant Ticketmaster and concert promotion conglomerate Clear Channel Entertainment, include a convenience fee, a facility fee and a handling charge.

Moreover, a hidden $3.50 parking fee is buried in the price of each ticket by Clear Channel, owner of the Verizon Amphitheater in Irvine. All told, the fees add a 116% markup to the cost of a $16.50 ticket. . . .

In recent years, Clear Channel has emerged as the dominant force in the $1.6-billion concert industry. . . .

"They can pretty much dictate the costs, ad rates and ticket prices," said Jon Stoll, president of Fantasma Productions, a competing promoter in West Palm Beach, Fla. "If one company controls the live-music industry, there's nobody that can really bring ticket prices down."

—Jeff Leeds

Source: *Los Angeles Times,* July 17, 2001. Copyright, 2001, Los Angeles Times. Reprinted with permission.

Analysis: Control of concert sites and ticket distribution allows Clear Channel and Ticketmaster to charge monopoly prices for live concerts.

Chapter 23, the lure of high profits brought about an enormous expansion of computer output and a steep decline in computer prices. In Figure 24.6 the long-run equilibrium of a competitive industry is indicated by point *V.* What then can we expect to happen in the computer market now that Universal has a monopoly position and is enjoying huge profits?

Remember that Universal is now assumed to have an exclusive patent on microprocessor chips and can use this patent as an impassable barrier to entry. Consequently, would-be competitors can swarm around Universal's profits until their wings drop off; Universal isn't about to let them in on the spoils. By locking out potential competition, Universal can prevent the surge in computer output that pushed prices down the market demand curve. As long as Universal is able to keep out the competition, only the more affluent consumers will be able to use computers. The same phenomenom explains why ticket prices for live concerts are so high. Because Clear Channel controls most concert venues and Ticketmaster is the exclusive ticket distributor, fans have to pay monopoly prices to see Godsmack, Bare Naked Ladies, Pearl Jam, or other live concerts (see News). A monopoly has no incentive to move from point *A* in Figure 24.6, and there's no competitive pressure to force such a move. Universal may discover ways to reduce the costs of production and thus lower prices, but there's no *pressure* on it to do so, as there was in the competitive situation.

A COMPARATIVE PERSPECTIVE OF MARKET POWER

The different outcomes of the computer industry under competitive and monopoly conditions illustrate basic features of market structures. We may summarize the sequence of events that occurs in each type of market structure as follows:

COMPETITIVE INDUSTRY	MONOPOLY INDUSTRY
• High prices and profits signal consumers' demand for more output.	• High prices and profits signal consumers' demand for more output.
• The high profits attract new suppliers.	• Barriers to entry are erected to exclude potential competition.
• Production and supplies expand.	• Production and supplies are constrained.
• Prices slide down the market demand curve.	• Prices don't move down the market demand curve.
• A new equilibrium is established wherein more of the desired product is produced, its price falls, average costs of production approach their minimum, and economic profits approach zero.	• No new equilibrium is established; average costs aren't necessarily at or near a minimum, and economic profits are at a maximum.
• Price equals marginal cost throughout the process.	• Price exceeds marginal cost at all times.
• Throughout the process, there's great pressure to keep ahead of the profit squeeze by reducing costs or improving product quality.	• There's no squeeze on profits and thus no pressure to reduce costs or improve product quality.

In our discussion, we assumed that the competitive industry and the monopoly both started from the same position—an initial equilibrium in which the price of computers is $1,000. In reality, an industry may manifest concentrations of market power *before* such an equilibrium is established. That is, the sequence of events we've depicted may be altered (with step 3 occurring first, for example). Nevertheless, the basic distinctions between competitive and monopolistic behavior are evident.

Productivity Advances. To the extent that monopolies behave as we've discussed, they affect not just the price and output of a specific product but broader economic outcomes as well. Remember that competitive industries tend, in the long run, to produce at minimum average costs. Competitive industries also pursue cost reductions and product improvements relentlessly. These pressures tend to expand our production possibilities. No such forces are at work in the monopoly we've discussed here. Hence, there's a basic tendency for monopolies to inhibit productivity advances and economic growth.

marginal cost pricing: The offer (supply) of goods at prices equal to their marginal cost.

The Mix of Output. Another important feature of competitive markets is their observed tendency toward **marginal cost pricing.** Marginal cost pricing is important to consumers because it permits rational choices among alternative goods and services. In particular, it informs consumers of the true opportunity costs of various goods, thereby allowing them to choose the mix of output that delivers the most utility with available resources. In our monopoly example, however, consumers end up getting fewer computers than they'd like, while the economy continues to produce other, less desired goods. Thus, the mix of output shifted away from computers when Universal took over the industry.

The power to influence prices and product flows may have far-reaching consequences for our economic welfare. Changes in prices and product flows directly influence the level and composition of output, employment and resource allocation, the level and distribution of income, and, of course, the level and structure of prices. Hence, firms that wield significant market power affect all dimensions of economic welfare.

Political Power. Market power isn't the only kind of power wielded in society, of course. Political power, for example, is a different kind of power and important in its own right. Indeed, the power to influence an election or to sway a Senate committee vote may ultimately be more important than the power to increase the price of laundry soap. Nevertheless, market power is a force that influences the way we live, the incomes we earn, and our relationships with other countries. Moreover, market power may be the basis for political power: The individual or firm with considerable market power is likely to have the necessary resources to influence an election or sway a vote on a congressional committee.

The Limits to Power

Even though market power enables a producer to manipulate market outcomes, there's a clear limit to the exercise of power. Even a monopolist can't get everything it wants. Universal, for example, would really like to sell q_m computers at a price of $1,500 each because that kind of price would bring it even greater profits. Yet, despite its monopoly position, Universal is constrained to sell that quantity of computers at the lower price of $1,100 each. Even monopolists have their little disappointments.

The ultimate limit to a monopolist's power is evident in Figure 24.6. Universal's attainment of a monopoly position allows it only one prerogative: the ability to alter the quantity of output *supplied* to the market. This is no small prerogative, but it's far from absolute power. Universal, and every other monopolist, must still contend with the market *demand* curve. Note again that the new equilibrium in Figure 24.6 occurs at a point on the *unchanged* market demand curve. In effect, ***a monopolist has the opportunity to pick any point on the market demand curve and designate it as the new market equilibrium.*** The point it selects will depend on its own perceptions of effort, profit, and risk (in this case point *A*, determined by the intersection of marginal revenue and marginal cost).

The ultimate constraint on the exercise of market power, then, resides in the market demand curve. How great a constraint the demand curve imposes depends largely on the **price elasticity of demand.** The greater the price elasticity of demand, the more a monopolist will be frustrated in attempts to establish both high prices and high volume. Consumers will simply reduce their purchases if price is increased. If, however, consumer demand is highly inelastic—if consumers need or want that product badly and few viable substitutes are available—the monopolist can reap tremendous profits from market power.

price elasticity of demand: The percentage change in quantity demanded divided by the percentage change in price.

Price Discrimination

Even in situations where the *market* demand is relatively elastic, a monopolist may be able to extract high prices. A monopolist has the power not only to raise the market price of a good (by reducing the quantity supplied) but also to charge various prices for the same good. Recall that the market demand curve reflects the combined willingness of many individuals to buy. Some of those individuals are willing to buy the good at prices higher than the market price, just as other individuals will buy only at lower prices. A monopolist may be able to increase total profits by selling each unit of the good separately, at a price each *individual* consumer is willing to pay. This practice is called **price discrimination.**

price discrimination: The sale of an identical good at different prices to different consumers by a single seller.

The airline industry has practiced price discrimination for many years. Basically, there are two distinct groups of travelers: business and nonbusiness travelers. Business executives must fly from one city to another on a certain day and at a particular time. They typically make flight arrangements on short notice and may have no other way to get to their destination. Nonbusiness travelers, such as people on vacation and students going home during semester break, usually have more flexible schedules. They may plan their trips weeks or months in advance and often have the option of traveling by car, bus, or train.

The different travel needs of business and vacation travelers are reflected in their respective demand curves. Business demand for air travel tends to be less price-elastic than the demand of nonbusiness travelers. Few business executives would stop flying if airfares increased. Higher airfares would, however, discourage air travel by nonbusiness travelers.

What should airlines do in this case? Should they *raise* airfares to take advantage of the relative price inelasticity of business demand, or should they *lower* airfares to attract more nonbusiness travelers?

They should do both. In fact, they *have* done both. The airlines offer a full-fare ride, available at any time, and a discount-fare ride, available only by purchasing a ticket in advance and agreeing to some restrictions on time of departure. The advance purchase and other restrictions on discount fares effectively exclude most business travelers, who end up paying full fare. The higher full fare doesn't, however, discourage most nonbusiness travelers, who can fly at a discount. Consequently, the airlines are able to sell essentially identical units of the same good (an airplane ride) at substantially different prices to different customers. This price discrimination enables the airlines to capture the highest possible *average* price for the quantity supplied. Doctors, lawyers, and car dealers commonly practice the same type of price discrimination.

Entry Barriers

It's the lack of competitors that gives monopolists such pricing power. Accordingly, ***the preservation of monopoly power depends on keeping potential competitors out of the market.*** A monopolist doesn't want anyone else to produce an *identical* product or even a *close substitute.* To do that, a monopoly must erect and maintain barriers to market entry. It was the absence of significant entry barriers that permitted iPod clones to attack Apple's profits (News, page 485). Some of the entry barriers used to repel such attacks include:

Patents. This was the critical barrier in the mythical Universal Electronics case. A government-awarded patent gives a producer 20 years of exclusive rights to produce a particular product. The Polaroid Corporation used its patents to keep Eastman Kodak and other potential rivals out of the market for instant development cameras.

Monopoly Franchises. The government also creates and maintains monopolies by giving a single firm the exclusive right to supply a particular good or service, even though other firms can produce it. Local cable TV stations and telephone companies are examples. Congress also bestows monopoly privileges to baseball teams and the U.S. Postal Service. Your campus bookstore may have exclusive rights to sell textbooks on campus.

Control of Key Inputs. A company may lock out competition by securing exclusive access to key inputs. Airlines need landing rights and terminal gates in order to compete. Oil and gas producers need pipelines to supply their product. Utility companies need transmission networks to supply consumers with electricity. Software vendors need to know the features of computer operating systems. If a single company controls these critical inputs, it can lock out potential competition. That's alleged to be a prime source of Microsoft's monopoly power (see The Economy Tomorrow).

Lawsuits. In the event that competitors actually surmount other entry barriers, a monopoly may sue them out of existence. Typically, start-up firms are rich in ideas but cash poor. They need to get their products to the market quickly to generate some cash. A timely lawsuit alleging patent or copyright infringement can derail such a company by absorbing critical management, cash, and time. Long before the merits of the lawsuit are adjudicated, the company may be forced to withdraw from the market.

Acquisition. When all else fails, a monopolist may simply purchase a potential competitor. As the accompanying cartoon suggests, mergers tend to raise consumer prices.

Analysis: Mergers and acquisitions reduce competition in an industry. The increased industry concentration may lead to higher prices.

Economies of Scale. Last but far from least, a monopoly may persist because of economies of scale. If large firms have a substantial cost advantage over smaller firms, the smaller firms may not be able to compete. We look at this entry barrier again in a moment.

PROS AND CONS OF MARKET POWER

Despite the strong case against market power, it's conceivable that monopolies could also benefit society. One argument made for concentrations of market power is that monopolies have greater ability to pursue research and development. Another argument is that the lure of market power creates a tremendous incentive for invention and innovation. A third argument in defense of monopoly is that large companies can produce goods more efficiently than smaller firms. Finally, it's argued that even monopolies have to worry about *potential* competition and will behave accordingly.

Research and Development

In principle, monopolies are well positioned to undertake valuable research and development. First, such firms are sheltered from the constant pressure of competition. Second, they have the resources (monopoly profits) with which to carry out expensive R&D functions. The manager of a perfectly competitive firm, by contrast, has to worry about day-to-day production decisions and profit margins. As a result, she is unable to take the longer view necessary for significant research and development and couldn't afford to purchase such a view even if she could see it.

The basic problem with the R&D argument is that it says nothing about *incentives.* Although monopolists have a clear financial advantage in pursuing research and development activities, they have no clear incentive to do so. Research and development aren't necessarily required for profitable survival. In fact, research and development that make existing plant and equipment technologically obsolete run counter to a monopolist's vested interest and so may actually be suppressed (see News). In contrast, a perfectly competitive firm can't continue to make significant profits unless it stays ahead of the competition. This pressure constitutes a significant incentive to discover new products or new and cheaper ways of producing existing products.

IN THE NEWS

Jury Rules Magnetek Unit Is Liable for Keeping Technology off Market

SAN FRANCISCO—Is a company liable if it deliberately keeps a technology off the market? Apparently so, judging from an unusual ruling by a California jury.

A county superior court jury in Oakland ordered a unit of Magnetek Inc. to pay $25.8 million to two California entrepreneurs and their companies. They charged that the unit had failed to bring the pair's energy-saving fluorescent-light technology to market in a profitable manner, suppressing it in favor of an outmoded technology.

The lawsuit reads like familiar legends of big business quashing inventions that threaten its interests. . . .

In 1984, the two entrepreneurs, C. R. Stevens and William R. Alling, charged that Universal Manufacturing Corp., now a unit of Los Angeles–based Magnetek, buried a technology through which fluorescent lights use 70 percent less energy. The two said they sold Universal the technology, called a solid-state ballast, in 1981 after the company promised to market it aggressively.

Instead, they charged, Universal suppressed the technology to protect its less-efficient existing ballast models. "They told us they were going to be first on the market with our tech, yet they planned otherwise," said Mr. Alling.

—Stephen Kreider Yoder

Source: *The Wall Street Journal,* January 10, 1990.

Analysis: A monopoly has little incentive (no competitive pressure) to pursue R&D. In fact, R&D that threatens established products or processes may be suppressed.

Entrepreneurial Incentives

The second defense of market power uses a novel incentive argument. Every business is out to make a buck, and it's the quest for profits that keeps industries running. Thus, it's argued, even greater profit prizes will stimulate more entrepreneurial activity. Little Horatio Algers will work harder and longer if they can dream of one day possessing a whole monopoly.

The incentive argument for market power is enticing but not entirely convincing. After all, an innovator can make substantial profits in a competitive market before the competition catches up. Recall that the early birds did get the worm in the competitive computer industry (see Chapter 23), even though profit margins were later squeezed. It's not evident that the profit incentives available in a competitive industry are at all inadequate.

We must also recall the arguments about research and development efforts. A monopolist has little incentive to pursue R&D. Furthermore, entrepreneurs who might pursue product innovation or technological improvements may be dissuaded by their inability to penetrate a monopolized market. The barriers to entry that surround market power may not only keep out potential competitors but also lock out promising ideas.

Economies of Scale

A third defense of market power is the most convincing. A large firm, it's argued, can produce goods at a lower unit (average) cost than a small firm. If such *economies of scale* exist, we could attain greater efficiency (higher productivity) by permitting firms to grow to market-dominating size.

We sidestepped this argument in our story about the Universal Electronics monopoly. We explicitly assumed that Universal confronted the same production costs as the competitive industry. We simply converted each typical competitive firm into a separate plant owned and operated by Universal. Universal wasn't able to produce computers any more cheaply than the competitive counterpart, and we concerned ourselves only with the different production decisions made by competitive and monopolistic firms.

A monopoly *could,* however, attain greater cost savings. By centralizing various functions it might be able to eliminate some duplicative efforts. It might also shut down some plants and concentrate production in fewer facilities. If these kinds of efficiencies are attained, a monopoly would offer attractive resource savings.

There's no guarantee, however, of such economies of scale. As we observed in Chapter 21, increasing the size (scale) of a plant may actually *reduce* operating efficiency (see Figure 21.10). In evaluating the economies-of-scale argument for market power, then, we must recognize that ***efficiency and size don't necessarily go hand in hand. Some firms and industries may be subject to economies of scale, but others won't.***

Even when economies of scale are present there is no guarantee that consumers will benefit. This is why the Justice Department opposed the merger of the nation's only two satellite radio companies in 2007 (see News). Even though there were substantial short-run economies of scale in eliminating duplicate facilities, the Justice Department concluded that even a little competition (two firms) was better than none (a monopoly) in the long run.

natural monopoly: An industry in which one firm can achieve economies of scale over the entire range of market supply.

Natural Monopolies. Industries that exhibit economies of scale over the entire range of market output are called **natural monopolies.** In these cases, one single firm can produce the entire market supply more efficiently than any large number of (smaller) firms. As the size (scale) of the one firm increases, its minimum average costs continue to fall. These economies of scale give the one large producer a decided advantage over would-be rivals. Hence, ***economies of scale act as a "natural" barrier to entry.***

Local telephone and utility services are classic examples of natural monopoly. A single telephone or utility company can supply the market more efficiently than a large number of competing firms.

Although natural monopolies are economically desirable, they may be abused. We must ask whether and to what extent consumers are reaping some benefit from the efficiency a

IN THE NEWS

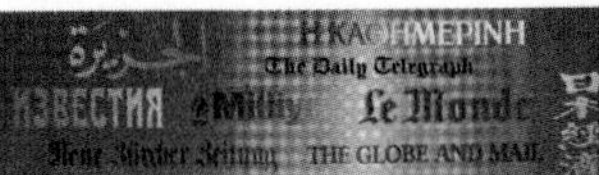
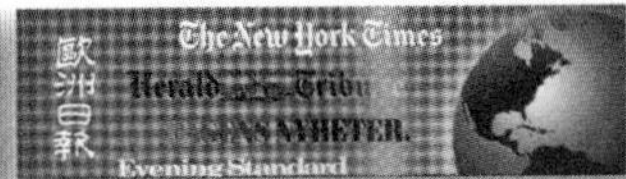

XM, Sirius Quit Head-to-Head Competition

Rivals Plan to Merge, but Where Does That Leave Consumers?

NEW YORK—The vision of a robustly competitive satellite radio business came crashing to Earth on Monday, as the industry's once bitter rivals—Sirius and XM Satellite Radio—agreed to merge, creating a company valued at $13 billion, including $1.6 billion in debt.

"The benefits of a merger are simply too good to pass up," Moffett says. "There are obvious financial synergies from the fact that these two companies run similar operations."

. . . Executives might find as much as $7 billion a year in savings that they say they can realize, for example by eliminating redundant channels and expenses for transmission and marketing. . . .

Antitrust officials will examine whether a satellite radio monopoly would have too much power to raise subscription fees and ad rates, and to force programmers to accept lower payments.

—David Lieberman

Source: *USA Today,* February 20, 2007, p. 1. Reprinted with permission.

Analysis: Monopolies may enjoy economies of scale. In the long run, however, consumers may benefit more from competitive pressures to reduce costs, improve product quality, and lower prices.

natural monopoly makes possible. Do consumers end up with lower prices, expanded output, and better service? Or does the monopoly keep most of the benefits for itself, in the form of higher prices and profits? Multiplex movie theaters, for example, achieve economies of scale by sharing operating and concession facilities among as many as 30 screens. But do moviegoers get lower prices for movies or popcorn? Not often. Because megamultiplex theaters tend to drive out competition, they don't have to reduce prices when costs drop. Under such circumstances, we may need government "trustbusters" to ensure that the benefits of increased efficiency are shared with consumers. (The potential and pitfalls of government regulation are examined in Chapter 27.)

Contestable Markets

Governmental regulators aren't necessarily the only force keeping monopolists in line. Even though a firm may produce the entire supply of a particular product at present, it may face *potential* competition from other firms. Potential rivals may be sitting on the sidelines, watching how well the monopoly fares. If it does too well, these rivals may enter the industry, undermining the monopoly structure and profits. In such **contestable markets,** monopoly behavior may be restrained by potential competition.

contestable market: An imperfectly competitive industry subject to potential entry if prices or profits increase.

How "contestable" a market is depends not so much on its structure as on entry barriers. If entry barriers are insurmountable, would-be competitors are locked out of the market. But if entry barriers are modest, they'll be surmounted when the lure of monopoly profits is irresistible. When CNN's profits reached irresistible proportions, both domestic and foreign companies decided to invade CNN's monopoly market (see World View on next page). Since then, CNN hasn't been nearly as profitable.

Structure vs. Behavior. From the perspective of contestable markets, the whole case against monopoly is misconceived. Market *structure* per se isn't a problem; what counts is market *behavior.* If potential rivals force a monopolist to behave like a competitive firm, then monopoly imposes no cost on consumers or on society at large.

The experience with the Model T Ford illustrates the basic notion of contestable markets. At the time Henry Ford decided to increase the price of the Model T and paint them all black, the Ford Motor Company enjoyed a virtual monopoly on mass-produced cars. But potential rivals saw the profitability of offering additional colors and features such as a self-starter and left-hand drive. When rivals began producing cars in volume, Ford's market power was greatly reduced. In 1926, the Ford Motor Company tried to regain its dominant position by again supplying cars in colors other than black. By that

webnote

Information on Federal Communications Commission regulation and deregulation can be found at www.fcc.gov

WORLD VIEW

New Competition May Mean Bad News for CNN

A growing crowd of media giants wants to make sure that most people don't get their news from Cable News Network. They're all gunning for the lucrative, Turner Broadcasting System unit with a host of rival 24-hour news networks, spurred by new technologies for delivering TV programs and shifting alliances in the cable business. . . .

Last year, with the market to itself, CNN and its related news businesses, including a Headline News channel, generated about $227 million in operating profit for Turner Broadcasting System Inc.

But CNN may not keep its monopoly for long. If the proposed services can overcome huge distribution hurdles caused by lack of space on crowded cable systems, their strong brand names and well-known correspondents and anchors may be enough to lure viewers away from CNN.

Capital Cities/ABC Inc., for example, said yesterday that it will launch a 24-hour news service in the U.S. in 1997, using ABC News's star talent and rerunning some of its popular shows. . . .

Other companies have similar ideas. General Electric Co.'s NBC for the past year has been putting together a detailed plan for launching its own national news network with a strong local component. . . .

Meanwhile, Britain's BBC is also trying to start a global news channel. And News Corp. Chairman Rupert Murdoch, whose British BSkyB service already offers a 24-hour news channel, said last week that he wants to launch a U.S. competitor to CNN. . . .

Behind all the expansion plans is a straightforward economic calculation: Companies already in the news business think they can squeeze out more profits with relatively little new cost by expanding to 24 hours of TV news.

—Elizabeth Jensen and John Lippman

Source: *The Wall Street Journal,* December 6, 1995.

Analysis: As a monopolist's profits grow, would-be competitors will try to overcome barriers to entry. If entry is possible, a monopolized market may be contestable.

time, however, consumers had more choices. Ford ceased production of the Model T in May 1927.

The experience with the Model T suggests that potential competition can force a monopoly to change its ways. Critics point out, however, that even contestable markets don't force a monopolist to act *exactly* like a competitive firm. There will always be a gap between competitive outcomes and those monopoly outcomes likely to entice new entry. That gap can cost consumers a lot. The absence of *existing* rivals is also likely to inhibit product and productivity improvements. From 1913 to 1926, all Model Ts were black, and consumers had few alternatives. Ford changed its behavior only after *potential* competition became *actual* competition. Even after 1927, when the Ford Motor Company could no longer act like a monopolist, it still didn't price its cars at marginal cost.

THE ECONOMY TOMORROW

MICROSOFT: BULLY OR GENIUS?

Ford Motor Company's experience is a useful reminder that monopolies rarely last forever. Potential competitors will always look for ways to enter a profitable market. Eventually they'll surmount entry barriers or develop substitute goods that supplant a monopolist's products.

Consumer advocates assert that we shouldn't have to wait for the invisible hand to dismantle a monopoly. They say the government should intervene to dismantle a monopoly or at least force it to change its behavior. Then consumers would get lower prices and better products a whole lot sooner.

IN THE NEWS  

Judge Says Microsoft Broke Antitrust Law

A federal judge yesterday found Microsoft Corp. guilty of violating antitrust law by waging a campaign to crush threats to its Windows monopoly, a severe verdict that opens the door for the government to seek a breakup of one of the most successful companies in history.

Saying that Microsoft put an "oppressive thumb on the scale of competitive fortune," U.S. District Judge Thomas Penfield Jackson gave the Justice Department and 19 states near-total victory in their lawsuit. His ruling puts a black mark on the reputation of a software giant that has been the starter engine of the "new economy."

"Microsoft mounted a deliberate assault upon entrepreneurial efforts that, left to rise or fall on their own merits, could well have enabled the introduction of competition into the market for Intelcompatible PC operating systems," Jackson said. . . .

In blunt language, Jackson depicted a powerful and predatory company that employed a wide array of tactics to destroy any innovation that posed a danger to the dominance of Windows. . . .

To crush the competitive threat posed by the Internet browser, Jackson ruled, Microsoft integrated its own Internet browser into its Windows operating system "to quell incipient competition," bullied computer makers into carrying Microsoft's browser by threatening to withhold price discounts and demanded that computer makers not feature rival Netscape's browser in the PC desktop as a condition of licensing the Windows operating system.

"Only when the separate categories of conduct are viewed, as they should be, as a single, well-coordinated course of action does the full extent of the violence that Microsoft has done to the competitive process reveal itself," Jackson wrote in the 43-page ruling.

—James V. Grimaldi

Source: *The Washington Post,* April 4, 2000. © **2000 *The Washington Post.* Excerpted with permission.** www.washingtonpost.com

Analysis: A federal court concluded that Microsoft followed the textbook script of monopoly: erecting entry barriers, suppressing innovation, and charging high prices.

Microsoft's dominant position in the computer industry highlights this issue. Microsoft produces the operating system (Windows) that powers 9 out of 10 personal computers. It also produces a huge share of applications software, including Internet browsers. Critics fear that this kind of monopoly power is a threat to consumers. They say Microsoft charges too much for its systems software, suppresses substitute technologies, and pushes potential competitors around. In short, Microsoft is a bully. In April 2000, a federal court accepted this argument (see News). To weaken Microsoft's grip on the computer market, the court considered forcing changes in both Microsoft's behavior and structure.

The AT&T Case. The federal government's authority to mend Microsoft's ways originates in the Sherman, the Clayton, and the Federal Trade Commission Acts. As noted in Table 24.1, these acts give the government broad **antitrust** authority to break up monopolies or compel them to change their behavior. The government used this authority in 1984 to dismantle American Telephone and Telegraph's (AT&T's) phone monopoly. AT&T then supplied 96 percent of all long-distance service and over 80 percent of local telephone service. AT&T kept long-distance charges high and compelled consumers to purchase hardware from its own subsidiary (Western Electric). Potential competitors claimed they could supply better and cheaper services if the government ended the AT&T monopoly. After 4 years of antitrust litigation, AT&T agreed to (1) separate its long-distance and local services and (2) turn over the local transmission networks to new "Baby Bell" companies. Since then there has been a competitive revolution in telephone hardware, services, and pricing.

antitrust: Government intervention to alter market structure or prevent abuse of market power.

The Microsoft Case. The U.S. Department of Justice filed a similar antitrust action against Microsoft. The first accusation leveled against Microsoft was that it thwarted competitors in operating systems by erecting entry barriers such as exclusive purchase agreements with computer manufacturers. These agreements either forbade manufacturers from

- ***The Sherman Act (1890).*** The Sherman Act prohibits "conspiracies in restraint of trade," including mergers, contracts, or acquisitions that threaten to monopolize an industry. Firms that violate the Sherman Act are subject to fines of up to $1 million, and their executives may be subject to imprisonment. In addition, consumers who are damaged—for example, via high prices—by a "conspiracy in restraint of trade" may recover treble damages. With this act as its principal "trustbusting" weapon, the U.S. Department of Justice has blocked attempted mergers and acquisitions, forced changes in price or output behavior, required large companies to sell some of their assets, and even sent corporate executives to jail for "conspiracies in restraint of trade."
- ***The Clayton Act (1914).*** The Clayton Act of 1914 was passed to outlaw specific antitrust behavior not covered by the Sherman Act. The principal aim of the act was to prevent the development of monopolies. To this end, the Clayton Act prohibited price discrimination, exclusive dealing agreements, certain types of mergers, and interlocking boards of directors among competing firms.
- ***The Federal Trade Commission Act (1914).*** The increased antitrust responsibilities of the federal government created the need for an agency that could study industry structures and behavior so as to identify anticompetitive practices. The Federal Trade Commission was created for this purpose in 1914.

Although the Sherman, Clayton, and FTC Acts create a legal basis for government antitrust activity, they leave some basic implementation issues unanswered. What, for example, constitutes a "monopoly" in the real world? Must a company produce 100 percent of a particular good to be a threat to consumer welfare? How about 99 percent? Or even 75 percent?

And what specific monopolistic practices should be prohibited? Should we be looking for specific evidence of price gouging? Or should we focus on barriers to entry and unfair market practices?

These kinds of questions determine how and when antitrust laws will be enforced. The first question relates to the *structure* of markets, the second to their *behavior.*

TABLE 24.1
Antitrust Laws

The legal foundations for antitrust intervention are contained in three landmark antitrust laws.

installing a rival operating system or made it prohibitively expensive. The second accusation against Microsoft was that it used its monopoly position in *operating* systems to gain an unfair advantage in the *applications* market. It did this by not disclosing operating features that make applications run more efficiently or by bundling software, thereby forcing consumers to accept Microsoft applications along with the operating system. When the latter occurs, consumers have little incentive to buy a competing product. Microsoft also prohibited computer manufacturers from displaying rival product icons on the Windows desktop. Finally, Microsoft was accused of thwarting competition by simply buying out promising rivals.

Microsoft's Defense. Bill Gates, Microsoft's chairman, scoffed at the government's charges. He contends that Microsoft dominates the computer industry only because it continues to produce the best products at attractive prices. Microsoft doesn't need to lock out potential competitors, he argues, because it can and does beat the competition with superior products. Furthermore, Gates argues, the software industry is a highly *contestable* market even if not a perfectly competitive one. So Microsoft has to behave like a competitive firm even though it supplies most of the industry's output. In short, Microsoft is a genius, not a bully. Therefore, the government should leave Microsoft alone and let the market decide who best serves consumers.

The Verdict. After 9 years of litigation, a federal court determined that Microsoft was more of a bully than a genius. The court concluded that Microsoft not only held a monopoly position in operating systems but had abused that position in a variety of anticompetitive ways. As a result, consumers were harmed. **The real economic issue, the court asserted, was not whether Microsoft was improving its products (it was) or reducing prices (it was) but instead how much *faster* products would have improved and prices fallen in a more competitive market.** By limiting consumer choices and stifling competition, Microsoft had denied consumers better and cheaper information technology.

WORLD VIEW 

Europe Fines Microsoft $357M

SEATTLE—The European Commission on Wednesday slammed Microsoft with a $357 million fine for defying its 2004 antitrust ruling, and threatened more fines if the company doesn't start toeing the line.

Microsoft missed a Dec 15 deadline to provide technical data required to help software applications from rival vendors work better on Windows servers. . . .

Microsoft has already paid a record $613 million fine and obeyed an order to supply Europe with a version of Windows with its media player stripped out. But the company has failed to meet a remedy calling for it to supply useful Windows server code to rivals.

With some $34 billion in cash and investments. Microsoft can easily absorb the fine.

—Byron Acohido

Source: USA Today, July 13, 2006, p. B1. Reprinted with permission.

Analysis: EU regulators are seeking to lower entry barriers for firms that want to compete for software applications.

The Remedy. The trial judge suggested that Microsoft might have to be broken into two companies—an operating software company and an applications software company—to ensure enough competition. Such a *structural* remedy would have resembled the court-ordered breakup of AT&T. In November 2001, however, the U.S. Department of Justice decided to seek *behavioral* remedies only. With Windows XP about to be launched, the Justice Department only required Microsoft to lower entry barriers for competing software applications (e.g., disclose middleware specifications, refrain from exclusive contracts, open desktops to competition). Although Microsoft reluctantly agreed to change its conduct in many ways, rivals complained that they still didn't have a fair chance of competing against the Microsoft monopoly. European regulators agreed, imposing still greater restrictions on Microsoft's business practices in 2004 and huge fines in 2004 and 2006 (see World View). Critics contend, however, that market *structure* is still the critical factor in determining market outcomes for the economy tomorrow.

SUMMARY 

- Market power is the ability to influence the market price of goods and services. The extreme case of market power is monopoly, a situation in which only one firm produces the entire supply of a particular product. LO1
- The distinguishing feature of any firm with market power is the fact that the demand curve it faces is downward-sloping. In the case of monopoly, the demand curve facing the firm and the market demand curve are identical. LO1
- The downward-sloping demand curve facing a monopolist creates a divergence between marginal revenue and price. To sell larger quantities of output, the monopolist must lower product prices. A firm without market power has no such problem. LO1
- Like other producers, a monopolist will produce at the rate of output at which marginal revenue equals marginal cost. Because marginal revenue is always less than price in monopoly, the monopolist will produce less output than a competitive industry confronting the same market demand and costs. That reduced rate of output will be sold at higher prices, in accordance with the (downward-sloping) market demand curve. LO2
- A monopoly will attain a higher level of profit than a competitive industry because of its ability to equate industry (that is, its own) marginal revenues and costs. By contrast, a competitive industry ends up equating marginal costs and price, because its individual firms have no control over market supply. LO2
- Because the higher profits attained by a monopoly will attract envious entrepreneurs, barriers to entry are needed to prohibit other firms from expanding market supplies. Patents are one such barrier to entry. LO2
- The defense of market power rests on (1) the alleged ability of large firms to pursue long-term research and development, (2) the incentives implicit in the chance to attain market power, (3) the efficiency that larger firms may attain, and (4) the contestability of even monopolized

markets. The first two arguments are weakened by the fact that competitive firms are under much greater pressure to innovate and can stay ahead of the profit game only if they do so. The contestability defense at best concedes some amount of monopoly exploitation. LO3

- A natural monopoly exists when one firm can produce the output of the entire industry more efficiently than can a number of small firms. This advantage is attained from economies of scale. Large firms aren't necessarily more efficient, however, because either constant returns to scale or diseconomies of scale may prevail. LO3
- Antitrust laws restrain the acquisition and abuse of monopoly power. Where barriers to entry aren't insurmountable, market forces may ultimately overcome a monopoly as well. LO3

Key Terms

market power
monopoly
profit-maximization rule
marginal revenue (MR)
barriers to entry
economies of scale
production decision
average total cost (ATC)
marginal cost pricing
price elasticity of demand
price discrimination
natural monopoly
contestable market
antitrust

Questions for Discussion

1. The objective in the game of Monopoly is to get all the property and then raise the rents. Can this power be explained with market supply and demand curves? LO1
2. Is single ownership of a whole industry necessary to exercise monopoly power? How might an industry with many firms achieve the same result? Can you think of any examples? LO1
3. Why don't monopolists try to establish "the highest price possible," as many people allege? What would happen to sales? To profits? LO1
4. In 1990, a federal court decided that Eastman Kodak had infringed on Polaroid's patent when it produced similar instant-photo cameras. The court then had to award Polaroid compensation for damages. What was the nature of the damages to Polaroid? How could you compute them? (The court awarded Polaroid a record $900 million!) LO2
5. What would have happened to iPod prices and features if Apple had not faced competition from iPod clones (Chapter 23)? LO1
6. What entry barriers helped protect the following? LO1
   (*a*) The Russian sable monopoly (see World View, page 492).
   (*b*) The Ticketmaster monopoly (see News, page 497).
   (*c*) The CNN monopoly (see World View, page 504).
7. What similarities exist between the AT&T and Microsoft antitrust cases? What should the government do? LO3
8. How might consumers benefit from a merger of XM and Sirius (News, page 503)? How might they lose? LO3
9. Do price reductions and quality enhancements on Microsoft products prove that Microsoft is a perfectly competitive firm? What should be the test of competitiveness? LO3
10. Why doesn't Microsoft comply fully with EU edicts about code sharing? (See World View, page 507.) LO1

problems The Student Problem Set at the back of this book contains numerical and graphing problems for this chapter.

web activities to accompany this chapter can be found on the Online Learning Center: **http://www.mhhe.com/economics/schiller11e**

25 Oligopoly

LEARNING OBJECTIVES

After reading this chapter, you should know:

LO1. The unique characteristics of oligopoly.

LO2. How oligopolies maximize profits.

LO3. How interdependence affects oligopolists' pricing decisions.

> People of the same trade seldom meet together, but the conversation ends in a conspiracy against the public, or in some diversion to raise prices.
>
> —Adam Smith, *The Wealth of Nations,* 1776

Although it's convenient to think of the economy as composed of the powerful and the powerless, market realities don't always provide such clear distinctions. There are very few perfectly competitive markets in the world, and few monopolies. Market power is an important phenomenon nonetheless; it's just that it's typically shared by several firms rather than monopolized by one. In the soft drink industry, for example, Coca-Cola and Pepsi share tremendous market power, even though neither company qualifies as a pure monopoly. The same kind of power is shared by Kellogg, General Mills, and General Foods in the breakfast cereals market, and by Sony, Nintendo, and Microsoft in the video game console market. Apple Computer, Inc., too, now has power in the digital music player market, which it shares with Microsoft, Sony, RealNetworks, and other firms.

These market structures fall between the extremes of perfect competition and pure monopoly; they represent *imperfect competition.* They contain some elements of competitive rivalry but also exhibit traces of monopoly. In many cases, imperfect competitors behave much like a monopoly, restricting output, charging higher prices, and reaping greater profits than firms in a competitive market. But behavior in imperfectly competitive markets is more complicated than in a monopoly because it involves a number of decision makers (firms) rather than only one.

This chapter focuses on one form of imperfect competition: *oligopoly.* We examine the nature of decision making in this market structure and the likely impacts on prices, production, and profits. What we want to know is:

- **What determines how much market power a firm has?**
- **How do firms in an oligopoly set prices and output?**
- **What problems does an oligopoly have in maintaining price and profit?**

MARKET STRUCTURE

As we saw in Chapter 24, Microsoft is virtually the sole supplier of computer operating systems; as a monopoly, it has tremendous market power. The corner grocery store, on the other hand, must compete with other stores and has less control over prices. But even the corner grocery isn't completely powerless. If it's the only grocery within walking distance, or the only one open on Sunday—it too exerts *some* influence on prices and product flows. The amount of power it possesses depends on the availability of *substitute goods,* that is, the proximity and convenience of alternative retail outlets.

Degrees of Power

market structure: The number and relative size of firms in an industry.

Between the extremes of monopoly and perfect competition are many gradations of market power (see Figure 22.1). To sort them out, we classify firms into five specific **market structures,** based on the number and relative size of firms in an industry.

Table 25.1 summarizes the characteristics of the five major market structures. At one extreme is the structure of *perfect competition,* the subject of Chapters 22 and 23. At the other extreme of the power spectrum is perfect *monopoly.* A perfect monopoly exists when only one firm is the exclusive supplier of a particular product. Our illustration of Universal Electronics (the imaginary computer monopolist in Chapter 24) exemplifies such a firm.

oligopoly: A market in which a few firms produce all or most of the market supply of a particular good or service.

Between the two extremes of perfect competition and perfect monopoly lies most of the real world, which we call *imperfectly competitive.* ***In imperfect competition, individual firms have some power in a particular product market.*** *Oligopoly* refers to one of these imperfectly competitive market structures. **Oligopoly** is a situation in which only a *few* firms have a great deal of power in a product market. An oligopoly may exist because only a few firms produce a particular product or because a few firms account for most, although not all, of a product's output.

Determinants of Market Power

The number of firms in an industry is a key characteristic of market structure. The amount of market power the firms possess, however, depends on several factors. ***The determinants of market power include***

- ***Number of producers.***
- ***Size of each firm.***
- ***Barriers to entry.***
- ***Availability of substitute goods.***

When only one or a few producers or suppliers exist, market power is automatically conferred. In addition to the number of producers, however, the size of each firm is also important. Over 800 firms supply long-distance telephone service in the United States. But just

	Market Structure				
Characteristic	Perfect Competition	Monopolistic Competition	Oligopoly	Duopoly	Monopoly
Number of firms	Very large number	Many	Few	Two	One
Barriers to entry	None	Low	High	High	High
Market power (control over price)	None	Some	Substantial	Substantial	Substantial
Type of product	Standardized	Differentiated	Standardized or differentiated	Standardized or differentiated	Unique

TABLE 25.1
Characteristics of Market Structures

Market structure varies, depending on the number of producers, their size, barriers to entry, and the availability of substitute goods.

An oligopoly is an imperfectly competitive structure in which a few firms dominate the market.

three of those firms (AT&T/Cingular, Verizon, and Nextel) account for 82 percent of all calls. Hence, it wouldn't make sense to categorize that industry on the basis of only the number of firms; relative size is also important.

A third and critical determinant of market power is the extent of barriers to entry. A highly successful monopoly or oligopoly arouses the envy of other profit maximizers. If it's a **contestable market,** potential rivals will seek to enter the market and share in the spoils. Should they succeed, the power of the former monopolist or oligopolists would be reduced. Accordingly, ease of entry into an industry limits the ability of a powerful firm to dictate prices and product flows. In Chapter 24 we saw how monopolies erect barriers to entry (e.g., patents) to maintain their power.

contestable market: An imperfectly competitive industry subject to potential entry if prices or profits increase.

A fourth determinant of market power is the availability of substitute goods. If a monopolist or other power baron sets the price of a product too high, consumers may decide to switch to close substitutes. Thus, the price of Coors is kept in check by the price of Coke, and the price of sirloin steak is restrained by the price of chicken and pork. By the same token, a lack of available substitute products keeps the prices of insulin and AZT high.

Measuring Market Power

Although there are many determinants of market power, most observers use just one yardstick to measure the extent of power in an industry.

Concentration Ratio. The standard measure of market power is the **concentration ratio.** This ratio tells the share of output (or combined market share) accounted for by the largest firms in an industry. Using this ratio one can readily distinguish between an industry composed of hundreds of small, relatively powerless firms and another industry also composed of hundreds of firms but dominated by a few that are large and powerful. Thus, ***the concentration ratio is a measure of market power that relates the size of firms to the size of the product market.***

concentration ratio: The proportion of total industry output produced by the largest firms (usually the four largest).

Table 25.2 gives the concentration ratios for selected products in the United States. The standard measure used here depicts the proportion of domestic production accounted for by the largest firms, usually the four largest. As is apparent from the table, the supply side of these product markets can be described as *oligopolies,* since most of the industry's output is produced by just three or four firms. Indeed, in some markets, one single firm is so large that an outright monopoly is nearly attained. For example, 70 percent of all canned soup is produced by Campbell. Eastman Kodak supplies two-thirds of all still cameras and film. Procter & Gamble makes 62 percent of this country's disposable diapers. In the satellite radio market, two *duopolists* (XM and Sirius) have 100 percent of the market (and they are trying to merge, as the News on page 503 discussed). All firms that have a market share of at least 40 percent are denoted by **boldface** type in Table 25.2.

webnote

The Federal Trade Commission publishes data on *industry,* not product concentration; check www.ftc.gov

Firm Size. We noted before that market power isn't necessarily associated with firm size—in other words, a small firm could possess a lot of power in a relatively small market. Table 25.2 on the next page, however, should be convincing testimony that we're not talking about small product markets here. Every one of the products listed enjoys a broad-based market. Even the chewing gum market (94 percent concentration ratio) rings up annual sales of $2 billion. The three oligopolists that produce video game consoles (Sony, Nintendo, Microsoft) have 100 percent of a $10 billion market. Accordingly, for most of the firms listed in the table, market power and firm size go hand in hand. Indeed, the largest firms enjoy sales volumes that exceed the entire output of most of the *countries* in the world (see World View on page 513).

Measurement Problems

A high concentration ratio or large firm size isn't the only way to achieve market power. The supply and price of a product can be altered by many firms acting in unison. Even 1,000 small producers can band together to change the quantity supplied to the market, thus exercising market power. Recall how our mythical Universal Electronics (Chapter 24) exercised market power by coordinating the production decisions of its many separate plants. Those plants could have attempted such coordination on their own even if they

Product	Largest Firms	Concentration Ratio (%)
Satellite radio	**XM Satellite, Sirius Satellite**	100%
Video game consoles	**Microsoft,** Nintendo, Sony	100
Baby food	**Gerber Products,** Heinz, Beech-Nut	100
Instant breakfast	**Carnation,** Pillsbury, Dean Foods	100
Laser eye surgery	**VISX,** Summit Technology	100
Tennis balls	**Gen Corp (Penn),** PepsiCo **(Wilson),** Dunlop, Spalding	100
Credit cards	**Visa,** MasterCard, American Express, Discover	99
Disposable diapers	**Procter & Gamble,** Kimberly-Clark, Curity, Romar Tissue Mills	99
Razor blades	**Gillette,** Warner-Lambert (Schick; Wilkinson), Bic, American Safety Razor	98
Sports drinks	**PepsiCo** (Gatorade), Coca-Cola (PowerAde), Monarch (All Sport)	98
Digital music players	**Apple,** Sony, Microsoft, Real Networks	97
Baseball cards	Topps, Upper Deck, Fleer, Leaf Inc. (Donruss)	96
Electric razors	**Norelco,** Remington, Warner-Lambert, Sunbeam	96
Sanitary napkins	**Johnson & Johnson,** Kimberly-Clark, Procter & Gamble	96
Batteries	**Duracell,** Eveready, Ray-O-Vac, Kodak	94
Camera, film	**Eastman Kodak,** Fuji, Polaroid	94
Chewing gum	**Wm. Wrigley,** Pfizer, Hershey	94
Soft drinks	**Coca-Cola,** Pepsico, Cadbury Schweppes (7-Up, Dr. Pepper, A&W), Royal Crown	93
Internet search engines	Google, Yahoo, AOL, Microsoft (MSN)	92
Breakfast cereals	General Mills, Kelloggs, Philip Morris (Kraft Foods), PepsiCo (Quaker Oats)	92
Computer printers	**Hewlitt-Packard,** Epson, Canon, Lexmark	91
Toothpaste	Colgate-Palmolive, Procter & Gamble, Church & Dwight, Beecham	91
Local phone service	AT&T, Verizon, Qwest	90
Detergents	**Procter & Gamble,** Lever Bros., Dial, Colgate-Palmolive	90
Art auctions	**Sotheby's, Christie's**	90
Cigarettes	**Philip Morris,** Reynolds American, Lorillard	89
Greeting cards	**Hallmark,** American Greetings, Gibson	88
Coffee	General Foods, Procter & Gamble, Nestlé, Philip Morris	86
Contact lens care	Bausch & Lomb, Allergan Optical, Alcon, Coopervision	86
Beer	**Anheuser-Busch,** Philip Morris (Miller), Coors, Pabst	85
Canned soup	**Campbell,** Progresso	85
Tires and tubes	Goodyear, Firestone, Uniroyal, B.F. Goodrich	85
Cable TV (for-pay)	TimeWarner (HBO), Viacom (Showtime), Cinemax, Movie Channel	83

Sources: Data from Federal Trade Commission, *The Wall Street Journal, Advertising Age, Financial World, Standard & Poor's, Fortune,* and industry sources.

Note: Individual corporations with a market share of at least 40 percent are designated in **boldface.** Market shares based on selected years, 2001–2007

TABLE 25.2
Power in U.S. Product Markets

The domestic production of many familiar products is concentrated among a few firms. These firms have substantial control over the quantity supplied to the market and thus over market price. The concentration ratio measures the share of total output produced by the largest producers in a given market.

hadn't all been owned by the same corporation. Lawyers and doctors exercise this kind of power by maintaining uniform fee schedules for members of the American Bar Association (ABA) and the American Medical Association (AMA).[1] Similarly, dairy farmers act jointly through three large cooperatives (the American Milk Producers, Mid-America Dairies, and Dairymen, Inc.), which together control 50 percent of all milk production.

[1]The courts have ruled that uniform fee schedules are illegal and that individual lawyers and doctors have the right to advertise their prices (fees). Nevertheless, a combination of inertia and self-interest has effectively maintained high fee schedules and inhibited advertising.

WORLD VIEW

Putting Size in Global Perspective

The largest firms in the United States are also the dominant forces in global markets. They export products to foreign markets and produce goods abroad for sale there or to import back into the United States. In terms of size alone, these business giants rival most of the world's nations. Wal-Mart's gross sales, for example, would make it the twenty-second largest "country" in terms of national GDP.

American corporations aren't the only giants in the global markets. Toyota (Japan) and Royal Dutch Shell (Netherlands) are among the foreign giants that contest global markets.

Rank	Country or Corporation	Sales or GDP
1	United States	$12,455
2	Japan	4,506
3	Germany	2,782
4	China	2,229
5	United Kingdom	2,193
6	France	2,110
7	Italy	1,723
8	Spain	1,124
9	Canada	1,115
10	Brazil	794
11	South Korea	788
12	India	786
13	Mexico	768
14	Russia	764
15	Australia	701
16	The Netherlands	595
17	Switzerland	366
18	Belgium	365
19	Turkey	363
20	Sweden	354

Rank	Country or Corporation	Sales or GDP
21	**ExxonMobil**	$340
22	**Wal-Mart Stores**	316
23	Saudi Arabia	310
24	**Royal Dutch/Shell**	307
25	Austria	305
26	Poland	299
27	Indonesia	287
28	Norway	284
29	**British Petroleum**	268
30	Denmark	254
31	South Africa	240
32	Greece	214
33	Iran	196
34	Finland	194
35	**General Motors**	193
36	**Chevron**	189
37	**Daimler/Chrysler**	186
38	**Toyota**	186
39	Hong Kong	178
40	**Ford Motor**	177

Sources: World Bank and *Fortune* magazine (2005 data in billions).

Analysis: Firm size is a determinant of market power. The size of the largest firms, as measured by total revenue, exceeds the value of total output in most of the world's 200-plus countries.

Finally, all the figures and corporations cited here refer to *national* markets. They don't convey the extent to which market power may be concentrated in a *local* market. In fact, many industries with low concentration ratios nationally are represented by just one or a few firms locally. Prime examples include milk, newspapers, and transportation (both public and private). For example, fewer than 60 cities in the United States have two or more independently owned daily newspapers, and nearly all those newspapers rely on only two news services (Associated Press and United Press International). Perhaps you've also noticed that most college campuses have only one bookstore. It may not be a *national* powerhouse, but it does have the power to influence what goods are available on campus and how much they cost.

OLIGOPOLY BEHAVIOR

With so much market power concentrated in so few hands, it's unrealistic to expect market outcomes to resemble those of perfect competition. As we observed in Chapter 24, ***market structure affects market behavior and outcomes.*** In that chapter we focused on the contrast

FIGURE 25.1
Initial Conditions in the Computer Market

As in Chapters 23 and 24, we assume that the initial equilibrium in the computer market occurs at a price of $1,000 and a quantity of 20,000 per month. How will an oligopoly alter these outcomes?

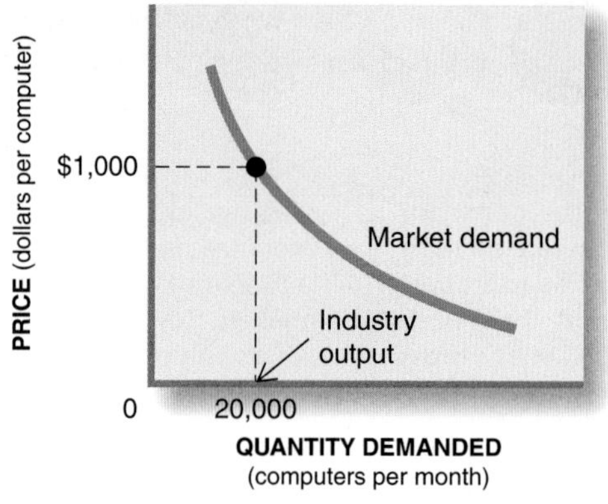

between monopoly and perfect competition. Now we focus on the behavior of a more common market structure: oligopoly.

To isolate the unique character of oligopoly, we'll return to the computer market. In Chapter 23 we observed that the computer market was highly competitive in its early stages, when entry barriers were low and hundreds of firms were producing similar products. In Chapter 24 we created an impassable barrier to entry (a patent on the electronic brain of the computer) that transformed the computer industry into a monopoly of Universal Electronics. Now we'll transform the industry again. This time we'll create an oligopoly by assuming that three separate firms (Universal, World, and International) all possess patent rights. The patent rights permit each firm to produce and sell all the computers it wants and to exclude all other would-be producers from the market. With these assumptions, we create three **oligopolists,** the firms that share an *oligopoly.* Our objective is to see how market outcomes would change in such a market structure.

oligopolist: One of the dominant firms in an oligopoly.

The Initial Equilibrium

As before, we'll assume that the initial conditions in the computer market are represented by a market price of $1,000 and market sales of 20,000 computers per month, as illustrated in Figure 25.1.

We'll also assume that the **market share** of each producer is accurately depicted in Table 25.3. Thus, Universal Electronics is assumed to be producing 8,000 computers per month, or 40 percent of total market supply. World Computers has a market share of 32.5 percent, while International Semiconductor has only a 27.5 percent share.

market share: The percentage of total market output produced by a single firm.

The Battle for Market Shares

The first thing to note about the computer oligopoly is that it's likely to exhibit great internal tension. Neither World Computers nor International Semiconductor is really happy playing second or third fiddle to Universal Electronics. Each company would like to be number one in this market. On the other hand, Universal too would like a larger market share, particularly in view of the huge profits being made on computers. As we observed in Chapter 23, the initial equilibrium in the computer industry yielded an *average* profit of $300 per computer, and total *industry* profits of $6 million per month (20,000 × $300). Universal would love to acquire the market shares of its rivals, thereby grabbing all this industry profit for itself.

TABLE 25.3
Initial Market Shares of Microcomputer Producers

The market share of a firm is the percentage of total market output it produces. These are hypothetical market shares of three fictional oligopolists.

Producer	Output (computers per month)	Market Share (%)
Universal Electronics	8,000	40.0%
World Computers	6,500	32.5
International Semiconductor	5,500	27.5
Total industry output	20,000	100.0%

But how does an oligopolist acquire a larger market share? In a truly competitive market, a single producer could expand production at will, with no discernible impact on market supply. That's not possible when there are only three firms in the market: ***In an oligopoly, increased sales on the part of one firm will be noticed immediately by the other firms.***

How do we know that increased sales will be noticed so quickly? Because increased sales by one firm will have to take place either at the existing market price ($1,000) or at a lower price. Either of these two events will ring an alarm at the corporate headquarters of the other two firms.

Increased Sales at the Prevailing Market Price. Consider first the possibility of Universal Electronics increasing its sales at the going price of $1,000 per computer. We know from the demand curve in Figure 25.1 that consumers are willing to buy *only* 20,000 microcomputers per month at that price. Hence, any increase in computer sales by Universal must be immediately reflected in *lower* sales by World or International. That is, ***increases in the market share of one oligopolist necessarily reduce the shares of the remaining oligopolists.*** If Universal were to increase its sales from 8,000 to 9,000 computers per month, the combined monthly sales of World and International would have to fall from 12,000 to 11,000 (see Table 25.3). The *quantity demanded* at $1,000 remains 20,000 computers per month (see Figure 25.1). Thus, any increased sales at that price by Universal must be offset by reduced sales by its rivals.

This interaction among the market shares of the three oligopolists ensures that Universal's sales success will be noticed. It won't be necessary for World Computers or International Semiconductor to engage in industrial espionage. These firms can quickly figure out what Universal is doing simply by looking at their own (declining) sales figures.

Increased Sales at Reduced Prices. Universal could pursue a different strategy. Specifically, Universal could attempt to increase its sales by lowering the price of its computers. Reduced prices would expand total market sales, possibly enabling Universal to increase its sales without directly reducing the sales of either World or International.

But this outcome is most unlikely. If Universal lowered its price from $1,000 to, say, $900, consumers would flock to Universal Computers, and the sales of World and International would plummet. After all, we've always assumed that consumers are rational enough to want to pay the lowest possible price for any particular good. It's unlikely that consumers would continue to pay $1,000 for a World or International machine when they could get basically the same computer from Universal for only $900. If there were no difference, either perceived or real, among the computers of the three firms, a *pure* oligopoly would exist. In that case, Universal would capture the *entire* market if it lowered its price below that of its rivals.

More often, consumers perceive differences in the products of rival oligopolists, even when the products are essentially identical. These perceptions (or any real differences that may exist) create a *differentiated* oligopoly. In this case, Universal would gain many but not all customers if it reduced the price of its computers. That's the outcome we'll assume here. In either case, there simply isn't any way that Universal can increase its sales at reduced prices without causing all the alarms to go off at World and International.

Retaliation

So what if all the alarms do go off at World Computers and International Semiconductor? As long as Universal Electronics is able to enlarge its share of the market and grab more profits, why should it care if World and International find out?

Universal *does* have something to worry about. World and International may not be content to stand by and watch their market shares and profits diminish. On the contrary, World and International are likely to take some action of their own once they discover what's going on.

There are two things World and International can do once they decide to act. In the first case, where Universal is expanding its market share at prevailing prices ($1,000), World and International can retaliate by

- Stepping up their own marketing efforts.
- Cutting prices on their computers.

IN THE NEWS

Pop Culture: RC Goes for the Youth Market

RC Cola, like the Brady Bunch and push-up bras, is attempting a '90s comeback. . . .

To that end, the company is spending $15 million on a new advertising campaign—the largest in RC's history—designed to cast the blue-collar drink of the Midwest and South as the hip alternative to "corporate colas," as it refers to market leaders Coke and Pepsi. Accompanying the ad blitz are new products, including a sour-tasting, Windex-colored Nehi and a long-neck brew called RC Draft, formulated specifically for younger palates.

"This company spent no money on advertising during the 1980s, and we lost an entire generation of cola drinkers who grew up in that decade," said John Carson, Royal Crown's chief executive. . . .

"Anybody in the soft drink business trying to compete with Pepsi and Coke has an uphill battle—they have huge amounts of marketing muscle, financial resources, experience and bottling agreements," said John Sicher, co-editor of Beverage Digest, an industry publication. "But RC's new tactics are smart. They are tossing out a bunch of beverages targeted toward younger drinkers. Against Coke and Pepsi, guerrilla warfare is the only thing that might work."

—Anthony Faiola

The U.S. Soda Market

Market share of soft drink makers, 2001.

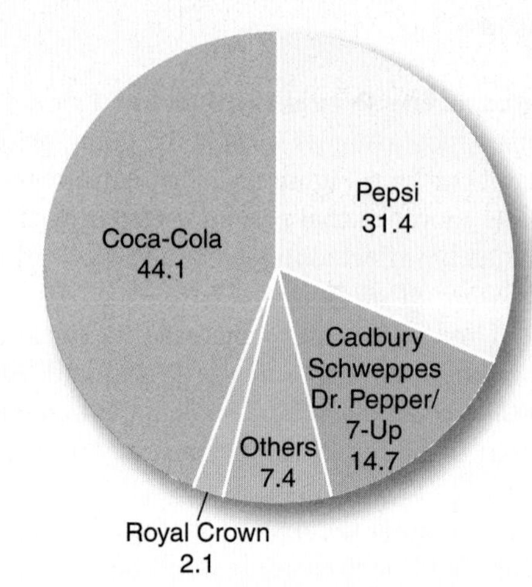

Source: *The Washington Post*, February 17, 1995. www.washingtonpost.com

Analysis: Because price competition is typically self-defeating in an oligopoly, rival firms in an oligopoly rely on advertising and product differentiation (nonprice competition) to gain market share.

product differentiation: Features that make one product appear different from competing products in the same market.

To step up their marketing efforts, World and International might increase their advertising expenditures, repackage their computers, put more sales representatives on the street, or sponsor a college homecoming week. This is the kind of behavior RC Cola used to gain market share from Coke and Pepsi (see News). Such attempts at **product differentiation** are designed to make one firm's products appear different and superior to those produced by other firms. If successful, such marketing efforts will increase RC Cola sales and market share or at least stop its rivals from grabbing larger shares.

An even quicker way to stop Universal from enlarging its market share is for World and International to lower the price of *their* computers. Such price reductions will destroy Universal's hopes of increasing its market share at the old price. In fact, this is the other side of a story we've already told. If the price of World and International computers drops to, say, $900, it's preposterous to assume that Universal will be able to expand its market share at a price of $1,000. Universal's market share will shrink if it maintains a price of $1,000 per computer after World and International drop their prices to $900. Hence, the threat to Universal's market share grab is that the other two oligopolists will retaliate by reducing *their* prices. Should they carry out this threat, Universal would be forced to cut computer prices too, or accept a greatly reduced market share.

The same kind of threat exists in the second case, where we assumed that Universal Electronics expands its sales by initiating a price reduction. World and International aren't going to just sit by and applaud Universal's marketing success. They'll have to respond with price cuts of their own. Universal would then have the highest price on the market, and computer buyers would flock to cheaper substitutes. Accordingly, it's safe to conclude that ***an attempt by one oligopolist to increase its market share by cutting prices will lead to a***

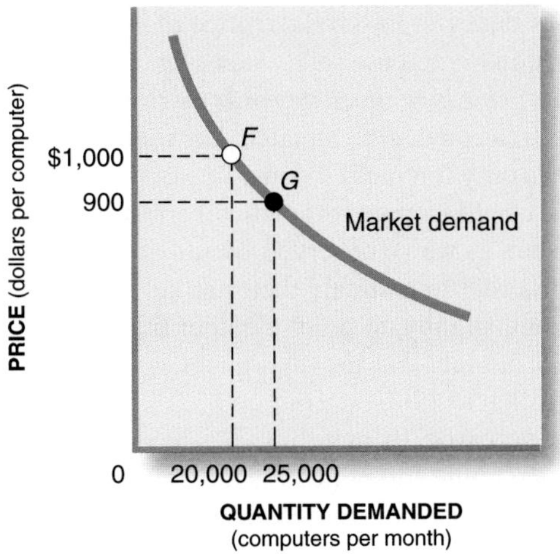

FIGURE 25.2
Rivalry for Market Shares Threatens an Oligopoly

If oligopolists start cutting prices to capture larger market shares, they'll be behaving much like truly competitive firms. The result will be a slide down the market demand curve to lower prices, increased output, and smaller profits. In this case, the market price and quantity would move from point *F* to point *G* if rival oligopolists cut prices to gain market shares.

general reduction in the market price. The three oligopolists will end up using price reductions as weapons in the battle for market shares, the kind of behavior normally associated with competitive firms. Should this behavior continue, not only will oligopoly become less fun, but it will also become less profitable as prices slide down the market demand curve (Figure 25.2). This is why ***oligopolists avoid price competition and instead pursue nonprice competition*** (e.g., advertising and production differentiation).

THE KINKED DEMAND CURVE

The close interdependence of oligopolists—and the limitations it imposes on individual price and output decisions—is the principal moral of this story. We can summarize the story with the aid of the kinked demand curve in Figure 25.3.

Recall that at the beginning of this oligopoly story Universal Electronics had a market share of 40 percent and was selling 8,000 computers per month at a price of $1,000 each. This output is represented by point *A* in Figure 25.3. The rest of the demand curve illustrates what would happen to Universal's unit sales if it changed its selling price. What we have to figure out is why this particular demand curve has such a strange "kinked" shape.

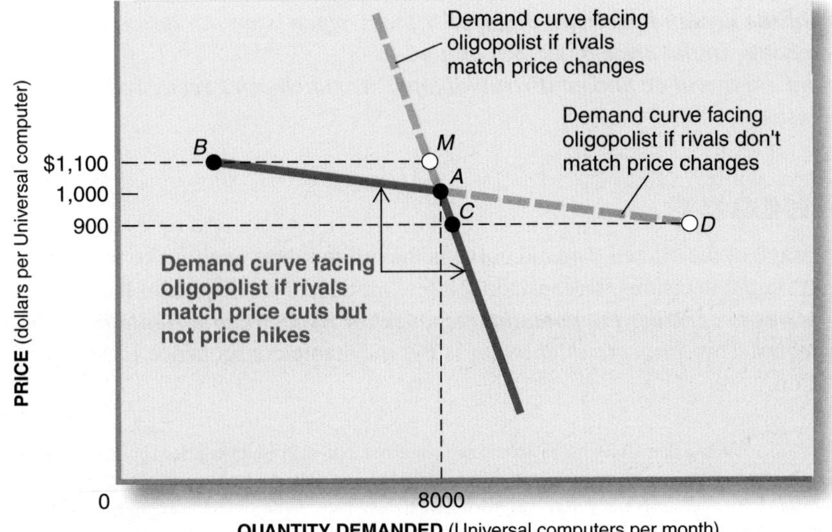

FIGURE 25.3
The Kinked Demand Curve Confronting an Oligopolist

The shape of the demand curve facing an oligopolist depends on the responses of its rivals to its price and output decisions. If rival oligopolists match price reductions but not price increases, the demand curve will be kinked.

Initially, the oligopolist is at point *A*. If it raises its price to $1,100 and its rivals don't raise their prices, it will be driven to point *B*. If its rivals match a price reduction (to $900), the oligopolist will end up at point *C*.

Rivals' Response to Price Reductions

Consider first what would happen to Universal's sales if it lowered the price of its computers to $900. In general, we expect a price reduction to increase sales. However, ***the degree to which an oligopolist's sales increase when its price is reduced depends on the response of rival oligopolists.*** Suppose World and International *didn't* match Universal's price reduction. In this case, Universal would have the only low-priced computer in the market. Consumers would flock to Universal, and sales would increase dramatically, from point *A* to point *D.* But point *D* is little more than a dream, as we've observed. World and International are sure to cut their prices to $900 too, in order to maintain their market shares. As a consequence, Universal's sales will expand only slightly, to point *C* rather than to point *D.* Universal's increased sales at point *C* reflect the fact that the total quantity demanded in the market has risen as the market price has fallen to $900 (see Figure 25.2). Thus, even though Universal's *market share* may not have increased, its monthly sales have.

The section of the demand curve that runs from point *A* to point *D* is unlikely to exist in an oligopolistic market. Instead, ***we expect rival oligopolists to match any price reductions*** that Universal initiates, forcing Universal to accept the demand curve that runs from point *A* through point *C.* The News illustrates such behavior in the airline industry, where rivals were forced to match price cuts introduced by Delta.

Rivals' Response to Price Increases

What about price increases? How will World and International respond if Universal raises the price of its computers to $1,100?

Recall that the demand for computers is assumed to be price-elastic in the neighborhood of $1,000 and that all computers are basically similar. Accordingly, if Universal raises its price and neither World nor International follows suit, Universal will be out there alone with a higher price and reduced sales. ***Rival oligopolists may choose not to match price increases.*** In terms of Figure 25.3, a price increase that isn't matched by rival oligopolists will drive Universal from point *A* to point *B.* At point *B,* Universal is selling very few computers at its price of $1,100 each.[2]

Is this a likely outcome? Suffice it to say that World Computers and International Semiconductor wouldn't be unhappy about enlarging their own market shares. Unless they see the desirability of an industrywide price increase, they're not likely to come to Universal's rescue with price increases of their own. This is why Northwest Airlines decided not to match the fare hikes announced by its rivals (see News).

Anything is possible, however, and World and International might match Universal's price increase. In this case, the *market price* would rise to $1,100 and the total quantity of computers demanded would diminish. Under such circumstances Universal's sales would diminish, too, in accordance with its (constant) share of a smaller market. This would lead us to point *M* in Figure 25.3.

We may draw two conclusions from Figure 25.3:

- ***The shape of the demand curve an oligopolist faces depends on the responses of its rivals to a change in the price of its own output.***
- ***That demand curve will be kinked if rival oligopolists match price reductions but not price increases.***

GAME THEORY

The central message of the kinked demand curve is that oligopolists can't make truly independent price or output decisions. Because only a few producers participate in the market, ***each oligopolist has to consider the potential responses of rivals when formulating price or output strategies.*** This *strategic interaction* is the inevitable consequence of their oligopolistic position.

[2]Notice again that we're assuming that Universal is able to sell some computers at a higher price (point *B*) than its rivals. The kinked demand curve applies primarily to differentiated oligopolies. As we'll discuss later, such differentiation may result from slight product variations, advertising, customer habits, location, friendly service, or any number of other factors. Most oligopolies exhibit some differentiation.

IN THE NEWS

Airlines Drop Fare Hikes

Major airlines abandoned fare increases of as much as $20 on one-way tickets after all carriers failed to match the increases . . .

Continental Airlines and AMR Corp.'s American Airlines yesterday became the last of the major airlines to roll back increases that were put in place last Tuesday and were matched initially by most airlines except Northwest Airlines.

—Gary McWilliams

Source: *The Wall Street Journal,* May 25, 2004. Reprinted by permission of *The Wall Street Journal,*

Delta Cuts Fares 25 Percent; Rival Lines Follow Suit

Major airlines slashed fares about 25 percent yesterday in the hope that leisure summer passengers will make up for the sharp decline in business travel that has pushed airline revenue down dramatically.

Delta Air Lines cut fares in the United States, Latin America and Asia. Other airlines such as United, American, Continental, Northwest and US Airways immediately said they would match Delta's 25 percent fare reductions in markets where they compete.

—Keith L. Alexander

Source: *The Washington Post,* June 26, 2001. www.washingtonpost.com

Analysis: If rivals match price cuts but not price increases, the demand curve confronting an oligopolist will be kinked. Prices will increase only when all firms agree to raise them at the same time.

Uncertainty and Risk. What makes oligopoly particularly interesting is the *uncertainty* of rivals' behavior. For example, Universal *would* want to lower its prices *if* it thought its rivals wouldn't retaliate with similar price cuts. But it can't be sure of that response. Universal must instead consider the odds of its rivals not matching a price cut. If the odds are low, Universal might decide *not* to initiate a price cut. Or maybe Universal might offer price discounts to just a few select customers, hoping World and International might not notice or react to small changes in market share.

The Payoff Matrix. Table 25.4 summarizes the strategic options each oligopolist confronts. In this case, let's assume that Universal is contemplating a price cut. The **payoff matrix** in the table summarizes the various profit consequences of such a move. One thing should be immediately clear: ***The payoff to an oligopolist's price cut depends on how its rivals respond.*** Indeed, the only scenario that increases Universal's profit is one in which Universal reduces its price and its rivals don't. We visualized this outcome earlier as a move from point *A* to point *D* in Figure 25.3. Note again that this scenario implies losses for Universal's two rival oligopolists.

payoff matrix: A table showing the risks and rewards of alternative decision options.

	Rivals' Actions	
Universal's Options	Reduce Price	Don't Reduce Price
Reduce price	Small loss for everyone	Huge gain for Universal; rivals lose
Don't reduce price	Huge loss for Universal; rivals gain	No change

TABLE 25.4
Oligopoly Payoff Matrix

The payoff to an oligopolist's price cut depends on its rivals' responses. Each oligopolist must assess the risks and rewards of each scenario before initiating a price change. Which option would you choose?

webnote

The "Prisoner's Dilemma" (who should confess) is a classic game theory problem. Try solving this and other games at www.princeton.edu/~mdaniels/pd/pd.html

The remaining cells in the payoff matrix show how profits change with other action/response scenarios. One thing is evident: If Universal *doesn't* reduce prices, it can't increase profits. In fact, it might end up as the Big Loser if its rivals reduce *their* prices while Universal stands pat.

The option of reducing price doesn't guarantee a profit, but at least it won't decimate Universal's market share or profits. If rivals match a Universal price cut, all three oligopolists will suffer small losses.

So what should Universal do? The *collective* interests of the oligopoly are protected if no one cuts the market price. But an individual oligopolist could lose big time if it holds the line on price when rivals reduce price. Hence each oligopolist might decide to play it safe by *initiating* a price cut.

Expected Gain (Loss). The decision to initiate a price cut boils down to an assessment of *risk.* If you thought the risk of a "first strike" was high, you'd be more inclined to reduce price. This kind of risk assessment is the foundation of game theory. You could in fact make that decision by *quantifying* the risks involved. Consider again the option of reducing price. As the first row of Table 25.4 shows, rivals can respond in one of only two ways. If they follow suit, a small loss is incurred by Universal. If they don't, there's a huge gain for Universal. To quantify the risk assessment, we need two pieces of information: (1) the size of each "payoff" and (2) the probability of its occurrence.

Suppose the "huge gain" is \$1 million and the "small loss" is \$20,000. What should Universal do? The huge gain looks enticing, but we now know it's not likely to happen. But *how* unlikely is it? What if there's only a 1 percent chance of rivals not matching a price reduction? In that case, the *expected* payoff to a Universal price cut is

$$\text{Expected value} = \left[\begin{matrix}\text{Probability of}\\\text{rivals matching}\end{matrix} \times \begin{matrix}\text{Size of}\\\text{loss from}\\\text{price cuts}\end{matrix}\right] + \left[\begin{matrix}\text{Probability}\\\text{of rivals}\\\text{not matching}\end{matrix} \times \begin{matrix}\text{Gain}\\\text{from lone}\\\text{price cut}\end{matrix}\right]$$

$$= [(0.99) \times (-\$20{,}000)] + [(0.01) \times (\$1 \text{ million})]$$

$$= -\$19{,}800 + \$10{,}000$$

$$= -\$9{,}800$$

Hence, it's not a good idea. Once potential payoffs and probabilities are taken into account, a unilateral price cut doesn't look promising. The odds say a unilateral price cut will result in a loss (−\$9,800).

These kinds of computations underlay the Cold War games that the world's one-time super powers played. Neither side was certain of the enemy's next move but knew a nuclear first strike could trigger retaliatory destruction. As a consequence, the United States and the former Soviet Union continually probed each other's responses but were quick to retreat from the brink whenever all-out retaliation was threatened. Oligopolists play the same kind of game on a much smaller scale, using price discounts and advertising rather than nuclear warheads as their principal weapons. The reward they receive for coexistence is the oligopoly profits that they continue to share. This reward, together with the threat of mutual destruction, leads oligopolists to limit their price rivalry. This explains why Coke and Pepsi quickly ended their brief price war (see News). After finger-pointing about who started the war, the companies pulled back from the brink of mutual profit destruction. Notice in the last paragraph of the News how Coke's CEO explicitly rejects price competition as a viable strategy for oligopolists.

game theory: The study of decision making in situations where strategic interaction (moves and countermoves) between rivals occurs.

This isn't to say oligopolists won't ever cut prices or use other means to gain market share. They might, given the right circumstances and certain expectations of how rivals will behave. Indeed, there are a host of different price, output, and marketing strategies an oligopolist might want to pursue. The field of **game theory** is dedicated to the study of how decisions are made when such strategic interaction exists, for example, when the outcome

IN THE NEWS   

Coke and Pepsi May Call Off Pricing Battle

ATLANTA—A brief but bitter pricing war within the soft-drink industry might be drawing to a close—all because no one wants to be blamed for having fired the first shot.

Coca-Cola Enterprises Inc., Coca-Cola Co.'s biggest bottler, said in a recent memorandum to executives that it will "attempt to increase prices" after July 4 amid concern that heavy price discounting in most of the industry is squeezing profit margins.

The memo is a response to statements made to analysts last week by top PepsiCo Inc. executives. Pepsi, of Purchase, N.Y., said "irrational" pricing in much of the soft-drink industry might temporarily squeeze domestic profits, and it laid the blame for the price cuts at Coke's door.

That clearly incensed executives at Coca-Cola and Coca-Cola Enterprises, which had no desire to be criticized for threatening profit margins for the entire industry. Indeed, industry analysts in the wake of Pepsi's statements expressed concern that profit margins for Pepsi and Coke bottlers may erode as a result of cutthroat pricing. . . .

In the June 5 memo, Summerfield K. Johnston Jr. and Henry A. Schimberg, the chief executive and the president of Coca-Cola Enterprises, respectively, said the bottler's plan is to "succeed based on superior marketing programs and execution rather than the short-term approach of buying share through price discounting. . . . We have absolutely no motivation to decrease prices except in response to a competitive initiative."

—Nikhil Deogun

Source: *The Wall Street Journal,* June 12, 1997.

Analysis: Price discounting can destroy oligopoly profits. When it occurs, rival oligopolists seek to end it as quickly as possible.

of a business strategy depends on the decisions rival firms make. Just as there are dozens of different moves and countermoves in a chess game, so too are there numerous strategies oligopolists might use to gain market share.

OLIGOPOLY VS. COMPETITION

While contemplating strategies for maximizing their *individual* profits, oligopolists are also mindful of their common interest in maximizing *joint* (industry) profits. They want to avoid behavior that destroys the very profits that they're vying for. Indeed, they might want to coordinate their behavior in a way that maximizes *industry* profits. If they do, how will market outcomes be affected?

Price and Output

Thus far we've focused on a single oligopolist's decision about whether to *change* the price of its output. But how was the initial (market) price determined? In this example, we assumed that the initial price was $1,000 per computer, the price that prevailed initially in a *competitive* market. But the market is no longer competitive. As we saw in the previous chapter, a change in industry structure will affect market outcomes. A monopolist, for example, would try to maximize *industry* profits, all of which it would keep. To do this, it would select that one rate of output where marginal revenue equals marginal cost, and it would charge whatever price consumers were willing and able to pay for that rate of output (see Figure 25.4).

An oligopoly would seek similar profits. An oligopoly is really just a *shared* monopoly. Hence, ***an oligopoly will want to behave like a monopoly, choosing a rate of industry output that maximizes total industry profit.***

The challenge for an oligopoly is to replicate monopoly outcomes. To do so, the firms in an oligopoly must find the monopoly price and maintain it. This is what the members of OPEC are trying to do when they meet to establish a common price for the oil they sell (see

webnote

To assess the effects of OPEC's 2004 agreement, check the trend of oil prices at www.eia.doe.gov

FIGURE 25.4
Maximizing Oligopoly Profits

An oligopoly strives to behave like a monopoly. Industry profits are maximized at the rate of output at which the industry's marginal cost equals the marginal revenue (point *J*). In a monopoly, this profit all goes to one firm; in an oligopoly, it must be shared among a few firms.

In an oligopoly, the MC and ATC curves represent the combined production capabilities of several firms, rather than only one. The industry MC curve is derived by horizontally summing the MC curves of the individual firms.

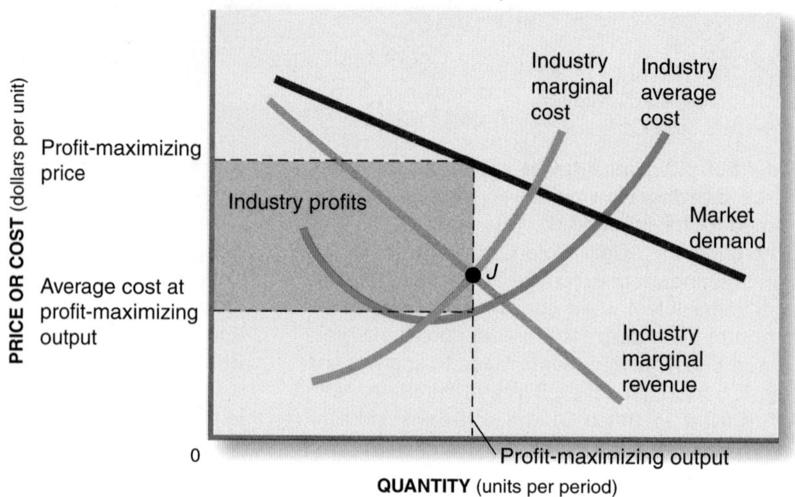

World View). To reach agreement requires a common view of the industry demand curve, satisfaction with respective market shares, and precise coordination.

Competitive industries would also like to reap monopoly-like profits. But competitive industries experience relentless pressure on profits, as individual firms expand output, reduce costs, and lower prices. To maximize industry profits, competitive firms would have to band together and agree to restrict output and raise prices. If they did, though, the industry would no longer be competitive. The potential for maximizing industry profits is clearly greater in an oligopoly because fewer firms are involved and each is aware of its dependence on the behavior of the others.

WORLD VIEW

OPEC's Cut Aims to Prop Up Prices

Plan to Pare Output by 1.9% Starting Feb. 1 Signals Bid to Halt Crude Oil's Decline

ABUJA, Nigeria—OPEC, in announcing it plans to slice its output by an additional 1.9% starting Feb. 1, is sending a strong signal that it will try to prevent oil prices from sliding further.

The real impact of the cartel's latest output move on oil markets remains unclear. The big unknown is whether members of the Organization of Petroleum Exporting Countries will actually implement the decision, which calls for a collective cut of 500,000 barrels a day. . . .

Oil prices rose yesterday, with light, sweet crude for January delivery up $1.14, or 1.9%, to $62.51 a barrel on the New York Mercantile Exchange.

—Bhushan Bahree

Analysis: An oligopoly tries to act like a shared monopoly. To maximize industry profit, the firms in an oligopoly must concur on what the monopoly price is and agree to maintain it by limiting output and allocating market shares.

COORDINATION PROBLEMS

A successful oligopoly will achieve monopoly-level profits by restricting industry output. As we've observed, however, this outcome depends on mutual agreement and coordination among the oligopolists. This may not come easy. ***There's an inherent conflict in the joint and individual interests of oligopolists.*** Their joint, or collective, interest is in maximizing industry profit. The individual interest of each oligopolist, however, is to maximize its own share of sales and profit. This conflict creates great internal tension within an oligopoly. Recall that each firm wants as large a market share as possible, at prevailing prices. But encroachments in the market shares of rival oligopolists threaten to bring retaliation, price reductions, and reduced industry profits. To avoid such self-destructive behavior, oligopolists must coordinate their production decisions so that

- *Industry* output and price are maintained at profit-maximizing levels.
- Each oligopolistic *firm* is content with its market share.

Price-Fixing

To bring about this happy outcome, rival oligopolists could discuss their common interests and attempt to iron out an agreement on both issues. Identifying the profit-maximizing rate of industry output would be comparatively simple, as Figure 25.4 illustrated. Once the optimal rate of output was found, the associated profit-maximizing price would be evident. The only remaining issue would be the division of industry output among the oligopolists, that is, the assignment of market shares.

The most explicit form of coordination among oligopolists is called **price-fixing.** In this case, the firms in an oligopoly explicitly agree to charge a uniform (monopoly) price. This is what the 12 OPEC member-nations do when they get together to set oil prices (previous World View). Some other examples of price-fixing include the following:

price-fixing: Explicit agreements among producers regarding the price(s) at which a good is to be sold.

Ivy League Colleges. For more than 30 years Ivy League schools worked together to offer a uniform financial-aid package for individual students, eliminating price competition. The Justice Department ordered the schools to end that practice in 1992.

Electric Generators. In 1961, General Electric and Westinghouse were convicted of fixing prices on $2 billion worth of electrical generators that they'd been selling to the Tennessee Valley Authority and commercial customers. Among the corporate executives, 7 went to prison and 23 others were put on probation. In addition, the companies were fined a total of $1.8 million and compelled to pay triple damages in excess of $500 million to their victimized customers. Nevertheless, another suit was filed against General Electric and Westinghouse in 1972, charging these same companies—still the only two U.S. manufacturers of turbine generators—with continued price-fixing.

School Milk. Between 1988 and 1991, the U.S. Justice Department filed charges against 50 companies for fixing the price of milk sold to public schools in 16 states. Dairy companies paid over $20 million in fines. In 1993, Borden Inc. paid $8 million in fines for fixing bids on milk sold to Texas Tech University, public schools, and hospitals.

Baby Formula. Two makers of baby formula (Bristol-Myers Squibb and American Home Products) agreed to pay $5 million in 1992 to settle Florida charges that they had fixed prices on baby formula. Three companies control 95 percent of this $1.3 billion national market.

Perfume. Thirteen companies—including Chanel, Dior, and Yves Saint Laurent—paid $55 million in penalties in 2006 for fixing prices.

Auction Commissions. Sotheby's and Christie's, who together control 90 percent of the world's art auction business, admitted in 2000 to fixing commission rates throughout the 1990s. They paid a $512 million fine when they got caught.

Music CDs. In 2001, the Federal Trade Commission charged AOL–TimeWarner and Universal Music with fixing prices on the best-selling "Three Tenors" CD. The FTC also forced

TimeWarner, Sony, Bertelsmann, and EMI to end prohibitions on the advertising of discounted CD prices. The companies paid a $67 million fine and gave away $76 million in free CDs in 2002 to settle the case.

Laser Eye Surgery. The FTC charged the two companies that sell the lasers used for corrective eye surgery (VISX and Summit Technology) with price-fixing that inflated the retail price of surgery by $500 per eye.

Memory Chips. In 2005, the world's largest memory-chip (DRAM) manufacturers (Samsung, Micron, Infineon, Hynix) admitted to fixing prices in the $16 billion-a-year DRAM market and paid nearly $700 million in criminal fines.

Elevators. In 2007 five companies were fined $1.3 *billion* for fixing prices on elevators and escalators in Europe for ten years.

Price Leadership

price leadership: An oligopolistic pricing pattern that allows one firm to establish the (market) price for all firms in the industry.

Although price-fixing agreements are still a reality in many product markets, oligopolies have discovered that they don't need *explicit* agreements to arrive at uniform prices; they can achieve the same outcome in more subtle ways. **Price leadership** rather than price-fixing will suffice. If all oligopolists in a particular product market follow the lead of one firm in raising prices, the result is the same as if they had all agreed to raise prices simultaneously. Instead of conspiring in motel rooms (as in the electrical products and soft drink cases), the firms can achieve their objective simply by reading *The Wall Street Journal* or industry publications and responding appropriately. This is apparently how Coke and Pepsi communicated their desire to end their 1997 price war (see News on page 521).

According to the U.S. Department of Justice, the major airlines developed a highly sophisticated form of price leadership. They used their shared computer reservation systems to signal *intended* price hikes. Rival oligopolists then responded with their own *intended* price changes. Only after it was clear that all the airlines would match a planned price increase was the price hike announced. The Justice Department argued that this "electronic dialogue" was equivalent to a price-fixing conspiracy that cost consumers $1.9 billion in excessive fares. In response, the major airlines agreed to stop using the reservations system to communicate *planned* fare hikes.

Allocation of Market Shares

Whenever oligopolists successfully raise the price of a product, the law of demand tells us that unit sales will decline. Even in markets with highly inelastic demand (such as those for school milk and generic drugs), *some* decrease in sales always accompanies an increase in price. When this happens in a monopolistic industry, the monopolist simply cuts back his rate of output. In an oligopoly, however, no single firm will wish to incur the whole weight of that cutback. Some form of accommodation is required by all the oligopolists.

The adjustment to the reduced sales volume can take many forms. Members of OPEC, for example, assign explicit quotas for the oil output of each member country (see World View on page 522). Such open and explicit production-sharing agreements transform an oligopoly into a **cartel.**

cartel: A group of firms with an explicit, formal agreement to fix prices and output shares in a particular market.

Because cartels openly violate U.S. antitrust laws, American oligopolies have to be more circumspect in divvying up shared markets. A particularly novel method of allocating market shares occurred in the price-fixing case involving General Electric and Westinghouse. Agreeing to establish high prices on electric generators wasn't particularly difficult. But how would the companies decide who was to get the restricted sales? Their solution was to designate one firm as the "low" bidder for a particular phase of the moon. The "low" bidder would charge the previously agreed-upon (high) price, with the other firms offering their products at even higher prices. The "low" bidder would naturally get the sale. Each time the moon entered a new phase, the order of "low" and "high" bidders changed. Each firm got a share of the business, and the price-fixing scheme hid behind a facade of "competitive" bidding.

IN THE NEWS  

Eliminating the Competition

On January 5, 2006 Independence Air ceased flying. CEO Kerry Skeen, armed with $300 million in start-up capital, had positioned Independence as a low-fare entrant at the profitable Washington, DC Dulles airport. At its launch in June 2004, Skeen observed that the Washington, DC area was "screaming" for low fares.

The major carriers didn't agree. United Airlines, with a hub at Dulles, slashed fares as soon as Independence took flight. The rest of the "Big Six" (Delta, American, Northwest, US Airways, Continental) did the same. The fare war kept Independence from gaining enough market share to survive. As CEO Skeen concluded, "It's a brutal industry."

The week after Independence ceased flying, the "walk-up" fare between Dulles and Atlanta jumped from $118 to $478. Other fares followed suit.

Source: "Flying Monopoly Air," McGraw-Hill News Flash, February 2006. Reprinted with permission.

Analysis: To protect their prices and profits, oligopolists must be able to eliminate potential competition. Predatory pricing can serve that purpose.

Such intricate systems for allocating market shares are more the exception than the rule. More often the oligopolists let the sales and output reduction be divided up according to consumer demands, intervening only when market shares are thrown markedly out of balance. At such times an oligopolist may take drastic action, such as **predatory pricing.** Predatory price cuts are temporary price reductions intended to drive out new competition or reestablish market shares. The sophisticated use of price cutting can also function as a significant barrier to entry, inhibiting potential competitors from trying to gain a foothold in the price cutter's market. The accompanying News feature describes how major airlines forced Independence Air out of their market with predatory pricing in 2006.

predatory pricing: Temporary price reductions designed to alter market shares or drive out competition.

IN THE NEWS 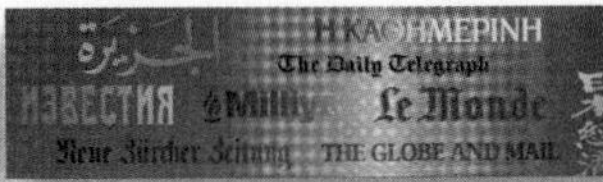 

RIM to Pay NTP $612.5 Million to Settle BlackBerry Patent Suit

With Pact, Tech Firm Avoids Court-Ordered Shutdown of Popular Wireless Device

Research In Motion Ltd., on the brink of a possible court-ordered shutdown of its widely used BlackBerry wireless email device, agreed to pay $612.5 million to settle its long-running legal battle with NTP Inc.

The settlement, announced after markets closed on Friday, ended all court proceedings in the nearly five-year legal battle that saw a tiny patent-holding firm take on one of technology's hottest companies and threaten to disrupt service to BlackBerry users in the U.S. . . .

The news was greeted with relief by BlackBerry customers. "It will continue to be business as usual with regard to sales and service of BlackBerry devices," said spokesman Matt Sullivan of Sprint Nextel Corp., one of the service's wireless carriers. . . .

RIM fought NTP for years with every legal tactic at its disposal. In particular, it succeeded in getting the U.S. Patent and Trademark Office to reexamine NTP's patents and take steps to overturn them. But NTP countered each of RIM's moves, promising to tie up the patent-office proceedings for years with appeals.

—Mark Heinzel and Amol Sharma

Source: *Wall Street Journal,* March 4, 2006, p. 1.

Analysis: Patents prevent potential competitors from entering a specific market—unless they are willing to pay for patent rights.

Barriers to Entry

If oligopolies succeed in establishing monopoly prices and profits, they'll attract the envy of would-be entrants. To keep potential competitors out of their industry, oligopolists must maintain **barriers to entry.** ***Above-normal profits can't be maintained over the long run unless barriers to entry exist.*** The entry barriers erected include those monopolists use (Chapter 24).

Patents

Patents are a very effective barrier to entry. Potential competitors can't set up shop until they either develop an alternative method for producing a product or receive permission from the patent holder to use the patented process. Such permission, when given, costs something, of course. In 2006, Research in Motion paid an extraordinary $612.5 million for the patent rights to produce Blackberries (see News).

Distribution Control

barriers to entry: Obstacles, such as patents, that make it difficult or impossible for would-be producers to enter a particular market.

Another way of controlling the supply of a product is to take control of distribution outlets. If a firm can persuade retail outlets not to peddle anyone else's competitive wares, it will increase its market power. This control of distribution outlets can be accomplished through selective discounts, long-term supply contracts, or expensive gifts at Christmas. Recall from Chapter 24 (see News, page 497) how Clear Channel and Ticketmaster locked up concert arenas. According to the U.S. Justice Department, Visa and MasterCard prevent banks that issue their credit cards from offering rival cards. Frito-Lay elbows out competing snack companies by paying high fees to "rent" shelf space in grocery stores (see the News). Such up-front costs create an entry barrier for potential rivals. Even if a potential rival can come up with the up-front money, the owner of an arena or grocery store chain may not wish to anger the firm that dominates the market.

New car warranties also serve as an entry barrier. The warranties typically require regular maintenance at authorized dealerships and the exclusive use of authorized parts. These provisions limit the ability of would-be competitors to provide cheaper auto parts and service. Frequent-flier programs have similar effects in the airline industry. MP3 players that restrict download options or retransmissions also curtail competition.

IN THE NEWS

Frito-Lay Devours Snack-Food Business

Once again, Frito-Lay is chewing up the competition.

The announcement Wednesday that Anheuser-Busch Cos. is selling off its Eagle Snacks business highlights the danger of trying to compete against Frito-Lay in the salty-snacks game. The company owns half of the $15 billion salty-snacks market.

"Frito's a fortress," says Michael Branca, an analyst at NatWest Securities. "And it continues to expand its realm. I'd tell anyone else trying to get into the business, don't try to expand, don't try to impinge on Frito's territory or you'll get crushed."

In fact, competitors say that it is Frito-Lay's tactics with retailers that make it an invincible foe. Because many retailers are charging more and more for shelf space—$40,000 a foot annually in some instances—many regional companies say Frito-Lay is paying retailers to squeeze out competing brands.

"Frito can afford it," says a regional snack company executive. "But we can't. It's become a real-estate business."

Frito-Lay can also afford to out-promote its competitors. In 1993, the company spent more than $60 million on advertising, while Eagle spent less than $2 million.

—Robert Frank

Snack-Food Giant

Frito-Lay's market share in various snack-food categories.

	Salty Snacks		Potato Chips		Tortilla Chips	
	1990	1995	1990	1995	1990	1995
Market share	43%	52%	45%	52%	63%	72%

Analysis: Barriers to entry such as self-space rental and advertising enable a firm to maintain market dominance. Acquisitions also reduce competition.

Mergers and Acquisition

Large and powerful firms can also limit competition by outright *acquisition.* A *merger* between two firms amounts to the same thing, although mergers often entail the creation of new corporate identities.

Perhaps the single most dramatic case of acquisition for this purpose occurred in the breakfast cereals industry. In 1946, General Foods acquired the cereal manufacturing facilities of Campbell Cereal Company, a substantial competitor. Following this acquisition, General Foods dismantled the production facilities of Campbell Cereal and shipped them off to South Africa!

Although the General Foods acquisition was more dramatic than most, acquisitions have been the most popular route to increased market power. General Motors attained a dominant share of the auto market largely by its success in merging with and acquiring two dozen independent manufacturers. In the cigarette industry, the American Tobacco Company attained monopoly powers by absorbing 250 independent companies. Later antitrust action (1911) split up the resultant tobacco monopoly into an oligopoly consisting of four companies, which continued to dominate the cigarette market until 2004, when R. J. Reynolds bought Brown & Williamson, leaving only three firms to dominate the cigarette industry. Other companies that came to dominate their product markets through mergers and acquisitions include U.S. Steel, U.S. Rubber, General Electric, United Fruit, National Biscuit Company, International Salt, and Ticketmaster. Frito-Lay's 1995 acquisitions of Eagle Snacks (see News) extended its already dominant control of the chip, pretzel, and nuts markets.

Government Regulation

The government often helps companies acquire and maintain control of market supply. Patents are issued by and enforced by the federal government and so represent one form of supply-restricting regulation. Barriers to international trade are another government-imposed barrier to entry. By limiting imports of everything from Chinese mushrooms to Japanese cars (see Chapter 35), the federal government reduces potential competition in U.S. product markets. Government regulation also limits *domestic* competition in many industries. From 1984 to 1990, the Federal Communications Commission (FCC) allowed only one company (GTE Corporation) to provide telephone service on airlines. When the FCC ended the monopoly in 1990, phone charges declined sharply.

New York City also limits competition—in this case, the number of taxicabs on the streets. The maximum number of cabs was set at 11,787 in 1937 and stayed at that ceiling until 1996. The city's Taxi and Limousine Commission raised the ceiling by a scant 400 cabs in 1996. That didn't do much to eliminate New York's perennial taxi shortage, much less reduce fares. As a result, license holders continue to reap monopoly-like profits. A good measure of those profits is the price of the medallions that the city sells as taxi licenses. The market price of a New York City taxi medallion—and thus the price of entry into the industry—was $415,000 in 2007. By contrast, a Washington, D.C., taxi license costs only $35, and fares are about half those in New York.

Nonprice Competition

Producers who control market supply can enhance their power even further by establishing some influence over market demand. The primary mechanism of control is *advertising.* To the extent that a firm can convince you that its product is essential to your well-being and happiness, it has effectively shifted your demand curve. ***Advertising not only strengthens brand loyalty but also makes it expensive for new producers to enter the market.*** A new entrant must buy both production facilities and advertising outlets.

The cigarette industry is a classic case of high concentration and product differentiation. As Table 25.2 shows, the top three cigarette companies produce 89 percent of all domestic output; small, generic firms produce the rest. Together, the three cigarette companies produce well over 100 brands. To solidify brand loyalties, the cigarette industry spent over $10 billion on advertising and promotions in 2006.

The breakfast cereals industry also uses nonprice competition to lock in consumers. Although the Federal Trade Commission has suggested that "a corn flake is a corn flake no matter who makes it," the four firms (Kellogg, General Mills, Philip Morris, and Quaker Oats) that supply more than 90 percent of all ready-to-eat breakfast cereals spend over $400 million a year—about $1 per box!—to convince consumers otherwise. During the last 20 years, more than 200 brands of cereal have been marketed by these companies. As the FTC has documented, the four companies "produce basically similar RTE [ready-to-eat] cereals, and then emphasize and exaggerate trivial variations such as color and shape . . . to differentiate cereal brands."[3]

Training In today's technology-driven markets, early market entry can create an important barrier to later competition. Customers of computer hardware and software, for example, often become familiar with a particular system or computer package. To switch to a new product may entail significant cost, including the retraining of user staff. As a consequence, would-be competitors will find it difficult to sell their products even if they offer better quality and lower prices.

Network Economies The widespread use of a particular product may also heighten its value to consumers, thereby making potential substitutes less viable. The utility of instant messaging—or even a telephone—depends on how many of your friends have computers or telephones. If no one else had a phone or computer, there'd be no reason to own one. In other words, the larger the network of users, the greater the value of the product. Such network economies help explain why software developers prefer to write Windows-based programs than programs for rival operating systems. Network economics also explains why Microsoft doesn't want computer manufacturers to display icons for rival instant-messaging services on the Windows XP desktop. Whichever instant-messaging service expands the quickest may achieve a network entry barrier.

THE ECONOMY TOMORROW

ANTITRUST ENFORCEMENT

Examples of market power at work in product markets could be extended to the closing pages of this book. The few cases cited here, however, are testimony enough to the fact that market power has some influence on our lives. Market power *does* exist; market power *is* used. Although market power may result in economies of scale, the potential for abuse is evident. Market power contributes to **market failure** when it leads to resource misallocation (restricted output) or greater inequity (monopoly profits; higher prices).

market failure: An imperfection in the market mechanism that prevents optimal outcomes.

What should we do about these abuses? Should we leave it to market forces to find ways of changing industry structure and behavior? Or should the government step in to curb noncompetitive practices?

Industry Behavior. Our primary concern is the *behavior* of market participants. What ultimately counts is the quantity of goods supplied to the market, their quality, and their price. Few consumers care about the underlying *structure* of markets; what we seek are good market *outcomes.*

In principle, the government could change industry behavior without changing industry structure. We could, for example, explicitly outlaw collusive agreements and cast a wary eye on industries that regularly exhibit price leadership. We could also dismantle barriers to entry and thereby promote contestable markets. We might also prohibit oligopolists from extending their market power via such mechanisms as acquisitions, excessive or deceptive advertising, and, alas, the financing of political campaigns. In fact, the existing **antitrust** laws—the Sherman Act, the Clayton Act, and the Federal Trade Commission Act (see Table 24.1)—explicitly forbid most of these practices.

antitrust: Government intervention to alter market structure or prevent abuse of market power.

There are several problems with this behavioral approach. The first limitation is scarce resources. Policing markets and penalizing noncompetitive conduct require more resources

[3]Complaint, *Kellogg Company et al.,* FTC Dkt. 8883 (1972).

than the public sector can muster. Indeed, the firms being investigated often have more resources than the public watchdogs. The advertising expenditures of just one oligopolist, Procter & Gamble, are more than 10 times as large as the *combined* budgets of both the Justice Department's Antitrust Division and the Federal Trade Commission.

The paucity of antitrust resources is partly a reflection of public apathy. Consumers rarely think about the connection between market power and the price of the goods they buy, the wages they receive, or the way they live. As Ralph Nader discovered, "Antitrust violations are part of a phenomenon which, to the public is too complex, too abstract, and supremely dull."[4] As a result, there's little political pressure to regulate market behavior.

The behavioral approach also suffers from the "burden-of-proof" requirement. How often will "trustbusters" catch colluding executives in the act? More often than not, the case for collusion rests on such circumstantial evidence as simultaneous price hikes, identical bids, or other market outcomes. The charge of explicit collusion is hard to prove. Even in the absence of explicit collusion, however, consumers suffer. If an oligopoly price is higher than what a competitive industry would charge, consumers get stuck with the bill whether or not the price was "rigged" by explicit collusions. The U.S. Supreme Court recognized that consumers may suffer from *tacit* collusion, even where no *explicit* collusion occurs.

Industry Structure. The concept of tacit collusion directs attention to the *structure* of an industry. It essentially says that oligopolists and monopolists will act in their own best interest. As former Supreme Court Chief Justice Earl Warren observed, "An industry which does not have a competitive structure will not have competitive behavior."[5] To expect an oligopolist to disavow profit opportunities or to ignore its interdependence with fellow oligopolists is naive. It also violates the basic motivations imputed to a market economy. As long as markets are highly concentrated, we must expect to observe oligopolistic behavior.

Judge Learned Hand used these arguments to dismantle the Aluminum Company of America (Alcoa) in 1945. Alcoa wasn't charged with any illegal *behavior.* Nevertheless, the company controlled over 90 percent of the aluminum supplied to the market. This monopoly structure, the Supreme Court concluded, was itself a threat to the public interest.

Corporate breakups are rarely pursued today. In 2001, the Justice Department withdrew a proposal to break up Microsoft into separate systems and applications companies. The prevalent feeling today, even among antitrust practitioners, is that the powerful firms are too big and too entrenched to make deconcentration a viable policy alternative.

Objections to Antitrust. Some people think *less* antitrust enforcement is actually a good thing. The companies challenged by the public "trustbusters" protest that they're being penalized for their success. Alcoa, for example, attained a monopoly by investing heavily in a new product before anyone else recognized its value. Other firms too have captured dominant market shares by being first, best, or most efficient. Having "won" the game fairly, why should they have to give up their prize? They contend that noncompetitive *behavior,* not industry *structure,* should be the only concern of antitrust enforcers.

Essentially the same argument is made for proposed mergers and acquisitions. The firms involved claim that the increased concentration will enhance productive efficiency (e.g., via economies of scale). They also argue that big firms are needed to maintain America's competitive position in international markets (which are themselves often dominated by foreign monopolies and oligopolies). Those same global markets, they contend, ensure that even highly concentrated domestic markets will be contested by international rivals.

Finally, critics of antitrust suggest that market forces themselves will ensure competitive behavior. Foreign firms and domestic entrepreneurs will stalk a monopolist's preserve.

[4]Mark J. Green et al., *The Closed Enterprise System: The Report on Antitrust Enforcement* (New York: Grossman, 1972), p. ix.
[5]Ibid., p. 7.

People will always be looking for ways to enter a profitable market. Monopoly or oligopoly power may slow entry but is unlikely to stop it forever. Eventually, competitive forces will prevail.

Structural Guidelines: The Herfindahl-Hirshman Index. There are no easy answers. In theory, competition is valuable, but some mergers and acquisitions undoubtedly increase efficiency. Moreover, some international markets may require a minimum firm size not consistent with perfect competition. Finally, our regulatory resources are limited; not every acquisition or merger is worthy of public scrutiny.

Where would we draw the line? Can a firm hold a 22 percent market share, but not 30 percent? Are five firms too few, but six firms in an industry enough? Someone has to make those decisions. That is, ***the broad mandates of the antitrust laws must be transformed into specific guidelines for government intervention.***

In 1982, the Antitrust Division of the U.S. Department of Justice adopted specific guidelines for intervention based on industry *structure* alone. They're based on an index that takes into account the market share of *each* firm rather than just the *combined* market share of the top four firms. Specifically, the **Herfindahl-Hirshman Index (HHI)** of market concentration is calculated as

Herfindahl-Hirshman Index (HHI): Measure of industry concentration that accounts for number of firms and size of each.

$$\text{HHI} = \sum_{i=1}^{n} = \begin{pmatrix}\text{share of}\\ \text{firm 1}\end{pmatrix}^2 + \begin{pmatrix}\text{share of}\\ \text{firm 2}\end{pmatrix}^2 + \cdots + \begin{pmatrix}\text{share of}\\ \text{firm } n\end{pmatrix}^2$$

Thus, a three-firm oligopoly like that described in Table 25.3 would have an HHI value of

$$\text{HHI} = (40.0)^2 + (32.5)^2 + (27.5)^2 = 3{,}412.5$$

where the numbers in parentheses indicate the market shares of the three fictional computer companies. The calculation yields an HHI value of 3,412.5.

webnote

For concentration ratios and HHIs in U.S. industries, go to www.census.gov/epdc/www/concentration.html

For policy purposes, the Justice Department decided it would draw the line at 1,800. Any merger that creates an HHI value over 1,800 will be challenged by the Justice Department. If an industry has an HHI value between 1,000 and 1,800, the Justice Department will challenge any merger that *increases* the HHI by 100 points or more. Mergers and acquisitions in industries with an HHI value of less than 1,000 won't be challenged.

The HHI is an arbitrary but workable tool for deciding when the government should intervene to challenge mergers and acquisitions. The Justice Department reviews about 2,500 mergers a year but challenges less than 50.

Contestability. Even when intervention is signaled, however, there are still decisions to make. Should a challenged merger be allowed? The same old questions arise. Will the proposed merger enhance efficiency in domestic and global markets? Or will it tend to constrain competitive forces, keeping consumer prices high?

In 1992, the Justice Department broadened its antitrust focus. Rather than just look at the *existing* market structure, the department decided to examine entry barriers as well. If entry barriers were low enough, even a highly concentrated industry might be compelled to behave more competitively. In other words, *contestability* as well as *structure* now motivates antitrust decisions.

Behavioral Guidelines: Cost Savings. In 1996, the Federal Trade Commission (FTC) moved even further away from strict *structural* (market share) criteria by deciding to take potential cost savings into account. Previously, the FTC and Justice Department had declined to consider greater efficiencies that might result from a merger. The focus was strictly on the structural threat to competition. Since 1996, the focus has shifted from the concept of "unfair competition" to an emphasis on consumer welfare. If companies can show how a merger or acquisition will result in greater efficiency and lower costs, they will get the green light from the trustbusters in the economy tomorrow.

SUMMARY 

- Imperfect competition refers to markets in which individual suppliers (firms) have some independent influence on the price at which their output is sold. Examples of imperfectly competitive market structures are duopoly, oligopoly, and monopolistic competition. LO1
- The extent of market power (control over price) depends on the number of firms in an industry, their size, barriers to entry, and the availability of substitutes. LO1
- The concentration ratio is a measure of market power in a particular product market. It equals the share of total industry output accounted for by the largest firms, usually the top four. LO1
- An oligopoly is a market structure in which a few firms produce all or most of a particular good or service; it's essentially a shared monopoly. LO1
- Because oligopolies involve several firms rather than only one, each firm must consider the effect of its price and output decisions on the behavior of rivals. Such firms are highly interdependent. LO3
- Game theory attempts to identify different strategies a firm might use, taking into account the consequences of rivals' moves and countermoves. LO3
- The kinked demand curve illustrates a pattern of strategic interaction in which rivals match a price cut but not a price hike. Such behavior reinforces the oligopolistic aversion to price competition. LO3
- A basic conflict exists between the desire of each individual oligopolist to expand its market share and the *mutual* interest of all the oligopolists in restricting total output so as to maximize industry profits. This conflict must be resolved in some way, via either collusion or some less explicit form of agreement (such as price leadership). LO3
- Oligopolists may use price-fixing agreements or price leadership to establish the market price. To maintain that price, the oligopolists must also agree on their respective market shares. LO3
- To maintain economic profits, an oligopoly must erect barriers to entry. Patents are one form of barrier. Other barriers include predatory price cutting (price wars), control of distribution outlets, government regulations, advertising (product differentiation), training, and network economies. Outright acquisition and merger may also eliminate competition. LO2
- Market power may cause market failure. The symptoms of that failure include increased prices, reduced output, and a transfer of income from the consuming public to a relatively few powerful corporations and the people who own them. LO2
- Government intervention may focus on either market structure or market behavior. In either case, difficult decisions must be made about when and how to intervene. LO1
- The Herfindahl-Hirshman Index is a measure of industry concentration that takes into account the number of firms and the size of each. It is used as a structural guideline to identify cases worthy of antitrust concern. LO1

Key Terms

market structure
oligopoly
contestable market
concentration ratio
oligopolist
market share
product differentiation
payoff matrix
game theory
price-fixing
price leadership
cartel
predatory pricing
barriers to entry
market failure
antitrust
Herfindahl-Hirshman Index (HHI)

Questions for Discussion

1. How many bookstores are on or near your campus? If there were more bookstores, how would the price of new and used books be affected? LO1
2. What entry barriers exist in (*a*) the fast-food industry, (*b*) cable television, (*c*) the auto industry, (*d*) illegal drug trade, and (*e*) beauty parlors? LO1
3. Why does RC Cola depend on advertising to gain market share? (See News, page 516.) Why not offer cheaper sodas than Coke or Pepsi? LO3
4. Why might OPEC members have a difficult time setting and maintaining a monopoly price? (See World View, page 522.) LO2

5. If an oligopolist knows rivals will match a price cut, would he ever reduce his price? LO3
6. How might the high concentration ratio in the credit card industry (Table 25.2) affect the annual fees and interest charges on credit card services? LO2
7. Identify three products you purchase that aren't listed in Table 25.2. What's the structure of those three markets? LO1
8. What reasons might Northwest Airlines have for *not* matching its rivals' fare increases? (See News, page 519.) LO3
9. The Ivy League schools defended their price-fixing arrangement (see page 523) by arguing that their coordination assured a fair distribution of scholarship aid. Who was hurt or helped by this arrangement? LO2
10. Using the payoff matrix in Table 25.4, decide whether Universal should cut its price. What factors will influence the decision? LO3
11. Dominos and Pizza Hut hold 66 percent of the delivered-pizza market. Should antitrust action be taken? LO1

problems The Student Problem Set at the back of this book contains numerical and graphing problems for this chapter.

web activities to accompany this chapter can be found on the Online Learning Center: **http://www.mhhe.com/economics/schiller11e**

26 Monopolistic Competition

LEARNING OBJECTIVES

After reading this chapter, you should know:

LO1. The unique characteristics of monopolistic competition.

LO2. How monopolistically competitive firms maximize profits.

LO3. Why economic profits tend toward zero in monopolistic competition.

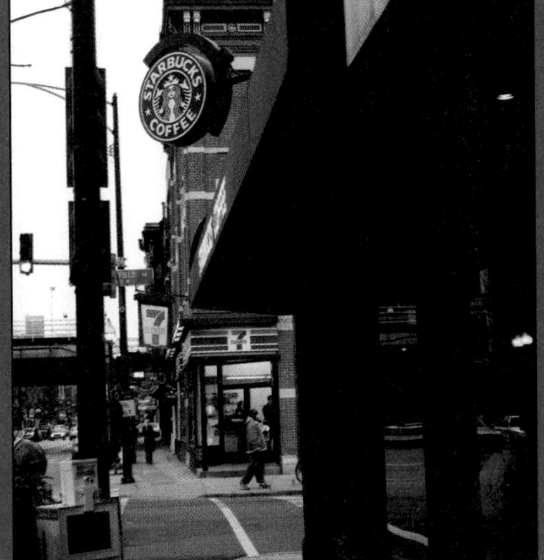

Starbucks is already the biggest coffee bar chain in the country, with roughly 13,000 locations on four continents. And the company is determined to keep growing by setting up coffee bars in airports, department stores, and just about anywhere consumers congregate. Even if Starbucks achieves such meteoric growth, however, it will never have great market power. There are more than 13,000 other coffee bars in the United States, not to mention a million or so other places you can buy a cup of coffee (e.g., Dunkin' Donuts). With so many other close substitutes, the best Starbucks can hope for is a little brand loyalty. If enough consumers think of Starbucks when they get the caffeine urge, Starbucks will at least be able to charge more for coffee than a perfectly competitive firm. It won't enjoy *monopoly* profits, or even share the kind of monopoly profits *oligopolies* sometimes achieve. It may, however, be able to maintain an economic profit for many years.

Starbucks is an example of yet another market structure—*monopolistic competition.* In this chapter we focus on how such firms make price and output decisions and the market outcomes that result. Our objective is to determine

- **The unique features of monopolistic competition.**
- **How market outcomes are affected by this market structure.**
- **The long-run consequences of different market structures.**

In this chapter we'll also see why we can't escape the relentless advertising that bombards us from every angle.

STRUCTURE

As we first noted in Table 25.1, the distinguishing structural characteristic of **monopolistic competition** is that there are *many* firms in an industry. "Many" isn't an exact specification, of course. It's best understood as lying somewhere between the few that characterize oligopoly and the hordes that characterize perfect competition.

Low Concentration

monopolistic competition: A market in which many firms produce similar goods or services but each maintains some independent control of its own price.

concentration ratio: The proportion of total industry output produced by the largest firms (usually the four largest).

A more precise way to distinguish monopolistic competition is to examine **concentration ratios.** Oligopolies have very high four-firm concentration ratios. As we saw in Chapter 25 (Table 25.2), concentration ratios of 70 to 100 percent are common in oligopolies. By contrast, there's much less concentration in monopolistic competition. A few firms may stand above the rest, but the combined market share of the top four firms will typically be in the range of 20 to 40 percent. Hence, ***low concentration ratios are common in monopolistic competition.***

Starbucks has less than 15 percent of the coffee bar business and a mere 7 percent of all coffee sales. The top four coffee bar outlets (Starbucks, Caribou, The Coffee Beanery, and Peet's) have a concentration ratio of only 28 percent (see Table 26.1). Other examples of monopolistic competition include banks, radio stations, health spas, apparel stores, convenience stores, night clubs, bars, and law firms. Notice in Table 26.1 that the personal computer market now has a monopolistically competitive structure as well. Even as large a firm as McDonald's might be regarded as a monopolistic competitor. Although "Mickey D's" has a huge share (40 percent) of the quickie *hamburger* market, its share of the much larger *fast-food* market is significantly smaller. The 13,000+ McDonald's outlets in the United States compete with over 200,000 fast-food outlets. If consumers regard pizzas, Chinese carry-outs, and delis as close substitutes for hamburgers, then the broader fast-food market is the appropriate basis for measuring market power and concentration.

Market Power

Although concentration rates are low in monopolistic competition, the individual firms aren't powerless. There is a *monopoly* aspect to monopolistic competition. Each producer

Product	Largest Firms (market share)	Concentration Ratio (%)
Personal computers	Hewlett-Packard (19%), Dell (15%), Lenova (6.7%), Acer (6.7%)	47%
Auto tires (replacement)	Goodyear (16%), Michelin (8%), Firestone (7.5%), General (5%)	36
Bottled water	PepsiCo (Aquafina 15.8%), Coca-Cola (Dasani 8.7%), Perrier (Poland Spring, 6.4%), Dannon (5.3%)	36
Toys	Hasbro (15%), Mattel (11%), Tyco (5%), Fisher-Price (4%)	35
Coffee bars	Starbucks (15%), Caribou (6%), Peet's (4%), Coffee Beanery (3%)	28
Drugs	Glaxo-Wellcome (5.8%), Hoechst-Marion Merrell Dow (4.4%), Merck (4.4%), American Home Products (3.8%)	18

Source: Industry sources and business publications (2003–2007 data).

TABLE 26.1
Monopolistic Competition

Monopolistically competitive industries are characterized by modest concentration ratios and low entry barriers. Contrast these four-firm concentration ratios with those of oligopoly (see Table 25.2).

IN THE NEWS  

What's Behind Starbucks' Price Hike?

The Coffee Company Will Raise Drink Prices in October, Even As Other Chains Crowd the Market with Similar (and Cheaper) Products

Starbucks has had a strange spate of troubles this summer—from tepid same-store sales, to a bungled foray into movies, to bad PR on some of its promotions. Such stumbles are entirely atypical of America's favorite coffee shop, and Starbucks (*SBUX*) came up with an unconventional response: It raised its drink prices.

Starting on Oct. 3, the prices on lattes, cappuccinos, drip coffee, and other drinks will go up 5 cents at company-operated stores in North America. Starbucks is also jacking up the price of its coffee beans by roughly 50 cents per pound, or an average of 3.9%. . . .

The timing is certainly odd. For a while now, Starbucks has been struggling with labor disputes. Rivals McDonald's, Dunkin' Donuts, and Canadian restaurant chain Tim Horton's are steaming into its turf. . . .

A CONFIDENT COMPANY. If Starbucks were really worried about any of these issues, the last thing its senior execs would consider is a price hike. In fact, Starbucks' dominant market position gives it unique pricing flexibility. Every week, the company succeeds in persuading nearly 40 million people to buy pricey espresso drinks.

"The company is selling a product that has become part of our daily lives, said Kristine Koerber, an analyst at JMP Securities. "Raising prices by a nickel is not going to meet any resistance."

Company officials say the higher prices are intended to offset higher labor and fuel costs. And while the price increases are small, they underscore just how confident Starbucks remains about its growth prospects and its ability to fend off new competitive threats. Koerber and many other analysts seem to support this optimism. "You're not going to raise prices if you have the competitive or macroeconomic environment going against you," she says.

—Stanley Holmes

Analysis: A monopolistically competitive firm has the power to increase price unilaterally. The greater the brand loyalty, the less unit sales will decline in response.

in monopolistic competition is large enough to have some **market power.** If a perfectly competitive firm increases the price of its product, it will lose all its customers. Recall that a perfectly competitive firm confronts a horizontal demand curve for its output. Competition is less intense in monopolistic competition. ***A monopolistically competitive firm confronts a downward-sloping demand curve for its output.*** When Starbucks increases the price of coffee, it loses some customers, but nowhere close to all of them (see News.) Starbucks, like other monopolistically competitive firms, has some control over the price of its output. This is the *monopoly* dimension of monopolistic competition.

market power: The ability to alter the market price of a good or service.

Independent Production Decisions

In an oligopoly, a firm that increased its price would have to worry about how rivals might respond. In monopolistic competition, however, there are many more firms. As a result, ***modest changes in the output or price of any single firm will have no perceptible influence on the sales of any other firm.*** This relative independence results from the fact that the effects of any one firm's behavior will be spread over many other firms (rather than only two or three other firms, as in an oligopoly).

The relative independence of monopolistic competitors means that they don't have to worry about retaliatory responses to every price or output change. As a result, they confront more traditional demand curves, with no kinks. The kink in the oligopolist's curve results from the likelihood that rival oligopolists would match any price reduction (to preserve market shares) but not necessarily any price increase (to increase their shares). In monopolistic competition, the market shares of rival firms aren't perceptibly altered by another firm's price changes.

barriers to entry: Obstacles, such as patents, that make it difficult or impossible for would-be producers to enter a particular market.

Low Entry Barriers

Another characteristic of monopolistic competition is the presence of *low* **barriers to entry**—it's relatively easy to get in and out of the industry. To become a coffee vendor, all you need is boiling water, some fresh beans, and cups. You can save on rent by using a pushcart to dispense the brew. These unusually low entry barriers keep Starbucks and other coffee bars on their toes. Low entry barriers also tend to push economic profits toward zero. This is the *competitive* dimension of monopolistic competition.

BEHAVIOR

Given the unique structural characteristics of monopolistic competition we should anticipate some distinctive behavior.

Product Differentiation

product differentiation: Features that make one product appear different from competing products in the same market.

One of the most notable features of monopolistically competitive behavior is **product differentiation.** A monopolistically competitive firm is distinguished from a purely competitive firm by its downward-sloping demand curve. Individual firms in a perfectly competitive market confront horizontal demand curves because consumers view their respective products as interchangeable (homogeneous). As a result, an attempt by one firm to raise its price will drive its customers to other firms.

Brand Image. In monopolistic competition, each firm has a distinct identity—a *brand image.* Its output is perceived by consumers as being somewhat different from the output of all other firms in the industry. Nowhere is this more evident than in the fast-growing bottled water industry. Pepsi and Coke have become the leaders in the bottled water market as a result of effective marketing (see News below). Although Aquafina (Pepsi) and Dasani (Coke) are just filtered municipal water, clever advertising campaigns have convinced consumers that these branded waters are different—and better—than hundreds of other bottled waters. As a result of such product differentiation, Pepsi and Coke can raise the price of their bottled waters without losing all their customers to rival firms.

Brand Loyalty

At first blush, the demand curve facing a monopolistically competitive firm looks like the demand curve confronting a monopolist. There's a profound difference, however. In a

IN THE NEWS

Water, Water Everywhere; Coke, Pepsi Unleash Flood of Ad Muscle

Water is water, at least until the marketers get hold of it.

Then a humble commodity that literally falls from the sky becomes something else. Something with "personality."

Not long ago, it would have been silly to think about branding water. But the big beverage companies are doing just that, and this summer marks the biggest-ever ad barrage for Dasani, Coke's water brand, and Aquafina, bottled by Pepsi-Cola Co.

Branding is an important issue in a category where sales grew by nearly 26 percent in 2000, to 807 million cases—the highest growth rate in the beverage industry. The challenge is getting attention in a highly fragmented market. There are hundreds of different water brands, and some are so small that they serve just a few towns.

"Consumers are trading up. They're willing to search for a brand," said Kellam Graitcer, Dasani brand manager at Coca-Cola. "We're trying to inject a little bit of personality into the category."

The two companies are likely to spend about $20 million each this year on ads.

—Scott Leith

Source: *Atlanta Journal–Constitution,* July 12, 2001. Copyright 2001 by *The Atlanta Journal–Constitution.* Reprinted with permission. www.accessatlanta.com/ajc

Analysis: By differentiating their products, monopolistic competitors establish brand loyalty. Brand loyalty gives producers greater control over the price of their products.

monopoly, there are no other firms. In monopolistic competition, ***each firm has a monopoly only on its brand image; it still competes with other firms offering close substitutes.*** This implies that the extent of power a monopolistically competitive firm has depends on how successfully it can differentiate its product from that of other firms. The more brand loyalty a firm can establish, the less likely consumers are to switch brands when price is increased. In other words, ***brand loyalty makes the demand curve facing the firm less price-elastic.***

Brand loyalty exists even when products are virtually identical. Gasoline of a given octane rating is a very standardized product. Nevertheless, most consumers regularly buy one particular brand. Because of that brand loyalty, Texaco can raise the price of its gasoline by a penny or two a gallon without losing its customers to competing companies. Brand loyalty is particularly high for cigarettes, toothpaste, and even laxatives. Consumers of those products say they'd stick with their accustomed brand even if the price of a competing brand was cut by 50 percent. In other words, ***brand loyalty implies low cross-price elasticity of demand.*** Brand loyalty is less strong (and cross-price elasticity higher) for paper towels and virtually nonexistent for tomatoes.

In the computer industry, product differentiation has been used to establish brand loyalty. Although virtually all computers use identical microprocessor "brains" and operating platforms, the particular mix of functions performed on any computer can be varied, as can its appearance (packaging). Effective advertising can convince consumers that one computer is "smarter," more efficient, or more versatile than another. Also, a single firm may differentiate itself by providing faster or more courteous customer service. If successful in any of these efforts, ***each monopolistically competitive firm will establish some consumer loyalty.*** With such loyalty a firm can alter its own price somewhat, without fear of great changes in unit sales (quantity demanded). In other words, the demand curve facing each firm will slope downward, as in Figure 26.1*a*.

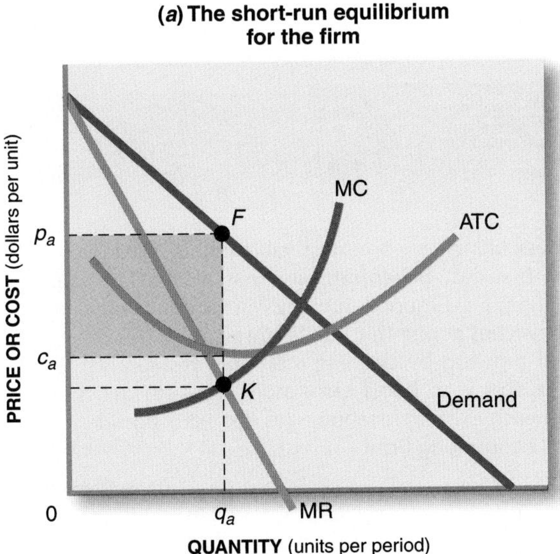

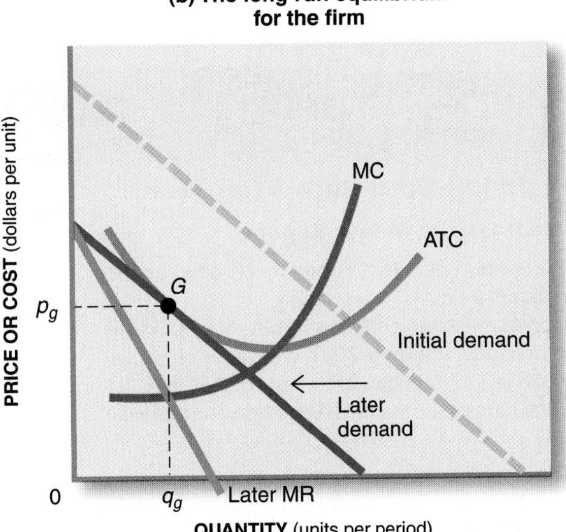

FIGURE 26.1
Equilibrium in Monopolistic Competition

(*a*) Short run In the short run, a monopolistically competitive firm equates marginal revenue and marginal cost (point *K*). In this case, the firm sells the resulting output at a price (point *F*) above marginal cost. Total profits are represented by the shaded rectangle.

(*b*) Long run In the long run, more firms enter the industry. As they do so, the demand curve facing each firm *shifts* to the left, as all market shares decline. Firms still equate MR and MC. Ultimately, however, the demand curve will be tangent to the ATC curve (point *G*), at which point price equals average total cost and no economic profits exist.

Repurchase Rates. One symptom of brand loyalty is consumers' tendency to repurchase the same brand. Nearly 9 out of 10 Apple Macintosh users stick with Apple products when they upgrade or replace computer components. Repurchase rates are 74 percent for Dell, 72 percent for Hewlett-Packard, and 66 percent for Gateway. Starbucks also counts on return customers.

To maintain such brand loyalty, monopolistically competitive firms must often expand services or product offerings. Remember that entry barriers are low. In the coffee business, it was relatively easy for fast-food companies like McDonald's and Dunkin' Donuts to enter once they saw how profitable Starbucks was. When they did, Starbucks had to expand its menu to maintain its market dominance. As the accompanying News relates, a "breakfast war" ensued as firms sought greater product differentiation. Although menu expansion is costly, firms often decide that increased service is more cost-effective than price competition, given the low cross-price elasticity of demand in monopolistically-competitive markets.

Price Premiums. Another symptom of brand loyalty is the price differences between computer brands. Consumers are willing to pay more for an HP- or Dell-branded computer than a no-name computer with identical features. For the same reason, consumers are willing to pay more for Starbucks coffee or Ben and Jerry's ice cream, even when virtually identical products are available at lower prices.

Short-Run Price and Output

production decision: The selection of the short-run rate of output (with existing plant and equipment).

The monopolistically competitive firm's **production decision** is similar to that of a monopolist. Both types of firms confront downward-sloping demand and marginal revenue curves. To maximize profits, both seek the rate of output at which marginal revenue equals marginal cost. This short-run profit-maximizing outcome is illustrated by point K in Figure 26.1a. That MC = MR intersection establishes q_a as the profit-maximizing rate of output. The demand curve indicates (point F) that q_a of output can be sold at the price of p_a. Hence q_a, p_a illustrates the short-run equilibrium of the monopolistically competitive firm.

IN THE NEWS

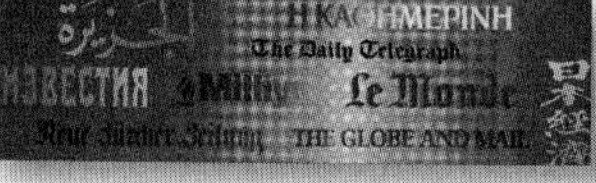

Fast-Food Rivals Suit Up for Breakfast War

Competition Heats Up as Menus Expand

Hamburgers, schmamburgers. Fast food's fiery new battleground is the breakfast table.

Just about everyone—even coffee kingpin Starbucks—is entering the hot-breakfast arena in 2007 with new offerings. At stake: a piece of the $77.6 billion breakfast market that, for the fast-food giants, can mean the difference between growth and stagnation.

Marketing

Starbucks, for the first time, is rolling out five hot breakfast sandwiches. Wendy's is expanding its breakfast rollout. Burger King this week launches a breakfast value menu. McDonald's, the current breakfast behemoth, also has a breakfast value menu in testing. Next month, Subway will introduce breakfast omelet sandwiches at one-third of its stores.

Instead of growing by building still more restaurants, the new growth goal is to boost same-store sales—to get more dollars from each existing location, says Ron Paul, president of Technomic, a consulting firm.

—Bruce Horovitz

Source: *USA Today*, February 20, 2007 p. 38. Reprinted with permission.

Analysis: Monopolistically competitive firms must differentiate their products to establish and maintain brand loyalty. Variations in products and services help create unique brand profiles.

Entry and Exit

Figure 26.1*a* indicates that this monopolistically competitive firm is earning an **economic profit:** Price (p_a) exceeds average total cost (c_a) at the short-run rate of output. These profits are of course a welcome discovery for the firm. They also portend increased competition, however.

economic profit: The difference between total revenues and total economic costs.

Entry Effects. If firms in monopolistic competition are earning an economic profit, other firms will flock to the industry. Remember that ***entry barriers are low in monopolistic competition so new entrants can't be kept out of the market.*** If they get wind of the short-run profits depicted in Figure 26.1*a*, they'll come running.

As new firms enter the industry, supply increases and prices will be pushed down the market demand curve, just as in competitive markets. Figure 26.2*a* illustrates these market changes. The initial price p_1 is set by the intersection of *industry* MC and MR. Because that price generates a profit, more firms enter. This entry shifts the *industry* cost structure to the right, creating a new equilibrium price, p_2.

The impact of this entry on the firms already in the market will be different from that in competitive markets, however. As new firms enter a monopolistically competitive industry, existing firms will lose customers. This is illustrated by the leftward shift of the demand curve facing each firm, as in Figure 26.2*b*. Accordingly, we conclude that ***when firms enter a monopolistically competitive industry,***

- ***The industry cost curves shift to the right, pushing down price*** (Figure 26.2*a*).
- ***The demand curves facing individual firms shift to the left*** (Figure 26.2*b*).

As the demand curve it faces shifts leftward, the monopolistically competitive firm will have to make a new production decision. It need not charge the same price as its rivals, however, or coordinate its output with theirs. Each monopolistically competitive firm has some independent power over its (shrinking numbers of) captive customers.

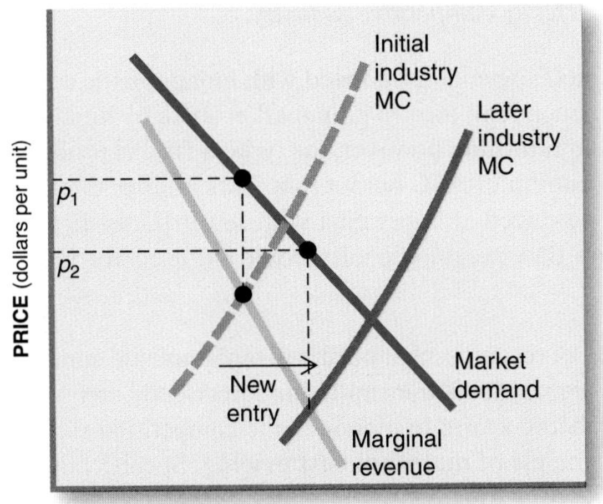

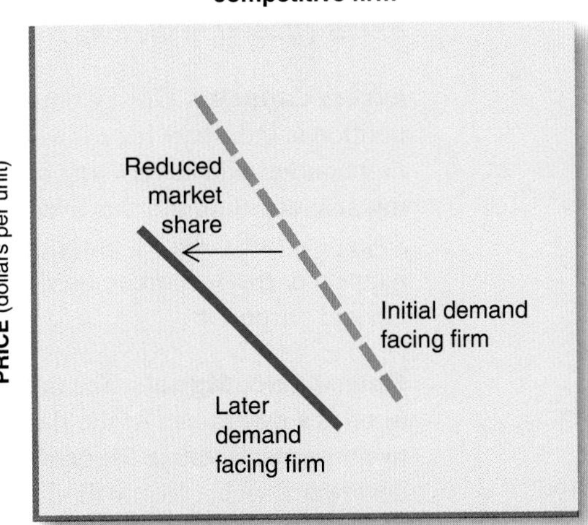

FIGURE 26.2
Market vs. Firm Effects of Entry

Barriers to entry are low in monopolistic competition. Hence, new firms will enter if economic profits are available.

(*a*) The Market The entry of new firms will shift the *market* cost curves to the right, as in part *a*. This pushes the average price down the *market* demand curve.

(*b*) The Firm The entry of new firms also affects the demand curve facing the typical firm. The *firm's* demand curve shifts to the left and becomes more elastic because more close substitutes (other firms) are available.

No Long-Run Profits

Although each firm has some control over its own pricing decisions, continued leftward shifts of its demand curve will ultimately eliminate economic profits.

Long-Run Equilibrium. Notice in Figure 26.1*b* where the firm eventually ends up. In long-run equilibrium (point *G*), marginal cost is again equal to marginal revenue (at the MR = MC intersection directly below *G*). At that rate of output (q_g), however, there are no economic profits. At that output, price (p_g) is exactly equal to average total cost. The profit-maximizing equilibrium (point *G*) occurs where the demand curve is tangent to the ATC curve. If the demand curve shifted any farther left, price would always be less than ATC and the firm would incur losses. If the demand curve were positioned farther to the right, price would exceed ATC at some rates of output. When the demand curve is *tangent* to the ATC curve, the firm's best possible outcome is to break even. At point *G* in Figure 26.1*b*, price equals ATC and economic profit is zero.

Will a monopolistically competitive firm end up at point *G*? As long as other firms can enter the industry, the disappearance of economic profits is inevitable. Firms will enter as long as the demand (price) line lies above ATC at some point. Firms will exit when the demand facing the firm lies to the left and below the ATC curve. Entry and exit cease when the firm's demand curve is *tangent* to the ATC curve. Once entry and exit cease, the long-run equilibrium has been established. ***In the long run, there are no economic profits in monopolistic competition.***

Inefficiency

The zero-profit equilibrium of firms in monopolistic competition, as illustrated in Figure 26.1*b*, differs from the perfectly competitive equilibrium. In perfect competition, long-run profits are also zero. But at that point, a competitive industry produces at the *lowest* point on the ATC curve and thus maximizes efficiency. In monopolistic competition, however, the demand curve facing each firm slopes downward. Hence, it can't be tangent to the ATC curve at its lowest point (the bottom of the U), as in perfect competition. Instead, the demand curve of a monopolistically competitive firm must touch the ATC curve on the *left* side of the U. Note in Figure 26.1*b* how point *G* lies above and to the left of the bottom of the ATC curve. This long-run equilibrium occurs at an output rate that is less than the minimum-cost rate of production. In long-run equilibrium, the monopolistically competitive industry isn't producing at minimum average cost. As a consequence, ***monopolistic competition tends to be less efficient in the long run than a perfectly competitive industry.***

Excess Capacity. One symptom of the inefficiencies associated with monopolistic competition is industrywide excess capacity. Each firm tries to gain market share by building more outlets and advertising heavily. In equilibrium, however, the typical firm is producing at a rate of output that's less than its minimum-ATC output rate. This implies that the *same* level of *industry* output could be produced at lower cost with fewer firms. If that happened, the resources used to develop that excess capacity could be used for more desired purposes.

Flawed Price Signals. The misallocation of resources that occurs in monopolistic competition is a by-product of the flawed price signal that is transmitted in imperfectly competitive markets. Because the demand curve facing a firm in monopolistic competition slopes downward, such a firm will violate the principle of **marginal cost pricing.** Specifically, it will always price its output above the level of marginal costs, just like firms in an oligopoly or monopoly. Notice in Figure 26.1 that price lies above marginal cost in both the short- and long-run equilibrium. As a consequence, price always exceeds the opportunity cost. Consumers respond to these flawed signals by demanding fewer goods from monopolistically competitive industries than they would otherwise. We end up with the wrong (suboptimal) mix of output and misallocated resources.

marginal cost pricing: The offer (supply) of goods at prices equal to their marginal cost.

Thus, ***monopolistic competition results in both production inefficiency (above-minimum average cost) and allocative inefficiency (wrong mix of output).*** This contrasts with the model of perfect competition, which delivers both minimum average total cost and efficient (MC-based) price signals.

THE ECONOMY TOMORROW

NO CEASE-FIRE IN ADVERTISING WARS

Models of oligopoly and monopolistic competition show how industry structure affects market behavior. Of particular interest is the way different kinds of firms "compete" for sales and profits. ***In truly (perfectly) competitive industries, firms compete on the basis of price.*** Competitive firms win by achieving greater efficiency and offering their products at the lowest possible price.

Firms in imperfectly competitive markets don't "compete" in the same way. In oligopolies, the kink commonly found in the demand curve facing each firm inhibits price reductions. In monopolistic competition, there's also a reluctance to engage in price competition. Because each firm has its own captive market—consumers who prefer its particular brand over competing brands—price reductions by one firm won't induce many consumers to switch brands. Thus, price reductions aren't a very effective way to increase sales or market share in monopolistic competition.

If imperfectly competitive firms don't compete on the basis of price, do they really compete at all? The answer is evident to anyone who listens to the radio, watches television, reads magazines or newspapers, or drives on the highway: ***Imperfectly competitive firms engage in nonprice competition.***

The most prominent form of *nonprice competition* is advertising. An imperfectly competitive firm typically uses advertising to enhance its own product's image, thereby increasing the size of its captive market (consumers who identify with a particular brand). The Coca-Cola Company hires rock stars to create the image that Coke is superior to other soft drinks (see News), thereby creating brand loyalty. In 2005, oligopolies and monopolistic competitive firms spent nearly $400 *billion* on advertising for such purposes. Procter & Gamble alone spent $8.2 billion (see Table 26.2). P&G hopes that these expenditures shift the demand for its products (e.g., Ivory Soap, Pampers, Jif peanut butter, Crest, Tide) to the right, while perhaps making it less price-elastic as well. America Online, Yahoo!, and Amazon.com spent hundreds of millions of dollars in the 1990s to establish brand loyalty in crowded dot.com markets. By contrast, perfectly competitive firms have no incentive to advertise because they can individually sell their entire output at the current market price.

IN THE NEWS

The Cola Wars: It's Not All Taste

American consumers gulp nearly 40 million soft drinks per day. The Coca-Cola Company produces about 40 percent of those soft drinks, while Pepsi-Cola produces about 30 percent of the market supply. With nearly 70 percent of the market between them, Pepsi and Coke wage fierce battles for market share.

The major weapon in these "cola wars" is advertising. Coke spends $2 billion a year to convince consumers that its products are superior. Pepsi spends almost as much to win the hearts and taste buds of American consumers. The advertisements not only tout the superior taste of their respective products but also try to create a particular image for each cola.

The advertising apparently works. Half of all soft drink consumers profess loyalty to either Coke or Pepsi. In their view, there's only one "real" cola, and that's the one they'll buy every time. Few of these loyalists can be persuaded to switch cola brands, even when offered lower prices for the "other" cola.

Ironically, few people can identify their favorite cola in blind taste tests. Seventy percent of the people who swore loyalty to either Coke or Pepsi picked the wrong cola in a taste test.

The moral of the story? That in imperfectly competitive markets, product *image* and *perceptions* may be as important as product quality and price in winning market shares.

Analysis: Advertising is intended to create brand loyalty. Loyal consumers are likely to buy the same brand all the time, even if competitors offer nearly identical products.

TABLE 26.2
Top 10 Advertisers

Firms with market power attempt to preserve and extend that power through advertising. A successful advertising campaign alters the demand curve facing the firm, thus increasing potential profits. Shown here are the advertising outlays of the biggest advertisers in 2005.

Company	Ad Spending in 2005 ($billion)
Procter & Gamble	$8.2 billion
Unilever	4.3
General Motors	4.2
Toyota	2.8
L'Oreal	2.8
Ford Motor	2.6
TimeWarner	2.5
DaimlerChrysler	2.1
Nestlé	2.0
Johnson & Johnson	2.0

Source: *Advertising Age,* November 20, 2006. Reprinted by permission. www.adage.com

A company that runs a successful advertising campaign can create enormous *goodwill* value. That value is reflected in stronger brand loyalty—as expressed in greater demand and smaller price elasticity. Often a successful brand image can be used to sell related products as well. According to the World View, the most valuable brand name in the world is Coca-Cola, whose worldwide name recognition is worth nearly $70 *billion.*

Advertising isn't the only form of nonprice competition. Before the airline industry was deregulated (1978), individual airlines were compelled to charge the same price for any

WORLD VIEW 

The Best Global Brands

A belief in the power of brands and brand management has spread far beyond the traditional consumer-goods marketers who invented the discipline. For companies in almost every industry, brands are important in a way they never were before. Why? For one thing, customers for everything from soda pop to software now have a staggering number of choices. And the Net can bring the full array to any computer screen with a click of the mouse. Without trusted brand names as touchstones, shopping for almost anything would be overwhelming. Meanwhile, in a global economy, corporations must reach customers in markets far from their home base. A strong brand acts as an ambassador when companies enter new markets or offer new products.

That's why companies that once measured their worth strictly in terms of tangibles such as factories, inventory, and cash have realized that a vibrant brand, with its implicit promise of quality, is an equally important asset. A brand has the power to command a premium price among customers and a premium stock price among investors. It can boost earnings and cushion cyclical downturns—and now, a brand's value can be measured.

The World's 10 Most Valuable Brands

Rank	Brand	2006 Brand Value ($billions)
1	Coca-Cola	67.5
2	Microsoft	56.9
3	IBM	56.2
4	GE	48.9
5	Intel	32.3
6	Nokia	30.1
7	Toyota	27.9
8	Disney	27.8
9	McDonald's	27.5
10	Mercedes-Benz	21.8

Data: Interbrand, Citigroup.

Source: *BusinessWeek,* August 7, 2006. © 2006 The McGraw-Hill Companies, Inc. Reprinted with permission. www.businessweek.com

Analysis: Brand names are valuable economic assets and assist a firm in maintaining a base of loyal customers. These brands have worldwide recognition as a result of heavy advertising.

given trip; hence, price competition was prohibited. But airlines did compete—not only by advertising, but also by offering "special" meals, movies, more frequent or convenient departures, and faster ticketing and baggage services.

Is there anything wrong with nonprice competition? Surely airline passengers enjoyed their "special" meals, "extra" services, and "more convenient" departure times. But these services weren't free. As always, there were opportunity costs. From an air traveler's perspective, the "special" services stimulated by nonprice competition substituted for cheaper fares. With more price competition, customers could have chosen travel more cheaply *or* in greater comfort.

From society's perspective, the resources used in advertising and other forms of nonprice competition could be used instead to produce larger quantities of desired goods and services (including airplane trips). Unless consumers are given the chance to *choose* between "more" service and lower prices, there's a presumption that nonprice competition leads to an undesirable use of our scarce resources. For example, marketing costs absorb over a third of the price of breakfast cereal. As a result of such behavior, consumers end up with more advertising but less cereal than they would otherwise. They could, of course, save money by buying store brand or generic cereals. But they've never seen athletes or cartoon characters endorse such products. So consumers pay the higher price for branded cereals.

Models of imperfect competition imply that advertising wars between powerful corporations won't end anytime soon. As long as markets have the *structure* of oligopoly or monopolistic competition, we expect the *behavior* of nonprice competition. Advertising jingles will be as pervasive in the economy tomorrow as they are today.

SUMMARY

- There are many (rather than few) firms in monopolistic competition. The concentration ratio in such industries tends to be low (20–40 percent). LO1
- Each monopolistically competitive firm enjoys some brand loyalty. This brand loyalty, together with its relatively small market share, gives each firm a high degree of independence in price and output decisions. LO1
- The amount of market share and power a monopolistically competitive firm possesses depends on how successfully it differentiates its product from similar products. Accordingly, monopolistically competitive firms tend to devote more resources to advertising. LO2
- Low entry barriers permit new firms to enter a monopolistically competitive industry whenever economic profits exist. Such entry eliminates long-run economic profit and reduces (shifts leftward) the demand for the output of existing firms. LO3
- Monopolistic competition results in resource misallocations (due to flawed price signals) and inefficiency (above-minimum average cost). LO2
- Monopolistic competition encourages nonprice competition instead of price competition. Because the resources used in nonprice competition (advertising, packaging, service, etc.) may have more desirable uses, these industry structures lead to resource misallocation. LO2

Key Terms

monopolistic competition
concentration ratio
market power
barriers to entry
product differentiation
production decision
economic profit
marginal cost pricing

Questions for Discussion

1. What is the source of Starbucks' "confidence" in the News on page 535? LO1
2. What are the entry barriers to the pizza business? Are they relatively high or low? LO3
3. If auto firms eliminated their advertising, could they reduce car prices? What would happen to unit sales? LO1
4. If one gas station reduces its prices, must other gas stations match the price reduction? Why or why not? LO2
5. The News article on page 541 suggests that most consumers can't identify their favorite cola in blind taste tests. Why then do people stick with one brand? What accounts for brand loyalty in bottled water (News, page 536)? LO1
6. How do new product offerings like breakfast sandwiches (News, page 538) affect Starbucks sales and profits? LO1
7. Why is the mix of output produced in competitive markets more desirable than that in monopolistically competitive markets? LO2
8. How would our consumption of cereal change if cereal manufacturers stopped advertising? Would we be better or worse off? LO2
9. Why are people willing to pay more for Dreyer's ice cream when it has a Starbucks brand on it? LO1
10. According to the World View on page 542, what gives brand names their value? LO1

problems The Student Problem Set at the back of this book contains numerical and graphing problems for this chapter.

! **web activities** to accompany this chapter can be found on the Online Learning Center: **http://www.mhhe.com/economics/schiller11e**

Regulatory Issues

Microeconomic theory provides insights into how prices and product flows are determined in unregulated markets. Sometimes those market outcomes are not optimal and the government intervenes to improve them. In this section we examine government regulation of natural monopolies (Chapter 27), environmental protection (Chapter 28), and farm output and prices (Chapter 29). The goal is to determine whether and how government regulation might improve market outcomes—or possibly worsen them.

(De)Regulation of Business

LEARNING OBJECTIVES

After reading this chapter, you should know:

LO1. The characteristics of natural monopoly.

LO2. The regulatory dilemmas posed by natural monopoly.

LO3. The costs associated with regulation.

The lights went out in California in 2001—not just once but repeatedly. Offices went dark, air conditioners shut down, assembly lines stopped, and TV screens went blank. The state governor blamed power-company "profiteers" for the rolling blackouts. He charged the companies with curtailing power supplies and hiking prices. He wanted *more* regulation of the power industry. Industry representatives responded that government regulation was itself responsible for throwing California into a new Dark Age. *Less* regulation, not more, would keep the lights on, they claimed.

The battle over government regulation of the power industry quickly spread to other states. Some states that were deregulating power companies suspended the process. Other states also put (de)regulation plans on hold until they could better assess what went wrong in California.

Everyone agrees that markets sometimes fail—that unregulated markets may produce the wrong mix of output, undesirable methods of production, or an unfair distribution of income. But government intervention can fail as well. Hence, we need to ask,

- **When is government regulation necessary?**
- **What form should that regulation take?**
- **When is it appropriate to deregulate an industry?**

In answering these questions we draw on economic principles as well as recent experience. This will permit us to contrast the theory of (de)regulation with reality.

ANTITRUST VS. REGULATION

A perfectly competitive market provides a model for economic efficiency. As we first observed in Chapter 3, the market mechanism can answer the basic economic questions of WHAT to produce, HOW to produce it, and FOR WHOM. Under ideal conditions, the market's answers may also be optimal—that is, they may represent the best possible mix of output. To achieve this **laissez-faire** ideal, all producers must be perfect competitors; people must have full information about tastes, costs, and prices; all costs and benefits must be reflected in market prices; and pervasive economies of scale must be absent.

laissez faire: The doctrine of "leave it alone," or nonintervention by government in the market mechanism.

In reality, these conditions are rarely, if ever, fully attained. Markets may be dominated by large and powerful producers. In wielding their power, these producers may restrict output, raise prices, stifle competition, and inhibit innovation. In other words, market power may cause **market failure,** leaving us with suboptimal market outcomes.

market failure: An imperfection in the market mechanism that prevents optimal outcomes.

Behavioral Focus

As we observed in Chapter 25, the government has two options for intervention where market power prevails. It may focus on the *structure* of an industry or on its *behavior.* **Antitrust** laws cover both options: They prohibit mergers and acquisitions that reduce potential competition (structures) and forbid market practices (behavior) that are anticompetitive.

antitrust: Government intervention to alter market structure or prevent abuse of market power.

Government **regulation** has a different focus. Instead of worrying about industry structure, regulation focuses almost exclusively on *behavior.* In general, regulation seeks to change market outcomes directly, by imposing specific limitations on price, output, or investment decisions.

regulation: Government intervention to alter the behavior of firms, for example, in pricing, output, or advertising.

NATURAL MONOPOLY

When a natural monopoly exists, the choice between structural remedies and behavioral remedies is simplified. A **natural monopoly** is a *desirable* market structure, because it generates pervasive economies of scale. Because of these scale economies, a natural monopoly can produce the products consumers want at the lowest possible price. A single cable company is more efficient than a horde of cable firms developing a maze of cable networks. The same is true of local telephone service and many utilities. In all of these cases, a single company can deliver products at lower cost than a bunch of smaller firms. Dismantling such a natural monopoly would destroy that cost advantage. Hence, *regulation,* not antitrust, is the more sensible intervention.

natural monopoly: An industry in which one firm can achieve economies of scale over the entire range of market supply.

Do we need to regulate natural monopolies? Even though a natural monopoly might enjoy economies of scale, it might not pass those savings along to consumers. In that case, the economies of scale don't do consumers any good, and the government might have to regulate the firm's behavior.

To determine whether regulation is desirable, we first have to determine how an *unregulated* natural monopoly will behave.

Declining ATC Curve

Figure 27.1 on the next page illustrates the unique characteristics of a natural monopoly. ***The distinctive characteristic of a natural monopoly is its downward-sloping average total cost (ATC) curve.*** Because unit costs keep falling as the rate of production increases, a single large firm can underprice any smaller firm. Ultimately, it can produce all the market supply at the lowest attainable cost. In an unregulated market, such a firm will "naturally" come to dominate the industry.

High Fixed Costs. Natural monopolies typically emerge in situations where the fixed costs of production are extremely large. To supply electricity, for example, you first need to build a power source (e.g., a coal-fired plant, hydroelectric dam, or nuclear generator), then a distribution network. It's the same thing with subways and railroads: A lot of infrastructure must be constructed before anyone gets a ride. As a consequence of these high fixed costs, the *average* total cost curve starts out very high (recall that ATC = AFC + AVC).

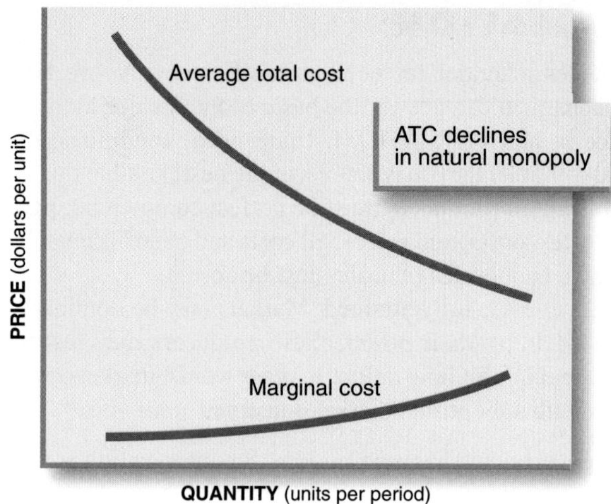

FIGURE 27.1
Declining ATC

A combination of high fixed costs and very low marginal costs generates a unique, downward-sloping ATC curve in natural monopoly. MC lies below ATC at all output levels.

Low Marginal Costs. Once productive capacity is built, the focus turns to *marginal costs.* In natural monopolies, marginal costs are typically low—*very low.* Supplying another kilowatt of electricity entails negligible marginal cost. Carrying one more passenger on a railroad or subway entails similarly negligible costs.

Even if marginal costs rise as production increases (the law of diminishing returns), marginal cost remains less than average total cost over the entire range of output. Notice in Figure 27.1 that ***the marginal cost (MC) curve lies below the ATC curve at all rates of output for a natural monopoly.*** The ATC curve never rises into its conventional U shape because marginal costs never exceed average costs. Hence, there is no force to pull average total costs up, as in conventional cost structures. The combination of high fixed costs and low (negligible) marginal costs gives the ATC curve a unique shape. The ATC curve starts out high (due to high AFC) and keeps declining as output increases (because MC < ATC at all times). ***The downward-sloping ATC curve is the hallmark of a natural monopoly.***

economies of scale: Reductions in minimum average costs that come about through increases in the size (scale) of plant and equipment.

The declining costs of a natural monopoly are of potential benefit to society. The **economies of scale** offered by a natural monopoly imply that no other market structure can supply the good as cheaply. Hence, ***natural monopoly is a desirable market structure.*** A competitive market structure—with many smaller firms—would have higher average cost.

Unregulated Behavior

Although the* structure *of a natural monopoly may be beneficial, its* behavior *may leave something to be desired. Natural monopolists have the same profit-maximizing motivations as other producers. Moreover, they have the monopoly power to achieve and maintain economic profits. Hence, there's no guarantee that consumers will reap the benefits of a natural monopoly. Critics charge that the monopolist tends to keep most of the benefits. This has been a recurrent criticism of cable TV operators: Consumers have complained about high prices, poor service, and a lack of programming choices from local cable monopolies.

Figure 27.2 illustrates the unregulated behavior of a natural monopolist. Like all other producers, the natural monopolist will maximize profits by producing at that rate of output where marginal revenue equals marginal cost. Point *A* in Figure 27.2 indicates that an unregulated monopoly will end up producing the quantity q_A and charging the price p_A.

marginal cost pricing: The offer (supply) of goods at prices equal to their marginal cost.

The natural monopolist's preferred outcome isn't the most desirable one for society. This price-output combination violates the competitive principle of **marginal cost pricing.** The monopoly price p_A greatly exceeds the marginal cost of producing q_A of output, as represented by MC_A in Figure 27.2. As a result of this gap, consumers aren't getting accurate

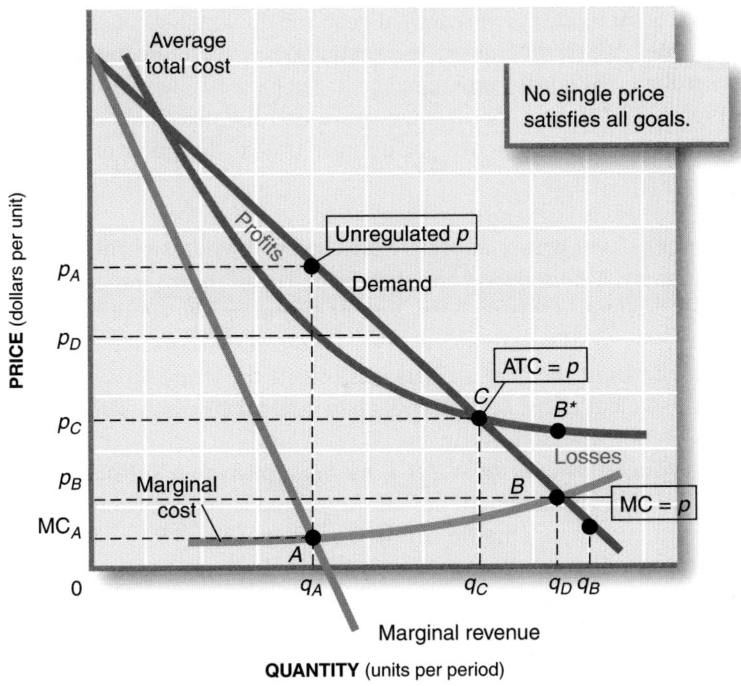

FIGURE 27.2
Natural Monopoly: Price Regulation

If unregulated, a natural monopoly will produce q_A and charge p_A, as determined by the intersection of the marginal cost and marginal revenue curves (point *A*).

Regulation designed to achieve efficient prices will seek point *B*, where p = MC. Still lower average costs (production efficiency) are attainable at higher rates of output, however. On the other hand, a zero-profit, zero-subsidy outcome exists only at point *C*.

Which price-output combination should be sought?

information about the **opportunity cost** of this product. This flawed price signal is the cause of market failure. We end up consuming less of this product (and more of other goods) than we would if charged its true opportunity cost. A suboptimal mix of output results.

opportunity cost: The most desired goods or services that are forgone in order to obtain something else.

The natural monopolist's profit-maximizing output (q_A) also fails to minimize average total cost. In a competitive industry, ATC is driven down to its minimum by relentless competition. In this case, however, reductions in ATC cease when the monopolist achieves the profit-maximizing rate of output (q_A). Were output to increase further, average total costs would fall.

Finally, notice that the higher price (p_A) associated with the monopolist's preferred output (q_A) ensures a fat profit. The **economic profit** may violate our visions of equity. In 2001, millions of Californians were convinced that this kind of "profiteering" was the root of their electricity woes.

economic profit: The difference between total revenues and total economic costs.

REGULATORY OPTIONS

The suboptimal outcomes likely to emerge from a free-swinging natural monopoly prompt consumers to demand government intervention. The market alone can't overcome the natural advantage of pervasive economies of scale. But the government could compel different outcomes. The question is, Which outcomes do we want? And how will we get them?

Price Regulation

For starters, we might consider price regulation. The natural monopolist's preferred price (p_A) is, after all, a basic cause of market failure. By regulating the firm, the government can compel a lower price. The California legislature did this in 1996 when it set a maximum retail price for electricity.

As is apparent from Figure 27.2 there are lots of choices in setting a regulated price. We start with the conviction that the unregulated price p_A is too high. But where on the demand curve below p_A do we want to be?

Price Efficiency (p = MC). One possibility is to set the price at a level consistent with opportunity costs. As we saw earlier, a monopolist's unregulated price sends out a flawed price signal. By charging a price in excess of marginal cost, the monopolist causes a suboptimal allocation of resources. We could improve market outcomes, therefore, by compelling the monopolist to set the price equal to marginal cost. Such an efficient price would lead us to point B in Figure 27.2, where the demand curve and the marginal cost curve intersect. At that price (p_B), consumers would get optimal use of the good or service produced.

Subsidy. Although the price p_B will ensure allocative efficiency, it will also bankrupt the producer. In a natural monopoly, MC is always less than ATC. Hence, ***marginal cost pricing by a natural monopolist implies a loss on every unit of output produced.*** In this case, the loss per unit is equal to $B^* - B$. If confronted with the regulated price p_B, the firm will ultimately shut down and exit from the market. This was one of the many problems that plagued California. Unable to charge a price high enough to cover their costs, some of the state's utility companies were forced into bankruptcy.

If we want to require efficient pricing (p = MC), we must provide a subsidy to the natural monopoly. In Figure 27.2 the amount of the subsidy would have to equal the anticipated loss at q_B, that is, the quantity q_B multiplied by the per-unit loss ($B^* - B$). Such subsidies are provided to subway systems. With subsidies, local subway systems can charge fees below *average* cost and closer to *marginal* cost. These subsidized fares increase ridership, thus ensuring greater use of very expensive transportation systems.

Despite the advantages of this subsidized pricing strategy, taxpayers always complain about the cost of such subsidies. Taxpayers are particularly loath to provide them for private companies. Hence, political considerations typically preclude efficient (marginal cost) pricing, despite the economic benefits of this regulatory strategy.

Production Efficiency (p = minATC). Even if it were possible to impose marginal cost pricing, we still wouldn't achieve maximum production efficiency. Production efficiency is attained at the lowest possible average total cost. At q_B we're producing a lot of output but still have some unused capacity. Since ATC falls continuously, we could achieve still lower average costs if we increased output beyond q_B. ***In a natural monopoly, production efficiency is achieved at capacity production, where ATC is at a minimum.***

Increasing output beyond q_B raises the same problems we encountered at that rate of output. At production rates in excess of q_B, ATC is always higher than price. Even MC is higher than price to the right of point B. Thus, ***no regulated price can induce the monopolist to achieve minimum average cost. A subsidy would be required to offset the market losses.***

Profit Regulation

Instead of price regulation, we could try profit regulation. If we choose not to subsidize a natural monopolist, we must permit it to charge a price high enough to cover all its costs, including a normal profit. We can achieve the result by mandating a price equal to average total cost. In Figure 27.2 this regulatory objective is achieved at point C. In this case, the rate of output is q_C and the regulated price is p_C.

Profit regulation looks appealing for two reasons. First, it eliminates the need to subsidize the monopolist. Second, it allows us to focus on profits only, thus removing the need to develop demand and cost curves. In theory, all we have to do is check the firm's annual profit-and-loss statement to confirm that it's earning a normal (average) profit. If its profits are too high, we can force the firm to reduce its price; if profits are too low, we may permit a price increase.

Bloated Costs. While beautiful in principle, profit regulation can turn out ugly in practice. In particular, profit regulation can lead to bloated costs and dynamic inefficiency. ***If a firm is permitted a specific profit rate (or rate of return), it has no incentive to limit costs.*** On the contrary, higher costs imply higher profits. If permitted to charge 10 percent over unit costs, a monopolist may be better off with average costs of \$6 rather than only \$5. The higher costs translate into 60 cents of profit per unit rather than only 50 cents. Hence,

IN THE NEWS

FCC: Nynex Padded Millions in Profits

Commission Urges Refunds, $1.4 Million Fine

Regional phone company Nynex Corp. overcharged its customers by tens of millions of dollars over a four-year period so that the company could pad its profits illegally, the Federal Communications Commission said yesterday.

The commission proposed refunds as well as a $1.4 million fine that would be the largest it has ever imposed.

Nynex, which provides phone service in New York and New England, denied wrongdoing, saying that the commission was applying newly passed rules retroactively. "There was no intent to overcharge," said Nynex Chairman William C. Ferguson. Under FCC rules, Nynex has 30 days in which to respond to the charges and seek dismissal of them.

The commission found that Nynex violated complex rules of accounting that are designed to keep telephone companies from subsidizing unregulated subsidiaries with money that they collect from customers of their monopoly phone service. This resulted, the FCC said, in a transfer of profits to a subsidiary whose bottom line is not regulated, boosting the overall profits of Nynex.

— John Burgess

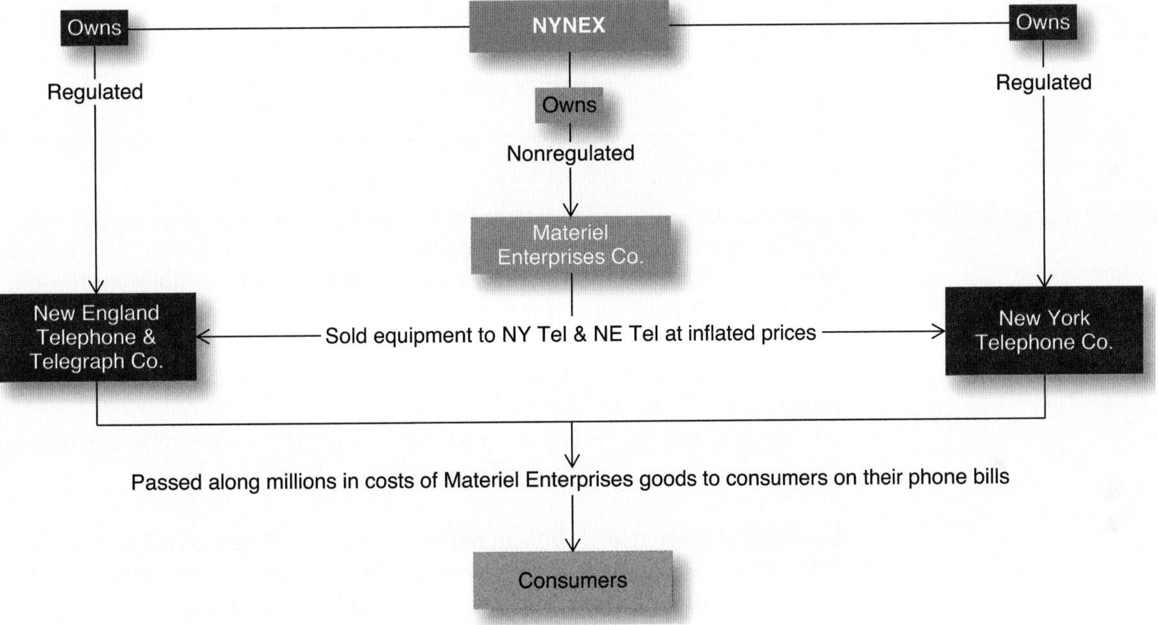

Analysis: Profit regulation creates incentives for a regulated firm to inflate ("pad") its costs. One way to accomplish that is to pay high prices for products purchased from unregulated subsidiaries.

there's an incentive to "pad costs." If those costs actually represent improvements in wages and salaries, fringe benefits, or the work environment, then cost increases are doubly attractive to the firm and its employees. Cost efficiency is as welcome as the plague under such circumstances.

Profit regulation can also motivate a firm to inflate its costs by paying above-market prices for products purchased from an unregulated subsidiary. This was the strategy AT&T used to increase its *regulated* cost base while ringing up high profits at Western Electric, its *unregulated* subsidiary (see Chapter 24). The FCC accused Nynex (the "Baby Bell" that provided phone service in New York and New England in the 1970s) of using the same strategy to pad its profits (see News).

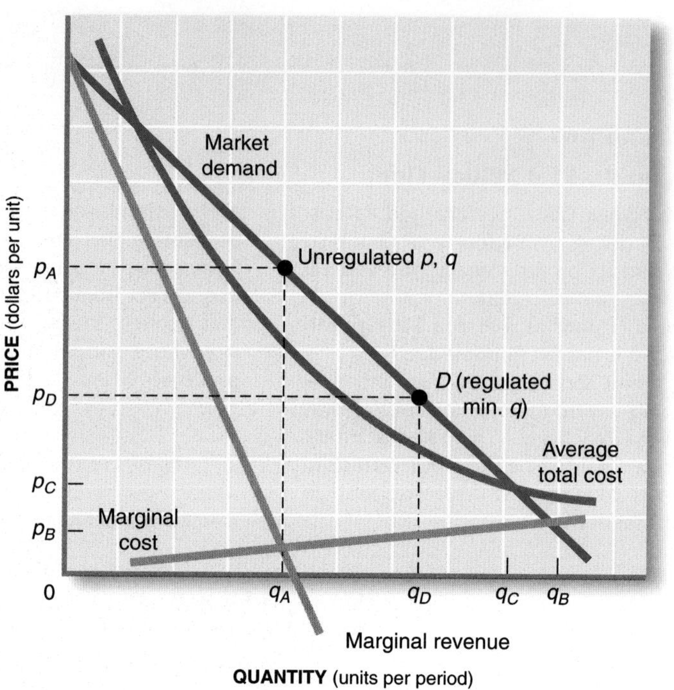

FIGURE 27.3
Minimum Service Regulation

Regulation may seek to ensure some minimal level of service. In this case, the required rate of output is arbitrarily set at q_D. Consumers are willing to pay p_D per unit for that output.

Regulated output q_D is preferable to the unregulated outcome (q_A,p_A) but may induce a decline in quality. Cost cutting is the only way to increase profits when the rate of output is fixed and price is on the demand curve.

Output Regulation

Given the difficulties in regulating prices and profits, regulators may choose to regulate output instead. The natural monopolist's preferred output rate is q_A, as illustrated again in Figure 27.3. We could compel this monopolist to provide a minimum level of service in excess of q_A. This regulated minimum is designated q_D in Figure 27.3. At q_D consumers get the benefit not only of more output but also of a lower price (p_D). At q_D total monopoly profit must also be less than at q_A, since q_A was the profit-maximizing rate of output.

It appears, then, that compelling any rate of output in excess of q_A can only benefit consumers. Moreover, output regulation is an easy rule to enforce.

Quality Deterioration. Unfortunately, minimum-service regulation can also cause problems. If forced to produce at the rate of q_D, the monopolist may seek to increase profits by cutting cost corners. This can be accomplished by deferring plant and equipment maintenance, reducing quality control, or otherwise lowering the quality of service. ***Regulation of the quantity produced may induce a decline in quality.*** Since a monopolist has no direct competition, consumers pretty much have to accept whatever quality the monopolist offers. This structural reality may explain why consumers complain so much about the services of local cable monopolies.

In addition to encouraging quality deterioration, output regulation at q_D also violates the principle of marginal cost pricing. Because an economic profit exists at q_D, equity goals may be jeopardized as well. Hence, minimum service (output) regulation isn't a panacea for the regulatory dilemma. In fact, there is no panacea: ***Goal conflicts are inescapable, and any regulatory rule may induce undesired producer responses.***

Imperfect Answers

The call for public regulation of natural monopolies is based on the recognition that the profit motive doesn't generate optimal outcomes in any monopoly environment. If unregulated, a natural monopolist will charge too much and produce too little. The regulatory remedy for these market failures isn't evident, however. Regulators can compel efficient prices or least-cost production only by offering a subsidy. Profit regulation is likely to induce cost-inflating responses. Output regulation is an incentive for quality deterioration. No matter which way we turn, regulatory problems result.

There's not much hope for transforming unregulated market failure into perfect regulated outcomes. In reality, regulators must choose a strategy that balances competing objectives (e.g., price efficiency and equity). A realistic goal for regulation is to *improve* market outcomes, not to *perfect* them. In the real world, ***the choice isn't between imperfect markets and flawless government intervention but rather between imperfect markets and imperfect intervention.***

The argument for *deregulation* rests on the observation that government regulation sometimes worsens market outcomes. In some cases, **government failure** may be worse than market failure. Specifically, regulation may lead to price, cost, or production outcomes that are inferior to those of an unregulated market.

government failure: Government intervention that fails to improve economic outcomes.

THE COSTS OF REGULATION

Improving outcomes in a particular market isn't adequate proof of regulatory success. We also have to consider the *costs* incurred to change market outcomes.

Administrative Costs

As we've observed, industry regulation entails various options and a host of trade-offs. Someone must sit down and assess these trade-offs. To make a sound decision, a regulatory administration must have access to lots of information. At a minimum, the regulator must have some clue as to the actual shape and position of the demand and cost curves depicted in Figures 27.2 and 27.3. Crude illustrations won't suffice when decisions about the prices, output, or costs of a multibillion-dollar industry are being made. The regulatory commission needs volumes of details about actual costs and demand and a platoon of experts to collect and analyze the needed data. All this labor represents a real cost to society, since the regulatory lawyers, accountants, and economists could be employed elsewhere.

webnote

The Weidenbaum Center on the Economy, Government, and Public Policy at Washington University tracks and analyzes regulation: http://csab.wustl.edu

As Table 27.1 on the next page illustrates, nearly 200,000 people are employed in regulatory agencies of the federal government. Thousands more have regulatory responsibilities in smaller agencies and the major executive departments. In addition to these federal workers, tens of thousands more people are employed by state and local regulatory agencies. All of these regulators are part of our limited labor resources. By using them to regulate private industry, we are forgoing their use in the production of desired goods and services. This is a significant economic cost.

Compliance Costs

The administrative costs of regulation focus on resources used in the public sector. By its very nature, however, regulation also changes resource use in the private sector. Regulated industries must expend resources to educate themselves about the regulations, to change their production behavior, and often to file reports with the regulatory authorities. The human and capital resources used for these purposes represent the *compliance* cost of regulation.

New rules on trucking illustrate how regulation can increase production costs. In 2003, the U.S. Department of Transportation reduced the amount of permitted driving time for interstate truckers (see News, page 555). This rule requires freight companies to use more trucks and more labor to transport goods, thereby raising economic costs. Although the resultant gain in safety is desired, the cost of achieving that gain is not inconsequential.

Efficiency Costs

Finally, we have to consider the potential costs of changes in output. Most regulation alters the mix of output, either directly or indirectly. Ideally, regulation will always improve the mix of output. But it's possible that bad decisions, incomplete information, or faulty implementation may actually *worsen* the mix of output. If this occurs, then the loss of utility associated with an inferior mix of output imposes a further cost on society, over and above administrative and compliance costs.

Efficiency costs may increase significantly over time. Consumer tastes change, demand and marginal revenue curves shift, costs change, and new technologies emerge. Can regulatory commissions respond to these changes as fast as the market mechanism does? If not, even optimal regulations may soon become obsolete and counterproductive. Worse still, the regulatory process itself may impede new technology, new marketing approaches, or

TABLE 27.1
Employment in Federal Regulatory Agencies

The human and capital resources the bureaucracy employs represent a real opportunity cost. The 242,376 people employed in 63 federal agencies—and tens of thousands more employed in state and local bureaucracies—could be producing other goods and services. These and other costs must be compared to the benefits of regulation.

Agency	Number of Employees
SOCIAL REGULATION	
Consumer Safety and Health	34,391
• Food and Drug Administration (FDA)	
• Food Safety and Inspection Service, etc.	
Homeland Security	122,324
• Transportation Security Adm. (TSA)	
• Customs and Border Security	
• Immigration and Customs, etc.	
Transportation	8,690
• Federal Aviation Adm. (FAA)	
• Federal Motor Carriers Safety Adm.	
• Federal Railroad Adm., etc.	
Workplace	7,406
• Occupational Safety and Health Adm. (OSHA)	
• Mine Safety and Health Adm.	
• Employment Standards Adm., etc.	
Environment	27,584
• Environmental Protection Agency (EPA)	
• Forest and Rangeland Research	
• Fish and Wildlife Service, etc.	
Energy	3,240
• Nuclear Regulatory Agency, etc.	
ECONOMIC REGULATION	
General Business	15,874
• Patent and Trademark Office	
• Securities and Exchange Commission (SEC)	
• Federal Trade Commission (FTC), etc.	
Finance and Banking	11,797
• Federal Reserve System	
• Federal Deposit Insurance Corporation (FDIC)	
• Comptroller of the Currency, etc.	
Industry-Specific Regulation	6,753
• Agricultural Marketing Service	
• Federal Communications Commission (FCC), etc.	
Total Employment:	242,376

Source: Melinda Warren, Weidenbaum Center on the Economy, Government, and Public Policy, Washington University, 2006.

improved production processes. These losses may be the most important. As Robert Hahn of the American Enterprise Institute observed:

> The measurable costs of regulation pale against the distortions that sap the economy's dynamism. The public never sees the factories that weren't built, the new products that didn't appear, or the entrepreneurial idea that drowned in a cumbersome regulatory process.[1]

[1]Cited in *Fortune,* October 19, 1992, p. 94.

IN THE NEWS 

Costs of Trucking Seen Rising under New Safety Rules

The first major changes in truck-driver work hours since 1939 are expected to reduce highway fatalities, but also contribute to the biggest increase in trucking rates in two decades. . . .

The new rules increase the time that truck drivers must set aside to rest in each 24-hour period to 10 hours from eight hours, and the total time a driver can be on duty will fall to 14 hours from 15 hours. . . .

The government estimates the new rules could cost trucking companies about $1.3 billion a year. . . .

Because trucks haul so much commerce, accounting for more than 81% of the nation's $571 billion freight-transportation bill last year, the effects could be far-reaching. Some users of truck transportation say higher trucking rates could lead to a broad-based increase in prices of goods from paper to chemicals, diapers to trash cans. . . .

Still, "there are about 410 fatalities a year attributed to fatigue-related truck crashes, and that's 410 very good reasons for changing the rule," says Annette Sandberg, administrator of the Transportation Department's Federal Motor Carrier Safety Administration. The agency expects the new rules to save up to 75 lives a year and prevent as many as 1,326 fatigue-related crashes a year.

—Daniel Machalaba

Analysis: Regulations designed to improve market outcomes typically impose higher costs. The challenge is to balance benefits and costs.

These kinds of dynamic efficiency losses are a drag on economic growth, limiting outward shifts of the production possibilities curve while perpetuating an increasingly undesired mix of output.

Balancing Benefits and Costs

The economic costs of regulation are a reminder of the "no free lunch" maxim. Although regulatory intervention may improve market outcomes, that intervention isn't without cost. The real resources used in the regulatory process could be used for other purposes. Hence, even if we could achieve perfect outcomes with enough regulation, the cost of achieving perfection might outweigh the benefits. ***Regulatory intervention must balance the anticipated improvements in market outcomes against the economic cost of regulation.*** In principle, the marginal benefit of regulation must exceed its marginal cost. If this isn't the case, then additional regulation isn't desirable, even if it would improve short-run market outcomes.

DEREGULATION IN PRACTICE

The push to *de*regulate was prompted by two concerns. The first concern focused on the dynamic inefficiencies that regulation imposes. It appeared that these inefficiencies had accumulated over time, rendering regulated industries less productive than desired. The other push for deregulation came from advancing technology, which destroyed the basis for natural monopoly in some industries. A brief review of the resulting deregulation illustrates the impact of these forces.

Railroads

The railroad industry was the federal government's first broad regulatory target. Railroads are an example of natural monopoly, with high fixed costs and negligible marginal costs. Furthermore, there were no airports or interstate highways to compete with the railroads in 1887, when Congress created the Interstate Commerce Commission (ICC). The ICC was established to limit monopolistic exploitation of this situation while assuring a fair profit to railroad owners. The ICC established rates and routes for the railroads while limiting both entry to and exit from the industry.

With the advent of buses, trucks, subways, airplanes, and pipelines as alternative modes of transportation, railroad regulation became increasingly obsolete. Regulated cargoes, routes, and prices prevented railroads from adapting their prices or services to meet changing consumer demands. With regulation-protected routes, they also had little incentive to invest in new technologies or equipment. As a result, railroad traffic and profits declined while other transportation industries flourished.

The Railroad Revitalization and Regulatory Reform Act of 1976 was a response to this crisis. Its major goal was to reduce the scope of government regulation. Reinforced by the Staggers Rail Act of 1980, railroads were granted much greater freedom to adapt their prices and service to market demands.

Railroad companies used that flexibility to increase their share of total freight traffic. Fresh fruits and vegetables, for example, were exempted from ICC rate regulation in 1979. Railroads responded by *reducing* their rates and improving service. In the first year of deregulated rates, fruits and vegetable shipments increased over 30 percent, a dramatic reversal of earlier trends. Deregulation of coal traffic (in 1980) and piggyback (trucks on railroad flatcars) traffic (in 1982) prompted similar turnarounds. The railroads prospered by reconfiguring routes and services, cutting operating costs, and offering lower rates. Between 1986 and 1993, the average cost of moving freight by rail dropped by 69 percent.

Not all rates have fallen. Indeed, one worrisome effect of deregulation is the increased concentration in the rail industry. After a series of mergers and acquisitions, the top four railroads moved nearly 90 percent of all rail freight (ton-miles) during 1998 and 1999. Moreover, these same firms held monopoly positions on specific routes. Shippers in these captive markets were paying rates 20 to 30 percent higher than in nonmonopoly routes.

Telephone Service

The telephone industry has long been the classic example of a natural monopoly. Although enormous fixed costs are necessary to establish a telephone network, the marginal cost of an additional telephone call approaches zero. Hence, it made economic sense to have a single network of telephone lines and switches rather than a maze of competing ones. Recognizing these economies of scale, Congress permitted AT&T to maintain a monopoly on both long-distance and most local telephone service. To assure that consumers would benefit from this natural monopoly, the Federal Communications Commission (FCC) regulated phone services and prices.

Once again, technology outpaced regulation. Communications satellites made it much easier and less costly for new firms to provide long-distance telephone service. Moreover, the rate structure that AT&T and the Federal Communications Commission had established made long-distance service highly profitable. Accordingly, start-up firms clamored to get into the industry, and consumers petitioned for lower rates.

Long Distance. In 1982, the courts put an end to AT&T's monopoly, transforming long-distance telecommunications into a more competitive industry with more firms and less regulation. Since then, over 800 firms have entered the industry, and long-distance telephone rates have dropped sharply. Between 1983 and 1990, long-distance telephone rates fell more than 40 percent. The quality of service also improved with fiber-optic cable, advanced switching systems, cell phones, and myriad new phone-line services such as fax transmissions, remote access, and Internet access. All these changes have contributed to a tripling of long-distance telephone use in the United States. The same kinds of changes have occurred around the world as other telephone monopolies have crumbled (see World View).

Local Service. The deregulation of long-distance services was so spectacularly successful that observers wondered whether local telephone service might be deregulated as well. As competition in *long-distance* services increased, the monopoly nature of *local* rates became

WORLD VIEW 

Demise of Telephone Monopolies

The breakup of AT&T was spurred by new technology that undercut the basis for natural monopoly. The same technological advances have transformed the telecommunications industry around the world:

- *Canada:* In 1994, the 10 regional phone companies were required to provide equal access to their transmission networks. Over 200 new companies entered the industry, and telephone rates fell by 40 percent.
- *Japan:* In 1984, the Japanese government ended the monopoly long held by Nippon Telegraph & Telephone (NTT). More than 500 companies have now entered the industry, chipping away at NTT's market share.
- *Great Britain:* The British government has privatized British Telecommunications and licensed another company to build a second, competing network.
- *France:* The French government has retained a single, state-owned network but opened the door to competition in equipment and services.
- *Germany:* The former state-owned monopoly was privatized in 1996. Competitive entry began in 1998.
- *Chile:* The long-established monopoly (Entel) was deregulated in 1994, and entry barriers dropped. Rates plunged and volume doubled. Within two years Entel's market share fell from 100 to 40 percent.
- *Brazil:* The state-owned monopoly (Telebras) was opened to competition in 1998.
- *Mexico:* In 1997, Mexico opened its telecommunications market to competition. New domestic and international fiber-optic networks have been built, and phone rates have dropped dramatically.
- *European Union:* At the beginning of 1998, all local and long-distance markets were opened to competition.
- *China:* At the end of 2001, China split its fixed-line monopoly into two regional companies.

Analysis: The deregulation of telephone industries has spurred price competition and innovation, while greatly increasing the volume of telephone service.

painfully apparent: Local rates kept increasing after 1983 while long-distance rates were tumbling.

The Baby Bells that held monopolies on local service defended their high rates based on the high costs of building and maintaining transmission networks. But new technologies permitted wireless companies to offer local service if they could gain access to the monopoly networks. Congress responded in 1996. The Telecommunications Act of 1996 required the Baby Bells to grant rivals access to their transmission networks. The Baby Bells kept rivals at bay, however, by charging excessive access fees, imposing overly complex access codes, requiring unnecessary capital equipment, and raising other entry barriers. The battle for local access continues (see News on next page).

webnote

Find out what has happened to the Telecommunications Act of 1996 at www.fcc.gov/telecom.html

Airlines

The Civil Aeronautics Board (CAB) was created in 1938 to regulate airline routes and fares. From its inception, the primary concern of the CAB was to ensure a viable system of air transportation for both large and small communities. Such a system would be ensured, the CAB believed, only if a fair level of profits was maintained by entry and price regulations. Thus, the focus of the CAB was on *profit* regulation.

Price Regulation. Initially, the CAB set airline fares at roughly the levels of Pullman rates for train travel. This implied that airfares would be proportional to distance, as they were for train travel. In the late 1930s, this fare structure wasn't unreasonable, as most flights were relatively short and planes were small.

As the airline industry grew, the CAB abandoned fare comparisons with trains but maintained the basic distance-based fare structure. To ensure fair profits, the CAB set fares in accordance with airline costs. This required the CAB to undertake intensive cost studies, based on accounting data provided by the airlines. Once the average cost of service and capital equipment was established, the CAB then set an average price that would ensure a fair rate of return (profit) (see point *C* in Figure 27.2).

IN THE NEWS

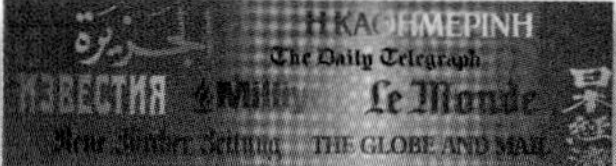

Bell Monopolies Push to Disconnect Competition

Seven years ago, Congress set out to break up the local Bell telephone monopolies and bring competition to consumers' homes. But just as states are finally figuring out how to make that promise a reality, and some communities are seeing phone bills drop, federal regulators may unplug the competitors at the behest of the four Bell monopolies.

The Bells want to gut rules spurring competition that were enacted in the wake of the 1996 Telecommunications Act. They require the Bells to rent their networks at reasonable prices to potential rivals that may want to offer local phone service but can't afford to set up their own phone networks.

For years, the law wasn't an issue because states let the Bells charge exorbitant fees that kept competitors out of their markets. Now that several states are ordering them to cut their network fees, competition is emerging, and phone rates are decreasing. On Monday, AT&T announced plans to compete in Washington, D.C., after the local government cut the charges for tapping into the network operated by Verizon. Nationwide, 11% of local phone lines were serviced by competitors through last June, nearly double their share two years earlier.

Faced with the first real threat to their grip on local service, Verizon and the other Bells are crying to the Federal Communications Commission (FCC) that they're forced to rent their networks at a loss. They want to go back to the way it was: higher fees for rivals and less choice for consumers.

—Marcy E. Mullins

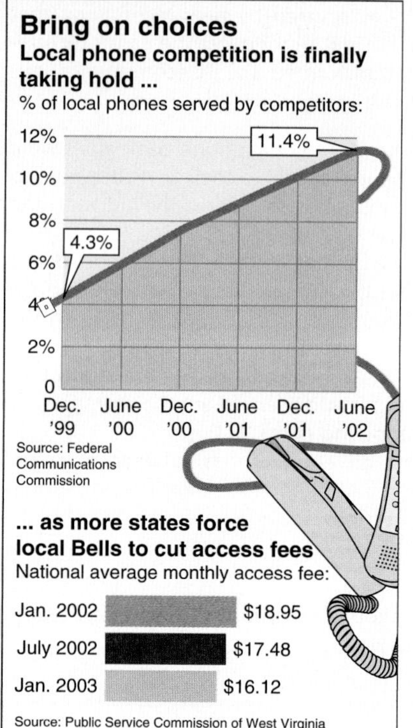

Source: *USA Today,* January 14, 2003. USA TODAY. Copyright 2003. Reprinted with permission.

Analysis: To enter local phone markets, would-be rivals must pay an access fee to the local phone monopoly. High fees are a substantial entry barrier.

A secondary objective of the CAB was to ensure air service to smaller, less traveled communities. Short hauls entail higher average costs and therefore justify higher fares. To avoid high fares on such routes, the CAB permitted airlines to charge prices well in excess of average costs on longer, more efficient routes as long as they maintained service on shorter, unprofitable routes. This **cross-subsidization** was similar to that of the telephone industry, in which long-distance profits helped keep local telephone charges low.

cross-subsidization: Use of high prices and profits on one product to subsidize low prices on another product.

To maintain this price and profit structure, the CAB had to regulate routes and limit entry into the airline industry. Otherwise, established carriers would abandon short, unprofitable routes, and new carriers would offer service only on more profitable routes. Unregulated entry thus threatened both cross-subsidization and the CAB's vision of a fair profit.

No Entry. The CAB was extremely effective in restricting entry into the industry. Would-be entrants had to demonstrate to the CAB that their proposed service was required by "public convenience and necessity" and was superior to that of established carriers. Established carriers could oppose a new application by demonstrating sufficient service, offering to expand their service, or claiming superior service. In view of the fact that new applicants had no airline experience, established carriers easily won the argument. From 1938 until 1977, the CAB *never* awarded a major route to a new entrant.

No Price Competition. The CAB also eliminated price competition between established carriers. The CAB fixed airfares on all routes. Airlines could reduce fares no more than 5 percent and couldn't increase them more than 10 percent without CAB approval.

Bloated Costs. Ironically, the established airlines failed to reap much profit from these high fares. Unable to compete on the basis of price, the established carriers had to engage in nonprice competition. The most costly form of nonprice competition was frequency of service. Once the CAB authorized service between any two cities, a regulated carrier could provide as many flights as desired. This enticed the regulated carriers to purchase huge fleets of planes and provide frequent departures. In the process, load factors (the percentage of seats filled with passengers) fell and average costs rose.

The regulated carriers also pursued **product differentiation** by offering special meals, first-run movies, free drinks, better service, and wider seats. This nonprice competition further inflated average costs and reduced profits.

product differentiation: Features that make one product appear different from competing products in the same market.

Profit regulation ultimately came to be regarded as a failure. The regulated airline industry was not as profitable as anticipated. And consumers weren't being offered very many price-service combinations.

New Entrants. The Airline Deregulation Act of 1978 changed the structure and behavior of the airline industry. Entry regulation was effectively abandoned. With the elimination of this **barrier to entry,** the number of carriers increased greatly. Between 1978 and 1985, the number of airline companies increased from 37 to 174! The new entrants intensified competition on nearly all routes. The share of domestic markets with four or more carriers grew from 13 percent in May 1978 to 73 percent in May 1981. All those new entrants pushed airfares down sharply, as Table 27.2 shows.

barriers to entry: Obstacles that make it difficult or impossible for would-be producers to enter a particular market, such as patents.

The CAB's authority over airfares ended January 1, 1983. Since then, airlines have been able to adapt their fares to market supply and demand. The CAB itself was eliminated at the end of 1984. Its remaining responsibilities—for foreign travel, mail service, mergers, and operating authority—were transferred to the U.S. Department of Transportation.

Increasing Concentration. Although airline deregulation is hailed as one of the greatest policy achievements of the 1980s, airline industry structure and behavior remain imperfect. Of particular concern has been the sharp increase in the industry's concentration ratio in the last 10 years. In the competitive fray spawned by deregulation, lots of new entrants and even some established airlines went broke. Unable to match lower fares and increased service, scores of airline companies exited the industry in the period 1985–95. In the process, a handful of major carriers increased their market share. The combined market share of the

TABLE 27.2
Airfare Reductions after Deregulation (deregulated fares as percentage of regulated levels)

Five years after being deregulated, fares on heavily used long-distance routes were 40 percent lower than those dictated by the CAB's pricing formula. Rates on previously subsidized short hauls were higher, however, as cross-subsidies disappeared.

	Percentage Change in Airfare by Market Density (passengers per day)			
Market Distance	10–50	51–200	201–500	500+
1–400 miles	+14	+12	−5	−29
401–1,500 miles	+10	−3	−13	−20
1,501+ miles	N/A	−25	−35	−40

Source: Civil Aeronautics Board, *Implementation of the Provisions of the Airline Deregulation Act of 1978,* January 1984.

three largest carriers (American, United, Delta) increased from 35 percent in 1985 to 60 percent in 2001. In many cases, firms gained near-monopoly power in specific hub airports; by 2005 1 out of 10 domestic routes was again monopolized. Not surprisingly, a study by the U.S. General Accounting Office found that ticket prices are 45 to 85 percent higher on monopolized routes than on routes where at least two airlines compete.

webnote

For a sense of how competition affects airfares, check the number of carriers serving each of the following routes and the cheapest available fare *per mile:* (*a*) Detroit–Boston, (*b*) Pittsburgh–Washington, (*c*) Minneapolis–Milwaukee, (*d*) Denver–Colorado Springs, (*e*) Charlotte–Atlanta, (*f*) Las Vegas–Los Angeles. For information on carriers and fares, check expedia.com or visit www.travelocity.com and set up a free user's account.

Entry Barriers. To exploit their hub dominance, major carriers must keep out rivals. One of the most effective entry barriers is their ownership of landing slots. Air traffic is limited by the number of these slots, or authorized landing permits. In 1998, United Airlines controlled 82 percent of the slots at Chicago's O'Hare, up from 66 percent in 1986. Delta controls 83 percent of the slots at New York's Kennedy Airport. Smaller airlines complain that they can't get access to these slots, even when the slots aren't being used.

Would-be foreign competitors also complain that they can't get access to U.S. routes. The Air Commerce Act of 1926 forbids "foreign control" of airlines flying domestic U.S. routes. The U.S. Department of Transportation used that law in 2007 to deny Virgin Air entry into the U.S. airline market (see World View). Had Virgin been allowed to enter the industry, the pressure on existing airlines to improve service and reduce fares would have increased.

Defenders of deregulation are quick to point out that despite increasing *industry* concentration, there's more competition in most airline markets. In 1979, about 22 percent of all traffic was in monopoly markets, where a single carrier supplied at least 90 percent of all traffic. By 1989, only 11 percent of all traffic was in such monopoly markets. Furthermore, entry is still easier today than it was before deregulation, as a flock of new entrants attests. Hence, the airline industry is more of a **contestable market,** even if not a perfectly competitive one. When entry barriers (including slot access) are lowered, consumers continue to enjoy the low fares deregulation has made possible (see News on the "JetBlue effect").

contestable market: An imperfectly competitive industry subject to potential entry if prices or profits increase.

WORLD VIEW

[Unfriendly Skies]
Branson Gets Grounded

Using a 1926 Law, Old-School U.S. Airlines Have Halted the Virgin Founder's Bid to Launch a Domestic Carrier.

With a business empire ranging from cola to cell-phones to condoms, Richard Branson was once dismissed by the jolly old British business establishment as a brash, attention-grabbing American-style entrepreneur.

But in his latest venture, Branson's problem is that he simply isn't American enough. His dream of launching Virgin America, a low-fare U.S. airline, has run into a xenophobic buzz saw—a 1926 federal law that bars foreigners from controlling domestic carriers—and a furious onslaught from the airline's would-be competitors.

Based in San Francisco, Virgin America has $177 million in financing, seasoned management, plans to fly coast to coast, and nine Airbus jets, to be equipped with comfy leather seats and personal video screens featuring live satellite TV, movies, and games. What it doesn't have is permission from the U.S. Department of Transportation to take off. In fact, on Dec. 27, the DOT "tentatively" rejected its application. . . .

The resistance is perhaps understandable: With fuel prices falling and the number of full flights rising, the industry is set to make a solid profit in 2007 after hemorrhaging money for years. The last thing it needs is another low-cost rival.

—Peter Elkind

Source: FORTUNE, February 5, 2007, p. 13.

Analysis: Regulations that block entry into an industry reduce potential competition and so keep prices higher and service levels lower. Virgin America received permission to fly in August, 2007.

IN THE NEWS  

The JetBlue Effect

When the carrier comes to town, fares go down, traffic goes up, and the airline ends up with a big chunk of the business.

Source: *BusinessWeek*, February 16, 2004. Reprinted by permission. Copyright 2004 by The McGraw-Hill Companies.

	Change in Daily Passengers	Change in Average Fare	JetBlue Local Traffic Share
New York to Miami/Fort Lauderdale	+14%	−17% to $121.50	23.1%
New York to Los Angeles Basin	+2%	−26% to $219.31	18%
New York to Buffalo	+94%	−40% to $86.09	61.2%

Figures as of second quarter, 2003.
Data: Back Aviation Solutions (www.backaviation.com).

Analysis: If entry barriers are low enough, new entrants will contest a market, keeping pressure on prices and service.

Cable TV

The cable TV industry offers examples of both deregulation and *re*regulation. Up until 1986, city and county governments had the authority to franchise (approve) local cable TV operators and regulate their rates. In almost all cases, local governments franchised only one operator, thus establishing local monopolies. The monopoly structure was justified by pervasive economies of scale and the desire to avoid the cost and disruption of laying multiple cable systems. The rationale behind local regulation of cable prices (rates) was to ensure that consumers shared in the benefits of natural monopoly.

Deregulation. By 1984, Congress was convinced that broadcast TV and emerging technologies (such as microwave transmissions and direct satellite broadcasts) offered sufficient competition to ensure consumers fair prices and quality service. The Cable Communications Policy Act of 1984 *de*regulated cable TV by stripping local governments of the authority to regulate prices. From 1986 to 1992, cable TV was essentially unregulated.

Soon after price regulation ended, cable companies began increasing their rates sharply. As Figure 27.4 shows, the rate of price acceleration nearly doubled after the cable industry was deregulated. Consumers also complained that local cable companies offered poor service. They demanded that Congress *re*regulate the industry.

Reregulation. In 1992, Congress responded with the Cable Television Consumer Protection and Competition Act. That act gave the Federal Communications Commission authority to reregulate cable TV rates. The FCC required cable operators to *reduce* prices by nearly 17 percent in 1993–94. It then issued 450 pages of new rules that would limit future price increases. As Figure 27.4 illustrates, these interventions had a dramatic effect on cable prices.

While consumers applauded the new price rules, cable operators warned of unwelcome long-term effects. The rate cuts reduced cable-industry revenues by nearly $4 billion between 1993 and 1995. The cable companies say they would have used that revenue to invest in improved networks and services. The cable companies also argued that increased

FIGURE 27.4
Annual Increase in Price of Basic Cable Service

After cable TV prices were deregulated in 1986, monthly charges moved up sharply. In 1992 Congress *re*regulated cable TV and prices stabilized. The Telecommunications Act of 1996 again deregulated prices and they surged, as shown in these annual averages.

Source: Industry publications.

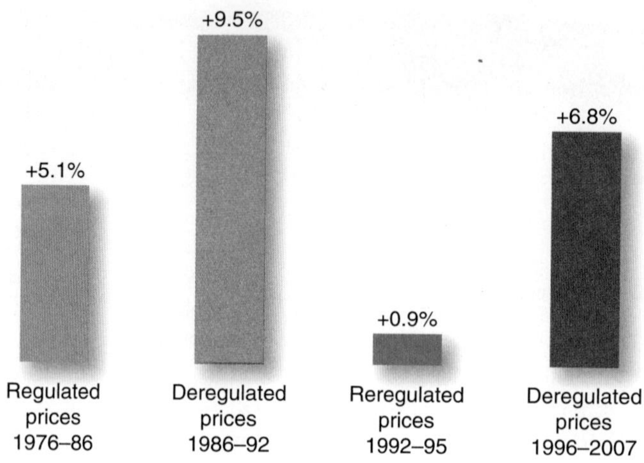

competition from satellite transmissions and the Internet made government regulation of (wired) cable TV increasingly unnecessary.

Deregulation. Congress responded to these industry complaints by *de*regulating the cable industry again. The Telecommunications Act of 1996 mandated that rate regulation be phased out and ended completely by March 1999. Almost immediately, cable prices soared again, as Figure 27.4 shows. Critics asserted that alternative technologies were still not viable competitors to local cable monopolies. Even where alternative technologies are available—e.g., in the fiber-optic lines of telephone companies—access to the video market has been highly restricted.

Electricity

The electric utility industry is the latest target for deregulation. Here again, the industry has long been regarded as a natural monopoly. The enormous fixed costs of a power plant and transmission network, combined with negligible marginal costs for delivering another kilowatt of electricity, gave electric utilities a downward-sloping average total cost curve. The focus of government intervention was therefore on rate regulation (behavior) rather than promoting competition (structure).

Bloated Costs, High Prices. Critics of local utility monopolies complained that local rate regulation wasn't working well enough. In order to get higher (retail) prices, the utility companies allowed costs to rise. They also had no incentive to pursue new technologies that would reduce the costs of power generation or distribution. Big power users like steel companies complained that high electricity prices were crippling their competitive position. The only viable option for consumers was to move from a state with a high-cost power monopoly to a state with low-cost power monopoly.

Demise of Power Plant Monopolies. Advances in transmission technology gave consumers a new choice. High-voltage transmission lines can carry power thousands of miles with negligible power loss. Utility companies used these lines to link their power grids, thereby creating backup power sources in the event of regional blackouts. In doing so, however, they created a new entry point for potential competition. Now a Kentucky power plant with surplus capacity can supply electricity to consumers in California. There's no longer any need to rely on a regional utility monopoly. At the wholesale level, utility companies have been trading electricity across state lines since 1992.

Local Distribution Monopolies. Although technology destroyed the basis for natural monopolies in power *production,* local monopolies in power *distribution* remain. Electricity reaches consumers through the wires attached to every house and business. As with TV cables, there is a natural monopoly in electricity distribution; competing wire grids would be costly and inefficient.

To deliver the benefits of competition in power *production,* rival producers must be able to access these local distribution grids. This is the same problem that has plagued competition in local telephone service. The local power companies that own the local distribution grids aren't anxious to open the wires to new competition. The central problem for electricity deregulation has been to assure wider access to local distribution grids.

California's Mistakes. The California legislature decided to resolve this problem by stripping local utility monopolies of their production capacity. By forcing utility companies to sell their power plants, California transformed its utilities into pure power *distributors.* This seemed to resolve the conflict between ownership and access to the distribution system. However, it also made California's utility companies totally dependent on third-party power producers, many of which were then out of state.

California also put a ceiling on the *retail* price its utilities could charge. But the state had no power to control the *wholesale* price of electricity in interstate markets. When wholesale prices rose sharply in 2000 (see News), California's utilities were trapped between rising costs and a fixed price ceiling. Fearful of a political backlash, the governor refused to raise the retail price ceiling. As a result, some of the utility companies were forced into bankruptcy and power supplies were interrupted. The state itself entered the utility business by buying power plants and more out-of-state power supplies. In the end, Californians ended up with very expensive electricity.

Better Strategies. Other states and countries have demonstrated how deregulation can generate much better results. Norway deregulated its electric industry in 1991, and prices soon declined by 20 percent. After the European Union started deregulating its electric industries in 1999, prices fell as well. In the United States, the 50 states are at various stages of deregulation, amassing lots of evidence on how best to use competition to reduce electricity costs and prices.

webnote

Visit the Center for the Advancement of Energy Markets at www.caem.org to see how states differ in the extent of electricity deregulation and price changes.

IN THE NEWS

Financial Woes Heating Up

Pacific Gas and Electric is in financial trouble because the cost of power it purchases on the wholesale market is soaring higher than the fixed rate it charges its customers:

—Suzy Parker

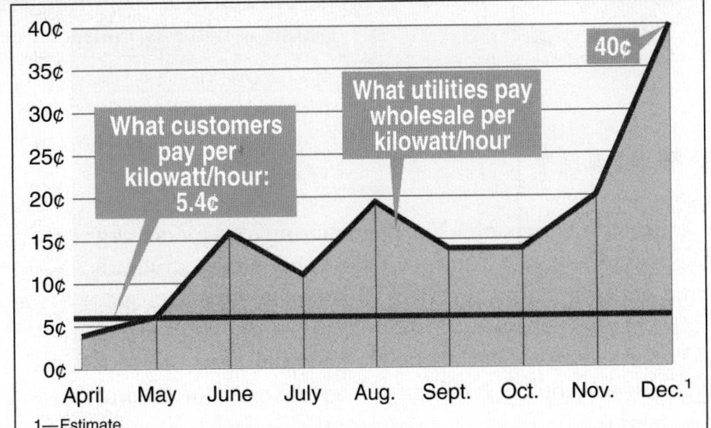

Source: Pacific Gas and Electric (www.pge.com).

Analysis: When wholesale prices for electricity rose above the retail price ceiling established by the California legislature, the state's utility companies lost money on every kilowatt supplied. It was a recipe for financial disaster.

THE ECONOMY TOMORROW

DEREGULATE EVERYTHING?

Deregulation of the railroad, telephone, airline, and electricity industries has yielded substantial benefits: more competition, lower prices, and improved services. Such experiences bolster the case for laissez faire. Nevertheless, we shouldn't jump to the conclusion that all regulation of business should be dismantled. All we know from experience is that the regulation of certain industries has become outmoded. Changing consumer demands, new technologies, and substitute goods had simply made existing regulations obsolete, even counterproductive. A combination of economic and political forces doomed them to extinction.

But were these regulations ever necessary? In the 1880s there were no viable alternatives to railroads for overland transportation. The forces of natural monopoly could easily have exploited consumers and retarded economic growth. The same was largely true for long-distance telephone service prior to the launching of communications satellites. Even the limitations on competition in trucking and banking made some sense in the depths of the Great Depression. One shouldn't conclude that regulatory intervention never made sense just because the regulations themselves later became obsolete.

webnote

The Brookings Institution and the American Enterprise Institute have a joint project to analyze regulatory programs at www.aei.brookings.org

Even today, most people recognize the need for regulation of many industries. The transmission networks for local telephone service and electricity delivery are still natural monopolies. The government can force owners to permit greater access. But an unregulated network owner could still extract monopoly profits through excessive prices. Hence, even a deregulated industry may still require some regulation at critical entry or supply junctures. Existing regulations may not be optimal, but they probably generate better outcomes than totally unregulated monopolies.

Likewise, few people seriously propose relying on competition and the good judgment of consumers to determine the variety or quality of drugs on the market. Regulations imposed by the Food and Drug Administration restrain competition in the drug industry, raise production costs, and inhibit new technology. But they also make drugs safer. Here, as in other industries, there's a trade-off between the virtues of competition and those of regulation. The basic policy issue, as always, is whether the benefits of regulation exceed their administrative, compliance, and efficiency costs. The challenge for public policy in the economy tomorrow is to adapt regulations—or to discard them (that is, deregulate)—as market conditions, consumer demands, or technology changes.

SUMMARY

- Antitrust and regulation are alternative options for dealing with market power. Antitrust focuses on market structure and anticompetitive practices. Regulation stipulates specific market behavior. LO2
- High fixed costs and negligible marginal costs create a downward-sloping ATC curve, the hallmark of natural monopoly. LO1
- Natural monopolies offer pervasive economies of scale. Because of this potential efficiency, a more competitive market *structure* may not be desirable. LO2
- Regulation of natural monopoly can focus on price, profit, or output *behavior*. Price regulation may require subsidies; profit regulation may induce cost escalation; and output regulation may lead to quality deterioration. These problems compel compromises and acceptance of second-best solutions. LO2
- The demand for deregulation rests on the argument that the costs of regulation exceed the benefits. These costs include the opportunity costs associated with regulatory administration and compliance as well as the (dynamic) efficiency losses that result from inflexible pricing and production rules. LO3
- Deregulation of the railroad, telephone, and airline industries has been a success. In all these industries, regulation became outmoded by changing consumer demands, products, and technology. As regulation was relaxed, these industries became more competitive, output increased, and prices fell. LO3

- Recent experiences with deregulation don't imply that all regulation should end. Regulation is appropriate if market failure exists *and* if the benefits of regulation exceed the costs. As benefits and costs change, decisions about what and how to regulate must be reevaluated. LO3

Key Terms

laissez faire
market failure
antitrust
regulation
natural monopoly
economies of scale
marginal cost pricing
opportunity cost
economic profit
government failure
cross-subsidization
product differentiation
barriers to entry
contestable market

Questions for Discussion

1. Given the inevitable limit on airplane landings, how should available airport slots be allocated? How would market outcomes be altered? LO2
2. Should the airline industry be reregulated? LO3
3. Prior to 1982, AT&T kept local phone rates low by subsidizing them from long-distance profits. Was such cross-subsidization in the public interest? Explain. LO1
4. In most cities local taxi fares are regulated. Should such regulation end? Who would gain or lose? LO3
5. The News story on page 551 describes how Nynex inflated its regulated costs. What advantage did Nynex gain from this practice? How else might a regulated company pad its costs? LO2
6. How could a local phone or cable company reduce service quality if forced to accept price ceilings? LO2
7. If cable TV were completely deregulated, would local monopolies ever confront effective competition? Does profit regulation inhibit or accelerate would-be competition? LO3
8. Why is there resistance to (*a*) local phone companies providing video and data services and (*b*) mergers of local cable and telephone companies? LO1
9. Will reregulation of cable TV prices slow or hasten competition from alternative technologies? LO3
10. Who gains or loses by denying Virgin Air permission to fly U.S. air routes (World View, page 560)? LO2

problems The Student Problem Set at the back of this book contains numerical and graphing problems for this chapter.

web activities to accompany this chapter can be found on the Online Learning Center: **http://www.mhhe.com/economics/schiller11e**

Environmental Protection

28

LEARNING OBJECTIVES

After reading this chapter, you should know:

LO1. How markets encourage pollution.

LO2. Why *zero* pollution may not be desirable.

LO3. Alternative strategies for reducing pollution.

> Progress in environmental problems is impossible without a clear understanding of how the economic system works in the environment and what alternatives are available to take away the many roadblocks to environmental quality.
>
> —Council on Environmental Quality, First Annual Report

> What good is a clean river if you've got no jobs?
>
> —Steelworkers Union Official in Youngstown, Ohio

A hole in the ozone layer is allowing increased ultraviolet radiation to reach the earth's surface. The hole is the result of excessive release of chlorine gases (chlorofluorocarbons, or CFCs) from air conditioners, plastic-foam manufacture, industrial solvents, and aerosol spray cans such as deodorants and insecticides. The resulting damage to the stratosphere is causing skin cancer, cataracts, and immune-system disorders.

Skin cancer may turn out to be one of our less serious problems. As carbon dioxide is building up in the atmosphere, it is creating a gaseous blanket around the earth that is trapping radiation and heating the atmosphere. Scientists predict that this greenhouse effect will melt the polar ice caps, raise sea levels, flood coastal areas, and turn rich croplands into deserts within 60 years.

Everyone wants a cleaner and safer environment. So why don't we stop polluting the environment with CFCs, carbon dioxide, toxic chemicals, and other waste? If we don't do it ourselves, why doesn't the government force people to stop polluting?

Economics is part of the answer. To reduce pollution, we have to change our patterns of production and consumption. This entails economic costs, in terms of restricted consumption choices, more expensive ways of producing goods, and higher prices. Thus, we have to weigh the benefits of a cleaner, safer environment against the costs of environmental protection.

Instinctively, most people don't like the idea of measuring the value of a cleaner environment in dollars and cents. But most people might also agree that spending $2 trillion to avoid a few cataracts is awfully expensive. There has to be *some* balance between the benefits of a cleaner environment and the cost of cleaning it up.

This chapter assesses our environmental problems from this economic perspective, considering three primary concerns:

- **How do (unregulated) markets encourage pollution?**
- **What are the costs of greater environmental protection?**
- **How can government policy best ensure an *optimal* environment?**

To answer these questions, we first survey the major types and sources of pollution. Then we examine the benefits and costs of environmental protection, highlighting the economic incentives that shape market behavior.

THE ENVIRONMENTAL THREAT

The hole in the ozone layer and the earth's rising temperature are at the top of the list of environmental concerns. The list is much longer, however, and very old as well. As early as A.D. 61, the statesman and philosopher Seneca was complaining about the smoky air emitted from household chimneys in Rome. Lead emissions from ancient Greek and Roman silver refineries poisoned the air in Europe and the remote Arctic. And historians are quick to remind us that open sewers running down the street were once the principal mode of urban waste disposal. Typhoid epidemics were a recurrent penalty for water pollution. So we can't say that environmental damage is a new phenomenon or that it's now worse than ever before.

But we do know more about the sources of environmental damage than our ancestors did, and we can better afford to do something about it. Our understanding of the economics of pollution has increased as well. We've come to recognize that pollution impairs health, reduces life expectancy, and thus reduces labor-force activity and output. Pollution also destroys capital (such as the effects of air pollution on steel structures) and diverts resources to undesired activities (like car washes, laundry, and cleaning). Not least of all, pollution directly reduces our social welfare by denying us access to clean air, water, and beaches.

Air Pollution

Air pollution is as familiar as a smoggy horizon. But smog is only one form of air pollution.

Acid Rain. Sulfur dioxide (SO_2) is an acrid, corrosive, and poisonous gas that's created by burning high-sulfur fuels such as coal. As a contributor to acid rain, it destroys vegetation and forests. Electric utilities and industrial plants that burn high-sulfur coal or fuel oil are the prime sources of SO_2. Coal burning alone accounts for about 60 percent of all emissions of sulfur oxides. As the World View on the next page illustrates, SO_2 pollution is a serious problem not only in U.S. cities but all over the world: The air is much dirtier in Beijing, Calcutta, Tokyo, and Rome than in New York City.

Smog. Nitrogen oxides (NO_x), another ingredient in the formation of acid rain, are also a principal ingredient in the formation of smog. Smog not only irritates the eyes and spoils the view, but it also damages plants, trees, and human lungs. Automobile emissions account for 40 percent of urban smog. Bakeries, dry cleaners, and production of other consumer goods account for an equal amount of smog. The rest comes from electric power plants and industrial boilers.

The Greenhouse Effect. The prime villain in the greenhouse effect is the otherwise harmless carbon dioxide (CO_2) that we exhale. Unfortunately, we and nature now release so much CO_2 that the earth's oceans and vegetation can no longer absorb it all. The excess CO_2 is creating a gaseous blanket around the earth that may warm the earth to disastrous levels. The burning of fossil fuels is a significant source of CO_2 buildup. The destruction of rain forests, which absorb CO_2, also contributes to the greenhouse effect.

Water Pollution

Water pollution is another environmental threat. Its effects are apparent in the contamination of drinking water, restrictions on swimming and boating, foul-smelling waterways, swarms of dead fish, and floating debris.

Organic Pollution. The most common form of water pollution occurs in the disposal of organic wastes from toilets and garbage disposals. The wastes that originate there are collected in sewer systems and ultimately discharged into the nearest waterway. The key question is whether the wastes are treated (separated and decomposed) before ultimate discharge. Sophisticated waste-treatment plants can reduce organic pollution up to 99 percent. Unfortunately, only 70 percent of the U.S. population is served by a system of sewers and adequate (secondary) treatment plants. Inadequate treatment systems often result in the closure of waterways and beaches—even in Hawaii (see News on page 569).

WORLD VIEW

Polluted Cities

The air in New York City may be unhealthy, but it's not nearly as polluted with sulfur dioxide (SO_2) as that in some other major cities.

© Brand X Pictures/Punchstock/DAL

SO_2 Micrograms per Cubic Meter of Air

City	SO_2
Havana, Cuba	1
London, England	25
New York, New York	26
Rome, Italy	35
Cairo, Egypt	69
Mexico City, Mexico	74
Yokohama, Japan	100
Moscow, Russia	109
Istanbul, Turkey	120
Rio de Janeiro, Brazil	129
Tehran, Iran	209
Guiyang, China	424

Source: World Bank, *World Development Indicators,* 2006, Table 3.13. Used with permission by the International Bank for Reconstruction and Development/The World Bank.

Analysis: Pollution is a worldwide phenomenon, with common origins and potential remedies.

webnote

Find out about pollution in your zip code area from the Environmental Defense Fund's Chemical Scoreboard at www.scorecard.org

In addition to household wastes, our waterways must also contend with industrial wastes. Over half the volume of industrial discharge comes from just a few industries—principally paper, organic chemicals, petroleum, and steel. Finally, there are all those farm animals: The 7.5 billion chickens and 161 million cows and hogs raised each year generate 1.4 billion tons of manure (whew!). If improperly managed, that organic waste will contaminate water supplies and trigger algae blooms that can choke waterways and kill fish. Animal wastes don't cause too great a problem in Boston or New York City, but they can wreak havoc on the water supplies of towns in California, Texas, Kansas, and Iowa.

Thermal Pollution. Thermal pollution is an increase in the temperature of waterways brought about by the discharge of steam or heated water. Heat discharges can kill fish, upset marine reproductive cycles, and accelerate biological and chemical processes in water, thereby reducing its ability to retain oxygen. Electric power plants account for over 80 percent of all thermal discharges, with primary metal, chemical, and petroleum-refining plants accounting for nearly all the rest.

Solid-Waste Pollution

Solid waste is yet another environmental threat. Solid-waste pollution is apparent everywhere, from the garbage can to litter on the streets and beaches, to debris in the water, to open dumps. According to EPA estimates, we generate over 5 billion tons of solid waste each year. This figure includes more than 30 billion bottles, 60 billion cans, 100 million tires, and millions of discarded automobiles and major appliances. Where do you think all this refuse goes?

Most solid wastes originate in agriculture (slaughter wastes, orchard prunings, harvest residues) and mining (slag heaps, mill tailings). The much smaller amount of solid waste

IN THE NEWS   

Kualoa Park Pollution: "It's Ridiculous"

KUALOA REGIONAL PARK—The city plans to fight a $300,000 fine levied by the state Health Department over pollution problems that have kept the beach at Kualoa Regional Park closed for months at a time over the past several years, officials said yesterday.

The state also ordered city officials to act immediately to fix the ongoing problem.

The issue goes back to at least 2000 when the Health Department cited the city for a sewage spill at the park. In 2003, the city proposed a new, $1.3 million wastewater system there. Construction stalled over cultural and other concerns, and work isn't likely to begin before the end of the year, city officials said yesterday.

News of the fine set off a new round of frustration in the community.

"I don't care who is responsible. I just want somebody to do something about it," said Wayne Panoke, a member of the Kahalu'u Neighborhood Board and the Ko'olauloa Hawaiian Civic Club. "It's ridiculous. Why are they taking so long? We've waited long enough. When is something going to get done?". . .

The city hopes to put a contract out to bid by the end of the year for permanent repairs to the wastewater system at the park.

—Mike Leidemann

Source: *Honolulu Advertiser,* March 8, 2007. Reprinted by permission.

Analysis: The pollution that closes beaches can be avoided with better sewage treatment facilities. Who should bear that cost?

originating in residential and commercial use is considered more dangerous, however, simply because it accumulates where people live. New York City alone generates 24,000 tons of trash a day. Because it has neither the land area nor the incinerators needed for disposal, it must ship its garbage to other states. Seattle ships its trash to Oregon; Los Angeles transports its trash to the Mojave Desert; New York City sludge is dumped in west Texas; and Philadelphia ships its garbage all the way to Panama.

POLLUTION DAMAGES

Shipping garbage to Panama is an expensive answer to our waste disposal problem. But even those costs are a small fraction of the total cost of environmental damage. Much greater costs are associated with the damage to our health (labor), buildings (capital), and land. Even the little things count, like being able to enjoy a clear sunset or take a deep breath.

Although many people don't like to put a price on the environment, some monetary measure of environmental damage is important in decision making. Unless we value the environment above everything else, we have to establish some method of ranking the importance of environmental damage. Although it's tempting to say that clean air is priceless, ***we won't get clean air unless we spend resources to get it.*** This economic reality suggests that we begin by determining how much cleaner air is worth to us.

Assigning Prices

In some cases, it's fairly easy to put a price on environmental damage. Scientists can measure the increase in cancer, heart attacks, and other disorders attributable to air pollution, as the EPA does for air toxins (see News on next page). Engineers can also measure the rate at which buildings decay or forests and lakes die. Economists can then estimate the dollar value of this damage by assessing the economic value of lives, forests, lakes, and other resources. For example, if people are willing to pay $5,000 for a cataract operation, then the avoidance of such eye damage is worth at least $5,000. Saving a tree is worth whatever the marketplace is willing to pay for the products of that tree. Using such computations, the EPA estimates that air pollution alone inflicts health, property, and vegetation damage in excess of $50 billion a year.

The Earth Policy Institute offers data on the costs of pollution at www.earth-policy.org

IN THE NEWS   

Dirty Air Can Shorten Your Life

The largest study ever conducted on the health effects of airborne particles from traffic and smokestacks has found that people in the nation's most polluted cities are 15 to 17 percent more likely to die prematurely than those in cities with the cleanest air.

This form of pollution is killing citizens even in areas that meet Environmental Protection Agency air quality standards, said study coauthor Douglas Dockery of the Harvard School of Public Health, who said "the impact on life and health is more pervasive than previously thought."

In Washington, where levels of airborne particles fall in the low middle range for U.S. cities, the average long-term resident loses approximately one year of life expectancy compared to the average for such relatively pristine places as Topeka, Kan., or Madison, Wis., Dockery said. In highly polluted places like Los Angeles or Salt Lake City, the toll is much greater: Compared to people in the cleanest metropolitan areas, those exposed to the highest concentrations of particles run a risk of premature death about one-sixth as great as if they had been smoking for 25 years.

—Curt Suplee

Source: *The Washington Post,* March 10, 1995. www.washingtonpost.com

Analysis: Pollution entails real costs, as measured by impaired health, reduced life spans, and other damages.

The job of pricing environmental damage is much more difficult with intangible losses like sunsets. Nevertheless, when governmental agencies and courts are asked to assess the damages of oil spills and other accidents, they must try to inventory *all* costs, including polluted sunsets, reduced wildlife, and lost recreation opportunities. The science of computing such environmental damage is very inexact. Nevertheless, crude but reasonable procedures generate damage estimates measured in hundreds of billions of dollars per year.

Cleanup Possibilities

One of the most frustrating things about all this environmental damage is that it can be avoided. The EPA estimates that *95 percent of current air and water pollution could be eliminated by known and available technology.* Nothing very exotic is needed: just simple things like auto-emission controls, smokestack cleaners, improved sewage and waste treatment facilities, and cooling towers for electric power plants. Even solid-waste pollution could be reduced by comparable proportions if we used less packaging, recycled more materials, or transformed our garbage into a useful (relatively low-polluting) energy source. The critical question here is, Why don't we do these things? Why do we continue to pollute so much?

MARKET INCENTIVES

Previous chapters emphasized how market incentives influence the behavior of individual consumers, firms, and government agencies. Incentives in the form of price reductions can be used to change consumer buying habits. Incentives in the form of high profit margins encourage production of desired goods and services. And market incentives in the form of cost differentials help allocate resources efficiently. Accordingly, we shouldn't be too surprised to learn that ***market incentives play a major role in pollution behavior.***

The Production Decision

production decision: The selection of the short-run rate of output (with existing plant and equipment).

Imagine that you're the majority stockholder and manager of an electric power plant. Such plants are responsible for a significant amount of air pollution (especially sulfur dioxide and particulates) and nearly all thermal water pollution. Hence, your position immediately puts you on the most-wanted list of pollution offenders. But suppose you're civic minded and would truly like to help eliminate pollution. Let's consider the alternatives.

As the owner-manager of an electric power plant, you'll strive to make a profit-maximizing **production decision.** That is, you'll seek the rate of output at which marginal revenue equals marginal cost. Let's assume that the electric power industry is still regulated by the

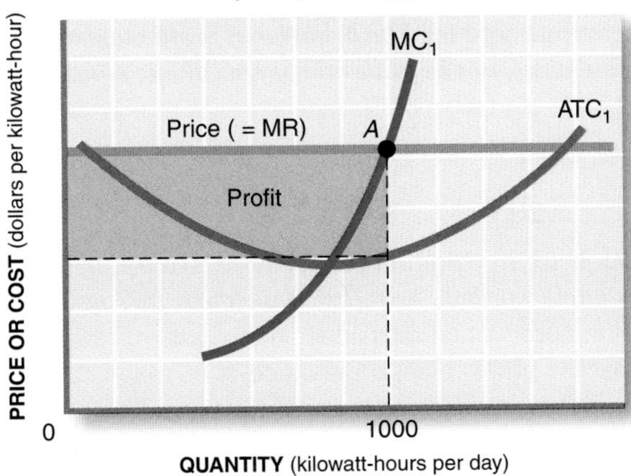

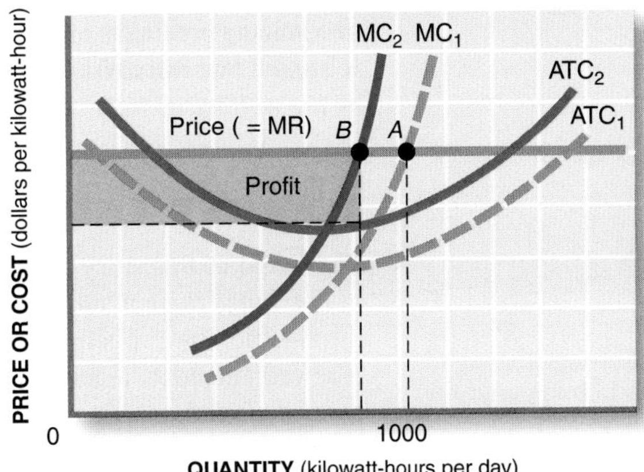

FIGURE 28.1
Profit Maximization in Electric Power Production

Production processes that control pollution may be more expensive than those that don't. If they are, the MC and ATC curves will shift upward (to MC_2 and ATC_2). At the new profit-maximizing rate of output (point *B*), output and total profit shrink. Hence, a producer has an incentive to continue polluting, using cheaper technology.

state power commission so that the price of electricity is fixed, at least in the short run. The effect of this assumption is to render marginal revenue equal to price, thus giving us a horizontal price line, as in Figure 28.1*a*.

Figure 28.1*a* also depicts the marginal and average total costs (MC and ATC) associated with the production of electricity. By equating marginal cost (MC) to price (marginal revenue, MR), we observe (point *A*) that profit maximization occurs at an output of 1,000 kilowatt-hours per day. Total profits are illustrated by the shaded rectangle between the price line and the average total cost (ATC) curve.

The Efficiency Decision

efficiency decision: The choice of a production process for any given rate of output.

The profits illustrated in Figure 28.1*a* are achieved in part by use of the cheapest available fuel under the boilers (which create the steam that rotates the generators). Recall that the construction of a marginal cost curve presumes some knowledge of alternative production processes. Recall too that the **efficiency decision** requires a producer to choose that production process (and its associated cost curve) that minimizes costs for any particular rate of output.

Costs of Pollution Abatement. Unfortunately, the efficiency decision in this case leads to the use of high-sulfur coal, the prime villain in SO_2 and particulate pollution. Other fuels, such as low-sulfur coal, fuel oil, and nuclear energy, cost considerably more. Were you to switch to one of them, the ATC and MC curves would both shift upward, as in Figure 28.1*b*. Under these conditions, the most profitable rate of output would be lower than before (point *B*), and total profits would decline (note the smaller profit rectangle in Figure 28.1*b*). Thus, ***pollution abatement can be achieved, but only at significant cost to the plant.***

The same kind of cost considerations lead the plant to engage in thermal pollution. Cool water must be run through an electric utility plant to keep the turbines from overheating. Once the water has run through the plant, it's too hot to recirculate. It must be either dumped back into the adjacent river or cooled off by being circulated through cooling towers. As you might expect, it's cheaper to simply dump the hot water in the river. The fish don't like it, but they don't have to pay the construction costs associated with cooling towers.

The big question here is whether you and your fellow stockholders would be willing to incur higher costs in order to cut down on pollution. Eliminating either the air pollution or the water pollution emanating from the electric plant will cost a lot of money. And to whose benefit? To the people who live downstream and downwind? We don't expect profit-maximizing producers to take such concerns into account. ***The behavior of profit maximizers is guided by comparisons of revenues and costs, not by philanthropy, aesthetic concerns, or the welfare of fish.***

MARKET FAILURE: EXTERNAL COSTS

The moral of this story—and the critical factor in pollution behavior—is that ***people tend to maximize their personal welfare, balancing private benefits against private costs.*** For the electric power plant, this means making production decisions on the basis of revenues received and costs incurred. The fact that the power plant imposes costs on others, in the form of air and water pollution, is irrelevant to its profit-maximizing decisions. Those costs are *external* to the firm and don't appear on its profit-and-loss statement. Those **external costs**—or *externalities*—are no less real, but they're incurred by society at large rather than by the firm.

external cost: Cost of a market activity borne by a third party; the difference between the social and private costs of a market activity.

Externalities in Production

Whenever external costs exist, a private firm won't allocate its resources and operate its plant in such a way as to maximize social welfare. In effect, society permits the power plant the free use of valued resources—clean air and clean water. The power plant has a tremendous incentive to substitute those resources for others (such as high-priced fuel or cooling towers) in the production process. The inefficiency of such an arrangement is obvious when we recall that the function of markets is to allocate scarce resources in accordance with the consumer's expressed demands. Yet here we are, proclaiming a high value for clean air and clean water and encouraging the power plant to use up both resources by offering them at zero cost to the firm.

The inefficiency of this market arrangement can be expressed in terms of a distinction between social costs and private costs. **Social costs** are the total costs of all the resources used in a particular production activity. On the other hand, **private costs** are the resource costs incurred by the specific producer.

social costs: The full resource costs of an economic activity, including externalities.

private costs: The costs of an economic activity directly borne by the immediate producer or consumer (excluding externalities).

Ideally, a producer's private costs will encompass all the attendant social costs, and production decisions will be consistent with our social welfare. Unfortunately, this happy identity doesn't always exist, as our experience with the power plant illustrates. ***When social***

"Where there's smoke, there's money."

Analysis: If a firm can substitute external costs for private (internal) costs, its profits may increase.

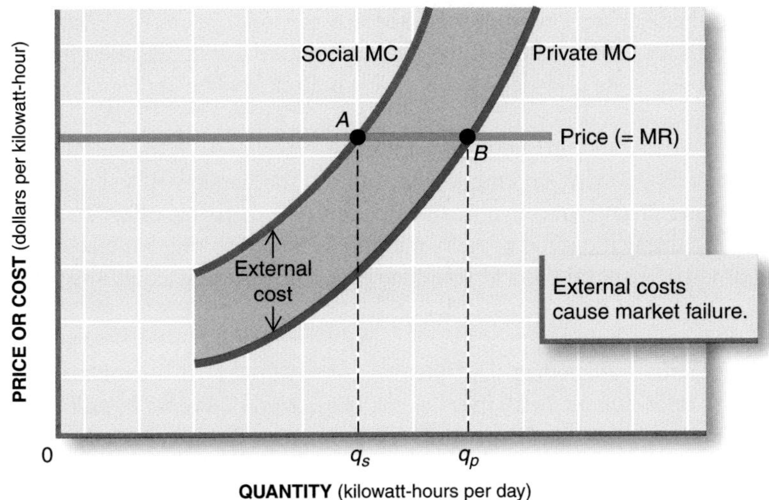

FIGURE 28.2
Market Failure

Social costs exceed private costs by the amount of external costs. Production decisions based on private costs alone will lead us to point *B,* where private MC = MR. At point *B,* the rate of output is q_p.

To maximize social welfare, we equate *social* MC and MR, as at point *A.* Only q_s of output is socially desirable. The failure of the market to convey the full costs of production keeps us from attaining this outcome.

costs differ from private costs, external costs exist. In fact, external costs are equal to the difference between the social and private costs—that is,

$$\text{External costs} = \text{social costs} - \text{private costs}$$

When external costs are present, the market mechanism won't allocate resources efficiently. This is a case of **market failure.** The price signal confronting producers is flawed. By not conveying the full (social) cost of scarce resources, the market encourages excessive pollution. We end up with a suboptimal mix of output (too much electricity, too little clean air) and the wrong production processes.

market failure: An imperfection in the market mechanism that prevents optimal outcomes.

The consequences of this market failure are illustrated in Figure 28.2, which again depicts the cost situation confronting the electric power plant. Notice that we use *two* different marginal cost curves this time. The lower one, the *private* MC curve, reflects the private costs incurred by the power plant when it operates on a profit-maximization basis, using high-sulfur coal and no cooling towers. It's identical to the MC curve in Figure 28.1*a*. We now know, however, that such operations impose external costs on others in the form of air and water pollution. These external costs must be added on to private marginal costs. When this is done, we get a *social* marginal cost curve that lies above the private MC curve.

To maximize profits, private firms seek the rate of output that equates private MC to MR (price). ***To maximize social welfare, we need to equate social marginal cost to marginal revenue (price).*** This social optimum occurs at point *A* in Figure 28.2 and results in output of q_s. By contrast, the firm's private profit maximization occurs at point *B*, where q_p is produced. Hence, the private firm ends up producing more output than socially desired, while earning more profit and causing more pollution. As a general rule, ***if pollution costs are external, firms will produce too much of a polluting good.***

Externalities in Consumption

A divergence between private and social costs can also be observed in consumption. Consumers try to maximize their personal welfare. We buy and use more of those goods and services that yield the highest satisfaction (marginal utility) per dollar expended. By implication (and the law of demand), we tend to use more of a product if we can get it at a discount—that is, pay less than the full price. Unfortunately, the "discount" often takes the form of an external cost imposed on neighbors and friends.

Automobile driving illustrates the problem. The amount of driving one does is influenced by the price of a car and the marginal costs of driving it. People buy smaller cars and drive less when the attendant marginal costs (for instance, gasoline prices) increase substantially. But automobile use involves not only *private costs* but *external costs* as well. Auto emissions (carbon monoxide, hydrocarbons, and nitrogen oxides) are a principal cause of air pollution. In effect, automobile drivers have been able to use a valued resource, clean air, at no cost to themselves. Few motorists see any personal benefit in installing exhaust control devices because the quality of the air they breathe would be little affected by their efforts. Hence, low private costs lead to excessive pollution when high social costs are dictating cleaner air.

A divergence between social and private costs can be observed even in the simplest of consumer activities, such as throwing an empty soda can out the window of your car. To hang on to the can and later dispose of it in a trash barrel involves personal effort and thus private marginal costs. To throw it out the window not only is more exciting but also effectively transfers the burden of disposal costs to someone else. The resulting externality ends up as roadside litter.

The same kind of divergence between private and social costs helps explain why people abandon old cars in the street rather than haul them to scrapyards. It also explains why people use vacant lots as open dumps. In all these cases, ***the polluter benefits by substituting external costs for private costs.*** In other words, market incentives encourage environmental damage.

REGULATORY OPTIONS

The failure of the market to include external costs in production and consumption decisions creates a basis for government intervention. As always, however, we confront a variety of policy options. We may define these options in terms of ***two general strategies for environmental protection:***

- ***Alter market incentives*** in such a way that they discourage pollution.
- ***Bypass market incentives*** with some form of regulatory intervention.

Market-Based Options

Insofar as market incentives are concerned, the key to environmental protection is to eliminate the divergence between private costs and social costs. The opportunity to shift some costs onto others lies at the heart of the pollution problem. If we could somehow compel producers to *internalize* all costs—pay for both private and previously external costs—the divergence would disappear, along with the incentive to pollute.

emission charge: A fee imposed on polluters, based on the quantity of pollution.

Emission Charges. One possibility is to establish a system of **emission charges,** direct costs attached to the act of polluting. Suppose that we let you keep your power plant and permit you to operate it according to profit-maximizing principles. The only difference is that we no longer supply you with clean air and cool water at zero cost. From now on, we'll charge you for these scarce resources. We might, say, charge 2 cents for every gram of noxious emission discharged into the air. In addition we might charge 3 cents for every gallon of water you use, heat, and discharge back into the river.

Confronted with such emission charges, you'd have to alter your production decision. ***An emission charge increases private marginal cost and encourages lower output and cleaner technology.*** Figure 28.3 illustrates this effect. Notice how the fee raises private marginal costs and induces a lower rate of (polluting) production (q_1 rather than q_0).

Once an emission fee is in place, a producer may also reevaluate the efficiency decision. Consider again the choice of fuels to be used in our fictional power plant. We earlier chose high-sulfur coal, for the very good reason that it was the cheapest fuel available. Now, however, there's an additional cost attached to burning such fuel, in the form of an emission charge. This added cost may encourage the firm to switch to cleaner sources of energy, which would increase private marginal costs but reduce emission fees.

An emission charge might also persuade a firm to incur higher fixed costs. Rather than pay emission charges, it might be more economical to install scrubbers and other smokestack controls that reduce the volume of emissions from the burning of high-sulfur coal. This would entail additional capital outlays for the necessary abatement equipment but might not alter marginal costs. In this case, the fee-induced change in fixed costs might reduce pollution without any reduction in output.

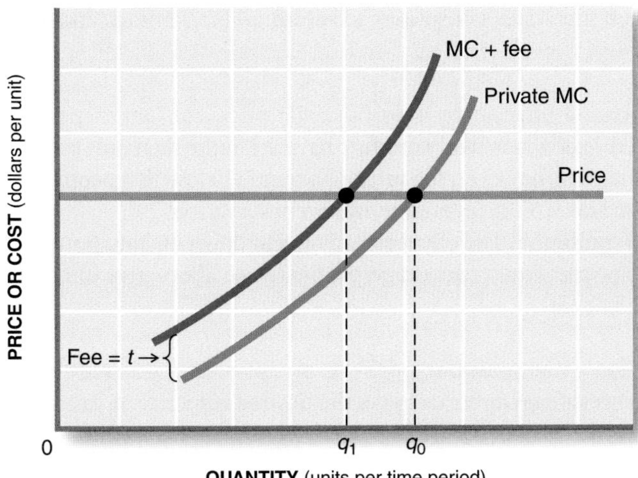

FIGURE 28.3
Emission Fees

Emission charges can be used to close the gap between marginal social costs and marginal private costs. Faced with an emission charge of t, a private producer will reduce output from q_0 to q_1. Emission charges may also induce different investment and efficiency decisions.

The actual response of producers will depend on the relative costs involved. If emission charges are too low, it may be more profitable to continue burning and polluting with high-sulfur coal and simply pay a nominal fee. This is a simple pricing problem. We could set the emission price higher, prompting the behavioral responses we desire.

The same kind of relative cost considerations would apply to the thermal pollution associated with the power plant. The choice heretofore has been between building expensive cooling towers (and not polluting) or not incurring such capital costs (and simply discharging the heated water into the river). The profit-maximizing choice was fairly obvious. Now, however, the choice is between building cooling towers or paying out a steady flow of emission charges. The profit-maximizing decision is no longer evident. The decisive factor will be how high we set the emission charges. If the emission charges are set high enough, the producer will find it unprofitable to pollute.

Economic incentives can also change consumer behavior. At one time, beverage producers imposed deposits to encourage consumers to bring the bottle back so it could be used again. But producers discovered that such deposits discouraged sales and yielded very little cost savings. Today, returnable bottles are rarely used. One result is the inclusion of over 30 billion bottles and 60 billion cans in our solid-waste disposal problem. We could reverse this trend by imposing a deposit on all beverage containers. Many states do this, at least for certain cans and bottles. Such deposits internalize pollution costs for the consumer and render the throwing of a soda can out the window equivalent to throwing away money.

Some communities have also tried to reduce solid-waste processing by charging a fee for each container of garbage collected. In Charlotte, Virginia, a fee of 80 cents per 32-gallon bag of garbage had a noticeable impact on consumer behavior. Economists Don Fullerton and Thomas Kinnaman observed that households reduced the weight of their garbage by 14 percent and the volume by 37 percent. As they noted, "Households somehow stomped their garbage to get more in a container and trim their garbage bill."

Recycling Materials. An important bonus that emission charges offer is an increased incentive for the recycling of materials. The glass and metal in used bottles and cans can be recycled to produce new bottles and cans. Such recycling not only eliminates a lot of unsightly litter but also diminishes the need to mine new resources from the earth, a process that often involves its own environmental problems. The critical issues are once again relative costs and market incentives. ***A container producer has no incentive to use recycled materials unless they offer superior cost efficiency and thus greater profits.*** The largest component in the costs of recycled materials is usually the associated costs of collection and transportation. In this regard, an emission charge such as the 5-cent container deposit

webnote

Trends in recycling are posted by the U.S. Environmental Protection Agency (EPA) at www.epa.gov/epaoswer/non-hw/muncpl/recycle.htm

lowers collection costs because it motivates consumers to return all their bottles and cans to a central location.

Higher User Fees. Another market alternative is to raise the price consumers pay for scarce resources. If people used less water, we wouldn't have to build so many sewage treatment plants. In most communities, however, the price of water is so low that people use it indiscriminately. Higher water fees would encourage water conservation.

A similar logic applies to auto pollution. The cheapest way to cut down on auto pollution is to drive less. Higher gasoline prices would encourage people to use alternative transportation and drive more fuel-efficient cars.

"Green" Taxes. Automakers don't want gasoline prices to go up; neither do consumers. So the government may have to impose *green taxes* to get the desired response. A green tax on gasoline, for example, raises the price of gasoline. The taxes not only curb auto emissions (less driving) but also create a revenue source for other pollution-abatement efforts. As the World View on the next page indicates, other nations impose far more green taxes than does the United States. Because public opinion polls show that a plurality of American consumers oppose such taxes, this disparity isn't likely to disappear.

Pollution Fines. Not far removed from the concept of emission and user charges is the imposition of fines or liability for cleanup costs. In some situations, such as an oil spill, the pollution is so sudden and concentrated that society has little choice but to clean it up quickly. The costs for such cleanup can be imposed on the polluter, however, through appropriate fines. Such fines place the cost burden where it belongs. In addition, they serve as an incentive for greater safety, for such things as double-hulled oil tankers and more efficient safety mechanisms on offshore oil wells. When Royal Caribbean Cruises was fined $9 million in 1998 for dumping garbage and oil from its cruise ships, the firm decided to monitor waste disposal practices more closely. In the absence of such fines, firms have little incentive to invest in environmental protection. The Comprehensive Environmental Response, Compensation, and Liability Act of 1980 allows the EPA to recoup *treble* damages from a firm that causes a hazardous spill but fails to help clean it up.

Tradable Pollution Permits

Another environmental policy option makes even greater use of market incentives. Rather than penalize firms that have already polluted, let firms *purchase* the right to continue polluting. As crazy as this policy might sound, it can be highly effective in limiting environmental damage.

The key to the success of pollution permits is that they're bought and sold among private firms. The system starts with a government-set standard for pollution reduction. Firms that reduce pollution by more than the standard earn pollution credits. They may then sell these credits to other firms, who are thereby relieved of cleanup chores. ***The principal advantage of pollution permits is their incentive to minimize the cost of pollution control.***

To see how the permits work, suppose the policy objective is to reduce sulfur dioxide emissions by 2 tons. There are only two major polluters in the community: a copper smelter and an electric utility. Should each company be required to reduce its SO_2 emissions by 1 ton? Or can the same SO_2 reduction be achieved more cheaply with marketable pollution rights?

Table 28.1 depicts the assumed cost of pollution abatement at each plant. The copper smelter would have to spend $200 to achieve a 1-ton reduction in SO_2 emissions. The utility can do it for only $100. Table 28.1 also indicates that the utility can attain a *second* ton of SO_2 abatement for $150. Even though its marginal cost of pollution control is increasing, the utility still has lower abatement costs than the smelter. This cost advantage creates an interesting economic opportunity.

Recall that the policy goal is to reduce emissions by 2 tons. The copper smelter would have to spend $200 to achieve its share. But the utility can abate that second ton for $150.

WORLD VIEW

Guess Who Taxes Pollution Least?

Making a Mess Costs Less in the U.S.

Economists have long argued that an efficient way to control pollution is to make those who cause it bear some of the costs via environmentally related or "green" taxes. These can run the gamut from retail taxes on gasoline to landfill charges on waste disposal.

By dint of its economic heft, the U.S. is commonly regarded as the world's biggest polluter. Yet the Organization for Economic Cooperation & Development reports that it imposes the lowest green taxes as a percent of gross domestic product of any industrial nation. While the average for OECD countries in 1998 was 2.7 percent of GDP, for example, the U.S. level was estimated at less than 1 percent.

Between 1994 and 1998, a majority of OECD members boosted their green-tax ratios, with Denmark's and Turkey's both rising by a full percentage point to 5 percent and 3 percent respectively. By contrast, the U.S., Germany, and France actually reduced their green-tax levels over the four-year period.

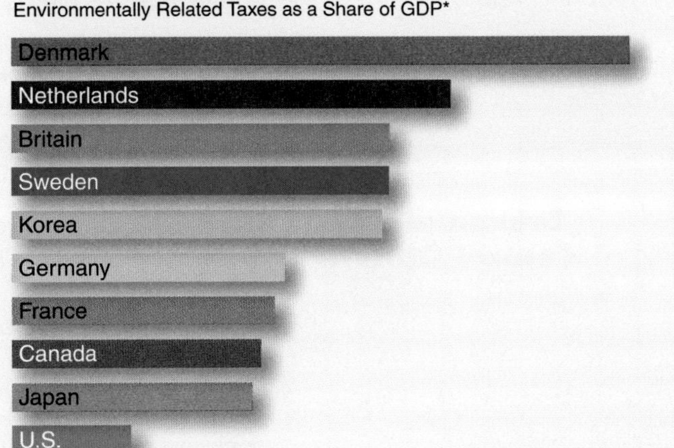

Source: *BusinessWeek,* September 17, 2001. © 2001 The McGraw-Hill Companies, Inc. Reprinted with permission. www.businessweek.com

Analysis: "Green" taxes can be used to reduce the level of polluting consumption or production activities. They are not popular in the United States, however.

Accordingly, the smelter would save money by *paying* the utility for additional pollution abatement.

How much would the smelter have to pay? The utility would want at least $150 to cover its own costs. The smelter would benefit at any price below $200. Accordingly, the price of this transaction would be somewhere between $150 (the utility's cost) and $200 (the smelter's cost). The smelter would continue to pollute, but total SO_2 emissions would still drop by 2 tons. Both firms and society would be better off.

At the first real auction of pollution credits the average price paid was $156. For this price a firm could pay someone else to reduce SO_2 emissions by 1 ton rather than curb its own emissions. The Carolina Power and Light Company spent $11.5 *million* buying such permits.

Since they first became available in 1992, tradable pollution permits ("allowances") have become a popular mechanism for pollution control. Millions of allowances are now traded in the open market every year. Moreover, the permit market has gotten increasingly efficient, with visible bid and ask prices, broker specialists, and low transaction costs. In

webnote

The Environmental Protection Agency has a Web site (www.epa.gov/acidrain) that explains the sulfur dioxide allowance trading system. The site also provides information on trading volume and prices. A private brokerage firm also offers a succinct explanation of permit trading and more timely prices; see www.emissionstrading.com

TABLE 28.1
Pricing Pollution Permits

If both firms reduce emissions by 1 ton each, the cost is $300. If the utility instead reduces emissions by 2 tons, the cost is only $250. A permit system allows the smelter to pay the utility for assuming the added abatement responsibility.

	Marginal Cost of Pollution Abatement	
Reduction in Emissions (in tons)	**Copper Smelter**	**Electric Utility**
1	$200	$100
2	250	150
3	300	200

2000, 12.7 *million* sulfur dioxide allowances were traded, each covering one ton of emission reduction. The price of a permit has also steadily declined, indicating that companies are discovering cheaper methods of pollution control. Entrepreneurs now have an incentive to discover cheaper methods for pollution abatement. They don't have to own a smelter or utility; they can now *sell* their pollution control expertise to the highest bidder. As the market for permits has expanded, the profit opportunities for environmental engineering firms have increased. This has accelerated productivity and reduced the cost of pollution abatement by 25 to 34 percent. In view of these results, the EPA extended the pollution-permit trading system to *water* pollution in 2003 and the European Union extended it to carbon dioxide emissions in 2005 (see World View).

Command-and-Control Options

Public policy needn't rely on tradable permits or other market incentives to achieve desired pollution abatement. The government could instead simply *require* firms to reduce pollutants by specific amounts and even specify which abatement technology must be used. This approach is often referred to as the "command-and-control" option. The government *commands* firms to reduce pollution and then *controls* the process for doing so.

The potential inefficiency of the command-and-control strategy was outlined earlier in Table 28.1. Had the government required *each* firm to reduce pollution by 1 ton, the total cost would have been $300. By allowing firms to use tradable permits, the cost of obtaining the same level of pollution abatement was only $250. The cost saving of $50 represents valuable resources that could be used to produce other desired goods and services.

Despite the superior efficiency of market-based environmental policies, the government often relies on the command-and-control approach. The Clean Air Acts of 1970 and 1990, for example, mandated not only fewer auto emissions but also specific processes such as catalytic converters and lead-free gasoline for attaining them. Specific processes and technologies are also required for toxic waste disposal and water treatment. Laws requiring the sorting and recycling of trash are other examples of process regulation.

Although such command-and-control regulation can be effective, this policy option also

WORLD VIEW

Paying to Pollute

System Would Limit Emission, Allow Trading of Credits

It costs nothing to pump greenhouse gases into the air. . . .

That is starting to change.

Driven by fears of global warming, countries and states are trying to place a price tag on emissions of carbon dioxide, the gas considered most responsible for rising temperatures.

They are turning to a system called "cap and trade," which limits the overall amount of carbon dioxide an area or industry can emit and then lets individual companies buy and sell credits to release specific amounts of the gas.

The cap-and-trade concept is considered an alternative to strict government mandates. It tries to use market dynamics to cut pollution, allowing flexibility on emission levels—for a price. Emissions that were free in the past, regardless of their environmental cost, now would cost an amount set by the market.

In theory at least, it allows businesses that emit carbon dioxide to choose the most cost-effective way to cut their emissions. And it gives them leeway in the speed of their cuts. . . .

Europe has a carbon dioxide market up and running, with release of a ton of gas now trading at 27 euros, about $32. New York and six other Eastern states plan to open one in 2009. California energy regulators last week took the first step toward such a system.

—David R. Baker

Source: *San Francisco Chronicle,* February 19, 2006, p. J1.

Analysis: Marketable pollution permits encourage firms with more efficient pollution control technologies to overachieve, thereby earning pollution permits that can be sold to firms with more expensive pollution control technologies. Such trades reduce the *average* cost of pollution control.

entails risks. By requiring all market participants to follow specific rules, the regulations may impose excessive costs on some activities and too low a constraint on others. Some communities may not need the level of sewage treatment the federal government prescribes. Individual households may not generate enough trash to make sorting and separate pickups economically sound. Some producers may have better or cheaper ways of attaining environmental standards. ***Excessive process regulation may raise the costs of environmental protection*** and discourage cost-saving innovation. There's also the risk of regulated processes becoming entrenched long after they are obsolete. When that happens we may end up with worse outcomes than a less regulated market would have generated—that is, **government failure.**

government failure: Government intervention that fails to improve economic outcomes.

BALANCING BENEFITS AND COSTS

Protecting the environment entails costs as well as benefits. Installing smokestack scrubbers on factory chimneys and catalytic converters on cars requires the use of scarce resources. Taking the lead out of gasoline wears out engines faster and requires expensive changes in technology. Switching to clean fuels requires enormous investments in technology, plant, and equipment. The EPA estimates that a 10-year program to achieve national air and water standards would cost more than $1 trillion. Restoring the ozone layer, removing hazardous wastes, and cleaning up the rest of the environment would cost trillions more.

Opportunity Costs

Although cleaning up the environment is a universally acknowledged goal, we must remind ourselves that those resources could be used to fulfill other goals as well. The multitrillion-dollar tab would buy a lot of subways and parks or build decent homes for the poor. If we choose to devote those resources instead to pollution-abatement efforts, we'll have to forgo some other goods and services. This isn't to say that environmental goals don't deserve that kind of priority but simply to remind us that any use of our scarce resources involves an **opportunity cost.**

opportunity cost: The most desired goods or services that are forgone in order to obtain something else.

Fortunately, the amount of additional resources required to clean up the environment is relatively modest in comparison to our productive capacity. Over a 10-year period we'll produce well over $150 trillion of goods and services (GDP). On this basis, the environmental expenditures contemplated by present environmental policies and goals represent only 1 to 3 percent of total output.

The Optimal Rate of Pollution

Spending even a small percentage of GDP on environmental protection entails value judgments. The **optimal rate of pollution** occurs at the point at which the opportunity costs of further pollution control equal the benefits of further reductions in pollution. To determine the optimal rate of pollution, we need to compare the marginal social benefits of additional pollution abatement with the marginal social costs of additional pollution control expenditure. The optimal rate of pollution is achieved when we've satisfied the following equality:

optimal rate of pollution: The rate of pollution that occurs when the marginal social benefit of pollution control equals its marginal social cost.

$$\text{Optimal rate of pollution}: \text{marginal benefit of pollution abatement} = \text{marginal cost of pollution abatement}$$

This formulation is analogous to the utility-maximizing rule in consumption. If another dollar spent on pollution control yields less than a dollar of social benefits, then additional pollution control expenditure isn't desirable. In such a situation, the goods and services that would be forsaken for additional pollution control are more valued than the environmental improvements that would result.

A 2003 White House study concluded that past efforts to clean up the air have yielded far more benefits than costs. As the accompanying News reports, the benefits of a 10-year (1992–2002) air pollution abatement program were five to seven times greater than its cost.

webnote

OMB's annual cost-benefit analysis of pollution control is at www.omb.gov.

Although pollution abatement has been an economic success, that doesn't mean *all* pollution controls are desirable. The focus must still be on *marginal* benefits and costs. In that context, a surprising conclusion emerges, namely ***a totally clean environment isn't economically desirable.*** The marginal benefit of achieving zero pollution is infinitesimally small. But

IN THE NEWS  

Study Finds Net Gain from Pollution Rules

A new White House study concludes that environmental regulations are well worth the costs they impose on industry and consumers, resulting in significant public health improvements and other benefits to society. . . .

The report, issued this month by the Office of Management and Budget, concludes that the health and social benefits of enforcing tough new clean-air regulations during the past decade were five to seven times greater in economic terms than were the costs of complying with the rules. The value of reductions in hospitalization and emergency room visits, premature deaths and lost workdays resulting from improved air quality were estimated between $120 billion and $193 billion from October 1992 to September 2002.

By comparison, industry, states and municipalities spent an estimated $23 billion to $26 billion to retrofit plants and facilities and make other changes to comply with new clean-air standards, which are designed to sharply reduce sulfur dioxide, fine-particle emissions and other health-threatening pollutants.

—Eric Pianin

Source: *The Washington Post,* September 27, 2003.

Analysis: The benefits of pollution abatement have generally exceeded its costs. However, *marginal* benefits and costs are critical in setting policy goals.

the marginal cost of eliminating that last particle of pollution will be very high. As we weigh the marginal benefits and costs, we'll conclude that *some* pollution is cost-effective.

Cost-Benefit Analysis

Although marginal analysis tells us that a zero-pollution goal isn't economically desirable, it doesn't really pinpoint the optimal level of pollution. To apply those guidelines we need to identify and evaluate the marginal benefits of any intervention and its marginal costs. Sometimes such calculations yield extraordinarily high cost-benefit ratios. According to researchers at the Harvard Center for Risk Analysis, the *median* cost per life-year saved by EPA regulations is $7.6 million. One of the highest cost-benefit ratios is attached to chloroform emission controls at pulp mills: The cost per life-year saved exceeds $99 billion. A human life may in fact be too precious to value in dollars and cents. But in a world of limited resources, the opportunity costs of every intervention need to be assessed. How many lives would be saved if we spent $99 billion on cancer or AIDS research?

Mayor Bloomberg performed the same kind of analysis for New York City's recycling program. Sure, everyone thinks recycling is a good idea. But Mayor Bloomberg started looking at the cost of the recycling program and decided it didn't make economic sense (see following News). He figured the city could use the $57 million for higher-priority programs, yielding greater (marginal) benefits to NYC residents.

Who Will Pay?

The costs of pollution control aren't distributed equally. In New York City, the cost of the recycling program is borne by those who end up with fewer city services and amenities (opportunity costs). A national pollution-abatement program would target the relatively small number of economic activities that account for the bulk of emissions and effluents. These activities will have to bear a disproportionate share of the cleanup burden.

To ascertain how the burden of environmental protection will be distributed, consider first the electric power plant discussed earlier. As we observed (Figure 28.2), the plant's output will decrease if production decisions are based on social rather than private marginal costs—that is, if environmental consequences are considered. If the plant itself is compelled to pay full social costs, in the form of either compulsory investment or emission charges, its profits will be reduced. Were no other changes to take place, the burden of environmental improvements would be borne primarily by the producer.

Such a scenario is unlikely, however. Rather than absorb all the costs of pollution controls themselves, producers will seek to pass on some of this burden to their customers in the form of higher prices. Their ability to do so will depend on the extent of competition in

webnote

Find out how economists measure the costs and benefits of environmental programs at www.epa.gov. Click on "Programs," then "Research," then "Office of Research and Development."

IN THE NEWS

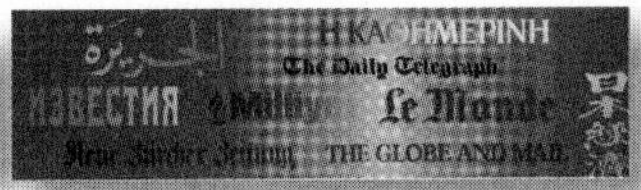

Forced Recycling Is a Waste

As New York City faces the possibility of painful cuts to its police and fire department budgets, environmentalists are bellyaching over garbage. Mayor Michael Bloomberg's proposed budget for 2003 would temporarily suspend the city's recycling of metal, glass and plastic, saving New Yorkers $57 million.

The city's recycling program—like many others around the country—has long hemorrhaged tax dollars. . . .

The city spends about $240 per ton to "recycle" plastic, glass, and metal, while the cost of simply sending waste to landfills is about $130 per ton.

You don't need a degree in economics to see that something is wrong here. Isn't recycling supposed to save money and resources? Some recycling does—when driven by market forces. Private parties don't voluntarily recycle unless they know it will save money, and, hence, resources. But forced recycling can be a waste of both because recycling itself entails using energy, water and labor to collect, sort, clean and process the materials. There are also air emissions, traffic and wear on streets from the second set of trucks prowling for recyclables. The bottom line is that most mandated recycling hurts, not helps the environment. . . .

"You could do a lot better things in the world with $57 million," says Mayor Bloomberg.

—Angela Logomasini

Analysis: Recycling uses scarce resources that could be employed elsewhere. The benefits of recycling may not exceed its (opportunity) costs.

their industry, their relative cost position in it, and the price elasticity of consumer demand. In reality, the electric power industry isn't very competitive as yet, and its prices are still subject to government regulation. In addition, consumer demand is relatively price-inelastic. Accordingly, the profit-maximizing producer will appeal to the state or local power commission for an increase in electricity prices based on the costs of pollution control. Electric power consumers are likely to end up footing part or all of the environmental bill. The increased prices will more fully reflect the social costs associated with electricity use.

In addition to the electric power industry, the automobile, paper, steel, and chemical industries will be adversely affected by pollution controls. In all of these cases, the prices of the related products will increase, in some instances by significant percentages. These price increases will help reduce pollution in two ways. First, they'll help pay for pollution control equipment. Second, they'll encourage consumers to change their expenditure patterns in the direction of less polluting goods.

THE ECONOMY TOMORROW

THE GREENHOUSE THREAT

Forget about littered beaches, smelly landfills, eye-stinging smog, and contaminated water. The really scary problem for the economy tomorrow is much more serious: Some scientists say that the carbon emissions we're now spewing into the air are warming the earth's atmosphere. If the earth's temperature rises only a few degrees, they contend, polar caps will melt, continents will flood, and weather patterns will go haywire (see World View on the next page). If things get bad enough, there may not be any economy tomorrow.

The Greenhouse Effect. The earth's climate is driven by solar radiation. The energy the sun absorbs must be balanced by outgoing radiation from the earth and the atmosphere. Scientists fear that a flow imbalance is developing. Of particular concern is a buildup of carbon dioxide (CO_2) that might trap heat in the earth's atmosphere, warming the planet.

The natural release of CO_2 dwarfs the emissions from human activities. But there's a concern that the steady increase in man-made CO_2 emissions—principally from burning fossil fuels like gasoline and coal—is tipping the balance.

The Skeptics. Other scientists are skeptical about both the temperature change and its causes. A 1988 National Oceanic and Atmospheric Administration study concluded that there's been no ocean warming in this past century. Furthermore, they say, the amount of CO_2 emitted into the atmosphere by human activity (about 7 billion tons per year) is only a tiny fraction of natural emissions from volcanoes, fires, and lightning (200 billion tons per year). Skeptics also point out that the same computer models predicting global warming in the next generation predicted a much larger increase in temperature for the previous century than actually occurred.

In mid-2001, the National Academy of Sciences resolved one of those issues. The Academy confirmed that the earth is warming, largely due to the increased buildup of greenhouse gas concentrations. A 2004 analysis by the National Center for Atmospheric Research concluded that natural climate changes were responsible for the earth's warming from 1900 to 1950, but could not explain the continuing rise in the earth's temperature since then. Human activity seemed to be the only possible culprit. In 2007, the United Nations concluded with 90 percent certainty that that was the case (see World View).

webnote

The 2004 White House report to Congress on climate change is at www.climatescience.gov

Global Externalities. The 2007 U.N. report doesn't lay out a plan of action for slowing global warming. One thing is certain, however: ***CO_2 emissions are a global externality*** of industrial production and fuel consumption. Without some form of government intervention, there's little likelihood that market participants will voluntarily reduce CO_2 emissions.

WORLD VIEW

Evidence Is Now "Unequivocal" That Humans Are Causing Global Warming

Changes in the atmosphere, the oceans and glaciers and ice caps now show unequivocally that the world is warming due to human activities, the United Nations Intergovernmental Panel on Climate Change (IPCC) said in new report released today in Paris. . . .

The IPCC, which brings together the world's leading climate scientists and experts, concluded that major advances in climate modelling and the collection and analysis of data now give scientists "very high confidence"—at least a 9 out of 10 chance of being correct—in their understanding of how human activities are causing the world to warm. This level of confidence is much greater than the IPCC indicated in their last report in 2001.

Today's report, the first of four volumes to be released this year by the IPCC, also confirms that it is "very likely" that humanity's emissions of carbon dioxide, methane, nitrous oxide and other greenhouse gases have caused most of the global temperature rise observed since the mid-20th century. The report says that it is likely that effect of human activity since 1750 is five times greater than the effect of fluctuations in the sun's output.

Susan Soloman, co-chair of the IPCC working group that produced the report, said records from ice cores, going back 10,000 years, show a dramatic rise in greenhouse gases from the onset of the industrial era. "There can be no question that the increase in these greenhouse gases are dominated by human activity." . . .

The report describes an accelerating transition to a warmer world—an increase of 3°C is expected this century—marked by more extreme temperatures including heat waves, new wind patterns, worsening drought in some regions, heavier precipitation in others, melting glaciers and Arctic ice, and rising global average sea levels.

Source: UN News Service, February 2, 2007. Reprinted with permission.

Analysis: The external costs of consumption and production activities contribute to global environmental problems. What should be done to curb these global external costs?

Kyoto Treaty. In December 1997, most of the world's industrialized nations pledged to reduce CO_2 emissions. The Kyoto treaty they initialed in 1997 expressed an international commitment to reduce greenhouse emissions during the period 2008–12. The world's industrialized nations promised to cut their emissions below 1990 levels. That would require some industries (e.g., autos, steel, paper, and electric power) to substantially alter production methods and, possibly, output. For their part, the developing nations of the world promised to curb their *growth* of emissions.

After 7 years of negotiations, 141 nations ratified the Kyoto treaty, with a start date of February 16, 2005. Under the treaty, the European Union agreed to cut CO_2 emissions 8 percent below 1990 levels; Japan and Canada agreed to a 6 percent cut; and Russia agreed to stay at 1990 levels. Developing nations are exempted from limits.

The United States, Australia, and other nations refused to ratify the treaty. President Bush argued that the implied curbs on production would cost the U.S. 5 million jobs and $400 billion of output annually. It would also put the U.S. and other industrial nations at a competitive disadvantage in global markets, relative to China, India, and other developing nations without CO_2 limits. The implied costs of mandatory CO_2 reductions, President Bush asserted, exceed the promised and uncertain benefits.

It is unlikely that the Kyoto treaty will attain its CO_2-reduction targets. Not just because the United States didn't sign it. But also because of the exceptionally fast economic growth of China, India, and other exempt nations. China and India are the second- and third-largest CO_2 emitters, behind the United States, and their emissions are increasing faster. As such, they have become a major source of tradable pollution credits for firms in Kyoto-bound nations. In 2006, for example, China sold roughly 200 million metric tons of CO_2 credits for $6–8 a ton per year. This allowed the European utilities and manufacturers who bought the credits to maintain CO_2 emission levels while financing CO_2 controls in China. In the process, the *growth* of CO_2 emissions is slowed, even if an outright emission *reduction* doesn't occur. Any progress in CO_2 control is welcome, however. Whether we will avert global catastrophe may be uncertain, but any reduction in emissions (growth) will at least give us cleaner air. A *universal* set of CO_2-reduction goals and *a global* tradable permit system might well accelerate that outcome in the economy tomorrow.

webnote

The United Nations provides information on climate change and emissions data for individual nations at www.unfccc.de

SUMMARY

- Air, water, and solid-waste pollution impose social and economic costs. The costs of pollution include the direct damages inflicted on our health and resources, the expense of cleaning up, and the general aesthetic deterioration of the environment. LO1
- Pollution is an external cost, a cost of a market activity imposed on someone (a third party) other than the immediate producer or consumer. LO1
- Producers and consumers generally operate on the basis of private benefits and costs. Accordingly, a private producer or consumer has an incentive to minimize his own costs by transforming private costs into external costs. One way of making such a substitution is to pollute—to use "free" air and water rather than install pollution control equipment, or to leave the job of waste disposal to others. LO1
- Social costs are the total amount of resources used in a production or consumption process. When social costs are greater than private costs, the market's price signals are flawed. This market failure will induce people to harm the environment by using suboptimal processes and products. LO1
- One way to correct the market inefficiency created by externalities is to compel producers and consumers to internalize all (social) costs. This can be done by imposing emission charges and higher user fees. Such charges create an incentive to invest in pollution abatement equipment, recycle reusable materials, and conserve scarce elements of the environment. LO3
- Tradable pollution permits help minimize the cost of pollution control by (*a*) promoting low-cost controls to substitute for high-cost controls and (*b*) encouraging innovation in pollution control technology. LO3
- An alternative approach to cleaning up the environment is to require specific pollution controls or to prohibit specific kinds of activities. Direct regulation runs the risk of higher cost and discouraging innovations in environmental protection. LO3

- The opportunity costs of pollution abatement are the most desired goods and services given up when factors of production are used to control pollution. The optimal rate of pollution is reached when the marginal social benefits of further pollution control equal associated marginal social costs. LO2
- In addition to diverting resources, pollution control efforts alter relative prices, change the mix of output, and redistribute incomes. These outcomes cause losses for particular groups and may thus require special economic or political attention. LO2
- The greenhouse effect represents a global externality. Reducing global emissions requires consensus on optimal pollution levels (i.e., the optimal balance of pollution-abatement costs and benefits) and the distribution of attendant costs. LO3

Key Terms

production decision
efficiency decision
external cost
social costs
private costs
market failure
emission charge
government failure
opportunity cost
optimal rate of pollution

Questions for Discussion

1. What are the *economic* costs of the externalities caused by air toxins? Or beach closings? (See News, page 569.) How would you measure their value? LO1
2. Should we try to eliminate *all* pollution? What economic considerations might favor permitting some pollution? LO2
3. Why would auto manufacturers resist exhaust control devices? How would their costs, sales, and profits be affected? LO1
4. Does anyone have an incentive to maintain auto-exhaust control devices in good working order? How can we ensure that they will be maintained? LO1
5. Suppose we established a $10,000 fine for water pollution. Would some companies still find that polluting was economical? Under what conditions? LO3
6. What economic costs are imposed by mandatory sorting of trash? LO3
7. "The issuance of a pollution permit is just a license to destroy the environment." Do you agree? Explain. LO3
8. If a high per-bag fee were charged for garbage collection, would illegal dumping increase? LO3
9. Should the United States have signed the Kyoto treaty? What are the arguments for and against U.S. participation? LO3
10. Might the exemption of China from Kyoto CO_2 limits give it an incentive to *increase* CO_2 emissions, whose later reduction it could sell (tradable permits)? LO1

problems The Student Problem Set at the back of this book contains numerical and graphing problems for this chapter.

web activities to accompany this chapter can be found on the Online Learning Center: **http://www.mhhe.com/economics/schiller11e**

29 The Farm Problem

LEARNING OBJECTIVES

After reading this chapter, you should know:

LO1. What makes the farm business different from others.

LO2. What mechanisms are used to prop up farm prices and incomes.

LO3. How subsidies affect farm prices, output, and incomes.

In 1996, the U.S. Congress charted a new future for U.S. farmers. No longer would they look to Washington, D.C., for decisions on what crops to plant or how much farmland to leave fallow. The Freedom to Farm Act would get the government out of the farm business and let "laissez faire" dictate farm outcomes. Farmers would lose their federal subsidies but could earn as much as they wanted in the marketplace. Taxpayers loved the idea. So did most farmers, who were enjoying high prices and bumper profits in 1996.

The Asian crisis that began in mid-1997 dealt farmers a severe blow. U.S. farms export 25–50 percent of all the wheat, corn, soybeans, and cotton they grow. When Asia's economies plunged into recession, those export sales plummeted. With sales, prices, and profits all declining, farmers lost their enthusiasm for the "freedom to farm"; they wanted Uncle Sam to jump back into the farm business with price and income guarantees. The U.S. Congress obliged by passing the Farm Security Act of 2001. That act not only increased farm subsidies, but also extended them to peanut farmers, hog farmers, and horse breeders. Between 2002 and 2012, these subsidies will cost taxpayers $15–20 billion per year.

This chapter examines the rationale for continuing farm subsidies and their effects on farm production, prices, and exports. In particular, we confront these questions:

- **Why do farmers need any subsidies?**
- **How do government subsidies affect farm production, prices, and incomes?**
- **Who pays for farm subsidies?**

DESTABILIZING FORCES

Competition in Agriculture

market power: The ability to alter the market price of a good or service.

barriers to entry: Obstacles, such as patents, that make it difficult or impossible for would-be producers to enter a particular market.

economic profit: The difference between total revenues and total economic costs.

The agriculture industry is one of the most competitive of all U.S. industries. First, there are 2 million farms in the United States. Although some of these farms are immense—with tens of thousands of acres—no single farm has the power to affect the market supply or price of farm products. That is, individual farmers have no **market power.**

Competition in agriculture is maintained by low **barriers to entry.** Although farmers need large acreages, expensive farm equipment, substantial credit, hard work, and hired labor, all these resources become affordable when farming is generating **economic profits.** When farming is profitable, existing farmers expand their farms and farmers' children are able to start new farms. It would be much harder to enter the automobile industry, the airline business, or even the farm machinery market than it would be to enter farming. Because of these low barriers to entry, economic profits don't last long in agriculture.

Given the competitive structure of U.S. agriculture, ***individual farmers tend to behave like perfect competitors.*** Individual farmers seek to expand their rate of output until marginal cost equals price. By following this rule, each farmer makes as much profit as possible from existing resources, prices, and technology.

Like other competitive firms, U.S. farmers can maintain economic profits only if they achieve continuing cost reductions. Above-normal profits obtained from current production techniques and prices aren't likely to last. Such economic profits will entice more people into agriculture and will stimulate greater output from existing farmers. That is exactly the kind of dilemma that confronted the early producers of microcomputers. To stay ahead, individual firms (farms) must continue to improve their productivity.

Technological Advance

The rate of technological advance in agriculture has, in fact, been spectacular. Since 1929, the farm labor force has shrunk by two-thirds, yet farm output has increased by 70 percent. Between the early 1950s and today,

- Annual egg production has jumped from 183 to 260 eggs per laying chicken.
- Milk output has increased from 5,400 to 19,576 pounds per cow annually.
- Wheat output has increased from 17.3 to 39 bushels per acre.
- Corn output has jumped from 39.4 to 156 bushels per acre.

Farm output per labor-hour has grown even faster, having increased 10 times over in the same period. Such spectacular rates of productivity advance rival those of our most high-tech industries. These technological advances resulted from the development of higher-yielding seeds (the "green revolution"), advanced machinery (mechanical feeders and milkers), improved animal breeding (crossbreeding), improved plants (rust-resistant wheat), better land-use practices (crop rotation and fertilizers), and computer-based management systems.

Inelastic Demand

price elasticity of demand: The percentage change in quantity demanded divided by the percentage change in price.

In most industries, continuous increases in technology and output would be most welcome. The agricultural industry, however, confronts a long-term problem. Simply put, there's a limit to the amount of food people want to eat.

This constraint on the demand for agricultural output is reflected in the relatively inelastic demand for food. Consumers don't increase their food purchases very much when farm prices fall. The **price elasticity** of food demand is low. As a consequence, when harvests are good, farmers must reduce prices a lot to induce a substantial increase in the quantity of food demanded. Even if the price elasticity of demand were as high as 0.2, the percentage change in price would have to be five times as large as the percentage change in quantity produced. Hence, prices would have to fall 25 percent in order to sell a bumper crop that was 5 percent larger than normal, that is,

$$\text{Required percentage change in price} = \frac{\text{percentage change in quantity (harvest)}}{\text{price elasticity of demand}}$$

so,

$$\%\,\Delta p = \frac{0.05}{0.20} = 0.25$$

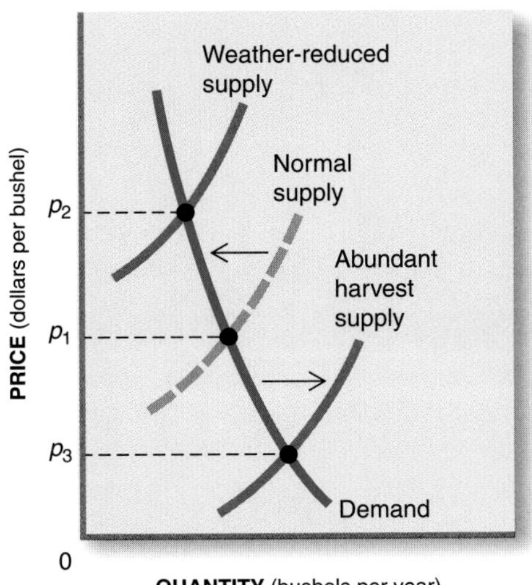

FIGURE 29.1
Short-Term Instability

Changes in weather cause abrupt shifts of the food supply curve. When combined with the relatively inelastic demand for food, these supply shifts result in wide price swings. Notice how the price of grain jumps from p_1 to p_2 when bad weather reduces the harvest. If good weather follows, prices may fall to p_3.

In 1998, the *corn* crop was 6 percent larger than the year before. In 1999, the corn crop *decreased* by 3.5 percent. As Figure 29.1 illustrates, ***with low price elasticity of demand, abrupt changes in farm output have a magnified effect on market prices.***

The **income elasticity** of food demand is also low. The income elasticity of demand for food refers to the responsiveness of food demand to changes in income. Specifically,

income elasticity of demand: Percentage change in quantity demanded divided by percentage change in income.

$$\text{Income elasticity of demand} = \frac{\text{\% change in quantity demanded (at constant price)}}{\text{\% change in income}}$$

Since 1929, per capita income has quadrupled. But per capita food consumption has increased only 85 percent. Hence, ***neither lower prices nor higher incomes significantly increase the quantity of food demanded.***

In the long run, then, the increasing ability of U.S. agriculture to produce food must be reconciled with very slow growth of U.S. demand for food. Over time, this implies that farm prices will fall, relative to nonfarm prices. And they have. Between the years 1910–14 and 2007, the ratio of farm prices to nonfarm prices fell 60 percent. In the absence of government price-support programs and foreign demand for U.S. farm products, farm prices would have fallen still further.

Abrupt Shifts of Supply

The long-term downtrend in (relative) farm prices is only one of the major problems confronting U.S. agriculture. The second major problem is short run in nature. Prices of farm products are subject to abrupt short-term swings. If the weather is good, harvests are abundant. Normally, this might be a good thing. In farming, however, abundant harvests imply a severe drop in prices. On the other hand, a late or early freeze, a drought, or an infestation by disease or insect pests can reduce harvests and push prices sharply higher (see Figure 29.1).

Response Lags. Natural forces aren't the only cause of short-term price instability. Time lags between the production decision and the resultant harvest also contribute to price instability. If prices are high one year, farmers have an incentive to increase their rate of output. In this sense, prices serve the same signaling function in agriculture as they do in nonfarm industries. What distinguishes the farmers' response is the lack of inventories and the fixed duration of the production process. In the computer industry, a larger quantity of output can be supplied to the market fairly quickly by drawing down inventories or stepping up the rate of production. In farming, supply can't respond so quickly. In the short run, the farmer can only till more land, plant additional seed, or breed more livestock. No additional food supplies will be available

webnote

Annual prices for farm products are compiled by the National Agricultural Statistics Service at the U.S. Department of Agriculture. Visit http://usda.mannlib.cornell.edu/MannUsda/viewdocumentInfo.do?document ID=1003-bb

FIGURE 29.2
Unstable Corn Prices

Most agricultural prices are subject to abrupt short-term changes. Notice how corn prices rose dramatically during World Wars I and II, then fell sharply. Poor harvests in the rest of the world increased demand for U.S. food in 1973–74. Since then prices have moved sharply in both directions.

Source: U.S. Department of Agriculture.

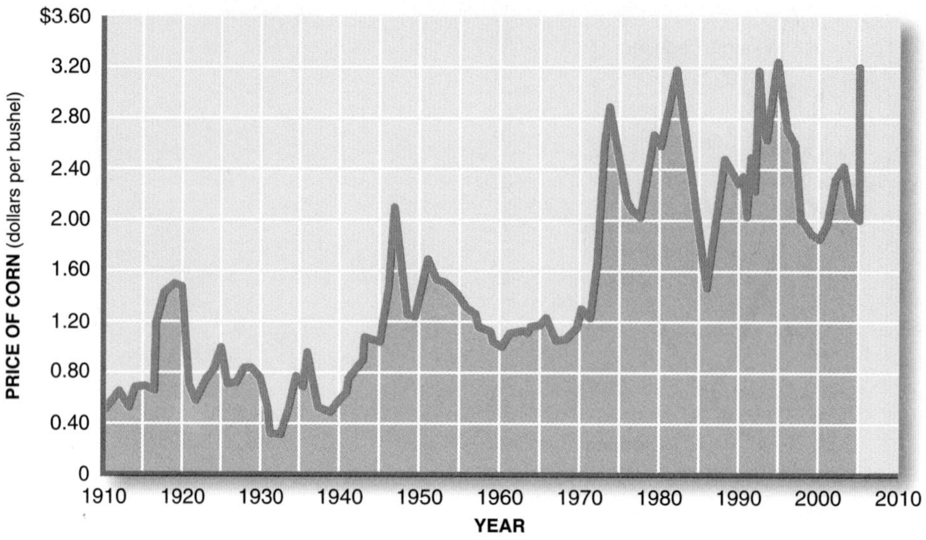

until a new crop or herd grows. Hence, the agricultural supply response to a change in prices is always one harvest (or breeding period) later.

The natural lag in responses of agricultural supplies intensifies short-term price swings. Suppose corn prices are exceptionally high at the end of a year, because of a reduced harvest. High prices will make corn farming appear unusually profitable. Farmers will want to expand their rate of output—plant more corn acreage—to share in these high profits. But the corn won't appear on the market until the following year. By that time, there's likely to be an abundance of corn on the market, as a result of both better weather and increased corn acreage. Hence, corn prices are likely to plummet (look again at Figure 29.1).

No single farmer can avoid the boom-or-bust movement of prices. Even a corn farmer who has mastered the principles of economics has little choice but to plant more corn when prices are high. If he doesn't plant additional corn, prices will fall anyway, because his own production decisions don't affect market prices. By not planting additional corn, he only denies himself a share of corn market sales. ***In a highly competitive market, each producer acts independently.***

Figure 29.2 demonstrates the historical instability of corn prices. Notice how corn prices repeatedly rise, then abruptly fall. This kind of price swing is particularly evident in 1915–20, 1935–37, 1946–48, 1973–76, 1980–84, and 1997–2000. In 2007, corn prices spiked again after President Bush proposed expanded use of corn-based ethanol as an alternative fuel source. Farmers rushed to plant additional acreage (see News), raising the specter of another boom-bust cycle.

THE FIRST FARM DEPRESSION, 1920–1940

The U.S. agricultural industry operated without substantial government intervention until the 1930s. In earlier decades, an expanding population, recurrent wars, and less advanced technology had helped maintain a favorable supply-demand relationship for farm products. There were frequent short-term swings in farm prices, but these were absorbed by a generally healthy farm sector. The period 1910–19 was particularly prosperous for farmers, largely because of the expanded foreign demand for U.S. farm products by countries engaged in World War I.

The two basic problems of U.S. agriculture grew to crisis proportions after 1920. In 1919, most farm prices were at historical highs (see Figures 29.2 and 29.3). After World War I ended, however, European countries no longer demanded as much American food. U.S. exports of farm products fell from nearly $4 billion in 1919 to $1.9 billion in 1921. Farm exports were further reduced in the following years by increasing restrictions on

IN THE NEWS

Corn Acres Expected to Soar in 2007, USDA Says Ethanol, Export Demand Lead to Largest Planted Area in 63 Years

WASHINGTON, Mar. 30, 2007—Driven by growing ethanol demand, U.S. farmers intend to plant 15 percent more corn acres in 2007, according to the *Prospective Plantings* report released today by the U.S. Department of Agriculture's National Agricultural Statistics Service (NASS). Producers plan to plant 90.5 million acres of corn, the largest area since 1944 and 12.1 million acres more than in 2006.

Expected corn acreage is up in nearly all states, due to favorable prices fueled by increased demand from ethanol producers as well as strong export sales.

The increase in intended corn acres is partially offset by a decrease in soybean acres in the Corn Belt and Great Plains, as well as fewer expected acres of cotton and rice in the Delta and Southeast.

Source: U.S. Dept. of Agriculture, National Agricultural Statistics Service

Analysis: Price swings motivate farmers to alter their production. The abrupt change in production may reverse the price movement in the next harvest, however.

international trade. At home, the end of the war implied an increased availability of factors of production and continuing improvement in farm technology.

The impact of reduced demand and increasing supply is evident in Figure 29.3. In 1919 farm prices were more than double their levels of the period 1910–14. Prices then fell abruptly. In 1921 alone, farm prices fell nearly 40 percent.

Farm prices stabilized in the mid-1920s but resumed a steep decline in 1930. In 1932 average farm prices were 75 percent lower than they had been in 1919. At the same time, the average income per farmer from farming fell from \$2,651 in 1919 to \$855 in 1932.

The Great Depression hit small farmers particularly hard. They had fewer resources to withstand consecutive years of declining prices and income. Even in good times, small farmers must continually expand output and reduce costs just to maintain their incomes. Hence, the Great Depression accelerated an exodus of small farmers from agriculture, a trend that continues today.

Table 29.1 shows that the number of small farms has declined dramatically. In 1910, there were 3.7 million farmers under 100 acres in size. Today, there are fewer than 1 million small farms. During the same period, the number of huge farms (1000 acres or more) has

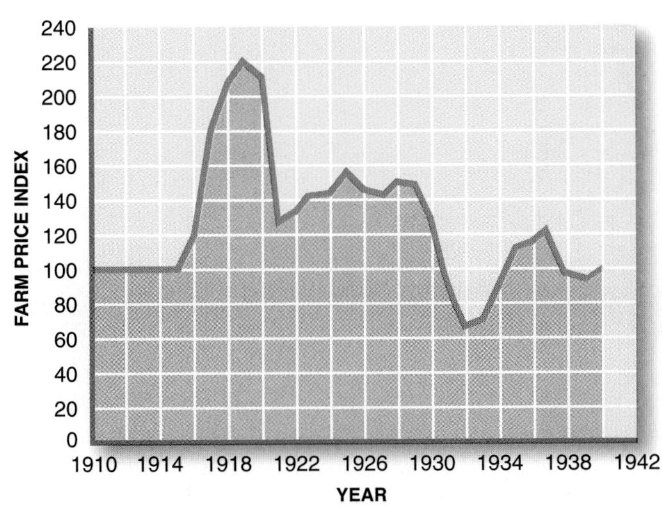

FIGURE 29.3
Farm Prices, 1910–1940 (1910–1914 = 100)

Farm prices are less stable than nonfarm prices. During the 1930s, relative farm prices fell 50 percent. This experience was the catalyst for government price supports and other agricultural assistance programs.

TABLE 29.1
Size Distribution of U.S. Farms, 1910 and 2002

Inelastic food demand, combined with increasing agricultural productivity, implies a declining number of farmers. Small farmers are particularly vulnerable because they don't have the resources to maintain a high rate of technological improvement. As a result, the number of small farms has declined dramatically, while the number of large farms has grown.

Size of Farm	Number, 1910	Percent	Number, 2002	Percent
Under 100 acres	3,691,611	58.0%	943,118	44.3%
100–499 acres	2,494,461	39.2	847,322	39.8
500–999 acres	125,295	2.0	161,552	7.6
1000 acres and over	50,135	0.8	176,990	8.3
Total	6,361,502	100.0%	2,128,982	100.0%

Source: U.S. Department of Agriculture.

more than tripled. This loss of small farmers, together with the increased mechanization of larger farms, has reduced the farm population by 23 million people since 1910.

U.S. FARM POLICY

The U.S. Congress has responded to these agricultural problems with a variety of programs. Most seek to raise and stabilize the price of farm products. Other programs seek to reduce the costs of production. When all else fails, the federal government also provides direct income support to farmers.

Price Supports

market surplus: The amount by which the quantity supplied exceeds the quantity demanded at a given price; excess supply.

parity: The relative price of farm products in the period 1910–14.

Price supports have always been the primary focus of U.S. farm policy. As early as 1926, Congress decreed that farm products should sell at a fair price. By "fair," Congress meant a price higher than the market equilibrium. The consequences of this policy are evident in Figure 29.4: ***A price floor creates a*** **market surplus.**

Once it set an above-equilibrium price for food, Congress had to find some way of disposing of the resultant food surplus. Initially, Congress proposed to get rid of this surplus by selling it abroad at world market prices. President Calvin Coolidge, a staunch opponent of government intervention, vetoed this legislation both times Congress passed it.

The notion of fair prices resurfaced in the Agricultural Adjustment Act of 1933. During the Great Depression farmers were going bankrupt in droves. To help them, Congress sought to restore the purchasing power of farm products to the 1909–14 level. The farm-nonfarm price relationships of 1909–14 were regarded by Congress as fair and came to be known as **parity** prices. If parity prices could be restored, Congress reasoned, farm incomes would improve.

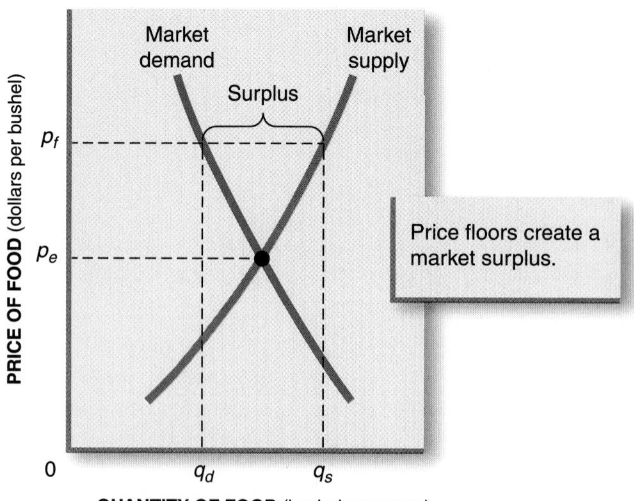

FIGURE 29.4
Fair Prices and Market Surplus

The interaction of market supply and demand establishes an equilibrium price (p_e) for any product, including food. If a higher price (p_f) is set, the quantity of food supplied (q_s) will be larger than the quantity demanded (q_d). Hence, attempts to establish a "fair" (higher) price for farm products must cope with resultant market surpluses.

Supply Restrictions

The goal of parity pricing couldn't be attained without altering market supply and demand in some way.

Set-Asides. The easiest way to increase farm prices without creating a surplus is to reduce the production of food. Congress does this by paying farmers for voluntary reductions in crop acreage. These **acreage set-asides** shift the food supply curve to the left. In 2007, nearly 40 *million* acres of farmland—one-sixth of the nation's wheat, corn, sorghum, rice, and cotton acreage—were idled by government set-asides. If farmers didn't agree to these set-asides, they couldn't participate in the price support programs.

acreage set-aside: Land withdrawn from production as part of policy to increase crop prices.

Dairy Termination Program. To prop up dairy prices, the federal government also started a Dairy Termination Program in 1985. This is analogous to a set-aside program. In this case, however, the government pays dairy farmers to slaughter or export dairy cattle. Between 1985 and 1987, the government paid dairy farmers over $1 billion to "terminate" 1.6 million cows. The reduction in dairy herds boosted prices for milk and other dairy products.

Marketing Orders. The federal government also permits industry groups to limit the quantity of output brought to market. By themselves, individual farmers can't raise the market price by withholding output. If they act collectively, however, they can. If a quantity greater than authorized is actually grown, the "surplus" is disposed of by individual farmers. In the 1980s, these *marketing orders* forced farmers to waste each year roughly 500 million lemons, 1 billion(!) oranges, 70 million pounds of raisins, 70 million pounds of almonds, and millions of plums, nectarines, and other fruits. This wholesale destruction of crops gave growers market power and kept farm prices artificially high.

Import Quotas. The market supply of farm products is also limited by import restrictions. Imports of sugar, dairy products, cotton, and peanuts are severely limited by import quotas. Imports of beef are limited by "voluntary" export limits in foreign countries. Import taxes (duties) limit the foreign supply of other farm products.

Demand Distortions

While trying to limit the *supply* of farm products, the government also inflates the *demand* for selected farm products.

Government Stockpiles. An executive order signed by President Franklin Roosevelt in 1933 altered the demand for farm products. The Commodity Credit Corporation (CCC) created at that time became a buyer of last resort for selected farm products.

The CCC becomes a buyer of last resort through its loan programs. Farmers can borrow money from the CCC at **loan rates** set by Congress (see Table 29.2). In 2007, for example, a wheat farmer could borrow $2.75 in cash for every bushel of wheat he relinquished to the CCC. If the market price of wheat went above $2.75, the farmer could sell the wheat, repay the CCC, and pocket the difference. If, instead, the price fell below the loan rate, the farmer

loan rate: The implicit price paid by the government for surplus crops taken as collateral for loans to farmers.

Commodity	Loan Rate
Corn	$1.95 per bushel
Sorghum	1.95
Barley	1.85
Oats	1.33
Wheat	2.75
Soybeans	5.00
Cotton (upland)	0.52 per pound
Rice	6.50 per hundredweight

Source: U.S. Department of Agriculture.

TABLE 29.2
2007 Loan Rates

The Commodity Credit Corporation lends money to farmers at fixed "loan rates" that are implicit price floors. If the market price falls below the CCC loan rate, the government keeps the crop as full payment of the loan or *pays* farmers a "loan deficiency payment."

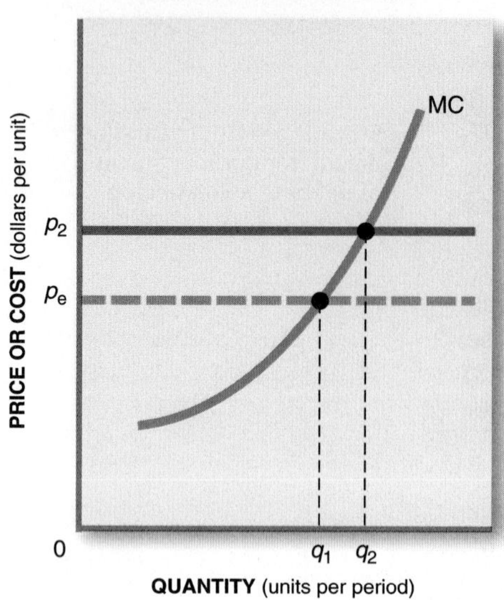

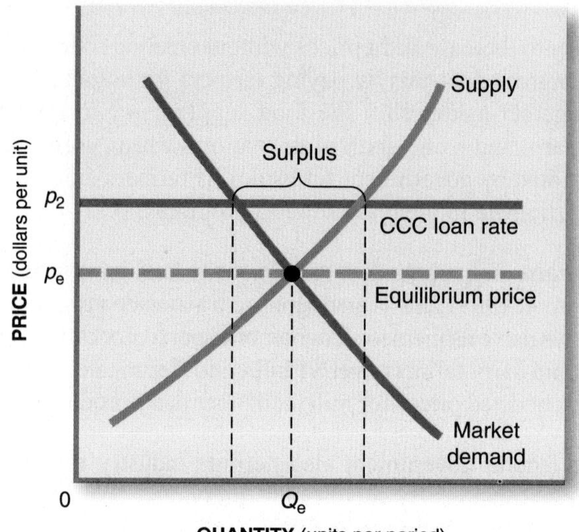

FIGURE 29.5
The Impact of Price Supports

In the absence of price supports, the price of farm products would be determined by the intersection of market supply and demand. In this case, the equilibrium price would be p_e, as shown in part *b*. All individual farmers would confront this price and produce up to the point where MC = p_e, as in part *a*.

Government price supports raise the price to p_2. By offering to buy (or "loan") unlimited quantities at this price, the government shifts the demand curve facing each farmer upward. Individual farmers respond by increasing their output from q_1 to q_2. As farmers increase their output, a market surplus develops (part *b*).

could simply let the CCC keep the wheat and repay nothing. Hence, ***whenever market prices are below CCC loan rates, the government ends up buying surplus crops.***

Figure 29.5 illustrates the effect of CCC price supports on individual farmers and the agricultural market. In the absence of price supports, competitive farmers would confront a horizontal demand curve at price p_e, itself determined by the intersection of market supply and demand (in part *b*). The CCC's offer to buy ("loan") unlimited quantities at a higher price shifts the demand curve facing each farmer upward, to the guaranteed price p_2. This higher price induces individual farmers to increase their rate of output, from q_1 to q_2.

As farmers respond to price supports, the agriculture market is pushed out of equilibrium. At the support level p_2, more output is supplied than demanded. The market surplus created by government price supports creates an additional policy dilemma. ***The market surplus induced by price supports must be eliminated in one of three ways:***

- ***Government purchases*** and stockpiling of surplus food.
- ***Export sales.***
- ***Restrictions on supply.***

Government purchases of surplus crops have led to massive stockpiles of wheat, cotton, corn, and dairy products. At one time, the excess wheat was stored in old ammunition bunkers in Nebraska and scrubbed-out oil tanks in Texas. More than 130 *million* pounds of surplus nonfat dry milk is now stored in limestone caverns under Kansas City, and surplus cotton fills warehouses in the South. Even today about one-fourth of U.S. farm output is destroyed or stored.

Deficiency Payments. To keep these stockpiles from growing further, Congress amended the CCC loan program in 2001. When market prices fall below CCC loan rates (Table 29.2), farmers don't have to turn over their crops to the government. Instead, the government pays

WORLD VIEW

EU Farm Subsidies

In Europe, believe it or not, the subsidy for every cow is greater than the personal income of half the people in the world.

—Former British Prime Minister Margaret Thatcher

United States farm policy isn't unique. Most industrialized countries go to even greater lengths to protect domestic agriculture. For example, France, Germany, and Switzerland all shield their farmers from international competition while subsidizing their exports. Japan protects its inefficient rice producers, while the Netherlands subsidizes greenhouse vegetable farmers.

The motivations for farm subsidies are pretty much the same in every country in the world. Every country wants a secure source of food in the event of war. Most nations also want to maintain a viable farm sector, which is viewed as a source of social stability. Finally, politicians in every country must be responsive to a well-established and vocal political constituency.

The European Union (EU) imposes high tariffs on imported food, keeping domestic prices high. The member governments also agree to purchase any surplus production. To get rid of the surplus, the governments then subsidize exports. In 2000, direct EU farm subsidies exceeded $45 billion, triple the size of U.S. farm subsidies. All this protection costs the average EU consumer over $200 a year.

Analysis: Farm subsidies are common around the world. Such subsidies alter not only domestic output decisions but international trade patterns as well.

them a *loan deficiency payment* equal to the *difference* between the loan rate and the market price. The farmer can then sell his crop on the open market. By dumping excess supply on the market rather than stockpiling it, this policy tends to aggravate downward price swings.

Because farm prices are artificially high in the United States, export sales are sometimes difficult. As a result, the federal government must give away lots of food to poor nations and even subsidize exports to developed nations. The United States isn't alone in this regard: The European Union maintains even higher prices and subsidies (see World View).

webnote

For more on the EU, see europa.eu.int/index-en.htm

Cost Subsidies

The market surplus induced by price supports is exacerbated by cost subsidies. Irrigation water, for example, is delivered to many farmers by federally funded reclamation projects. The price farmers pay for the water is substantially below the cost of delivering it; the difference amounts to a subsidy. In 1986, this water subsidy cost taxpayers over $500 million. The Department of Agriculture has distributed an additional $150 million to $200 million a year to farmers to help defray the costs of fertilizer, drainage, and other production costs.

The federal government has also provided basic research, insurance, marketing, grading, and inspection services to farmers at subsidized prices. All these subsidies serve to lower fixed or variable costs. Their net impact is to stimulate additional output, as illustrated in Figure 29.6.

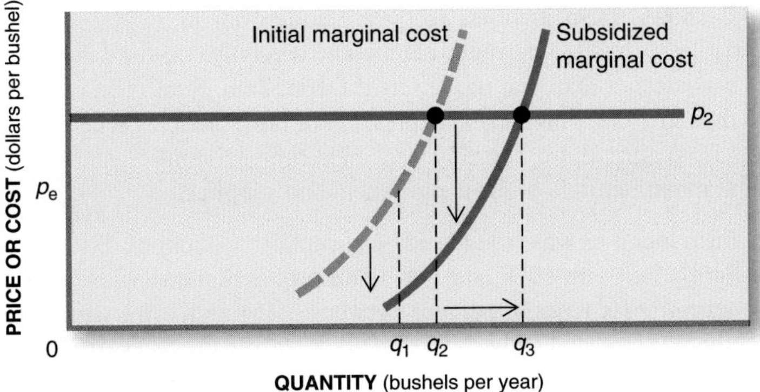

FIGURE 29.6
The Impact of Cost Subsidies

Cost subsidies lower the marginal cost of producing at any given rate of output, thereby shifting the marginal cost curve downward. The lower marginal costs make higher rates of output more profitable and thus increase output. At price p_2, lower marginal costs increase the farmer's profit-maximizing rate of output from q_2 to q_3.

TABLE 29.3
2004 Target Prices

Congress sets target prices for selected commodities. If the market price falls below the target price, a *deficiency payment* is made directly to the farmer.

Commodity	Target Price
Corn	$ 2.63 per bushel
Sorghum	2.57
Barley	2.24
Oats	1.44
Wheat	3.92
Soybeans	5.80
Cotton (upland)	0.7240 per pound
Rice	10.50 per hundredweight

Source: U.S. Department of Agriculture.

Direct Income Support

Price supports, cost subsidies, and supply restrictions are designed to stabilize agricultural markets and assure farmers an adequate income. As we've seen, however, they entail significant distortions of market outcomes. The Congressional Budget Office estimates that the milk price supports alone have increased retail dairy prices 3 to 6 percent, reduced consumption 1 to 5 percent, and encouraged excessive dairy production. Because of such distortions, direct income supports were authorized by the Agriculture and Consumer Protection Act of 1973. ***The advantage of direct income supports is that they achieve the goal of income security without distortions of market prices and output.***

counter-cyclical payment: Income transfer paid to farmers for difference between target and market prices.

The principal form of direct income support is so-called **counter-cyclical payments.** Congress identifies specific "target prices" for selected crops. In 2004, the target price for wheat was $3.92 a bushel (see Table 29.3). If market prices fall below these targets, the government makes up the difference. Target prices are another form of price floor. Unlike the case of CCC loan rates, however, target prices don't trigger government purchases of surplus crops. The target price is only used to compute the amount of the "counter-cyclical" payment paid directly to farmers.

In principle, direct income payments are a more efficient mechanism for subsidizing farm incomes. But farmers don't like them. Five thousand angry farmers drove their tractors to Washington, D.C., in February 1979 to protest this policy approach. Their rallying cry was "parity, not charity." They wanted higher price supports (an indirect subsidy) rather than more direct payments (a direct subsidy).

THE SECOND FARM DEPRESSION, 1980–1986

With so many price supports, supply restrictions, cost subsidies, and income transfers, one would think that farming is a riskless and profitable business. But this hasn't been the case. Incomes remain low and unstable, especially for small farmers. In fact, the entire agricultural sector experienced another setback in the 1980s. In 1980, the net income of U.S. farmers fell 42 percent. As Figure 29.7 shows, farm incomes recovered somewhat in 1981 but then resumed their steep decline in 1982. In 1983, farmers' net income was only one-third the level of 1979. This income loss was steeper than that of the Great Depression. Real farm income was actually lower in 1983 than in 1933. This second depression of farm incomes accelerated the exodus of small farmers from agriculture, severely weakened rural economies, and bankrupted many farm banks and manufacturers of farm equipment and supplies.

The Cost Squeeze

profit: The difference between total revenue and total cost.

This second depression of farm incomes was not caused by abrupt price declines. Prices for farm products increased slightly between 1979 and 1983. But production costs rose much faster. Average farm production costs rose 30 percent between 1979 and 1983 while the average price of farm products increased only 1.5 percent. As a result, the **profit** (net income) of farmers fell abruptly.

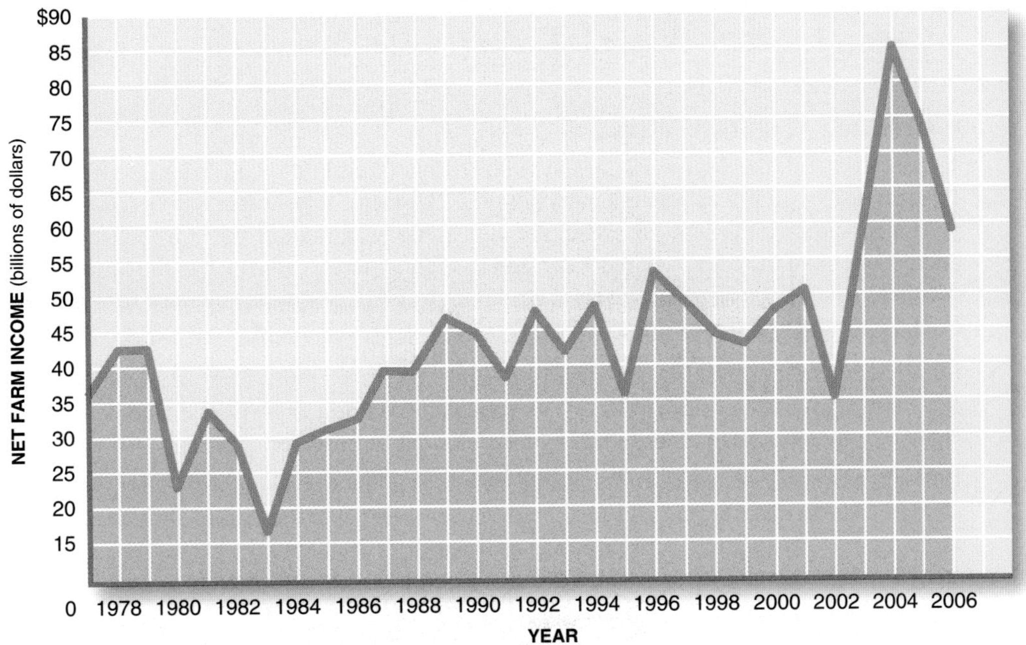

FIGURE 29.7
Net Farm Income, 1977–2006

Between 1979 and 1983 net farm income fell 64 percent. This decline was steeper than the income slide that occurred during the Great Depression (when net farm income fell 45 percent between 1929 and 1933). Farm incomes rose sharply from 1983 to 1989 but were unstable throughout the 1990s.

Source: *Economic Report of the President, 2007.*

Fuel Costs. The cost squeeze on farm incomes started with an abrupt increase in fuel (oil) prices in 1979–80 that made it more expensive to operate farm equipment.

Fertilizer Costs. The increase in crude oil prices also pushed up the price of fertilizer, which is manufactured from a petroleum base. Fertilizer prices rose in tandem with fuel prices, increasing 24 percent in 1980.

Interest Rates. The third, and perhaps most devastating, source of the farmers' cost squeeze was an increase in interest rates. Farming is extremely land- and capital-intensive. Many of these assets (such as land and machinery) are purchased with borrowed funds, often at variable interest rates. Farmers also borrow money for planting and harvesting. When interest rates skyrocketed—the prime rate rose from 9 percent in 1978 to over 20 percent in 1980—the cost of servicing this debt jumped.

Declining Land Values. High interest rates and declining incomes also reduced the value of farmers' most important asset—their land. Falling land prices made it more difficult and expensive for farmers to get needed credit.

Declining Exports. The farmers' plight was worsened still further by declining export sales. In 1980, in response to the Soviet invasion of Afghanistan, President Jimmy Carter imposed an embargo on grain sales to the Soviet Union. This directly reduced wheat sales by 15,000 to 20,000 tons per year.

Export sales were reduced even further by the strong value of the U.S. dollar. Between 1980 and 1984, the international value of the dollar rose a staggering 50 percent. This made it much more expensive for global consumers to buy U.S. farm output. As a result, the quantity of exports declined.

THE ECONOMY TOMORROW

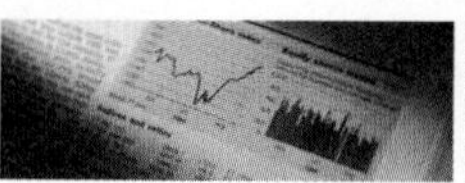

FARMERS ON THE DOLE

To a large extent, the farm crisis of the 1980s had nothing to do with federal farm policy. The increase in oil prices was initiated by OPEC. Higher interest rates were a reflection of macroeconomic conditions. Likewise, the high value of the dollar was a response to U.S. interest rates and the economic recovery, and its effects weren't confined to the farm sector. All these adverse forces were reversed in the mid-1980s, and farm incomes rose sharply from their 1983 lows (see Figure 29.7).

Steps toward Deregulation. The post-1983 recovery of the farm sector created an opportunity to redesign farm policy. With production, prices, exports, and incomes all rising, the timing was perfect for the deregulation of the farm sector.

1985 Farm Act. The Farm Security Act of 1985 took a few steps in that direction. The core feature of the act was a gradual reduction in government support prices. For example, the support price ("loan rate") for wheat was reduced from \$3.30 per bushel in 1986 to \$1.95 in 1990. By reducing the support price, the government hoped to discourage overproduction and recurrent market surpluses.

Another feature of the 1985 act was to limit the government purchase of market surpluses. Rather than buying surpluses at the guaranteed loan rate, the government encouraged farmers to sell their surpluses at market prices. The government then used deficiency payments to reimburse the farmers for the difference between the guaranteed (support) price and the market price.

The 1990 Act. By the time the authority of the 1985 act expired (in 1990), crop prices, farm incomes, and the price of farmland had all risen significantly, thanks to the continued expansion of the U.S. economy, declining oil and fertilizer costs, and strong foreign demand for U.S. farm products.

Despite the increased prosperity of farming during the 1985–90 period, the basic structure of farm subsidies was continued in the 1990 Farm Act. Indeed, loan rates were *increased,* effectively raising the price floor for farm products. At the same time, however, Congress reduced the amount of set-aside acreage by 15 percent. It also gave farmers more discretion to farm on unsubsidized acreage. Target prices were reduced and frozen for 5 years.

The net effect of the 1990 legislation was to move farming another small step closer to market realities. A bit more acreage was freed from government regulation, target prices were set closer to market prices, and more market surpluses were sold rather than stored in government warehouses.

The 1996 Freedom to Farm Act. In 1996, Congress moved farmers considerably further down the road toward deregulation with two radical changes in farm policy. The first change was the phaseout of deficiency payments. Target prices (Table 29.3) and their associated deficiency payments were terminated. In their place, farmers were offered "market transition payments." The size of the transition payments wasn't dependent on commodity prices but instead was fixed by Congress for a period of 7 years. In this way, Congress focused on stabilizing farm *incomes* rather than farm *prices.* In 2002, all such income support was scheduled to end, leaving farmers the "freedom to farm" (off the dole).

The 1996 act also eliminated many restrictions on acreage set-asides. Up to 36.4 million acres were still eligible for "production flexibility contract payments" (set-asides). But farmers no longer had to keep set-aside acreage completely idle or to grow only specific commodities. Markets, not politicians, would decide what to grow.

Back from the Brink. At first, farmers loved the 1996 policy reforms. In the 1996–97 crop year, commodity prices were up and farm incomes were at an all-time high (Figure 29.7). Yet farmers were still getting billions of dollars in taxpayer subsidies. What a great deal!

The Asian Crisis. Then the farm economy turned sour again. The Asian crisis that began in July 1997 was the principal cause. When the currencies of Thailand, Korea, Indonesia, Malaysia, and other Asian nations tumbled, the foreign price of U.S. farm output soared. When the economies of these Asian nations stumbled into recession, their ability to buy American farm products was further diminished. As a result, U.S. farm exports fell sharply during 1997 and 1998 and farm prices tumbled.

Renewed Subsidies. When farm prices and incomes plunged, farmers again demanded federal aid. Just prior to the November 1998 elections, Congress increased market transition payments by 50 percent. Congress also authorized the early payment of $5 billion in farm aid not due until 1999. Finally, Congress approved $500 million in "disaster payments"—a new form of aid—to offset falling prices and exports.

The 2002 Farm Act. The intent of the 1996 Farm Act ostensibly had been to wean farmers off the dole, making them more reliant on market forces. That isn't how it worked out, however. When the market for farm products went bad, farmers expected more federal aid, not more freedom to farm.

Farmers got more permanent aid in 2001. Even before the 1996 Freedom to Farm Act had expired, farm lobbyists petitioned Congress not only to continue deficiency payments (based on target prices) but also to increase loan rates. The September 11, 2001, terrorist attacks enhanced the chances of congressional approval by highlighting the need for secure food supplies. Congress responded by increasing farm subsidies and creating new ones for sugar growers, peanut farmers, hog operators, and even horse breeders.

The 2007 Farm Act. Rising commodity prices in 2006–7 created another opportunity to wean farmers off the dole. As alternatives to so many subsidies, critics suggested that farmers make greater use of crop insurance and futures markets to stabilize their incomes. But those proposals never got much of a hearing. With the 2008 presidential elections on the horizon, no politician wanted to offend the farm bloc, least of all the farmers in Iowa, where the first presidential primary vote is held. As the 2007 Farm Act was being drafted, there was little enthusiasm for reducing, much less eliminating, farm subsidies. So it appears that farmers will remain on the dole in the economy tomorrow..

webnote

The U.S. Department of Agriculture makes available a broad array of statistics on the U.S. farm sector at www.usda.gov

webnote

See the latest U.S. House of Representatives Agriculture Committee at www.house.gov/agriculture

SUMMARY

- The agricultural sector has a highly competitive structure, with approximately 2 million farms. Many crops are regulated, however, by government restrictions and subsidies. LO1
- Most farm output is produced by the small percentage of large farms that enjoy economies of scale. Most small farmers rely on nonfarm employment for their income. LO1
- In a free market, farm prices tend to decline over time because of increasing productivity and low income elasticity of demand. Variations in harvests, combined with a low price elasticity of demand, make farm prices unstable. LO1
- Most of today's farm policies originated during the Great Depression, in response to low farm prices and incomes. LO3
- The government uses price supports and cost subsidies to raise farm prices and profits. These policies cause resource misallocations and create market surpluses of specific commodities. LO2
- Direct income support in the form of counter-cyclical payments also generates excess supply, but can be targeted more to income needs. LO2
- Farm incomes declined sharply between 1979 and 1983, causing a second depression in the farm sector. The drop was caused by sharp increases in fuel, fertilizer, and interest costs. The Asian crisis that began in 1997 caused another farm crisis. LO1
- The 1996 Farm Act called for a phaseout of farm subsidies. Falling prices and incomes during 1997–2001 stalled and eventually reversed that process. LO2
- Government regulation not only risks design flaws but creates moral hazards that may reduce efficiency. LO3

Key Terms

market power
barriers to entry
economic profit
price elasticity of demand
income elasticity of demand
market surplus
parity
acreage set-aside
loan rate
counter-cyclical payment
profit

Questions for Discussion

1. Would the U.S. economy be better off without government intervention in agriculture? Who would benefit? Who would lose? LO3
2. Are large price movements inevitable in agricultural markets? What other mechanisms might be used to limit such movement? LO1
3. Why doesn't the United States just give its crop surpluses to poor countries? What problems might such an approach create? LO3
4. Farmers can eliminate the uncertainties of fluctuating crop prices by selling their crops in futures markets (agreeing to a fixed price for crops to be delivered in the future). Who gains or loses from this practice? LO2
5. Why do farmers prefer price supports to direct payments? LO2
6. If two-thirds of all U.S. farms fail to earn a profit, why do they stay in business? LO3
7. You need a government permit (allotment) to grow tobacco. Who gains or loses from such regulation? LO2

problems The Student Problem Set at the back of this book contains numerical and graphing problems for this chapter.

web activities to accompany this chapter can be found on the Online Learning Center: **http://www.mhhe.com/economics/schiller11e**

PART 11 Factor Markets: Basic Theory

Factor markets operate like product markets, with supply and demand interacting to determine prices and quantities. In factor markets, however, resource inputs rather than products are exchanged. Those exchanges determine the wages paid to workers and the rent, interest, and profits paid to other inputs. The micro theories presented in Chapters 30 through 32 explain how those factor payments are determined.

The Labor Market

LEARNING OBJECTIVES

After reading this chapter, you should know:

LO1. What factors shape labor supply and demand.

LO2. How market wage rates are established.

LO3. How wage floors alter labor-market outcomes.

In 2004, the CEO of Walt Disney Company was ending a 10-year contract that could have paid him as much as $771 million for his services. LeBron James was in the second year of a Nike endorsement contract worth at least $90 million. Yet the president of the United States was paid only $400,000. And the secretary who typed the manuscript of this book was paid just $19,000. What accounts for these tremendous disparities in earnings?

Why does the average college graduate earn over $50,000 while the average high school graduate earns just $27,000? Are such disparities simply a reward for enduring 4 years of college, or do they reflect real differences in talent?

Surely we can't hope to explain these earnings disparities on the basis of the willingness to work. After all, my secretary would be more than willing to work day and night for $77 million per year. For that matter, so would I. Accordingly, the earnings disparities can't be attributed to differences in the quantity of labor supplied. If we're going to explain why some people earn a great deal of income while others earn very little, we must consider both the *supply* and the *demand* for labor. In this regard, the following questions arise:

- **How do people decide how much time to spend working?**
- **What determines the wage rate an employer is willing to pay?**
- **Why are some workers paid so much and others so little?**

To answer these questions, we must examine the behavior of labor *markets*.

LABOR SUPPLY

The following two ads recently appeared in the campus newspaper of a well-known university:

Will do ANYTHING for money: able-bodied liberal-minded male needs money, will work to get it. Have car. Call Josh 765-3210.

Web architect. Experienced website designer. Looking for part-time or consulting position on or off campus. Please call Danielle, ext. 0872, 9–5.

Although placed by individuals of very different talents, the ads clearly expressed Josh's and Danielle's willingness to work. Although we don't know how much money they were asking for their respective talents, or whether they ever found jobs, we can be sure that they were prepared to take a job at some wage rate. Otherwise, they wouldn't have paid for the ads in the "Jobs Wanted" column of their campus newspaper.

The advertised willingness to work represents a **supply of labor.** These individuals are offering to sell their time and talents to anyone who's willing to pay the right price. Their explicit offers are similar to those of anyone who looks for a job. Job seekers who check the current job openings at the student employment office or e-mail résumés to potential employers are demonstrating a willingness to accept employment—that is, to *supply* labor. The 25,000 people who applied for jobs at Wal-Mart (see News) were also offering to supply labor.

labor supply: The willingness and ability to work specific amounts of time at alternative wage rates in a given time period, *ceteris paribus.*

Our first concern in this chapter is to explain these labor supply decisions. How do people decide how many hours to supply at any given wage rate? Do people try to maximize their total wages? If they did, we'd all be holding three jobs and sleeping on the commuter bus. Since most of us don't behave this way, other motives must be present.

Income vs. Leisure

The reward for working comes in two forms: (1) the intrinsic satisfaction of working and (2) a paycheck. MBA grads say they care more about the intrinsic satisfaction than the pay (see News on the next page). They also get huge paychecks, however. Those big paychecks are explained in part by the quantity of labor supplied: MBA grads often end up working 60 or more hours a week. The reason people are willing to work so many hours is that they want more income.

Not working obviously has some value, too. In part, we need some nonwork time just to recuperate from working. We also want some leisure time to watch television, go to a soccer game, or enjoy other goods and services we've purchased.

Our conflicting desires for income and leisure create a dilemma: The more time we spend working, the more income we have but also less time to enjoy it. Working, like all activities, involves an opportunity cost. Generally, we say that ***the opportunity cost of working is the amount of leisure time that must be given up in the process.***

The inevitable trade-off between labor and leisure explains the shape of individual labor supply curves. As we work more hours, our leisure time becomes more scarce—and thus

IN THE NEWS

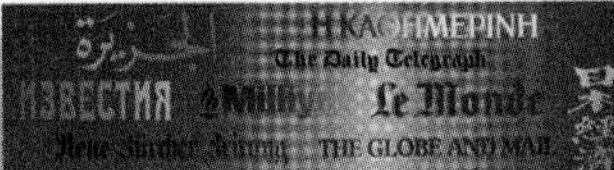

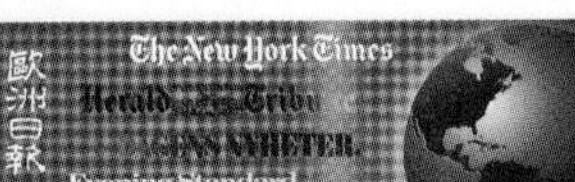

Wal-Mart Gets 25,000 Applications for Evergreen Park Store

Interest for 325 Jobs Biggest in Company's History

(Crain's)—The new Wal-Mart Stores Inc. location opening Friday in suburban Evergreen Park received a record 25,000 applications for 325 positions, the highest for any one location in the retailer's history, a company official says. . . .

He said the 325 jobs include cashier, stocking, sales and back office positions. The average pay for non-management full-time positions is $10.99 an hour.

—Shruti Dale Singh

Source: *Chicago Business,* January 25, 2006. Reprinted with permission.

Analysis: The quantity of labor supplied at any given wage rate depends on the value of leisure and the desire for income. Even a seemingly low wage offer attracted a huge quantity of labor in Chicago.

IN THE NEWS 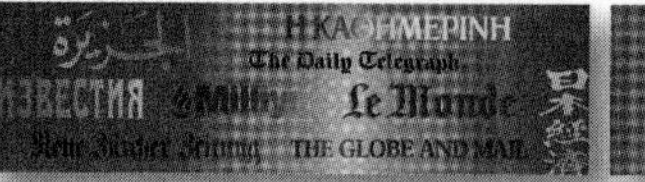 

MBA Grads Seek Challenge at Work, Not Just Big Bucks

Cynics might argue, but money apparently isn't what drives most graduate business students, *Inc.* magazine says. . . .

Inc. talked to 907 graduating MBA students at 10 schools this spring. Just 12 percent of those questioned said they went into graduate school primarily because of big salaries down the road. Only 24 percent rated a high salary as one of the most important considerations in choosing their next job.

Those answers don't surprise Teresa Miles, 23, who just earned her MBA at Duke University's Fuqua School of Business. "There are definitely some students who fit that greedy mold," says Miles, a native of Greenwich, Conn. "But it's such a stereotype I have to laugh at it."

Miles, who starts work June 15 at the Bank of New York's commercial lending department, will earn about $60,000 annually. But it was "a challenging experience and something that will do something for me" that led her to accept the bank's offer.

Most students think along those lines, says Associate Dean Dennis Weidenear at Purdue University's Krannert School of Management. "I don't think you should discount the pay they'll be getting because it is important," he says. "But they're not willing to walk over their grandmothers just to get a better salary."

Other poll results:

Challenging work was rated a "most important" job characteristic by 75 percent of the students; 44 percent ranked atmosphere first; 40 percent, location. . . .

—Mark Memmott

What MBAs at Some Top Schools Earn

School	Starting Salaries in 2006
Stanford	$126,661
Harvard	125,527
Univ. of Pennsylvania	122,708
Columbia	119,280
MIT	118,779
Dartmouth	118,201
Chicago	115,499
Northwestern	114,457

Source: *U.S. News & World Report,* April 16, 2007. Copyright 2007 U.S. News & World Report, L.P. Reprinted with permission. www.usnews.com

Source: *USA Today,* May 28, 1987. USA TODAY. Copyright 1987. Reprinted with permission (updated in 2001 by author). www.usatoday.com

Analysis: The quantity of labor supplied depends on the intrinsic satisfaction of working and the wages paid. MBA grads apparently work long hours for both high wages and job satisfaction. Would they work just as hard for *less* pay?

more valuable. Hence, ***higher wage rates are required to compensate for the increasing opportunity cost of labor.*** We'll supply a larger quantity of labor only if offered a higher wage rate. This is reflected in the labor supply curve in Figure 30.1.

The upward slope of the labor supply curve may be reinforced with the changing value of income. Those first few dollars earned on the job are really precious, especially if you have bills to pay. As you work and earn more, however, your most urgent needs will be satisfied. You may still want more things, but the urgency of your consumption desires is

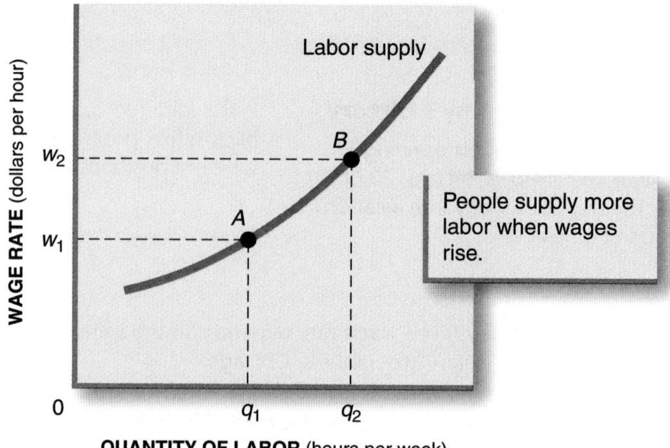

FIGURE 30.1
The Supply of Labor

The quantity of any good or service offered for sale typically increases as its price rises. Labor supply responds in the same way. At the wage rate w_1, the quantity of labor supplied is q_1 (point *A*). At the higher wage w_2, workers are willing to work more hours per week, that is, to supply a larger quantity of labor (q_2).

likely to be diminished. In other words, ***the marginal utility of income may decline as you earn more.*** If this happens, the wages offered for more work lose some of their allure. You may not be willing to work more hours unless offered a higher wage rate.

The upward slope of an individual's labor supply curve is thus a reflection of two potential phenomena:

- The increasing opportunity cost of labor as leisure time declines.
- The decreasing marginal utility of income as a person works more hours.

Money isn't necessarily the only thing that motivates people to work. People *do* turn down higher-paying jobs in favor of lower-wage jobs that they like. Many parents forgo high-wage "career" jobs in order to have more flexible hours and time at home. Volunteers offer their services just for the sense of contributing to their communities; they don't need a paycheck. Even MBA graduates say they're motivated more by the challenge of high-paying jobs than the money (see News). But money almost always makes a difference: ***People do supply more labor when offered higher wages.***

A Backward Bend?

The force that drives people up the labor supply curve is the lust for more income. Higher wages enable people to buy more goods and services. To achieve higher levels of consumption people decide to *substitute* labor for leisure.

At some point, however, additional goods and services will lose their allure. Individuals with extremely high incomes already have lots of toys. If they are offered a higher wage rate, the **substitution effect of wages** may not be persuasive. Rather than supplying *more* labor, they might even *reduce* the number of hours they work, thereby maintaining a high income *and* increasing their leisure. While you might do cartwheels for $50 an hour, Bill Gates or Brad Pitt might not lift a finger for such a paltry sum. Muhammad Ali once announced that he wouldn't spend an hour in the ring for less than $1 million and would box *less,* not more, as the pay for his fights exceeded $3 million. For him, the added income from one championship fight was so great that he felt he didn't have to fight more to satisfy his income and consumption desires.

substitution effect of wages: An increased wage rate encourages people to work more hours (to substitute labor for leisure).

A low-wage worker might also respond to higher wage rates by working *less,* not more. People receiving very low wages (such as migrant workers, household help, and babysitters) have to work long hours just to pay the rent. The increased income made possible by higher wage rates might permit them to work *fewer* hours. These *negative* labor supply responses to increased wage rates are referred to as the **income effect** of a wage increase.

income effect of wages: An increased wage rate allows a person to reduce hours worked without losing income.

The conflict between income and substitution effects shapes an individual's labor-supply curve. The *substitution effect* of high wages encourages people to work more hours. The *income effect,* on the other hand, allows them to reduce work hours without losing income. If substitution effects dominate, the labor supply curve will be upward-sloping. ***If income effects outweigh substitution effects, an individual will supply* less *labor at higher wages.*** This kind of reaction is illustrated by the backward-bending portion of the supply curve in Figure 30.2.

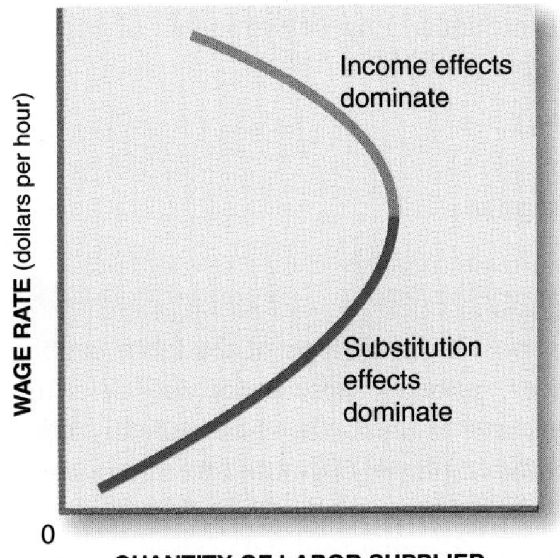

FIGURE 30.2
The Backward-Bending Supply Curve

Increases in wage rates make additional hours of work more valuable, but also less necessary. Higher wage rates increase the quantity of labor supplied as long as substitution effects outweigh income effects. At the point where income effects begin to outweigh substitution effects, the labor supply curve starts to bend backward.

WORLD VIEW

Your Money or Your Life

Would you rather have more time or more money? Here's how people in six countries answered.

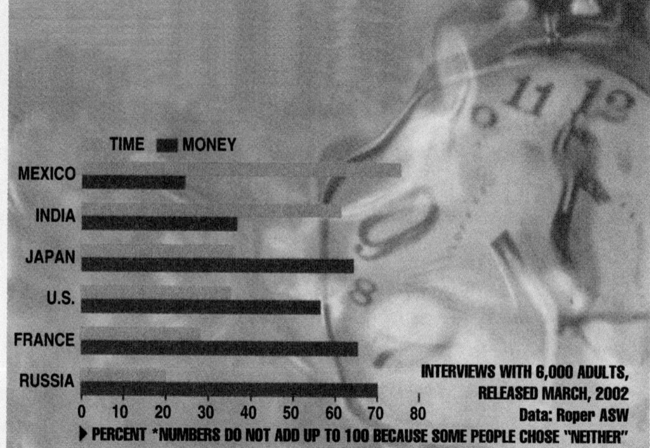

Source: Reprinted from the May 26, 2003, issue of *BusinessWeek* by permission. Copyright 2003 by The McGraw-Hill Companies.

Analysis: Despite already high incomes, Americans are still willing to sacrifice leisure for more income; *substitution effects* outweigh *income effects.*

market supply of labor: The total quantity of labor that workers are willing and able to supply at alternative wage rates in a given time period, *ceteris paribus.*

Backward-bending labor supply curves are more the exception than the rule. Most Americans do want more leisure. But given the choice between more leisure or more income, Americans choose added income (see World View). In other words, substitution effects outweigh income effects in the U.S. labor force. This explains why Americans work such long hours despite their comparatively high incomes. Workers in Mexico and India, by contrast, appear to covet more leisure rather than more income.

MARKET SUPPLY

The **market supply of labor** represents the sum of all individual labor supply decisions. Although some individuals have backward-bending supply curves, these negative responses to higher wages are swamped by positive responses from the 150 million individuals who participate in the U.S. labor market. As a result, the *market* supply curve is upward-sloping.

Courtesy of Monster.com

The labor market includes people looking for jobs and employees looking for workers.

The upward slope of the labor supply curve doesn't imply that we'll all be working longer hours in the future. As time passes, the labor supply curve can *shift.* And it will whenever one of the underlying determinants of supply changes. ***The determinants of labor supply include***

- ***Tastes*** (for leisure, income, and work).
- ***Income and wealth.***
- ***Expectations*** (for income or consumption).
- ***Prices*** of consumer goods.
- ***Taxes.***

These shift factors determine the position and slope of the labor supply curve at any point in time. As time passes, however, these underlying determinants change, causing the labor supply curve to shift. This has evidently happened. In 1890, the average U.S. worker was employed 60 hours a week at a wage rate of 20 cents an hour. In 2007, the average worker worked less than 34 hours per week at a wage rate of $18 an hour. Contributing to this long-run leftward shift has been (1) the spectacular rise in living standards (a change in income and wealth), (2) the growth of income transfer programs that provide economic security when one isn't working (a change in income and expectations), and (3) the increased diversity and attractiveness of leisure activities (a change in tastes and other goods).

Elasticity of Labor Supply

Despite the evident *long*-run shifts of the labor supply curve, workers still respond positively to higher wage rates in the *short* run. To measure the resulting movements along the labor supply curve, we use the concept of elasticity. Specifically, **elasticity of labor supply** is the percentage change in the quantity of labor supplied divided by the percentage change in the wage rate—that is,

elasticity of labor supply: The percentage change in the quantity of labor supplied divided by the percentage change in wage rate.

$$\text{Elasticity of labor supply} = \frac{\%\text{ change in quantity of labor supplied}}{\%\text{ change in wage rate}}$$

The elasticity of labor tells us how much more labor will be available if a higher wage is offered. If the elasticity of labor is 0.2, a 10 percent increase in wage rates will induce a 2 percent increase in the quantity of labor supplied.

The actual responsiveness of workers to a change in wage rates depends on the determinants of labor supply. Time is also important for labor supply elasticity, as individuals can't always adjust their schedules or change jobs instantaneously.

Institutional Constraints

The labor supply curve and its related elasticities tell us how much time people would like to allocate to work. We must recognize, however, that people seldom have the opportunity to adjust their hours of employment at will. True, a Bill Gates or a Britney Spears can easily choose to work more or fewer hours. Most workers, however, face more rigid choices. They must usually choose to work at a regular job for 8 hours a day, 5 days a week, or not to work at all. Very few firms are flexible enough to accommodate a desire to work only between the hours of 11 A.M. and 3 P.M. on alternate Thursdays. Adjustments in work hours are more commonly confined to choices about overtime work or secondary jobs (moonlighting) and vacation and retirement. Families may also alter the labor supply by varying the number of family members sent into the labor force at any given time. Students, too, can often adjust their work hours. The flow of immigrants into the U.S. labor market also increases when U.S. wages rise.

LABOR DEMAND

demand for labor: The quantities of labor employers are willing and able to hire at alternative wage rates in a given time period, *ceteris paribus.*

Regardless of how many people are *willing* to work, it's up to employers to decide how many people will *actually* work. That is, there must be a **demand for labor.** What determines the number of workers employers are willing to hire at various wage rates?

Derived Demand

In earlier chapters we emphasized that employers are profit maximizers. In their quest for maximum profits, firms seek the rate of output at which marginal revenue equals marginal cost. Once they've identified the profit-maximizing rate of output, firms enter factor markets to purchase the required amounts of labor, equipment, and other resources. Thus, ***the quantity of resources purchased by a business depends on the firm's expected sales and output.*** In this sense, the demand for factors of production, including labor, is a **derived demand;** it's derived from the demand for goods and services.

derived demand: The demand for labor and other factors of production results from (depends on) the demand for final goods and services produced by these factors.

Consider the plight of strawberry pickers. Strawberry pickers are paid very low wages and are employed only part of the year. But their plight can't be blamed on the greed of the strawberry growers. Strawberry growers, like most producers, would love to sell more strawberries at higher prices. If they did, the growers would hire more pickers and might even pay them higher wages. But the growers must contend with the market demand for strawberries: Consumers aren't willing to buy more strawberries at higher prices. As a consequence, the growers can't afford to hire more pickers or pay them

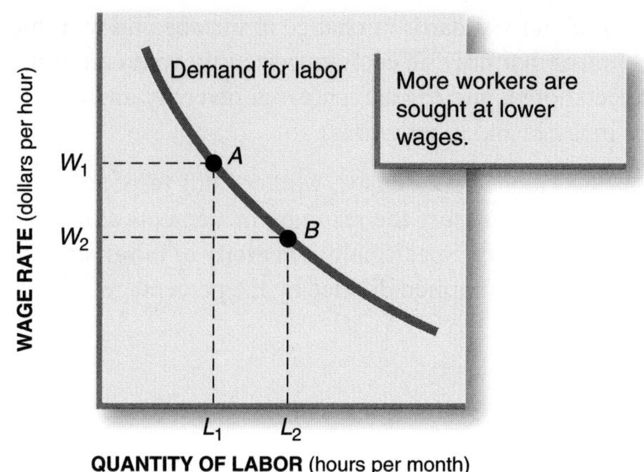

FIGURE 30.3
The Demand for Labor

The higher the wage rate, the smaller the quantity of labor demanded (*ceteris paribus*). At the wage rate W_1, only L_1 of labor is demanded. If the wage rate falls to W_2, a larger quantity of labor (L_2) will be demanded. The labor demand curve obeys the law of demand.

webnote

Average earnings by occupation can be obtained from the U.S. Bureau of Labor Statistics at www.stats.bls.gov. Under "Wages, Earnings, and Benefits" choose "Wages by Area and Occupation."

higher wages. In contrast, information-technology (IT) firms are always looking for more workers and offer very high wages to get them. This helps explain why college students who major in engineering, math, or computer science get paid a lot more than philosophy majors. IT specialists benefit from the growing demand for Internet services, while philosophy majors suffer because the search for the meaning of life is not a growth industry.

The principle of derived demand suggests that if consumers really want to improve the lot of strawberry pickers, they should eat more strawberries. An increase in the demand for strawberries will motivate growers to plant more berries and hire more labor to pick them. Until then, the plight of the pickers isn't likely to improve.

The Labor Demand Curve

The number of strawberry pickers hired by the growers isn't completely determined by the demand for strawberries. The number of pickers hired will also depend on the wage rate. That is, ***the quantity of labor demanded depends on its price (the wage rate).*** In general, we expect that strawberry growers will be *willing to hire* more pickers at low wages than at higher wages. Hence, the demand for labor looks very much like the demand for any good or service (see Figure 30.3).

Marginal Physical Product

The fact that the demand curve for labor slopes downward doesn't tell us what quantity of labor will be hired. Nor does it tell us what wage rate will be paid. To answer such questions, we need to know what determines the particular shape and position of the labor demand curve.

A strawberry grower will be willing to hire another picker only if that picker contributes more to output than he or she costs. Growers, as rational businesspeople, recognize that *every* sale, *every* expenditure has some impact on total profits. Hence, the truly profit-maximizing grower will evaluate each picker's job application in terms of the applicant's potential contribution to profits.

Fortunately, a strawberry picker's contribution to output is easy to measure; it's the number of boxes of strawberries he or she picks. Suppose for the moment that Marvin, a college dropout with three summers of experience as a canoe instructor, is able to pick 5 boxes per hour. These 5 boxes represent Marvin's **marginal physical product (MPP).** In other words, Marvin's MPP is the *addition* to total output that occurs when the grower hires him for an hour:

marginal physical product (MPP): The change in total output associated with one additional unit of input.

$$\text{Marginal physical product} = \frac{\text{change in total output}}{\text{change in quantity of labor}}$$

Marginal physical product establishes an *upper* limit to the grower's willingness to pay. Clearly the grower can't afford to pay Marvin more than 5 boxes of strawberries for an hour's work; the grower won't pay Marvin more than he produces.

Marginal Revenue Product

Most strawberry pickers don't want to be paid in strawberries. At the end of a day in the fields, the last thing a picker wants to see is another strawberry. Marvin, like the rest of the pickers, wants to be paid in cash. To find out how much cash he might be paid, we need to know what a box of strawberries is worth. This is easy to determine. The market value of a box of strawberries is simply the price at which the grower can sell it. Thus, Marvin's contribution to output can be measured by either marginal physical product (5 boxes per hour) or the dollar value of that product.

The dollar value of a worker's contribution to output is called **marginal revenue product (MRP).** Marginal revenue product is the *change* in total revenue that occurs when more labor is hired—that is,

marginal revenue product (MRP): The change in total revenue associated with one additional unit of input.

$$\text{Marginal revenue product} = \frac{\text{change in total revenue}}{\text{change in quantity of labor}}$$

In Marvin's case, the "change in quantity of labor" is 1 extra hour of picking strawberries. The "change in total revenue" is the *value* of the extra 5 boxes of berries Marvin picks in that hour. If the grower can sell strawberries for $2 a box, Marvin's marginal revenue product is simply 5 boxes per hour × $2 per box, or $10 per hour. We could have come to the same conclusion by multiplying marginal *physical* product times *price,* that is

$$\text{MRP} = \text{MPP} \times p$$

or

$$\$10 \text{ per hour} = 5 \text{ boxes per hour} \times \$2 \text{ per box}$$

In compliance with the rule about not paying anybody more than he or she contributes, the profit-maximizing grower should be willing to pay Marvin *up to* $10 an hour. In other words, ***marginal revenue product sets an upper limit to the wage rate an employer will pay.***

But what about a lower limit? Suppose the pickers aren't organized and that Marvin is desperate for money. Under such circumstances, he might be willing to work—to supply labor—for only $4 an hour.

Should the grower hire Marvin for such a low wage? The profit-maximizing answer is obvious. If Marvin's marginal revenue product is $10 an hour and his wages are only $4 an hour, the grower will be eager to hire him. The difference between Marvin's marginal revenue product ($10) and his wage ($4) implies additional profits of $6 an hour. In fact, the grower will be so elated by the economics of this situation that he'll want to hire everybody he can find who's willing to work for $4 an hour. After all, if the grower can make $6 an hour by hiring Marvin, why not hire 1,000 pickers and accumulate profits at an even faster rate?

The Law of Diminishing Returns

The exploitive possibilities suggested by Marvin's picking are too good to be true. It isn't at all clear, for example, how the grower could squeeze 1,000 workers onto 1 acre of land and have any room left over for strawberry plants. There must be some limit to the profit-making potential of this situation.

A few moments' reflection on the absurdity of trying to employ 1,000 people to pick 1 acre of strawberries should be ample warning of the limits to profits here. You don't need 2 years of business school to recognize this. But some grasp of economics may help explain exactly why the grower's eagerness to hire additional pickers will begin to fade long before 1,000 are hired. The operative concept here is *marginal productivity.*

Diminishing MPP. The decision to hire Marvin originated in his marginal physical product—that is, the 5 boxes of strawberries he can pick in an hour's time. To assess the wisdom of hiring still more pickers, we have to ***consider how total output will change if additional labor is employed.*** To do so, we need to keep track of marginal physical product.

Figure 30.4 shows how strawberry output changes as additional pickers are hired. Marvin picks 5 boxes of strawberries per hour. Total output and his marginal physical product are identical, because he's initially the only picker employed. When the grower hires

FIGURE 30.4
Diminishing Marginal Physical Product

The marginal physical product of labor is the increase in total production that results when one additional worker is hired. Marginal physical product tends to fall as additional workers are hired in any given production process. This decline occurs because each worker has increasingly less of other factors (e.g., land) with which to work.

When the second worker (George) is hired, total output increases from 5 to 10 boxes per hour. Hence, the second worker's MPP equals 5 boxes per hour. Thereafter, capital and land constraints diminish marginal physical product.

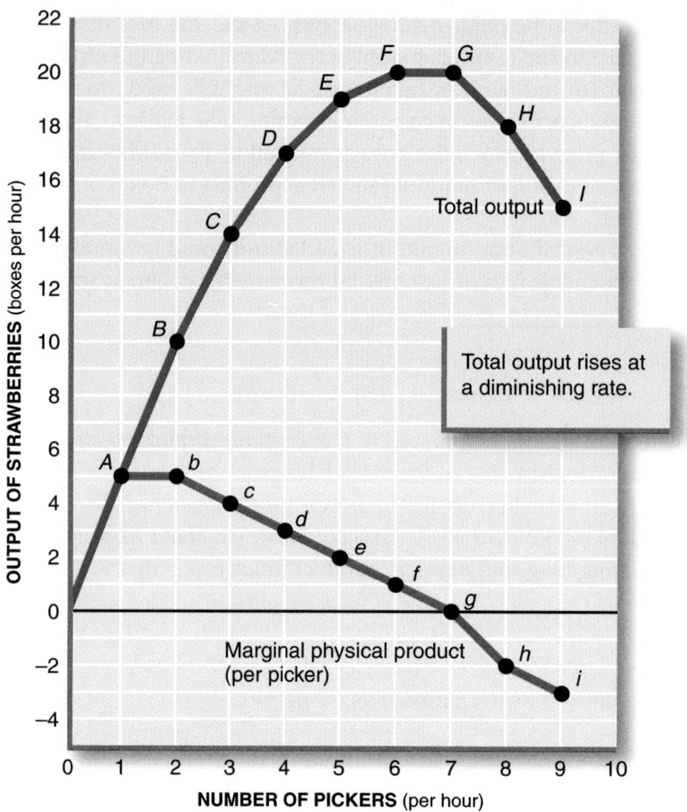

	Number of Pickers (per hour)	Total Strawberry Output (boxes per hour)	Marginal Physical Product (boxes per hour)
A	1 (Marvin)	5	5
B	2 (George)	10	5
C	3	14	4
D	4	17	3
E	5	19	2
F	6	20	1
G	7	20	0
H	8	18	–2
I	9	15	–3

George, Marvin's old college roommate, we observe the total output increases to 10 boxes per hour (point *B* in Figure 30.4). This figure represents another increase of 5 boxes per hour. Accordingly, we may conclude that George's *marginal physical product* is 5 boxes per hour, the same as Marvin's. Given such productivity, the grower will want to hire George and continue looking for more pickers.

As more workers are hired, total strawberry output continues to increase but not nearly as fast. Although the later hires work just as hard, the limited availability of land and capital constrain their marginal physical product. One problem is the number of boxes. There are only a dozen boxes, and the additional pickers often have to wait for an empty box. The time spent waiting depresses marginal physical product. The worst problem is space: As additional workers are crowded onto the 1-acre patch, they begin to get in one another's way. The picking process is slowed, and marginal physical product is further depressed. Note that the MPP of the fifth picker is 2 boxes per hour, while the MPP of the sixth picker is only 1 box per hour. By the time we get to the seventh picker, marginal physical product actually falls to zero, as no further increases in total strawberry output take place.

Things get even worse if the grower hires still more pickers. If 8 pickers are employed, total output actually *declines.* The pickers can no longer work efficiently under such crowded conditions. The MPP of the eighth worker is *negative,* no matter how ambitious or hardworking this person may be. Figure 30.4 illustrates this decline in marginal physical product.

Our observations on strawberry production are similar to those made in most industries. In the short run, the availability of land and capital is limited by prior investment decisions. Hence, additional workers must share existing facilities. As a result, ***the marginal physical product of labor eventually declines as the quantity of labor employed increases.*** This is the **law of diminishing returns** we first encountered in Chapter 21. It's based on the simple observation that an increasing number of workers leaves each worker with less land and capital to work with. At some point, this "crowding" causes MPP to decline.

law of diminishing returns: The marginal physical product of a variable factor declines as more of it is employed with a given quantity of other (fixed) inputs.

Diminishing MRP. As marginal *physical* product diminishes, so does marginal *revenue* product (MRP). As noted earlier, marginal revenue product is the increase in the *value* of total output associated with an added unit of labor (or other input). In our example, it refers to the increase in strawberry revenues associated with one additional picker and is calculated as MPP × *p.*

The decline in marginal revenue product mirrors the drop in marginal physical product. Recall that a box of strawberries sells for $2. With this price and the output statistics in Figure 30.4, we can readily calculate marginal revenue product, as summarized in Table 30.1. As the growth of output diminishes, so does marginal revenue product. Marvin's marginal revenue product of $10 an hour has fallen to $6 by the time 4 pickers are employed and reaches zero when 7 pickers are employed.[1]

Number of Pickers (per hour)	Total Strawberry Output (in boxes per hour)	×	Price of Strawberries (per box)	=	Total Strawberry Revenue (per hour)	Marginal Revenue Product
0	0		$2		0	—
1 (Marvin)	5		2		$10	$10
2 (George)	10		2		20	10
3	14		2		28	8
4	17		2		34	6
5	19		2		38	4
6	20		2		40	2
7	20		2		40	0
8	18		2		36	−4
9	15		2		30	−6

TABLE 30.1
Diminishing Marginal Revenue Product

Marginal revenue product (MRP) measures the change in total revenue that occurs when one additional worker is hired. At constant product prices, MRP equals MPP × price. Hence, MRP declines along with MPP.

[1]Marginal revenue product would fall even faster if the price of strawberries declined as increasing quantities were supplied. We're assuming that the grower's output doesn't influence the market price of strawberries and hence that the grower is a *competitive* producer.

A FIRM'S HIRING DECISION

The tendency of marginal revenue product to diminish will cool the strawberry grower's eagerness to hire 1,000 pickers. We still don't know, however, how many pickers will be hired.

The Firm's Labor Supply

Our earlier discussion of labor supply indicated that more workers are available only at higher wage rates. But that's true only for the *market* supply. A single producer may be able to hire an unlimited number of workers at the prevailing wage rate—if the firm is perfectly competitive in the labor market. In other words, ***a firm that's a perfect competitor in the labor market can hire all the labor it wants at the prevailing market wage.***

Let's assume that the strawberry grower is so small that his hiring decisions have no effect on local wages. As far as he's concerned, there's an unlimited supply of strawberry pickers willing to work for $4 an hour. His only decision is how many of these willing pickers to hire at that wage rate.

MRP = Firm's Labor Demand

webnote

The AFL-CIO has computed how much less income a woman earns as a result of the gender gap in pay. For lively illustrations, visit www.aflcio.org/issues/jobseconomy/women/equalpay/index.cfm

Figure 30.5 provides the answer. We already know that the grower is eager to hire pickers whose marginal revenue product exceeds their wage. He'll therefore hire at least 1 worker at that wage, because the MRP of the first picker is $10 an hour (point *A* in Figure 30.5). A second worker will be hired as well, because that picker's MRP (point *B* in Figure 30.5) also exceeds the going wage rate. In fact, ***the grower will continue hiring pickers until the MRP has declined to the level of the market wage rate.*** Figure 30.5 indicates that this intersection (point *C*) occurs when 5 pickers are employed. We can conclude that the grower will be willing to hire—will *demand*—5 pickers if wages are $4 an hour.

The folly of hiring more than 5 pickers is also apparent in Figure 30.5. The marginal revenue product of the sixth worker is only $2 an hour (point *D*). Hiring a sixth picker will cost more in wages than the picker brings in as revenue. The *maximum* number of pickers the grower will employ at prevailing wages is 5 (point *C*).

The law of diminishing returns also implies that all 5 pickers will be paid the same wage. Once 5 pickers are employed, we can't say that any single picker is responsible for the observed decline in marginal revenue product. Marginal revenue product of labor diminishes because each worker has less capital and land to work with, not because the last worker hired is less able than the others. Accordingly, the "fifth" picker can't be identified as any particular individual. Once 5 pickers are hired, Marvin's MRP is no higher than any other picker's. ***Each (identical) worker is worth no more than the marginal revenue product of the last worker hired, and all workers are paid the same wage rate.***

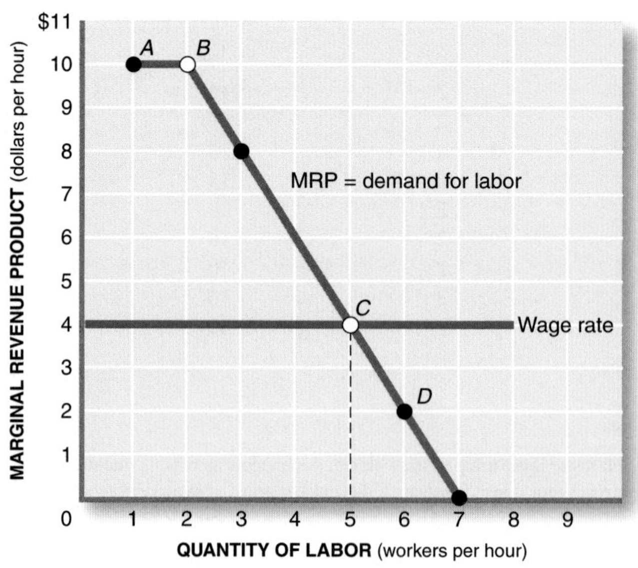

FIGURE 30.5
The Marginal Revenue Product Curve Is the Labor Demand Curve

The MRP curve tells us how many workers an employer would want to hire at various wage rates. An employer is willing to pay a worker no more than the marginal revenue product. In this case, a grower would gladly hire a second worker, because that worker's MRP (point *B*) exceeds the wage rate ($4). The sixth worker won't be hired at that wage rate, however, since the MRP (at point *D*) is less than $4. The MRP curve is the labor demand curve.

IN THE NEWS 

A-Rod Takes the Stage in New York

NEW YORK—Alex Rodriguez is catching on fast in the Big Apple.

After investing $112 million on Rodriguez, the New York Yankees introduced their new third baseman Tuesday. If the buzz at Yankee Stadium is any indicator, the acquisition is paying off.

The Yankees usually sell 14,000 tickets a day, but on Monday, the day the trade that brought Rodriguez to the Yankees from Texas became official, the team sold 22,000 tickets. That puts them 75,000 ahead of their pace from last season, when they drew a team record 3.4 million.

Internet hits on the team's Web site have soared from 500,000 to 2.5 million a day. The Yankees, who also added Gary Sheffield, Kevin Brown and Javier Vazquez in the offseason, have sold 24,300 season tickets, 100 more than last season.

A couple of hundred fans were standing outside the Yankee Stadium souvenir shop before it opened Tuesday, watching employees hang Rodriguez T-shirts and his No. 13 pinstripe jersey. . . .

Two hours after the shop opened, more than a dozen of 72 jerseys had sold for $115 each. Also, 70 blue Rodriguez T-shirts sold at $25 each.

—Mel Antonen

Source: *USA Today,* February 18, 2004.

Analysis: Marginal revenue product measures what a worker is worth to an employer. The New York Yankees are expecting a high MRP from A-Rod.

The principles of marginal revenue product apply to baseball players as well as strawberry pickers. The New York Yankees are paying Alex Rodriguez $112 million to play baseball. As the News reports, the Yankees expect "A-Rod" to generate at least that much added revenue in extra ticket sales, merchandise sales, and ad revenue. The Yankees think A-Rod's MRP justifies his extraordinarily high salary.

Whatever the explanation for the disparity between the incomes of baseball players and strawberry pickers, the enormous gap between them seems awfully unfair. An obvious question then arises: Can't the number of pickers or their wages be increased?

Changes in Wage Rates

Suppose the government were to set a minimum wage for strawberry pickers at $6 an hour. At first glance this action would appear to boost the wages of pickers, who have been earning only $4 an hour. This isn't all good news for the strawberry pickers, however. ***There's a trade-off between wage rates and the number of workers demanded.*** If wage rates go up, growers will hire fewer pickers.

Figure 30.6 illustrates this trade-off. The grower's earlier decision to hire 5 pickers was based on a wage of $4 an hour (point *C*). If the wage jumps to $6 an hour, it no longer makes economic sense to keep 5 pickers employed. The MRP of the fifth worker is only $4 an hour. The grower will respond to higher wage rates by moving up the labor demand curve to point *G*. At point *G*, only 4 pickers are hired and MRP again equals the wage rate. If more workers are to be hired, the wage rate must drop.

Changes in Productivity

The downward slope of the labor demand curve doesn't doom strawberry pickers to low wages. It does emphasize, however, the inevitable link between workers' productivity and wages. ***To get higher wages without sacrificing jobs, productivity (MRP) must increase.***

Suppose Marvin and his friends all enroll in a local agricultural extension course and learn new methods of strawberry picking. With these new methods, the marginal physical product of each picker increases by 1 box per hour. With the price of strawberries still at $2 a box, this productivity improvement implies an increase in marginal *revenue* product of $2 per worker. This change causes an upward *shift* of the labor demand (MRP) curve, as in Figure 30.6*b*.

Notice how the improvement in productivity has altered the value of strawberry pickers. The MRP of the fifth picker is now $6 an hour (point *F*) rather than $4 (point *C*). Hence, the grower can now afford to pay higher wages. Or the grower could employ more pickers

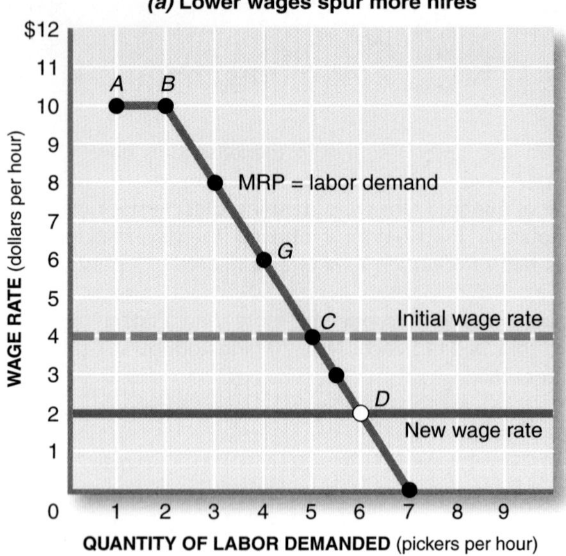

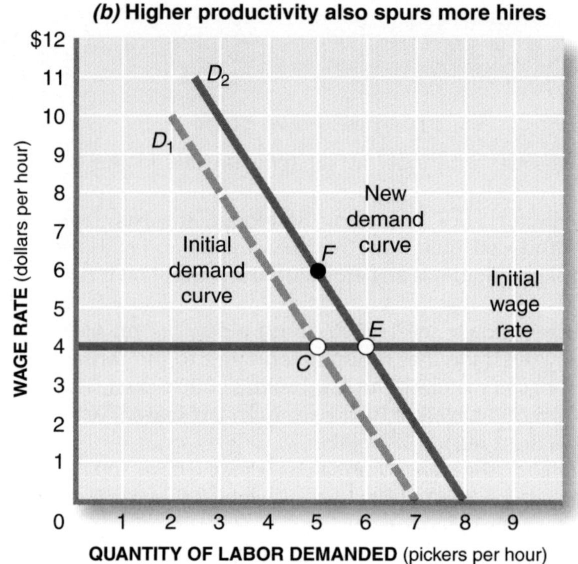

FIGURE 30.6
Incentives to Hire

(*a*) **Lower wage** If the wage rate drops, an employer will be willing to hire more workers, *ceteris paribus.* At $4 an hour, only 5 pickers per hour would be demanded (point *C*). If the wage rate dropped to $2 an hour, 6 pickers per hour would be demanded (point *D*).

(*b*) **Higher productivity** If the marginal revenue product of labor improves, the employer will hire a greater quantity of labor at any given wage rate. The labor demand curve will shift up (from D_1 to D_2). In this case, an increase in MRP leads the employer to hire 6 workers (point *E*) rather than only 5 workers (point *C*) at $4 per hour.

than before, moving from point *C* to point *E*. ***Increased productivity implies that workers can get higher wages without sacrificing jobs or more employment without lowering wages.*** Historically, increased productivity has been the most important source of rising wages and living standards.

Changes in Price

An increase in the price of strawberries would also help the pickers. Marginal revenue product reflects the interaction of productivity and product prices. If strawberry prices were to double, strawberry pickers would become twice as valuable, even without an increase in physical productivity. Such a change in product prices depends, however, on changes in the market supply and demand for strawberries.

MARKET EQUILIBRIUM

The principles that guide the hiring decisions of a single strawberry grower can be extended to the entire labor market. This suggests that ***the market demand for labor depends on***

- ***The number of employers.***
- ***The marginal revenue product of labor in each firm and industry.***

Increases in either the demand for final products or the productivity of labor will tend to increase marginal revenue productivity and therewith the demand for labor.

On the supply side of the labor market we have already observed that ***the market supply of labor depends on***

- ***The number of available workers.***
- ***Each worker's willingness to work at alternative wage rates.***

The supply decisions of each worker are in turn a reflection of tastes, income, wealth, expectations, other prices, and taxes.

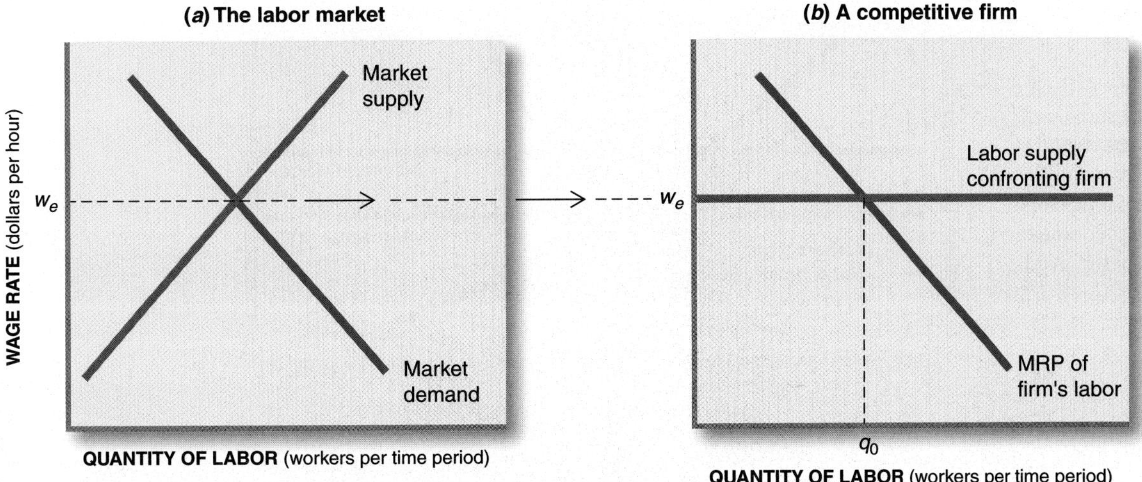

FIGURE 30.7
Equilibrium Wage

The intersection of *market* supply and demand determines the equilibrium wage in a competitive labor market. All the firms in the industry can then hire as much labor as they want at that equilibrium wage. In this case, the firm can hire all the workers it wants at the equilibrium wage, w_e. It chooses to hire q_0 workers, as determined by their marginal revenue product within the firm.

Equilibrium Wage

equilibrium wage: The wage rate at which the quantity of labor supplied in a given time period equals the quantity of labor demanded.

Figure 30.7 brings these market forces together. ***The intersection of the market supply and demand curves establishes the* equilibrium wage.** This is the only wage rate at which the quantity of labor supplied equals the quantity of labor demanded. Everyone who's willing and able to work for this wage will find a job.

If the labor market is perfectly competitive, all employers will be able to hire as many workers as they want at the equilibrium wage. Like our strawberry grower, every competitive firm is assumed to have no discernible effect on market wages. ***Competitive employers act like price takers with respect to wages as well as prices.*** This phenomenon is also portrayed in Figure 30.7.

Minimum Wages

Some people will be unhappy with the equilibrium wage. Employers may grumble that wages are too high. Workers may complain that wages are too low. They may seek government intervention to change market outcomes. This is the goal of Congress when it establishes a *minimum* wage (see Table 30.2).

Figure 30.8 illustrates the effects of such government intervention. The equilibrium wage is W_e, and q_e workers are employed. A minimum wage of W_M is then set, above the market equilibrium. The wage W_M encourages more low-skilled workers to seek employment; the

Oct. '38	$0.25	Jan. '78	$2.65
Oct. '39	0.30	Jan. '79	2.90
Oct. '45	0.40	Jan. '80	3.10
Jan. '50	0.75	Jan. '81	3.35
Mar. '56	1.00	Apr. '90	3.80
Sept. '61	1.15	Apr. '91	4.25
Sept. '63	1.25	Oct. '96	4.75
Feb. '67	1.40	Sept. '97	5.15
Feb. '68	1.60	July '07	5.85
May '74	2.00	July '08	6.55
Jan. '75	2.10	July '09	7.25
Jan. '76	2.30		

TABLE 30.2
Minimum Wage History

The federal minimum wage has been increased periodically since first set in 1938. In 2007 Congress raised the minimum to $7.25 by 2009.

FIGURE 30.8
Minimum Wage Effects

If the minimum wage exceeds the equilibrium wage, a labor surplus will result: More workers will be willing to work at that wage rate than employers will be willing to hire. Some workers will end up with higher wages, but others will end up unemployed.

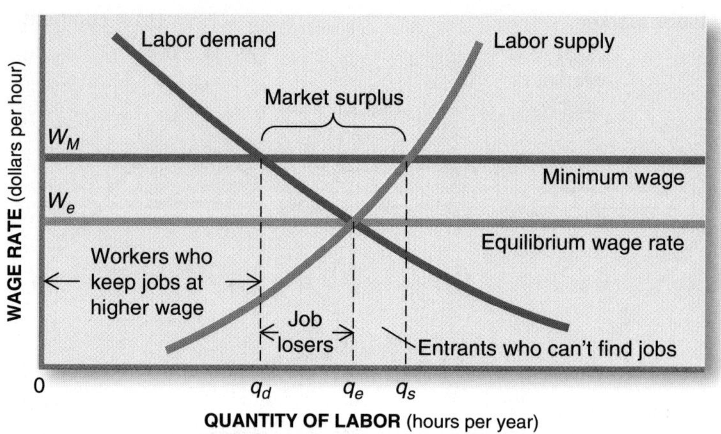

quantity supplied increases from q_e to q_s. At the same time, however, the number of available jobs declines from q_e to q_d. This leaves a market surplus at the wage W_M. As a result of the increased wage, some workers have lost jobs ($q_e - q_d$) and some new entrants fail to find employment ($q_s - q_e$). Only those workers who remain employed (q_d) benefit from the higher wage.

Government-imposed wage floors thus have two distinct effects: ***A minimum wage***

- ***Reduces the quantity of labor demanded.***
- ***Increases the quantity of labor supplied.***
- ***Creates a market surplus.***

webnote

For pros and cons of raising the minimum wage, see the Electronic Policy Network (pro) at www.movingideas.org/issuesindepth and Employment Policies Institute (con) at www.epionline.org/index_mw.cfm

The extent of job loss resulting from a minimum wage hike is hotly debated. How many jobs are lost obviously depends on how far the minimum wage is raised. The elasticity of labor demand is also important. Democrats argue that labor demand is inelastic, so few jobs will be lost. Republicans assert that labor demand is elastic, so more jobs will be lost. In the early 1980s, the elasticity of labor demand was found to be 0.10. Hence, a 10 percent increase in the minimum wage would cause a 1 percent reduction in employment. Between

IN THE NEWS

Congress Approves Minimum Wage Hike

With little fanfare, Congress yesterday approved the first increase in the federal minimum wage in nearly a decade, voting to boost wages for America's lowest-paid workers from $5.15 to $7.25 an hour over the next two years. . . .

According to the Bureau of Labor Statistics, about 1.7 million workers, or 2 percent of the hourly workforce, were earning $5.15 an hour or less last year. About half were under age 25, and nearly three-quarters were employed in food preparation or other service jobs. . . .

Workers would get their first raise, to $5.85 an hour, 60 days after the measure is signed by Bush. A year later, the minimum wage would rise to $6.55 an hour, and it would hit $7.25 a year after that.

—Lori Montgomery

Source: *The Washington Post,* May 25, 2007, D01. www.washingtonpost.com.

Analysis: A higher minimum wage encourages firms to hire fewer workers. How many jobs are lost depends on the size of the wage hike and the price elasticity of labor demand.

1981 and 1990, however, the minimum was stuck at $3.35 an hour while average wages increased 30 percent. By 1989, the federal minimum may have actually been *below* the equilibrium wage for low-skilled labor. When the minimum wage is below the equilibrium wage, an increase in the minimum may have little or no adverse employment effects. This appeared to be the case again in 1996. Because the federal minimum hadn't been raised for 5 years (see Table 30.2), the 50-cent-per-hour hike in October 1996 caused few job losses. According to Federal Reserve estimates, the 1997 wage hike may have reduced employment growth by only 100,000 to 200,000 jobs.

The same situation existed again in 2007. By then, the federal minimum of $5.15 hadn't been lifted for 10 years (Table 30.2) and had fallen below equilibrium levels (McDonald's and other fast-food outlets were paying $6.50 and more in 2007). When Congress raised the minimum to $5.85 (see News), the legislated floor still lagged behind market wages. Further hikes, to $7.25 an hour, would probably cause some job losses, however. In general, ***the further the minimum wage rises above the market's equilibrium wage, the greater the job loss.***

webnote

For historical data on the federal minimum wage, in real and nominal terms, visit the U.S. Department of Labor at www.dol.gov/esa/whd/flsa

CHOOSING AMONG INPUTS

One of the options employers have when wage rates rise is to utilize more machinery in place of labor. In most production processes there are possibilities for substituting capital inputs for labor inputs. In the long run, there are still more possibilities for redesigning the whole production process. Given these options, how should the choice of inputs be made?

Suppose a mechanical strawberry picker can pick berries twice as fast as Marvin. Who will the grower hire, Marvin or the mechanical picker? At first it would seem that the grower would choose the mechanical picker. But the choice isn't so obvious. So far, all we know is that the mechanical picker's MPP is twice as large as Marvin's. But we haven't said anything about the *cost* of the mechanical picker.

Cost Efficiency

Suppose that a mechanical picker can be rented for $10 an hour, while Marvin is still willing to work for $4 an hour. Will this difference in hourly cost change the grower's input choice?

To determine the relative desirability of hiring Marvin or renting the mechanical picker, the grower must compare the ratio of their marginal physical products to their cost. This ratio of marginal product to cost expresses the **cost efficiency** of an input—that is,

cost efficiency: The amount of output associated with an additional dollar spent on input; the MPP of an input divided by its price (cost).

$$\text{Cost efficiency} = \frac{\text{marginal physical product of an input}}{\text{cost of an input}}$$

Marvin's MPP is 5 boxes of strawberries per hour and his cost (wage) is $4. Thus, the return on each dollar of wages paid to Marvin is

$$\text{Cost efficiency of labor} = \frac{\text{MPP}_{\text{labor}}}{\text{cost}_{\text{labor}}} = \frac{5 \text{ boxes}}{\$4} = 1.25 \text{ boxes per } \$1 \text{ of cost}$$

By contrast, the mechanical picker has an MPP of 10 boxes per hour and costs $10 per hour; thus

$$\text{Cost efficiency of mechanical picker} = \frac{\text{MPP of mechanical picker}}{\text{cost of mechanical picker}} = \frac{10 \text{ boxes}}{\$10} = 1 \text{ box per } \$1 \text{ of cost}$$

These calculations indicate that Marvin is more cost-effective than the mechanical picker. From this perspective, the grower is better off hiring Marvin than renting a mechanical picker.

From the perspective of cost efficiency, the cheapness of a productive input is measured not by its price but by the amount of output it delivers for that price. Thus, ***the most cost-efficient factor of production is the one that produces the most output per dollar.***

The concept of cost efficiency helps explain why American firms don't move en masse to Haiti, where peasants are willing to work for as little as 80 cents an hour. Although this wage rate is far below the minimum wage in the United States, the marginal physical product of Haitian peasants is even further below American standards. American workers remain more cost-efficient than the "cheap" labor available in Haiti, making it unprofitable to **outsource** U.S. jobs. So long as U.S. workers deliver more output per dollar of wages, they will remain cost-effective in global markets.

outsourcing: The relocation of production to foreign countries.

Alternative Production Processes

Typically a producer doesn't choose between individual inputs but rather between alternative production processes. General Motors, for example, can't afford to compare the cost efficiency of each job applicant with the cost efficiency of mechanical tire mounters. Instead, GM compares the relative desirability of a **production process** that is labor-intensive (uses a lot of labor) with others that are less labor-intensive. GM ignores individual differences in marginal revenue product. Nevertheless, the same principles of cost efficiency guide the decision.

production process: A specific combination of resources used to produce a good or service.

The Efficiency Decision

Let's return to the strawberry patch to see how the choice of an entire production process is made. We again assume that strawberries can be picked by either human or mechanical hands. Now, however, we assume that 1 ton of strawberries can be produced by only one of the three production processes described in Table 30.3. Process A is most *labor-intensive;* it uses the most labor and thus keeps more human pickers employed. By contrast, process C is *capital-intensive;* it uses the most mechanical pickers and provides the least employment to human pickers. Process B falls between these two extremes.

Which of these three production processes should the grower use? If he used labor-intensive process A, he'd be doing the pickers a real favor. But his goal is to maximize profits, so we assume he'll choose the production process that best serves this objective. That is, he'll choose the *least-cost* process to produce 1 ton of strawberries.

But which of the production processes in Table 30.3 is least expensive? We really can't tell on the basis of the information provided. To determine the relative cost of each process—and thus to understand the producer's choice—we must know something more about input costs. In particular, we have to know how much an hour of mechanical picking costs and how much an hour of human picking (labor) costs. Then we can determine which combination of inputs is least expensive in producing 1 ton of strawberries—that is, which is most *cost-efficient.* Note that we don't have to know how much the land costs, because the same amount of land is used in all three production processes. Thus, land costs won't affect our efficiency decision.

Suppose that strawberry pickers are still paid $4 an hour and that mechanical pickers can be rented for $10 an hour. The acre of land rents for $500 per year. With this information we can now calculate the total dollar cost of each production process and quickly determine the most cost-efficient. Table 30.4 summarizes the required calculations.

The calculations performed in Table 30.4 clearly identify process C as the least expensive way of producing 1 ton of strawberries. Process A entails a total cost of $2,230, whereas the capital-intensive process C costs only $1,560 to produce the same quantity of output.

TABLE 30.3
Alternative Production Processes

One ton of strawberries can be produced with varying input combinations. Which process is most efficient? What information is missing?

	Alternative Processes for Producing One Ton of Strawberries		
Input	Process A	Process B	Process C
Labor (hours)	400	270	220
Machinery (hours)	13	15	18
Land (acres)	1	1	1

TABLE 30.4
The Least-Cost Combination

A producer wants to produce a given rate of output for the least cost. Choosing the least expensive production process is the efficiency decision. In this case, process C represents the most cost-efficient production process for producing 1 ton of strawberries.

Input	Cost Calculation
Process A	
Labor	400 hours at $4 per hour = $1,600
Machinery	13 hours at $10 per hour = 130
Land	1 acre at $500 = 500
	Total cost $2,230
Process B	
Labor	270 hours at $4 per hour = $1,080
Machinery	15 hours at $10 per hour = 150
Land	1 acre at $500 = 500
	Total cost $1,730
Process C	
Labor	220 hours at $4 per hour = $ 880
Machinery	18 hours at $10 per hour = 180
Land	1 acre at $500 = 500
	Total cost $1,560

As a profit maximizer, the grower will choose process C, even though it implies less employment for strawberry pickers.

The choice of an appropriate production process—the decision about *how* to produce—is called the **efficiency decision.** As we've seen, a producer seeks to use the combination of resources that produces a given rate of output for the least cost. The efficiency decision requires the producer to find that particular least-cost combination.

efficiency decision: The choice of a production process for any given rate of output.

THE ECONOMY TOMORROW

CAPPING CEO PAY

At the beginning of this chapter we noted that Michael Eisner, the CEO of Walt Disney Company, signed a 10-year contract that could have paid him an astronomical $771 million. When challenged to defend his pay, Disney's CEO asserted he had earned every penny of it by enhancing the value of the company's stock.

Critics of CEO pay don't accept this explanation. They make three points. First, the rise in the price of Disney's *stock* is not a measure of marginal revenue product. Only part of the increase in share prices was due to the company's performance; the rest was caused by a general upswing in the stock market. Second, the revenues of the Walt Disney Company probably wouldn't have been $771 million lower in the absence of Eisner. Hence, his marginal revenue product is less than $771 million. Finally, Eisner probably would have worked just as hard for, say, a mere $400 million or so. Therefore, his actual pay was more than required to elicit the desired supply response.

Critics conclude that many CEO paychecks are out of line with realities of supply and demand (see cartoon on next page). They want corporations to reduce CEO pay and revise the process used for setting CEO pay levels.

webnote

Motivated by money? Check out the highest-paying occupations at www.acinet.org/acinet

Unmeasured MRP. One of the difficulties in determining the appropriate level of CEO pay is the elusiveness of marginal revenue product. It's easy to measure the MRP of a strawberry picker or even a salesclerk who sells Disney toys. But a corporate CEO's contributions are less well defined. A CEO is supposed to provide strategic leadership and a sense of mission. These are critical to a corporation's success but hard to quantify.

Congress confronts the same problem in setting the president's pay. We noted earlier that the president of the United States is paid $400,000 a year. Can we argue that this salary

"O.K. guys, now lets go and earn that four hundred times our workers' salaries."

Analysis: The wages of top corporate officers may not be fully justified by their marginal revenue product.

represents the president's marginal revenue product? The News on the next page suggests that the president's pay would be in the range of $38–58 million if he were paid on performance (MRP). The wage we actually pay a president is less a reflection of contribution to total output than a matter of custom. The salary also reflects the price voters believe is required to induce competent individuals to forsake private-sector jobs and assume the responsibilities of the presidency. In this sense, the wage paid to the president and other public officials is set by their **opportunity wage**—that is, the wage they could earn in private industry.

opportunity wage: The highest wage an individual would earn in his or her best alternative job.

The same kinds of considerations influence the wages of college professors. The marginal revenue product of a college professor isn't easy to measure. Is it the number of students she teaches, the amount of knowledge conveyed, or something else? Confronted with such problems, most universities tend to pay college professors according to their opportunity wage—that is, the amount the professors could earn elsewhere.

Opportunity wages also help explain the difference between the wage of the CEO of Disney and the workers who peddle its products. The lower wage of salesclerks reflects not only their marginal revenue product at Disney stores but also the fact that they're not trained for many other jobs. That is, their opportunity wages are low. By contrast, Disney's CEO has impressive managerial skills that are in demand by many corporations; his opportunity wages are high.

Opportunity wages help explain CEO pay but don't fully justify such high pay levels. If Disney's CEO pay is justified by opportunity wages, that means that another company would be willing to pay him that much. But what would justify such high pay at another company? Would his MRP be any easier to measure? Maybe *all* CEO paychecks have been inflated.

Critics of CEO pay conclude that the process of setting CEO pay levels should be changed. All too often, executive pay scales are set by self-serving committees composed of executives of the same or similar corporations. Critics want a more independent assessment of pay scales, with nonaffiliated experts and stockholder representatives. Some critics want to go a step further and set mandatory "caps" on CEO pay. President Clinton rejected legislated caps but convinced Congress to limit the tax deductibility of CEO pay. Any "unjustified" CEO pay in excess of $1 million a year can't be treated as a business expense but instead must be paid out of after-tax profits. This change puts more pressure on corporations to examine the rationale for multimillion-dollar paychecks.

webnote

Read more about top CEO salaries and check CEO/worker pay ratios at www.aflcio.org/paywatch

If markets work efficiently, such government intervention shouldn't be necessary. Corporations that pay their CEOs excessively will end up with smaller profits than companies

IN THE NEWS 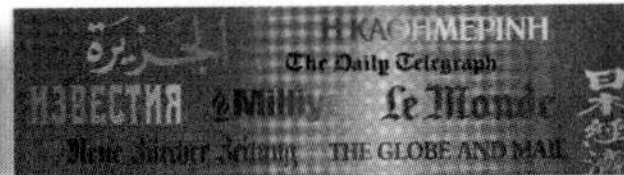  

What's a President Worth?

So what if the president were paid like a CEO? Based on performance, a president would be worth up to $58 million a year—if he meets certain goals, compensation experts say. What those goals might be are shown below.

If the nation's president and chief executive were running a major corporation, he probably would find a proposed pay raise to $400,000 laughable.

Compared with what Jack Welch makes at General Electric and Lou Gerstner makes at IBM, that's pocket change.

In the private sector, a CEO running a huge corporation would earn $34 million to $58 million a year, much of it from incentive bonuses and stock options, says compensation expert Graef Crystal of the on-line newsletter *crystal-report.com.*

At $200,000 a year, the president makes more than 99 percent of all workers. But he oversees a budget of $1.8 trillion, 11 times the annual revenue of the nation's largest company, General Motors. He's boss of 4.2 million employees, both civilian and military, six times as many as the largest private employer, Wal-Mart.

Yet he would have to work 2,878 years to bring home the $576 million that Walt Disney CEO Michael Eisner made last year, largely from exercising stock options he was granted as incentives.

In 1980, *Fortune* 500 CEOs averaged $625,000 a year, a little more than three times what President Carter was making. By 1990, the average CEO was making 10 times more than President Bush. And last year, in the wake of generous stock options awarded in a booming market, the CEO-to-president ratio swelled to 53-to-1.

—Del Jones and Gary Strauss

Source: *USA Today,* May 27, 1999. USA TODAY. Copyright 1999. Reprinted with permission. www.usatoday.com

	Possible payout
Inflation A key to everything from credit card rates to grocery prices. Say the annualized rate is 2.5% or less.	**$10 million to $14 million**
Economic growth A growing economy means prosperity from Wall Street to Main Street. Gross National Product growth of 3% or more.	**$15 million to $23 million**
Crime Reduction in murders, robberies, and other serious crimes.	**$5 million to $8 million**
Employment Cut unemployment to 4%.	**$3 million to $5 million**
Intangibles Foreign policy successes, lowering the trade deficit, environmental issues, cutting the costs of government.	**$5 million to $8 million**

Total annual potential pay: $38 million to $58 million

Analysis: If the nation's president were paid on the basis of his marginal revenue product, his salary would be a lot higher than $400,000.

who pay market-based wages. Over time, "lean" companies will be more competitive than "fat" companies, and excessive pay packages will be eliminated. Legislated CEO pay caps imply that CEO labor markets aren't efficient or that the adjustment process is too slow. To forestall more government intervention in pay decisions, companies may tie executive pay more explicitly to performance (marginal revenue product) in the economy tomorrow.

SUMMARY

- The motivation to work arises from social, psychological, and economic forces. People need income to pay their bills, but they also need a sense of achievement. As a consequence, people are willing to work—to supply labor. LO1
- There's an opportunity cost involved in working—namely, the amount of leisure time one sacrifices. By the same token, the opportunity cost of not working (leisure) is the income and related consumption possibilities thereby forgone. Thus each person confronts a trade-off between leisure and income. LO1
- Increases in wage rates induce people to work more—that is, to substitute labor for leisure. But this substitution effect may be offset by an income effect. Higher wages also enable a person to work fewer hours with no loss of income. When income effects outweigh substitution effects, the labor supply curve bends backward. LO2
- A firm's demand for labor reflects labor's marginal revenue product. A profit-maximizing employer won't pay a worker more than the worker produces. LO2
- The marginal revenue product of labor diminishes as additional workers are employed on a particular job (the law of diminishing returns). This decline occurs because additional workers have to share existing land and capital, leaving each worker with less land and capital to work with. LO2
- A producer seeks to get the most output for every dollar spent on inputs. This means getting the highest ratio of marginal product to input price. A profit-maximizing producer will choose the most cost-efficient input (not necessarily the one with the cheapest price). LO1
- The efficiency decision involves the choice of the least-cost productive process and is also made on the basis of cost efficiency. A producer seeks the least expensive process to produce a given rate of output. LO3
- Differences in marginal revenue product are an important explanation of wage inequalities. But the difficulty of measuring MRP in some jobs leaves many wage rates to be determined by opportunity wages or other mechanisms. LO3

Key Terms

labor supply
substitution effect of wages
income effect of wages
market supply of labor
elasticity of labor supply
demand for labor
derived demand
marginal physical product (MPP)
marginal revenue product (MRP)
law of diminishing returns
equilibrium wage
cost efficiency
outsourcing
production process
efficiency decision
opportunity wage

Questions for Discussion

1. Why are you doing this homework? What are you giving up? What utility do you expect to gain? LO1
2. Would you continue to work after winning a lottery prize of $50,000 a year for life? Would you change schools, jobs, or career objectives? What factors besides income influence work decisions? LO1
3. According to the World View on page 604 does the substitution effect or the income effect dominate in India? In Russia? Why might this be the case? LO1
4. Explain why marginal physical product would diminish as
   (*a*) More secretaries are hired in an office.
   (*b*) More professors are hired in the economics department.
   (*c*) More construction workers are hired to build a school. LO2
5. Is this course increasing your marginal productivity? If so, in what way? LO2

6. How might you measure the marginal revenue product of (*a*) a quarterback and (*b*) the team's coach? LO2
7. Who is hurt and who is helped by an increase in the legal minimum wage? Under what circumstances might a higher minimum *not* reduce employment? LO3
8. In 2006 the chancellor of the University of Texas was paid $693,677 and the football coach was paid $2.6 million. Does this make any sense? LO2
9. Is it possible that the president of the United States is overpaid? How should his MRP be measured? LO2
10. The minimum wage in Mexico is less than $1 an hour. Does this make Mexican workers more cost-effective than U.S. workers? Explain. LO2
11. Is "excessive" CEO pay a *public* issue or a *private* issue? LO2

problems The Student Problem Set at the back of this book contains numerical and graphing problems for this chapter.

web activities to accompany this chapter can be found on the Online Learning Center: **http://www.mhhe.com/economics/schiller11e**

Labor Unions

LEARNING OBJECTIVES

After reading this chapter, you should know:

LO1. How unions secure higher wages.

LO2. What factors affect the outcomes of collective bargaining.

LO3. How unions affect nonunion wages.

The United Auto Workers Union (UAW) launched a strike against Caterpillar, Inc., in November 1991. The union wanted the manufacturer of construction machinery to increase pay, benefits, and job security. *Four years* later, Caterpillar hadn't budged; it continued to operate with replacement workers, management crews, and union members who crossed the picket line. The union finally capitulated in December 1995, sending its 8,700 members back to work with neither higher pay nor even a new contract. The union struck again in 1996 but relented after 17 months. Seven years after their first strike, the Caterpillar workers still had no contract.

To many observers, the failed UAW strike at Caterpillar climaxed a steady decline in the power of labor unions. But the union movement is far from dead. Labor unions are even expanding in some sectors (especially government employment). Many unions still have **market power**—the ability to alter market outcomes. This chapter focuses on how power in the labor market affects wages, employment, and other economic outcomes. We address the following questions:

- **How do large and powerful employers affect market wages?**
- **How do labor unions alter wages and employment?**
- **What outcomes are possible from collective bargaining between management and unions?**

In the process of answering these questions, we look at the nation's most powerful unions and their actual behavior.

THE LABOR MARKET

To gauge the impact of labor market power, we must first observe how a competitive labor market sets wages and employment. On the supply side, we have all those individuals who are willing to work—to supply labor—at various wage rates. By counting the number of individuals willing to work at each and every wage rate, we can construct a *market* **labor supply** curve, as in Figure 31.1.

market power: The ability to alter the market price of a good or service.

labor supply: The willingness and ability to work specific amounts of time at alternative wage rates in a given time period, *ceteris paribus*.

The willingness of producers (firms) to hire labor is reflected in the market labor demand curve. The curve itself is constructed by counting the number of workers each firm says it is willing and able to hire at each and every wage rate. The curve illustrates the market **demand for labor.**

Competitive Equilibrium

The intersection of the labor supply and labor demand curves (point *C* in Figure 31.1) reveals the **equilibrium wage** rate (w_e): the wage rate at which the quantity of labor supplied equals the quantity demanded. At this wage rate, every job seeker who's willing and able to work for the wage w_e is employed. In addition, firms are able to acquire all the labor they're willing and able to hire at that wage.

demand for labor: The quantities of labor employers are willing and able to hire at alternative wages in a given time period, *ceteris paribus*.

Not everyone is employed in equilibrium. Workers who demand wages in excess of w_e are unable to find jobs. By the same token, employers who refuse to pay a wage as high as w_e are unable to attract workers.

Local Labor Markets

Figure 31.1 appears to suggest that there's only *one* labor market and thus only one equilibrium wage. This is a gross oversimplification. If you were looking for a job in Tulsa, you'd have little interest in employment prospects or power configurations in New York City. You'd be more concerned about the available jobs and wages in Tulsa—that is, the condition of the *local* labor market.

equilibrium wage: The wage rate at which the quantity of labor supplied in a given time period equals the quantity of labor demanded.

Even within a particular geographical area, interest usually focuses on particular occupations and workers rather than on all the people supplying or demanding labor. If you were looking for work as a dancer, you'd have little interest in the employment situation for carpenters or dentists. Rather, you'd want to know how many nightclubs or dance troupes had job vacancies, and what wages and working conditions they offered.

The distinction among various geographical, occupational, and industrial labor markets provides a more meaningful basis for analyzing labor market power. The tremendous size of the national labor market, with over 150 million workers, precludes anyone from acquiring control of the entire market. The largest employer in the United States (Wal-Mart) employs less than 0.8 percent of the labor force. General Motors employs fewer than that, and the top 500 industrial corporations employ less than 20 percent of all workers. The

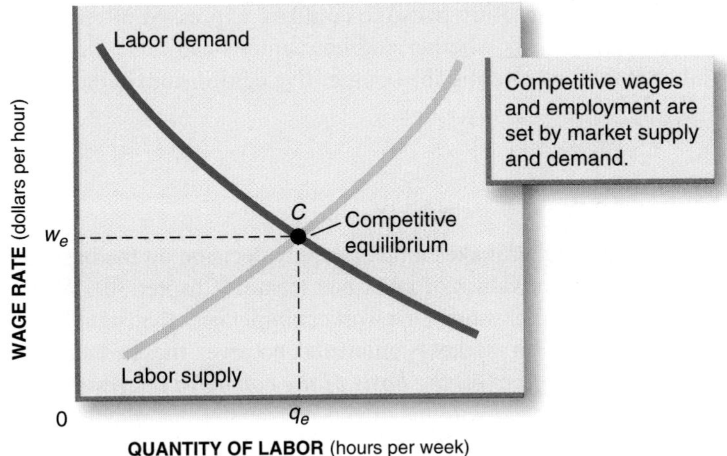

FIGURE 31.1
Competitive Equilibrium in the Labor Market

The market labor supply curve includes all persons willing to work at various wage rates. The labor demand curve tells us how many workers employers are willing to hire. In a competitive market, the intersection of the labor supply and labor demand curves (point *C*) determines the equilibrium wage (w_e) and employment (q_e) levels.

situation on the supply side is similar. The largest labor union (the Teamsters) represents less than 1 percent of all workers in the country. All unions together represent only one-eighth of the labor force. This doesn't mean that particular employers or unions have no influence on our economic welfare. It does suggest, however, that ***power in labor markets is likely to be more effective in specific areas, occupations, and industries.***

LABOR UNIONS

Types of Unions

The immediate objective of labor unions is to alter the equilibrium wage and employment conditions in specific labor markets. ***To be successful, unions must be able to exert control over the market supply curve.*** That's why workers have organized themselves along either industry or occupational craft lines. *Industrial unions* include workers in a particular industry (the United Auto Workers, for example). *Craft unions* represent workers with a particular skill (like the International Brotherhood of Electrical Workers), regardless of the industry in which they work.

The purpose of both types of labor unions is to coordinate the actions of thousands of individual workers, thereby achieving control of market supply. If a union is able to control the supply of workers in a particular industry or occupation, the union acquires a *monopoly* in that market. Like most monopolies, unions attempt to use their market power to increase their incomes.

Union Objectives

A primary objective of unions is to raise the wages of union members. In the 2005 dispute between pro hockey team owners and players, money was the sole issue. The players, who were already getting an average paycheck of $1.8 million per season, were resisting a salary cap that would restrain wages. The team owners wanted to limit total player salaries to 53–55 percent of league revenues.

webnote

For an overview and update on UAW activity, visit the organization's Web site at www.uaw.org

An exclusive focus on wages is somewhat unusual. Union objectives also include improved working conditions, job security, and other nonwage forms of compensation, such as retirement (pension) benefits, vacation time, and health insurance. The Players Association and the National Football League have bargained about the use of artificial turf, early retirement, player fines, television revenues, game rules, and the use of team doctors, drug tests, pensions, and the number of players permitted on a team. A recurring concern of the United Auto Workers is job security. Consequently, they focus on work rules that may eliminate jobs and unemployment benefits for laid-off workers.

Although union objectives tend to be as broad as the concerns of union members, we focus here on just one objective, wage rates. This isn't too great a simplification, because most nonwage issues can be translated into their effective impact on wage rates. In 2003, for example, the UAW and GM agreed to nearly two dozen different job provisions, ranging from job security to child care (see following News). It was possible, however, to figure out the cost of these many provisions ($4,625 per worker per year). Hence, the "bottom line" of the compensation package could be expressed in terms of wage costs. What we seek to determine is whether and how unions can raise effective wage rates in a specific labor market by altering the competitive equilibrium depicted in Figure 31.1.

THE POTENTIAL USE OF POWER

In a competitive labor market, each worker makes a labor supply decision on the basis of his or her own perceptions of the relative values of labor and leisure (Chapter 30). Whatever decision is made won't alter the market wage. One worker simply isn't that significant in a market composed of thousands. Once a market is unionized, however, these conditions no longer hold. A ***union evaluates job offers on the basis of the collective interests of its members.*** In particular, it must be concerned with the effects of increased employment on the wage rate paid to its members.

IN THE NEWS  

What Autoworkers Won

After two months of negotiations, the UAW and GM signed a new four-year contract in October 2003. The contract included these provisions.

- **Wages** $3,000 lump-sum payments in 2003 and 2004 plus 2 percent increase in 2005 and 3% in 2006.
- **Holidays** Increased to 67 days with addition of a National Election Day in November 2005.
- **Pensions** Increased by $4.20 per month for each year of service.
- **Tool Allowance** Increased by 30 cents per hour.
- **Eye care** Coverage extended to LASIK.
- **Vehicle vouchers** $1,000 each in first and third years.
- **Contraceptives** Newly covered.
- **Job security** Requires new employees to be hired as attrition replacements.
- **Tuition assistance** Increased from $4,200 to $4,600 per year.
- **Dental services** Benefit increased from $1,600 to $1,700 per year.
- **Supplemental unemployment benefits** Increased from $175 to $190 per week.
- **Relocation allowance** Increased from $23,500 to $25,000.
- **Life insurance** Survivor benefit increased by $50 per month.

Analysis: Labor unions bargain with management over a variety of employment conditions. Most issues, however, can be expressed in terms of their impact on wage costs.

The Marginal Wage

Like all monopolists, unions have to worry about the downward slope of the demand curve. In the case of labor markets, a larger quantity of labor can be "sold" only at lower wage rates. Suppose the workers in a particular labor market confront the market labor demand schedule depicted in Figure 31.2. This schedule tells us that employers aren't willing to hire any workers at a wage rate of $6 per hour (row *S*) but will hire 1 worker per hour if the wage rate is $5 (row *T*). At still lower rates, the quantity of labor demanded increases; five workers per hour are demanded at a wage of $1 per hour.

An individual worker offered a wage of $1 an hour would have to decide whether such wages merited the sacrifice of an hour's leisure. But a union would evaluate the offer differently. A union must consider how the hiring of one more worker will affect the wages of all the workers.

Total Wages Paid. Notice that when four workers are hired at a wage rate of $2 an hour (row *W*), total wages are $8 per hour. In order for a fifth worker to be employed, the wage rate must drop to $1 an hour (row *X*). At wages of $1 per hour, the *total* wages paid to the five workers amount to only $5 per hour. Thus, total wages paid to the workers actually *fall* when a fifth worker is employed. Collectively the workers would be better off sending only four people to work at the higher wage of $2 an hour and paying the fifth worker $1 an hour to stay home!

The basic mandate of a labor union is to evaluate wage and employment offers from this *collective* perspective. To do so, ***a union must distinguish the marginal wage from the market wage.*** The market wage is simply the current wage rate paid by the employer; it's the wage received by individual workers. The **marginal wage,** on the other hand, is the change in *total* wages paid (to all workers) when an additional worker is hired—that is,

marginal wage: The change in total wages paid associated with a one-unit increase in the quantity of labor employed.

$$\text{Marginal wage} = \frac{\text{change in total wages paid}}{\text{change in quantity of labor employed}}$$

The distinction between marginal wages and market wages arises from the downward slope of the labor demand curve. It's analogous to the distinction we made between marginal revenue and price for monopolists in product markets. The distinction simply reflects the law of demand: As wages fall, the number of workers hired increases.

FIGURE 31.2
The Marginal Wage

The *marginal wage* is the change in *total wages* (paid to all workers) associated with the employment of an additional worker. If the wage rate is $4 per hour, only two workers will be hired (point *U*). The wage rate must fall to $3 per hour if three workers are to be hired (point *V*). In the process, *total* wages paid rise from $8 ($4 × 2 workers) to $9 ($3 × 3 workers). The *marginal* wage of the third worker is only $1 (point *v*).

The graph illustrates the relationship of the marginal wage to labor demand. The marginal wage curve lies below the labor demand curve, because the marginal wage is less than the nominal wage. Compare the marginal wage (point *v*) and the nominal wage (point *V*) of the third worker.

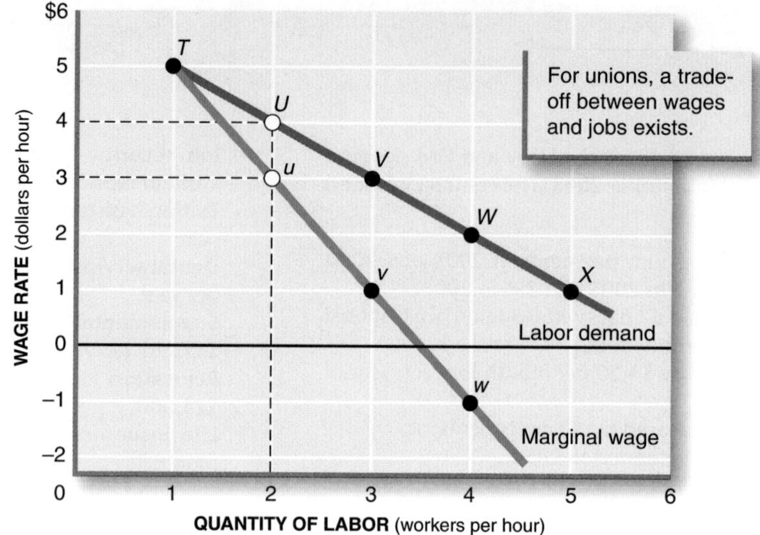

	Wage Rate (per hour)	×	Number of Workers Demanded (per hour)	=	Total Wages Paid (per hour)		Marginal Wage (per labor hour)
S	$6		0		$0		
						>	$5
T	5		1		5		
						>	3
U	4		2		8		
						>	1
V	3		3		9		
						>	−1
W	2		4		8		
						>	−3
X	1		5		5		

The impact of increased employment on marginal wages is also illustrated in Figure 31.2. According to the labor demand curve, one worker will be hired at a wage rate of $5 an hour (point *T*); two workers will be hired only if the market wage falls to $4 an hour (point *U*), at which point the first and second workers will each be getting $4 an hour. Thus, the increased wages of the second worker (from zero to $4) will be partially offset by the reduction in the wage rate paid to the first worker (from $5 to $4). *Total* wages paid will increase by only $3; this is the *marginal* wage (point *u*). The marginal wage actually becomes negative at some point, when the implied wage loss to workers already on the job begins to exceed the wage of a new hired worker.

The Union Wage Goal

A union never wants to accept a negative marginal wage, of course. At such a point, union members would be better off paying someone to stay home. The question, then, is what level of (positive) marginal wage the union should accept.

We can answer this question by looking at the labor supply curve. The labor supply curve tells us how much labor workers are *willing to supply* at various wage rates. Hence, the labor supply curve defines the lowest wage *individual* union members would accept. If the union adopts a *collective* perspective on the welfare of its members, however, it will view the wage offer differently. From their collective perspective, the wage that union members are getting for additional labor is the *marginal* wage, not the nominal (market) wage. Hence, the marginal wage curve, not the labor demand curve, is decisive in the union's assessment of wage offers.

If the union wants to maximize the *total* welfare of its members, it will seek the level of employment that equates the marginal wage with the supply preferences of union members.

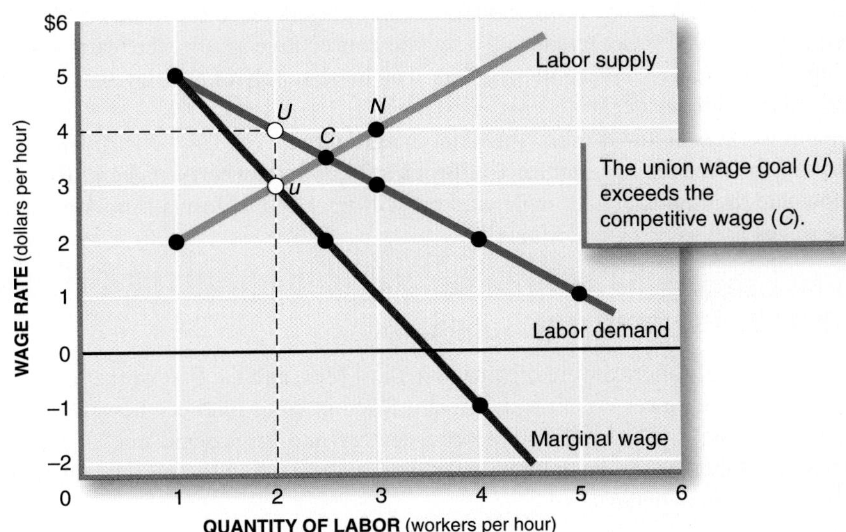

FIGURE 31.3
The Union Wage Objective

The intersection of the marginal wage and labor supply curves (point *u*) determines the union's desired employment. Employers are willing to pay a wage rate of $4 per hour for that many workers, as revealed by point *U* on the labor demand curve.

More workers (*N*) are willing to work at $4 per hour than employers demand (*U*). To maintain that wage rate, the union must exclude some workers from the market. In the absence of such power, wages would fall to the competitive equilibrium (point *C*).

In Figure 31.3, ***the intersection of the marginal wage curve with the labor supply curve identifies the desired level of employment for the union.*** This intersection occurs at point *u,* yielding total employment of two workers per hour.

The marginal wage at point *u* is $3. However, the union members will get paid an actual wage higher than that. Look up from point *u* on the marginal wage curve to point *U* on the employer's labor demand curve. Point *U* tells us that the employer is *willing to pay* a wage rate of $4 an hour to employ two workers. The union knows it can demand and get $4 an hour if it supplies only two workers to the firm.

What the union is doing here is choosing a point on the labor demand curve that the union regards as the optimal combination of wages and employment. In a competitive market, point *C* would represent the equilibrium combination of wages and employment. But the union forces employers to point *U,* thereby attaining a higher wage rate and reducing employment.

Exclusion

The union's ability to maintain a wage rate of $4 an hour depends on its ability to exclude some workers from the market. Figure 31.3 suggests that three workers are willing and able to work at the union wage of $4 an hour (point *N*), whereas only two are hired (point *U*). If the additional worker were to offer his services, the wage rate would be pushed down the labor demand curve (to $3 per hour). Hence, ***to maintain a noncompetitive wage, the union must be able to exercise some control over the labor supply decisions of individual workers.*** The essential force here is union solidarity. Once unionized, the individual workers must agree not to compete among themselves by offering their labor at nonunion wage rates. Instead, the workers must agree to withhold labor—to strike, if necessary—if wage rates are too low, and to supply labor only at the union-set wage.

Unions can solidify their control of the labor supply by establishing **union shops,** workplaces where workers must join the union within 30 days after being employed. In this way, the unions gain control of all the workers employed in a particular company or industry, thereby reducing the number of replacement workers available for employment during a strike. Stiff penalties (such as loss of seniority or pension rights) and general union solidarity ensure that only nonunion workers will "fink" or "scab"—take the job of a worker on strike.

union shop: An employment setting in which all workers must join the union within 30 days after being employed.

Replacement Workers. Even union shops, however, are subject to potential competition from substitute labor. When the UAW struck Caterpillar in 1991, the company advertised nationally for replacement workers and set up a toll-free phone line for applicants. In the midst of a recession the company got a huge response. The resulting flow of replacement workers crippled the UAW strike. Professional baseball players faced the same problem in 1995. When the continued strike threatened a second consecutive season, the team owners started hiring new players to replace the regulars. The huge supply of aspiring ball players forced the strikers to reconsider.

Replacement workers are even more abundant in agriculture. The United Farm Workers has been trying for decades to organize California's 20,000 strawberry pickers. But the workers know that thousands of additional workers will flock to California from Mexico if they protest wages and working conditions.

THE EXTENT OF UNION POWER

Early Growth

The first labor unions in America were organized in the 1780s, and the first worker protests as early as 1636. Union power wasn't a significant force in labor markets, however, until the 1900s, when heavily populated commercial centers and large-scale manufacturing became common. Only then did large numbers of workers begin to view their employment situations from a common perspective.

The period 1916–20 was one of particularly fast growth for labor unions, largely because of the high demand for labor resulting from World War I. All these membership gains were lost, however, when the Great Depression threw millions of people out of work. By 1933, union membership had dwindled to the levels of 1915.

As the Depression lingered on, public attitudes and government policy changed. Too many people had learned the meaning of layoffs, wage cuts, and prolonged unemployment. In 1933, the National Industrial Recovery Act (NIRA) established the right of employees to bargain collectively with their employers. When the NIRA was declared unconstitutional by the Supreme Court in 1935, its labor provisions were incorporated into a new law, the Wagner Act. With this legislative encouragement, union membership doubled between 1933 and 1937. Unions continued to gain in strength as the production needs of World War II increased the demand for labor. Figure 31.4 reflects the tremendous spurt of union activity between the depths of the Depression and the height of World War II.

Union Power Today

unionization ratio: The percentage of the labor force belonging to a union.

Union membership stopped increasing in the 1950s, even though the labor force kept growing. As a result, the unionized percentage of the labor force—the **unionization rate**—has been in steady decline for more than 40 years. The current unionization rate of 12.5 percent is less than half of its post–World War II peak and far below unionization rates in other industrialized nations (see World View on the next page).

Private- vs. Public-Sector Trends. The decline in the *national* unionization rate conceals two very different trends. Union representation of *private*-sector workers has plunged even more sharply than Figure 31.4 suggests. In the last 10 years, the unionization rate in the private sector has fallen from 11.5 percent to only 7.9 percent. At the same time, union

FIGURE 31.4
Changing Unionization Rates

Unions grew most rapidly during the decade 1935–1945. Since that time, the growth of unions hasn't kept pace with the growth of the U.S. labor force. Most employment growth has occurred in service industries that have traditionally been nonunion.

Source: U.S. Department of Labor.

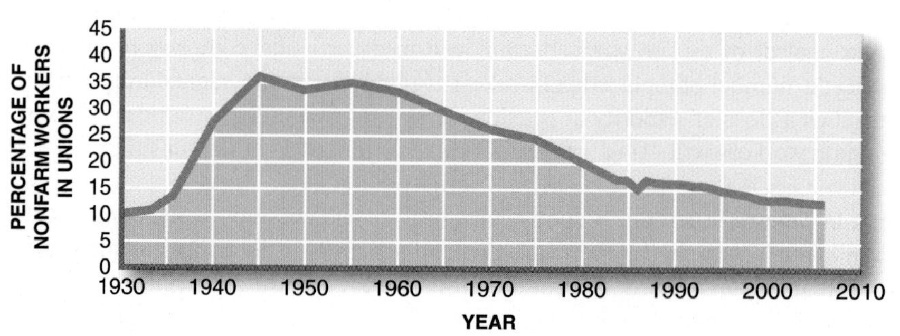

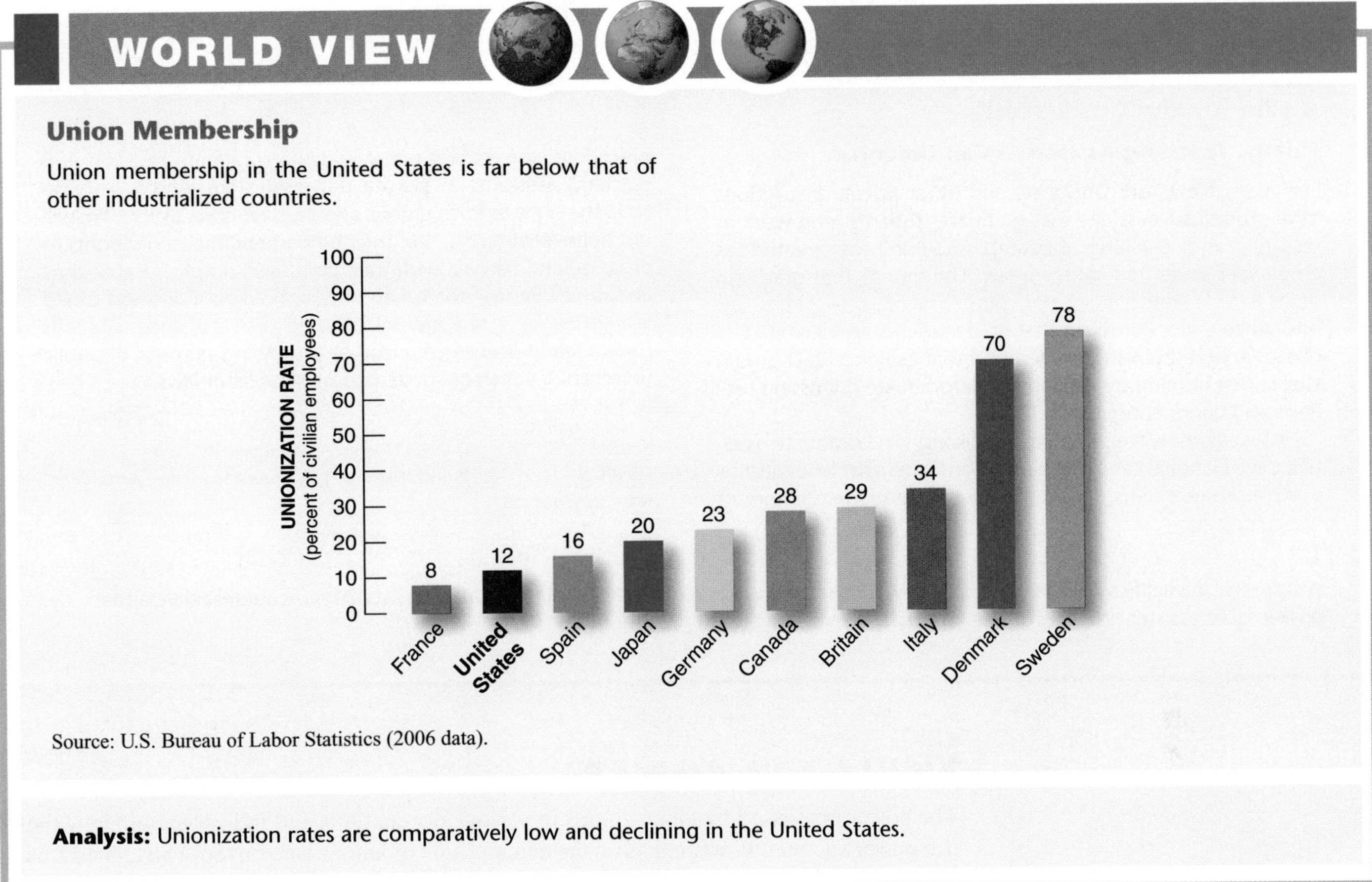

membership has increased sharply among teachers, government workers, and nonprofit employees. As of 2007, over 36 percent of workers on government payrolls were union members. ***The old industrial unions are being supplanted by unions of service workers, especially those employed in the public sector.***

Although industrial unions have been in general decline, they still possess significant pockets of market power. The Teamsters, the UAW, the United Mine Workers, the Union of Needletrades and Textile Employees, and the Food Workers all have substantial representation in their respective markets. Their strength in those specific markets, not national averages, determines their ability to alter market outcomes.

The AFL-CIO. One labor organization with a decidedly national focus is the AFL-CIO (the American Federation of Labor–Congress of Industrial Organizations). The AFL-CIO is not a separate union but a representational body of more than 50 national unions, representing 9 million workers. It doesn't represent or negotiate for any particular group of workers but focuses instead on issues of general labor interest. The AFL-CIO acts as an advocate for the labor movement and represents labor's interest in legislative areas. It's the primary vehicle for political action. In addition, the AFL-CIO may render economic assistance to member unions or to groups of workers who wish to organize.

webnote

The AFL-CIO's Web site offers a brief mission statement and a map of affiliated unions; visit www.aflcio.org

Change to Win Coalition. The AFL-CIO's political activity upset member unions who favored more focus on traditional union interests, particularly union organizing. In September 2005, some of these unions (including teamsters, garment workers, food workers, service workers) quit the AFL-CIO and formed a new multiunion organization, the Change to Win Coalition.

IN THE NEWS

A Win for the Graduate(s)

Finally, Teaching Assistants Can Unionize

For years, New York University and other private institutions have argued successfully that graduate students who work as research and teaching assistants shouldn't be treated as employees under federal labor law. The money that grad students earn is financial aid, not compensation, universities say. And while critics complain that grad students are exploited as cheap labor, administrators respond that aspiring Ph.D.'s gain vital career training by teaching undergraduate discussion sections and conducting research.

Last week, however, in a case involving NYU graduate assistants, the National Labor Relations Board gave a decisive thumbs down to these claims. Overturning nearly a quarter century of precedent, the federal panel said that graduate research and teaching assistants at private universities are employees who have the right to form unions and bargain collectively. "We will not deprive workers . . . of their fundamental statutory rights to organize and bargain with their employer, simply because they also are students," the ruling said, upholding a decision issued last spring by a regional NLRB director. Grad student unions have already been recognized at a growing number of public universities, which are governed by state labor laws.

—Ben Wildavsky

Source: *U.S. News & World Report.* November 13, 2000. www.usnews.com

Analysis: Universities have monopsony power in setting wage and workloads for graduate assistants. To counterbalance that power, grad assistants may organize and bargain collectively.

EMPLOYER POWER

The power possessed by labor unions in various occupations and industries seldom exists in a power vacuum. Power exists on the demand side of labor markets, too. The United Auto Workers confront GM, Ford, and Chrysler; the Steelworkers confront U.S. Steel, International Steel Group, and AK Steel; the Teamsters confront the Truckers' Association; the Communications Workers confront AT&T; and so on. An imbalance of power often exists on one side of the market or the other (as with, say, the Carpenters versus individual construction contractors). Labor markets with significant power on both sides, however, are common. To understand how wage rates and employment are determined in such markets, we have to assess the market power possessed by employers.

Monopsony

monopsony: A market in which there's only one buyer.

Power on the demand side of a market belongs to a *buyer* who is able to influence the market price of a good. With respect to labor markets, market power on the demand side implies the ability of a single employer to alter the market wage rate. The extreme case of such power is a **monopsony,** a situation in which one employer is the only buyer in a particular market. The classic example of a monopsony is a company town—that is, a town that depends for its livelihood on the decisions of a single employer.

Graduate teaching assistants have complained that the universities that employ them are much like company towns. Once they've started taking graduate classes at one university, it's difficult to transfer to another. As they see it, there is only one local labor market for graduate students. They complain that their monopsony employer compels them to work long hours at low wages. In 1998, University of California graduate students went out on strike to protest those conditions. In 1999, over 10,000 of those graduate students affiliated with the United Auto Workers to gain more power. In November 2000, the National Labor Relations Board decreed that graduate research and teaching assistants are employees with the right to organize and strike (see News).

Before 1976, professional sports teams also had monopsony power. Sports contracts prohibited pro players from moving from one team (employer) to another without permission. This gave team owners a lot of power to set wages and working conditions. That power was diluted when players got the right to be "free agents" and bargain with more than one team (see News on next page).

IN THE NEWS

Free Agents in Sports: A Threat to Monopsony

Before 1976, the owners of professional baseball, football, and basketball teams enjoyed monopsonistic power. This power was bestowed by the "reserve clause" included in player contracts. Individual players were permitted to negotiate with only one team. Once signed, they couldn't move to another team without their owner's permission. The player's only option was to "take it or leave"—that is, to accept his team's wage offer or quit playing altogether for at least one season. Team owners used the reserve clause to hold down player salaries far below their marginal revenue product.

In 1976, baseball players won the right to become free agents—to negotiate and play for any team—after six years of major-league experience. In 1977, pro football players also won the right to become free agents, but under more restrictive conditions (the team losing a free agent had to be "compensated" with draft choices). Pro basketball players became true free agents in 1980.

The weakening of monopsonistic power led to dramatically higher player salaries. The average baseball salary soared from about $51,000 in 1976 to $900,000 in 1992 and surpassed $2 million in 2006.

Analysis: Because "reserve clauses" limited competing wage offers, they conferred monopsony power on team owners. This kept athletes' wages below competitive equilibrium. Free agency changed that.

There are many degrees of market power, and they can be defined in terms of *buyer concentration.* When buyers are many and of limited market power, the demand for resources is likely to be competitive. When only one buyer has access to a particular resource market, a monopsony exists. Between the two extremes lie the various degrees of imperfect competition, including the awkward-sounding but empirically important case of *oligopsony.* In an oligopsony (e.g., the auto industry), only a few firms account for most of the industry's employment.

The Potential Use of Power

Firms with power in labor markets generally have the same objective as all other firms—to maximize profits. What distinguishes them from competitive (powerless) firms is their ability to attain and keep economic profits. In labor markets, this means using fewer workers and paying them lower wages.

The distinguishing characteristic of labor market monopsonies is that their hiring decisions influence the market wage rate. In a competitive labor market, no single employer has any direct influence on the market wage rate; each firm can hire as much labor as it needs at the prevailing wage. But a monopsonist confronts the *market* labor supply curve. As a result, any increase in the quantity of labor demanded will force the monopsonist to climb up the labor supply curve in search of additional workers. In other words, ***a monopsonist can hire additional workers only if it offers a higher wage rate.***

Marginal Factor Cost. Any time the price of a resource (or product) changes as a result of a firm's purchases, a distinction between marginal cost and price must be made. Making this distinction is one of the little headaches—and potential sources of profit—of a monopsonist. For labor, we distinguish between the **marginal factor cost (MFC)** of labor and its wage rate.

marginal factor cost (MFC): The change in total costs that results from a one-unit increase in the quantity of a factor employed.

Suppose that Figure 31.5 accurately described the labor supply schedule confronting a monopsonist. It's evident that the monopsonist will have to pay a wage of at least $2 an hour if it wants any labor. But even at that wage rate (row *F* of the supply schedule), only one worker will be willing to work. If the firm wants more labor, it will have to offer higher wages.

Two things happen when the firm raises its wage offer to $3 an hour (row *G*). First, the quantity of labor supplied increases (to two workers per hour). Second, the total wages paid

FIGURE 31.5
Marginal Factor Cost

More workers can be attracted only if the wage rate is increased. As it rises, all workers must be paid the higher wage. Consequently, the change in *total* wage costs exceeds the actual wage paid to the last worker. In the table, notice that in row *I*, for example, the marginal factor cost of the fourth worker ($8) exceeds the wage actually paid to that worker ($5). Thus, the marginal factor cost curve lies above the labor supply curve.

In the graph, the intersection of the marginal factor cost and labor demand curves (point *U*) indicates the quantity of labor a monopsonist will want to hire. The labor supply curve (at point *G*) indicates the wage rate that must be paid to attract the desired number of workers. This is the monopsonist's desired wage ($3). In the absence of market power, an employer would end up at point *C* (the competitive equilibrium), paying a higher wage and employing more workers.

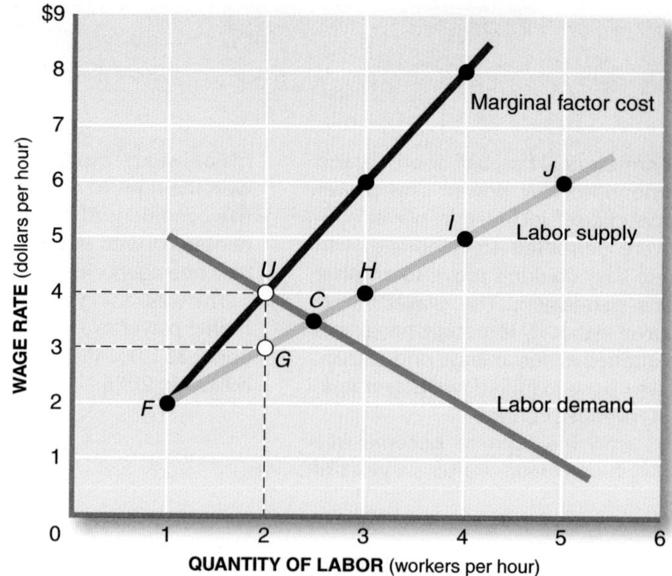

	Wage Rate (per hour)	×	Quantity of Labor Supplied (workers per hour)	=	Total Wage Cost (Per hour)		Marginal Factor Cost (per labor-hour)
D	$0		0		$0		
E	1		0		0		
F	2		1		2	>	2
G	3		2		6	>	4
H	4		3		12	>	6
I	5		4		20	>	8
J	6		5		30	>	10

rise by $4. This *marginal* cost of labor is attributable to the fact that the first worker's wages rise when the wage rate is increased to attract additional workers. If all the workers perform the same job, the first worker will demand to be paid the new (higher) wage rate. Thus, ***the marginal factor cost exceeds the wage rate, because additional workers can be hired only if the wage rate for all workers is increased.***

The Monopsony Firm's Goal. The marginal factor cost curve confronting this monopsonist is shown in the upper half of Figure 31.5. It starts at the bottom of the labor supply curve and rises above it. The monopsonist must now decide how many workers to hire, given the impact of its hiring decision on the market wage rate.

Remember from Chapter 30 that the labor demand curve is a reflection of labor's **marginal revenue product,** that is, the increase in total revenue attributable to the employment of one additional worker.

marginal revenue product (MRP): The change in total revenue associated with one additional unit of input.

As we've emphasized, the profit-maximizing producer always seeks to equalize marginal revenue and marginal cost. Accordingly, the monopsonistic employer will seek to hire the amount of labor at which the marginal revenue product of labor equals its marginal factor cost—that is,

$$\text{Profit-maximizing level of input use}: \text{marginal revenue product of input (MRP)} = \text{marginal factor cost of input (MFC)}$$

In Figure 31.5, this objective is illustrated by the intersection of the marginal factor cost and labor demand curves at point *U.*

At point *U* the monopsonist is *willing to hire* two workers per hour at a wage rate of $4. But the firm doesn't have to pay this much. The labor supply curve informs us that two workers are *willing to work* for only $3 an hour. Hence, the firm first decides how many workers it wants to hire (at point *U*) and then looks at the labor supply curve (point *G*) to see what it has to pay them. As we suspected, a monopsonistic employer ends up hiring fewer workers at a lower wage rate than would prevail in a competitive market (point *C*).

COLLECTIVE BARGAINING

The potential for conflict between a powerful employer and a labor union should be evident:

- ***The objective of a labor union is to establish a wage rate that's* higher *than the competitive wage (Figure 31.3).***
- ***A monopsonist employer seeks to establish a wage rate that's* lower *than competitive standards (Figure 31.5).***

The resultant clash generates intense bargaining that often spills over into politics, the courts, and open conflict.

The confrontation of power on both sides of the labor market is a situation referred to as **bilateral monopoly.** In such a market, wages and employment aren't determined simply by supply and demand. Rather, economic outcomes must be determined by **collective bargaining**—that is, direct negotiations between employers and labor unions for the purpose of determining wages, employment, working conditions, and related issues.

bilateral monopoly: A market with only one buyer (a monopsonist) and one seller (a monopolist).

collective bargaining: Direct negotiations between employers and unions to determine labor market outcomes.

Possible Agreements

In a typical labor-business confrontation, the two sides begin by stating their preferences for equilibrium wages and employment. The *demands* laid down by the union are likely to revolve around point *U* in Figure 31.6; the *offer* enunciated by management is likely to be at point *G.*[1] Thus the boundaries of a potential settlement—a negotiated final equilibrium—are usually established at the outset of collective bargaining. The accompanying News summarizes the points of contention in the 1991–98 dispute between Caterpillar and the UAW.

The interesting part of collective bargaining isn't the initial bargaining positions but the negotiation of the final settlement. The speed with which a settlement is reached and the

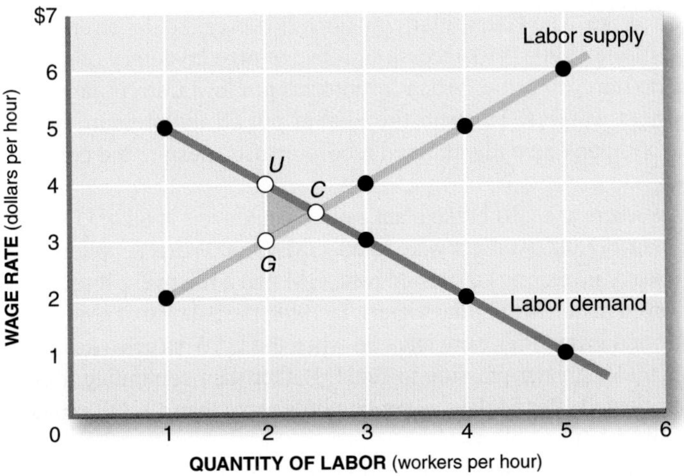

FIGURE 31.6
The Boundaries of Collective Bargaining

Firms with power in the labor market seek to establish wages and employment levels corresponding to point *G* (from Figure 31.5). Unions, on the other hand, seek to establish an equilibrium at point *U* (from Figure 31.3). The competitive equilibrium is at point *C*. The function of collective bargaining is to identify a compromise between these points—that is, to locate an equilibrium somewhere in the shaded area.

[1]Even though points *U* and *G* may not be identical to the initial bargaining positions, they represent the positions of maximum attainable benefit for both sides. Points outside the demand or supply curve will be rejected out of hand by one side or the other.

IN THE NEWS

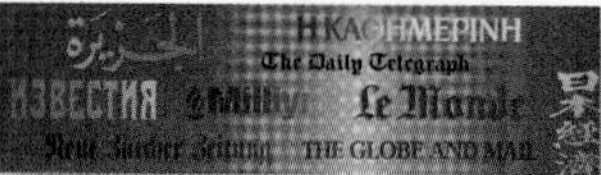

Caterpillar vs. the UAW

What Separates the Two Sides

	Company Proposal	**Union Proposal**
Wages	One 3% wage hike for 12,800 of Cat's 16,500 union workers	One 3% wage hike for all workers, plus two one-time payments of 3% each
	Lower pay for new hires at parts-distribution centers	Same wage scales for all union workers
Benefits	Medical co-payments and a preferred-provider plan	A traditional plan with no co-payments
Job security	Employment levels can fall by attrition	Guaranteed number of union jobs

Source: Reprinted from the March 23, 1992, issue of *BusinessWeek* by permission. Copyright 1992 by The McGraw-Hill Companies, Inc. www.businessweek.com

Analysis: Collective bargaining begins with a set of union demands and management offers. The outcome depends on the relative strength and tactics of the two parties.

terms of the resulting compromise depend on the patience, tactics, and resources of the negotiating parties. ***The fundamental source of negotiating power for either side is its ability to withhold labor or jobs.*** The union can threaten to strike, thereby cutting off the flow of union labor to the employer. The employer can impose a lockout, thereby cutting off jobs and paychecks. The effectiveness of those threats depends on the availability of substitute workers or jobs.

The Pressure to Settle

Labor and management both suffer from either a strike or a lockout, no matter who initiates the work stoppage. The strike benefits paid to workers are rarely comparable to wages they would otherwise have received, and the payment of those benefits depletes the union treasury. By the same token, the reduction in labor costs and other expenses rarely compensates the employer for lost profits.

When the UAW was unable to attain its bargaining goals with Caterpillar, it instructed its 12,600 workers to go out on strike. The Caterpillar company, however, held a strong bargaining position. As a result of the 1990–1991 recession, it had a huge inventory of unsold farm equipment and was in no hurry to settle. When inventories got low, Caterpillar found a willing supply of replacement workers. This substitute labor put all the pressure on the union to settle. In 1994, the company actually attained record profits, despite the continuing strike.

In 1996, a strike by UAW workers at a GM brake plant caused shutdowns at all of GM's 29 U.S. assembly plants. More than 175,000 workers were idled. GM's 1,600 parts suppliers also had to lay off workers. With heavy inventories of unsold cars, GM had a relatively strong bargaining position. The UAW caved in quickly (17 days later). In 1998, the balance of power was different. Car sales were brisk and inventories were lean. So when the UAW struck a key parts plant in June 1998, GM was under greater pressure to settle. Rather than continuing to lose over $100 million a day, GM relented after 54 days, accepting little more than a UAW promise not to strike again for a year and a half.

The 2004–5 National Hockey League bargaining didn't end so well. Unable to compromise on the level of salary caps (team budgets for player pay), the NHL *canceled* the entire 2004–5 hockey season. That cancellation cost the players $1 billion in lost pay and the team owners more than $200 million.

Because potential income losses are usually high, both labor and management try to avoid a strike or lockout if they can. In fact, over 90 percent of the 20,000 collective bargaining agreements negotiated each year are concluded without recourse to a strike and often without even the explicit threat of one.

The Final Settlement

The built-in pressures for settlement help resolve collective bargaining. They don't tell us, however, what the dimensions of that final settlement will be. All we know is that the settlement will be located within the boundaries established in Figure 31.6. The relative pressures on each side will determine whether the final equilibrium is closer to the union or the management position.

The final settlement almost always necessitates hard choices on both sides. The union usually has to choose between an increase in job security or higher pay. A union must also consider how management will react in the long run to higher wages, perhaps by introducing new technology that reduces its dependence on labor. The employer has to worry whether productivity will suffer if workers are dissatisfied with their pay package.

webnote

For information about recent union contracts and strikes, see the U.S. Bureau of Labor Statistics at www.bls.gov. Click on "Collective Bargaining" under the "Wages, Earnings, and Benefits" heading.

THE IMPACT OF UNIONS

We know that unions tend to raise wage rates in individual companies, industries, and occupations. But can we be equally sure that unions have raised wages in general? If the UAW is successful in raising wages in the automobile industry, what, if anything, happens to car prices? If car prices rise in step with UAW wage rates, labor and management in the auto industry will get proportionally larger slices of the economic pie. At the same time, workers in other industries will be burdened with higher car prices.

Relative Wages

One measure of union impact is *relative* wages—the wages of union members in comparison with those of nonunion workers. As we've noted, unions seek to control the supply of labor in a particular industry or occupation. This forces the excluded workers to seek work elsewhere. As a result of this labor supply imbalance, wages tend to be higher in unionized industries than in nonunionized industries. Figure 31.7 illustrates this effect.

Although the theoretical impact of union exclusionism on relative wages is clear, empirical estimates of that impact are fairly rare. We do know that union wages in general are

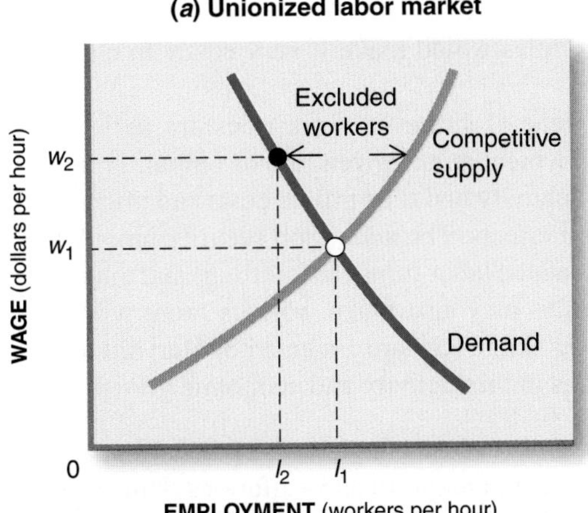

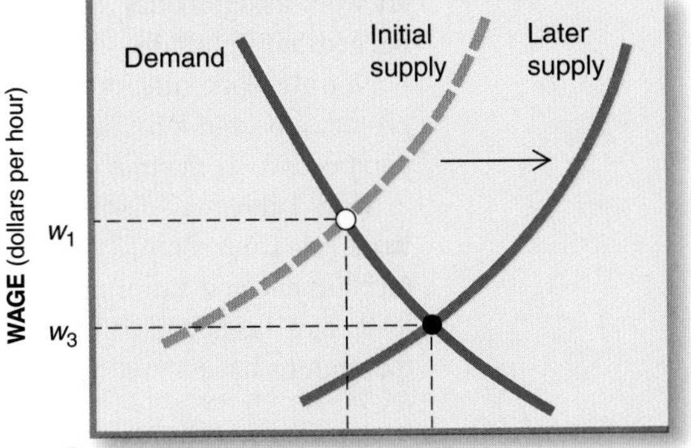

FIGURE 31.7
The Effect of Unions on Relative Wages

In the absence of unions, the average wage rate would be equal to w_1. As unions take control of the market, however, they seek to raise wage rates to w_2, in the process reducing the amount of employment in that market from l_1 to l_2. The workers displaced from the unionized market will seek work in the nonunionized market, thereby shifting the nonunion supply curve to the right. The result will be a reduction of wage rates (to w_3) in the nonunionized market. Thus, union wages end up higher than nonunion wages.

significantly higher than nonunion wages ($833 versus $642 per week in 2006). But part of this differential is due to the fact that unions are more common in industries that have always been more capital-intensive and paid relatively high wages. When comparisons are made within particular industries or sectors, the differential narrows considerably. Nevertheless, there's a general consensus that unions have managed to increase their relative wages from 15 to 20 percent.

Labor's Share of Total Income

Even though unions have been successful in redistributing some income from nonunion to union workers, the question still remains as to whether they've increased labor's share of *total* income. The *labor share* of total income is the proportion of income received by all workers, in contrast to the share of income received by owners of capital (the *capital share*). The labor share of total income will rise only if the gains to union workers exceed the losses to the (excluded) nonunion workers.

Evidence of unions' impact on labor's share is almost as difficult to assemble as evidence on relative wages, and for much the same reasons. Labor's share has risen dramatically, from only 56 percent in 1919 to 75 percent in 2007. But there have been tremendous changes in the mix of output during that same period. The proportion of output composed of personal services (accountants, teachers, electricians) is much larger now than it was in 1919. The labor share of income derived from personal services is and always was close to 100 percent. Accordingly, ***most of the rise in labor's share of total income is due to changes in the structure of the economy rather than to unionization.***

Prices

One way firms can protect their profits in the face of rising union wages is to raise product prices. If firms raise prices along with union wages, then consumers end up footing the bill. In that case, profits and the capital share of total income might not be reduced.

The ability of firms to pass along increased union wages depends on the structure of product markets as well as labor markets. If a firm has power in both markets, it's better able to protect itself in this way. There's little evidence, however, that unions have contributed significantly to general cost-push inflation.

Productivity

productivity: Output per unit of input, such as output per labor-hour.

Unions also affect prices indirectly, via changes in **productivity.** Unions bargain not only for wages but also for work rules that specify how goods should be produced. Work rules may limit the pace of production, restrict the type of jobs a particular individual can perform, or require a minimum number of workers to accomplish a certain task. A factory carpenter, for example, may not be permitted to change a lightbulb that burns out in his shop area. And the electrician who is summoned may be required to have an apprentice on all work assignments. Such restrictive work rules would make it very costly to change a burned-out lightbulb.

Not all work rules are so restrictive. In general, however, work rules are designed to protect jobs and maximize the level of employment at any given rate of output. From this perspective, work rules directly restrain productivity and thus inflate costs and prices.

Work rules may also have some beneficial effects. The added job security provided by work rules and seniority provisions tends to reduce labor turnover (quitting) and thus saves recruitment and training costs. Protective rules may also make workers more willing to learn new tasks and to train others in specific skills. Richard Freeman of Harvard asserts that unions have actually accelerated advances in productivity and economic growth.

Political Impact

Perhaps more important than any of these specific union effects is the general impact the union movement has had on our economic, social, and political institutions. Unions are a major political force in the United States. They've not only provided critical electoral and financial support for selected political candidates, but they've also fought hard for important legislation. Unions have succeeded in establishing minimum wage laws, work and safety rules, and retirement benefits. They've also actively lobbied for civil rights legislation and health and education programs. Whatever one may think of any particular union or specific union action, it's clear that our institutions and national welfare would be very different in their absence.

THE ECONOMY TOMORROW

MERGING TO SURVIVE

Unions have been in retreat for nearly a generation. As shown in Figure 31.4, the unionized share of the labor force has fallen from 35 percent in 1950 to less than 13 percent today. Even that modest share has been maintained only by the spread of unionism among public school teachers and other government employees. In the private sector, the unionization rate is closer to 9 percent and still declining. The Teamsters, the Auto Workers, and the Steelworkers have lost over 1 million members in the last 15 years.

The decline in unionization is explained by three phenomena. Most important is the relative decline in manufacturing, coupled with rapid growth in high-tech service industries (like computer software, accounting, and medical technology). The second force is the downsizing of major corporations and the relatively faster growth of smaller companies. These structural changes have combined to shrink the traditional employment base of labor unions.

webnote

For trends in union membership, see www.aflcio.org/joinaunion/why/uniondifference/index.cfm

The third cause of shrinking unionization is increased global competition. The decline of worldwide trade and investment barriers has made it easier for firms to import products from low-wage nations and even to relocate production plants. With more options, firms can more easily resist noncompetitive wage demands.

The labor-union movement is fully aware of these forces and determined to resist them. To increase their power, unions are merging across craft and industry lines. In 1995, the Rubber Workers merged with the Steelworkers, the two major textile unions combined forces, and the Food Workers and Retail Clerks formed a new union. In 1999, the Grain Millers merged with the Paperworkers Union. By merging, the unions hope to increase representation, gain financial strength, and enhance their political clout. They're also seeking to broaden their appeal by organizing low-wage workers in the service industries. These efforts, together with their political strength, will help unions to play a continuing role in the economy tomorrow, even if their share of total employment continues to shrink.

SUMMARY

- Power in labor markets is the ability to alter market wage rates. Such power is most evident in local labor markets defined by geographical, occupational, or industrial boundaries. LO1
- Power on the supply side of labor markets is manifested by unions, organized along industry or craft lines. The basic function of a union is to evaluate employment offers in terms of the *collective* interest of its members. LO1
- The downward slope of the labor demand curve creates a distinction between the marginal wage and the market wage. The marginal wage is the change in *total* wages occasioned by employment of one additional worker and is less than the market wage. LO1
- Unions seek to establish that rate of employment at which the marginal wage curve intersects the labor supply curve. The desired union wage is then found on the labor demand curve at that level of employment. LO1
- Power on the demand side of labor markets is manifested in buyer concentrations such as monopsony and oligopsony. Such power is usually found among the same firms that exercise market power in product markets. LO2
- By definition, power on the demand side implies some direct influence on market wage rates; additional hiring by a monopsonist will force up the market wage rate. Hence, a monopsonist must recognize a distinction between the marginal factor cost of labor and its (lower) market wage rate. LO2
- The goal of a monopsonistic employer is to hire the number of workers at which the marginal factor cost of labor equals its marginal revenue product. The employer then looks at the labor supply curve to determine the wage rate that must be paid for that number of workers. LO2
- The desire of unions to establish a wage rate that's higher than competitive wages directly opposes the desire of powerful employers to establish lower wage rates. In bilateral monopolies unions and employers engage in collective bargaining to negotiate a final settlement. LO2
- The impact of unions on the economy is difficult to measure. It appears, however, that they've increased their own relative wages and contributed to rising prices. They've also had substantial political impact. LO3

Key Terms

market power
labor supply
demand for labor
equilibrium wage
marginal wage
union shop
unionization ratio
monopsony
marginal factor cost (MFC)
marginal revenue product (MRP)
bilateral monopoly
collective bargaining
productivity

Questions for Discussion

1. Collective bargaining sessions often start with unreasonable demands and categorical rejections. Why do unions and employers tend to begin bargaining from extreme positions? LO2
2. Does a strike for a raise of 5 cents an hour make any sense? What kinds of long-term benefits might a union gain from such a strike? LO1
3. Are large and powerful firms easier targets for union organization than small firms? Why or why not? LO1
4. Nonunionized firms tend to offer wage rates that are close to rates paid by unionized firms in the same industry. How do you explain this? LO3
5. Why are farm workers much less successful than airplane machinists in securing higher wages? LO2
6. In 1998, teaching assistants at the University of California struck for higher wages and union recognition, something they had sought for 14 years. How did the availability of replacement workers affect their power? LO2
7. A key issue in the 1998 GM strike involved "peg rates" that allow workers to go home or get paid overtime wages once production reaches a specified level. How do peg rates affect productivity and costs? LO1
8. How will union mergers affect the market power of unions? LO2

problems The Student Problem Set at the back of this book contains numerical and graphing problems for this chapter.

web activities to accompany this chapter can be found on the Online Learning Center: **http://www.mhhe.com/economics/schiller11e**

32 Financial Markets

LEARNING OBJECTIVES

After reading this chapter, you should know:

LO1. The difference between stocks and bonds.

LO2. Key financial parameters for stocks and bonds.

LO3. How risks and rewards are reflected in current values.

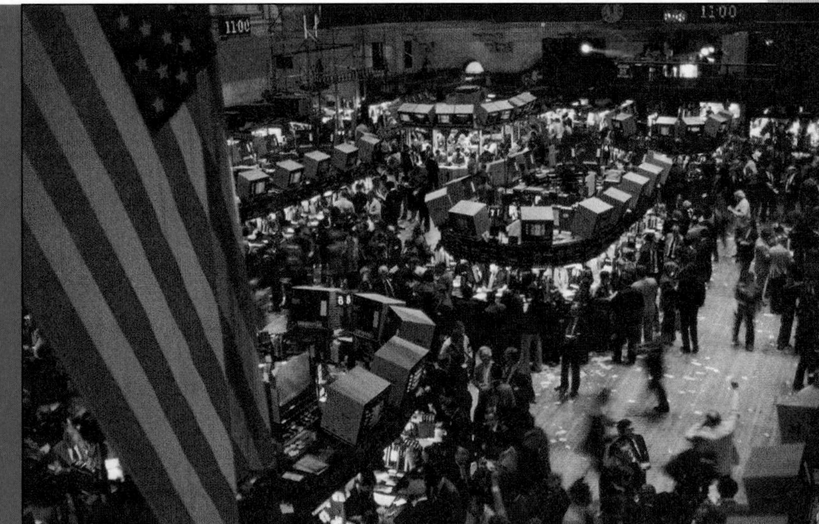

Christopher Columbus had a crazy entrepreneurial idea: He was certain he could find a new route to the Indies by sailing not east from Europe but west—around the world. Such a route, he surmised, would give Europe quicker access to the riches of the East Indies. Whoever discovered that western route could become very, very rich.

To find that route, Columbus needed ships, sailors, and tons of provisions. He couldn't afford to supply these resources himself. He needed financial backers who would put up the money. For several years he tried to convince King Ferdinand of Spain to provide the necessary funds. But the king didn't want to risk so much wealth on a single venture. Twice he'd turned Columbus down.

Fortunately, Genoese merchant bankers in Seville came to Columbus's rescue. Convinced that Columbus's "enterprise of the Indies" might bring back "pearls, precious stones, gold, silver, spiceries," and other valuable merchandise, they guaranteed repayment of any funds lent to Columbus. With that guarantee in hand, the Duke of Medina Sidonia, in April 1492, offered to lend 1,000 maravedis (about $5,000 in today's dollars) to Queen Isabella for the purpose of funding Columbus's expedition. With no personal financial risk, King Ferdinand then granted Columbus the funds and authority for a royal expedition.

Columbus's experience in raising funds for his expedition illustrates a critical function of financial markets, namely, the management of *risk.* This chapter examines how financial markets facilitate economic activities (like Columbus's expedition) by managing the risks of failure. Three central questions guide the discussion:

- **What is traded in financial markets?**
- **How do the financial markets affect the economic outcomes of WHO, WHAT, and FOR WHOM?**
- **Why do financial markets fluctuate so much?**

THE ROLE OF FINANCIAL MARKETS

A central question for every economy is WHAT to produce. In 1492, all available resources were employed in farming, fishing, food distribution, metalworking, and other basic services. For Columbus to pursue his quest, he needed some of those resources. To get them, he needed money to bid scarce resources from other pursuits and employ them on his expedition.

Financial Intermediaries

Entrepreneurs who don't have great personal wealth must get start-up funds from other people. There are two possibilities: either *borrow* the money, or invite other people to *invest* in the new venture.

How might you pursue these options? You could ask your relatives for a loan or go door-to-door in your neighborhood seeking investors. But such direct fund-raising is costly, inefficient, and often unproductive. Columbus went hat in hand to the Spanish royal court twice, but each time he came back empty-handed.

financial intermediary: Institution (e.g., bank or the stock market) that makes savings available to dissavers (e.g., investors).

The task of raising start-up funds is made much easier by the existence of **financial intermediaries**—institutions that steer the flow of savings to cash-strapped entrepreneurs and other investors. Funds flow into banks, pension funds, bond markets, stock markets, and other financial intermediaries from businesses, households, and government entities that have some unspent income. This pool of national savings is then passed on to entrepreneurs, expanding businesses, and other borrowers by these same institutions (see Figure 32.1).

Financial intermediaries provide several important services: They greatly reduce the cost of locating loanable funds. Their pool of savings offers a clear economy of scale compared to the alternative of door-to-door solicitations. They also reduce the cost to savers of finding suitable lending or investment opportunities. Few individuals have the time, resources, or interest to do the searching on their own. With huge pools of amassed savings, however, financial intermediaries have the incentive to acquire and analyze information about lending and investment opportunities. Hence, ***financial intermediaries reduce search and information costs*** in the financial markets. In so doing, they make the allocation of resources more efficient.

Although financial intermediaries make the job of acquiring start-up funds a lot easier, there's no guarantee that the funds needed will be acquired. First, there must be an adequate supply of funds available. Second, financial intermediaries must be convinced that they should allocate some of those funds to a project.

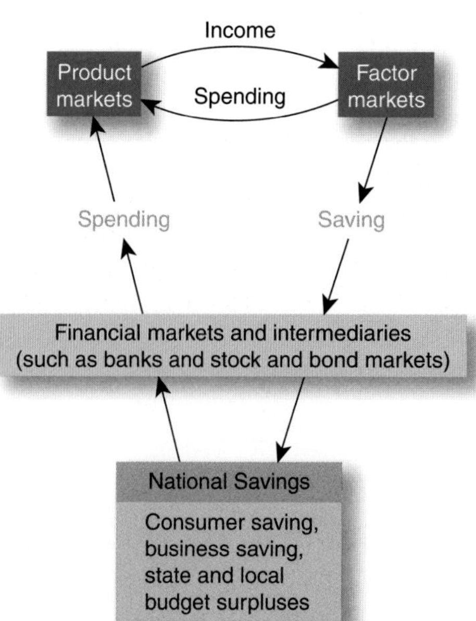

FIGURE 32.1
Mobilizing Savings

The central economic function of financial markets is to channel national savings into new investment and other desired expenditure. Financial intermediaries such as banks, insurance companies, and stockbrokers help transfer purchasing power from savers to spenders.

The Supply of Loanable Funds

As noted, the supply of loanable funds originates in the decisions of market participants to not spend all their current income. Those saving decisions are influenced by time preferences and interest rates.

Time Preferences. In deciding to *save* rather than *spend,* people effectively reallocate their spending over time. That is, people save *now* in order to spend more *later.* How much to save, then, depends partly on *time preference.* If a person doesn't give any thought to the future, she's likely to save little. If, by contrast, a person wants to buy a car, a vacation, or a house in the future, she's more inclined to save some income now.

Interest Rates. Interest rates also affect saving decisions. If interest rates are high, the future payoff to every dollar saved is greater. A higher return on savings translates into more future income for every dollar of current income saved. Hence, ***higher interest rates increase the quantity of available savings (loanable funds).***

Risk. In early 2007, banks in Zimbabwe were offering interest rates on savings accounts of more than 100 percent a year. In Latin America, banks have offered similarly higher interest rates on occasion. Yet few people rushed to deposit their savings in these banks. People worried that the banks might fail, wiping out their savings in the process. In other words, there was a high *risk* attached to those high interest rates.

Anyone who contemplated lending funds to Columbus confronted a similar risk. That was the dilemma King Ferdinand confronted. He had enough funds to finance Columbus's expedition, but he didn't want to risk losing so much on a single venture.

Risk Management. This is why the Genoese bankers were so critical: These financial intermediaries could spread the risk of failure among many individuals. Each investor could put up just a fraction of the needed funds. No one had to put all his eggs in one basket. Once the consortium of bankers agreed to share the risks of Columbus's expedition, the venture had wings. The Genoese merchant bankers could afford to take portions of the expedition's risks because they also financed many less risky projects. By diversifying their portfolios, they could attain whatever degree of *average* risk they preferred. That is the essence of risk management.

Risk Premiums. Even though diversification permits greater risk management, lenders will want to be compensated for any above-average risks they take. Money lent to local merchants must have seemed a lot less risky than lending funds to Columbus. Thus no one would have stepped forward to finance Columbus unless promised an *above-average* return upon the expedition's success. The difference between the rates of return on a safe (certain) investment and a risky (uncertain) one is called the **risk premium.** Risk premiums compensate people who finance risky ventures that succeed. Because these ventures are risky, however, investors often lose their money in such ventures too.

risk premium: The difference in rates of return on risky (uncertain) and safe (certain) investments.

Risk premiums help explain why blue-chip corporations such as Microsoft can borrow money from a bank at the low "prime" rate while ordinary consumers have to pay much higher interest rates on personal loans. Corporate loans are less risky because corporations typically have plenty of revenue and assets to cover their debts. Consumers often get overextended, however, and can't pay all their bills. As a result, there's a greater risk that consumers' loans won't be paid back. Banks charge higher interest rates on consumer loans to compensate for this risk.

THE PRESENT VALUE OF FUTURE PROFITS

In deciding whether to assume the *risk* of supplying funds to a new venture, financial intermediaries assess the potential *rewards.* In Columbus's case, the rewards were the fabled treasures of the East Indies. Even if he found those treasures, however, the rewards would only come long after the expedition was financed. When Columbus proposed his East Indies expedition, he envisioned a round trip that would last at least 6 months. If he located the treasures he sought, he planned subsequent trips to acquire and transport his precious cargoes back home. Although King Ferdinand granted Columbus only one-tenth of any profits from the first expedition, Columbus had a claim on one-eighth of the profits of any subsequent voyages. Hence, even if Columbus succeeded in finding a shortcut to the East, he wouldn't generate any substantial profit for perhaps 2 years or more.

Suppose for the moment that Columbus expected no profit from the first expedition but a profit of $1,000 at the end of 2 years from a second voyage. How much was that future profit worth to Columbus in 1492?

Time Value of Money

To assess the present value of *future* receipts, we have to consider the *time value* of money. A dollar received today is worth more than a dollar received 2 years from today. Why? Because a dollar received today can earn *interest.* If you have a dollar today and put it in an interest-bearing account, in 2 years you'll have your original dollar *plus* accumulated interest. ***As long as interest-earning opportunities exist, present dollars are worth more than future dollars.***

In 1492, there were plenty of opportunities to earn interest. Indeed, the Genoese bankers were charging high interest rates on their loans and guarantees. If Columbus had had the cash, he too could have lent money to others and earned interest on his funds.

To calculate the present value of future dollars, this forgone interest must be taken into account. This computation is essentially interest accrual in reverse. ***We "discount" future dollars by the opportunity cost of money***—that is, the market rate of interest.

present discounted value (PDV): The value today of future payments, adjusted for interest accrual.

Suppose the market rate of interest in 1492 was 10 percent. To compute the **present discounted value (PDV)** of future payment, we discount as follows:

$$\text{PDV} = \frac{\text{future payment}_N}{(1 + \text{interest rate})^N}$$

where N refers to the number of years into the future when a payment is to be made. If the future payment is to be made in 1 year, the N in the equation equals 1, and we have

$$\text{PDV} = \frac{\$1{,}000}{1.10}$$

$$= \$909.09$$

Hence, the present discounted value of $1,000 to be paid 1 year from today is $909.09. If $909.09 were received today, it could earn interest. In a year's time, the $909.09 would grow to $1,000 with interest accrued at the rate of 10 percent per year.

Suppose it would have taken Columbus 2 years to complete his expeditions and collect his profits. In that case, the present value of the $1,000 payment would be lower. The N in the formula would be 2 and the present value would be

$$\text{PDV} = \frac{\$1{,}000}{(1.10)^2} = \frac{\$1{,}000}{1.21} = \$826.45$$

Hence, ***the longer one has to wait for a future payment, the less present value it has.***

Lottery winners often have to choose between present and future values. In July 2004, for example, Geraldine Williams, a 68-year-old housekeeper in Lowell, Massachusetts, won a $294 million MegaMillions lottery. The $294 million was payable in 26 annual installments of $11.3 million. If the lucky winner wanted to get her prize sooner, she could accept an immediate but smaller payout rather than 25 future installments.

Table 32.1 shows how the lottery officials figured the present value of the $294 million prize. The first installment of $11.3 million would be paid immediately. Mrs. Williams would have had to wait 1 year for the second check, however. At the then-prevailing interest rate of 4.47 percent, the *present* value of that second $11.3 million check was only $10.82 million. The *last* payoff check had even less present value since it wasn't due to be paid for

Years in the Future	Future Payment ($ millions)	Present Value ($ millions)
0	$ 11.3	$ 11.30
1	11.3	10.82
2	11.3	10.35
3	11.3	9.91
4	11.3	9.49
5	11.3	8.04
*	*	*
*	*	*
*	*	*
25	11.3	3.79
	$294.0	$168.0

Note: The general formula for computing present values is $\text{PDV} = \Sigma \frac{\text{payment in year } N}{(1 + r)^N}$, where r is the prevailing rate.

TABLE 32.1
Computing Present Value

The present value of a future payment declines the longer one must wait for a payment. At an interest rate of 4.47 percent, $11.3 million payable in 1 year is worth only $10.82 million today. A payout of $11.3 million 25 years from now has a present value of only $3.79 million. A string of $11.3 million payments spread out over 25 years has a present value of $168 million (at 4.47 percent interest).

25 years. With so much time for interest to accrue, that final $11.3 million payment had a present value of only $3.79 million. The calculations in Table 32.1 convinced lottery officials to offer an immediate payout of only $168 million on the $294 million prize. Mrs. Williams wasn't too disappointed.

Interest Rate Effects

The winner would have received even less money had interest rates been higher. At the time Mrs. Williams won the lottery, the interest rate on bonds was 4.47 percent. Had the rate been higher, the discount for immediate payment would have been higher as well. Table 32.2 indicates that Mrs. Williams would have received only $107 million had the prevailing interest rate been 10 percent. What Tables 32.1 and 32.2 illustrate, then, is that ***the present discounted value of a future payment declines with***

- ***Higher interest rates.***
- ***Longer delays in future payment.***

Uncertainty

The valuation of future payments must also consider the possibility of *non*payment. State governments are virtually certain to make promised lottery payouts, so there's little risk in accepting a promised payout of 25 annual installments. But what about the booty from Columbus's expeditions? There was great uncertainty that Columbus would ever return from his expeditions, much less bring back the "pearls, precious stones, gold, silver, spiceries"

Interest Rate (%)	Present Discounted Value of $294 Million Lottery Prize ($ millions)
5.0%	$166.3
6.0	150.8
7.0	137.5
8.0	126.0
9.0	115.9
10.0	107.1

TABLE 32.2
Higher Interest Rates Reduce Present Values

Higher interest rates raise the *future* value of current dollars. The rates therefore reduce the *present* value of future payments. Shown here is the present discounted value of the July 2004 MegaMillions lottery prize of $294 million at different interest rates.

that people coveted. Investing in those expeditions was far riskier than deferring a lottery payment.

expected value: The probable value of a future payment, including the risk of nonpayment.

Expected Value. Whenever an anticipated future payment is uncertain, a risk factor should be included in present-value computations. This is done by calculating the **expected value** of a future payment. Suppose there was only a 50:50 chance that Columbus would bring back the bacon. In that event, the expected payoff would be

$$\text{Expected value} = (1 - \text{risk factor}) \times \text{present discounted value}$$

With a 50:50 chance of failure, the expected value of Columbus's first-year profits would have been

$$\text{Expected value} = (1 - 0.5) \times \$909.09$$
$$= \$454.55$$

Expected values also explain why people buy more lottery tickets when the prize is larger. The odds of winning the multistate Powerball lottery are 80 *million*:1. That's about the same odds as getting struck by lightning *14 times* in the same year! So it makes almost no sense to buy a ticket. With a $16 million prize, the *undiscounted* expected value of a $1 lottery ticket is only 20 cents. When the lottery prize increases, however, the expected value of a ticket grows as well (there are still only 80 million possible combinations of numbers). When the grand prize reached $250 million in July 1998, the undiscounted expected value of a lone winning ticket jumped to over $3. Millions of people decided that the expected value was high enough to justify buying a $1 lottery ticket. People took off from work, skipped classes, and drove across state lines to queue up for lottery tickets. So many people bought tickets on the last day that the lottery grand prize swelled to $295 million. (Thirteen machinists from Ohio had the winning ticket and chose the present discounted value of $165.6 million.) When the prize is only $10 million, far fewer people buy tickets.

The Demand for Loanable Funds

People rarely borrow money to buy lottery tickets. But entrepreneurs and other market participants often use other people's funds to finance their ventures. ***How much loanable funds are demanded depends on***

- ***The expected rate of return.***
- ***The cost of funds.***

The higher the expected return, or the lower the cost of funds, the greater will be the amount of loanable funds demanded.

Figure 32.2 offers a general view of the loanable funds market that emerges from these considerations. From the entrepreneur's perspective, the prevailing interest rate represents

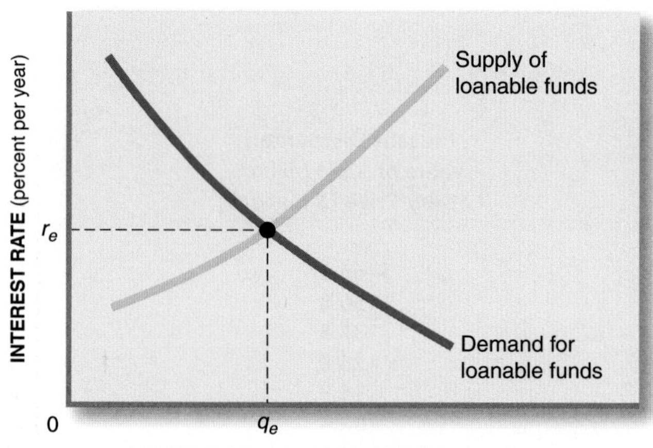

FIGURE 32.2
The Loanable Funds Market

The market rate of interest (r_e) is determined by the intersection of the curves representing supply of and demand for loanable funds. The rate of interest represents the price paid for the use of money.

the cost of funds. From the perspective of savers, the interest rate represents the payoff to savings. When interest rates rise, the quantity of funds supplied goes up and the quantity demanded goes down. The prevailing (equilibrium) interest rate is set by the intersection of these supply and demand curves.

THE STOCK MARKET

The concept of a loanable funds market sounds a bit alien. But the same principles of supply, demand, and risk management go a long way in explaining the action in stock markets. Suppose you had $1,000 to invest. Should you invest it all in lottery tickets that offer a multimillion-dollar payoff? Put it in a savings account that pays next to nothing? Or how about the stock market? The stock market can reward you handsomely; or it can wipe out your savings if the stocks you own tumble. Hence, ***stocks offer a higher average return than bank accounts but also entail greater average risk.*** People who bought Amazon.com stock in May 1997 got a 1,000 percent profit on their stock in only 2 years. But people who bought Amazon.com stock in December 1999 lost 90 percent of their investment in even less time.

Corporate Stock

When people buy a share of stock, they're buying partial ownership of a corporation. The three legal forms of business entities are

- Corporations
- Partnerships
- Proprietorships

Limited Liability. Proprietorships are businesses owned by a single individual. The owner-proprietor is entirely responsible for the business, including repayment of any debts. Members of a partnership are typically liable for all business debts and activities as well. By contrast, a **corporation** is a limited liability form of business. The corporation itself, not its individual shareholders, is responsible for all business activity and debts. As a result of this limited liability, you can own a piece of a corporation without worrying about being sued for business mishaps (like environmental damage) or nonpayment of debt. This feature significantly reduces the risk of owning corporate stock.

corporation: A business organization having a continuous existence independent of its members (owners) and power and liabilities distinct from those of its members.

Shared Ownership. The ownership of a corporation is defined in terms of stock shares. Each share of **corporate stock** represents partial ownership of the business. Chipmaker Intel, for example, has nearly 7 *billion* shares of stock outstanding (that is, shares held by the public). Hence, each share of Intel stock represents less than one-seventh of one-billionth ownership of the corporation. Potentially, this means that as many as 7 billion people could own the Intel Corporation. In reality, however, many individuals own hundreds of shares, and institutions may own thousands. Indeed, some of the largest pension funds in the United States own over a million shares of Intel.

corporate stock: Shares of ownership in a corporation.

In principle, the owners of corporate stock collectively run the business. In practice, the shareholders select a board of directors to monitor corporate activity and protect their interests. The day-to-day business of running a corporation is the job of managers who report to the board of directors.

Stock Returns

If shareholders don't have any direct role in running a corporation, why would they want to own a piece of it? Essentially, for the same reason that the Genoese bankers agreed to finance Columbus's expedition: profits. Owners (shareholders) of a corporation hope to share in the profits the corporation earns.

Dividends. Shareholders rarely receive their full share of the company's profits in cash. Corporations typically use some of the profits for investment in new plants or equipment. They may also want to retain some of the profits for operational needs or unforeseen contingencies. ***Corporations may choose to retain earnings or pay them out to shareholders***

dividend: Amount of corporate profits paid out for each share of stock.

retained earnings: Amount of corporate profits not paid out in dividends.

***as* dividends.** Any profits not paid to shareholders are referred to as **retained earnings.** Thus,

$$\text{Dividends} = \text{corporate profits} - \text{retained earnings}$$

In 2006, Intel paid quarterly dividends amounting to 40 cents per share for the year. But the company earned profits equal to 87 cents per share. Thus, shareholders received less than 50 percent of their accrued profits in dividend checks; Intel retained the remaining $0.47 per-share profit earned in 2006 for future investments.

capital gain: An increase in the market value of an asset.

Capital Gains. If Intel invests its retained earnings wisely, the corporation may reap even larger profits in the future. As a company grows and prospers, each share of ownership may become more valuable. This increase in value would be reflected in higher market prices for shares of Intel stock. Any increase in the value of a stock represents a **capital gain** for shareholders. Capital gains directly increase shareholder wealth.

Total Return. People who own stocks can thus get two distinct payoffs: dividends and capital gains. Together, these payoffs represent the total return on stock investments. Hence, ***the higher the expected total return (future dividends and capital gains), the greater the desire to buy and hold stocks.*** If a stock paid no dividends and had no prospects for price appreciation (capital gain) you'd probably hold your savings in a different form (such as another stock or maybe an interest-earning bank account).

Initial Public Offering

initial public offering (IPO): The first issuance (sale) to the general public of stock in a corporation.

When a corporation is formed, its future sales and profits are most uncertain. When shares are first offered to the public, the seller of stock is the company itself. By *going public,* the corporation seeks to raise funds for investment and growth. A true *start-up* company may have nothing more than a good idea, a couple of dedicated employees, and Big Plans. To fund these plans, it sells shares of itself in an **initial public offering (IPO).** People who buy the newly issued stock are putting their savings directly into the corporation's accounts.[1] As new owners, they stand to profit from the corporation's business or take their lumps if the corporation fails.

In 2004, Google was still a relatively new company. Although the company had been in operation since 1999, its search-engine capacities were limited. To expand, it needed more computers, more employees, and more technology. To finance this expansion, Google needed more money. The company could have *borrowed* money from a bank or other financial institution, but that would have saddled the company with debt and forced it to make regular interest payments.

Rather than borrow money, Google's directors elected to sell ownership shares in the company. In August 2004, the company raised $1.7 *billion* in cash by selling 19.6 million shares for $85 per share in its initial public offering.

Secondary Trading

Why were people eager to buy shares in Google? They certainly weren't buying the stock with expectations of high dividends. The company hadn't earned much profit in its first 5 years and didn't expect substantial profits for at least another few years.

price/earnings (P/E) ratio: The price of a stock share divided by earnings (profit) per share.

P/E Ratio. In 2003, Google had earned only 41 cents of profit per share. In 2004, it would earn $1.46 per share. So people who were buying Google stock for $85 per share in August 2004 were paying a comparatively high price for relatively little profit. This can be seen by computing the **price/earnings (P/E) ratio:**

$$\text{P/E ratio} = \frac{\text{price of stock share}}{\text{earnings (profit) per share}}$$

[1]In reality, some of the initial proceeds will go to stockbrokers and investment bankers as compensation for their services as financial intermediaries. The entrepreneur who starts the company, other company employees, and any venture capitalists who help fund the company before the public offering may also get some of the IPO receipts by selling shares they acquired before the company went public.

For Google in 2004,

$$\text{P/E ratio} = \frac{\$85}{\$1.46} = 58.2$$

In other words, investors were paying $58.20 for every $1 of profits. That implies a rate of return of 1 ÷ $58.20, or only 1.7 percent. Compared to the interest rates banks were paying on deposit balances, Google shares didn't look like a very good buy.

Profit Expectations. People weren't buying Google stock just to get a piece of *current* profits. What made Google attractive was its *growth* potential. The company projected that revenues and profits would grow rapidly as its search capabilities expanded, more people used its services, and, most important, more advertisers clamored to get premium spots on the company's Web pages. Given these expectations, investors projected that Google's profits would jump from $1.46 per share in 2004 to roughly $10 in 4 years. From that perspective, the *projected* P/E ratio looked cheap.

Investors who wanted a piece of those future profits rushed to buy Google stock after its IPO. On the first day of trading, the share price rose from the IPO price of $85 to $100. Within a month the price rose to $120. Two years later Google's stock sold for more than $450 a share.

That post-IPO rise in Google's stock price had no direct effect on the company. A corporation reaps the proceeds of stock sales only when it sells shares to the public (the initial public offering). After the IPO, the company's stock is traded among individuals in the "after market." Virtually, all the trading activity on major stock exchanges consists of such after-market sales. Mr. Dow sells his Google share to Ms. Jones, who may later sell them to Brad Pitt. Such *secondary* trades may take place at the New York Stock Exchange (NYSE) on Wall Street or in the computerized over-the-counter market (e.g., NASDAQ).

Market Fluctuations

The price of a stock at any moment is the outcome of supply-and-demand interactions. I wouldn't mind owning a piece of Google. But since I think the current share price is too high, I'll buy the stock only if the price falls substantially. Even though I'm not buying any Google stock now, I'm part of the *market demand.* That is, all the people who are willing and able to buy Google stock at *some* price are included in the demand curve in Figure 32.3. The cheaper the stock, the more people will want to buy it, *ceteris paribus.* The opposite is true on the supply side of the market: Ever-higher prices are necessary to induce more shareholders to part with their shares.

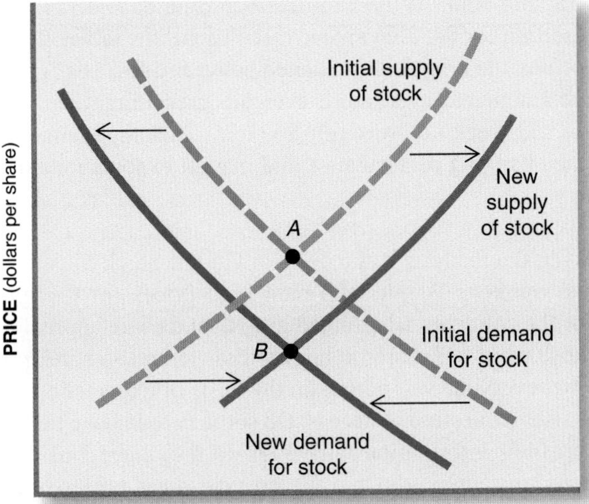

FIGURE 32.3
Worsened Expectations

The supply and demand for stocks is fueled in part by expectations of future profits. When investors concluded that Google's future profit potential wasn't so great, demand for the stock decreased, supply increased, and the share price fell.

52 Weeks											
Hi	Lo	Stock	Sym	Div	Yld%	P/E	Vol 100s	Hi	Lo	Close	Net Chg
22.50	16.75	Intel	INTC	.40	2.36	21.95	713755	19.42	19.05	19.10	–.13
513.00	331.55	Google	GOOG	N/A	N/A	45.57	61153	458.40	450.10	452.96	–1.76

The information provided by this quotation includes:

52-Weeks Hi and Lo: The highest and lowest prices paid for a share of stock in the previous year.

Stock: The name of the corporation whose shares are being traded.

Sym: The symbol used as a shorthand description for the stock.

Div: A dividend is the amount of profit paid out by the corporation in the preceding year for each share of stock.

Yld%: The yield is the dividend paid per share divided by the price of a share.

P/E: The price of the stock (P) divided by the earnings (profit) per share (E). This indicates how much a purchaser is effectively paying for each dollar of profits.

Vol 100s: The number of shares traded in hundreds.

Hi: The highest price paid for a share of stock on the previous day.

Lo: The lowest price paid for a share of stock on the previous day.

Close: The price paid in the last trade of the day as the market was closing.

Net Chg: The change in the closing price yesterday vs. the previous day's closing price.

Source: CNN.money.com

TABLE 32.3
Reading Stock Quotes

The financial pages of the daily newspaper summarize the trading activity in corporate stocks. The quotation above summarizes trading in Intel and Google shares on March 9, 2007.

webnote

How is *your* stock doing? Find current and past stock prices at http://finance.yahoo.com

Changing Expectations. In early 2006, investors reevaluated the profit prospects for Google and other Internet companies. Several years of experience had shown that earning profits in e-commerce wasn't so easy. Projections of advertising-sales growth and future profits were sharply reduced. In 2 months' time Google's stock price fell from $470 to $340. Figure 32.3 illustrates how this happened. Higher perceived risk reduced the demand for Google stock and increased the willingness of existing shareholders to sell. Such ***changes in expectations imply shifts in supply and demand for a company's stock.*** As Figure 32.3 illustrates, these combined shifts sent Google stock plummeting.

Table 32.3 summarizes the action in Google stock on a single day. On that day over 6 million shares of Google were bought and sold. At the end of the trading day (4 P.M., in New York City) Google shares were selling for $452.96 apiece (see "Close" in Table 32.3). Along the path to that closing equilibrium, the price had fluctuated between $450.10 ("Lo") and $458.40 ("Hi"). The stock price fluctuated even more over the preceding year, the "52-week Hi" was $513.00, while the "52-week Lo" was only $331.55. This huge range in the price of Google shares reflects the changing performance and market expectations for the company.

The Value of Information. The wide fluctuations in the price of Google stock illustrate the value of *information* in financial markets. People who paid high prices for Google shares had optimistic expectations for the company's continued growth and share appreciation (see News on the next page). Those who *sold* shares at high prices weren't so sure. No one *knew* what future profits would be; everyone was acting on the basis of expectations.

The evident value of information raises a question of access. Do some people have better information than others? Do they get their information fairly? Or do they have "inside" sources (such as company technicians, managers, directors) who give them preferential access to information? If so, these insiders would have an unfair advantage in the market-

IN THE NEWS   

Growth Undergirds Google's Pricey IPO But Can It Keep Up?

INVESTORS HAD BETTER be feeling lucky about **Google** Inc.'s growth prospects.

Now that the Internet-search company has trotted out its own $35 billion or so estimate of its value, the challenge for those pondering whether to participate in Google's initial public offering of stock next month is to figure out how much longer the good times will last. Sure, the company is making money hand over fist, and it has juicy margins and profits that are expanding rapidly. But with its IPO shares likely to begin trading at expensive levels, Google is attractive only if it can maintain impressive growth.

In the near term, the acceleration likely will continue, analysts and industry specialists say. But some are concerned that growth in the search business and related advertising is slowing from its heady clip. Fewer people will be going online for the first time, they say, and those already on the Internet probably won't radically increase the number of searches they conduct. In the long run, Google likely will have to prove that it can continue to come up with new ways to profit from its dominant position in the Web-search business for its shares to be big winners.

—Gregory Zuckerman and Kevin J. Delaney

Analysis: People who buy a company's stock are betting on future sales and profits. If expectations change, the price of the stock will change as well.

place and could alter the distribution of income and wealth in their favor. This is the kind of "insider trading" that got Martha Stewart into trouble (and jail).

The value of information also explains the demand for information services. People pay hundreds and even thousands of dollars for newsletters, wire services, and online computer services that provide up-to-date information on companies and markets. They also pay for the services of investment bankers, advisers, and brokers to help keep them informed. These services help disseminate information quickly, thereby helping financial markets operate efficiently.

webnote

You can retrieve the latest news about a company and its stock from various online brokerage and investment-advice services, including cnnfin.com. You can also retrieve charts showing how a stock price has fluctuated during the day or over longer periods. Free charts on individual stocks are available at www.bigcharts.com

Booms and Busts. If stock markets are so efficient at computing the present value of future profits, why does the entire market make abrupt moves every so often? Fundamentally, the same factors that determine the price of a single stock influence the broader stock market averages as well. An increase in interest rates, for example, raises the opportunity cost of holding stocks. Hence, higher interest rates should cause stock prices to fall, *ceteris paribus.* Stocks might decline even further if higher interest rates are expected to curtail investment and consumption, thus reducing future sales and profits. Such a double whammy could cause the whole stock market to tumble.

Other factors also affect the relative desirability of holding stock. Congressional budget and deficit decisions, monetary policy, consumer confidence, business investment plans, international trade patterns, and new inventions are just a few of the factors that may alter present and future profits. These ***broad changes in the economic outlook tend to push all stock prices up or down at the same time.***

Broad changes in the economic outlook, however, seldom occur overnight. Moreover, these changes are rarely of a magnitude that could precipitate a stock market boom or bust. In reality, the stock market often changes more abruptly than the economic outlook. These exaggerated movements in the stock market are caused by sudden and widespread changes in expectations. Keep in mind that the value of the stock depends on anticipated *future* profits and expectations for interest rates and the economic outlook. No elements of the future are certain. Instead, people use present clues to try to discern the likely course of future events. In other words, ***all information must be filtered through people's expectations.***

webnote

Think you can make a profit in the stock market? Try the Stock Market Game, an electronic simulation of Wall Street trading, at www.smg2000.org

Just a normal day at the nation's most important financial institution . . .

Analysis: Sudden changes in expectations can substantially alter stock prices.

The central role of expectations implies that the economy can change more gradually than the stock market. If, for example, interest rates rise, market participants may regard the increase as temporary or inconsequential: Their expectations for the future may not change. If interest rates keep rising, however, investors may have greater doubts. At some point, the market participants may revise their expectations. Stock prices may falter, triggering an adjustment in expectations. A herding instinct may surface, sending expectations for stock prices abruptly lower (see cartoon).

Shocks. The September 11, 2001, terrorist attacks on the World Trade Center and the Pentagon illustrated how much faster expectations can change than does the real economy. The attacks paralyzed the U.S. economy for several days and made people fearful for both their physical and economic security. People wanted to withdraw from the marketplace, taking their assets with them. When the U.S. stock exchanges opened several days after the attacks, stocks tumbled. The Dow Jones industrial average (see Table 32.4) fell 685 points—its biggest loss ever. The NASDAQ Composite (Table 32.4) also plunged by more than 7 percent in 1 day. Within 10 days, the value of U.S. stocks had declined by more than $1 *trillion.*

The economy didn't fare nearly as badly as the stock market. Although the attacks were tragic in human terms, they made only a tiny dent in the economy's productive capacity. Quick responses by the government in defending the financial markets also dispelled fears of a financial meltdown. As people's worst fears subsided, the demand for stocks picked up again. Within a month's time, the stock markets had fully recovered their post-attack losses. Along the way, however, changing expectations caused wild gyrations in stock prices.

Resource Allocations

Although it's fascinating and sometimes fun to watch stock market gyrations, we shouldn't lose sight of the *economic* role of financial markets. Columbus needed *real* resources—ships, men, equipment—for his expeditions. Five centuries later, Google also needed real resources—computers, labor, technology—to expand. To find the necessary economic

TABLE 32.4
Stock Market Averages

Over 1,600 stocks are listed (traded) on the New York Stock Exchange, and many times that number are traded in other stock markets. To gauge changes in so many stocks, people refer to various indices, such as the Dow Jones industrial average. The Dow and similar indexes help us keep track of the market's ups and downs. Some of the most frequently quoted indexes are

Dow Jones

Industrial average: An arithmetic average of the prices of 30 blue-chip industrial stocks traded on the New York Stock Exchange (NYSE) and by computers of the National Association of Securities Dealers (NASD).

Transportation average: An average of 20 transportation stocks traded on the NYSE.

Utilities average: An average of 15 utility stocks traded on the NYSE.

S&P 500: An index compiled by Standard and Poor of 500 stocks drawn from major stock exchanges as well as over-the-counter stocks. The S&P 500 is made up of 400 industrial companies, 40 utilities, 20 transportation companies, and 40 financial institutions.

NASDAQ Composite: Index of stocks traded in the over-the-counter market among securities dealers.

New York Stock Exchange composite index: The "Big Board" index, which includes all 1,600-plus stocks traded on the NYSE.

Nikkei index: An index of 225 stocks traded on the Tokyo stock market.

resources, both Columbus and Google had to convince society to reallocate resources from other activities to their new ventures.

Financial markets facilitate resource reallocations. In Columbus's case, the Genoese bankers lent the funds that Columbus used to buy scarce resources. The funds obtained from Google's 2004 initial public offering served the same purpose. In both cases, the funds obtained in the financial markets helped change the mix of output. If the financial markets hadn't supplied the necessary funding, neither Columbus nor Google would have been able to go forth. The available resources would have been used to produce other goods.

THE BOND MARKET

The bond market is another mechanism for transferring the pool of national savings into the hands of would-be spenders. It operates much like the stock market. The major difference is the kind of paper traded. ***In the stock market, people buy and sell shares of corporate ownership. In the bond market, people buy and sell promissory notes (IOUs).*** A **bond** is simply an IOU, a written promise to repay a loan. The bond itself specifies the terms of repayment, noting both the amount of interest to be paid each year and the maturity date (the date on which the borrower is to repay the entire debt). The borrower may be a corporation (corporate bonds), local governments (municipal bonds), the federal government (Treasury bonds), or other institutions.

bond: A certificate acknowledging a debt and the amount of interest to be paid each year until repayment; an IOU.

Bond Issuance

A bond is first issued when an institution wants to borrow money. Recall the situation Google faced in 2004. The company needed additional funds to expand its Internet operations. Rather than sell equity shares in itself, Google could have *borrowed* funds. The advantage of borrowing funds rather than issuing stock is that the owners can keep control of their company. ***Lenders aren't owners, but shareholders are.*** The disadvantage of borrowing funds is that the company gets saddled with a repayment schedule. Lenders want to be paid back—with interest. For a new company like Google, the burden of interest payments may be too great.

Ignoring these problems momentarily, let's assume that Google decided in 2004 to borrow funds rather than sell stock in itself. To do so, it would have *issued* bonds. This simply par value: The face value of a bond; the amount to be repaid when the bond is due.

means that it would have printed formal IOUs called bonds. Typically, each bond certificate would have a **par value** (face value) of $1,000. The bond certificate would also specify the rate of interest to be paid and the promised date of repayment. A Google bond issued in 2004, for example, might specify repayment in 10 years, with annual interest payments of $100. The individual who bought the bond from Google would lend $1,000 for 10 years and receive annual interest payments of $100. Thus, ***the initial bond purchaser lends funds directly to the bond issuer.*** The borrower (such as Google, General Motors, or the U.S. Treasury) can then use those funds to acquire real resources. Thus, the bond market also functions as a financial intermediary, transferring available savings (wealth) to those who want to acquire more resources (invest).

As in the case of IPOs of stock, the critical issue here is the *price* of the bond. How many people are willing and able to lend funds to the company? What rate of interest will they charge?

default: Failure to make scheduled payments of interest or principal on a bond.

As we observed in Figure 32.2, the quantity of loanable funds supplied depends on the interest rate. At low interest rates no one is willing to lend funds to the company. Why lend your savings to a risky venture like Google when more secure bonds and even banks pay higher interest rates? Google might not catch on and may later **default** (not pay) on its obligations. Potential lenders would want to be compensated for this extra risk with above-average interest rates, that is, a risk premium. Remember that lenders don't share in any profits Google might earn; they get only interest payments. Hence, they'd want a hefty premium to compensate them for the risk of default.

coupon rate: Interest rate set for a bond at time of issuance.

Suppose that market participants will lend the desired amount of money to Google only at 16 percent interest. In this case, Google may agree to pay an interest rate—the so-called **coupon rate**—of 16 percent to secure start-up funding of $50 million. That means Google agrees to pay $160 of interest each year for every $1,000 borrowed and to repay the entire $50 million at the end of 10 years.

Bond Trading

liquidity: The ability of an asset to be converted into cash.

Once a bond has been issued, the initial lenders don't have to wait 10 years to get their money back. They can't go back to the company and demand early repayment, but they can sell their bonds to someone else. This **liquidity** is an important consideration for prospective bondholders. If a person had no choice but to wait 10 years for repayment, he or she might be less willing to buy a bond (lend funds). ***By facilitating resales, the bond market increases the availability of funds to new ventures and other borrowers.*** As is the case with stocks, most of the action in the bond markets consists of such after-market trades, that is, the buying and selling of bonds issued at some earlier time. The company that first issued the bonds doesn't participate in these trades.

The portfolio decision in the bond market is motivated by the same factors that influence stock purchases. The *opportunity cost* of buying and selling bonds is the best alternative rate of return—for example, the interest rate on other bonds or money market mutual funds. *Expectations* also play a role, in gauging both likely changes in opportunity costs and the ability of the borrower to redeem (pay off) the bond when it's due. ***Changes in expectations or opportunity costs shift the bond supply and demand curves,*** thereby altering market interest rates.

Current Yields

We've assumed that Google would have had to offer 16 percent interest to induce enough people to lend the company (buy bonds worth) $50 million. This was far higher than the 6 percent the U.S. Treasury was paying on its bonds (borrowed funds). This large risk premium reflected the fear that Google might not succeed and end up defaulting on it loans.

Suppose that Google actually took off. The risk of a bond default would diminish, and people would be more willing to lend it funds. This change in the availability of loanable funds is illustrated in the rightward shift of the supply curve in Figure 32.4.

According to the new supply curve in Figure 32.4, Google could now borrow $50 million at 10 percent interest (point *B*) rather than paying 16 percent (point *A*). Unfortunately, Google already borrowed the funds and is obliged to continue paying $160 per year in interest on each bond. Hence, the company doesn't benefit directly from the supply shift.

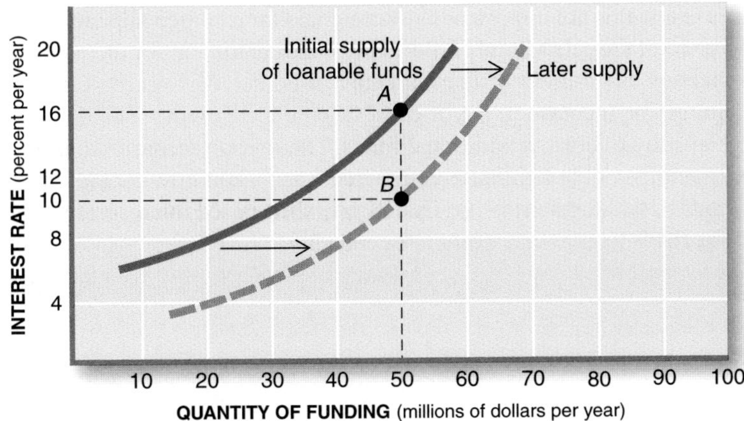

FIGURE 32.4
Shifts in Funds Supply

If lenders decide that a company's future is less risky, they will be more willing to lend it money or hold its bonds. The resulting shift of the loanable funds supply curve reduces the current yield on a bond by raising its price.

The change in the equilibrium value of Google bonds must show up somewhere, however. People who hold Google bonds continue to get $160 per year in interest (16 percent of $1,000). Now there are lots of people who would be willing to lend funds to Google at that rate. These people want to hold Google bonds themselves. To get them, they'll have to buy the bonds in the market from existing bondholders. Thus, the ***increased willingness to lend funds is reflected in an increased demand for bonds.*** This increased demand will push up the price of Google bonds. As bond prices rise, their implied effective interest rate **(current yield)** falls. Table 32.5 illustrates this relationship.

current yield: The rate of return on a bond; the annual interest payment divided by the bond's price.

Price of Bond	Annual Interest Payment	Current Yield
$ 600	$150	25.0%
800	150	18.8
1,000	150	15.0
1,200	150	12.5

The annual interest payments on a bond are fixed at the time of issuance. Accordingly, only the market (resale) prices of the bond can change. An increase in the price of the bond lowers its *effective* interest rate, or yield. The formula for computing the current yield on a bond is

$$\text{Current yield} = \frac{\text{annual interest payment}}{\text{market (resale) price of bond}}$$

Thus, higher bond prices imply lower yields (effective interest rates), as confirmed in the table above. Bond prices and yields vary with changes in expectations and opportunity costs.

The newspaper quotation below shows how changing bond prices and yields are reported. This General Motors (GM) bond was issued with a coupon rate (nominal interest rate) of 8⅜ percent. Hence, GM promised to pay $83.75 in interest each year until it redeemed (paid off) the $1,000 bond in the year 2033. In July 2004, however, the market price of the bond was $1,032.40 (103.24). This created a yield of 8.08 percent.

Bond	Current Yield	Volume	Close
GM 8⅜ 33	8.083	142	103.24

TABLE 32.5
Bond Price and Yields Move in Opposite Directions

Changing bond prices and yields are important market signals for resource allocation. In our example, the rising price of Google's bonds reflects increased optimism for the company's prospects. The collective assessment of the marketplace is that Web search engines will be a profitable venture. The increase in the price of Google bonds will make it easier and less costly for the company to borrow additional funds. The reverse scenario unfolded in 2000–2001. When investors concluded that e-commerce wasn't going to generate fast profits, the supply of funds to dot.coms dried up. That supply shift raised interest rates and made it more difficult for firms to expand e-commerce capacity.

THE ECONOMY TOMORROW

VENTURE CAPITALISTS—FINANCING TOMORROW'S PRODUCTS

One of the proven paths to high incomes and wealth is entrepreneurship. Most of the great American fortunes originated in entrepreneurial ventures, for example, building railroads, mass-producing automobiles, introducing new computers, or perfecting mass-merchandising techniques. These successful ventures all required more than just a great idea. To convert the original idea into actual output requires the investment of real resources.

Recall that Apple Computer started in a garage, with a minimum of resources (Chapter 23). The idea of packaging a personal computer was novel, and few resources were required to demonstrate that it could be done. But Steven Jobs couldn't have become a multimillionaire by building just a few dozen computers a month. To reap huge economic profits from his idea, he needed much greater production capacity. He also needed resources for marketing the new Apples to a broader customer base. In other words, Steven Jobs needed lots of economic resources—land, labor, and capital—to convert his entrepreneurial dream into a profit-making reality.

Steven Jobs and his partner, Steve Wozniak, had few resources of their own. In fact, they'd sold Jobs's Volkswagen and Wozniak's scientific calculator to raise the finances for the first computer. To go any further, they needed financial support from others. Loans were hard to obtain since the company had no assets, no financial history, and no certainty of success. Jobs needed people who were willing to share the *risks* associated with a new venture. He found one such person in A. C. Markkula, who put up $250,000 and became a partner in the new venture. Shortly thereafter, other venture capitalists provided additional financing. With this start-up financing, Jobs was able to acquire more resources and make the Apple Computer Company a reality.

This is a classic case study in venture capitalism. As the accompanying News documents, most business start-ups are created with shoestring budgets, averaging $10,000 (Apple started with even less). The initial seed money typically comes from an entrepreneur's own assets or credit, with a little help from family and friends. If the idea pans out, entrepreneurs need a lot more money to develop their product. This is where venture capitalists come in. Venture capitalists provide initial funding for entrepreneurial ventures. In return for their financial backing, the venture capitalists are entitled to a share of any profits that result. If the venture fails, however, they get nothing. Thus, ***venture capitalists provide financial support for entrepreneurial ideas and share in the risks and rewards.*** Even Christopher Columbus needed venture capitalists to fund his risky expeditions to the New World.

Venture capital is as important to the economy tomorrow as it was to Columbus. For technology and entrepreneurship to continue growing, market conditions and tax provisions must be amenable to venture capitalists.

IN THE NEWS

Where Do Start-Ups Get Their Money?

SAN FRANCISCO—YouTube landed millions in venture-capital money in its first year to expand so fast that its founders were able to sell the video-sharing company to Google last week for $1.7 billion.

For most entrepreneurs, however, venture capital isn't an option. VCs, investing for institutions and rich individuals, likely will invest in fewer than 3,400 of the USA's more than 20 million small firms this year.

Instead, a majority of founders reach into their own pockets or turn to family members, who provide nearly $60 billion a year in start-up and expansion funding. Today's typical new business sells a service, such as bookkeeping, so requires little more than an inexpensive computer, a fax machine and a home office. Even trendy start-ups such as YouTube get going with a handful of computers lashed together in a garage.

Banking giant Wells Fargo found in a recent survey of owners that their start-up costs averaged just $10,000. . . .

—Jim Hopkins

Source: *USA Today,* October 18, 2006, p. 3B. Reprinted with permission.

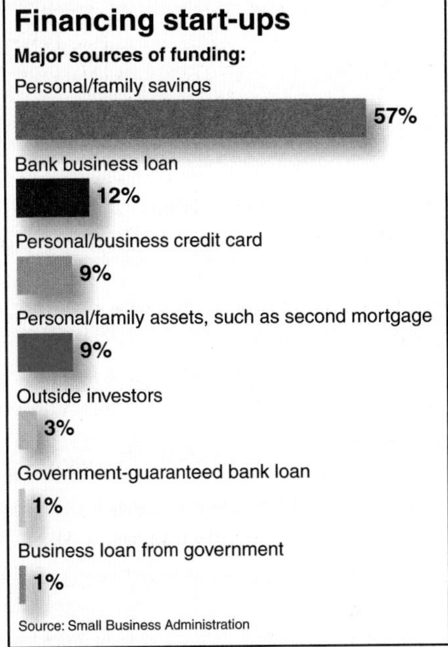

Source: Alejandro Gonzalez, *USA Today,* October 18, 2006, p. 3B.

Analysis: Business start-ups need outside financing to transform hot new ideas into market reality. Venture capitalists provide speculative funding to acquire needed resources.

SUMMARY

- The primary economic function of financial markets is to help allocate scarce resources to desired uses. They do this by providing access to the pool of national savings for entrepreneurs, investors, and other would-be spenders. LO3
- Financial markets enable individuals to manage risk by holding different kinds of assets. Financial intermediaries also reduce the costs of information and search, thereby increasing market efficiency. LO3
- Future returns on investments must be discounted to present value. The present discounted value (PDV) of a future payment adjusts for forgone interest accrual. LO2
- Future returns are also uncertain. The *expected* value of future payments must also reflect the risk of nonpayment. LO3
- Shares of stock represent ownership in a corporation. The shares are initially issued to raise funds and are then traded on the stock exchanges. LO1
- Changes in the value of a corporation's stock reflect changing expectations and opportunity costs. Share price changes, in turn, act as market signals to direct more or fewer resources to a company. LO3
- Bonds are IOUs issued when a company (or government agency) borrows funds. After issuance, bonds are traded in the after (secondary) market. LO1
- The interest (coupon) rate on a bond is fixed at the time of issuance. The price of the bond itself, however, varies with changes in expectations (perceived risk) and opportunity cost. Yields vary inversely with bond prices. LO2

Key Terms

financial intermediary
risk premium
present discounted value (PDV)
expected value
corporation
corporate stock
dividend
retained earnings
capital gain
initial public offering (IPO)
price/earnings (P/E) ratio
bond
par value
default
coupon rate
liquidity
current yield

Questions for Discussion

1. If there were no organized financial markets, how would an entrepreneur acquire resources to develop and produce a new product? LO1
2. Why would anyone buy shares of a corporation that had no profits and paid no dividends? What's the highest price a person would pay for such a stock? LO2
3. Why would anyone sell a bond for less than its face (par) value? LO2
4. If you could finance a new venture with either a stock issue or bonds, which option would you choose? What are their respective (dis)advantages? LO1
5. Why is it considered riskier to own stock in a software company than to hold U.S. Treasury savings bonds? Which asset will generate a higher return? LO3
6. How does a successful IPO affect WHAT, HOW, and FOR WHOM the economy produces? LO1
7. What considerations might have created the difference between the coupon rate and current yield on GM bonds (Table 32.5)? LO2
8. What is the price of Google stock now? What has caused the change in price since its 2004 IPO at $85 a share (News, page 649). LO3

problems The Student Problem Set at the back of this book contains numerical and graphing problems for this chapter.

web activities to accompany this chapter can be found on the Online Learning Center: **http://www.mhhe.com/economics/schiller11e**

Distributional Issues

Of the three core questions in economics, the FOR WHOM issue is often the most contentious. Should the market decide who gets the most output? Or should the government intervene and redistribute market incomes to achieve greater equity?

Tax and transfer systems are designed to redistribute market incomes. The next two chapters survey these systems. In the process, we assess not only how effective they are in achieving greater *equity,* but also what impacts they have on *efficiency.* High taxes and generous transfer payments may blunt work incentives and so reduce the size of the pie being resliced. This creates a fundamental conflict between the goals of equity and efficiency. Chapters 33 and 34 examine this conflict.

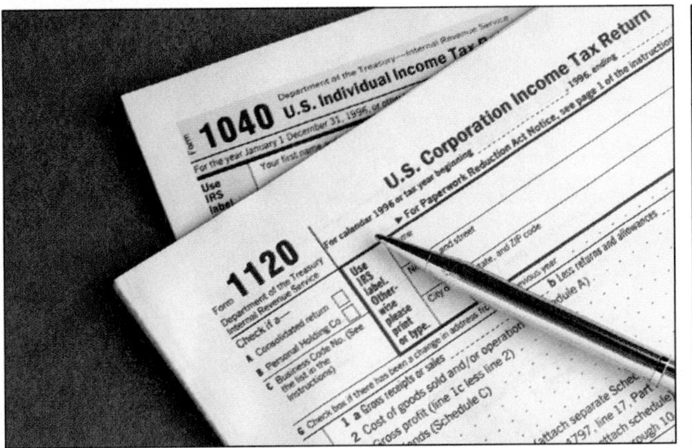

Taxes: Equity versus Efficiency

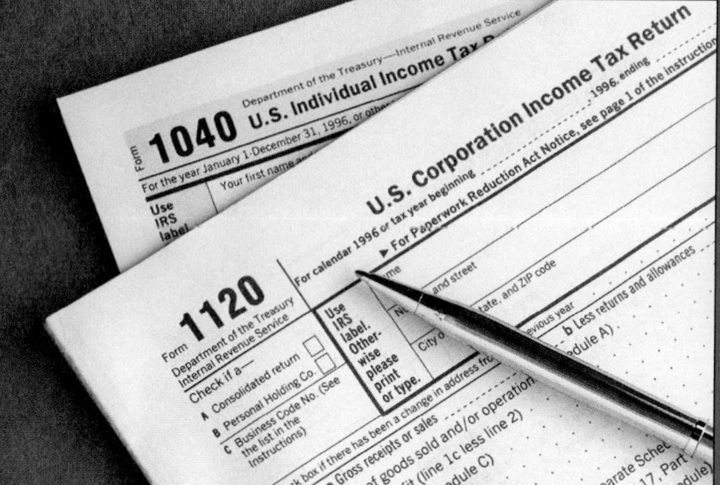

LEARNING OBJECTIVES

After reading this chapter, you should know:

LO1. How the U.S. tax system is structured.

LO2. What makes taxes more or less progressive.

LO3. The nature of the equity-efficiency trade-off.

Insistence on carving the pie into equal slices would shrink the size of the pie. That fact poses the trade-off between economic equality and economic efficiency.

—Arthur M. Okun

Steve Jobs, chairman of Apple Computer, earned a whopping $647 million in 2006. That would have been enough income to lift nearly 350,000 poor persons out of poverty. But Jobs didn't share his good fortune with those people, and they remained poor.

The market mechanism generated both Steve Jobs's extraordinary income and that of so many poor families. Is this the way we want the basic FOR WHOM question to be settled? Should some people own vast fortunes while others seek shelter in abandoned cars? Or do the inequalities that emerge in product and factor markets violate our notions of equity? If the market's answer to the FOR WHOM question isn't right, some form of government intervention to redistribute incomes may be desired.

The tax system is the government's primary lever for redistributing income. But taxing Peter to pay Paul may affect more than just income shares. If taxed too heavily, Peter may stop producing so much. Paul, too, may work less if assured of government support. The end result may be *less* total income to share. In other words: ***Taxes affect production as well as distribution. This creates a potential trade-off between the goal of equity and the goal of efficiency.***

This chapter examines this equity-efficiency trade-off, with the following questions as a guide:

- **How are incomes distributed in the United States?**
- **How do taxes alter that distribution?**
- **How do taxes affect the rate and mix of output?**

After addressing these questions, we examine the allure of a "flat tax."

WHAT IS *INCOME?*

Before examining the distribution of income in the United States, let's decide what to count as *income.* There are several possibilities. The most obvious choice is **personal income (PI)**—the flow of annual income received by households before payment of personal income taxes. Personal income includes wages and salaries, corporate dividends, rent, interest, Social Security benefits, welfare payments, and any other form of money income.

Personal Income

personal income (PI): Income received by households before payment of personal taxes.

in-kind income: Goods and services received directly, without payment in a market transaction.

Personal income isn't a complete measure of income, however. Many goods and services are distributed directly as **in-kind income** rather than through market purchases. Many poor people, for example, live in public housing and pay little or no rent. As a consequence, they receive a larger share of total output than their money incomes imply. People with low incomes also receive food stamps that allow them to purchase more food than their money incomes would allow. In this sense, food stamp recipients are better off than the distribution of personal income (which omits food stamps) implies.

In-kind benefits aren't limited to low-income households. Students who attend public schools and colleges consume more goods and services than they directly pay for; public education is subsidized by all taxpayers. People over age 65 also get medical services through Medicare that they don't directly pay for. And middle-class workers get noncash fringe benefits (like health insurance, paid vacations, pension contributions) that don't show up in their paychecks or on their tax returns.

So long as some goods and services needn't be purchased in the marketplace, ***the distribution of money income isn't synonymous with the distribution of goods and services.*** This measurement problem is particularly important when comparisons are made over time. For example, the federal government officially classifies people as "poor" if their money income is below a certain threshold. By this standard, we've made no progress against poverty. The Census Bureau counted nearly 37 million Americans as "poor" in 2005, more than it counted in 1965. In both years the Census Bureau counted only money incomes. In 1965 that approach was acceptable, since little income was transferred in kind. In 2005, however, the federal government spent over $30 billion on food stamps, $22 billion on housing subsidies, and nearly $300 billion on Medicaid. Had all this in-kind income been counted, 7 million fewer Americans would have been counted poor in 2005. Although that would still leave a lot of people in poverty, at least more progress in eliminating poverty would be evident.

webnote

The Census Bureau compiles data on poverty from each year's March household survey. For the most recent data, visit www.census.gov/hhes/www/poverty.html

Wealth

wealth: The market value of assets.

If our ultimate concern is access to goods and services, the distribution of wealth is also important. **Wealth** refers to the market value of assets (such as houses and bank accounts) people own. Hence, ***wealth represents a stock of potential purchasing power; income statistics tell us only how this year's flow of purchasing power (income) is being distributed.*** Accordingly, to provide a complete answer to the FOR WHOM question, we have to know how wealth, as well as income, is distributed. In general, wealth tends to be distributed much less equally than income. The Internal Revenue Service estimates that 3 percent of the adult population owns 30 percent of all personal wealth in the United States but gets less than 20 percent of total income.

THE SIZE DISTRIBUTION OF INCOME

size distribution of income: The way total personal income is divided up among households or income classes.

Although incomes aren't a perfect measure of access to goods and services (much less happiness), they're the best single indicator of the FOR WHOM outcomes. The **size distribution of income** tells us how large a share of total personal income is received by various households, grouped by income class. Imagine for the moment that the entire population is lined up in order of income, with lowest-income recipients in front and highest-income recipients at the end of the line. We want to know how much income the people in front get in comparison with those at the back.

We first examined the size distribution of income in Chapter 2. Figure 2.5 showed that households in the lowest quintile received less than $19,000 apiece in 2005. As a group,

income share: The proportion of total income received by a particular group.

this class received only 3.4 percent of total income, despite the fact that it included 20 percent of all households (the lowest fifth). Thus, the **income share** of the people in the lowest group (3.4 percent) was much smaller than their proportion in the total population (20 percent).

Moving back to the end of the line, we observed that a household needed $92,000 to make it into the highest income class in 2005. Many families in that class made much more than $92,000—some even millions of dollars. But $92,000 was at least enough to get into the top fifth (quintile).

The top quintile ended up with half of total U.S. income and, by implication, that much of total output.

The Lorenz Curve

Lorenz curve: A graphic illustration of the cumulative size distribution of income; contrasts complete equality with the actual distribution of income.

The size distribution of income provides the kind of information we need to determine how total income (and output) is distributed. The **Lorenz curve** is a convenient summary of that information; it is a graphical illustration of the size distribution.

Figure 33.1 is a Lorenz curve for the United States. Our lineup of individuals is on the horizontal axis, with the lowest-income earners on the left. On the vertical axis we depict the cumulative share of income received by people in our income line. Consider the lowest quintile of the distribution again. They're represented on the horizontal axis at 20 percent. If their share of income was identical to their share of population, they'd get 20 percent of total income. This would be represented by point *C* in the figure. In fact, the lowest quintile gets only 3.4 percent, as indicated by point *A*. Point *B* tells us that the *cumulative* share of income received by the lowest *three*-fifths of the population was 26.6 percent.

The really handy feature of the Lorenz curve is the way it contrasts the actual distribution of income with an absolutely equal one. If incomes were distributed equally, the first 20 percent of the people in line would be getting exactly 20 percent of all income. In that case, the Lorenz curve would run through point *C*. Indeed, the Lorenz "curve" would be a straight line along the diagonal. The actual Lorenz curve lies below the diagonal because our national income isn't distributed equally. In fact, the area between the diagonal and the actual Lorenz curve (the shaded area in Figure 33.1) is a convenient measure of the degree of inequality. ***The greater the area between the Lorenz curve and the diagonal, the more inequality exists.***

Gini coefficient: A mathematical summary of inequality based on the Lorenz curve.

The visual summary of inequality the Lorenz curve provides is also expressed in a mathematical relationship. The ratio of the shaded area in Figure 33.1 to the area of the triangle formed by the diagonal is called the **Gini coefficient.** The higher the Gini coefficient, the

FIGURE 33.1
The Lorenz Curve

The Lorenz curve illustrates the extent of income inequality. If all incomes were equal, each fifth of the population would receive one-fifth of total income. In this case, the diagonal line through point C would represent the cumulative size distribution of income. In reality, incomes aren't distributed equally. Point *A*, for example, indicates that the 20 percent of the population with the lowest income receives only 3.4 percent of total income.

Source: Figure 2.5.

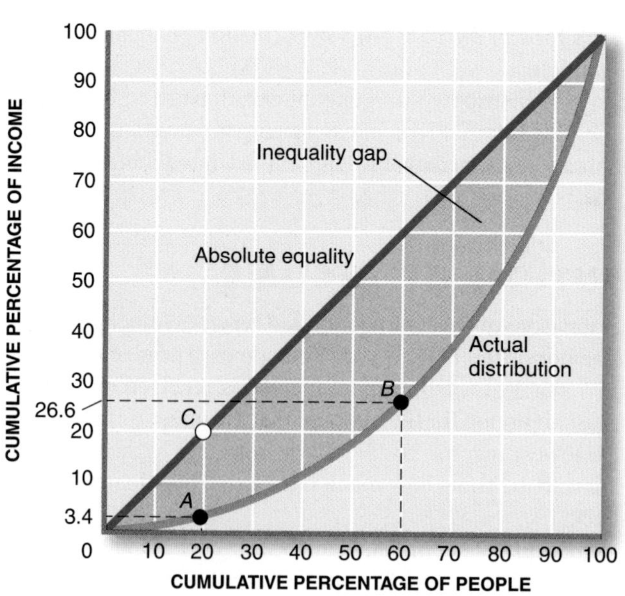

Robert Graysmith, Graysmith.

Analysis: An increase in the size of the economic pie doesn't ensure everyone a larger slice. A goal of the tax system is to attain a fairer distribution of the economic pie.

greater the degree of inequality. Between 1980 and 2005, the Gini coefficient rose from 0.403 to 0.469. In other words, the shaded area in Figure 33.1 expanded by about 16 percent, indicating *increased* inequality. Although the size of the economic pie (real GDP) more than *doubled* between 1980 and 2005, some people's slices got a lot bigger while other people saw little improvement, or even less (see cartoon).

The Call for Intervention

To many people, large and increasing inequality represents a form of **market failure:** The market is generating a suboptimal (unfair) answer to the FOR WHOM question. As in other instances of market failure, the government is called on to intervene. The policy lever in this case is taxes. **By levying taxes on the rich and providing transfer payments to the poor, the government *redistributes* market incomes.**

market failure: An imperfection in the market mechanism that prevents optimal outcomes.

THE FEDERAL INCOME TAX

The federal income tax is designed for this redistributional purpose. Specifically, the federal income tax is designed to be **progressive**—that is, to impose higher tax *rates* on high incomes than on low ones. Progressivity is achieved by imposing increasing **marginal tax rates** on higher incomes. The *marginal* tax rate refers to the tax rate imposed on the last (marginal) dollar of income.

progressive tax: A tax system in which tax rates rise as incomes rise.

marginal tax rate: The tax rate imposed on the last (marginal) dollar of income.

In 2006, the tax code specified the six tax brackets shown in Table 33.1. For an individual with less than $7,550 of income, the tax rate was 10 percent. Any income in excess of $7,550 was taxed at a *higher* rate of 15 percent. If an individual's income rose above $74,200, the amount between $74,200 and $154,800 was taxed at 28 percent. Any income greater than $336,550 was taxed at 35 percent.

To understand the efficiency and equity effects of taxes, we must distinguish between the *marginal* tax rate and the *average* tax rate. A person who earned $350,000 in 2006 paid the 35 percent tax only on the income in excess of $336,550, that is, the last (marginal) $13,450. The first $7,550 was taxed at a marginal rate of only 10 percent.

TABLE 33.1
Progressive Taxes

The federal income tax is progressive because it levies higher tax rates on higher incomes. The 2006 marginal tax rate started out at 10 percent for incomes below $7,550 and rose to 35 percent for incomes above $336,550.

Tax Bracket	Marginal Tax Rate
$0–7,550	10%
$7,550–30,650	15
$30,650–74,200	25
$74,200–154,800	28
$154,800–336,550	33
Over $336,550	35

Source: Internal Revenue Service (tax rates for single individuals).

webnote

Current tax rate schedules are available from the Internal Revenue Service at www.irs.gov/formspubs/article/0,,id=164272,00.html

Hence this individual's tax bill was

Marginal Tax Rate	Income		Tax
10% of	$ 7,550	=	$ 755.50
15% of	23,100	=	3,465.00
25% of	43,550	=	10,887.50
28% of	80,600	=	22,568.00
33% of	181,750	=	57,977.50
35% of	13,450	=	4,707.50
	$350,000		$100,361.00

The total tax of $100,361 represented only 26.7 percent of this individual's income. Hence, this person had a

- *Marginal* tax rate of 35 percent.
- *Average* tax rate of 26.7 percent.

By contrast, a person with only $20,000 of income would pay a *marginal* tax of only 15 percent and an *average* tax of 13 percent. The rationale behind this progressive system is to tax ever-larger percentages of higher incomes, thereby reducing income inequalities. This makes the *after-tax* distribution of income more equal than the *before-tax* distribution. This is how ***progressive taxes reduce inequality.***

Efficiency Concerns

Although the redistributive intent of a progressive tax system is evident, it raises concerns about efficiency. As noted in the chapter-opening quote, attempts to reslice the pie may end up reducing the size of the pie. The central issue here is incentives. Chapter 30 emphasized that the supply of labor is motivated by the pursuit of income. If Uncle Sam takes away ever-larger chunks of income, won't that dampen the desire to work? If so, ***the incentive to work more, produce more, or invest more is reduced by higher marginal tax rates.*** This suggests that as marginal tax rates increase, total output shrinks, creating a basic conflict between the goals of equity (more progressive taxes) and efficiency (more output).

Tax Elasticity of Supply. How great the conflict is between the equity and efficiency depends on how responsive market participants are to higher tax rates. The Rolling Stones left Great Britain off their 1998–99 world tour because the British marginal tax rate was so high (see World View). Many other businesses relocate to low-tax nations for the same reason. For the typical household, however, the response to higher tax rates is limited to reducing hours worked. In all cases we can summarize the response with **the tax elasticity of supply;** that is,

tax elasticity of supply: The percentage change in quantity supplied divided by the percentage change in tax rates.

$$\text{Tax elasticity of supply} = \frac{\text{\% change in quantity supplied}}{\text{\% change in tax rate}}$$

If the tax elasticity of supply were zero, there'd be no conflict between equity and efficiency. But a zero tax elasticity would also imply that people would continue to work, produce, and invest even if Uncle Sam took *all* their income in taxes. In today's range of taxes,

WORLD VIEW 

Stones Keep England off '98 Tour to Avoid Tax

MUNICH, Germany, June 11—Mick Jagger said today that the Rolling Stones were disappointed they would not be playing in England this year, but the band looked forward to coming home for a series of concerts in 1999.

Lambasted by the British press for calling off a four-date tour at home because of a new tax law, members of the Stones said they opted out because the band stood to lose $19.6 million in taxes.

Under the previous tax code, Britons who lived and worked abroad for more than a year were exempt from British taxes on their earnings so long as they did not spend more than 62 days on native soil.

But the Labor government elected a year ago has scrapped that arrangement for everyone except some 10,000 seafarers. Now any citizen who works in Britain at all must pay tax on his or her entire year's earnings.

More than 300,000 tickets had been sold for the four British dates, which have been rescheduled for June 1999.

—Dorothee Stoewahse

Source: *The Washington Post,* June 12, 1998. © Reuters. Used with permission.

Analysis: High tax rates deter people from supplying resources—in this case, staging a concert.

the average household's elasticity of labor supply is between 0.15 and 0.30. Hence, if tax *rates* go up by 20 percent, the quantity of labor supplied would decline by 3 to 6 percent. In other words, the size of the pie being resliced would shrink by 3–6 percent. Figure 33.2 confirms that the top marginal tax rate has changed by much more than 20 percent in the past, thereby significantly altering the size of the economic pie.

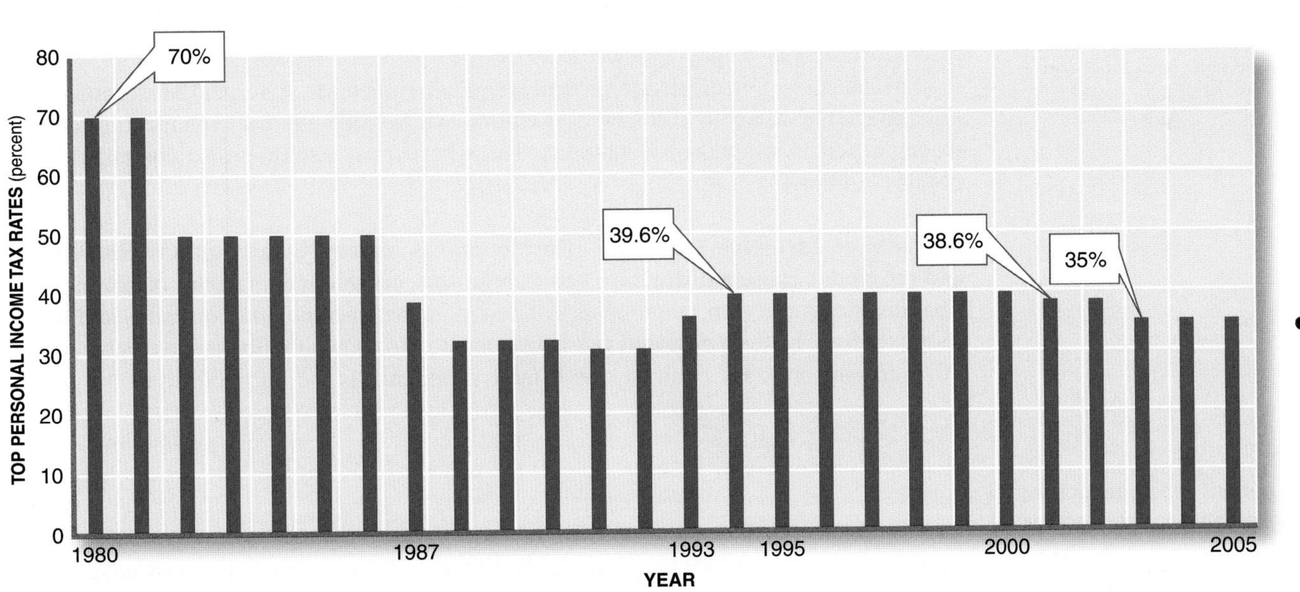

FIGURE 33.2
Changes in Marginal Tax Rates

During the past 25 years, Congress revised the federal income tax system many times. The top marginal tax rates were steadily reduced from 70 percent in 1980 to 28 percent in 1992. They were raised in 1993–95. The Bush tax cuts of 2001–4 reduced marginal tax rates again.

Source: Internal Revenue Service.

Equity Concerns

As if the concern about efficiency weren't enough, critics also raise questions about how well the federal income tax promotes equity. What appears to be a fairly progressive tax in theory turns out to be a lot less progressive in practice. Hundreds of people with $1 million incomes pay no taxes. They aren't necessarily breaking any laws, just taking advantage of loopholes in the tax system.

Loopholes. The progressive ***tax rates described in the tax code apply to "taxable" income, not to all income.*** The so-called loopholes in the system arise from the way Congress defines taxable income. The tax laws permit one to subtract certain exemptions and deductions from gross income in computing taxable income; that is,

$$\frac{\text{Taxable}}{\text{income}} = \frac{\text{gross}}{\text{income}} - \text{exemptions and deductions}$$

Exemptions are permitted for dependent children, spouses, old age, and disabilities. Prior to the 1986 law, deductions were permitted for home mortgage interest, work-related expenses, child care, depreciation of investments, oil exploration, interest payments, union dues, medical expenses, and many other items.

The purpose of these many *itemized deductions* was to encourage specific economic activities and reduce potential hardship. The deduction for mortgage interest payments, for example, encourages people to buy their own homes. The deduction for medical expenses helps relieve the financial burden of illness.

Whatever the merits of specific exemptions and deductions, they create potential inequities. ***People with high incomes can avoid high taxes by claiming large exemptions and deductions.*** Each year the Internal Revenue Service discovers individuals earning million-dollar incomes and paying little or no taxes. They aren't doing anything illegal, just taking advantage of the many deductions Congress permits. Nevertheless, this means that some people with high incomes could end up paying *less* tax than people with lower incomes. This would violate the principle of **vertical equity,** the progressive intent of taxing people on the basis of their ability to pay.

vertical equity: Principle that people with higher incomes should pay more taxes.

Table 33.2 illustrates vertical *in*equity. Mr. Jones has an income three times larger than Ms. Smith's. However, Mr. Jones also has huge deductions that reduce his *taxable* income dramatically. In fact, Mr. Jones ends up with less *taxable* income than Ms. Smith. As a result, he also ends up paying lower taxes.

horizontal equity: Principle that people with equal incomes should pay equal taxes.

The deductions that create the vertical inequity between Mr. Jones and Ms. Smith could also violate the principle of **horizontal equity**—as people with the *same* incomes end up paying different amounts of income tax. These horizontal *in*equities also contradict basic notions of fairness.

nominal tax rate: Taxes paid divided by taxable income.

effective tax rate: Taxes paid divided by total income.

Nominal vs. Effective Tax Rates. The "loopholes" created by exemptions, deductions, and tax credits cause a distinction between gross economic income and taxable income. That distinction, in turn, requires us to distinguish between *nominal* tax rates and *effective* tax rates. The term **nominal tax rate** refers to the taxes actually paid as a percentage of *taxable* income. By contrast, the **effective tax rate** is the tax paid divided by *total*

TABLE 33.2
Vertical Inequity

Tax exemptions and deductions create a gap between total income and *taxable* income. In this case, Mr. Jones has both a higher income and extensive deductions. He ends up with less taxable income than Ms. Smith and so pays less taxes. This vertical inequity is reflected in the lower effective tax rate paid by Mr. Jones.

	Mr. Jones	Ms. Smith
1. Total income	$90,000	$30,000
2. Less exemptions and deductions	−$70,000	−$ 5,000
3. Taxable income	$20,000	$25,000
4. Tax	$ 4,000	$ 5,500
5. Nominal tax rate (= row 4 ÷ row 3)	20%	22%
6. Effective tax rate (= row 4 ÷ row 1)	4.4%	18.3%

economic income without regard to exemptions, deductions, or other intricacies of the tax laws.

As Table 33.2 illustrates, someone with a gross income of \$90,000 might end up with a much lower *taxable* income, thanks to various tax deductions and exemptions. Mr. Jones ended up with a taxable income of only \$20,000 and a tax bill of merely \$4,000. As a result, we can characterize Mr. Jones's tax burden in two ways:

$$\text{Nominal tax rate} = \frac{\text{tax paid}}{\text{taxable income}} = \frac{\$4{,}000}{\$20{,}000} = 20 \text{ percent}$$

or, alternatively,

$$\text{Effective tax rate} = \frac{\text{tax paid}}{\text{total economic income}} = \frac{\$4{,}000}{\$90{,}000} = 4.4 \text{ percent}$$

This huge gap between the nominal tax rate (20 percent) and the effective tax rate (4.4 percent) is a reflection of loopholes in the tax code. It's also the source of the vertical and horizontal inequities discussed earlier. Notice that Ms. Smith, with much less gross income, ends up with an effective tax rate (18.3 percent) that's more than four times higher than Mr. Jones's (4.4 percent).

Tax-Induced Misallocations. Tax loopholes not only foster inequity but encourage inefficiency as well. The optimal mix of output is the one that balances consumer preferences and opportunity costs. Tax loopholes, however, encourage a different mix of output. By offering preferential treatment for some activities, the tax code reduces their relative accounting cost. In so doing, ***tax preferences induce resource shifts into tax-preferred activities.***

These resource allocations are a principal objective of tax preferences. By 1986, however, the accumulation of exemptions, deductions, and credits had become so unwieldy and complex that tax considerations were overwhelming economic considerations in many investment and consumption decisions. The resulting mix of output, many observers felt, was decidedly inferior to a *pure* market outcome. From this viewpoint, the federal income tax was promoting both inequity and inefficiency.

A Shrinking Tax Base. Loopholes in the tax code create yet another problem. As the **tax base** gets smaller and smaller, it becomes increasingly difficult to sustain, much less increase, tax revenues. The tax arithmetic is simple:

tax base: The amount of income or property directly subject to nominal tax rates.

$$\text{Tax revenue} = \frac{\text{average}}{\text{tax rate}} \times \frac{\text{tax}}{\text{base}}$$

As deductions, exemptions, and credits accumulate, the tax base (taxable income) keeps shrinking. To keep tax rates low—or to reduce them further—Congress had to stop this erosion of the tax base.

The 1986 Tax Reform Act

Rising discontent with a shrinking tax base, horizontal and vertical inequities, and tax-distorted resource allocations led to a major reform of federal taxes in 1986. The basic features of the Tax Reform Act (TRA) of 1986 included

- ***Loophole closing.*** Major loopholes were closed or reduced.
- ***Reductions in marginal tax rates.*** The top marginal tax rate was reduced from 50 to 28 percent.
- ***Fewer tax brackets.*** The number of tax brackets dropped from 16 to 2.

IN THE NEWS

The President's Taxes

President and Mrs. Bush received nearly $800,000 of income in 2006. Taxable income was reduced by deductions, however. Their $186,378 tax bill represented 29 percent of *taxable* income (the *nominal* tax rate) but only 24 percent of *total* income (the *effective* rate).

Income	
Wages	$397,768
Interest	285,734
Dividends	38,201
Capital gain	42,075
Partnership gain	2,023
Adjusted gross income	$765,801

Deductions	
Charitable contributions	78,100
Investment expenses	27,428
State, local etc taxes	27,474
Limit on deductions	(12,306)
Total deductions	$120,696
Taxable income	$642,905
Tax	$186,376

Source: The White House. www.whitehouse.gov

Analysis: Taxes are levied on *taxable* income, not total income. Various deductions and exemptions reduce taxable income and *effective* tax rates.

- ***Tax relief for the poor.*** Increases in the personal exemption and standard deduction removed nearly 5 million poor people from the tax rolls.
- ***Shift from personal to corporate taxes.*** The direct tax burden on individuals was reduced while the corporate tax burden was increased.

webnote

To view tax returns of U.S. presidents and to review the history of tax features, visit www.taxhistory.org. Click on "Presidential Tax Returns."

Base Broadening. The elimination or reduction of scores of tax preferences increased the tax base almost 25 percent. By broadening the tax base to encompass more economic income, the TRA eliminated the source of many horizontal and vertical inequities. This loophole closing also made the tax system more progressive, since tax preferences disproportionately benefited higher-income families.

Rate Reductions. By broadening the tax base, the TRA made it possible to reduce tax rates. This was of particular concern to those who feared that high marginal tax rates were inhibiting labor supply, investment, and production. The cut in the top marginal tax rate from 50 to 28 percent was intended to stimulate a greater supply of labor and capital and thus promote efficiency.

1990 and 1993 Tax Increases

Although the 1986 reforms increased the progressivity of the tax system, some critics claimed that the reforms were a "giveaway" to the rich. In 1990, Congress responded to this sentiment by raising the top marginal tax rate from 28 to 31 percent. President Clinton pushed Congress to raise taxes even further in 1993. Two more tax brackets were added, with marginal tax rates of 36 and 39.6 percent. In the process, the tax system became a bit more progressive.

The Bush Tax Cuts (2001–2010)

President Bush worried that the higher marginal tax rates created in 1993–95 would slow economic growth. He also felt that low-income households would gain more from faster economic growth than from progressive tax and transfer policies. After his 2000 election, he made tax *cuts* one of his highest priorities.

Reduced Marginal Rates. Initially, President Bush wanted the top marginal tax rate of 39.6 percent reduced to 33 percent. Compromises with Congress achieved a smaller rate reduction, however, phased in over several years. As Figure 33.2 illustrated, the 2001 Tax Relief Act reduced the highest marginal tax rate in three steps, to 35 percent. That act also reduced the marginal tax rate for the *lowest* income class to only 10 percent (from 15 percent). The goal of this rate cut was to increase the disposable income of low-wage workers (equity) while giving them more incentive to work (efficiency). In 2003, Bush convinced Congress to accelerate the rate cuts to further boost production and employment.

New "Loopholes." Aside from encouraging more *work,* President Bush also sought to encourage more *education.* The biggest incentive was a tuition tax deduction of $3,000 per year. This allows students, or their parents, to reduce their taxable income by the amount of tuition payments. In effect, Uncle Sam ends up paying part of the first $3,000 in tuition. In addition, the 2001 legislation allows people to save more money for college in tax-free accounts.

webnote

Check out the lastest tax deductions for college expenses at http://www.irs.gov. Click on "Individuals" then "Students," then "TaxTrails."

As welcome as these "loopholes" are to college students, they raise the same kind of efficiency and equity concerns as other tax preferences. If most of the students who take the tax deduction would have gone to college anyway, the deduction isn't very efficient in promoting education. Furthermore, most of the deductions go to middle-class families who itemize deductions. Hence, the tuition deduction introduces new vertical inequities. Few students have protested this particular loophole, however.

President Bush also sought to use the tax code to promote "family values." To encourage marital stability, the "marriage penalty" of the standard deduction was phased out (allowing a married couple to have twice the standard deduction of a single person). To defray the cost of raising children, the child tax credit was increased in 2001 and again in 2003.

The Tax Relief Act of 2001 also encouraged people to save more by raising the ceiling on deductions for retirement savings accounts (IRA, 401(k) plans). The estate tax was also targeted for phase-out.

The creation of these and other tax preferences raises all the same issues about equity and efficiency. ***The greater the number of loopholes, the wider the distinction between gross incomes and taxable incomes.*** Although President Bush himself used only a handful of deductions in 2006, those provisions reduced his effective tax rate substantially, as the accompanying News illustrates. When the Democrats won a Congressional majority in the 2006 elections, they vowed to revise the tax code in ways that would foster greater equity.

PAYROLL, STATE, AND LOCAL TAXES

The federal income tax is only one of many taxes the average taxpayer must pay. For many families, in fact, the federal income tax is the smallest of many tax bills. Other tax bills come from the Social Security Administration and from state and local governments. These taxes also affect both efficiency and equity.

Sales and Property Taxes

Sales taxes are the major source of revenue for state governments. Many local governments also impose sales taxes, but most cities rely on *property taxes* for the bulk of their tax receipts. Both taxes are **regressive:** They impose higher tax rates on lower incomes.

regressive tax: A tax system in which tax rates fall as incomes rise.

At first glance, a 5 percent sales tax doesn't look very regressive. After all, the same 5 percent tax is imposed on virtually all goods. But we're interested in *people,* not goods and services, so ***we gauge tax burdens in relation to people's incomes.*** A tax is regressive if it imposes a proportionally *larger* burden on *lower* incomes.

This is exactly what a uniform sales tax does. To understand this concept, we have to look not only at how much tax is levied on each dollar of consumption but also at *what percentage of income* is spent on consumer goods.

Low-income families spend everything they've got (and sometimes more) on basic consumption. As a result, most of their income ends up subject to sales tax. By contrast, higher-income families save more. As a result, a smaller proportion of their income is subject to a sales tax. Table 33.3 illustrates this regressive feature of a sales tax. Notice that the low-income family ends up paying a larger fraction of its income (4.7 percent) than does the high income family (3 percent).

TABLE 33.3
The Regressivity of Sales Taxes

A sales tax is imposed on consumer purchases. Although the sales tax itself is uniform (here at 5 percent), the taxes paid represent different proportions of high and low incomes. In this case, the low-income family's *sales tax* bill equals 4.7 percent of its *income.* The high-income family has a sales tax bill equal to only 3 percent of its income.

	High-Income Family	Low-Income Family
Income	$50,000	$15,000
Consumption	$30,000	$14,000
Saving	$20,000	$ 1,000
Sales tax paid (5% of consumption)	$ 1,500	$ 700
Effective tax rate (sales tax ÷ income)	3.0%	4.7%

Property taxes are regressive also and for the same reason. Low-income families spend a higher percentage of their incomes for shelter. A uniform property tax thus ends up taking a larger fraction of their income than it does of the incomes of high-income families.

Tax Incidence. It may sound strange to suggest that low-income families bear the brunt of property taxes. After all, the tax is imposed on the landlords who *own* property, not on people who *rent* apartments and houses. However, here again we have to distinguish between the apparent payee and the individual whose income is actually reduced by the tax. **Tax incidence** refers to the actual burden of a tax—that is, who really ends up paying it.

tax incidence: Distribution of the real burden of a tax.

In general, people who rent apartments pay higher rents as a result of property taxes. In other words, landlords pass along to tenants any property taxes they must pay. Thus, to a large extent ***the burden of property taxes is reflected in higher rents.*** Tenants pay property taxes *indirectly* via these higher rents. The incidence of the property tax thus falls on renters, in the form of higher rents, rather than on the landlords who write checks to the local tax authority.

Payroll Taxes

Payroll taxes also impose effective tax burdens quite different from their nominal appearance. Consider, for example, the Social Security payroll tax, the second-largest source of federal tax revenue (see Figure 4.6). Every worker sees a Social Security (FICA) tax taken out of his or her paycheck. The nominal tax rate on workers is 7.65 percent. But there's a catch: Only wages below a legislated ceiling are taxable. In 2007, the taxable wage ceiling was $97,500. Hence, a worker earning $200,000 paid no more tax than a worker earning $97,500. As a result, the effective tax *rate* (tax paid ÷ total wages) is lower for high-income workers than low- and middle-income workers. That's a *regressive* tax.

There is another problem in gauging the impact of the Social Security payroll tax. Nominally, the Social Security payroll tax consists of two parts: half paid by employees and half by employers. But do employers really pay their half? Or do they end up paying lower wages to compensate for their tax share? If so, employees end up paying *both* halves of the Social Security payroll tax.

Figure 33.3 illustrates how the tax incidence of the payroll tax is distributed. The supply of labor reflects the ability and willingness of people to work for various wage rates. Labor demand reflects the **marginal revenue product (MRP)** of labor; it sets a *limit* to the wage an employer is willing to pay.

marginal revenue product (MRP): The change in total revenue associated with one additional unit of input.

The employer's half of the payroll tax increases the nominal cost of labor. Thus, the S + tax curve lies *above* the labor supply curve. It incorporates the wages that must be paid to workers *plus* the payroll tax that must be paid to the Social Security Administration. This total labor cost is the one that will determine how many workers are hired. Specifically, the intersection of the S + tax curve and the labor demand curve determines the equilibrium level of employment (L_1). The employer will pay the amount w_1 for this much labor. But part of that outlay ($w_1 - w_2$) will go to the public treasury in the form of payroll taxes. Workers will receive only w_2 in wages. This is less than they'd get in the absence of the payroll tax (compare w_0 and w_2). Thus, ***fewer workers are employed, and the net wage is reduced when a payroll tax is imposed.***

What Figure 33.3 reveals is how the true incidence of payroll taxes is distributed. The employer share of the Social Security tax is $w_1 - w_2$. This is the amount sent to the Social

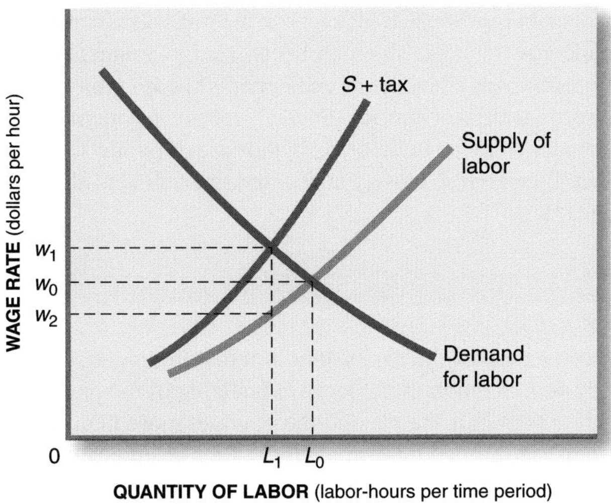

FIGURE 33.3
The Incidence of a Payroll Tax

Some portion of a payroll tax imposed on employers may actually be borne by workers. The tax raises the cost of labor and so imposes a tax-burdened supply curve (S + tax) on employers. The intersection of this tax-burdened supply curve with the labor demand curve determines a new equilibrium of employment (L_1). At that level, employers pay w_1 in wages and taxes, but workers get only w_2 in wages. The wage reduction from w_0 to w_2 is a real burden of the payroll tax, and it is borne by workers.

Security Administration for every hour of labor. Of this amount, the employer incurs higher labor costs ($w_1 - w_0$) and workers lose ($w_0 - w_2$) in the wage rate. Hence, workers end up paying *their* share (7.65 percent) of the Social Security tax *plus* a sizable part ($w_0 - w_2$) of the employer's share ($w_1 - w_2$).

These reflections on tax incidence don't imply that payroll taxes are necessarily bad. They do emphasize, however, that ***the apparent taxpayer isn't necessarily the individual who bears the real burden of a tax.***

TAXES AND INEQUALITY

A Proportional System

The regressivity of the Social Security payroll tax and of many state and local taxes offsets most of the progressivity of the federal income tax. The top 1 percent of income recipients gets 19 percent of total income and pays 37 percent of federal income tax (see Figure 33.4). Hence, the federal income tax is still progressive, despite rampant loopholes. Other federal taxes (Social Security, excise), however, reduce the tax share of the rich to only 18 percent. State and local tax incidence reduces their tax share still further. The final result is that ***the tax system as a whole ends up being nearly proportional.*** High-income families end up paying roughly the same percentage of their income in taxes as do low-income families. The tax system does reduce inequality somewhat, but the redistributive impact is quite small.

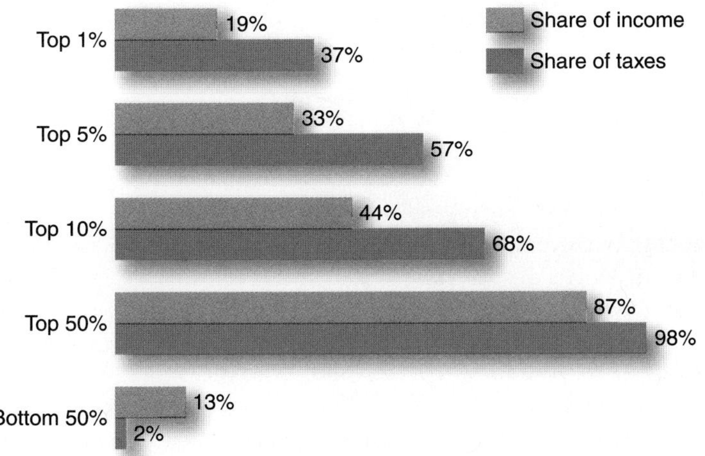

FIGURE 33.4
Income Tax Shares

Despite loopholes, the federal income tax remains highly progressive. The richest 1% of households pay over a third of all federal income taxes, though they receive less than a fifth of all income.

Source: Internal Revenue Service. (2004 data)

The Impact of Transfers

income transfers: Payments to individuals for which no current goods or services are exchanged, for example, Social Security, welfare, and unemployment benefits.

The tax system tells only half the redistribution story. It tells whose income was taken away. Equally important is who gets the income the government collects. The government completes the redistribution process by *transferring* income to consumers. The **income transfers** may be explicit, as in the case of welfare benefits, Social Security payments, and unemployment insurance. Or the transfers may be indirect, as in the case of public schools, farm subsidies, and student loans. We'll look more closely at how income transfers alter the distribution of income in the next chapter.

WHAT IS *FAIR*?

government failure: Government intervention that fails to improve economic outcomes.

To many people, the apparent ineffectiveness of the tax system in redistributing income is a mark of **government failure.** They want a much more decisive reslicing of the pie—one in which the top quintile gets a *lot* less than half the pie and the poor get more than 4 percent (Figure 2.5). But how much redistribution should we attempt? Rich people can rattle off as many good reasons for preserving income inequalities as poor people can recite for eliminating them.

Economists aren't uniquely qualified to overcome self-interest, much less to divine what a fair distribution of income might look like. But economists can assess some of the costs and benefits of altering the distribution of income.

The Costs of Greater Equality

The greatest potential cost of a move toward greater equality is the reduced incentives it might leave in its wake. People *are* motivated by income. In factor markets, higher wages call forth more workers and induce them to work longer hours. In fields where earnings are very high, as in the medical and legal professions, people are willing to spend many years and thousands of dollars acquiring the skills such earnings require. Could we really expect people to make such sacrifices in a market that paid everyone the same wage?

The same problem exists in product markets. The willingness of producers to supply goods and services depends on their expectation of profits. Why should they work hard and take risks to produce goods and services if their efforts won't make them any better off? If incomes were distributed equally, producers might just as well sit back and enjoy the fruits of someone else's labor.

The essential economic problem absolute income equality poses is that it breaks the market link between effort and reward. If all incomes were equal, it would no longer pay to make an above-average effort. If people stopped making such efforts, total output would

"I suppose one could say it favors the rich, but, on the other hand it's a great incentive for everyone to make two hundred grand a year."

Analysis: Inequalities are an incentive for individuals to work and invest more.

Top Tax Rates

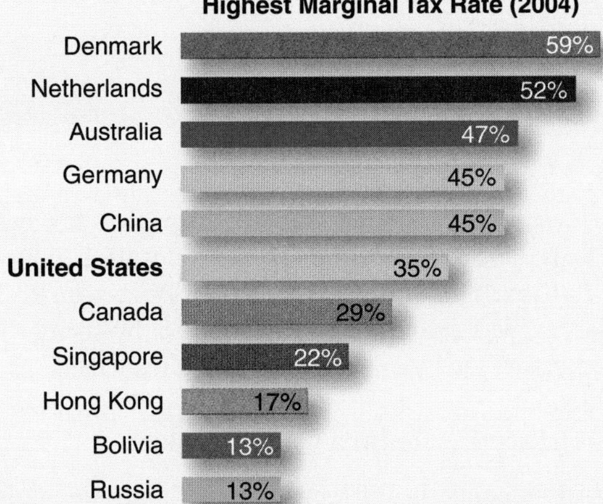

Source: World Bank, *World Development Indicators,* 2006. Used with permission by the International Bank for Reconstruction and Development/The World Bank.

Analysis: The highest marginal tax rate in the United States is lower than in most industrial nations. Some nations offer even lower tax rates, however.

decline, and we'd have less income to share (a smaller pie). Not that all high incomes are attributable to great skill or effort. Such factors as luck, market power, and family connections also influence incomes. It remains true, however, that the promise of higher income encourages work effort. Absolute income equality threatens those conditions.

The argument for preserving income inequalities is thus anchored in a concern for productivity. From this perspective, income inequalities are the driving force behind much of our production. By preserving inequalities, we not only enrich the fortunate few, but also provide incentives to take risks, invest more, and work harder (see cartoon). In so doing, we enlarge the economic pie, including the slices available to lower-income groups. Thus, everyone is potentially better off, even if only a few end up rich. This is the rationale that keeps the top marginal tax rate in the United States below that in most other countries (see World View).

The Benefits of Greater Equality

Although the potential benefits of inequality are impressive, ***there's a trade-off between efficiency and equality.*** Moreover, many people are convinced that the terms of the trade-off are exaggerated and the benefits of greater equality are ignored. These rebuttals take the form of economic and noneconomic arguments.

The economic arguments for greater equality also focus on incentives. The first argument is that the present degree of inequality is more than necessary to maintain work incentives. Upper-class incomes needn't be 14 times as large as those of the lowest-income classes; perhaps 4 times as large would do as well.

The second argument is that low-income earners might actually work harder if incomes were distributed more fairly. As matters now stand, the low-income worker sees little chance of making it big. Extremely low income can also inhibit workers' ability to work by subjecting them to poor health, malnutrition, or inadequate educational opportunities. Accordingly, some redistribution of income to the poor might improve the productivity of low-income workers and compensate for reduced productivity among the rich.

Finally, we noted that the maze of loopholes that preserves inequality also distorts economic incentives. Labor and investment decisions are influenced by tax considerations, not just economic benefits and costs. If greater equality were achieved via tax simplification, a more efficient allocation of resources might result.

THE ECONOMY TOMORROW

A FLAT TAX?

Widespread dissatisfaction with the present tax system has spawned numerous reform proposals. One of the most debated proposals is to replace the current federal income tax with a **flat tax.** First proposed by Nobel Prize winner Milton Friedman in the early 1960s, the flat tax was championed in Congress by former majority leader (and former economics professor) Dick Armey. The concept resurfaced as a political issue in the 2004 presidential election.

flat tax: A single-rate tax system.

The key features of a flat tax include

- Replacing the current system of multiple tax brackets and rates with a single (flat) tax rate that would apply to all taxable income.
- Eliminating all deductions, credits, and most exemptions.

Simplicity. A major attraction of the flat tax is its simplicity. The current 1,600-page tax code that details all the provisions of the present system would be scrapped. The 437 different IRS tax forms now in use would be replaced by a single, postcard-sized form.

Fairness. Flat-tax advocates also emphasize its fairness. They point to the rampant vertical and horizontal inequities created by the current tangle of tax loopholes. By scrapping all those deductions, the flat tax would treat everyone equally.

Some progressivity could also be preserved with a flat tax. In the version proposed by Dick Armey, the flat tax rate would be 17 percent, but one personal exemption would be maintained. Every adult would get a personal exemption of $13,100 and each child an exemption of $5,300. Accordingly, a family of four would have personal exemptions of $36,800. Hence, a family earning less than that amount would pay no income tax. *Effective* tax rates would increase along with rising incomes above that threshold.

Efficiency. Proponents of a flat tax claim it enhances efficiency as well as equity. Taxpayers now spend over a billion hours a year preparing tax returns. Legions of lobbyists, accountants, and lawyers devote their energy to tax analysis and avoidance. With a simplified flat tax, all those labor resources could be put to more productive use.

A flat tax would also change the mix of output. Consumption and investment decisions would be made on the basis of economic considerations, not tax consequences.

The Critique. As alluring as a flat tax appears, it has aroused substantial opposition. As proposed by Dick Armey, the flat tax would not apply to all income. Income on savings and investments (such as interest and dividends, capital gains) wouldn't be taxed. The purpose of that exemption would be to encourage greater saving, investment, and economic growth. At the same time, however, such a broad exemption creates a whole new set of horizontal and vertical inequities. Someone receiving $1 million in interest and dividends could escape all income taxes, while a family earning $50,000 would have to pay.

Critics also object to the wholesale elimination of all deductions and credits. Many of those loopholes are expressly designed to encourage desired economic activity. The Bush tax cuts were explicitly designed to encourage education, family stability, and savings. By discarding all tax preferences, the flat tax significantly reduces the government's ability to alter the mix of output. Even if the current maze of loopholes exceeds the threshold of government failure, complete reliance on the market mechanism isn't necessarily appropriate.

A careful pruning of the tax code rather than a complete uprooting might yield better results.

Finally, critics point out that the transition to a flat tax would entail a wholesale reshuffling of wealth and income. Home values would fall precipitously if the tax preference for homeownership were eliminated. That would hit the middle class particularly hard. State and local governments would have greater difficulty raising their own revenues if the federal deduction for state and local taxes were eliminated. Millionaires might benefit by sharply reduced tax burdens. Confronted with such consequences, many people begin to have second thoughts about the desirability of adopting a flat tax in the economy tomorrow. Taxpayers seem to like the *principle* of a flat tax more than its actual provisions.

SUMMARY

- The distribution of income is a vital economic issue because incomes largely determine access to the goods and services we produce. Wealth distribution is important for the same reason. LO3
- The size distribution of income tells us how incomes are divided up among individuals. The Lorenz curve is a graphic summary of the cumulative size distribution of income. The Gini coefficient is a mathematical summary. LO3
- Personal incomes are distributed quite unevenly in the United States. At present, the highest quintile (the top 20 percent) gets nearly half of all cash income, and the bottom quintile gets less than 4 percent. LO3
- The trade-off between equity and efficiency is rooted in supply incentives. The tax elasticity of supply measures how the quantity of resources (labor and capital) declines when tax rates rise. LO3
- The progressivity of the federal income tax is weakened by various loopholes (exemptions, deductions, and credits), which create a distinction between nominal and effective tax rates and cause vertical and horizontal inequities. LO2
- The Tax Reform Act of 1986 broadened the tax base (by eliminating many deductions), reduced tax rates, and shifted more of the tax burden onto corporations. The reforms made federal taxes a bit more progressive. LO2
- Tax rates and brackets were increased in 1990 and 1993, reversing earlier trends. LO1
- The 2001–4 Bush tax cuts reduced marginal tax rates and created new tax preferences for education, marriage, and saving. LO1
- Mildly progressive federal income taxes are offset by regressive payroll, state, and local taxes. Overall, the tax system redistributes little income; most redistribution occurs through transfer payments. LO2
- Tax incidence refers to the real burden of a tax. In many cases, reductions in wages, increases in rent, or other real income changes represent the true burden of a tax. LO2
- There is a trade-off between efficiency and equality. If all incomes are equal, there's no economic reward for superior productivity. On the other hand, a more equal distribution of incomes might increase the productivity of lower income groups and serve important noneconomic goals as well. LO3
- A flat tax is a nominally proportional tax system. A personal exemption and the exclusion of capital income can render a flat tax progressive or regressive, however. A flat tax reduces the government's role in resource allocation (the WHAT and HOW questions). LO1

Key Terms

personal income (PI)
in-kind income
wealth
size distribution of income
income share
Lorenz curve
Gini coefficient
market failure
progressive tax
marginal tax rate
tax elasticity of supply
vertical equity
horizontal equity
nominal tax rate
effective tax rate
tax base
regressive tax
tax incidence
marginal revenue product (MRP)
income transfers
government failure
flat tax

Questions for Discussion

1. What goods or services do you and your family receive without directly paying for them? How do these goods affect the distribution of economic welfare? LO2
2. Why are incomes distributed so unevenly? Identify and explain three major causes of inequality. LO3
3. Do inequalities stimulate productivity? In what ways? Provide two specific examples. LO3
4. What loopholes reduced the president's tax bill (see News, page 666)? What's the purpose of those loopholes? How else might those purposes be achieved? LO1
5. How might a flat tax affect efficiency? Fairness? LO3
6. If a new tax system encouraged more output but also created greater inequality, would it be desirable? LO3
7. If the tax elasticity of supply were zero, how high could the tax rate go before people reduced their work effort? How do families vary the quantity of labor supplied when tax rates change? LO3
8. Is a tax deduction for tuition likely to increase college enrollments? How will it affect horizontal and vertical equities? LO3
9. If tax breaks for the rich really stimulated investment and growth, wouldn't everyone benefit from them? Why would anyone oppose them? LO3
10. What share of taxes *should* the rich pay (see Figure 33.4)? LO3

problems The Student Problem Set at the back of this book contains numerical and graphing problems for this chapter.

web activities to accompany this chapter can be found on the Online Learning Center: **http://www.mhhe.com/economics/schiller11e**

34 Transfer Payments: Welfare and Social Security

LEARNING OBJECTIVES

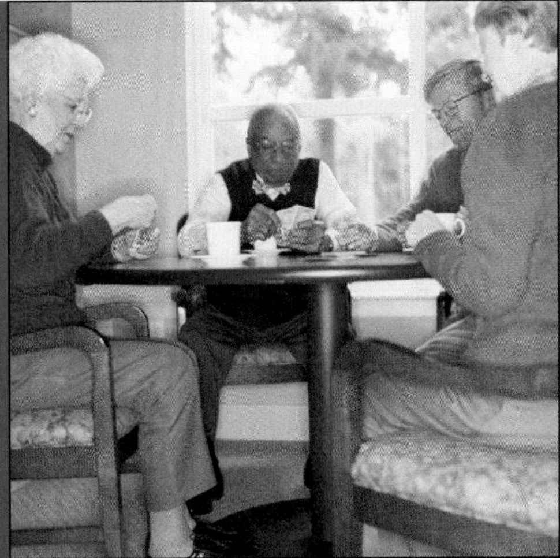

After reading this chapter, you should know:

LO1. The major income transfer programs.

LO2. How transfer programs affect labor supply and total output.

LO3. The trade-offs between benefit levels, marginal tax rates, and costs.

Americans are compassionate. Public opinion polls reveal that an overwhelming majority of the public wants to "help the needy." Most Americans say they're even willing to pay more taxes to help fund aid to the poor. But their compassion is tempered by caution: Taxpayers don't want to be ripped off. They want to be sure their money is helping the "truly needy," not being squandered by deadbeats, drug addicts, shirkers, and "welfare queens."

The conflict between compassion and resentment affects not only welfare programs for the poor but also Social Security for the aged, unemployment insurance benefits for the jobless, and even disability benefits for injured workers. In every one of these programs, people are getting money without working. **Transfer payments** are payments to individuals for which no current goods or services are exchanged. In effect, they're a "free ride."

The risk of providing a free ride is that some of the people who take it could have gotten by without it. As the humorist Dave Barry observed, if the government offers $1 million to people with six toes, a lot of people will try to grow a sixth toe or claim they have one. Income transfers create similar incentives: They encourage people to change their behavior in order to get a free ride.

This chapter focuses on how income transfer programs change not only the distribution of income, but also work incentives and behavior. Central questions include

- **How much income do income transfer programs redistribute?**
- **How are transfer benefits computed?**
- **How do transfer payments alter market behavior?**

MAJOR TRANSFER PROGRAMS

transfer payments: Payments to individuals for which no current goods or services are exchanged, like Social Security, welfare, and unemployment benefits.

Roughly 50 cents out of every federal tax dollar now is devoted to income transfers (see Figure 4.4). That amounts to roughly *$1.5 trillion* a year in transfer payments. Who gets all this money?

The easy answer to this question is that almost every household gets some of the transfer money. There are over 100 federal income transfer programs. Students get tuition grants and subsidized loans. Farmers get crop assistance. Homeowners get disaster relief when their homes are destroyed. Veterans get benefit checks and subsidized health care. People over age 65 get Social Security benefits and subsidized health care. And poor people get welfare checks, food stamps, and subsidized housing.

Although income transfers are widely distributed, not everyone shares equally in the tax-paid bounty. As Figure 34.1 shows, just three of the myriad transfer programs account for 85 percent of total outlays. Social Security, the largest program, alone accounts for 41 percent of the transfer budget. Medicare and Medicaid benefits absorb another 44 percent. By contrast, welfare checks account for only 4 percent of all income transfers.

Cash vs. In-Kind Benefits

Income transfer doesn't always entail cash payments. The Medicare program, for example, is a health insurance subsidy program that pays hospital and doctor bills for people over age 65. The 48 million people who receive Medicare benefits don't get checks from Uncle Sam; instead, Uncle Sam pays the bills for the medical *services* they receive. The same is true for the 58 million people who get Medicaid. Poor people get free health care from the Medicaid program; their benefits are paid *in-kind,* not in cash. Such programs provide **in-kind transfers,** that is, direct transfers of goods and services rather than cash. Food stamps, rent subsidies, legal aid, and subsidized school lunches are all in-kind transfer programs. By contrast, Social Security is a **cash transfer** because it mails benefit checks, not services, to recipients.

in-kind transfers: Direct transfers of goods and services rather than cash; examples include food stamps, Medicaid benefits, and housing subsidies.

cash transfers: Income transfers that entail direct cash payments to recipients, for example, Social Security, welfare, and unemployment benefits.

The provision of in-kind benefits rather than cash is intended to promote specific objectives. Few taxpayers object to feeding the hungry. But they bristle at the thought that welfare recipients might spend the income they receive on something potentially harmful like liquor or drugs or on nonessentials like cars or fancy clothes. To minimize that risk, taxpayers offer electronic food stamps, not cash, thereby limiting the recipient's consumption choices. This helps reassure taxpayers that their assistance is being well spent.

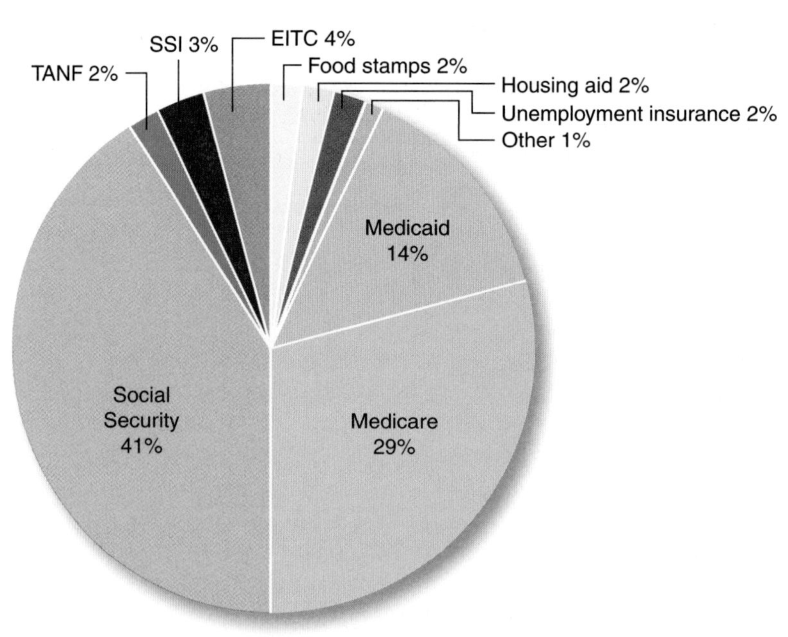

FIGURE 34.1
Income Transfer Program

There are nearly 100 different federal income transfer programs. However, just three programs—Social Security, Medicare, and Medicaid—account for nearly 80 percent of all transfers. Cash welfare benefits (TANF, SSI) absorb only 5 percent of all income transfers.

Source: U.S. Office of Management and Budget (FY 2008 data).

Similar considerations shape the Medicare program. Taxpayers could "cash out" Medicare by simply mailing older people the $450 billion now spent on the program. But then some healthy older Americans would get cash they didn't need. Some sick people might not get as much money as *they* needed. Or they might choose to spend their new-found income on something other than health care. The end result would be a smaller health care gain than in-kind transfers facilitate.

The **target efficiency** of a transfer program refers to how well income transfers attain their intended purpose. In-kind medical transfers are more target-efficient than cash transfers because recipients would use equivalent cash transfers for other purposes. Food stamps are more target-efficient than cash in reducing hunger for the same reason. If given cash rather than food stamps, recipients would spend less than 70 cents of each dollar on food.

target efficiency: The percentage of income transfers that go to the intended recipients and purposes.

Social Insurance vs. Welfare

You may have noted by now that not all income transfers go to the poor. A lot of student loans go to middle-class college students. And disaster relief helps rebuild both mansions and trailer parks. Such income transfers are triggered by specific *events,* not the recipient's income. By contrast, welfare checks are *means-tested:* They go only to families with little income and fewer assets.

Welfare programs always entail some kind of income eligibility test. To receive welfare payments, a family must prove that it has too little income to fend for itself. Medicaid is an in-kind **welfare program** because only poor people are eligible for the health care benefits of that program. To get food stamps, another in-kind welfare program, a family must also pass an income test.

welfare programs: Means-tested income transfer programs, for example, welfare and food stamps.

Social Security and Medicare aren't *welfare* programs because recipients don't have to be poor. To get Social Security or Medicare benefits you just have to be old enough. The *event* of reaching age 62 makes people eligible for Social Security retirement benefits. At age 65 everyone—whether rich or poor—gets Medicare benefits. These event-conditioned benefits are the hallmark of **social insurance programs:** They insure people against the costs of old age, illness, disability, unemployment, and other specific problems. As Figure 34.2 illustrates, ***most income transfers are for social insurance programs, not welfare.***

social insurance programs: Event-conditioned income transfers intended to reduce the costs of specific problems, for example, Social Security and unemployment insurance.

Transfer Goals

If the market sliced up the economic pie in a manner that society deemed fair, there would be no need for all these government-provided income transfers. Hence, the mere existence of such programs implies a **market failure**—an unfair market-generated distribution of income. When the market alone slices up the pie, some people get too much and others get too little. To redress this inequity, we ask the government to play Robin Hood—taking income from the rich and giving it to the poor. Thus, ***the basic goal of income transfer programs is to reduce income inequalities.***

market failure: An imperfection in the market mechanism that prevents optimal outcomes.

FIGURE 34.2
Social Insurance vs. Welfare

Social insurance programs provide *event*-based transfers—for example, upon reaching age 65 or becoming unemployed or disabled. Welfare programs offer benefits only to those in need; they're *means-tested.* Social insurance transfers greatly outnumber welfare transfers.

Source: U.S. Office of Management and Budget.

FOR WHOM. Transfer programs do in fact significantly change the distribution of income. Social Security alone redistributes $600 billion a year from workers to retirees. Those Social Security checks account for 40 percent of all the income older people receive. Without those checks, nearly half of the elderly population would be poor. More generally, income transfers reduce U.S. inequality by at least 20 percent (as measured by the Gini coefficient).

WHAT to Produce. In the process of redistributing incomes, income transfers also change the mix of output. The goal of food stamps, for example, is to increase food consumption by the poor. The strategy isn't to take food off rich people's plates, however. Instead, it is expected that the additional food purchases of the poor will encourage more food *production,* thereby changing the mix of output. Housing subsidies and free health care have similar effects on the mix of output. So do student loans: If more students end up going to college, the mix of output changes in favor of educational services.

Unintended Consequences

Although income transfers change the distribution of income and mix of output in desired ways, they are not costless interventions. The Law of Unintended Consequences rears its ugly head here: ***Income transfers often change market behavior and outcomes in unintended (and undesired) ways.***

Reduced Output. First, the provision of transfer payments may dull work incentives. If you can get paid for *not* working (via a transfer payment), why would you go to work? Why endure 40 hours of toil for a paycheck when you can stay home and collect a welfare check, an unemployment check, or Social Security? If the income transfers are large enough, I'll stay home too. When people reduce their **labor supply** in response to income transfers, total output will shrink. Figure 34.3 shows that ***attempts to redistribute income may reduce total income.*** In other words, the pie shrinks when we try to reslice it.

labor supply: The willingness and ability to work specific amounts of time at alternative wage rates in a given time period, *ceteris paribus.*

Undesirable Behavior. A reduction in labor supply isn't the only unintended consequence of income transfer programs. People may also change their *nonwork* behavior. Welfare benefits give a (small) incentive to women to have more children and to teen moms to establish their own households. Medicare and Medicaid encourage people to overuse health care services and neglect the associated costs. Unemployment benefits encourage workers to stay jobless longer. And, as Dave Berry noted at the beginning of the chapter, disability payments encourage people to grow a sixth toe. Although the actual response to these incentives is hotly debated, the existence of the undesired incentives is unambiguous.

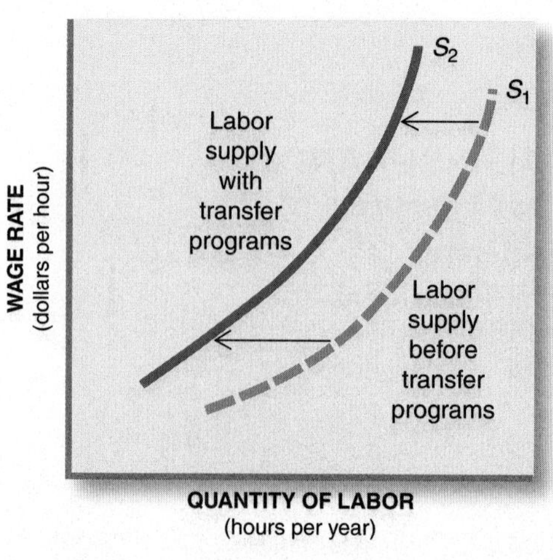

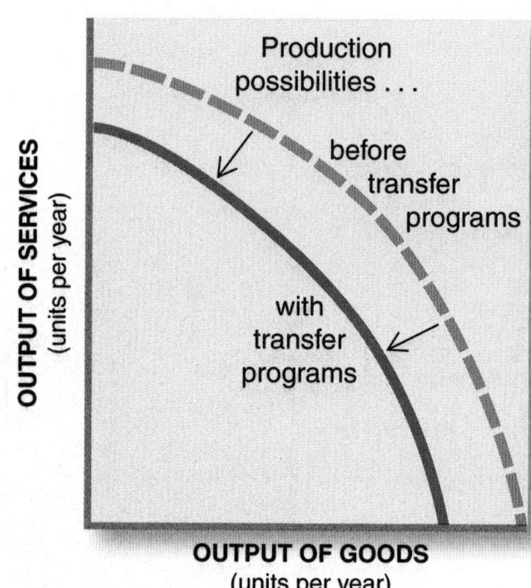

FIGURE 34.3
Reduced Labor Supply and Output

Transfer payments may induce people to supply less labor at any market wage rate. If this happens, the supply of labor shifts to the left and the economy's production possibilities shrink. We end up with less total output.

WELFARE PROGRAMS

To understand how income transfer programs change market behavior and outcomes, let's look closer at how welfare programs operate. The largest federal cash welfare program is called Temporary Aid to Needy Families (TANF). The TANF program was created by congressional welfare reforms in 1996 and replaced an earlier program (AFDC) that had operated since 1935. The new program offers states much discretion to decide who gets welfare, under what conditions, and for how long. States can also supplement their federal TANF block grants with their own tax revenues and even establish supplementary programs. However, all such programs confront a central dilemma: how to help the poor without encouraging undesired market behavior.

webnote

Compare federal welfare programs before and after the major 1996 reform at http://aspe.os.dhhs.gov/hsp/isp/reform.htm

Benefit Determination

The first task of the TANF program is to identify potential recipients. In principle, this task is easy: Find out who is poor. To do this, the federal government has established a poverty line that specifies how much cash income families of different sizes need just to buy basic necessities. In 2006, the federal government estimated that a family of four was poor if its income was less than $20,600. Table 34.1 shows how this poverty threshold varies by family size.

According to Table 34.1, a four-person family with $18,000 of income in 2006 would have been considered poor. In their case, the **poverty gap**—the shortfall between actual income and the poverty threshold—was $2,600. The Jones family needed at least that much additional income to purchase what the government deems a "minimally adequate" standard of living.

poverty gap: The shortfall between actual income and the poverty threshold.

So how much welfare should the government give this family? Should it give $2,600 to this family, thereby closing its poverty gap? As simple as that proposition sounds, it creates some unintended problems.

The Work Incentive Problem

Suppose we guaranteed all families enough income to reach their respective poverty line. Any family earning less than the poverty line would receive a welfare check in the amount of their poverty gap. In that case, poor people would get enough welfare to escape poverty. No one would be poor.

There are two potential problems with such a welfare policy. First, people who *weren't* poor would have a strong incentive to become poor. Why try to support a family of four with a paycheck of $25,000 when you can quit and get $20,600 in welfare checks? Recall from Chapter 30 that the decision to work is largely a response to both the financial and psychological rewards associated with employment. People in dull, dirty, low-paying jobs get little of either. By quitting their jobs, declaring themselves poor, and accepting a guaranteed income transfer, they would gain much more leisure at little financial or psychological cost. In the process, total output would shrink (Figure 34.3).

webnote

Current statistics on poverty are available from the U.S. Census Bureau at www.census.gov/hhes/www/poverty.html

The second potential problem affects the work behavior of people who were poor to begin with. We assumed that the Jones family was earning $18,000 before they got a welfare check. The question now is whether the welfare check will change their work behavior.

Number of Family Members	Family Income
1	$10,300
2	13,200
3	16,000
4	20,600
5	24,400
6	27,600
7	31,200
8	34,700

Source: U.S. Department of Commerce, Bureau of the Census (rounded to 100s).

TABLE 34.1
Poverty Lines

The official definition of poverty relates current income to the minimal needs of a family. Poverty thresholds vary with family size. In 2006, a family of four was considered poor if it had less than $20,600 of income.

Suppose that family gets an opportunity to earn an extra $1,000 a year by working overtime. Should they seize that opportunity? Consider the effect of the higher *wages* on the family's *income*. Before working overtime, the Jones family earned

INCOME WITHOUT OVERTIME WAGES	
Wages	$18,000
Welfare benefits	2,600
Total income	$20,600

If they now work overtime, their income is

INCOME WITH OVERTIME WAGES	
Wages	$19,000
Welfare benefits	1,600
Total income	$20,600

Something is wrong here: Although *wages* have gone up, the family's *income* hasn't.

Implicit Marginal Tax Rates. The failure of income to rise with wages is the by-product of how welfare benefits were computed. ***If welfare benefits are set equal to the poverty gap, every additional dollar of wages reduces welfare benefits by the same amount.*** In effect, the Jones family confronts a **marginal tax rate** of 100 percent: Every dollar of wages results in a lost dollar of benefits. Uncle Sam isn't literally raising the family's taxes by a dollar. By reducing benefits dollar for dollar, however, the end result is the same.

marginal tax rate: The tax rate imposed on the last (marginal) dollar of income.

With a 100 percent marginal tax rate, a family can't improve its income by working more. In fact, this family might as well work *less*. As wages decline, welfare benefits increase by the same amount. Thus, we end up with a conflict between compassion and work incentives. By guaranteeing a poverty-level income, we destroy the economic incentive of low-income workers to support themselves. This creates a **moral hazard** for welfare recipients; that is, we encourage undesirable behavior. The moral hazard here is the temptation not to support oneself by working—choosing welfare checks instead.

moral hazard: An incentive to engage in undesirable behavior.

Less Compassion

To reduce this moral hazard, Congress and the states changed the way benefits are computed. First, they set a much lower ceiling on welfare benefits. States don't offer to close the poverty gap; instead, they set a maximum benefit far below the poverty line. Hence, we have the amended benefit formula:

$$\text{Welfare benefit} = \text{maximum benefit} - \text{wages}$$

In 2006, the typical state set a maximum benefit of about $8,000 for a family of four. Hence, a family without any other income couldn't get enough money from welfare to stay out of poverty. As a result, ***a family totally dependent on welfare is unquestionably poor.*** Although the lower benefit ceiling is less compassionate, it reduces the risk of climbing on the welfare wagon for a free ride.

More Incentives

To encourage welfare recipients to lift their own incomes above the poverty line, welfare departments made another change in the benefit formula. As we saw above, ***the rate at which benefits are reduced as wages increase is the marginal tax rate.*** The dollar-for-dollar benefit cuts illustrated above destroyed the financial incentive to work. To give recipients more incentive to work, the marginal tax rate was cut from 100 to 67 percent. So we now have a new benefit formula:

$$\text{Welfare benefit} = \text{maximum benefit} - \frac{2}{3}[\text{wages}]$$

Figure 34.4 illustrates how a lower marginal tax rate alters the relationship of total income to wages. The black line in the figure shows the total wages Mrs. Jones could earn at $8 per hour. She could earn nothing by not working or as much as $16,000 per year by working full time (point *F* in the figure).

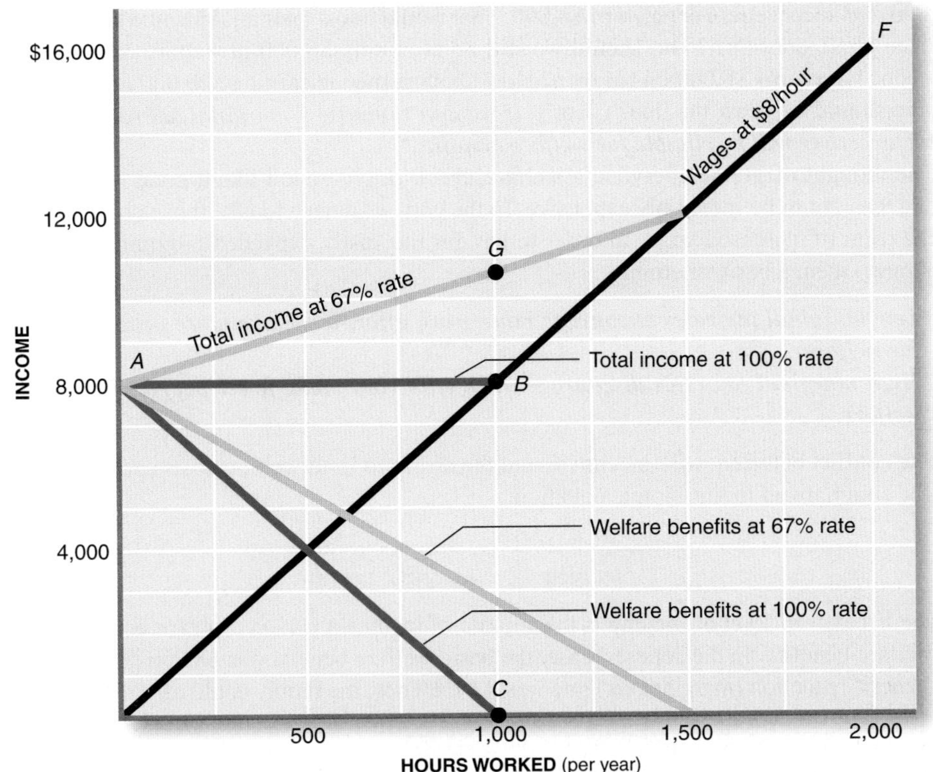

FIGURE 34.4
Work (Dis)Incentives

If welfare benefits are reduced dollar for dollar as wages increase, the implied marginal tax rate is 100 percent. In that case, total income remains at the benefit limit of $8,000 (point *A*) as work effort increases from 0 to 1,000 hours (point *B*). There is no incentive to work in this range.

When the marginal tax rate is reduced to 67 percent, total income starts increasing as soon as the welfare recipient starts working. At 1,000 hours of work, total income is $10,226 (point *G*).

The blue lines in the figure show what happens to her welfare benefits and total income when a 100 percent marginal tax rate is imposed. At point *A* she gets $8,000 in welfare benefits and total income because she's not working at all.

Now consider what happens to the family's total income if Mrs. Jones goes to work. If she works 1,000 hours per year (essentially half-time), she could earn $8,000 (point *B*). But what would happen to her income? If the welfare department cuts her benefit by $1 for every dollar she earns, her benefit check slides down the blue "welfare benefits" line to point *C*, where she gets nothing from welfare. By working 1,000 hours per year, all Mrs. Jones has done is replace her welfare check with a paycheck. That might make taxpayers smile, but Mrs. Jones will wonder why she bothered to go to work. With a 100 percent tax rate, her total income doesn't rise above $8,000 until she works more than 1,000 hours.

The green lines in Figure 34.4 show how work incentives improve with a lower marginal tax rate. Now welfare benefits are reduced by only 67 cents for every $1 of wages earned. As a result, total income starts rising as soon as Mrs. Jones goes to work. If she works 1,000 hours, her total income will include

Wages	$ 8,000	
Welfare benefit	2,667	= $8,000 − 2/3 ($8,000)
Total income	$10,667	

Point *G* on the graph illustrates this outcome.

Incentives vs. Costs

It may be comforting to know that the Jones family can now increase its income from $8,000 when not working to $10,667 by working 1,000 hours per year. But they still face a higher marginal tax rate (67 percent) than rich people (the top marginal tax rate on federal income taxes is 35 percent). Why not lower their marginal tax rate even further, thus increasing both their work incentives and their total income?

Unfortunately, a reduction in the marginal tax rate would also increase welfare costs. Suppose we eliminated the marginal tax rate altogether. Then, the Jones family could earn

$8,000 *and* keep welfare benefits of $8,000. That would boost their total income to $16,000. Sounds great, doesn't it? But should we still be providing $8,000 in welfare payments to someone who earns $8,000 on her own? How about someone earning $20,000 or $30,000? Where should we draw the line? Clearly, ***if we don't impose a marginal tax rate at some point, everyone will be eligible for welfare benefits.***

The thought of giving everyone a welfare check might sound like a great idea, but it would turn out to be incredibly expensive. In the end, we'd have to take those checks back, in the form of increased taxes, in order to pay for the vastly expanded program. We must recognize, then, a basic dilemma:

- ***Low marginal tax rates encourage more work effort but make more people eligible for welfare.***
- ***High marginal tax rates discourage work effort but make fewer people eligible for welfare.***

The conflict between work incentives and the desire to limit welfare costs and eligibility can be summarized in this simple equation:

$$\text{Breakeven level of income} = \frac{\text{basic benefits}}{\text{marginal tax rate}}$$

breakeven level of income: The income level at which welfare eligibility ceases.

The **breakeven level of income** is the amount of income a person can earn before losing all welfare benefits. In the Joneses' case, the basic welfare benefit was $8,000 per year and the benefit-reduction (marginal tax) rate was 0.67. Hence, the family could earn as much as

$$\text{Breakeven level of income} = \frac{\$8{,}000}{0.67} \text{ per year}$$
$$= \$12{,}000$$

before losing all welfare benefits. Thus, ***low marginal tax rates encourage work but make it hard to get completely off welfare.***

If the marginal tax rate were 100 percent, as under the old welfare system, the breakeven point would be $8,000 divided by 1.00. In that case, people who earned $8,000 on their own would get no assistance from welfare. Fewer people would be eligible for welfare, but those who drew benefits would have no incentive to work. If the marginal tax rate were lowered to 0, the breakeven point would rise to infinity ($8,000 divided by 0)—and we'd all be on welfare.

As this arithmetic shows, ***there's a basic conflict between work incentives (low marginal tax rates) and welfare containment (smaller welfare rolls and outlays).*** We can achieve a lower breakeven level of income (less welfare eligibility) only by sacrificing low marginal tax rates or higher income floors (basic benefits). Hence, welfare costs can be minimized only if we sacrifice income provision or work incentives.

tax elasticity of labor supply: The percentage change in quantity of labor supplied divided by the percentage change in tax rates.

Tax Elasticity of Labor Supply. The terms of the trade-off between more welfare and less work depend on how responsive people are to marginal tax rates. As we first noted in Chapter 33, the **tax elasticity of labor supply** measures the response to changes in tax rates; that is,

$$\text{Tax elasticity of labor supply} = \frac{\text{\% change in quantity of labor supplied}}{\text{\% change in tax rate}}$$

If the tax elasticity of labor supply were zero, it wouldn't matter how high the marginal tax rate was: People would work for nothing (100 percent tax rate). In reality, the tax elasticity of labor supply among low-wage workers is more in the range of 0.2 to 0.3, so marginal tax rates *do* affect work effort.

Time Limits. The 1996 welfare reforms sidestepped this dilemma by setting time limits on welfare eligibility. TANF recipients *must* engage in some sort of employment-related activity (e.g., a job, job search, or training) within 2 years of first receiving benefits. There is also a 5-year lifetime limit on welfare eligibility. States, however, can still use their own (non-federal) funds to extend welfare benefits beyond those time limits.

SOCIAL SECURITY

Like welfare programs, the Social Security program was developed to redistribute incomes. In the case of Social Security, however, *age,* not low income, is the primary determinant of eligibility. The program seeks to provide a financial prop under retirement incomes. Here again, however, we have to confront policy conflicts between the goals of compassion, work incentives, and program costs.

Program Features

The Social Security program is actually a mix of three separate income transfers. The main program is for retired workers, the second for survivors of deceased workers, and the third for disabled workers. Created in 1935, this combined Old Age Survivors and Disability Insurance (OASDI) program is now so large that it accounts for over 40 percent of all federal income transfers. The monthly benefit checks distributed to 50 million recipients are financed with a payroll tax on workers and employees.

Retirement Age. As Figure 34.5 confirms, the retirement program is by far the largest component of OASDI. Individuals become eligible for Social Security retirement benefits when they reach certain ages. People can choose either "early" retirement (at age 62 to 64) or "normal" retirement (at age 65 to 67). Those who choose early retirement receive a smaller monthly benefit because they're expected to live longer in retirement.

For people born after 1940, the age threshold for "normal" retirement is increasing each year. By the year 2022, the age threshold for normal retirement will be age 67. This delay in benefit eligibility is intended to keep aging Baby Boomers working longer, thereby curtailing a surge in benefit outlays.

Progressive Benefits. Retirement benefits are based on an individual's wages. In 2006, the median Social Security retirement benefit for an individual was about $14,000. But high-wage workers could get nearly $25,000 and low-wage workers as little as $7,000 a year.

Although high-wage workers receive larger benefit checks than low-wage workers, the *ratio* of benefits to prior wages isn't constant. Instead, the ***Social Security benefits formula is progressive*** because the ratio of benefits to prior wages declines as wages increase.

Who Pays Social Security Taxes

Payroll taxes

7.65% paid by workers

7.65% paid by employers

Who Gets Social Security Checks

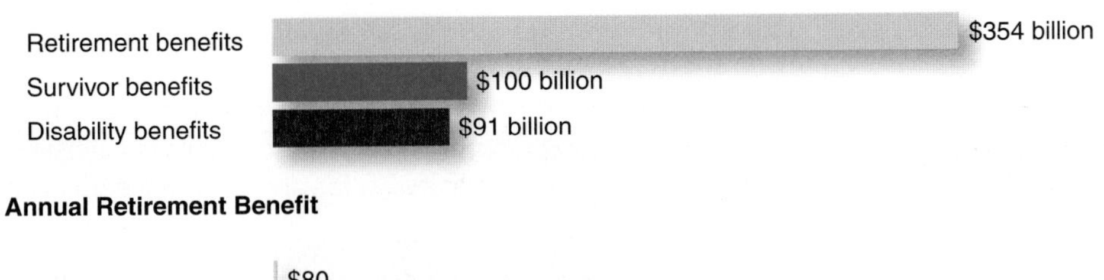

FIGURE 34.5
Social Security Finances

The Social Security retirement, survivor, and disability programs are financed with payroll taxes. Most benefits go to retired workers, who get a median transfer of $14,000 per year.

Source: U.S. Social Security Administration (2006 data).

TABLE 34.2
Progressive Benefits

Social Security redistributes income progressively by replacing a larger share of low wages than high wages. Shown here are the wage-replacement rates for 2006 (adjusted annually for inflation).

Wage-Replacement Rate (%)	For Average Monthly Wages of
90%	$1–656
32	656–3,955
15	over $3,955

Source: U.S. Social Security Administration.

wage-replacement rate: The percentage of base wages paid out in benefits.

Social Security replaces 90 percent of the first $656 of prior average monthly earnings but only 15 percent of monthly wages above $3,955 (see Table 34.2). The declining **wage-replacement rate** ensures that low-wage workers receive *proportionately* greater benefits. Thus, retirement benefits end up more equally distributed than wages.

The Earnings Test

In reality, a worker doesn't have to *retire* in order to receive Social Security benefits. But the government imposes an *earnings test* to determine how much retirement benefits an older person can collect while still working. The earnings test is very similar to the formula used to compute welfare benefits. The formula establishes a maximum benefit amount and a marginal tax rate that reduces benefits as wages increase:

$$\frac{\text{Benefit}}{\text{amount}} = \frac{\text{maximum}}{\text{award}} - 0.5\,(\text{wages in excess of ceiling})$$

Consider the case of Leonard, a 62-year-old worker contemplating retirement. Suppose Leonard's wage history entitles him to a maximum award of $12,000 per year. But he wants to keep working to supplement Social Security benefits with wages. What happens to his benefits if he continues to work?

In 2006, the wage "ceiling" for workers 62 to 64 was $12,480. Hence, the benefit formula was

$$\frac{\text{Benefit}}{\text{amount}} = \$12{,}000 - 0.5\,(\text{wage} > \$12{,}480)$$

As a result, a person could earn as much as $12,480 and still get maximum retirement benefits ($12,000), putting the total income at $24,480.

The Work Disincentive

Suppose Leonard wants a bit more income than that. Can he increase his total income by working more? Yes, but not by much. He faces the same kind of work incentives the Jones family had when on welfare. The formula says benefits will drop by 50 cents for every $1 of wages earned over $12,480. Hence, the implicit marginal tax rate is 50 percent. Uncle Sam is effectively getting half of any wages Leonard earns in excess of $12,480 per year. Figure 34.6 illustrates this sorry state of affairs. Notice in particular how *income* rises half as fast as *wages* after point *C*.

In reality, the marginal tax rate on Leonard's wages is even higher. If he works, Leonard will have to pay the Social Security payroll tax (7.65 percent) as well as federal, state, and local income taxes (say, another 15 percent). Hence, the full burden of taxes and benefit losses includes

ITEM	MARGINAL TAX RATE
Social security benefitloss	50.00%
Payroll tax	7.65
Income taxes	15.00
Total	72.65%

As a consequence, Leonard's income goes up by only 27.35 cents with every $1 he earns. The remaining 72.65 cents of every wage dollar is lost to taxes or reduced Social Security benefits.

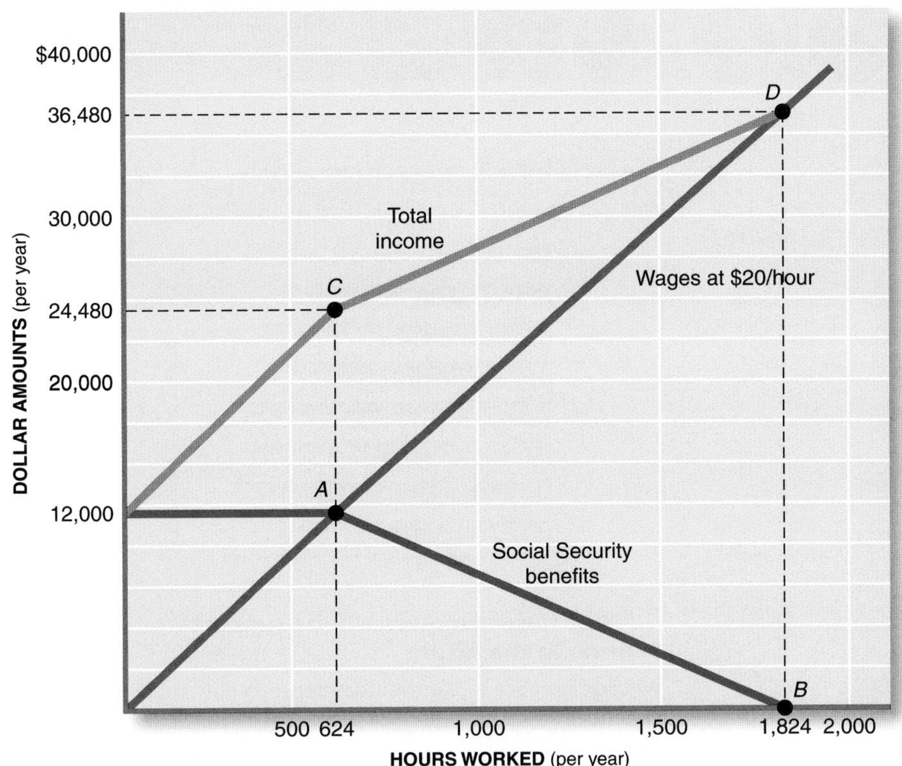

FIGURE 34.6
The Social Security Work Test

A worker aged 62–64 can earn up to $12,480 (point *A*) without losing any Social Security benefits. If wages increase beyond $12,480, however, Social Security benefits decline by 50 cents for every $1 earned. After point *C*, income rises only half as fast as wages. At the breakeven point *D*, earnings and income are $36,480, and there are no Social Security benefits (point *B*).

Declining Labor Supply

Like welfare recipients, older people are quick to realize that work no longer pays. Not surprisingly, they've exited the labor market in droves. The **labor-force participation rate** measures the percentage of the population that is either employed or actively seeking a job (unemployed). Figure 34.7 shows how precipitously the labor-force participation rate has declined among older Americans. As the World View on the next page illustrates, this problem isn't unique to the United States. The relative size of the over-65 population is growing everywhere, and more older people are retiring earlier.

labor-force participation rate: The percentage of the working-age population working or seeking employment.

Prior to the creation of the Social Security system, most older people had to continue working until advanced age. Many "died with their boots on" because they had no other means of support. Just a generation ago, over 75 percent of men 62 to 64 were working. Today, less than 50 percent of that group are working.

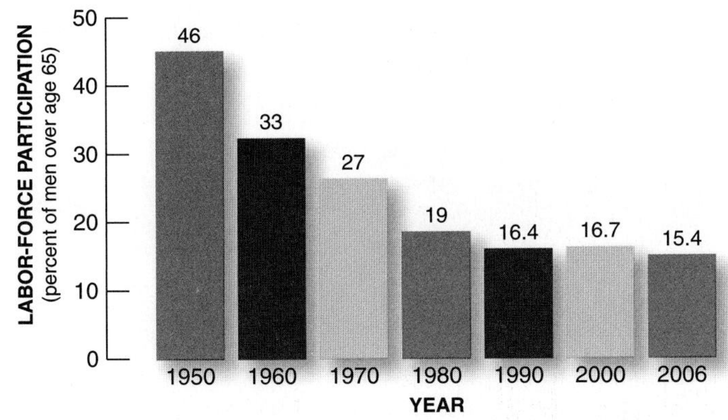

FIGURE 34.7
Declining Labor-Force Participation

In the 1960s and 1970s, the eligibility age for Social Security was lowered for men and benefits were increased. This convinced an increased percentage of older men to leave the labor force and retire. In a single generation the labor-force participation rate of men over age 65 was halved.

Source: U.S. Bureau of Labor Statistics.

WORLD VIEW

An Aging World

Richer Countries Aging Fastest

The whole world is aging, but the trend is most pronounced in developed countries, where elders already outnumber youths next year.

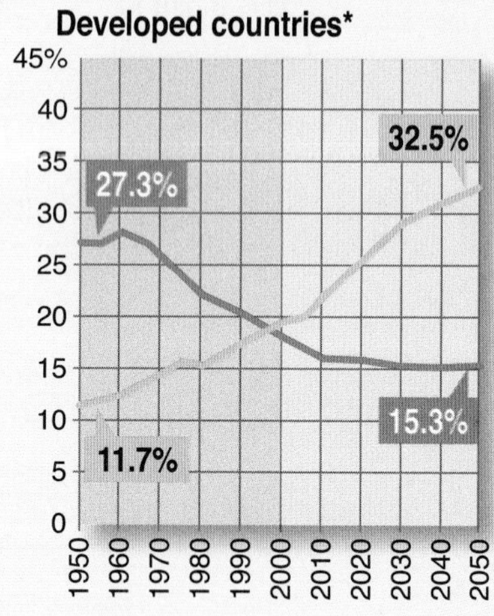

*(Includes North America, Japan, Europe, Australia, New Zealand)

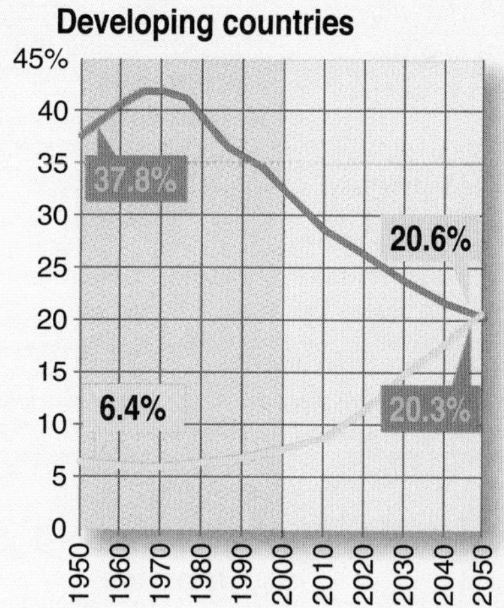

Source: *U.S. News & World Report,* March 1, 1999. Copyright 1999 U.S. News & World Report, L. P. Reprinted with permission. www.usnews.com

Workers have been retiring earlier . . .

Average age of retirement for men in industrialized countries

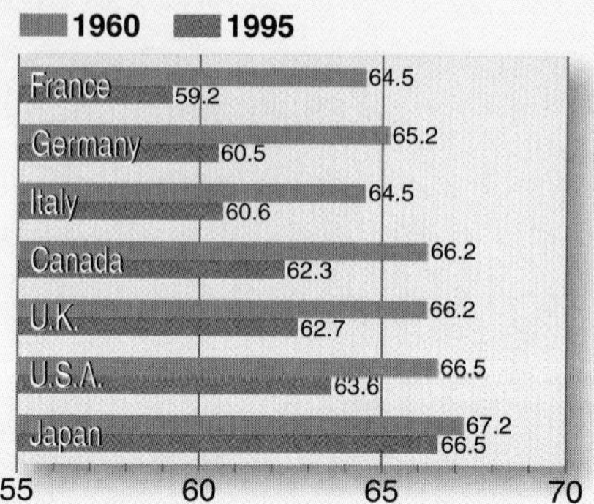

. . . but fewer workers will be supporting retirees in the future . . .

Average number of contributors per retiree in public pension systems

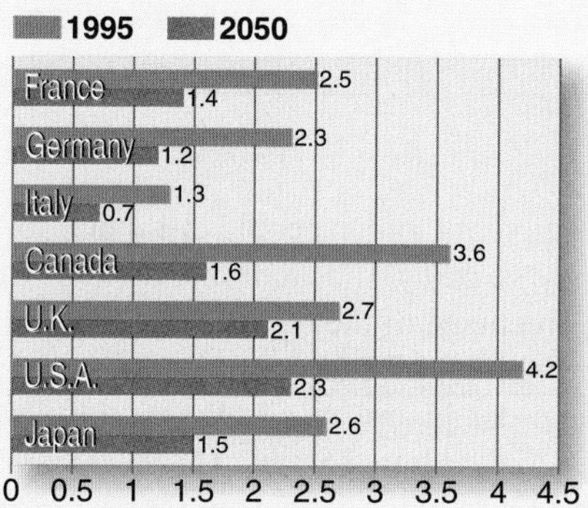

. . . which could lead to higher taxes

Projected payroll tax rates needed to cover all retirees

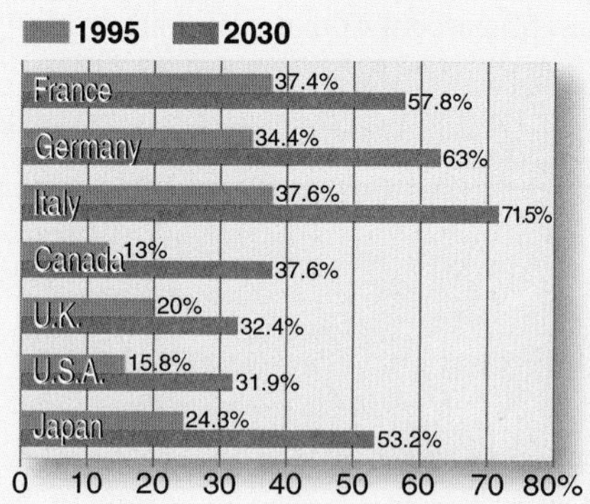

Analysis: The aging of the world's population implies an increasing income transfer burden. As older workers choose to retire earlier, the burden increases still further.

Compassion, Incentives, and Cost

The primary economic cost of the Social Security program isn't the benefits it pays but the reduction in total output that occurs when workers retire early. In the absence of Social Security benefits, millions of older workers would still be on the job, contributing to the output of goods and services. When they instead retire—or simply work less—total output shrinks.

The economic cost of Social Security is increased further by a labor supply reduction among *younger* workers. Recall how all those retirement benefits are *financed* (Figure 34.5). The payroll taxes levied on employees and employers increase the cost of labor and discourage people from working more, which further reduces total output. As the behavior of both older and younger workers changes, ***the economic pie shrinks as we try to redistribute it from younger to older workers.***

webnote

Read about the future of Social Security as analyzed by the Social Security Administration at www.ssa.gov/qa.htm

Trade-Offs. Just because the intergenerational redistribution is expensive doesn't mean we shouldn't do it. Going to college is expensive too, but you're doing it. The real economic issue is benefits versus costs. Compassion for older workers is what motivates Social Security transfers. Presumably, society gains from the more equitable distribution of income that results (a revised FOR WHOM). The economic concern is that we *balance* this gain against the implied costs.

One way of reducing the economic cost of the Social Security program would be to eliminate the earnings test. The American Association of Retired Persons (AARP) has advocated this option for many years. If the earnings test were eliminated, the marginal tax rate on the wages of older workers would drop from 50 percent to 0. In a flash, the work disincentive would vanish, and older workers would produce more goods and services.

There's a downside to this reform, however. If the earnings test were eliminated, all older individuals would get their full retirement benefit, even if they continued to work. This would raise the budgetary cost of the program substantially. To cover that cost, payroll taxes would have to increase. Higher payroll taxes would in turn reduce supply and demand for *younger* workers. Hence, the financial burden of eliminating the earnings test might actually *increase* the economic cost of Social Security.

There's also an equity issue here. Should we increase payroll taxes on younger low-income workers in order to give higher Social Security benefits to older workers who still command higher salaries? In 2000, Congress gave a very qualified "yes" to this question. The earnings test was eliminated for workers over age 70 and raised to $30,000 for workers aged 65–69. The marginal tax rate for workers aged 65–69 was also reduced to 33.3 percent. The lower earnings test and 50 percent marginal tax rate were left intact, however, for people aged 62–64, the ones for whom the retirement decision is most pressing. The *budget* cost of greater work incentives for "early retirees" was regarded as too high.

THE ECONOMY TOMORROW

PRIVATIZE SOCIAL SECURITY?

As we saw, all income transfer programs entail a redistribution of income. In the case of Social Security, the redistribution is largely intergenerational: Payroll taxes levied on younger workers finance retirement benefits for older workers. The system is financed on a pay-as-you-go basis; future benefits depend on future taxes. This is very different from private pension plans, whereby you salt away some wages while working to finance your own eventual benefits. Such private plans are advance-*funded.*

Many people say we should run the Social Security system the same way. They want to "privatize" Social Security by permitting workers to establish their own retirement plans. Instead of paying payroll taxes to fund someone else's benefits, you'd make a contribution to your own pension fund.

FIGURE 34.8
A Declining Tax Base

Because Social Security benefits are financed by payroll taxes, the ratio of workers to retirees is a basic measure of the program's fiscal health. That ratio has declined dramatically, and it will decline even more as the Baby Boomers now start retiring.

Source: U.S. Social Security Administration.

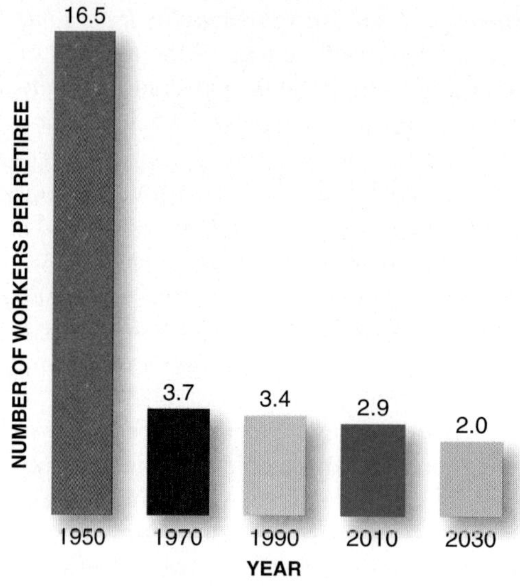

The case for privatizing Social Security is based on both efficiency and equity. The efficiency argument reflects the core laissez-faire argument that markets know best. In a privatized system, individuals would have the freedom to tailor their consumption and saving choices. The elimination of mandatory payroll taxes and the earnings test would also lessen work disincentives. People would work harder and longer, maximizing total output.

Advocates of privatization also note how inequitable the existing program is for younger workers. The people now retired are getting a great deal: They paid relatively low payroll taxes when young and now receive substantial benefits. In part this high payoff is due to demographics. Thirty years ago there were four workers for every retired person. By the time the post–World War II baby boomers retire, the ratio of workers to retirees will be a lot lower. By the year 2030, there will be only two workers for every retiree (see Figure 34.8). As a result, the tax burden on tomorrow's workers will have to be a lot higher, or the Baby Boomers will have to accept much lower Social Security benefits. Either way, some generation of workers will get a lot less than everyone else. If Social Security is privatized, tomorrow's workers won't have to bear such a demographic tax burden.

As alluring as these suggestions sound, the privatization of Social Security would foster other inequities. The primary goal of Social Security is to fend off poverty among the aged. Social Security does this in two ways: by (1) transferring income from workers to retirees and (2) redistributing income from high-wage workers to low-wage workers in retirement with progressive wage-replacement rates. By contrast, a privatized system would let the market alone determine FOR WHOM goods are produced. Low-income workers and other people who saved little while working would end up poor in their golden years. In a privatized system, even some high earners and savers might end up poor if their investments turned sour. Would we turn our collective backs on these people? If not, then the government would have to intervene with *some* kind of transfer program. The real issue, therefore, may not be whether a privatized Social Security system would work but what kind of *public* transfer program we'd have to create to supplement it. Then the choice would be either (1) Social Security or (2) a privatized retirement system plus a public welfare program for the aged poor. Framed in this context, the choice for the economy tomorrow is a lot more complex.

U.S. TRADE PATTERNS

The United States is by far the largest player in global product and resource markets. In 2006, we purchased 20 percent of the world's exports and sold 15 percent of the same total.

Imports

In dollar terms, our imports in 2006 exceeded $2.2 trillion. These **imports** included the consumer items mentioned earlier as well as capital equipment, raw materials, and food. Table 35.1 is a sampler of the goods and services we purchase from foreign suppliers.

imports: Goods and services purchased from international sources.

Although imports represent only 17 percent of total GDP, they account for larger shares of specific product markets. Coffee is a familiar example. Since virtually all coffee is imported (except for a tiny amount produced in Hawaii), Americans would have a harder time staying awake without imports. Likewise, there'd be no aluminum if we didn't import bauxite, no chrome bumpers if we didn't import chromium, no tin cans without imported tin, and a lot fewer computers without imported components. We couldn't even play the all-American game of baseball without imports, since baseballs are no longer made in the United States.

We import *services* as well as *goods.* If you fly to Europe on Virgin Airways you're importing transportation services. If you stay in a London hotel, you're importing lodging services. When you go to Barclay's Bank to cash traveler's checks, you're importing foreign financial services. These and other services now account for one-sixth of U.S. imports.

Exports

While we're buying goods (merchandise) and services from the rest of the world, global consumers are buying our **exports.** In 2006, we exported $1 trillion of *goods,* including farm products (wheat, corn, soybeans), tobacco, machinery (computers), aircraft, automobiles

exports: Goods and services sold to foreign buyers.

Country	Imports from	Exports to
Australia	Beef Alumina Autos	Airplanes Computers Auto parts
Belgium	Jewelry Cars Optical glass	Cigarettes Airplanes Diamonds
Canada	Cars Trucks Paper	Auto parts Cars Computers
China	Toys Shoes Clothes	Fertilizer Airplanes Cotton
Germany	Cars Engines Auto parts	Airplanes Computers Cars
Japan	Cars Computers Telephones	Airplanes Computers Timber
Russia	Oil Platinum Artworks	Corn Wheat Oil seeds
South Korea	Shoes Cars Computers	Airplanes Leather Iron ingots and oxides

Source: U.S. Department of Commerce.

TABLE 35.1
A U.S. Trade Sampler

The United States imports and exports a staggering array of goods and services. Shown here are the top exports and imports with various countries. Notice that we export many of the same goods we import (such as cars and computers). What's the purpose of trading goods we produce ourselves?

WORLD VIEW

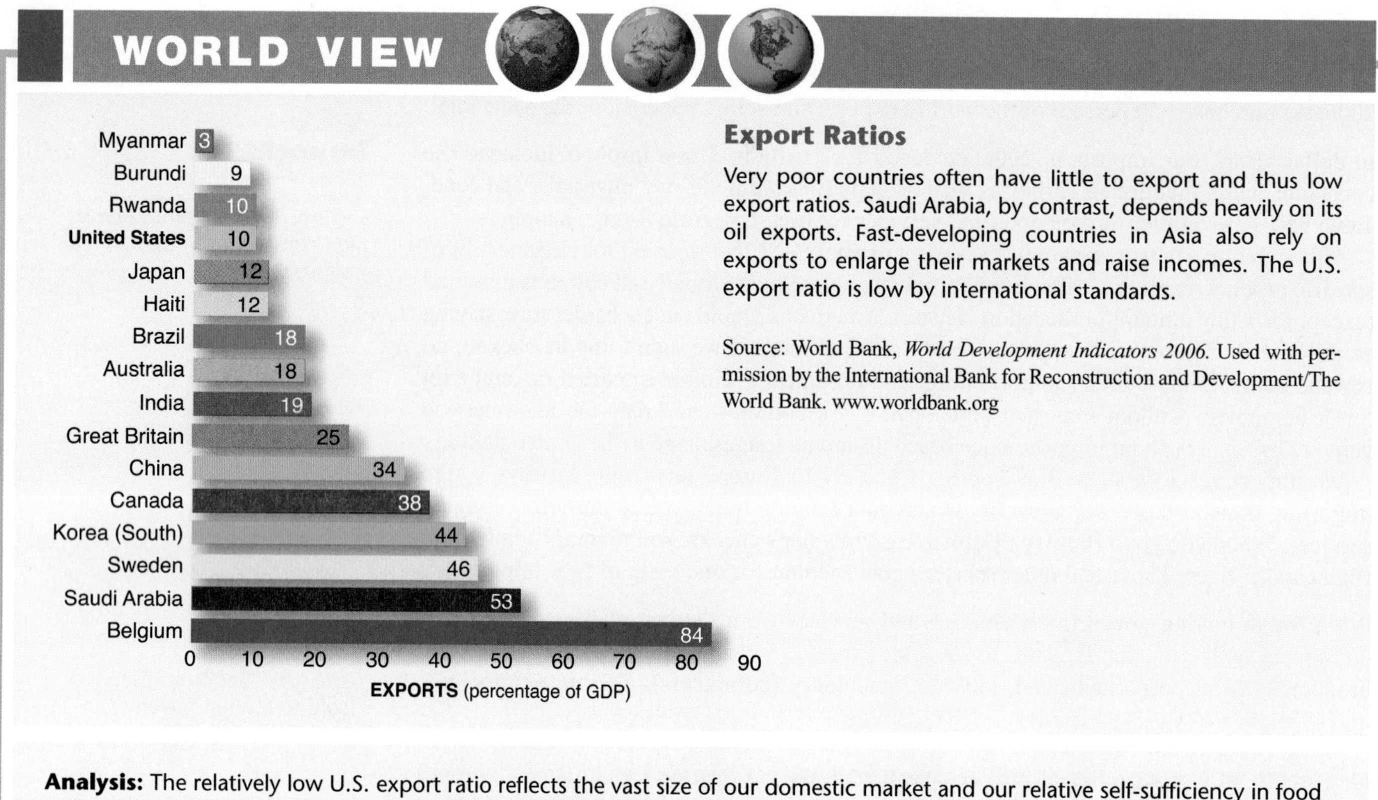

Export Ratios

Very poor countries often have little to export and thus low export ratios. Saudi Arabia, by contrast, depends heavily on its oil exports. Fast-developing countries in Asia also rely on exports to enlarge their markets and raise incomes. The U.S. export ratio is low by international standards.

Source: World Bank, *World Development Indicators 2006.* Used with permission by the International Bank for Reconstruction and Development/The World Bank. www.worldbank.org

Analysis: The relatively low U.S. export ratio reflects the vast size of our domestic market and our relative self-sufficiency in food and resources. European nations are smaller and highly interdependent.

and auto parts, raw materials (lumber, iron ore), and chemicals (see Table 35.1 for a sample of U.S. merchandise exports). We also exported $431 billion of services (movies, software licenses, tourism, engineering, financial services, etc.).

Although the United States is the world's largest exporter of goods and services, exports represent a relatively modest fraction of our total output. As the World View illustrates, other nations export much larger proportions of their GDP. Belgium is one of the most export-oriented countries, with tourist services and diamond exports pushing its export ratio to an incredible 84 percent. By contrast, Myanmar (Burma) is basically a closed economy, with few exports (other than opium and other drugs traded in the black market).

webnote

Find the most recent trends in trade statistics at www.whitehouse.gov/fsbr/international.html

The low U.S. export ratio (10 percent) disguises our heavy dependence on exports in specific industries. We export 25 to 50 percent of our rice, corn, and wheat production each year, and still more of our soybeans. Clearly, a decision by international consumers to stop eating U.S. agricultural products could devastate a lot of American farmers. Such companies as Boeing (planes), Caterpillar Tractor (construction and farm machinery), Weyerhaeuser (logs, lumber), Eastman Kodak (film), Dow (chemicals), and Sun Microsystems (computer workstations) sell over one-fourth of their output in foreign markets. McDonald's sells hamburgers to over 50 million people a day in 128 countries around the world; to do so, the company exports management and marketing services (as well as frozen food) from the United States. The Walt Disney Company produces the most popular TV shows in Russia and Germany, publishes Italy's best-selling weekly magazine, and has the most popular tourist attraction in Japan (Tokyo Disneyland). The 500,000 foreign students attending U.S. universities are purchasing $5 billion of American educational services. All these activities are part of America's service exports.

Trade Balances

Although we export a lot of products, we usually have an imbalance in our trade flows. The trade balance is the difference between the value of exports and imports; that is,

$$\text{Trade balance} = \text{exports} - \text{imports}$$

Product Category	Exports ($ billions)	Imports ($ billions)	Surplus (Deficit) ($ billions)
Merchandise	$1,035	$1,880	$(845)
Services	431	349	82
Total trade	$1,466	$2,229	$(763)

Source: U.S. Department of Commerce.

TABLE 35.2
Trade Balances

Both merchandise (goods) and services are traded between countries. The United States typically has a merchandise deficit and a services surplus. When combined, an overall trade deficit remained in 2006.

During 2006, we imported much more than we exported and so had a negative trade balance. A negative trade balance is called a **trade deficit.**

trade deficit: The amount by which the value of imports exceeds the value of exports in a given time period.

Although the overall trade balance includes both goods and services, these flows are usually reported separately, with the *merchandise* trade balance distinguished from the *services* trade balance. As Table 35.2 shows, the United States had a merchandise (goods) trade deficit of $845 billion in 2006 and a *services* trade *surplus* of $82 billion, leaving the overall trade balance in the red.

When the United States has a trade deficit with the rest of the world, other countries must have an offsetting **trade surplus.** On a global scale, imports must equal exports, since every good exported by one country must be imported by another. Hence, ***any imbalance in America's trade must be offset by reverse imbalances elsewhere.***

trade surplus: The amount by which the value of exports exceeds the value of imports in a given time period.

Whatever the overall balance in our trade accounts, bilateral balances vary greatly. Table 35.3 shows, for example, that our 2006 aggregate trade deficit ($763 billion) incorporated huge bilateral trade deficits with Japan and China. In the same year, however, we had trade surpluses with the Netherlands, Belgium, Australia, Hong Kong, and the United Arab Emirates.

webnote

For more data on bilateral trade, visit the U.S. Census Bureau at www.census.gov/foreign-trade/www

MOTIVATION TO TRADE

Many people wonder why we trade so much, particularly since (1) we import many of the things we also export (like computers, airplanes, clothes), (2) we *could* produce many of the other things we import, and (3) we worry so much about trade imbalances. Why not just import those few things that we can't produce ourselves, and export just enough to balance that trade?

Country	Exports to ($ billions)	Imports from ($ billions)	Trade Balance ($ billions)
Top Deficit Countries			
China	$ 55	$288	−$233
Japan	60	148	−88
Canada	230	303	−73
Mexico	134	198	−64
Germany	41	89	−48
Top Surplus Countries			
Netherlands	31	17	+14
United Arab Emirates	12	1	+11
Australia	18	8	+10
Hong Kong	18	8	+10
Belgium	21	14	+7

Source: U.S. Census Bureau, Foreign Trade Division.

TABLE 35.3
Bilateral Trade Balances

The U.S. trade deficit is the net result of bilateral deficits and surpluses. We had huge trade deficits with Japan and China in 2006, for example, but small trade surpluses with the Netherlands, Belgium, Australia, and Hong Kong. International trade is *multi*national, with surpluses in some countries being offset by trade deficits elsewhere.

Specialization

Although it might seem strange to be importing goods we could produce ourselves, such trade is entirely rational. Our decision to trade with other countries arises from the same considerations that motivate individuals to specialize in production: satisfying their remaining needs in the marketplace. Why don't you become self-sufficient, growing all your own food, building your own shelter, recording your own songs? Presumably because you've found that you can enjoy a much higher standard of living (and better music) by working at just one job and then buying other goods in the marketplace. When you do so, you're no longer self-sufficient. Instead, you are *specializing* in production, relying on others to produce the array of goods and services you want. When countries trade goods and services, they are doing the same thing—*specializing* in production, and then *trading* for other desired goods. Why do they do this? Because ***specialization increases total output.***

To see how nations benefit from trade, we'll examine the production possibilities of two countries. We want to demonstrate that two countries that trade can together produce more output than they could in the absence of trade. If they can, ***the gain from trade is increased world output and a higher standard of living in all trading countries.*** This is the essential message of the *theory of comparative advantage.*

Production and Consumption without Trade

production possibilities: The alternative combinations of final goods and services that could be produced in a given time period with all available resources and technology.

Consider the production and consumption possibilities of just two countries—say, the United States and France. For the sake of illustration, assume that both countries produce only two goods: bread and wine. Let's also set aside worries about the law of diminishing returns and the substitutability of resources, thus transforming the familiar **production possibilities** curve into a straight line, as in Figure 35.1.

The "curves" in Figure 35.1 suggest that the United States is capable of producing much more bread than France. With our greater abundance of labor, land, and other resources, we assume that the United States is capable of producing up to 100 zillion loaves of bread per year. To do so, we'd have to devote all our resources to that purpose. This capability is indicated by point *A* in Figure 35.1*a* and in row *A* of the accompanying production possibilities schedule. France (Figure 35.1*b*), on the other hand, confronts a *maximum* bread production of only 15 zillion loaves per year (point *G*) because it has little available land, less fuel, and fewer potential workers.

The capacities of the two countries for wine production are 50 zillion barrels for us (point *F*) and 60 zillion for France (point *L*), largely reflecting France's greater experience in tending vines. Both countries are also capable of producing alternative *combinations* of bread and wine, as evidenced by their respective production possibilities curves (points *A*–*F* for the United States and *G*–*L* for France).

closed economy: A nation that doesn't engage in international trade.

consumption possibilities: The alternative combinations of goods and services that a country could consume in a given time period.

A nation that doesn't trade with other countries is called a **closed economy.** In the absence of contact with the outside world, the production possibilities curve for a closed economy also defines its **consumption possibilities.** Without imports, a country cannot consume more than it produces. Thus, the only immediate issue in a closed economy is which mix of output to choose—*what* to produce and consume—out of the domestic choices available.

Assume that Americans choose point *D* on their production possibilities curve, producing and consuming 40 zillion loaves of bread and 30 zillion barrels of wine. The French, on the other hand, prefer the mix of output represented by point *I* on their production possibilities curve. At that point they produce and consume 9 zillion loaves of bread and 24 zillion barrels of wine.

To assess the potential gain from trade, we must focus the *combined* output of the United States and France. In this case, total world output (points *D* and *I*) comes to 49 zillion loaves of bread and 54 zillion barrels of wine. What we want to know is whether world output would increase if France and the United States abandoned their isolation and started trading. Could either country, or both, consume more output by engaging in a little trade?

Production and Consumption with Trade

Because both countries are saddled with limited production possibilities, trying to eke out a little extra wine and bread from this situation might not appear very promising. Such a conclusion is unwarranted, however. Take another look at the production possibilities

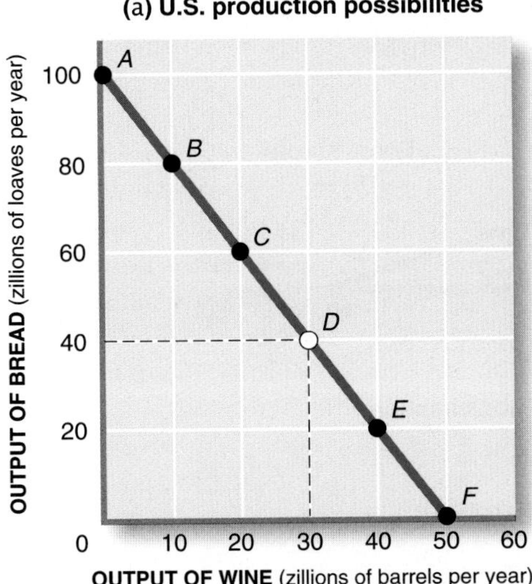

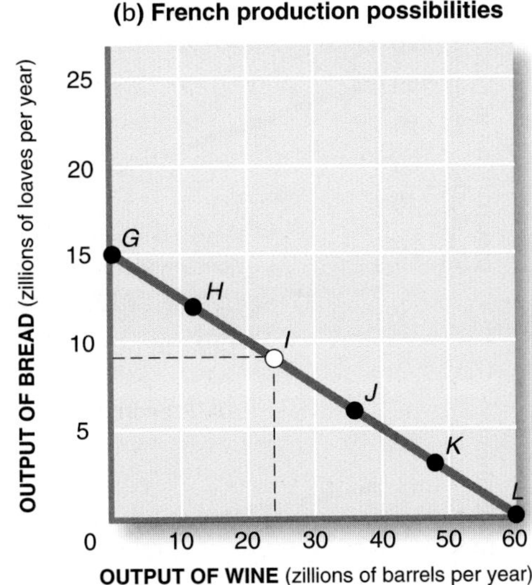

U.S. Production Possibilities

	Bread (zillions of loaves)	+	Wine (zillions of barrels)
A	100	+	0
B	80	+	10
C	60	+	20
D	40	+	30
E	20	+	40
F	0	+	50

French Production Possibilities

	Bread (zillions of loaves)	+	Wine (zillions of barrels)
G	15	+	0
H	12	+	12
I	9	+	24
J	6	+	36
K	3	+	48
L	0	+	60

FIGURE 35.1
Consumption Possibilities without Trade

In the absence of trade, a country's consumption possibilities are identical to its production possibilities. The assumed production possibilities of the United States and France are illustrated in the graphs and the corresponding schedules. Before entering into trade, the United States chose to produce and consume at point *D*, with 40 zillion loaves of bread and 30 zillion barrels of wine. France chose point *I* on its own production possibilities curve. By trading, each country hopes to increase its consumption beyond these levels.

confronting the United States, as reproduced in Figure 35.2. Suppose the United States were to produce at point *C* rather than point *D*. At point *C* we could produce 60 zillion loaves of bread and 20 zillion barrels of wine. That combination is clearly possible, since it lies on the production possibilities curve. We didn't choose that point earlier because we assumed the mix of output at point *D* was preferable. The mix of output at point *C* could be produced, however.

We could also change the mix of output in France. Assume that France moved from point *I* to point *K*, producing 48 zillion barrels of wine and only 3 zillion loaves of bread.

Two observations are now called for. The first is simply that output mixes have changed in each country. The second, and more interesting, is that total world output has

FIGURE 35.2
Consumption Possibilities with Trade

A country can increase its consumption possibilities through international trade. Each country alters its mix of domestic output to produce more of the good it produces best. As it does so, total world output increases, and each country enjoys more consumption. In this case, trade allows U.S. consumption to move from point *D* to point *N*. France moves from point *I* to point *M*.

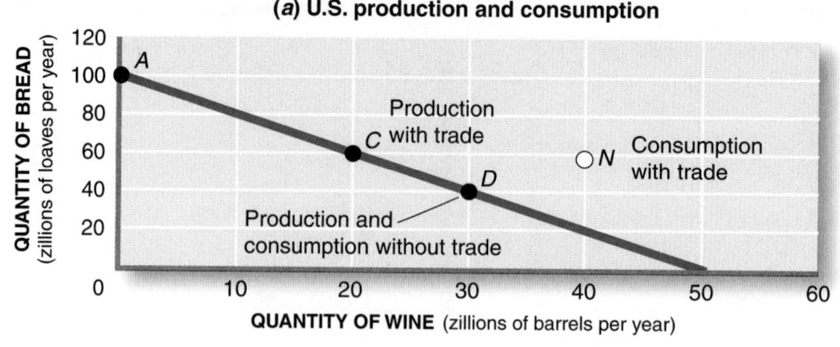

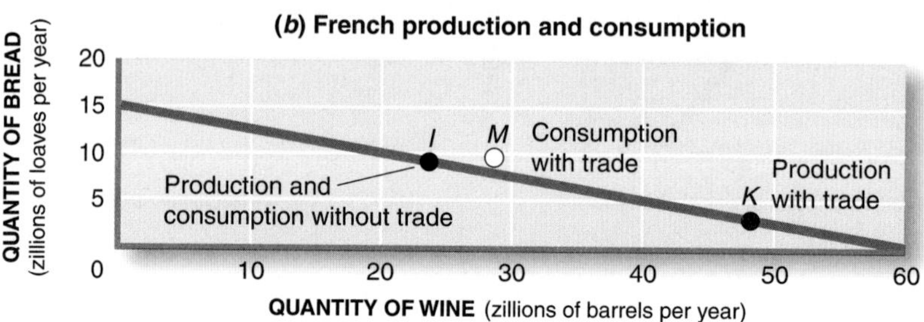

increased. When the United States and France were at points *D* and *I*, their *combined* output consisted of

	Bread (zillions of loaves)	Wine (zillions of barrels)
United States (at point *D*)	40	30
France (at point *I*)	9	24
Total pretrade output	49	54

After moving along their respective production possibilities curves to points *C* and *K*, the combined world output becomes

	Bread (zillions of loaves)	Wine (zillions of barrels)
United States (at point *C*)	60	20
France (at point *K*)	3	48
Total output with trade	63	68

Total world output has increased by 14 zillion loaves of bread and 14 zillion barrels of wine. ***Just by changing the mix of output in each country, we've increased total world output.*** This additional output creates the potential for making both countries better off than they were in the absence of trade.

The United States and France weren't producing at points *C* and *K* before because they simply didn't want to *consume* those particular output combinations. Nevertheless, our discovery that points *C* and *K* allow us to produce *more* output suggests that everybody can consume more goods and services if we change the mix of output in each country. This is our first clue as to how specialization and trade can benefit an **open economy**—a nation that engages in international trade.

open economy: A nation that engages in international trade.

Suppose we're the first to discover the potential benefits from trade. Using Figure 35.2 as our guide, we suggest to the French that they move their mix of output from point *I* to point *K*. As an incentive for making such a move, we promise to give them 6 zillion loaves of bread in exchange for 20 zillion barrels of wine. This would leave them at point *M*, with as much bread to consume as they used to have, plus an extra 4 zillion barrels of wine. At point *I* they had 9 zillion loaves of bread and 24 zillion barrels of wine. At point *M* they can have 9 zillion loaves of bread and 28 zillion barrels of wine. Thus, by altering their mix of output (from point *I* to point *K*) and then trading (point *K* to point *M*), the French end up with more goods and services than they had in the beginning. Notice in particular that this new consumption possibility (point *M*) lies *outside* France's domestic production possibilities curve.

The French will be quite pleased with the extra output they get from trading. But where does this leave us? Does France's gain imply a loss for us? Or do we gain from trade as well?

Mutual Gains

As it turns out, *both* the United States and France gain by trading. The United States, too, ends up consuming a mix of output that lies outside our production possibilities curve.

Note that at point *C* we produce 60 zillion loaves of bread per year and 20 zillion barrels of wine. We then export 6 zillion loaves to France. This leaves us with 54 zillion loaves of bread to consume.

In return for our exported bread, the French give us 20 zillion barrels of wine. These imports, plus our domestic production, permit us to *consume* 40 zillion barrels of wine. Hence, we end up consuming at point *N*, enjoying 54 zillion loaves of bread and 40 zillion barrels of wine. Thus, by first changing our mix of output (from point *D* to point *C*), then trading (point *C* to point *N*), we end up with 14 zillion more loaves of bread and 10 zillion more barrels of wine than we started with. International trade has made us better off, too.

Table 35.4 recaps the gains from trade for both countries. Notice that U.S. imports match French exports and vice versa. Also notice how the trade-facilitated consumption in each country exceeds no-trade levels.

There's no sleight of hand going on here; the gains from trade are due to specialization in production. When each country goes it alone, it's a prisoner of its own production possibilities curve; it must make production decisions on the basis of its own consumption desires. When international trade is permitted, however, each country can concentrate on the exploitation of its production capabilities. ***Each country produces those goods it makes best and then trades with other countries to acquire the goods it desires to consume.***

	Production and Consumption with Trade								Production and Consumption with No Trade
	Production	+	Imports	−	Exports	=	Consumption		
United States at . . .	Point C						Point N		Point D
Bread	60	+	0	−	6	=	54		40
Wine	20	+	20	−	0	=	40		30
France at . . .	Point K						Point M		Point I
Bread	3	+	6	−	0	=	9		9
Wine	48	+	0	−	20	=	28		24

TABLE 35.4
Gains from Trade

When nations specialize in production, they can export one good and import another and end up with more total goods to consume than they had without trade. In this case, the United States specializes in bread production. Notice how U.S. *consumption* of both goods increases.

The resultant specialization increases total world output. In the process, each country is able to escape the confines of its own production possibilities curve, to reach beyond it for a larger basket of consumption goods. ***When a country engages in international trade, its consumption possibilities always exceed its production possibilities.*** These enhanced consumption possibilities are emphasized by the positions of points *N* and *M* outside the production possibilities curves (Figure 35.2). If it weren't possible for countries to increase their consumption by trading, there'd be no incentive for trading, and thus no trade.

PURSUIT OF COMPARATIVE ADVANTAGE

Although international trade can make everyone better off, it's not so obvious which goods should be traded, or on what terms. In our previous illustration, the United States ended up trading bread for wine in terms that were decidedly favorable to us. Why did we export bread rather than wine, and how did we end up getting such a good deal?

Opportunity Costs

comparative advantage: The ability of a country to produce a specific good at a lower opportunity cost than its trading partners.

opportunity cost: The most desired goods or services that are forgone in order to obtain something else.

The decision to export bread is based on **comparative advantage,** that is, the *relative* cost of producing different goods. Recall that we can produce a maximum of 100 zillion loaves of bread per year or 50 zillion barrels of wine. Thus, the domestic **opportunity cost** of producing 100 zillion loaves of bread is the 50 zillion barrels of wine we forsake in order to devote our resources to bread production. In fact, at every point on the U.S. production possibilities curve (Figure 35.2*a*), the opportunity cost of a loaf of bread is $\frac{1}{2}$ barrel of wine. We're effectively paying half a barrel of wine to get a loaf of bread.

Although the cost of bread production in the United States might appear outrageous, even higher opportunity costs prevail in France. According to Figure 35.2*b*, the opportunity cost of producing a loaf of bread in France is a staggering 4 barrels of wine. To produce a loaf of bread, the French must use factors of production that could otherwise be used to produce 4 barrels of wine.

Comparative Advantage. A comparison of the opportunity costs prevailing in each country exposes the nature of comparative advantage. The United States has a comparative advantage in bread production because less wine has to be given up to produce bread in the United States than in France. In other words, the opportunity costs of bread production are lower in the United States than in France. ***Comparative advantage refers to the relative (opportunity) costs of producing particular goods.***

A country should specialize in what it's *relatively* efficient at producing, that is, goods for which it has the lowest opportunity costs. In this case, the United States should produce bread because its opportunity cost ($\frac{1}{2}$ barrel of wine) is less than France's (4 barrels of wine). Were you the production manager for the whole world, you'd certainly want each country to exploit its relative abilities, thus maximizing world output. Each country can arrive at that same decision itself by comparing its own opportunity costs to those prevailing elsewhere. ***World output, and thus the potential gains from trade, will be maximized when each country pursues its comparative advantage.*** Each country does so by exporting goods that entail relatively low domestic opportunity costs and importing goods that involve relatively high domestic opportunity costs. That's the kind of situation depicted in Table 35.4.

Absolute Costs Don't Count

absolute advantage: The ability of a country to produce a specific good with fewer resources (per unit of output) than other countries.

In assessing the nature of comparative advantage, notice that we needn't know anything about the actual costs involved in production. Have you seen any data suggesting how much labor, land, or capital is required to produce a loaf of bread in either France or the United States? For all you and I know, the French may be able to produce both a loaf of bread and a barrel of wine with fewer resources than we're using. Such an **absolute advantage** in production might exist because of their much longer experience in cultivating both grapes and wheat or simply because they have more talent.

We can envy such productivity, and even try to emulate it, but it shouldn't alter our production or trade decisions. All we really care about are *opportunity costs*—what *we* have to give up in order to get more of a desired good. If we can get a barrel of wine for less bread in trade than in production, we have a comparative advantage in producing bread. As long as we have a *comparative* advantage in bread production we should exploit it. It doesn't matter to us whether France could produce either good with fewer resources. For that matter, even if France had an absolute advantage in *both* goods, we'd still have a *comparative* advantage in bread production, as we've already confirmed. The absolute costs of production were omitted from the previous illustration because they were irrelevant.

To clarify the distinction between absolute advantage and comparative advantage, consider this example. When Charlie Osgood joined the Willamette Warriors football team, he was the fastest runner ever to play football in Willamette. He could also throw the ball farther than most people could see. In other words, he had an *absolute advantage* in both throwing and running. Charlie would have made the greatest quarterback or the greatest end ever to play football. *Would have.* The problem was that he could play only one position at a time. Thus, the Willamette coach had to play Charlie either as a quarterback or as an end. He reasoned that Charlie could throw only a bit farther than some of the other top quarterbacks but could far outdistance all the other ends. In other words, Charlie had a *comparative advantage* in running and was assigned to play as an end.

TERMS OF TRADE

It definitely pays to pursue one's comparative advantage by specializing in production. It may not yet be clear, however, how we got such a good deal with France. We're clever traders but, beyond that, is there any way to determine the **terms of trade,** the quantity of good A that must be given up in exchange for good B? In our previous illustration, the terms of trade were very favorable to us; we exchanged only 6 zillion loaves of bread for 20 zillion barrels of wine (Table 35.4). The terms of trade were thus 6 loaves = 20 barrels.

terms of trade: The rate at which goods are exchanged; the amount of good A given up for good B in trade.

Limits to the Terms of Trade

The terms of trade with France were determined by our offer and France's ready acceptance. But why did France accept those terms? France was willing to accept our offer because the terms of trade permitted France to increase its wine consumption without giving up any bread consumption. Our offer of 6 loaves for 20 barrels was an improvement over France's domestic opportunity costs. France's domestic possibilities required it to give up 24 barrels of wine in order to produce 6 loaves of bread (see Figure 35.2*b*). Getting bread via trade was simply cheaper for France than producing bread at home. France ended up with an extra 4 zillion barrels of wine (Table 35.4).

Our first clue to the terms of trade, then, lies in each country's domestic opportunity costs. ***A country won't trade unless the terms of trade are superior to domestic opportunities.*** In our example, the opportunity cost of 1 barrel of wine in the United States is 2 loaves of bread. Accordingly, we won't export bread unless we get at least 1 barrel of wine in exchange for every 2 loaves of bread we ship overseas.

All countries want to gain from trade. Hence, we can predict that ***the terms of trade between any two countries will lie somewhere between their respective opportunity costs in production.*** That is, a loaf of bread in international trade will be worth at least $\frac{1}{2}$ barrel of wine (the U.S. opportunity cost) but no more than 4 barrels (the French opportunity cost). In our example, the terms of trade ended up at 1 loaf = 3.33 barrels (that is, at 6 loaves = 20 barrels). This represented a very large gain for the United States and a small gain for France. Figure 35.3 illustrates this outcome and several other possibilities.

The Role of Markets and Prices

Relatively little trade is subject to such direct negotiations between countries. More often than not, the decision to import or export a particular good is left up to the market decisions of individual consumers and producers.

Individual consumers and producers aren't much impressed by such abstractions as comparative advantage. Market participants tend to focus on prices, always trying to allocate their resources in order to maximize profits or personal satisfaction. Consumers tend to buy the products that deliver the most utility per dollar of expenditure, while producers try to get the most output per dollar of cost. Everybody's looking for a bargain.

So what does this have to do with international trade? Well, suppose that Henri, an enterprising Frenchman, visited the United States before the advent of international trade.

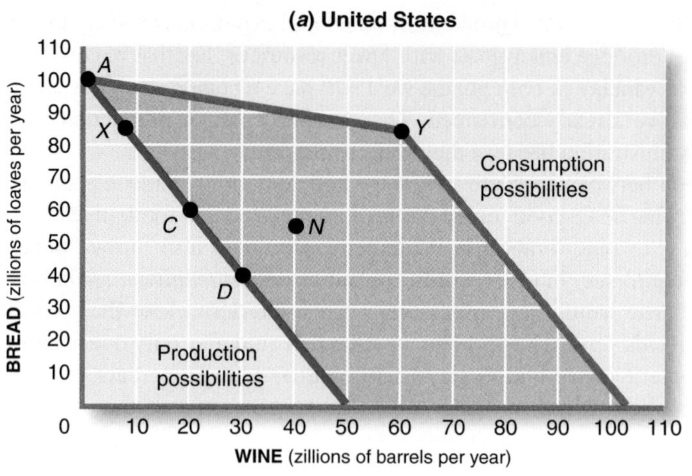

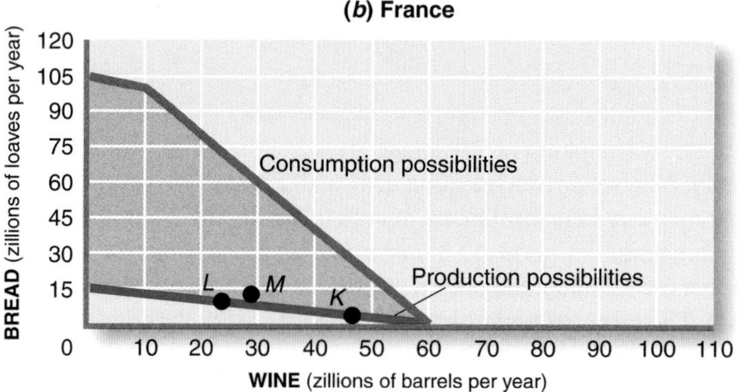

FIGURE 35.3
Searching for the Terms of Trade

Assume the United States can produce 100 zillion loaves of bread per year (point *A*). If we reduce output to only 85 zillion loaves, we could move to point *X*. At point *X* we have 7.5 zillion barrels of wine and 85 zillion loaves of bread.

Trade increases consumption possibilities. If we continued to produce 100 zillion loaves of bread, we could trade 15 zillion loaves to France in exchange for as much as 60 zillion barrels of wine. This would leave us *producing* at point *A* but *consuming* at point *Y*. At point *Y* we have more wine and no less bread than we had at point *X*.

A country will end up on its consumption possibilities curve only if it gets *all* the gains from trade. It will remain on its production possibilities curve only if it gets *none* of the gains from trade. The terms of trade determine how the gains from trade are distributed, and thus at what point in the shaded area each country ends up.

Note: The kink in the consumption possibilities curve at point *Y* occurs because France is unable to produce more than 60 zillion barrels of wine.

He observed that bread was relatively cheap while wine was relatively expensive—the opposite of the price relationship prevailing in France. These price comparisons brought to his mind the opportunity for making a fast euro. All he had to do was bring over some French wine and trade it in the United States for a large quantity of bread. Then he could return to France and exchange the bread for a greater quantity of wine. *Alors!* Were he to do this a few times, he'd amass substantial profits.

Henri's entrepreneurial exploits will not only enrich him but will also move each country toward its comparative advantage. The United States ends up exporting bread to France, and France ends up exporting wine to the United States, exactly as the theory of comparative advantage suggests. The activating agent isn't the Ministry of Trade and its 620 trained economists but simply one enterprising French trader. He's aided and encouraged, of course, by consumers and producers in each country. American consumers are happy to

webnote

Find out more about trade patterns and policy from the International Trade Commission at dataweb.usitc.gov trade their bread for his wines. They thereby end up paying less for wine (in terms of bread) than they'd otherwise have to. In other words, the terms of trade Henri offers are more attractive than the prevailing (domestic) relative prices. On the other side of the Atlantic, Henri's welcome is equally warm. French consumers are able to get a better deal by trading their wine for his imported bread than by trading with the local bakers.

Even some producers are happy. The wheat farmers and bakers in the United States are eager to deal with Henri. He's willing to buy a lot of bread and even to pay a premium price for it. Indeed, bread production has become so profitable in the United States that a lot of people who used to grow and mash grapes are now growing wheat and kneading dough. This alters the mix of U.S. output in the direction of more bread, exactly as suggested in Figure 35.2*a*.

In France, the opposite kind of production shift is taking place. French wheat farmers are planting more grape vines so they can take advantage of Henri's generous purchases. Thus, Henri is able to lead each country in the direction of its comparative advantage while raking in a substantial profit for himself along the way.

Where the terms of trade and the volume of exports and imports end up depends partly on how good a trader Henri is. It will also depend on the behavior of the thousands of individual consumers and producers who participate in the market exchanges. In other words, trade flows depend on both the supply and the demand for bread and wine in each country. ***The terms of trade, like the price of any good, depend on the willingness of market participants to buy or sell at various prices.*** All we know for sure is that the terms of trade will end up somewhere between the limits set by each country's opportunity costs.

PROTECTIONIST PRESSURES

Although the potential gains from world trade are impressive, not everyone will smile at the Franco-American trade celebration. On the contrary, some people will be upset about the trade routes that Henri has established. They'll not only boycott the celebration but actively seek to discourage us from continuing to trade with France.

Microeconomic Pressures

Consider, for example, the winegrowers in western New York. Do you think they're going to be happy about Henri's entrepreneurship? Americans can now buy wine more cheaply from France than they can from New York. Before long we may hear talk about unfair foreign competition or about the greater nutritional value of American grapes (see News). The

IN THE NEWS

California Grape Growers Protest Mixing Foreign Wine

California wine grape growers are growing increasingly frustrated and angry at each market percentage point gain of foreign wine in the U.S. wine market.

By the end of the year, burgeoning wine imports are expected to account for 30 percent of the U.S. market.

As the overall wine market in the U.S. grows at a healthy 2 percent to 5 percent annual clip, California grape growers continue to rip out vineyards. More than 100,000 acres in the Central Valley have been destroyed in the past five years. Growers are beyond weary of prices offered less than production costs. . . .

Rubbing salt into the open economic sore this season includes record bulk, inexpensive wine imports that are being blended with California wines and sold by California wineries as "American" appellation wine. . . .

"California grape growers made a significant investment in wine grape vineyards on the signals from wineries that there was a bright future in California wine." Those same growers are seeing at least some of that bright future being taken by imports.

—Harry Cline

Source: *Western Farm Press,* December 6, 2006. Reprinted with permission.

Analysis: Although trade increases consumption possibilities, imports typically compete with a domestic industry. The affected industries will try to restrict imports in order to preserve their own jobs and incomes.

New York winegrowers may also emphasize the importance of maintaining an adequate grape supply and a strong wine industry at home, just in case of terrorist attacks.

Import-Competing Industries. Joining with the growers will be the farm workers and the other producers and merchants whose livelihood depends on the New York wine industry. If they're clever enough, the growers will also get the governor of the state to join their demonstration. After all, the governor must recognize the needs of his people, and his people definitely don't include the wheat farmers in Kansas who are making a bundle from international trade. New York consumers are of course benefiting from lower wine prices, but they're unlikely to demonstrate over a few cents a bottle. On the other hand, those few extra pennies translate into millions of dollars for domestic wine producers.

The wheat farmers in France are no happier about international trade than are the winegrowers in the United States. They'd dearly love to sink all those boats bringing wheat from America, thereby protecting their own market position.

If we're to make sense of trade policies, then, we must recognize one central fact of life: Some producers have a vested interest in restricting international trade. In particular, ***workers and producers who compete with imported products—who work in import-competing industries—have an economic interest in restricting trade.*** This helps explain why GM, Ford, and Chrysler are unhappy about auto imports and why workers in Massachusetts want to end the importation of Italian shoes. It also explains why textile producers in South Carolina think China is behaving irresponsibly when it sells cotton shirts and dresses in the United States.

Export Industries. Although imports typically mean fewer jobs and less income for some domestic industries, exports represent increased jobs and income for other industries. Producers and workers in export industries gain from trade. Thus, on a microeconomic level there are identifiable gainers and losers from international trade. ***Trade not only alters the mix of output but also redistributes income from import-competing industries to export industries.*** This potential redistribution is the source of political and economic friction.

Net Gain. We must be careful to note, however, that the microeconomic gains from trade are greater than the microeconomic losses. It's not simply a question of robbing Peter to enrich Paul. We must remind ourselves that consumers in general enjoy a higher standard of living as a result of international trade. As we saw earlier, trade increases world efficiency and total output. Accordingly, we end up slicing up a larger pie rather than just reslicing the same old smaller pie.

The gains from trade will mean nothing to workers who end up with a smaller slice of the (larger) pie. It's important to remember, however, that the gains from trade are large enough to make everybody better off. Whether we actually choose to distribute the gains from trade in this way is a separate question, to which we shall return shortly. Note here, however, that ***trade restrictions designed to protect specific microeconomic interests reduce the total gains from trade.*** Trade restrictions leave us with a smaller pie to split up.

Additional Pressures

Import-competing industries are the principal obstacle to expanded international trade. Selfish micro interests aren't the only source of trade restrictions, however. Other arguments are also used to restrict trade.

National Security. The national security argument for trade restrictions is twofold. We can't depend on foreign suppliers to provide us with essential defense-related goods, it is said, because that would leave us vulnerable in time of war. The machine tool industry used this argument to protect itself from imports. In 1991, the Pentagon again sided with the toolmakers, citing the need for the United States to "gear up military production quickly in case of war," a contingency that couldn't be assured if weapons manufacturers relied on imported lathes, milling machines, and other tools. After the September 11, 2001, terrorist attacks on the World Trade Center and Pentagon, U.S. farmers convinced

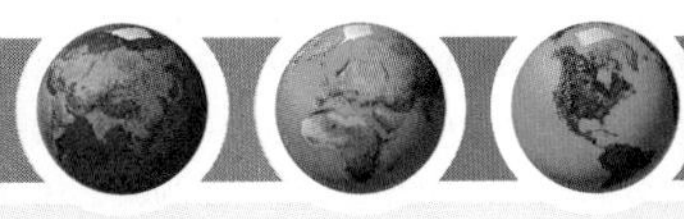

China Accuses Corning of "Dumping"

Corning Inc., the big U.S. fiber-optic and glass maker, said the Chinese government has charged it with selling optical-fiber products in China at an unfairly low price that damaged Chinese producers, a practice known as dumping.

Corning denied the charge, which followed a nearly yearlong investigation by China's Ministry of Commerce after two Chinese companies alleged that optical-fiber imports were priced below what market conditions justified. . . .

Since it joined the WTO, China has brought about 25 dumping cases against foreign companies, according to a King & Spalding estimate. In that same period, U.S. companies have brought 24 dumping cases against China, according to the International Trade Commission. . . .

Recent U.S. trade actions against China, most notably an antidumping case launched in October against $1 billion worth of Chinese wood and bedroom furniture imports, have likely played a role, too, according to trade experts.

The high-profile U.S. furniture case against China and China's charge against fiber makers such as Corning also exemplify the chief economic concerns in each economy: The U.S. is preoccupied with protecting workers in its hard-hit manufacturing sector, while China is interested in nurturing its technology industry. . . .

With the filing of the Chinese charges, Corning customers in China will have to pay a 16% deposit on the purchase price of the company's products, starting immediately. That money will be held in an escrow account until the matter is resolved.

Source: *The Wall Street Journal,* June 17, 2004.

Analysis: *Dumping* means that a foreign producer is selling exports at prices below cost or below prices in the home market, putting import-competing industries at a competitive disadvantage. *Accusations* of dumping are an effective trade barrier.

Congress to safeguard the nation's food supply with additional subsidies (see Chapter 29). The steel industry emphasized the importance of not depending on foreign suppliers.

Dumping. Another argument against free trade arises from the practice of **dumping.** Foreign producers "dump" their goods when they sell them in the United States at prices lower than those prevailing in their own country, perhaps even below the costs of production.

> **dumping:** The sale of goods in export markets at prices below domestic prices.

Dumping may be unfair to import-competing producers, but it isn't necessarily unwelcome to the rest of us. As long as foreign producers continue dumping, we're getting foreign products at low prices. How bad can that be? There's a legitimate worry, however. Foreign producers might hold prices down only until domestic producers are driven out of business. Then we might be compelled to pay the foreign producers higher prices for their products. In that case, dumping could consolidate market power and lead to monopoly-type pricing. The fear of dumping, then, is analogous to the fear of predatory pricing.

The potential costs of dumping are serious. It's not always easy to determine when dumping occurs, however. Those who compete with imports have an uncanny ability to associate any and all low prices with predatory dumping. The United States has used dumping *charges* to restrict imports of Chinese shrimp, furniture, lingerie, and other products in which China has an evident comparative advantage. The Chinese have retaliated with dozens of their own dumping investigations, including the fiber-optic cable case. As the accompanying World View explains, such actions slow imports and protect domestic producers.

Infant Industries. Actual dumping threatens to damage already established domestic industries. Even normal import prices, however, may make it difficult or impossible for a new domestic industry to develop. Infant industries are often burdened with abnormally high start-up costs. These high costs may arise from the need to train a whole workforce and the expenses of establishing new marketing channels. With time to grow, however, an infant industry might experience substantial cost reductions and establish a comparative advantage. When this is the case, trade restrictions might help nurture an industry in its infancy. Trade restrictions are justified, however, only if there's tangible evidence that the industry can develop a comparative advantage reasonably quickly.

Improving the Terms of Trade. A final argument for restricting trade rests on how the gains from trade are distributed. As we observed, the distribution of the gains from trade depends on the terms of trade. If we were to buy fewer imports, foreign producers might lower their prices. If that happened, the terms of trade would move in our favor, and we'd end up with a larger share of the gains from trade.

One way to bring about this sequence of events is to put restrictions on imports, making it more difficult or expensive for Americans to buy foreign products. Such restrictions will reduce the volume of imports, thereby inducing foreign producers to lower their prices. Unfortunately, this strategy can easily backfire: Retaliatory restrictions on imports, each designed to improve the terms of trade, will ultimately eliminate all trade and therewith all the gains people were competing for in the first place.

BARRIERS TO TRADE

The microeconomic losses associated with imports give rise to a constant clamor for trade restrictions. People whose jobs and incomes are threatened by international trade tend to organize quickly and air their grievances. The World View depicts the efforts of farmers in the Czech Republic to limit imports of Austrian pork in 2007. They hope to convince their government to impose restrictions on imports. More often than not, governments grant the wishes of these well-organized and well-financed special interests.

Embargoes

embargo: A prohibition on exports or imports.

The surefire way to restrict trade is simply to eliminate it. To do so, a country need only impose an embargo on exports or imports, or both. An **embargo** is nothing more than a prohibition against trading particular goods.

In 1951, Senator Joseph McCarthy convinced the U.S. Senate to impose an embargo on Soviet mink, fox, and five other furs. He argued that such imports helped finance world communism. Senator McCarthy also represented the state of Wisconsin, where most U.S. minks are raised. The Reagan administration tried to end the fur embargo in 1987 but met with stiff congressional opposition. By then, U.S. mink ranchers had developed a $120 million per year industry.

The United States has also maintained an embargo on Cuban goods since 1959, when Fidel Castro took power there. This embargo severely damaged Cuba's sugar industry and deprived American smokers of the famed Havana cigars. It also fostered the development of U.S. sugar beet and tobacco farmers, who now have a vested interest in maintaining the embargo.

tariff: A tax (duty) imposed on imported goods.

Tariffs

A more frequent trade restriction is a **tariff,** a special tax imposed on imported goods. Tariffs, also called *customs duties,* were once the principal source of revenue for governments.

WORLD VIEW

Meat Imports "Threaten" Farmers

Around 200 Czech farmers held a protest action March 26 on the Czech-Austrian border crossing in Dolni Dvořiště, South Bohemia, against meat imports. The protest was to draw attention to the situation of Czech pig breeders who claim they are threatened by growing pork imports to Czech retail chains and low purchasing prices.

Representatives of the Agricultural Chamber (AK) said it was a token protest, but didn't rule out further actions.

"We will . . . send an appeal to the Ministry of Agriculture, the Chamber of Deputies and the Senate, asking them for public support of Czech farmers and Czech food," said Jan Veleba, president of the AK. . . .

Minister of Agriculture Petr Gandalovič said blockades won't resolve the situation and would probably only worsen relations between the Czech Republic and Austria.

Source: *Czech Business Weekly,* April 2, 2007. Used with permission.

Analysis: Import-competing industries cite lots of reasons for restricting trade. Their primary concern, however, is to protect their own jobs and profits.

In the eighteenth century, tariffs on tea, glass, wine, lead, and paper were imposed on the American colonies to provide extra revenue for the British government. The tariff on tea led to the Boston Tea Party in 1773 and gave added momentum to the American independence movement. In modern times, tariffs have been used primarily as a means to protect specific industries from import competition. The current U.S. tariff code specifies tariffs on over 9,000 different products—nearly 50 percent of all U.S. imports. Although the average tariff is less than 5 percent, individual tariffs vary widely. The tariff on cars, for example, is only 2.5 percent, while cotton sweaters confront a 17.8 percent tariff.

The attraction of tariffs to import-competing industries should be obvious. ***A tariff on imported goods makes them more expensive to domestic consumers and thus less competitive with domestically produced goods.*** Among familiar tariffs in effect in 2007 were $0.50 per gallon on Scotch whiskey and 76 cents per gallon on imported champagne. These tariffs made American-produced spirits look relatively cheap and thus contributed to higher sales and profits for domestic distillers and grape growers. In the same manner, imported baby food is taxed at 34.6 percent, maple sugar at 9.4 percent, golf shoes at 8.5 percent, and imported sailboats at 1.5 percent. In each case, domestic producers in import-competing industries gain. The losers are domestic consumers, who end up paying higher prices. The tariff on orange juice, for example, raises the price of drinking orange juice by $525 million a year. Tariffs also hurt foreign producers, who lose business, and world efficiency, as trade is reduced.

webnote

The tariff schedule for imported products is available online from the U.S. International Trade Commission. Go to www.usitc.gov and click on "Publications" then "Harmonized Tariff Schedule."

"Beggar Thy Neighbor." Microeconomic interests aren't the only source of pressure for tariff protection. Imports represent leakage from the domestic circular flow and a potential loss of jobs at home. From this perspective, the curtailment of imports looks like an easy solution to the problem of domestic unemployment. Just get people to "buy American" instead of buying imported products, so the argument goes, and domestic output and employment will surely expand.

Congressman Willis Hawley used this argument in 1930. He assured his colleagues that higher tariffs would "bring about the growth and development in this country that has followed every other tariff bill, bringing as it does a new prosperity in which all people, in all sections, will increase their comforts, their enjoyment, and their happiness."[1] Congress responded by passing the Smoot-Hawley Tariff Act of 1930, which raised tariffs to an average of nearly 60 percent, effectively cutting off most imports.

Tariffs designed to expand domestic employment are more likely to fail than to succeed. If a tariff wall does stem the flow of imports, it effectively transfers the unemployment problem to other countries, a phenomenon often referred to as "beggar thy neighbor." The resultant loss of business in other countries leaves them less able to purchase our exports. The imported unemployment also creates intense political pressures for retaliatory action. That's exactly what happened in the 1930s. Other countries erected trade barriers to compensate for the effects of the Smoot-Hawley tariff. World trade subsequently fell from $60 billion in 1928 to a mere $25 billion in 1938. This trade contraction increased the severity of the Great Depression (see World View on next page).

Quotas

Tariffs reduce the flow of imports by raising import prices. The same outcome can be attained more directly by imposing import **quotas,** numerical restrictions on the quantity of a particular good that may be imported. The United States limits the quantity of ice cream imported from Jamaica to 950 gallons a year. Only 1.4 million kilograms of Australian cheddar cheese and no more than 7,730 tons of Haitian sugar can be imported. Textile quotas are imposed on every country that wants to ship textiles to the U.S. market. According to the U.S. Department of State, approximately 12 percent of our imports are subject to import quotas.

quota: A limit on the quantity of a good that may be imported in a given time period.

Comparative Effects

Quotas, like all barriers to trade, reduce world efficiency and invite retaliatory action. Moreover, their impact can be even more damaging than tariffs. To see this, we may compare market outcomes in four different contexts: no trade, free trade, tariff-restricted trade, and quota-restricted trade.

[1] *The New York Times,* June 15, 1930, p. 25.

WORLD VIEW 

"Beggar-Thy-Neighbor" Policies in the 1930s

President Herbert Hoover, ignoring the pleas of 1,028 economists to veto it, signed the Smoot-Hawley Tariff Act on June 17, 1930. It was a hollow celebration. The day before, anticipating the signing, the stock market suffered its worst collapse since November 1929, and the law quickly helped push the Great Depression deeper.

The new tariffs, which by 1932 rose to an all-time high of 59 percent of the average value of imports (today it's 5 percent), were designed to save American jobs by restricting foreign competition. Economists warned that angry nations would retaliate, and they did.

- Spain passed the Wais tariff in July in reaction to U.S. tariffs on grapes, oranges, cork, and onions.
- Switzerland, objecting to new U.S. tariffs on watches, embroideries, and shoes, boycotted American exports.
- Italy retaliated against tariffs on hats and olive oil with high tariffs on U.S. and French automobiles in June 1930.
- Canada reacted to high duties on many food products, logs, and timber by raising tariffs threefold in August 1932.
- Australia, Cuba, France, Mexico, and New Zealand also joined in the tariff wars.

From 1930 to 1931 U.S. imports dropped 29 percent, but U.S. exports fell even more, 33 percent, and continued their collapse to a modern-day low of $2.4 billion in 1933. World trade contracted by similar proportions, spreading unemployment around the globe.

In 1934 the U.S. Congress passed the Reciprocal Trade Agreements Act to empower the president to reduce tariffs by half the 1930 rates in return for like cuts in foreign duties on U.S. goods. The "beggar-thy-neighbor" policy was dead. Since then, the nations of the world have been reducing tariffs and other trade barriers.

Source: World Bank, *World Development Report 1987.* Used with permission by the International Bank for Reconstruction and Development/The World Bank; and *The Wall Street Journal,* April 28, 1989. Copyright 1989 by DOW JONES & COMPANY, INC. Reproduced with permission of DOW JONES & COMPANY, INC. in the format Textbook via Copyright Clearance Center.

Analysis: Tariffs inflict harm on foreign producers. If foreign countries retaliate with tariffs of their own, world trade will shrink and unemployment will increase in all countries.

equilibrium price: The price at which the quantity of a good demanded in a given time period equals the quantity supplied.

From *Herbert At Large* by Herbert Block.*

Analysis: Trade restrictions that protect import-competing industries also raise consumer prices.

* Used by permission of Pantheon Books, a division of Random House, Inc. Also, reprinted with permission of S11/Sterling Lord Literistic, Inc. Copyright by Herbert Block.

No-Trade Equilibrium. Figure 35.4*a* depicts the supply-and-demand relationships that would prevail in an economy that imposed a trade *embargo* on foreign textiles. In this situation, the **equilibrium price** of textiles is completely determined by domestic demand and supply curves. The no-trade equilibrium price is p_1, and the quantity of textiles consumed is q_1.

Free-Trade Equilibrium. Suppose now that the embargo is lifted. The immediate effect of this decision will be a rightward shift of the market supply curve, as foreign supplies are added to domestic supplies (Figure 35.4*b*). If an unlimited quantity of textiles can be bought in world markets at a price of p_2, the new supply curve will look like S_2 (infinitely elastic at p_2). The new supply curve (S_2) intersects the old demand curve (D_1) at a new equilibrium price of p_2 and an expanded consumption of q_2. At this new equilibrium, domestic producers are supplying the quantity q_d while foreign producers are supplying the rest ($q_2 - q_d$). Comparing the new equilibrium to the old one, we see that ***free trade results in reduced prices and increased consumption.***

Domestic textile producers are unhappy, of course, with their foreign competition. In the absence of trade, the domestic producers would sell more output (q_1) and get higher prices (p_1). Once trade is opened up, the willingness of foreign producers to sell unlimited quantities of textiles at the price p_2 puts a lid on domestic prices.

Tariff-Restricted Trade. Figure 35.4*c* illustrates what would happen to prices and sales if the United Textile Producers were successful in persuading the government to impose a tariff. Assume that the tariff raises imported textile prices from p_2 to p_3, making it more difficult for foreign producers to undersell domestic producers. Domestic production expands from q_d to q_1, imports are reduced from $q_2 - q_d$ to $q_3 - q_t$, and the market price of textiles rises. Domestic textile producers are clearly better off, whereas consumers and foreign producers are worse off. In addition, the U.S. Treasury will collect increased tariff revenues.

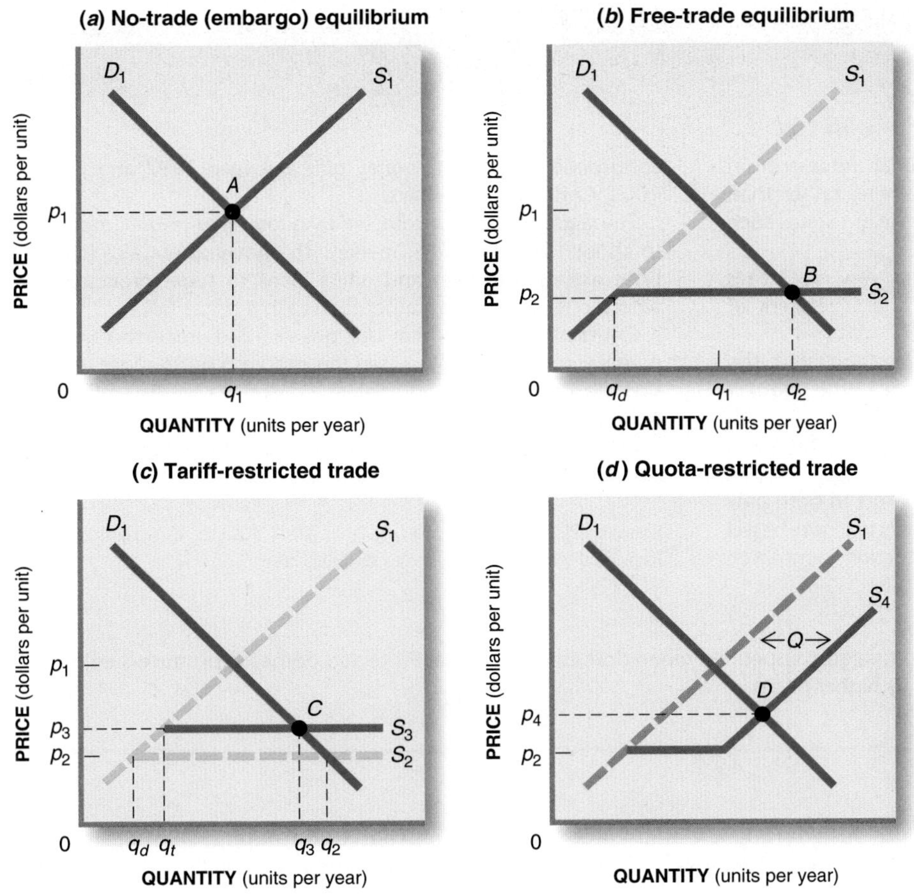

FIGURE 35.4
The Impact of Trade Restrictions

In the *absence of trade,* the domestic price and sales of a good will be determined by domestic supply and demand curves (point *A* in part *a*). Once trade is permitted, the market supply curve will be altered by the availability of imports. With *free trade* and unlimited availability of imports at price p_2, a new market equilibrium will be established at world prices (point *B*).

Tariffs raise domestic prices and reduce the quantity sold (point *C*). *Quotas* put an absolute limit on imported sales and thus give domestic producers a great opportunity to raise the market price (point *D*).

Quota-Restricted Trade. Now consider the impact of a textile *quota.* Suppose we eliminate tariffs but decree that imports can't exceed the quantity *Q*. Because the quantity of imports can never exceed *Q*, the supply curve is effectively shifted to the right by that amount. The new curve S_4 (Figure 35.4*d*) indicates that no imports will occur below the world price p_2 and above that price the quantity *Q* will be imported. Thus, the *domestic* demand curve determines subsequent prices. Foreign producers are precluded from selling greater quantities as prices rise further. This outcome is in marked contrast to that of tariff-restricted trade (Figure 35.4*c*), which at least permits foreign producers to respond to rising prices. Accordingly, ***quotas are a greater threat to competition than tariffs, because quotas preclude additional imports at any price.*** The actual quotas on textile imports raise the prices of shirts, towels, and other textile products by 58 percent. As a result, a $10 shirt ends up costing consumers $15.80. All told, U.S. consumers end up paying an extra $25 billion a year for textile products.

The sugar industry is one of the greatest beneficiaries of quota restrictions. By limiting imports to 15 percent of domestic consumption, sugar quotas keep U.S. prices artificially high (see News on next page). This costs consumers nearly $2 billion a year in higher prices. Candy and soda producers lose sales and profits. Foreign sugar producers (mainly in poor nations) lose sales and income. Who gains? Domestic sugar producers—who, coincidently, are highly concentrated in key electoral states.

webnote

Differing views on the cost of sugar quotas are offered by The Foundation for American Communications at www.facsnet.org and by the Sugar Alliance at www.sugaralliance.org and at www.opensecrets.org

voluntary restraint agreement (VRA): An agreement to reduce the volume of trade in a specific good; a voluntary quota.

Voluntary Restraint Agreements

A slight variant of quotas has been used in recent years. Rather than impose quotas on imports, the U.S. government asks foreign producers to "voluntarily" limit their exports. These so-called **voluntary restraint agreements** have been negotiated with producers in Japan, South Korea, Taiwan, China, the European Union, and other countries. Korea, for example, agreed to reduce its annual shoe exports to the United States from 44 million pairs to 33 million pairs. Taiwan reduced its shoe exports from 156 million pairs to 122 million

IN THE NEWS 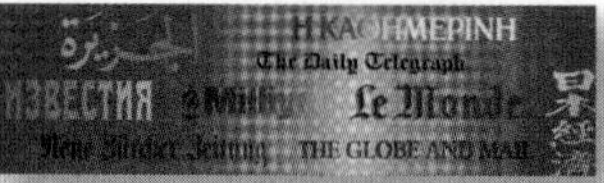 

Some See Bush Sheltering Sugar for Votes

The Bush administration is shielding the sugar industry from competition in a new trade pact with Australia, rather than damage the president's re-election hopes in swing states such as Florida and Michigan, industry groups say. . . .

"It all boils down to electoral politics. It's very raw," says Sarah Thorn, a lobbyist at the Grocery Manufacturers of America. . . .

President Bush edged Al Gore four years ago after the Supreme Court ruled on the vote in Florida, the biggest sugar-producing state. Michigan and Minnesota, home to thousands of sugar beet growers, are considered up for grabs this fall.

The industry is among the largest contributors to both parties. Growers and processors, along with makers of corn-based sweetener, made $25.5 million in political action committee contributions and soft money gifts between 1997 and June 2003, Common Cause says.

The sugar industry is protected by quotas that restrict imports to about 15% of the U.S. market. The government also has a price-support program and offers loans to sugar processors, who can repay in sugar rather than cash if prices fall. . . .

Critics of the program say U.S. growers and processors aren't globally competitive. They say the program hurts sugar users such as candymakers and forces consumers to pay inflated prices. U.S. sugar prices last year were 21.4 cents a pound, nearly three times the world price of 7.5 cents a pound.

—James Cox

Source: *USA Today,* February 11, 2004. USA TODAY. Copyright 2004. Reprinted with permission. www.usatoday.com

Analysis: Import quotas preclude increased foreign competition when domestic prices rise. Protected domestic producers enjoy higher prices and profits while consumers pay higher prices.

pairs per year. In 2005, China agreed to slow its exports of clothing, limiting its sales growth to 8–17 percent a year. For their part, the Japanese agreed to reduce sales of color TV sets in the United States from 2.8 million to 1.75 million per year. In 2006, Mexico agreed to limit its cement exports to the U.S. to 3 million tons a year.

All these voluntary export restraints, as they're often called, represent an informal type of quota. The only difference is that they're negotiated rather than imposed. But these differences are lost on consumers, who end up paying higher prices for these goods. The voluntary limit on Japanese auto exports to the United States alone cost consumers $15.7 billion in only four years.

Nontariff Barriers

Tariffs and quotas are the most visible barriers to trade, but they're only the tip of the iceberg. Indeed, the variety of protectionist measures that have been devised is testimony to the ingenuity of the human mind. At the turn of the century, the Germans were committed to a most-favored-nation policy, a policy of extending equal treatment to all trading partners. The Germans, however, wanted to lower the tariff on cattle imports from Denmark without extending the same break to Switzerland. Such a preferential tariff would have violated the most-favored-nation policy. Accordingly, the Germans created a new and higher tariff on "brown and dappled cows reared at a level of at least 300 meters above sea level and passing at least one month in every summer at an altitude of at least 800 meters." The new tariff was, of course, applied equally to all countries. But Danish cows never climb that high, so they weren't burdened with the new tariff.

With the decline in tariffs over the last 20 years, nontariff barriers have increased. The United States uses product standards, licensing restrictions, restrictive procurement practices, and other nontariff barriers to restrict roughly 15 percent of imports. In 1999–2000, the European Union banned imports of U.S. beef, arguing that the use of hormones on U.S. ranches created a health hazard for European consumers. Although both the U.S. government and the World Trade Organization disputed that claim, the ban was a highly effective nontariff trade barrier. The United States responded by slapping 100 percent tariffs on dozens of European products. In 2001, the U.S. Congress suspended an agreement to give Mexican trucking companies access to U.S. roads. U.S.

WORLD VIEW 

U.S. to Allow Mexican Trucks

Pilot Program Resolves Nafta Issue but Upsets Teamsters, Lawmakers

WASHINGTON—Following a decade of dispute, the U.S. will open its highways to Mexican cargo trucks, in a move that could alter the economics of the domestic trucking industry and is already uniting some American lawmakers, unions and trucking companies to oppose the change.

The Transportation Department on Friday said it is starting a pilot program that could begin as soon as April that will allow 100 Mexican trucking companies unfettered access to U.S. roads. Under the program, both drivers and trucks must first pass certain safety checks designed and overseen by U.S. officials in Mexico. The program could eventually be expanded to include additional Mexican trucking firms.

Open Road

A pilot program will give a number of drivers and trucks from Mexico full access to U.S. roads, so U.S.-bound goods will no longer have to be offloaded to American trucks near the border.

If the trial succeeds, the U.S. trucking industry could change drastically. Mexican drivers are paid one-third to 40% less than their U.S. counterparts, who make an average of about $40,000 a year. An influx of Mexican truckers would be a boon for U.S. businesses with production lines in Mexico, by decreasing costs and delays from the current need to shift U.S.-bound goods at the border to American trucks from Mexican ones. According to the Census Bureau, the U.S. imported $198 billion of goods from Mexico in 2006.

Some trucking companies in the U.S. vowed to block the move, which they say will hurt them.

—Robert Guy Matthews

Source: *The Wall Street Journal*, February 24, 2007, p. A3.

Analysis: Nontariff barriers like extraordinary safety requirements on Mexican trucks limit import competition.

trucking companies and the Teamsters union argued that Mexican trucks were unsafe, caused excessive pollution, and would facilitate illegal immigration. The U.S. government responded with nontariff barriers that kept Mexican competitors off U.S. roads. Six *years* after the "open roads" agreement was to be implemented, only a pilot program was initiated (see World View).

THE ECONOMY TOMORROW 

AN INCREASINGLY GLOBAL MARKET

Proponents of free trade and representatives of special interests that profit from trade protection are in constant conflict. But most of the time the trade-policy deck seems stacked in favor of the special interests. Because the interests of import-competing firms and workers are highly concentrated, they're quick to mobilize politically. By contrast, the benefits of freer trade are less direct and spread over millions of consumers. As a consequence, the beneficiaries of freer trade are less likely to monitor trade policy—much less lobby actively to change it. Hence, the political odds favor the spread of trade barriers.

Multilateral Trade Pacts. Despite these odds, the long-term trend is toward *lowering* trade barriers, thereby increasing global competition. Two forces encourage this trend. The principal barrier to protectionist policies is worldwide recognition of the gains from freer trade. Since world nations now understand that trade barriers are ultimately self-defeating, they're more willing to rise above the din of protectionist cries and dismantle trade barriers. They diffuse political opposition by creating across-the-board trade pacts that seem to spread the pain (and gain) from freer trade across a broad swath of industries. Such pacts also incorporate multiyear timetables that give affected industries time to adjust.

Trade liberalization has also been encouraged by firms that *export* products or use imported inputs in their own production. Tariffs on imported steel raise product costs for U.S.-based auto producers and construction companies. In 2007 the European Union eliminated a tariff on frozen Chinese strawberries, largely due to complaints from EU yogurt and jam producers.

Global Pacts: GATT and WTO. The granddaddy of the multilateral, multiyear free-trade pacts was the 1947 *General Agreement on Tariffs and Trade (GATT).* Twenty-three nations pledged to reduce trade barriers and give all GATT nations equal access to their domestic markets.

Since the first GATT pact, seven more "rounds" of negotiations have expanded the scope of GATT: 117 nations signed the 1994 pact. As a result of these GATT pacts, average tariff rates in developed countries have fallen from 40 percent in 1948 to less than 4 percent today.

WTO. The 1994 GATT pact also created the *World Trade Organization (WTO)* to enforce free-trade rules. If a nation feels its exports are being unfairly excluded from another country's market, it can file a complaint with the WTO. This is exactly what the United States did when the EU banned U.S. beef imports. The WTO ruled in favor of the United States. When the EU failed to lift its import ban, the WTO authorized the United States to impose retaliatory tariffs on European exports.

The EU turned the tables on the United States in 2003. It complained to the WTO that U.S. tariffs on steel violated trade rules. The WTO agreed and gave the EU permission to impose retaliatory tariffs on $2.2 billion of U.S. exports. That prompted the Bush administration to scale back the tariffs in December 2003.

In effect, the WTO is now the world's trade police force. It is empowered to cite nations that violate trade agreements and even to impose remedial action when violations persist. Why do sovereign nations give the WTO such power? Because they are all convinced that free trade is the surest route to GDP growth.

WTO Protests. Although freer trade clearly boosts economic growth, some people say that it does more harm than good. Environmentalists question the very desirability of continued economic growth. They worry about the depletion of resources, congestion and pollution, and the social friction that growth often promotes. Labor organizations worry that global competition will depress wages and working conditions. And many Third World nations are concerned about playing by trade rules that always seem to benefit rich nations (e.g., copyright protection, import protection, farm subsidies).

Despite some tumultuous street protests (e.g., Seattle in 1999, Hong Kong in 2005), WTO members continue the difficult process of dismantling trade barriers. The latest round of negotiations began in Doha, Qatar, in 2001. The key issue in the "Doha Round" has been farm subsidies in rich nations. Poor nations protest that farm subsidies in the United States and Europe not only limit their exports but also lower global farm prices (hurting farmers in developing nations). After 6 *years* of negotiations, the industrial nations had still not agreed to reduce those farm subsidies significantly.

Regional Pacts. Because worldwide trade pacts are so complex, many nations have also pursued *regional* free-trade agreements.

NAFTA. In December 1992, the United States, Canada, and Mexico signed the *North American Free Trade Agreement (NAFTA),* a 1,000-page document covering more than 9,000 products. The ultimate goal of NAFTA is to eliminate all trade barriers between these three countries. At the time of signing, intraregional tariffs averaged 11 percent in Mexico, 5 percent in Canada, and 4 percent in the United States. NAFTA requires that all tariffs between the three countries be eliminated. The pact also requires the elimination of specific nontariff barriers.

The NAFTA-initiated reduction in trade barriers substantially increased trade flows between Mexico, Canada, and the United States. It also prompted a wave of foreign investment in Mexico, where both cheap labor and NAFTA access were available. Overall,

IN THE NEWS

NAFTA Reallocates Labor: Comparative Advantage at Work

More Jobs in These Industries		but . . .	Few Jobs in These Industries	
Agriculture	+10,600		Construction	−12,800
Metal products	+6,100		Medicine	−6,000
Electrical appliances	+5,200		Apparel	−5,900
Business services	+5,000		Lumber	−1,200
Motor vehicles	+5,000		Furniture	−400

Source: Congressional Budget Office.

The lowering of trade barriers between Mexico and the United States is changing the mix of output in both countries. New export opportunities create jobs in some industries while increased imports eliminate jobs in other industries. (Estimated gains and losses are during the first five years of NAFTA.)

Analysis: The specialization encouraged by free trade creates new jobs in export but reduces employment in import-competing industries. In the process, total world output increases.

NAFTA accelerated economic growth and reduced inflationary pressures in all three nations. Some industries (like construction and apparel) suffered from the freer trade, but others (like trucking, farming, and finance) reaped huge gains (see News).

webnote

To see how detailed a trade pact can be, access the NAFTA pact at www.nafta-sec-alena.org.

CAFTA. The success of NAFTA prompted a similar 2005 agreement between the United States and Central American nations. The Central American Free Trade Agreement (CAFTA) aims to standardize trade and investment policies in CAFTA nations, while eliminating tariffs on thousands of products.

European Union. The *European Union* is another regional pact, but one that virtually eliminates national boundaries among 27 countries. The EU not only eliminates trade barriers but also enhances full intercountry mobility of workers and capital. In effect, Europe has become one large, unified market.

As trade barriers continue to fall around the world, the global marketplace is likely to become more like an open bazaar as well. The resulting increase in competition should spur efficiency and growth in the economy tomorrow.

SUMMARY

- International trade permits each country to specialize in areas of relative efficiency, increasing world output. For each country, the gains from trade are reflected in consumption possibilities that exceed production possibilities. LO2
- One way to determine where comparative advantage lies is to compare the quantity of good A that must be given up in order to get a given quantity of good B from domestic production. If the same quantity of B can be obtained for less A by engaging in world trade, we have a comparative advantage in the production of good A. Comparative advantage rests on a comparison of relative opportunity costs. LO1
- The terms of trade—the rate at which goods are exchanged—are subject to the forces of international supply and demand. The terms of trade will lie somewhere between the opportunity costs of the trading partners. The terms of trade determine how the gains from trade are shared. LO2
- Resistance to trade emanates from workers and firms that must compete with imports. Even though the country as a whole stands to benefit from trade, these individuals and companies may lose jobs and incomes in the process. LO3

- Trade barriers take many forms. Embargoes are outright prohibitions against import or export of particular goods. Quotas limit the quantity of a good imported or exported. Tariffs discourage imports by making them more expensive. Other nontariff barriers make trade too costly or time-consuming. LO3
- The World Trade Organization (WTO) seeks to reduce worldwide trade barriers and enforce trade rules. Regional accords such as the European Union (EU), the North American Free Trade Agreement (NAFTA), and the Central American Free Trade Agreement (CAFTA) pursue similar objectives among fewer countries. LO3

Key Terms

imports
exports
trade deficit
trade surplus
production possibilities
closed economy
consumption possibilities
open economy
comparative advantage
opportunity cost
absolute advantage
terms of trade
dumping
embargo
tariff
quota
equilibrium price
voluntary restraint agreement (VRA)

Questions for Discussion

1. Suppose a lawyer can type faster than any secretary. Should the lawyer do her own typing? Can you demonstrate the validity of your answer? LO1
2. What would be the effects of a law requiring bilateral trade balances? LO2
3. If a nation exported much of its output but imported little, would it be better or worse off? How about the reverse, that is, exporting little but importing a lot? LO2
4. How does international trade restrain the price behavior of domestic firms? LO3
5. Suppose we refused to sell goods to any country that reduced or halted its exports to us. Who would benefit and who would lose from such retaliation? Can you suggest alternative ways to ensure import supplies? LO2
6. Domestic producers often base their claim for import protection on the fact that workers in country X are paid substandard wages. Is this a valid argument for protection? LO1
7. On the basis of News on page 713, how do U.S. furniture manufacturers feel about NAFTA? How about farmers? LO3
8. What is the "bright future" referred to in the News on page 703? How do wine imports affect it? LO3
9. Who pays for sugar quotas? (See News, page 710.) How could the quotas be eliminated? LO3
10. Which consumers benefited from the dumping cases mentioned in the World View on page 705? LO3

problems The Student Problem Set at the back of this book contains numerical and graphing problems for this chapter.

web activities to accompany this chapter can be found on the Online Learning Center:
http://www.mhhe.com/economics/schiller11e

36 International Finance

LEARNING OBJECTIVES

After reading this chapter, you should know:

LO1. The sources of foreign-exchange demand and supply.

LO2. How exchange rates are established.

LO3. How changes in exchange rates affect prices, output, and trade flows.

U.S. textile, furniture, and shrimp producers want China to increase the value of the yuan. They say China's undervalued currency makes Chinese exports too cheap, undercutting American firms. On the other hand, Wal-Mart thinks a cheap yuan is a good thing, as it keeps prices low for the $16 *billion* of toys, tools, linens, and other goods it buys from China each year. Those low import prices help Wal-Mart keep its prices low and sales volume high.

This chapter examines how currency values affect trade patterns and ultimately the core questions of WHAT, HOW, and FOR WHOM to produce. We focus on the following questions:

- **What determines the value of one country's money as compared to the value of another's?**
- **What causes the international value of currencies to change?**
- **Should governments intervene to limit currency fluctuations?**

EXCHANGE RATES: THE GLOBAL LINK

As we saw in Chapter 35, the United States exports and imports a staggering volume of goods and services. Although we trade with nearly 200 nations around the world, we seldom give much thought to where imports come from and much less to how we acquire them. Most of the time, all we want to know is which products are available and at what price.

Suppose you want to buy a Magnavox DVD player. You don't have to know that Magnavox players are produced by the Dutch company Philips Electronics. And you certainly don't have to fly to the Netherlands to pick it up. All you have to do is drive to the nearest electronics store; or you can just "click and buy" at the Internet's virtual mall.

But you may wonder how the purchase of an imported product was so simple. Dutch companies sell their products in euros, the currency of Europe. But you purchase the DVD player in dollars. How is such an exchange possible?

There's a chain of distribution between your dollar purchase in the United States and the euro-denominated sale in the Netherlands. Somewhere along that chain someone has to convert your dollars into euros. The critical question for everybody concerned is how many euros we can get for our dollars—that is, what the **exchange rate** is. If we can get two euros for every dollar, the exchange rate is 2 euros = 1 dollar. Alternatively, we could note that the price of a euro is 50 U.S. cents when the exchange rate is 2 to 1. Thus, ***an exchange rate is the price of one currency in terms of another.***

exchange rate: The price of one country's currency expressed in terms of another's; the domestic price of a foreign currency.

FOREIGN-EXCHANGE MARKETS

Most exchange rates are determined in foreign-exchange markets. Stop thinking of money as some sort of magical substance, and instead view it as a useful commodity that facilitates market exchanges. From that perspective, an exchange rate—the price of money—is subject to the same influences that determine all market prices: demand and supply.

The Demand for Dollars

When Toshiba Corporation bought Westinghouse Electric Co. in 2006, it paid $5.4 billion. When the Sony Corporation bought Columbia Pictures, it also needed dollars—over 3 billion of them! In both cases, the objective of the foreign investor was to acquire an American business. To attain their objectives, however, the buyers first had to buy *dollars.* The Japanese buyers had to exchange their own currency for American dollars.

Canadian tourists also need American dollars. Few American restaurants or hotels accept Canadian currency as payment for goods and services; they want to be paid in U.S. dollars. Accordingly, Canadian tourists must buy American dollars if they want to see the United States.

Europeans love iPods. The Apple Corporation, however, wants to be paid in U.S. dollars. Hence, European consumers must exchange their euros for U.S. dollars if they want an iPod. Individual consumers can spend euros at their local electronics store. When they do so, however, they're initiating a series of market transactions that will end when Apple Corporation gets paid in U.S. dollars. In this case, some intermediary exchanges the European currency for American dollars.

Some foreign investors also buy U.S. dollars for speculative purposes. When the ruble collapsed, Russians feared that the value of the ruble would drop further and preferred to hold U.S. dollars. Barclay's Bank also speculates in dollars on occasions when it fears that the value of the British pound will drop.

All these motivations give rise to a demand for U.S. dollars. Specifically, ***the market demand for U.S. dollars originates in***

- ***Foreign demand for American exports*** (including tourism).
- ***Foreign demand for American investments.***
- ***Speculation.***

Governments may also create a demand for dollars through currency *swaps* and other activities.

The Supply of Dollars

The *supply* of dollars arises from similar sources. On the supply side, however, it's Americans who initiate most of the exchanges. Suppose you take a trip to Mexico. You'll need to buy Mexican pesos at some point. When you do, you'll be offering to *buy* pesos by offering to *sell* dollars. In other words, ***the* demand *for foreign currency represents a* supply *of U.S. dollars.***

When Americans buy BMW cars, they also supply U.S. dollars. American consumers pay for their BMWs in dollars. Somewhere down the road, however, those dollars will be exchanged for European euros. At that exchange, dollars are being *supplied* and euros *demanded.*

American corporations demand foreign exchange too. General Motors builds cars in Germany, Coca-Cola produces Coke in China, Exxon produces and refines oil all over the world. In nearly every such case, the U.S. firm must first build or buy some plant and equipment, using another country's factors of production. This activity requires foreign currency and thus becomes another component of our demand for foreign currency.

We may summarize these market activities by noting that ***the supply of dollars originates in***

- ***American demand for imports*** (including tourism).
- ***American investments in foreign countries.***
- ***Speculation.***

As on the demand side, government intervention can also contribute to the supply of dollars.

The Value of the Dollar

Whether American consumers will choose to buy an imported BMW depends partly on what the car costs. The price tag isn't always apparent in international transactions. Remember that the German BMW producer and workers want to be paid in their own currency. Hence, the *dollar* price of an imported BMW depends on two factors: (1) the German price of a BMW and (2) the *exchange rate* between U.S. dollars and euros. Specifically, the U.S. price of a BMW is

$$\text{Dollar price of BMW} = \text{euro price of BMW} \times \text{dollar price of euro}$$

Suppose the BMW company is prepared to sell a German-built BMW for 100,000 euros and that the current exchange rate is 2 euros = \$1. At these rates, a BMW will cost you

$$\text{Dollar price of BMW} = 100{,}000 \text{ euros} \times \frac{\$1}{2 \text{ euros}}$$

$$= \$50{,}000$$

If you're willing to pay this much for a shiny new German-built BMW, you may do so at current exchange rates.

Now suppose the exchange rate changes from 2 euros = \$1 to 1 euro = \$1. ***A higher dollar price for euros will raise the dollar costs of European goods.*** In this case, the dollar price of a euro increases from \$0.50 to \$1. At this new exchange rate, the BMW plant in Germany is still willing to sell BMWs at 100,000 euros apiece. And German consumers continue to buy BMWs at that price. But this constant euro price now translates into a higher *dollar* price. Thus a BMW now costs you \$100,000.

As the dollar price of a BMW rises, the number of BMWs sold in the United States will decline. As BMW sales decline, the quantity of euros demanded may decline as well. Thus, the quantity of foreign currency demanded declines when the exchange rate rises because foreign goods become more expensive and imports decline.[1] When the dollar price of European currencies actually increased in 1992, BMW decided to start producing cars in South Carolina. A year later Mercedes-Benz decided to produce cars in the United States as well.

webnote

What's a euro? Read more about the European currency at www.europe-euro.com

[1]The extent to which imports decline as the cost of foreign currency rises depends on the *price elasticity of demand.*

FIGURE 36.1
The Foreign-Exchange Market

The foreign-exchange market operates like other markets. In this case, the "good" bought and sold is dollars (foreign exchange). The price and quantity of dollars actually exchanged are determined by the intersection of market supply and demand.

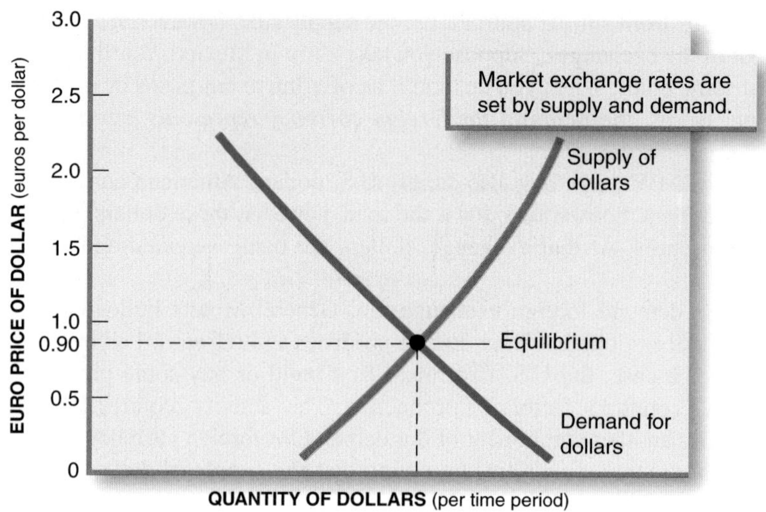

Sales of American-made BMWs and Mercedes no longer depend on the exchange rate of the U.S. dollars.

The Supply Curve. These market responses suggest that the supply of dollars is upward-sloping. If the value of the dollar rises, Americans will be able to buy more euros. As a result, the dollar price of imported BMWs will decline. American consumers will respond by demanding more imports, thereby supplying a larger quantity of dollars. The supply curve in Figure 36.1 shows how the quantity of dollars supplied rises as the value of the dollar increases.

The Demand Curve. The demand for dollars can be explained in similar terms. Remember that the demand for dollars arises from the foreign demand for U.S. exports and investments. If the exchange rate moves from 2 euros = \$1 to 1 euro = \$1, the euro price of dollars falls. As dollars become cheaper for Germans, all American exports effectively fall in price. Germans will buy more American products (including trips to Disney World) and therefore demand a greater quantity of dollars. In addition, foreign investors will perceive in a cheaper dollar the opportunity to buy U.S. stocks, businesses, and property at fire-sale prices. Accordingly, they join foreign consumers in demanding more dollars. Not all these behavioral responses will occur overnight, but they're reasonably predictable over a brief period of time.

Equilibrium

equilibrium price: The price at which the quantity of a good demanded in a given time period equals the quantity supplied.

Given market demand and supply curves, we can predict the **equilibrium price** of any commodity, that is, the price at which the quantity demanded will equal the quantity supplied. This occurs in Figure 36.1 where the two curves cross. At that equilibrium, the value of the dollar (the exchange rate) is established. In this case, the euro price of the dollar turns out to be 0.90.

The value of the dollar can also be expressed in terms of other currencies. The following World View displays a sampling of dollar exchange rates in March 2007. (Notice how many Indonesian rupiah you could buy for \$1.) The *average* value of the dollar is a weighted mean of the exchange rates between the U.S. dollar and all these currencies. The value of the dollar is "high" when its foreign-exchange price is above recent levels, "low" when it is below recent averages.

The Balance of Payments

The equilibrium depicted in Figure 36.1 determines not only the *price* of the dollar but also a specific *quantity* of international transactions. Those transactions include the exports, imports, international investments, and other sources of dollar supply and

WORLD VIEW 

Foreign-Exchange Rates

The foreign-exchange mid-range rates below show (a) how many U.S. dollars are needed to buy one unit of foreign currency and (b) how many units of foreign currency are needed to buy one U.S. dollar.

Country	(a) U.S. Dollar per Unit (dollar price of foreign currency)	(b) Currency per U.S. Dollar (foreign price of U.S. dollar)
Brazil (real)	0.4852	2.0610
Britain (pound)	1.9621	0.5096
Canada (dollar)	0.8614	1.1609
China (yuan)	0.1293	7.7325
Indonesia (rupiah)	0.0001	9107.00
Japan (yen)	0.0085	118.064
Mexico (peso)	0.0907	11.0217
Russia (ruble)	0.0384	26.055
Euroland (euro)	1.3289	0.7525

Source: March 23, 2007, data from Federal Reserve Board of Governors.

Analysis: The exchange rates between currencies are determined by supply and demand in foreign-exchange markets. The rates reported here represent the equilibrium exchange rates on a particular day.

demand. A summary of all those international money flows is contained in the **balance of payments**—an accounting statement of all international money flows in a given period of time.

balance of payments: A summary record of a country's international economic transactions in a given period of time.

Trade Balance. Table 36.1 depicts the U.S. balance of payments for 2006. Notice first how the millions of separate transactions are classified into a few summary measures. The trade balance is the difference between exports and imports of goods (merchandise) and services. In 2006, the United States imported over $2.2 trillion of goods and services but exported less than $1.5 trillion. This created a **trade deficit** of $763 billion. That trade deficit represents a net outflow of dollars to the rest of the world.

trade deficit: The amount by which the value of imports exceeds the value of exports in a given time period.

$$\text{Trade balance} = \text{exports} - \text{imports}$$

The excess supply of dollars created by the trade gap widened further by other net outflows. U.S. government grants to foreign nations (line 7 in Table 36.1) contributed $28 billion to the net *supply* of dollars.

Current-Account Balance. The current-account balance is a subtotal in Table 36.1. It includes the merchandise, services, and investment balances as well as government grants and private transfers such as wages sent home by foreign citizens working in the United States.

$$\begin{matrix}\text{Current-account} \\ \text{balance}\end{matrix} = \begin{matrix}\text{trade} \\ \text{balance}\end{matrix} + \begin{matrix}\text{unilateral} \\ \text{transfers}\end{matrix}$$

The current-account balance is the most comprehensive summary of our trade relations. As indicated in Table 36.1, the United States had a current-account deficit of $856 billion in 2006.

TABLE 36.1
The U.S. Balance of Payments

The balance of payments is a summary statement of a country's international transactions. The major components of that activity are the trade balance (merchandise exports minus merchandise imports), the current-account balance (trade, services, and transfers), and the capital-account balance. The net total of these balances must equal zero, since the quantity of dollars paid must equal the quantity received.

Item	Amount ($ billions)
1. Merchandise exports	$1,035
2. Merchandise imports	(1,880)
3. Service exports	431
4. Service imports	(349)
Trade balance (items 1–4)	−763
5. Income from U.S. overseas investments	621
6. Income outflow for foreign-owned U.S. investments	(630)
7. Net U.S. government grants	(28)
8. Net private transfers and pensions	(56)
Current-account balance (items 1–8)	−856
9. U.S. capital inflow	1,464
10. U.S. capital outflow	(1,043)
11. Increase in U.S. official reserves	2
12. Increase in foreign official assets in U.S.	300
Capital-account balance (items 9–12)	723
13. Statistical discrepancy	133
Net balance (items 1–13)	0

Source: U.S. Department of Commerce (2006 data).

webnote

The latest statistics on the balance of payments are available from the Bureau of Economic Analysis at www.bea.gov

Capital-Account Balance. The current-account deficit is offset by the capital-account surplus. The capital-account balance takes into consideration assets bought and sold across international borders; that is,

$$\text{Capital-account balance} = \text{foreign purchases of U.S. assets} - \text{U.S. purchases of foreign assets}$$

As Table 36.1 shows, foreign consumers demanded nearly \$1.5 trillion in 2006 to buy farms and factories as well as U.S. bonds, stocks, and other investments (item 9). This exceeded the flow of U.S. dollars going overseas to purchase foreign assets (item 10). In addition, the United States and foreign governments bought and sold dollars, creating an additional outflow of dollars (items 11 and 12).

The net capital inflows were essential in financing the U.S. trade deficit (negative trade balance). As in any market, the number of dollars demanded must equal the number of dollars supplied. Thus, ***the capital-account surplus must equal the current-account deficit.*** In other words, there can't be any dollars left lying around unaccounted for. Item 13 in Table 36.1 reminds us that our accounting system isn't perfect—that we can't identify every transaction. Nevertheless, all the accounts must eventually "balance out":

$$\text{Net balance of payments} = \text{current-account balance} + \text{capital-account balance} = 0$$

That's the character of a market *equilibrium:* The quantity of dollars demanded equals the quantity of dollars supplied.

MARKET DYNAMICS

The interesting thing about markets isn't their character in equilibrium but the fact that prices and quantities are always changing in response to shifts in demand and supply. The U.S. demand for BMWs shifted overnight when Japan introduced a new line of sleek, competitively priced cars (e.g., Lexus). The reduced demand for BMWs shifted the supply

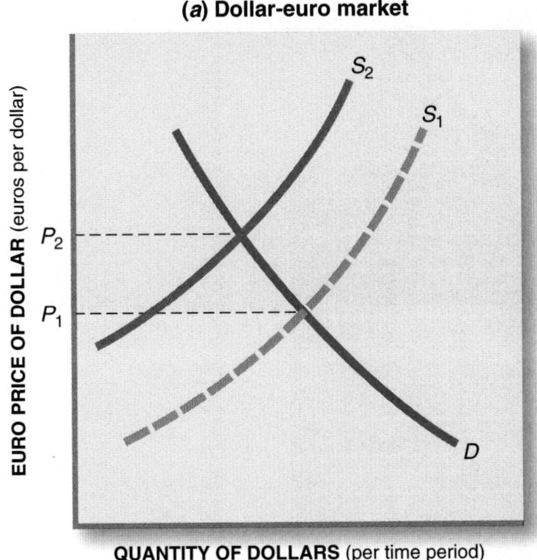

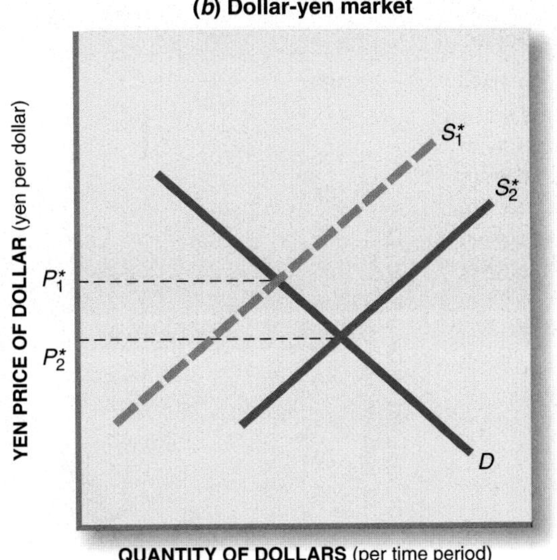

FIGURE 36.2
Shifts in Foreign-Exchange Markets

When the Japanese introduced luxury autos into the United States, the American demand for German cars fell. As a consequence, the supply of dollars in the dollar-euro market (part *a*) shifted to the left and the euro value of the dollar rose. At the same time, the increased American demand for Japanese cars shifted the dollar supply curve in the yen market (part *b*) to the right, reducing the yen price of the dollar.

of dollars leftward. That supply shift raised the value of the dollar vis-à-vis the euro, as illustrated in Figure 36.2. (It also increased the demand for Japanese yen, causing the yen value of the dollar to *fall.*)

Depreciation and Appreciation

Exchange-rate changes have their own terminology. **Depreciation** of a currency occurs when one currency becomes cheaper in terms of another currency. In our earlier discussion of exchange rates, for example, we assumed that the exchange rate between euros and dollars changed from 2 euros = $1 to 1 euro = $1, making the euro price of a dollar cheaper. In this case, the dollar *depreciated* with respect to the euro.

depreciation (currency): A fall in the price of one currency relative to another.

The other side of depreciation is **appreciation,** an increase in value of one currency as expressed in another country's currency. ***Whenever one currency depreciates, another currency must appreciate.*** When the exchange rate changed from 2 euros = $1 to 1 euro = $1, not only did the euro price of a dollar fall, but also the dollar price of a euro rose. Hence, the euro appreciated as the dollar depreciated.

appreciation: A rise in the price of one currency relative to another.

Figure 36.3 illustrates actual changes in the exchange rate of the U.S. dollar since 1980. The trade-adjusted value of the U.S. dollar is the (weighted) average of all exchange rates for the dollar. Between 1980 and 1985, the U.S. dollar appreciated over 80 percent. This appreciation greatly reduced the price of imports and thus increased their quantity. At the same time, the dollar appreciation raised the foreign price of U.S. exports and so reduced their volume. U.S. farmers, aircraft manufacturers, and tourist services suffered huge sales losses. The trade deficit ballooned.

How much are 100 Japanese yen worth in U.S. dollars? Find out at the currency converter at www.oanda.com/site/cc_index.shtml

The value of the dollar reversed course after 1985. This brief dollar depreciation set in motion forces that reduced the trade deficit in the late 1980s. Then the dollar started appreciating again, slowing export growth and increasing imports throughout the 1990s. After a long steep appreciation, the dollar started losing value in 2003. This was good for U.S. exporters, but bad for U.S. tourists and foreign producers (see World View).

FIGURE 36.3
Changing Values of U.S. Dollar

Since 1973, exchange rates have been flexible. As a result, the value of the U.S. dollar has fluctuated with international differences in inflation, interest rates, and economic growth. U.S. economic stability has given the U.S. dollar increasing value over time.

Source: Federal Reserve Board of Governers

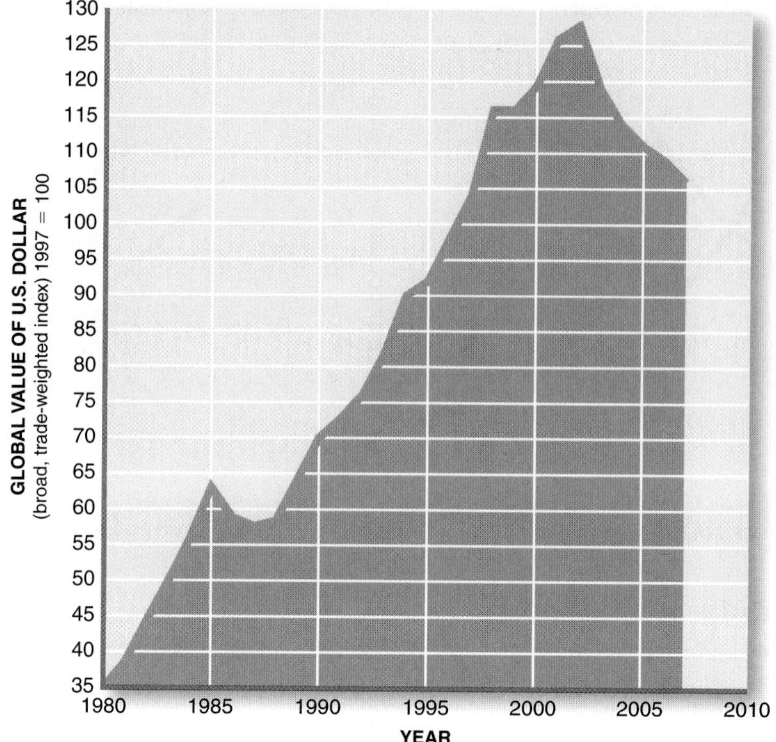

Weak Dollar Helps U.S. Firms

The dollar's precipitous decline against European currencies has brought overseas customers to Al Lubrano's small Rhode Island manufacturing firm that he hasn't heard from in five years.

Gerry Letendre's manufacturing plant in New Hampshire just hired five employees to keep up with growing European demand, two and a half years after Letendre laid off a quarter of his work force.

The dollar's slide has made U.S. goods far cheaper for European consumers, and European exports considerably more expensive here. Letendre's Diamond Casting and Machine Co. in Hollis, N.H., has already boosted shipments of its circuit board printing equipment and industrial valves to Europe by 30 percent. Lubrano, president of Technical Materials Inc., in Lincoln, R.I., said his export business should jump as much as 25 percent this year.

"On balance, the weak dollar has been tremendous for us," Lubrano said.

—Jonathan Weisman

Source: *The Washington Post,* January 26, 2004. **© 2004 *The Washington Post.* Excerpted with permission.**

Dollar's Fall Puts Big Crimp in European Tourism

ROME—As the euro continues to strengthen against the battered U.S. dollar, tourists, businesses and Americans living abroad complain that Europe is pricing itself out of the market.

"It has become so expensive it almost makes me ill," says Nancy Oliveira, 55, an American living in Rome on what she says was once a "comfortable fixed income." . . .

The Italian National Tourist office reports a 15% decline in the number of Americans visiting from 2000 to 2002. . . .

Companies that rely on tourists and visitors estimate business is down 20% to 30%. . . .

Sales at Florence Moon, a leather store in Rome that caters primarily to Americans, are down 50%, says Farshad Shahabadi, whose family owns the store. "If it's bad for us, then it must be bad for everyone else, too," Shahabadi says.

—Ellen Hale

Source: *USA Today,* February 20, 2004. USA TODAY. Copyright 2004. Reprinted with permission. www.usatoday.com

Analysis: Depreciation of a nation's currency is good for that nation's exporters but bad for that nation's importers (including its tourists).

Market Forces

Exchange rates change for the same reasons that any market price changes: The underlying supply or demand (or both) has shifted. Among the more important sources of such shifts are

- ***Relative income changes.*** If incomes are increasing faster in country A than in country B, consumers in A will tend to spend more, thus increasing the demand for B's exports and currency. B's currency will appreciate.
- ***Relative price changes.*** If domestic prices are rising rapidly in country A, consumers will seek out lower-priced imports. The demand for B's exports and currency will increase. B's currency will appreciate.
- ***Changes in product availability.*** If country A experiences a disastrous wheat crop failure, it will have to increase its food imports. B's currency will appreciate.
- ***Relative interest rate changes.*** If interest rates rise in country A, people in country B will want to move their deposits to A. Demand for A's currency will rise and it will appreciate.
- ***Speculation.*** If speculators anticipate an increase in the price of A's currency, for the preceding reasons or any other, they'll begin buying it, thus pushing its price up. A's currency will appreciate.

All these various changes are taking place every minute of every day, thus keeping **foreign-exchange markets** active. On an average day, over *$1 trillion* of foreign exchange is bought and sold in the market. Significant changes occur in currency values, however, only when several of these forces move in the same direction at the same time. This is what caused the Asian crisis of 1997–98.

foreign-exchange markets: Places where foreign currencies are bought and sold.

The Asian Crisis of 1997–98

In July 1997, the Thai government decided the baht was overvalued and let market forces find a new equilibrium. Within days, the dollar prices of the baht plunged 25 percent. This sharp decline in the value of the Thai baht simultaneously increased the Thai price of the U.S. dollar. As a consequence, Thais could no longer afford to buy as many American products.

The devaluation of the baht had a domino effect on other Asian currencies. The plunge in the baht shook confidence in the Malaysian ringget, the Indonesian rupiah, and even the Korean won. People wanted to hold "hard" currencies like the U.S. dollar. As people rushed to buy U.S. dollars with their local currencies, the value of those currencies plunged. At one point the Indonesian rupiah had lost 80 percent of its dollar value, making U.S. exports five times more expensive for Indonesians. As a result, Indonesians could no longer afford to buy imported rice, machinery, cars, or pork. Indonesian students attending U.S. colleges could no longer afford to pay tuition. The sudden surge in prices and scarcity of goods led to street demonstrations and a change in government. Similar problems erupted throughout Southeast Asia.

webnote

Check out the latest exchange rates for the euro and the baht at www.x-rates.com

The "Asian contagion" unfortunately wasn't confined to that area of the world. Hog farmers in the United States saw foreign demand for their pork evaporate. Koreans stopped taking vacations in Hawaii. Thai Airways canceled orders for Boeing jets. And Japanese consumers bought fewer Washington state apples and California oranges. This loss of export markets slowed economic growth in the United States, Europe, Japan, and other nations.

RESISTANCE TO EXCHANGE-RATE CHANGES

Given the scope and depth of the Asian crisis of 1997–98, it's easy to understand why people crave *stable* exchange rates. The resistance to exchange-rate fluctuations originates in various micro- and macroeconomic interests.

Micro Interests

The microeconomic resistance to changes in the value of the dollar arises from two concerns. First, people who trade or invest in world markets want a solid basis for forecasting future costs, prices, and profits. Forecasts are always uncertain, but they're even less dependable when the value of money is subject to change. An American firm that invests $2 million in a ski factory in Sweden expects not only to make a profit on the production there but also to return that profit to the United States. If the Swedish krona depreciates sharply in the interim, however, the profits amassed in Sweden may dwindle to a mere

WORLD VIEW 

Nobel Prize Was Nobler in October

STOCKHOLM—Winners of the four Nobel science awards said yesterday that the honor is more important than the money, so it does not matter much that each award has lost $242,000 in value since October.

"If we had been more intelligent, we would have done some hedging," said Gary S. Becker, 61, a University of Chicago professor and a Nobel economics laureate. Sweden's decision last month to let the krona float caused the prizes' value to drop from $1.2 million each when announced in October to $958,000 when King Carl XVI Gustaf presents them Thursday.

The recipients are Becker; American Rudolph A. Marcus, the chemistry laureate; Frenchman Georges Charpak, the physics laureate; and medicine prize winners Edmond Fischer and Edwin Krebs of the University of Washington in Seattle.

—Associated Press

Source: *Boston Globe,* December 8, 1992. Reprinted with permission of The Associated Press. www.ap.org

Analysis: Currency depreciation reduces the external value of domestic income and assets. The dollar value of the Nobel Prize fell when the Swedish krona depreciated.

trickle, or even a loss, when the kronor are exchanged back into dollars. Even the Nobel Prize loses a bit of its luster when the krona depreciates (see World View). From this view, the uncertainty associated with fluctuating exchange rates is an unwanted burden.

Even when the direction of an exchange rate move is certain, those who stand to lose from the change are prone to resist. ***A change in the price of a country's money automatically alters the price of all its exports and imports.*** When the Russian ruble and Japanese yen depreciated in 2000–2001, for example, the dollar price of Russian and Japanese steel declined as well. This prompted U.S. steelmakers to accuse Russia and Japan of "dumping" steel. Steel companies and unions appealed to Washington to protect their sales and jobs.

Even in the country whose currency becomes cheaper, there'll be opposition to exchange-rate movements. When the U.S. dollar appreciates, Americans buy more foreign products. This increased U.S. demand for imports may drive up prices in other countries. In addition, foreign firms may take advantage of the reduced American competition by raising their prices. In either case, some inflation will result. The consumer's insistence that the government "do something" about rising prices may turn into a political force for "correcting" foreign-exchange rates.

Macro Interests

Any microeconomic problem that becomes widespread enough can turn into a macroeconomic problem. The huge U.S. trade deficits of the 1980s effectively exported jobs to foreign nations. Although the U.S. economy expanded rapidly in 1983–85, the unemployment rate stayed high, partly because American consumers were spending more of their income on imports. Yet fear of renewed inflation precluded more stimulative fiscal and monetary policies.

The U.S. trade deficits of the 1980s were offset by huge capital-account surpluses. Foreign investors sought to participate in the U.S. economic expansion by buying land, plant, and equipment and by lending money in U.S. financial markets. These capital inflows complicated monetary policy, however, and greatly increased U.S. foreign debt and interest costs.

U.S. a Net Debtor

The inflow of foreign investment also raised anxieties about "selling off" America. As Japanese and other foreign investors increased their purchases of farmland, factories, and real estate (e.g., Rockefeller Center), many Americans worried that foreign investors were taking control of the U.S. economy.

Fueling these fears was the dramatic change in America's international financial position. From 1914 to 1984, the United States had been a net creditor in the world economy.

We owned more assets abroad than foreign investors owned in the United States. Our financial position changed in 1985. Continuing trade deficits and offsetting capital inflows transformed the United States into a net debtor in that year. Since then, foreigners have owned more U.S. assets than Americans own of foreign assets.

America's new debtor status can complicate domestic policy. A sudden flight from U.S. assets could severely weaken the dollar and disrupt the domestic economy. To prevent that from occurring, policymakers must consider the impact of their decisions on foreign investors. This may necessitate difficult policy choices.

There's a silver lining to this cloud, however. The inflow of foreign investment is a reflection of confidence in the U.S. economy. Foreign investors want to share in our growth and profitability. In the process, their investments (like BMW's auto plant) expand America's production possibilities and stimulate still more economic growth.

Foreign investors actually assume substantial risk when they invest in the United States. If the dollar falls, the foreign value of *their* U.S. investments will decline. Hence, foreigners who've already invested in the United States have no incentive to start a flight from the dollar. On the contrary, a strong dollar protects the value of their U.S. holdings.

EXCHANGE-RATE INTERVENTION

Given the potential opposition to exchange-rate movements, governments often feel compelled to intervene in foreign-exchange markets. The intervention is usually intended to achieve greater exchange-rate stability. But such stability may itself give rise to undesirable micro- and macroeconomic effects.

Fixed Exchange Rates

One way to eliminate fluctuations in exchange rates is to fix the rate's value. To fix exchange rates, each country may simply proclaim that its currency is worth so much in relation to that of other countries. The easiest way to do this is for each country to define the worth of its currency in terms of some common standard. Under a **gold standard,** each country determines that its currency is worth so much gold. In so doing, it implicitly defines the worth of its currency in terms of all other currencies, which also have a fixed gold value. In 1944, the major trading nations met at Bretton Woods, New Hampshire, and agreed that each currency was worth so much gold. The value of the U.S. dollar was defined as being equal to 0.0294 ounce of gold, while the British pound was defined as being worth 0.0823 ounce of gold. Thus, the exchange rate between British pounds and U.S. dollars was effectively fixed at $1 = 0.357 pound, or 1 pound = $2.80 (or $2.80/0.0823 = $1/0.0294).

gold standard: An agreement by countries to fix the price of their currencies in terms of gold; a mechanism for fixing exchange rates.

Balance-of-Payments Problems. It's one thing to proclaim the worth of a country's currency; it's quite another to *maintain* the fixed rate of exchange. As we've observed, foreign-exchange rates are subject to continual and often unpredictable changes in supply and demand. Hence, two countries that seek to stabilize their exchange rate at some fixed value are going to find it necessary to compensate for such foreign-exchange market pressures.

Suppose the exchange rate officially established by the United States and Great Britain is equal to e_1, as illustrated in Figure 36.4. As is apparent, that particular exchange rate is consistent with the then-prevailing demand and supply conditions in the foreign-exchange market (as indicated by curves D_1 and S_1).

Now suppose that Americans suddenly acquire a greater taste for British cars and start spending more income on Jaguars and the like. Although Ford Motor owns Jaguar, the cars are still produced in Great Britain. Hence, as U.S. purchases of British goods increase, the demand for British currency will *shift* from D_1 to D_2 in Figure 36.4. Were exchange rates allowed to respond to market influences, the dollar price of a British pound would rise, in this case to the rate e_2. But we've assumed that government intervention has fixed the exchange rate at e_1. Unfortunately, at e_1, American consumers want to buy more pounds (q_D) than the British are willing to supply (q_S). The difference between the quantity demanded and the quantity supplied in the market at the rate e_1 represents a **market shortage** of British pounds.

market shortage: The amount by which the quantity demanded exceeds the quantity supplied at a given price; excess demand.

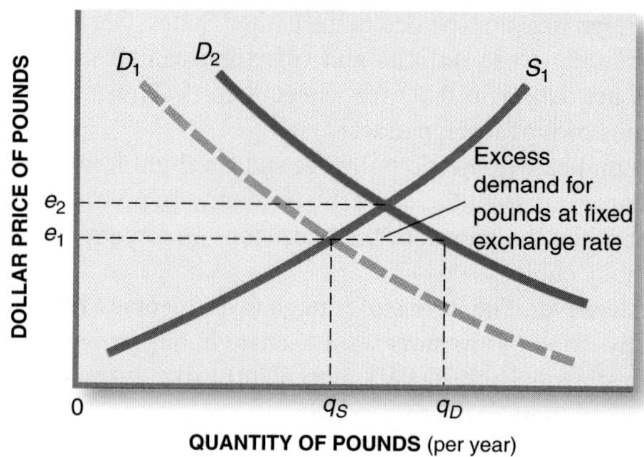

FIGURE 36.4
Fixed Rates and Market Imbalance

If exchange rates are fixed, they can't adjust to changes in market supply and demand. Suppose the exchange rate is initially fixed at e_1. When the demand for British pounds increases (shifts to the right), an excess demand for pounds emerges. More pounds are demanded (q_D) at the rate e_1 than are supplied (q_S). This causes a balance-of-payments deficit for the United States.

balance-of-payments deficit: An excess demand for foreign currency at current exchange rates.

balance-of-payments surplus: An excess demand for domestic currency at current exchange rates.

The excess demand for pounds implies a **balance-of-payments deficit** for the United States: More dollars are flowing out of the country than into it. The same disequilibrium represents a **balance-of-payments surplus** for Britain, because its outward flow of pounds is less than its incoming flow.

Basically, there are only two solutions to balance-of-payments problems brought about by the attempt to fix exchange rates:

- Allow exchange rates to rise to e_2 (Figure 36.4), thereby eliminating the excess demand for pounds.
- Alter market supply or demand so that they intersect at the fixed rate e_1.

Since fixed exchange rates were the initial objective of policy, only the second alternative is of immediate interest.

foreign-exchange reserves: Holdings of foreign exchange by official government agencies, usually the central bank or treasury.

The Need for Reserves. One way to alter market conditions would be for someone simply to supply British pounds to American consumers. The U.S. Treasury could have accumulated a reserve of foreign exchange in earlier periods. By selling some of those **foreign-exchange reserves** now, the Treasury could help to stabilize market conditions at the officially established exchange rate. The rightward shift of the pound supply curve in Figure 36.5 illustrates the sale of accumulated British pounds—and related purchase of U.S. dollars—by the U.S. Treasury. (In 2006, the U.S. Treasury increased foreign-exchange reserves by $2 billion; see item 11 in Table 36.1.)

Although foreign-exchange reserves can be used to fix exchange rates, such reserves may not be adequate. Indeed, Figure 36.6 should be testimony enough to the fact that

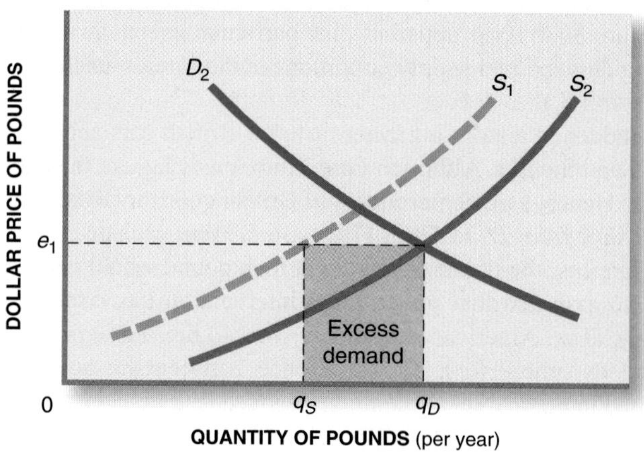

FIGURE 36.5
The Impact of Monetary Intervention

If the U.S. Treasury holds reserves of British pounds, it can use them to buy U.S. dollars in foreign-exchange markets. As it does so, the supply of pounds will shift to the right, to S_2, thereby maintaining the desired exchange rate, e_1. The Bank of England could bring about the same result by offering to buy U.S. dollars with pounds.

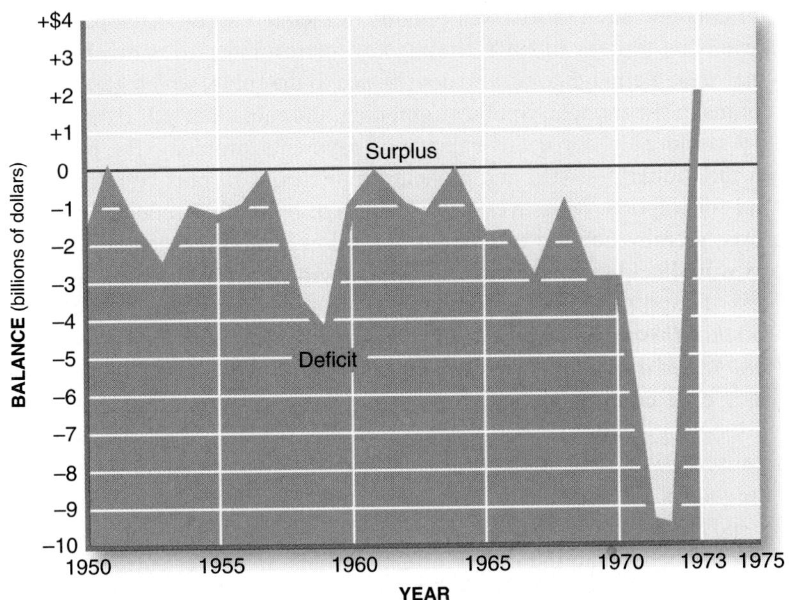

FIGURE 36.6
The U.S. Balance of Payments, 1950–1973

The United States had a balance-of-payments deficit for 22 consecutive years. During this period, the foreign-exchange reserves of the U.S. Treasury were sharply reduced. Fixed exchange rates were maintained by the willingness of foreign countries to accumulate large reserves of U.S. dollars. However, neither the Treasury's reserves nor the willingness of foreigners to accumulate dollars was unlimited. In 1973, fixed exchange rates were abandoned.

today's deficit isn't always offset by tomorrow's surplus. A principal reason that fixed exchange rates didn't live up to their expectations is that the United States had balance-of-payments deficits for 22 consecutive years. This long-term deficit overwhelmed our stock of foreign-exchange reserves.

The Role of Gold. Gold reserves are a potential substitute for foreign-exchange reserves. As long as each country's money has a value defined in terms of gold, we can use gold to buy British pounds, thereby restocking our foreign-exchange reserves. Or we can simply use the gold to purchase U.S. dollars in foreign-exchange markets. In either case, the exchange value of the dollar will tend to rise. However, we must have **gold reserves** available for this purpose. Unfortunately, the continuing U.S. balance-of-payments deficits recorded in Figure 36.6 exceeded even the hoards of gold buried under Fort Knox. As a consequence, our gold reserves lost their credibility as a potential guarantee of fixed exchange rates.

gold reserves: Stocks of gold held by a government to purchase foreign exchange.

Domestic Adjustments. The supply and demand for foreign exchange can also be shifted by changes in basic fiscal, monetary, or trade policies. With respect to trade policy, ***trade protection can be used to prop up fixed exchange rates.*** We could eliminate the excess demand for pounds (Figure 36.4), for example, by imposing quotas and tariffs on British goods. Such trade restrictions would reduce British imports to the United States and thus the demand for British pounds. In August 1971, President Nixon imposed an emergency 10 percent surcharge on all imported goods to help reduce the payments deficit that fixed exchange rates had spawned. Such restrictions on international trade, however, violate the principle of comparative advantage and thus reduce total world output. Trade protection also invites retaliatory trade restrictions.

Fiscal policy is another way out of the imbalance. An increase in U.S. income tax rates will reduce disposable income and have a negative effect on the demand for all goods, including imports. A reduction in government spending will have similar effects. In general, ***deflationary (or restrictive) policies help correct a balance-of-payments deficit by lowering domestic incomes and thus the demand for imports.***

Monetary policies in a deficit country could follow the same restrictive course. A reduction in the money supply will tend to raise interest rates. The balance of payments will benefit in two ways. The resultant slowdown in spending will reduce import demand. In addition, higher interest rates may induce international investors to move some of their funds into the deficit country. Such moves will provide immediate relief to the payments imbalance.[2] Russia tried this strategy in 1998, tripling key interest rates (to as much as 150 percent). But even that wasn't enough to restore confidence in the ruble, which kept depreciating. Within 3 months of the monetary policy tightening, the ruble lost half its value.

A surplus country could help solve the balance-of-payments problem. By pursuing expansionary—even inflationary—fiscal and monetary policies, a surplus country could stimulate the demand for imports. Moreover, any inflation at home will reduce the competitiveness of exports, thereby helping to restrain the inflow of foreign demand. Taken together, such efforts would help reverse an international payments imbalance.

Even under the best of circumstances, domestic economic adjustments entail significant costs. In effect, ***domestic adjustments to payments imbalances require a deficit country to forsake full employment and a surplus country to forsake price stability.*** China has had to grapple with these domestic consequences of fixing the value of its currency. The artificially low value of the yuan promoted Chinese exports and accelerated China's GDP growth. It has also caused prices in China to rise faster than the government desires, however. To maintain the yuan's fixed exchange rate, the Chinese government had to adopt restrictive monetary and fiscal policies to keep inflation in check. The Chinese government also had to be willing to accumulate the inflow of U.S. dollars and other currencies. By 2007, China's foreign-exchange reserves exceeded $1 trillion (see World View). There's no easy way out of this impasse. Market imbalances caused by fixed exchange rates can be corrected only with abundant supplies of foreign-exchange reserves or deliberate changes in fiscal, monetary, or trade policies. At some point, it may become easier to let a currency adjust to market equilibrium.

The Euro Fix. As noted earlier in the chapter, the original 12 nations of the European Monetary Union (EMU) did fix their exchange rates in 1999. They went far beyond the kind of exchange-rate fix we're discussing here. Members of the EMU *eliminated* their national currencies, making the euro the common currency of Euroland. They don't have to worry about reserve balances or domestic adjustments. However, they do have to reconcile their varied national interests to a single monetary authority, which may prove to be difficult politically in times of economic stress.

Flexible Exchange Rates

flexible exchange rates: A system in which exchange rates are permitted to vary with market supply-and-demand conditions; floating exchange rates.

Balance-of-payments problems wouldn't arise in the first place if exchange rates were allowed to respond to market forces. Under a system of **flexible exchange rates** (often called floating exchange rates), the exchange rate moves up or down to choke off any excess supply of or demand for foreign exchange. Notice again in Figure 36.4 that the exchange-rate move from e_1 to e_2 prevents any excess demand from emerging. ***With flexible exchange rates, the quantity of foreign exchange demanded always equals the quantity supplied,*** and there's no imbalance. For the same reason, there's no need for foreign-exchange reserves.

Although flexible exchange rates eliminate balance-of-payments and foreign-exchange reserves problems, they don't solve all of a country's international trade problems. ***Exchange-rate movements associated with flexible rates alter relative prices and may disrupt import and export flows.*** As noted before, depreciation of the dollar raises the price of all imported goods. The price increases may contribute to domestic cost-push inflation. Also, domestic businesses that sell imported goods or use them as production inputs may suffer sales losses. On the other hand, appreciation of the dollar raises the foreign price of U.S. goods and reduces the sales of American exporters. Hence, ***someone is always hurt, and others are helped, by exchange-rate movements.*** The resistance to flexible exchange rates originates in these potential losses. Such resistance creates pressure for official intervention in foreign-exchange markets or increased trade barriers.

[2]Before 1930, not only were foreign-exchange rates fixed, but domestic monetary supplies were tied to gold stocks as well. Countries experiencing a balance-of-payments deficit were thus forced to contract their money supply, and countries experiencing a payments surplus were forced to expand their money supply by a set amount. Monetary authorities were powerless to control domestic money supplies except by erecting barriers to trade. The system was abandoned when the world economy collapsed into the Great Depression.

WORLD VIEW 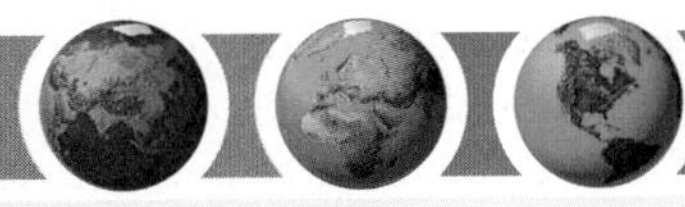

Foreign Currency Piles Up in China

SHANGHAI, Jan. 16—China's state media on Monday reported that the country's foreign currency reserves swelled by more than one-third last year to a record $819 billion as its factories churned out goods for markets around the world, heightening the likelihood of fresh trade tensions with the United States.

Coupled with news only days earlier that China's world trade surplus tripled last year, to $102 billion, the country's burgeoning foreign exchange reserves seemed certain to intensify demands that China increase the value of its currency, the yuan, the worth of which is linked to the dollar. U.S. manufacturing groups argue that China's currency is priced too low, making its goods unfairly cheap on world markets. . . .

China is loath to increase the yuan enough to dampen growth in its coastal factories. Exports are a key source of jobs in a country that must find tens of millions of them for poor farmers and workers laid off by bankrupt state factories in the continued transition from communism to capitalism. . . .

Still, some economists said China's reserves were now growing so huge as to compel the central bank to deliver a significant revaluation. Otherwise, China risks that its reserves will leak into the banking system and be lent out for speculative investments that will only worsen a feared glut of real estate and factory capacity.

"The renminbi [yuan] is fundamentally undervalued," said Ha Jiming, chief economist at China International Capital Corp., a giant state-owned investment bank. "As foreign exchange continues to grow, it will force a revaluation."

—Peter S. Goodman

Source: *Washington Post,* January 17, 2006, p. D1. **© 2006, The Washington Post. Excerpted with permission.**

Analysis: When a currency is deliberately undervalued, strong export demand may kindle inflation. The trade surplus that results also increases foreign-exchange reserves.

The United States and its major trading partners abandoned fixed exchange rates in 1973. Although exchange rates are now able to fluctuate freely, it shouldn't be assumed that they necessarily undergo wild gyrations. On the contrary, experience with flexible rates since 1973 suggests that some semblance of stability is possible even when exchange rates are free to change in response to market forces.

Speculation. One force that often helps maintain stability in a flexible exchange-rate system is speculation. Speculators often counteract short-term changes in foreign-exchange supply and demand. If an exchange rate temporarily rises above its long-term equilibrium, speculators will move in to sell foreign exchange. By selling at high prices and later buying at lower prices, speculators hope to make a profit. In the process, they also help stabilize foreign-exchange rates.

"Damn it! How can I relax, knowing that out there, somewhere, somehow, someone's attacking the dollar?"

Analysis: A "weak" dollar reduces the buying power of American tourists.

Speculation isn't always stabilizing, however. Speculators may not correctly gauge the long-term equilibrium. Instead, they may move "with the market" and help push exchange rates far out of kilter. This kind of destabilizing speculation sharply lowered the international value of the U.S. dollar in 1987, forcing the Reagan administration to intervene in foreign-exchange markets, borrowing foreign currencies to buy U.S. dollars. In 1997, the Clinton administration intervened for the opposite purpose: stemming the rise in the U.S. dollar. The Bush administration was more willing to stay on the sidelines, letting global markets set the exchange rates for the U.S. dollar.

Managed Exchange Rates. Governments can intervene in foreign-exchange markets without completely fixing exchange rates. That is, they may buy and sell foreign exchange for the purpose of *narrowing* rather than *eliminating* exchange-rate movements. Such limited intervention in foreign-exchange markets is often referred to as **managed exchange rates,** or, popularly, "dirty floats."

managed exchange rates: A system in which governments intervene in foreign-exchange markets to limit but not eliminate exchange-rate fluctuations; "dirty floats."

The basic objective of exchange-rate management is to provide a stabilizing force. The U.S. Treasury, for example, may use its foreign-exchange reserves to buy dollars when they're depreciating too much. Or it may buy foreign exchange if the dollar is rising too fast. From this perspective, exchange-rate management appears as a fail-safe system for the private market. Unfortunately, the motivation for official intervention is sometimes suspect. Private speculators buy and sell foreign exchange for the sole purpose of making a profit. But government sales and purchases may be motivated by other considerations. A falling exchange rate increases the competitive advantage of a country's exports. A rising exchange rate makes international investment less expensive. Hence, a country's efforts to manage exchange-rate movements may arouse suspicion and outright hostility in its trading partners.

Although managed exchange rates would seem to be an ideal compromise between fixed rates and flexible rates, they can work only when some acceptable "rules of the game" and mutual trust have been established. As Sherman Maisel, a former governor of the Federal Reserve Board, put it, "Monetary systems are based on credit and faith: If these are lacking, a . . . crisis occurs."[3]

THE ECONOMY TOMORROW

CURRENCY BAILOUTS

The world has witnessed a string of currency crises, including the one in Asia during 1997–98, the Brazilian crisis of 1999, the Argentine crisis of 2001–2, recurrent ruble crises in Russia, and periodic panics in Mexico and South America. In every instance, the country in trouble pleads for external help. In most cases, a currency "bailout" is arranged, whereby global monetary authorities lend the troubled nation enough reserves (such as U.S. dollars) to defend its currency. Typically, the International Monetary Fund (IMF) heads the rescue party, joined by the central banks of the strongest economies.

The Case for Bailouts. The argument for currency bailouts typically rests on the domino theory. Weakness in one currency can undermine another. This seemed to be the case during the 1997–98 Asian crisis. After the **devaluation** of the Thai baht, global investors began worrying about currency values in other Asian nations. Choosing to be safe rather than sorry, they moved funds out of Korea, Malaysia, and the Philippines and invested in U.S. and European markets (notice in Figure 36.3 the 1997–98 appreciation of the U.S. dollar).

devaluation: An abrupt depreciation of a currency whose value was fixed or managed by the government.

[3]Sherman Maisel, *Managing the Dollar* (New York: W. W. Norton, 1973), p. 196.

The initial baht devaluation also weakened the competitive trade position of these same economies. Thai exports became cheaper, diverting export demand from other Asian nations. To prevent loss of export markets, Thailand's neighbors felt they had to devalue as well. Speculators who foresaw these effects accelerated the domino effect by selling the region's currencies.

When Brazil devalued its currency (the *real*) in January 1999, global investors worried that a "samba effect" might sweep across Latin America. The domino effect could reach across the ocean and damage U.S. and European exports as well. Hence, the industrial countries often offer a currency bailout as a form of self-defense.

The Case against Bailouts. Critics of bailouts argue that such interventions are ultimately self-defeating. They say that once a country knows for sure that currency bailouts are in the wings, it doesn't have to pursue the domestic policy adjustments that might stabilize its currency. A nation can avoid politically unpopular options such as high interest rates, tax hikes, or cutbacks in government spending. It can also turn a blind eye to trade barriers, monopoly power, lax lending policies, and other constraints on productive growth. Hence, the expectation of readily available bailouts may foster the very conditions that cause currency crises.

Future Bailouts? The decision to bail out a depreciating currency isn't as simple as it appears. To minimize the ill effects of bailouts, the IMF and other institutions typically require the crisis nation to pledge more prudent monetary, fiscal, and trade policies. Usually there's a lot of debate about what kinds of adjustments will be made—and how soon. As long as the crisis nation is confident of an eventual bailout, however, it has a lot of bargaining power to resist policy changes. Only after the IMF finally said no to further bailouts in 2001 did Argentina devalue its currency and pursue more domestic reforms.

SUMMARY

- Money serves the same purposes in international trade as it does in the domestic economy, namely, to facilitate productive specialization and market exchanges. The basic challenge of international finance is to create acceptable standards of value from the various currencies maintained by separate countries. LO1
- Exchange rates are the basic mechanism for translating the value of one national currency into the equivalent value of another. An exchange rate of $1 = 2 euros means that one dollar is worth two euros in foreign-exchange markets. LO2
- Foreign currencies have value because they can be used to acquire goods and resources from other countries. Accordingly, the supply of and demand for foreign currency reflect the demands for imports and exports, for international investment, and for overseas activities of governments. LO1
- The balance of payments summarizes a country's international transactions. Its components are the trade balance, the current-account balance, and the capital-account balance. The current and capital accounts must offset each other. LO1
- The equilibrium exchange rate is subject to any and all shifts of supply and demand for foreign exchange. If relative incomes, prices, or interest rates change, the demand for foreign exchange will be affected. A depreciation is a change in market exchange rates that makes one country's currency cheaper in terms of another currency. An appreciation is the opposite kind of change. LO2
- Changes in exchange rates are often resisted. Producers of export goods don't want their currencies to rise in value (appreciate); importers and people who travel dislike it when their currencies fall in value (depreciate). LO3
- Under a system of fixed exchange rates, changes in the supply and demand for foreign exchange can't be expressed in exchange-rate movements. Instead, such shifts will be reflected in excess demand for or excess supply of foreign exchange. Such market imbalances are referred to as balance-of-payments deficits or surpluses. LO2
- To maintain fixed exchange rates, monetary authorities must enter the market to buy and sell foreign exchange. In order to do so, deficit countries must have foreign-exchange reserves. In the absence of sufficient reserves, a country can maintain fixed exchange rates only if it's willing to alter basic fiscal, monetary, or trade policies. LO3
- Flexible exchange rates eliminate balance-of-payments problems and the crises that accompany them. But complete flexibility can lead to excessive changes. To avoid this contingency, many countries prefer to adopt managed exchange rates, that is, rates determined by the market but subject to government intervention. LO3

Key Terms

exchange rate
equilibrium price
balance of payments
trade deficit
depreciation (currency)
appreciation
foreign-exchange markets
gold standard
market shortage
balance-of-payments deficit
balance-of-payments surplus
foreign-exchange reserves
gold reserves
flexible exchange rates
managed exchange rates
devaluation

Questions for Discussion

1. Why would a decline in the value of the dollar prompt foreign manufacturers such as BMW to build production plants in the United States? LO3
2. How do changes in the foreign value of the U.S. dollar affect foreign enrollments at U.S. colleges? LO3
3. How would rapid inflation in Canada alter our demand for travel to Canada and for Canadian imports? Does it make any difference whether the exchange rate between Canadian and U.S. dollars is fixed or flexible? LO2
4. Under what conditions would a country welcome a balance-of-payments deficit? When would it *not* want a deficit? LO3
5. In what sense do fixed exchange rates permit a country to "export its inflation"? LO1
6. In the World View on page 722, who is Farshad Shahabadi referring to as "everyone else"? LO1
7. If a nation's currency depreciates, are the reduced export prices that result "unfair"? LO3
8. How would each of these events affect the supply or demand for Japanese yen? LO1
   (*a*) Stronger U.S. economic growth.
   (*b*) A decline in Japanese interest rates.
   (*c*) Higher inflation in the USA.
9. Is a stronger dollar good or bad for America? Explain. LO3
10. Who will gain and who will lose if China revalues the yuan? LO3

problems The Student Problem Set at the back of this book contains numerical and graphing problems for this chapter.

web activities to accompany this chapter can be found on the Online Learning Center: **http://www.mhhe.com/economics/schiller11e**

37 Global Poverty

LEARNING OBJECTIVES

After reading this chapter, you should know:

LO1. How U.S. and global poverty are defined.

LO2. How many people in the world are poor.

LO3. How global poverty can be reduced.

Bono, the lead singer for the rock group U2, has performed concerts around the world to raise awareness of global poverty. He doesn't have a specific agenda for eradicating poverty. He does believe, though, that greater awareness of global poverty will raise assistance levels and spawn more ideas for combating global hunger, disease, and isolation.

The dimensions of global poverty are staggering. According to the World Bank, roughly a third of the world's population lacks even the barest of life's necessities. *Billions* of people are persistently malnourished, poorly sheltered, minimally clothed, and at constant risk of debilitating diseases. Life expectancies among the globally poor population still hover in the range of 40–50 years, far below the norm (70–80 years) of the rich, developed nations.

In this chapter we follow Bono's suggestion and take a closer look at global poverty. The issues we address include

- **What income thresholds define "poverty"?**
- **How many people are poor?**
- **What actions can be taken to reduce global poverty?**

In the process of answering these questions, we get another opportunity to examine what makes economies "tick"—particularly what forces foster faster economic growth for some nations and slower economic growth for others.

AMERICAN POVERTY

Poverty, like beauty, is often in the eye of the beholder. Many Americans feel "poor" if they can't buy a new car, live in a fancy home, or take an exotic vacation. Indeed, the average American asserts that a family needs at least $35,000 a year "just to get by." With that much income, however, few people would go hungry or be forced to live in the streets.

Official Poverty Thresholds

To develop a more objective standard of poverty, the U.S. government assessed how much money a U.S. family needs to purchase a "minimally adequate" diet. Back in 1963, they concluded that $1,000 per year was needed for that purpose alone. Then they asked how much income was needed to purchase other basic necessities like housing, clothes, transportation, etc. They figured all those *non*food necessities would cost twice as much as the food staples. So they concluded that a budget of $3,000 per year would fund a "minimally adequate" living standard for a U.S. family of four. That standard became the official **U.S. poverty threshold** in 1963.

poverty threshold (U.S.): Annual income of less than $20,000 for a family of four (2007, inflation adjusted).

Inflation Adjustments. Since 1963, prices have risen every year. As a result, the price of the poverty "basket" has risen as well. In 2007, it cost roughly $20,000 to purchase those same basic necessities for a family of four that cost only $3,000 in 1963.

Twenty thousand dollars might sound like a lot of money, especially if you're not paying your own rent or feeding a family. If you break the budget down, however, it doesn't look so generous. Only a third of the budget goes for food. And that portion has to feed four people. So the official U.S. poverty standard provides only $4.80 per day for an individual's food. That just about covers a single Big Mac combo at McDonald's. There's no money in the poverty budget for dining out. And the implied rent money is only $600–$700 a month (for the whole family). So the official U.S. poverty standard isn't that generous—certainly not by *American* standards (where the *average* family has an income of roughly $75,000 per year and eats outside their $260,000 home three times a week).

U.S. Poverty Count

The Census Bureau counted over 35 million Americans as "poor" in 2006 according to the official U.S. thresholds (as adjusted for family size). This was one out of eight U.S. households, for a **poverty rate** of roughly 12.5 percent. According to the Census Bureau, the official U.S. poverty rate has been in a narrow range of 11–15 percent for the last 40 years.

poverty rate: Percentage of the population counted as poor.

How Poor Is U.S. "Poor"?

Many observers criticize these official U.S. poverty statistics. They say that far fewer Americans meet the government standard of poverty and even fewer are really destitute.

In-Kind Income. A major flaw in the official tally is that the government counts only *cash* income in defining poverty. Since the 1960s, however, the U.S. has developed an extensive system of **in-kind transfers** that augment cash incomes. Food stamps, for example, can be used just as easily as cash to purchase groceries. Medicaid and Medicare pay doctor and hospital bills, reducing the need for cash income. Government rent subsidies and public housing allow poor families to have more housing than their cash incomes would permit. These in-kind transfers allow "poor" families to enjoy a higher living standard than their cash incomes imply. Adding those transfers to cash incomes would bring the U.S. poverty count down into the 9–11 percent range.

in-kind transfers: Direct transfers of goods and services rather than cash, e.g., food stamps, Medicaid benefits, and housing subsidies.

Material Possessions. Even those families who remain "poor" after counting in-kind transfers aren't necessarily destitute. Over 40 percent of America's "poor" families own their own home, 70 percent own a car or truck, and 30 percent own at least *two* vehicles. Telephones, color TVs, dishwashers, clothes dryers, air conditioners, and microwave ovens are commonplace in America's poor households.

America's poor families themselves report few acute problems in everyday living. Fewer than 14 percent report missing a rent or mortgage payment, and fewer than 8 percent report a food deficiency. So American poverty isn't synonymous with homelessness, malnutrition, chronic illness, or even social isolation. These problems exist among America's poverty population, but don't define American poverty.

GLOBAL POVERTY

Poverty in the rest of the world is much different from poverty in America. ***American poverty is more about* relative *deprivation than* absolute *deprivation. In the rest of the world, poverty is all about* absolute *deprivation.***

Low Average Incomes

As a starting point for assessing global poverty consider how *average* incomes in the rest of the world stack up against U.S. levels. By global standards, the U.S. is unquestionably a very rich nation. As we observed in Chapter 2 (World View, p. 28), U.S. GDP per capita is five times larger than the world average. Over three-fourths of the world's population lives in what the World Bank calls "low-income" or "lower-middle-income" nations. In those nations the *average* income is under $4,000 a year, less than *one-tenth* of America's per capita GDP. Average incomes are lower yet in Haiti, Nigeria, Ethiopia, and other desperately poor nations. By American standards, virtually all the people in these nations would be poor. By *their* standards, no American would be poor.

World Bank Poverty Thresholds

Because national poverty lines are so diverse and culture-bound, the World Bank decided to establish a uniform standard for assessing global poverty. And it set the bar amazingly low. In fact, the World Bank regularly uses two thresholds, namely $1 per day for **"extreme" poverty** and a higher $2 per day standard for less "severe" poverty.

extreme poverty (world): World Bank income standard of less than $1 per day per person (inflation adjusted).

The World Bank thresholds are incomprehensively low by American standards. How much could you buy for $1 a day? A little rice, maybe, and perhaps some milk? Certainly not a Big Mac. And part of that dollar would have to go for rent. Clearly, this isn't going to work. Doubling the World Bank standard to $2 per day **(severe poverty)** doesn't reach a whole lot further.

severe poverty (world): World Bank income standard of $2 per day per person (inflation adjusted).

The World Bank, of course, wasn't defining "poverty" in the context of American affluence. They were instead trying to define a rock-bottom threshold of absolute poverty—a threshold of physical deprivation that people everywhere would acknowledge as the barest "minimum"—a condition of "unacceptable deprivation."

Inflation Adjustments. The World Bank lines were established in the context of 1985 prices and translated into local currencies (based on purchasing power equivalents, not official currency exchange rates). Like official U.S. poverty lines, the World Bank's global poverty lines are adjusted each year for inflation. They are also recalculated on occasion (e.g., 1993) to reflect changing consumption patterns. In today's dollars, the "$1" standard of 1985 is actually about $1.50 per day in U.S. currency. That works out to $2,190 per year for a family of four—about a tenth of the official U.S. poverty threshold. Despite continuing inflation adjustments, the World Bank standard is still referred to as the "dollar-a-day" index of extreme poverty.

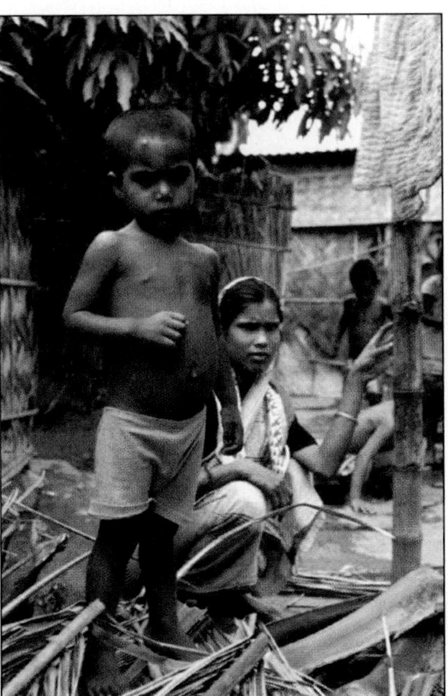

Analysis: Global poverty is defined in terms of absolute deprivation.

FIGURE 37.1
Geography of Extreme Poverty

Over a billion people around the world are in "extreme" poverty. In smaller, poor nations, deprivation is commonplace.

Source: World Bank, *World Development Report 2007* (New York: Oxford University Press, 2007).

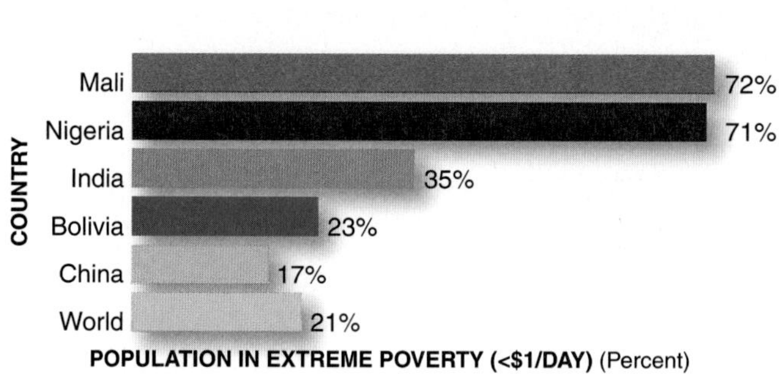

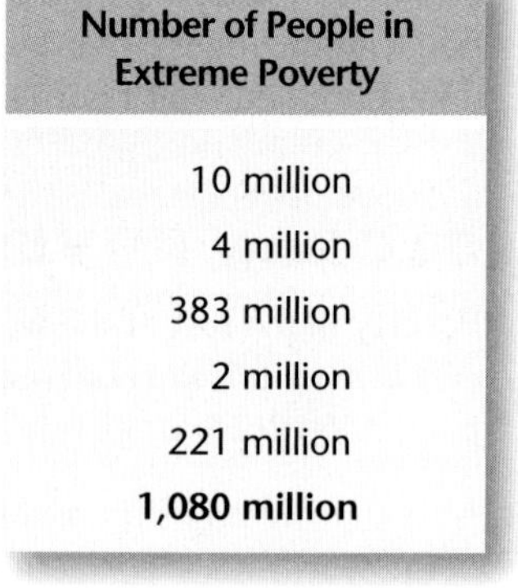

Number of People in Extreme Poverty
10 million
4 million
383 million
2 million
221 million
1,080 million

Global Poverty Counts

On the basis of household surveys in over 100 nations, ***the World Bank classifies over a* billion *people as being in "extreme" poverty (<$1/day) and nearly 3 billion people as being in "severe" poverty (<$2/day).***

Figure 37.1 shows where concentrations of extreme poverty are the greatest. Concentrations of extreme poverty are alarmingly high in dozens of smaller, less developed nations like Mali, Haiti, and Zambia, where average incomes are also shockingly low. However, the greatest *number* of extremely poor people reside in the world's largest countries. China and India alone contain a third of the world's population and over half of the world's extreme poverty.

Table 37.1 reveals that the distribution of severe poverty (<$2/day) is similar. The incidence of this higher poverty threshold is, of course, much greater. Severe poverty afflicts over 80 percent of the population in dozens of nations and even reaches over 90 percent of the population in some (e.g. Nigeria). By contrast, less than 13 percent of the U.S. population falls below the official *American* poverty threshold and virtually no American household has an income below the *global* poverty threshold.

Social Indicators

The levels of poverty depicted in Figure 37.1 and Table 37.1 imply levels of physical and social deprivation few Americans can comprehend. Living on less than a dollar or two a day means always being hungry, malnourished, ill-clothed, dirty, and unhealthy. The problems associated with such deprivation begin even before birth. Pregnant women often fail to get enough nutrition or medical attention. In low-income countries only a third of all births are attended by a skilled health practitioner. If something goes awry, both the mother and the baby are at fatal risk. Nearly all of the children in global poverty are in a state of chronic malnutrition. At least 1 out of 10 children in low-income nations will actually die before reaching age five. In the

TABLE 37.1
Population in Severe Poverty (<$2/day)

Nearly half the world's population has income of less than $2 per person per day. Such poverty is pervasive in low-income nations.

Country	Percent	Number
Nigeria	92%	129 million
Mali	91	11 million
Bangladesh	83	117 million
India	80	864 million
Ethiopia	78	55 million
China	47	611 million
World	**54%**	**2,700 million**

Source: World Bank, *World Development Report 2007.* Used with permission by the International Bank for Reconstruction and Development/The World Bank.

poorest sectors of the population infant and child mortality rates are often two to three times higher than that. Children often remain unimmunized to preventable diseases. And AIDS is rampant among both children and adults in the poorest nations. All of these factors contribute to a frighteningly short life expectancy—less than half that in the developed nations.

Fewer than one out of two children from extremely poor households is likely to stay in school past the eighth grade. Women and minority ethnic and religious groups are often wholly excluded from educational opportunities. As a consequence, great stocks of human capital remain undeveloped: In low-income nations only one out of two women is literate and only two out of three men.

Persistent Poverty

Global poverty is not only more desperate than American poverty, but also more permanent. In India, a rigid caste system still defines differential opportunities for millions of rich and poor villagers. Studies in Brazil, South Africa, Peru, and Ecuador document barriers that block access to health care, education, and jobs for children of poor families. Hence, inequalities in poor nations are not only more severe than in developed nations but also tend to be more permanent.

Economic stagnation also keeps a lid on upward mobility. President John F. Kennedy observed that "a rising tide lifts all boats," referring to the power of a growing economy to raise everyone's income. In a growing economy, one person's income *gain* is not another person's *loss*. By contrast, a stagnant economy intensifies class warfare, with everyone jealously protecting whatever gains they have made. The *haves* strive to keep the *have-nots* at bay. Unfortunately, this is the reality in many low-income nations. As we observed in Chapter 2 (Table 2.1), in some of the poorest nations in the world output grows more slowly than the population, intensifying the competition for resources.

GOALS AND STRATEGIES

The U.N. Millennium Goal

Global poverty is so extensive that no policy approach offers a quick solution. Even the World Bank doesn't see an end to global poverty. The United Nations set a much more modest goal back in 2000. The U.N. established a **Millennium Poverty Goal** of cutting the incidence of extreme global poverty in half by 2015 (from 30 percent in 1990 to 15 percent in 2015). Even that seemingly modest goal wouldn't greatly decrease the *number* of people in poverty. The world's population keeps growing at upward of 80–100 million people a year. By the year 2015, there will be close to 7.2 billion people on this planet. Fifteen percent of that population would still leave over a *billion* people in extreme global poverty.

> **Millennium Poverty Goal:** United Nations goal of reducing global rate of extreme poverty to 15 percent by 2015.

Why should we care? After all, America has its own poverty problems and a slew of other domestic concerns. So why should an American—or, for that matter, an affluent Canadian, French, or German citizen—embrace the U.N.'s Millennium Poverty Goal? For starters, one might embrace the notion that a poor child in sub-Saharan Africa or Borneo is no less worthy than a poor child elsewhere. And a child's death in Bangladesh is just as tragic as a child's death in Buffalo, New York. In other words, humanitarianism is a starting point for *global* concern for poor people. Then there are pragmatic concerns. Poverty and inequality sow the seeds of social tension both within and across national borders. Poverty in other nations also limits potential markets for international trade. Last but not least, undeveloped human capital anywhere limits human creativity. For all these reasons, the U.N. feels the Millennium Poverty Goal should be universally embraced.

Policy Strategies

To reach even this modest goal will be difficult, however. In principle, ***there are only two general approaches to global poverty reduction, namely,***

- ***Redistribution*** of incomes within and across nations.
- ***Economic growth*** that raises average incomes.

The following sections explore the potential of these strategies for eliminating global poverty.

WORLD VIEW

Glaring Inequalities

Inequality tends to diminish as a country develops. In poor nations, the richest tenth of the population typically gets 40 to 50 percent of all income—sometimes, even more. In developed countries, the richest tenth gets 20 to 30 percent of total income.

Source: World Bank, *World Development Indicators, 2006*. Used with permission by the International Bank for Reconstruction and Development/The World Bank.

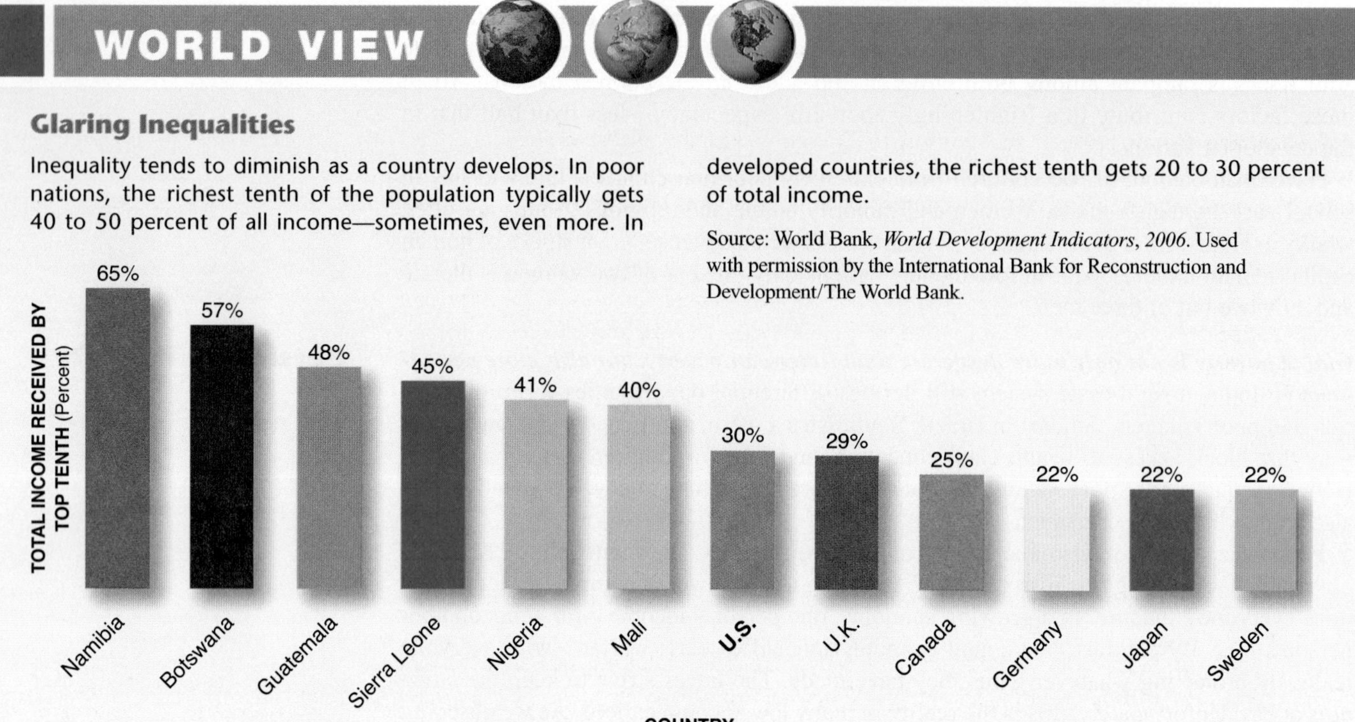

Analysis: The FOR WHOM question is reflected in the distribution of income. Although the U.S. income distribution is very unequal, inequalities loom even larger in most poor countries.

INCOME REDISTRIBUTION

Many people suggest that the quickest route to eliminating global poverty is simply to *redistribute* incomes and assets, both within and across countries. The potential for redistribution is often exaggerated, however, and its risks underestimated.

Within-Nation Redistribution

Take another look at those nations with the highest concentrations of extreme poverty. Mali tops the list in Figure 37.1, with an incredible 72 percent of its population in extreme poverty and 91 percent in severe poverty. Yet the other 9 percent of the population lives fairly well, taking in 40 percent of that nation's income (see World View above). So what would happen if we somehow forced Mali's richest households to share that wealth? Sure, Mali's poorest households would be better off. But the gains wouldn't be spectacular: the *average* income in Mali is less than $1,000 a year. Nigeria, Haiti, Zambia, and Madagascar also have such low *average* incomes that outright redistribution doesn't hold great hope for income gains by the poor.

Economic Risks. Then there's the downside to direct redistribution. How is the income pie going to be resliced? Will the incomes or assets of the rich be confiscated? How will underlying jobs, stocks, land, and businesses be distributed to the poor? How will *total* output (and income) be affected by the redistribution? If savings are confiscated, people will no longer want to save and invest. If large, efficient farms are divided up into small parcels, who will manage them? After Zimbabwe confiscated and fragmented that nation's farms in 2000, its agricultural productivity plummeted. If the government expropriates factories, mills, farms, or businesses, who will run them? If the *rewards* to saving, investment, entrepreneurship, and management are expropriated, who will undertake these economic activities?

This is not to suggest that *no* redistribution of income or assets is appropriate. More progressive taxes and land reforms can reduce inequalities and poverty. But the potential of direct within-nation redistribution is often exaggerated. Historically, nations have often been forced to reverse land, tax, and property reforms that have slowed economic growth and reduced average incomes.

Expenditure Reallocation. In addition to directly redistributing private income and wealth, governments can also reduce poverty by reallocating direct government expenditures. As we observed in Chapter 1 (Figure 1.3), some poor nations devote a large share of output to the military. If more of those resources were channeled into schools, health services, and infrastructure, the poor would surely benefit. Governments in poor nations also tend to give priority to urban development (where the government and middle class reside), to the neglect of rural development (where the poor reside). Redirecting more resources to rural development and core infrastructure (roads, electricity, and water) would accelerate poverty reduction.

Across-Nation Redistribution

Redistribution *across* national borders could make even bigger dents in global poverty. After all, the United States and other industrialized nations are so rich that they could transfer a lot of income to the globally poor if they chose to.

Foreign Aid. Currently, developed nations give poorer nations $80–$100 billion a year in "official development assistance." That's a lot of money. But even if it were distributed exclusively to globally poor households, it would amount to less than $35 per year per person.

Developed nations have set a goal of delivering more aid. The United Nations' **Millennium Aid Goal** is to raise foreign aid levels to 0.7 percent of donor-country GDP. That may not sound too ambitious, but it's a much larger flow than at present. As Table 37.2 reveals, few "rich" nations now come close to this goal. Although the United States is by far the world's largest aid donor, its aid equals only 0.17 percent of U.S. total output. For all developed nations, the aid ratio averages around 0.25 percent—just over a third of the U.N. goal.

Millennium Aid Goal: United Nations goal of raising foreign aid levels to 0.7 percent of donor-country GDP.

Given the history of foreign aid, the U.N. goal is unlikely to be met anytime soon. But what if it were? What if foreign aid *tripled*? Would that cure global poverty? No. Tripling foreign aid would generate only $100 a year for each of the nearly 3 billion people now in global poverty. Even that figure is optimistic, as it assumes all aid is distributed to the poor in a form (e.g., food, clothes, and medicine) that directly addresses their basic needs.

Nongovernmental Aid. Official development assistance is augmented by private charities and other nongovernmental organizations (NGOs). The Gates Foundation, for example, spends upward of $1 billion a year on health care for the globally poor, focusing on treatable diseases like malaria, tuberculosis, and HIV infection (see World View on the next page). Religious organizations operate schools and health clinics in areas of extreme poverty. The International Red Cross brings medical care, shelter, and food in emergencies.

TABLE 37.2
Foreign Aid

Rich nations give roughly $80–$100 billion to poor nations every year. This is a tiny fraction of donor GDP, however.

Country	Total Aid ($millions)	Percent of Donor Total Income
Australia	$1,460	0.25%
Canada	2,599	0.27
Denmark	2,037	0.85
France	8,473	0.41
Japan	8,906	0.19
Italy	2,462	0.15
Norway	2,199	0.87
United Kingdom	7,883	0.36
United States	19,705	0.17
22-Nation Total	**$79,512**	**0.25%**

Source: World Bank, *World Development Indicators 2006* (2004 data). Used with permission by the International Bank for Reconstruction and Development/The World Bank.

WORLD VIEW

The Way We Give

Philanthropy Can Step In Where Market Forces Don't

One day my wife, Melinda, and I were reading an article about millions of children in poor countries who die from diseases that have been eliminated in this country. . . .

Take malaria, for example. The world has known about malaria for a long time. In the early 1900s, Nobel Prizes were given for advances in understanding the malaria parasite and how it was transmitted. But 100 years later malaria is setting records, infecting more than 400 million people every year, killing over a million people every year. That's more than 2,000 children every day. . . .

This same basic story extends to tuberculosis, yellow fever, acute diarrheal illnesses, and respiratory illnesses. Millions of children die from these diseases every year, and yet the advances we have in biology have not been applied, because rich countries don't have these diseases. The private sector hasn't been involved in developing vaccines and medicines for these diseases, because the developing countries can't buy them.

So more than 90% of the money devoted to health research is spent on those who are the healthiest. About $1 billion is spent each year to combat baldness. That's great for some people, but if we're setting priorities, perhaps baldness should rank behind malaria.

Philanthropy can step in when market forces aren't doing the job. It can draw in experts. It can give awards, it can make novel arrangements with private companies, it can partner with universities. Every year the platform of science that we have to do on this gets better.

—Bill Gates

Source: *Fortune,* January 22, 2007, p. 42. Reprinted with permission.

Analysis: When markets fail to provide for basic human needs, additional institutions and incentives may be needed.

As with official development assistance, the content of NGO aid can be as important as its level. Relatively low-cost immunizations, for example, can improve health conditions more than an expensive, high-tech health clinic can. Teaching basic literacy to a community of young children can be more effective than equipping a single high school with Internet capabilities. Distributing drought-resistant seeds to farmers can be more effective than donating advanced farm equipment (which may become useless when it needs to be repaired).

ECONOMIC GROWTH

No matter how well designed foreign aid and philanthropy might be, across-nation transfers alone cannot eliminate global poverty. As Bill Gates observed, the entire endowment of the Gates Foundation would meet the health needs of the globally poor for only 1 year. The World Bank concurs: "Developing nations hold the keys to their prosperity; global action cannot substitute for equitable and efficient domestic policies and institutions."[1] So as important as international assistance is, it will never fully suffice.

Increasing Total Income

The "key" to ending global poverty is, of course, **economic growth.** As we've observed, ***redistributing existing incomes doesn't do the job;* total *income has to increase.*** This is what economic growth is all about.

economic growth: An increase in output (real GDP); an expansion of production possibilities.

Unique Needs. The generic prescription for economic growth is simple: more resources and better technology. But this growth formula takes on a new meaning in the poorest nations. Rich nations can focus on research, technology, and the spread of "brain power." Poor nations need the basics—the "bricks and mortar" elements of an economy such as water systems, roads, schools, and legal systems. Bill Gates learned this firsthand in his early philanthropic efforts. In 1996 Microsoft donated a computer for a community center in Soweto, one of the poorest areas in South Africa. When he visited the center in 1997 he

[1]World Bank, *World Development Report, 2006* (Washington, DC: World Bank, 2006)., p. 206.

discovered the center had no electricity. He quickly realized that growth-policy priorities for poor nations are different from those for rich nations.

Growth Potential

The potential of economic growth to reduce poverty in poor nations is impressive. The 61 nations classified as "low-income" by the World Bank have a combined output of nearly $1.5 trillion. "Lower-middle-income" nations like China, Brazil, Egypt, and Sri Lanka produce another $4 trillion or so of annual output. Hence, every one percentage point of economic growth increases total income in these combined nations by roughly $55 billion. According to the World Bank, if these nations could grow their economies by just 3.8 percent a year (an extra $200 billion of output in the first year and increasing thereafter), global poverty *could* be cut in half by 2015.

China has demonstrated just how effective economic growth can be in reducing poverty. Since 1990, China has been the world's fastest-growing economy, with annual GDP growth rates routinely in the 8–10 percent range. This sensational growth has not only raised *average* incomes, but has also dramatically reduced the incidence of poverty. In fact, ***the observed success in reducing global poverty from 30 percent in 1990 to 21 percent in 2006 is almost entirely due to the decline in Chinese poverty.*** By contrast, slow economic growth in Africa, Latin America, and South Asia has *increased* their respective poverty populations.

Reducing Population Growth

China not only has enjoyed exceptionally fast GDP growth, but also has benefited from relatively slow population growth (now around 0.9 percent a year). This has allowed *aggregate* GDP growth to lift *average* incomes more quickly. In other poor nations, population growth is much faster, making poverty reduction more difficult. As Table 37.3 shows, population growth is in the range of 2–3 percent in some of the poorest nations (e.g., Ethiopia, Nigeria, Angola, Mali, Niger, and Somalia). ***Reducing population growth rates in the poorest nations is one of the critical keys to reducing global poverty.***

Birth control in some form may have to be part of any antipoverty strategy. In the poorest population groups in the poorest nations, contraceptives are virtually nonexistent. As Figure 37.2 illustrates, within those same nations contraceptive use is much more common in the richest segments of the population. This suggests that limited access, not cultural norms or religious values, constrains the use of contraceptives. To encourage more birth control, China also used tax incentives and penalties to limit families to one child.

	Average Annual Growth Rate (2000–2005) of		
	GDP	Population	Per Capita GDP
High-income countries			
United States	2.8	1.0	1.8
Canada	2.6	1.0	1.6
Japan	1.3	0.2	1.1
France	1.5	0.6	0.9
Low-income countries			
China	9.6	0.9	8.7
India	6.9	1.5	5.4
Nigeria	5.9	2.3	3.6
Ethiopia	4.2	2.1	2.1
Kenya	2.8	2.2	0.6
Venezuela	1.3	1.8	−0.5
Paraguay	1.8	2.4	−0.6
Haiti	−0.5	1.4	−1.9
Zimbabwe	−6.1	0.6	−6.7

Source: World Bank, *World Development Report, 2007.* Used with permission by the International Bank for Reconstruction and Development/The World Bank.

TABLE 37.3
Growth Rates in Selected Countries, 2000–2005

The relationship between GDP growth and population growth is very different in rich and poor countries. The populations of rich countries are growing very slowly, and gains in per capita GDP are easily achieved. In the poorest countries, population is still increasing rapidly, making it difficult to raise living standards. Notice how per capita incomes are declining in many poor countries (such as Venezuela, Zimbabwe, and Haiti).

FIGURE 37.2
Contraceptive Use

Contraceptive use by women aged 15–49 is low in poor nations, but not uniformly so. This suggests that economic barriers may impede birth control.

Source: World Bank, *World Development Indicators 2005*, Table 2.6. Used with permission by the International Bank for Reconstruction and Development/The World Bank.

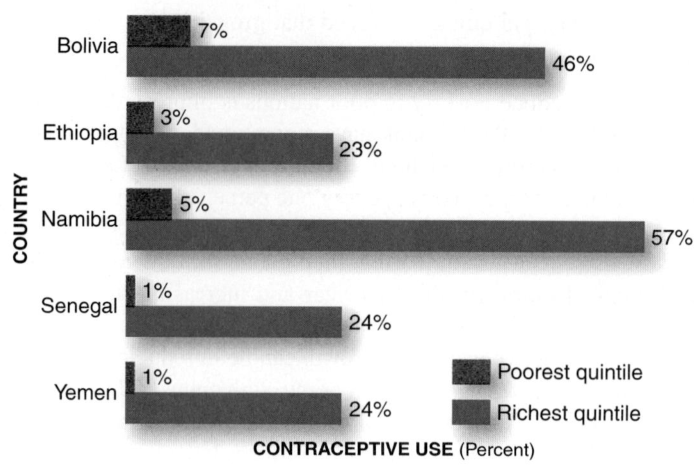

Human Capital Development

Reducing population growth makes poverty reduction easier, but not certain. The next key is to make the existing population more productive, that is, to increase **human capital.**

human capital: The knowledge and skills possessed by the workforce.

Education. In poor nations, the need for human capital development is evident. Only 71 percent of the population in low-income nations complete even elementary school. Even fewer people are *literate,* that is, able to read and write a short, simple statement about everyday life (e.g., "We ate rice for breakfast"). Educational deficiencies are greatest for females, who are often prevented from attending school by cultural, social, or economic concerns (see World View). In Chad and Liberia, fewer than one out of six girls completes primary school. Primary-school completion rates for girls are in the 25–35 percent range in most of the poor nations of sub-Saharan Africa.

In Niger and Mali, only one out of five *teenage* girls is literate. This lack of literacy creates an **inequality trap** that restricts the employment opportunities for young women to simple, routine, manual jobs (e.g., carpet weaving and sewing). With so few skills and little education, they are destined to remain poor.

inequality trap: Institutional barriers that impede human and physical capital investment, particularly by the poorest segments of society.

WORLD VIEW

The Female "Inequality Trap"

In many poor nations, women are viewed as such a financial liability that female fetuses are aborted, female infants are killed, and female children are so neglected that they have significantly higher mortality rates. The "burden" females pose results from social norms that restrict the ability of women to earn income, accumulate wealth, or even decide their own marital status. In many of the poorest nations, women

- have restricted property rights,
- can't inherit wealth,
- are prohibited or discouraged from working outside the home,
- are prohibited or discouraged from going to school,
- are prevented from voting,
- are denied the right to divorce,
- are paid less than men if they do work outside the home,
- are often expected to bring a financial dowry to the marriage,
- may be beaten if they fail to obey their husbands.

These social practices create an "inequality trap" that keeps returns on female human capital investment low. Without adequate education or training, they can't get productive jobs. Without access to good jobs, they have no incentive to get an education or training. This kind of vicious cycle creates an inequality trap that keeps women and their communities poor.

Source: World Bank, *World Development Report 2006,* pp. 51–54. Used with permission by the International Bank for Reconstruction and Development/The World Bank.

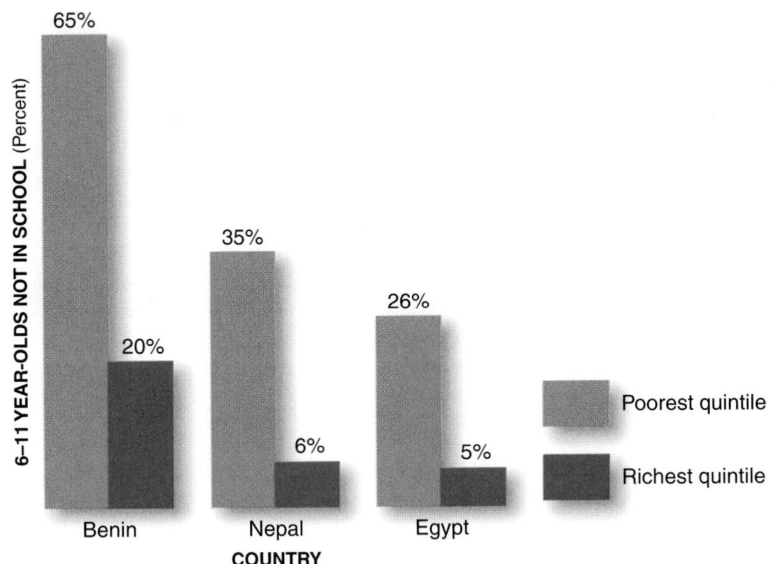

FIGURE 37.3
School Attendance

In developing countries the poorest children often don't attend school at all. Illiteracy is common in these extremely poor families.

Source: World Bank, *World Development Indicators 2005*, Table 2.11a. Used with permission by the International Bank for Reconstruction and Development/The World Bank.

The already low levels of *average* education are compounded by unequal access to schools. Families in extreme poverty typically live in rural areas, with primitive transportation and communication facilities. *Physical* access to schools itself is problematic. On top of that, the poorest families often need their children to work, either within the family or in paid employment. As Figure 37.3 shows, these forces often foreclose school attendance for the poorest children.

Health. In poor nations, basic health care is also a critical dimension of human capital development. Immunizations against measles, diphtheria, and tetanus are more the exception than the rule in Somalia, Nigeria, Afghanistan, Congo, the Central African Republic, and many other poor nations. For all low-income nations taken together, the child immunization rate is only 67 percent (versus 96 percent in the United States). Access and education—not money—are the principal barriers to greater immunizations.

Water and sanitation facilities are also in short supply. The World Bank defines "adequate water access" as a protected water source of at least 20 liters per person a day within 1 kilometer of the home dwelling. We're not limited to indoor plumbing with this definition: A public water pipe a half a mile from one's home is considered adequate. Yet, only three out of four households in low-income nations even meet this minimum threshold of water adequacy (see World View on next page). In Afghanistan, Ethiopia, and Somalia only one out of four households has even that much water access. Access to sanitation facilities (ranging from pit latrines to flush toilets) is less common still (on average one out of three low-income-nation households). In Ethiopia, only 6 percent of the population is so privileged.

When illness strikes, professional health care is hard to find. In the United States, there is one doctor for every 180 people. In Sierra Leone, there is one doctor for every 10,000 people! For low-income nations as a group, there are 2,500 people for every available doctor.

These glaring inadequacies in health conditions breed high rates of illness and death. In the United States, only 8 out of every 1,000 children die before age five. In Angola, 260 of every 1,000 children die that young. For all low-income nations, the under-five mortality rate is 12.2 percent (one out of eight). Those children who live are commonly so malnourished (either severely underweight and/or short) that they can't develop fully (another inequality trap).

Associated Press

Analysis: Unsafe water is a common problem for the globally poor.

WORLD VIEW

Dying for a Drink of Clean Water

In the United States and Europe, people take it for granted that when they turn on their taps, clean water will flow out. But for those living in U.S. cities devastated by Hurricane Katrina, as in large parts of the world, obtaining safe water requires a constant struggle.

Water is essential to all aspects of life, yet 99 percent of water on Earth is unsafe or unavailable to drink. About 1.2 billion people lack safe water to consume and 2.6 billion do not have access to adequate sanitation. There are also stark comparisons: Just one flush of a toilet in the West uses more water than most Africans have to perform an entire day's washing, cleaning, cooking, and drinking.

Unsafe water and sanitation is now the single largest cause of illness worldwide, just as it has been a major threat to the health people affected by Hurricane Katrina. A recent U.N. report estimated that:

- At least 2 million people, most of them children, die annually from water-borne diseases such as diarrhea, cholera, dysentery, typhoid, guinea worm and hepatitis as well as such illnesses as malaria and West Nile virus carried by mosquitoes that breed in stagnant water.
- Many of the 10 million child deaths that occurred last year were linked to unsafe water and lack of sanitation. Children can't fight off infections if their bodies are weakened by water-borne diseases.
- Over half of the hospital beds in the developing world are occupied by people suffering from preventable diseases caused by unsafe water and inadequate sanitation.

When poor people are asked what would most improve their lives, water and sanitation is repeatedly one of the highest priorities. We should heed their call.

—Jan Eliasson and Susan Blumenthal

Source: *Washington Post,* September 20, 2005, p. A23. From *The Washington Post*, September 20, 2005. Reprinted with permission by Jan Eliasson through Monica Lundkrist.

Analysis: Access to safe water and sanitation is one of the most basic foundations for economic growth. The U.N.'s millennium water goal is to reduce by 2015 half the percentage of people without safe water.

AIDS takes a huge toll as well. Only 0.6 percent of the U.S. adult population has HIV. In Botswana, Lesotho, Swaziland, and Zimbabwe, over 25 percent of the adult population is HIV-infected. As a result of these problems, life expectancies are inordinately low. In Zambia, only 16 percent of the population live to age 65. In Botswana, life expectancy at birth is 35 years (versus 77 years in the United States). For low-income nations as a group, life expectancy is a mere 59 years.

Rostow's 5 Stages of Development

In view of these glaring human-capital deficiencies, one might wonder how poor nations could possibly grow enough to reduce their extreme poverty. After surveying diverse growth experiences, Walt Rostow, an M.I.T. economist, discerned five distinct stages in the development process, as summarized in Table 37.4. Many of the poorest nations are still stuck in stage 1, the "traditional society," with minimal core infrastructure, especially in the rural areas where the poorest households reside. To get beyond that stage, poor nations have to

TABLE 37.4
Five Stages of Economic Development

Walt Rostow distinguished these five sequential stages of economic development:

- Stage 1: *Traditional society.* Rigid institutions, low productivity, little infrastructure, dependence on subsistence agriculture.
- Stage 2: *Preconditions for takeoff.* Improved institutional structure, increased agricultural productivity, emergence of an entrepreneurial class.
- Stage 3: *Takeoff into sustained growth.* Increased saving and investment, rapid industrialization, growth-enhancing policies.
- Stage 4: *Drive to maturity.* Spread of growth process to lagging industrial sectors.
- Stage 5: *High mass consumption.* High per capita GDP attained and accessible to most of population.

Source: World Bank, *World Development Indicators 2005,* Table 2.11a. Used with permission by the International Bank for Reconstruction and Development/The World Bank.

create the "preconditions for takeoff"—to channel more resources into basic education and health services, while dismantling critical inequality traps.

Meeting Basic Needs. ***To get beyond Rostow's stage 1, poor nations must substantially improve the health and education of the mass of poor people.*** Cuba was highly successful in following this approach. Although Cuba was a very poor country when Fidel Castro took power in 1959, his government placed high priority on delivering basic educational and health services to the entire population. Within a decade, health and educational standards approached that of industrialized nations.

Implied Costs. The amount of money needed to meet the basic needs of poor nations is surprisingly modest. Malaria vaccinations cost less than 20 cents a shot. Bringing safe water to the poor would cost around $4 billion per year. Bringing both safe water and sanitation would cost about $23 billion annually. Providing universal primary education would cost about $8 billion a year. These costs aren't prohibitive. After all, U.S. consumers spend $15 billion a year on pet food and $100 billion on alcohol. The challenge for poor nations is to get the necessary resources applied to their basic needs.

Capital Investment

To reach stages 2 and 3 in Rostow's scenario, poor nations also need sharply increased capital investment, in both the public and private sectors. Transportation and communications systems must be expanded and upgraded so that markets can function. Capital equipment and upgraded technology must flow into both agricultural and industrial enterprises.

Internal Financing. Acquiring the capital resources needed to boost productivity and accelerate economic growth is not an easy task. Domestically, freeing up scarce resources for capital investment requires cutbacks in domestic consumption. In the 1920s, Stalin used near-totalitarian powers to cut domestic consumption in Russia (by limiting output of consumer goods) and raise Russia's **investment rate** to as much as 30 percent of output. This elevated rate of investment pushed Russia into stage 3, but at a high cost in terms of consumer deprivation.

investment rate: The percentage of total output (GDP) allocated to the production of new plant, equipment, and structures

Other nations haven't had the power or the desire to make such a sacrifice. China spent two decades trying to raise consumption standards before it gave higher priority to investment. Once it did so, however, economic growth accelerated sharply. Table 37.5 documents the low investment rates that continue to plague other poor nations.

Pervasive poverty in poor nations sharply limits the potential for increased savings. Nevertheless, governments can encourage more saving with improved banking facilities, transparent capital markets, and education and saving incentives. And there is mounting evidence that even small dabs of financing can make a big difference. Extending a small loan that enables a poor farmer to buy improved seeds or a plow can have substantial effects on productivity. Financing small equipment or inventory for an entrepreneur can get a new business rolling. Such **"microfinance"** can be a critical key to escaping poverty (see World View, next page).

microfinance: The granting of small ("micro"), unsecured loans to small business and entrepreneurs.

Some nations have also used inflation as a tool for shifting resources from consumption to investment. By financing public works projects and private investment with an increased money supply, governments can increase the inflation rate. As prices rise faster than

Angola	13%
Central African Republic	7
Congo	14
Tajikistan	14
West Bank and Gaza	3
Bolivia	12
China	39
India	30

Source: World Bank, *World Development Report 2007* (2005 data). Used with permission by the International Bank for Reconstruction and Development/The World Bank.

TABLE 37.5
Low Investment Rates

Low investment rates limit economic growth. China has attained gross investment rates as high as 45 percent—and exceptionally fast economic growth.

WORLD VIEW

Muhammad Yunus: Microloans

Teach a man to fish, and he'll eat for a lifetime. But only if he can afford the fishing rod. More than 30 years ago in Bangladesh, economics Professor Muhammad Yunus recognized that millions of his countrymen were trapped in poverty because they were unable to scrape together the tiny sums they needed to buy productive essentials such as a loom, a plow, an ox, or a rod. So he gave small loans to his poor neighbors, secured by nothing more than their promise to repay.

Microcredit, as it's now known, became a macro success in 2006, reaching two huge milestones. The number of the world's poorest people with outstanding microloans—mostly in amounts of $15 to $150—was projected to reach 100 million. And Yunus, 66, shared the Nobel Peace Prize with the Grameen Bank he founded. The Nobel Committee honored his grassroots strategy as "development from below."

You know an idea's time has come when people start yanking it in directions its originator never imagined. Some, like Citigroup, are making for-profit loans, contrary to Yunus' break-even vision. Others, like Bangladesh's BRAC, are nonprofit but have a more holistic vision than Grameen, offering health care and social services in addition to loans.

Source: *BusinessWeek*, December 18, 2006, p. 102.

Analysis: "Microloans" focus on tiny loans to small businesses and farmers that enable them to increase output and productivity.

consumer incomes, households are forced to curtail their purchases. This "inflation tax" ultimately backfires, however, when both domestic and foreign market participants lose confidence in the nation's currency. Periodic currency collapses have destabilized many South and Central American economies and governments. Inflation financing also fails to distinguish good investment ideas from bad ones.

External Financing. Given the constraints on internal financing, poor nations have to seek external funding to lift their investment rate. In fact, Columbia University economist Jeffrey Sachs has argued that external financing is not only necessary but, if generous enough, also sufficient for *eliminating* global poverty (see World View below). As we've observed, however, actual foreign aid flows are far below the "Big Money" threshold that

WORLD VIEW

Jeffrey Sachs: Big Money, Big Plans

Columbia University economics professor Jeffrey Sachs has seen the ravages of poverty around the world. As director of the UN Millennium Project, he is committed to attaining the UN's goal of reducing global poverty rates by half by 2015. In fact, Professor Sachs thinks we can do even better: the complete *elimination* of extreme poverty by 2025.

How will the world do this? First, rich nations must double their foreign aid flows now, and then double them again in ten years. Second, poor nations must develop full-scale, comprehensive plans for poverty reduction. This "shock therapy" approach must address all dimensions of the poverty problem simultaneously and quickly, sweeping all inequality traps out of the way.

Critics have called Sachs's vision utopian. They point to the spotty history of foreign aid projects and the failure of many top-down, Big Plan development initiatives. But they still applaud Sachs for mobilizing public opinion and economic resources to fight global poverty.

Source: Jeffrey Sachs, *The End of Poverty*, Penguin, 2006.

Analysis: World poverty can't be eliminated without committing far more resources. Jeff Sachs favors an externally financed, comprehensive Big Plan approach.

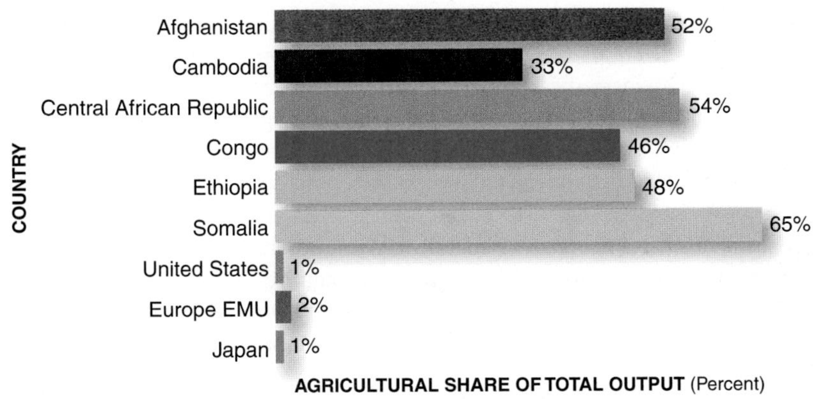

FIGURE 37.4
Agricultural Share of Output

In poor nations, agriculture accounts for a very large share of total output.

Source: World Bank (2005 data). Used with permission by the International Bank for Reconstruction and Development/The World Bank.

Sachs envisions. Skeptics also question whether more foreign aid would really solve the problem, given the mixed results of previous foreign aid flows. They suggest that more emphasis should be placed on increasing *private* investment flows. Private investment typically entails *direct foreign investment* in new plants, equipment, and technology, or the purchase of ownership stakes in existing enterprises.

Agricultural Development

When we think about capital investment, we tend to picture new factories, gleaming office buildings, and computerized machinery. In discussing global poverty, however, we have to remind ourselves of how dependent poor nations are on agriculture. As Figure 37.4 illustrates, 65 percent of Somalia's income originates in agriculture. Agricultural shares in the range of 35–65 percent are common in the poorest nations. By contrast, only 1 percent of America's output now comes from farms.

Low Farm Productivity. What keeps poor nations so dependent on agriculture is their incredibly low **productivity.** Subsistence farmers are often forced to plow their own fields by hand, with wooden plows. Irrigation systems are primitive and farm machinery is scarce or nonexistent. While high-tech U.S. farms produce nearly $37,000 of output per worker, Ethiopian farms produce a shockingly low $118 of output per worker (see Figure 37.5). Farmers in Zimbabwe produce only 676 kilograms of cereal per hectare, compared with 6,444 kilos per hectare in the United States.

productivity: Output per unit of input, e.g., output per labor-hour.

To grow their economies—to rise out of stage 1—poor nations have to invest in agricultural development. Farm productivity has to rise beyond subsistence levels so that workers can migrate to other industries and expand production possibilities. One of the catapults to China's growth was an exponential increase in farm productivity that freed up labor for industrial production. (China now produces nearly 5,000 kilos of cereal per hectare.) To achieve greater farm productivity, poor nations need capital investment, technological know-how, and improved infrastructure.

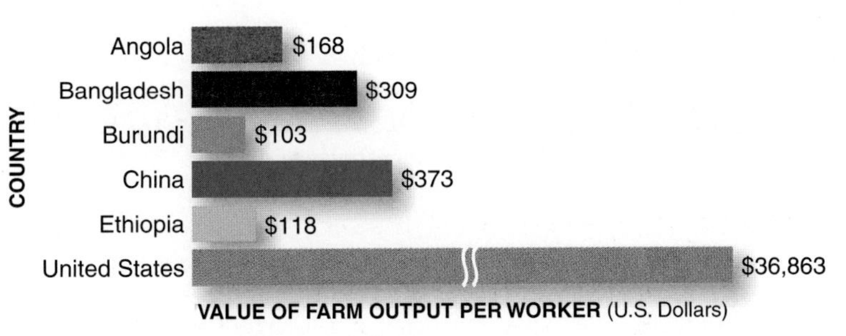

FIGURE 37.5
Low Agricultural Productivity

Farmers in poor nations suffer from low productivity. They are handicapped by low education, inferior technology, primitive infrastructure, and a lack of machinery.

Source: World Bank (2004 data). Used with permission by the International Bank for Reconstruction and Development/The World Bank.

Institutional Reform

The five stages of economic growth envisioned by Rostow imply significant discontinuities in the development process. Nations need some critical mass—some spark—to jump from one stage to the next. That's where the kind of "shock therapy" envisioned by Jeff Sachs comes in. But not everyone embraces this view. Surely, economic growth won't occur automatically, as centuries of global poverty make clear. But growth doesn't necessarily have to follow the sequence of Rostow's five stages either. Moreover, even a series of capital infusions (rather than one massive shock) might promote development.

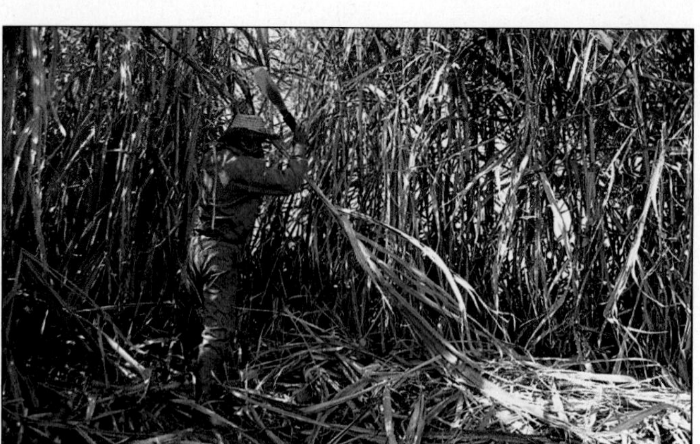

Punchstock/DAL

Analysis: Lack of capital, technology, and markets keeps farm productivity low.

The critical thing is to get enough resources and use them in the best possible way. To do that, ***a nation needs an institutional structure that promotes economic growth.***

Property Rights. Land, property, and contract rights have to be established before farmers will voluntarily improve their land or invest in agricultural technology. China saw how agricultural productivity jumped when it transformed government-run communal farms into local enterprises and privately managed farms, beginning in 1978. China is using the lessons of that experience to now extend ownership rights to farmers.

Entrepreneurial Incentives. Unleashing the "animal spirits" of the marketplace is also critical. People *do* respond to incentives. If farmers see the potential for profit—and the opportunity to keep that profit—they will pursue productivity gains with more vigor. To encourage that response, governments need to assure the legitimacy of profits and their fair tax treatment. In 1992 the Chinese government acknowledged the role of profits and entrepreneurship in fostering economic advancement. Before then, successful entrepreneurs ran the risk of offending the government with conspicuous consumption that highlighted growing inequalities. The government even punished some entrepreneurs and confiscated their wealth. Once "profits" were legitimized, however, entrepreneurship and foreign investment accelerated, pushing China well into Rostow's stage 3.

Cuba stopped short of legitimizing private property and profits. Although Fidel Castro periodically permitted some private enterprises (e.g., family restaurants), he always withdrew that permission when entrepreneurial ventures succeeded. As a consequence, Cuba didn't advance from stage 2 to stage 3. Venezuela has recently moved further in that direction, expropriating and nationalizing private enterprises (see World View below), thereby discouraging private investment and entrepreneurship.

WORLD VIEW

Chávez Sets Plans for Nationalization

BOGOTA, Colombia, Jan. 8—Venezuelan President Hugo Chávez on Monday announced plans to nationalize the country's electrical and telecommunications companies, take control of the once-independent Central Bank and seek special constitutional powers permitting him to pass economic laws by decree.

"We're heading toward socialism, and nothing and no one can prevent it," Chávez, who won a third term in a landslide election in December, said in a speech in Caracas, in the Venezuelan capital.

Chávez also said Monday that the government would soon exert more control over the Central Bank, one of the few Venezuelan institutions that has shown itself to be independent of the Chávez administration. Two of the seven directors of the bank's board, including Domingo Maza Zavala, who often criticized government economic policy, are on their way out.

"The Central Bank must not be autonomous," Chávez said. "That is a neoliberal idea."

—Juan Forero

Source: *Washington Post,* January 9, 2007, p. A10.

Analysis: By restricting private ownership, governments curb the entrepreneurship and investment that may be essential for economic development.

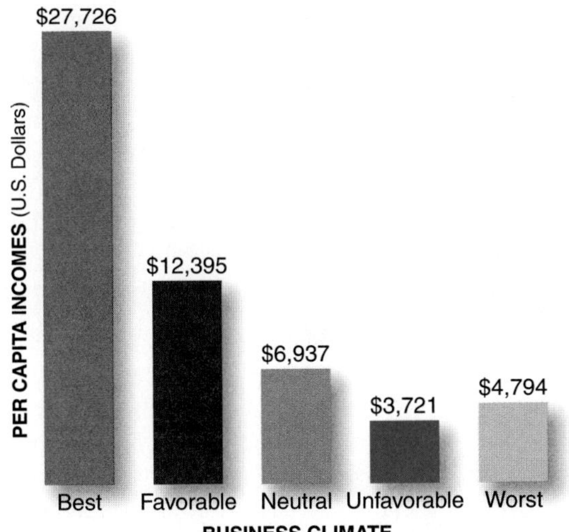

Note: Business climate in 157 nations gauged by 50 measures of government tax, regulatory, and legal policy.

FIGURE 37.6
Business Climates Affect Growth

Nations that offer more secure property rights, less regulation, and lower taxes grow faster and enjoy higher per capita incomes.

Source: Adapted from Heritage Foundation, *2007 Index of Economic Freedom*, p. 7. Washington, DC. Used with permission.

Equity. What disturbed both Castro and Venezuelan President Chávez was the way capitalism intensified income inequalities. Entrepreneurs got rich while the mass of people remained poor. For Castro, the goal of equity was more important than the goal of efficiency. A nation where everyone was equally poor was preferred to a nation of Haves and Have-nots. Chávez thought he could pursue both equity and efficiency with government-managed enterprises.

In many of today's poorest nations policy interests are not so noble. A small elite often holds extraordinary political power and uses that power to protect its privileges. Greed restricts the flow of resources to the poorest segments of the population, leaving them to fend for themselves. These inequalities in power, wealth, and opportunity create inequality traps that restrain human capital development, capital investment, entrepreneurship, and, ultimately, economic growth.

Business Climate. To encourage capital investment and entrepreneurship, governments have to assure a secure and supportive business climate. Investors and business start-ups want to know what the rules of the game are and how they will be enforced. They also want assurances that contracts will be enforced and that debts can be collected. They want their property protected from crime and government corruption. They want minimal interference from government regulation and taxes.

As the annual surveys by the Heritage Foundation document, nations that offer a more receptive business climate grow at a faster pace. Figure 37.6 illustrates this connection. Notice that nations with the most pro-business climate (e.g., Hong Kong, Singapore, Iceland, USA, and Denmark) enjoy living standards far superior to those in nations with hostile business climates (e.g., North Korea, Congo, Sudan, Zimbabwe, and Myanmar). This is no accident; ***pro-business climates encourage the capital investment, the entrepreneurship, and the human capital investment that drive economic growth.***

Unfortunately, some of the poorest nations still fail to provide a pro-business environment. Figure 37.7 illustrates how specific dimensions of the business climate differ across fast-growing nations (China) and perpetually poor ones (Cambodia and Kenya). A biannual survey of 26,000 international firms elicits their views of how different government policies restrain their investment decisions. Notice how China offers a more certain policy environment, less corruption, more secure property rights, and less crime. Given these business conditions, where would you invest?

The good news about the business climate is that it doesn't require huge investments to fix. It does require, however, a lot of political capital.

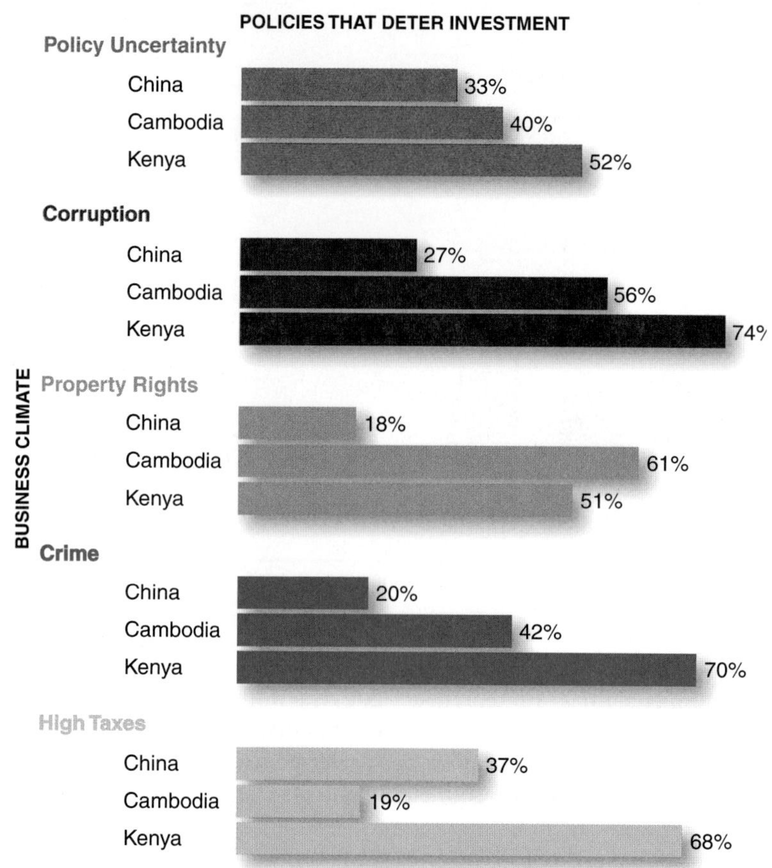

FIGURE 37.7
Investment Climate

International investors gravitate toward nations with business-friendly policies. Shown here are the percentages of international firms citing specific elements of the business climate that deter their investment in the named countries.

Source: World Bank, *World Development Indicators 2006*. Used with permission by the International Bank for Reconstruction and Development/The World Bank.

World Trade

comparative advantage: The ability of a country to produce a specific good at a lower opportunity cost than its trading partners.

import quota: A limit on the quantity of a good that may be imported in a given time period.

When it comes to political capital, poor nations have a complaint of their own. They say that rich nations lock them out of their most important markets—particularly agricultural export markets. Poor nations typically have a **comparative advantage** in the production of agricultural products. Their farm productivity may be low (see Figure 37.5), but their low labor costs keep their farm output competitive. They can't fully exploit that advantage in export markets, however. The United States, the European Union, and Japan heavily subsidize their own farmers. This keeps farm prices low in the rich nations, eliminating the cost advantage of farmers in poor nations. To further protect their own farmers from global competition, rich nations erect trade barriers to stem the inflow of Third World products. The United States, for example, enforces an **import quota** on foreign sugar. This trade barrier has fostered a high-cost, domestic beet-sugar industry (see World View, p. 751), while denying poor nations the opportunity to sell more sugar and grow their economies faster.

Poor nations need export markets. Export sales generate the hard currency (dollars, euros, and yen) that is needed to purchase capital equipment in global markets. Export sales also allow farmers in poor nations to expand production, exploit economies of scale, and invest in improved technology. Ironically, ***trade barriers in rich nations impede poor nations from pursuing the agricultural development that is a* prerequisite *for growth.*** The latest round of multilateral trade negotiations (the "Doha" round; see p. 712) dragged on forever because of the resistance of rich nations to open their agricultural markets. Poor nations plead that "trade, not aid" is their surest path to economic growth.

A 2004 study estimated that 440 million people would be lifted out of severe poverty if all trade barriers were dismantled.[2] China has demonstrated how a vibrant export sector can propel economic growth; South Korea, Taiwan, Malaysia, India, and Costa Rica have also

[2]William Cline, *Trade Policy and Global Poverty* (Washington, DC: Institute for International Economics, 2004).

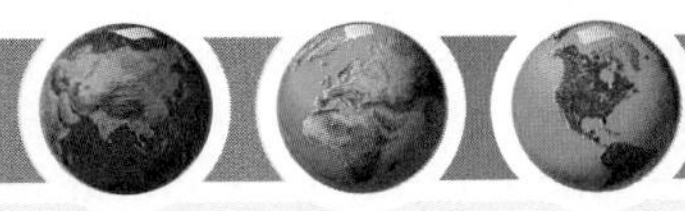

WORLD VIEW

African Sugar Production Ramps Up

EU Plan to Cut Tariffs Shows How Developing Nations Can Benefit

BRUSSELS—The developing world has been adamant that rich nations abandon farm subsidies in order to get a global trade deal both sides say they want. A flood of investment pouring into Southern Africa's sugar industry demonstrates why the poor countries won't back down on this demand.

The hundreds of millions of dollars being spent to ramp up African sugar production is a direct response to European Union plans to slash import duties and subsidies that for years have locked out farmers in developing countries. . . .

The expansion shows how the EU's gradual opening of its farm sector can boost production in some developing countries. . . .

The impact of the planned opening of the EU's sugar market suggests those changes could trigger significant investment in some of the world's poorest rural economies.

Sugar concern Tongaat-Hulett Group Ltd. of South Africa says it will spend $180 million over the next two years to plant roughly an additional 21,250 acres of sugar cane, install modern technology in existing mills and hire 8,800 more workers. . . .

"It's not easy to find reasons to invest in countries like Mozambique," said Tongaat-Hulett Chief Executive Peter Staude in an interview. "The civil war just ended, and there are land mines and machine guns all over." One of the company's executives was shot at recently when his plane landed near the sugar mill in Xinavane.

Two things made the investment possible, he said. One is that Mozambique has two functional harbors connected to rail lines, infrastructure that doesn't exist in many other poor African countries, Mr. Staude said. The other was the planned changes to EU sugar tariffs and subsidies. "Above all, we want a platform to sell into the EU," he said.

—John W. Miller

Source: *The Wall Street Journal,* February 12, 2007, p. A4.

Analysis: Poor nations need access to markets in rich nations in order to encourage investment in domestic production. They demand "trade, not aid."

successfully used exports to advance into the higher stages of economic growth. Mozambique is demonstrating how even a small window of export opportunity can make a real difference in investment and productivity rates (see World View). Other poor nations want the same opportunity.

THE ECONOMY TOMORROW

UNLEASHING ENTREPRENEURSHIP

The traditional approach to economic development emphasizes the potential for government policy to reallocate resources and increase capital investment. External financing of capital investment was always at or near the top of the policy agenda (see World View, bottom of p. 746). This approach has been criticized for neglecting the power of people and markets.

One of the most influential critics is the Peruvian economist Hernando de Soto. When he returned to his native Peru after years of commercial success in Europe, he was struck by the dichotomy in his country. The "official" economy was mired in bureaucratic red tape and stagnant. Most of the vitality of the Peruvian economy was contained in the unofficial "underground" economy. The underground economy included trade in drugs but was overwhelmingly oriented to meeting the everyday demands of Peruvian consumers and households. The

© David Zurich/DAL

Analysis: Markets exist but struggle in poor nations.

underground economy wasn't hidden from view; it flourished on the streets, in outdoor markets, and in transport services. The only thing that forced this thriving economy underground was the failure of the government to recognize it and give it legitimate status. Government restrictions on prices, business activities, finance, and trade—a slew of inequality traps—forced entrepreneurs to operate "underground."

De Soto concluded that countries like Peru could grow more quickly if governments encouraged rather than suppressed these entrepreneurial resources. In his best-selling book, *The Other Path*, he urged poor countries to refocus their development policies. This "other path" entails improving the business climate by

- Reducing bureaucratic barriers to free enterprise.
- Spreading private ownership.
- Developing and enforcing legal safeguards for property, income, and wealth.
- Developing infrastructure that facilitates business activity.

Yunus's "microloans" (World View, p. 746) would also fit comfortably on this other path.

De Soto's book has been translated into several languages and has encouraged market-oriented reforms in Peru, Argentina, Mexico, Russia, Vietnam, and elsewhere. In India the government is drastically reducing both regulation and taxes in order to pursue De Soto's other path. The basic message of his other path is that poor nations should exploit the one resource that is abundant in even the poorest countries—entrepreneurship.

SUMMARY

- Definitions of "poverty" are culturally based. Poverty in the United States is defined largely in *relative* terms, whereas global poverty is tied more to *absolute* levels of subsistence. LO1
- About 12 percent of the U.S. population (35–36 million people) are officially counted as poor. Poor people in America suffer from *relative* deprivation, not *absolute* deprivation, as in global poverty. LO1
- Global poverty thresholds are about one-tenth of U.S. standards. "Extreme" poverty is defined as less than $1 per day per person; "severe" poverty is less than $2 per day (inflation adjusted). LO1
- One billion people around the world are in extreme poverty; close to 3 billion are in severe poverty. In low-income nations global poverty rates are as high as 70–90 percent. LO2
- The United Nations' Millennium Poverty Goal is to cut the global poverty rate in half, to 15 percent by 2015. LO3
- Redistribution of incomes *within* poor nations doesn't have much potential for reducing poverty, given their low *average* incomes. *Across*-nation redistributions (e.g., foreign aid) can make a small dent, however. LO3
- Economic growth is the key to global poverty reduction. Many poor nations are stuck in stage 1 of development, with undeveloped human capital, primitive infrastructure, and subsistence agriculture. To grow more quickly, they need to meet basic human needs (health and education) increase agricultural productivity, and encourage investment. LO3
- To move into sustained economic growth, poor nations need capital investment and institutional reforms that promote both equity and entrepreneurship. LO3
- Poor nations also need "trade, not aid," that is, access to rich-nation markets, particularly in farm products. LO3

Key Terms

poverty threshold (U.S.)
poverty rate
in-kind transfers
extreme poverty (world)
severe poverty (world)
Millennium Poverty Goal
Millennium Aid Goal
economic growth
human capital
inequality trap
investment rate
microfinance
productivity
comparative advantage
import quota

Questions for Discussion

1. Why should Americans care about extreme poverty in Haiti, Ethiopia, or Bangladesh? LO2
2. If you had only $14 to spend per day (the U.S. poverty threshold), how would you spend it? What if you had only $2 a day (the World Bank "severe poverty" threshold)? LO1
3. If a poor nation must choose between building an airport, some schools, or a steel plant, which one should it choose? Why? LO3
4. Why are incomes so much more unequal in poor nations than in developed ones? (See World View, p. 758.) LO1
5. How do more children per family either restrain or expand income-earning potential? LO3
6. Are property rights a perquisite for economic growth? Explain. LO3
7. How do unequal rights for women affect economic growth? LO3
8. Identify "inequality traps" that might inhibit economic growth. LO3
9. Could a nation reorder Rostow's five stages of development and still grow? Explain. LO3
10. How does microfinance alter prospects for economic growth? The distribution of political power? LO3
11. Can poor nations develop without substantial increases in agricultural productivity? (See Figure 37.4.) How? LO3
12. Would you invest in Cambodia or Kenya on the basis of the information in Figure 37.7? LO3
13. How might Bolivia match China's investment rate? (See Table 37.5.) LO2
14. Why do economists put so much emphasis on entrepreneurship? How can poor nations encourage it? LO3
15. How do nations expect nationalization of basic industries to foster economic growth? LO3
16. If economic growth reduced poverty but widened inequalities, would it still be desirable? LO3
17. What market failure does Bill Gates (World View, p. 740) cite as the motivation for global philanthropy? LO3

problems The Student Problem Set at the back of this book contains numerical and graphing problems for this chapter.

web activities to accompany this chapter can be found on the Online Learning Center: **http://www.mhhe.com/economics/schiller11e**

PHOTO CREDITS

Chapter 1: p.1 (left), p.2 Photo by Time Life Pictures/JPL/NASA/Time Life Pictures/Getty Images.
Chapter 2: p.1 (center), p.26 RF/CORBIS/DAL
Chapter 3: p.1 (right), p.42 Rob Melnychuk/Getty Images/DAL
Chapter 4: p.66 Hisham F. Ibrahim/Getty Images/DAL
Chapter 5: p.85 (left), p.86 Kim Steele/Getty Images/DAL
Chapter 6: p.85 (center), p.106 Dado Galdieri/AP
Chapter 7: p.85 (right), p.123 ©Photolink/Getty Images/DAL
Chapter 8: p.143 (left), p.144 Associated Press
Chapter 9: p.143 (center), p.166 ©Photolink/Getty Images/DAL
Chapter 10: p.143 (right), p.192 C. McIntyre/Photolink/Getty Images/DAL
Chapter 11: p.211 (left), p.212 ©Alan Schein/zefa/Corbis
Chapter 12: p.211 (right), p.231 ©Michael Newman/PhotoEdit-All rights reserved.
Chapter 13: p.253 (center), p.254 Keith Brofsky/Getty Images/DAL
Chapter 14: p.253 (left), p.272 ©Eyewire/Photodisc/Punchstock/DAL
Chapter 15: p.253 (right), p.288 ©Paul Conklin/PhotoEdit
Chapter 16: p.311 (left), p.312 Skip Nall/Getty Images/DAL
Chapter 17: p.311 (right), p.332 Public Domain/DAL
Chapter 18: p.351 (left), p.352 Keith Brofsky/Getty Images/DAL
Chapter 19: p.351 (right), p.367 The McGraw-Hill Companies, Inc. /Lars A. Niki, photographer
Chapter 20: p.389 (left), p.390 Photolink/Getty Images
Chapter 21: p.389 (right), p.421 RF/Corbis/DAL
Chapter 22: p.445 (left), p.446 The McGraw-Hill Companies, Inc. /Lars A. Niki, photographer
Chapter 23: p.445 (center), p.468 DigitalVision/Punchstock/DAL
Chapter 24: p.445 (right), p.488 Public Domain/DAL
Chapter 25: p.509 The McGraw-Hill Companies/Andrew Resek, photographer
Chapter 26: p.533 The McGraw-Hill Companies/Jill Braaten, photographer
Chapter 27: p.545 (left), p.546 RF/Corbis/DAL
Chapter 28: p.545 (middle), p.566 RF/Corbis/DAL
Chapter 29: p.545 (right), p.585 Corbis
Chapter 30: p.599 (left), p.600 Associated Press
Chapter 31: p.599 (middle), p.622 ©Mark Richards/PhotoEdit
Chapter 32: p.599 (right), p.639 RF/Corbis/DAL
Chapter 33: p.657 (left), p.658 RF/Corbis/DAL
Chapter 34: p.657 (right) Ryan McVay/Getty Images/DAL
Chapter 35: p.691 (left), p.692 F. Schussier/Photolink/Getty Images/DAL
Chapter 36: p.691 (middle), p.715 Getty Images/DAL
Chapter 37: p.691 (right), p. 733 AFP/Getty Images

GLOSSARY

Note: Numbers in parenthesis indicate the chapters in which the definitions appear.

absolute advantage: The ability of a country to produce a specific good with fewer resources (per unit of output) than other countries. (35)
acreage set-aside: Land withdrawn from production as part of policy to increase crop prices. (29)
AD excess: The amount by which aggregate demand must be reduced to achieve full employment equilibrium after allowing for price-level changes. (11)
AD shortfall: The amount of additional aggregate demand needed to achieve full employment after allowing for price-level changes. (11)
adjustable-rate mortgage (ARM): A mortgage (home loan) that adjusts the nominal interest rate to changing rates of inflation. (7)
aggregate demand (AD): The total quantity of output (real GDP) demanded at alternative price levels in a given time period, *ceteris paribus.* (8, 9, 10, 11, 13, 15)
aggregate expenditure: The rate of total expenditure desired at alternative levels of income, *ceteris paribus.* (9)
aggregate supply (AS): The total quantity of output (real GDP) producers are willing and able to supply at alternative price levels in a given time period, *ceteris paribus.* (8, 9, 10, 11, 16)
antitrust: Government intervention to alter market structure or prevent abuse of market power. (4, 24, 25, 27)
appreciation: A rise in the price of one currency relative to another. (36)
arithmetic growth: An increase in quantity by a constant amount each year. (17)
asset: Anything having exchange value in the marketplace; wealth. (12)
automatic stabilizer: Federal expenditure or revenue item that automatically responds countercyclically to changes in national income, like unemployment benefits, income taxes. (12, 19)
average fixed cost (AFC): Total fixed cost divided by the quantity produced in a given time period. (21)
average propensity to consume (APC): Total consumption in a given period divided by total disposable income. (9)
average total cost (ATC): Total cost divided by the quantity produced in a given time period. (21, 23, 24)
average variable cost (AVC): Total variable cost divided by the quantity produced in a given time period. (21)

balance of payments: A summary record of a country's international economic transactions in a given period of time. (36)
balance-of-payments deficit: An excess demand for foreign currency at current exchange rates. (36)
balance-of-payments surplus: An excess demand for domestic currency at current exchange rates. (36)
bank reserves: Assets held by a bank to fulfill its deposit obligations. (13)
barriers to entry: Obstacles such as patents that make it difficult or impossible for would-be producers to enter a particular market. (23, 24, 25, 26, 27, 28, 29)
barter: The direct exchange of one good for another, without the use of money. (13)
base period: The time period used for comparative analysis; the basis for indexing, e.g., of price changes. (5, 7, 17)
bilateral monopoly: A market with only one buyer (a monopsonist) and one seller (a monopolist). (31)
bond: A certificate acknowledging a debt and the amount of interest to be paid each year until repayment; an IOU. (14, 32)
bracket creep: The movement of taxpayers into higher tax brackets (rates) as nominal incomes grow. (7)
breakeven level of income: The income level at which welfare eligibility ceases. (34)
budget constraint: A line depicting all combinations of goods that are affordable with a given income and given prices. (20)
budget deficit: Amount by which government spending exceeds government revenue in a given time period. (12)
budget surplus: An excess of government revenues over government expenditures in a given time period. (12)
business cycle: Alternating periods of economic growth and contraction. (8, 9, 19)

capital: Final goods produced for use in the production of other goods, e.g., equipment, structures. (1)
capital deficit: The amount by which the capital outflow exceeds the capital inflow in a given time period. (18)
capital gain: An increase in the market value of an asset. (32)
capital-intensive: Production processes that use a high ratio of capital to labor inputs. (2)
capital surplus: The amount by which the capital inflow exceeds the capital outflow in a given time period. (18)
cartel: A group of firms with an explicit, formal agreement to fix prices and output shares in a particular market. (25)
cash transfers: Income transfers that entail direct cash payments to recipients, e.g., Social Security, welfare, and unemployment benefits. (34)
categorical grants: Federal grants to state and local governments for specific expenditure purposes. (4)
ceteris paribus: The assumption of nothing else changing. (1, 3, 20)
closed economy: A nation that doesn't engage in international trade. (35)
collective bargaining: Direct negotiations between employers and unions to determine labor market outcomes. (31)
comparative advantage: The ability of a country to produce a specific good at a lower opportunity cost than its trading partners. (2, 18, 35, 37)
competitive firm: A firm without market power, with no ability to alter the market price of the goods it produces. (22)
competitive market: A market in which no buyer or seller has market power. (23)
complementary goods: Goods frequently consumed in combination; when the price of good *x* rises, the demand for good *y* falls, *ceteris paribus.* (3, 20)
concentration ratio: The proportion of total industry output produced by the largest firms (usually the four largest). (25, 26)
constant returns to scale: Increases in plant size do not affect minimum average cost; minimum per-unit costs are identical for small plants and large plants. (21)
Consumer Price Index (CPI): A measure (index) of changes in the average price of consumer goods and services. (7)
consumption: Expenditure by consumers on final goods and services. (9)
consumption function: A mathematical relationship indicating the rate of desired consumer spending at various income levels. (9)
consumption possibilities: The alternative combinations of goods and services that a country could consume in a given time period. (35)
contestable market: An imperfectly competitive industry subject to potential entry if prices or profits increase. (24, 25, 27)
core inflation rate: Changes in the CPI, excluding food and energy prices. (7)
corporate stock: Shares of ownership in a corporation. (32)
corporation: A business organization having a continuous existence independent of its members (owners) and power and liabilities distinct from those of its members. (32)

cost efficiency: The amount of output associated with an additional dollar spent on input; the MPP of an input divided by its price (cost). (30)
cost-of-living adjustment (COLA): Automatic adjustments of nominal income to the rate of inflation. (7)
countercyclical payment: Income transfer paid to farmers for difference between target and support prices. (29)
coupon rate: Interest rate set for a bond at time of issuance. (32)
cross-price elasticity of demand: Percentage change in the quantity demanded of *X* divided by percentage change in price of *Y.* (20)
cross-subsidization: Use of high prices and profits on one product to subsidize low prices on another product. (27)
crowding in: An increase in private-sector borrowing (and spending) caused by decreased government borrowing. (12, 17)
crowding out: A reduction in private-sector borrowing (and spending) caused by increased government borrowing. (11, 12, 15, 17, 18)
current yield: The rate of return on a bond; the annual interest payment divided by the bond's price. (32)
cyclical deficit: That portion of the budget deficit attributable to unemployment or inflation. (12)
cyclical unemployment: Unemployment attributable to a lack of job vacancies, that is, to inadequate aggregate demand. (6, 9, 10)

debt ceiling: An explicit, legislated limit on the amount of outstanding national debt. (12)
debt service: The interest required to be paid each year on outstanding debt. (12)
default: Failure to make scheduled payments of interest or principal on a bond. (32)
deficit ceiling: An explicit, legislated limitation on the size of the budget deficit. (12)
deficit spending: The use of borrowed funds to finance government expenditures that exceed tax revenues. (12)
deflation: A decrease in the average level of prices of goods and services. (7)
demand: The willingness and ability to buy specific quantities of a good at alternative prices in a given time period, *ceteris paribus.* (3, 20)
demand curve: A curve describing the quantities of a good a consumer is willing and able to buy at alternative prices in a given time period, *ceteris paribus.* (3, 20)
demand for labor: The quantities of labor employers are willing and able to hire at alternative wage rates in a given time period, *ceteris paribus.* (30, 31)
demand for money: The quantities of money people are willing and able to hold at alternative interest rates, *ceteris paribus.* (15)
demand-pull inflation: An increase in the price level initiated by excessive aggregate demand. (9, 10)
demand schedule: A table showing the quantities of a good a consumer is willing and able to buy at alternative prices in a given time period, *ceteris paribus.* (3)
deposit creation: The creation of transactions deposits by bank lending. (13)
depreciation: The consumption of capital in the production process; the wearing out of plant and equipment. (5)
depreciation (currency): A fall in the price of one currency relative to another. (36)
derived demand: The demand for labor and other factors of production results from (depends on) the demand for final goods and services produced by these factors. (30)
devaluation: An abrupt depreciation of a currency whose value was fixed or managed by the government. (36)
discount rate: The rate of interest the Federal Reserve charges for lending reserves to private banks. (14)
discounting: Federal Reserve lending of reserves to private banks. (14)
discouraged worker: An individual who isn't actively seeking employment but would look for or accept a job if one were available. (6)
discretionary fiscal spending: Those elements of the federal budget not determined by past legislative or executive commitments. (12)
disposable income (DI): After-tax income of households; personal income less personal taxes. (5, 9, 11)
dissaving: Consumption expenditure in excess of disposable income; a negative saving flow. (9)
dividend: Amount of corporate profits paid out for each share of stock. (32)
dumping: The sale of goods in export markets at prices below domestic prices. (35)

economic cost: The value of all resources used to produce a good or service; opportunity cost. (21, 22)
economic growth: An increase in output (real GDP); an expansion of production possibilities. (1, 2, 6, 17, 37)
economic profit: The difference between total revenues and total economic costs. (22, 23, 26, 27, 29)
economics: The study of how best to allocate scarce resources among competing uses. (1)
economies of scale: Reductions in minimum average costs that come about through increases in the size (scale) of plant and equipment. (21, 24, 27)
effective tax rate: Taxes paid divided by total income. (33)
efficiency: Maximum output of a good from the resources used in production. (1, 21, 23)
efficiency decision: The choice of a production process for any given rate of output. (28, 30)
elasticity of labor supply: The percentage change in the quantity of labor supplied divided by the percentage change in wage rate. (30)
embargo: A prohibition on exports or imports. (35)
emission charge: A fee imposed on polluters, based on the quantity of pollution. (28)
employment rate: The percentage of the adult population that is employed. (17)
entrepreneurship: The assembling of resources to produce new or improved products and technologies. (1)
equation of exchange: Money supply (M) times velocity of circulation (V) equals level of aggregate spending ($P \times Q$). (15, 16)
equilibrium (macro): The combination of price level and real output that is compatible with both aggregate demand and aggregate supply. (8, 9, 11)
equilibrium GDP: The value of total output (real GDP) produced at macro equilibrium (AS–AD). (9, 10)
equilibrium price: The price at which the quantity of a good demanded in a given time period equals the quantity supplied. (3, 23, 35, 36)
equilibrium rate of interest: The interest rate at which the quantity of money demanded in a given time period equals the quantity of money supplied. (15)
equilibrium wage: The wage rate at which the quantity of labor supplied in a given time period equals the quantity of labor demanded. (30, 31)
excess reserves: Bank reserves in excess of required reserves. (13, 14)
exchange rate: The price of one country's currency expressed in terms of another's; the domestic price of a foreign currency. (18, 36)
expected value: The probable value of a future payment, including the risk of nonpayment. (32)
expenditure equilibrium: The rate of output at which desired spending equals the value of output. (9)
explicit costs: A payment made for the use of a resource. (21, 22)
exports: Goods and services sold to foreign buyers. (2, 5, 18, 35)
external costs: Costs of a market activity borne by a third party; the difference between the social and private costs of a market activity. (28)
external debt: U.S. government debt (Treasury bonds) held by foreign households and institutions. (12)
externalities: Costs (or benefits) of a market activity borne by a third party; the difference between the social and private costs (benefits) of a market activity. (2, 4, 28)
extreme poverty (world): World Bank income standard of less than $1 per day per person (inflation adjusted). (37)

factor market: Any place where factors of production (e.g., land, labor, capital) are bought and sold. (3)

factors of production: Resource inputs used to produce goods and services, e.g., land, labor, capital, entrepreneurship. (1, 2, 21)
federal funds rate: The interest rate for interbank reserve loans. (14, 15)
financial intermediary: Institution (e.g., a bank or the stock market) that makes savings available to dissavers (e.g., investors). (32)
fine-tuning: Adjustments in economic policy designed to counteract small changes in economic outcomes; continuous responses to changing economic conditions. (19)
fiscal policy: The use of government taxes and spending to alter macroeconomic outcomes. (8, 11, 12, 19)
fiscal restraint: Tax hikes or spending cuts intended to reduce (shift) aggregate demand. (11, 12, 19)
fiscal stimulus: Tax cuts or spending hikes intended to increase (shift) aggregate demand. (11, 12, 19)
fiscal year (FY): The 12-month period used for accounting purposes; begins October 1 for the federal government. (12)
fixed costs: Costs of production that don't change when the rate of output is altered, e.g., the cost of basic plant and equipment. (21, 22)
flat tax: A single-rate tax system. (33)
flexible exchange rates: A system in which exchange rates are permitted to vary with market supply-and-demand conditions; floating exchange rates. (36)
foreign-exchange markets: Places where foreign currencies are bought and sold. (36)
foreign-exchange reserves: Holdings of foreign exchange by official government agencies, usually the central bank or treasury. (36)
free rider: An individual who reaps direct benefits from someone else's purchase (consumption) of a public good. (4)
frictional unemployment: Brief periods of unemployment experienced by people moving between jobs or into the labor market. (6)
full employment: The lowest rate of unemployment compatible with price stability; variously estimated at between 4 and 6 percent unemployment. (6, 10)
full-employment GDP: The value of total market output (real GDP) produced at full employment. (8, 9, 10)

game theory: The study of decision making in situations where strategic interaction (moves and countermoves) occurs between rivals. (25)
GDP deflator: A price index that refers to all goods and services included in GDP. (7)
GDP gap (real): The difference between full-employment GDP and equilibrium GDP. (10, 11, 19)
GDP per capita: Total GDP divided by total population; average GDP. (5, 17)
geometric growth: An increase in quantity by a constant proportion each year. (17)
Gini coefficient: A mathematical summary of inequality based on the Lorenz curve. (33)
gold reserves: Stocks of gold held by a government to purchase foreign exchange. (36)
gold standard: An agreement by countries to fix the price of their currencies in terms of gold; a mechanism for fixing exchange rates. (36)
government failure: Government intervention that fails to improve economic outcomes. (1, 4, 27, 28, 33)
gross business saving: Depreciation allowances and retained earnings. (10)
gross domestic product (GDP): The total market value of all final goods and services produced within a nation's borders in a given time period. (2, 5)
gross investment: Total investment expenditure in a given time period. (5)
growth rate: Percentage change in real output from one period to another. (17)
growth recession: A period during which real GDP grows but at a rate below the long-term trend of 3 percent. (8, 19)

Herfindahl-Hirshman Index (HHI): Measure of industry concentration that accounts for number of firms and size of each. (25)
horizontal equity: Principle that people with equal incomes should pay equal taxes. (33)
human capital: The knowledge and skills possessed by the workforce. (2, 16, 17)
hyperinflation: Inflation rate in excess of 200 percent, lasting at least one year. (7)
implicit cost: The value of resources used, even when no direct payment is made. (21, 22)
imports: Goods and services purchased from international sources. (2, 5, 18, 35)
import quota: A limit on the quantity of a good that may be imported in a given time period. (37)
income effect of wages: An increased wage rate allows a person to reduce hours worked without losing income. (30)
income elasticity of demand: Percentage change in quantity demanded divided by percentage change in income. (20, 29)
income quintile: One-fifth of the population, rank-ordered by income (e.g., top fifth). (2)
income share: The proportion of total income received by a particular group. (33)
income transfers: Payments to individuals for which no current goods or services are exchanged, e.g., Social Security, welfare, unemployment benefits. (2, 11, 12, 33)
income velocity of money: (V) The number of times per year, on average, a dollar is used to purchase final goods and services; $PQ \div M$. (15)
indifference curve: A curve depicting alternative combinations of goods that yield equal satisfaction. (20)
indifference map: The set of indifference curves that depicts all possible levels of utility attainable from various combinations of goods. (20)
inequality trap: Institutional barriers that impede human and physical capital investment, particularly by the poorest segments of society. (37)
inferior good: Good for which demand decreases when income rises. (20)
inflation: An increase in the average level of prices of goods and services. (4, 5, 7, 8)
inflation rate: The annual percentage rate of increase in the average price level. (7)
inflation targeting: The use of an inflation ceiling ("target") to signal the need for monetary-policy adjustments. (15)
inflationary GDP gap: The amount by which equilibrium GDP exceeds full employment GDP. (9, 10, 11, 19)
infrastructure: The transportation, communications, education, judicial, and other institutional systems that facilitate market exchanges. (16)
initial public offering (IPO): The first issuance (sale) to the general public of stock in a corporation. (32)
injection: An addition of spending to the circular flow of income. (10)
in-kind income: Goods and services received directly, without payment, in a market transaction. (33)
in-kind transfers: Direct transfers of goods and services rather than cash; examples include food stamps, Medicaid benefits, and housing subsidies. (34)
interest rate: The price paid for the use of money. (15)
intermediate goods: Goods or services purchased for use as input in the production of final goods or in services. (5)
internal debt: U.S. government debt (Treasury bonds) held by U.S. households and institutions. (12)
investment: Expenditures on (production of) new plant, equipment, and structures (capital) in a given time period, plus changes in business inventories. (2, 5, 9, 16)
investment decision: The decision to build, buy, or lease plant and equipment; to enter or exit an industry. (22, 23)
investment rate: The percentage of total output (GDP) allocated to the production of new plant, equipment, and structures, (37)
item weight: The percentage of total expenditure spent on a specific product; used to compute inflation indexes. (7)

labor force: All persons over age 16 who are either working for pay or actively seeking paid employment. (6, 17)
labor-force participation rate: The percentage of the working-age population working or seeking employment. (6, 34)
labor productivity: Amount of output produced by a worker in a given period of time; output per hour (or day, etc.). (16)
labor supply: The willingness and ability to work specific amounts of time at alternative wage rates in a given time period, *ceteris paribus.* (30, 31, 34)

laissez faire: The doctrine of "leave it alone," of nonintervention by government in the market mechanism. (l, 8, 27)
law of demand: The quantity of a good demanded in a given time period increases as its price falls, *ceteris paribus.* (3, 8, 20)
law of diminishing marginal utility: The marginal utility of a good declines as more of it is consumed in a given time period. (20)
law of diminishing returns: The marginal physical product of a variable input declines as more of it is employed with a given quantity of other (fixed) inputs. (21, 30)
law of supply: The quantity of a good supplied in a given time period increases as its price increases, *ceteris paribus.* (3)
leakage: Income not spent directly on domestic output but instead diverted from the circular flow, e.g., saving, imports, taxes. (10, 18)
liability: An obligation to make future payment; debt. (12)
liquidity: The ability of an asset to be converted into cash. (32)
liquidity trap: The portion of the money demand curve that is horizontal; people are willing to hold unlimited amounts of money at some (low) interest rate. (15)
loan rate: The implicit price paid by the government for surplus crops taken as collateral for loans to farmers. (29)
long run: A period of time long enough for all inputs to be varied (no fixed costs). (21, 22)
long-run competitive equilibrium: p = MC = minimum ATC. (23)
Lorenz curve: A graphic illustration of the cumulative size distribution of income; contrasts complete equality with the actual distribution of income. (33)

macroeconomics: The study of aggregate economic behavior, of the economy as a whole. (1, 8)
managed exchange rates: A system in which governments intervene in foreign-exchange markets to limit but not eliminate exchange-rate fluctuations; "dirty floats." (36)
marginal cost (MC): The increase in total cost associated with a one-unit increase in production. (21, 22, 23)
marginal cost pricing: The offer (supply) of goods at prices equal to their marginal cost. (23, 24, 26, 27)
marginal factor cost (MFC): The change in total costs that results from a one-unit increase in the quantity of a factor employed. (31)
marginal physical product (MPP): The change in total output associated with one additional unit of input. (21, 30)
marginal propensity to consume (MPC): The fraction of each additional (marginal) dollar of disposable income spent on consumption; the change in consumption divided by the change in disposable income. (9, 10, 11)
marginal propensity to import (MPM): The fraction of each additional (marginal) dollar of disposable income spent on imports. (18)
marginal propensity to save (MPS): The fraction of each additional (marginal) dollar of disposable income not spent on consumption; 1 – MPC. (9, 18)
marginal rate of substitution: The rate at which a consumer is willing to exchange one good for another; the relative marginal utilities of two goods. (20)
marginal revenue (MR): The change in total revenue that results from a one-unit increase in the quantity sold. (22, 24, 25)
marginal revenue product (MRP): The change in total revenue associated with one additional unit of input. (30, 31, 33)
marginal tax rate: The tax rate imposed on the last (marginal) dollar of income. (16, 33, 34)
marginal utility: The change in total utility obtained by consuming one additional (marginal) unit of a good or service. (20)
marginal wage: The change in total wages paid associated with a one-unit increase in the quantity of labor employed. (31)
market demand: The total quantities of a good or service people are willing and able to buy at alternative prices in a given time period; the sum of individual demands. (3)
market failure: An imperfection in the market mechanism that prevents optimal outcomes. (1, 4, 25, 27, 28, 33, 34)
market mechanism: The use of market prices and sales to signal desired outputs (or resource allocations). (1, 3, 4, 23, 32)
market power: The ability to alter the market price of a good or service. (4, 22, 24, 26, 29, 31)
market share: The percentage of total market output produced by a single firm. (25)
market shortage: The amount by which the quantity demanded exceeds the quantity supplied at a given price; excess demand. (3, 36)
market structure: The number and relative size of firms in an industry. (22, 25)
market supply: The total quantities of a good that sellers are willing and able to sell at alternative prices in a given time period, *ceteris paribus.* (3, 23)
market supply of labor: The total quantity of labor that workers are willing and able to supply at alternative wage rates in a given time period, *ceteris paribus.* (30)
market surplus: The amount by which the quantity supplied exceeds the quantity demanded at a given price; excess supply. (3, 29)
merit good: A good or service society deems everyone is entitled to some minimal quantity of. (4)
microeconomics: The study of individual behavior in the economy, of the components of the larger economy. (1)
microfinance: The granting of small ("micro") unsecured loans to small business and enterpreneurs. (37)
Millennium Aid Goal: United Nations goal of raising foreign aid levels to 0.7 percent of donor-country GDP. (37)
Millennium Poverty Goal: United Nations goal of reducing global rate of extreme poverty to 15 percent by 2015. (37)
mixed economy: An economy that uses both market signals and government directives to allocate goods and resources. (1)
monetary policy: The use of money and credit controls to influence macroeconomic outcomes. (8, 14, 15, 19)
money: Anything generally accepted as a medium of exchange. (13)
money illusion: The use of nominal dollars rather than real dollars to gauge changes in one's income or wealth. (7)
money multiplier: The number of deposit (loan) dollars that the banking system can create from $1 of excess reserves; equal to 1 ÷ required reserve ratio. (13, 14)
money supply (M1): Currency held by the public, plus balances in transactions accounts. (13, 14, 15)
money supply (M2): M1 plus balances in most savings accounts and money market funds. (13, 14, 15)
monopolistic competition: A market in which many firms produce similar goods or services but each maintains some independent control of its own price. (26)
monopoly: A firm that produces the entire market supply of a particular good or service. (2, 4, 22, 24)
monopsony: A market in which there's only one buyer. (31)
moral hazard: An incentive to engage in undesirable behavior. (29, 34)
multiplier: The multiple by which an initial change in aggregate spending will alter total expenditure after an infinite number of spending cycles; 1/(1 – MPC). (10, 11, 18, 19)

national debt: Accumulated debt of the federal government. (12)
national income (NI): Total income earned by current factors of production: NDP less depreciation and indirect business taxes; plus net foreign factor income. (5)
national-income accounting: The measurement of aggregate economic activity, particularly national income and its components. (5)
natural monopoly: An industry in which one firm can achieve economies of scale over the entire range of market supply. (4, 24, 27)
natural rate of unemployment: Long-term rate of unemployment determined by structural forces in labor and product markets. (6, 15, 19)
net domestic product (NDP): GDP less depreciation. (5)
net exports: The value of exports minus the value of imports: $(X - M)$. (2, 5, 18)
net investment: Gross investment less depreciation. (5, 17)
nominal GDP: The value of final output produced in a given period, measured in the prices of that period (current prices). (5, 7)

nominal income: The amount of money income received in a given time period, measured in current dollars. (7)
nominal tax rate: Taxes paid divided by taxable income. (33)
normal good: Good for which demand increases when income rises. (20)
normal profit: The opportunity cost of capital: zero economic profit. (22)

Okun's Law: 1 percent more unemployment is estimated to equal 2 percent less output. (6)
oligopolist: One of the dominant firms in an oligopoly. (25)
oligopoly: A market in which a few firms produce all or most of the market supply of a particular good or service. (25)
open economy: A nation that engages in international trade. (35)
open market operations: Federal Reserve purchases and sales of government bonds for the purpose of altering bank reserves. (14)
opportunity cost: The most desired goods or services that are forgone in order to obtain something else. (1, 3, 4, 12, 20, 21, 23, 27, 28, 35)
opportunity wage: The highest wage an individual would earn in his or her best alternative job. (30)
optimal consumption: The mix of consumer purchases that maximizes the utility attainable from available income. (20)
optimal mix of output: The most desirable combination of output attainable with existing resources, technology, and social values. (4, 12)
optimal rate of pollution: The rate of pollution that occurs when the marginal social benefit of pollution control equals its marginal social cost. (28)
outsourcing: The relocation of production to foreign countries. (6, 30)

par value: The face value of a bond; the amount to be repaid when the bond is due. (32)
parity: The relative price of farm products in the period 1910–14. (29)
per capita GDP: The dollar value of GDP divided by total population; average GDP. (2, 17)
perfect competition: A market in which no buyer or seller has market power. (22)
personal income (PI): Income received by households before payment of personal taxes. (5, 33)
Phillips curve: An historical (inverse) relationship between the rate of unemployment and the rate of inflation; commonly expresses a trade-off between the two. (16)
portfolio decision: The choice of how (where) to hold idle funds. (14, 15)
poverty gap: The shortfall between actual income and the poverty threshold. (34)
poverty rate: Percentage of the population counted as poor. (37)
poverty threshold (U.S.): Annual income of less than $20,000 for family of four (2007, inflation adjusted). (37)
precautionary demand for money: Money held for unexpected market transactions or for emergencies. (15)
predatory pricing: Temporary price reductions designed to alter market shares or drive out competition. (25)
present discounted value (PDV): The value today of future payments, adjusted for interest accrual. (32)
price ceiling: Upper limit imposed on the price of a good. (3)
price discrimination: The sale of an identical good at different prices to different consumers by a single seller. (24)
price/earnings (P/E) ratio: The price of a stock share divided by earnings (profit) per share. (32)
price elasticity of demand: The percentage change in quantity demanded divided by the percentage change in price. (20, 24, 29)
price-fixing: Explicit agreements among producers regarding the price(s) at which a good is to be sold. (25)
price floor: Lower limit set for the price of a good. (3)
price leadership: An oligopolistic pricing pattern that allows one firm to establish the (market) price for all firms in the industry. (25)
price stability: The absence of significant changes in the average price level; officially defined as a rate of inflation of less than 3 percent. (7)
private costs: The costs of an economic activity directly borne by the immediate producer or consumer (excluding externalities). (28)
private good: A good or service whose consumption by one person excludes consumption by others. (4)
product differentiation: Features that make one product appear different from competing products in the same market. (25, 26, 27)
product market: Any place where finished goods and services (products) are bought and sold. (3)
production decision: The selection of the short-run rate of output (with existing plant and equipment). (22, 23, 24, 26, 28)
production function: A technological relationship expressing the maximum quantity of a good attainable from different combinations of factor inputs. (21)
production possibilities: The alternative combinations of final goods and services that could be produced in a given time period with all available resources and technology. (1, 5, 6, 17, 35)
production process: A specific combination of resources used to produce a good or service. (30)
productivity: Output per unit of input, e.g., output per labor-hour. (2, 17, 18, 21, 31)
profit: The difference between total revenue and total cost. (21, 22, 29)
profit-maximization rule: Produce at that rate of output where marginal revenue equals marginal cost. (22, 24, 25)
profit per unit: Total profit divided by the quantity produced in a given time period; price minus average total cost. (23)
progressive tax: A tax system in which tax rates rise as incomes rise. (4, 33)
proportional tax: A tax that levies the same rate on every dollar of income. (4)
public choice: Theory of public-sector behavior emphasizing rational self-interest of decision makers and voters. (4)
public good: A good or service whose consumption by one person does not exclude consumption by others. (4, 27)
quota: A limit on the quantity of a good that may be imported in a given time period. (35)

rational expectations: Hypothesis that people's spending decisions are based on all available information, including the anticipated effects of government intervention. (19)
real GDP: The value of final output produced in a given period, adjusted for changing prices. (5, 7, 8, 17)
real income: Income in constant dollars; nominal income adjusted for inflation. (7)
real interest rate: The nominal interest rate minus the anticipated inflation rate. (7, 15)
recession: A decline in total output (real GDP) for two or more consecutive quarters. (8)
recessionary GDP gap: The amount by which equilibrium GDP falls short of fullemployment GDP. (9, 10, 11, 19)
refinancing: The issuance of new debt in payment of debt issued earlier. (12)
regressive tax: A tax system in which tax rates fall as incomes rise. (4, 33)
regulation: Government intervention to alter the behavior of firms, e.g., in pricing, output, or advertising. (27)
relative price: The price of one good in comparison with the price of other goods. (7)
required reserves: The minimum amount of reserves a bank is required to hold; equal to required reserve ratio times transactions deposits. (13, 14)
reserve ratio: The ratio of a bank's reserves to its total transactions deposits. (13)
retained earnings: Amount of corporate profits not paid out in dividends. (32)
risk premium: The difference in rates of return on risky (uncertain) and safe (certain) investments. (32)

saving: That part of disposable income not spent on current consumption; disposable income less consumption. (5, 9, 16)
Say's Law: Supply creates its own demand. (8)
scarcity: Lack of enough resources to satisfy all desired uses of those resources. (1)
seasonal unemployment: Unemployment due to seasonal changes in employment or labor supply. (6)

severe poverty (world): World Bank income standard of $2 per day per person (inflation adjusted). (37)
shift in demand: A change in the quantity demanded at any (every) given price. (3, 20)
short run: The period in which the quantity (and quality) of some inputs can't be changed. (21, 22)
short-run competitive equilibrium: p = MC. (23)
shutdown point: The rate of output where price equals minimum AVC. (22, 23)
size distribution of income: The way total personal income is divided up among households or income classes. (33)
social costs: The full resource costs of an economic activity, including externalities. (28)
social insurance programs: Event-conditioned income transfers intended to reduce the cost of specific problems, e.g., Social Security and unemployment insurance. (34)
speculative demand for money: Money held for speculative purposes, for later financial opportunities. (15)
stagflation: The simultaneous occurrence of substantial unemployment and inflation. (16, 19)
structural deficit: Federal revenues at full employment minus expenditures at full employment under prevailing fiscal policy. (12, 19)
structural unemployment: Unemployment caused by a mismatch between the skills (or location) of job seekers and the requirements (or location) of available jobs. (6, 16)
substitute goods: Goods that substitute for each other; when the price of good x rises, the demand for good y increases, *ceteris paribus.* (3, 20)
substitution effect of wages: An increased wage rate encourages people to work more hours (to substitute labor for leisure). (30)
supply: The ability and willingness to sell (produce) specific quantities of a good at alternative prices in a given time period, *ceteris paribus.* (3)
supply curve: A curve describing the quantities of a good a producer is willing and able to sell (produce) at alternative prices in a given time period, *ceteris paribus.* (22)
supply-side policy: The use of tax incentives, (de)regulation, and other mechanisms to increase the ability and willingness to produce goods and services. (8, 19)
target efficiency: The percentage of income transfers that go to the intended recipients and purposes. (34)
tariff: A tax (duty) imposed on imported goods. (35)
tax base: The amount of income or property directly subject to nominal tax rates. (33)
tax elasticity of labor supply: The percentage change in quantity of labor supplied divided by the percentage change in tax rates. (34)
tax elasticity of supply: The percentage change in quantity supplied divided by the percentage change in tax rates. (16, 33)
tax incidence: Distribution of the real burden of a tax. (33)
tax rebate: A lump-sum refund of taxes paid. (16)
terms of trade: The rate at which goods are exchanged; the amount of good A given up for good B in trade. (35)
total cost: The market value of all resources used to produce a good or service. (21)
total revenue: The price of a product multiplied by the quantity sold in a given time period: $p \times q$. (20, 22)
total utility: The amount of satisfaction obtained from entire consumption of a product. (20)
trade deficit: The amount by which the value of imports exceeds the value of exports in a given time period (negative net exports). (18, 35, 36)
trade surplus: The amount by which the value of exports exceeds the value of imports in a given time period (positive net exports). (18, 35)
transactions account: A bank account that permits direct payment to a third party, for example, with a check. (13)
transactions demand for money: Money held for the purpose of making everyday market purchases. (15)
transfer payments: Payments to individuals for which no current goods or services are exchanged, like Social Security, welfare, unemployment benefits. (4, 16, 34)
Treasury bonds: Promissory notes (IOUs) issued by the U.S. Treasury. (12)
underemployment: People seeking full-time paid employment who work only part-time or are employed at jobs below their capability. (6)
unemployment: The inability of labor-force participants to find jobs. (4, 6)
unemployment rate: The proportion of the labor force that is unemployed. (6)
union shop: An employment setting in which all workers must join the union within 30 days after being employed. (31)
unionization ratio: The percentage of the labor force belonging to a union. (31)
unit labor cost: Hourly wage rate divided by output per labor-hour. (21)
user charge: Fee paid for the use of a public-sector good or service. (4)
utility: The pleasure or satisfaction obtained from a good or service. (20)

value added: The increase in the market value of a product that takes place at each stage of the production process. (5)
variable costs: Costs of production that change when the rate of output is altered, e.g., labor and material costs. (21, 22)
velocity of money: (V) The number of times per year, on average, that a dollar is used to purchase final goods and services; $PQ \div M$. (19)
vertical equity: Principle that people with higher incomes should pay more taxes. (33)
voluntary restraint agreement (VRA): An agreement to reduce the volume of trade in a specific good; a "voluntary" quota. (35)

wage-replacement rate: The percentage of base wages paid out in benefits. (34)
wealth: The market value of assets. (33)
wealth effect: A change in consumer spending caused by a change in the value of owned assets. (9)
welfare programs: Means-tested income transfer programs, e.g., welfare and food stamps. (34)

yield: The rate of return on a bond; the annual interest payment divided by the bond's price. (14)

INDEX

Page numbers followed by n indicate material found in notes.

D

E

F

G

M

N

O

T

U

V

W

X

Y

Z

PROBLEM SETS

PROBLEM SETS

PROBLEMS FOR CHAPTER 1

Name: ____________________

LO1 1. According to Table 1.1 (or Figure 1.1), what is the opportunity cost of the
   (*a*) Fourth truck?
   (*b*) Fifth truck?

LO2 2. (*a*) According to Figure 1.2, what is the opportunity cost of North Korea's military force at point *N*?
   (*b*) How much of a peace dividend would North Korea get if it cut the military establishment from OD to OH?

LO2 3. How much of a peace dividend is generated in a $14 trillion economy when defense spending is cut from 4.0 percent to 3.8 percent of total output? $

LO1 4. What is the opportunity cost (in dollars) to attend an hour-long econ lecture for
   (*a*) A minimum-wage teenager $
   (*b*) A $100,000 per year corporate executive $

LO1 5. Suppose either computers or televisions can be assembled with the following labor inputs:

Units produced	1	2	3	4	5	6	7	8	9	10
Total labor used	3	7	12	18	25	33	42	54	70	90

   (*a*) Draw the production possibilities curve for an economy with 54 units of labor. Label it P54.
   (*b*) What is the opportunity cost of the eighth computer?
   (*c*) Suppose immigration brings in 36 more workers. Redraw the production possibilities curve to reflect this added labor. Label the new curve P90.
   (*d*) Suppose advancing technology (e.g., the miniaturization of electronic circuits) increases the productivity of the 90-laborer workforce by 20 percent. Draw a third production possibilities curve (PT) to illustrate this change.

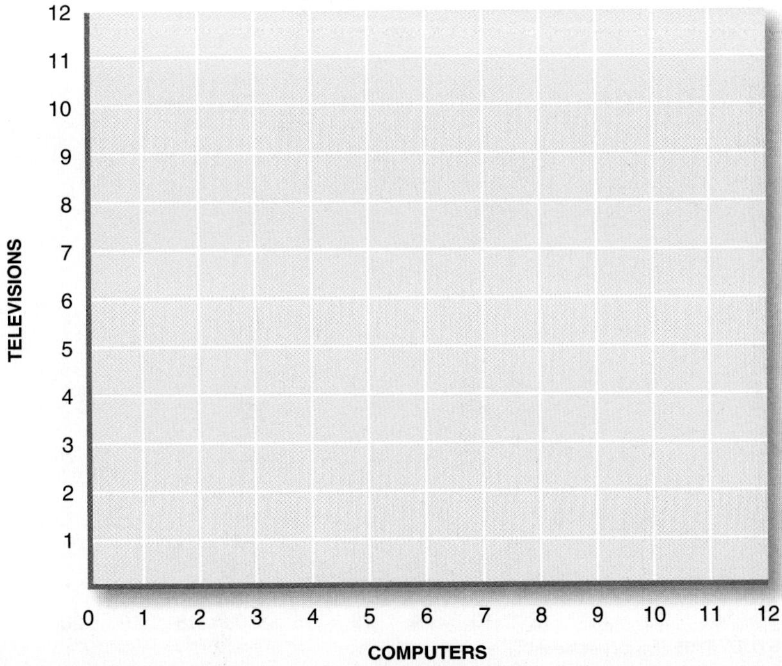

LO3 6. According to the World View on p. 14, which nation has
   (*a*) the most faith in the market system?
   (*b*) the least faith in the market system?

 Name: ______________________

LO1 7. Suppose there's a relationship of the following sort between study time and grades:

	(a)	*(b)*	*(c)*	*(d)*	*(e)*
Study time (hours per week)	0	2	6	12	20
Grade-point average	0	1.0	2.0	3.0	4.0

If you have only 20 hours per week to use for either study time or fun time,

(*a*) Draw the (linear) production possibilities curve on the graph below that represents the alternative uses of your time.

(*b*) What is the cost, in lost fun time, of raising your grade-point average from 2.0 to 3.0? Illustrate this effort on the graph (point *C* to point *D*). __________

(*c*) What is the opportunity cost of increasing your grades from 3.0 to 4.0? Illustrate as point *D* to point *E*. __________

(*d*) Why does the opportunity cost change? ______________________

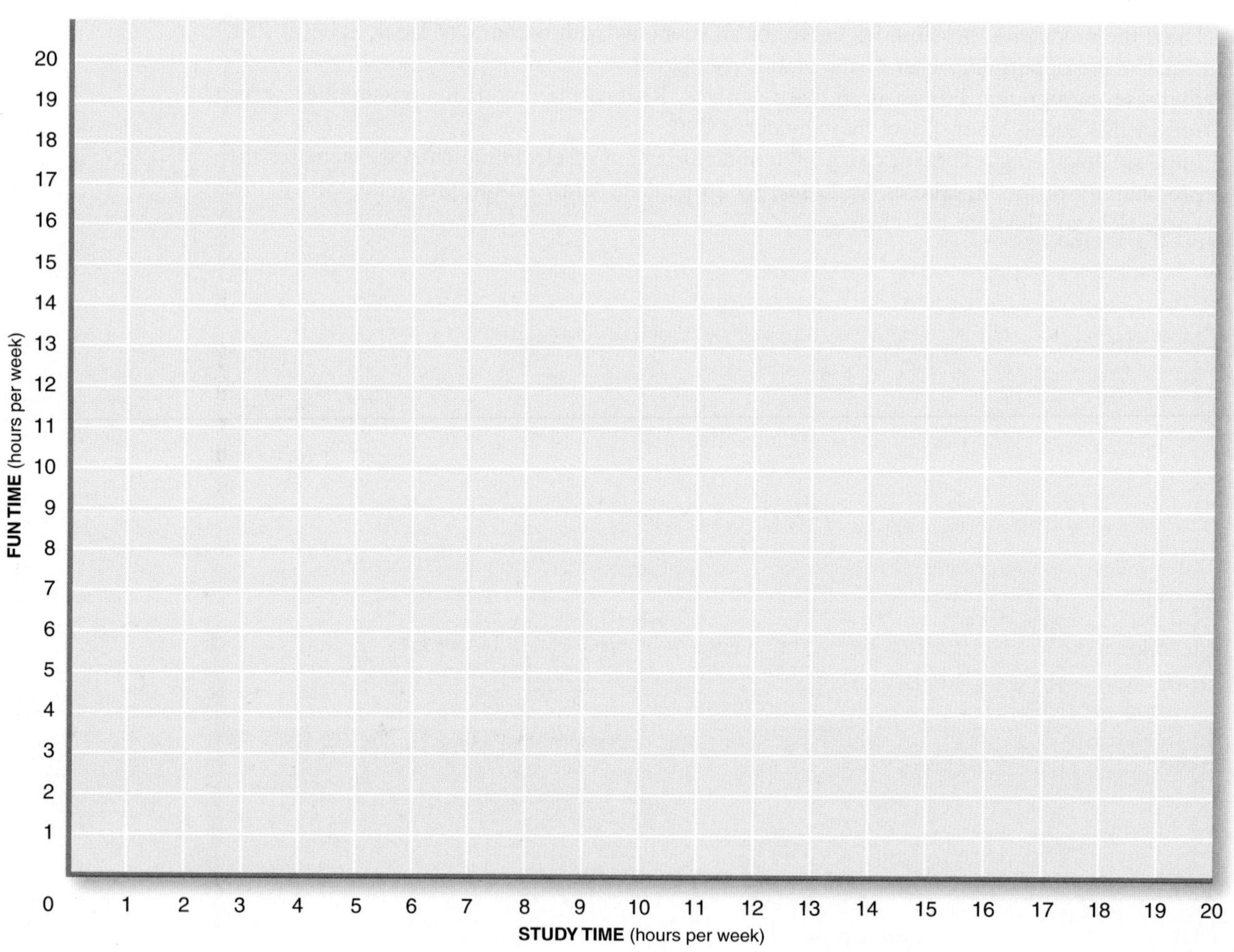

PROBLEMS FOR CHAPTER 2

Name: ______________________

LO1 1. In 2005, the world's total output (real GDP) was roughly $60 trillion. What percent of this total was produced by the three largest economies (World View, p. 27)? ______%

LO3 2. According to the World View on p. 28, what percentage of America's GDP per capita is available to the average citizen of

(*a*) Mexico ______%
(*b*) China ______%
(*c*) Ethiopia ______%

LO3 3. According to Table 2.1, how fast does total output have to grow in order to raise per capita GDP in

(*a*) Japan? ______
(*b*) Paraguay? ______

LO3 4. If Haiti's per capita GDP of roughly $1,800 were to increase as fast as China's (see Table 2.1), what would its per capita GDP be in

(*a*) 10 years? $______
(*b*) 20 years? $______

LO1 5. U.S. real gross domestic product increased from $9 trillion in 1995 to $13 trillion in 2005. During that same decade the share of manufactured goods (e.g., cars, appliances) fell from 16 percent to 12 percent. What was the dollar value of manufactured output

(*a*) In 1995? $______
(*b*) In 2005? $______
(*c*) By how much did durable output change? ______%

LO3 6. Using the data in Figure 2.5,

(*a*) Compute the average income of U.S. households. $______
(*b*) If all incomes were equalized by government taxes and transfer payments, how much would the average household in each income quintile gain (via transfers) or lose (via taxes)?

(*i*) Highest fifth $______
(*ii*) Second fifth $______
(*iii*) Third fifth $______
(*iv*) Fourth fifth $______
(*v*) Lowest fifth $______

(*c*) What is the implied tax rate on the highest quintile? ______%

LO2 7. If 140 million workers produced America's GDP in 2005 (World View, p. 27), how much output did the average worker produce? $______

LO3 8. How much more output (income) per year will have to be produced in the world

(*a*) Just to provide the 2.7 billion "severely" poor population with $1 more output per day? $______
(*b*) To raise the incomes of the world's "severely poor" population to the official threshold of U.S. poverty (roughly $5,000 per year)? $______

 Name: ____________

LO1 9. **(Macro course only)** Using the data from the endpapers of this book, complete the following table.

Sector	Share of Total Output 1980	Share of Total Output 2000
Consumption	______	______
Investment	______	______
Government purchases	______	______
Exports	______	______
Imports	______	______

(*a*) Which sector share has increased the most? ______

(*b*) Which sector share has decreased the most? ______

LO1 10. **(Macro course only)** Using data from the endpapers, illustrate on the graph below

(*a*) The federal government's share of the total output.

(*b*) The state/local government's share of total output.

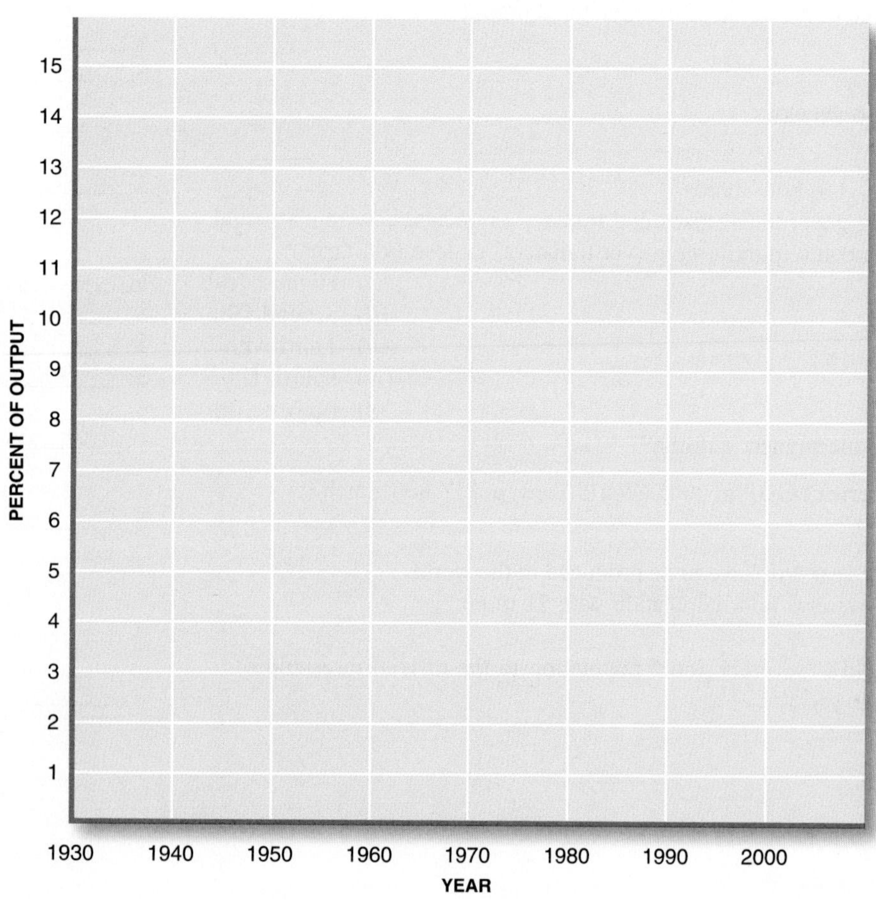

PROBLEMS FOR CHAPTER 3

Name: ____________________

LO1 1. According to Figure 3.3, at what price would Tom buy 15 hours of Web tutoring?
(*a*) Without a lottery win. ________
(*b*) With a lottery win. ________

LO2 2. According to Figures 3.5 and 3.6, what would the new equilibrium price of tutoring services be if Ann decided to stop tutoring? ________

LO2 3. Given the following data, identify the amount of shortage or surplus that would exist at a price of
(*a*) $5.00 ________
(*b*) $3.00 ________
(*c*) $1.00 ________

A. Price	$5.00	$4.00	$3.00	$2.00	$1.00
B. Quantity demanded					
Al	1	2	3	4	5
Betsy	0	1	1	1	2
Casey	2	2	3	3	4
Daisy	1	3	4	4	6
Eddie	1	2	2	3	5
Market total	__	__	__	__	__

	$5.00	$4.00	$3.00	$2.00	$1.00
C. Quantity supplied					
Alice	3	3	3	3	3
Butch	7	5	4	4	2
Connie	6	4	3	3	1
Dutch	6	5	4	3	0
Ellen	4	2	2	2	1
Market total	__	__	__	__	__

LO3 4. As a result of Katrina damage (News, p. 55), which of the following changed:
(*a*) Demand ________
(*b*) Quantity demanded ________
(*c*) Price ________

LO2 5. In the World View on page 61, menu prices are continuously adjusted. Graph the initial and final (adjusted) prices for the following situations. Be sure to label axes and graph completely.

(*a*) Customers are ordering too little haddock.

(*b*) The kitchen is running out of beef ribs.

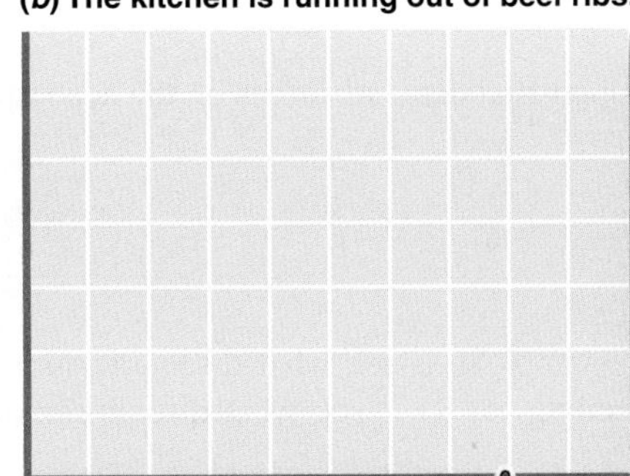

LO4 6. In Figure 3.8 how many more people would live if the prohibition on selling human organs were lifted? ________

 Name: ______________________

LO4 7. In Figure 3.8, when a price prohibition is imposed on the organ market by how much does
   (*a*) The quantity of organs demanded increase? ________
   (*b*) The quantity of organs supplied decrease? ________
   (*c*) How large is the resulting shortage? ________

LO3 8. On the basis of the World View on p. 60, illustrate on the graphs below:
   (*a*) The rise in the price of gasoline.
   (*b*) The change in the quantity of gasoline demanded.
   (*c*) The new equilibrium in the bus market.
   (*d*) What determinant of bus demand changed? ________________

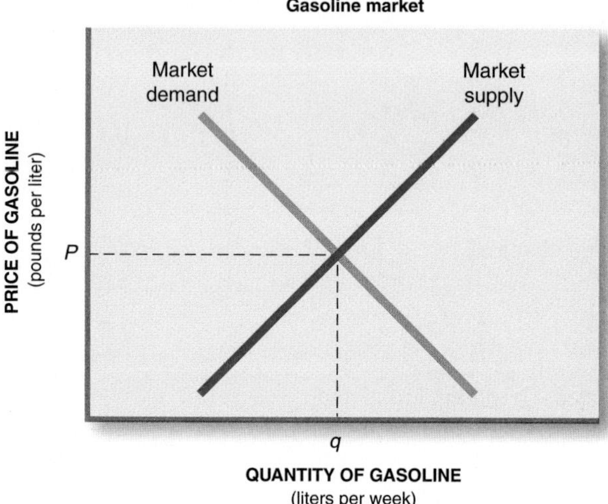

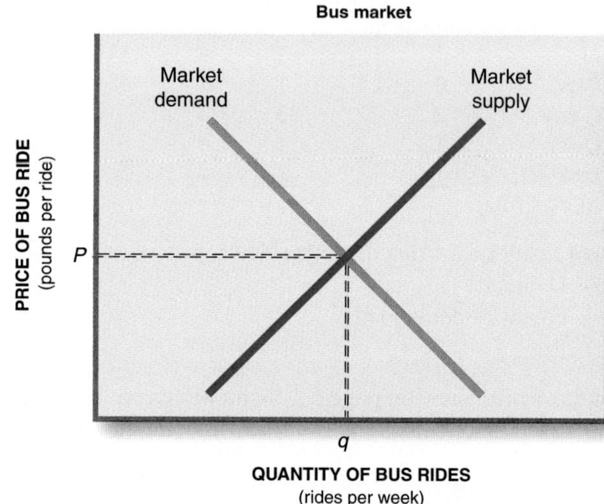

LO2 9. Use the following data to draw supply and demand curves on the accompanying graph.

Price	$ 8	7	6	5	4	3	2	1
Quantity demanded	2	3	4	5	6	7	8	9
Quantity supplied	10	9	8	7	6	5	4	3

   (*a*) What is the equilibrium price? ________
   (*b*) If a *minimum* price (price floor) of $6 is set, what disequilibrium results? ________
   (*c*) If a *maximum* price (price ceiling) of $3 is set, what disequilibrium results? ________

   Illustrate these answers.

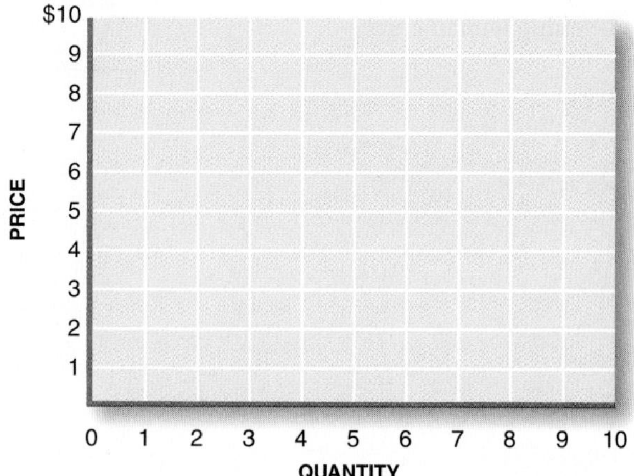

PROBLEMS FOR CHAPTER 4

Name: ______________________

LO1 1. In Figure 4.2, by how much is the market
(*a*) Overproducing private goods? (*a*) ________
(*b*) Underproducing public goods? (*b*) ________

LO1 2. Use Figure 4.3 to illustrate on the accompanying production possibilities curve
(*a*) The market mix of output (*M*).
(*b*) The optimal mix of output (*X*).

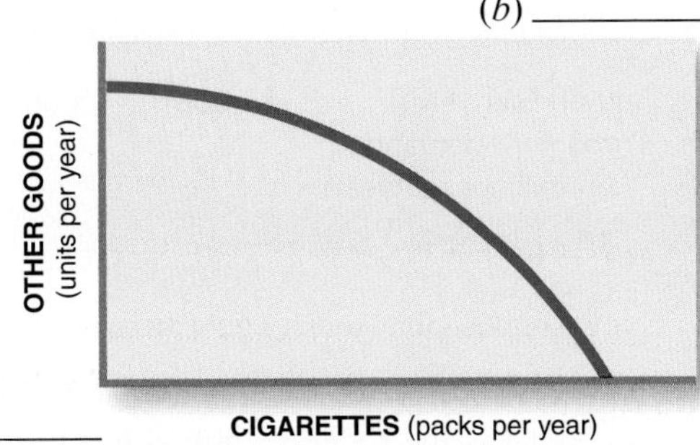

LO1 3. Assume that the product depicted below generates external costs in consumption of $5 per unit.
(*a*) Draw the social demand curve.
(*b*) What is the socially optimal output? (*b*) ________
(*c*) By how much does the market overproduce this good? (*c*) ________

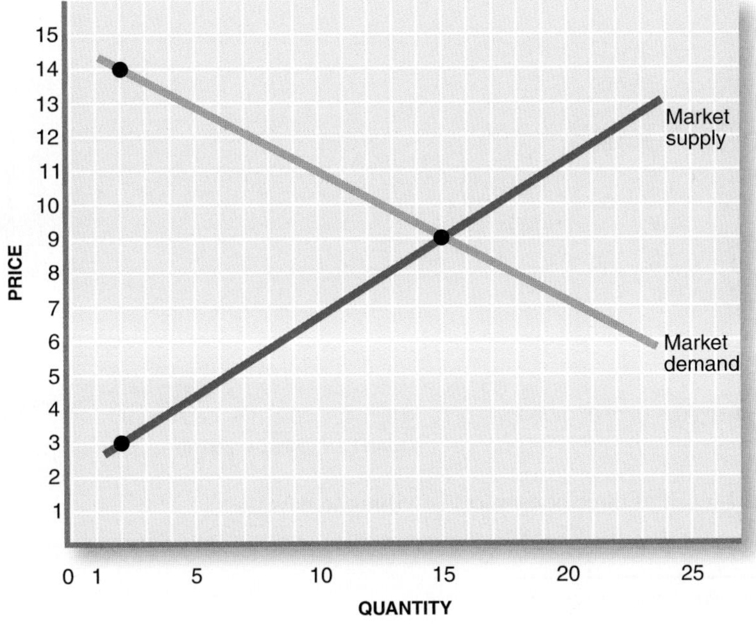

LO1 4. In the previous problem's market equilibrium, what is
(*a*) The market value of the good? ________
(*b*) The social value of the good? ________

LO1 5. If the average adult produces $80,000 of output per year, how much output is lost as a result of secondhand smoke, according to the News on p. 70? $________

LO2 6. (*a*) Assuming a 10 percent sales tax is levied on all consumption, complete the following table:

Income	Consumption	Sales Tax	Percent of Income Paid in Taxes
$10,000	$10,000	________	________
20,000	19,000	________	________
40,000	36,000	________	________
80,000	68,000	________	________

(*b*) Is the sales tax progressive or regressive? ________

 Name: ________________

LO2 7. If a new home can be constructed for $120,000, what is the opportunity cost of federal defense spending, measured in terms of private housing? (Assume a defense budget of $600 billion.) ________

LO1 8. Suppose the following data represent the market demand for college education:

Tuition (per year)	$1,000	2,000	3,000	4,000	5,000	6,000	7,000	8,000
Enrollment demanded (in millions per year)	8	7	6	5	4	3	2	1

(*a*) If tuition is set at $5,000, how many students will enroll? ________

Now suppose that society gets an external benefit of $1,000 for every enrolled student.

(*b*) Draw the social and market demand curves for this situation on the graph below (left).
(*c*) What is the socially optimal level of enrollments at the same tuition price of $5,000? ________
(*d*) How can this optimal enrollment level be achieved? ________________

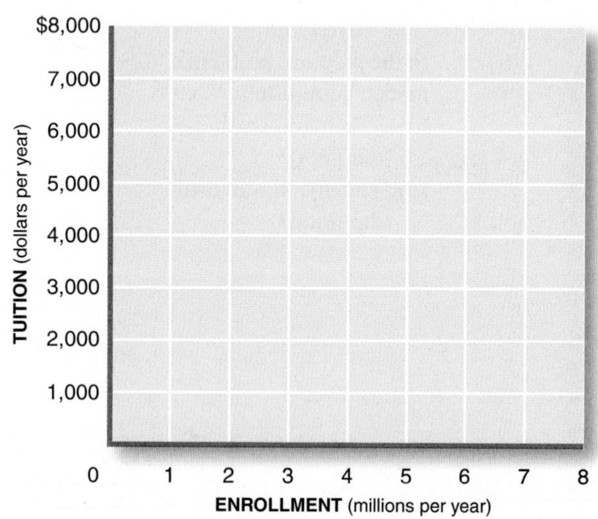

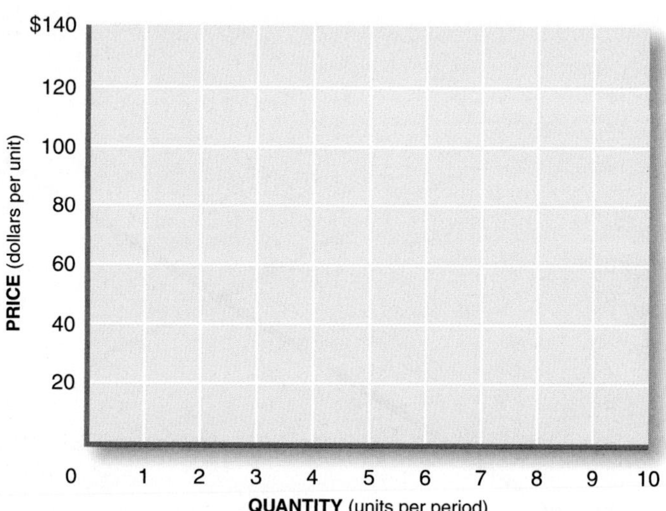

LO1 9. Suppose the following data represent the prices that each of three consumers is willing to pay:

Quantity	Consumer A	Consumer B	Consumer C
1	$50	$40	$30
2	30	20	20
3	20	15	10

(*a*) Construct the market demand curve for this good on the graph above (right).
(*b*) If this good were priced in the market at $40, how many units would be demanded? ________
(*c*) Now suppose that this is a public good, in the sense that all consumers receive satisfaction from the good even if only one person buys it. Under these conditions, what is the social value of the
(*i*) First unit? ________
(*ii*) Second unit? ________

LO2 10. According to the News on p. 78, what percent of income is spent on lottery tickets by
(*a*) A poor family with income of $18,000 per year? ________
(*b*) An affluent family with income of $40,000 per year? ________

PROBLEMS FOR CHAPTER 5

Name: ________________

LO1 1. Suppose that furniture production encompasses the following stages:

Stage 1: Trees sold to lumber company	$1,000
Stage 2: Lumber sold to furniture company	$1,700
Stage 3: Furniture company sells furniture to retail store	$3,200
Stage 4: Furniture store sells furniture to consumer	$5,995

(*a*) What is the value added at each stage?

Stage 1: ________
Stage 2: ________
Stage 3: ________
Stage 4: ________

(*b*) How much does this output contribute to GDP? ________

(*c*) How would answer *b* change if the lumber were imported from Canada? ________

LO1 2. If real GDP increases by 5 percent next year and the price level goes up by 3 percent, what will happen to nominal GDP? ________

LO1 3. What was real per capita GDP in 1933 measured in 2003 prices? (Use the data in Table 5.4 to compute your answer.) ________

LO3 4. (*a*) Calculate national income from the following figures:

Consumption	$200 billion
Depreciation	20
Retained earnings	12
Gross investment	30
Imports	40
Social Security taxes	25
Exports	50
Indirect business taxes	15
Government purchases	60
Personal income taxes	40

NI: ________

(*b*) If there were 80 million people in this country, what would the GDP per capita be? ________

(*c*) If all prices were to double overnight, what would happen to the values of real and nominal GDP per capita?

Change in real GDP: ________
Change in nominal GDP: ________

LO3 5. What is the value of net investment in Problem 4? ________

LO3 6. What share of total income consists of

(*a*) Wages and salaries ________

(*b*) Corporate profits ________

(*Note:* See Table 5.5 for data)

LO1 7. (*a*) Compute real GDP for 1995 using average prices of 1985 as the base year. (On the inside covers of this book you'll find data for GDP and the GDP "price deflator" used to measure inflation.)

(*b*) By how much did real GDP increase between 1985 and 1995? ________

(*c*) By how much did nominal GDP increase between 1985 and 1995? ________

LO3 8. Suppose all the dollar values in Problem 4 were in 1990 dollars. Use the Consumer Price Index shown on the end cover of this book to convert the numbers to 2006 dollars. What is the value of national income in 2006 dollars? (You'll be converting the figures from their nominal to their real values, with 2006 as the base year.) ________

 Name: ______________

LO1 9. On the accompanying graph, illustrate (*A*) nominal per capita GDP and (*B*) real per capita GDP for each year. (The necessary data appear on the endpapers of this book.)

(*a*) By what percent did nominal per capita GDP increase in the 1990s? ______

(*b*) By what percent did real per capita GDP increase in the 1990s? ______

(*c*) In how many years did nominal per capita GDP decline? ______

(*d*) In how many years did real per capita GDP decline? ______

(*e*) What explains the divergence between nominal and real growth rates? ______

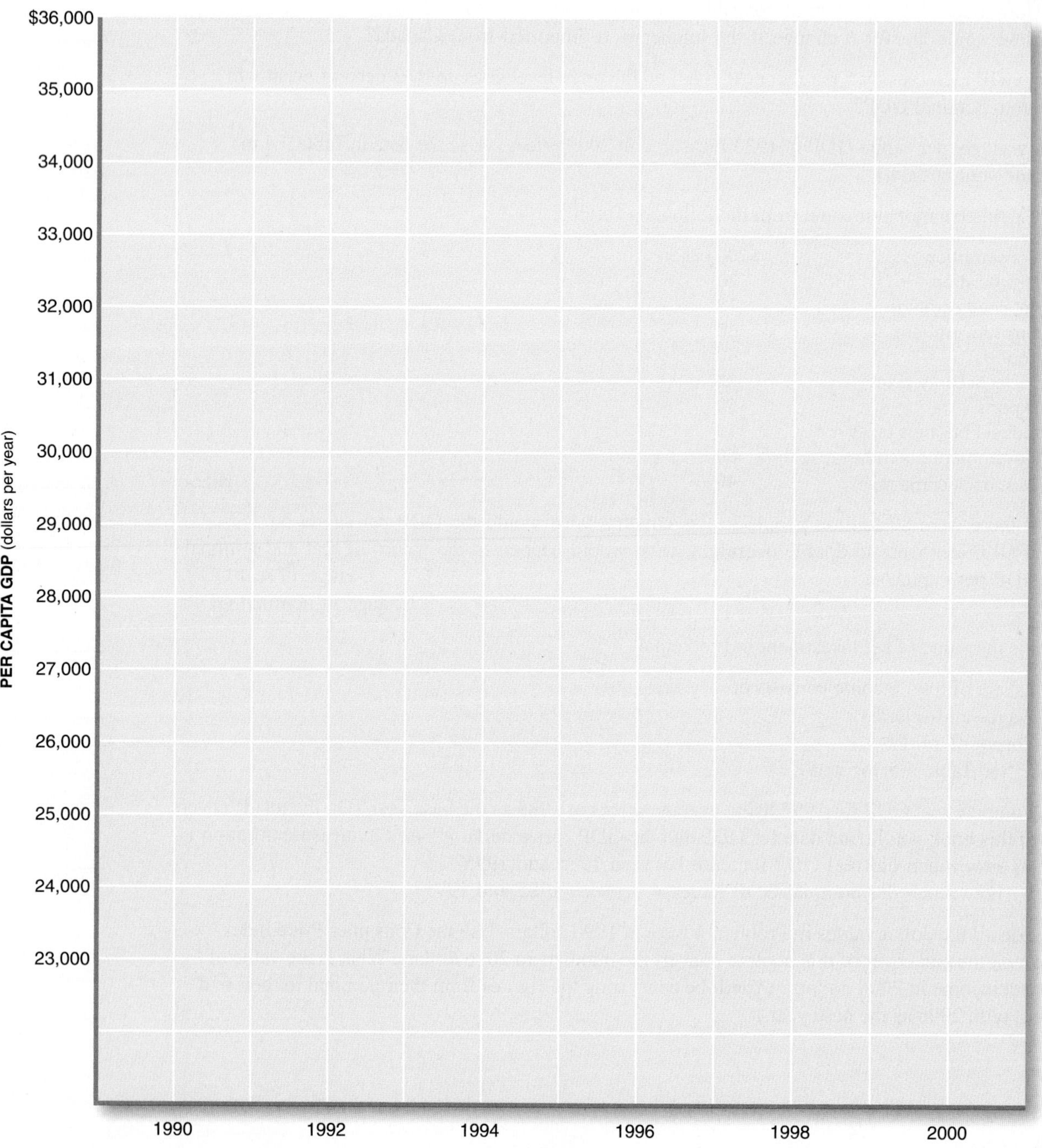

PROBLEMS FOR CHAPTER 6

Name: ______________________

LO1 1. According to Figure 6.1, what percent of the civilian labor force was
(*a*) Employed? ________%
(*b*) Unemployed? ________%
(*c*) What percent of the *population* was employed in civilian jobs? ________%

LO1 2. Between 2000 and 2005, by how much did
(*a*) The labor force increase? ________%
(*b*) Total output (real GDP) increase? ________%
(*c*) The national unemployment rate change? ________
(*Note:* Data on inside covers of the text.)

LO1 3. If the labor force is growing by 1.5 percent per year, how many new jobs have to be created each *month* to keep unemployment from increasing? ________
Web query: By how much did U.S. employment actually increase last month (www.bls.gov)? ________

LO1 4. Between 1980 and 2006, by how much did the labor-force participation rate (Figure 6.2) of
(*a*) Men fall? ________
(*b*) Women rise? ________

LO1 5. According to Okun's Law, how much output (real GDP) was lost in 2002 when the nation's unemployment rate increased from 4.7 percent to 5.8 percent? $________

LO1 6. Suppose the following data describe a nation's population:

	Year 1	Year 2
Population	200 million	203 million
Labor force	120 million	125 million
Unemployment rate	6 percent	6 percent

(*a*) How many people are unemployed in each year? Year 1: ________ Year 2: ________

(*b*) How many people are employed in each year? Year 1: ________ Year 2: ________

(*c*) Compute the employment rate (i.e., number employed ÷ population) in each year. Year 1: ________ Year 2: ________

(*d*) How can the employment rate rise when the *un*employment rate is constant?

____

LO1 7. Based on the data in the previous problem, what happens to each of the following numbers in Year 2 when 1 million jobseekers become "discouraged workers"?
(*a*) Number of unemployed persons. ________
(*b*) Unemployment rate. ________
(*c*) Employment rate. ________

LO2 8. According to the News on p. 118, how many additional people became *under*employed in September/October 2001? ________

LO1 9. In 2006 how many of the 800,000 black teenagers who participated in the labor market
(*a*) Were unemployed? ________
(*b*) Were employed? ________
(*c*) Would have been employed if they had the same unemployment rate as white teenagers? ________
(See Figure 6.4 for needed info.)

PROBLEMS FOR CHAPTER 6 (cont'd)

Name: ____________________

LO3 10. On the accompanying graph, illustrate both the unemployment rate and the percentage change in real GDP (output) for each year. (The data required for this exercise are on the inside cover of this book.)

(*a*) In how many years was "full employment" achieved? (Use current benchmark.) ________

(*b*) Unemployment and growth rates tend to move in opposite directions. Which appears to change direction first? ________

(*c*) Does the unemployment rate ever increase even when output is expanding? ________

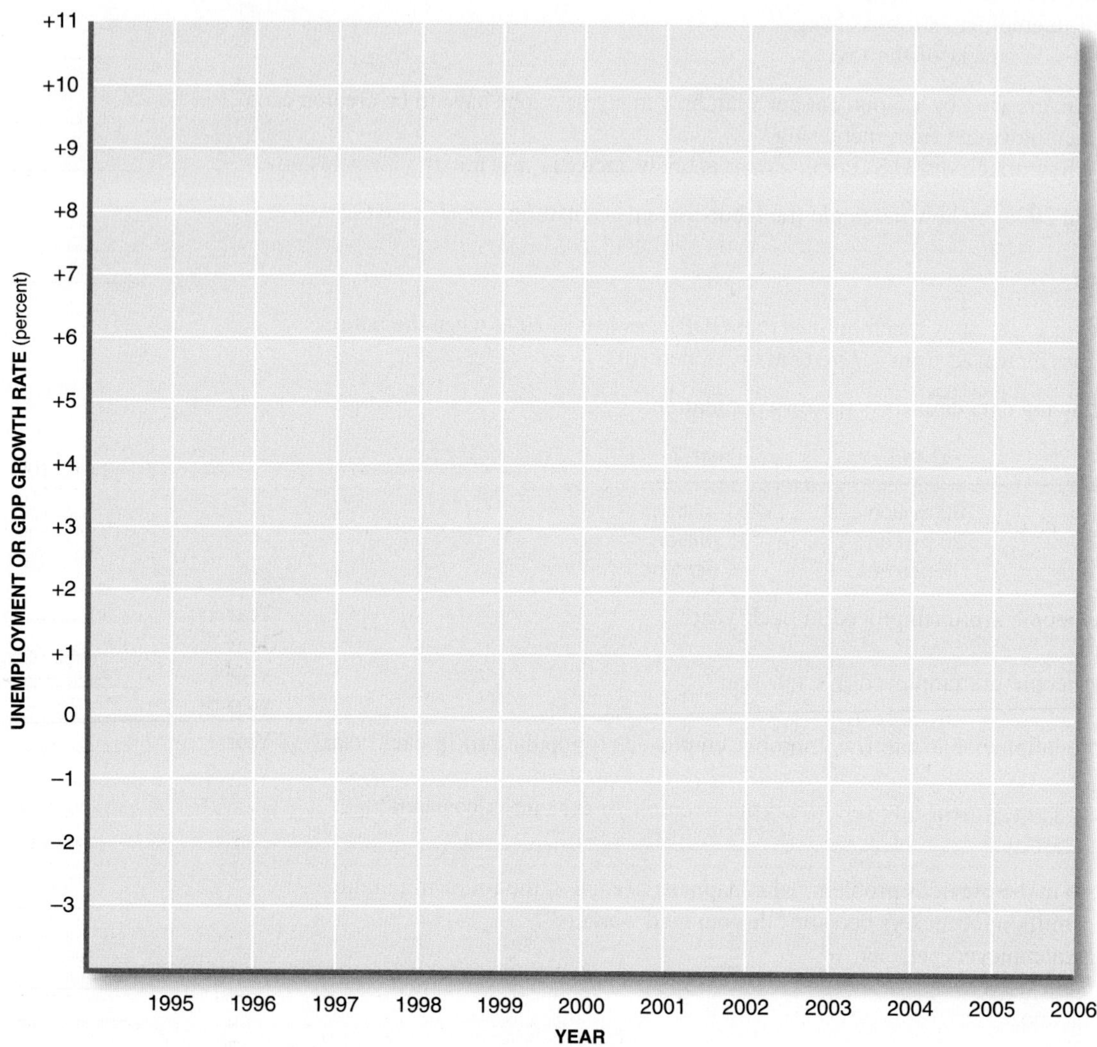

PROBLEMS FOR CHAPTER 7

Name: ____________________

LO2 1. If tuition keeps increasing at the same rate as in 2006 (see News, page 125), what will it cost to attend a 4-year private college in 2011? ________

LO1 2. Suppose you'll have an annual nominal income of $40,000 for each of the next 3 years, and the inflation rate is 5 percent per year.

(*a*) Find the real value of your $40,000 salary for each of the next 3 years.
Year 1: ________
Year 2: ________
Year 3: ________

(*b*) If you have a COLA in your contract, and the inflation rate is 5 percent, what is the real value of your salary for each year?
Year 1: ________
Year 2: ________
Year 3: ________

LO1 3. In the World View on page 139, what was the real rate of interest in Zimbabwe in 2007? ________

LO2 4. Suppose you borrow $1,000 of principal that must be repaid at the end of 2 years, along with interest of 5 percent a year. If the annual inflation rate turns out to be 10 percent,

(*a*) What is the real value of the principal repayment? ________
(*b*) What is the real rate of interest on the loan? ________
(*c*) Whose real wealth is diminished in this case? ________

LO1 5. Assuming that the following table describes a typical consumer's complete budget, compute the item weights for each product.

Item	Quantity	Unit Price	Item Weight:
Coffee	20 pounds	$ 3	________
Tuition	1 year	4,000	________
Pizza	100 pizzas	8	________
DVD rental	75 days	15	________
Vacation	2 weeks	300	________
		Total:	________

LO1 6. Suppose the prices listed in the table for Problem 5 changed from one year to the next, as shown below. Use the rest of the table to compute the average inflation rate.

	Unit Price						
Item	Last Year	This Year	Percent Change in Price	×	Item Weight	=	Inflation Impact
Coffee	$ 3	$ 4	________		________		________
Tuition	4,000	7,000	________		________		________
Pizza	8	10	________		________		________
DVD rental	15	10	________		________		________
Vacation	300	500	________		________		________
					Average inflation:		________

LO1 7. Use the item weights in Figure 7.2 to determine the percentage change in the CPI that would result from a

(*a*) 10 percent increase in entertainment prices. ________
(*b*) 6 percent decrease in transportation costs. ________
(*c*) Doubling of clothing prices. ________
(*Note:* Review Table 7.4 for assistance.)

LO1 8. Use the GDP deflator data on the inside cover of this book to compute real GDP in 1990 at 2005 prices. ________

LO1 9. According to Table 7.3, what happened during the period shown to the
(*a*) Nominal price of gold? ______
(*b*) Real price of gold? ______

LO3 10. On the accompanying graph, illustrate for each year (*A*) the nominal interest rate (use the prime rate of interest), (*B*) the CPI inflation rate, and (*C*) the real interest rate (adjusted for same-year CPI inflation). The required data appear on the inside cover of the book.
(*a*) In what years was the official goal of price stability met? ______
(*b*) In what years was the inflation rate lowest? ______
(*c*) In the most recent of those years, what was the
(*i*) Nominal interest rate? ______
(*ii*) Real interest rate? ______
(*d*) What was the range of rates during this period for
(*i*) Nominal interest rates? ______
(*ii*) Real interest rates? ______
(*e*) On a year-to-year basis which varies more, nominal or real interest rates? ______

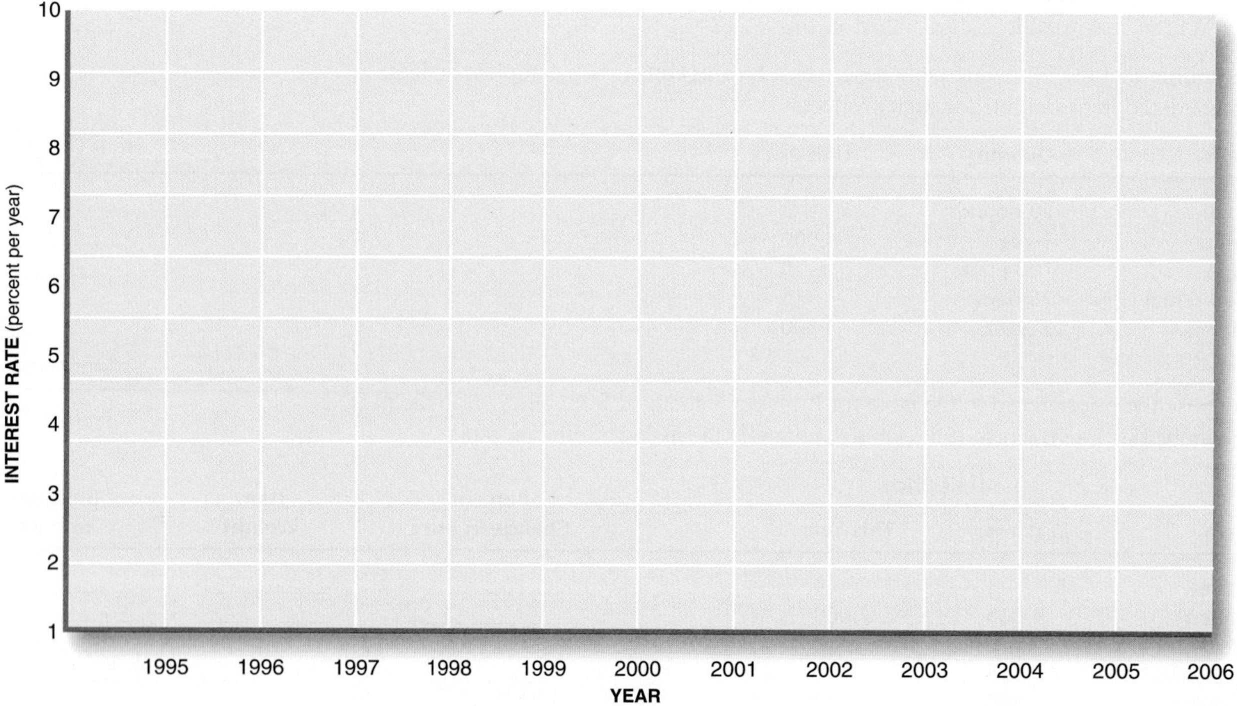

PROBLEMS FOR CHAPTER 8

Name: ______________________

LO1 1. (*a*) How much output is unsold at the price level P_l in Figure 8.7? ______
(*b*) At what price level is all output produced sold? ______

LO1 2. Suppose you have $500 in savings when the price level index is at 100.
(*a*) If inflation pushes the price level up by 20 percent, what will be the real value of your savings? ______
(*b*) What is the real value of your savings if the price level *declines* by 10 percent? ______

LO2 3. Use the following information to draw aggregate demand and aggregate supply curves on the graph below. Both curves are assumed to be straight lines.

Average Price	Real Output Demanded (per year)	Real Output Supplied (per year)
$1,000	0	$1,000
100	$900	100

(*a*) At what price level does equilibrium occur? ______
(*b*) What curve would have shifted if a new equilibrium were to occur at an output level of 700 and a price level of 700? ______
(*c*) What curve would have shifted if a new equilibrium were to occur at an output level of 700 and a price level of 500? ______
(*d*) What curve would have shifted if a new equilibrium were to occur at an output level of 700 and a price level of 300? ______
(*e*) Compared to the initial equilibrium (*a*), how have price levels or output changed in
(*b*) Output: ______ Price level: ______
(*c*) Output: ______ Price level: ______
(*d*) Output: ______ Price level: ______

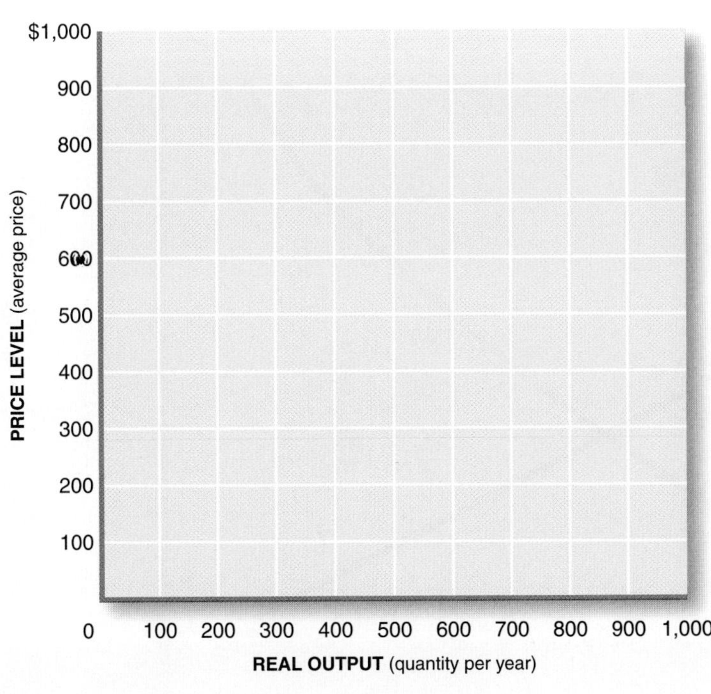

LO3 4. According to the News on p. 159, which curve shifted to cause a recession? ______

 Name: ____________

LO3 5. Illustrate these events with AS or AD shifts:

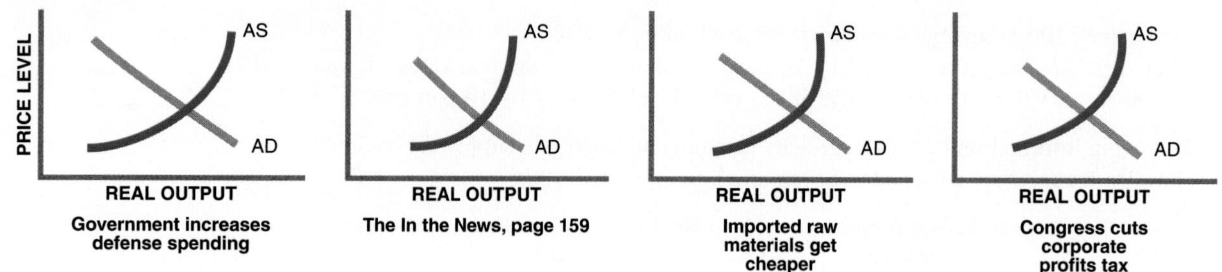

LO3 6. Assume that the accompanying graph depicts aggregate supply and demand conditions in an economy. Full employment occurs when $6 trillion of real output is produced.

(*a*) What is the equilibrium rate of output? ________

(*b*) How far short of full employment is the equilibrium rate of output? ________

(*c*) Illustrate a shift of aggregate demand that would change the equilibrium rate of output to $6 trillion. Label the new curve AD_2.

(*d*) What is the price level at the new equilibrium? ________

(*e*) Illustrate a shift of aggregate supply (AS_2) that would, when combined with AD_1, move equilibrium output to $6 trillion.

(*f*) What is the price level at this new equilibrium? ________

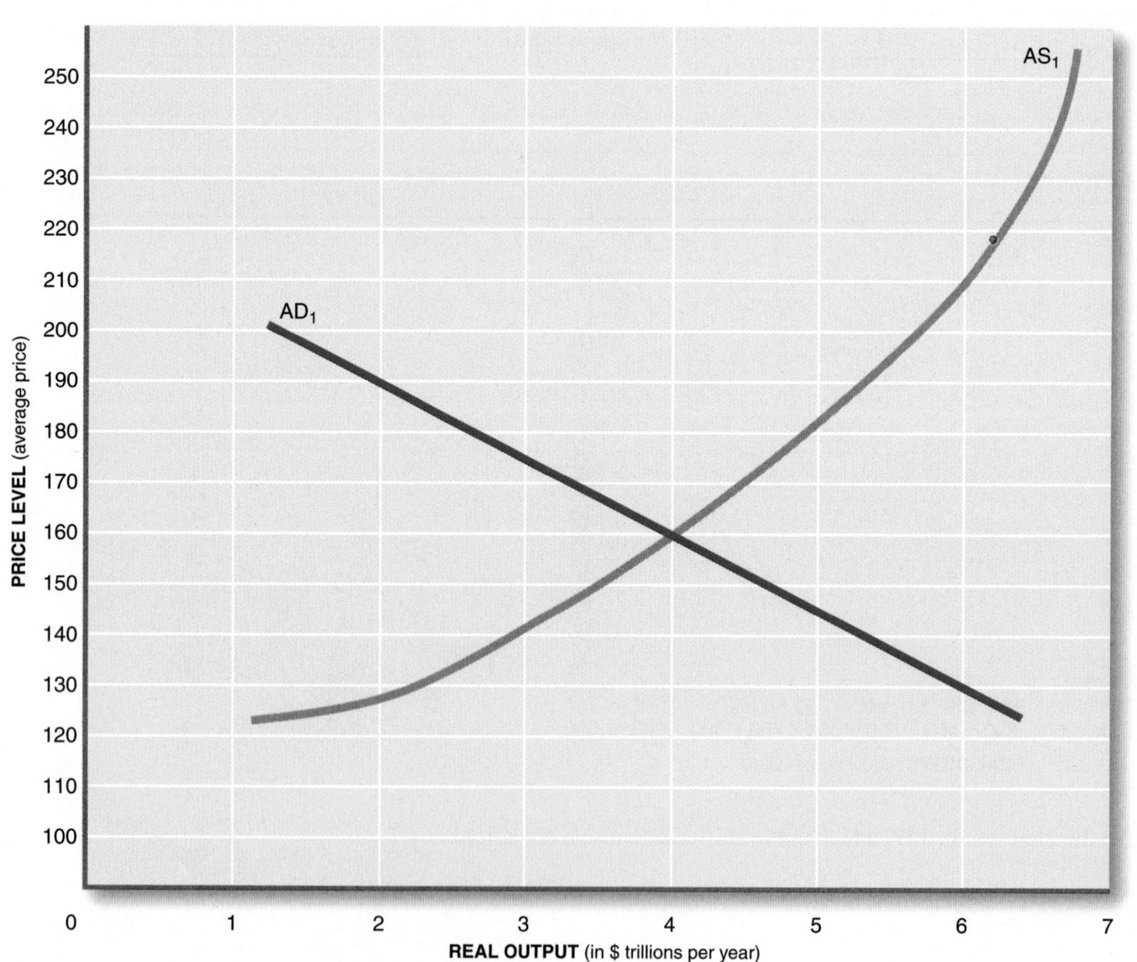

PROBLEMS FOR CHAPTER 9

Name: ______________________

LO1 1. (*a*) What is the implied MPC in the News on p. 175? ______
(*b*) What is the implied APC? ______

LO1 2. On the accompanying graph, draw the consumption function $C = \$150 + 0.8Y_D$.
(*a*) At what level of income do households begin to save? Designate that point on the graph with the letter *A*. ______
(*b*) By how much does consumption increase when income rises \$200 beyond point *A*? Designate this new level of consumption with point *B*. ______
(*c*) Illustrate the impact on consumption of the change in consumer confidence described in the News on page 175.

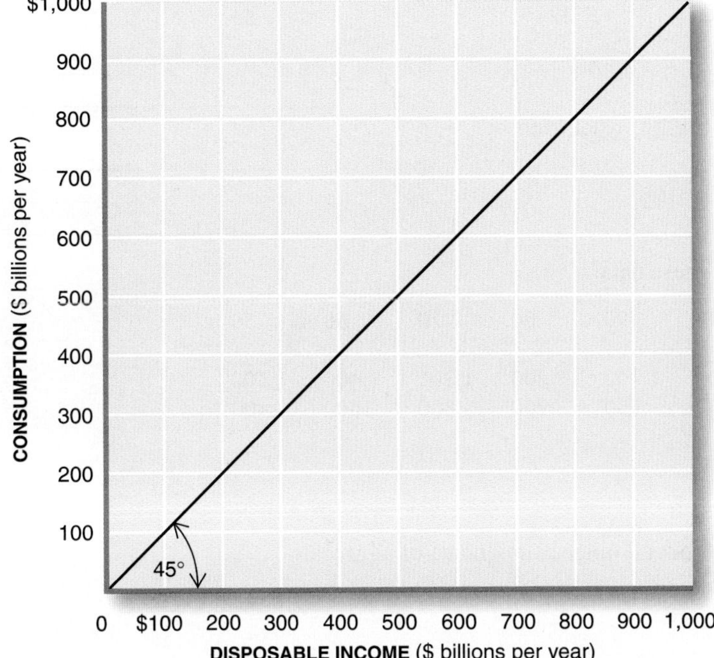

LO2 3. Illustrate on the following two graphs the wealth effect from rising home prices (discussed on p. 176.)

(*a*)

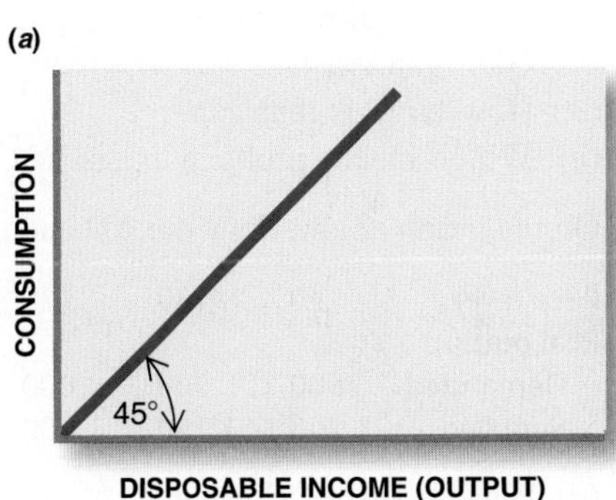

(*b*)

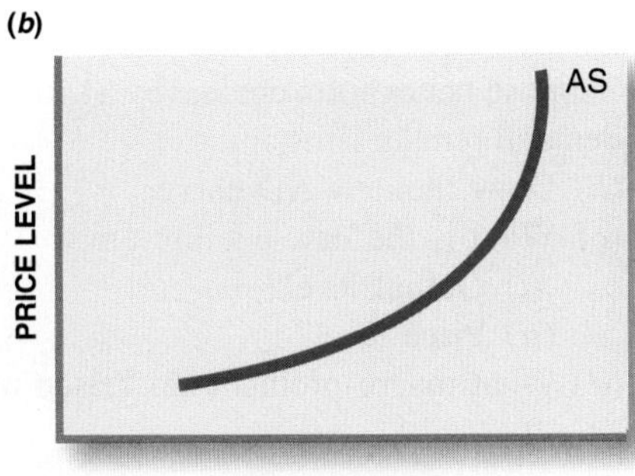

LO2 4. Illustrate on the following graph what was happening to aggregate demand in Canada according to the World View on page 180.

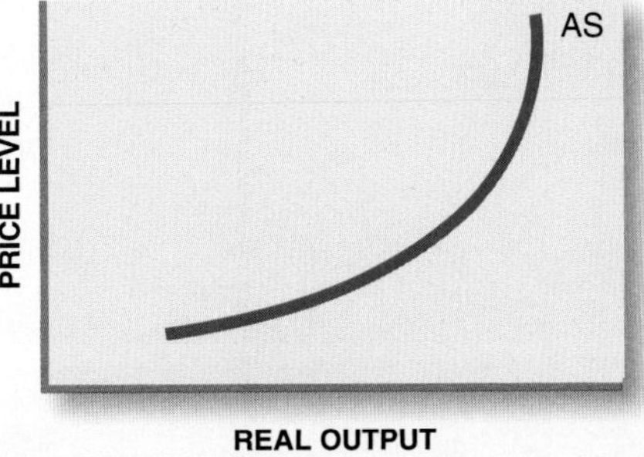

LO2 5. What was the range, in percentage points, of the variation in quarterly growth rates between 1999 and 2003 of
(*a*) Consumer spending ______
(*b*) Investment spending ______
(*Note:* See Figure 9.8 for data.)

LO3 6. Complete the following table:

	Real Output Demanded (in $ billions) by:								
Price Level	Consumers	+	Investors	+	Government	+	Net Exports	=	Aggregate Demand	Aggregate Supply
120	80		15		20		10		___	170
110	92		16		20		12		___	160
100	104		17		20		14		___	150
90	116		18		20		16		___	140
80	128		19		20		18		___	120
70	140		20		20		20		___	95
60	154		21		20		22		___	65

(*a*) What is the level of equilibrium GDP? ________
(*b*) What is the equilibrium price level? ________
(*c*) If full employment occurs at real GDP = $165 billion, what kind of GDP gap exists? ________
(*d*) How large is that gap? ________
(*e*) Which macro problem exists here? ________

LO3 7. On the graph below, draw the AD and AS curves with these data:

Price level	140	130	120	110	100	90	80	70	60	50
Real output										
Demanded	600	700	800	900	1,000	1,100	1,200	1,300	1,400	1,500
Supplied	1,200	1,150	1,100	1,050	1,000	950	900	800	600	400

(*a*) What is the equilibrium
(*i*) Real output level? ________
(*ii*) Price level? ________

Suppose net exports decline by $150 at all price levels, but all other components of aggregate demand remain constant.

(*b*) Draw the new AD curve.
(*c*) What is the new equilibrium
(*i*) Output level? ________
(*ii*) Price level? ________
(*d*) What macro problem has arisen in this economy? ________

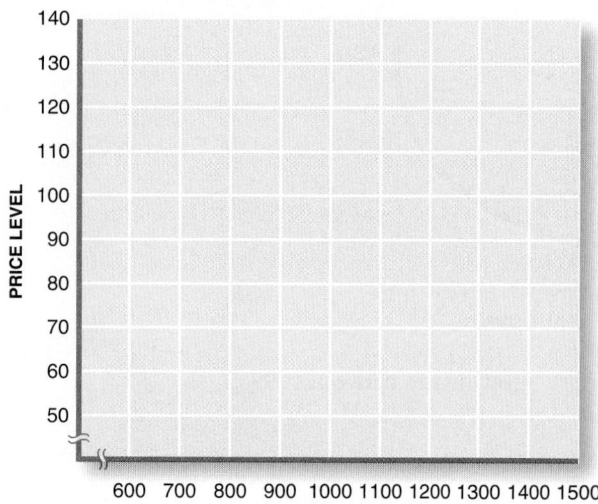

LO2 8. If every $1,000 increase in the real price of homes adds 5 cents to annual consumer spending, how large was the wealth effect from the $6-trillion increase in home prices (1997–2006)? ________

PROBLEMS FOR CHAPTER 10

Name: ____________________

LO1 1. From 1929 to 2006, in how many years did
   (a) real consumption decline? ______
   (b) real investment decline? ______
   (c) real government spending increase at least $100 billion? (Data on end covers of text.) ______

LO1 2. If the consumption function is $C = \$200 + 0.9Y$,
   (a) What does the saving function look like? ______
   (b) What is the rate of desired saving when disposable income equals
      (i) $500? ______
      (ii) $1,000? ______

LO2 3. What is the value of the multiplier when the marginal propensity to consume is
   (a) 0.10 ______
   (b) 0.25 ______

LO2 4. Suppose that investment demand increases by $100 billion in a closed and private economy (no government or foreign trade). Assume further that households have a marginal propensity to consume of 90 percent.
   (a) Compute four rounds of multiplier effects:

	Changes in This Cycle's Spending	Cumulative Change in Spending
First cycle	______	______
Second cycle	______	______
Third cycle	______	______
Fourth cycle	______	______

   (b) What will be the final cumulative impact on spending? ______
   (c) Compare your results with those in Table 10.1. With a higher marginal propensity to consume, does the cumulative change in expenditure become larger or smaller? ______

LO3 5. Illustrate in the graph on the left below the impact of a sudden decline in consumer confidence that reduces autonomous consumption by $50 billion at the price level P_F. Assume $MPC = 0.8$.
   (a) What is the new equilibrium level of real output? (Don't forget the multiplier.) ______
   (b) How large is the real GDP gap? ______
   (c) What has happened to average prices? ______

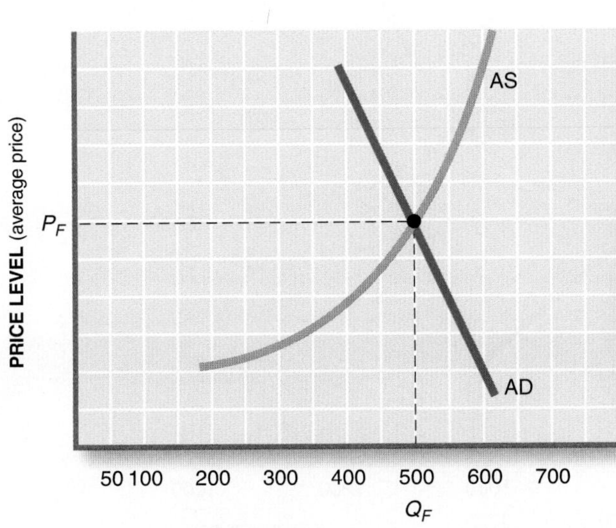

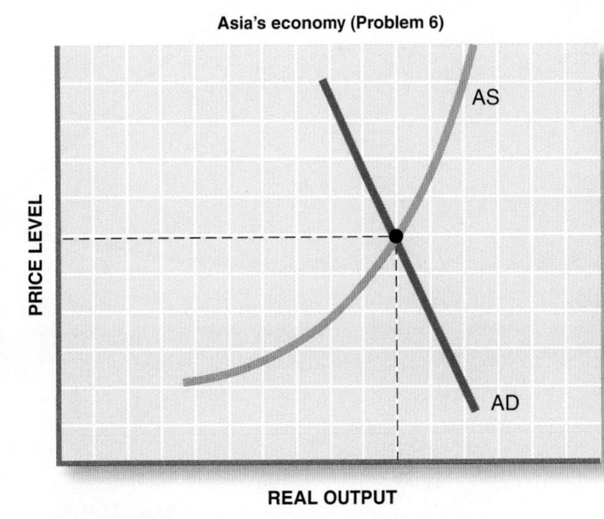

 Name: ______________________

LO2 LO3 6. (*a*) Show on the previous graph (right) the effects of the U.S. slump on Asia's economy (World View, p. 202).
(*b*) If Asian net exports to the U.S. declined by $40 billion per year, by how much would *total* Asian spending decline if Asian consumers have an MPC of 0.90? ________

LO3 7. According to World Bank estimates (see p. 207), by how much did consumer spending decline as a result of the post-Katrina, September 2005 drop in consumer confidence (see News, p. 175 in Chapter 9)? ________

LO3 8. How large is the inflationary GDP gap in Figure 10.9?

LO2 LO3 9. The accompanying graph depicts a macro equilibrium. Answer the questions based on the information in the graph.
(*a*) What is the equilibrium rate of GDP? ________
(*b*) If full-employment real GDP is $1,200, what problem does this economy have? ________
(*c*) How large is the real GDP gap? ________
(*d*) If the multiplier were equal to 4, how much additional investment would be needed to increase aggregate demand by the amount of the initial GDP gap? ________
(*e*) Illustrate the changes in autonomous investment and induced consumption that occur in *d*.
(*f*) What happens to prices when aggregate demand increases by the amount of the initial GDP gap? ________
(*g*) Is full employment restored by the AD shift? ________

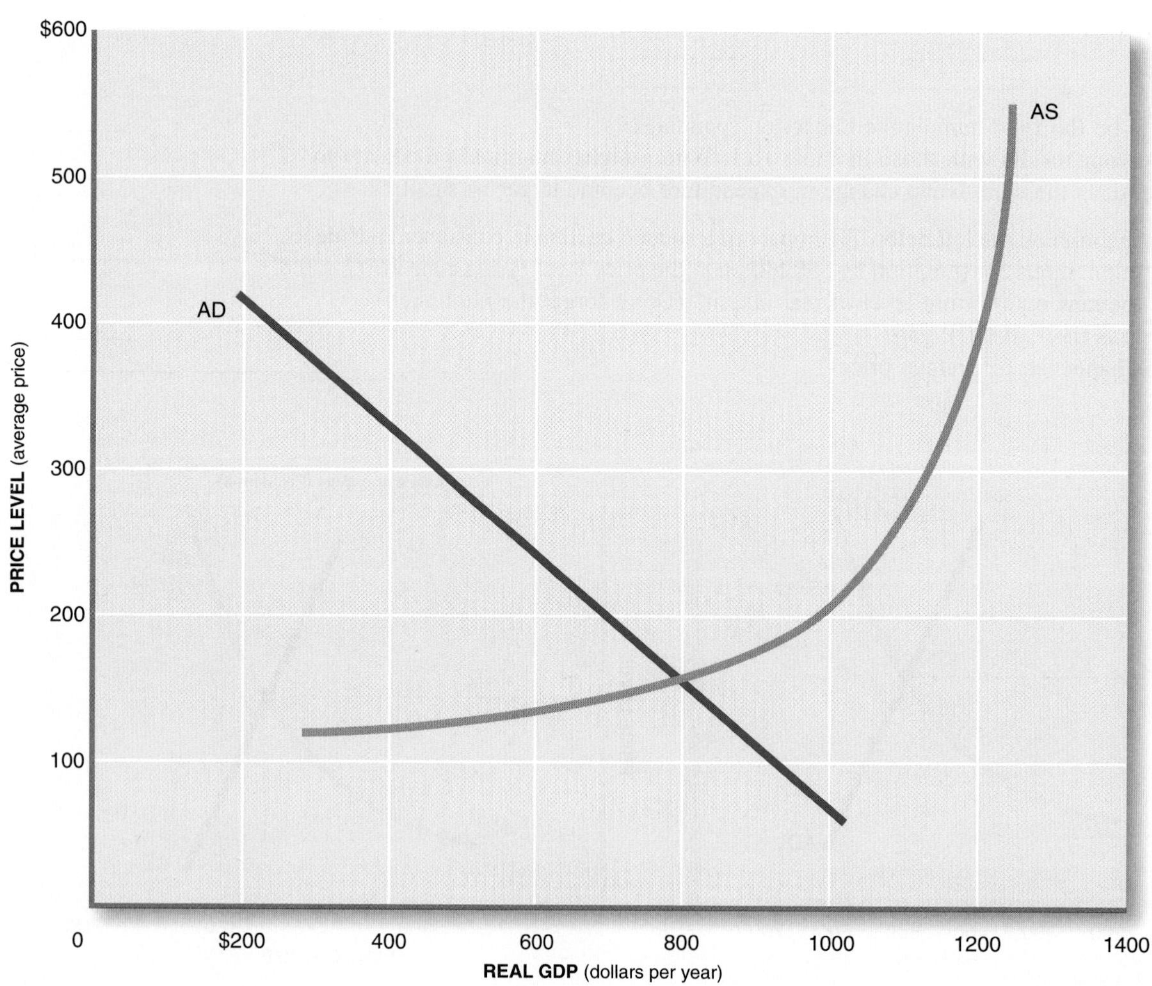

PROBLEMS FOR CHAPTER 11

Name: ______________________

LO2 1. In the tax-cut example on pp. 219–220,

(*a*) By how much does consumer saving increase initially? ________

(*b*) What is the marginal propensity to save? ________

LO2 2. Suppose the consumption function is

$$C = \$400 \text{ billion} + 0.8Y$$

and the government wants to stimulate the economy. By how much will aggregate demand at current prices shift initially (before multiplier effects) with

(*a*) A \$50 billion increase in government purchases? ________

(*b*) A \$50 billion tax cut? ________

(*c*) A \$50 billion increase in income transfers? ________

What will the cumulative AD shift be for

(*d*) The increased G? ________

(*e*) The tax cut? ________

(*f*) The increased transfers? ________

LO3 3. Suppose the government decides to increase taxes by \$20 billion in order to increase Social Security benefits by the same amount. How will this combined tax-transfer policy affect aggregate demand at current prices? ________________

LO1 4. On the accompanying graph, identify and label

(*a*) Macro equilibrium.

(*b*) The real GDP gap.

(*c*) The AD excess or shortfall.

(*d*) The new equilibrium that would occur with appropriate fiscal policy.

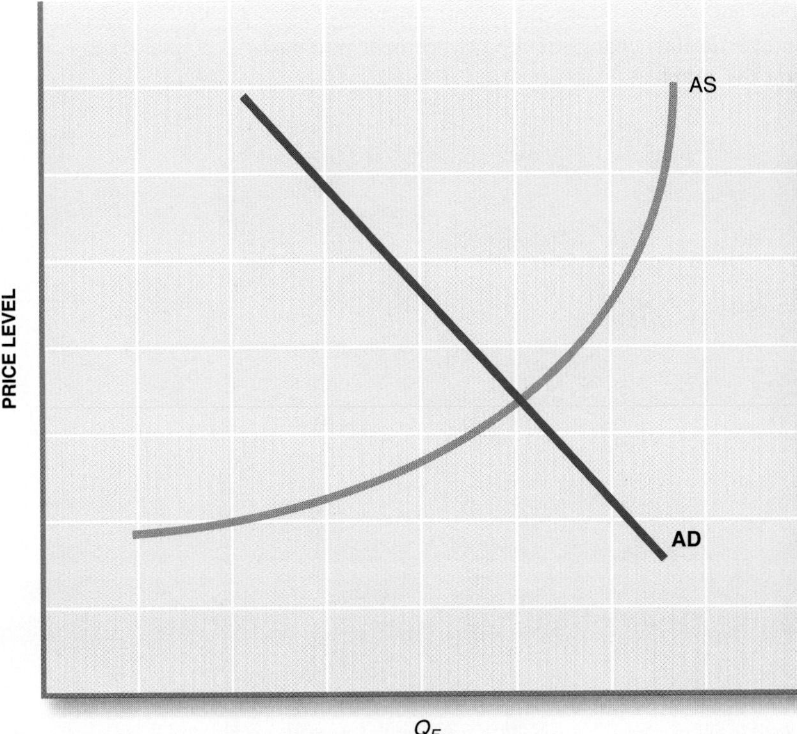

 Name: ________________

LO3 5. According to the World View on page 218,
(*a*) By how much did South Korea's government *increase* public-works spending? ______
(*b*) By how much might this fiscal stimulus have increased aggregate demand if the marginal propensity to consume was 0.9? ______

LO3 6. (*a*) According to the News on page 221, by how much were tax cuts expected to boost consumer spending in 2001? ______
(*b*) By how much would total spending have changed as a result of such an initial consumption surge? ______

LO2 7. Suppose that an increase in income transfers rather than government spending was the preferred policy for stimulating the economy depicted in Figure 11.4. By how much would transfers have to increase to attain the desired shift of AD? ______

LO3 8. If the marginal propensity to consume was 0.9, how large would each of the following need to be in order to restore a full-employment equilibrium in Figure 11.6?
(*a*) A tax increase. ______
(*b*) A government spending cut. ______
(*c*) A cut in income transfers. ______

LO1 LO3 9. Use the following data to complete the graph and to answer the following questions:

Price level	10	20	30	40	50	60	70	80	90	100
Real GDP supplied	$500	600	680	750	820	880	910	940	960	970
Real GDP demanded	$960	920	880	840	800	760	720	680	640	600

(*a*) If full employment occurs at a real output rate of $880, how large is the real GDP gap? ______
(*b*) How large is the AD shortfall? ______
(*c*) What will happen to prices if AD increases enough to restore full employment? ______
(*d*) Assuming MPC = 0.75, how will macro equilibrium change if the government purchases increase by $20? Illustrate your answer on the graph. ______

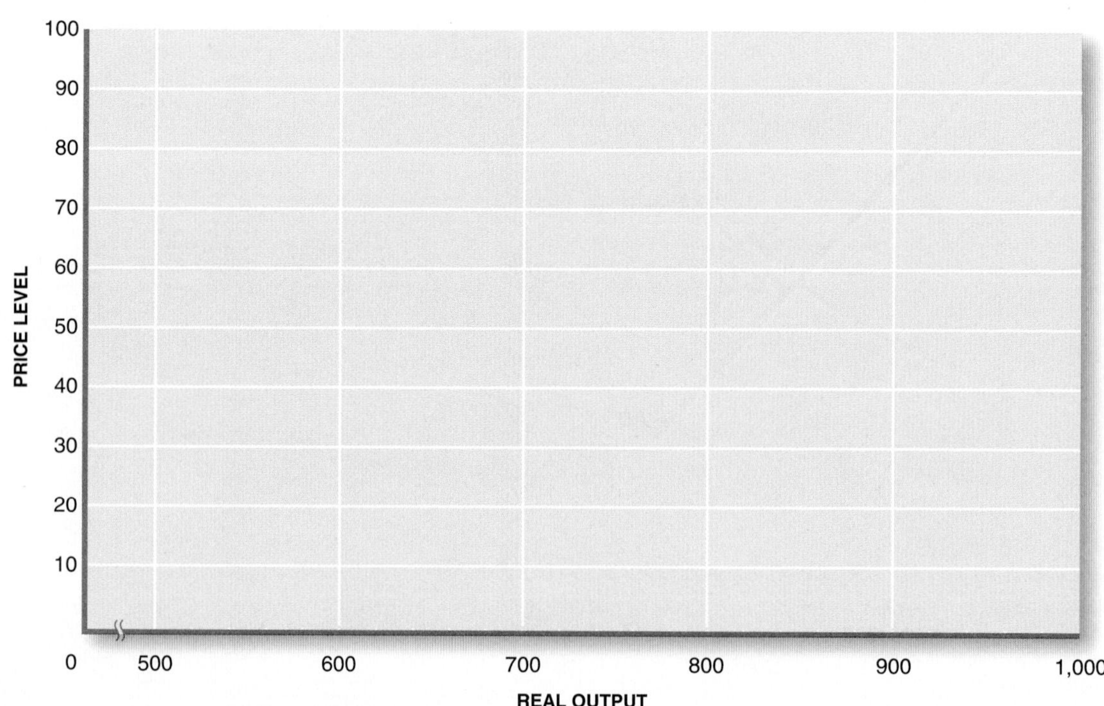

PROBLEMS FOR CHAPTER 12

Name: ______________________

LO1 1. From 2002 to 2003 how did each of the following change?
(*a*) Tax revenue ________
(*b*) Government spending ________
(*c*) Budget deficit ________
(*Note:* See Table 12.1.)

LO1 2. Since 1970, in how many years has the federal budget had a surplus? (See Figure 12.1.) ________

3. What country had the largest budget defichit (as percent of GDP) in 2006? ________

LO1 4. What would happen to the budget deficit if the
(*a*) GDP growth rate jumped from 1 percent to 3 percent? ________
(*b*) Inflation rate increased by 2 percentage points? ________
(*Note:* See Table 12.2 for clues.)

LO1 5. Use Table 12.3 to determine how much fiscal stimulus or restraint occured between
(*a*) 2000 and 2001 ________
(*b*) 2001 and 2002 ________

LO1 6. Suppose a government has no debt and a balanced budget. Suddenly it decides to spend \$10 billion while raising only \$8 billion worth of taxes.
(*a*) What will be the government's deficit? ________
(*b*) If the government finances the deficit by issuing bonds, what amount of bonds will it issue? ________
(*c*) At a 10 percent rate of interest, how much interest will the government pay each year? ________
(*d*) Add the interest payment to the government's \$10 billion expenditures for the next year, and assume that taxes remain at \$8 billion. In the second year, compute the
(*i*) Deficit. ________
(*ii*) Amount of new debt (bonds) issued. ________
(*iii*) Debt-service requirement. ________
(*e*) Repeat these calculations for the third, fourth, and fifth years, assuming that the government taxes at a rate of \$8 billion each year and has noninterest expenditures of \$10 billion annually.

	Year 3	Year 4	Year 5
Deficit	________	________	________
New debt	________	________	________
Debt service	________	________	________

(*f*) What is the ratio of interest payments, relative to the deficit, with each passing year? ________

Year 2	Year 3	Year 4	Year 5
________	________	________	________

(*g*) What will happen to the ratio of government debt to government expenditure with each passing year? ________

LO1 7. (*a*) According to the News on page 238, how much fiscal restraint occurred between 1931 and 1933? ________
(*b*) By how much did this policy reduce aggregate demand if the MPC was 0.8? ________

LO3 8. In Figure 12.5, what is the opportunity cost of increasing government spending from g_1 to g_2 if
(*a*) No external financing is available? ____________
(*b*) Complete external financing is available? ____________

LO3 9. (*a*) How much U.S. debt do foreigners hold? ________
(*b*) If the interest rate on U.S. Treasury debt is 5 percent, how much interest do foreigners collect each year? ________

LO1 10. Use the accompanying graph to illustrate *changes* in the structural and total deficits for fiscal years 2000–2006 (data in Table 12.3). Why do the two measures move in different directions?

____

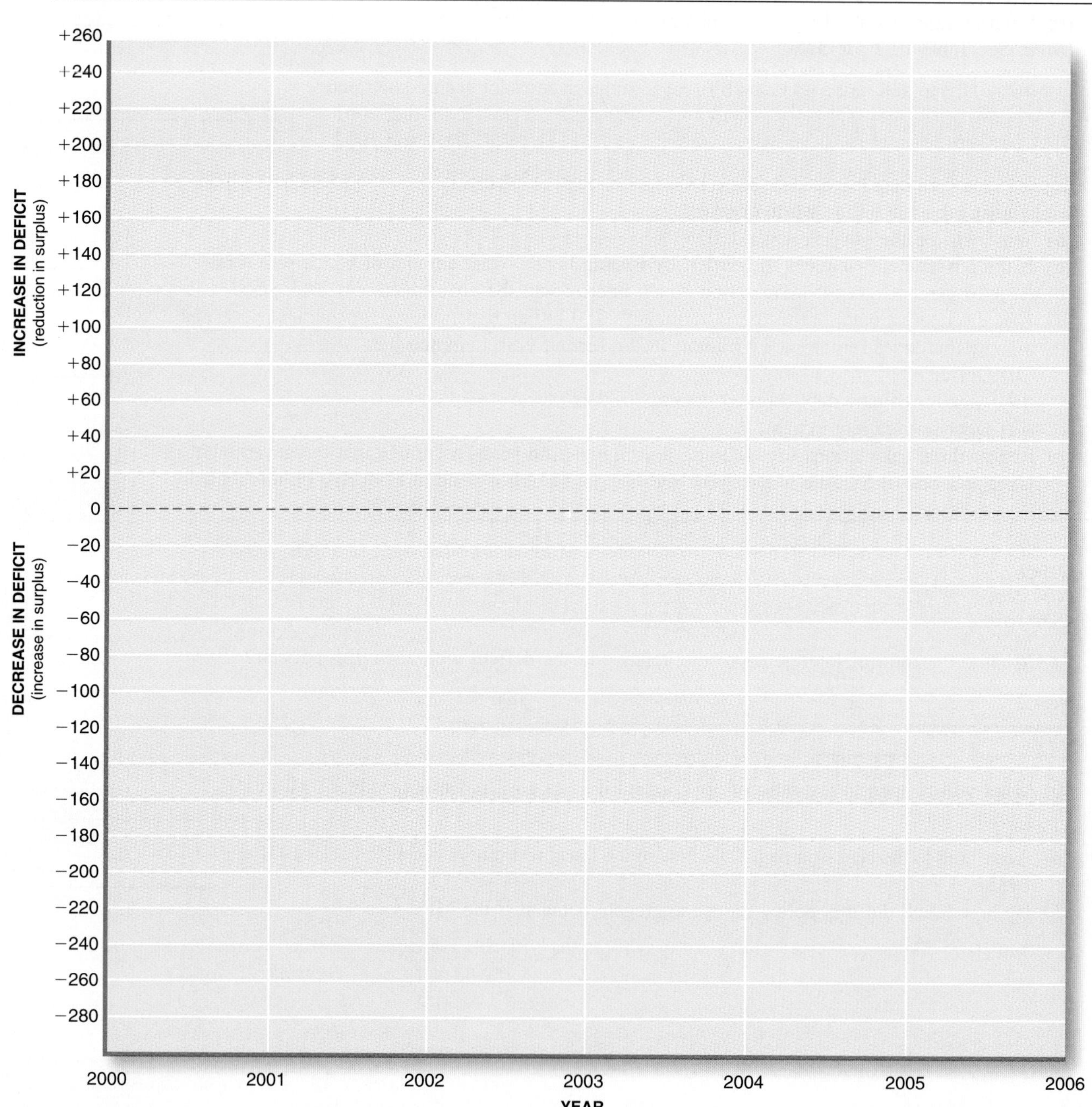

PROBLEMS FOR CHAPTER 13

Name: ____________________

LO1 LO2 1. If you cash a $50 traveler's check at a bank, by how much does

(*a*) M1 change? ________

(*b*) M2 change? ________

(*c*) bank reserves change? ________

If you deposit the traveler's check in your bank account, by how much does

(*d*) M1 change? ________

(*e*) M2 change? ________

(*f*) bank reserves change? ________

LO2 2. Suppose a bank's balance sheet looks as follows:

Assets		Liabilities	
Reserves	$350	Deposits	$4,000

and banks are required to hold reserves equal to 10 percent of deposits.

(*a*) How much excess reserves does the bank hold? (*a*) ________

(*b*) How much more can this bank lend? (*b*) ________

LO2 3. Suppose a bank's balance sheet looks like this:

Assets		Liabilities	
Reserves		Deposits	$500
Excess	$ 70		
Required	30		
Loans	400		
Total	$500	Total	$500

What is the required reserve ratio? ________

LO3 4. What is the value of the money multiplier when the required reserve ratio is

(*a*) 10 percent? ________

(*b*) 4 percent? ________

LO2 5. In December 1994, a man in Ohio decided to deposit all of the 8 *million* pennies he'd been saving for nearly 65 years. (His deposit weighed over 48,000 pounds!) With a reserve requirement of 5 percent, what will be the cumulative change for the banking system in

(*a*) Transactions deposits? ________

(*b*) Total reserves? ________

(*c*) Lending capacity? ________

LO2 6. (*a*) When the reserve requirement changes, which of the following will change for the bank that receives the initial deposit (Bank *A*)? (Check those items that will change.)

Transactions deposits ________

Total reserves ________

Required reserves ________

Excess reserves ________

Lending capacity ________

(*b*) When the reserve requirement changes, which of the following will experience a cumulative change in the total banking system? (Check all that apply.)

Transactions deposits ________

Total reserves ________

Required reserves ________

Excess reserves ________

Lending capacity ________

LO2 7. In Table 13.3, how much unused lending capacity does Eternal Savings have at step 4? ________

 Name: ______________________

LO2 LO3 8. Suppose that a lottery winner deposits $10 million in cash into her transactions account at the Bank of America (B of A). Assume a reserve requirement of 25 percent and no excess reserves in the banking system prior to this deposit.

(*a*) Use step 1 in the T-accounts below to show how her deposit affects the balance sheet at B of A.

(*b*) Has the money supply been changed by her deposit? ______

(*c*) Use step 2 below to show the changes at B of A after B of A fully uses its new lending capacity.

(*d*) Has the money supply been changed in step 2? ______

(*e*) In step 3 the new borrower(s) writes a check for the amount of the loan. That check is deposited at another bank, and B of A pays the other bank when the check clears. What does the B of A balance sheet look like now?

(*f*) After the entire banking system uses the lending capacity of the initial ($10 million) deposit, by how much will the following have changed?

Total reserves ______
Total deposits ______
Total loans ______
Cash held by public ______
The money supply ______

Step 1: Winnings Deposited
Bank of America

Assets (in millions)		**Liabilities (in millions)**	
Reserves:		Deposits	____
Required	____		
Excess	____		
Subtotal	____		
Loans	____		
Total assets	____	Total liabilities	____

Step 2: Loans Made
Bank of America

Assets (in millions)		**Liabilities (in millions)**	
Reserves:		Deposits	____
Required	____		
Excess	____		
Subtotal	____		
Loans	____		
Total assets	____	Total liabilities	____

Step 3: Check Clears
Bank of America

Assets (in millions)		**Liabilities (in millions)**	
Reserves:		Deposits	____
Required	____		
Excess	____		
Subtotal	____		
Loans	____		
Total assets	____	Total liabilities	____

PROBLEMS FOR CHAPTER 14

Name: ____________________

LO2 1. What is the money multiplier when the reserve requirement is:

(*a*) 0.100 ________
(*b*) 0.125 ________

LO2 2. In Table 14.1, what would the following values be if the required reserve ratio fell to 0.125?

Total deposits ________
(*b*) Total reserves ________
(*c*) Required reserves ________
(*d*) Excess reserves ________
(*e*) Money multiplier ________
(*f*) Unused lending capacity ________

LO2 3. Assume that the following data describe the condition of the banking system:

Total reserves	$200 billion
Transactions deposits	$800 billion
Cash held by public	$100 billion
Reserve requirement	0.20

(*a*) How large is the money supply (M1)? (*a*) ________
(*b*) How large are *required* reserves? (*b*) ________
(*c*) How large are *excess* reserves? (*c*) ________
(*d*) By how much could the banks increase their lending activity? (*d*) ________

LO2 4. In Problem 3, suppose the Fed wanted to stop further lending activity. To do this, what reserve requirement should the Fed impose? ________

LO2 5. According to the News on page 276, and World View on page 284, what was the money multiplier in

(*a*) The United States? ________
(*b*) China? ________

LO2 6. Assume the banking system contains

Total reserves	$60 billion
Transactions deposits	$600 billion
Cash held by public	$100 billion
Reserve requirement	0.10

(*a*) Are the banks fully utilizing their lending capacity? ________
(*b*) What would happen to the money supply *initially* if the public deposited another $50 billion of cash in transactions accounts? ________
(*c*) What would the lending capacity of the banking system be after such a portfolio switch? ________
(*d*) How large would the money supply be if the banks fully utilized their lending capacity? ________
(*e*) What three steps could the Fed take to offset that potential growth in M1? ________
____
____

LO3 7. Assume that a $1,000 bond issued in 2007 pays $100 in interest each year. What is the current yield on the bond if it can be purchased for

(*a*) $1,200? ________
(b) $1,000? ________
(c) $800? ________

LO3 8. Suppose a $1,000 bond pays $50 per year in interest.
(*a*) What is the contractual interest rate on the bond? ________
(*b*) If market interest rates rise to 10 percent, what price will the bond sell for? ________

LO3 9. By how much did the Fed reduce the fed funds rate in August 2001 (News, p. 279) ________

LO3 10. If the GM bond described on p. 280 was resold for $800, what would its yield be? ________

LO3 11. Suppose a banking system with the following balance sheet has no excess reserves. Assume that banks will make loans in the full amount of any excess reserves that they acquire and will immediately be able to eliminate loans from their portfolio to cover inadequate reserves.

Assets (in billions)		Liabilities (in billions)	
Total reserves	$ 30	Transactions accounts	$300
Securities	90		
Loans	180		
Total	$300	Total	$300

(*a*) What is the reserve requirement? ________

(*b*) Suppose the reserve requirement is changed to 5 percent. Reconstruct the balance sheet of the total banking system after all banks have fully utilized their lending capacity.

Assets (in billions)		Liabilities (in billions)	
Total reserves	________	Transactions accounts	________
Securities	________		
Loans	________		
Total	________	Total	________

(*c*) By how much has the money supply changed as a result of the lower reserve requirement (step *b*)? ________

(*d*) Suppose the Fed now buys $10 billion of securities directly from the banks. What will the banks' books look like after this purchase?

Assets (in billions)		Liabilities (in billions)	
Total reserves	________	Transactions accounts	________
Securities	________		
Loans	________		
Total	________	Total	________

(*e*) How much excess reserves do the banks have now? ________

(*f*) By how much can the money supply now increase? ________

PROBLEMS FOR CHAPTER 15

Name: ______________________

LO1 1. Suppose homeowners owe $4 trillion in mortgage loans.

(*a*) If the mortgage interest rate is 9 percent, approximately how much are homeowners paying in annual mortgage interest? ________

(*b*) If the interest rate drops to 8 percent, by how much will annual interest payments drop? ________

(*c*) What are homeowners likely to do with their interest rate "savings"? ________

LO1 2. If all of the "cash out" described in the News on p. 293 was spent on consumption, by how much did AD shift

(a) initially? ________

(b) cumulatively? ________

LO1 3. Illustrate the effects on investment of

(*a*) An interest-rate hike (point *A*).

(*b*) An interest-rate hike accompanied by increased sales expectations (point *B*).

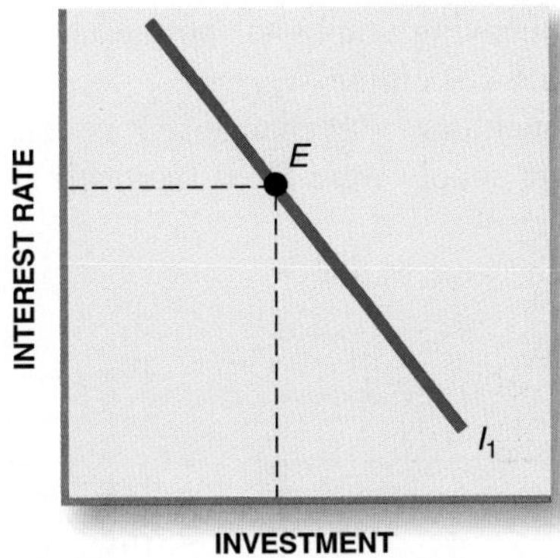

LO2 LO3 4. Suppose that an economy is characterized by

$$M = \$4{,}000 \text{ billion}$$

$$V = 2$$

$$P = 100$$

(*a*) What is the real value of output (*Q*)? ________

Now assume that the Fed increases the money supply by 10 percent and velocity remains unchanged.

(*b*) If the price level remains constant, what will happen to real output? ________

(*c*) If, instead, real output is fixed at the natural level of unemployment, what will happen when *M* increases? ________

(*d*) By how much would *V* have to fall to offset the increase in *M*? ________

LO1 5. If the nominal rate of interest is 8 percent and the real rate of interest is 3 percent, what rate of inflation is anticipated? ________

LO1 LO2 6. Suppose the Fed decided to purchase $20 billion worth of government securities in the open market. What impact would this action have on the economy? Specifically, answer the following questions:

(*a*) How will M1 be affected initially? ________

(*b*) How will the banking system's lending capacity be affected if the reserve requirement is 25 percent? ________

(*c*) How will banks induce investors to utilize this expanded lending capacity? ________

(*d*) How will aggregate demand be affected if investors borrow and spend all the newly available credit? ________

(*e*) Under what circumstances would the Fed be pursuing such an open market policy? ________

(*f*) How could those same objectives be achieved through changes in the discount rate or reserve requirement?

____

____

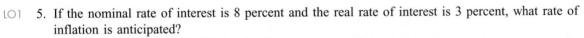

 Name: ____________

LO1 LO2 7. According to Greenspan's rule of thumb, how much fiscal restraint would be equivalent to a 2-point hike in long-term interest rates? ________

LO2 LO3 8. The following data describe market conditions:

Money supply (in billions)	$100	$200	$300	$400	$ 500	$ 600	$ 700
Interest rate	8.0	7.5	7.0	6.5	6.0	5.5	5.5
Rate of investment (in billions)	$ 12	$ 12	$ 15	$ 16	$16.5	$16.5	$16.5

(*a*) At what rate of interest does the liquidity trap emerge? ________

(*b*) At what rate of interest does investment demand become totally inelastic? ________

LO3 9. Use the accompanying graphs to show what happens in the economy when M increases from $300 billion to $400 billion.

(*a*) By how much does PQ change if V is constant? ________

(*b*) If aggregate supply were fixed (vertical) at the initial output level, what would happen to the price level? ________

(*c*) What is the value of V? ________

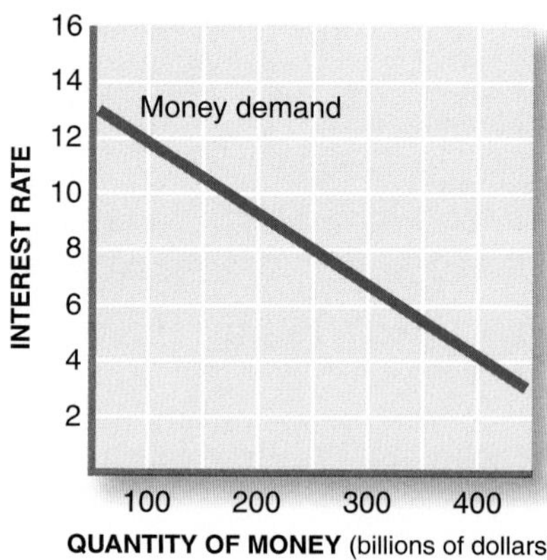

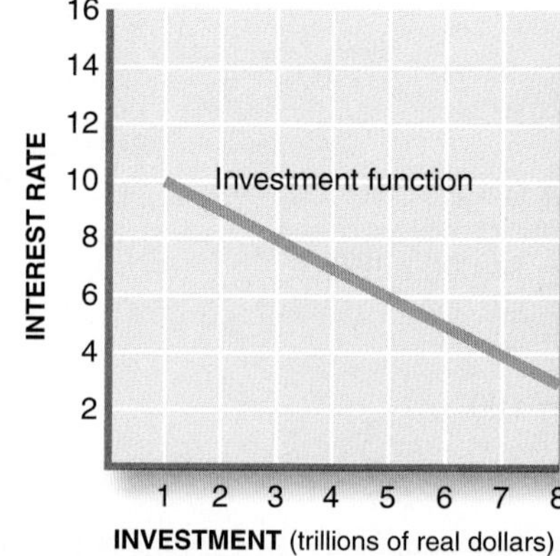

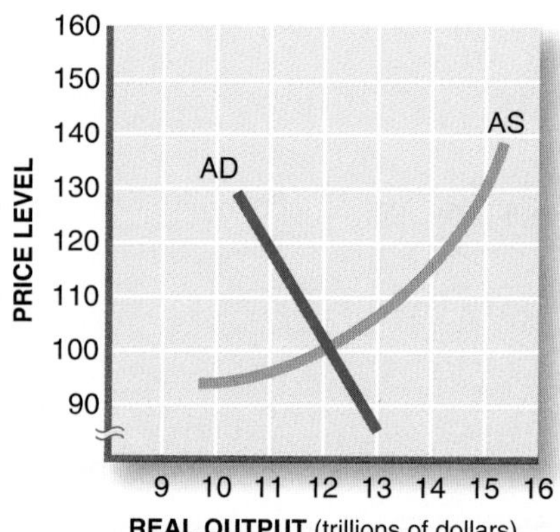

LO2 10. Use the newspaper and the Internet (e.g., www.CBO.gov) to determine

(*a*) The interest rate on 10-year Treasury bonds. ________

(*b*) The U.S. inflation rate. ________

(*c*) The real rate of interest. ________

PROBLEMS FOR CHAPTER 16

Name: ______________________________

LO1 1. On the graph below, draw the (*A*) Keynesian, (*B*) Monetarist, and (*C*) hybrid AS curves, all intersecting AD at point *E*. If AD shifts rightward, which AS curve generates
(*a*) The biggest increase in output? ________
(*b*) The biggest increase in prices? ________

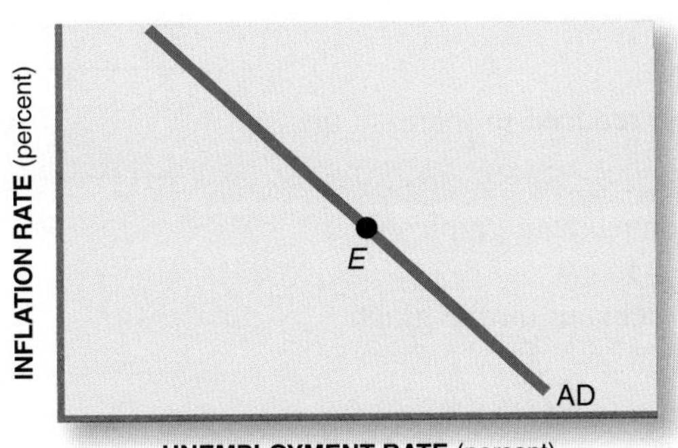

LO1 2. The Economy Tomorrow section provides estimates of time spent in traffic delays. If the average worker produces $40 of output per hour, what is the opportunity cost of
(*a*) Current traffic delays? $________
(*b*) Estimated delays in 10 years? $________

LO3 3. Suppose taxpayers are required to pay a base tax of $50 plus 30 percent on any income over $100, as in the initial tax system *B* in Table 16.1. Suppose further that the taxing authority wishes to raise by $20 the taxes of people with incomes of $200.
(*a*) If marginal tax rates are to remain unchanged, what will the new base tax have to be? $________
(*b*) If the base tax of $50 is to remain unchanged, what will the marginal tax rate have to be? ________%

LO3 4. Suppose households supply 230 billion hours of labor per year and have a tax elasticity of supply of 0.20. If the tax rate is increased by 10 percent, by how many hours will the supply of labor decline? ________

LO3 5. By how much did the disposable income of rich people increase as a result of the 2001–4 reduction in the top marginal tax rate from 39.6 to 35 percent? Assume they have $2 trillion of income in the highest bracket. ________

LO2 6. According to Figure 16.5, what inflation rate would occur if the unemployment rate fell to 4 percent, with
(*a*) *PC*1? ________
(*b*) *PC*2? ________

LO2 7. On the following graph, plot the unemployment and inflation rates for the years 1996–2006. Is there any evidence of a Phillips curve trade-off? ________

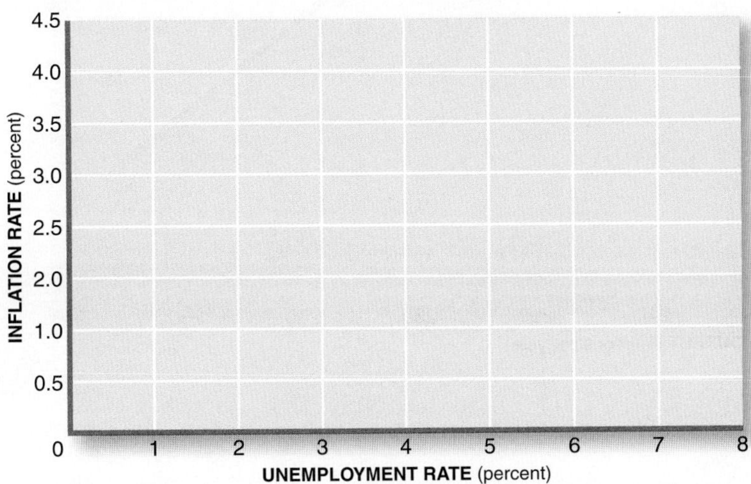

 Name: ____________

LO3 8. If the tax elasticity of labor supply is 0.20, by how much will the quantity of labor supplied increase in response to
   (*a*) A $1,000 per person income-tax rebate? ______
   (*b*) A 2-percent reduction in marginal tax rates? ______

LO3 9. If the tax elasticity of supply is 0.10, by how much do taxes have to be reduced to increase the labor supply by 3 percent? ______

LO3 10. Suppose an economy is characterized by the AS/AD curves in the accompanying graph. A decision is then made to increase infrastructure spending by $20 billion a year.
   (*a*) Illustrate the direct impact of the increased spending on aggregate demand on the graph (ignore multiplier effects).
   (*b*) If AS is unaffected, what is the new equilibrium rate of output? ______
   (*c*) What is the new equilibrium price level? ______
   (*d*) Now assume that the infrastructure investments increase aggregate supply by $30 billion a year (from the initial equilibrium), Illustrate this effect on the graph.
   (*e*) After both demand and supply adjustments occur, what is the final equilibrium
      (*i*) Rate of output? ______
      (*ii*) Price level? ______

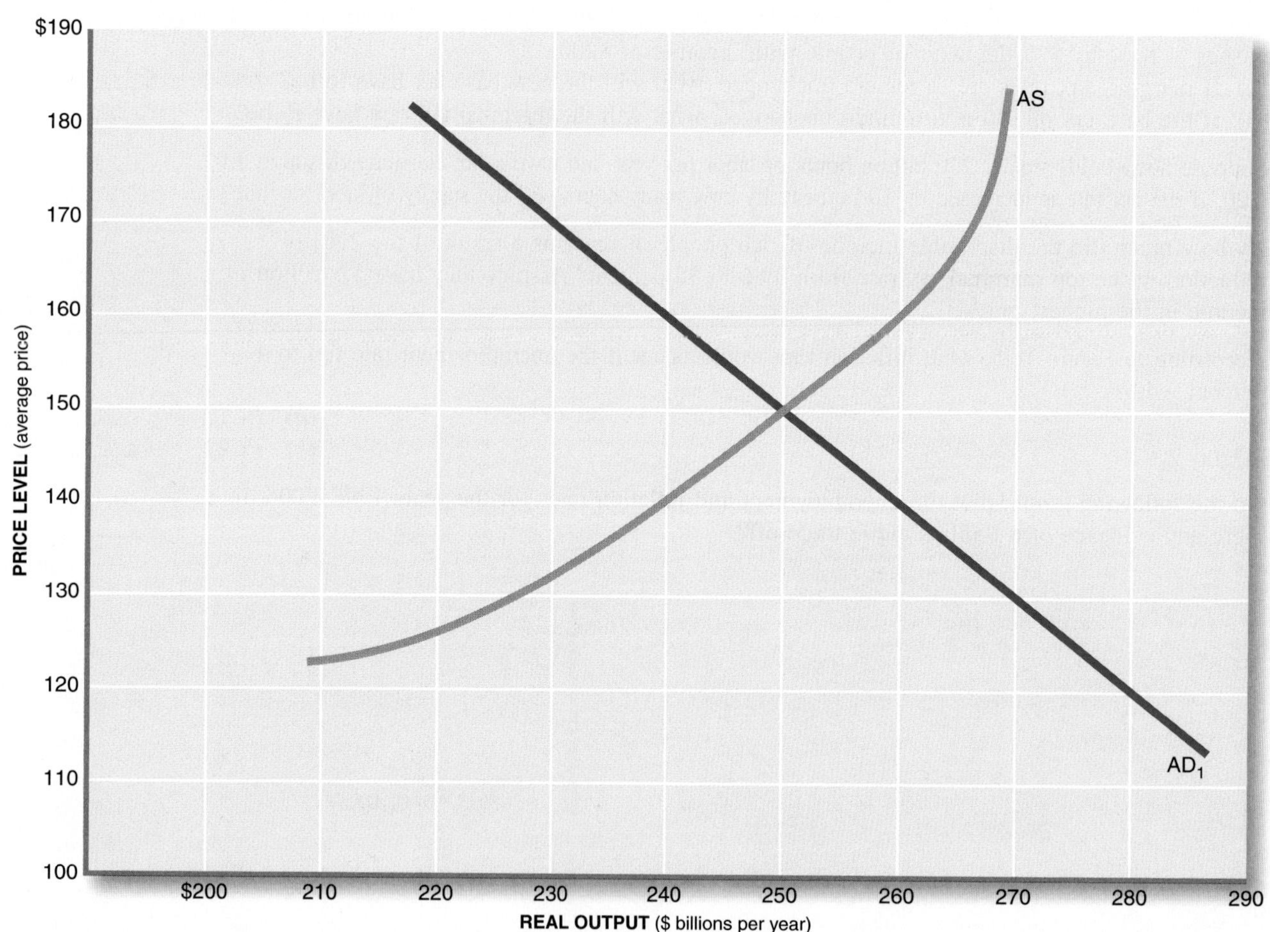

PROBLEMS FOR CHAPTER 17

Name: ____________________

LO1 1. According to the rule of 72 (Table 17.1), how many years will it take for GDP to double if the economy is growing at:

(*a*) 3 percent a year? ______
(*b*) 4.5 percent a year? ______

LO1 2. According to the Rule of 72 (Table 17.1) and recent growth rates (World View, p. 340) how long will it be before GDP doubles in

(*a*) The United States? ______
(*b*) China? ______
(*c*) Uruguay? ______

LO1 3. If real GDP is growing at 3 percent a year, how long will it take for

(*a*) Real GDP to double? ______
(*b*) Real GDP per capita to double if the population is increasing each year by
(*i*) 0 percent? ______
(*ii*) 1 percent? ______
(*iii*) 2 percent? ______

LO3 4. According to Figure 17.3, in how many years since 1960 has GDP grown

(*a*) Faster than the population? ______
(b) Slower than the population? ______

LO1 5. If the labor force increases by 1 percent each year and productivity increases by 2 percent, how fast will output grow? ______

LO1 6. In 2006, approximately 62 percent of the adult population (230 million) was employed. If the employment rate increased to 65 percent,

(*a*) How many more people would be working? ______
(*b*) By how much would output increase if per worker GDP is $80,000? ______

LO1 7. If output per worker is now $80,000 per year, how much will the average worker produce 10 years from now if productivity improves by

(*a*) 1.0 percent per year? ______
(*b*) 2.0 percent per year? ______

LO1 8. The real (inflation-adjusted) value of U.S. manufacturing output and related manufacturing employment was

	Output	**Employment**
1974	$576 billion	18,514,000
2004	$1,420 billion	14,329,000

(*a*) How many manufacturing jobs were lost between 1974 and 2004? ______
(*b*) What happened to output? ______
(*c*) What was average manufacturing productivity in
(*i*) 1974? ______
(*ii*) 2004? ______

LO1 9. What is the annual rate of productivity advance implied by Moore's Law (News, p. 342)? ______

LO1 10. Suppose that every additional five percentage points in the investment rate ($I \div$ GDP) boost economic growth by one percentage point. Assume also that all investment must be financed with consumer saving. The economy is now assumed to be fully employed at

GDP	\$6 trillion
Consumption	5 trillion
Saving	1 trillion
Investment	1 trillion

If the goal is to raise the growth rate by 1 percent,

(*a*) By how much must investment increase? ______

(*b*) By how much must consumption decline for this to occur? ______

LO3 11. Using data from the endcovers of this book, graph real GDP and population growth since 1997, setting 1997 values to an index base of 100.

Lowest ______

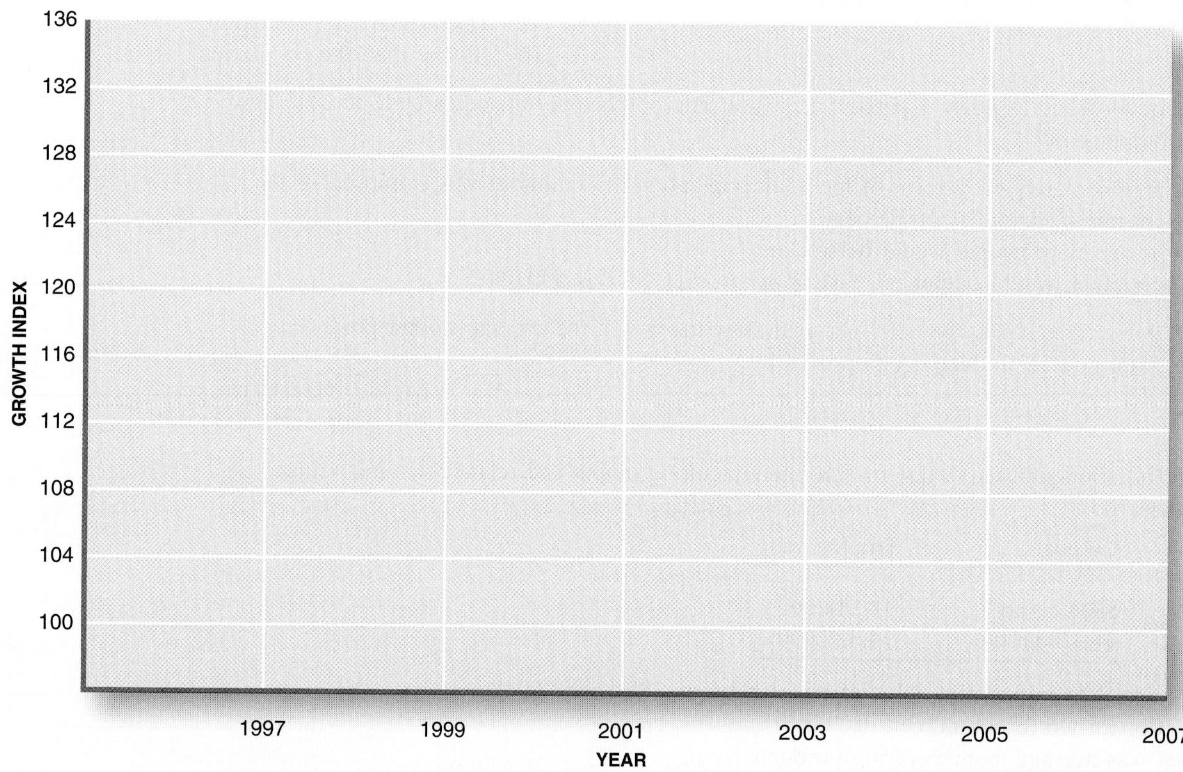

PROBLEMS FOR CHAPTER 18

Name: ____________________

LO1 1. Using the data from the inside front cover and the first page of this book, compute the
(*a*) Import/GDP ratio in 2006. ________
(*b*) Export/GDP ratio in 2006. ________

LO1 2. (*a*) If the marginal propensity to save in a closed (no-trade) economy is 0.05, what is the value of the multiplier? ________
(*b*) If this same economy opens up to trade and exhibits a marginal propensity to import of 0.10, what does the value of the multiplier become? ________

LO1 3. According to the World View on page 353,
(*a*) What percent of European exports goes to the United States? ________
(*b*) By how much does European GDP growth accelerate if U.S. GDP growth increases by two percentage points? ________

LO1 4. According to the World View on page 356, what is the marginal propensity to import for capital investment? ________

LO1 5. How much less income did the 110 million U.S. households have to spend on nonoil products in 2006 as a result of the jump in oil prices (World View, p. 359)? ________

LO1 6. Use data from the inside cover to compute the marginal propensity to import between 2005 and 2006. ________

LO1 7. Suppose that the expenditure patterns of a country are as follows:

$$C = \$60 \text{ million per year} + 0.8Y$$

$$I = \$100 \text{ billion per year}$$

$$G = 0 \text{ (no taxes either)}$$

$$\text{Exports} = \text{imports} = \$10 \text{ billion per year}$$

(*a*) What is the value of equilibrium GDP? ________
(*b*) As a result of higher oil prices, this country must now spend an additional $10 billion per year on imported oil. Assuming that prices of other goods do not change, what impact will the higher oil prices have on equilibrium GDP? ________

LO1 8. Recompute the answer to Problem 7 by assuming that the marginal propensity to import equals 0.1 (and thus that the MPC for domestic goods is 0.7). ________

LO1 9. Using the data from the inside front cover and the first page of this text, compute the 2002–2006 percentage growth for the following:
(*a*) Consumption ________
(*b*) Investment ________
(*c*) Government spending ________
(*d*) Exports ________
(*e*) What was the fastest-growing component of aggregate demand? ________
(*f*) If the average U.S. worker produces $80,000 of output per year, how many jobs were created by that fastest-growing component? ________

 Name: ______________________

LO1 10. On the graph plot (*a*) U.S. exports, (*b*) U.S. imports, and (*c*) nominal GDP growth for each year. Which trade flow is more related to GDP growth? ________

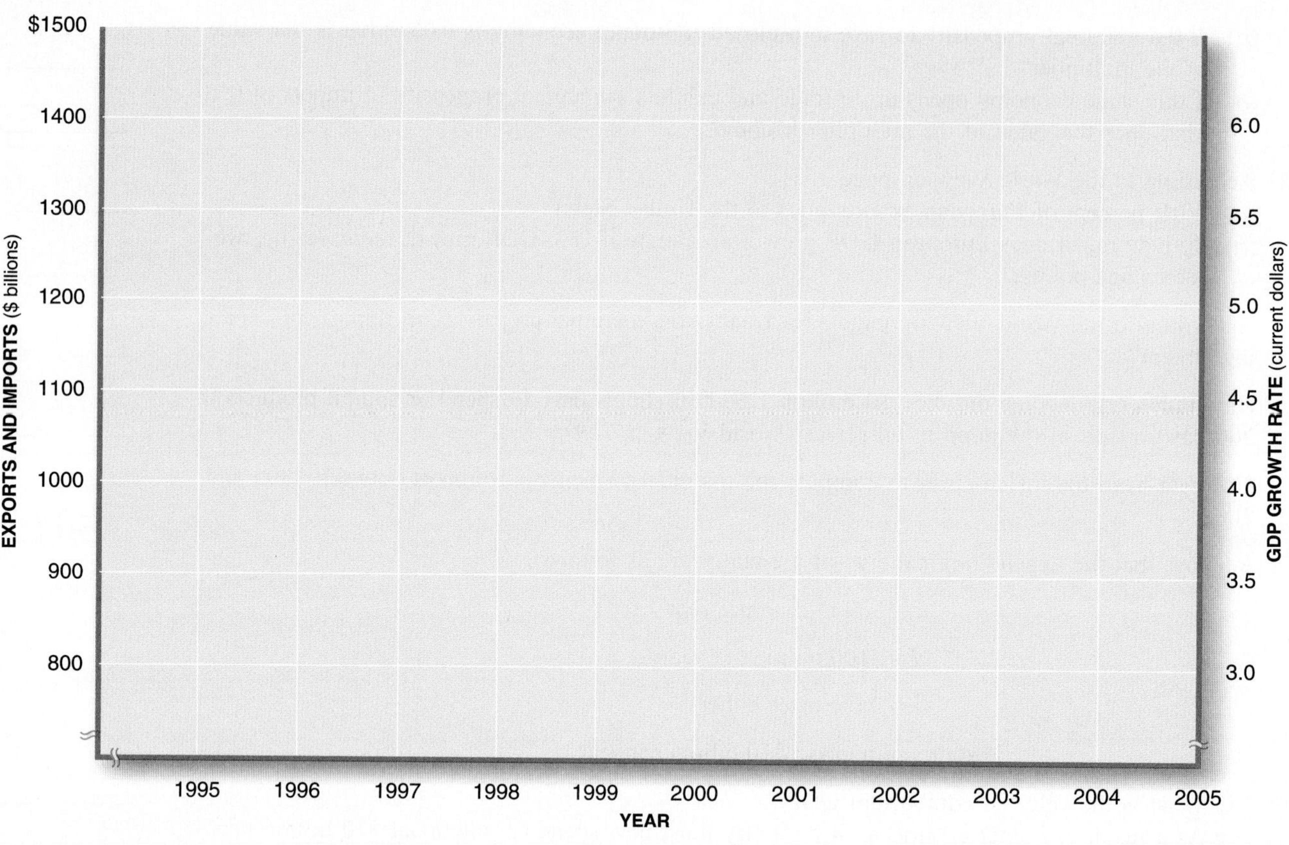

LO3 11. Illustrate on the graphs below the impact of monetary stimulus in

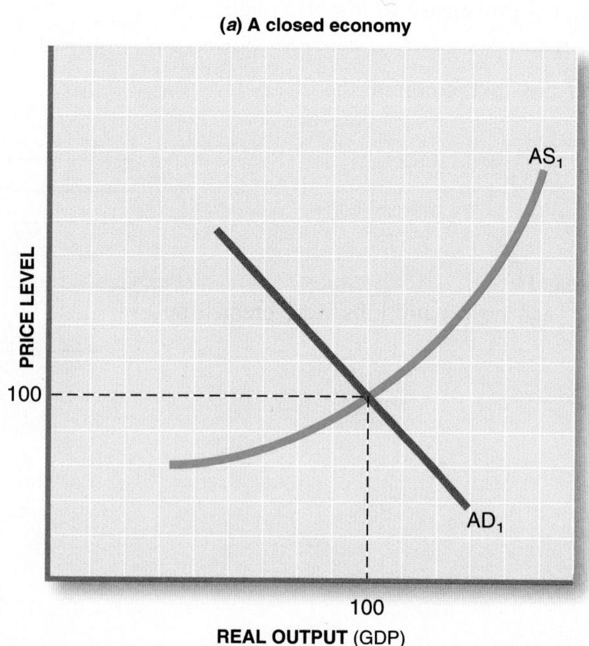

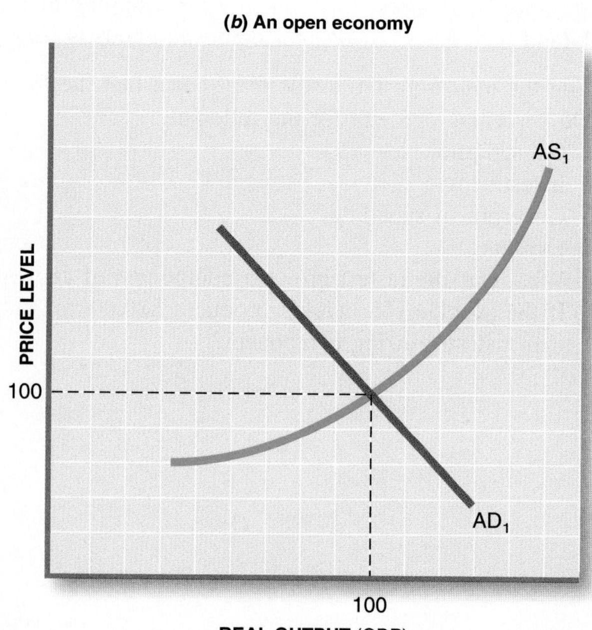

PROBLEMS FOR CHAPTER 19

Name: ____________________

LO3 1. If the Congressional Budget Office makes its average error this year, by how much will it underestimate next year's budget deficit? (See News on page 380) ________

LO1 2. If the unemployment rate stays two percentage points above full employment for an entire year,
(*a*) How many jobs will be lost? ________
(*b*) If the average worker produces $80,000 of output, how much output will be lost? ________

LO1 3. According to the World View on page 375,
(*a*) Which country had the greatest macro misery in the 2000s? (Compute the "misery in the index" from Chapter 16.) ________
(*b*) Who had the fastest growth? ________

LO2 4. Complete the following chart by summarizing the policy prescriptions of various economic theories:

	Policy Prescription for	
Policy Approach	**Recession**	**Inflation**
Fiscal	________	________
Classical	________	________
Keynesian	________	________
Monetarist	________	________
Monetary	________	________
Keynesian	________	________
Monetarist	________	________
Supply Side	________	________

 Name: ______________________

LO3 5. The following table displays Congressional Budget Office forecasts of federal budget balances for the following year. Graph these forecasts on the graph below, along with *actual* surplus and deficits for those same years (see Table 12.3 for data).

Year:	2000	2001	2002	2003	2004	2005	2006	2007
Budget balance forecast (in billions of dollars)	+161	+268	+176	−315	−480	−348	−314	−285

(*a*) In how many years was CBO too optimistic (underestimating the deficit or overestimating the surplus)? ______________________

(*b*) In how many years was CBO too pessimistic? ______________________

(*c*) Why was the forecast so wrong in 2002?

____

____

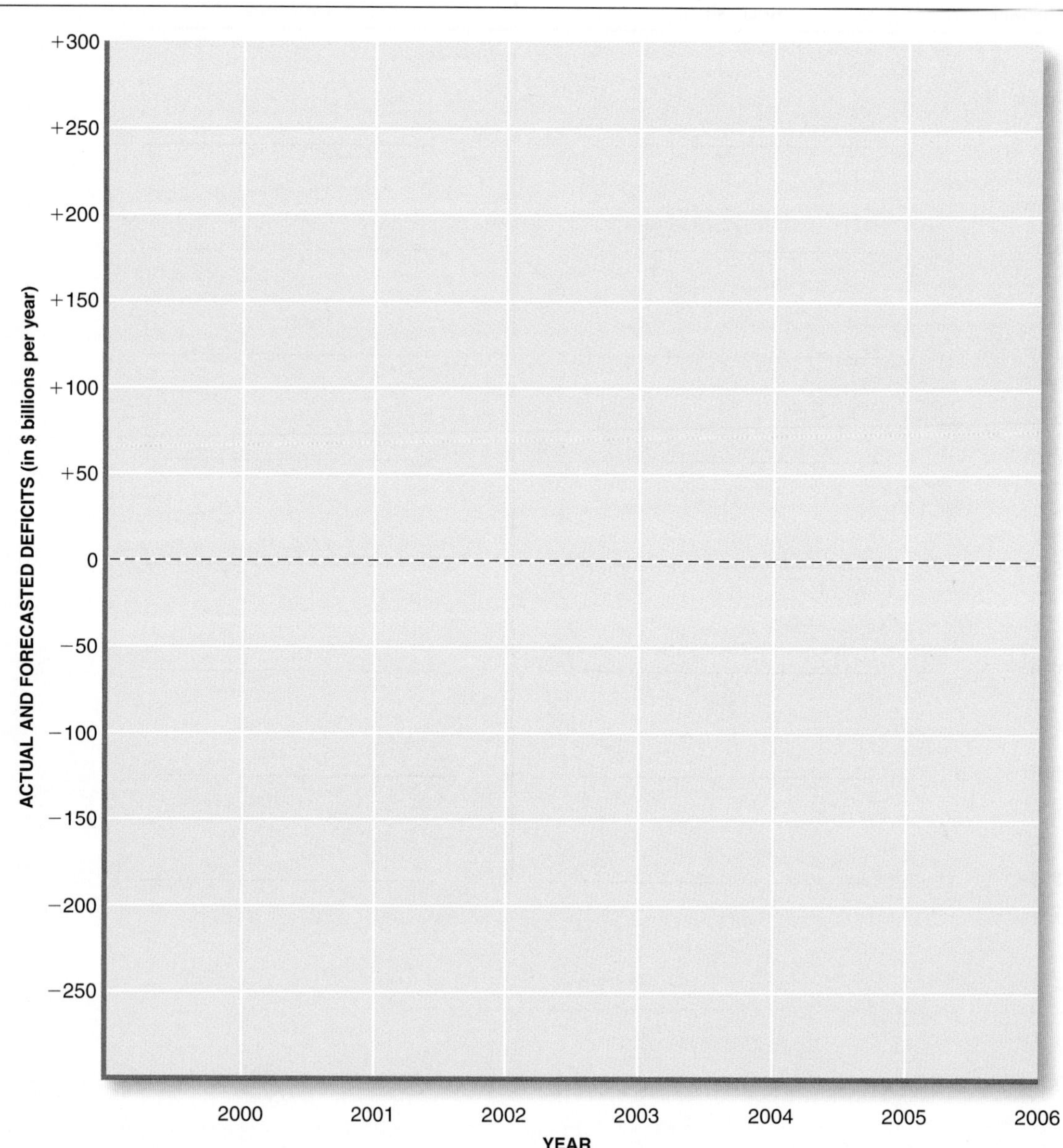

PROBLEMS FOR CHAPTER 20

Name: ______________________

LO1 1. Illustrate the following demand on the accompanying graph:

Price (per pair)	$100	$80	$60	$40	$20
Quantity demanded (pairs per day)	10	14	18	22	26

(*a*) How many pairs will be demanded when the price is $70? ________

(b) How much money will be spent on shoes at a price of

(*i*) $50 ________

(*ii*) $90 ________

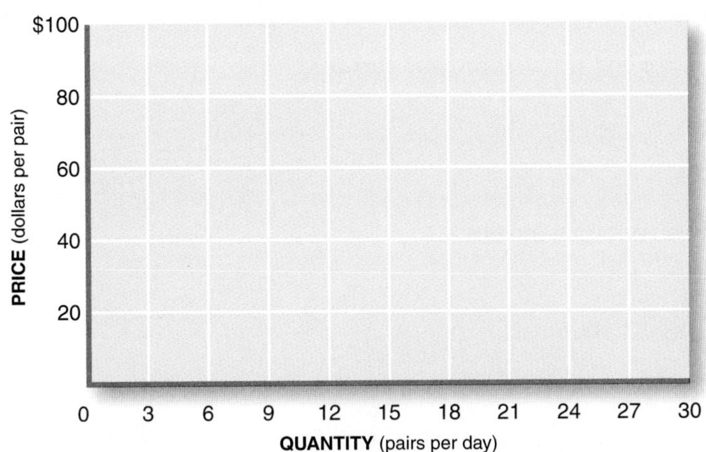

LO2 2. If the price elasticity of demand for iPhones were 1.6, by how much would iPhone unit sales have increased if the launch price had been $399 instead of $499? ________%

LO1 3. According to the News stories on pages 399 and 400, by how much would cigarette prices have to rise to get a 50 percent reduction in smoking by

(*a*) Teenagers? ________%

(*b*) Adults (short-run)? ________%

LO2 4. Suppose consumers buy 20 million packs of cigarettes per month at a price of $2 per pack. If a $1 tax is added to that price,

(*a*) By what percent does price change? (Use midpoint formula on p. 396.) ________%

(*b*) By what percent will cigarette sales decline in the short run? (See Table 20.1 for clue.) ________%

(c) According to Gary Becker, by how much will sales decline in the long run? (See News, page 400.) ________%

LO2 5. From Figure 20.3, compute (*a*) the price elasticity between each of the following points and (*b*) the total revenue at each point.

	Price Elasticity		Total Revenue
Point *D* to *E*	________	At point *D*	________
		E	________
G to *H*	________	*G*	________
		H	________

LO2 6. What is the price elasticity of demand for New York City cigarettes? (See News, page 400.) ________

LO2 7. According to the calculation on page 404, by how much will popcorn sales increase if average income goes up by 5 percent? ________%

LO2 8. Use the following table to compute the income elasticity of the demand for air travel:

Income (per year)	Vacations (per year)		Income Elasticity of Demand
a. $ 20,000	0		
b. 50,000	1	*b* to *c*	________
c. 100,000	3	*c* to *d*	________
d. 200,000	5		

 Name: ________________

LO3 9. Suppose the following table reflects the total satisfaction derived from consumption of pizza slices and Pepsis. Assume that pizza costs $1 per slice and a large Pepsi costs $2. With $20 to spend, what c onsumption mix will maximize satisfaction?

Quantity consumed	1	2	3	4	5	6	7	8	9	10	11	12	13	14
Total units of pleasure from pizza slices	47	92	132	166	196	224	251	271	288	303	313	315	312	300
Total units of pleasure from Pepsis	111	200	272	336	386	426	452	456	444	408	340	217	92	−17

LO1 LO2 10. Use the following data to illustrate the (*a*) demand curve and (*b*) total revenue curve:

Price	$ 1	2	3	4	5	6	7	8	9	10
Quantity	18	16	14	12	10	8	6	4	2	0

(*a*) At what price is total revenue maximized? $________

(*b*) At that price what is the elasticity of demand? E = ________

(c) Indicate the elastic and inelastic regions of each curve on the graphs.

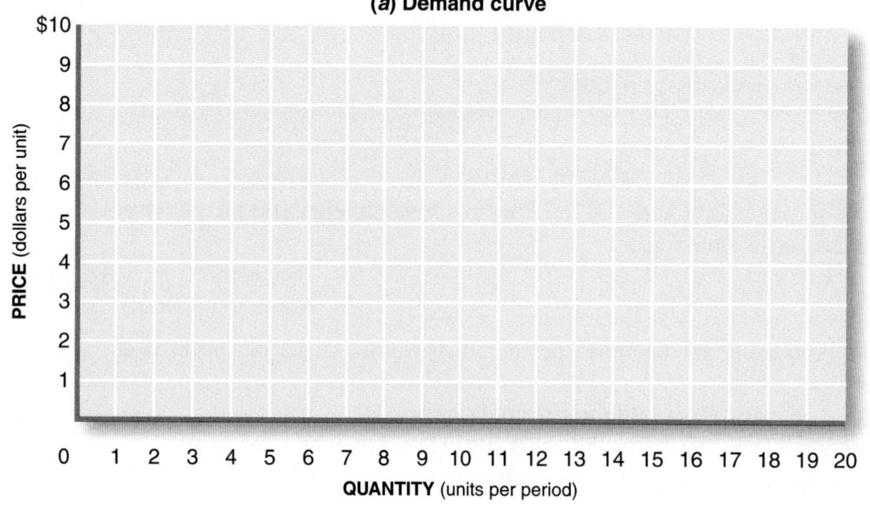

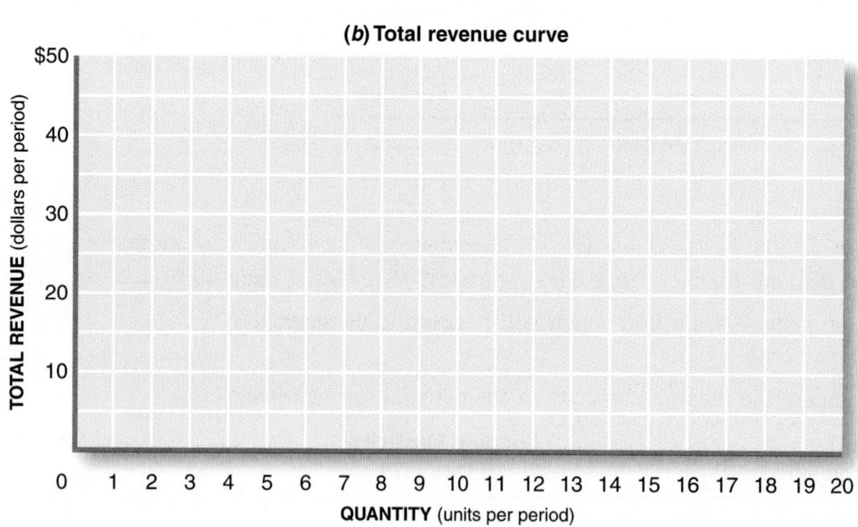

PROBLEMS FOR CHAPTER 21

Name: ______________________

LO3 1. (a) Complete the following cost schedule:

Rate of Output	Total Cost	Marginal Cost	Average Fixed Cost	Average Variable Cost	Average Total Cost
0	$1000	______	______	______	______
1	1100	______	______	______	______
2	1300	______	______	______	______
3	1650	______	______	______	______
4	2200	______	______	______	______
5	3000	______	______	______	______

(*b*) Use the cost data to plot the ATC and MC curves on the accompanying graph.

(*c*) At what output rate is ATC minimized? ______

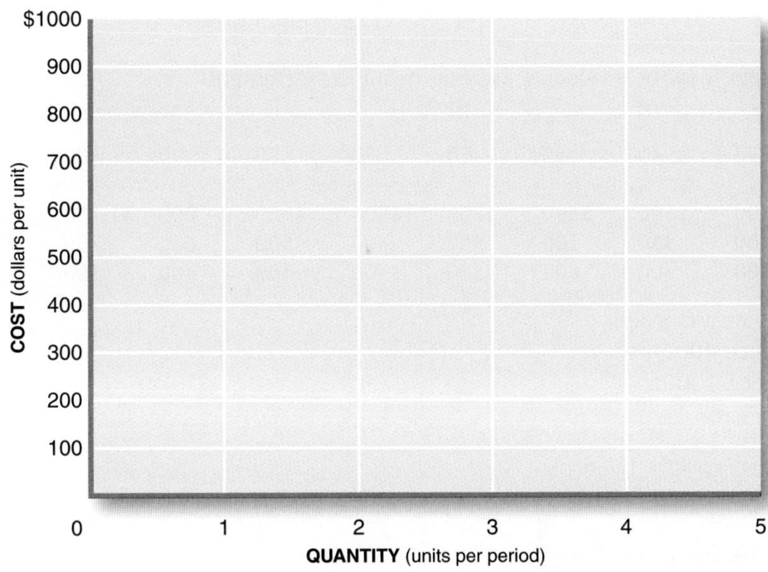

LO3 2. Based on the News on page 439, what is the ATC per dollar of sales at a

(*a*) Large funeral home? ______

(*b*) Small funeral home? ______

LO3 3. Suppose a company incurs the following costs: labor, $600; equipment, $200; and materials, $100. The company owns the building, so it doesn't have to pay the usual $800 in rent.

(*a*) What is the total accounting cost? ______

(*b*) What is the total economic cost? ______

(*c*) How would accounting and economic costs change if the company sold the building and then leased it back? ______

LO1 LO2 4. Refer to the production table for jeans (Table 21.1). Suppose a firm had three sewing machines and could vary only the amount of labor input.

(*a*) Graph the production function for jeans given the three sewing machines.

(*b*) Compute and graph the marginal physical product curve.

(*c*) At what amount of labor input does the law of diminishing returns first become apparent in your graph of marginal physical product? ______

(*d*) Is total output still increasing when MPP begins to diminish? ______

(*e*) When total output stops increasing, what is the value of MPP? ______

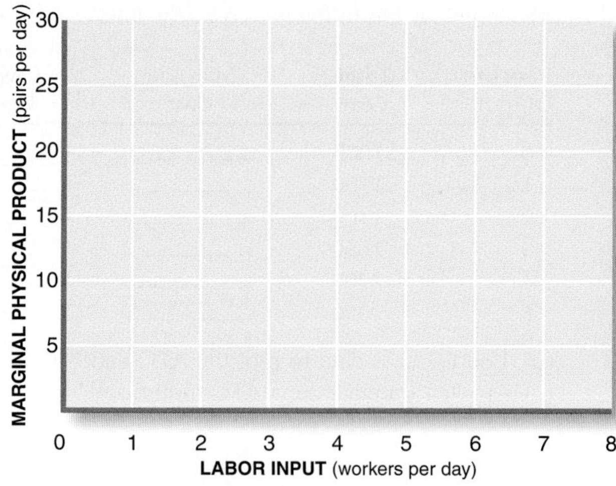

LO3 5. The following table indicates the average total cost of producing varying quantities of output from three different plants:

Rate of output	10	20	30	40	50	60	70	80	90	100
Average total cost										
Small firm	$ 600	$500	$400	$500	$600	$700	$800	$900	$1,000	$1,100
Medium firm	800	650	500	350	200	300	400	500	600	700
Large firm	1,000	900	800	700	600	500	400	300	400	500

(*a*) Plot the ATC curves for all three firms on the graph.

(*b*) Which plant(s) should be used to produce 40 units? ________

(*c*) Which plant(s) should be used to produce 100 units? ________

(*d*) Are there economies of scale in these plant-size choices? ________

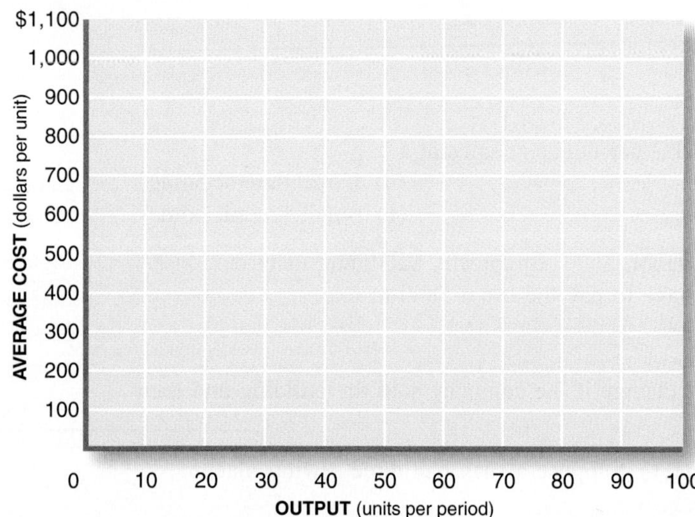

LO3 6. According to the World View on page 442, which nation had the biggest loss of competitive position in years 1995–2005? ________

LO3 7. Suppose (*A*) the hourly wage rate is $16 in the United States and $1 in China, and (*B*) productivity is 20 units per hour in the U.S. and 1 unit per hour in China. What are unit labor costs in

(*a*) The United States? ________

(*b*) China? ________

PROBLEMS FOR CHAPTER 22

Name: ____________________

LO2 1. If the owner of the Table 22.1 drugstore hired a manager for \$10 an hour to take his place, how much of a change would show up in

(*a*) Accounting profits? ________
(*b*) Economic profits? ________

LO2 2. If the price of catfish fell from \$13 to \$7 per bushel, use Figure 22.7 to determine the

(*a*) Profit-maximizing output. ________
(*b*) Profit or loss per bushel. ________
(*c*) Total profit or loss. ________

LO2 3. (*a*) Complete the following cost and revenue schedules:

Quantity	Price	Total Revenue	Total Cost	Marginal Cost
0	\$60	________	\$ 50	________
1	60	________	70	________
2	60	________	110	________
3	60	________	170	________
4	60	________	240	________
5	60	________	330	________

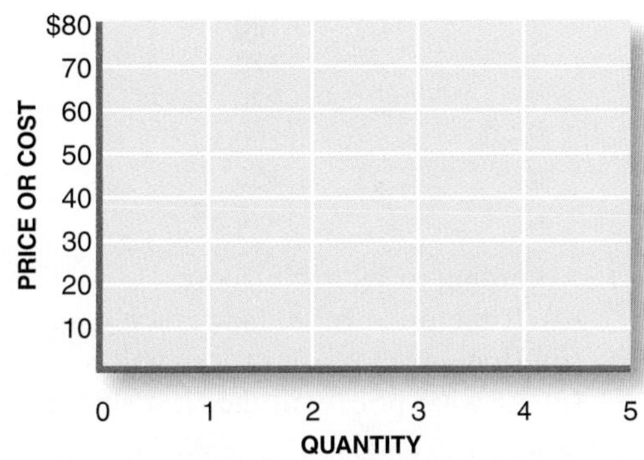

(*b*) Graph MC and P.
(*c*) What rate of output maximizes profit? ________
(*d*) What is MC at that rate of output? ________

LO2 4. Complete the following cost schedules:

Quantity	0	1	2	3	4	5	6	7
Total cost	\$9	\$12	\$16	\$21	\$30	\$40	\$52	\$66
ATC	____	____	____	____	____	____	____	____
MC	____	____	____	____	____	____	____	____

Assuming the price of this product is \$10, at what output rate is

(*a*) Total revenue maximized? ________
(*b*) ATC minimized? ________
(*c*) Profit per unit maximized? ________
(*d*) Total profit maximized? ________

LO2 5. Assume that the price of silk ties in a perfectly competitive market is \$15 and that the typical firm confronts the following costs:

Quantity (ties per day)	0	1	2	3	4	5	6	7	8	9	10
Total Cost	\$10	\$17	\$26	\$37	\$50	\$65	\$82	\$101	\$122	\$145	\$170

(*a*) What is the profit-maximizing rate of output for the firm? ________
(*b*) How much profit does the firm earn at that rate of output? ________
(*c*) If the price of ties fell to \$11, how many ties should the firm produce? ________
(*d*) At what price should the firm shut down? ________

LO3 6. Using the data from Problem 5 (at the original price of \$15), determine how many ties the producer would supply if

(*a*) A tax of \$2 per tie were collected from the producer. ________
(*b*) A property tax of \$2 was levied. ________
(*c*) Profits were taxed at 50 percent. ________

LO2 7. Suppose labor is the only variable cost in fish farming and that a new minimum-wage law increases wages by 40 percent.
(*a*) What will the new output rate be for the firm in Figure 22.7? ______
(*b*) How much profit will it make? ______

LO2 8. Complete the following table:

Output	Total Cost	Marginal Cost	Average Total Cost	Average Variable Cost
0	$100	______	______	______
5	110	______	______	______
10	130	______	______	______
15	170	______	______	______
20	220	______	______	______
25	290	______	______	______
30	380	______	______	______
35	490	______	______	______

According to the table above,
(*a*) If the price is $8, how much output will the firm supply? ______
(*b*) How much profit or loss will it make? ______
(*c*) At what price will the firm shut down? ______

LO2 9. A firm has leased plant and equipment to produce video game cartridges, which can be sold in unlimited quantities at $21 each. The following figures describe the associated costs of productions:

Rate of output (per day)	0	1	2	3	4	5	6	7	8
Total cost (per day)	$50	$55	$62	$75	$96	$125	$162	$203	$248

(*a*) How much are fixed costs? ______
(*b*) Draw total revenue and cost curves on the graphs below.
(*c*) Draw the average total cost (ATC), marginal cost (MC), and demand curves of the firm.
(*d*) What is the profit-maximizing rate of output? ______
(*e*) Should the producer stay in business? ______
(*f*) What is the size of the loss if production continues? ______
(*g*) How much is lost if the firm shuts down? ______

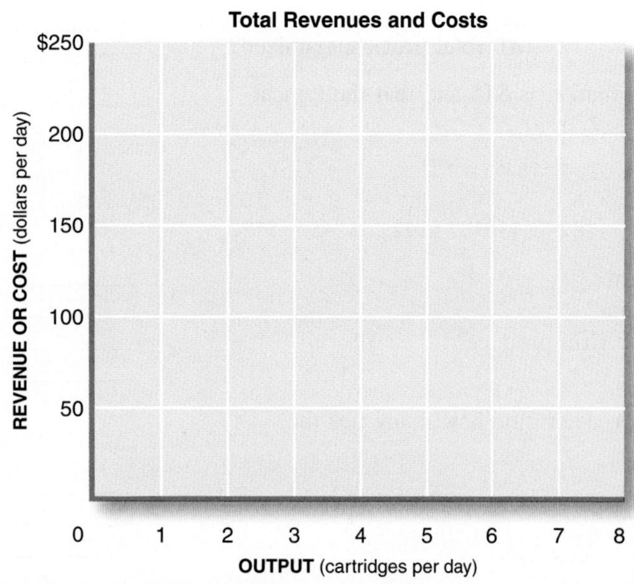

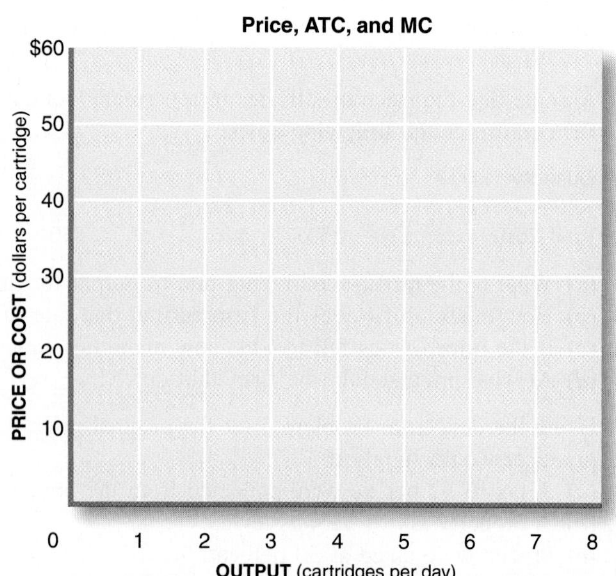

PROBLEMS FOR CHAPTER 23

Name: ______________________

LO1 1. According to Table 23.1,

(*a*) What were the fixed costs of production for the firm? ________

(*b*) At what rate of output was profit per computer maximized? ________

(*c*) At what output rate was total profit maximized? ________

LO1 2. Suppose the following data summarize the costs of a perfectly competitive firm:

Quantity	0	1	2	3	4	5	6	7	8
Total cost	$100	102	105	109	114	120	127	135	144

(*a*) Draw the firm's MC curve on the graph on the left below.

(*b*) Draw the market supply curve on the right graph, assuming 8 firms identical to the one above.

(*c*) What is the equilibrium price in this market? ________

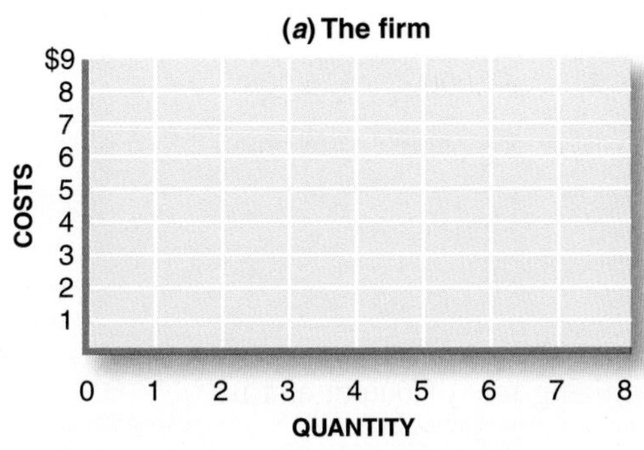

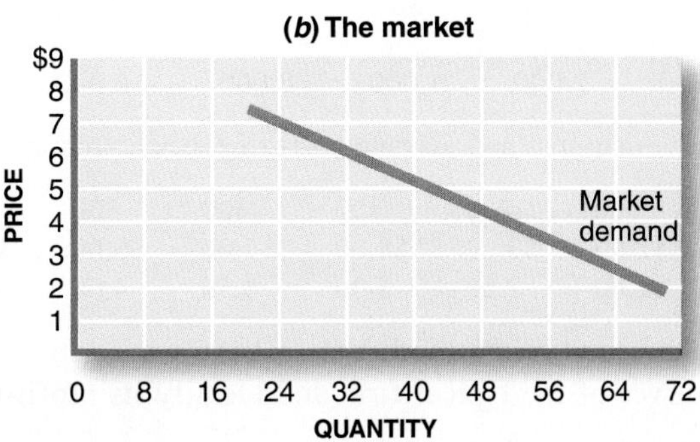

LO1 3. Suppose the following data describe the demand for liquid-diet beverages:

Price	$11	$10	$9	$8	$7	$6	$5	$4	$3	$2
Quantity demanded	9	12	15	18	21	24	27	30	33	36

Four identical, perfectly competitive firms are producing these beverages. The cost of producing these beverages at each firm are the following:

Quantity produced	0	1	2	3	4	5	6	7	8	9	10
Total cost	$5	$8	$10	$13	$17	$22	$28	$36	$45	$55	$67

(*a*) What price will prevail in this market? ________

(*b*) What quantity is produced? ________

(*c*) How much profit (loss) does each firm make? ________

(*d*) What happens to price if two more identical firms enter the market? ________

LO2 4. Suppose the typical catfish farmer was incurring an economic loss at the prevailing price p_1. (*a*) Illustrate these losses on the firm and market graphs. (*b*) What forces would raise the price? What price would prevail in long-term equilibrium? Illustrate your answers on the graphs.

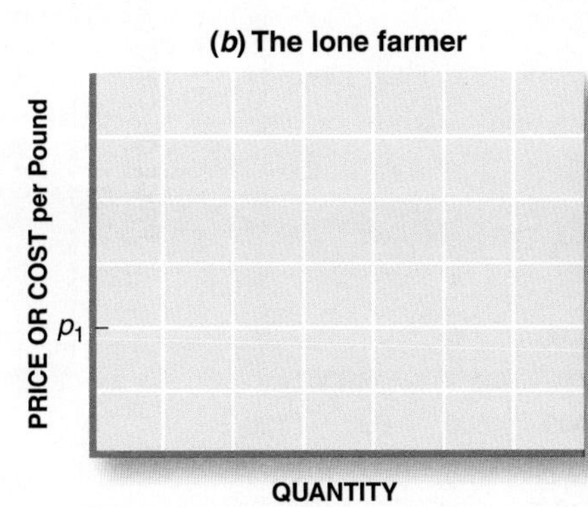

LO2 5. According to Table 23.1,
  (*a*) What was the prevailing computer price in 1978? ______
  (*b*) How much total profit did the typical firm earn? ______
  (*c*) At what price would profits have been zero? ______
  (*d*) At what price would the firm have shut down? ______

LO2 6. According to the World View on page 472,
  (*a*) How many brands entered the flat-panel TV market between 2002 and 2007? ______
  (*b*) Where will long-run economic profit end up? ______
  (*c*) Will more firms enter the market between now and then? ______

LO2 7. Suppose that the monthly market demand schedule for Frisbees is

Price	$8	$7	$6	$5	$4	$3	$2	$1
Quantity demanded	1,000	2,000	4,000	8,000	16,000	32,000	64,000	128,000

Suppose further that the marginal and average costs of Frisbee production for every competitive firm are

Rate of output	100	200	300	400	500	600
Marginal cost	$2.00	$3.00	$4.00	$5.00	$6.00	$7.00
Average total cost	2.00	2.50	3.00	3.50	4.00	4.50

Finally, assume that the equilibrium market price is $6 per Frisbee.
  (*a*) Draw the cost curves of the typical firm and identify its profit-maximizing rate of output and its total profits.
  (*b*) Draw the market demand curve and identify market equilibrium.
  (*c*) How many Frisbees are being sold? ______
  (*d*) How many (identical) firms are initially producing Frisbees? ______
  (*e*) How much profit is the typical firm making? ______
  (*f*) In view of the profits being made, more firms will want to get into Frisbee production. In the long run, these new firms will shift the market supply curve to the right and push price down to average total cost, thereby eliminating profits. At what equilibrium price are all profits eliminated? ______
  (*g*) How many firms will be producing Frisbees at this price? ______

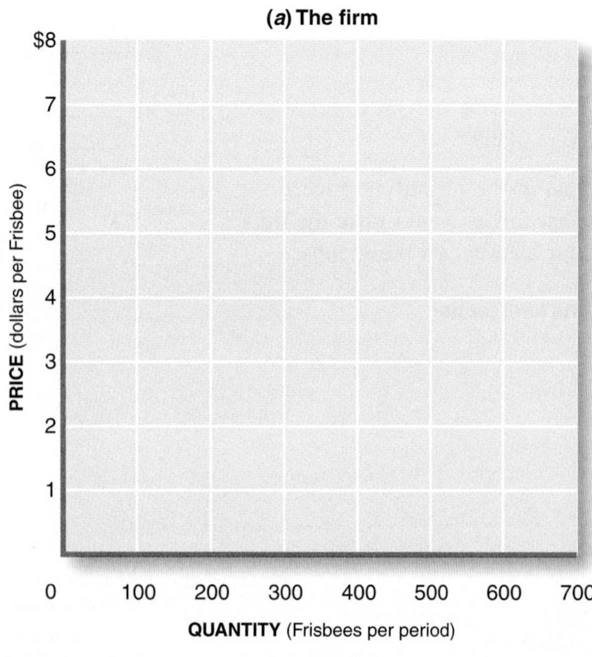

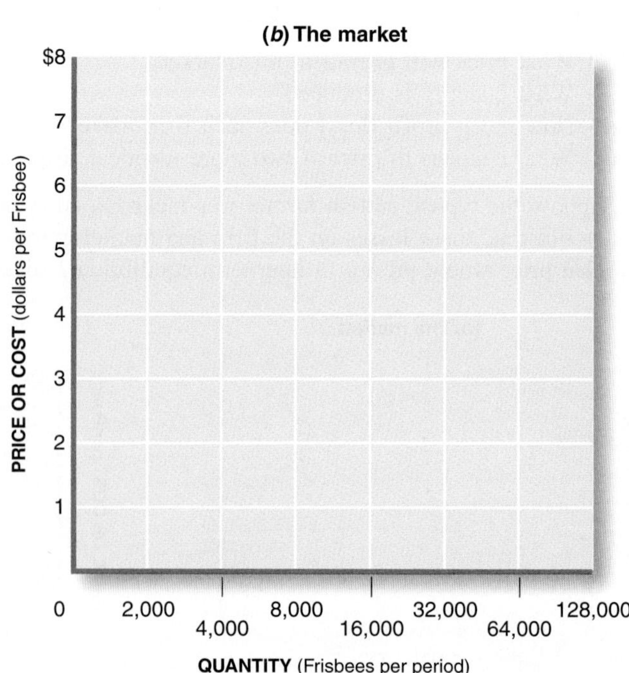

PROBLEMS FOR CHAPTER 24

Name: ____________________

LO1 1. Use Figures 24.2 and 24.3 to answer the following questions:
   (*a*) What is the highest price the monopolist could charge and still sell fish? ________
   (*b*) What is total revenue at that highest price? ________
   (*c*) What rate of output maximizes total revenue? ________
   (*d*) What is marginal revenue at that rate of output? ________
   (*e*) What is price at that rate of output? ________
   (*f*) What rate of output maximizes total profit? ________
   (*g*) What is MR at that rate of output? ________
   (*h*) What is price? ________

LO1 2. (*a*) Complete the following table:

Price	$15	$13	$11	$9	$7	$5	$3	$1
Quantity demanded	1	2	3	4	5	6	7	8
Marginal revenue	____	____	____	____	____	____	____	____

   (*b*) If marginal cost is constant at $3, what is the profit-maximizing rate of output? ________
   (*c*) What price should be charged at that rate of output? ________
   (*d*) Are profits higher or lower at the highest price possible? ________

LO1 3. The following table indicates the prices various buyers are willing to pay for a Miata sports car:

Buyer	Maximum Price	Buyer	Maximum Price
Buyer A	$50,000	Buyer D	$20,000
Buyer B	40,000	Buyer E	10,000
Buyer C	30,000		

The cost of producing the cars includes $50,000 of fixed costs and a constant marginal cost of $10,000.
   (*a*) Graph below the demand, marginal revenue, and marginal cost curves.
   (*b*) What is the profit-maximizing rate of output and price for a monopolist? How much profit does the monopolist make?
   Output ________
   Price ________
   Profit ________
   (*c*) If the monopolist can price-discriminate, how many cars will he sell? ________
   (*d*) How much profit will he make? ________

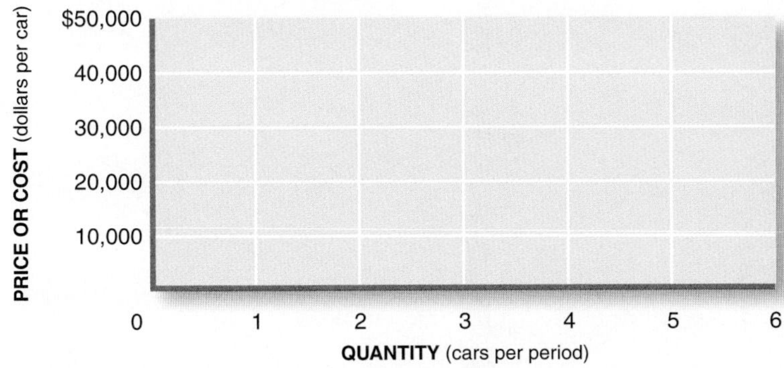

LO2 4. If the on-campus demand for soda is as follows:

Price (per can)	$0.25	0.50	0.75	1.00	1.25	1.50	1.75	2.00
Quantity demanded (per day)	100	90	80	70	60	50	40	30

and the marginal cost of supplying a soda is 50 cents, what price will students end up paying in
   (*a*) A perfectly competitive market? ________
   (*b*) A monopolized market? ________

 Name: ______________________

LO2 5. The following table summarizes the weekly sales and cost situation confronting a monopolist:

Price	Quantity Demanded	Total Revenue	Marginal Revenue	Total Cost	Marginal Cost	Average Total Cost
$20	0			$ 6		
18	1			12		
16	2			20		
14	3			30		
12	4			42		
10	5			56		
8	6			72		
6	7			90		
4	8			110		
2	9			145		

(*a*) Complete the table.
(*b*) Graph the demand, MR, and MC curves on the graph below.
(*c*) At what rate of output is total revenue maximized within this range? ________
(*d*) What are the values of MR and MC at the revenue-maximizing rate of output? MR ________ MC ________
(*e*) At what rate of output are profits maximized within this range? ________
(*f*) What are the values of MR and MC at the profit-maximizing rate of output? MR ________ MC ________
(*g*) What are total profits at that output rate? ________
(*h*) If a competitive industry confronted the same demand and costs, how much output would it produce in the short run? ________
(*i*) What would happen to long-run price if the market became perfectly competitive?

____

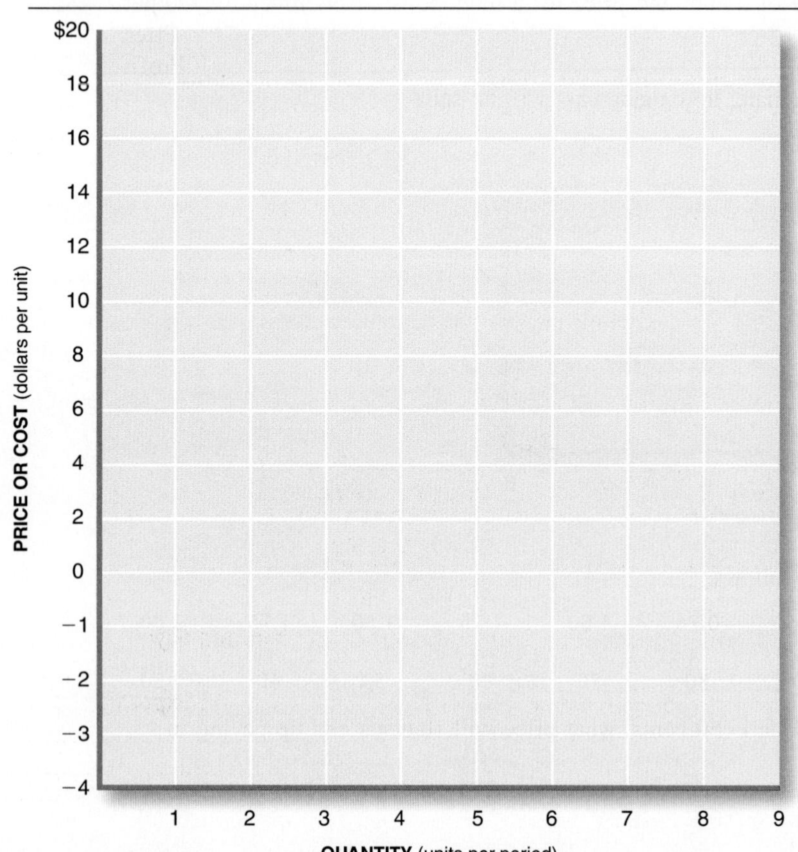

PROBLEMS FOR CHAPTER 25

Name: ______________________

LO1 1. According to Table 25.2, in which markets do fewer than four firms produce at least 90 percent of total output?

______________ ______________ ______________

______________ ______________ ______________

______________ ______________ ______________

LO1 2. According to the News on page 516,
(*a*) What is the concentration ratio in the U.S. soda market? ________
(*b*) What is the *maximum* value of the Herfindahl-Hirshman Index? ________

LO2 LO3 3. Assume an oligopolist confronts *two* possible demand curves for its own output, as illustrated below. The first (*A*) prevails if other oligopolists don't match price changes. The second (*B*) prevails if rivals *do* match price changes.

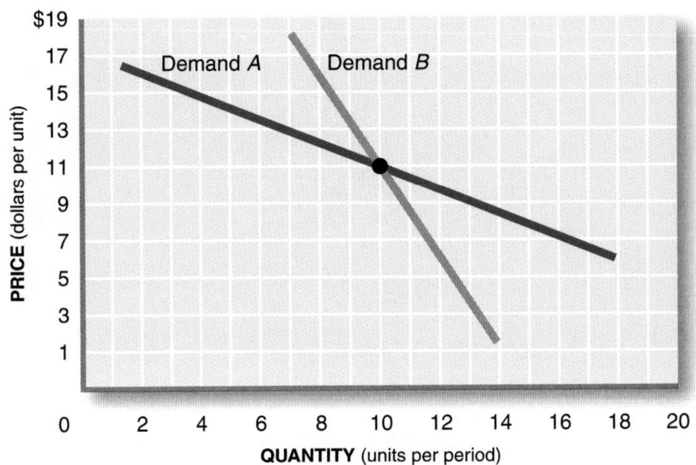

(*a*) By how much does quantity demanded change if price is reduced from $11 to $7 and
(*i*) Rivals match price cut? ________
(*ii*) Rivals don't match price cut? ________
(*b*) By how much does quantity demanded change when price is raised from $11 to $15 and
(*i*) Rivals match price hike? ________
(*ii*) Rivals don't match price hike? ________

LO3 4. How large would the probability of a "don't match" outcome have to be to make a Universal price cut statistically worthwhile? (See expected payoff, page 520.) ________

LO3 5. Suppose the payoff to each of four strategic interactions is as follows:

	Rival Response	
Action	**Reduce Price**	**Don't Reduce Price**
Reduce price	Loss = $300	Gain = $30,000
Don't reduce price	Loss = $5,000	No loss or gain

(*a*) If the probability of rivals matching a price reduction is 99 percent, what is the expected payoff to a price cut? ________
(*b*) If the probability of rivals reducing price even though you don't is 5 percent, what is the expected payoff to *not* reducing price? ________
(*c*) What should you do? ______________

 Name: ______________________

LO2 6. Suppose that the following schedule summarizes the sales (demand) situation confronting an oligopolist:

Price (per unit)	$8	$10	$12	$14	$16	$17	$18	$19	$20
Quantity demanded (units per period)	10	9	8	7	6	5	4	3	2

Using the graph below,

(*a*) Draw the demand and marginal revenue curves facing the firm.

(*b*) Identify the profit-maximizing rate of output in a situation where marginal cost is constant at $10 per unit. ________

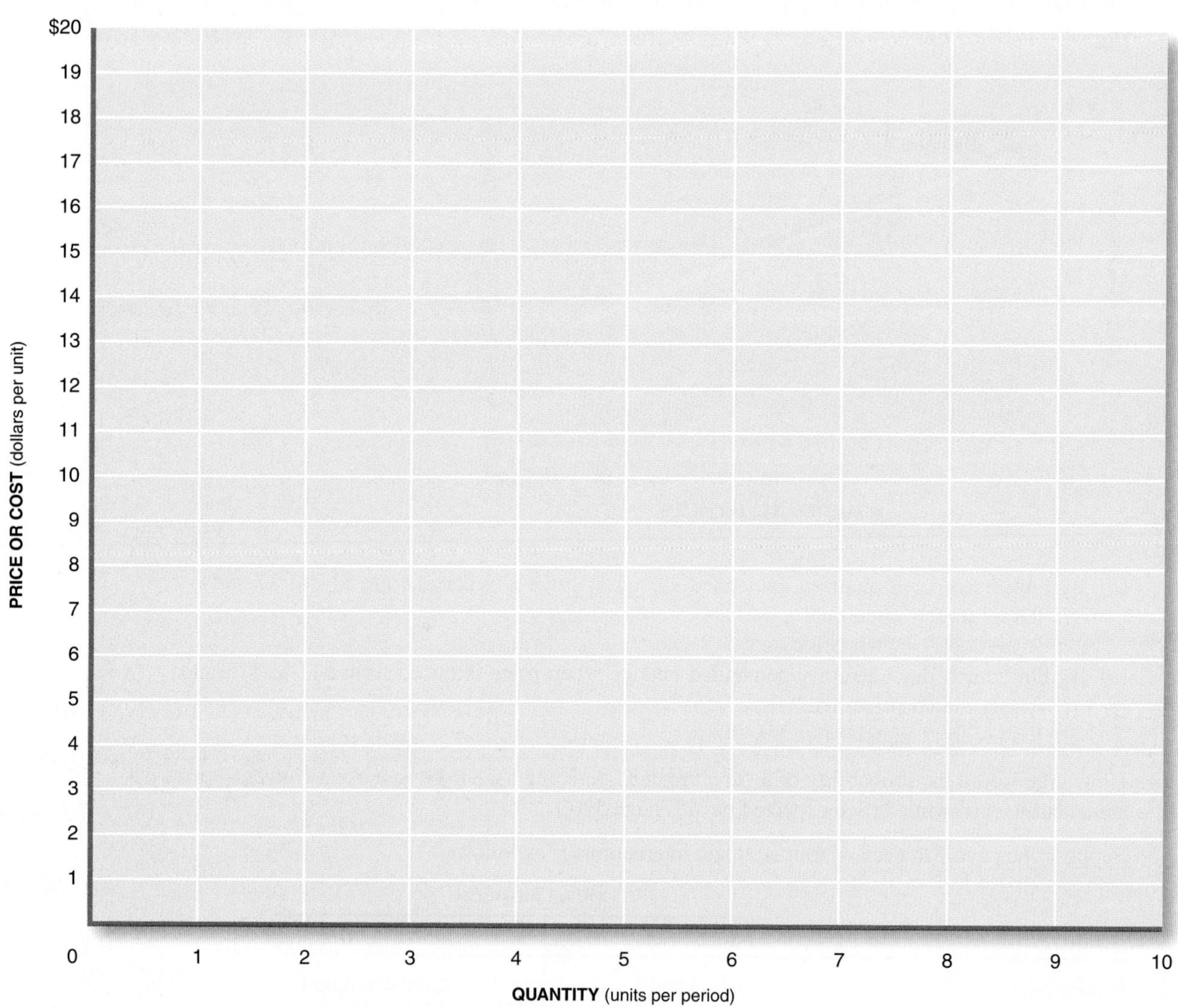

LO2 7. What is the price elasticity of demand in Figure 25.2? ________

PROBLEMS FOR CHAPTER 26

Name: ____________________

LO3 1. In Figure 26.1(b),

(*a*) At what output rate is economic profit equal to zero? ________

(*b*) At what output rate(s) are positive economic profits available? ________

(*c*) At what output rate(s) do economic losses occur? ________

LO2 LO3 2. (*a*) Use the accompanying graph to illustrate the short-run equilibrium of a monopolistically competitive firm.

(*b*) At that equilibrium, what is

(*i*) Price? ________

(*ii*) Output? ________

(*iii*) Total profit? ________

(*c*) Identify the long-run equilibrium of the same firm.

(*d*) In long-run equilibrium, what is (approximately)

(*i*) Price? ________

(*ii*) Output? ________

(*iii*) Total profit? ________

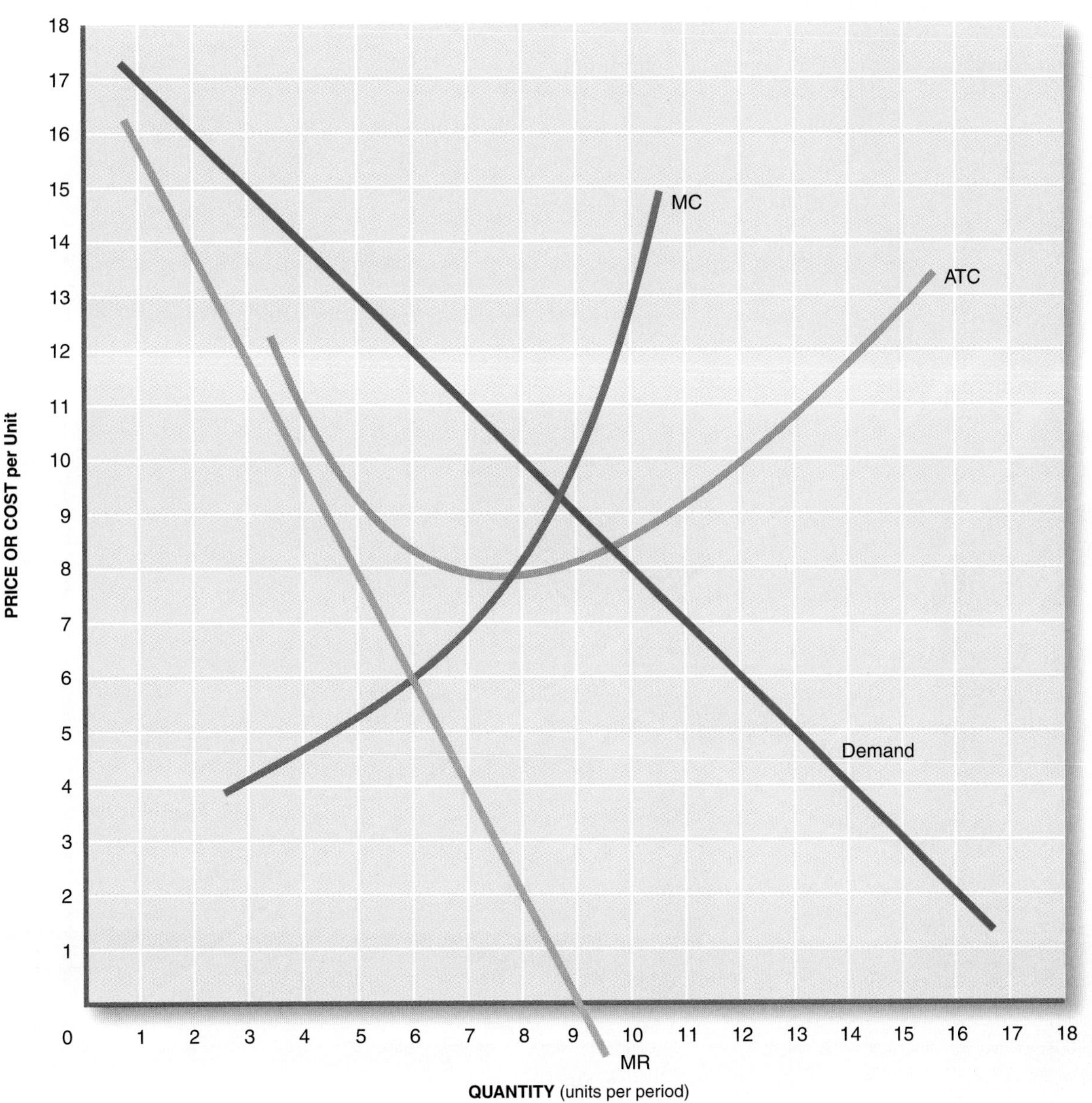

 Name: ____________________

LO2 LO3 3. (*a*) In the *short*-run equilibrium of the previous problem, what is
(*i*) The price of the product? ________
(*ii*) The opportunity cost of producing the last unit? ________
(*b*) In *long*-run equilibrium what is
(*i*) The price of the product? ________
(*ii*) The opportunity cost of producing the last unit? ________

LO2 4. According to the News on page 535,
(*a*) By how much could unit sales at Starbucks decline after the 2006 price increase without reducing total revenue? ________%
(*b*) If the price elasticity of demand for Starbucks is 0.10, by how much would unit sales have fallen? ________%

LO3 5. On the accompanying graph, identify each of the following *market* outcomes:
(*a*) Short-run equilibrium output in competition.
(*b*) Long-run equilibrium output in competition.
(*c*) Long-run equilibrium output in monopoly.
(*d*) Long-run equilibrium output in monopolistic competition.

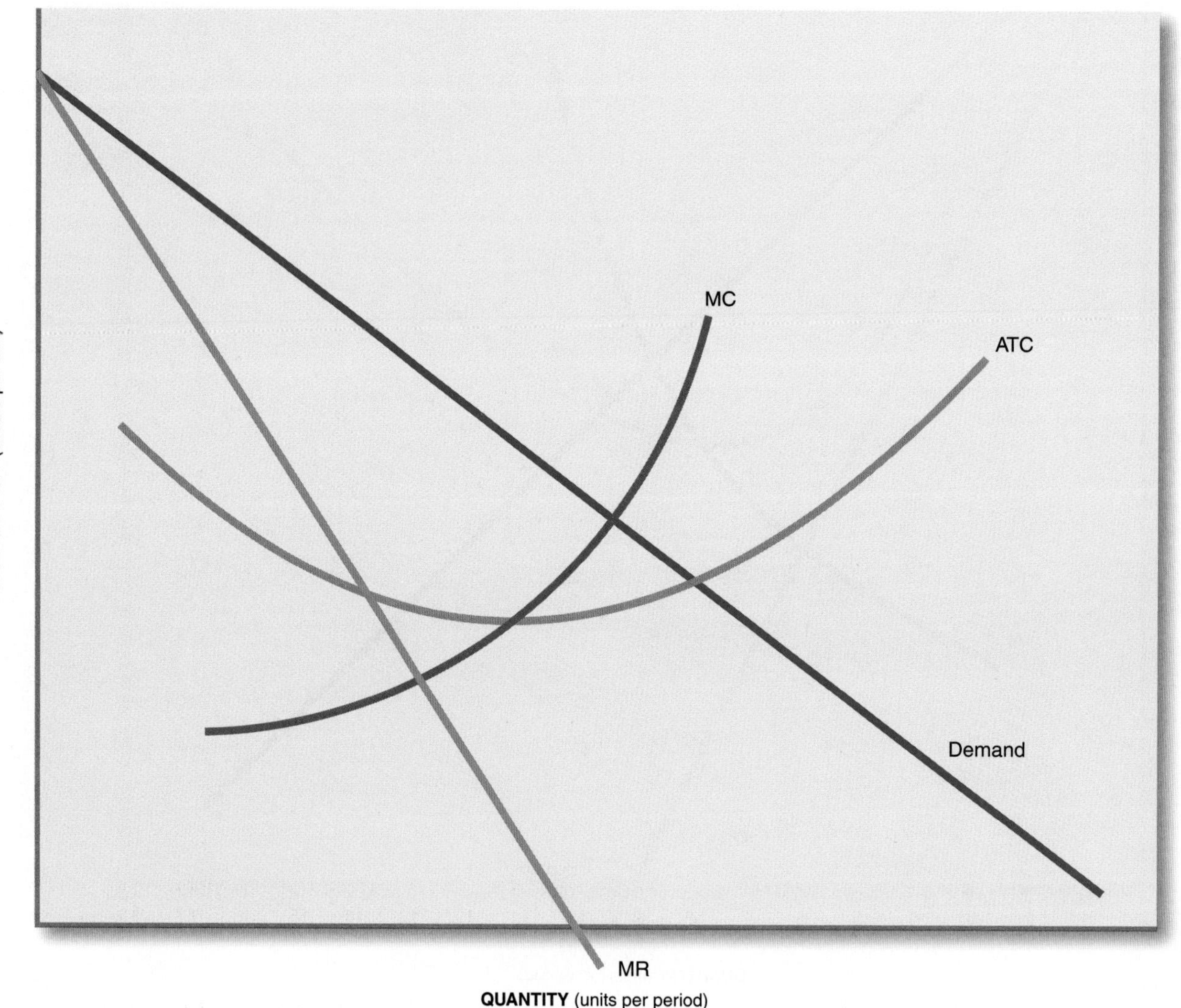

PROBLEMS FOR CHAPTER 27

Name: ____________

LO2 1. In Figure 27.2,

(*a*) How much profit does an unregulated monopolist earn? ______

(*b*) How much profit would be earned if MC pricing was imposed? ______

LO1 LO2 2. What happens to total profits when new technology reduces average total costs (shifts ATC downward in Figure 27.2) in

(*a*) An unregulated natural monopoly? ______

(*b*) A price-regulated natural monopoly? ______

(*c*) A profit-regulated natural monopoly? ______

LO1 LO2 3. Suppose a natural monopolist has fixed costs of \$20 and a constant marginal cost of \$2. The demand for the product is as follows:

Price (per unit)	\$10	\$9	\$8	\$7	\$6	\$5	\$4	\$3	\$2	\$1
Quantity demanded (units per day)	0	2	4	6	8	10	12	14	16	18

Under these conditions,

(*a*) What price and quantity will prevail if the monopolist isn't regulated? ______

(*b*) What price-output combination would exist with efficient pricing (MC = *p*)? ______

(*c*) What price-output combination would exist with profit regulation (zero economic profits)? ______

Illustrate your answers on the graph below.

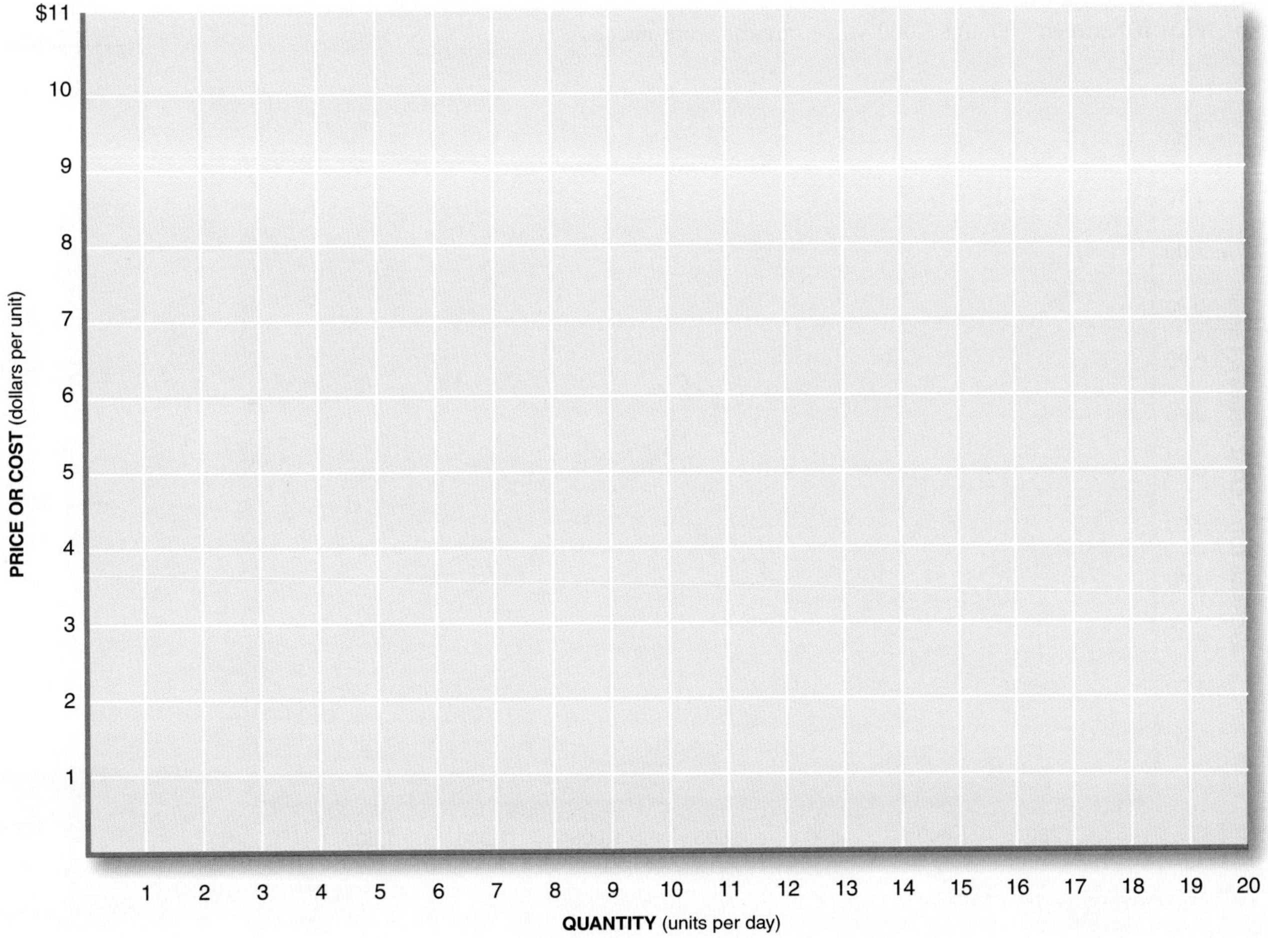

LO3 4. According to the News on page 555, how much will annual shipping costs increase for each saved life? ______

LO1 5. In the long-distance telephone industry, three new transmission technologies—microwaves, satellites, and fiber-optic cable—have replaced the traditional coaxial cable made of copper. The following schedule indicates the costs of the different technologies. (Although similar to the actual figures, the data have been altered to ease calculation and graphing.) Voice circuits indicate the number of phone conversations that can be carried simultaneously. Costs are given in thousands of dollars per month.

Number of voice circuits	50	100	500	1,000	1,500
Total cost of					
Fiber-optic cable	$60	$100	$250	$300	$337
Microwave	40	45	150	250	375
Satellite	35	50	200	350	525

(*a*) Compute and graph (in a single diagram) the average costs of each technology.

(*b*) Draw the long-run average cost curve facing a long-distance telecommunication company that's deciding what transmission technology to use.

(*c*) Are there economies, diseconomies, or constant returns to scale? ______

(*d*) In the long run, how many firms would you expect to provide long-distance service over any given route between two cities? (Base your answer on the long-run average cost curve you drew.) ______

(*e*) With microwave technology, what would be the smallest number of voice circuits that a company could provide and still achieve minimum average cost? ______

(*f*) What kind of technology would be most appropriate if only 50 voice circuits were needed between two towns? ______

(*g*) What if between 100 and 1,000 voice circuits were needed? ______

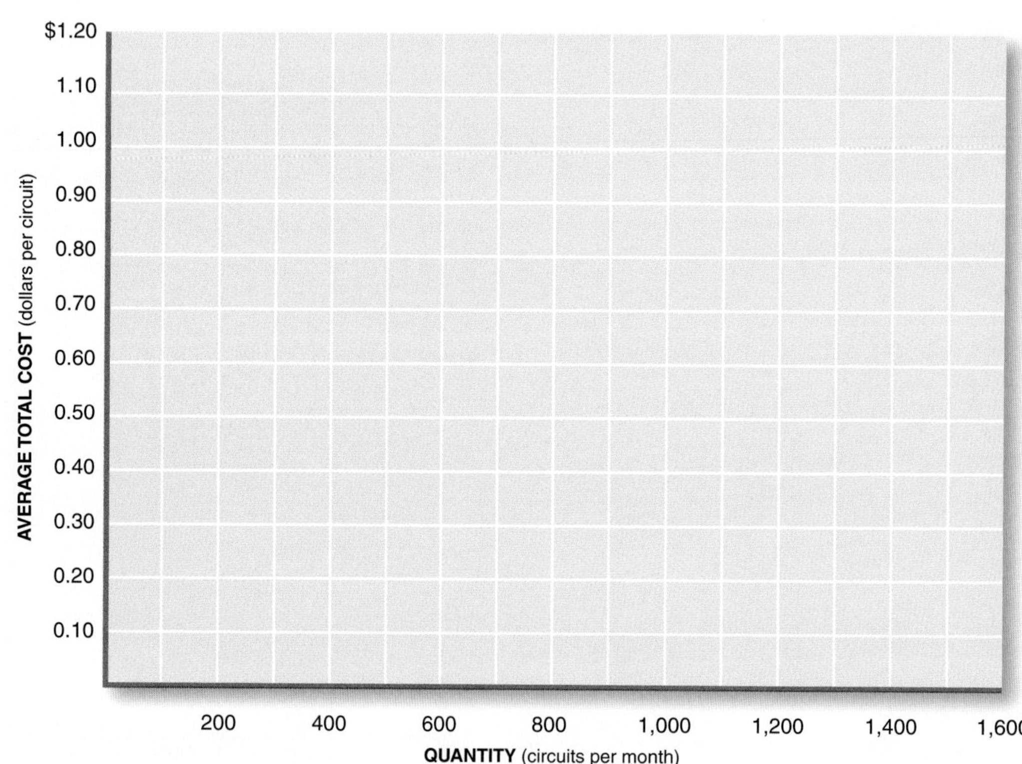

PROBLEMS FOR CHAPTER 28

Name: ______________________

LO1 1. How high would its pollution-control costs have to be before a firm would "pay to pollute" carbon dioxide? (see World View, page 578) $ ________

LO2 2. In some states, mining for coal leaves large mounds of rubble, which poses flooding problems, causes land damage, and is unsightly. The following table shows the estimated annual social benefits and costs of restoring various amounts of such land:

Land restored (in acres)	0	100	200	300	400	500
Social benefits of restoring land	0	$70	$120	$160	$190	$220
Social costs of restoring land	0	$10	$40	$80	$140	$230

(*a*) Compute the marginal social benefits and the marginal social costs for each restoration level.

Land restored (in acres)	0	100	200	300	400500	
Marginal benefit	____	____	____	____	____	____
Marginal cost	____	____	____	____	____	____

(*b*) What is the optimal rate of restoration? ________

LO1 LO3 3. Most people pay nothing for each extra pound of garbage they create. Yet the garbage imposes external costs on a community. In view of this factor, what's an appropriate price for garbage collection? Answer the questions based on the following graph.

(*a*) What is the quantity of garbage collection now demanded? ________

(*b*) How much would be demanded if a fee of $3 per pound were charged? ________

(*c*) Draw the social demand curve when an external benefit of $2 per pound exists.

(*d*) If the marginal cost of collecting garbage were constant at $5 per pound, what would be the optimal level of garbage collection? ________

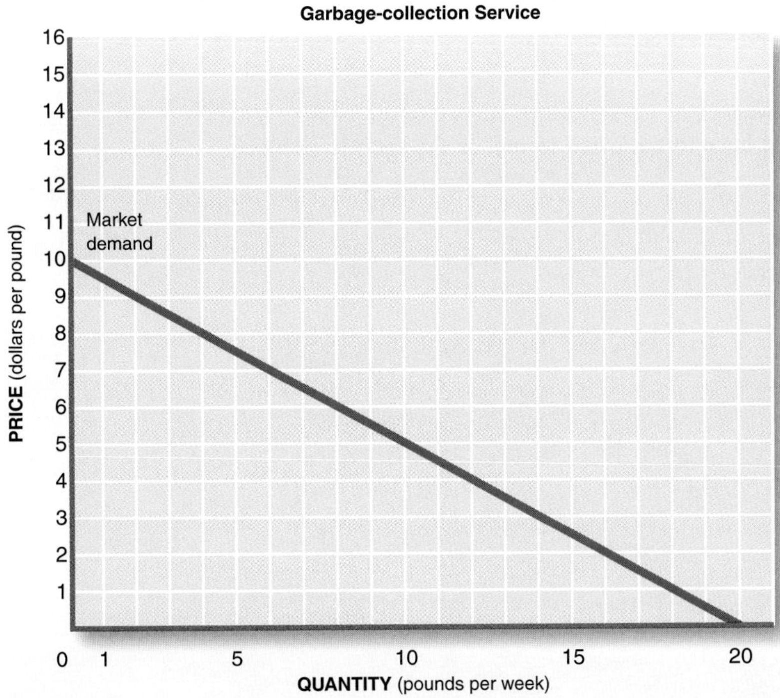

LO3 4. Using the *high* estimate of costs and *low* estimate of benefits for pollution controls (News, page 580), what is the average benefit per dollar spent? ________

LO2 LO3 5. How much more per ton is New York City paying to recycle rather than just dump its garbage (News, page 581)? ________

LO3 6. Suppose three firms confront the following costs for pollution control:

Emissions Reduction (tons per year)	Total Costs of Control		
	Firm A	Firm B	Firm C
1	$ 50	$ 60	$ 40
2	105	140	150
3	175	230	300
4	300	350	600

(*a*) If each firm must reduce emissions by 1 ton, how much will be spent? ________

(*b*) If the firms can trade pollution rights, what would be the cheapest way of attaining a net 3-ton reduction? ________

(*c*) How much would a pollution permit trade for? ________

Now suppose the goal is to reduce pollution by 6 tons.

(*d*) If each firm must reduce emissions by 2 tons, how much will be spent? ________

(*e*) If the firms can trade permits, what is the cheapest way of attaining a 6-ton reduction? ________

(*f*) How much will a permit cost? ________

LO1 LO3 7. The following cost schedule depicts the private and social costs associated with the daily production of apacum, a highly toxic fertilizer. The sales price of apacum is $18 per ton.

Output (in tons)	0	1	2	3	4	5	6	7	8
Total private cost	$5	7	13	23	37	55	77	103	133
Total social cost	$7	13	31	61	103	157	223	301	391

Answer the questions using this schedule, and graph on the figure below.

(*a*) Graph the private and social marginal costs associated with apacum production.

(*b*) What is the profit-maximizing rate of output for this competitive firm? ________

(*c*) How much profit is earned at that output level? ________

(*d*) What is the socially optimal rate of output? ________

(*e*) How much profit is there at that output level? ________

(*f*) How much of a "green tax" per ton would have to be levied to induce the firm to produce the socially optimal rate of output? ________

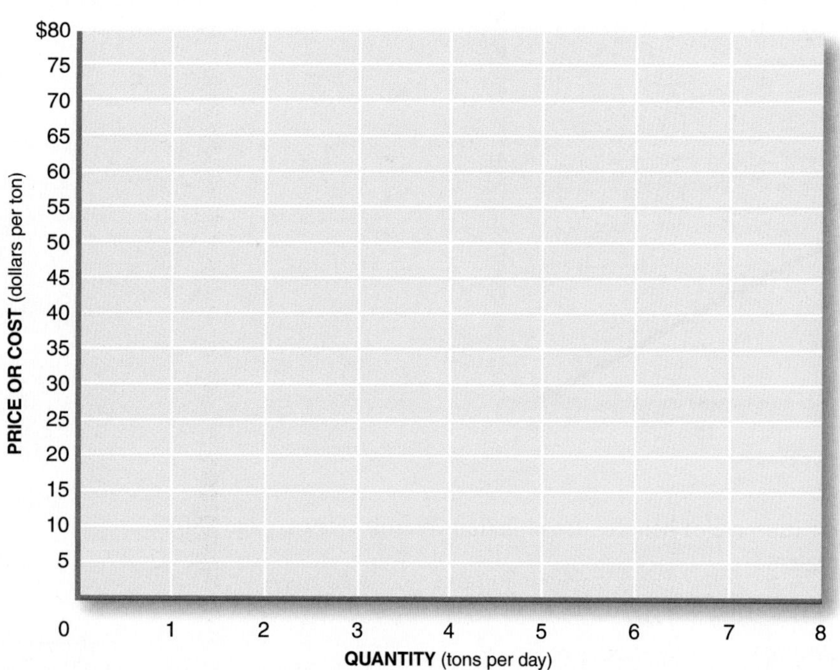

PROBLEMS FOR CHAPTER 29

Name: ____________________

LO2 LO3 1. Suppose the market price of wheat was $3 per bushel.

(*a*) Would a farmer have sold wheat to the market or to the government (CCC)? (See Table 29.2.) ________

(*b*) How much of a counter-cyclical payment would the farmer have received? (See Table 29.3.) ________

(*c*) If the market price fell to $2.50, what would the farmer do with his wheat? ________

LO1 2. Suppose that consumers' incomes fall 20 percent, which results in a 2 percent drop in consumption of farm goods without change in prices. What is the income elasticity of demand for farm goods? ________

LO1 LO3 3. Assume that the unregulated supply schedule for milk is the following:

Price (per pound)	5¢	7¢	8¢	10¢	14¢
Quantity supplied (billions of pounds per year)	42	53	63	76	103

(*a*) Draw the supply and demand curves for milk, assuming that the demand for milk is perfectly inelastic and consumers will buy 53 billion pounds of it. What is the equilibrium price? ________

(*b*) Suppose that the farmers' response to the government's offer to pay them for not producing milk results in the following supply schedule:

Price (per pound)	5¢	7¢	8¢	10¢	14¢
Quantity supplied (billions of pounds per year)	19	30	40	53	80

(*c*) Draw this new supply curve on the same set of axes as the supply curve prior to the government's action. What is the equilibrium price following the government's action? ________

(*d*) How much more money would consumers pay for the 53 billion pounds of milk because of the higher equilibrium price? ________

(*e*) Shade in the area in your diagram that represents how much more consumers will pay because of the government-sponsored cutbacks.

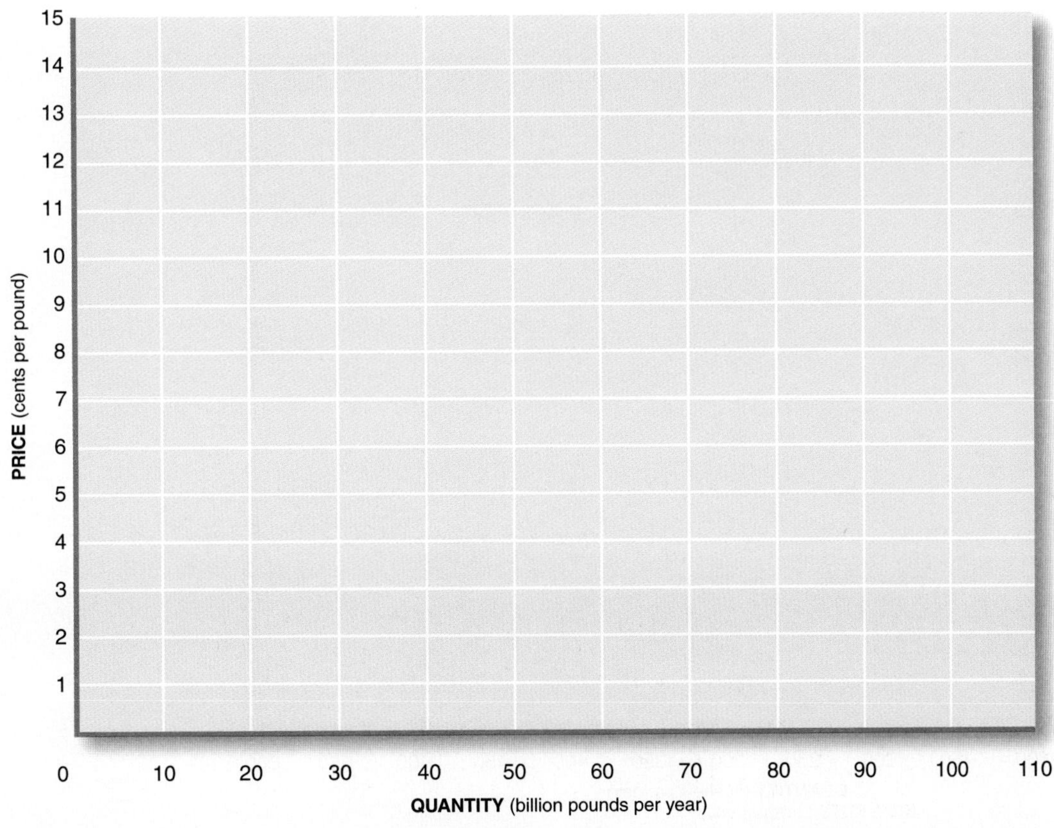

LO1 LO2 LO3 4. Suppose there are 100 grain farmers, each with identical cost structures as shown in the following table:

Production Costs (per farm)		Demand	
Output (bushels per day)	**Total Cost (per day)**	**Price (per bushel)**	**Quantity Demanded (bushels per day)**
0	$ 5	$1	600
1	7	2	500
2	10	3	400
3	14	4	300
4	19	5	200
5	25	6	100
6	33	7	50

Under these circumstances, graph the market supply and demand.

(*a*) What is the equilibrium price for grain? ____________

(*b*) How much grain will be produced at the equilibrium price? ____________

(*c*) How much profit will each farmer earn at that price? ____________

(*d*) If the government gives farmers a cost subsidy equal to $1 a bushel, what will happen to

(*i*) Output? ____________

(*ii*) Price? ____________

(*iii*) Profit? ____________

(*e*) What will happen to total output if the government additionally guarantees a price of $5 per bushel? ____________

(*f*) What price is required to sell this output? ____________

(*g*) What is the cost to the government in *d*? ____________

(*h*) Show your answers on the graph below.

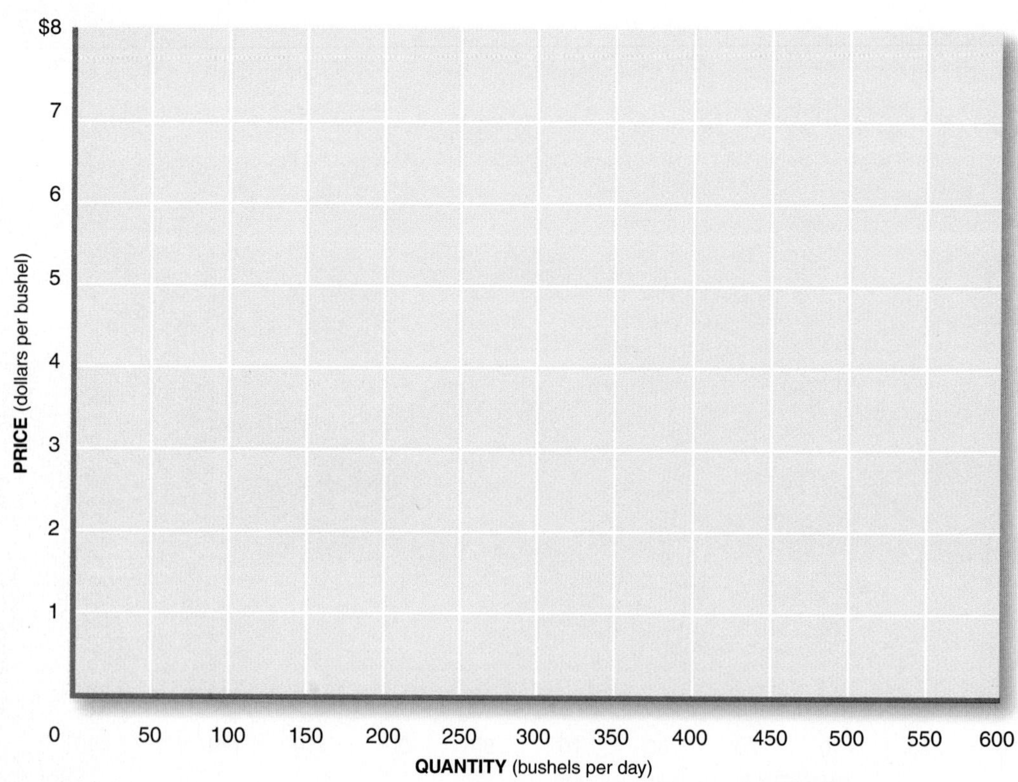

PROBLEMS FOR CHAPTER 30

Name: ______________________

LO3 1. (*a*) What was the federal minimum wage the year you were born? ______
(*b*) What is it now? ______

LO3 2. (*a*) In Figure 30.8, how many workers are unemployed at the equilibrium wage? ______
(*b*) How many workers are unemployed at the minimum wage? ______

LO1 3. Suppose a wage increase from $11 to $13 an hour increases the number of job applicants from 42 to 56. What is the price elasticity of labor supply? ______

LO2 4. According to the News on p. 601, what is the *equilibrium* wage at Wal-Mart? ______

LO2 5. According to the News on page 611, how much more ticket revenue are the Yankees bringing in since signing A-Rod? ______

LO2 6. If the price of strawberries doubled, how many pickers would be hired at $4 an hour, according to Table 30.1? ______

LO1 7. Apples can be harvested by hand or machine. Handpicking yields 40 pounds per hour, mechanical pickers yield 70 pounds per hour. If the wage rate of human pickers is $8 an hour and the rental on a mechanical picker is $16 an hour,
(*a*) Which is more cost-effective? ______
(*b*) If the wage rate increased to $10 an hour, which would be more cost-effective? ______

LO1 LO2 LO3 8. Assume that the following data describe labor-market conditions:

Wage rate (per hour)	$3	$4	$5	$6	$7	$8	$9	$10
Labor demanded	50	45	40	35	30	25	20	15
Labor supplied	20	30	40	50	60	70	80	90

On the graph below, illustrate
(*a*) The equilibrium wage.
(*b*) A government-set minimum wage of $6 per hour when the minimum wage is implemented.
(*c*) How many workers lose jobs? ______
(*d*) How many additional workers seek jobs? ______
(*e*) How many workers end up unemployed? ______

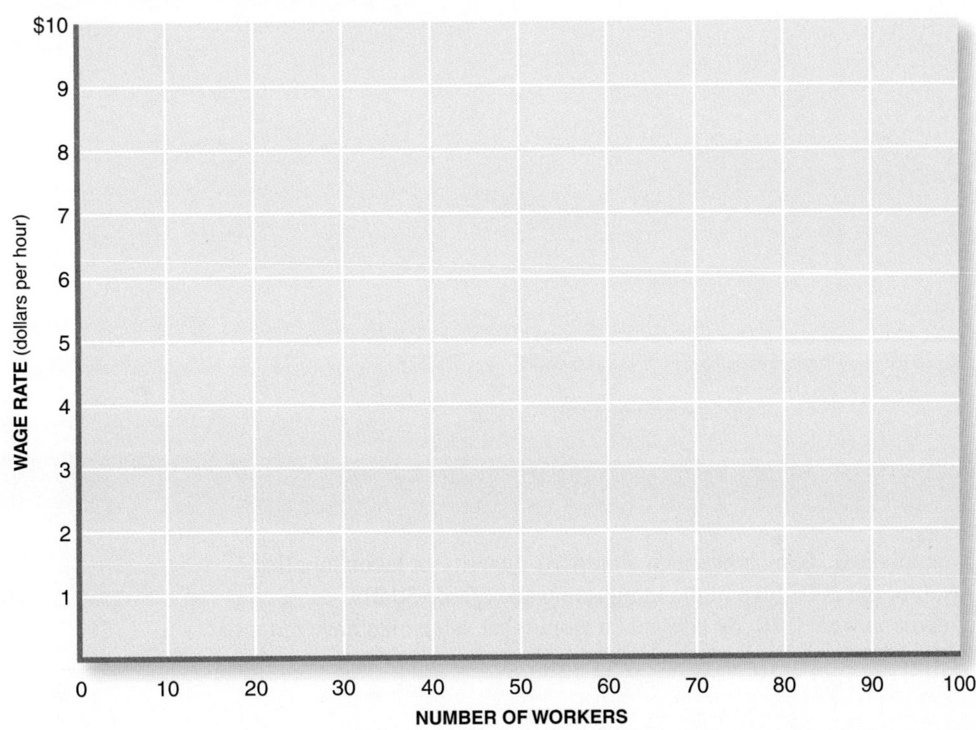

LO1 LO2 9. The following table depicts the number of grapes that can be picked in an hour with varying amounts of labor:

Number of pickers (per hour)	1	2	3	4	5	6	7	8
Output of grapes (in flats)	20	38	53	64	71	74	74	70

(*a*) Illustrate the supply and demand of labor for a single farmer, assuming that the local wage rate is $6 an hour and a flat of grapes sells for $2.

(*b*) How many pickers will be hired? __________

(*c*) If the wage rate doubles, how many pickers will be hired? __________

(*d*) If the productivity of all workers doubles, how many pickers will be hired at a wage of $12 an hour? __________

(*e*) Illustrate your answers on the graph below.

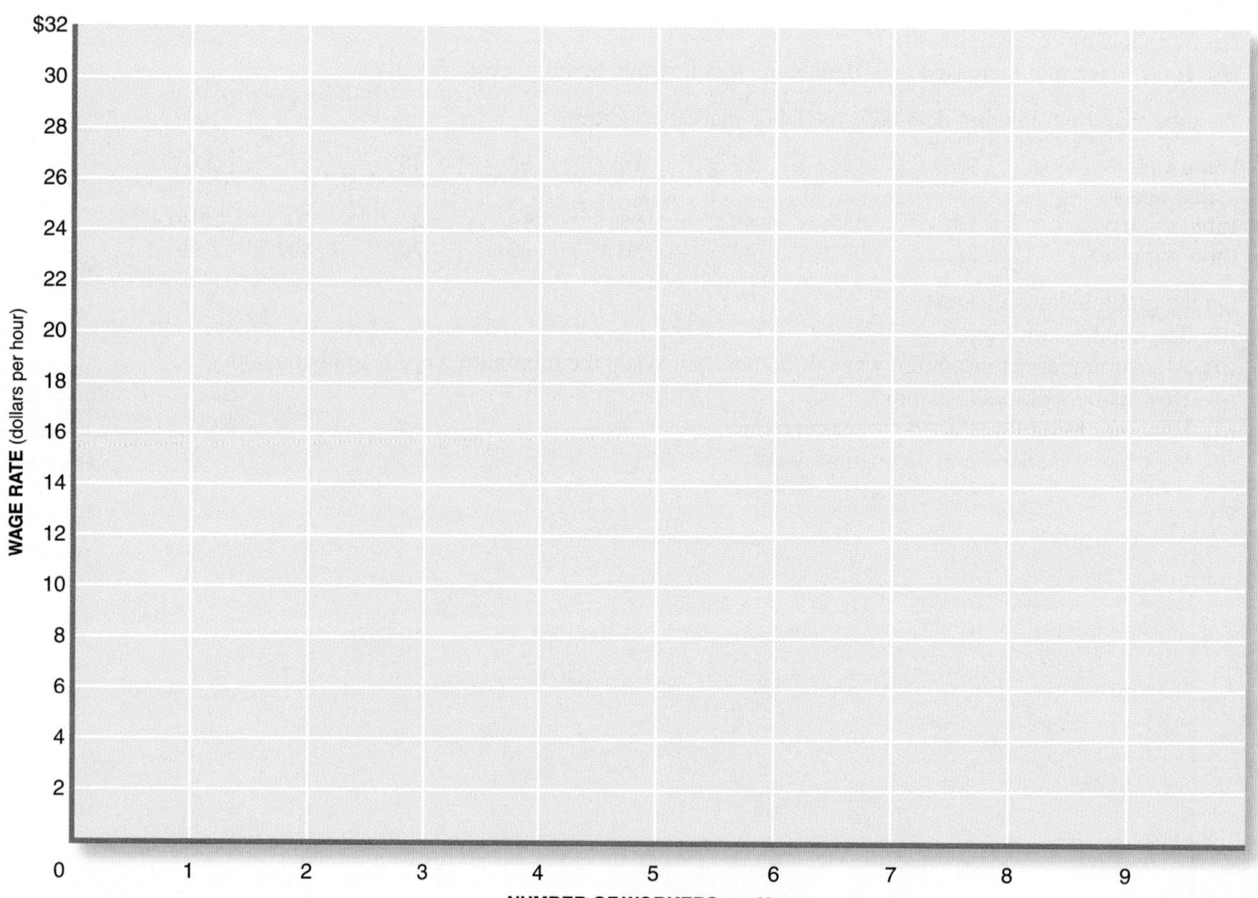

LO3 10. (*a*) If the elasticity of labor supply is 0.20, by how much would the quantity of labor supplied have increased as the result of the 2008 hike in the minimum wage (Table 30.2)? __________%

(*b*) If the elasticity of labor demand were 0.10, by how much would that same hike have reduced the quantity of labor demanded? __________%

PROBLEMS FOR CHAPTER 31

Name: ____________

LO1 LO2 1. Complete the following table:

Wage rate	$14	$13	$12	$11	$10	$9	$8	$7
Quantity of labor demanded	0	5	20	50	75	95	110	120
Marginal wage		—	—	—	—	—	—	—

(*a*) At what wage rate(s) is the marginal wage below the nominal wage? ____________

(*b*) At what wage rate does the marginal wage first become negative? ____________

LO1 LO2 2. Complete the following table:

Wage rate	$5	$6	$7	$8	$9	$10	$11
Quantity of labor supplied	80	120	155	180	200	210	215
Marginal factor cost	—	—	—	—	—	—	—

LO1 LO2 3. Based on the data in problems (1) and (2) above,

(*a*) What is the competitive wage rate? ____________

(*b*) Approximately what wage will the union seek? ____________

(*c*) How many workers will the union have to exclude in order to get that wage? ____________

LO2 4. At the time of the National Football League strike in 1987, the football owners made available the following data:

	Revenue	
Source of Revenue	**Before the Strike**	**During the Strike**
Television	$973,000	$973,000
Stadium gate	526,000	126,000
Luxury box seats	255,000	200,000
Concessions	60,000	12,000
Radio	40,000	40,000
Players' salaries and costs	854,000	230,000
Nonplayer costs (coaches' salaries)	200,000	200,000

(*a*) Compute total revenues, total expenses, and profits both before and during the strike.

	Before Strike	During Strike
Total revenue	____________	____________
Total expense	____________	____________
Total profit	____________	____________

(*b*) Why would the owners ever agree to settle the strike under these conditions?

LO1 LO2 LO3 5. Suppose the following supply-and-demand schedules apply in a particular labor market:

Wage rate (per hour)	$4	$5	$6	$7	$8	$9	$10
Quantity of labor supplied (workers per hour)	2	3	4	5	6	7	8
Quantity of labor demanded (workers per hour)	6	5	4	3	2	1	0

Graph the relevant curves and identify the

(*a*) Competitive wage rate. ____________

(*b*) Union wage rate. ____________

(*c*) Monopsonist's wage rate. ____________

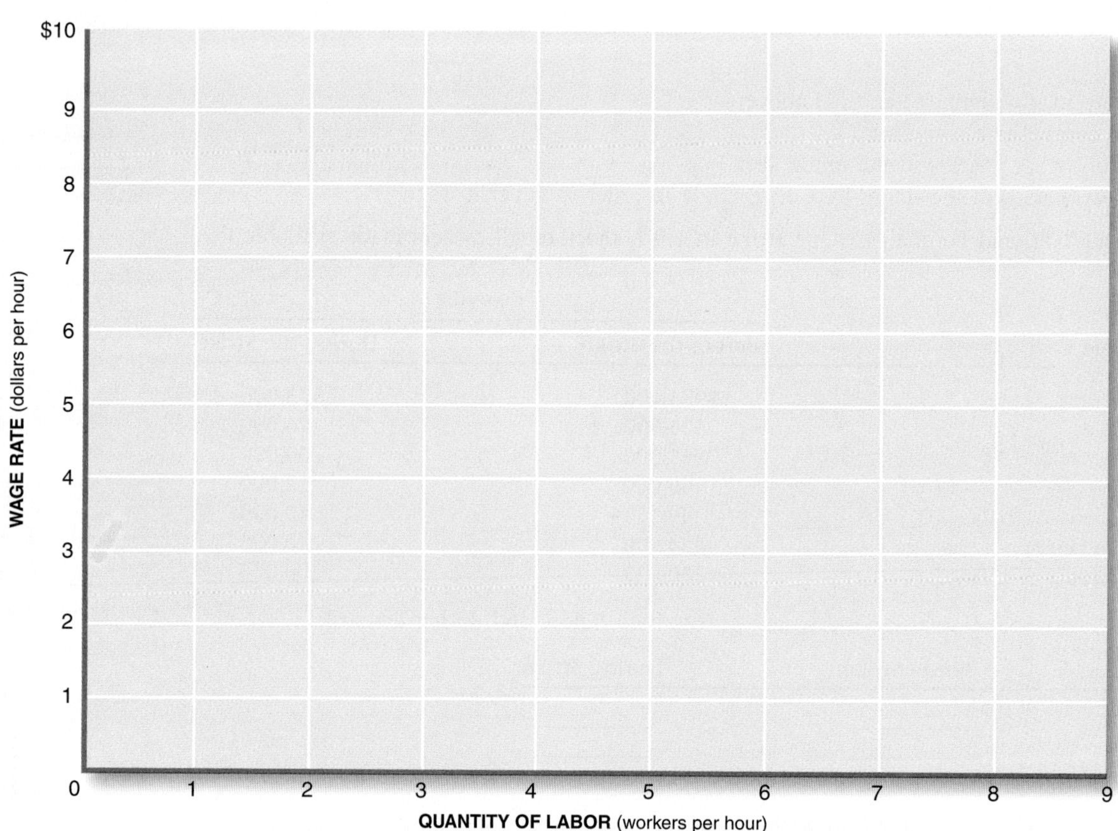

PROBLEMS FOR CHAPTER 32

Name: ________________________

LO2 1. If a \$48 stock pays a quarterly dividend of \$1, what is the implied annual rate of return? ______%

LO2 2. If a \$32 per share stock has a P/E ratio of 20 and pays out 40 percent of its profits in dividends,
(*a*) How large is its dividend? \$ ______
(*b*) What is the implied rate of return? ______%

LO2 3. According to the data in Table 32.3,
(*a*) How much profit per share did Google earn in 2006? \$ ______
(*b*) How much of that profit did it pay out in dividends? \$ ______

LO2 4. According to the data in Table 32.3,
(*a*) How much profit per share did Intel earn in 2006? \$ ______
(*b*) How much of that profit did it pay out in dividends? \$ ______

LO3 5. If the market rate of interest is 5 percent, what is the present discounted value of \$1,000 that will be paid in
(*a*) 1 year? ______
(*b*) 5 years? ______
(*c*) 10 years? ______

LO3 6. What is the present discounted value of \$10,000 that is to be received in 5 years if the market rate of interest is
(*a*) 0 percent? ______
(*b*) 5 percent? ______
(*c*) 10 percent? ______

LO3 7. Compute the expected return on Columbus's expedition assuming that he had a 50 percent chance of discovering valuables worth \$1 million, a 25 percent chance of bringing home only \$10,000, and a 25 percent chance of sinking. ______

LO2 8. Locate the stock quotation for General Motors Corporation in today's newspaper (traded on the New York Stock Exchange). From the information provided, determine
(*a*) Yesterday's percentage change in the price of GM stock. ______
(*b*) How much profit (earnings) GM made last year for each share of stock. ______
(*c*) How much of that profit was paid out in dividends. ______
(*d*) How much profit GM retained for investment. ______

LO2 9. Compute the market price of the GM bonds described in Table 32.5 if the yield goes to 9 percent. ______

LO2 LO3 10. What is the current yield on a \$1,000 bond with a 6 percent coupon if its market price is
(*a*) \$900? ______
(*b*) \$1,000? ______
(*c*) \$1,100? ______

LO3 11. How much interest accrued each day on the cash payoff of the MegaMillions jackpot? (See Table 32.1.) ______

 Name: ____________________

LO2 LO3 12. Illustrate the impact of the following events on stock prices:

(*a*) A federal court finds Microsoft guilty of antitrust violations.

Microsoft stock

PRICE (dollars per share)

QUANTITY (shares per day)

(*b*) Intel announces a new and faster processor.

Intel stock

PRICE (dollars per share)

QUANTITY (shares per day)

(*c*) Corporate executives announce they intend to sell a large block of stock.

Company stock

PRICE (dollars per share)

QUANTITY (shares per day)

(*d*) Microsoft enhances its search capabilities.

Google stock

PRICE (dollars per share)

QUANTITY (shares per day)

PROBLEMS FOR CHAPTER 33

Name: ______________________

LO1 LO2 1. How much income tax would President Bush have paid in 2006 (News, page 666) if there were no tax deductions? (Use tax rates in Table 33.1.) $______

LO1 LO2 2. Use Table 33.1 to compute the taxes on a taxable income of $160,000.
(*a*) What is the marginal tax rate? ______%
(*b*) What is the average tax rate? ______%

LO1 LO2 3. Using Table 33.1, compute the taxable income and taxes for the following taxpayers:

Taxpayer	Gross Income	Exemptions and Deductions	Taxable Income	Tax
A	$ 20,000	$ 7,000	______	______
B	30,000	4,000	______	______
C	40,000	28,000	______	______
D	70,000	32,000	______	______
E	200,000	80,000	______	______

Which taxpayer has
(*a*) The highest nominal tax rate? ______
(*b*) The highest effective tax rate? ______
(*c*) The highest marginal tax rate? ______

LO3 4. If the tax elasticity of supply is 0.20, by how much will the quantity supplied decrease when the marginal tax rate increases from 40 to 50 percent? ______%

LO3 5. By how much would the quantity of labor supplied have increased from the Bush tax cuts of 2001–4 if the tax elasticity of supply were 0.15 and the marginal tax rate fell from 22 to 19 percent? ______%

LO3 6. If the tax elasticity of labor supply were 0.16, by how much would the quantity of labor supplied increase among people in the top U.S. tax bracket if the highest marginal tax rate in the United States were reduced to the level of Hong Kong's (World View, page 671)? ______%

LO1 LO2 7. What percentage of income is paid in Social Security taxes by a worker earning
(*a*) $20,000? ______%
(*b*) $90,000? ______%
(*c*) $200,000? ______%
(*d*) What kind of tax is this? ______

LO2 LO3 8. What is the effective tax rate with Dick Armey's proposed flat tax for a family of four with earnings of
(*a*) $30,000? ______%
(*b*) $60,000? ______%
(*c*) $90,000? ______%

LO3 9. Following are hypothetical data on the size distribution of income and wealth for each quintile (one-fifth) of a population:

Quintile	Lowest	Second	Third	Fourth	Highest
Income	5%	10%	15%	25%	45%
Wealth	2%	8%	12%	20%	58%

(*a*) On the graph on the next page, draw the line of absolute equity; then draw a Lorenz curve for income, and shade the area between the two curves.
(*b*) In the same diagram, draw a Lorenz curve for wealth. Is there more inequality in the distribution of wealth than of income, or less? How do you know? ______
(*c*) The difference in inequality between income and wealth is quite typical of most economies. What might be the reason? ______

 Name: ____________

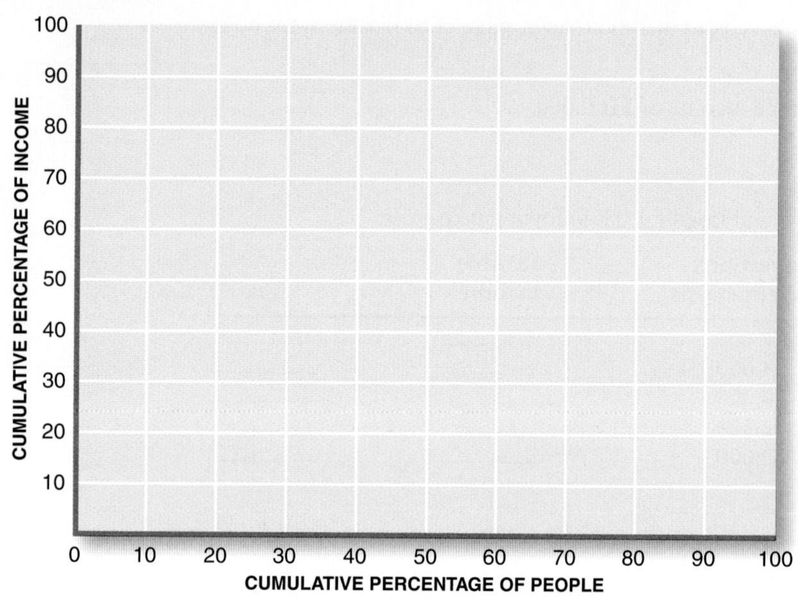

LO3 10. (*a*) On the graph below, draw the supply and demand for labor represented by the following data:

Wage	$1	2	3	4	5	6	7	8	9	10	11	12
Quantity of labor												
Supplied	1	2	3	4	5	6	8	10	12	14	17	20
Demanded	20	18	16	14	12	10	8	6	5	4	3	2

(*b*) How many workers are employed in equilibrium? ________

(*c*) What wage are they paid? ________

(*d*) Now suppose a payroll tax of $2 per worker is imposed on the employer. Draw the "supply + tax" graph that results.

(*e*) How many workers are now employed? ________

(*f*) How much is the employer paying for each worker? ________

(*g*) How much is each worker receiving? ________

For the incidence of this tax,

(*h*) What is the increase in unit labor cost to the employer? ________

(*i*) What is the reduction in the wage paid to labor? ________

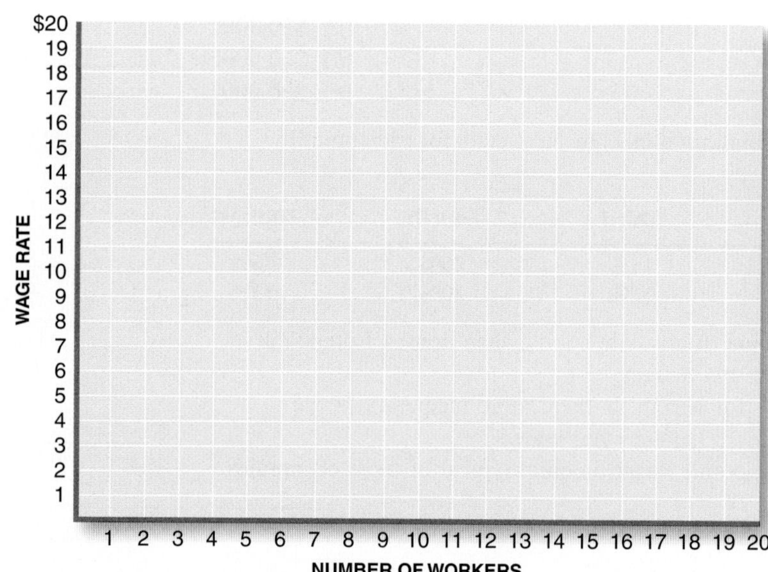

PROBLEMS FOR CHAPTER 34

Name: ______________________

LO3 1. Suppose the welfare benefit formula is

$$\text{Benefit} = \$4{,}800 - 2/3\ (\text{wages} > \$4{,}000)$$

(*a*) What is the marginal tax rate? ________

(*b*) How large is the benefit if wages equal

(*i*) \$0? ________

(*ii*) \$4,000? ________

(*iii*) \$9,000? ________

(*c*) What is the breakeven level of income in this case? ________

LO2 LO3 2. A welfare recipient can receive food stamps as well as cash welfare benefits. If the food stamp allotment is set as follows,

$$\text{Food stamps} = \$4{,}000 - 0.30\ (\text{wages})$$

(*a*) How high can wages rise before all food stamps are eliminated? ________

(*b*) If the welfare check formula in Problem 1 applies, what is the *combined* marginal tax rate of both welfare and food stamps for wages above \$4,000? ________

LO3 3. Draw a graph showing how benefits, total income, and wages change under the following conditions:

$$\text{Wage rate} = \$10 \text{ per hour}$$

$$\text{Welfare benefit} = \$6{,}000 - 0.5\ (\text{wages} > \$3{,}000)$$

Label the following points:
A—welfare benefit when wages = 0
B—welfare benefit when wages = \$10,000
C—breakeven level of income

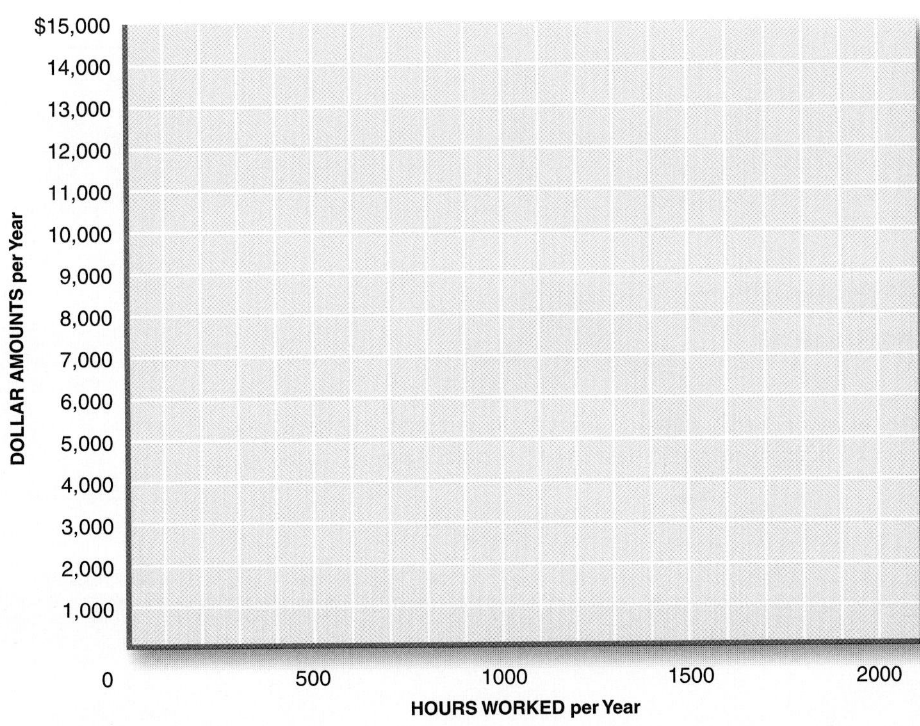

LO1 4. What is the breakeven level of income for Social Security as depicted in Figure 34.6? ________

LO3 5. According to the benefit formula in Table 34.2, how large will the Social Security benefit be for a worker who had earned

(*a*) $20,000 a year? ________
(*b*) $60,000 a year? ________

What is the marginal wage replacement rate for

(*c*) The $20,000 per year worker? ________
(*d*) The $60,000 per year worker? ________

LO3 6. How large a monthly Social Security check will a retiree get if her maximum benefit is $1,600 per month and she continues working for wages of $2,000 per month? ________

LO2 LO3 7. (*a*) On the graph below, depict the wages, income, and Social Security benefits at different hours of work for a worker aged 62–64 who earns $15 per hour and is eligible for $12,000 in Social Security benefits.

(*b*) What is total income if the person works 1,000 hours per year? ________
(*c*) What is the breakeven level of income? ________

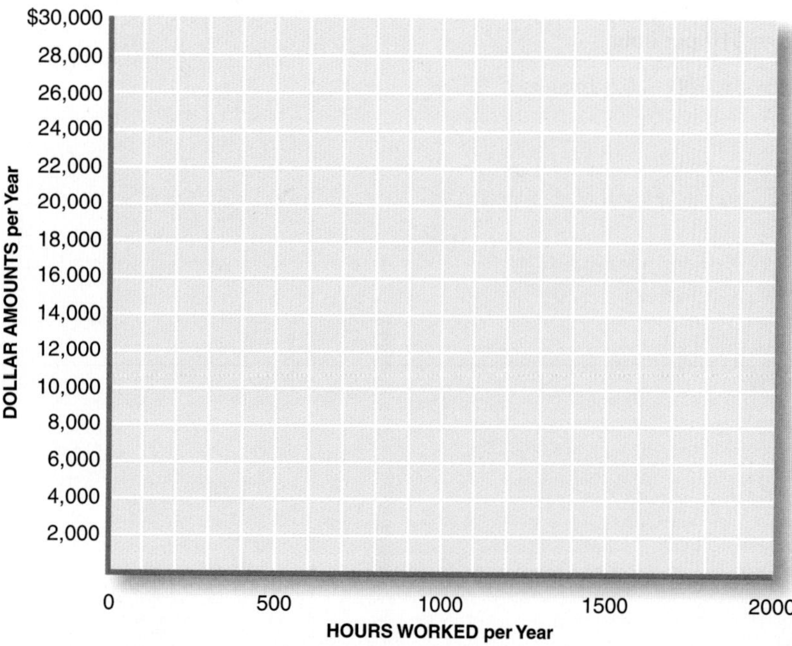

LO2 8. If older workers have a tax elasticity of labor supply equal to 0.20, by how much will their work activity decline when they hit the Social Security earnings-test limit? (Assume explicit taxes of 30 percent below that limit.) ________%

PROBLEMS FOR CHAPTER 35

Name: ____________________

LO2 1. Which countries are the two largest export markets for the United States? (See Table 35.3.) 1. ________ 2. ________

LO1 2. Suppose a country can produce a maximum of 10,000 jumbo airliners or 6000 aircraft carriers.

(*a*) What is the opportunity cost of an aircraft carrier? ________

(*b*) If another country offers to trade six planes for four aircraft carriers, should the offer be accepted? ________

(*c*) What are the implied terms of trade? ________

LO1 3. If it takes 48 farm workers to harvest one ton of strawberries and 12 farm workers to harvest one ton of wheat, what is the opportunity cost of five tons of strawberries? ________

LO1 LO2 4. Alpha and Beta, two tiny islands off the east coast of Tricoli, produce pearls and pineapples. The following production possibilities schedules describe their potential output in tons per year.

Alpha		Beta	
Pearls	**Pineapples**	**Pearls**	**Pineapples**
0	30	0	20
2	25	10	16
4	20	20	12
6	15	30	8
8	10	40	4
10	5	45	2
12	0	50	0

(*a*) Graph the production possibilities confronting each island.

(*b*) What is the opportunity cost of pineapples on each island (before trade)? Alpha: ________ Beta: ________

(*c*) Which island has a comparative advantage in pearl production? ________

(*d*) Graph the consumption possibilities of each island with free trade.

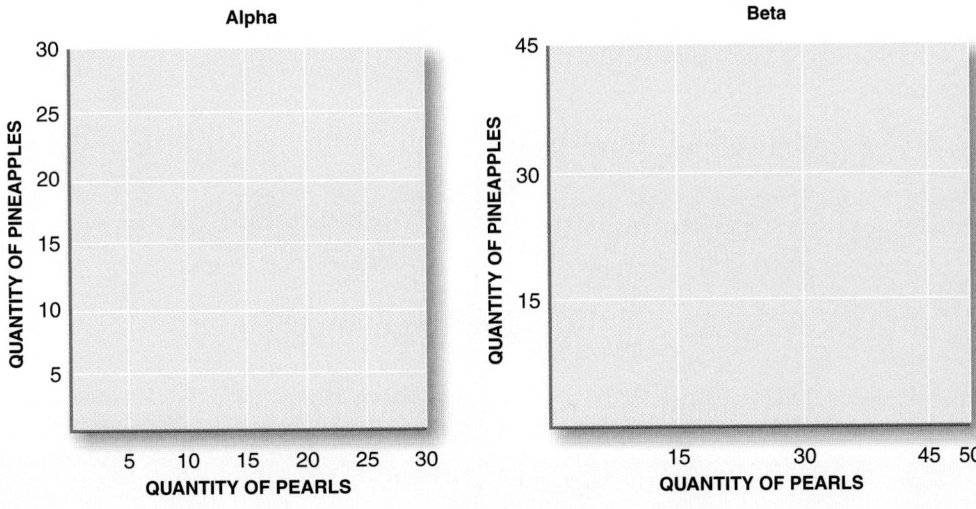

LO3 5. (*a*) How much more are U.S. consumers paying for the 20 billion pounds of sugar they consume each year as a result of the quotas on sugar imports? (See News, page 710.) ________

(*b*) How much sales revenue are foreign sugar producers losing as a result of those same quotas? ________

 Name: ____________________

LO2 6. Suppose the two islands in Problem 4 agree that the terms of trade will be one for one and exchange 10 pearls for 10 pineapples.

(*a*) If Alpha produced 6 pearls and 15 pineapples while Beta produced 30 pearls and 8 pineapples before they decided to trade, how much would each be producing after trade? Assume that the two countries specialize just enough to maintain their consumption of the item they export, and make sure each island follows its comparative advantage. Alpha: ________ Beta: ________

(*b*) How much would each island be consuming after specializing and trading? Alpha: ________ Beta: ________

(*c*) How much would the combined production of pineapples increase for the two islands due to trade? ____________________

(*d*) How much would the combined production of pearls increase? ____________________

(*e*) How could both countries produce and consume even more? ____________________

____

(*f*) Assume the two islands are able to trade as much as they want with the rest of the world, with the terms of trade at one pineapple for one pearl. Draw the ultimate consumption possibilities curve for each island.

LO2 LO3 7. Suppose the following table reflects the domestic supply and demand for compact disks (CDs):

Price ($)	18	16	14	12	10	8	6	4
Quantity supplied	8	7	6	5	4	3	2	1
Quantity demanded	2	4	6	8	10	12	14	16

(*a*) Graph these market conditions and identify the equilibrium price and sales. Price/sales: ________

(*b*) Now suppose that foreigners enter the market, offering to sell an unlimited supply of CDs for $6 apiece. Illustrate and identify

(*i*) The market price ________

(*ii*) Domestic consumption ________

(*iii*) Domestic production ________

(*c*) If a tariff of $2 per CD is imposed, what will happen to

(*i*) The market price? ________

(*ii*) Domestic consumption? ________

(*iii*) Domestic production? ________

Graph your answers.

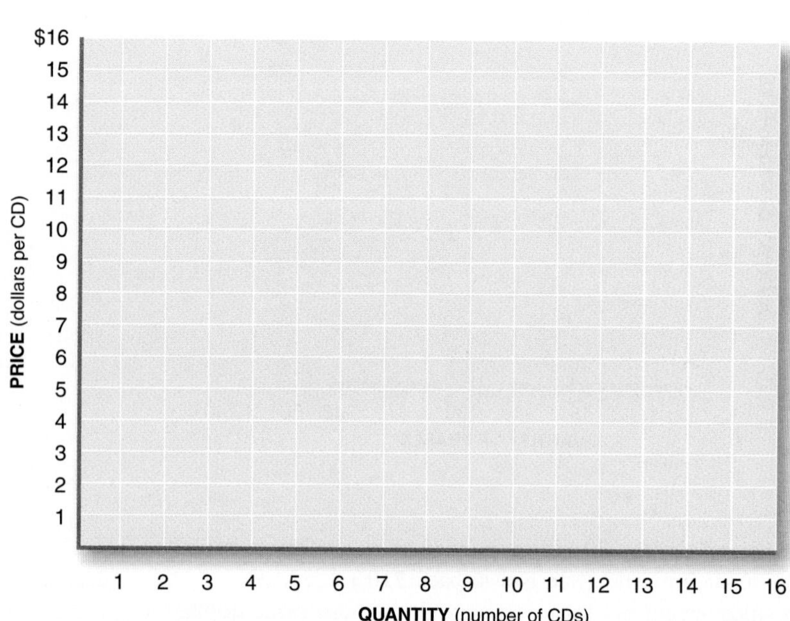

PROBLEMS FOR CHAPTER 36

Name: ______________________________

LO2 1. If a euro is worth $1.25, what is the euro price of a dollar? ________

LO3 2. If a pound of U.S. pork cost 40 rupiah in Indonesia before the Asian crisis, how much did it cost when the dollar value of the rupiah fell by 80 percent? ________

LO2 3. If a PlayStation 3 costs 20,000 yen in Japan, how much will it cost in U.S. dollars if the exchange
LO3 rate is

(*a*) 120 yen = $1? ________
(*b*) 1 yen = $0.00833? ________
(*c*) 100 yen = $1? ________

LO2 4. Between 1980 and 2000,
LO3 (*a*) By how much did the dollar appreciate (Figure 36.3)? ________%
(*b*) How did that appreciation affect the relative price of U.S. exports? ________________

LO1 5. If inflation raises U.S. prices by 3 percent and the U.S. dollar appreciates by 2 percent, by how
LO3 much does the foreign price of U.S. exports change? ________%

LO2 6. According to the World View on page 719, what was the peso price of a euro in March 2007? ________

LO1 7. For each of the following possible events, indicate whether the demand or supply curve for dollars
LO2 would shift, the direction of the shift, the determinant of the change, the inflow or outflow effect
LO3 on the balance of payments (and the specific account that would be affected), and the resulting movement of the equilibrium exchange rate for the value of the dollar.

(*a*) American cars become suddenly more popular abroad. ________________________________

(*b*) Inflation rates in the United States accelerate. ________________________________

(*c*) The United States falls into a depression. ________________________________

(*d*) Interest rates in the United States drop. ________________________________

(*e*) The United States suddenly experiences rapid increases in productivity. ________________

(*f*) Anticipating a return to the gold standard, Americans suddenly rush to buy gold from the two big producers, South Africa and the Soviet Union. ________________________________

(*g*) War is declared in the Middle East. ________________________________

(*h*) The stock markets in the United States suddenly collapse. ________________________________

LO1 LO2 LO3 8. The following schedules summarize the supply and demand for trifflings, the national currency of Tricoli:

Triffling price (U.S. dollars per triffling)	0	$4	$8	$12	$16	$20	$24
Quantity demanded (per year)	40	38	36	34	32	30	28
Quantity supplied (per year)	1	11	21	31	41	51	61

Use the above schedules for the following:

(*a*) Graph the supply and demand curves.

(*b*) Determine the equilibrium exchange rate. ________

(*c*) Determine the size of the excess supply or excess demand that would exist if the Tricolian government fixed the exchange rate at $22 = 1 triffling. ________

(*d*) How might this imbalance be remedied?

____

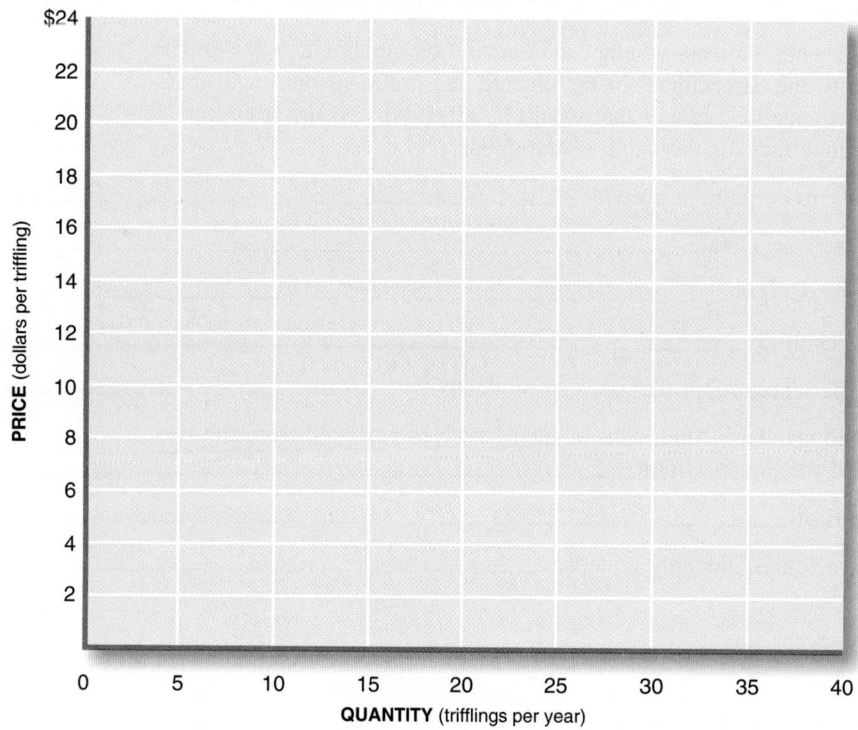

PROBLEMS FOR CHAPTER 37

Name: ______________________

LO1 1. Adjusted for inflation, the World Bank's threshold for "extreme" poverty is now close to $1.50 per person per day.

(a) How much *annual* income does this imply? $______

(b) What portion of the official U.S. poverty threshold (roughly $20,000 for a family of four) is met by the Bank's measure? ______%

LO2 2. Close to half the world's population of 6 billion people is in "severe" poverty with less than $3 of income per day (with inflation adjustments).

(a) What is the maximum *combined* income of this "severely" poor population? $______

(b) What percentage of the world's *total* income (roughly $60 trillion) does this represent? ______%

LO2 3. In Namibia,

(a) What percent of total output is received by the richest 10 percent of households? (See World View, p. 738.) ______%

(b) How much output did this share amount to in 2005, when Namibia's GDP was $6 billion? $______

(c) With a total population of 2 million, what was the implied per capita income of

(i) the richest 10 percent of the population? $______

(ii) the remaining 90 percent? $______

LO3 4. (a) How much foreign aid does the U.S. now provide? $______

(b) How much is required to satisfy the U.N.'s Millennium Aid Goal? $______

LO3 5. If the industrialized nations were to satisfy the U.N.'s Millennium Aid Goal, how much *more* foreign aid would they give annually? (See Table 37.2.) $______

LO3 6. According to Table 37.3, how many years will it take for per capita GDP to double in

(a) China? ______

(b) Kenya? ______

(c) Zimbabwe? ______

LO3 7. (a) Which low-income nation in Table 37.3 has GDP growth equal to Japan's? ______

(b) How much faster is that nation's population growth? ______%

(c) How much lower is its per capita GDP growth? ______%

LO3 8. According to the World View on p.740,

(a) How much money is spent annually to combat baldness? $______

(b) How much medical care would that money buy for each child who dies from malaria each year? $______